D0080742

Fifth Edition

PRINCIPLES OF ELECTRIC CIRCUITS

Electron Flow Version

THOMAS L. FLOYD

PRENTICE HALL
Upper Saddle River, New Jersey   **Columbus, Ohio**

Cover Photo: © Uniphoto
Editor: Scott Sambucci
Developmental Editor: Katie E. Bradford
Production Editor: Rex Davidson
Design Coordinator: Karrie Converse-Jones
Text Designer: John Edeen
Cover Designer: Brian Deep
Production Buyer: Patricia A. Tonneman
Marketing Manager: Ben Leonard
Illustrations: Jane Lopez and Steve Botts

Library of Congress Cataloging-in-Publication Data

Floyd, Thomas L.
    Principles of electric circuits : electron flow version /
Thomas L. Floyd.—5th ed.
      p. cm.
    Includes index.
    ISBN 0-13-095998-7
    1. Electric circuits.   I. Title.
TK454.F57   2000
621.319'2—dc21
                          99-36154
                              CIP

This book was set in Times Roman by The Clarinda Company and was printed and bound by R. R. Donnelley & Sons Company. The cover was printed by Phoenix Color Corp.

© 2000, 1997, 1993 by Prentice-Hall, Inc.
Pearson Education
Upper Saddle River, New Jersey 07458

All rights reserved. No part of this book may be reproduced, in any form or by any means, without permission in writing from the publisher.

Earlier editions © 1990, 1983 by Merrill Publishing Company

Printed in the United States of America

10 9 8 7 6 5 4 3 2 1

ISBN   0-13-095998-7

Prentice-Hall International (UK) Limited, *London*
Prentice-Hall of Australia Pty. Limited, *Sydney*
Prentice-Hall Canada Inc., *Toronto*
Prentice-Hall Hispanoamericana, S. A., *Mexico*
Prentice-Hall of India Private Limited, *New Delhi*
Prentice-Hall of Japan, Inc., *Tokyo*
Prentice-Hall (Singapore) Pte. Ltd., *Singapore*
Editora Prentice-Hall do Brasil, Ltda., *Rio de Janeiro*

PREFACE

Principles of Electric Circuits: Electron Flow Version, Fifth Edition, provides comprehensive, practical coverage of basic electrical concepts and circuits. Material is presented in a readable style complemented by numerous examples and illustrations. As in previous editions, the text includes strong coverage of troubleshooting and applications. This edition has been thoroughly reviewed and a tremendous effort has been made to ensure that the coverage is accurate and up-to-date.

New Software and Internet-Related Features

- Electronics Workbench® (EWB) tutorials for most chapters are now available on the Internet at www.prenhall.com/floyd
- PSpice tutorials for each chapter and a selection of PSpice circuits are now available on the Internet at www.prenhall.com/floyd. (PSpice student demonstration software can be downloaded from www.orcad.com).

The CD-ROM packaged with the text contains the following three items:

1. Approximately 100 EWB circuits for the textbook's Troubleshooting and Analysis Problems. EWB software version 5.X or higher is required to view these circuits.
2. Limited demonstration version of EWB version 5.X software. This allows the reader access to 15 of the circuits on the CD-ROM.
3. A full student version of EWB version 5.X. This is available for purchase by contacting Interactive Image Technologies.

Users should direct all technical questions about the CD-ROM to Interactive Image Technologies at (800) 263-5552 or www.interactiv.com.

Other New Features

- Troubleshooting and Analysis Problems at the end of most chapters coordinate with EWB circuits on the CD-ROM that comes with the textbook. Answers are in the Instructor's Resource Manual.
- Revised organization of the chapters on reactive circuits (Chapters 16, 17, and 18) that facilitates two popular approaches to the subject matter
- Safety notes in some chapters
- Historical Notes at the opening of many chapters
- Expanded use of calculator solutions
- Identification of the most difficult end-of-chapter problems

Other Features

- Functional full-color format
- TECHnology Theory Into Practice (Tech TIP) sections in most chapters
- Chapter Overview and Objectives at the opening of each chapter
- Introduction and Objectives at the beginning of each section in a chapter
- Many worked examples, each with a related problem
- Reviews at the end of each chapter section

- Chapter summaries
- List of chapter formulas
- Chapter glossaries (comprehensive glossary at the end of the book.)
- Chapter self-tests
- Sectionalized chapter problem sets
- Electron flow direction is used. (An alternate version of this text uses conventional current direction.)
- Ancillary package that includes
  - Lab Manual: *Experiments in Basic Circuits: Theory and Application,* by Dave Buchla. Solutions manual available.
  - Lab Manual: *Experiments in Electric Circuits,* by Brian Stanley. Solutions manual available.
  - PowerPoint slides
  - Test Item File (printed testbank)
  - Prentice Hall Test Manager (electronic testbank)
  - Instructor's Resource Manual
  - Bergwall Videos

Illustration of Chapter Features

Chapter Opener   Each chapter begins with a two-page opener as shown in Figure A. A typical chapter opener contains a section list, a reference to the Electronics Workbench (EWB) and PSpice tutorials on the website at www.prenhall.com/floyd, a chapter overview, chapter objectives, and associated art related to the TECHnology Theory Into Practice (Tech TIP) section and, in some chapters, one or two Historical Notes related to the chapter.

EWB and PSpice Tutorials   The website tutorials correspond to chapters in the text-book, and a tutorial is referenced at the beginning of most chapters. If your course covers EWB or PSpice, you can study the tutorial for a given chapter just as if it were another section in the text. Of course, the other textbook material is not affected if these tutorials are not used; they are strictly optional.

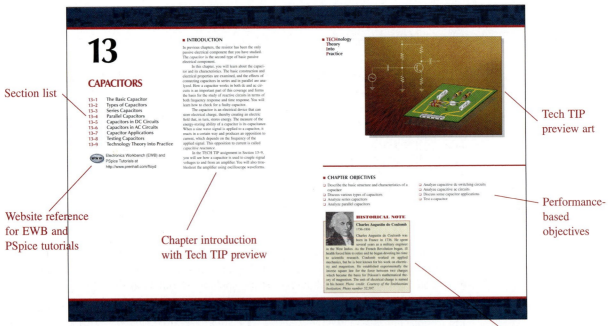

FIGURE A
Chapter opener.

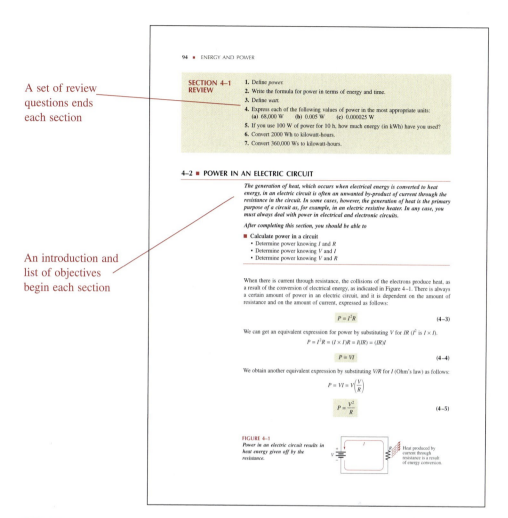

The following content appears within Figure B:

SECTION 4–1 REVIEW

1. Define *power*.
2. Write the formula for power in terms of energy and time.
3. Define *watt*.
4. Express each of the following values of power in the most appropriate units:
   (a) 68,000 W   (b) 0.005 W   (c) 0.000025 W
5. If you use 100 W of power for 10 h, how much energy (in kWh) have you used?
6. Convert 2000 Wh to kilowatt-hours.
7. Convert 360,000 Ws to kilowatt-hours.

4–2 ■ POWER IN AN ELECTRIC CIRCUIT

The generation of heat, which occurs when electrical energy is converted to heat energy, in an electric circuit is often an unwanted by-product of current through the resistance in the circuit. In some cases, however, the generation of heat is the primary purpose of a circuit as, for example, in an electric resistive heater. In any case, you must always deal with power in electrical and electronic circuits.

After completing this section, you should be able to

■ **Calculate power in a circuit**
  • Determine power knowing I and R
  • Determine power knowing V and I
  • Determine power knowing V and R

When there is current through resistance, the collisions of the electrons produce heat, as a result of the conversion of electrical energy, as indicated in Figure 4–1. There is always a certain amount of power in an electric circuit, and it is dependent on the amount of resistance and on the amount of current, expressed as follows:

$$P = I^2R \qquad (4\text{–}3)$$

We can get an equivalent expression for power by substituting V for IR (I^2 is $I \times I$).

$$P = I^2R = (I \times I)R = I(IR) = (IR)I$$

$$P = VI \qquad (4\text{–}4)$$

We obtain another equivalent expression by substituting V/R for I (Ohm's law) as follows:

$$P = VI = V\left(\frac{V}{R}\right)$$

$$P = \frac{V^2}{R} \qquad (4\text{–}5)$$

FIGURE 4–1
Power in an electric circuit results in heat energy given off by the resistance.

Heat produced by current through resistance is a result of energy conversion.

FIGURE B
Section opener and section review.

Section Opener   Each section in a chapter begins with a brief introduction that provides the essence of the section and a list of section objectives. A typical section opener is shown in Figure B.

Section Review   Each section ends with a review consisting of questions and/or exercises that focus on the main concepts covered in the section. Answers to these section reviews are at the end of the chapter. A typical section review is also shown in Figure B.

Worked Examples and Related Problems   Numerous examples help to illustrate and clarify basic concepts or demonstrate specific procedures. Each example concludes with a related problem that reinforces or expands on the topic covered in the example. Some of the related problems require a repetition of the calculations in the example using different values or conditions. Others focus on a more limited part of the example or encourage further thought. Answers to the related problems are found at the end of the chapter. A typical worked example and the related problem are shown in Figure C.

Troubleshooting Sections   Many chapters include troubleshooting sections emphasizing troubleshooting techniques and the use of test instruments as they apply to situations related to chapter topics.

FIGURE C
An example and related problem.

Each example is enclosed in a box

Calculator key sequences are found in some examples

Each example contains a related problem

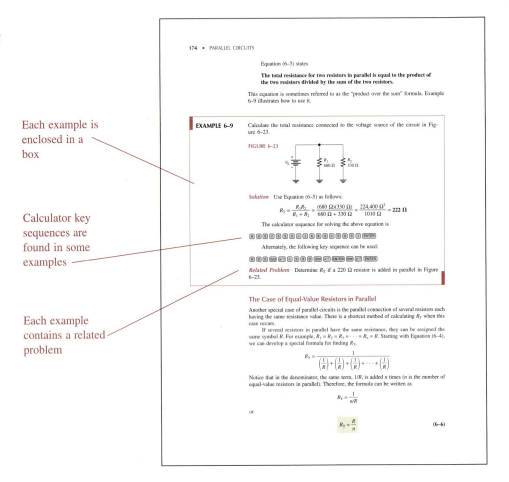

Equation (6–5) states

The total resistance for two resistors in parallel is equal to the product of the two resistors divided by the sum of the two resistors.

This equation is sometimes referred to as the "product over the sum" formula. Example 6–9 illustrates how to use it.

EXAMPLE 6–9   Calculate the total resistance connected to the voltage source of the circuit in Figure 6–23.

FIGURE 6–23

Solution   Use Equation (6–5) as follows:

$$R_T = \frac{R_1 R_2}{R_1 + R_2} = \frac{(680\ \Omega)(330\ \Omega)}{680\ \Omega + 330\ \Omega} = \frac{224,400\ \Omega^2}{1010\ \Omega} = 222\ \Omega$$

The calculator sequence for solving the above equation is

Alternately, the following key sequence can be used:

Related Problem   Determine R_T if a 220 Ω resistor is added in parallel in Figure 6–23.

The Case of Equal-Value Resistors in Parallel

Another special case of parallel circuits is the parallel connection of several resistors each having the same resistance value. There is a shortcut method of calculating R_T when this case occurs.

If several resistors in parallel have the same resistance, they can be assigned the same symbol R. For example, $R_1 = R_2 = R_3 = \cdots = R_n = R$. Starting with Equation (6–4), we can develop a special formula for finding R_T.

$$R_T = \frac{1}{\left(\dfrac{1}{R}\right) + \left(\dfrac{1}{R}\right) + \left(\dfrac{1}{R}\right) + \cdots + \left(\dfrac{1}{R}\right)}$$

Notice that in the denominator, the same term, 1/R, is added n times (n is the number of equal-value resistors in parallel). Therefore, the formula can be written as

$$R_T = \frac{1}{n/R}$$

or

$$R_T = \frac{R}{n} \qquad (6\text{–}6)$$

Opener

Basic description of circuit and application

Schematic

Circuit board

Test setup

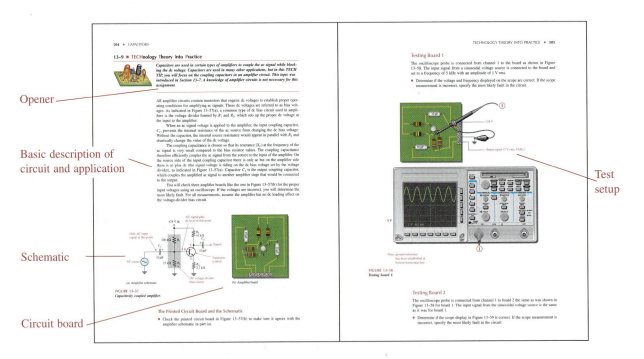

13–9 ■ TECHnology Theory Into Practice

Capacitors are used in certain types of amplifiers to couple the ac signal while blocking the dc voltage. Capacitors are used in many other applications, but in this TECH TIP, you will focus on the coupling capacitors in an amplifier circuit. This topic was introduced in Section 13–7. A knowledge of amplifier circuits is not necessary for this assignment.

All amplifier circuits contain transistors that require dc voltages to establish proper operating conditions for amplifying ac signals. These dc voltages are referred to as bias voltages. As indicated in Figure 13–57(a), a common type of dc bias circuit used in amplifiers is the voltage divider formed by R_1 and R_2, which sets up the proper dc voltage at the input to the amplifier.

When an ac signal voltage is applied to the amplifier, the input coupling capacitor, C_1, prevents the internal resistance of the ac source from changing the dc bias voltage. Without the capacitor, the internal source resistance would appear in parallel with R_2 and drastically change the value of the dc voltage.

The coupling capacitance is chosen so that its reactance (X_C) at the frequency of the ac signal is very small compared to the bias resistor values. The coupling capacitance therefore efficiently couples the ac signal from the source to the input of the amplifier. On the source side of the input coupling capacitor there is only ac but on the amplifier side there is ac plus dc (the signal voltage is riding on the dc bias voltage set by the voltage divider), as indicated in Figure 13–57(a). Capacitor C_2 is the output coupling capacitor, which couples the amplified ac signal to another amplifier stage that would be connected to the output.

You will check three amplifier boards like the one in Figure 13–57(b) for the proper input voltages using an oscilloscope. If the voltages are incorrect, you will determine the most likely fault. For all measurements, assume the amplifier has no dc loading effect on the voltage-divider bias circuit.

FIGURE 13–57
Capacitively coupled amplifier.

The Printed Circuit Board and the Schematic

■ Check the printed circuit board in Figure 13–57(b) to make sure it agrees with the amplifier schematic in part (a).

Testing Board 1

The oscilloscope probe is connected from channel 1 to the board as shown in Figure 13–58. The input signal from a sinusoidal voltage source is connected to the board and set to a frequency of 5 kHz with an amplitude of 1 V rms.

■ Determine if the voltage and frequency displayed on the scope are correct. If the scope measurement is incorrect, specify the most likely fault in the circuit.

FIGURE 13–58
Testing board 1.

Testing Board 2

The oscilloscope probe is connected from channel 1 to board 2 the same as was shown in Figure 13–58 for board 1. The input signal from the sinusoidal voltage source is the same as it was for board 1.

■ Determine if the scope display in Figure 13–59 is correct. If the scope measurement is incorrect, specify the most likely fault in the circuit.

FIGURE D
Representative pages from a typical TECHnology Theory Into Practice (Tech TIP) section.

TECHnology Theory Into Practice (Tech TIP)   The last section of each chapter (except Chapters 1 and 22) presents a practical application of certain material presented in the chapter. Each Tech TIP includes a series of activities, many of which involve comparing circuit board layouts with schematics, analyzing circuits, using measurements to determine circuit operation, and in some cases, developing simple test procedures. Results and answers to Tech TIPs are found in the Instructor's Resource Manual. A typical Tech TIP section is illustrated in Figure D.

Chapter End Matter   Each chapter ends with a summary, glossary, formula list, multiple-choice self-test, and extensive sectionalized problem set including EWB Troubleshooting and Analysis problems. The most difficult problems are indicated by an asterisk. Also, answers to section reviews, related problems, and self-tests are at the end of each chapter. Terms that appear **boldface** in the text are defined in the end-of-chapter glossaries.

Book End Matter   Appendices at the end of the book consist of a table of standard resistor values, a brief coverage of batteries, derivations of selected text equations, and coverage of capacitor color coding. Following the appendices are answers to selected odd-numbered problems (solutions to all end-of-chapter problems are in the Instructor's Resource Manual), comprehensive glossary, and index.

Suggestions for Teaching with *Principles of Electric Circuits*

Selected Course Emphasis and Flexibility of the Text   This textbook is designed primarily for use in a two-term course sequence in which dc topics (Chapters 1 through 10) are covered in the first term and ac topics (Chapters 11 through 22) are covered in the second term. A one-term course covering dc and ac topics is possible but would require very selective and abbreviated coverage of many topics.

If time limitations or course emphasis restricts the topics that can be covered, as is usually the case, there are several options for selective coverage. The following suggestions for light treatment or omission do not necessarily imply that a certain topic is less important than others but that, in the context of a specific program, the topic may not require the emphasis that the more fundamental topics do. Because course emphasis, level, and available time vary from one program to another, the omission or abbreviated treatment of selected topics must be made on an individual basis. Therefore, the following suggestions are intended only as a general guide.

1. Chapters that may be considered for omission or selective coverage:
   - Chapter 8, Circuit Theorems and Conversions
   - Chapter 9, Branch, Mesh, and Node Analysis
   - Chapter 10, Magnetism and Electromagnetism
   - Chapter 19, Basic Filters
   - Chapter 20, Circuit Theorems in AC Analysis
   - Chapter 21, Pulse Response of Reactive Circuits
   - Chapter 22, Polyphase Systems in Power Applications

2. The Tech Tip and troubleshooting sections can be omitted without affecting other material.
3. Other specific topics may be omitted or covered lightly on a section-by-section basis at the discretion of the instructor.

The order in which certain topics appear in the text can be altered at the instructor's discretion. For example, the topics of capacitors and inductors (Chapter 13 and 14) can be covered at the end of the dc course in the first term by delaying coverage of the ac topics in Sections 13–6, 13–7, 14–6, and 14–7 until the ac course in the second term. Another possibility is to cover Chapters 13 and 14 in the second term but cover Chapter 16 (*RC* Circuits) immediately after Chapter 13 (Capacitors) and cover Chapter 17 (*RL* Circuits) immediately after Chapter 14 (Inductors).

Tech TIPS These sections are useful for motivation and for introducing applications of basic concepts and components. Suggestions for using these sections are:

- As an integral part of the chapter to illustrate how the concepts and components can be applied in a practical situation. The activities can be assigned for homework.
- As extra credit assignments.
- As in-class activities to promote discussion and interaction and to help students understand why they need to know the material.

Coverage of Reactive Circuits Chapters 16, 17, and 18 have been designed to facilitate two approaches to teaching these topics on reactive circuits.

The first approach is to cover the topics on the basis of components. That is, first cover all of Chapter 16 (*RC* Circuits), then all of Chapter 17 (*RL* Circuits), and, finally, all of Chapter 18 (*RLC* Circuits and Resonance).

The second approach is to cover the topics on the basis of circuit type. That is, first cover all topics related to series reactive circuits, then all topics related to parallel reactive circuits, and finally, all topics related to series-parallel reactive circuits. To facilitate this second approach, each of the chapters have been divided into the following parts: *Part 1: Series Reactive Circuits, Part 2: Parallel Reactive Circuits, Part 3: Series-Parallel Reactive Circuits,* and *Part 4: Special Topics.* So, for series reactive circuits, cover Part 1 of all three chapters in sequence. For parallel reactive circuits, cover Part 2 of all three chapters in sequence. For series-parallel reactive circuits, cover Part 3 of all three chapters in sequence. Finally, cover Part 4 of all three chapters.

A Brief History of Electronics

It is always good to have a sense of the history of your career field. So, before you begin your study of electric circuits, let's briefly look at the beginnings of electronics and some of the important developments that have led to the electronics technology that we have today. The names of many of the early pioneers in electricity and electromagnetics still live on in terms of familiar units and quantities. Names such as Ohm, Ampere, Volta, Farad, Henry, Coulomb, Oersted, and Hertz are some of the better known examples. More widely known names such as Franklin and Edison are also very significant in the history of electricity and electronics because of their tremendous contributions. Brief biographies of many of these appear in Historical Notes at the beginning of the appropriate chapters.

The Beginning of Electronics The early experiments in electronics involved electric currents in glass vacuum tubes. One of the first to conduct such experiments was a German named Heinrich Geissler (1814–1879). Geissler removed most of the air from a glass tube and found that the tube glowed when there was an electric current through it. Around 1878, British scientist Sir William Crookes (1832–1919) experimented with tubes similar to those of Geissler. In his experiments, Crookes found that the current in the vacuum tubes seemed to consist of particles.

Thomas Edison (1847–1931), experimenting with the carbon-filament light bulb he had invented, made another important finding. He inserted a small metal plate in the bulb. When the plate was positively charged, there was a current from the filament to the plate. This device was the first thermionic diode. Edison patented it but never used it.

The electron was discovered in the 1890s. The French physicist Jean Baptiste Perrin (1870–1942) demonstrated that the current in a vacuum tube consisted of the movement of negatively charged particles in a given direction. Some of the properties of these particles were measured by Sir Joseph Thompson (1856–1940), a British physicist, in experiments he performed between 1895 and 1897. These negatively charged particles later became known as electrons. The charge on the electron was accurately measured by an American physicist, Robert A. Millikan (1868–1953), in 1909. As a result of these discoveries, electrons could be controlled, and the electronic age was ushered in.

Putting the Electron to Work In 1904 a British scientist, John A. Fleming, constructed a vacuum tube that allowed electric current in only one direction. The tube was used to detect electromagnetic waves. Called the Fleming valve, it was the forerunner of the more recent vacuum diode tubes. Major progress in electronics, however, awaited the development of a device that could boost, or amplify, a weak electromagnetic wave or radio signal. This device was the audion, patented in 1907 by Lee deForest, an American. It was a triode vacuum tube capable of amplifying small electrical ac signals.

Two other Americans, Harold Arnold and Irving Langmuir, made great improvements in the triode vacuum tube between 1912 and 1914. About the same time, deForest and Edwin Armstrong, an electrical engineer, used the triode tube in an oscillator circuit. In 1914, the triode was incorporated in the telephone system and made the transcontinental telephone network possible. In 1916 Walter Schottky, a German, invented the tetrode tube. The tetrode, along with the pentode (invented in 1926 by Dutch engineer Tellegen), greatly improved the triode. The first television picture tube, called the kinescope, was developed in the 1920s by Vladimir Zworykin, an American researcher.

During World War II, several types of microwave tubes were developed that made possible modern microwave radar and other communications systems. In 1939, the magnetron was invented in Britain by Henry Boot and John Randall. In that same year, the klystron microwave tube was developed by two Americans, Russell Varian and his brother Sigurd Varian. The traveling-wave tube (TWT) was invented in 1943 by Rudolf Komphner, an Austrian-American.

Solid-State Electronics   The crystal detectors used in early radios were the forerunners of modern solid-state devices. However, the era of solid-state electronics began with the invention of the transistor in 1947 at Bell Labs. The inventors were Walter Brattain, John Bardeen, and William Shockley.

In the early 1960s, the integrated circuit (IC) was developed. It incorporated many transistors and other components on a single small chip of semiconductor material. Integrated circuit technology has been continuously developed and improved, allowing increasingly more complex circuits to be built on smaller chips.

Around 1965, the first integrated general-purpose operational amplifier was introduced. This low-cost, highly versatile device incorporated nine transistors and twelve resistors in a small package. It proved to have many advantages over comparable discrete component circuits in terms of reliability and performance. Since this introduction, the IC operational amplifier has become a basic building block for a wide variety of linear systems.

Applications

Electricity and electronics are very broad and diverse fields and almost anything you can think of somehow uses electricity or electronics. The following are some of the major application areas.

Computers   As everyone knows, computers are used just about everywhere and their applications are almost unlimited. For example, computers are used in business for record keeping, accounting, payroll, inventory control, market analysis, and statistics. In industry, computers are used for controlling and monitoring manufacturing processes. Information, communications, navigation, medical, military, law enforcement, and domestic applications are some of the other broad areas where computers are found.

Communications   Electronic communications involves a wide variety of specialized fields that include telephone systems, satellites, radio, television, data communications, and radar, to name a few.

Automation   Electronic systems are used extensively in the control of manufacturing processes. For example, the robotic systems used in the assembly of automobiles are electronically controlled. A few other applications are the control of ingredient mixes in food processing, the operation of machine tools, distribution of power, and printing.

Transportation   Electronics is an integral part of most types of transportation equipment and systems. One example is the electronics found in most modern automobiles for entertainment, brake controls, ignition controls, engine monitoring, and communications. The airline industry would be completely shut down without electronics for navigation, communication, and scheduling purposes. Also, trucks, trains, and boats depend on electronics for much of their operation.

Medicine   Electronic systems are used in the medical field for many things. For example, the monitoring of patient functions such as heart rate, blood pressure, temperature, and respiration is accomplished electronically. Diagnostic tools such as the CAT scan, EKG, X-ray, and ultrasound are all electronic-based systems.

Consumer Electronics   Products used directly by the consumer constitute a large segment of the electronics market. There are systems for entertainment and information such as radios, televisions, VCRs, computers, sound systems, and electronic games. There are systems for communications such as cellular phones, pagers, recorders, intercoms, CB radio, short-wave radio, and computers. Also, many products that do work in the home such as washing machines, dryers, refrigerators, ranges, and security systems have electronic controls.

Acknowledgments

Many very capable people have been involved with this Fifth Edition of *Principles of Electric Circuits: Electron Flow Version.* It has been completely reviewed and checked for both content and accuracy. Those at Prentice Hall who have been instrumental in moving this project through its many phases include Rex Davidson, Katie Bradford, and Scott Sambucci. They deserve much credit.

My appreciation, once again, to Lois Porter who has done another wonderful job of editing the manuscript. Also, thanks to Jane Lopez for the great job on the graphics art used in the text. Chuck Garbinski has been my accuracy checker on this project and I commend him for his outstanding work. In addition, Chuck created the EWB circuit files for the Electronics Workbench features that are new to this edition. Last but certainly not least, thanks to my colleague Dave Buchla for his consultations on many topics and his thorough review of the manuscript. As always, we depend on expert input from many users and nonusers of *Principles of Electric Circuits.* My thanks to the following reviewers who made many valuable suggestions and provided much constructive criticism.

Herbert Hall, Lakeland Community College

Leslie E. Johnson, Delaware Tech and Community College

Steve Kuchler, Ivy Tech State College

Stuart Peterson, Ridgewater College

Charles R. Morgan, Denver Technical College

Jon Speer, Northwest State Community College, Archbold, OH

Victor L. Stateler, Kirkwood Community College

Thomas L. Floyd

CONTENTS

1

COMPONENTS, QUANTITIES, AND UNITS

 PSpice Tutorials available at
http://www.prenhall.com/floyd

■ INTRODUCTION

This chapter presents a basic introduction to the field of electronics. An overview of electrical and electronic components and instruments gives you a preview of the types of things you will study throughout this book.

You must be familiar with the units used in electronics and know how to express electrical quantities in various ways using metric prefixes. Scientific notation is an indispensable tool whether you use a computer, a calculator, or do computations the old-fashioned way.

■ **TECH**nology
   Theory
   Into
   Practice

Fluke 867 graphical multimeter (courtesy of John Fluke Manufacturing Co.)

■ CHAPTER OBJECTIVES

❏ Recognize some common components and measuring instruments

❏ List the electrical and magnetic quantities and their units

❏ Use scientific notation (powers of ten) to express quantities

❏ Use metric prefixes to express large and small numbers

❏ Convert from one metric unit to another

1–1 ■ ELECTRICAL COMPONENTS AND MEASURING INSTRUMENTS

In this book, you will study many types of electrical components and several instruments. A thorough background in dc and ac fundamentals provides the foundation for understanding complex electronic devices and circuits. A preview of the basic types of electrical and electronic components and instruments that you will be studying in detail later in this and in other courses is provided in this section.

After completing this section, you should be able to

■ **Recognize some common components and measuring instruments**
  • State the purpose of a resistor
  • State the purpose of a capacitor
  • State the purpose of an inductor
  • State the purpose of a transformer
  • List some basic types of electronic test and measuring instruments

Resistors

Resistors resist, or limit, electric current in a circuit. Several common types of resistors are shown in Figure 1–1 through Figure 1–4.

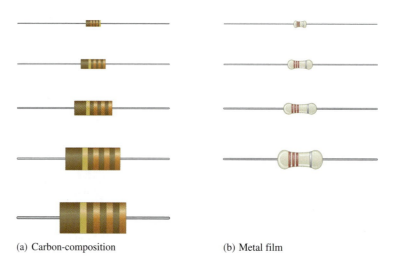

(a) Carbon-composition   (b) Metal film

FIGURE 1–1
Two common types of individual fixed resistors with axial leads.

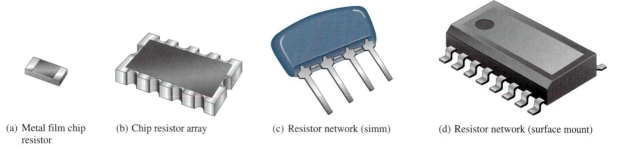

(a) Metal film chip   (b) Chip resistor array   (c) Resistor network (simm)   (d) Resistor network (surface mount)
    resistor

FIGURE 1–2
Chip resistor and resistor networks.

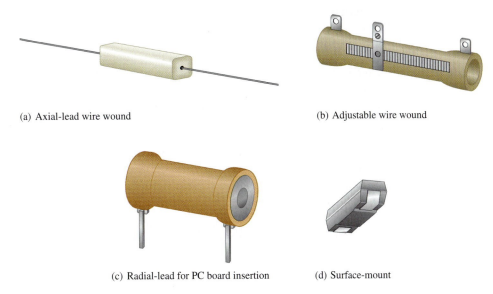

(a) Axial-lead wire wound

(b) Adjustable wire wound

(c) Radial-lead for PC board insertion

(d) Surface-mount

FIGURE 1–3
Common types of power resistors.

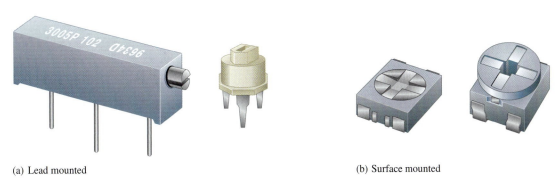

(a) Lead mounted

(b) Surface mounted

FIGURE 1–4
Common types of variable resistors.

Capacitors

Capacitors store electrical charge; they are found in most types of electronic circuits. Figure 1–5 and Figure 1–6 show several typical capacitors.

Inductors

Inductors, also known as *coils,* are used to store energy in an electromagnetic field; they serve many useful functions in an electrical circuit. Figure 1–7 on page 5 shows several typical inductors.

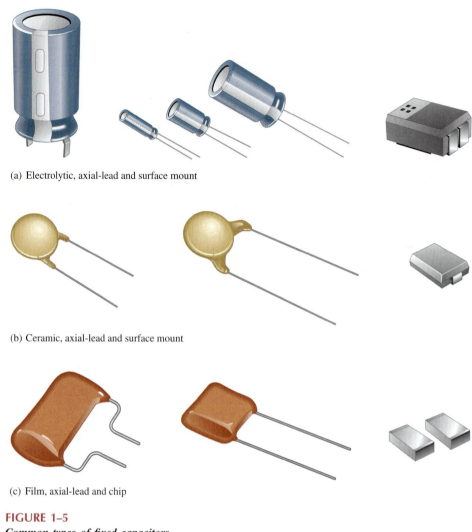

(a) Electrolytic, axial-lead and surface mount

(b) Ceramic, axial-lead and surface mount

(c) Film, axial-lead and chip

FIGURE 1–5
Common types of fixed capacitors.

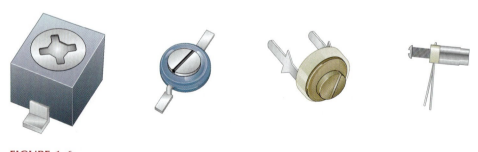

FIGURE 1–6
Typical variable capacitors.

Transformers

Transformers are used to magnetically couple ac voltages from one point in a circuit to another, or to increase or decrease the ac voltage. Several types of small transformers are shown in Figure 1–8. Utility companies use huge transformers to change voltages for high-voltage transmission lines.

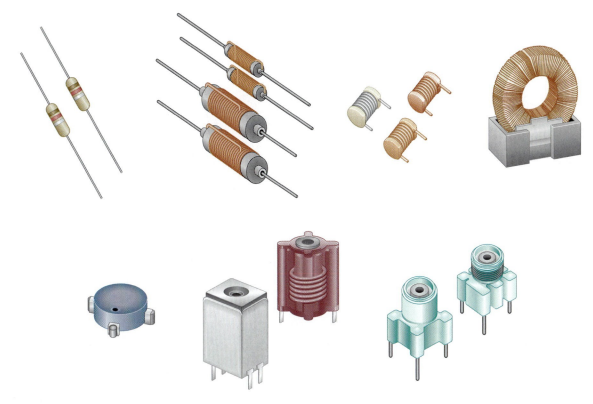

FIGURE 1–7
Some fixed and variable inductors.

FIGURE 1–8
Typical transformers.

Semiconductor Devices

Several varieties of diodes, transistors, and integrated circuits are shown in Figure 1–9.

Electronic Instruments

Figure 1–10 shows a variety of instruments that are discussed throughout the text. Typical instruments include the power supply, for providing voltage and current; the voltmeter, for measuring voltage; the ammeter, for measuring current; the ohmmeter, for measuring resistance; the wattmeter, for measuring power; and the oscilloscope for observing and measuring ac voltages. The voltmeter, ammeter, and ohmmeter are available in a single instrument called a *multimeter.*

FIGURE 1–9
*An assortment of
semiconductor devices.*

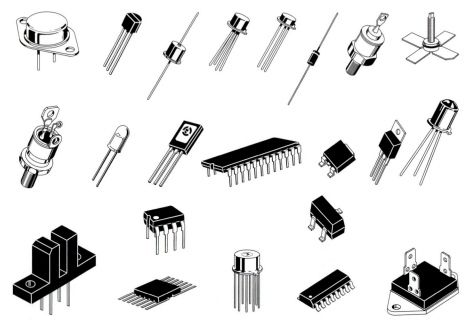

(a)

(b)

(c)

(d)

FIGURE 1–10

Typical instruments. (a) DC power supply. (b) Analog multimeter. (c) Digital multimeter (d) Digital storage oscilloscope. (Photography courtesy of B&K Precision Corp.)

SECTION 1–1 REVIEW

Answers to section reviews are found at the end of the chapter.

1. Name four types of common electrical components.
2. What instrument is used for measuring electrical current?
3. What instrument is used for measuring resistance?
4. What instrument is used for measuring voltage?
5. What is a multimeter?

1–2 ■ ELECTRICAL AND MAGNETIC UNITS

In electronics, you must deal with measurable quantities. For example, you must be able to express how many volts are measured at a certain point in a circuit, how much current there is through a wire or a component, or how much power a certain amplifier produces. In this section, you are introduced to the units and symbols for most of the electrical and magnetic quantities that are used in this book.

After completing this section, you should be able to

■ **List the electrical and magnetic quantities and their units**
  • Specify the symbol for each quantity
  • Specify the symbol for each unit

Letter symbols are used in electronics to represent both quantities and their units. One symbol is used to represent the name of the quantity, and another symbol is used to represent the unit of measurement of that quantity. For example, P stands for *power,* and W stands for *watt,* which is the unit of power. Another example is voltage. In this case, the same letter stands for both the quantity and its unit. Italic V represents voltage and nonitalic V represents the volt, which is the unit of voltage. As a rule, italic letters stand for the quantity and nonitalic letters represent the unit of that quantity.

Table 1–1 lists the most important electrical quantities, along with their SI units and symbols. The term *SI* is the French abbreviation for *International System (Système International* in French). Table 1–2 lists magnetic quantities, along with their SI units and symbols.

TABLE 1–1

Electrical quantities and units with SI symbols.

Quantity	Symbol	Unit	Symbol
capacitance	C	farad	F
charge	Q	coulomb	C
conductance	G	siemens	S
current	I	ampere	A
energy	W	joule	J
frequency	f	hertz	Hz
impedance	Z	ohm	Ω
inductance	L	henry	H
power	P	watt	W
reactance	X	ohm	Ω
resistance	R	ohm	Ω
time	t	second	s
voltage	V	volt	V

TABLE 1–2

Magnetic quantities and units with SI symbols.

Quantity	Symbol	Unit	Symbol
flux density	B	tesla	T
magnetic flux	ϕ	weber	Wb
magnetizing force	H	ampere-turns/meter	At/m
magnetomotive force	F_m	ampere-turn	At
permeability	μ	webers/ampere-turns-meter	Wb/Atm
reluctance	$\mathcal{R}$	ampere-turns/weber	At/Wb

SECTION 1–2 REVIEW

1. What does *SI* stand for?
2. Without referring to Table 1–1, list as many electrical quantities as possible, including their symbols, units, and unit symbols.
3. Without referring to Table 1–2, list as many magnetic quantities as possible, including their symbols, units, and unit symbols.

1–3 ▪ SCIENTIFIC NOTATION

In the field of electronics, you will encounter both very small and very large quantities. For example, it is common to have electric current values of only a few thousandths or even a few millionths of an ampere. On the other hand, you will find resistance values of several thousand or several million ohms. This range of values is typical of many other electrical quantities also.

After completing this section, you should be able to

▪ Use scientific notation (powers of ten) to express quantities
  • Express any number using a power of ten
  • Perform calculations with powers of ten

Scientific notation provides an easy method to express large and small numbers and to perform calculations involving such numbers. In scientific notation, a quantity is expressed as a product of a number and a power of ten. In *standard* scientific notation, the number has an absolute value between 1 and 10. For example, the quantity 150,000 would be expressed in scientific notation as 1.5×10^5.

Powers of Ten

Table 1–3 lists some powers of ten, both positive and negative, and the corresponding decimal numbers. The power of ten is expressed as an exponent of the base 10 in each case. The exponent indicates the number of places that the decimal point is moved to the right or left to produce the decimal number. If the power of ten is positive, the decimal point is moved to the right to get the equivalent decimal number. For example,

$$10^4 = 1 \times 10^4 = 1.0000. = 10,000$$

TABLE 1–3
Some positive and negative powers of ten.

$10^6 = 1,000,000$	$10^{-6} = 0.000001$
$10^5 = 100,000$	$10^{-5} = 0.00001$
$10^4 = 10,000$	$10^{-4} = 0.0001$
$10^3 = 1,000$	$10^{-3} = 0.001$
$10^2 = 100$	$10^{-2} = 0.01$
$10^1 = 10$	$10^{-1} = 0.1$
$10^0 = 1$	

If the power of ten is negative, the decimal point is moved to the left to get the equivalent decimal number. For example,

$$10^{-4} = 1 \times 10^{-4} = .0001. = 0.0001$$

EXAMPLE 1–1

Express each number in scientific notation as a number between 1 and 10 times a positive power of ten:
(a) 200   (b) 5000   (c) 85,000   (d) 3,000,000

Solution
(a) $200 = \mathbf{2 \times 10^2}$ (b) $5000 = \mathbf{5 \times 10^3}$
(c) $85,000 = \mathbf{8.5 \times 10^4}$ (d) $3,000,000 = \mathbf{3 \times 10^6}$

Related Problem* Express 4750 in scientific notation as a number between 1 and 10 times a positive power of ten.

EXAMPLE 1–2

Express each number in scientific notation as a number between 1 and 10 times a negative power of ten:
(a) 0.2   (b) 0.005   (c) 0.00063   (d) 0.000015

Solution
(a) $0.2 = \mathbf{2 \times 10^{-1}}$ (b) $0.005 = \mathbf{5 \times 10^{-3}}$
(c) $0.00063 = \mathbf{6.3 \times 10^{-4}}$ (d) $0.000015 = \mathbf{1.5 \times 10^{-5}}$

Related Problem Express 0.00738 in scientific notation as a number between 1 and 10 times a negative power of ten.

EXAMPLE 1–3

Express each of the following as a regular decimal number:
(a) 1×10^5 (b) 2×10^3 (c) 3.2×10^{-2} (d) 250×10^{-6}

Solution
(a) $1 \times 10^5 = \mathbf{100,000}$ (b) $2 \times 10^3 = \mathbf{2000}$
(c) $3.2 \times 10^{-2} = \mathbf{0.032}$ (d) $250 \times 10^{-6} = \mathbf{0.000250}$

Related Problem Express 9.12×10^3 as a regular decimal number.

---

* Answers to related problems for examples are found at the end of the chapter.

Calculations Using Powers of Ten

The advantage of scientific notation is in addition, subtraction, multiplication, and division of very small or very large numbers.

Addition The steps for adding numbers using powers of ten are as follows:

1. Express the numbers to be added in the same power of ten.
2. Add the numbers without their powers of ten to get the sum.
3. Bring down the common power of ten, which is the power of ten of the sum.

EXAMPLE 1–4 Add 2×10^6 and 5×10^7 and show the result for each step.

Solution
1. Express both numbers in the same power of ten: $(2 \times 10^6) + (50 \times 10^6)$.
2. Add $2 + 50 = 52$.
3. Bring down the common power of ten (10^6), and the sum is 52×10^6.

Related Problem Add 3.1×10^3 and 0.55×10^4.

Subtraction The steps for subtracting numbers using powers of ten are as follows:

1. Express the numbers to be subtracted in the same power of ten.
2. Subtract the numbers without their powers of ten to get the difference.
3. Bring down the common power of ten, which is the power of ten of the difference.

EXAMPLE 1–5 Subtract 25×10^{-12} from 75×10^{-11} and show the result for each step.

Solution
1. Express each number in the same power of ten: $(750 \times 10^{-12}) - (25 \times 10^{-12})$.
2. Subtract $750 - 25 = 725$.
3. Bring down the common power of ten (10^{-12}), and the difference is 725×10^{-12}.

Related Problem Subtract 98×10^{-2} from 1530×10^{-3}.

Multiplication The steps for multiplying numbers using powers of ten are as follows:

1. Multiply the numbers directly without their powers of ten.
2. Add the powers of ten algebraically (the powers do not have to be the same).

EXAMPLE 1–6 Multiply 5×10^{12} and 3×10^{-6}.

Solution Multiply the numbers, and algebraically add the powers.

$$(5 \times 10^{12})(3 \times 10^{-6}) = 15 \times 10^{12 + (-6)} = 15 \times 10^6$$

Related Problem Multiply 3.2×10^6 and 1.5×10^{-3}.

Division The steps for dividing numbers using powers of ten are as follows:

1. Divide the numbers directly without their powers of ten.
2. Subtract the power of ten in the denominator from the power of ten in the numerator (the powers do not have to be the same).

EXAMPLE 1–7

Divide 50×10^8 by 25×10^3.

Solution The division problem is written with a numerator and denominator as

$$\frac{50 \times 10^8}{25 \times 10^3}$$

Divide the numbers and subtract 3 from 8.

$$\frac{50 \times 10^8}{25 \times 10^3} = 2 \times 10^{8-3} = \mathbf{2 \times 10^5}$$

Related Problem Divide 100×10^{12} by 4×10^6.

SECTION 1–3 REVIEW

1. Scientific notation uses both positive and negative powers of ten. (T or F)
2. Express 100 as a power of ten.
3. Do the following operations:
   (a) $(1 \times 10^5) + (2 \times 10^5)$ (b) $(3 \times 10^6)(2 \times 10^4)$
   (c) $(8 \times 10^3) \div (4 \times 10^2)$ (d) $(25 \times 10^{-6}) - (130 \times 10^{-7})$

1–4 ■ METRIC PREFIXES

In electrical and electronics applications, certain powers of ten are used more often than others. It is common practice to use metric prefixes to represent these quantities. You can think of the metric prefix as a shorthand way to express a large or small number.

After completing this section, you should be able to

■ **Use metric prefixes to express large and small numbers**
  • List the metric prefixes
  • Change a power of ten to a metric prefix
  • Use a calculator for numbers with metric prefixes
  • Use engineering notation

Table 1–4 lists the metric prefix for each of the commonly used powers of ten.

Use of Metric Prefixes

Now some examples will illustrate the use of metric prefixes. The number 2000 can be expressed in scientific notation as 2×10^3. Suppose you wish to represent 2000 watts (W) with a metric prefix. Since $2000 = 2 \times 10^3$, the metric prefix *kilo* (k) is used for 10^3. So you can express 2000 W as 2 kW (2 kilowatts).

As another example, 0.015 ampere (A) can be expressed as 15×10^{-3} A. The metric prefix *milli* (m) is used for 10^{-3}. So 0.015 A becomes 15 mA (15 milliamperes).

TABLE 1–4
Commonly used metric prefixes and their symbols.

Metric Prefix	Metric Symbol	Power of Ten	Value
tera	T	10^{12}	one trillion
giga	G	10^9	one billion
mega	M	10^6	one million
kilo	k	10^3	one thousand
milli	m	10^{-3}	one-thousandth
micro	μ	10^{-6}	one-millionth
nano	n	10^{-9}	one-billionth
pico	p	10^{-12}	one-trillionth

EXAMPLE 1–8

Express each quantity using a metric prefix:
(a) 50,000 V (b) 25,000,000 Ω (c) 0.000036 A

Solution
(a) 50,000 V = 50×10^3 V = **50 kV**
(b) 25,000,000 Ω = 25×10^6 Ω = **25 MΩ**
(c) 0.000036 A = 36×10^{-6} A = **36 μA**

Related Problem Express using metric prefixes:
(a) 56,000,000 Ω (b) 0.000470 A

Entering Numbers with Metric Prefixes on a Calculator

To enter a number expressed in scientific notation on a calculator, use the EE key (the EXP key on some calculators). Example 1–9 shows how to enter numbers with metric prefixes on a TI-85 scientific calculator. Consult the user's manual for your particular calculator.

EXAMPLE 1–9

(a) Enter 3.3 kΩ (3.3×10^3 Ω) on your calculator.
(b) Enter 450 μA (450×10^{-6} A) on your calculator.

Solution
(a) Step 1: Enter ③ ⦁ ③. The display shows 3.3.
    Step 2: Press [EE]. The display shows 3.3E.
    Step 3: Enter ③. The display shows 3.3E3.
(b) Step 1: Enter ④ ⑤ ⓪. The display shows 450.
    Step 2: Press [EE]. The display shows 450E.
    Step 3: Press [(−)]. Enter ⑥. The display shows 450E−6.

Related Problem Enter 259 mA on your calculator.

Engineering Notation

Engineering notation is a term that refers to the application of powers of ten in which the powers of ten are limited to multiples of three, such as 10^3, 10^{-3}, 10^6, 10^{-6}, 10^9, 10^{-9}, 10^{12}, and 10^{-12}. The reason for this is that all units used in the fields of engineering and technology, such as ohms, amps, volts, and watts, are expressed with prefixes of k (kilo, 10^3), m (milli, 10^{-3}), M (mega, 10^6), μ (micro, 10^{-6}), G (giga, 10^9), n (nano, 10^{-9}), T (tera, 10^{12}), and p (pico, 10^{-12}).

SECTION 1–4 REVIEW

1. List the metric prefix for each of the following powers of ten: 10^6, 10^3, 10^{-3}, 10^{-6}, 10^{-9}, and 10^{-12}.
2. Use an appropriate metric prefix to express 0.000001 A.
3. Use an appropriate metric prefix to express 250,000 W.

1–5 ■ METRIC UNIT CONVERSIONS

It is often necessary or convenient to convert a quantity from one metric-prefixed unit to another, such as from milliamperes (mA) to microamperes (μA). A metric prefix conversion is accomplished by moving the decimal point in the number an appropriate number of places to the left or to the right, depending on the particular conversion.

After completing this section, you should be able to

■ **Convert from one metric unit to another**
  • Convert between milli, micro, nano, and pico
  • Convert between kilo and mega

The following basic rules apply to metric unit conversions:

1. When converting from a larger unit to a smaller unit, move the decimal point to the right.
2. When converting from a smaller unit to a larger unit, move the decimal point to the left.
3. Determine the number of places that the decimal point is moved by finding the difference in the powers of ten of the units being converted.

For example, when converting from milliamperes (mA) to microamperes (μA), move the decimal point three places to the right because there is a three-place difference between the two units (mA is 10^{-3} A and μA is 10^{-6} A). The following examples illustrate a few conversions.

EXAMPLE 1–10

Convert 0.15 milliampere (0.15 mA) to microamperes (μA).

Solution Move the decimal point three places to the right.
$$0.15 \text{ mA} = 0.15 \times 10^{-3} \text{ A} = 150 \times 10^{-6} \text{ A} = \mathbf{150 \ \mu A}$$

Related Problem Convert 1 mA to microamperes.

EXAMPLE 1–11

Convert 4500 microvolts (4500 μV) to millivolts (mV).

Solution Move the decimal point three places to the left.
$$4500 \ \mu V = 4500 \times 10^{-6} \text{ V} = 4.5 \times 10^{-3} \text{ V} = \mathbf{4.5 \ mV}$$

Related Problem Convert 1000 μV to millivolts.

EXAMPLE 1–12   Convert 5000 nanoamperes (5000 nA) to microamperes (μA).

Solution   Move the decimal point three places to the left.

$$5000 \text{ nA} = 5000 \times 10^{-9} \text{ A} = 5 \times 10^{-6} \text{ A} = \textbf{5 } \boldsymbol{\mu}\textbf{A}$$

Related Problem   Convert 893 nA to microamperes.

EXAMPLE 1–13   Convert 47,000 picofarads (47,000 pF) to microfarads (μF).

Solution   Move the decimal point six places to the left.

$$47,000 \text{ pF} = 47,000 \times 10^{-12} \text{ F} = 0.047 \times 10^{-6} \text{ F} = \textbf{0.047 } \boldsymbol{\mu}\textbf{F}$$

Related Problem   Convert 0.0022 μF to picofarads.

EXAMPLE 1–14   Convert 0.00022 microfarad (0.00022 μF) to picofarads (pF).

Solution   Move the decimal point six places to the right.

$$0.00022 \text{ } \mu\text{F} = 0.00022 \times 10^{-6} \text{ F} = 220 \times 10^{-12} \text{ F} = \textbf{220 pF}$$

Related Problem   Convert 10,000 pF to microfarads.

EXAMPLE 1–15   Convert 1800 kilohms (1800 kΩ) to megohms (MΩ).

Solution   Move the decimal point three places to the left.

$$1800 \text{ k}\Omega = 1800 \times 10^{3} \text{ } \Omega = 1.8 \times 10^{6} \text{ } \Omega = \textbf{1.8 M}\boldsymbol{\Omega}$$

Related Problem   Convert 2.2 kΩ to megohms.

When adding (or subtracting) quantities with different metric prefixes, first convert one of the quantities to the same prefix as the other as the next example shows.

EXAMPLE 1–16   Add 15 mA and 8000 μA and express the sum in milliamperes.

Solution   Convert 8000 μA to 8 mA and add.

$$15 \text{ mA} + 8000 \text{ } \mu\text{A} = 15 \times 10^{-3} \text{ A} + 8000 \times 10^{-6} \text{ A}$$
$$= 15 \times 10^{-3} \text{ A} + 8 \times 10^{-3} \text{ A} = 15 \text{ mA} + 8 \text{ mA} = \textbf{23 mA}$$

Related Problem   Add 2873 mA to 10,000 μA; express the sum in milliamperes.

SECTION 1–5 REVIEW

1. Convert 0.01 MV to kilovolts (kV).
2. Convert 250,000 pA to milliamperes (mA).
3. Add 0.05 MW and 75 kW.

**S A F E T Y
N O T E**

Safety is the first concern when working with electricity. The possibility of an electric shock is always present, so caution should always be used. Electrical current through your body resistance is what causes shock and other effects. Your body provides a current path when voltage is applied across two points of your body. For example, if one hand touches a positive voltage and the other hand touches a negative voltage or ground, there will be current from one hand to the other through your body. You can feel as little as 10 microamps of current and around 10 milliamps can be very painful. For current between 10 milliamps and 50 milliamps, there can be severe physical effects such as temporary paralysis, severe shock, and breathing difficulty—any of which could be fatal. Current above about 100 milliamps can be and usually is fatal.

■ SUMMARY

- Resistors limit electric current.
- Capacitors store electrical charge.
- Inductors (also known as coils) store energy electromagnetically.
- Transformers magnetically couple ac voltages from one point in a circuit to another.
- Semiconductor devices include diodes, transistors, and integrated circuits.
- Power supplies provide current and voltage.
- Voltmeters measure voltage.
- Ammeters measure current.
- Ohmmeters measure resistance.
- A multimeter measures voltage, current, and resistance.
- Metric prefixes are a convenient method of expressing both large and small quantities.
- In scientific notation, a quantity is expressed as a number times a power of ten.

■ SELF-TEST

Answers are found at the end of the chapter.

1. Which of the following is not an electrical quantity?
   (a) current   (b) voltage   (c) time   (d) power
2. The unit of current is
   (a) volt   (b) watt   (c) ampere   (d) joule
3. The unit of voltage is
   (a) ohm   (b) watt   (c) volt   (d) farad
4. The unit of resistance is
   (a) ampere   (b) henry   (c) hertz   (d) ohm
5. 15,000 W is the same as
   (a) 15 mW   (b) 15 kW   (c) 15 MW   (d) 15 μW
6. The quantity 4.7×10^3 is the same as
   (a) 470   (b) 4700   (c) 47,000   (d) 0.0047
7. The quantity 56×10^{-3} is the same as
   (a) 0.056   (b) 0.560   (c) 560   (d) 56,000
8. The number 3,300,000 can be expressed as
   (a) 3300×10^3 (b) 3.3×10^{-6} (c) 3.3×10^6 (d) either answer (a) or (c)
9. Ten milliamperes can be expressed as
   (a) 10 MA   (b) 10 μA   (c) 10 kA   (d) 10 mA
10. Five thousand volts can be expressed as
    (a) 5000 V   (b) 5 MV   (c) 5 kV   (d) either answer (a) or (c)
11. Twenty million ohms can be expressed as
    (a) 20 mΩ (b) 20 MW   (c) 20 MΩ (d) 20 $\mu\Omega$
12. Hertz is the unit of
    (a) power   (b) inductance   (c) frequency   (d) time

■ PROBLEMS

Answers to most odd-numbered problems are found at the end of the book.

SECTION 1–3   Scientific Notation

1. Express each of the following numbers in scientific notation as a number between 1 and 10 times a positive power of ten:
   (a) 3000   (b) 75,000   (c) 2,000,000

2. Express each number in scientific notation as a number between 1 and 10 times a negative power of ten:
   (a) 1/500   (b) 1/2000   (c) 1/5,000,000

3. Express each of the following numbers in three ways, using 10^3, 10^4, and 10^5:
   (a) 8400   (b) 99,000   (c) 0.2×10^6

4. Express each of the following numbers in three ways, using 10^{-3}, 10^{-4}, and 10^{-5}:
   (a) 0.0002   (b) 0.6   (c) 7.8×10^{-2}

5. Express each of the following in regular decimal form:
   (a) 2.5×10^{-6} (b) 50×10^2 (c) 3.9×10^{-1}

6. Express each of the following in regular decimal form:
   (a) 45×10^{-6} (b) 8×10^{-9} (c) 40×10^{-12}

7. Add the following numbers:
   (a) $(92 \times 10^6) + (3.4 \times 10^7)$ (b) $(5 \times 10^{-3}) + (85 \times 10^{-2})$
   (c) $(560 \times 10^{-8}) + (460 \times 10^{-9})$

8. Perform the following subtractions:
   (a) $(3.2 \times 10^{12}) - (1.1 \times 10^{12})$ (b) $(26 \times 10^8) - (1.3 \times 10^9)$
   (c) $(150 \times 10^{-12}) - (8 \times 10^{-11})$

9. Perform the following multiplications:
   (a) $(5 \times 10^3)(4 \times 10^5)$ (b) $(12 \times 10^{12})(3 \times 10^2)$
   (c) $(2.2 \times 10^{-9})(7 \times 10^{-6})$

10. Divide the following:
    (a) $(10 \times 10^3) \div (2.5 \times 10^2)$ (b) $(250 \times 10^{-6}) \div (50 \times 10^{-8})$
    (c) $(4.2 \times 10^8) \div (2 \times 10^{-5})$

11. Express each of the following numbers as a number having a power of ten of 10^{-6}:
    (a) 2.37×10^{-3} (b) 0.001856×10^{-2}
    (c) 5743.89×10^{-12} (d) 100×10^3

12. Perform the following indicated operations:
    (a) $(2.8 \times 10^3)(3 \times 10^2)/(2 \times 10^2)$ (b) $(46)(10^{-3})(10^5)/10^6$
    (c) $(7.35)(0.5 \times 10^{12})/[(2)(10 \times 10^{10})]$ (d) $(30)^2(5)^3/10^{-2}$

13. Perform each operation:
    (a) $(49 \times 10^6)/(4 \times 10^{-8})$ (b) $(3 \times 10^3)^2/(1.8 \times 10^3)$
    (c) $(1.5 \times 10^{-6})^2(4.7 \times 10^6)$ (d) $1/[(5 \times 10^{-3})(0.01 \times 10^{-6})]$

SECTION 1–4   Metric Prefixes

14. Express each of the following as a quantity having a metric prefix:
    (a) 31×10^{-3} A   (b) 5.5×10^3 V   (c) 200×10^{-12} F

15. Express the following using metric prefixes:
    (a) 3×10^{-6} F   (b) $3.3 \times 10^6 \, \Omega$ (c) 350×10^{-9} A

16. Express the following quantities using powers of ten:
    (a) 258 mA   (b) 0.022 μF   (c) 1200 kV

17. Express each of the following quantities as a metric unit:
    (a) 2.4×10^{-5} A   (b) $970 \times 10^4 \, \Omega$ (c) 0.003×10^{-9} W

18. Complete the following operations:
    (a) $(50 \, \mu A)(6.8 \, k\Omega) =$ _____ V   (b) 24 V/1.2 MΩ = _____ A
    (c) 12 kV/20 mA = _____ Ω

19. Complete the following operations and express the results using metric prefixes:
    (a) $(100 \, \mu A)^2(8.2 \, k\Omega) =$ _____ μW   (b) $(30 \, kV)^2/2 \, M\Omega =$ _____ W

SECTION 1–5   Metric Unit Conversions

20. Perform the indicated conversions:

(a) 5 mA to microamperes   (b) 3200 μW to milliwatts

(c) 5000 kV to megavolts   (d) 10 MW to kilowatts

21. Determine the following:

(a) The number of microamperes in 1 milliampere

(b) The number of millivolts in 0.05 kilovolt

(c) The number of megohms in 0.02 kilohm

(d) The number of kilowatts in 155 milliwatts

■ **ANSWERS TO SECTION REVIEWS**

Section 1–1

1. Common electrical components are resistors, capacitors, inductors, and transformers.

2. The ammeter measures current.

3. The ohmmeter measures resistance.

4. The voltmeter measures voltage.

5. A multimeter is an instrument that measures voltage, current, and resistance.

Section 1–2

1. SI is the abbreviation for Système International.

2. Refer to Table 1–1 after you have compiled your list of electrical quantities.

3. Refer to Table 1–2 after you have compiled your list of magnetic quantities.

Section 1–3

1. True

2. $100 = 1 \times 10^2$

3. (a) $(1 \times 10^5) + (2 \times 10^5) = 3 \times 10^5$ (b) $(3 \times 10^6)(2 \times 10^4) = 6 \times 10^{10}$

(c) $(8 \times 10^3) \div (4 \times 10^2) = 2 \times 10^1$ (d) $(25 \times 10^{-6}) - (130 \times 10^{-7}) = 12 \times 10^{-6}$

Section 1–4

1. 10^6 = mega (M), 10^3 = kilo (k), 10^{-3} = milli (m), 10^{-6} = micro (μ), 10^{-9} = nano (n), and 10^{-12} = pico (p)

2. 0.000001 A = 1 μA (one microampere)

3. 250,000 W = 250 kW (250 kilowatts)

Section 1–5

1. 0.01 MV = 10 kV   **2.** 250,000 pA = 0.00025 mA

3. 0.05 MW + 75 kW = 50 kW + 75 kW = 125 kW

■ **ANSWERS TO RELATED PROBLEMS FOR EXAMPLES**

1–1 4.75×10^3	**1–7** 25×10^6		**1–13** 2200 pF
1–2 7.38×10^{-3}	**1–8** (a) 56 MΩ	(b) 470 μA	**1–14** 0.010 μF
1–3 9120	**1–9** ⎡2⎤⎡5⎤⎡9⎤⎡EE⎤⎡(–)⎤⎡3⎤		**1–15** 0.0022 MΩ
1–4 8.6×10^3	**1–10** 1000 μA		**1–16** 2883 mA
1–5 55×10^{-2}	**1–11** 1 mV		
1–6 4.8×10^3	**1–12** 0.893 μA		

■ **ANSWERS TO SELF-TEST**

1. (c)   **2.** (c)   **3.** (c)   **4.** (d)   **5.** (b)   **6.** (b)   **7.** (a)   **8.** (d)

9. (d)   **10.** (d)   **11.** (c)   **12.** (c)

2

VOLTAGE, CURRENT, AND RESISTANCE

 Electronics Workbench (EWB) and PSpice Tutorials available at http://www.prenhall.com/floyd

■ INTRODUCTION

The useful application of electronics technology to practical situations requires that you first understand the theory on which a given application is based. Once the theory is mastered, you can learn to apply it in practice. In this chapter and throughout the rest of the book, you will learn the basics of putting technology theory into practice.

The theoretical concepts of electrical current, voltage, and resistance are introduced in this chapter. You will learn how to express each of these quantities in the proper units and how each quantity is measured. The essential elements that form a basic electric circuit and how they are put together are covered.

You will be introduced to the types of devices that generate voltage and current. In addition, you will see a variety of components that are used to introduce resistance into electric circuits. The operation of protective devices such as fuses and circuit breakers are discussed, and mechanical switches that are commonly used in electric circuits are introduced. Also, you will learn how to control and measure voltage, current, and resistance using measuring instruments.

Voltage is essential in any kind of electric circuit. Voltage is the potential energy of electrical charge required to make the circuit work. Current is also necessary for electric circuits to operate, but it takes voltage to produce the current. Current is the movement of electrons through a circuit. Resistance in a circuit limits the amount of current. A water system can be used as an analogy for a simple circuit. Voltage can be considered the pressure required to force water through the pipes. Current through wires can be thought of as the water moving through the pipes. Resistance can be thought of as the restriction on the water flow produced by adjusting a valve.

In the TECH TIP in Section 2–8, you will see how the theory presented in this chapter is applicable to a practical circuit that simulates part of your car's lighting system. Your automobile lights are examples of simple types of electric circuits. When you turn on your headlights and taillights, you are connecting the light bulbs to the battery, which provides the voltage and produces current through each bulb. The current causes the bulbs to emit light. The light bulbs themselves have resistance that limits the amount of current. The instrument panel light in most cars can be adjusted for brightness. When you make this adjustment by turning the knob, you are actually changing the resistance in the circuit, thereby causing the current to change. The amount of current through the light bulb determines its brightness.

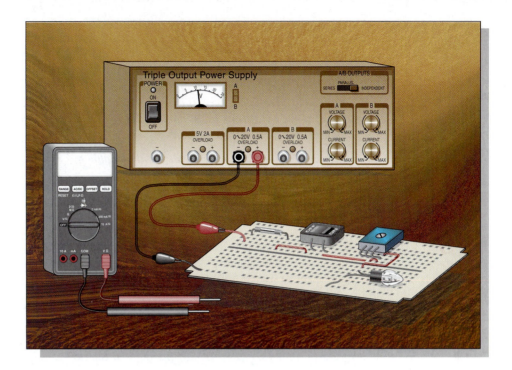

■ CHAPTER OBJECTIVES

- ❏ Discuss the basic structure of atoms
- ❏ Explain the concept of electrical charge
- ❏ Define *voltage* and discuss its characteristics
- ❏ Define *current* and discuss its characteristics

- ❏ Define *resistance* and discuss its characteristics
- ❏ Describe a basic electric circuit
- ❏ Make basic circuit measurements

HISTORICAL NOTES

André Marie Ampère
1775–1836

André Marie Ampère was born in Lyon, France, in 1775. It is claimed that he was a child prodigy who had mastered all known mathematics by age 12. He became a professor of physics and chemistry at Bourg in 1801 and was appointed professor of mathematics at the Ecole Polytechnique in 1809. In the early 1820s, Ampère developed a theory of electricity and magnetism which became fundamental for 19th century developments in the field. He was the first to build an instrument to measure charge flow (current). The unit of electrical current is named in his honor. *Photo credit: AIP Emilio Segrè Visual Archives.*

Alessandro Volta
1745–1827

Alessandro Volta was born in Como, Italy, in 1745. He was a physicist who invented a device to generate static electricity, discovered methane gas, and was appointed professor of natural philosophy at Pavia in 1778. Inspired by the work of his friend, Luigi Galvani, Volta investigated reactions between dissimilar metals and developed the first battery in 1800. Today his name is given to the unit for electrical potential, the volt. Further in his honor, electrical potential is more commonly known as voltage. *Photo credit: AIP Emilio Segrè Visual Archives, Lande Collection.*

2–1 ■ ATOMIC STRUCTURE

All matter is made of atoms; and all atoms are made of electrons, protons, and neutrons. In this section, you will learn about the structure of the atom, electron orbits and shells, valence electrons, ions, and types of materials used in electronics. Semiconductive material such as silicon or germanium is important because the configuration of certain electrons in an atom is the key factor in determining how a given material conducts electric current.

After completing this section, you should be able to

■ Describe the basic structure of atoms
  * Define *nucleus, proton, neutron,* and *electron*
  * Define *atomic number*
  * Define *shell*
  * Explain what a valence electron is
  * Describe ionization
  * Explain what a free electron is
  * Define *conductor, semiconductor,* and *insulator*

An **atom** is the smallest particle of an **element** that retains the characteristics of that element. Each of the known 109 elements has atoms that are different from the atoms of all other elements. This gives each element a unique atomic structure. According to the classic Bohr model, atoms have a planetary type of structure that consists of a central nucleus surrounded by orbiting electrons, as illustrated in Figure 2–1. The **nucleus** consists of positively charged particles called **protons** and uncharged particles called **neutrons.** The basic particles of negative charge are called **electrons.**

Each type of atom has a certain number of electrons and protons that distinguishes it from the atoms of all other elements. For example, the simplest atom is that of hydrogen, which has one proton and one electron, as pictured in Figure 2–2(a). As another example, the helium atom, shown in Figure 2–2(b), has two protons and two neutrons in the nucleus and two electrons orbiting the nucleus.

FIGURE 2–1

The Bohr model of an atom showing electrons in orbits around the nucleus. The "tails" on the electrons indicate they are moving.

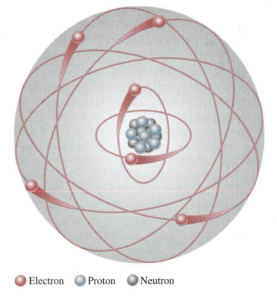

● Electron ● Proton ○ Neutron

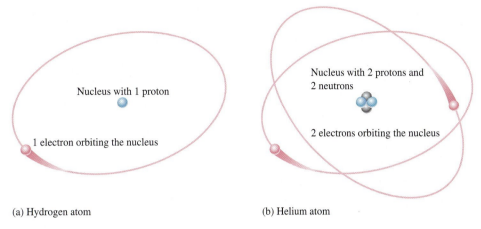

(a) Hydrogen atom   (b) Helium atom

FIGURE 2–2
The two simplest atoms, hydrogen and helium.

Atomic Number

All elements are arranged in the periodic table of the elements in order according to their **atomic number.** The atomic number equals the number of protons in the nucleus, which is the same as the number of electrons in an electrically balanced (neutral) atom. For example, hydrogen has an atomic number of 1 and helium has an atomic number of 2. In their normal (or neutral) state, all atoms of a given element have the same number of electrons as protons; the positive charges cancel the negative charges, and the atom has a net charge of zero.

Electron Shells and Orbits

Electrons orbit the nucleus of an atom at certain distances from the nucleus. Electrons near the nucleus have less energy than those in more distant orbits. It is known that only discrete (separate and distinct) values of electron energies exist within atomic structures. Therefore, electrons must orbit only at discrete distances from the nucleus.

Energy Levels   Each discrete distance (orbit) from the nucleus corresponds to a certain energy level. In an atom, the orbits are grouped into energy bands known as **shells.** A given atom has a fixed number of shells. Each shell has a fixed maximum number of electrons at permissible energy levels (orbits). The differences in energy levels within a shell are much smaller than the difference in energy between shells. The shells are designated 1, 2, 3, and so on, with 1 being closest to the nucleus. This energy band concept is illustrated in Figure 2–3, which shows the 1st shell with one energy level and the 2nd shell with two energy levels. Additional shells may exist in other types of atoms, depending on the element.

Valence Electrons

Electrons that are in orbits farther from the nucleus have higher energy and are less tightly bound to the atom than those closer to the nucleus. This is because the force of attraction between the positively charged nucleus and the negatively charged electron decreases with increasing distance from the nucleus. Electrons with the highest energy levels exist in the outermost shell of an atom and are relatively loosely bound to the atom. This outermost shell is known as the **valence** shell and electrons in this shell are called **valence electrons.** These valence electrons contribute to chemical reactions and bonding within the structure of a material and determine its electrical properties.

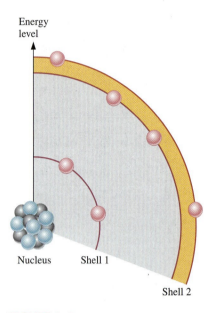

FIGURE 2–3
Energy levels increase as the distance from the nucleus increases.

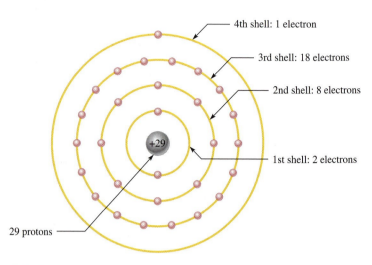

FIGURE 2–4
The copper atom.

Ionization

When an atom absorbs energy from a heat source or from light, for example, the energy levels of the electrons are raised. The valence electrons possess more energy and are more loosely bound to the atom than inner electrons, so they can easily jump to higher orbits within the valence shell when external energy is absorbed.

If a valence electron acquires a sufficient amount of energy, it can actually escape from the outer shell and the atom's influence. The departure of a valence electron leaves a previously neutral atom with an excess of positive charge (more protons than electrons). The process of losing a valence electron is known as **ionization,** and the resulting positively charged atom is called a *positive ion.* For example, the chemical symbol for hydrogen is H. When a neutral hydrogen atom loses its valence electron and becomes a positive ion, it is designated H^+. The escaped valence electron is called a **free electron.** When a free electron loses energy and falls into the outer shell of a neutral hydrogen atom, the atom becomes negatively charged (more electrons than protons) and is called a *negative ion,* designated H^-.

The Copper Atom

Because copper is the most commonly used metal in **electrical** applications, let's examine its atomic structure. The copper atom has 29 electrons that orbit the nucleus in four shells. The number of electrons in each shell follows a predictable pattern according to the formula, $2N^2$, where N is the number of the shell. The first shell of any atom can have up to 2 electrons, the second shell up to 8 electrons, the third shell up to 18 electrons, and the fourth shell up to 32 electrons.

A copper atom is represented in Figure 2–4. Notice that the fourth or outermost shell, the valence shell, has only 1 valence electron. When the valence electron in the outer shell of the copper atom gains sufficient energy from the surrounding medium, it can break away from the parent atom and become a free electron. The free electrons in the copper material are capable of moving from one atom to another in the material. In other words, they drift randomly from atom to atom within the copper. Free electrons make electric current possible.

Categories of Materials

Three categories of materials are used in electronics: conductors, semiconductors, and insulators.

Conductors **Conductors** are materials that readily allow current. They have a large number of free electrons and are characterized by one to three valence electrons in their structure. Most metals are good conductors. Silver is the best conductor, and copper is next. Copper is the most widely used conductive material because it is less expensive than silver. Copper wire is commonly used as a conductor in electric circuits.

Semiconductors **Semiconductors** are classed below the conductors in their ability to carry current because they have fewer free electrons than do conductors. Semiconductors have four valence electrons in their atomic structures. However, because of their unique characteristics, certain semiconductor materials are the basis for modern **electronic** devices such as the diode, transistor, and integrated circuit. Silicon and germanium are common semiconductive materials.

Insulators Insulating materials are poor conductors of electric current. In fact, **insulators** are used to prevent current where it is not wanted. Compared to conductive materials, insulators have very few free electrons and are characterized by more than four valence electrons in their atomic structures.

SECTION 2–1 REVIEW	**1.** What is the basic particle of negative charge?
	2. Define *atom*.
	3. What does a typical atom consist of?
	4. Define *atomic number*.
	5. Do all elements have the same types of atoms?
	6. What is a free electron?
	7. What is a shell in the atomic structure?
	8. Name two conductive materials.

2–2 ■ ELECTRICAL CHARGE

As you learned in the last section, the two types of charge are positive charge and negative charge. The electron is the smallest particle that exhibits negative electrical charge. When an excess of electrons exists in a material, there is a net negative electrical charge. When a deficiency of electrons exists, there is a net positive electrical charge.

After completing this section, you should be able to

■ **Explain the concept of electrical charge**
  • Name the unit of charge
  • Name the types of charge
  • Discuss attractive and repulsive forces
  • Determine the amount of charge on a given number of electrons

The **charge** of an electron and that of a proton are equal in magnitude. Electrical charge is symbolized by Q. Static electricity is the presence of a net positive or negative charge in a material. Everyone has experienced the effects of static electricity from time to time, for example, when attempting to touch a metal surface or another person or when the clothes in a dryer cling together.

Materials with charges of opposite polarity are attracted to each other, and materials with charges of the same polarity are repelled, as indicated in Figure 2–5. A force acts between charges, as evidenced by the attraction or repulsion. This force, called an *electric field*, consists of invisible lines of force, as shown in Figure 2–6.

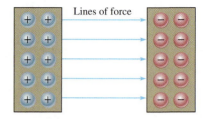

FIGURE 2–6
Electric field between oppositely charged surfaces.

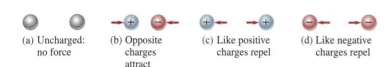

(a) Uncharged: no force

(b) Opposite charges attract

(c) Like positive charges repel

(d) Like negative charges repel

FIGURE 2–5
Attraction and repulsion of electrical charges.

Coulomb: The Unit of Charge

Electrical charge (Q) is measured in **coulombs,** abbreviated C.

One coulomb is the total charge possessed by 6.25×10^{18} electrons.

A single electron has a charge of 1.6×10^{-19} C. The unit of charge is named for Charles Coulomb (1736–1806), a French scientist. The total charge in a given number of electrons is stated in the following formula:

$$Q = \frac{\text{number of electrons}}{6.25 \times 10^{18} \text{ electrons/C}} \qquad (2\text{–}1)$$

Positive and Negative Charge

Consider a neutral atom—that is, one that has the same number of electrons and protons and thus has no net charge. If a valence electron is pulled away from the atom by the application of energy, the atom is left with a net positive charge (more protons than electrons) and becomes a positive ion. If an atom acquires an extra electron in its outer shell, it has a net negative charge and becomes a negative ion.

The amount of energy required to free a valence electron is related to the number of electrons in the outer shell. An atom can have up to eight valence electrons. The more complete the outer shell, the more stable the atom and thus the more energy is required to release an electron. Figure 2–7 illustrates the creation of a positive and a negative ion when a hydrogen atom gives up its single valence electron to a chloride atom, forming gaseous hydrogen chloride (HCl). When the gaseous HCl is dissolved in water, hydrochloric acid is formed.

EXAMPLE 2–1   How many coulombs do 93.75×10^{16} electrons represent?

Solution

$$Q = \frac{\text{number of electrons}}{6.25 \times 10^{18} \text{ electrons/C}} = \frac{93.75 \times 10^{16} \text{ electrons}}{6.25 \times 10^{18} \text{ electrons/C}} = 15 \times 10^{-2} \text{ C} = \mathbf{0.15\ C}$$

Related Problem   How many electrons does it take to have 3 C of charge?

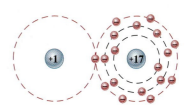

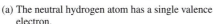

Hydrogen atom
(1 proton, 1 electron)

Chloride atom
(17 protons, 17 electrons)

(a) The neutral hydrogen atom has a single valence electron.

(b) The atoms combine by sharing the valence electron to form gaseous hydrogen chloride (HCl).

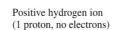

Positive hydrogen ion
(1 proton, no electrons)

Negative chloride ion
(17 protons, 18 electrons)

(c) When dissolved in water, hydrogen chloride gas separates into positive hydrogen ions and negative chloride ions. The chloride atom retains the electron given up by the hydrogen atom forming both positive and negative ions in the same solution.

FIGURE 2–7
Example of the formation of positive and negative ions.

SECTION 2–2 REVIEW	
	1. What is the symbol for charge?
	2. What is the unit of charge, and what is the unit symbol?
	3. What causes positive and negative charge?
	4. How much charge, in coulombs, is there in 10×10^{12} electrons?

2–3 ■ VOLTAGE

As you have seen, a force of attraction exists between a positive and a negative charge. A certain amount of energy must be exerted, in the form of work, to overcome the force and move the charges a given distance apart. All opposite charges possess a certain potential energy because of the separation between them. The difference in potential energy per charge is the potential difference or voltage. Voltage is the driving force in electric circuits and is what establishes current.

After completing this section, you should be able to

■ **Define** *voltage* **and discuss its characteristics**
  • State the formula for voltage
  • Name and define the unit of voltage
  • Describe basic sources of voltage

Consider a water tank that is supported several feet above the ground. A given amount of energy must be exerted in the form of work to pump water up to fill the tank. Once the water is stored in the tank, it has a certain potential energy which, if released, can be used to perform work. For example, the water can be allowed to fall down a chute to turn a water wheel.

The difference in potential energy per charge in electrical terms is called **voltage** (V) and is expressed as energy or work (W) per unit charge (Q).

$$V = \frac{W}{Q}$$ (2–2)

where W is expressed in **joules** (J) and Q is in coulombs (C).

Volt: The Unit of Voltage

The unit of voltage is the **volt,** symbolized by V.

> **One volt is the potential difference (voltage) between two points when one joule of energy is used to move one coulomb of charge from one point to the other.**

EXAMPLE 2–2   If 50 J of energy are available for every 10 C of charge, what is the voltage?

Solution $$V = \frac{W}{Q} = \frac{50 \text{ J}}{10 \text{ C}} = \textbf{5 V}$$

Related Problem   How much energy is used to move 50 C from one point to another when the voltage between the two points is 12 V?

Sources of Voltage

Batteries   A voltage **source** is a source of electrical potential energy or *electromotive force,* more commonly known as voltage. A **battery** is a type of voltage source that converts chemical energy into electrical energy. A battery consists of one or more electrochemical cells that are electrically connected. A cell consists of four basic components: a positive electrode, a negative electrode, electrolyte, and a separator. The *positive electrode* has a deficiency of electrons due to chemical reaction, the *negative electrode* has a surplus of electrons due to chemical reaction, the *electrolyte* provides a mechanism for charge flow between positive and negative electrodes, and the *separator* electrically isolates the positive and negative electrodes. A basic diagram of a battery cell is shown in Figure 2–8.

The voltage of a battery cell is determined by the materials used in it. The chemical reacton at each of the electrodes produces a fixed potential at each electrode. For

FIGURE 2–8
Diagram of a battery cell.

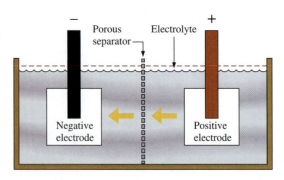

example, in a lead-acid cell, a potential of −1.685 V is produced at the positive electrode and a potential of +0.365 V is produced at the negative electrode. This means that the voltage between the two electrodes of a cell is 2.05 V, which is the standard lead-acid electrode potential. Factors such as acid concentration will affect this value to some degree so that the typical voltage of a commercial lead-acid cell is 2.15 V. The voltage of any battery cell depends on the cell chemistry. Nickel-cadmium cells are about 1.2 V and lithium cells can be as high as almost 4 V.

Although the voltage of a battery cell is fixed by its chemistry, the capacity is variable and depends on the quantity of materials in the cell. Essentially, the *capacity* of a cell is the number of electrons that can be obtained from it and is measured by the amount of current (defined in Section 2–4) that can be supplied over time.

Batteries normally consist of multiple cells that are electrically connected together internally. The way that the cells are connected and the type of cells determine the voltage and capacity of the battery. If the positive electrode of one cell is connected to the negative electrode of the next and so on, as illustrated in Figure 2–9(a), the battery voltage is the sum of the individual cell voltages. This is called a series connection. To increase battery capacity, the positive electrodes of several cells are connected together and all the negative electrodes are connected together, as illustrated in Figure 2–9(b). This is called a parallel connection. Also, by using larger cells, which have a greater quantity of material, the capacity can be increased but the voltage is not affected.

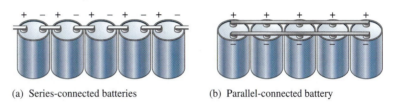

(a) Series-connected batteries   (b) Parallel-connected battery

FIGURE 2–9
Cells connected to form batteries.

Batteries are divided into two major classes, primary and secondary. Primary batteries are used once and discarded because their chemical reactions are irreversible. Secondary batteries can be recharged and reused many times because they are characterized by reversible chemical reactions. A further discussion of batteries is given in Appendix B.

Solar Cells   The operation of solar cells is based on the photovoltaic effect, which is the process whereby light energy is converted directly into electrical energy. A basic solar cell consists of two layers of different types of semiconductive materials joined together to form a junction. When one layer is exposed to light, many electrons acquire enough energy to break away from their parent atoms and cross the junction. This process forms negative ions on one side of the junction and positive ions on the other, and thus a potential difference (voltage) is developed. Figure 2–10 shows the construction of a basic solar cell.

FIGURE 2–10
Construction of a basic solar cell.

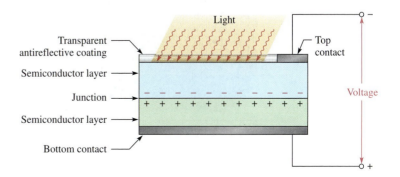

Generator Electrical **generators** convert mechanical energy into electrical energy using a principle called *electromagnetic induction* (see Chapter 10). A conductor is rotated through a magnetic field, and a voltage is produced across the conductor. A typical generator is pictured in Figure 2–11.

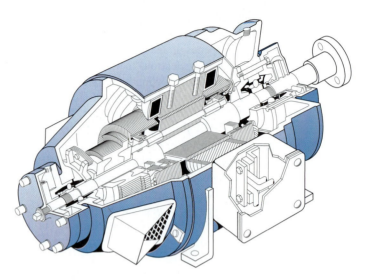

FIGURE 2–11
Cutaway view of a dc generator.

The Electronic Power Supply Electronic **power supplies** do not produce electrical energy from some other form of energy. They simply convert the ac voltage from the wall outlet to a constant (dc) voltage that is available across two terminals, as indicated in Figure 2–12(a). Typical commercial power supplies are shown in Figure 2–12(b).

FIGURE 2–12
Electronic power supplies (photography courtesy of B&K Precision Corp.).

1. Define *voltage*.

2. What is the unit of voltage?

3. How much is the voltage when there are 24 joules of energy for 10 coulombs of charge?

4. List four sources of voltage.

2–4 ■ CURRENT

Voltage provides energy to electrons which allows them to move through a circuit. This movement of electrons is the current, which results in work being done in an electric circuit.

After completing this section, you should be able to

■ **Define *current* and discuss its characteristics**

• Explain the movement of electrons

• State the formula for current

• Name and define the unit of current

As you have learned, free electrons are available in all conductive and semiconductive materials. These electrons drift randomly in all directions, from atom to atom, within the structure of the material, as indicated in Figure 2–13.

Now, if a voltage is placed across the conductive or semiconductive material, one end becomes positive and the other negative, as indicated in Figure 2–14. The repulsive force produced by the negative voltage at the left end causes the free electrons (negative charges) to move toward the right. The attractive force produced by the positive voltage at the right end pulls the free electrons to the right. The result is a net movement of the free electrons from the negative end of the material to the positive end, as shown in Figure 2–14.

The movement of these free electrons from the negative end of the material to the positive end is the electrical **current,** symbolized by *I.*

Electrical current is the rate of flow of charge.

Current in a conductive material is determined by the number of electrons (amount of charge, Q) that flow past a point in a unit of time.

$$I = \frac{Q}{t}$$

$$(2–3)$$

where I is current in amperes, Q is the charge of the electrons in coulombs, and t is the time in seconds.

Randomly drifting free electron

FIGURE 2–13
Random motion of free electrons in a material.

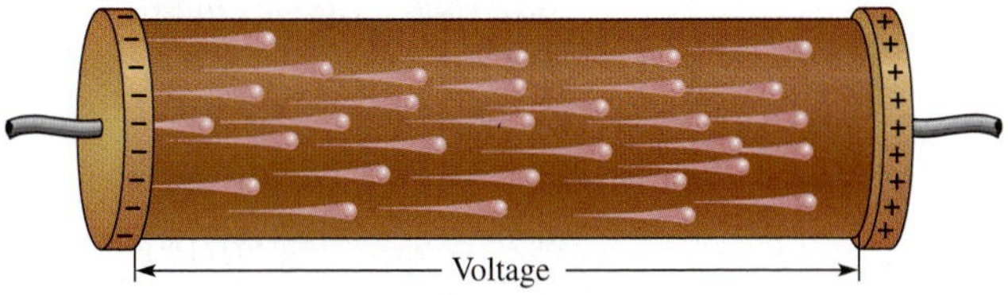

FIGURE 2–14
Electrons flow from negative to positive when a voltage is applied across a conductive or semiconductive material.

Ampere: The Unit of Current

Current is measured in a unit called the **ampere** or *amp* for short, symbolized by A.

> **One ampere (1 A) is the amount of current that exists when a number of electrons having a total charge of one coulomb (1 C) move through a given cross-sectional area in one second (1 s).**

See Figure 2–15. Remember, one coulomb is the charge carried by 6.25×10^{18} electrons.

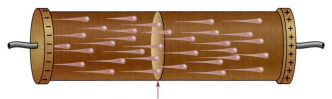

When a number of electrons having 1 coulomb of charge pass through this cross-sectional area in 1 second, there is 1 ampere of current.

FIGURE 2–15
Illustration of one ampere of current in a material (1 C/s).

EXAMPLE 2–3	Ten coulombs of charge flow past a given point in a wire in 2 s. What is the current in amperes?

Solution

$$I = \frac{Q}{t} = \frac{10\ \text{C}}{2\ \text{s}} = 5\ \text{A}$$

Related Problem
many coulombs of charge move through the filament in 1.5 s?

SECTION 2–4 REVIEW

1. Define *current* and state its unit.
2. How many electrons make up one coulomb of charge?
3. What is the current in amperes when 20 C flow past a point in a wire in 4 s?

2–5 ■ RESISTANCE

When there is current in a conductive material, the free electrons move through the material and occasionally collide with atoms. These collisions cause the electrons to lose some of their energy, and thus their movement is restricted. The more collisions, the more the flow of electrons is restricted. This restriction varies and is determined by the type of material. The property of a material that restricts the flow of electrons is called resistance.

After completing this section, you should be able to

■ Define *resistance* and discuss its characteristics
  • Name and define the unit of resistance
  • Describe basic types of resistors
  • Identify resistance by color code or labeling

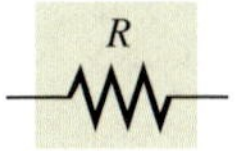

FIGURE 2–16
Resistance/resistor symbol.

Resistance is the opposition to current.

The schematic symbol for **resistance** is shown in Figure 2–16.

When there is current through any material that has resistance, heat is produced by the collisions of free electrons and atoms. Therefore, wire, which typically has a very small resistance, becomes warm when there is sufficient current through it.

Ohm: The Unit of Resistance

Resistance, *R,* is expressed in **ohms,** named after Georg Simon Ohm (1787–1854) and symbolized by the Greek letter omega (Ω).

One ohm (1 Ω) of resistance exists if there is one ampere (1 A) of current in a material when one volt (1 V) is applied across the material.

Conductance   The reciprocal of resistance is **conductance,** symbolized by *G.* It is a measure of the ease with which current is established. The formula is

$$G = \frac{1}{R} \tag{2–4}$$

The unit of conductance is the **siemens,** abbreviated S. For example, the conductance of a 22 kΩ resistor is $G = 1/22$ k$\Omega = 45.5$ μS. Occasionally, the earlier unit of mho is still used.

Resistors

Components that are specifically designed to have a certain amount of resistance are called **resistors.** The principal applications of resistors are to limit current, to divide voltage, and, in certain cases, to generate heat. Although a variety of different types of resistors come in many shapes and sizes, they can all be placed in one of two main categories: fixed or variable.

Fixed Resistors   Fixed resistors are available with a large selection of resistance values that are set during manufacturing and cannot be changed easily. They are constructed using various methods and materials. Figure 2–17 shows several common types.

One common fixed resistor is the carbon-composition type, which is made with a mixture of finely ground carbon, insulating filler, and a resin binder. The ratio of carbon to insulating filler sets the resistance value. The mixture is formed into rods, and conductive lead connections are made. The entire resistor is then encapsulated in an insulated coating for protection. Figure 2–18(a) shows the construction of a typical carbon-composition resistor.

The chip resistor is another type of fixed resistor and is in the category of SMT (surface mount technology) components. It has the advantage of a very small size for compact assemblies. Figure 2–18(b) shows the construction of a chip resistor.

Other types of fixed resistors include carbon film, metal film, and wirewound. In film resistors, a resistive material is deposited evenly onto a high-grade ceramic rod. The resistive film may be carbon (carbon film) or nickel chromium (metal film). In these types of resistors, the desired resistance value is obtained by removing part of the resistive material in a helical pattern along the rod using a spiraling technique as shown in Figure 2–19(a). Very close **tolerance** can be achieved with this method. Film resistors are also available in the form of resistor networks as shown in Figure 2–19(b).

Wirewound resistors are constructed with resistive wire wound around an insulating rod and then sealed. Normally, wirewound resistors are used in applications requiring higher power ratings.

Resistor Color Codes   Fixed resistors with value tolerances of 5%, 10%, or 20% are color coded with four bands to indicate the resistance value and the tolerance. This color-code band system is shown in Figure 2–20, and the color code is listed in Table 2–1.

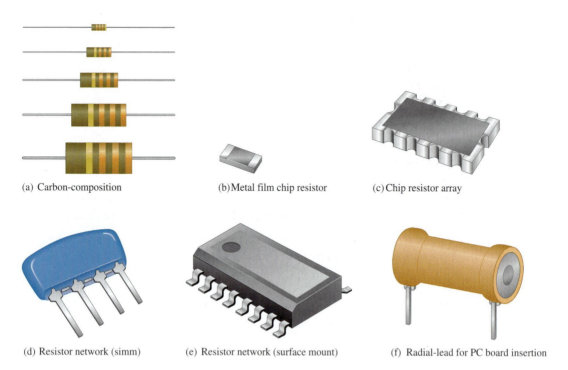

(a) Carbon-composition

(b) Metal film chip resistor

(c) Chip resistor array

(d) Resistor network (simm)

(e) Resistor network (surface mount)

(f) Radial-lead for PC board insertion

FIGURE 2–17
Typical fixed resistors.

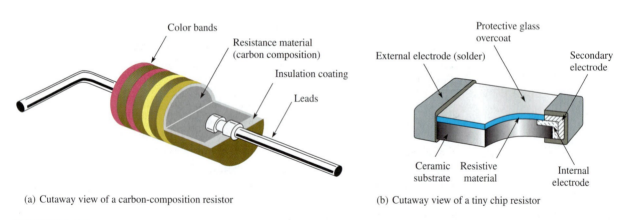

Color bands

Resistance material
(carbon composition)

Insulation coating

Leads

(a) Cutaway view of a carbon-composition resistor

Protective glass
overcoat

External electrode (solder)

Secondary
electrode

Ceramic
substrate

Resistive
material

Internal
electrode

(b) Cutaway view of a tiny chip resistor

FIGURE 2–18
Two types of fixed resistors (not to scale).

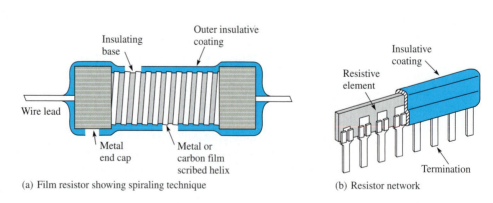

Insulating
base

Outer insulative
coating

Insulative
coating

Resistive
element

Wire lead

Metal
end cap

Metal or
carbon film
scribed helix

Termination

(a) Film resistor showing spiraling technique

(b) Resistor network

FIGURE 2–19
Construction views of typical film resistors.

FIGURE 2–20
Color-code bands on a resistor.

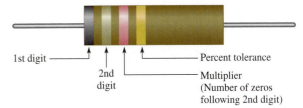

1st digit
2nd digit
Percent tolerance
Multiplier
(Number of zeros
following 2nd digit)

TABLE 2–1
Resistor color code.

	Digit	Color
Resistance value, first three bands: First band—1st digit Second band—2nd digit Third band—multipler (number of zeros following 2nd digit)	0 1 2 3 4 5 6 7 8 9	Black Brown Red Orange Yellow Green Blue Violet Gray White
Tolerance, fourth band	5% 10% 20%	Gold Silver No band

The color code is read as follows:

1. Start with the band closest to one end of the resistor. The first band is the first digit of the resistance value. If it is not clear which is the banded end, start from the end that does not begin with a gold or silver band.

2. The second band is the second digit of the resistance value.

3. The third band is the number of zeros following the second digit, or multiplier.

4. The fourth band indicates the tolerance and is usually gold or silver.

For example, a 5% tolerance means that the *actual* resistance value is within ±5% of the color-coded value. Thus, a 100 Ω resistor with a tolerance of ±5% can have acceptable values as low as 95 Ω and as high as 105 Ω.

For resistance values less than 10 Ω, the *third* band is either gold or silver. Gold represents a multiplier of 0.1, and silver represents 0.01. For example, a color code of red, violet, gold, and silver represents 2.7 Ω with a tolerance of ±10%. A table of standard resistance values is in Appendix A.

EXAMPLE 2–4

Find the resistance value in ohms and the percent tolerance for each of the color-coded resistors shown in Figure 2–21.

(a)　　　　　　　　(b)　　　　　　　　(c)

FIGURE 2–21

Solution

(a) First band is red = 2, second band is violet = 7, third band is orange = 3 zeros, fourth band is silver = 10% tolerance.

$$R = 27,000 \ \Omega \ \pm \ 10\%$$

(b) First band is brown = 1, second band is black = 0, third band is brown = 1 zero, fourth band is silver = 10% tolerance.

$$R = 100 \ \Omega \ \pm \ 10\%$$

(c) First band is green = 5, second band is blue = 6, third band is green = 5 zeros, fourth band is gold = 5% tolerance.

$$R = 5,600,000 \ \Omega \ \pm \ 5\%$$

Related Problem   A certain resistor has a yellow first band, a violet second band, a red third band, and no fourth band. Determine its value in ohms.

Certain precision resistors with tolerances of 1% or 2% are color coded with five bands. Beginning at the banded end, the first band is the first digit of the resistance value, the second band is the second digit, the third band is the third digit, the fourth band is the multiplier, and the fifth band indicates the tolerance. Table 2–1 applies, except that brown indicates 1% and red indicates 2%.

Numerical labels are often used on certain types of resistors where the resistance value and tolerance are stamped on the body of the resistor. For example, a common system uses R to designate the decimal point and letters to indicate tolerance as follows:

$$F = \pm1\%, \qquad G = \pm2\%, \qquad J = \pm5\%, \qquad K = \pm10\%, \qquad M = \pm20\%$$

For values above 100 Ω, three digits are used to indicate resistance value, followed by a fourth digit that specifies the number of zeros. For values less than 100 Ω, R indicates the decimal point.

Some examples are as follows: 6R8M is a 6.8 Ω ±20% resistor; 3301F is a 3300 Ω ±1% resistor; and 2202J is a 22,000 Ω ±5% resistor.

Resistor Reliability Band   The fifth band on some color-coded resistors indicates the resistor's reliability in percent of failures per 1000 hours of use. The fifth-band reliability color code is listed in Table 2–2. For example, a brown fifth band means that if a group of like resistors are operated under standard conditions for 1000 hours, 1% of the resistors in that group will fail.

TABLE 2–2

Fifth-band reliability color code.

Color	Failures (%) during 1000 Hours of Operation
Brown	1.0%
Red	0.1%
Orange	0.01%
Yellow	0.001%

Variable Resistors   Variable resistors are designed so that their resistance values can be changed easily with a manual or an automatic adjustment.

Two basic uses for variable resistors are to divide voltage and to control current. The variable resistor used to divide voltage is called a **potentiometer.** The variable resistor used to control current is called a **rheostat.** Schematic symbols for these types are shown in Figure 2–22. The potentiometer is a three-terminal device, as indicated in part

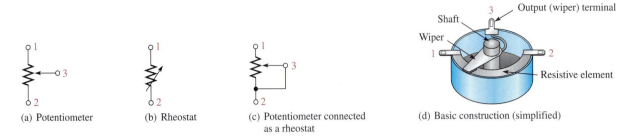

(a) Potentiometer (b) Rheostat (c) Potentiometer connected as a rheostat (d) Basic construction (simplified)

FIGURE 2–22
Potentiometer and rheostat symbols and basic construction of one type of potentiometer.

(a). Terminals 1 and 2 have a fixed resistance between them, which is the total resistance. Terminal 3 is connected to a moving contact **(wiper).** You can vary the resistance between 3 and 1 or between 3 and 2 by moving the contact up or down.

Figure 2–22(b) shows the rheostat as a two-terminal variable resistor. Part (c) shows how you can use a potentiometer as a rheostat by connecting terminal 3 to either terminal 1 or terminal 2. Parts (b) and (c) are equivalent symbols. Part (d) shows a simplified construction diagram of a potentiometer (which can also be configured as a rheostat). Some typical potentiometers are pictured in Figure 2–23.

FIGURE 2–23
Typical potentiometers and two construction views.

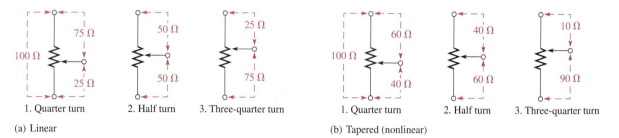

(a) Linear

(b) Tapered (nonlinear)

FIGURE 2–24

Examples of (a) linear and (b) tapered potentiometers.

Potentiometers and rheostats can be classified as linear or tapered, as shown in Figure 2–24, where a potentiometer with a total resistance of 100 Ω is used as an example. As shown in part (a), in a linear potentiometer, the resistance between either terminal and the moving contact varies linearly with the position of the moving contact. For example, one-half of the total contact movement results in one-half the total resistance. Three-quarters of the total movement results in three-quarters of the total resistance between the moving contact and one terminal, or one-quarter of the total resistance between the other terminal and the moving contact.

In the **tapered** potentiometer, the resistance varies nonlinearly with the position of the moving contact, so that one-half of a turn does not necessarily result in one-half the total resistance. This concept is illustrated in Figure 2–24(b), where the nonlinear values are arbitrary.

The potentiometer is used as a voltage-control device because when a fixed voltage is applied across the end terminals, a variable voltage is obtained at the wiper contact with respect to either end terminal. The rheostat is used as a current-control device because the current can be changed by changing the wiper position.

Two Types of Automatically Variable Resistors   A **thermistor** is a type of variable resistor that is temperature-sensitive. When its temperature coefficient is negative, the resistance changes inversely with temperature. When its temperature coefficient is positive, the resistance changes directly with temperature.

The resistance of a **photoconductive cell** changes with a change in light intensity. This cell also has a negative temperature coefficient. Symbols for both of these devices are shown in Figure 2–25.

FIGURE 2–25

Symbols for resistive devices with sensitivities to temperature and light.

(a) Thermistor

(b) Photoconductive cell

✳ **S A F E T Y   N O T E**   As stated earlier, electrical shock will result if sufficient current passes through your body. Typically, you will begin to feel pain at about 10 mA of current. In order to have current, there must be a voltage between two points on your body. It's the current, not the voltage, that causes physical pain and damage, although voltage is required to produce current. Resistance of the human body is typically between 10 kΩ and 50 kΩ and depends on the two points between which it is measured. As little as 100 volts will cause a significant shock because it will produce 10 mA of current, assuming a body resistance of 10 kΩ.

**SECTION 2–5
REVIEW**

1. Define *resistance* and name its unit.
2. What are the two main categories of resistors? Briefly explain the difference between them.
3. In the resistor color code, what does each band represent?
4. Determine the resistance and tolerance for each of the resistors in Figure 2–26.

FIGURE 2–26

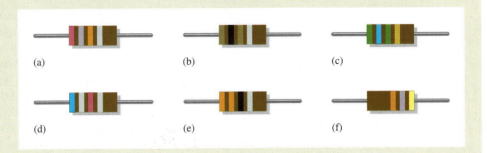

(a) (b) (c)

(d) (e) (f)

5. From the selection of resistors in Figure 2–27, select the following values: 330 Ω, 2.2 kΩ, 56 kΩ, 100 kΩ, and 39 kΩ.

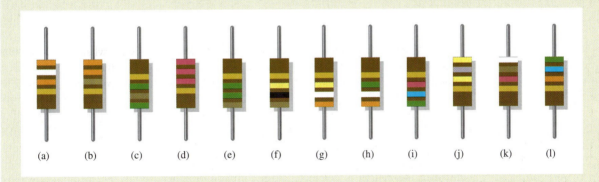

(a) (b) (c) (d) (e) (f) (g) (h) (i) (j) (k) (l)

FIGURE 2–27

6. What is the basic difference between a rheostat and a potentiometer?
7. What is a thermistor?

2–6 ■ THE ELECTRIC CIRCUIT

A basic electric circuit is an arrangement of physical components that use voltage, current, and resistance to perform some useful function.

After completing this section, you should be able to

■ **Describe a basic electric circuit**
  • Relate a schematic to a physical circuit
  • Define *open circuit* and *closed circuit*
  • Describe various types of protective devices
  • Describe various types of switches
  • Explain how wire sizes are related to gage numbers
  • Define *ground*

Direction of Current

For a few years after the discovery of electricity, people assumed all current consisted of moving positive charges. However, in the 1890s, the electron was identified as the charge carrier for current in conductive materials.

Today, there are two accepted conventions for the direction of electrical current. *Electron flow direction,* preferred by many in the fields of electrical and electronics technology, assumes for analysis purposes that current is out of the negative terminal of a voltage source, through the circuit, and into the positive terminal of the source. *Conventional current direction* assumes for analysis purposes that current is out of the positive terminal of a voltage source, through the circuit, and into the negative terminal of the source. By following the direction of conventional current, there is a rise in voltage across a source (negative to positive) and a drop in voltage across a resistor (positive to negative).

Since you cannot actually see current, only its effects, it actually makes no difference which direction of current is assumed as long as it is used *consistently.* The results of electric circuit analysis are not affected by the direction of current that is assumed for analytical purposes. The direction used for analysis is largely a matter of preference, and there are many proponents for each approach.

Electron flow direction is used widely in electronics technology and is the approach used in this book. Conventional current direction is also used in electronics technology and at the engineering level. An alternate version of this text that uses conventional current direction is also available.

The Basic Circuit

Basically, an electric **circuit** consists of a voltage source, a load, and a path for current between the source and the **load.** Figure 2–28 shows in pictorial form an example of a simple electric circuit: a battery connected to a lamp with two conductors (wires). The battery is the voltage source, the lamp is the load on the battery because it draws current from the battery, and the two wires provide the current path from the negative terminal of the battery to the lamp and back to the positive terminal of the battery. Current goes through the filament of the lamp (which has a resistance), causing it to emit visible light. Current through the battery occurs by chemical action. In many practical cases, one terminal of the battery is connected to a common or ground point. For example, in most automobiles, the negative battery terminal is connected to the metal chassis of the car. The chassis is the ground for the automobile electrical system and acts as a conductor which completes the circuit.

The Electric Circuit Schematic

An electric circuit can be represented by a **schematic** using standard symbols for each element, as shown in Figure 2–29 for the simple circuit in Figure 2–28. The purpose of a schematic is to show in an organized manner how the various components in a given circuit are interconnected so that the operation of the circuit can be determined.

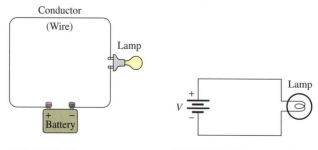

FIGURE 2–28
A simple electric circuit.

FIGURE 2–29
Schematic for the circuit in Figure 2–28.

Closed and Open Circuits

The example circuit in Figure 2–28 illustrated a **closed circuit**—that is, a circuit in which the current has a complete path. When the current path is broken, the circuit is called an **open circuit.**

Switches **Switches** are commonly used for controlling the opening or closing of circuits by either mechanical or electronic means. For example, a switch is used to turn a lamp on or off as illustrated in Figure 2–30. Each circuit pictorial is shown with its associated schematic. The type of switch indicated is a single-pole–single-throw (SPST) toggle switch.

Figure 2–31 shows a somewhat more complicated circuit using a single-pole–double-throw (SPDT) type of switch to control the current to two different lamps. When one lamp is on, the other is off, and vice versa, as illustrated by the two schematics in parts (b) and (c), which represent each of the switch positions.

The term *pole* refers to the movable arm in a switch, and the term *throw* indicates the number of contacts that are affected (either opened or closed) by a single switch action (a single movement of a pole).

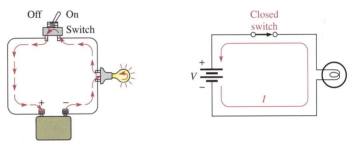

(a) There is current in a *closed* circuit (switch is ON or in the *closed* position).

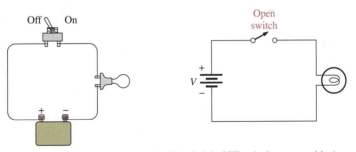

(b) There is no current in an *open* circuit (switch is OFF or in the *open* position).

FIGURE 2–30
Basic closed and open circuits using an SPST switch for control.

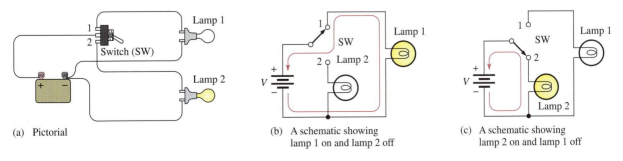

(a) Pictorial

(b) A schematic showing lamp 1 on and lamp 2 off

(c) A schematic showing lamp 2 on and lamp 1 off

FIGURE 2–31
An example of an SPDT switch controlling two lamps.

In addition to the SPST and the SPDT switches (symbols are shown in Figure 2–32(a) and (b)), the following other types are important:

- *Double-pole–single throw (DPST).* The DPST switch permits simultaneous opening or closing of two sets of contacts. The symbol is shown in Figure 2–32(c). The dashed line indicates that the contact arms are mechanically linked so that both move with a single switch action.
- *Double-pole–double-throw (DPDT).* The DPDT switch provides connection from one set of contacts to either of two other sets. The schematic symbol is shown in Figure 2–32(d).
- *Push-button (PB).* In the normally open push-button switch (NOPB), shown in Figure 2–32(e), connection is made between two contacts when the button is depressed, and connection is broken when the button is released. In the normally closed push-button switch (NCPB), shown in Figure 2–32(f), connection between the two contacts is broken when the button is depressed.
- *Rotary.* In a rotary switch, a knob is turned to make connection between one contact and any one of several others. A symbol for a simple six-position rotary switch is shown in Figure 2–32(g).

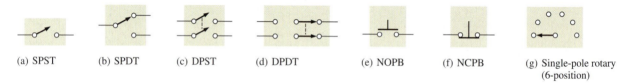

(a) SPST   (b) SPDT   (c) DPST   (d) DPDT   (e) NOPB   (f) NCPB   (g) Single-pole rotary (6-position)

FIGURE 2–32
Switch symbols.

Figure 2–33 shows several varieties of switches and Figure 2–34 shows the construction view of a typical toggle switch.

Protective Devices **Fuses** and **circuit breakers** are used to deliberately create an open circuit when the current exceeds a specified number of amperes due to a malfunction or other abnormal condition in a circuit. For example, a 20 A fuse or circuit breaker will open a circuit when the current exceeds 20 A.

The basic difference between a fuse and a circuit breaker is that when a fuse is "blown," it must be replaced; but when a circuit breaker opens, it can be reset and reused repeatedly. Both of these devices protect against damage to a circuit due to excess current or prevent a hazardous condition created by the overheating of wires and other components when the current is too great. Several typical fuses and circuit breakers, along with their schematic symbols, are shown in Figure 2–35 on page 42.

Wires

Wires are the most common form of conductive material used in electrical applications. They vary in diameter and are arranged according to standard gage numbers, called **American Wire Gage (AWG)** sizes. The larger the gage number is, the smaller the wire diameter is. The size of a wire is also specified in terms of its cross-sectional area, as illustrated in Figure 2–36. A unit of cross-sectional area used for wires is the **circular mil,** abbreviated CM. One circular mil is the area of a wire with a diameter of 0.001 inch (1 mil). You can find the cross-sectional area by expressing the diameter in thousandths of an inch (mils) and squaring it, as follows:

$$A = d^2 \tag{2–5}$$

where A is the cross-sectional area in circular mils and d is the diameter in mils. Table 2–3 on page 43 lists the AWG sizes with their corresponding cross-sectional area and resistance in ohms per 1000 ft at 20°C.

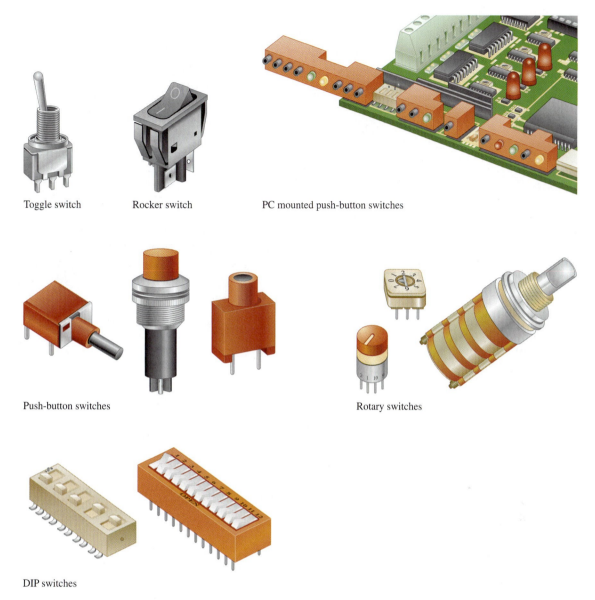

Toggle switch   Rocker switch   PC mounted push-button switches

Push-button switches   Rotary switches

DIP switches

FIGURE 2–33
Typical mechanical switches.

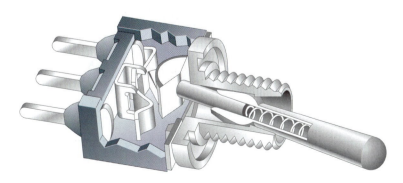

FIGURE 2–34
Construction view of a typical toggle switch.

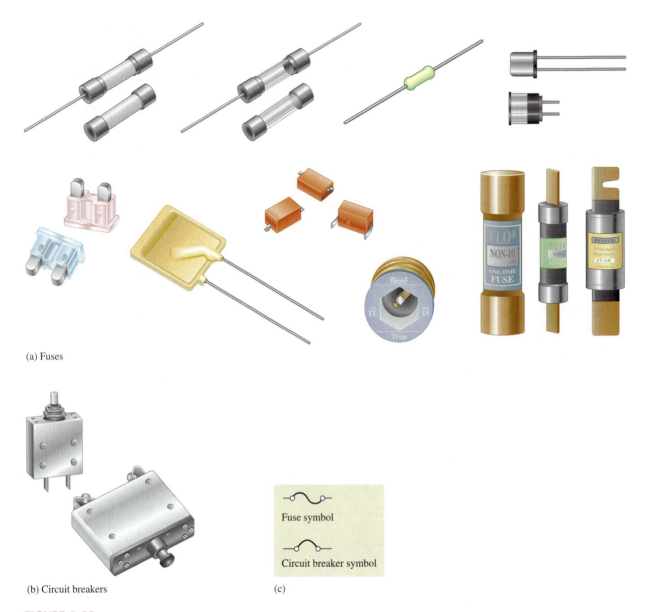

(a) Fuses

(b) Circuit breakers

(c)

Fuse symbol

Circuit breaker symbol

FIGURE 2–35
Typical fuses and circuit breakers and their symbols.

Cross-sectional area, *A*

0.001 in.

A = 1 CM

FIGURE 2–36
Cross-sectional area of a wire.

TABLE 2–3
American Wire Gage (AWG) sizes for solid round copper.

AWG #	Area (CM)	Ω/1000 ft at 20°C	AWG #	Area (CM)	Ω/1000 ft at 20°C
0000	211,600	0.0490	19	1,288.1	8.051
000	167,810	0.0618	20	1,021.5	10.15
00	133,080	0.0780	21	810.10	12.80
0	105,530	0.0983	22	642.40	16.14
1	83,694	0.1240	23	509.45	20.36
2	66,373	0.1563	24	404.01	25.67
3	52,634	0.1970	25	320.40	32.37
4	41,742	0.2485	26	254.10	40.81
5	33,102	0.3133	27	201.50	51.47
6	26,250	0.3951	28	159.79	64.90
7	20,816	0.4982	29	126.72	81.83
8	16,509	0.6282	30	100.50	103.2
9	13,094	0.7921	31	79.70	130.1
10	10,381	0.9989	32	63.21	164.1
11	8,234.0	1.260	33	50.13	206.9
12	6,529.0	1.588	34	39.75	260.9
13	5,178.4	2.003	35	31.52	329.0
14	4,106.8	2.525	36	25.00	414.8
15	3,256.7	3.184	37	19.83	523.1
16	2,582.9	4.016	38	15.72	659.6
17	2,048.2	5.064	39	12.47	831.8
18	1,624.3	6.385	40	9.89	1049.0

EXAMPLE 2–5

What is the cross-sectional area of a wire with a diameter of 0.005 inch?

Solution

$$d = 0.005 \text{ in.} = 5 \text{ mils}$$
$$A = d^2 = 5^2 = \textbf{25 CM}$$

Related Problem   What is the cross-sectional area of a 0.0015 in. diameter wire?

Wire Resistance

Although copper wire conducts electricity extremely well, it still has some resistance, as do all conductors. The resistance of a wire depends on three physical characteristics: (a) type of material, (b) length of wire, and (c) cross-sectional area. In addition, temperature can also affect the resistance.

Each type of conductive material has a characteristic called its *resistivity, ρ*. For each material, ρ is a constant value at a given temperature. The formula for the resistance of a wire of length l and cross-sectional area A is

$$R = \frac{\rho l}{A} \tag{2–6}$$

This formula shows that resistance increases with resistivity and length and decreases with cross-sectional area. For resistance to be calculated in ohms, the length must be in feet, the cross-sectional area in circular mils, and the resistivity in CM-Ω/ft.

EXAMPLE 2–6 Find the resistance of a 100 ft length of copper wire with a cross-sectional area of 810.1 CM. The resistivity of copper is 10.4 CM-Ω/ft.

Solution

$$R = \frac{\rho l}{A} = \frac{(10.4 \text{ CM-}\Omega\text{/ft})(100 \text{ ft})}{810.1 \text{ CM}} = \textbf{1.284 }\Omega$$

Related Problem What is the resistance of a 1000 ft length of copper wire that has a diameter of 0.0015 in.?

As mentioned, Table 2–3 lists the resistance of the various standard wire sizes in ohms per 1000 feet at 20°C. For example, a 1000 ft length of 14 gage copper wire has a resistance of 2.525 Ω. A 1000 ft length of 22 gage wire has a resistance of 16.14 Ω. For a given length, the smaller wire has more resistance. Thus, for a given voltage, larger wires can carry more current than smaller ones.

Ground

The term *ground* comes from the method used in ac power distribution where one side of the power line is neutralized by connecting it to a metal rod driven into the ground. This method of grounding is called *earth ground.*

In electrical and electronic systems, the metal chassis that houses the assembly or a large conductive area on a printed circuit board is used as the electrical reference point and is called *chassis ground* or *circuit ground.* Circuit ground may or may not be connected to earth ground. For example, the negative terminal of the battery and one side of all the electrical circuits in most cars are connected to the metal chassis.

Ground is the reference point in electric circuits and has a potential of 0 V with respect to other points in the circuit. All of the ground points in a circuit are electrically the same and are therefore common points. Two ground symbols are shown in Figure 2–37. The symbol in part (a) is commonly used in schematic drawings to represent a reference ground, and the one in part (b) represents a chassis ground. The one in part (a) will be used throughout this textbook.

FIGURE 2–37
Symbols for ground.

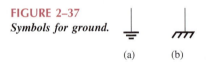

(a)   (b)

Figure 2–38 illustrates a simple circuit with ground connections. The current is from the negative terminal of the 12 V source, through the ground connection, through the lamp, and back to the positive terminal of the source. Ground provides a return path for the current back to the source because all of the ground points are electrically the same point. The voltage at the top of the circuit is +12 V with respect to ground.

FIGURE 2–38
A simple circuit with ground connections.

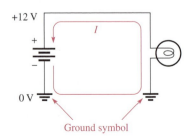

Ground symbol

1. What are the basic elements of an electric circuit?

2. What is an open circuit?

3. What is a closed circuit?

4. What is the resistance across an open switch? Ideally, what is the resistance across a closed switch?

5. What is the difference between a fuse and a circuit breaker?

6. Which wire is larger in diameter, AWG 3 or AWG 22?

7. What is ground in an electric circuit?

2–7 ■ BASIC CIRCUIT MEASUREMENTS

An electronics technician cannot function without knowing how to measure voltage, current, and resistance.

After completing this section, you should be able to

■ **Make basic circuit measurements**
  • Properly place a voltmeter in a circuit
  • Properly place an ammeter in a circuit
  • Properly connect an ohmmeter to measure resistance
  • Set up and read basic meters

Voltage, current, and resistance measurements are commonly required in electronics work. Special types of instruments are used to measure these basic electrical quantities.

The instrument used to measure voltage is a **voltmeter,** the instrument used to measure current is an **ammeter,** and the instrument used to measure resistance is an **ohmmeter.** Commonly, all three instruments are combined into a single instrument such as a **multimeter** or a VOM (volt-ohm-milliammeter), in which you can choose what specific quantity to measure by selecting the switch setting.

Figure 2–39 shows typical multimeters. Part (a) shows an analog meter with a needle pointer, and part (b) shows a digital multimeter (DMM), which provides a digital readout of the measured quantity plus graphing capability.

FIGURE 2–39
Typical portable multimeters (photography courtesy of B&K Precision Corp.).

(a)   (b)

Meter Symbols

Throughout this book, certain symbols will be used in circuits to represent meters, as shown in Figure 2–40. You may see any of four types of symbols for voltmeters, ammeters, or ohmmeters, depending on which symbol most effectively conveys the information required. We will use the bar graph meter symbol and sometimes the needle meter symbol to illustrate the operation of a circuit when *relative* measurements or changes in quantities, rather than specific values, need to be depicted. A changing quantity may be indicated by an arrow in the display showing an increase or decrease. The digital meter symbol is used when specific values are to be indicated in a circuit. The general symbol is used to indicate placement of meters in a circuit when no values or value changes need to be shown.

| (a) Bar graph | (b) Digital | (c) Needle | (d) General |

FIGURE 2–40
Examples of meter symbols used in this book. V, A, or Ω indicate voltmeter, ammeter, or ohmmeter, respectively, for each symbol.

Measuring Current with an Ammeter

Figure 2–41 illustrates how to measure current with an ammeter. Part (a) shows the simple circuit in which the current through the resistor is to be measured. First make sure the range setting of the ammeter is greater than the expected current and then connect the ammeter in

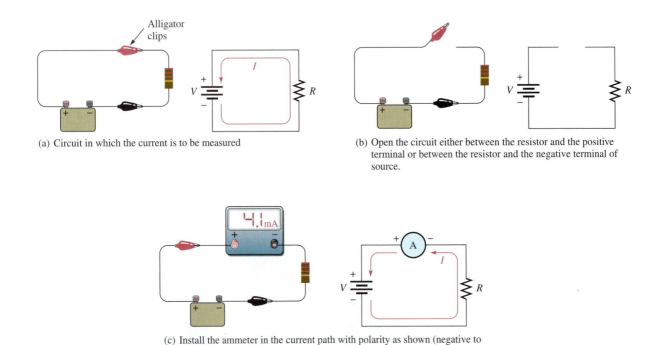

(a) Circuit in which the current is to be measured

(b) Open the circuit either between the resistor and the positive terminal or between the resistor and the negative terminal of source.

(c) Install the ammeter in the current path with polarity as shown (negative to negative, positive to positive).

FIGURE 2–41
Example of an ammeter connection in a simple circuit to measure current.

the current path by first opening the circuit, as shown in part (b). Then insert the meter as shown in part (c). Such a connection is a series connection. The polarity of the meter must be such that the current is in at the negative terminal and out at the positive terminal.

Measuring Voltage with a Voltmeter

To measure voltage, connect the voltmeter across the component for which the voltage is to be found. Such a connection is a parallel connection. The negative terminal of the meter must be connected to the negative side of the circuit, and the positive terminal of the meter must be connected to the positive side of the circuit. Figure 2–42 shows a voltmeter connected to measure the voltage across the resistor.

FIGURE 2–42

Example of a voltmeter connection in a simple circuit to measure voltage.

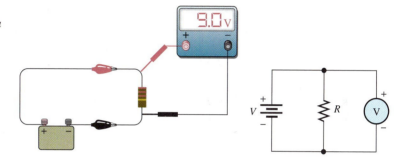

Measuring Resistance with an Ohmmeter

To measure resistance, first turn off the power and disconnect one end or both ends of the resistor from the circuit; then connect the ohmmeter across the resistor. This procedure is shown in Figure 2–43.

FIGURE 2–43

Example of using an ohmmeter to measure resistance.

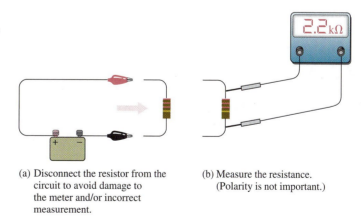

(a) Disconnect the resistor from the circuit to avoid damage to the meter and/or incorrect measurement.

(b) Measure the resistance. (Polarity is not important.)

Reading Analog Multimeters

A representation of a typical analog multimeter is shown in Figure 2–44. This particular instrument can be used to measure both direct current (dc) and alternating current (ac) quantities as well as resistance values. It has four selectable functions: dc volts (DC VOLTS), dc milliamperes (DC mA), ac volts (AC VOLTS), and OHMS. Most analog multimeters are similar to this one.

FIGURE 2–44
A typical analog multimeter.

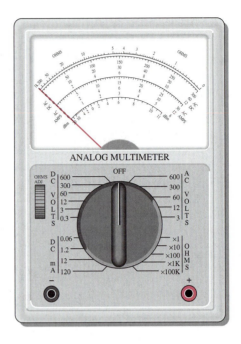

Within each function there are several ranges, as indicated by the brackets around the selector switch. For example, the DC VOLTS function has 0.3 V, 3 V, 12 V, 60 V, 300 V, and 600 V ranges. Thus, dc voltages from 0.3 V full-scale to 600 V full-scale can be measured. On the DC mA function, direct currents from 0.06 mA full-scale to 120 mA full-scale can be measured. On the ohm scale, the settings are ×1, ×10, ×100, ×1000, and ×100,000.

The Ohm Scale   Ohms are read on the top scale of the meter. This scale is nonlinear; that is, the values represented by each division (large or small) vary as you go across the scale. In Figure 2–44, notice how the scale becomes more compressed as you go from right to left.

To read the actual value in ohms, multiply the number on the scale as indicated by the pointer by the factor selected by the switch. For example, when the switch is set at ×100 and the pointer is at 20, the reading is 20 × 100 = 2000 Ω.

As another example, assume that the switch is at ×10 and the pointer is at the seventh small division between the 1 and 2 marks, indicating 17 Ω (1.7 × 10). Now, if the meter remains connected to the same resistance and the switch setting is changed to ×1, the pointer will move to the second small division between the 15 and 20 marks. This, of course, is also a 17 Ω reading, illustrating that a given resistance value can often be read at more than one range switch setting. However, the meter should be *zeroed* each time the range is changed by touching the leads together and adjusting the needle.

The AC-DC Scales   The second, third, and fourth scales from the top, labeled "AC" and "DC," are used in conjunction with the DC VOLTS, DC mA, and AC VOLTS functions. The upper ac-dc scale ends at the 300 mark and is used with the range settings that are multiples of three, such as 0.3, 3, and 300. For example, when the switch is at 3 on the DC VOLTS function, the 300 scale has a full-scale value of 3 V. At the range setting of 300, the full-scale value is 300 V, and so on.

The middle ac-dc scale ends at 60. This scale is used in conjunction with range settings that are multiples of 6, such as 0.06, 60, and 600. For example, when the switch is at 60 on the DC VOLTS function, the full-scale value is 60 V.

The lower ac-dc scale ends at 12 and is used in conjunction with switch settings that are multiples of 12, such as 1.2, 12, and 120.

EXAMPLE 2–7 In parts (a), (b), and (c) of Figure 2–45, determine the quantity that is being measured and its value.

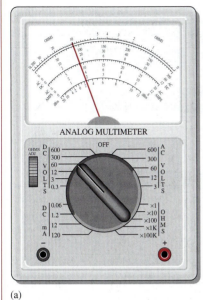

(a)

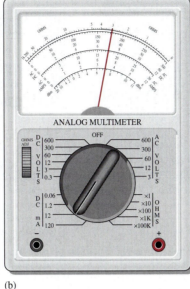

(b)

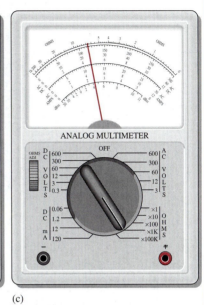

(c)

FIGURE 2–45

Solution

(a) The switch in Figure 2–45(a) is set on the DC VOLTS function and the 60 V range. The reading taken from the middle ac-dc scale is 18 V.

(b) The switch in Figure 2–45(b) is set on the DC mA function and the 12 mA range. The reading taken from the lower ac-dc scale is approximately 7.2 mA.

(c) The switch in Figure 2–45(c) is set on the OHMS function and the ×1000 range. The reading taken from the ohm scale (top scale) is approximately 7 kΩ.

Related Problem In Figure 2–42 (c) the switch is moved to the ×100 setting. Assuming that the same resistance is being measured, what will the needle do?

Digital Multimeters (DMMs)

DMMs are the most widely used type of electronic measuring instrument. Generally, DMMs provide more functions, better accuracy, greater ease of reading, and greater reliability than do many analog meters. Analog meters have at least one advantage over DMMs, however. They can track short-term variations and trends in a measured quantity that many DMMs are too slow to respond to. Figure 2–46 shows typical DMMs.

DMM Functions The basic functions found on most DMMs include the following:

■ Ohms
■ DC voltage and current
■ AC voltage and current

Some DMMs provide special functions such as transistor or diode tests, power measurement, and decibel measurement for audio amplifier tests. Some meters require manual selection of the ranges for the functions. Many meters provide automatic range selection and are called *autoranging*.

FIGURE 2–46
Typical digital multimeters (DMMs) (photography courtesy of B&K Precision Corp.).

DMM Displays　DMMs are available with either LCD (liquid-crystal display) or LED (light-emitting diode) readouts. The LCD is the most commonly used readout in battery-powered instruments because it requires only very small amounts of current. A typical battery-powered DMM with an LCD readout operates on a 9 V battery that will last from a few hundred hours to 2000 hours and more. The disadvantages of LCD readouts are that (a) they are difficult or impossible to see in low-light conditions and (b) they are relatively slow to respond to measurement changes. LEDs, on the other hand, can be seen in the dark and respond quickly to changes in measured values. LED displays require much more current than LCDs, and, therefore, battery life is shortened when they are used in portable equipment.

Both LCD and LED DMM displays are in a 7-segment format. Each digit in a display consists of seven separate segments as shown in Figure 2–47(a). Each of the ten decimal digits is formed by activation of appropriate segments, as illustrated in Figure 2–47(b). In addition to the seven segments, there is also a decimal point.

FIGURE 2–47
Seven-segment display.

(a)　　　　　　　　(b)

Resolution　The resolution of a meter is the smallest increment of a quantity that the meter can measure. The smaller the increment, the better the resolution. One factor that determines the resolution of a meter is the number of digits in the display.

Because many meters have $3\frac{1}{2}$ digits in their display, we will use this case for illustration. A $3\frac{1}{2}$-digit multimeter has three digit positions that can indicate from 0 through 9, and one digit position that can indicate only a value of 0 or 1. This latter digit, called the *half-digit,* is always the most significant digit in the display. For example, suppose that a DMM is reading 0.999 V, as shown in Figure 2–48(a). If the voltage increases by 0.001 V to 1 V, the display correctly shows 1.000 V, as shown in part (b). The "1" is the half-digit. Thus, with $3\frac{1}{2}$ digits, a variation of 0.001 V, which is the resolution, can be observed.

(a) Resolution: 0.001 V   (b) Resolution: 0.001 V   (c) Resolution: 0.001 V   (d) Resolution: 0.01 V

FIGURE 2–48
A 3½-digit DMM illustrates how the resolution changes with the number of digits in use.

Now, suppose that the voltage increases to 1.999 V. This value is indicated on the meter as shown in Figure 2–48(c). If the voltage increases by 0.001 V to 2 V, the half-digit cannot display the "2," so the display shows 2.00. The half-digit is blanked and only three digits are active, as indicated in part (d). With only three digits active, the resolution is 0.01 V rather than 0.001 V as it is with 3½ active digits. The resolution remains 0.01 V up to 19.99 V. The resolution goes to 0.1 V for readings of 20.0 V to 199.9 V. At 200 V, the resolution goes to 1 V, and so on.

The resolution capability of a DMM is also determined by the internal circuitry and the rate at which the measured quantity is sampled. DMMs with displays of 4½ through 8½ digits are also available.

Accuracy   The accuracy is the degree to which a measured value represents the true or accepted value of a quantity. The accuracy of a DMM is established strictly by its internal circuitry. For typical meters, accuracies range from 0.01% to 0.5%, with some precision laboratory-grade meters going to 0.002%.

SECTION 2–7 REVIEW

1. Name the meters for measurement of (a) current, (b) voltage, and (c) resistance.
2. Place two ammeters in the circuit of Figure 2–31 to measure the current through either lamp (be sure to observe the polarities). How can the same measurements be accomplished with only one ammeter?
3. Show how to place a voltmeter to measure the voltage across lamp 2 in Figure 2–31.
4. The multimeter in Figure 2–44 is set on the 3 V range to measure dc voltage. The pointer is at 150 on the upper ac-dc scale. What voltage is being measured?
5. How do you set up the meter in Figure 2–44 to measure 275 V dc, and on what scale do you read the voltage?
6. If you expect to measure a resistance in excess of 20 kΩ, where do you set the switch?
7. List two common types of DMM displays, and discuss the advantages and disadvantages of each.
8. Define *resolution* in a DMM.

2–8 ■ TECHnology Theory Into Practice

In this TECH TIP section, a dc voltage is applied to a circuit in order to produce current through a lamp and produce light. You will see how the current is controlled by resistance. The circuit that you will be working with simulates the instrument illumination circuit in your car, which allows you to increase or decrease the amount of light on the instruments.

The instrument panel illumination circuit in an automobile operates from the 12 V battery that is the voltage source for the circuit. The circuit uses a potentiometer connected as a rheostat, controlled by a knob on the instrument panel, which is used to set the amount of current through the lamp to back-light the instruments. The brightness of the lamp is proportional to the amount of current through the lamp. The switch used to turn the lamp on and off is the same one used for the headlights. There is a fuse for circuit protection in case of a short circuit.

Figure 2–49 shows the schematic for the illumination circuit. Figure 2–50 shows a breadboarded circuit which simulates the illumination circuit by using components that are functionally equivalent but not physically the same as those in a car. A laboratory dc power supply is used in the place of an actual automobile battery. The circuit board in Figure 2–50 is a type that is commonly used for constructing circuits on the test bench.

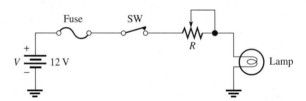

FIGURE 2–49
Basic automobile panel illumination circuit schematic.

The Test Bench

Figure 2–50 shows the breadboarded circuit, a dc power supply, and a digital multimeter. The power supply is connected to provide 12 V to the circuit. The multimeter is used to measure current, voltage, and resistance in the circuit.

■ Identify each component in the circuit and check the breadboarded circuit to make sure it is connected as the schematic in Figure 2–49 indicates.
■ Explain the purpose of each component in the circuit.

As shown in Figure 2–51, the typical circuit board consists of rows of small sockets into which component leads and wires are inserted. In this particular configuration, all five sockets in each row are connected together and are effectively one electrical point as shown in the bottom view. All sockets arranged on the outer edges of the board are typically connected together as shown.

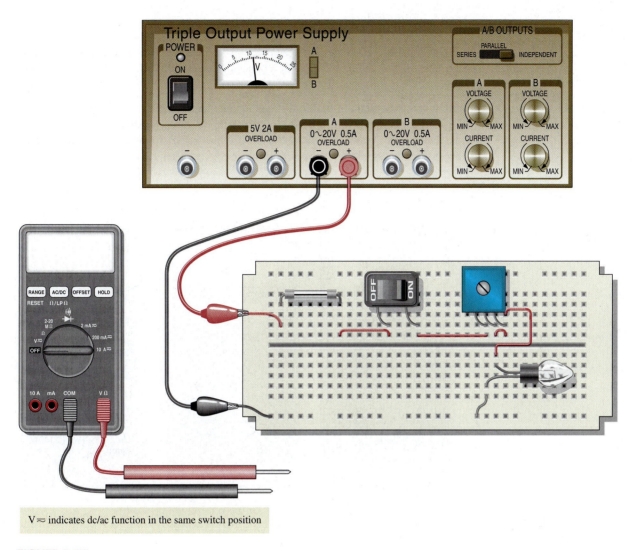

V≈ indicates dc/ac function in the same switch position

FIGURE 2–50
Test bench setup for simulating the automobile panel illumination circuit.

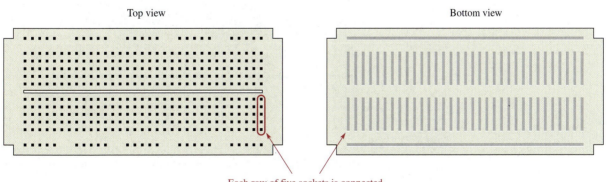

Top view   Bottom view

Each row of five sockets is connected
by a common strip on the bottom.

FIGURE 2–51
A typical circuit board used for breadboarding.

Measuring Current with the Multimeter

The meter must be set to the ammeter function to measure current. The circuit must be broken in order for the ammeter to be connected in series to measure current. Refer to Figure 2–52.

■ Redraw the schematic in Figure 2–49 to include the ammeter.
■ For which measurement (A, B, or C) is the lamp brightest? Explain.
■ List the change(s) in the circuit that can cause the ammeter reading to go from A to B.
■ List the circuit condition(s) that will produce the ammeter reading in C.

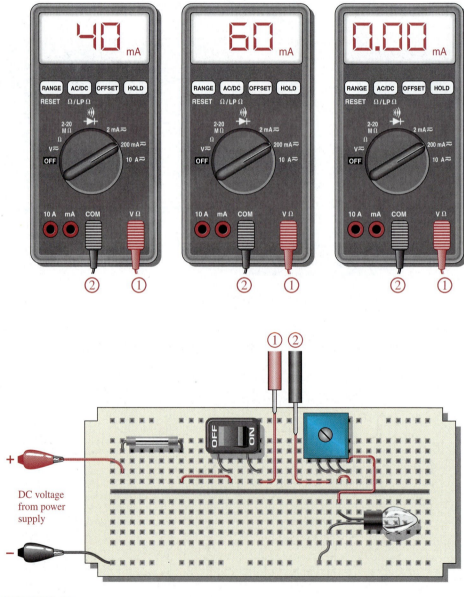

FIGURE 2–52
Current measurements. The circled numbers indicate the meter-to-circuit connections.

Measuring Voltage with the Multimeter

The meter must be set to the voltmeter function to measure voltage. The voltmeter must be connected to the two points across which the voltage is to be measured. Refer to Figure 2–53.

- Redraw the schematic in Figure 2–49 to include the voltmeter.
- Across which component is the voltage measured?
- For which measurement (A or B) is the lamp brighter? Explain.
- List the change(s) in the circuit that can cause the voltmeter reading to go from A to B.

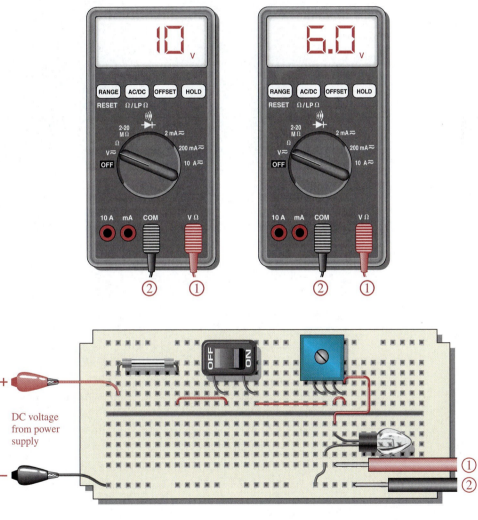

FIGURE 2–53
Voltage measurements.

Measuring Resistance with the Multimeter

The meter must be set to the ohmmeter function to measure resistance. Before the ohmmeter is connected, the resistance to be measured must be disconnected from the circuit. Before disconnecting any component, first turn the power supply off. Refer to Figure 2–54.

■ For which component is the resistance measured?
■ For which measurement (A or B) will the lamp be brighter when the circuit is reconnected and the power turned on? Explain.

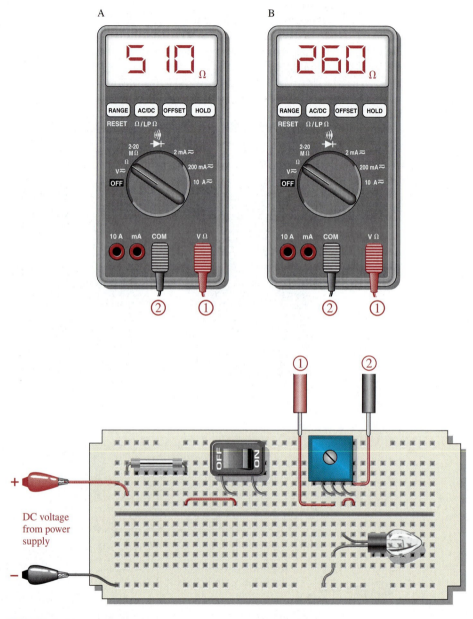

FIGURE 2–54
Resistance measurements.

**SECTION 2–8
REVIEW**

1. If the dc supply voltage in the panel illumination circuit is reduced, how is the
amount of light produced by the lamp affected? Explain.
2. Should the potentiometer be adjusted to a higher or lower resistance for the circuit
to produce more light?

■ SUMMARY

- An atom is the smallest particle of an element that retains the characteristics of that element.
- When electrons in the outer orbit of an atom (valence electrons) break away, they become free electrons.
- Free electrons make current possible.
- Like charges repel each other, and opposite charges attract each other.
- Voltage must be applied to a circuit to produce current.
- Resistance limits the current.
- Basically, an electric circuit consists of a source, a load, and a current path.
- An open circuit is one in which the current path is broken.
- A closed circuit is one which has a complete current path.
- An ammeter is connected in line with the current path.
- A voltmeter is connected across the current path.
- An ohmmeter is connected across a resistor (resistor must be removed from circuit).
- One coulomb is the charge of 6.25×10^{18} electrons.
- One volt is the potential difference (voltage) between two points when one joule of energy is used to move one coulomb from one point to the other.
- One ampere is the amount of current that exists when one coulomb of charge moves through a given cross-sectional area of a material in one second.
- One ohm is the resistance when there is one ampere of current in a material with one volt applied across the material.
- Figure 2–55 shows the electrical symbols introduced in this chapter.

FIGURE 2–55

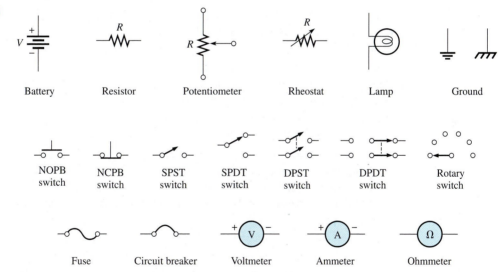

■ GLOSSARY

These terms are also in the end-of-book glossary.

American wire gage (AWG)   A standardization based on wire diameter.

Ammeter   An electrical instrument used to measure current.

Ampere (A)   The unit of electrical current.

Atom   The smallest particle of an element possessing the unique characteristics of that element.

Atomic number   The number of protons in a nucleus.

Battery   An energy source that uses a chemical reaction to convert chemical energy into electrical energy.

Charge   An electrical property of matter that exists because of an excess or a deficiency of electrons. Charge can be either positive or negative.

Circuit   An interconnection of electrical components designed to produce a desired result. A basic circuit consists of a source, a load, and an interconnecting current path.

Circuit breaker   A resettable protective device used for interrupting excessive current in an electric circuit.

Circular mil (CM)   A unit of the cross-sectional area of a wire.

Closed circuit   A circuit with a complete current path.

Conductance   The ability of a circuit to allow current. The unit is the siemens (S).

Conductor   A material in which electric current is easily established. An example is copper.

Coulomb (C)   The unit of electrical charge.

Current   The rate of flow of charge (electrons).

Electrical   Related to the use of electrical voltage and current to achieve desired results.

Electron   The basic particle of electrical charge in matter. The electron possesses negative charge.

Electronic   Related to the movement and control of free electrons in semiconductors or vacuum devices.

Element   One of the unique substances that make up the known universe. Each element is characterized by a unique atomic structure.

Free electron   A valence electron that has broken away from its parent atom and is free to move from atom to atom within the atomic structure of a material.

Fuse   A protective device that burns open when there is excessive current in a circuit.

Generator   An energy source that produces electrical signals.

Ground   The common or reference point in a circuit.

Ionization   The removal or addition of an electron from or to a neutral atom so that the resulting atom (called an ion) has a net positive or negative charge.

Insulator   A material that does not allow current under normal conditions.

Joule (J)   The unit of energy.

Load   The device in a circuit upon which work is done.

Multimeter   An instrument that measures voltage, current, and resistance.

Neutron   An atomic particle having no electrical charge.

Nucleus   The central part of an atom containing protons and neutrons.

Ohm (Ω)   The unit of resistance.

Ohmmeter   An instrument for measuring resistance.

Open circuit   A circuit in which there is not a complete current path.

Photoconductive cell   A type of variable resistor that is light-sensitive.

Potentiometer   A three-terminal variable resistor.

Power supply   An electronic instrument that produces voltage, current, and power from the ac power line or batteries in a form suitable for use in powering electronic equipment.

Proton   A positively charged atomic particle.

Resistance   Opposition to current. The unit is the ohm (Ω).

Resistor   An electrical component designed specifically to provide resistance.

Rheostat   A two-terminal variable resistor.

Schematic   A symbolized diagram of an electrical or electronic circuit.

Semiconductor   A material that has a conductance value between that of a conductor and an insulator. Silicon and germanium are examples.

Shell   An energy band in which electrons orbit the nucleus of an atom.

Siemens (S)   The unit of conductance.

Source   A device that produces electrical energy.

Switch   An electrical device for opening and closing a current path.

Tapered   Nonlinear, such as a tapered potentiometer.

Thermistor   A type of variable resistor.

Tolerance   The limits of variation in the value of a component.

Valence   Related to the outer shell or orbit of an atom.

Valence electron   An electron that is present in the outermost shell of an atom.

Volt The unit of voltage or electromotive force.

Voltage The amount of energy per charge available to move electrons from one point to another in an electric circuit.

Voltmeter An instrument used to measure voltage.

Wiper The sliding contact in a potentiometer.

■ FORMULAS

(2–1) $Q = \dfrac{\text{number of electrons}}{6.25 \times 10^{18} \text{ electrons/C}}$ Charge

(2–2) $V = \dfrac{W}{Q}$ Voltage equals energy divided by charge.

(2–3) $I = \dfrac{Q}{t}$ Current equals charge divided by time.

(2–4) $G = \dfrac{1}{R}$ Conductance is the reciprocal of resistance.

(2–5) $A = d^2$ Cross-sectional area equals the diameter squared.

(2–6) $R = \dfrac{\rho l}{A}$ Resistance is resistivity times length divided by cross-sectional area.

■ SELF-TEST

1. A neutral atom with an atomic number of three has how many electrons?

    (a) 1   **(b)** 3   **(c)** none   **(d)** depends on the type of atom

2. Electron orbits are called

    (a) shells   **(b)** nuclei   **(c)** waves   **(d)** valences

3. Materials in which there is no current when voltage is applied are called

    (a) filters   **(b)** conductors   **(c)** insulators   **(d)** semiconductors

4. When placed close together, a positively charged material and a negatively charged material will

    (a) repel   **(b)** become neutral   **(c)** attract   **(d)** exchange charges

5. The charge on a single electron is

    (a) 6.25×10^{-18} C   **(b)** 1.6×10^{-19} C   **(c)** 1.6×10^{-19} J   **(d)** 3.14×10^{-6} C

6. *Potential difference* is another term for

    (a) energy

    (b) voltage

    (c) distance of an electron from the nucleus

    (d) charge

7. The unit of energy is the

    (a) watt   **(b)** coulomb   **(c)** joule   **(d)** volt

8. Which one of the following is not a type of energy source?

    (a) battery   **(b)** solar cell   **(c)** generator   **(d)** potentiometer

9. Which one of the following is not a possible condition in an electric circuit?

    (a) voltage and no current   **(b)** current and no voltage

    (c) voltage and current   **(d)** no voltage and no current

10. Electrical current is defined as

    (a) free electrons

    (b) the rate of flow of free electrons

    (c) the energy required to move electrons

    (d) the charge on free electrons

11. There is no current in a circuit when
    (a) a switch is closed   (b) a switch is open   (c) there is no voltage
    (d) answers (a) and (c)   (e) answers (b) and (c)

12. The primary purpose of a resistor is to
    (a) increase current   (b) limit current
    (c) produce heat   (d) resist current change

13. Potentiometers and rheostats are types of
    (a) voltage sources   (b) variable resistors   (c) fixed resistors   (d) circuit breakers

14. The current in a given circuit is not to exceed 22 A. Which value of fuse is best?
    (a) 10 A   (b) 25 A   (c) 20 A   (d) a fuse is not necessary

---

■ PROBLEMS

More difficult problems are indicated by an asterisk (*).

SECTION 2–2   Electrical Charge

1. How many coulombs of charge do 50×10^{31} electrons possess?
2. How many electrons does it take to make 80 μC (microcoulombs) of charge?

SECTION 2–3   Voltage

3. Determine the voltage in each of the following cases:
    (a) 10 J/C   (b) 5 J/2 C   (c) 100 J/25 C
4. Five hundred joules of energy are used to move 100 C of charge through a resistor. What is the voltage across the resistor?
5. What is the voltage of a battery that uses 800 J of energy to move 40 C of charge through a resistor?
6. How much energy does a 12 V battery use to move 2.5 C through a circuit?
7. If a resistor with a current of 2 A through it converts 1000 J of electrical energy into heat energy in 15 s, what is the voltage across the resistor?

SECTION 2–4   Current

8. Determine the current in each of the following cases:
    (a) 75 C in 1 s   (b) 10 C in 0.5 s   (c) 5 C in 2 s
9. Six-tenths coulomb passes a point in 3 s. What is the current in amperes?
10. How long does it take 10 C to flow past a point if the current is 5 A?
11. How many coulombs pass a point in 0.1 s when the current is 1.5 A?
12. 5.74×10^{17} electrons flow through a wire in 250 ms. What is the current in amperes?

SECTION 2–5   Resistance

13. Determine the resistance values for the following:
    (a) Red, violet, orange, gold   (b) Brown, gray, red, silver
14. Find the minimum and the maximum resistance within the tolerance limits for each resistor in Problem 13.
15. Determine the color bands for each of the following values: 330 Ω, 2.2 kΩ, 56 kΩ, 100 kΩ, and 39 kΩ.
16. The adjustable contact of a linear potentiometer is set at the mechanical center of its adjustment. If the total resistance is 1000 Ω, what is the resistance between each end terminal and the adjustable contact?
17. Find the conductance for each of the following resistance values:
    (a) 5 Ω (b) 25 Ω (c) 100 Ω
18. Find the resistance corresponding to the following conductances:
    (a) 0.1 S   (b) 0.5 S   (c) 0.02 S

FIGURE 2–56

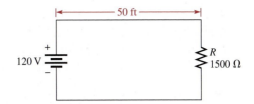

*19. A 120 V source is to be connected to a 1500 Ω resistive load by two lengths of wire as shown in Figure 2–56. The voltage source is to be located 50 ft from the load. Determine the gage number of the *smallest* wire that can be used if the *total* resistance of the two lengths of wire is not to exceed 6 Ω. Refer to Table 2–3.

20. Determine the resistance and tolerance of each resistor labeled as follows:

(a) 4R7J   (b) 5602M   (c) 1501F

SECTION 2–6   The Electric Circuit

21. Trace the current path in Figure 2–57(a) with the switch in position 2.

22. With the switch in either position, redraw the circuit in Figure 2–57(d) with a fuse connected to protect the circuit against excessive current.

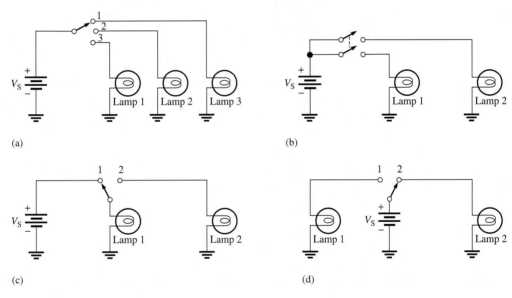

(a)   (b)

(c)   (d)

FIGURE 2–57

23. There is only one circuit in Figure 2–57 in which it is possible to have all lamps on at the same time. Determine which circuit it is.

24. Through which resistor in Figure 2–58 is there always current, regardless of the position of the switches?

FIGURE 2–58

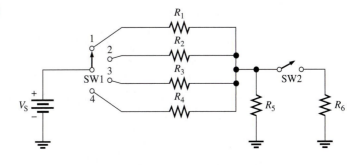

*25. Devise a switch arrangement whereby two voltage sources (V_{S1} and V_{S2}) can be connected simultaneously to either of two resistors (R_1 and R_2) as follows:

$$V_{S1} \text{ connected to } R_1 \text{ and } V_{S2} \text{ connected to } R_2$$

or $\qquad V_{S1} \text{ connected to } R_2 \text{ and } V_{S2} \text{ connected to } R_1$

26. The different sections of a stereo system are represented by the blocks in Figure 2–59. Show how a single switch can be used to connect the phonograph, the CD (compact disk) player, the tape deck, the AM tuner, or the FM tuner to the amplifier by a single knob control. Only one section can be connected to the amplifier at any time.

FIGURE 2–59

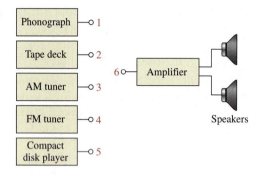

SECTION 2–7 Basic Circuit Measurements

27. Show the placement of an ammeter and a voltmeter to measure the current and the source voltage in Figure 2–60.

FIGURE 2–60

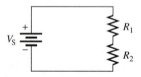

28. Explain how you would measure the resistance of R_2 in Figure 2–60.

29. In Figure 2–61, how much voltage does each meter indicate when the switch is in position 1? In position 2?

30. In Figure 2–61, indicate how to connect an ammeter to measure the current from the voltage source regardless of the switch position.

31. In Figure 2–58, show the proper placement of ammeters to measure the current through each resistor and the current out of the battery.

FIGURE 2–61

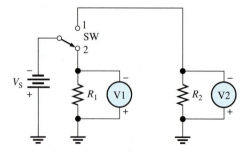

32. Show the proper placement of voltmeters to measure the voltage across each resistor in Figure 2–58.

33. What are the voltage readings in Figures 2–62(a) and 2–62(b)?

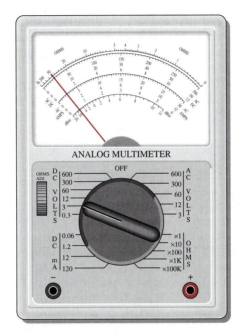
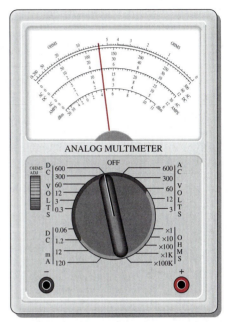

FIGURE 2–62

34. How much resistance is the ohmmeter in Figure 2–63 measuring?

FIGURE 2–63

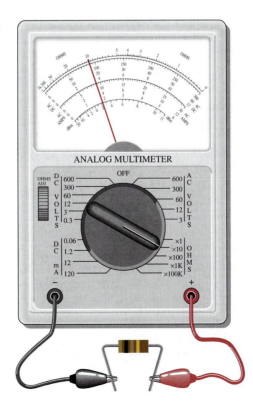

35. Determine the resistance indicated by each of the following ohmmeter readings and range settings:

   (a) pointer at 2, range setting at ×10

   (b) pointer at 15, range setting at ×100,000

   (c) pointer at 45, range setting at ×100

36. What is the maximum resolution of a 4½-digit DMM?

37. Indicate how you would connect the multimeter in Figure 2–63 to the circuit in Figure 2–64 to measure each of the following quantities. In each case indicate the appropriate function and range.

   (a) I_1 **(b)** V_1 **(c)** R_1

FIGURE 2–64

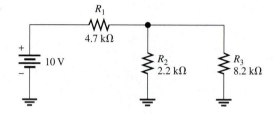

▪ **ANSWERS TO SECTION REVIEWS**

Section 2–1

1. The electron is the basic particle of negative charge.

2. An atom is the smallest particle of an element that retains the unique characteristics of the element.

3. An atom is a positively charged nucleus surrounded by orbiting electrons.

4. Atomic number is the number of protons in a nucleus.

5. No, each element has a different type of atom.

6. A free electron is an outer-shell electron that has drifted away from the parent atom.

7. Shells are energy bands in which electrons orbit the nucleus of an atom.

8. Copper and silver

Section 2–2

1. Q = charge

2. Unit of charge is the coulomb; C

3. Positive or negative charge is caused by the loss or acquisition respectively of an outer-shell (valence) electron.

4. $Q = \dfrac{10 \times 10^{12} \text{ electrons}}{6.25 \times 10^{18} \text{ electrons/C}} = 1.6 \times 10^{-6} \text{ C} = 1.6 \ \mu\text{C}$

Section 2–3

1. Voltage is energy per unit charge.

2. Volt is the unit of voltage.

3. $V = W/Q = 24 \text{ J/10 C} = 2.4 \text{ V}$

4. Battery, power supply, solar cell, and generator are voltage sources.

Section 2–4

1. Current is the rate of flow of electrons; its unit is the ampere (A).

2. electrons/coulomb = 6.25×10^{18}

3. $I = Q/t = 20 \text{ C/4 s} = 5 \text{ A}$

Section 2–5

1. Resistance is opposition to current; its unit is the ohm (Ω)
2. Two resistor categories are fixed and variable. The value of a fixed resistor cannot be changed, but that of a variable resistor can.
3. *First band:* first digit of resistance value. *Second band:* second digit of resistance value. *Third band:* multiplier (number of zeros following the second digit). *Fourth band:* % tolerance.
4. (a) $27 \text{ k}\Omega \pm 10\%$ (b) $100 \ \Omega \pm 10\%$
   (c) $5.6 \text{ M}\Omega \pm 5\%$ (d) $6.8 \text{ k}\Omega \pm 10\%$
   (e) $33 \ \Omega \pm 10\%$ (f) $47 \text{ k}\Omega \pm 20\%$
5. $330 \ \Omega$: (b), $2.2 \text{ k}\Omega$: (d), $56 \text{ k}\Omega$: (e), $100 \text{ k}\Omega$: (f), $39 \text{ k}\Omega$: (a)
6. A rheostat has two terminals; a potentiometer has three terminals.
7. A thermistor is a temperature-sensitive resistor.

Section 2–6

1. An electric circuit consists of a source, load, and current path between source and load.
2. An open circuit is one that has no path for current.
3. A closed circuit is one that has a complete path for current.
4. Infinite resistance across an open switch; zero resistance across a closed switch
5. A fuse is not resettable, a circuit breaker is.
6. AWG 3 is larger.
7. Ground is the common or reference point.

Section 2–7

1. (a) An ammeter measures current.
   (b) A voltmeter measures voltage.
   (c) An ohmmeter measures resistance.
2. See Figure 2–65.

FIGURE 2–65

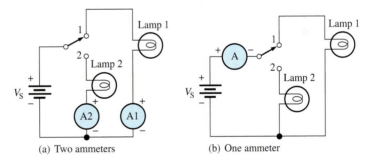

(a) Two ammeters   (b) One ammeter

3. See Figure 2–66.

FIGURE 2–66

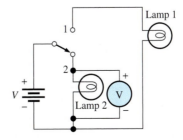

4. 1.5 V

5. Set the range switch to 600 and read on the middle ac-dc scale. The number read is multiplied by 10.

6. ×1000 range

7. Two types of DMM displays are liquid-crystal display (LCD) and light-emitting display (LED). The LCD requires little current, but it is difficult to see in low light and is slow to respond. The LED can be seen in the dark, and it responds quickly. However, it requires much more current than does the LCD.

8. Resolution is the smallest increment of a quantity that the meter can measure.

Section 2–8

1. Less voltage causes less light because the current is reduced.

2. A lower resistance will result in more light.

■ **ANSWERS TO RELATED PROBLEMS FOR EXAMPLES**

2–1 1.88×10^{19} electrons

2–2 600 J

2–3 12 C

2–4 4700 $\Omega \pm 20\%$

2–5 2.25 CM

2–6 4.62 kΩ

2–7 The needle will move left to the "70" mark.

■ **ANSWERS TO SELF-TEST**

1. (b) **2.** (a) **3.** (c) **4.** (c) **5.** (b) **6.** (b) **7.** (c) **8.** (d)

9. (b) **10.** (b) **11.** (e) **12.** (b) **13.** (b) **14.** (c)

3

OHM'S LAW

Electronics Workbench (EWB) and
PSpice Tutorials available at
http://www.prenhall.com/floyd

■ INTRODUCTION

In Chapter 2, you studied the concepts of voltage, current, and resistance. You also were introduced to a basic electric circuit. In this chapter, you will learn how voltage, current, and resistance are interrelated. You will also learn how to analyze a simple electric circuit.

Ohm's law is perhaps the single most important tool for the analysis of electric circuits. There are many other laws, theorems, and rules—some of which you can live without; however, you *must* know and be able to apply Ohm's law.

In 1826 Georg Simon Ohm found that current, voltage, and resistance are related in a specific and predictable way. Ohm expressed this relationship with a formula that is known today as Ohm's law. In this chapter, you will learn Ohm's law and how to use it in solving circuit problems. Ohm's law is one of the basic foundation elements upon which the rest of your study and work in electronics will be built.

In the TECH TIP, Section 3–6, you will see how Ohm's law is applicable to a practical circuit. Visualize the following situation: On the job, you are assigned to test a resistance box that has been constructed for use in the lab. The resistance box provides several decades of resistance (10 Ω, 100 Ω, 1.0 kΩ, etc.) that are switch selectable. This is a rush job and the resistance box is urgently needed in a product test setup. Checking out the box is simple enough. All you have to do is measure the resistance between the two terminals for each setting of the selector switch and verify that the resistance is correct. After connecting the multimeter and selecting the ohmmeter function, you discover that it is not functioning as an ohmmeter. This is the only meter in the lab that is available immediately. The boss wants this done right away, so what do you do?

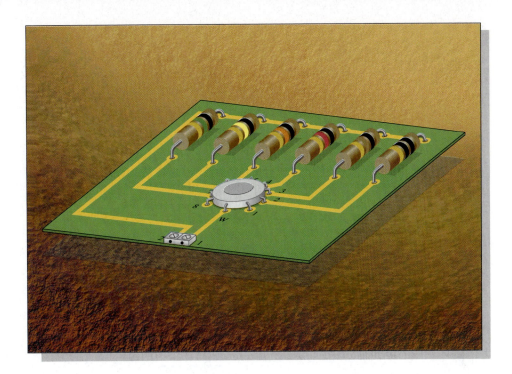

■ CHAPTER OBJECTIVES

❏ Explain Ohm's law
❏ Calculate current in a circuit
❏ Calculate voltage in a circuit

❏ Calculate resistance in a circuit
❏ Explain the proportional relationship of current, voltage, and resistance

HISTORICAL NOTE

Georg Simon Ohm
1787–1854

Georg Simon Ohm was a physicist born in Erlangen, Bavaria, in 1787. After a long struggle to gain recognition for his work in formulating the relationship of current, voltage (electromotive force), and resistance, he became a professor at Nuremburg from 1833 to 1849 and at Munich from 1849 to 1854. The mathematical relationship of the basic electrical quantities that he developed is known today as Ohm's law and the unit of resistance is the ohm (Ω). *Photo credit: Library of Congress, LC-USZ62-40943.*

3–1 ■ OHM'S LAW

Ohm's law describes mathematically how voltage, current, and resistance in a circuit are related. Ohm's law is used in three equivalent forms depending on which quantity you need to determine. In this section, you will learn each of these forms.

After completing this section, you should be able to

■ **Explain Ohm's law**
  • Describe how V, I, and R are related
  • Express I as a function of V and R
  • Express V as a function of I and R
  • Express R as a function of V and I

Ohm determined experimentally that if the voltage across a resistor is increased, the current through the resistor will also increase; and, likewise, if the voltage is decreased, the current will decrease. For example, if the voltage is doubled, the current will double. If the voltage is halved, the current will also be halved. This relationship is illustrated in Figure 3–1, with relative meter indications of voltage and current.

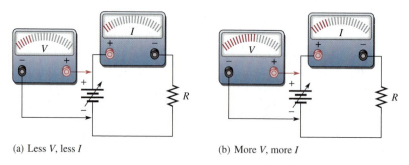

(a) Less V, less I (b) More V, more I

FIGURE 3–1
Effect on the current of changing the voltage with the resistance at a constant value.

Ohm's law also states that if the voltage is kept constant, less resistance results in more current, and, also, more resistance results in less current. For example, if the resistance is halved, the current doubles. If the resistance is doubled, the current is halved. This concept is illustrated by the meter indications in Figure 3–2, where the resistance is increased and the voltage is held constant.

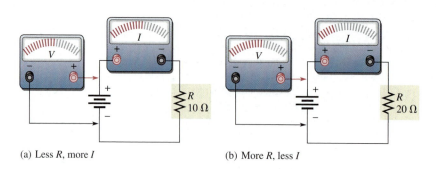

(a) Less R, more I (b) More R, less I

FIGURE 3–2
Effect on the current of changing the resistance with the voltage at a constant value.

Formula for Current

Ohm's law can be stated as follows:

$$I = \frac{V}{R}$$

(3–1)

This formula describes what was indicated by the circuits of Figures 3–1 and 3–2. For a constant value of R, if the value of V is increased, the value of I increases; if V is decreased, I decreases. Also notice in Equation (3–1) that if V is constant and R is increased, I decreases. Similarly, if V is constant and R is decreased, I increases.

Using Equation (3–1), you can calculate the current if the values of voltage and resistance are known.

Formula for Voltage

Ohm's law can also be stated another way. By multiplying both sides of Equation (3–1) by R and transposing terms, you obtain an equivalent form of Ohm's law, as follows:

$$V = IR$$

(3–2)

With this equation, you can calculate voltage if the current and resistance are known.

Formula for Resistance

There is a third equivalent way to state Ohm's law. By dividing both sides of Equation (3–2) by I and transposing terms, you obtain

$$R = \frac{V}{I}$$

(3–3)

This form of Ohm's law is used to determine resistance if voltage and current values are known.

Remember, the three formulas—Equations (3–1), (3–2) and (3–3)—are all equivalent. They are simply three different ways of expressing Ohm's law.

SECTION 3–1 REVIEW

1. Ohm's law defines how three basic quantities are related. What are these quantities?
2. Write the Ohm's law formula for current.
3. Write the Ohm's law formula for voltage.
4. Write the Ohm's law formula for resistance.
5. If the voltage across a fixed-value resistor is tripled, does the current increase or decrease, and by how much?
6. If the voltage across a fixed resistor is cut in half, how much will the current change?
7. There is a fixed voltage across a resistor, and you measure a current of 1 A. If you replace the resistor with one that has twice the resistance value, how much current will you measure?
8. In a circuit the voltage is doubled and the resistance is cut in half. Would the current increase or decrease, and if so, by how much?

3–2 ▪ CALCULATING CURRENT

In this section, you will learn to use Ohm's law to determine current values when you know the values of voltage and resistance. You will also see how to use quantities expressed with metric prefixes in circuit calculations.

After completing this section, you should be able to

▪ **Calculate current in a circuit**
- Use Ohm's law to find current when voltage and resistance are known
- Use voltage and resistance values expressed with metric prefixes

In the following examples, the formula $I = V/R$ is used. In order to get current in amperes, you must express the value of voltage in volts and the value of resistance in ohms.

EXAMPLE 3–1 How many amperes of current are in the circuit of Figure 3–3?

FIGURE 3–3

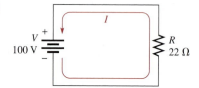

Solution Use the formula $I = V/R$, and substitute 100 V for V and 22 Ω for R.

$$I = \frac{V}{R} = \frac{100\ \text{V}}{22\ \Omega} = \textbf{4.55 A}$$

There are 4.55 A of current in this circuit.

Related Problem If R is changed to 33 Ω in Figure 3–3, what is the current?

EXAMPLE 3–2 If the resistance in Figure 3–3 is changed to 47 Ω and the voltage to 50 V, what is the new value of current?

Solution Substitute $V = 50$ V and $R = 47$ Ω into the formula $I = V/R$.

$$I = \frac{V}{R} = \frac{50\ \text{V}}{47\ \Omega} = \textbf{1.06 A}$$

Related Problem If $V = 5$ V and $R = 1000$ Ω, what is the current?

Larger Units of Resistance (kΩ and MΩ)

In electronics, resistance values of thousands of **ohms** or even millions of ohms are common. As you learned in Chapter 1, large values of resistance are indicated by the metric system prefixes *kilo* (k) and *mega* (M). Thus, thousands of ohms are expressed in kilohms (kΩ), and millions of ohms in megohms (MΩ). The following examples illustrate how to use kilohms and megohms when you calculate current.

EXAMPLE 3–3

Calculate the current in Figure 3–4.

FIGURE 3–4

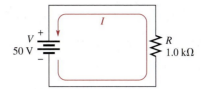

Solution   Remember that 1.0 kΩ is the same as 1×10^3 Ω. Use the formula $I = V/R$ and substitute 50 V for V and 1×10^3 Ω for R.

$$I = \frac{V}{R} = \frac{50\text{ V}}{1.0\text{ k}\Omega} = \frac{50\text{ V}}{1 \times 10^3\text{ }\Omega} = 50 \times 10^{-3}\text{ A} = \textbf{50 mA}$$

⑤ ⓪ ÷ ① EE ③ ENTER

Related Problem   Calculate the current in Figure 3–4 if R is changed to 10 kΩ.

In Example 3–3, 50×10^{-3} A is expressed as 50 milliamperes (50 mA). This can be used to advantage when you divide volts by kilohms. The current will be in milliamperes, as Example 3–4 illustrates.

EXAMPLE 3–4

How many milliamperes are in the circuit of Figure 3–5?

FIGURE 3–5

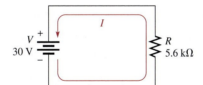

Solution   When you divide volts by kilohms, you get current in milliamperes.

$$I = \frac{V}{R} = \frac{30\text{ V}}{5.6\text{ k}\Omega} = \textbf{5.36 mA}$$

Related Problem   What is the current in milliamperes if R is changed to 2.2 kΩ?

If volts are applied when resistance values are in megohms, the current is in microamperes (μA), as Example 3–5 shows.

EXAMPLE 3–5

Determine the amount of current in the circuit of Figure 3–6.

FIGURE 3–6

Solution Recall that 4.7 MΩ equals 4.7×10^6 Ω. Substitute 25 V for V and 4.7×10^6 Ω for R.

$$I = \frac{V}{R} = \frac{25 \text{ V}}{4.7 \text{ M}\Omega} = \frac{25 \text{ V}}{4.7 \times 10^6 \text{ }\Omega} = 5.32 \times 10^{-6} \text{ A} = \textbf{5.32 }\boldsymbol{\mu}\textbf{A}$$

Related Problem What is the current if V is increased to 100 V in Figure 3–6?

EXAMPLE 3–6

Change the value of R in Figure 3–6 to 1.8 MΩ. What is the new value of current?

Solution When you divide volts by megohms, you get current in microamperes.

$$I = \frac{V}{R} = \frac{25 \text{ V}}{1.8 \text{ M}\Omega} = \textbf{13.9 }\boldsymbol{\mu}\textbf{A}$$

Related Problem If R is doubled in the circuit of Figure 3–6, what is the new value of current?

Larger Units of Voltage (kV)

Small voltages, usually less than 50 V are common in semiconductor circuits. Occasionally, however, large voltages are encountered. For example, the high-voltage supply in a television receiver is around 20,000 V (20 kilovolts, or 20 kV), and transmission voltages generated by the power companies may be as high as 345,000 V (345 kV). The following two examples illustrate how to use voltage values in the kilovolt range when you calculate current.

EXAMPLE 3–7

How much current is produced by a voltage of 24 kV across a 12 kΩ resistance?

Solution Since kilovolts are divided by kilohms, the prefixes cancel; therefore, the current is in amperes.

$$I = \frac{V}{R} = \frac{24 \text{ kV}}{12 \text{ k}\Omega} = \frac{24 \times 10^3 \text{ V}}{12 \times 10^3 \text{ }\Omega} = \textbf{2 A}$$

Related Problem What is the current in mA produced by 1 kV across a 27 kΩ resistance?

EXAMPLE 3–8

How much current is there through a 100 MΩ resistor when 50 kV are applied?

Solution In this case, divide 50 kV by 100 MΩ to get the current. Substitute 50×10^3 V for 50 kV and 100×10^6 Ω for 100 MΩ.

$$I = \frac{V}{R} = \frac{50 \text{ kV}}{100 \text{ M}\Omega} = \frac{50 \times 10^3 \text{ V}}{100 \times 10^6 \text{ }\Omega} = 0.5 \times 10^{-3} \text{ A} = \textbf{0.5 mA}$$

Remember that the power of ten in the denominator is subtracted from the power of ten in the numerator. So 50 was divided by 100, giving 0.5, and 6 was subtracted from 3, giving 10^{-3}.

[5][0][EE][3][÷][1][0][0][EE][6][ENTER]

Related Problem How much current is there through a 6.8 MΩ resistor when 10 kV are applied?

SECTION 3–2
REVIEW

In Problems 1–4, calculate I.

1. $V = 10$ V and $R = 5.6\ \Omega$.

2. $V = 100$ V and $R = 560\ \Omega$.

3. $V = 5$ V and $R = 2.2$ kΩ.

4. $V = 15$ V and $R = 4.7$ MΩ.

5. If a 4.7 MΩ resistor has 20 kV across it, how much current is there?

6. How much current will 10 kV across 2.2 kΩ produce?

3–3 ■ CALCULATING VOLTAGE

In this section, you will learn to use Ohm's law to determine voltage values when you know the values of current and resistance. You will also see how to use quantities expressed with metric prefixes in circuit calculations. After completing this section, you should be able to

■ **Calculate voltage in a circuit**
  • Use Ohm's law to find voltage when current and resistance are known
  • Use current and resistance values expressed with metric prefixes

In the following examples, the formula $V = IR$ is used. To obtain voltage in volts, you must express the value of I in amperes and the value of R in ohms.

EXAMPLE 3–9

In the circuit of Figure 3–7, how much voltage is needed to produce 5 A of current?

FIGURE 3–7

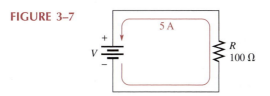

Solution Substitute 5 A for I and 100 Ω for R into the formula $V = IR$.

$$V = IR = (5\text{ A})(100\ \Omega) = \textbf{500 V}$$

Thus, 500 V are required to produce 5 A of current through a 100 Ω resistor.

Related Problem In Figure 3–7, how much voltage is required to produce 12 A of current?

Smaller Units of Current (mA and μA)

The following two examples illustrate how to use current values in the milliampere (mA) and microampere (μA) ranges when you calculate voltage.

EXAMPLE 3–10   How much voltage will be measured across the resistor in Figure 3–8?

FIGURE 3–8

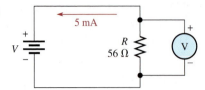

Solution   Five milliamperes equals 5×10^{-3} A. Substitute the values for I and R into the formula $V = IR$.

$$V = IR = (5 \text{ mA})(56 \text{ } \Omega) = (5 \times 10^{-3} \text{ A})(56 \text{ } \Omega) = 280 \times 10^{-3} \text{ V} = \textbf{280 mV}$$

When milliamperes are multiplied by ohms, you get millivolts.

Related Problem   How much voltage is measured across R if $R = 33 \text{ } \Omega$ and $I = 1.5$ mA in Figure 3–8?

EXAMPLE 3–11   Suppose that there is a current of 8 μA through a 10 Ω resistor. How much voltage is across the resistor?

Solution   Eight microamperes equals 8×10^{-6} A. Substitute the values for I and R into the formula $V = IR$.

$$V = IR = (8 \text{ } \mu\text{A})(10 \text{ } \Omega) = (8 \times 10^{-6} \text{ A})(10 \text{ } \Omega) = 80 \times 10^{-6} \text{ V} = \textbf{80 } \boldsymbol{\mu}\textbf{V}$$

When microamperes are multiplied by ohms, you get microvolts.

Related Problem   If there are 3.2 μA through a 47 Ω resistor, what is the voltage across the resistor?

These examples have shown that when you multiply milliamperes and ohms, you get millivolts. When you multiply microamperes and ohms, you get microvolts.

Larger Units of Resistance (kΩ and MΩ)

The following two examples illustrate how to use resistance values in the kilohm (kΩ) and megohm (MΩ) ranges when you calculate voltage.

EXAMPLE 3–12   The circuit in Figure 3–9 has a current of 10 mA. What is the voltage?

FIGURE 3–9

Solution   Ten milliamperes equals 10×10^{-3} A and 3.3 kΩ equals 3.3×10^3 Ω. Substitute these values into the formula $V = IR$.

$$V = IR = (10 \text{ mA})(3.3 \text{ k}\Omega) = (10 \times 10^{-3} \text{ A})(3.3 \times 10^3 \text{ } \Omega) = \textbf{33 V}$$

Notice that 10^{-3} and 10^3 cancel. Therefore, milliamperes cancel kilohms when multiplied, and the result is volts.

$$\boxed{1}\,\boxed{0}\,\boxed{\text{EE}}\,\boxed{(-)}\,\boxed{3}\,\boxed{\times}\,\boxed{3}\,\boxed{\cdot}\,\boxed{3}\,\boxed{\text{EE}}\,\boxed{3}\,\boxed{\text{ENTER}}$$

Related Problem   If the current in Figure 3–9 is 25 mA, what is the voltage?

EXAMPLE 3–13

If there is a current of 50 μA through a 4.7 MΩ resistor, what is the voltage?

Solution   Fifty microamperes equals 50×10^{-6} A and 4.7 MΩ is 4.7×10^6 Ω. Substitute these values into the formula $V = IR$.

$$V = IR = (50\ \mu\text{A})(4.7\ \text{M}\Omega) = (50 \times 10^{-6}\ \text{A})(4.7 \times 10^6\ \Omega) = \textbf{235 V}$$

Notice that 10^{-6} and 10^6 cancel. Therefore, microamperes cancel megohms when multiplied, and the result is volts.

Related Problem   If there are 450 μA through a 3.9 MΩ resistor, what is the voltage?

SECTION 3–3 REVIEW

In Problems 1–7, calculate V.

1. $I = 1$ A and $R = 10$ Ω.
2. $I = 8$ A and $R = 470$ Ω.
3. $I = 3$ mA and $R = 100$ Ω.
4. $I = 25$ μA and $R = 56$ Ω.
5. $I = 2$ mA and $R = 1.8$ kΩ.
6. $I = 5$ mA and $R = 100$ MΩ.
7. $I = 10$ μA and $R = 2.2$ MΩ.
8. How much voltage is required to produce 100 mA through 4.7 kΩ?
9. What voltage do you need to cause 3 mA of current in a 3.3 kΩ resistance?
10. A battery produces 2 A of current into a 6.8 Ω resistive load. What is the battery voltage?

3–4 ▪ CALCULATING RESISTANCE

In this section, you will learn to use Ohm's law to determine resistance values when you know the values of current and voltage. You will also see how to use quantities expressed with metric prefixes in circuit calculations.

After completing this section, you should be able to

▪ **Calculate resistance in a circuit**
   • Use Ohm's law to find resistance when voltage and current are known
   • Use current and voltage values expressed with metric prefixes

In the following examples, the formula $R = V/I$ is used. To get resistance in ohms, you must express the value of I in amperes and the value of V in volts.

EXAMPLE 3–14   In the circuit of Figure 3–10, how much resistance is needed to draw 3.08 A of current from the battery?

FIGURE 3–10

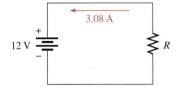

Solution   Substitute 12 V for V and 3.08 A for I into the formula $R = V/I$.

$$R = \frac{V}{I} = \frac{12 \text{ V}}{3.08 \text{ A}} = \mathbf{3.90 \ \Omega}$$

Related Problem   In Figure 3–10, to what value must R be changed for a current of 5.45 A?

Smaller Units of Current (mA and μA)

The following two examples illustrate how to use current values in the milliampere (mA) and microampere (μA) ranges when you calculate resistance.

EXAMPLE 3–15   Suppose that the ammeter in Figure 3–11 indicates 4.55 mA of current and the voltmeter reads 150 V. What is the value of R?

FIGURE 3–11

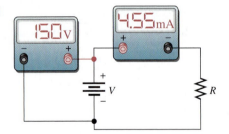

Solution   4.55 mA equals 4.55×10^{-3} A. Substitute the voltage and current values into the formula $R = V/I$.

$$R = \frac{V}{I} = \frac{150 \text{ V}}{4.55 \text{ mA}} = \frac{150 \text{ V}}{4.55 \times 10^{-3} \text{ A}} = 33 \times 10^3 \ \Omega = \mathbf{33 \ k\Omega}$$

When volts are divided by milliamperes, the resistance is in kilohms.

Related Problem   If the ammeter indicates 1.10 mA and the voltmeter reads 75 V, what is the value of R?

EXAMPLE 3–16

Suppose that the value of the resistor in Figure 3–11 is changed. If the battery voltage is still 150 V and the ammeter reads 68.2 μA, what is the new resistor value?

Solution   68.2 μA equals 68.2×10^{-6} A. Substitute V and I values into the equation for R.

$$R = \frac{V}{I} = \frac{150 \text{ V}}{68.2 \text{ } \mu\text{A}} = \frac{150 \text{ V}}{68.2 \times 10^{-6} \text{ A}} = 2.2 \times 10^6 \text{ } \Omega = \mathbf{2.2 \text{ M}\Omega}$$

When volts are divided by microamperes, the resistance has units of megohms.

Related Problem   If the resistor is changed in Figure 3–11 so that the ammeter reads 45.5 μA, what is the new resistor value? Assume $V = 150$ V.

SECTION 3–4 REVIEW

In Problems, 1–5, calculate R.

1. $V = 10$ V and $I = 2.13$ A.
2. $V = 270$ V and $I = 10$ A.
3. $V = 20$ kV and $I = 5.13$ A.
4. $V = 15$ V and $I = 2.68$ mA.
5. $V = 5$ V and $I = 2.27$ μA.
6. You have a resistor across which you measure 25 V, and your ammeter indicates 53.2 mA of current. What is the resistor's value in kilohms? In ohms?

3–5 ▪ THE RELATIONSHIP OF CURRENT, VOLTAGE, AND RESISTANCE

Ohm's law describes how current is related to voltage and resistance. Current and voltage are linearly proportional; current and resistance are inversely related. Because voltage is the "driving force," it is not dependent on the resistance when used as a source. When it is a voltage drop, it is directly proportional to the resistance for a given current.

After completing this section, you should be able to

▪ **Explain the proportional relationship of current, voltage, and resistance**
  • Show graphically that I and V are directly proportional
  • Show graphically that I and R are inversely proportional
  • Explain why I and V are linearly proportional

The Linear Relationship of Current and Voltage

Current and voltage are **linearly** proportional; that is, if one is increased or decreased by a certain percentage, the other will increase or decrease by the same percentage, assuming that the resistance is constant in value. For example, if the voltage across a resistor is tripled, the current will triple.

EXAMPLE 3–17   Show that if the voltage in the circuit of Figure 3–12 is increased to three times its present value, the current will triple in value.

FIGURE 3–12

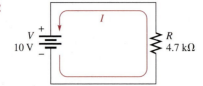

Solution   With 10 V, the current is

$$I = \frac{V}{R} = \frac{10\ \text{V}}{4.7\ \text{k}\Omega} = \textbf{2.13 mA}$$

If the voltage is increased to 30 V, the current will be

$$I = \frac{V}{R} = \frac{30\ \text{V}}{4.7\ \text{k}\Omega} = \textbf{6.38 mA}$$

The current went from 2.13 mA to 6.38 mA when the voltage was tripled to 30 V.

Related Problem   If the voltage in Figure 3–12 is quadrupled, will the current also quadruple?

A Graph of Current Versus Voltage

Let's take a constant value of resistance, for example, 10 Ω, and calculate the current for several values of voltage ranging from 10 V to 100 V. The current values obtained are shown in Figure 3–13(a). The graph of the *I* values versus the *V* values is shown in Figure 3–13(b). Note that it is a straight line graph. This graph tells us that a change in voltage results in a linearly proportional change in current. No matter what value *R* is, assuming that *R* is constant, the graph of *I* versus *V* will always be a straight line.

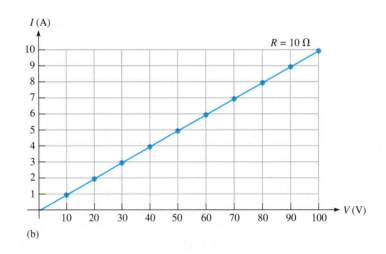

V	I
10 V	1 A
20 V	2 A
30 V	3 A
40 V	4 A
50 V	5 A
60 V	6 A
70 V	7 A
80 V	8 A
90 V	9 A
100 V	10 A

$$I = \frac{V}{10\ \Omega}$$

(a)

(b)

FIGURE 3–13
Graph of current versus voltage for R = 10 Ω.

Example 3–18 illustrates a use for the linear relationship between voltage and current in a resistive circuit.

EXAMPLE 3–18

Assume that you are measuring the current in a circuit that is operating with 25 V. The ammeter reads 50 mA. Later, you notice that the current has dropped to 40 mA. Assuming that the resistance did not change, you must conclude that the voltage source has changed. How much has the voltage changed, and what is its new value?

Solution The current has dropped from 50 mA to 40 mA, which is a decrease of 20%. Since the voltage is linearly proportional to the current, the voltage has decreased by the same percentage that the current did. Taking 20% of 25 V, you get

$$\text{Change in voltage} = (0.2)(25\text{ V}) = \textbf{5 V}$$

Subtract this change from the original voltage to get the new voltage.

$$\text{New voltage} = 25\text{ V} - 5\text{ V} = \textbf{20 V}$$

Notice that you did not need the resistance value in order to find the new voltage.

Related Problem If the current drops to 0 A under the same conditions stated in the example, what is the voltage?

Current and Resistance Are Inversely Related

As you have seen, current varies inversely with resistance as expressed by Ohm's law, $I = V/R$. When the resistance is reduced, the current goes up; when the resistance is increased, the current goes down. For example, if the source voltage is held constant and the resistance is halved, the current doubles in value; when the resistance is doubled, the current is reduced by half.

Let's take a constant value of voltage, for example, 10 V, and calculate the current for several values of resistance ranging from 10 Ω to 100 Ω. The values obtained are shown in Figure 3–14(a). The graph of the I values versus the R values is shown in Figure 3–14(b).

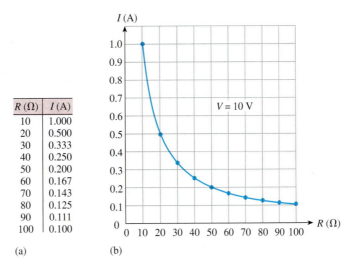

$R\ (\Omega)$	$I\ (A)$
10	1.000
20	0.500
30	0.333
40	0.250
50	0.200
60	0.167
70	0.143
80	0.125
90	0.111
100	0.100

(a)

(b)

FIGURE 3–14

Graph of current versus resistance for V = 10 V.

SECTION 3–5
REVIEW

1. What does *linearly proportional* mean?
2. In a circuit, $V = 2$ V and $I = 10$ mA. If V is changed to 1 V, what will I equal?
3. If $I = 3$ A at a certain voltage, what will it be if the voltage is doubled?
4. By how many volts must you increase a 12 V source in order to increase the current in a circuit by 50%?

3–6 ■ TECHnology Theory Into Practice

In this TECH TIP, an existing resistance box that is to be used as part of a test setup in the lab is to be checked out and modified. Your task is to modify the circuit so that it will meet the requirements of the new application. You will have to apply your knowledge of Ohm's law in order to complete this assignment.

The specifications are as follows:

1. *Each resistor is switch selectable and only one resistor is selected at a time.*
2. *The lowest resistor value is to be 10 Ω.*
3. *Each successively higher resistance in the switch sequence must be a decade (10 times) increase over the previous one.*
4. *The maximum resistor value must be 1.0 MΩ.*
5. *The maximum voltage across any resistor in the box will be 4 V.*
6. *Two additional resistors are required, one to limit the current to 10 mA ± 10% and the other to limit the current to 5 mA ± 10% with a 4 V drop.*

The Existing Resistor Circuit

The existing resistance box is shown in both top and bottom views in Figure 3–15. The switch is a rotary type.

(a) Top view

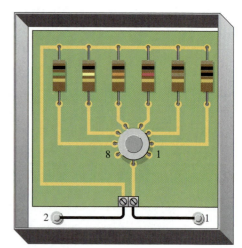

(b) Bottom view

FIGURE 3–15

The Schematic

■ From Figure 3–15, determine the resistor values and draw the schematic for the existing circuit so that you will know what you have to work with. Determine the resistor numbering from the *R* labels on the top view.

The Schematic for the New Requirements

■ Draw the schematic for a circuit that will accomplish the following:

1. One resistor at a time is to be connected by the switch between terminals 1 and 2 of the box.

2. Provide switch selectable resistor values beginning with 10 Ω and increasing in decade increments to 1.0 MΩ.

3. Each of the resistors must be selectable by a sequence of adjacent switch positions in ascending order.

4. There must be two switch-selectable resistors, one is in switch position 1 (shown in Figure 3–15, bottom view) and must limit the current to 10 mA ± 10% with a 4 V drop and the other is in switch position 8 and must limit the current to 5 mA ± 10% with a 4 V drop.

5. All the resistors must be standard values with 10% tolerance.

■ Determine the modifications that must be made to the existing circuit board to meet the specifications and develop a detailed list of the changes including resistance values, wiring, and new components. You should number each point in the schematic for easy reference.

A Test Procedure

■ After the resistance box has been modified to meet the new specifications, it must be tested to see if it is working properly. Determine how you would test the resistance box and what instruments you would use. Then detail your test procedure in a step-by-step format.

Troubleshooting the Circuit

■ When an ohmmeter is connected across terminals 1 and 2 of the resistance box, determine the most likely fault in each of the following cases:

1. The ohmmeter shows an infinitely high resistance when the switch is in position 3.

2. The ohmmeter shows an infinitely high resistance in all switch positions.

3. The ohmmeter shows an incorrect value of resistance when the switch is in position 6.

SECTION 3–6 REVIEW

1. Explain how you applied Ohm's law to this application assignment.

2. Determine the current through each resistor when 4 V is applied across it.

■ SUMMARY

■ Voltage and current are linearly proportional.
■ Ohm's law gives the relationship of voltage, current, and resistance.
■ Current is directly proportional to voltage.

■ Current is inversely proportional to resistance.

■ A kilohm (kΩ) is one thousand ohms.

■ A megohm (MΩ) is one million ohms.

■ A microampere (μA) is one-millionth of an ampere.

■ A milliampere (mA) is one-thousandth of an ampere.

■ Use $I = V/R$ when calculating the current.

■ Use $V = IR$ when calculating the voltage.

■ Use $R = V/I$ when calculating the resistance.

■ Figure 3–16 is a memory aid for the Ohm's law relationships.

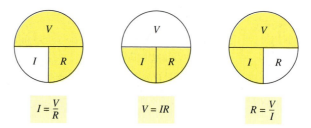

FIGURE 3–16

■ GLOSSARY

These terms are also in the end-of-book glossary.

Linear   Characterized by a straight-line relationship.

Ohm (Ω)   The unit of resistance.

Ohm's law   A law stating that current is directly proportional to voltage and inversely proportional to resistance.

■ FORMULAS

(3–1) $I = \dfrac{V}{R}$ Ohm's law for current

(3–2) $V = IR$ Ohm's law for voltage

(3–3) $R = \dfrac{V}{I}$ Ohm's law for resistance

■ SELF-TEST

1. Ohm's law states that
   (a) current equals voltage times resistance
   (b) voltage equals current times resistance
   (c) resistance equals current divided by voltage
   (d) voltage equals current squared times resistance
2. When the voltage across a resistor is doubled, the current will
   (a) triple   (b) halve   (c) double   (d) not change
3. When 10 V are applied across a 20 Ω resistor, the current is
   (a) 10 A   (b) 0.5 A   (c) 200 A   (d) 2 A
4. When there are 10 mA of current through a 1.0 kΩ resistor, the voltage across the resistor is
   (a) 100 V   (b) 0.1 V   (c) 10 kV   (d) 10 V
5. If 20 V are applied across a resistor and there are 6.06 mA of current, the resistance is
   (a) 3.3 kΩ   (b) 33 kΩ   (c) 330 Ω   (d) 3.03 kΩ
6. A current of 250 μA through a 4.7 kΩ resistor produces a voltage drop of
   (a) 53.2 V   (b) 1.18 mV   (c) 18.8 V   (d) 1.18 V

7. A resistance of 2.2 MΩ is connected across a 1 kV source. The resulting current is approximately
   (a) 2.2 mA   (b) 0.455 mA   (c) 45.5 μA   (d) 0.455 A

8. How much resistance is required to limit the current from a 10 V battery to 1 mA?
   (a) 100 Ω   (b) 1.0 kΩ   (c) 10 Ω   (d) 10 kΩ

9. An electric heater draws 2.5 A from a 110 V source. The resistance of the heating element is
   (a) 275 Ω   (b) 22.7 mΩ   (c) 44 Ω   (d) 440 Ω

10. The current through a flashlight bulb is 20 mA and the total battery voltage is 4.5 V. The resistance of the bulb is
   (a) 90 Ω   (b) 225 Ω   (c) 4.44 Ω   (d) 45 Ω

■ PROBLEMS

More difficult problems are indicated by an asterisk (*).

SECTION 3–1   Ohm's law

1. In a circuit consisting of a voltage source and a resistor, describe what happens to the current when
   (a) the voltage is tripled
   (b) the voltage is reduced by 75%
   (c) the resistance is doubled
   (d) the resistance is reduced by 35%
   (e) the voltage is doubled and the resistance is cut in half
   (f) the voltage is doubled and the resistance is doubled

2. State the formula used to find I when the values of V and R are known.

3. State the formula used to find V when the values of I and R are known.

4. State the formula used to find R when the values of V and I are known.

SECTION 3–2   Calculating Current

5. Determine the current in each case:
   (a) $V = 5$ V, $R = 1.0$ Ω   (b) $V = 15$ V, $R = 10$ Ω
   (c) $V = 50$ V, $R = 100$ Ω   (d) $V = 30$ V, $R = 15$ kΩ
   (e) $V = 250$ V, $R = 5.6$ MΩ

6. Determine the current in each case:
   (a) $V = 9$ V, $R = 2.7$ kΩ   (b) $V = 5.5$ V, $R = 10$ kΩ
   (c) $V = 40$ V, $R = 68$ kΩ   (d) $V = 1$ kV, $R = 2.2$ kΩ
   (e) $V = 66$ kV, $R = 10$ MΩ

7. A 10 Ω resistor is connected across a 12 V battery. What is the current through the resistor?

8. A certain resistor has the following color code: orange, orange, red, gold. Determine the maximum and minimum currents you should expect to measure when a 12 V source is connected across the resistor.

9. A resistor is connected across the terminals of a 25 V source. Determine the current in the resistor if the color code is yellow, violet, orange, silver.

*10. The potentiometer connected as a rheostat in Figure 3–17 is used to control the current to a heating element. When the rheostat is adjusted to a value of 8 Ω or less, the heating element can burn out. What is the rated value of the fuse needed to protect the circuit if the voltage across the heating element at the point of maximum current is 100 V and the voltage across the rheostat is the difference between the heating element voltage and the source voltage?

FIGURE 3–17

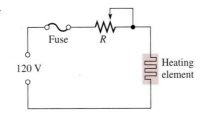

SECTION 3–3 Calculating Voltage

11. Calculate the voltage for each value of I and R:

    (a) $I = 2$ A, $R = 18$ Ω (b) $I = 5$ A, $R = 56$ Ω

    (c) $I = 2.5$ A, $R = 680$ Ω   (d) $I = 0.6$ A, $R = 47$ Ω

    (e) $I = 0.1$ A, $R = 560$ Ω

12. Calculate the voltage for each value of I and R:

    (a) $I = 1$ mA, $R = 10$ Ω   (b) $I = 50$ mA, $R = 33$ Ω

    (c) $I = 3$ A, $R = 5.6$ kΩ   (d) $I = 1.6$ mA, $R = 2.2$ kΩ

    (e) $I = 250$ μA, $R = 1.0$ kΩ   (f) $I = 500$ mA, $R = 1.5$ MΩ

    (g) $I = 850$ μA, $R = 10$ MΩ   (h) $I = 75$ μA, $R = 47$ Ω

13. Three amperes of current are measured through a 27 Ω resistor connected across a voltage source. How much voltage does the source produce?

14. Assign a voltage value to each source in the circuits of Figure 3–18 to obtain the indicated amounts of current.

FIGURE 3–18

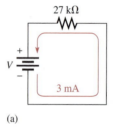
(a)

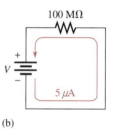
(b)

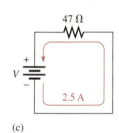
(c)

15. A 6 V source is connected to a 100 Ω resistor by two 12 ft lengths of 18 gage copper wire. The total resistance is found by adding the resistance of both wires to the 100 Ω resistor. Determine the following:

    (a) Current

    (b) Resistor voltage drop

    (c) Voltage drop across each length of wire

SECTION 3–4 Calculating Resistance

16. Calculate the resistance of a rheostat for each value of V and I:

    (a) $V = 10$ V, $I = 2$ A (b) $V = 90$ V, $I = 45$ A

    (c) $V = 50$ V, $I = 5$ A (d) $V = 5.5$ V, $I = 10$ A

    (e) $V = 150$ V, $I = 0.5$ A

17. Calculate the resistance of a rheostat for each set of V and I values:

    (a) $V = 10$ kV, $I = 5$ A (b) $V = 7$ V, $I = 2$ mA

    (c) $V = 500$ V, $I = 250$ mA   (d) $V = 50$ V, $I = 500$ μA

    (e) $V = 1$ kV, $I = 1$ mA

18. Six volts are applied across a resistor. A current of 2 mA is measured. What is the value of the resistor?

19. The filament of a light bulb in the circuit of Figure 3–19(a) has a certain amount of resistance, represented by an equivalent resistance in Figure 3–19(b). If the bulb operates with 120 V and 0.8 A of current, what is the resistance of its filament when it is on?

FIGURE 3–19

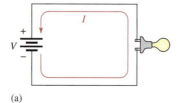
(a)

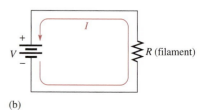
(b)

20. A certain electrical device has an unknown resistance. You have available a 12 V battery and an ammeter. How would you determine the value of the unknown resistance? Draw the necessary circuit connections.

21. By varying the rheostat (variable resistor) in the circuit of Figure 3–20, you can change the amount of current. The setting of the rheostat is such that the current is 750 mA. What is the resistance value of this setting? To adjust the current to 1 A, to what resistance value must you set the rheostat? What is the problem with this circuit?

FIGURE 3–20

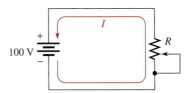

22. A 120 V lamp-dimming circuit is controlled by a rheostat and protected from excessive current by a 2 A fuse. To what minimum resistance value can the rheostat be set without blowing the fuse? Assume a lamp resistance of 15 Ω.

Section 3–5 The Relationship of Current, Voltage, and Resistance

23. A variable voltage source is connected to the circuit of Figure 3–21. Start at 0 V and increase the voltage in 10 V steps up to 100 V. Determine the current at each voltage point, and plot a graph of V versus I. Is the graph a straight line? What does the graph indicate?

FIGURE 3–21

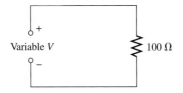

24. In a certain circuit, $I = 5$ mA when $V = 1$ V. Determine the current for each of the following voltages in the same circuit:
    (a) $V = 1.5$ V   (b) $V = 2$ V   (c) $V = 3$ V
    (d) $V = 4$ V   (e) $V = 10$ V

25. Figure 3–22 is a graph of voltage versus current for three resistance values. Determine R_1, R_2, and R_3.

FIGURE 3–22

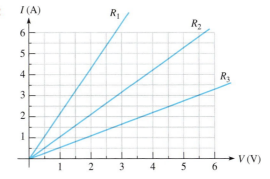

26. Which circuit in Figure 3–23 has the most current? The least current?

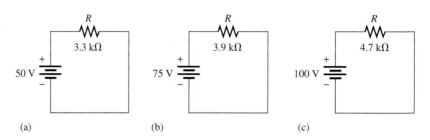

(a)   (b)   (c)

FIGURE 3–23

*27. You are measuring the current in a circuit that is operated on a 10 V battery. The ammeter reads 50 mA. Later, you notice that the current has dropped to 30 mA. Eliminating the possibility of a resistance change, you must conclude that the voltage has changed. How much has the voltage of the battery changed, and what is its new value?

*28. If you wish to increase the amount of current in a resistor from 100 mA to 150 mA by changing the 20 V source, by how many volts should you change the source? To what new value should you set it?

29. Plot a graph of current versus voltage for voltage values ranging from 10 V to 100 V in 10 V steps for each of the following resistance values:

    (a) 1.0 Ω   **(b)** 5.0 Ω   **(c)** 20 Ω   **(d)** 100 Ω

EWB Troubleshooting and Analysis

These problems require your EWB compact disk.

30. Open file PRO03-30.EWB on your EWB disk and determine which one of the three circuits is not working properly?

31. Open file PRO03-31.EWB and measure the resistance values of the resistors.

32. Open file PRO03-32.EWB and determine the values of the current and voltage.

33. Open file PRO03-33.EWB and determine the value of the source voltage and the resistance.

34. Open file PRO03-34.EWB and find the problem with the circuit.

■ **ANSWERS TO SECTION REVIEWS**

Section 3–1

1. Current, voltage, and resistance

2. $I = V/R$

3. $V = IR$

4. $R = V/I$

5. When voltage is tripled, current increases by three times.

6. When voltage is halved, current reduces to one-half of original value.

7. 0.5 A

8. The current would increase by four times if the voltage doubles and the resistance is halved.

Section 3–2

1. $I = 10 \text{ V}/5.6 \ \Omega = 1.79$ A

2. $I = 100 \text{ V}/560 \ \Omega = 179$ mA

3. $I = 5 \text{ V}/2.2 \text{ k}\Omega = 2.27$ mA

4. $I = 15 \text{ V}/4.7 \text{ M}\Omega = 3.19 \ \mu$A

5. $I = 20 \text{ kV}/4.7 \text{ M}\Omega = 4.26$ mA

6. $I = 10 \text{ kV}/2.2 \text{ k}\Omega = 4.55$ A

Section 3–3

1. $V = (1\ A)(10\ \Omega) = 10\ V$
2. $V = (8\ A)(470\ \Omega) = 3.76\ kV$
3. $V = (3\ mA)(100\ \Omega) = 300\ mV$
4. $V = (25\ \mu A)(56\ \Omega) = 1.4\ mV$
5. $V = (2\ mA)(1.8\ k\Omega) = 3.6\ V$
6. $V = (5\ mA)(100\ M\Omega) = 500\ kV$
7. $V = (10\ \mu A)(2.2\ M\Omega) = 22\ V$
8. $V = (100\ mA)(4.7\ k\Omega) = 470\ V$
9. $V = (3\ mA)(3.3\ k\Omega) = 9.9\ V$
10. $V = (2\ A)(6.8\ \Omega) = 13.6\ V$

Section 3–4

1. $R = 10\ V/2.13\ A = 4.7\ \Omega$
2. $R = 270\ V/10\ A = 27\ \Omega$
3. $R = 20\ kV/5.13\ A = 3.9\ k\Omega$
4. $R = 15\ V/2.68\ mA = 5.6\ k\Omega$
5. $R = 5\ V/2.27\ \mu A = 2.2\ M\Omega$
6. $R = 25\ V/53.2\ mA = 0.47\ k\Omega = 470\ \Omega$

Section 3–5

1. Linearly proportional means that the same percentage change occurs in two quantities.
2. $I = 5\ mA$
3. $I = 6\ A$
4. $\Delta V = 6\ V$

Section 3–6

1. For the new resistors, $R = V/I$.
2. $I = 4\ V/10\ \Omega = 400\ mA;\ I = 4\ V/100\ \Omega = 40\ mA;\ I = 4\ V/1.0\ k\Omega = 4\ mA;$
   $I = 4\ V/10\ k\Omega = 400\ \mu A;\ I = 4\ V/100\ k\Omega = 40\ \mu A;\ I = 4\ V/1.0\ M\Omega = 4\ \mu A.$

■ **ANSWERS TO RELATED PROBLEMS FOR EXAMPLES**

3–1 3.03 A	**3–10** 49.5 mV
3–2 0.005 A	**3–11** 0.150 mV
3–3 0.005 A	**3–12** 82.5 V
3–4 13.6 mA	**3–13** 1755 V
3–5 21.3 μA	**3–14** 2.20 Ω
3–6 2.66 μA	**3–15** 68.2 kΩ
3–7 37.0 mA	**3–16** 3.30 MΩ
3–8 1.47 mA	**3–17** Yes
3–9 1200 V	**3–18** 0 V

■ **ANSWERS TO SELF-TEST**

1. (b)   **2.** (c)   **3.** (b)   **4.** (d)   **5.** (a)   **6.** (d)   **7.** (b)   **8.** (d)
9. (c)   **10.** (b)

4

ENERGY AND POWER

 Electronics Workbench (EWB) and PSpice Tutorials available at http://www.prenhall.com/floyd

■ INTRODUCTION

From Chapter 3, you know the relationship of current, voltage, and resistance as stated by Ohm's law. The existence of these three quantities in an electric circuit results in the fourth basic quantity known as power. A specific relationship exists between power and I, V, and R, as you will learn.

Energy is the ability to do work, and power is the rate at which energy is used. Current carries electrical energy through a circuit. As the free electrons pass through the resistance of the circuit, they give up their energy when they collide with atoms in the resistive material. The electrical energy given up by the electrons is converted into heat energy. The rate at which the electrical energy is used is the power in the circuit.

In the TECH TIP, Section 4–6, you will see how the theory learned in this chapter is applicable to the resistance box introduced in the last chapter. Suppose your supervisor tells you that the resistance box is to be used in testing a circuit in which there will be a maximum of 4 V across all the resistors. You are asked to evaluate the power rating of each resistor and, if it is not sufficient, to replace the resistor with one that has an adequate power rating.

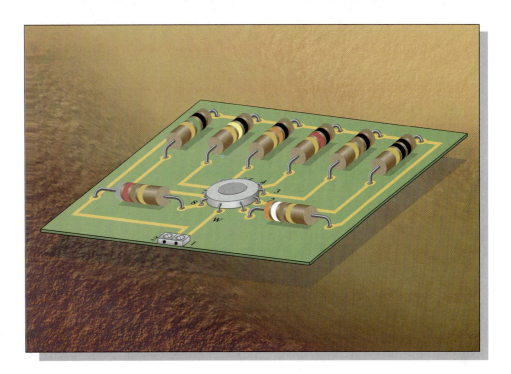

■ CHAPTER OBJECTIVES

❏ Define *energy* and *power*
❏ Calculate power in a circuit
❏ Properly select resistors based on power consideration

❏ Explain energy conversion and voltage drop
❏ Discuss power supplies and their characteristics

HISTORICAL NOTES

James Prescott Joule
1818–1889

James Prescott Joule was a British physicist who was born in Salford, Lancashire, in 1818. Joule is known for his research in electricity and thermodynamics. He formulated the relationship that states that the amount of heat energy produced by an electric current in a conductor is related to the conductor's resistance and the time (energy = power × time). The unit of energy is named in his honor. *Photo credit: Library of Congress.*

James Watt
1736–1819

James Watt was a Scottish inventer and mechanical engineer who was born in Greenock in 1736. He is renowned for his improvements to the steam engine which made it practical for industrial use. Watt designed a separate condensing chamber that prevented enormous loss of steam in the cylinder and enhanced the vacuum conditions. Watt's first patent was on this device, but he also patented several other inventions, including the rotary engine. The unit of power is named in his honor. *Photo credit: Library of Congress.*

4–1 ■ ENERGY AND POWER

When there is current through a resistance, electrical energy is converted to heat or other form of energy, such as light. A common example of this is a light bulb that becomes too hot to touch. The current through the filament that produces light also produces unwanted heat because the filament has resistance. Power is a measure of how fast energy is being used; electrical components must be able to dissipate a certain amount of energy in a given period of time.

After completing this section, you should be able to

■ Define *energy* and *power*
  • Express power in terms of energy
  • State the unit of power
  • State the common units of energy
  • Perform energy and power calculations

By definition,

> **Energy is the ability to do work; and power is the rate at which energy is used.**

In other words, **power,** symbolized by *P,* is a certain amount of **energy** used in a certain length of time, expressed as follows:

$$\text{Power} = \frac{\text{energy}}{\text{time}}$$

$$P = \frac{W}{t} \qquad (4\text{–}1)$$

Energy is measured in **joules** (J), time is measured in seconds (s), and power is measured in **watts** (W). Note that an italic *W* is used to represent energy in the form of work and a nonitalic W is used for watts, the unit of power.

Energy in joules divided by time in seconds gives power in watts. For example, if 50 J of energy are used in 2 s, the power is 50 J/2 s = 25 W. By definition,

> **One watt is the amount of power when one joule of energy is used in one second.**

Thus, the number of joules used in one second is always equal to the number of watts. For example, if 75 J are used in 1 s, the power is 75 W.

EXAMPLE 4–1

An amount of energy equal to 100 J is used in 5 s. What is the power in watts?

Solution

$$P = \frac{\text{energy}}{\text{time}} = \frac{W}{t} = \frac{100 \text{ J}}{5 \text{ s}} = \textbf{20 W}$$

Related Problem   If 100 W of power occurs for 30 s, how much energy, in joules, is used?

Amounts of power much less than one watt are common in certain areas of electronics. As with small current and voltage values, metric prefixes are used to designate small amounts of power. Thus, milliwatts (mW), microwatts (μW), and even picowatts (pW) are commonly found in some applications.

In the electrical utilities field, kilowatts (kW) and megawatts (MW) are common units. Radio and television stations also use large amounts of power to transmit signals.

EXAMPLE 4–2

Express the following values of electrical power using appropriate metric prefixes:
(a) 0.045 W **(b)** 0.000012 W **(c)** 3500 W **(d)** 10,000,000 W

Solution
(a) 0.045 W = **45 mW** **(b)** 0.000012 W = **12 μW**
(c) 3500 W = **3.5 kW** **(d)** 10,000,000 W = **10 MW**

Related Problem Express the following amounts of power in watts without metric prefixes:
(a) 1 mW **(b)** 1800 μW **(c)** 1000 mW **(d)** 1 μW

The Kilowatt-hour (kWh) Unit of Energy

Since power is the rate at which energy is used, as expressed in Equation (4–1), power utilized over a period of time represents energy consumption. If you multiply power and time, you have energy, *W.*

Energy = power × time

$$W = Pt \qquad (4\text{–}2)$$

Previously, the joule was defined as a unit of energy. However, there is another way to express energy. Since power is expressed in watts and time in seconds, units of energy called the watt-second (Ws), watt-hour (Wh), and kilowatt-hour (kWh) can be used.

When you pay your electric bill, you are charged on the basis of the amount of energy you use, not the power. Because power companies deal in huge amounts of energy, the most practical unit is the **kilowatt-hour.** You use a kilowatt-hour of energy when you use one thousand watts of power for one hour. For example, a 100 W light bulb burning for 10 h uses 1 kWh of energy.

$$W = Pt = (100\text{ W})(10\text{ h}) = 1000\text{ Wh} = 1\text{ kWh}$$

EXAMPLE 4–3

Determine the number of kilowatt-hours (kWh) for each of the following energy consumptions:
(a) 1400 W for 1 h **(b)** 2500 W for 2 h **(c)** 100,000 W for 5 h

Solution
(a) 1400 W = 1.4 kW **(b)** 2500 W = 2.5 kW
  $W = Pt = (1.4\text{ kW})(1\text{ h}) = $ **1.4 kWh** $W = (2.5\text{ kW})(2\text{ h}) = $ **5 kWh**
(c) 100,000 W = 100 kW
  $W = (100\text{ kW})(5\text{ h}) = $ **500 kWh**

Related Problem How many kilowatt-hours are used by a 250 W bulb burning for 8 h?

SECTION 4–1
REVIEW

1. Define *power.*

2. Write the formula for power in terms of energy and time.

3. Define *watt.*

4. Express each of the following values of power in the most appropriate units:
   (a) 68,000 W   **(b)** 0.005 W   **(c)** 0.000025 W

5. If you use 100 W of power for 10 h, how much energy (in kWh) have you used?

6. Convert 2000 Wh to kilowatt-hours.

7. Convert 360,000 Ws to kilowatt-hours.

4–2 ■ POWER IN AN ELECTRIC CIRCUIT

The generation of heat, which occurs when electrical energy is converted to heat energy, in an electric circuit is often an unwanted by-product of current through the resistance in the circuit. In some cases, however, the generation of heat is the primary purpose of a circuit as, for example, in an electric resistive heater. In any case, you must always deal with power in electrical and electronic circuits.

After completing this section, you should be able to

■ Calculate power in a circuit
  • Determine power knowing I and R
  • Determine power knowing V and I
  • Determine power knowing V and R

When there is current through resistance, the collisions of the electrons produce heat, as a result of the conversion of electrical energy, as indicated in Figure 4–1. There is always a certain amount of power in an electric circuit, and it is dependent on the amount of resistance and on the amount of current, expressed as follows:

$$P = I^2R \qquad (4–3)$$

We can get an equivalent expression for power by substituting V for IR (I^2 is $I \times I$).

$$P = I^2R = (I \times I)R = I(IR) = (IR)I$$

$$P = VI \qquad (4–4)$$

We obtain another equivalent expression by substituting V/R for I (Ohm's law) as follows:

$$P = VI = V\left(\frac{V}{R}\right)$$

$$P = \frac{V^2}{R} \qquad (4–5)$$

FIGURE 4–1

Power in an electric circuit results in heat energy given off by the resistance.

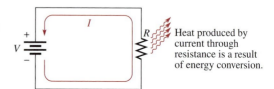

Heat produced by current through resistance is a result of energy conversion.

The relationships expressed in the preceding formulas are known as **Watt's law.** In each case, I must be in amps, V in volts, and R in ohms.

Using the Appropriate Power Formula

To calculate the power in a resistance, you can use any one of the three power formulas, depending on what information you have. For example, assume that you know the values of current and voltage. In this case you calculate the power with the formula $P = VI$. If you know I and R, use the formula $P = I^2R$. If you know V and R, use the formula $P = V^2/R$.

EXAMPLE 4–4

Calculate the power in each of the three circuits of Figure 4–2.

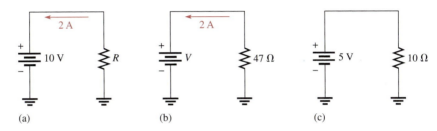

FIGURE 4–2

Solution   In circuit (a), V and I are known. Therefore, use Equation (4–4).

$$P = VI = (10 \text{ V})(2 \text{ A}) = \textbf{20 W}$$

In circuit (b), I and R are known. Therefore, use Equation (4–3).

$$P = I^2R = (2 \text{ A})^2(47 \text{ } \Omega) = \textbf{188 W}$$

In circuit (c), V and R are known. Therefore, use Equation (4–5).

$$P = \frac{V^2}{R} = \frac{(5 \text{ V})^2}{10 \text{ } \Omega} = \textbf{2.5 W}$$

Related Problem   Determine P in each circuit of Figure 4–2 for the following changes:
Circuit (a): I doubled and V remains the same
Circuit (b): R doubled and I remains the same
Circuit (c): V halved and R remains the same

EXAMPLE 4–5

A 100 W light bulb operates on 120 V. How much current does it require?

Solution   Use the formula $P = VI$ and solve for I by first transposing the terms to get I on the left of the equation.

$$VI = P$$

Divide both sides of the equation by V to get I by itself.

$$\frac{\cancel{V}I}{\cancel{V}} = \frac{P}{V}$$

The V's cancel on the left, leaving

$$I = \frac{P}{V}$$

Substituting 100 W for P and 120 V for V yields

$$I = \frac{P}{V} = \frac{100 \text{ W}}{120 \text{ V}} = 0.833 \text{ A} = \textbf{833 mA}$$

Related Problem A light bulb draws 545 mA from a 110 V source. What is the power?

SECTION 4–2 REVIEW

1. If there are 10 V across a resistor and a current of 3 A through it, what is the power?
2. How much power does the source in Figure 4–3 generate? What is the power in the resistor? Are the two values the same? Why?

FIGURE 4–3

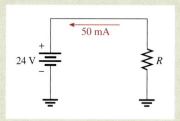

3. If there is a current of 5 A through a 56 Ω resistor, what is the power?
4. How much power is dissipated by 20 mA through a 4.7 kΩ resistor?
5. Five volts are applied to a 10 Ω resistor. What is the power?
6. How much power does a 2.2 kΩ resistor with 8 V across it dissipate?
7. What is the resistance of a 75 W bulb that takes 0.5 A?

4–3 ■ RESISTOR POWER RATINGS

As you already know, a resistor gives off heat when there is current through it. The limit to the amount of heat that a resistor can give off is specified by its power rating.

After completing this section, you should be able to

■ **Properly select resistors based on power consideration**
  • Define *power rating*
  • Explain how physical characteristics of resistors determine their power rating
  • Check for resistor failure with an ohmmeter

The **power rating** is the maximum amount of power that a resistor can dissipate without being damaged by excessive heat buildup. The power rating is not related to the ohmic value (resistance) but rather is determined mainly by the physical composition, size, and shape of the resistor. All else being equal, the larger the surface area of a resistor, the more power it can dissipate. Ignoring the area of the ends, *the surface area of a cylindrically shaped resistor is equal to the length (l) times the circumference (c),* as indicated in Figure 4–4.

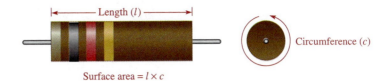

FIGURE 4–4

The power rating of a resistor is directly related to its surface area.

Metal-film resistors are available in standard power ratings from ⅛ W to 1 W, as shown in Figure 4–5. Available power ratings for other types of resistors vary. For example, wirewound resistors have ratings up to 225 W or greater. Figure 4–6 shows some of these resistors.

FIGURE 4–5

Relative sizes of metal-film resistors with standard power ratings of ⅛, W, ¼ W, ½ W, and 1 W.

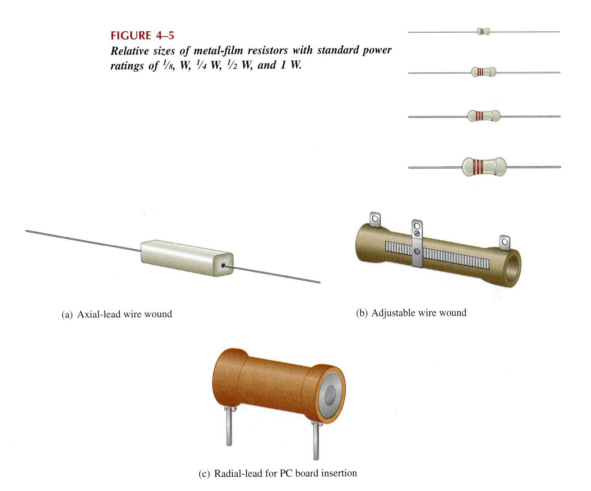

(a) Axial-lead wire wound

(b) Adjustable wire wound

(c) Radial-lead for PC board insertion

FIGURE 4–6

Typical resistors with high power ratings.

Selecting the Proper Power Rating for an Application

When a resistor is used in a circuit, its power rating must be greater than the maximum power that it will have to handle. For example, if a resistor is to dissipate 0.75 W in a circuit application, its rating should be at least the next higher standard value which is 1 W. *Ideally, a rating that is approximately twice the actual power should be used when possible.*

EXAMPLE 4–6   Choose an adequate power rating for each of the metal-film resistors in Figure 4–7 ($\frac{1}{8}$ W, $\frac{1}{4}$ W, $\frac{1}{2}$ W, or 1 W).

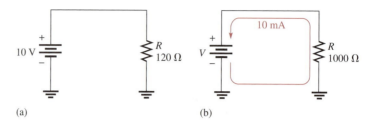

FIGURE 4–7

Solution   In Figure 4–7(a), the actual power is

$$P = \frac{V^2}{R} = \frac{(10 \text{ V})^2}{120 \text{ } \Omega} = \frac{100 \text{ V}^2}{120 \text{ } \Omega} = \textbf{0.833 W}$$

Select a resistor with a power rating higher than the actual power. In this case, a 1 W resistor should be used.

In Figure 4–7(b), the actual power is

$$P = I^2 R = (10 \text{ mA})^2 (1000 \text{ } \Omega) = (10 \times 10^{-3} \text{ A})^2 (1000 \text{ } \Omega) = \textbf{0.1 W}$$

At least a $\frac{1}{8}$ W (0.125 W) resistor should be used in this case.

Related Problem   A certain resistor is required to dissipate 0.25 W. What standard rating should be used?

Resistor Failures

When the power in a resistor is greater than its rating, the resistor will become excessively hot. As a result, either the resistor will burn open or its resistance value will be greatly altered.

A resistor that has been damaged because of overheating can often be detected by the charred or altered appearance of its surface. If there is no visual evidence, a resistor that is suspected of being damaged can be checked with an ohmmeter for an open or incorrect resistance value. Recall that one or both leads of a resistor should be removed from a circuit to measure resistance.

Checking a Resistor with an Ohmmeter

A typical analog multimeter (VOM) and a digital multimeter are shown in Figures 4–8(a) and 4–8(b), respectively. The large switch on the analog meter is called a range switch. Notice the resistance (OHMS) settings on both meters. For the analog meter in part (a), each setting indicates the amount by which the ohms scale (top scale) on the meter is to be multiplied. For example, if the pointer is at 50 on the ohms scale and the range switch is set at ×10, the resistance being measured is 50 × 10 Ω = 500 Ω. *If the resistor is open, the pointer will stay at full left scale (∞ means infinite) regardless of the range switch setting.*

For the digital meter in Figure 4–8(b), you use the range switch to select the appropriate setting for the value of resistance being measured. You do not have to multiply to get the correct reading because you have a direct digital readout of the resistance value.

(a)   (b)

FIGURE 4–8

Typical portable multimeters (photography courtesy of B&K Precision (Corp.).

EXAMPLE 4–7   Determine whether the resistor in each circuit of Figure 4–9 has possibly been damaged by overheating.

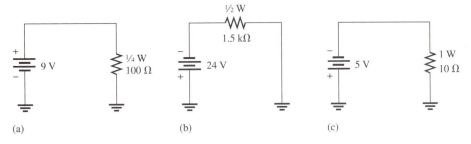

(a)   (b)   (c)

FIGURE 4–9

Solution   In the circuit in Figure 4–9(a),

$$P = \frac{V^2}{R} = \frac{(9 \text{ V})^2}{100 \text{ }\Omega} = 0.810 \text{ W} = \textbf{810 mW}$$

The rating of the resistor is ¼ W (0.25 W), which is insufficient to handle the power. The resistor has been overheated and may be burned out, making it an open.

In the circuit of Figure 4–9(b),

$$P = \frac{V^2}{R} = \frac{(24 \text{ V})^2}{1.5 \text{ k}\Omega} = 0.384 \text{ W} = \textbf{384 mW}$$

The rating of the resistor is ½ W (0.5 W), which is sufficient to handle the power.

In the circuit of Figure 4–9(c),

$$P = \frac{V^2}{R} = \frac{(5 \text{ V})^2}{10 \text{ }\Omega} = \textbf{2.5 W}$$

The rating of the resistor is 1 W, which is insufficient to handle the power. The resistor has been overheated and may be burned out, making it an open.

Related Problem A 0.25 W, 1.0 kΩ resistor is connected across a 12 V battery. Is the power rating adequate?

SECTION 4–3 REVIEW

1. Name two important values associated with a resistor.
2. How does the physical size of a resistor determine the amount of power that it can handle?
3. List the standard power ratings of metal-film resistors.
4. A resistor must handle 0.3 W. What minimum power rating of a metal-film resistor should be used to dissipate the energy properly?

4–4 ■ ENERGY CONVERSION AND VOLTAGE DROP IN RESISTANCE

As you have seen, when there is current through a resistance, electrical energy is converted to heat energy. This heat is caused by collisions of the free electrons within the atomic structure of the resistive material. When a collision occurs, heat is given off; and the electron loses some of its acquired energy.

After completing this section, you should be able to

■ **Explain energy conversion and voltage drop**
  • Discuss the cause of energy conversion in a circuit
  • Define *voltage drop*
  • Explain the relationship between energy conversion and voltage drop

In Figure 4–10, electrons are flowing out of the negative terminal of the battery. They have acquired energy from the battery and are at their highest energy level at the negative side of the circuit. As the electrons move through the resistor, they lose energy. The electrons emerging from the upper end of the resistor are at a lower energy level than those entering the lower end because some of the energy they had has been converted to heat. The drop in energy level of the electrons as they move through the resistor creates a potential difference, or **voltage drop,** across the resistor having the polarity shown in Figure 4–10. Notice that the upper end of the resistor in Figure 4–10 is less negative (more positive) than the lower end.

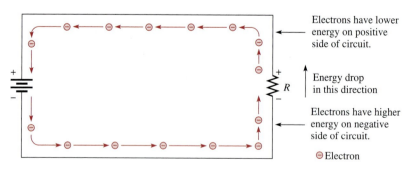

FIGURE 4–10
Electron flow in a simple circuit.

1. What is the basic reason for energy conversion in a resistor?

2. What is a voltage drop?

4–5 ■ POWER SUPPLIES

In general, a power supply is a device that provides power to a load. A load is any electrical device or circuit that is connected to the output of the power supply and draws current from the supply.

After completing this section, you should be able to

■ **Discuss power supplies and their characteristics**
  • Define *ampere-hour rating* of batteries
  • Discuss electronic power supply efficiency

Figure 4–11 shows a block diagram of a power supply with a loading device connected to it. The load can be anything from a light bulb to a computer. The power supply produces a voltage across its two output terminals and provides current through the load, as indicated in the figure. The product IV_{OUT} is the amount of power produced by the supply and consumed by the load. For a given output voltage (V_{OUT}), more current drawn by the load means more power from the supply.

FIGURE 4–11
Block diagram of power supply and load.

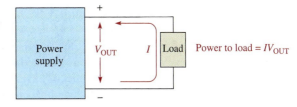

Power to load = IV_{OUT}

Power supplies range from simple batteries to regulated electronic circuits where an accurate output voltage is automatically maintained. A battery is a dc power supply that converts chemical energy into electrical energy. Electronic power supplies normally convert 110 V ac (alternating current) from a wall outlet into a regulated dc (direct current) voltage at a level suitable for electronic components.

Ampere-hour Ratings of Batteries

Batteries convert chemical energy into electrical energy. Because of their limited source of chemical energy, batteries have a certain capacity that limits the amount of time over which they can produce a given power level. This capacity is measured in ampere-hours (Ah). The **ampere-hour rating** determines the length of time that a battery can deliver a certain amount of current to a load at the rated voltage.

A rating of one ampere-hour means that a battery can deliver one ampere of current to a load for one hour at the rated voltage output. This same battery can deliver two amperes for one-half hour. The more current the battery is required to deliver, the shorter is the life of the battery. In practice, a battery usually is rated for a specified current level and output voltage. For example, a 12 V automobile battery may be rated for 70 Ah at 3.5 A. This means that it can produce 3.5 A for 20 h at the rated voltage.

EXAMPLE 4–8

For how many hours can a battery deliver 2 A if it is rated at 70 Ah?

Solution The ampere-hour rating is the current times the number of hours (x).

$$70 \text{ Ah} = (2 \text{ A})(x \text{ h})$$

Solving for the number of hours, x, yields

$$x = \frac{70 \text{ Ah}}{2 \text{ A}} = \textbf{35 h}$$

Related Problem A certain battery delivers 10 A for 6 h. What is its Ah rating?

Efficiency of Electronic Power Supplies

An important characteristic of electronic power supplies is efficiency. **Efficiency** is the ratio of the output power to the input power.

$$\text{Efficiency} = \frac{\text{output power}}{\text{input power}}$$

$$\text{Efficiency} = \frac{P_{\text{OUT}}}{P_{\text{IN}}} \qquad (4\text{–}6)$$

Efficiency is often expressed as a percentage. For example, if the input power is 100 W and the output power is 50 W, the efficiency is (50 W/100 W) × 100% = 50%.

All electronic power supplies require that power be put into them. For example, an electronic power supply generally uses the ac power from a wall outlet as its input. Its output is usually a regulated dc voltage. The output power is *always* less than the input power because some of the total power must be used internally to operate the power supply circuitry. This amount is normally called the *power loss*. The output power is the input power minus the amount of internal power loss.

$$P_{\text{OUT}} = P_{\text{IN}} - P_{\text{LOSS}} \qquad (4\text{–}7)$$

High efficiency means that little power is lost and there is a higher proportion of output power for a given input power.

EXAMPLE 4–9

A certain electronic power supply unit requires 25 W of input power. It can produce an output power of 20 W. What is its efficiency, and what is the power loss?

Solution

$$\text{Efficiency} = \left(\frac{P_{\text{OUT}}}{P_{\text{IN}}}\right)100\% = \left(\frac{20 \text{ W}}{25 \text{ W}}\right)100\% = \textbf{80\%}$$

$$P_{\text{LOSS}} = P_{\text{IN}} - P_{\text{OUT}} = 25 \text{ W} - 20 \text{ W} = \textbf{5 W}$$

Related Problem A power supply has an efficiency of 92%. If P_{IN} is 50 W, what is P_{OUT}?

**SECTION 4–5
REVIEW**

1. When a loading device draws an increased amount of current from a power supply, does this change represent a greater or a smaller load on the supply?

2. A power supply produces an output voltage of 10 V. If the supply provides 0.5 A to a load, what is the power to a load?

3. If a battery has an ampere-hour rating of 100 Ah, how long can it provide 5 A to a load?

4. If the battery in Question 3 is a 12 V device, what is its power to a load for the specified value of current?

5. An electronic power supply used in the lab operates with an input power of 1 W. It can provide an output power of 750 mW. What is its efficiency? Determine the power loss.

4–6 ■ TECHnology Theory Into Practice

In this TECH TIP section, the resistance box that you modified in Chapter 3 is back on your bench. The last time, you verified that all the resistor values were correct. This time you must make sure each resistor has a sufficient power rating; and if the power rating is insufficient, replace the resistor with one that is adequate.

Power Ratings

Assume the power rating of each resistor in the resistance box as modified in Chapter 3 is ⅛ W. The box is shown in Figure 4–12.

(a) Top view

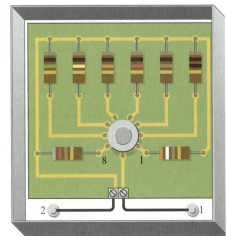

(b) Bottom view

FIGURE 4–12

■ Determine if the power rating of each resistor is adequate for a maximum of 4 V.
■ If a rating is not adequate, determine the lowest rating required to handle the maximum power. Choose from standard ratings of ¼ W, ½ W, 1 W, 2 W, and 5 W.
■ Add the power rating of each resistor to the schematic developed in Chapter 3.

<table>
<tr>
<td>

SECTION 4–6
REVIEW

</td>
<td>

1. How many resistors were replaced because of inadequate power ratings?

2. If the resistance must operate with 10 V maximum, which resistors must be changed and to what minimum power ratings?

</td>
</tr>
</table>

■ SUMMARY

- The power rating in watts of a resistor determines the maximum power that it can handle safely.
- Resistors with a larger physical size can dissipate more power in the form of heat than smaller ones.
- A resistor should have a power rating higher than the maximum power that it is expected to handle in the circuit.
- Power rating is not related to resistance value.
- A resistor normally opens when it burns out.
- Energy is the ability to do work and is equal to power multiplied by time.
- The kilowatt-hour is a unit of energy.
- One kilowatt-hour equals one thousand watts used for one hour or any other combination of watts and hours that has a product of one.
- A power supply is an energy source used to operate electrical and electronic devices.
- A battery is one type of power supply that converts chemical energy into electrical energy.
- An electronic power supply converts commercial energy (ac from the power company) to regulated dc at various voltage levels.
- The output power of a supply is the output voltage times the load current.
- A load is a device that draws current from the power supply.
- The capacity of a battery is measured in ampere-hours (Ah).
- One ampere-hour equals one ampere used for one hour, or any other combination of amperes and hours that has a product of one.
- A circuit with a high efficiency wastes less power than one with a lower efficiency.

■ GLOSSARY

These terms are also in the end-of-book glossary.

Ampere-hour rating A number given in ampere-hours (Ah) determined by multiplying the current (A) times the length of time (h) a battery can deliver that current to a load.

Efficiency The ratio of the output power to the input power of a circuit, expressed as a percent.

Energy The ability to do work.

Joule (J) The unit of energy.

Kilowatt-hour (kWh) A common unit of energy used mainly by utility companies.

Power The rate of energy usage.

Power rating The maximum amount of power that a resistor can dissipate without being damaged by excessive heat buildup.

Voltage drop The drop in energy level through a resistor.

Watt (W) The unit of power. One watt is the power when 1 J of energy is used in 1 s.

Watt's law A law that states the relationships of power to current, voltage, and resistance.

■ FORMULAS

(4–1)	$P = \dfrac{W}{t}$	Power equals energy divided by time.
(4–2)	$W = Pt$	Energy equals power multiplied by time.
(4–3)	$P = I^2 R$	Power equals current squared times resistance.
(4–4)	$P = VI$	Power equals voltage times current.

$$(4\text{–}5) \qquad P = \frac{V^2}{R} \qquad\qquad \text{Power equals voltage squared divided by resistance.}$$

$$(4\text{–}6) \qquad \text{Efficiency} = \frac{P_{OUT}}{P_{IN}} \qquad\qquad \text{Power supply efficiency}$$

$$(4\text{–}7) \qquad P_{OUT} = P_{IN} - P_{LOSS} \qquad\qquad \text{Output power is input power less power loss.}$$

■ SELF-TEST

1. Power can be defined as
   (a) energy (b) heat
   (c) the rate at which energy is used (d) the time required to use energy
2. Two hundred joules of energy are consumed in 10 s. The power is
   (a) 2000 W (b) 10 W (c) 20 W (d) 2 W
3. If it takes 300 ms to use 10,000 J of energy, the power is
   (a) 33.3 kW (b) 33.3 W (c) 33.3 mW
4. In 50 kW, there are
   (a) 500 W (b) 5000 W (c) 0.5 MW (d) 50,000 W
5. In 0.045 W, there are
   (a) 45 kW (b) 45 mW (c) 4,500 μW (d) 0.00045 MW
6. For 10 V and 50 mA, the power is
   (a) 500 mW (b) 0.5 W (c) 500,000 μW (d) answers (a), (b), and (c)
7. When the current through a 10 kΩ resistor is 10 mA, the power is
   (a) 1 W (b) 10 W (c) 100 mW (d) 1000 μW
8. A 2.2 kΩ resistor dissipates 0.5 W. The current is
   (a) 15.1 mA (b) 0.227 mA (c) 1.1 mA (d) 4.4 mA
9. A 330 Ω resistor dissipates 2 W. The voltage is
   (a) 2.57 V (b) 660 V (c) 6.6 V (d) 25.7 V
10. If you used 500 W of power for 24 h, you have used
    (a) 0.5 kWh (b) 2400 kWh (c) 12,000 kWh (d) 12 kWh
11. How many watt-hours represent 75 W used for 10 h?
    (a) 75 Wh (b) 750 Wh (c) 0.75 Wh (d) 7500 Wh
12. A 100 Ω resistor must carry a maximum current of 35 mA. Its rating should be at least
    (a) 35 W (b) 35 mW (c) 123 mW (d) 3500 mW
13. The power rating of a resistor that is to handle up to 1.1 W should be
    (a) 0.25 W (b) 1 W (c) 2 W (d) 5 W
14. A 22 Ω half-watt resistor and a 220 Ω half-watt resistor are connected across a 10 V source. Which one(s) will overheat?
    (a) 22 Ω (b) 220 Ω (c) both (d) neither
15. When the needle of an analog ohmmeter indicates infinity, the resistor being measured is
    (a) overheated (b) shorted (c) open (d) reversed
16. A 12 V battery is connected to a 600 Ω load. Under these conditions, it is rated at 50 Ah. How long can it supply current to the load?
    (a) 2500 h (b) 50 h (c) 25 h (d) 4.16 h
17. A given power supply is capable of providing 8 A for 2.5 h. Its ampere-hour rating is
    (a) 2.5 Ah (b) 20 Ah (c) 8 Ah
18. A power supply produces a 0.5 W output with an input of 0.6 W. Its percentage of efficiency is
    (a) 50% (b) 60% (c) 83.3% (d) 45%

■ PROBLEMS

More difficult problems are indicated by an asterisk (*).

SECTION 4–1   Energy and Power

1. What is the power when energy is consumed at the rate of 350 J/s?
2. How many watts are used when 7500 J of energy are consumed in 5 h?
3. How many watts does 1000 J in 50 ms equal?
4. Convert the following to kilowatts:
   (a) 1000 W   (b) 3750 W   (c) 160 W   (d) 50,000 W
5. Convert the following to megawatts:
   (a) 1,000,000 W   (b) 3×10^6 W   (c) 15×10^7 W   (d) 8700 kW
6. Convert the following to milliwatts:
   (a) 1 W   (b) 0.4 W   (c) 0.002 W   (d) 0.0125 W
7. Convert the following to microwatts:
   (a) 2 W   (b) 0.0005 W   (c) 0.25 mW   (d) 0.00667 mW
8. Convert the following to watts:
   (a) 1.5 kW   (b) 0.5 MW   (c) 350 mW   (d) 9000 μW
9. A particular electronic device uses 100 mW of power. If it runs for 24 h, how many joules of energy does it consume?
*10. A certain appliance uses 300 W. If it is allowed to run continuously for 30 days, how many kilowatt-hours of energy does it consume?
*11. At the end of a 31 day period, your utility bill shows that you have used 1500 kWh. What is your average daily power?
12. Convert 5×10^6 watt-minutes to kWh.
13. Convert 6700 watt-seconds to kWh.
14. For how many seconds must there be 5 A of current through a 47 Ω resistor in order to consume 25 J?

SECTION 4–2   Power in an Electric Circuit

15. If a 75 V source is supplying 2 A to a load, what is the resistance value of the load?
16. If a resistor has 5.5 V across it and 3 mA through it, what is the power?
17. An electric heater works on 120 V and draws 3 A of current. How much power does it use?
18. How much power is produced by 500 mA of current through a 4.7 kΩ resistor?
19. Calculate the power handled by a 10 kΩ resistor carrying 100 μA.
20. If there are 60 V across a 680 Ω resistor, what is the power?
21. A 56 Ω resistor is connected across the terminals of a 1.5 V battery. What is the power dissipation in the resistor?
22. If a resistor is to carry 2 A of current and handle 100 W of power, how many ohms must it be? Assume that the voltage can be adjusted to any required value.
23. A 12 V source is connected across a 10 Ω resistor.
   (a) How much energy is used in two minutes?
   (b) If the resistor is disconnected after one minute, is the power greater than, less than, or equal to the power during the two minute interval?

SECTION 4–3   Resistor Power Ratings

24. A 6.8 kΩ resistor has burned out in a circuit. You must replace it with another resistor with the same resistance value. If the resistor carries 10 mA, what should its power rating be? Assume that you have available resistors in all the standard power ratings.
25. A certain type of power resistor comes in the following ratings: 3 W, 5 W, 8 W, 12 W, 20 W. Your particular application requires a resistor that can handle approximately 8 W. Which rating would you use? Why?

SECTION 4–4   Energy Conversion and Voltage Drop in Resistance

26. For each circuit in Figure 4–13, assign the proper polarity for the voltage drop across the resistor.

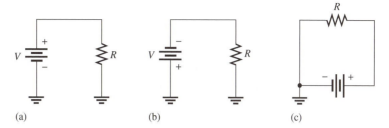

(a)   (b)   (c)

FIGURE 4–13

SECTION 4–5   Power Supplies

27. A 50 Ω load uses 1 W of power. What is the output voltage of the power supply?

28. A battery can provide 1.5 A of current for 24 h. What is its ampere-hour rating?

29. How much continuous current can be drawn from an 80 Ah battery for 10 h?

30. If a battery is rated at 650 mAh, how much current will it provide for 48 h?

31. If the input power is 500 mW and the output power is 400 mW, how much power is lost? What is the efficiency of this power supply?

32. To operate at 85% efficiency, how much output power must a source produce if the input power is 5 W?

*33. A certain power supply provides a continuous 2 W to a load. It is operating at 60% efficiency. In a 24 h period, how many kilowatt-hours does the power supply use?

EWB Troubleshooting and Analysis

These problems require your EWB compact disk.

34. Open file PRO04-34.EWB and determine the current, voltage, and resistance. Using the measured values, calculate the power.

35. Open file PRO04-35.EWB and determine the current voltage, and resistance. Calculate the power from these values.

36. Open file PRO04-36.EWB. Measure the current in the lamp and determine if the value agrees with that determined using the power and voltage rating of the lamp.

■ **ANSWERS TO SECTION REVIEWS**

Section 4–1

1. Power is the rate at which energy is used.

2. $P = W/t$

3. Watt is the unit of power. One watt is the power when 1 J of energy is used in 1 s.

4. **(a)** 68,000 W = 68 kW   **(b)** 0.005 W = 5 mW   **(c)** 0.000025 W = 25 μW

5. $W = (0.1 \text{ kW}) (10 \text{ h}) = 1 \text{ kWh}$

6. 2000 Wh = 2 kWh

7. 360,000 Ws = 0.1 kWh

Section 4–2

1. $P = (10 \text{ V})(3 \text{ A}) = 30 \text{ W}$

2. $P = (24 \text{ V})(50 \text{ mA}) = 1.2 \text{ W}$; 1.2 W; the values are the same because all energy generated by the source is dissipated by the resistance.

3. $P = (5 \text{ A})^2(56 \text{ }\Omega) = 1400 \text{ W}$

4. $P = (20 \text{ mA})^2(4.7 \text{ k}\Omega) = 1.88 \text{ W}$

5. $P = (5 \text{ V})^2/10 \text{ }\Omega = 2.5 \text{ W}$

6. $P = (8 \text{ V})^2/2.2 \text{ k}\Omega = 29.1 \text{ mW}$

7. $R = 75 \text{ W}/(0.5 \text{ A})^2 = 300 \text{ }\Omega$

Section 4–3

1. Resistors have resistance and a power rating.

2. A larger surface area of a resistor dissipates more power.

3. 0.125 W, 0.25 W, 0.5 W, 1 W

4. A 0.5 W rating should be used for 0.3 W.

Section 4–4

1. Energy conversion in a resistor is caused by collisions of the free electrons within the atomic structure.

2. A voltage drop is the potential difference between two points due to energy conversion.

Section 4–5

1. More current means a greater load.

2. $P = (10 \text{ V})(0.5 \text{ A}) = 5 \text{ W}$

3. $t = 100 \text{ Ah}/5 \text{ A} = 20 \text{ h}$

4. $P = (12 \text{ V})(5 \text{ A}) = 60 \text{ W}$

5. Eff $= (0.75 \text{ W}/1 \text{ W})100\% = 75\%$; $P_{\text{LOSS}} = 1000 \text{ mW} - 750 \text{ mW} = 250 \text{ mW}$

Section 4–6

1. Two   **2.** 10 Ω, 10 W; 100 Ω, 1 W; 400 Ω, ¼ W

■ **ANSWERS TO RELATED PROBLEMS FOR EXAMPLES**

4–1 3000 J

4–2 **(a)** 0.001 W   **(b)** 0.0018 W   **(c)** 1 W   **(d)** 0.000001 W

4–3 2 kWh

4–4 **(a)** 40 W   **(b)** 376 W   **(c)** 625 mW

4–5 60 W

4–6 0.5 W

4–7 Yes

4–8 60 Ah

4–9 46 W

■ **ANSWERS TO SELF-TEST**

1. (c)   **2.** (c)   **3.** (a)   **4.** (d)   **5.** (b)   **6.** (d)   **7.** (a)   **8.** (a)

9. (d)   **10.** (d)   **11.** (b)   **12.** (c)   **13.** (c)   **14.** (a)   **15.** (c)   **16.** (a)

17. (b)   **18.** (c)

5

SERIES CIRCUITS

 Electronics Workbench (EWB) and PSpice Tutorials available at http://www.prenhall.com/floyd

■ INTRODUCTION

In Chapter 3 you learned about Ohm's law, and in Chapter 4 you learned about power in resistors. In this chapter, those concepts are applied to circuits in which resistors are connected in a series arrangement.

Resistive circuits can be of two basic forms: series and parallel. In this chapter, series circuits are studied. Parallel circuits are covered in Chapter 6, and combinations of series and parallel resistors are examined in Chapter 7. In this chapter, you will see how Ohm's law is used in series circuits; and you will learn another important circuit law, Kirchhoff's voltage law. Also, several applications of series circuits, including voltage dividers, are presented.

When resistors are connected in series and a voltage is applied across the series connection, there is only one path for current; and, therefore, each resistor in series has the same amount of current through it. All of the resistances in series add together to produce a total resistance. The voltage drops across each of the resistors add up to the voltage applied across the entire series connection.

In the TECH TIP, Section 5–11, you are asked to evaluate a voltage-divider circuit board that will be connected to a 12 V battery to provide a selection of fixed reference voltages for use with an electronic instrument.

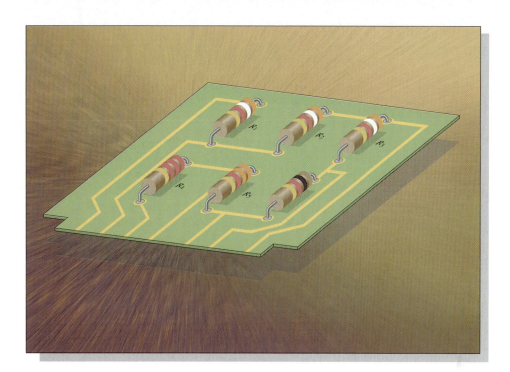

TECHnology
Theory
Into
Practice

■ CHAPTER OBJECTIVES

❑ Identify a series circuit
❑ Determine the current in a series circuit
❑ Determine total series resistance
❑ Apply Ohm's law in series circuits
❑ Determine the total effect of voltage sources in series

❑ Apply Kirchhoff's voltage law
❑ Use a series circuit as a voltage divider
❑ Determine power in a series circuit
❑ Determine and identify ground in a circuit
❑ Troubleshoot series circuits

5–1 ■ RESISTORS IN SERIES

When connected in series, resistors form a "string" in which there is only one path for current.

After completing this section, you should be able to

■ **Identify a series circuit**
  • Translate a physical arrangement of resistors into a schematic

The schematic in Figure 5–1(a) shows two resistors connected in **series** between point *A* and point *B*. Part (b) of the figure shows three resistors in series, and part (c) shows four in series. Of course, there can be any number of resistors in a series circuit.

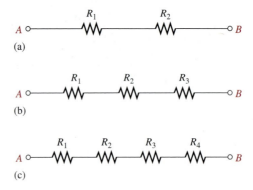

FIGURE 5–1
Resistors in series.

The only way for electrons to get from point *A* to point *B* in any of the connections of Figure 5–1 is to go through each of the resistors. The following is an important way to identify a series circuit.

> **A series circuit provides only one path for current between two points so that the current is the same through each series resistor.**

Identifying Series Circuits

In an actual circuit diagram, a series circuit may not always be as easy to visually identify as those in Figure 5–1. For example, Figure 5–2 shows series resistors drawn in other ways. Remember, if there is only one current path between two points, the resistors between those two points are in series, no matter how they appear in a diagram.

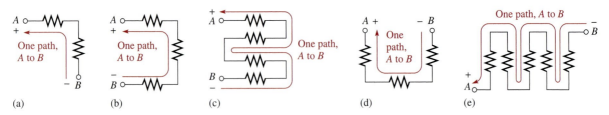

FIGURE 5–2
Some examples of series circuits. Notice that the current is the same at all points.

EXAMPLE 5–1

Suppose that there are five resistors positioned on a circuit board as shown in Figure 5–3. Wire them together in series so that, starting from the positive (+) terminal, R_1 is first, R_2 is second, R_3 is third, and so on. Draw a schematic showing this connection.

FIGURE 5–3

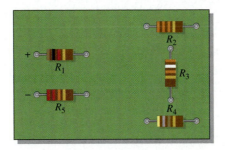

Solution   The wires are connected as shown in Figure 5–4(a), which is the assembly diagram. The schematic is shown in Figure 5–4(b). Note that the schematic does not necessarily show the actual physical arrangement of the resistors as does the assembly diagram. The schematic shows how components are connected electrically; the assembly diagram shows how components are arranged and interconnected physically.

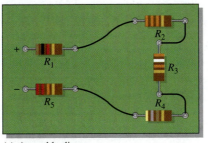

(a) Assembly diagram

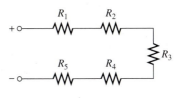

(b) Schematic

FIGURE 5–4

Related Problem   (a) Show how you would rewire the circuit board in Figure 5–4(a) so that all the odd-numbered resistors come first followed by the even-numbered ones. (b) Determine the resistance value of each resistor.

EXAMPLE 5–2

Describe how the resistors on the printed circuit (PC) board in Figure 5–5 are related electrically. Determine the resistance value of each resistor.

FIGURE 5–5

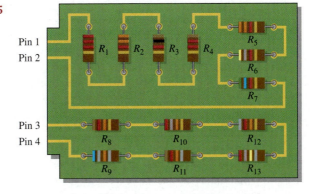

Solution Resistors R_1 through R_7 are in series with each other. This series combination is connected between pins 1 and 2 on the PC board.

Resistors R_8 through R_{13} are in series with each other. This series combination is connected between pins 3 and 4 on the PC board.

The values of the resistors are $R_1 = 2.2$ kΩ, $R_2 = 3.3$ kΩ, $R_3 = 1.0$ kΩ, $R_4 = 1.2$ kΩ, $R_5 = 3.3$ kΩ, $R_6 = 4.7$ kΩ, $R_7 = 5.6$ kΩ, $R_8 = 12$ kΩ, $R_9 = 68$ kΩ, $R_{10} = 27$ kΩ, $R_{11} = 12$ kΩ, $R_{12} = 82$ kΩ, and $R_{13} = 270$ kΩ.

Related Problem How is the circuit changed when pin 2 and pin 3 in Figure 5–5 are connected?

SECTION 5–1 REVIEW

1. How are the resistors connected in a series circuit?
2. How can you identify a series circuit?
3. Complete the schematics for the circuits in each part of Figure 5–6 by connecting each group of resistors in series in numerical order from terminal A to B.
4. Connect each group of series resistors in Figure 5–6 in series with each other.

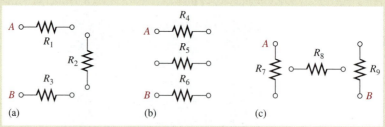

(a)   (b)   (c)

FIGURE 5–6

5–2 ■ CURRENT IN A SERIES CIRCUIT

The current is the same through all points in a series circuit. The current through each resistor in a series circuit is the same as the current through all the other resistors that are in series with it.

After completing this section, you should be able to

■ **Determine the current in a series circuit**
   • Show that the current is the same at all points in a series circuit

Figure 5–7 shows three resistors connected in series to a dc voltage source. *At any point in this circuit, the current into that point must equal the current out of that point,* as illustrated by the current directional arrows at points *A, B, C,* and *D* in part (b). Notice also that the current out of each resistor must equal the current into each resistor because there is no place where part of the current can branch off and go somewhere else. Therefore, the current in each section of the circuit is the same as the current in all other sections. It has only one path going from the negative (−) side of the source to the positive (+) side.

Let's assume that the battery in Figure 5–7 supplies two amperes of current to the series resistance. There are two amperes of current out of the battery's negative terminal. When ammeters are connected at several points in the circuit as shown in Figure 5–8, each meter reads two amperes.

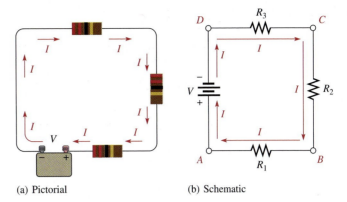

(a) Pictorial (b) Schematic

FIGURE 5–7
Current into any point in a series circuit is the same as the current out of that point.

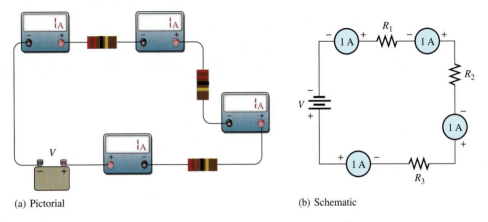

(a) Pictorial (b) Schematic

FIGURE 5–8
Current is the same at all points in a series circuit.

**SECTION 5–2
REVIEW**

1. In a circuit with a 10 Ω and a 4.7 Ω resistor in series, there is 1 A of current through the 10 Ω resistor. How much current is through the 4.7 Ω resistor?

2. A milliammeter is connected between points A and B in Figure 5–9. It measures 50 mA. If you move the meter and connect it between points C and D, how much current will it indicate? Between E and F?

3. In Figure 5–10, how much current does ammeter 1 indicate? How much current does ammeter 2 indicate?

4. What statement can you make about the amount of current in a series circuit?

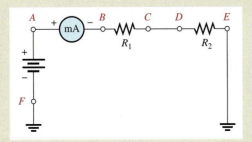

FIGURE 5–9

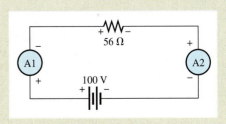

FIGURE 5–10

5–3 ■ TOTAL SERIES RESISTANCE

The total resistance of a series circuit is equal to the sum of the resistances of each individual series resistor.

After completing this section, you should be able to

■ **Determine total series resistance**
  - Explain why resistance values add when resistors are connected in series
  - Apply the series resistance formula

Series Resistor Values Add

When resistors are connected in series, the resistor values add because each resistor offers opposition to the current in direct proportion to its resistance. A greater number of resistors connected in series creates more opposition to current. More opposition to current implies a higher value of resistance. Thus, every time a resistor is added in series, the total resistance increases.

Figure 5–11 illustrates how series resistances add to increase the total resistance. Figure 5–11(a) has a single 10 Ω resistor. Figure 5–11(b) shows another 10 Ω resistor connected in series with the first one, making a total resistance of 20 Ω. If a third 10 Ω resistor is connected in series with the first two, as shown in Figure 5–11(c), the total resistance becomes 30 Ω.

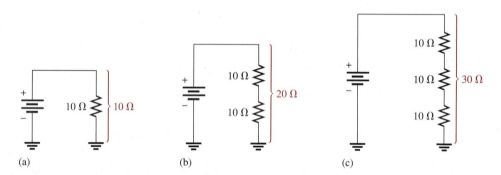

FIGURE 5–11
Total resistance increases with each additional series resistor.

Series Resistance Formula

For any number of individual resistors connected in series, the total resistance is the sum of each of the individual values.

$$R_T = R_1 + R_2 + R_3 + \cdots + R_n \qquad (5–1)$$

where R_T is the total resistance and R_n is the last resistor in the series string (n can be any positive integer equal to the number of resistors in series). For example, if there are four resistors in series ($n = 4$), the total resistance formula is

$$R_T = R_1 + R_2 + R_3 + R_4$$

If there are six resistors in series ($n = 6$), the total resistance formula is

$$R_T = R_1 + R_2 + R_3 + R_4 + R_5 + R_6$$

To illustrate the calculation of total series resistance, let's determine R_T in the circuit of Figure 5–12, where V_S is the source voltage. The circuit has five resistors in series. To get the total resistance, simply add the values as follows:

$$R_T = 56\ \Omega + 100\ \Omega + 27\ \Omega + 10\ \Omega + 47\ \Omega = 240\ \Omega$$

Note in Figure 5–12 that the order in which the resistances are added does not matter. You can physically change the positions of the resistors in the circuit without affecting the total resistance.

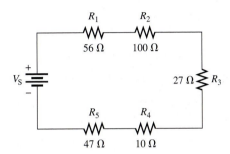

FIGURE 5–12
Example of five resistors in series.

EXAMPLE 5–3

Connect the resistors in Figure 5–13 in series, and determine the total resistance, R_T.

FIGURE 5–13

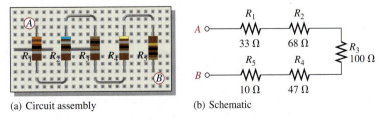

Solution The resistors are connected as shown in Figure 5–14. Find the total resistance by adding all the values as follows:

$$R_T = R_1 + R_2 + R_3 + R_4 + R_5 = 33\ \Omega + 68\ \Omega + 100\ \Omega + 47\ \Omega + 10\ \Omega = \mathbf{258\ \Omega}$$

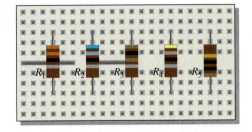

(a) Circuit assembly   (b) Schematic

FIGURE 5–14

Related Problem Determine the total resistance in Figure 5–14(a) if the positions of R_2 and R_4 are interchanged.

EXAMPLE 5–4   What is the total resistance (R_T) in the circuit of Figure 5–15?

FIGURE 5–15

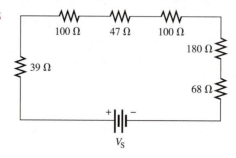

Solution   Sum all the values.

$$R_T = 39 \ \Omega + 100 \ \Omega + 47 \ \Omega + 100 \ \Omega + 180 \ \Omega + 68 \ \Omega = \textbf{534 } \mathbf{\Omega}$$

Related Problem   What is the total resistance for the following series resistors: 1.0 kΩ, 2.2 kΩ, 3.3 kΩ, and 5.6 kΩ?

EXAMPLE 5–5   Determine the value of R_4 in the circuit of Figure 5–16.

FIGURE 5–16

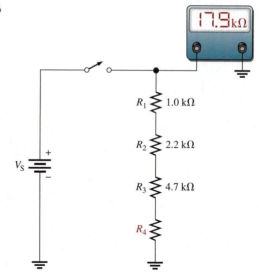

Solution   From the ohmmeter reading, $R_T = 17.9$ kΩ.

$$R_T = R_1 + R_2 + R_3 + R_4$$

Solving for R_4 yields

$$R_4 = R_T - (R_1 + R_2 + R_3) = 17.9 \text{ k}\Omega - (1.0 \text{ k}\Omega + 2.2 \text{ k}\Omega + 4.7 \text{ k}\Omega) = \textbf{10 k}\mathbf{\Omega}$$

The calculator sequence for determining R_4 is

[1] [7] [•] [9] [EE] [3] [–] [(] [(] [1] [EE] [3] [+] [2] [•] [2] [EE] [3]
[+] [4] [•] [7] [EE] [3] [)] [=]

Related Problem   Determine the value of R_4 in Figure 5–16 if the ohmmeter reading is 14.7 kΩ.

Equal-Value Series Resistors

When a circuit has more than one resistor of the same value in series, there is a shortcut method to obtain the total resistance: Simply multiply the resistance value by the number of equal-value resistors that are in series. This method is essentially the same as adding the values. For example, five 100 Ω resistors in series have an R_T of 5(100 Ω) = 500 Ω. In general, the formula is expressed as

$$R_T = nR \qquad\qquad (5\text{-}2)$$

where n is the number of equal-value resistors and R is the resistance value.

EXAMPLE 5-6

Find the R_T of eight 22 Ω resistors in series.

Solution   Find R_T by adding the values.

$$R_T = 22\ \Omega + 22\ \Omega + 22\ \Omega + 22\ \Omega + 22\ \Omega + 22\ \Omega + 22\ \Omega + 22\ \Omega = \textbf{176 } \boldsymbol{\Omega}$$

However, it is much easier to multiply to get the same result.

$$R_T = 8(22\ \Omega) = \textbf{176 } \boldsymbol{\Omega}$$

Related Problem   Find R_T for three 1.0 kΩ resistors and two 720 Ω resistors in series.

SECTION 5-3 REVIEW

1. The following resistors (one each) are in series: 1.0 Ω, 2.2 Ω, 3.3 Ω, and 4.7 Ω. What is the total resistance?

2. The following resistors are in series: one 100 Ω, two 56 Ω, four 12 Ω, and one 330 Ω. What is the total resistance?

3. Suppose that you have one resistor each of the following values: 1.0 kΩ, 2.7 kΩ, 5.6 kΩ, and 560 Ω. To get a total resistance of approximately 13.8 kΩ, you need one more resistor. What should its value be?

4. What is the R_T for twelve 56 Ω resistors in series?

5. What is the R_T for twenty 5.6 kΩ resistors and thirty 8.2 kΩ resistors in series?

5-4 ■ OHM'S LAW IN SERIES CIRCUITS

The use of Ohm's law and the basic concepts of series circuits are applied in several examples.

After completing this section, you should be able to

■ **Apply Ohm's law in series circuits**
  • Find the current in a series circuit
  • Find the voltage across each resistor in series

EXAMPLE 5–7

Find the current in the circuit of Figure 5–17.

FIGURE 5–17

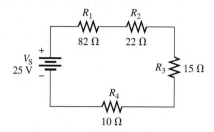

Solution The current is determined by the voltage and the total resistance. First, calculate the total resistance.

$$R_T = R_1 + R_2 + R_3 + R_4 = 82\ \Omega + 22\ \Omega + 15\ \Omega + 10\ \Omega = 129\ \Omega$$

Next, use Ohm's law to calculate the current.

$$I = \frac{V_S}{R_T} = \frac{25\ \text{V}}{129\ \Omega} = 0.194\ \text{A} = \textbf{194 mA}$$

Remember, the same current exists at all points in the circuit. Thus, each resistor has 194 mA through it.

Related Problem What is the current in Figure 5–17 if R_4 is changed to 100 Ω?

EXAMPLE 5–8

The current in the circuit of Figure 5–18 is 1 mA. For this amount of current, what must the source voltage V_S be?

FIGURE 5–18

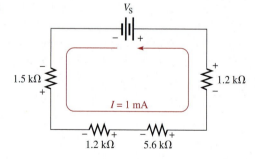

Solution In order to calculate V_S, first determine R_T.

$$R_T = 1.2\ \text{k}\Omega + 5.6\ \text{k}\Omega + 1.2\ \text{k}\Omega + 1.5\ \text{k}\Omega = 9.5\ \text{k}\Omega$$

Next, use Ohm's law to get V_S.

$$V_S = IR_T = (1\ \text{mA})(9.5\ \text{k}\Omega) = \textbf{9.5 V}$$

Related Problem Calculate V_S if the 5.6 kΩ resistor is changed to 3.9 kΩ with the current the same.

EXAMPLE 5–9   Calculate the voltage across each resistor in Figure 5–19, and find the value of V_S. To what maximum value can V_S be raised before the fuse blows?

FIGURE 5–19

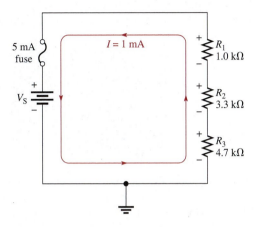

Solution   By Ohm's law, the voltage across each resistor is equal to its resistance multiplied by the current through it. Use the Ohm's law formula $V = IR$ to determine the voltage across each of the resistors. Keep in mind that there is the same current through each series resistor. The fuse is effectively like a wire and has negligible resistance. The voltage across R_1 (designated V_1) is

$$V_1 = IR_1 = (1 \text{ mA})(1.0 \text{ k}\Omega) = \textbf{1 V}$$

The voltage across R_2 is

$$V_2 = IR_2 = (1 \text{ mA})(3.3 \text{ k}\Omega) = \textbf{3.3 V}$$

The voltage across R_3 is

$$V_3 = IR_3 = (1 \text{ mA})(4.7 \text{ k}\Omega) = \textbf{4.7 V}$$

To find the value of V_S, first determine R_T.

$$R_T = 1.0 \text{ k}\Omega + 3.3 \text{ k}\Omega + 4.7 \text{ k}\Omega = 9 \text{ k}\Omega$$

The source voltage V_S is equal to the current times the total resistance.

$$V_S = IR_T = (1 \text{ mA})(9 \text{ k}\Omega) = \textbf{9 V}$$

Notice that if you add the voltage drops of the resistors, they total 9 V, which is the same as the source voltage.

   The fuse has a rating of 5 mA; thus V_S can be increased to a value where $I = 5$ mA. Calculate the maximum value of V_S as follows:

$$V_{S(max)} = IR_T = (5 \text{ mA})(9 \text{ k}\Omega) = \textbf{45 V}$$

Related Problem   Repeat the calculations for V_1, V_2, V_3, V_S, and $V_{S(max)}$ if $R_3 = 2.2 \text{ k}\Omega$ and I is maintained at 1 mA.

EXAMPLE 5–10   Some resistors are not color coded with bands but have the values stamped on the resistor body. When the circuit board shown in Figure 5–20 was assembled, the resistors were erroneously mounted with the labels turned down, and there is no documentation showing the resistor values. Without removing the resistors from the board, use Ohm's law to determine the resistance of each one. Assume that a voltmeter, ammeter, and power supply are readily available, but no ohmmeter is available.

FIGURE 5–20

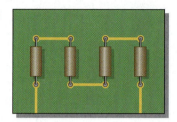

Solution   The resistors are all in series, so the current is the same through each one. Measure the current by connecting a 12 V source (arbitrary value) and an ammeter as shown in Figure 5–21. Measure the voltage across each resistor by placing the voltmeter across the first resistor. Then repeat this measurement for the other three resistors. For illustration, the voltage values indicated on the board are assumed to be the measured values.

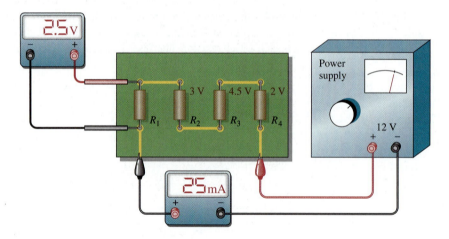

FIGURE 5–21
The voltmeter readings across each resistor are indicated.

Determine the resistance of each resistor by substituting the measured values of current and voltage into the Ohm's law formula.

$$R_1 = \frac{V_1}{I} = \frac{2.5\ \text{V}}{25\ \text{mA}} = 100\ \Omega$$

$$R_2 = \frac{V_2}{I} = \frac{3\ \text{V}}{25\ \text{mA}} = 120\ \Omega$$

$$R_3 = \frac{V_3}{I} = \frac{4.5\ \text{V}}{25\ \text{mA}} = 180\ \Omega$$

$$R_4 = \frac{V_4}{I} = \frac{2\ \text{V}}{25\ \text{mA}} = 80\ \Omega$$

Notice that the largest-value resistor has the largest voltage drop across it.

Related Problem   What is an easier way to determine the resistance values?

1. A 10 V battery is connected across three 100 Ω resistors in series. What is the current through each resistor?

2. How much voltage is required to produce 5 A through the circuit of Figure 5–22?

FIGURE 5–22

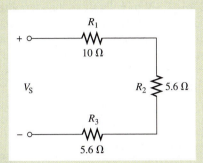

3. How much voltage is dropped across each resistor in Figure 5–22 when the current is 5 A?

4. There are four equal-value resistors connected in series with a 5 V source. A current of 4.63 mA is measured. What is the value of each resistor?

5–5 ■ VOLTAGE SOURCES IN SERIES

A voltage source is an energy source that provides a constant voltage to a load. Batteries and electronic power supplies are practical examples of dc voltage sources.

After completing this section, you should be able to

■ **Determine the total effect of voltage sources in series**
  • Determine the total voltage of series sources with the same polarities
  • Determine the total voltage of series sources with opposite polarities

When two or more voltage sources are in series, the total voltage is equal to the algebraic sum of the individual source voltages. The algebraic sum means that the polarities of the sources must be included when the sources are combined in series. Sources with opposite polarities have voltages with opposite signs.

$$V_{S(tot)} = V_{S1} + V_{S2} + \cdots + V_{Sn}$$

When the voltage sources are all in the same direction in terms of their polarities, as in Figure 5–23(a), all of the voltages have the same sign when added; there is a total of 4.5 V from terminal A to terminal B with A more positive than B.

$$V_{AB} = 1.5 \text{ V} + 1.5 \text{ V} + 1.5 \text{ V} = +4.5 \text{ V}$$

The voltage has a double subscript, AB, to indicate that it is the voltage at point A with respect to point B.

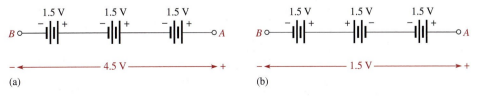

(a)   (b)

FIGURE 5–23
Voltage sources in series add algebraically.

In Figure 5–23(b), the middle voltage source is opposite to the other two; so its voltage has an opposite sign when added to the others. For this case the total voltage from *A* to *B* is

$$V_{AB} = +1.5 \text{ V} - 1.5 \text{ V} + 1.5 \text{ V} = +1.5 \text{ V}$$

Terminal *A* is 1.5 V more positive than terminal *B*.

A familiar example of voltage sources in series is the flashlight. When you put two 1.5 V batteries in your flashlight, they are connected in series, giving a total of 3 V. When connecting batteries or other voltage sources in series to increase the total voltage, always connect from the positive (+) terminal of one to the negative (−) terminal of another. Such a connection is illustrated in Figure 5–24.

FIGURE 5–24
Connection of three 6 V batteries to obtain 18 V.

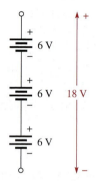

The following two examples illustrate calculation of total source voltage.

EXAMPLE 5–11   What is the total source voltage ($V_{S(tot)}$) in Figure 5–25?

FIGURE 5–25

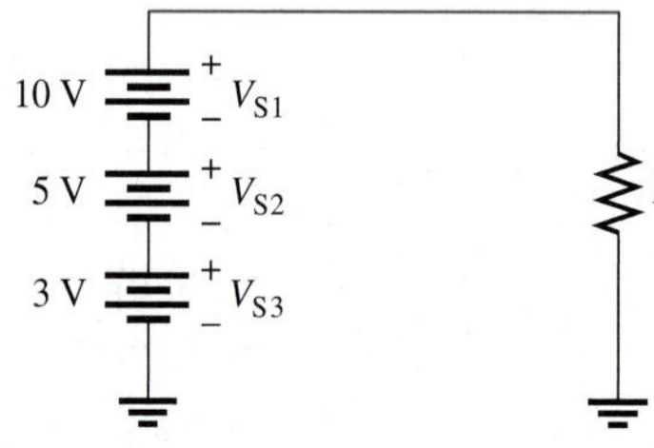

Solution   The polarity of each source is the same (the sources are connected in the same direction in the circuit). So add the three voltages to get the total.

$$V_{S(tot)} = V_{S1} + V_{S2} + V_{S3} = 10 \text{ V} + 5 \text{ V} + 3 \text{ V} = \textbf{18 V}$$

The three individual sources can be replaced by a single equivalent source of 18 V with its polarity as shown in Figure 5–26.

FIGURE 5–26

18 V ⎓ $V_{S(tot)}$ R

Related Problem   If the V_{S3} source in Figure 5–25 is reversed, what is the total source voltage?

EXAMPLE 5–12   Determine $V_{S(tot)}$ in Figure 5–27.

FIGURE 5–27

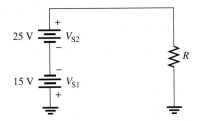

Solution   These sources are connected in opposing directions. If you go clockwise around the circuit, you go from plus to minus through V_{S1}, and minus to plus through V_{S2}. The total voltage is the difference of the two source voltages (algebraic sum of oppositely signed values). The total voltage has the same polarity as the larger-value source. Here we will choose V_{S2} to be positive.

$$V_{S(tot)} = V_{S2} - V_{S1} = 25 \text{ V} - 15 \text{ V} = \textbf{10 V}$$

The two sources in Figure 5–27 can be replaced by a single 10 V equivalent source with polarity as shown in Figure 5–28.

FIGURE 5–28

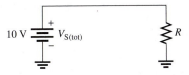

Related Problem   If an 8 V source in the direction of V_{S1} is added in series in Figure 5–27, what is $V_{S(tot)}$?

SECTION 5–5 REVIEW

1. Four 1.5 V flashlight batteries are connected in series plus to minus. What is the total voltage of all four cells?

2. How many 12 V batteries must be connected in series to produce 60 V? Sketch a schematic that shows the battery connections.

3. The resistive circuit in Figure 5–29 is used to bias a transistor amplifier. Show how to connect two 15 V power supplies in order to get 30 V across the two resistors.

4. Determine the total source voltage in each circuit of Figure 5–30.

5. Sketch the equivalent single-source circuit for each circuit of Figure 5–30.

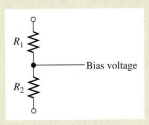

FIGURE 5–29

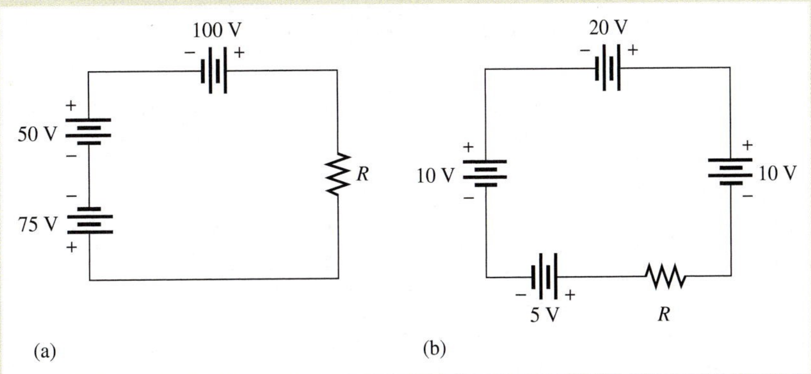

FIGURE 5–30

5–6 ■ KIRCHHOFF'S VOLTAGE LAW

Kirchhoff's voltage law is a fundamental circuit law that states that the algebraic sum of all the voltages around a closed path is zero or, in other words, the sum of the voltage drops equals the total source voltage.

After completing this section, you should be able to

■ **Apply Kirchhoff's voltage law**
  • State Kirchhoff's voltage law
  • Determine the source voltage by adding the voltage drops
  • Determine an unknown voltage drop

In an electric circuit, the voltages across the resistors (voltage drops) *always* have polarities opposite to the source voltage polarity. For example, in Figure 5–31, follow a counterclockwise loop around the circuit and note that the source polarity is plus-to-minus and each voltage drop is minus-to-plus.

Also notice in Figure 5–31 that the current is out of the negative side of the source and through the resistors as indicated by the arrows. The current is into the negative side of each resistor and out the positive side. The drop in energy level across a resistor creates a potential difference, or voltage drop, with a minus-to-plus polarity in the direction of the current.

Notice that the voltage from point A to point B in the circuit of Figure 5–31 equals the source voltage, V_S. Also, the voltage from A to B is the sum of the series resistor voltage drops. Therefore, the source voltage is equal to the sum of the three voltage drops.

This discussion is an example of **Kirchhoff's voltage law,** which is generally stated as follows:

> **The sum of all the voltage drops around a single closed loop in a circuit is equal to the total source voltage in that loop.**

The general concept of Kirchhoff's voltage law is illustrated in Figure 5–32 and expressed by Equation (5–3).

$$V_S = V_1 + V_2 + V_3 + \cdots + V_n \tag{5–3}$$

where the subscript n represents the number of voltage drops.

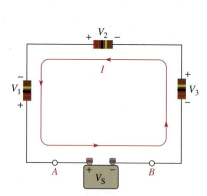

FIGURE 5–31
Kirchhoff's voltage law: The sum of the voltage drops equals the source voltage.

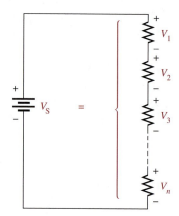

FIGURE 5–32
Sum of n voltage drops equals the source voltage.

Another Way to State Kirchhoff's Voltage Law

If all the voltage drops around a closed loop are added and then this total is subtracted from the source voltage, the result is zero. This result occurs because the sum of the voltage drops always equals the source voltage.

The algebraic sum of all voltages (both source and drops) around a closed path is zero.

Therefore, another way of expressing Kirchhoff's voltage law is as follows:

$$V_S - V_1 - V_2 - V_3 = 0 \qquad \textbf{(5–4)}$$

You can verify Kirchhoff's voltage law by connecting a circuit and measuring each resistor voltage and the source voltage as illustrated in Figure 5–33. When the resistor voltages are added together, their sum will equal the source voltage. Any number of resistors can be added.

FIGURE 5–33

Experimental verification of Kirchhoff's voltage law.

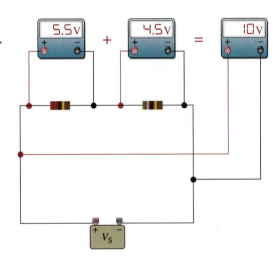

The following three examples use Kirchhoff's voltage law to solve circuit problems.

EXAMPLE 5–13 Determine the source voltage V_S in Figure 5–34 where the two voltage drops are given. There is no voltage drop across the fuse.

FIGURE 5–34

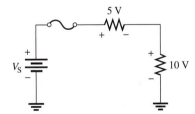

Solution By Kirchhoff's voltage law, (Eq. 5–3), the source voltage (applied voltage) must equal the sum of the voltage drops. Adding the voltage drops gives the value of the source voltage.

$$V_S = 5 \text{ V} + 10 \text{ V} = \textbf{15 V}$$

Related Problem If V_S is increased to 30 V, determine the two voltage drops.

EXAMPLE 5–14   Determine the unknown voltage drop, V_3, in Figure 5–35.

FIGURE 5–35

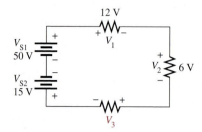

Solution   By Kirchhoff's voltage law (Eq. 5–4), the algebraic sum of all the voltages around the circuit is zero. The value of each voltage drop except V_3 is known. Substitute these values into the equation.

$$-V_{S2} + V_{S1} - V_1 - V_2 - V_3 = 0$$
$$-15 \text{ V} + 50 \text{ V} - 12 \text{ V} - 6 \text{ V} - V_3 = 0 \text{ V}$$

Next, combine the known values. Transpose 17 V to the right side of the equation, and cancel the minus signs.

$$17 \text{ V} - V_3 = 0 \text{ V}$$
$$-V_3 = -17 \text{ V}$$
$$V_3 = \mathbf{17 \text{ V}}$$

The voltage drop across R_3 is 17 V, and its polarity is as shown in Figure 5–35.

Related Problem   Determine V_3 if the polarity of V_{S2} is reversed in Figure 5–35.

EXAMPLE 5–15   Find the value of R_4 in Figure 5–36.

FIGURE 5–36

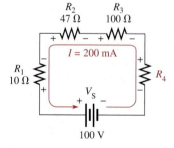

Solution   In this problem you will use both Ohm's law and Kirchhoff's voltage law. First, use Ohm's law to find the voltage drop across each of the known resistors.

$$V_1 = IR_1 = (200 \text{ mA})(10 \text{ } \Omega) = 2.0 \text{ V}$$
$$V_2 = IR_2 = (200 \text{ mA})(47 \text{ } \Omega) = 9.4 \text{ V}$$
$$V_3 = IR_3 = (200 \text{ mA})(100 \text{ } \Omega) = 20 \text{ V}$$

Next, use Kirchhoff's voltage law to find V_4, the voltage drop across the unknown resistor.

$$V_S - V_1 - V_2 - V_3 - V_4 = 0 \text{ V}$$
$$100 \text{ V} - 2.0 \text{ V} - 9.4 \text{ V} - 20 \text{ V} - V_4 = 0 \text{ V}$$
$$68.6 \text{ V} - V_4 = 0 \text{ V}$$
$$V_4 = 68.6 \text{ V}$$

Now that you know V_4, use Ohm's law to calculate R_4 as follows:

$$R_4 = \frac{V_4}{I} = \frac{68.6 \text{ V}}{200 \text{ mA}} = \textbf{343 } \boldsymbol{\Omega}$$

This is most likely a 330 Ω resistor because 343 Ω is within a standard tolerance range (+5%) of 330 Ω.

Related Problem   Determine R_4 in Figure 5–36 for V_S = 150 V and I = 200 mA.

SECTION 5–6 REVIEW

1. State Kirchhoff's voltage law in two ways.

2. A 50 V source is connected to a series resistive circuit. What is the total of the voltage drops in this circuit?

3. Two equal-value resistors are connected in series across a 10 V battery. What is the voltage drop across each resistor?

4. In a series circuit with a 25 V source, there are three resistors. One voltage drop is 5 V, and the other is 10 V. What is the value of the third voltage drop?

5. The individual voltage drops in a series string are as follows: 1 V, 3 V, 5 V, 8 V, and 7 V. What is the total voltage applied across the series string?

5–7 ■ VOLTAGE DIVIDERS

A series circuit acts as a voltage divider. You will learn what this term means and why voltage dividers are an important application of series circuits.

After completing this section, you should be able to

■ **Use a series circuit as a voltage divider**
  • Apply the voltage-divider formula
  • Use the potentiometer as an adjustable voltage divider
  • Describe some voltage-divider applications

To illustrate how a series string of resistors acts as a voltage divider, let's examine Figure 5–37 where there are two resistors in series. There are two voltage drops across the resistors: one across R_1 and one across R_2. These voltage drops are V_1 and V_2, respectively, as indicated in the schematic.

FIGURE 5–37
Two-resistor voltage divider.

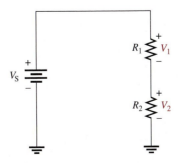

Since each resistor has the same current, the voltage drops are proportional to the resistance values. For example, if the value of R_2 is twice that of R_1, then the value of V_2 is twice that of V_1. In other words, *the total voltage drop divides among the series resistors in amounts directly proportional to the resistance values.*

For example, in Figure 5–37, if V_S is 10 V, R_1 is 50 Ω, and R_2 is 100 Ω, then V_1 is one-third the total voltage, or 3.33 V, because R_1 is one-third the total resistance of 150 Ω. Likewise, V_2 is two-thirds V_S, or 6.67 V.

Voltage-Divider Formula

With a few steps, a formula for determining how the voltages divide among series resistors can be developed. Let's assume that we have several resistors in series as shown in Figure 5–38. This figure shows five resistors as an example, but there can be any number.

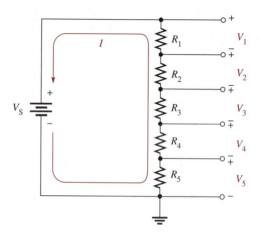

FIGURE 5–38
Five-resistor voltage divider.

Let's call the voltage drop across any one of the resistors V_x, where x represents the number of a particular resistor (1, 2, 3, and so on). By Ohm's law, the voltage drop across any of the resistors in Figure 5–38 can be written as follows:

$$V_x = IR_x$$

where x = 1, 2, 3, 4, or 5.

The current is equal to the source voltage divided by the total resistance ($I = V_S/R_T$). For the example circuit of Figure 5–38, the total resistance is $R_1 + R_2 + R_3 + R_4 + R_5$. Substituting V_S/R_T for I in the expression for V_x results in

$$V_x = \left(\frac{V_S}{R_T}\right)R_x$$

Rearranging the terms yields

$$V_x = \left(\frac{R_x}{R_T}\right)V_S \tag{5–5}$$

Equation (5–5) is the general voltage-divider formula. It can be stated as follows:

The voltage drop across any resistor or combination of resistors in a series circuit is equal to the ratio of that resistance value to the total resistance, multiplied by the source voltage.

The following three examples illustrate use of the voltage-divider formula.

EXAMPLE 5–16   Determine V_1 (the voltage across R_1) and V_2 (the voltage across R_2) in the voltage divider in Figure 5–39.

FIGURE 5–39

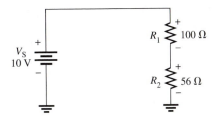

Solution   To determine V_1, use the voltage-divider formula, $V_x = (R_x/R_T)V_S$, where $x = 1$. The total resistance is

$$R_T = R_1 + R_2 = 100\ \Omega + 56\ \Omega = 156\ \Omega$$

R_1 is 100 Ω and V_S is 10 V. Substitute these values into the voltage-divider formula.

$$V_1 = \left(\frac{R_1}{R_T}\right)V_S = \left(\frac{100\ \Omega}{156\ \Omega}\right)10\ \text{V} = \textbf{6.41 V}$$

There are two ways to find the value of V_2: Kirchhoff's voltage law or the voltage-divider formula. If you use Kirchhoff's voltage law ($V_S = V_1 + V_2$), substitute the values for V_S and V_1 as follows:

$$V_2 = V_S - V_1 = 10\ \text{V} - 6.41\ \text{V} = \textbf{3.59 V}$$

A second way to find V_2 is to use the voltage-divider formula where $x = 2$.

$$V_2 = \left(\frac{R_2}{R_T}\right)V_S = \left(\frac{56\ \Omega}{156\ \Omega}\right)10\ \text{V} = \textbf{3.59 V}$$

You get the same result either way.

Related Problem   Find the voltages across R_1 and R_2 in Figure 5–39 if R_2 is changed to 180 Ω.

EXAMPLE 5–17   Calculate the voltage drop across each resistor in the voltage divider of Figure 5–40.

FIGURE 5–40

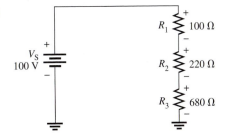

Solution   Look at the circuit for a moment and consider the following: The total resistance is 1000 Ω. Ten percent of the total voltage is across R_1 because it is 10% of the total resistance (100 Ω is 10% of 1000 Ω). Likewise, 22% of the total voltage is dropped across R_2 because it is 22% of the total resistance (220 Ω is 22% of 1000 Ω). Finally, R_3 drops 68% of the total voltage because 680 Ω is 68% of 1000 Ω.

Because of the convenient values in this problem, it is easy to figure the voltages mentally. ($V_1 = 0.10 \times 100$ V $= 10$ V, $V_2 = 0.22 \times 100$ V $= 22$ V, and $V_3 = 0.68 \times 100$ V $= 68$ V). Such is not always the case, but sometimes a little thinking will produce a result more efficiently and eliminate some calculating. This is also a good way to roughly estimate what your results should be so that you will recognize an unreasonable answer as a result of a calculation error.

Although you have already reasoned through this problem, the calculations will verify your results.

$$V_1 = \left(\frac{R_1}{R_T}\right)V_S = \left(\frac{100\ \Omega}{1000\ \Omega}\right)100\ \text{V} = \mathbf{10\ V}$$

$$V_2 = \left(\frac{R_2}{R_T}\right)V_S = \left(\frac{220\ \Omega}{1000\ \Omega}\right)100\ \text{V} = \mathbf{22\ V}$$

$$V_3 = \left(\frac{R_3}{R_T}\right)V_S = \left(\frac{680\ \Omega}{1000\ \Omega}\right)100\ \text{V} = \mathbf{68\ V}$$

Notice that the sum of the voltage drops is equal to the source voltage, in accordance with Kirchhoff's voltage law. This check is a good way to verify your results.

Related Problem If R_1 and R_2 in Figure 5–40 are changed to 680 Ω, what are the voltage drops?

EXAMPLE 5–18

Determine the voltages between the following points in the voltage divider of Figure 5–41:

(a) *A* to *B*   **(b)** *A* to *C*   **(c)** *B* to *C* .   **(d)** *B* to *D*   **(e)** *C* to *D*

FIGURE 5–41

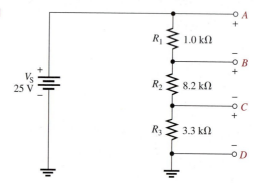

Solution First, determine R_T.

$$R_T = R_1 + R_2 + R_3 = 1.0\ \text{k}\Omega + 8.2\ \text{k}\Omega + 3.3\ \text{k}\Omega = 12.5\ \text{k}\Omega$$

Next, apply the voltage-divider formula to obtain each required voltage.
(a) The voltage *A* to *B* is the voltage drop across R_1.

$$V_{AB} = \left(\frac{R_1}{R_T}\right)V_S = \left(\frac{1.0\ \text{k}\Omega}{12.5\ \text{k}\Omega}\right)25\ \text{V} = \mathbf{2\ V}$$

(b) The voltage from *A* to *C* is the combined voltage drop across both R_1 and R_2. In this case, R_x in the general formula given in Equation (5–5) is $R_1 + R_2$.

$$V_{AC} = \left(\frac{R_1 + R_2}{R_T}\right)V_S = \left(\frac{9.2\ \text{k}\Omega}{12.5\ \text{k}\Omega}\right)25\ \text{V} = \mathbf{18.4\ V}$$

(c) The voltage from B to C is the voltage drop across R_2.

$$V_{BC} = \left(\frac{R_2}{R_T}\right)V_S = \left(\frac{8.2 \text{ k}\Omega}{12.5 \text{ k}\Omega}\right)25 \text{ V} = \textbf{16.4 V}$$

(d) The voltage from B to D is the combined voltage drop across both R_2 and R_3. In this case, R_x in the general formula is $R_2 + R_3$.

$$V_{BD} = \left(\frac{R_2 + R_3}{R_T}\right)V_S = \left(\frac{11.5 \text{ k}\Omega}{12.5 \text{ k}\Omega}\right)25 \text{ V} = \textbf{23 V}$$

(e) Finally, the voltage from C to D is the voltage drop across R_3.

$$V_{CD} = \left(\frac{R_3}{R_T}\right)V_S = \left(\frac{3.3 \text{ k}\Omega}{12.5 \text{ k}\Omega}\right)25 \text{ V} = \textbf{6.6 V}$$

If you connect this voltage divider in the lab, you can verify each of the calculated voltages by connecting a voltmeter between the appropriate points in each case.

Related Problem Determine each of the previously calculated voltages if V_S is doubled.

The Potentiometer as an Adjustable Voltage Divider

Recall from Chapter 2 that a potentiometer is a variable resistor with three terminals. A potentiometer connected to a voltage source is shown in Figure 5–42(a) with the schematic shown in part (b). Notice that the two end terminals are labeled 1 and 2. The adjustable terminal or wiper is labeled 3. The potentiometer acts as a voltage divider, which can be illustrated by separating the total resistance into two parts, as shown in Figure 5–42(c). The resistance between terminal 1 and terminal 3 (R_{13}) is one part, and the resistance between terminal 3 and terminal 2 (R_{32}) is the other part. So this potentiometer is equivalent to a two-resistor voltage divider that can be manually adjusted.

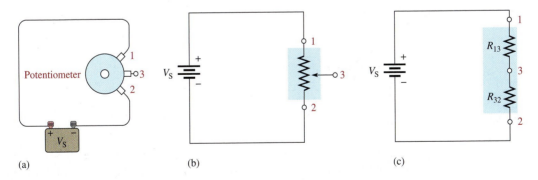

FIGURE 5–42
The potentiometer is a voltage divider.

Figure 5–43 shows what happens when the wiper terminal (3) is moved. In part (a) of Figure 5–43, the wiper is exactly centered, making the two resistances equal. If you measure the voltage across terminals 3 to 2 as indicated by the voltmeter symbol, you have one-half of the total source voltage. When the wiper is moved up, as in Figure 5–43(b), the resistance between terminals 3 and 2 increases, and the voltage across it increases proportionally. When the wiper is moved down, as in Figure 5–43(c), the resistance between terminals 3 and 2 decreases, and the voltage decreases proportionally.

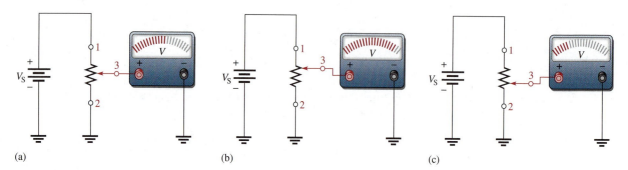

(a)   (b)   (c)

FIGURE 5–43
Adjusting the voltage divider.

Applications of Voltage Dividers

The volume control of radio or TV receivers is a common application of a potentiometer used as a voltage divider. Since the loudness of the sound is dependent on the amount of voltage associated with the audio signal, you can increase or decrease the volume by adjusting the potentiometer, that is, by turning the knob of the volume control on the set. The block diagram in Figure 5–44 shows how a potentiometer can be used for volume control in a typical receiver.

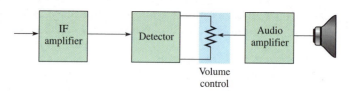

FIGURE 5–44
A voltage divider used for volume control.

Another application of a voltage divider is illustrated in Figure 5–45, which depicts a potentiometer voltage divider as a fuel-level sensor in an automobile gas tank. As shown in part (a), the float moves up as the tank is filled and moves down as the tank empties. The float is mechanically linked to the wiper arm of a potentiometer, as shown in part (b). The output voltage varies proportionally with the position of the wiper arm. As the fuel in the tank decreases, the sensor output voltage also decreases. The output voltage goes to the indicator circuitry, which controls the fuel gauge or digital readout to show the fuel level. The schematic of this system is shown in part (c).

Still another application for voltage dividers is in setting the dc operating voltage (bias) in transistor amplifiers. Figure 5–46 shows a voltage divider used for this purpose. You will study transistor amplifiers and biasing later, so it is important that you understand the basics of voltage dividers at this point.

These examples are only three out of many possible applications of voltage dividers.

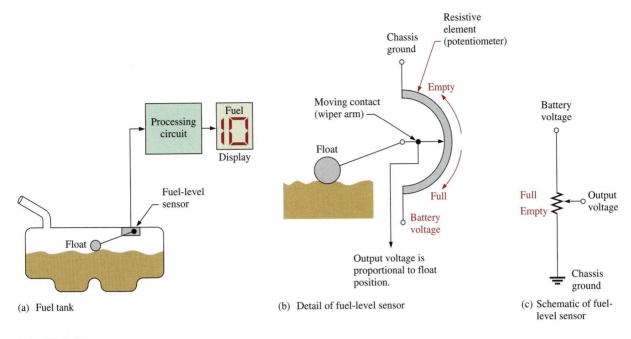

(a) Fuel tank

(b) Detail of fuel-level sensor

(c) Schematic of fuel-
level sensor

FIGURE 5–45
A potentiometer voltage divider used as an automotive fuel-level sensor.

FIGURE 5–46
The voltage divider is a bias circuit for a transistor amplifier, where the voltage at the base of the transistor is determined by the voltage divider as $V_{BASE} = (R_2/(R_1 + R_2))V_S$.

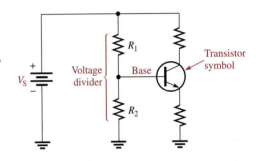

**SECTION 5–7
REVIEW**

1. What is a voltage divider?
2. How many resistors can there be in a series voltage-divider circuit?
3. Write the general formula for voltage dividers.
4. If two series resistors of equal value are connected across a 10 V source, how much voltage is there across each resistor?
5. A 47 Ω resistor and an 82 Ω resistor are connected as a voltage divider. The source voltage is 100 V. Sketch the circuit, and determine the voltage across each of the resistors.
6. The circuit of Figure 5–47 is an adjustable voltage divider. If the potentiometer is linear, where would you set the wiper in order to get 5 V from *A* to *B* and 5 V from *B* to *C*?

FIGURE 5–47

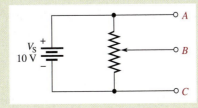

5–8 ■ POWER IN A SERIES CIRCUIT

The power dissipated by each individual resistor in a series circuit contributes to the total power in the circuit. The individual powers are additive.

After completing this section, you should be able to

■ Determine power in a series circuit

The total amount of power in a series resistive circuit is equal to the sum of the powers in each resistor in series.

$$P_T = P_1 + P_2 + P_3 + \cdots + P_n \tag{5–6}$$

where P_T is the total power and P_n is the power in the last resistor in series. In other words, the powers are additive.

The power formulas that you learned in Chapter 4 are, of course, directly applicable to series circuits. Since there is the same current through each resistor in series, the following formulas are used to calculate the total power:

$$P_T = V_S I$$
$$P_T = I^2 R_T$$
$$P_T = \frac{V_S^2}{R_T}$$

where V_S is the total source voltage across the series connection and R_T is the total resistance. Example 5–19 illustrates how to calculate total power in a series circuit.

EXAMPLE 5–19   Determine the total amount of power in the series circuit in Figure 5–48.

FIGURE 5–48

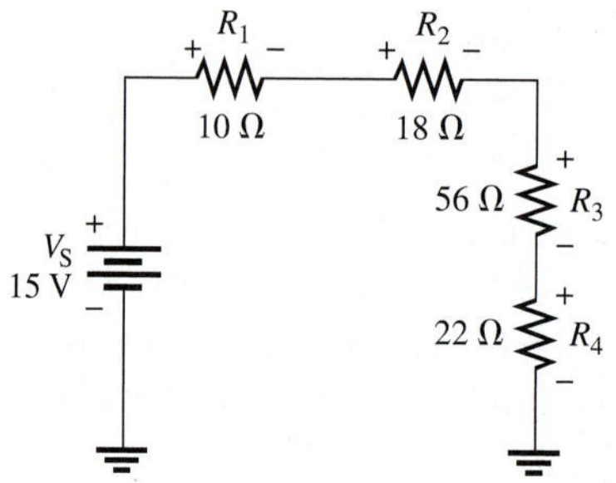

Solution   The source voltage is 15 V. The total resistance is

$$R_T = R_1 + R_2 + R_3 + R_4 = 10\ \Omega + 18\ \Omega + 56\ \Omega + 22\ \Omega = 106\ \Omega$$

The easiest formula to use is $P_T = V_S^2/R_T$ since you know both V_S and R_T.

$$P_T = \frac{V_S^2}{R_T} = \frac{(15\ \text{V})^2}{106\ \Omega} = \frac{225\ \text{V}^2}{106\ \Omega} = 2.12\ \text{W}$$

If you determine the power in each resistor separately and all of these powers are added, you obtain the same result. Calculate the power for each resistor using $P = I^2 R$, where $I = V_S / R_T$.

$$P_1 = I^2 R_1 = \left(\frac{V_S}{R_T}\right)^2 R_1 = \left(\frac{15\ \text{V}}{106\ \Omega}\right)^2 (10\ \Omega) = 0.200\ \text{W}$$

$$P_2 = I^2 R_2 = \left(\frac{V_S}{R_T}\right)^2 R_2 = \left(\frac{15\ \text{V}}{106\ \Omega}\right)^2 (18\ \Omega) = 0.360\ \text{W}$$

$$P_3 = I^2 R_3 = \left(\frac{V_S}{R_T}\right)^2 R_3 = \left(\frac{15\ \text{V}}{106\ \Omega}\right)^2 (56\ \Omega) = 1.121\ \text{W}$$

$$P_4 = I^2 R_4 = \left(\frac{V_S}{R_T}\right)^2 R_4 = \left(\frac{15\ \text{V}}{106\ \Omega}\right)^2 (22\ \Omega) = 0.441\ \text{W}$$

Then, add these powers to get the total power.

$$P_T = P_1 + P_2 + P_3 + P_4 = 0.200\ \text{W} + 0.360\ \text{W} + 1.121\ \text{W} + 0.441\ \text{W} = \mathbf{2.12\ W}$$

This result compares to the total power as determined previously by the formula $P_T = V_S^2/R_T$.

Related Problem   What is the power in the circuit of Figure 5–48 if V_S is increased to 30 V?

The amount of power in a resistor is important because the power rating of the resistors must be high enough to handle the expected power in the circuit. The following example illustrates practical considerations relating to power in a series circuit.

EXAMPLE 5–20

Determine if the indicated power rating (½ W) of each resistor in Figure 5–49 is sufficient to handle the actual power. If a rating is not adequate, specify the required minimum rating.

FIGURE 5–49

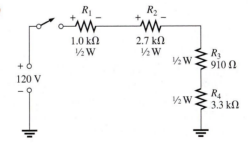

Solution   First determine the total resistance.

$$R_T = R_1 + R_2 + R_3 + R_4 = 1.0\ \text{k}\Omega + 2.7\ \text{k}\Omega + 910\ \Omega + 3.3\ \text{k}\Omega = 7.91\ \text{k}\Omega$$

Then calculate the power in each resistor.

$$P_1 = I^2 R_1 = \left(\frac{V_S}{R_T}\right)^2 R_1 = \left(\frac{120\ \text{V}}{7.91\ \text{k}\Omega}\right)^2 (1.0\ \text{k}\Omega) = \mathbf{230\ mW}$$

$$P_2 = I^2 R_2 = \left(\frac{V_S}{R_T}\right)^2 R_2 = \left(\frac{120\ \text{V}}{7.91\ \text{k}\Omega}\right)^2 (2.7\ \text{k}\Omega) = \mathbf{621\ mW}$$

$$P_3 = I^2 R_3 = \left(\frac{V_S}{R_T}\right)^2 R_3 = \left(\frac{120\ \text{V}}{7.91\ \text{k}\Omega}\right)^2 (910\ \Omega) = \mathbf{209\ mW}$$

$$P_4 = I^2 R_4 = \left(\frac{V_S}{R_T}\right)^2 R_4 = \left(\frac{120\ \text{V}}{7.91\ \text{k}\Omega}\right)^2 (3.3\ \text{k}\Omega) = \mathbf{759\ mW}$$

R_2 and R_4 do not have a rating sufficient to handle the actual power, which exceeds ½ W in each of these two resistors, and they may burn out if the switch is closed. These resistors should be replaced by 1 W resistors.

Related Problem Determine the minimum power rating required for each resistor in Figure 5–49 if the source voltage is increased to 240 V.

SECTION 5–8 REVIEW

1. If you know the power in each resistor in a series circuit, how can you find the total power?
2. The resistors in a series circuit dissipate the following powers: 2 W, 5 W, 1 W, and 8 W. What is the total power in the circuit?
3. A circuit has a 100 Ω, a 330 Ω, and a 680 Ω resistor in series. There is a current of 1 A through the circuit. What is the total power?

5–9 ■ CIRCUIT GROUND

Voltage is relative. That is, the voltage at one point in a circuit is always measured relative to another point. For example, if we say that there are +100 V at a certain point in a circuit, we mean that the point is 100 V more positive than some designated reference point in the circuit. This reference point is usually the ground point.

After completing this section, you should be able to

■ **Determine and identify ground in a circuit**
  • Measure voltage with respect to ground
  • Define the term circuit ground

The concept of *ground* was introduced in Chapter 2. In most electronic equipment, a large conductive area on a printed circuit board or the metal housing is used as the common or reference point, called **circuit ground** or *chassis ground,* as illustrated in Figure 5–50.

Ground has a potential of zero volts (0 V) with respect to all other points in the circuit that are referenced to it, as illustrated in Figure 5–51. In part (a), the negative side of the source is grounded, and all voltages indicated are positive with respect to ground. In part (b), the positive side of the source is ground. The voltages at all other points are therefore negative with respect to ground. Recall that all points shown grounded in a circuit are connected together through ground and are effectively the same point electrically.

Measuring Voltages with Respect to Ground

When voltages are measured with respect to ground in a circuit, one meter lead is connected to the circuit ground, and the other to the point at which the voltage is to be measured. In a negative ground circuit, the negative meter terminal is connected to the circuit ground. The positive terminal of the voltmeter is then connected to the positive voltage point. Measurement of positive voltage is illustrated in Figure 5–52, where the meter reads the positive voltage at point *A* with respect to ground.

For a circuit with a positive ground, the positive voltmeter lead is connected to ground, and the negative lead is connected to the negative voltage point, as indicated in Figure 5–53. Here the meter reads the negative voltage at point *A* with respect to ground.

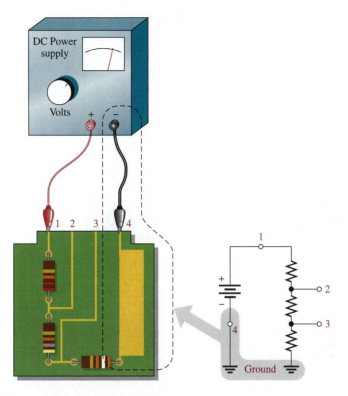

FIGURE 5–50
Simple illustration of circuit ground.

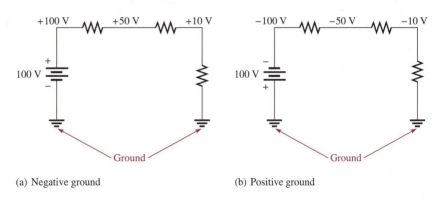

(a) Negative ground   (b) Positive ground

FIGURE 5–51
Example of negative and positive grounds.

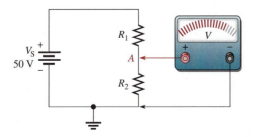

FIGURE 5–52
Measuring a voltage with respect to negative ground.

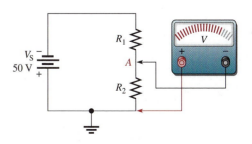

FIGURE 5–53
Measuring a voltage with respect to positive ground.

When voltages must be measured at several points in a circuit, the ground lead can be clipped to ground at one point in the circuit and left there. The other lead is then moved from point to point as the voltages are measured. This method is illustrated pictorially in Figure 5–54 and in equivalent schematic form in Figure 5–55.

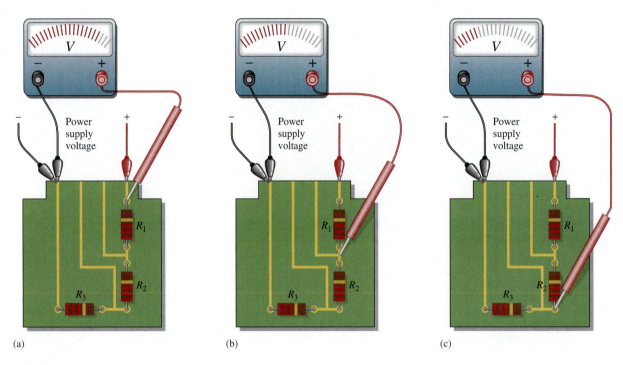

(a) (b) (c)

FIGURE 5–54
Measuring voltages at several points in a circuit with respect to ground.

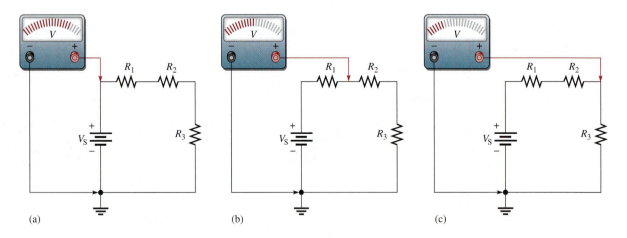

(a) (b) (c)

FIGURE 5–55
Equivalent schematics for Figure 5–54.

Measuring Voltage Across an Ungrounded Resistor

Voltage can normally be measured across a resistor, as shown in Figure 5–56, even though neither side of the resistor is connected to circuit ground. In some rare cases, when the meter is not isolated from power line ground, the negative lead of the meter will ground one side of the resistor and alter the operation of the circuit. In this situation, another method must be used, as illustrated in Figure 5–57. The voltages on each side of the resistor are measured with respect to ground. The difference of these two measurements is the voltage drop across the resistor.

FIGURE 5–56
Measuring voltage across a resistor.

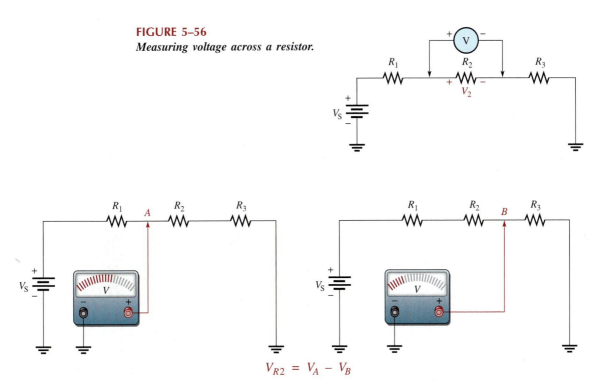

$$V_{R2} = V_A - V_B$$

FIGURE 5–57
Measuring voltage across a resistor with two separate measurements to ground.

EXAMPLE 5–21   Determine the voltages of each of the indicated points in each circuit of Figure 5–58. Assume that 25 V are dropped across each resistor.

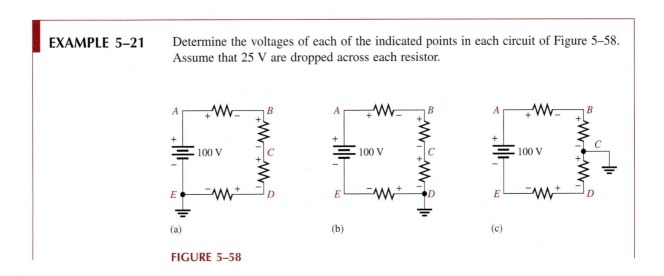

(a)   (b)   (c)

FIGURE 5–58

Solution   In circuit (a), the voltage polarities are as shown. Point *E* is ground. Single-letter subscripts denote voltage at a point with respect to ground. The voltages with respect to ground are as follows:

$$V_E = \mathbf{0\ V}$$
$$V_D = \mathbf{+25\ V}$$
$$V_C = \mathbf{+50\ V}$$
$$V_B = \mathbf{+75\ V}$$
$$V_A = \mathbf{+100\ V}$$

In circuit (b), the voltage polarities are as shown. Point *D* is ground. The voltages with respect to ground are as follows:

$$V_E = \mathbf{-25\ V}$$
$$V_D = \mathbf{0\ V}$$
$$V_C = \mathbf{+25\ V}$$
$$V_B = \mathbf{+50\ V}$$
$$V_A = \mathbf{+75\ V}$$

In circuit (c), the voltage polarities are as shown. Point *C* is ground. The voltages with respect to ground are as follows:

$$V_E = \mathbf{-50\ V}$$
$$V_D = \mathbf{-25\ V}$$
$$V_C = \mathbf{0\ V}$$
$$V_B = \mathbf{+25\ V}$$
$$V_A = \mathbf{+50\ V}$$

Related Problem   If the ground is at point *A* in the circuit in Figure 5–58, what are the voltages at each of the points with respect to ground?

SECTION 5–9 REVIEW

1. What is the common reference point in a circuit called?
2. Voltages in a circuit are generally referenced to ground.   (T or F)
3. The housing or chassis is often used as circuit ground.   (T or F)
4. What is the symbol for ground?

5–10 ■ TROUBLESHOOTING

Open resistors or contacts and one point shorted to another are common problems in all circuits including series circuits.

After completing this section, you should be able to

■ **Troubleshoot series circuits**
   • Check for an open circuit
   • Check for a short circuit
   • Identify primary causes of shorts

Open Circuit

The most common failure in a series circuit is an open. For example, when a resistor or a lamp burns out, it causes a break in the current path and creates an **open circuit** as illustrated in Figure 5–59.

An open in a series circuit prevents current.

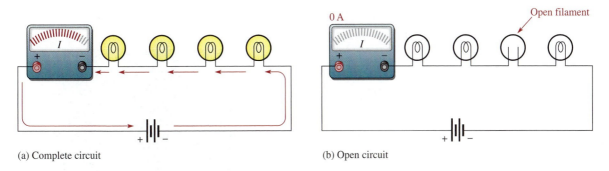

(a) Complete circuit

(b) Open circuit

FIGURE 5–59
An open circuit prevents current.

Checking for an Open Element Sometimes a visual check will reveal a charred resistor or an open lamp filament. However, it is possible for a resistor or connection to open without showing visible signs. In this situation, a voltage check of the series circuit may be required. A general procedure is as follows: *Measure the voltage across each resistor in series. The voltage across all of the good resistors will be zero. The voltage across the open resistor will equal the source voltage.*

This condition occurs because an open resistor or connection will prevent current through the series circuit. With no current, there can be no voltage drop across any of the good resistors. Since $IR = (0 \text{ A})R = 0 \text{ V}$, in accordance with Ohm's law, the voltage on each side of a good resistor is the same if there is no current. The total voltage must then appear across the open resistor or connection in accordance with Kirchhoff's voltage law, as illustrated in Figure 5–60. To fix the circuit, replace the open resistor or repair the open connection.

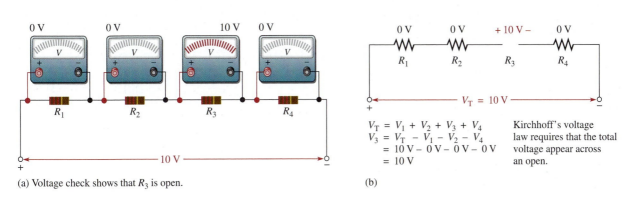

(a) Voltage check shows that R_3 is open.

(b)

$$V_T = V_1 + V_2 + V_3 + V_4$$
$$V_3 = V_T - V_1 - V_2 - V_4$$
$$= 10 \text{ V} - 0 \text{ V} - 0 \text{ V} - 0 \text{ V}$$
$$= 10 \text{ V}$$

Kirchhoff's voltage law requires that the total voltage appear across an open.

FIGURE 5–60
Troubleshooting a series circuit for an open element.

Short Circuit

Sometimes an unwanted **short circuit** occurs when two conductors touch or a foreign object such as solder or a wire clipping accidentally connects two sections of a circuit together. This situation is particularly common in circuits with a high component density. Several potential causes of short circuits are illustrated on the PC board in Figure 5–61.

When there is a short, a portion of the series resistance is bypassed (all of the current goes through the short), thus reducing the total resistance as illustrated in Figure 5–62. Notice that the current increases as a result of the short.

A short in a series circuit causes more current than normal.

FIGURE 5–61
Examples of shorts on a PC board.

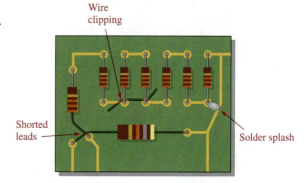

FIGURE 5–62
Example of the effect of a short in a series circuit.

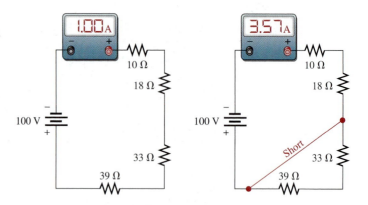

SECTION 5–10 REVIEW

1. Define *short circuit*.

2. Define *open circuit*.

3. What happens when a series circuit opens?

4. Name two general ways in which an open circuit can occur in practice. What may cause a short circuit to occur?

5. When a resistor fails, it will normally fail open.   (T or F)

6. The total voltage across a string of series resistors is 24 V. If one of the resistors is open, how much voltage is there across it? How much is there across each of the good resistors?

5–11 ■ TECHnology Theory Into Practice

For this TECH TIP assignment, you have been given a voltage-divider circuit board to evaluate and modify if necessary. It will be used to obtain five different voltage levels from a 12 V battery that has a 6.5 Ah rating. The voltage divider is to be used to provide positive reference voltages to an electronic circuit in an analog-to-digital converter. Your task will be to check the circuit to see if it provides the following voltages

within a tolerance of ±5% with respect to the negative side of the battery: 10.4 V, 8.0 V, 7.3 V, 6.0 V, and 2.7 V. If the existing circuit does not provide the specified voltages, you will modify it so that it does. Also, you must make sure that the power ratings of the resistors are adequate for the application and determine how long the battery will last with the voltage divider connected to it.

The Schematic of the Circuit

■ Use Figure 5–63 to determine the resistor values and draw the schematic of the voltage-divider circuit so you will know what you are working with. All the resistors on the board are $\frac{1}{4}$ W.

FIGURE 5–63

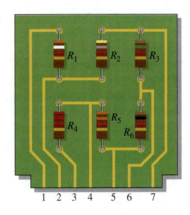

The Voltages

■ Determine the voltage at each pin on the circuit board with respect to the negative side of the battery when the positive side of the 12 V battery is connected to pin 3 and the negative side is connected to pin 1. Compare the existing voltages to the following specifications:

Pin 1: negative terminal of 12 V battery

Pin 2: 2.7 V ± 5%

Pin 3: positive terminal of 12 V battery

Pin 4: 10.4 V ± 5%

Pin 5: 8.0 V ± 5%

Pin 6: 7.3 V ± 5%

Pin 7: 6.0 V ± 5%

■ If the output voltages of the existing circuit are not the same as those stated in the specifications, make the necessary changes in the circuit to meet the specifications. Draw a schematic of the modified circuit showing resistor values and adequate power ratings.

The Battery

■ Find the total current drawn from the 12 V battery when the voltage-divider circuit is connected and determine how many days the 6.5 Ah battery will last.

A Test Procedure

■ Determine how you would test the voltage-divider circuit board and what instruments you would use. Then detail your test procedure in a step-by-step format.

Troubleshooting

■ Determine the most likely fault for each of the following cases (voltages are with respect to the negative battery terminal (pin 1 on the circuit board):

1. No voltage at any of the pins on the circuit board
2. 12 V at pins 3 and 4. All other pins have 0 V.
3. 12 V at all pins except 0 V at pin 1
4. 12 V at pin 6 and 0 V at pin 7
5. 3.3 V at pin 2

SECTION 5–11 REVIEW

1. What is the total power dissipated by the voltage-divider circuit in Figure 5–63 with a 12 V battery?
2. What are the output voltages from the voltage divider if the positive terminal of a 6 V battery is connected to pin 3 and the negative terminal to pin 1?
3. When the voltage-divider board is connected to the electronic circuit to which it is providing positive reference voltages, which pin on the board should be connected to the ground of the electronic circuit?

■ SUMMARY

■ The current is the same at all points in a series circuit.
■ The total series resistance is the sum of all resistors in the series circuit.
■ The total resistance between any two points in a series circuit is equal to the sum of all resistors connected in series between those two points.
■ If all of the resistors in a series circuit are of equal value, the total resistance is the number of resistors multiplied by the resistance value.
■ Voltage sources in series add algebraically.
■ Kirchhoff's voltage law: The sum of all the voltage drops around a single closed loop in a circuit is equal to the total source voltage in that loop.
■ Alternative statement of Kirchhoff's voltage law: The algebraic sum of all voltages (both source and drops) around a closed path is zero.
■ The voltage drops in a circuit are always opposite in polarity to the total source voltage.
■ Current is out of the negative side of a source and into the positive side.
■ Current is into the negative side of each resistor and out of the positive side.
■ A voltage divider is a series arrangement of resistors.
■ A voltage divider is so named because the voltage drop across any resistor in the series circuit is divided down from the total voltage by an amount proportional to that resistance value in relation to the total resistance.
■ A potentiometer can be used as an adjustable voltage divider.
■ The total power in a resistive circuit is the sum of all the individual powers of the resistors making up the series circuit.
■ Ground is zero volts with respect to all points referenced to it in the circuit.

- *Negative ground* is the term used when the negative side of the source is grounded.
- *Positive ground* is the term used when the positive side of the source is grounded.
- The voltage across an open series element equals the source voltage.

■ **GLOSSARY**

These terms are also in the end-of-book glossary

Circuit ground   A method of grounding whereby the metal chassis that houses the assembly or a large conductive area on a printed circuit board is used as the common or reference point; also called chassis ground.

Kirchhoff's voltage law   A law stating that (1) the sum of the voltage drops around a closed loop equals the source voltage or (2) the algebraic sum of all the voltages (drops and source) around a closed loop is zero.

Open circuit   A circuit in which the current path is broken.

Series   In an electric circuit, a relationship of components in which the components are connected such that they provide a single current path between two points.

Short circuit   A circuit in which there is a zero or abnormally low resistance path between two points; usually an inadvertent condition.

■ **FORMULAS**

(5–1)	$R_T = R_1 + R_2 + R_3 + \cdots + R_n$	Total resistance of n resistors in series
(5–2)	$R_T = nR$	Total resistance of n equal-value resistors in series
(5–3)	$V_S = V_1 + V_2 + V_3 + \cdots + V_n$	Kirchhoff's voltage law
(5–4)	$V_S - V_1 - V_2 - V_3 = 0$	Kirchhoff's voltage law
(5–5)	$V_x = \left(\dfrac{R_x}{R_T} \right) V_S$	Voltage-divider formula
(5–6)	$P_T = P_1 + P_2 + P_3 + \cdots + P_n$	Total power

■ **SELF-TEST**

1. Five resistors are connected in series and there is a current of 2 A into the first resistor. The amount of current out of the second resistor is
    (a) equal to 2 A   **(b)** less than 2 A   **(c)** greater than 2 A

2. To measure the current out of the third resistor in a circuit consisting of four series resistors, an ammeter can be placed
    (a) between the third and fourth resistors   **(b)** between the second and third resistors
    (c) at the positive terminal of the source   **(d)** at any point in the circuit

3. When a third resistor is connected in series with two series resistors, the total resistance
    (a) remains the same   **(b)** increases
    (c) decreases   **(d)** increases by one-third

4. When one of four series resistors is removed from a circuit and the circuit reconnected, the current
    (a) decreases by the amount of current through the removed resistor
    (b) decreases by one-fourth
    (c) quadruples
    (d) increases

5. A series circuit consists of three resistors with values of 100 Ω, 220 Ω, and 330 Ω. The total resistance is
    (a) less than 100 Ω   **(b)** the average of the values   **(c)** 550 Ω   **(d)** 650 Ω

6. A 9 V battery is connected across a series combination of 68 Ω, 33 Ω, 100 Ω, and 47 Ω resistors. The amount of current is
    (a) 36.3 mA   **(b)** 27.6 A   **(c)** 22.3 mA   **(d)** 363 mA

7. While putting four 1.5 V batteries in a flashlight, you accidentally put one of them in backward. The voltage across the bulb will be
   (a) 6 V   (b) 3 V   (c) 4.5 V   (d) 0 V

8. If you measure all the voltage drops and the source voltage in a series circuit and add them together, taking into consideration the polarities, you will get a result equal to
   (a) the source voltage
   (b) the total of the voltage drops
   (c) zero
   (d) the total of the source voltage and the voltage drops

9. There are six resistors in a given series circuit and each resistor has 5 V dropped across it. The source voltage is
   (a) 5 V   (b) 30 V
   (c) dependent on the resistor values   (d) dependent on the current

10. A series circuit consists of a 4.7 kΩ, a 5.6 kΩ, and a 10 kΩ resistor. The resistor that has the most voltage across it is
    (a) the 4.7 kΩ   (b) the 5.6 kΩ
    (c) the 10 kΩ   (d) impossible to determine from the given information

11. Which of the following series combinations dissipates the most power when connected across a 100 V source?
    (a) One 100 Ω resistor   (b) Two 100 Ω resistors
    (c) Three 100 Ω resistors   (d) Four 100 Ω resistors

12. The total power in a certain circuit is 10 W. Each of the five equal-value series resistors making up the circuit dissipates
    (a) 10 W   (b) 50 W   (c) 5 W   (d) 2 W

13. When you connect an ammeter in a series-resistive circuit and turn on the source voltage, the meter reads zero. You should check for
    (a) a broken wire   (b) a shorted resistor
    (c) an open resistor   (d) answers (a) and (c)

14. While checking out a series-resistive circuit, you find that the current is higher than it should be. You should look for
    (a) an open circuit   (b) a short
    (c) a low resistor value   (d) answers (b) and (c)

■ PROBLEMS   *More difficult problems are indicated by an asterisk (*).*

SECTION 5–1   Resistors in Series

1. Connect each set of resistors in Figure 5–64 in series between points A and B.

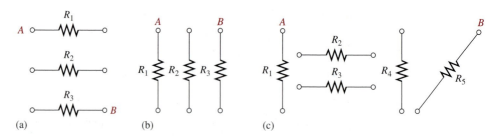

FIGURE 5–64

2. Determine which resistors in Figure 5–65 are in series. Show how to interconnect the pins to put all the resistors in series.

FIGURE 5–65

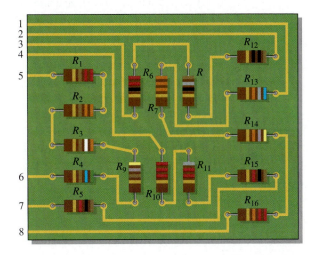

3. On the double-sided PC board in Figure 5–66, identify each group of series resistors. Note that many of the interconnections feed through the board from the top side to the bottom side.

FIGURE 5–66

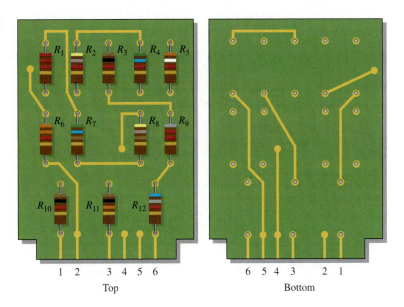

SECTION 5–2   Current in a Series Circuit

4. What is the current through each resistor in a series circuit if the total voltage is 12 V and the total resistance is 120 Ω?

5. The current from the source in Figure 5–67 is 5 mA. How much current does each milliammeter in the circuit indicate?

FIGURE 5–67

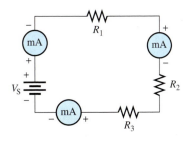

6. Show how to connect a voltage source and an ammeter to the PC board in Figure 5–65 to measure the current in R_1. Which other resistor currents are measured by this setup?

*7. Using 1.5 V batteries, a switch, and three lamps, devise a circuit to apply 4.5 V across either one lamp, two lamps in series, or three lamps in series with a single-control switch. Draw the schematic.

SECTION 5–3 Total Series Resistance

8. The following resistors (one each) are connected in a series circuit: 1.0 Ω, 2.2 Ω, 5.6 Ω, 12 Ω, and 22 Ω. Determine the total resistance.

9. Find the total resistance of each of the following groups of series resistors:
   (a) 560 Ω and 1000 Ω **(b)** 47 Ω and 56 Ω
   (c) 1.5 kΩ, 2.2 kΩ, and 10 kΩ   **(d)** 1.0 MΩ, 470 kΩ, 1.0 kΩ, 2.2 MΩ

10. Calculate R_T for each circuit of Figure 5–68.

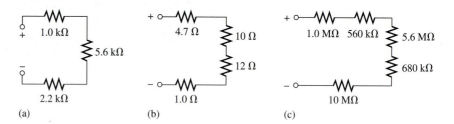

(a) 1.0 kΩ 5.6 kΩ 2.2 kΩ

(b) 4.7 Ω 10 Ω 12 Ω 1.0 Ω

(c) 1.0 MΩ 560 kΩ 5.6 MΩ 680 kΩ 10 MΩ

FIGURE 5–68

11. What is the total resistance of twelve 5.6 kΩ resistors in series?

12. Six 56 Ω resistors, eight 100 Ω resistors, and two 22 Ω resistors are all connected in series. What is the total resistance?

13. If the total resistance in Figure 5–69 is 17.4 kΩ, what is the value of R_5?

FIGURE 5–69

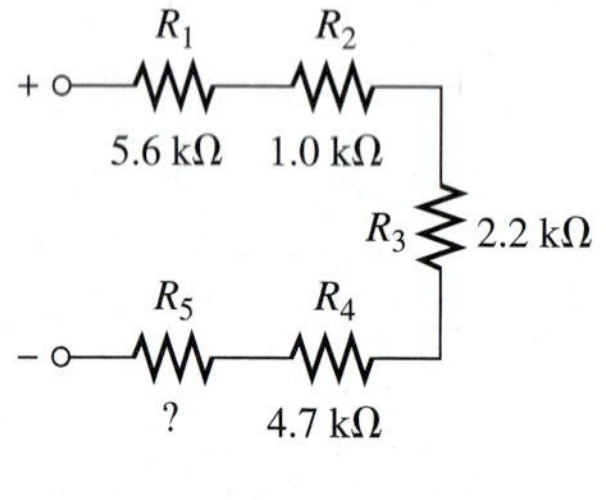

R_1 5.6 kΩ R_2 1.0 kΩ R_3 2.2 kΩ R_5 ? R_4 4.7 kΩ

14. You have the following resistor values available to you in the lab in unlimited quantities: 10 Ω, 100 Ω, 470 Ω, 560 Ω, 680 Ω, 1.0 kΩ, 2.2 kΩ, and 5.6 kΩ. All of the other standard values are out of stock. A project that you are working on requires an 18 kΩ resistance. What combinations of the available values would you use in series to achieve this total resistance?

15. Find the total resistance in Figure 5–68 if all three circuits are connected in series.

16. What is the total resistance from A to B for each switch position in Figure 5–70?

FIGURE 5–70

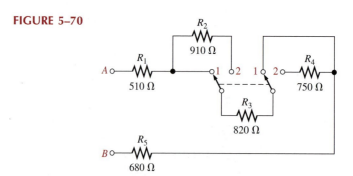

R_2 910 Ω R_1 510 Ω R_4 750 Ω R_3 820 Ω R_5 680 Ω

SECTION 5–4 Ohm's Law in Series Circuits

17. What is the current in each circuit of Figure 5–71?

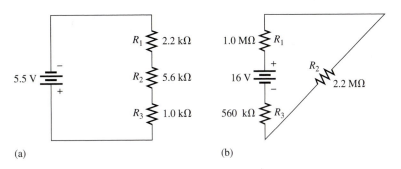

(a)   (b)

FIGURE 5–71

18. Determine the voltage drop across each resistor in Figure 5–71.

19. Three 470 Ω resistors are connected in series with a 500 V source. How much current is in the circuit?

20. Four equal-value resistors are in series with a 5 V battery, and 2.23 mA are measured. What is the value of each resistor?

21. What is the value of each resistor in Figure 5–72?

22. Determine V_{R1}, R_2, and R_3 in Figure 5–73.

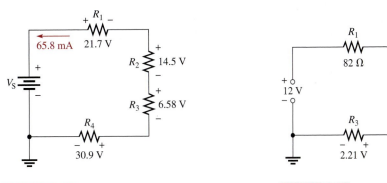

FIGURE 5–72   **FIGURE 5–73**

23. Determine the current measured by the meter in Figure 5–74 for each switch position.

24. Determine the current measured by the meter in Figure 5–75 for each position of the ganged switch.

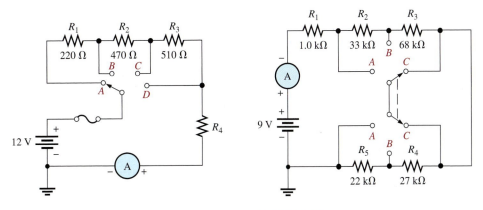

FIGURE 5–74   **FIGURE 5–75**

SECTION 5–5   Voltage Sources in Series

25. *Series aiding* is a term sometimes used to describe voltage sources of the same polarity in series. If a 5 V and a 9 V source are connected in this manner, what is the total voltage?

26. The term *series opposing* means that sources are in series with opposite polarities. If a 12 V and a 3 V battery are series opposing, what is the total voltage?

27. Determine the total source voltage in each circuit of Figure 5–76.

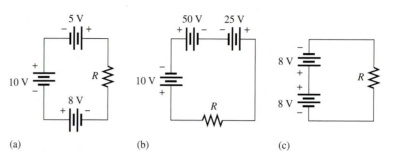

(a)   (b)   (c)

FIGURE 5–76

SECTION 5–6   Kirchhoff's Voltage Law

28. The following voltage drops are measured across three resistors in series: 5.5 V, 8.2 V, and 12.3 V. What is the value of the source voltage to which these resistors are connected?

29. Five resistors are in series with a 20 V source. The voltage drops across four of the resistors are 1.5 V, 5.5 V, 3 V, and 6 V. How much voltage is dropped across the fifth resistor?

30. Determine the unspecified voltage drop(s) in each circuit of Figure 5–77. Show how to connect a voltmeter to measure each unknown voltage drop.

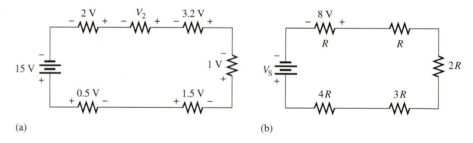

(a)   (b)

FIGURE 5–77

31. In the circuit of Figure 5–78, determine the resistance of R_4.

32. Find R_1, R_2, and R_3 in Figure 5–79.

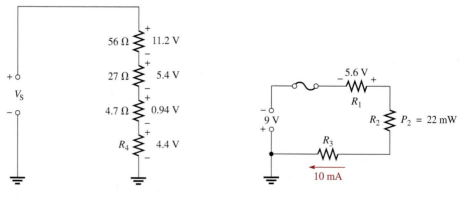

FIGURE 5–78   **FIGURE 5–79**

33. Determine the voltage across R_5 for each position of the switch in Figure 5–80. The current in each position is as follows: A, 3.35 mA; B, 3.73 mA; C, 4.50 mA; D, 6.00 mA.

34. Using the result of Problem 33, determine the voltage across each resistor in Figure 5–80 for each switch position.

FIGURE 5–80

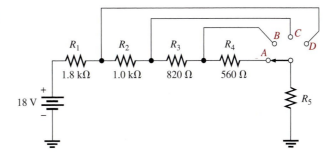

SECTION 5–7 Voltage Dividers

*35. The total resistance of a circuit is 560 Ω. What percentage of the total voltage appears across a 27 Ω resistor that makes up part of the total series resistance?

36. Determine the voltage between points A and B in each voltage divider of Figure 5–81.

FIGURE 5–81

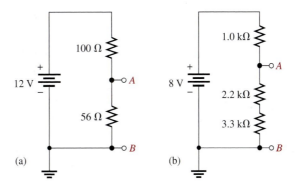

*37. What is the voltage across each resistor in Figure 5–82? R is the lowest-value resistor, and all others are multiples of that value as indicated.

38. Determine the voltage at each point in Figure 5–83 with respect to the negative side of the battery.

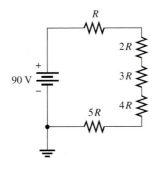

FIGURE 5–82

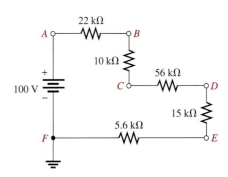

FIGURE 5–83

39. If there are 10 V across R_1 in Figure 5–84, what is the voltage across each of the other resistors?

*40. With the table of standard resistor values given in Appendix A, design a voltage divider to provide the following approximate voltages with respect to ground using a 30 V source: 8.18 V, 14.7 V, and 24.6 V. The current drain on the source must be limited to no more than 1 mA. The number of resistors, their values, and their wattage ratings must be specified. A schematic showing the circuit arrangement and resistor placement must be provided.

*41. Design a variable voltage divider to provide an output voltage adjustable from a minimum of 10 V to a maximum of 100 V within ±1% using a 120 V source. The maximum voltage must occur at the maximum resistance setting of the potentiometer, and the minimum voltage must occur at the minimum resistance (zero) setting. The maximum current is to be 10 mA.

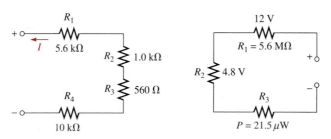

FIGURE 5–84   **FIGURE 5–85**

SECTION 5–8   Power in a Series Circuit

42. Five series resistors each handle 50 mW. What is the total power?

43. What is the total power in the circuit in Figure 5–84? Use the results of Problem 39.

44. The following ¼ W resistors are in series: 1.2 kΩ, 2.2 kΩ, 3.9 kΩ, and 5.6 kΩ. What is the maximum voltage that can be applied across the series resistors without exceeding a power rating? Which resistor will burn out first if excessive voltage is applied?

45. Find R_T in Figure 5–85.

46. A certain series circuit consists of a ⅛ W resistor, a ¼ W resistor and a ½ W resistor. The total resistance is 2400 Ω. If each of the resistors is operating in the circuit at its maximum power dissipation, determine the following:

    (a) I **(b)** V_T **(c)** The value of each resistor

SECTION 5–9   Circuit Ground

47. Determine the voltage at each point with respect to ground in Figure 5–86.

48. In Figure 5–87, how would you determine the voltage across R_2 by measuring, without connecting a meter directly across the resistor?

49. Determine the voltage at each point with respect to ground in Figure 5–87.

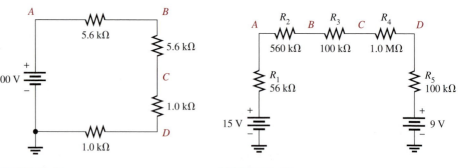

FIGURE 5–86   **FIGURE 5–87**

SECTION 5–10 Troubleshooting

50. A string of five series resistors is connected across a 12 V battery. Zero volts is measured across all of the resistors except R_2. What is wrong with the circuit? What voltage will be measured across R_2?

51. By observing the meters in Figure 5–88, determine the types of failures in the circuits and which components have failed.

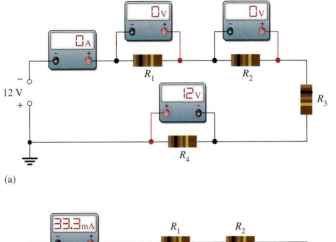

(a)

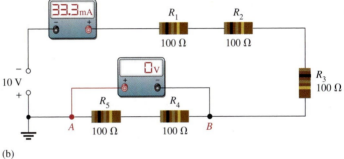

(b)

FIGURE 5–88

52. What current would you measure in Figure 5–88(b) if only R_2 were shorted?

*53. Table 5–1 shows the results of resistance measurements on the PC board in Figure 5–89. Are these results correct? If not, identify the possible problems.

TABLE 5–1

Between Pins	Resistance
1 and 2	∞
1 and 3	∞
1 and 4	4.23 kΩ
1 and 5	∞
1 and 6	∞
2 and 3	23.6 kΩ
2 and 4	∞
2 and 5	∞
2 and 6	∞
3 and 4	∞
3 and 5	∞
3 and 6	∞
4 and 5	∞
4 and 6	∞
5 and 6	19.9 kΩ

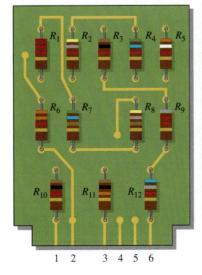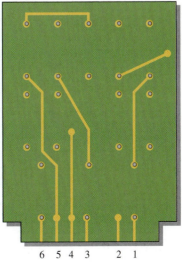

FIGURE 5–89

*54. You measure 15 kΩ between pins 5 and 6 on the PC board in Figure 5–89. Does this indicate a problem? If so, identify it.

*55. In checking out the PC board in Figure 5–89, you measure 17.83 kΩ between pins 1 and 2. Also, you measure 13.6 kΩ between pins 2 and 4. Does this indicate a problem on the PC board? If so, identify the fault.

*56. The three groups of series resistors on the PC board in Figure 5–89 are connected in series with each other to form a single series circuit by connecting pin 2 to pin 4 and pin 3 to pin 5. A voltage source is connected across pins 1 and 6 and an ammeter is placed in series. As you increase the source voltage, you observe the corresponding increase in current. Suddenly, the current drops to zero and you smell smoke. All resistors are ½ W.

   (a) What has happened?

   (b) Specifically, what must you do to fix the problem?

   (c) At what voltage did the failure occur?

EWB Troubleshooting and Analysis

These problems require your EWB compact disk.

57. Open file PRO05-57.EWB and measure the total series resistance.

58. Open file PRO05-58.EWB and determine by measurement if there is an open resistor and, if so, which one.

59. Open file PRO05-59.EWB and determine the unspecified resistance value.

60. Open file PRO05-60.EWB and determine the the unspecified source voltage.

61. Open file PRO05-61.EWB and find the shorted resistor if there is one.

■ **ANSWERS TO SECTION REVIEWS**

Section 5–1

1. Series resistors are connected end-to-end in a "string" with each lead of a given resistor connected to a different resistor.

2. There is a single current path in a series circuit.

3. See Figure 5–90.

FIGURE 5–90

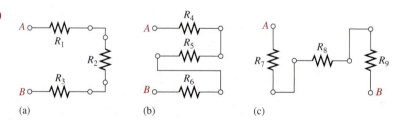

(a)   (b)   (c)

4. See Figure 5–91.

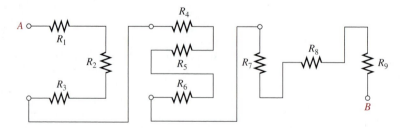

FIGURE 5–91

Section 5–2

1. $I = 1$ A
2. The ammeter measures 50 mA between C and D and 50 mA between E and F.
3. $I = 100$ V/56 $\Omega = 1.79$ A; 1.79 A
4. In a series circuit, current is the same at all points.

Section 5–3

1. $R_T = 1.0\ \Omega + 2.2\ \Omega + 3.3\ \Omega + 4.7\ \Omega = 11.2\ \Omega$
2. $R_T = 100\ \Omega + 2(56\ \Omega) + 4(12\ \Omega) + 330\ \Omega = 590\ \Omega$
3. $R = 13.8\ k\Omega - (1.0\ k\Omega + 2.7\ k\Omega + 5.6\ k\Omega + 560\ \Omega) = 3.9\ k\Omega$
4. $R_T = 12(56\ \Omega) = 672\ \Omega$
5. $R_T = 20(5.6\ k\Omega) + 30(8.2\ k\Omega) = 358\ k\Omega$

Section 5–4

1. $I = 10$ V/300 $\Omega = 33.3$ mA
2. $V_S = (5$ A)(21.2 $\Omega) = 106$ V
3. $V_1 = (5$ A)(10 $\Omega) = 50$ V; $V_2 = (5$ A)(5.6 $\Omega) = 28$ V; $V_3 = (5$ A)(5.6 $\Omega) = 28$ V
4. $R = (\frac{1}{4})(5$ V/4.63 mA) $= 270\ \Omega$

Section 5–5

1. $V_T = 4(1.5$ V) $= 6.0$ V
2. 60 V/12 V = 5; see Figure 5–92.

FIGURE 5–92

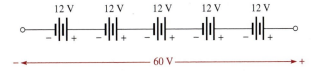

3. See Figure 5–93.
4. (a) $V_{S(tot)} = 100$ V $+ 50$ V $- 75$ V $= 75$ V
   (b) $V_{S(tot)} = 20$ V $+ 10$ V $- 10$ V $- 5$ V $= 15$ V
5. See Figure 5–94.

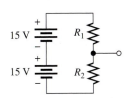

FIGURE 5–93

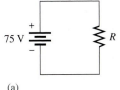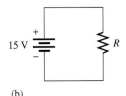

(a)   (b)

FIGURE 5–94

Section 5–6

1. (a) Kirchhoff's law states the sum of the voltages around a closed path is zero;
   (b) Kirchhoff's law states the sum of the voltage drops equals the total source voltage.
2. $V_T = V_S = 50$ V
3. $V_{R1} = V_{R2} = 5$ V
4. $V_R = 25$ V $- 10$ V $- 5$ V $= 10$ V
5. $V_S = 1$ V $+ 3$ V $+ 5$ V $+ 8$ V $+ 7$ V $= 24$ V

Section 5–7

1. A voltage divider is a circuit with two or more series resistors in which the voltage taken across any resistor or combination of resistors is proportional to the value of that resistance.

2. Two or more resistors form a voltage divider.

3. $V_x = (R_x/R_T)V_S$

4. $V_R = 10 \text{ V}/2 = 5 \text{ V}$

5. $V_{47} = (47 \ \Omega/129 \ \Omega)100 \text{ V} = 36.4 \text{ V}$; $V_{82} = (82 \ \Omega/129 \ \Omega)100 \text{ V} = 63.6 \text{ V}$; see Figure 5–95.

6. Set the wiper at the midpoint.

FIGURE 5–95

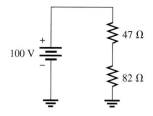

100 V   47 Ω   82 Ω

Section 5–8

1. Add the power in each resistor to get total power.

2. $P_T = 2 \text{ W} + 5 \text{ W} + 1 \text{ W} + 8 \text{ W} = 16 \text{ W}$

3. $P_T = (1 \text{ A})^2(1110 \ \Omega) = 1110 \text{ W}$

Section 5–9

1. The common reference point in a circuit is ground.

2. True

3. True

4. See Figure 5–96.

FIGURE 5–96

Section 5–10

1. A short circuit is a zero resistance path that bypasses a portion of a circuit.

2. An open circuit is a break in the current path.

3. When a circuit opens, current ceases.

4. An open can be created by a switch or by a component failure. A short can be created by a switch or, unintentionally, by a wire clipping or solder splash.

5. True, a resistor normally fails open.

6. 24 V across the open R; 0 V across the other Rs

Section 5–11

1. $P_T = (12 \text{ V})^2/16.6 \text{ k}\Omega = 8.67 \text{ mW}$

2. Pin 2: 1.41 V; Pin 6: 3.65 V; Pin 5: 4.01 V; Pin 4: 5.20 V; Pin 7: 3.11 V

3. Pin 3 connects to ground.

■ **ANSWERS TO RELATED PROBLEMS FOR EXAMPLES**

5–1 (a) See Figure 5–97.

(b) $R_1 = 1.0$ kΩ, $R_2 = 33$ kΩ, $R_3 = 39$ kΩ, $R_4 = 470$ Ω, $R_5 = 22$ kΩ

FIGURE 5–97

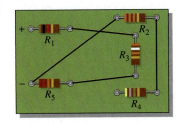

5–2 All resistors on the board are in series.

5–3 258 Ω

5–4 12.1 kΩ

5–5 6.8 kΩ

5–6 4440 Ω

5–7 114 mA

5–8 7.8 V

5–9 $V_1 = 1$ V, $V_2 = 3.3$ V, $V_3 = 2.2$ V; $V_S = 6.5$ V; $V_{S(max)} = 32.5$ V

5–10 Use an ohmmeter.

5–11 12 V

5–12 2 V

5–13 10 V and 20 V

5–14 47 V

5–15 593 Ω

5–16 $V_1 = 3.57$ V; $V_2 = 6.43$ V

5–17 $V_1 = V_2 = V_3 = 33.3$ V

5–18 $V_{AB} = 4$ V; $V_{AC} = 36.8$ V; $V_{BC} = 32.8$ V; $V_{BD} = 46$ V; $V_{CD} = 13.2$ V

5–19 8.49 W

5–20 $P_1 = 0.92$ W (1 W); $P_2 = 2.49$ W (5 W); $P_3 = 0.838$ W (1 W); $P_4 = 3.04$ W (5 W)

5–21 $V_A = 0$ V; $V_B = -25$ V; $V_C = -50$ V; $V_D = -75$ V; $V_E = -100$ V

■ **ANSWERS TO SELF-TEST**

1. (a)   **2.** (d)   **3.** (b)   **4.** (d)   **5.** (d)   **6.** (a)   **7.** (b)   **8.** (c)

9. (b)   **10.** (c)   **11.** (a)   **12.** (d)   **13.** (d)   (d)

6

PARALLEL CIRCUITS

 Electronics Workbench (EWB) and
PSpice Tutorials available at
http://www.prenhall.com/floyd

■ **INTRODUCTION**

In Chapter 5, you learned about series circuits and how to apply Ohm's law and Kirchhoff's voltage law. You also saw how a series circuit can be used as a voltage divider to obtain several specified voltages from a single source voltage. The effects of opens and shorts in series circuits were also examined.

In this chapter, you will see how Ohm's law is used in parallel circuits; and you will learn Kirchhoff's current law. Also, several applications of parallel circuits, including automotive lighting, residential wiring, and the internal wiring of analog ammeters are presented. You will learn how to determine total parallel resistance and how to troubleshoot for open resistors.

When resistors are connected in parallel and a voltage is applied across the parallel circuit, each resistor provides a separate path for current. The total resistance of a parallel circuit is reduced as more resistors are connected in parallel. The voltage across each of the parallel resistors is equal to the voltage applied across the entire parallel circuit.

In the TECH TIP, Section 6–11, imagine you are employed by an electronic instruments company. Your first job is to troubleshoot any defective instrument that fails the routine line check. In this particular assignment, you must determine the problem(s) with a defective five-range milliammeter so that it can be repaired. The knowledge of parallel circuits and of basic ammeters that you will acquire in this chapter plus your understanding of Ohm's law, current dividers, and the resistor color code will be put to good use.

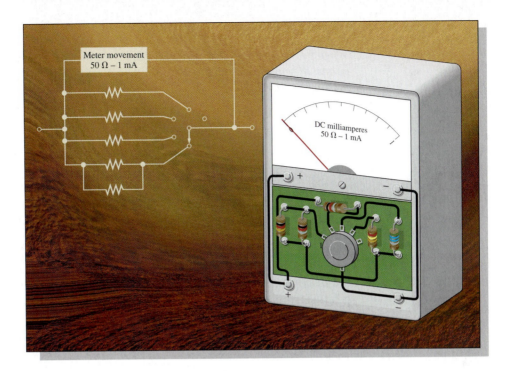

Meter movement
50 Ω − 1 mA

DC milliamperes
50 Ω − 1 mA

■ **CHAPTER OBJECTIVES**

❑ Identify a parallel circuit
❑ Determine the voltage across each parallel branch
❑ Apply Kirchhoff's current law
❑ Determine total parallel resistance
❑ Apply Ohm's law in a parallel circuit

❑ Determine the total effect of current sources in parallel
❑ Use a parallel circuit as a current divider
❑ Determine power in a parallel circuit
❑ Describe some basic applications of parallel circuits
❑ Troubleshoot parallel circuits

HISTORICAL NOTE

Ernst Werner von Siemens
1816–1872

Ernst Werner von Siemens was born in 1816 in Prussia. While in prison for acting as a second in a duel, he began to experiment with chemistry. These experiments eventually led to his invention of the first electroplating system. In 1837, Siemens began making improvements in the early telegraph and contributed greatly to the development of telegraphic systems. Ernst had a younger brother, Wilhelm, who was also a noted engineer. After moving to England, Wilhelm founded the company which today bears the family name. Unfortunately, it is not certain for which brother the unit of conductance is named, although it is most likely Ernst. *Photo credit: AIP Emilio Segrè Visual Archives, E. Scott Barr Collection.*

6–1 ■ RESISTORS IN PARALLEL

When two or more resistors are individually connected between the same two separate points, they are in parallel with each other. A parallel circuit provides more than one path for current.

After completing this section, you should be able to

■ **Identify a parallel circuit**
  • Translate a physical arrangement of resistors into a schematic

Each current path is called a **branch.** A **parallel** circuit is one that has more than one branch. Two resistors connected in parallel are shown in Figure 6–1(a). As shown in part (b), the current out of the source divides when it gets to point *B*. Part of it goes through R_1 and part through R_2. If additional resistors are connected in parallel with the first two, more current paths are provided between point *A* and point *B*, as shown in Figure 6–1(c). All points along the top shown in blue are electrically the same as point *A*, and all points along the bottom shown in green are electrically the same as point *B*.

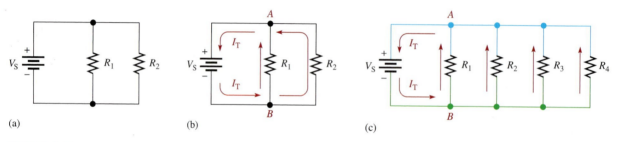

(a)   (b)   (c)

FIGURE 6–1
Resistors in parallel.

Identifying Parallel Circuits

In Figure 6–1, it is obvious that the resistors are connected in parallel. Often, in actual circuit diagrams, the parallel relationship is not as clear. It is important that you learn to recognize parallel circuits regardless of how they may be drawn.

A rule for identifying parallel circuits is as follows:

If there is more than one current path (branch) between two separate points (nodes), then there is a parallel circuit between those two points.

Figure 6–2 shows parallel resistors drawn in different ways between two separate points labeled *A* and *B.* Notice that in each case, the current "travels" two paths going from *B* to *A,* and the voltage across each branch is the same. Although these examples in Figure 6–2 show only two parallel paths, there can be any number of resistors in parallel.

FIGURE 6–2

Examples of circuits with two parallel paths.

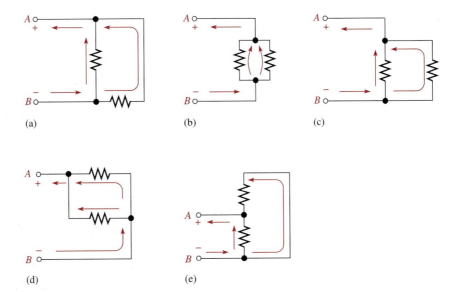

(a)　　　　(b)　　　　(c)

(d)　　　　(e)

EXAMPLE 6–1

Suppose that there are five resistors positioned on a circuit board as shown in Figure 6–3. Show the wiring required to connect all of the resistors in parallel, keeping in mind the positions of the + and − signs. Draw a schematic and label each of the resistors with its value.

FIGURE 6–3

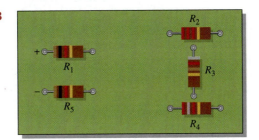

Solution   Wires are connected as shown in the assembly diagram of Figure 6–4(a). The schematic is shown in Figure 6–4(b). Again, note that the schematic does not necessarily have to show the actual physical arrangement of the resistors. The schematic shows how components are connected electrically.

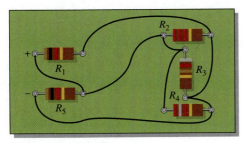

(a) Assembly wiring diagram

(b) Schematic

R_1 1.0 kΩ R_2 2.2 kΩ R_3 820 Ω R_4 2.7 kΩ R_5 1.0 kΩ

FIGURE 6–4

Related Problem   How would the circuit have to be rewired if R_2 is removed?

EXAMPLE 6–2 Determine the parallel groupings in Figure 6–5 and the value of each resistor.

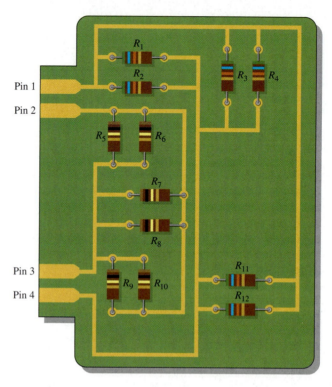

FIGURE 6–5

Solution Resistors R_1 through R_4 and R_{11} and R_{12} are all in parallel. This parallel combination is connected to pins 1 and 4. Each resistor in this group is 56 kΩ.

Resistors R_5 through R_{10} are all in parallel. This combination is connected to pins 2 and 3. Each resistor in this group is 100 kΩ.

Related Problem How would you connect all of the resistors in Figure 6–5 in parallel?

SECTION 6–1 REVIEW

1. How are the resistors connected in a parallel circuit?
2. How do you identify a parallel circuit?
3. Complete the schematics for the circuits in each part of Figure 6–6 by connecting the resistors in parallel between points *A* and *B*.
4. Now connect each group of parallel resistors in Figure 6–6 in parallel with each other.

FIGURE 6–6

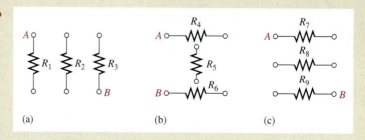

(a)   (b)   (c)

6–2 ■ VOLTAGE DROP IN PARALLEL CIRCUITS

As mentioned in the previous section, each current path in a parallel circuit is called a branch. The voltage across any given branch of a parallel circuit is equal to the voltage across each of the other branches in parallel.

After completing this section, you should be able to

■ **Determine the voltage across each parallel branch**
 • Explain why the voltage is the same across all parallel resistors

To illustrate voltage drop in a parallel circuit, let's examine Figure 6–7(a). Points *A, B, C,* and *D* along the left side of the parallel circuit are electrically the same point and form one node because the voltage is the same along this line. You can think of all of these points as being connected by a single wire to the negative terminal of the battery. The points *E, F, G,* and *H* along the right side of the circuit form another node and are all at a voltage equal to that of the positive terminal of the source. Thus, voltage across each parallel resistor is the same, and each is equal to the source voltage.

Figure 6–7(b) is the same circuit as in part (a), drawn in a slightly different way. Here the left side of each resistor is connected to a single point, which is the negative battery terminal. The right side of each resistor is connected to a single point, which is the positive battery terminal. The resistors are still all in parallel across the source.

In Figure 6–8, a 12 V battery is connected across three parallel resistors. When the voltage is measured across the battery and then across each of the resistors, the readings are the same. As you can see, the same voltage appears across each branch in a parallel circuit.

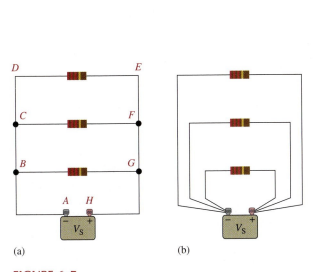

(a)   (b)

FIGURE 6–7
Voltage across parallel branches is the same.

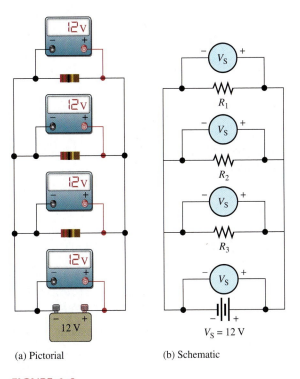

(a) Pictorial   (b) Schematic

FIGURE 6–8
The same voltage appears across each resistor in parallel.

EXAMPLE 6–3   Determine the voltage across each resistor in Figure 6–9.

FIGURE 6–9

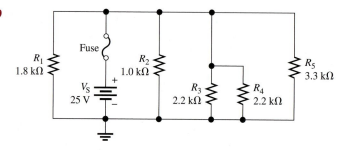

Solution   The five resistors are in parallel, so the voltage drop across each one is equal to the applied source voltage. There is insignificant voltage drop across the fuse.

$$V_1 = V_2 = V_3 = V_4 = V_5 = V_S = 25 \text{ V}$$

Related Problem   If R_4 is removed from the circuit, what is the voltage across R_3?

SECTION 6–2 REVIEW

1. A 10 Ω and a 22 Ω resistor are connected in parallel with a 5 V source. What is the voltage across each of the resistors?
2. A voltmeter is connected across R_1 in Figure 6–10. It measures 118 V. If you move the meter and connect it across R_2, how much voltage will it indicate? What is the source voltage?
3. In Figure 6–11, how much voltage does voltmeter 1 indicate? Voltmeter 2?
4. How are voltages across each branch of a parallel circuit related?

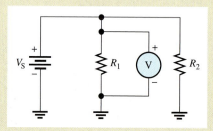

FIGURE 6–10

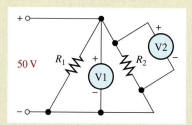

FIGURE 6–11

6–3 ▪ KIRCHHOFF'S CURRENT LAW

In the last chapter, you learned Kirchhoff's voltage law that dealt with voltages in a closed series circuit. Now, you will learn Kirchhoff's current law that deals with currents in a parallel circuit.

After completing this section, you should be able to

▪ **Apply Kirchhoff's current law**
  • State Kirchhoff's current law
  • Determine the total current by adding the branch currents
  • Determine an unknown branch current

Kirchhoff's current law, often abbreviated KCL, is stated as follows:

The sum of the currents into a junction (total current in) is equal to the sum of the currents out of that junction (total current out).

A **junction** is any point in a circuit where two or more components are connected. So, in a parallel circuit, a junction is where the parallel branches come together. For example, in the circuit of Figure 6–12, point *A* is one junction and point *B* is another. Let's start at the negative terminal of the source and follow the current. The total current I_T from the source is *into* the junction at point *B*. At this point, the current splits up among the three branches as indicated. Each of the three branch currents (I_1, I_2, and I_3) is *out of* junction *B*. Kirchhoff's current law says that the total current into junction *B* is equal to the total current out of junction *B;* that is,

$$I_T = I_1 + I_2 + I_3$$

Now, following the currents in Figure 6–12 through the three branches, you see that they come back together at point *A*. Currents I_1, I_2, and I_3 are into junction *A*, and I_T is out of junction *A*. Kirchhoff's current law formula at this junction is therefore the same as at junction *B*.

$$I_T = I_1 + I_2 + I_3$$

FIGURE 6–12

Total current into junction B equals the sum of currents out of junction B. The sum of currents into junction A equals the total current out of junction A.

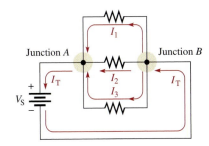

General Formula for Kirchhoff's Current Law

The previous discussion used a specific example to illustrate Kirchhoff's current law. Figure 6–13 shows a generalized circuit junction where a number of branches are connected to a point in the circuit. Currents $I_{IN(1)}$ through $I_{IN(n)}$ are into the junction (*n* can be any num-

FIGURE 6–13

Generalized circuit junction illustrating Kirchhoff's current law.

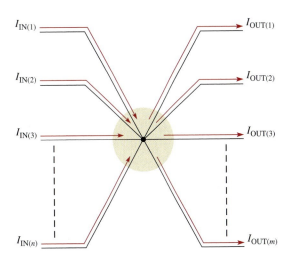

$$I_{IN(1)} + I_{IN(2)} + I_{IN(3)} + \cdots + I_{IN(n)} = I_{OUT(1)} + I_{OUT(2)} + I_{OUT(3)} + \cdots I_{OUT(m)}$$

ber). Currents $I_{\text{OUT}(1)}$ through $I_{\text{OUT}(m)}$ are out of the junction (m can be any number, but not necessarily equal to n). By Kirchhoff's current law, the sum of the currents into a junction must equal the sum of the currents out of the junction. With reference to Figure 6–13, the general formula for Kirchhoff's current law is

$$I_{\text{IN}(1)} + I_{\text{IN}(2)} + \cdots + I_{\text{IN}(n)} = I_{\text{OUT}(1)} + I_{\text{OUT}(2)} + \cdots + I_{\text{OUT}(m)} \qquad \textbf{(6–1)}$$

If all the terms on the right side of Equation (6–1) are brought over to the left side, their signs change to negative, and a zero is left on the right side as follows:

$$I_{\text{IN}(1)} + I_{\text{IN}(2)} + \cdots + I_{\text{IN}(n)} - I_{\text{OUT}(1)} - I_{\text{OUT}(2)} - \cdots - I_{\text{OUT}(m)} = 0$$

Kirchhoff's current law can also be stated in this way:

The algebraic sum of all the currents entering and leaving a junction is equal to zero.

You can verify Kirchhoff's current law by connecting a circuit and measuring each branch current and the total current from the source, as illustrated in Figure 6–14. When the branch currents are added together, their sum will equal the total current. This rule applies for any number of branches.

The following three examples illustrate use of Kirchhoff's current law.

FIGURE 6–14

Illustration of verifying Kirchhoff's current law.

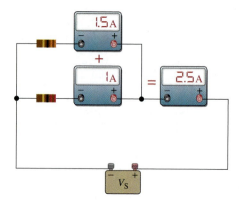

EXAMPLE 6–4

The branch currents in the circuit of Figure 6–15 are known. Determine the total current entering junction B and the total current leaving junction A.

FIGURE 6–15

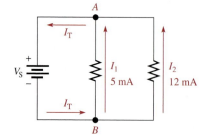

Solution The total current out of junction B is the sum of the two branch currents. So the total current into B is

$$I_T = I_1 + I_2 = 5 \text{ mA} + 12 \text{ mA} = \textbf{17 mA}$$

The total current entering junction A is the sum of the two branch currents. So the total current out of A is

$$I_T = I_1 + I_2 = 5 \text{ mA} + 12 \text{ mA} = \mathbf{17 \text{ mA}}$$

The calculator sequence is

⑤ EE (−) ③ ⊕ ① ② EE (−) ③ ENTER

Related Problem If a third branch is added to the circuit in Figure 6–15, and its current is 3 mA, what is the total current into junction B and out of junction A?

EXAMPLE 6–5   Determine the current I_2 through R_2 in Figure 6–16.

FIGURE 6–16

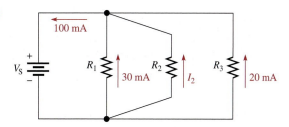

Solution The total current out of the junction of the three branches is $I_T = I_1 + I_2 + I_3$. From Figure 6–16, you know the total current and the branch currents through R_1 and R_3. Solve for I_2 as follows:

$$I_2 = I_T - I_1 - I_3 = 100 \text{ mA} - 30 \text{ mA} - 20 \text{ mA} = \mathbf{50 \text{ mA}}$$

Related Problem Determine I_T and I_2 if a fourth branch is added to the circuit in Figure 6–16 and it has 12 mA through it.

EXAMPLE 6–6   Use Kirchhoff's current law to find the current measured by ammeters A1 and A2 in Figure 6–17.

FIGURE 6–17

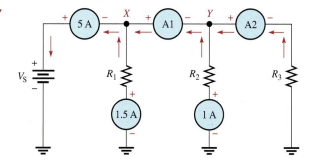

Solution The total current out of junction X is 5 A. Two currents are into junction X: 1.5 A through resistor R_1 and the current through A1. Kirchhoff's current law applied at junction X gives

$$5 \text{ A} = 1.5 \text{ A} + I_{A1}$$

Solving for I_{A1} yields

$$I_{A1} = 5 \text{ A} - 1.5 \text{ A} = \textbf{3.5 A}$$

The total current out of junction Y is $I_{A1} = 3.5$ A. Two currents are into junction Y: 1 A through resistor R_2 and the current through A2 and R_3. Kirchhoff's current law applied at junction Y gives

$$3.5 \text{ A} = 1 \text{ A} + I_{A2}$$

Solving for I_{A2} yields

$$I_{A2} = 3.5 \text{ A} - 1 \text{ A} = \textbf{2.5 A}$$

Related Problem How much current will an ammeter measure when it is placed in the circuit right below R_3? Below the negative battery terminal?

SECTION 6–3 REVIEW

1. State Kirchhoff's current law in two ways.
2. There is a total current of 2.5 A into the junction of three parallel branches. What is the sum of all three branch currents?
3. In Figure 6–18, 100 mA and 300 mA are out of the junction. What is the amount of current into the junction?
4. Determine I_1 in the circuit of Figure 6–19.
5. Two branch currents enter a junction, and two branch currents leave the same junction. One of the currents entering the junction is 1 A, and one of the currents leaving the junction is 3 A. The total current entering and leaving the junction is 8 A. Determine the value of the unknown current entering the junction and the value of the unknown current leaving the junction.

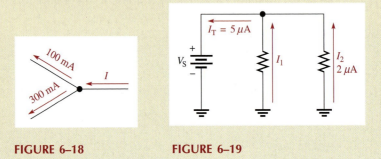

FIGURE 6–18   **FIGURE 6–19**

6–4 ■ TOTAL PARALLEL RESISTANCE

When resistors are connected in parallel, the total resistance of the circuit decreases. The total resistance of a parallel circuit is always less than the value of the smallest resistor. For example, if a 10 Ω resistor and a 100 Ω resistor are connected in parallel, the total resistance is less than 10 Ω.

After completing this section, you should be able to

■ **Determine total parallel resistance**
   • Explain why resistance decreases as resistors are connected in parallel
   • Apply the parallel-resistance formula

The Number of Current Paths Affects Total Resistance

As you know, when resistors are connected in parallel, the current has more than one path. The number of current paths is equal to the number of parallel branches.

For example, in Figure 6–20(a), there is only one current path since it is a series circuit. There is a certain amount of current, I_1, through R_1. If resistor R_2 is connected in parallel with R_1, as shown in Figure 6–20(b), there is an additional amount of current, I_2, through R_2. The total current from the source has increased with the addition of the parallel resistor. Assuming that the source voltage is constant, an increase in the total current from the source means that the total resistance has decreased, in accordance with Ohm's law. Additional resistors connected in parallel will further reduce the resistance and increase the total current.

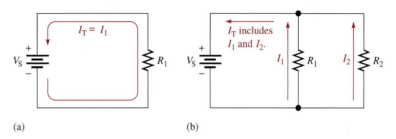

(a)   (b)

FIGURE 6–20
Addition of resistors in parallel reduces total resistance and increases total current.

Formula for Total Parallel Resistance

The circuit in Figure 6–21 shows a general case of n resistors in parallel (n can be any number). From Kirchhoff's current law, the current equation is

$$I_T = I_1 + I_2 + I_3 + \cdots + I_n$$

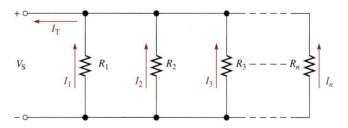

FIGURE 6–21
Circuit with n resistors in parallel.

Since V_S is the voltage across each of the parallel resistors, by Ohm's law, $I_1 = V_S/R_1$, $I_2 = V_S/R_2$, and so on. By substitution into the current equation,

$$\frac{V_S}{R_T} = \frac{V_S}{R_1} + \frac{V_S}{R_2} + \frac{V_S}{R_3} + \cdots + \frac{V_S}{R_n}$$

The term V_S can be factored out of the right side of the equation and canceled with V_S on the left side, leaving only the resistance terms.

$$\frac{1}{R_T} = \frac{1}{R_1} + \frac{1}{R_2} + \frac{1}{R_3} + \cdots + \frac{1}{R_n} \qquad \textbf{(6–2)}$$

Recall that the reciprocal of resistance ($1/R$) is called *conductance* and is symbolized by G. The unit of conductance is the siemens (S). Equation (6–2) can be expressed in terms of conductance as

$$G_T = G_1 + G_2 + G_3 + \cdots + G_n \qquad (6\text{–}3)$$

Solve for R_T in Equation (6–2) by taking the reciprocal of (that is, by inverting) both sides of the equation.

$$R_T = \cfrac{1}{\left(\dfrac{1}{R_1}\right) + \left(\dfrac{1}{R_2}\right) + \left(\dfrac{1}{R_3}\right) + \cdots + \left(\dfrac{1}{R_n}\right)} \qquad (6\text{–}4)$$

Equation (6–4) shows that to find the total parallel resistance, add all the $1/R$ (or conductance, G) terms and then take the reciprocal of the sum. Example 6–7 shows how to use the formula in a specific case, and Example 6–8 shows how to use a calculator to determine parallel resistances.

EXAMPLE 6–7

Calculate the total parallel resistance between points A and B of the circuit in Figure 6–22.

FIGURE 6–22

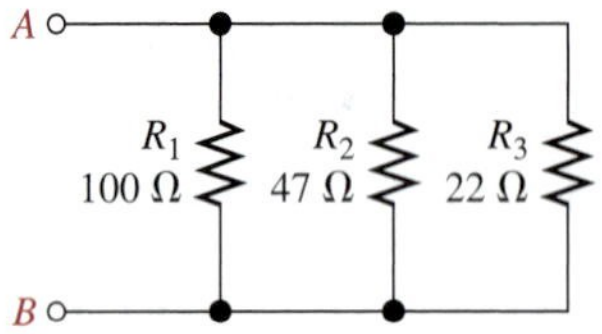

Solution Use Equation (6–4) to calculate the total parallel resistance when you know the individual resistances. First, find the conductance, which is the reciprocal of the resistance, of each of the three resistors.

$$G_1 = \frac{1}{R_1} = \frac{1}{100\ \Omega} = 10\ \text{mS}$$

$$G_2 = \frac{1}{R_2} = \frac{1}{47\ \Omega} = 21.3\ \text{mS}$$

$$G_3 = \frac{1}{R_3} = \frac{1}{22\ \Omega} = 45.5\ \text{mS}$$

Next, calculate R_T by adding G_1, G_2, and G_3 and taking the reciprocal of the sum.

$$R_T = \frac{1}{10\ \text{mS} + 21.3\ \text{mS} + 45.5\ \text{mS}} = \frac{1}{76.8\ \text{mS}} = \textbf{13.0}\ \boldsymbol{\Omega}$$

For a quick accuracy check, notice that the value of R_T (13.0 Ω) is smaller than the smallest value in parallel, which is R_3 (22 Ω), as it should be.

Related Problem If a 33 Ω resistor is connected in parallel in Figure 6–22, what is the new value of R_T?

Calculator Solution

The parallel-resistance formula is easily solved on a calculator. The general procedure is to enter the value of R_1 and then take its reciprocal ($1/R_1$ or R_1^{-1}) by pressing the [2nd] [x^{-1}] keys. (The reciprocal is not a secondary function on some calculators.) Next press the [+] key; then enter the value of R_2 and take its reciprocal. Repeat this procedure until all of the resistor values have been entered; then press [ENTER]. The final step is to press the [2nd] [x^{-1}] [ENTER] keys to convert $1/R_T$ to R_T. The total parallel resistance is now on the display.

EXAMPLE 6–8

Show the steps required for a TI-85 calculator solution of Example 6–7.

Solution
Step 1: Enter 100. Display shows 100.
Step 2: Press [2nd] [x^{-1}]. Display shows 100^{-1}.
Step 3: Press [+]. Display shows 100^{-1} +.
Step 4: Enter 47. Display shows 100^{-1} + 47.
Step 5: Press [2nd] [x^{-1}]. Display shows $100^{-1} + 47^{-1}$.
Step 6: Press [+]. Display shows $100^{-1} + 47^{-1}$ +.
Step 7: Enter 22. Display shows $100^{-1} + 47^{-1}$ + 22.
Step 8: Press [2nd] [x^{-1}]. Display shows $100^{-1} + 47^{-1} + 22^{-1}$.
Step 9: Press [ENTER]. Display shows a result of .076731141199.
Step 10: Press [2nd] [x^{-1}] and then [ENTER]. Display shows a result of 13.0325182758.
The number displayed in Step 10 is the total resistance in ohms. Round it to **13.0 Ω**.

Related Problem Show the additional calculator steps for R_T when a 33 Ω resistor is placed in parallel in the circuit of Example 6–7.

The Case of Two Resistors in Parallel

Equation (6–4) is a general formula for finding the total resistance for any number of resistors in parallel. It is often useful to consider only two resistors in parallel because this setup occurs commonly in practice. Also, any number of resistors in parallel can be broken down into pairs as an alternate way to find the R_T. Based on Equation (6–4), the formula for the total resistance of two resistors in parallel is

$$R_T = \frac{1}{\left(\dfrac{1}{R_1}\right) + \left(\dfrac{1}{R_2}\right)}$$

Combining the terms in the denominator yields

$$R_T = \frac{1}{\left(\dfrac{R_1 + R_2}{R_1 R_2}\right)}$$

which can be rewritten as follows:

$$R_T = \frac{R_1 R_2}{R_1 + R_2} \tag{6–5}$$

Equation (6–5) states

The total resistance for two resistors in parallel is equal to the product of the two resistors divided by the sum of the two resistors.

This equation is sometimes referred to as the "product over the sum" formula. Example 6–9 illustrates how to use it.

EXAMPLE 6–9

Calculate the total resistance connected to the voltage source of the circuit in Figure 6–23.

FIGURE 6–23

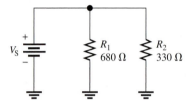

Solution   Use Equation (6–5) as follows:

$$R_T = \frac{R_1 R_2}{R_1 + R_2} = \frac{(680 \ \Omega)(330 \ \Omega)}{680 \ \Omega + 330 \ \Omega} = \frac{224{,}400 \ \Omega^2}{1010 \ \Omega} = \mathbf{222 \ \Omega}$$

The calculator sequence for solving the above equation is

6 8 0 × 3 3 0 ÷ (6 8 0 + 3 3 0) ENTER

Alternately, the following key sequence can be used:

6 8 0 2nd x⁻¹ + 3 3 0 2nd x⁻¹ ENTER 2nd x⁻¹ ENTER

Related Problem   Determine R_T if a 220 Ω resistor is added in parallel in Figure 6–23.

The Case of Equal-Value Resistors in Parallel

Another special case of parallel circuits is the parallel connection of several resistors each having the same resistance value. There is a shortcut method of calculating R_T when this case occurs.

If several resistors in parallel have the same resistance, they can be assigned the same symbol R. For example, $R_1 = R_2 = R_3 = \cdots = R_n = R$. Starting with Equation (6–4), we can develop a special formula for finding R_T.

$$R_T = \frac{1}{\left(\dfrac{1}{R}\right) + \left(\dfrac{1}{R}\right) + \left(\dfrac{1}{R}\right) + \cdots + \left(\dfrac{1}{R}\right)}$$

Notice that in the denominator, the same term, $1/R$, is added n times (n is the number of equal-value resistors in parallel). Therefore, the formula can be written as

$$R_T = \frac{1}{n/R}$$

or

$$R_T = \frac{R}{n} \tag{6–6}$$

Equation (6–6) says that when any number of resistors (n), all having the same resistance (R), are connected in parallel, R_T is equal to the resistance divided by the number of resistors in parallel. Example 6–10 shows how to use this formula.

EXAMPLE 6–10

Four 8 Ω speakers are connected in parallel to the output of an amplifier. What is the total resistance across the output of the amplifier?

Solution There are four 8 Ω resistors in parallel. Use Equation (6–6) as follows:

$$R_T = \frac{R}{n} = \frac{8\ \Omega}{4} = \mathbf{2\ \Omega}$$

Related Problem If two of the speakers are removed, what is the resistance across the output?

Determining an Unknown Parallel Resistor

Sometimes you need to determine the values of resistors that are to be combined to produce a desired total resistance. For example, two parallel resistors are used to obtain a known total resistance. If one resistor value is known or arbitrarily chosen, then the second resistor value can be calculated using Equation (6–5) for two parallel resistors. The formula for determining the value of an unknown resistor R_x is developed as follows:

$$\frac{1}{R_T} = \frac{1}{R_A} + \frac{1}{R_x}$$

$$\frac{1}{R_x} = \frac{1}{R_T} - \frac{1}{R_A}$$

$$\frac{1}{R_x} = \frac{R_A - R_T}{R_A R_T}$$

$$R_x = \frac{R_A R_T}{R_A - R_T} \qquad\qquad (6–7)$$

where R_x is the unknown resistor and R_A is the known or selected value. Example 6–11 illustrates use of this formula.

EXAMPLE 6–11

Suppose that you wish to obtain a resistance as close to 150 Ω as possible by combining two resistors in parallel. There is a 330 Ω resistor available. What other value do you need?

Solution $R_T = 150\ \Omega$ and $R_A = 330\ \Omega$. Therefore,

$$R_x = \frac{R_A R_T}{R_A - R_T} = \frac{(330\ \Omega)(150\ \Omega)}{330\ \Omega - 150\ \Omega} = 275\ \Omega$$

The closest standard value is **270 Ω.**

Related Problem If you need to obtain a total resistance of 130 Ω, what value can you add in parallel to the parallel combination of 330 Ω and 270 Ω? First find the value of 330 Ω and 270 Ω in parallel and treat that value as a single resistor.

Notation for Parallel Resistors

Sometimes, for convenience, parallel resistors are designated by two parallel vertical marks. For example, R_1 in parallel with R_2 can be written as $R_1 \parallel R_2$. Also, when several resistors are in parallel with each other, this notation can be used. For example,

$$R_1 \parallel R_2 \parallel R_3 \parallel R_4 \parallel R_5$$

indicates that R_1 through R_5 are all in parallel.

This notation is also used with resistance values. For example,

$$10 \text{ k}\Omega \parallel 5 \text{ k}\Omega$$

means that a 10 kΩ resistor is in parallel with a 5 kΩ resistor.

SECTION 6–4 REVIEW	**1.** Does the total resistance increase or decrease as more resistors are connected in parallel?
	2. The total parallel resistance is always less than _____.
	3. Write the general formula for R_T with any number of resistors in parallel.
	4. Write the special formula for two resistors in parallel.
	5. Write the special formula for any number of equal-value resistors in parallel.
	6. Calculate R_T for Figure 6–24.
	7. Determine R_T for Figure 6–25.
	8. Find R_T for Figure 6–26.

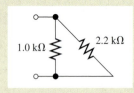

FIGURE 6–24

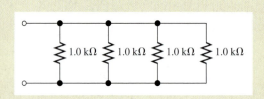

FIGURE 6–25

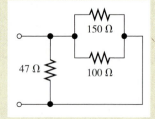

FIGURE 6–26

6–5 ■ OHM'S LAW IN PARALLEL CIRCUITS

In this section, examples illustrate how Ohm's law can be applied to parallel circuit analysis.

After completing this section, you should be able to

- **Apply Ohm's law in a parallel circuit**
  - Find the total current in a parallel circuit
  - Find each branch current in a parallel circuit
  - Find the voltage across a parallel circuit
  - Find the resistance in a parallel circuit

The following examples illustrate how to apply Ohm's law to determine the total current, branch currents, voltage, and resistance in parallel circuits.

EXAMPLE 6–12   Find the total current produced by the battery in Figure 6–27.

FIGURE 6–27

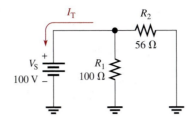

Solution   The battery "sees" a total parallel resistance which determines the amount of current that it generates. First, calculate R_T.

$$R_T = \frac{R_1 R_2}{R_1 + R_2} = \frac{(100\ \Omega)(56\ \Omega)}{100\ \Omega + 56\ \Omega} = \frac{5600\ \Omega^2}{156\ \Omega} = 35.9\ \Omega$$

The battery voltage is 100 V. Use Ohm's law to find I_T.

$$I_T = \frac{V_S}{R_T} = \frac{100\ \text{V}}{35.9\ \Omega} = \textbf{2.79 A}$$

Related Problem   What is I_T in Figure 6–27 if R_2 is changed to 120 Ω? What is the current through R_1?

EXAMPLE 6–13   Determine the current through each resistor in the parallel circuit of Figure 6–28.

FIGURE 6–28

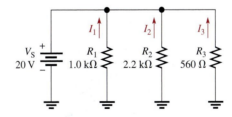

Solution   The voltage across each resistor (branch) is equal to the source voltage. That is, the voltage across R_1 is 20 V, the voltage across R_2 is 20 V, and the voltage across R_3 is 20 V. The current through each resistor is determined as follows:

$$I_1 = \frac{V_S}{R_1} = \frac{20\ \text{V}}{1.0\ \text{k}\Omega} = \textbf{20 mA}$$

$$I_2 = \frac{V_S}{R_2} = \frac{20\ \text{V}}{2.2\ \text{k}\Omega} = \textbf{9.09 mA}$$

$$I_3 = \frac{V_S}{R_3} = \frac{20\ \text{V}}{560\ \Omega} = \textbf{35.7 mA}$$

Related Problem   If an additional resistor of 910 Ω is connected in parallel to the circuit in Figure 6–28, determine all of the branch currents.

EXAMPLE 6–14   Find the voltage V_S across the parallel circuit in Figure 6–29.

FIGURE 6–29

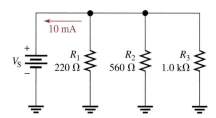

Solution   The total current into the parallel circuit is 10 mA. If you know the total resistance, then you can apply Ohm's law to get the voltage. The total resistance is

$$R_T = \cfrac{1}{\left(\dfrac{1}{R_1}\right)+\left(\dfrac{1}{R_2}\right)+\left(\dfrac{1}{R_3}\right)} = \cfrac{1}{\left(\dfrac{1}{220\ \Omega}\right)+\left(\dfrac{1}{560\ \Omega}\right)+\left(\dfrac{1}{1.0\ k\Omega}\right)}$$

$$= \frac{1}{4.55\ \text{mS} + 1.79\ \text{mS} + 1\ \text{mS}} = \frac{1}{7.34\ \text{mS}} = 136\ \Omega$$

Therefore, the source voltage is

$$V_S = I_T R_T = (10\ \text{mA})(136\ \Omega) = \textbf{1.36 V}$$

Related Problem   Find the voltage if R_3 is decreased to 680 Ω in Figure 6–29 and I_T is 10 mA.

EXAMPLE 6–15   The circuit board in Figure 6–30 has three resistors in parallel used for setting the gain of an instrumentation amplifier. The values of two of the resistors are known from the color codes, but the top resistor is not clearly marked (maybe the bands are worn off from handling). Determine the value of the unknown resistor R_1 using only an ammeter and a dc power supply.

FIGURE 6–30

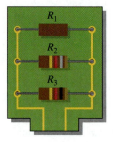

Solution   If you can determine the total resistance of the three resistors in parallel, then you can use the parallel-resistance formula to calculate the unknown resistance. You can use Ohm's law to find the total resistance if voltage and total current are known.

In Figure 6–31, a 12 V source (arbitrary value) is connected across the resistors, and the total current is measured. Using these measured values, find the total resistance.

$$R_T = \frac{V}{I_T} = \frac{12\ \text{V}}{24.1\ \text{mA}} = 498\ \Omega$$

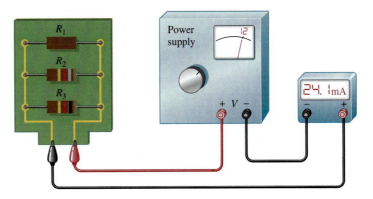

FIGURE 6–31

Use Equation (6–2) to find the unknown resistance as follows:

$$\frac{1}{R_T} = \frac{1}{R_1} + \frac{1}{R_2} + \frac{1}{R_3}$$

$$\frac{1}{R_1} = \frac{1}{R_T} - \frac{1}{R_2} - \frac{1}{R_3} = \frac{1}{498\ \Omega} - \frac{1}{1.8\ k\Omega} - \frac{1}{1.0\ k\Omega} = 453\ \mu S$$

$$R_1 = \frac{1}{453\ \mu S} = \textbf{2.21 k}\boldsymbol{\Omega}$$

The calculator sequence for R_1 is

4 9 8 2nd x^{-1} − 1 · 8 EE 3 2nd x^{-1} − 1 EE 3 2nd x^{-1} ENTER 2nd x^{-1} ENTER

Related Problem Is there an easier way to determine the value of R_1? If so, what is it?

SECTION 6–5 REVIEW

1. A 10 V battery is connected across three 68 Ω resistors that are in parallel. What is the total current from the battery?

2. How much voltage is required to produce 2 A of current through the circuit of Figure 6–32?

3. How much current is there through each resistor of Figure 6–32?

4. There are four equal-value resistors in parallel with a 12 V source, and 5.85 mA of current from the source. What is the value of each resistor?

5. A 1.0 kΩ and a 2.2 kΩ resistor are connected in parallel. There is a total of 100 mA through the parallel combination. How much voltage is dropped across the resistors?

FIGURE 6–32

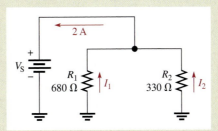

6–6 ■ CURRENT SOURCES IN PARALLEL

A current source is a type of energy source that provides a constant current to a load even if the resistance of that load changes. A transistor can be used as a current source; therefore, current sources are important in electronic circuits. At this point, you are not prepared to study transistors, but you do need to understand how current sources act in parallel.

After completing this section, you should be able to

■ **Determine the total effect of current sources in parallel**
   • Determine the total current from parallel sources having the same direction
   • Determine the total current from parallel sources having opposite directions

In general, the total current produced by current sources in parallel is equal to the algebraic sum of the individual current sources. The algebraic sum means that you must consider the direction of current when you combine the sources in parallel. For example, in Figure 6–33(a), the three current sources in parallel provide current in the same direction (out of point A). So the total current out of point A is

$$I_T = 1 \text{ A} + 2 \text{ A} + 2 \text{ A} = 5 \text{ A}$$

In Figure 6–33(b), the 1 A source provides current in a direction opposite to the other two. The total current out of point A in this case is

$$I_T = 2 \text{ A} + 2 \text{ A} - 1 \text{ A} = 3 \text{ A}$$

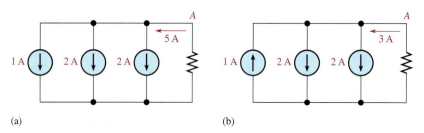

(a)   (b)

FIGURE 6–33

EXAMPLE 6–16   Determine the current through R_L in Figure 6–34.

FIGURE 6–34

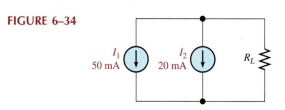

Solution   The two current sources are in the same direction; so the current through R_L is

$$I_L = I_1 + I_2 = 50 \text{ mA} + 20 \text{ mA} = \textbf{70 mA}$$

Related Problem   Determine the current through R_L if the direction of I_2 is reversed.

SECTION 6–6 REVIEW

1. Four 0.5 A current sources are connected in parallel in the same direction. What current will be produced through a load resistor?

2. How many 1 A current sources must be connected in parallel to produce a total current output of 3 A? Sketch a schematic showing the sources connected.

3. In a transistor amplifier circuit, the transistor can be represented by a 10 mA current source, as shown in Figure 6–35. In a certain transistor amplifier the transistors act in parallel. How much current is there through the resistor R_E?

FIGURE 6–35

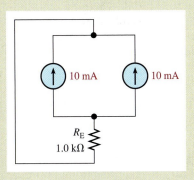

6–7 ▪ CURRENT DIVIDERS

A parallel circuit acts as a current divider because the current entering the junction of parallel branches "divides" up into several individual branch currents.

After completing this section, you should be able to

▪ **Use a parallel circuit as a current divider**
  • Apply the current-divider formula
  • Determine an unknown branch current

In a parallel circuit, the total current into the junction of parallel branches divides among the branches. Thus, a parallel circuit acts as a current divider. This current-divider principle is illustrated in Figure 6–36 for a two-branch parallel circuit in which part of the total current I_T goes through R_1 and part through R_2.

FIGURE 6–36
Total current divides between two branches.

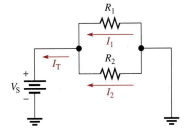

Since the same voltage is across each of the resistors in parallel, the branch currents are inversely proportional to the values of the resistors. For example, if the value of R_2 is twice that of R_1, then the value of I_2 is one-half that of I_1. In other words,

> **The total current divides among parallel resistors into currents with values inversely proportional to the resistance values.**

The branches with higher resistance have less current, and the branches with lower resistance have more current, in accordance with Ohm's law. If all the branches have the same resistance, the branch currents are all equal.

Figure 6–37 shows specific values to demonstrate how the currents divide according to the branch resistances. Notice that in this case the resistance of the upper branch is one-tenth the resistance of the lower branch, but the upper branch current is ten times the lower branch current.

FIGURE 6–37

The branch with the lowest resistance has the most current, and the branch with the highest resistance has the least current.

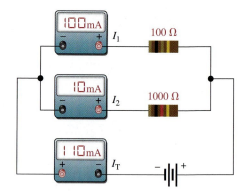

Current-Divider Formulas for Two Branches

Two parallel resistors are often found in practical circuits. Let's start by restating Equation (6–5), the formula for the total resistance of two parallel branches.

$$R_T = \frac{R_1 R_2}{R_1 + R_2}$$

When there are two parallel resistors, as in Figure 6–38, you may want to find the current through either or both of the branches. To do this, you need two special formulas.

FIGURE 6–38

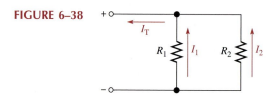

The formulas for I_1 and I_2 can be written as follows:

$$I_1 = \left(\frac{R_T}{R_1}\right)I_T \qquad \text{and} \qquad I_2 = \left(\frac{R_T}{R_2}\right)I_T$$

Substituting $R_1 R_2 / (R_1 + R_2)$ for R_T and canceling result in

$$I_1 = \frac{\left(\dfrac{R_1 R_2}{R_1 + R_2}\right)}{R_1}I_T \qquad \text{and} \qquad I_2 = \frac{\left(\dfrac{R_1 R_2}{R_1 + R_2}\right)}{R_2}I_T$$

Therefore, the current-divider formulas for two branches are the following:

$$I_1 = \left(\frac{R_2}{R_1 + R_2}\right)I_T \qquad \qquad (6\text{–}8)$$

$$I_2 = \left(\frac{R_1}{R_1 + R_2}\right)I_T \qquad (6\text{–}9)$$

Note that in Equations (6–8) and (6–9), the current in one of the branches is equal to the opposite branch resistance divided by the sum of the two resistors, all multiplied by the total current. In all applications of the current-divider equations, you must know the total current into the parallel branches. Example 6–17 illustrates application of these special current-divider formulas.

EXAMPLE 6–17   Find I_1 and I_2 in Figure 6–39.

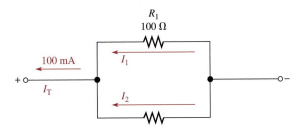

FIGURE 6–39

Solution   Use Equation (6–8) to determine I_1.

$$I_1 = \left(\frac{R_2}{R_1 + R_2}\right)I_T = \left(\frac{47\ \Omega}{147\ \Omega}\right)100\ \text{mA} = \mathbf{32.0\ mA}$$

Use Equation (6–9) to determine I_2.

$$I_2 = \left(\frac{R_2}{R_1 + R_2}\right)I_T = \left(\frac{100\ \Omega}{147\ \Omega}\right)100\ \text{mA} = \mathbf{68.0\ mA}$$

Related Problem   If $R_1 = 56\ \Omega$, and $R_2 = 82\ \Omega$ in Figure 6–39 and I_T stays the same, what will each branch current be?

General Current-Divider Formula for Any Number of Parallel Branches

With a few steps, a formula for determining how currents divide among parallel resistors can be developed. Let's assume that we have *n* resistors in parallel, as shown in Figure 6–40, where *n* can be any number.

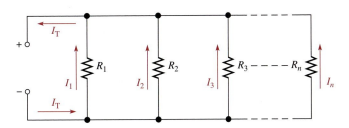

FIGURE 6–40
Generalized parallel circuit with n branches.

Let's call the current through any one of the parallel resistors I_x, where x represents the number of a particular resistor (1, 2, 3, and so on). By Ohm's law, the current through any one of the resistors in Figure 6–40 can be written as follows:

$$I_x = \frac{V_S}{R_x}$$

The source voltage, V_S, appears across each of the parallel resistors, and R_x represents any one of the parallel resistors. The total source voltage, V_S, is equal to the total current times the total parallel resistance.

$$V_S = I_T R_T$$

Substituting $I_T R_T$ for V_S in the expression for I_x results in

$$I_x = \frac{I_T R_T}{R_x}$$

Rearranging terms yields

$$I_x = \left(\frac{R_T}{R_x}\right) I_T \qquad\qquad \textbf{(6–10)}$$

where $x = 1, 2, 3$, etc. Equation (6–10) is the general current-divider formula and applies to a parallel circuit with any number of branches.

The current (I_x) through any branch equals the total parallel resistance (R_T) divided by the resistance (R_x) of that branch, and then multiplied by the total current (I_T) into the junction of parallel branches.

EXAMPLE 6–18   Determine the current through each resistor in the circuit of Figure 6–41.

FIGURE 6–41

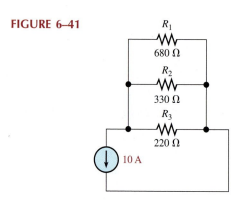

Solution   First calculate the total parallel resistance.

$$R_T = \frac{1}{\left(\dfrac{1}{R_1}\right) + \left(\dfrac{1}{R_2}\right) + \left(\dfrac{1}{R_3}\right)} = \frac{1}{\left(\dfrac{1}{680\ \Omega}\right) + \left(\dfrac{1}{330\ \Omega}\right) + \left(\dfrac{1}{220\ \Omega}\right)} = 111\ \Omega$$

The total current is 10 A. Use Equation (6–10) to calculate each branch current.

$$I_1 = \left(\frac{R_T}{R_1}\right)I_T = \left(\frac{111\ \Omega}{680\ \Omega}\right)10\ \text{A} = \textbf{1.63 A}$$

$$I_2 = \left(\frac{R_T}{R_2}\right)I_T = \left(\frac{111\ \Omega}{330\ \Omega}\right)10\ \text{A} = \textbf{3.36 A}$$

$$I_3 = \left(\frac{R_T}{R_3}\right)I_T = \left(\frac{111\ \Omega}{220\ \Omega}\right)10\ \text{A} = \textbf{5.05 A}$$

Related Problem Determine the current through each resistor in Figure 6–41 if R_3 is removed.

SECTION 6–7 REVIEW

1. Write the two special formulas for calculating each branch current for a two-branch circuit.
2. Write the general current-divider formula.
3. A parallel circuit has the following resistors in parallel: 220 Ω, 100 Ω, 82 Ω, 47 Ω, and 22 Ω. Which resistor has the most current through it? The least current?
4. Find I_1 and I_2 in the circuit of Figure 6–42.
5. Determine the current through R_3 in Figure 6–43.

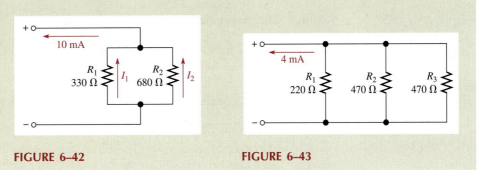

FIGURE 6–42   **FIGURE 6–43**

6–8 ▪ POWER IN PARALLEL CIRCUITS

Total power in a parallel circuit is found by adding up the powers of all the individual resistors, the same as you did for series circuits.

After completing this section, you should be able to

▪ **Determine power in a parallel circuit**

Equation (6–11) states the formula for finding total power in a concise way for any number of resistors in parallel.

$$P_T = P_1 + P_2 + P_3 + \cdots + P_n \qquad \text{(6–11)}$$

where P_T is the total power and P_n is the power in the last resistor in parallel. As you can see, the powers are additive, just as in the series circuit.

The power formulas in Chapter 4 are directly applicable to parallel circuits. The following formulas are used to calculate the total power P_T:

$$P_T = VI_T$$
$$P_T = I_T^2 R_T$$
$$P_T = \frac{V^2}{R_T}$$

where V is the voltage across the parallel circuit, I_T is the total current into the parallel circuit, and R_T is the total resistance of the parallel circuit. Example 6–19 shows how total power can be calculated in a parallel circuit.

EXAMPLE 6–19

Determine the total amount of power in the parallel circuit in Figure 6–44.

FIGURE 6–44

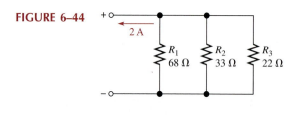

Solution   The total current is 2 A. The total resistance is

$$R_T = \cfrac{1}{\left(\cfrac{1}{68\ \Omega}\right) + \left(\cfrac{1}{33\ \Omega}\right) + \left(\cfrac{1}{22\ \Omega}\right)} = 11.1\ \Omega$$

The easiest power formula to use is $P_T = I_T^2 R_T$ because you know both I_T and R_T.

$$P_T = I_T^2 R_T = (2\ \text{A})^2 (11.1\ \Omega) = \textbf{44.4 W}$$

To demonstrate that if the power in each resistor is determined and if all of these values are added together, you will get the same result, let's work through another calculation. First, find the voltage across each branch of the circuit.

$$V = I_T R_T = (2\ \text{A})(11.1\ \Omega) = 22.2\ \text{V}$$

Remember that the voltage across all branches is the same.
   Next, use $P = V^2/R$ to calculate the power for each resistor.

$$P_1 = \frac{(22.2\ \text{V})^2}{68\ \Omega} = 7.25\ \text{W}$$

$$P_2 = \frac{(22.2\ \text{V})^2}{33\ \Omega} = 14.9\ \text{W}$$

$$P_3 = \frac{(22.2\ \text{V})^2}{22\ \Omega} = 22.4\ \text{W}$$

Add these powers to get the total power.

$$P_T = 7.25\ \text{W} + 14.9\ \text{W} + 22.4\ \text{W} = 44.6\ \text{W}$$

This calculation shows that the sum of the individual powers is equal (approximately) to the total power as determined by one of the power formulas. Rounding to three significant figures accounts for the difference.

Related Problem   Find the total power in Figure 6–44 if the total current is doubled.

EXAMPLE 6–20   The amplifier in one channel of a stereo system as shown in Figure 6–45 drives four speakers. If the maximum voltage to the speakers is 15 V, how much power must the amplifier be able to deliver to the speakers?

FIGURE 6–45

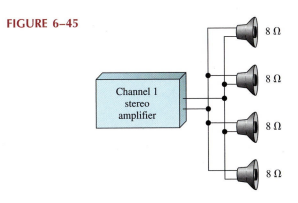

Solution   The speakers are connected in parallel to the amplifier output, so the voltage across each is the same. The maximum power to each speaker is

$$P_{max} = \frac{V_{max}^2}{R} = \frac{(15 \text{ V})^2}{8 \text{ }\Omega} = 28.1 \text{ W}$$

The total power that the amplifier must be capable of delivering to the speaker system is four times the power in an individual speaker because the total power is the sum of the individual powers.

$$P_{T(max)} = P_{(max)} + P_{(max)} + P_{(max)} + P_{(max)} = 4P_{(max)} = 4(28.1 \text{ W}) = \textbf{112.4 W}$$

Related Problem   If the amplifier can produce a maximum of 18 V, what is the maximum total power to the speakers?

SECTION 6–8 REVIEW

1. If you know the power in each resistor in a parallel circuit, how can you find the total power?
2. The resistors in a parallel circuit dissipate the following powers: 2.38 W, 5.12 W, 1.09 W, and 8.76 W. What is the total power in the circuit?
3. A circuit has a 1.0 kΩ, a 2.7 kΩ, and a 3.9 kΩ resistor in parallel. There is a total current of 1 A into the parallel circuit. What is the total power?

6–9 ■ EXAMPLES OF PARALLEL CIRCUIT APPLICATIONS

Parallel circuits are found in some form in virtually every electronic system. In many of these applications, the parallel relationship of components may not be obvious until you have covered some advanced topics that you will study later. For now, we will look at some common and familiar applications of parallel circuits.

After completing this section, you should be able to

■ **Describe some basic applications of parallel circuits**
  • Discuss the lighting system in automobiles
  • Discuss residential wiring
  • Describe how current through a heating element is controlled
  • Explain basically how a multiple-range ammeter works

Automotive

One advantage of a parallel circuit over a series circuit is that when one branch opens, the other branches are not affected. For example, Figure 6–46 shows a simplified diagram of an automobile lighting system. When one headlight on a car goes out, it does not cause the other lights to go out, because they are all in parallel.

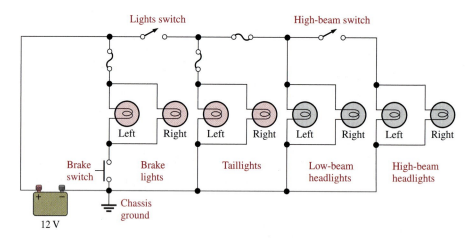

FIGURE 6–46

Simplified diagram of the exterior light system of an automobile. All lights are off when the switches are in the positions shown.

Notice that the brake lights are switched on independently of the headlights and taillights. They come on only when the driver closes the brake light switch by depressing the brake pedal. When the lights switch is closed, both low-beam headlights and both taillights are on. The high-beam headlights are on only when both the lights switch and the high-beam switch are closed. If any one of the lights burns out (opens), there is still current in each of the other lights.

Residential

Another common use of parallel circuits is in residential electrical systems. All the lights and appliances in a home are wired in parallel. Figure 6–47(a) shows a typical room wiring arrangement with two switch-controlled lights and three wall outlets in parallel.

Figure 6–47(b) shows a simplified parallel arrangement of four heating elements on an electric range. The four-position switches in each branch allow the user to control the amount of current through the heating elements by selecting the appropriate limiting resistor. The lowest resistor value (H setting) allows the highest amount of current for maximum heat. The highest resistor value (L setting) allows the least amount of current for minimum heat; M designates the medium settings.

Ammeters

Another example in which parallel circuits are used is the familiar analog (needle-type) ammeter or milliammeter. Parallel circuits are an important part of the operation of the ammeter because they allow the user to select various ranges in order to measure many different current values.

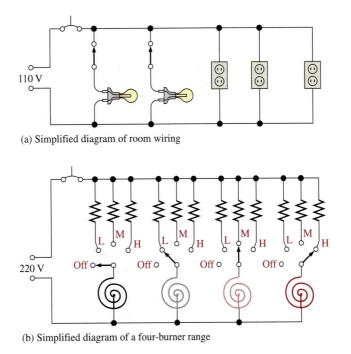

(a) Simplified diagram of room wiring

(b) Simplified diagram of a four-burner range

FIGURE 6–47

Examples of parallel circuits in residential wiring and appliances.

The mechanism in an ammeter that causes the pointer to move in proportion to the current is called the *meter movement,* which is based on a magnetic principle that you will learn later. Right now, it is sufficient to know that a meter movement has a certain resistance and a maximum current. This maximum current, called the *full-scale deflection current,* causes the pointer to go all the way to the end of the scale. For example, a certain meter movement has a 50 Ω resistance and a full-scale deflection current of 1 mA. A meter with this particular movement can measure currents of 1 mA or less as indicated in Figure 6–48(a) and (b). Currents greater than 1 mA will cause the pointer to "peg" (or stop) at full scale as indicated in part (c), which can damage the meter.

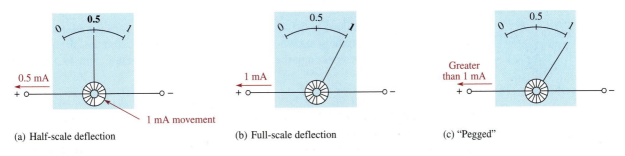

(a) Half-scale deflection

(b) Full-scale deflection

(c) "Pegged"

FIGURE 6–48

A 1 mA meter.

Figure 6–49 shows a simple ammeter with a resistor in parallel with the meter movement; this resistor is called a *shunt resistor.* Its purpose is to bypass a portion of current around the meter movement to extend the range of currents that can be measured. The figure specifically shows 9 mA through the shunt resistor and 1 mA through the meter movement. Thus, up to 10 mA can be measured. To find the actual current value, simply multiply the reading on the scale by 10.

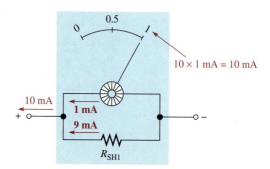

FIGURE 6–49
A 10 mA meter.

A practical ammeter has a range switch that permits the selection of several full-scale current settings. In each switch position, a certain amount of current is bypassed through a parallel resistor as determined by the resistance value. In our example, the current though the movement is never greater than 1 mA.

Figure 6–50 illustrates a meter with three ranges: 1 mA, 10 mA, and 100 mA. When the range switch is in the 1 mA position, all of the current into the meter goes through the meter movement. In the 10 mA setting, up to 9 mA goes through R_{SH1} and up to 1 mA through the movement. In the 100 mA setting, up to 99 mA goes through R_{SH2}, and the movement can still have only 1 mA for full-scale.

FIGURE 6–50
A milliammeter with three ranges.

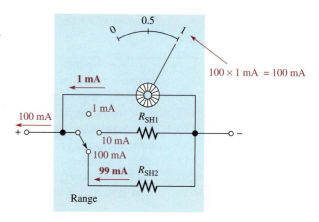

For example, in Figure 6–50, if 50 mA of current are being measured, the needle points at the 0.5 mark on the scale; you must multiply 0.5 by 100 to find the current value. In this situation, 0.5 mA is through the movement (half-scale deflection) and 49.5 mA are through R_{SH2}.

Effect of the Ammeter on a Circuit As you know, an ammeter is connected in series to measure the current in a circuit. Ideally, the meter should not alter the current that it is intended to measure. In practice, however, the meter unavoidably has some effect on the circuit because its internal resistance is connected in series with the circuit resistance. However, in most cases, the meter's internal resistance is so small compared to the circuit resistance that it can be neglected.

For example, if the meter has a 50 Ω movement (R_M) and a 100 μA full-scale current (I_M), the voltage dropped across the movement is

$$V_M = I_M R_M = (100 \ \mu A)(50 \ \Omega) = 5 \ mV$$

The shunt resistance (R_{SH}) for the 10 mA range, for example, is

$$R_{SH} = \frac{V_M}{I_{SH}} = \frac{5 \ mV}{9.9 \ mA} = 0.505 \ \Omega$$

As you can see, the total resistance of the ammeter on the 10 mA range is the resistance of the movement in parallel with the shunt resistance.

$$R_M \parallel R_{SH} = 50 \ \Omega \parallel 0.505 \ \Omega = 0.5 \ \Omega$$

EXAMPLE 6–21   How much does an ammeter with a 100 μA, 50 Ω movement affect the current in the circuit of Figure 6–51?

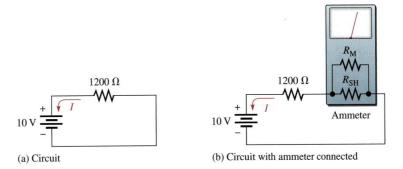

(a) Circuit   (b) Circuit with ammeter connected

FIGURE 6–51

Solution   The original current in the circuit (with no meter) is

$$I_{orig} = \frac{10 \ V}{1200 \ \Omega} = 8.3333 \ mA$$

The meter is set on the 10 mA range in order to measure this particular amount of current. It was found that the meter's resistance on the 10 mA range is 0.5 Ω. When the meter is connected in the circuit, its resistance is in series with the 1200 Ω resistor. Thus, there is a total of 1200.5 Ω.

The current in the circuit is reduced by inserting the meter to a new value of

$$I_{meas} = \frac{10 \ V}{1200.5 \ \Omega} = 8.3299 \ mA$$

The current with the presence of the meter differs from the original circuit current by only **3.4 μA** or **0.04%.**

Therefore, the meter does not significantly alter the current value, a situation which, of course, is necessary because the measuring instrument should not change the quantity that is to be measured accurately.

Related Problem   How much will the measured current differ from the original current if the circuit resistance in Figure 6–51 is 12 kΩ rather than 1200 Ω?

SECTION 6–9 REVIEW

1. For the ammeter in Figure 6–51, what is the maximum resistance that the meter will have when connected in a circuit? What is the maximum current that can be measured at the setting?

2. Do the shunt resistors have resistance values considerably less than or more than that of the meter movement? Why?

6–10 ■ TROUBLESHOOTING

In this section, you will see how an open in a parallel branch affects the parallel circuit.

After completing this section, you should be able to

■ **Troubleshoot parallel circuits**
  • Check for an open circuit

Open Branches

Recall that an open circuit is one in which the current path is interrupted and there is no current. In this section we examine what happens when a branch of a parallel circuit opens.

If a switch is connected in a branch of a parallel circuit, as shown in Figure 6–52, an open or a closed path can be made by the switch. When the switch is closed, as in Figure 6–52(a), R_1 and R_2 are in parallel. The total resistance is 50 Ω (two 100 Ω resistors in parallel). Current is through both resistors. If the switch is opened, as in Figure 6–52(b), R_1 is effectively removed from the circuit, and the total resistance is 100 Ω. Current is now only through R_2. In general,

> **When an open circuit occurs in a parallel branch, the total resistance increases, the total current decreases, and the same current continues through each of the remaining parallel paths.**

The decrease in total current equals the amount of current that was previously in the open branch. The other branch currents remain the same.

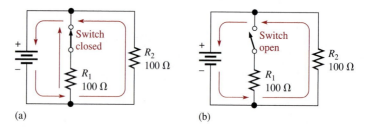

FIGURE 6–52
When switch opens, total current decreases and current through R_2 remains unchanged.

Consider the lamp circuit in Figure 6–53. There are four bulbs in parallel with a 120 V source. In part (a), there is current through each bulb. Now suppose that one of the bulbs burns out, creating an open path as shown in Figure 6–53(b). This light will go out because there is no current through the open path. Notice, however, that current continues through all the other parallel bulbs, and they continue to glow. The open branch does not change the voltage across the parallel branches; it remains at 120 V.

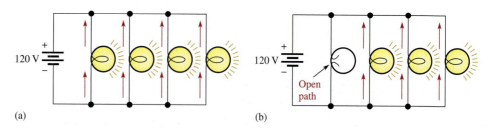

FIGURE 6–53
When one lamp opens, total current decreases and other branch currents remain unchanged.

You can see that a parallel circuit has an advantage over a series circuit in lighting systems because if one or more of the parallel bulbs burn out, the others will stay on. In a series circuit, when one bulb goes out, all of the others go out also because the current path is completely interrupted.

When a resistor in a parallel circuit opens, the open resistor cannot be located by measurement of the voltage across the branches because the same voltage exists across all the branches. Thus, there is no way to tell which resistor is open by simply measuring voltage. The good resistors will always have the same voltage as the open one, as illustrated in Figure 6–54 (note that the middle resistor is open).

If a visual inspection does not reveal the open resistor, it must be located by current measurements. In practice, measuring current is more difficult than measuring voltage because you must insert the ammeter in series to measure the current. Thus, a wire or a PC board connection must be cut or disconnected, or one end of a component must be lifted off the circuit board, in order to connect the ammeter in series. This procedure, of course, is not required when voltage measurements are made because the meter leads are simply connected across a component.

FIGURE 6–54

Parallel branches (open or not) have the same voltage.

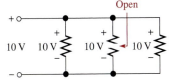

Finding an Open Branch by Current Measurement

In a parallel circuit, the total current should be measured. *When a parallel resistor opens, the total current, I_T, is always less than its normal value.* Once I_T and the voltage across the branches are known, a few calculations will determine the open resistor when all the resistors are of different resistance values.

Consider the two-branch circuit in Figure 6–55(a). If one of the resistors opens, the total current will equal the current in the good resistor. Ohm's law quickly tells you what the current in each resistor should be.

$$I_1 = \frac{50 \text{ V}}{560 \text{ }\Omega} = 89.3 \text{ mA}$$

$$I_2 = \frac{50 \text{ V}}{100 \text{ }\Omega} = 500 \text{ mA}$$

If R_2 is open, the total current is 89.3 mA, as indicated in Figure 6–55(b). If R_1 is open, the total current is 500 mA, as indicated in Figure 6–55(c).

This procedure can be extended to any number of branches having unequal resistances. If the parallel resistances are all equal, the current in each branch must be checked until a branch is found with no current. This is the open resistor.

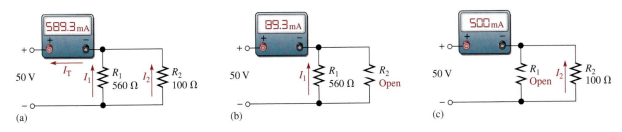

(a)　　　　　　　　　　　　　(b)　　　　　　　　　　　　　(c)

FIGURE 6–55

Finding an open path by current measurement.

EXAMPLE 6–22

In Figure 6–56, there is a total current of 31.09 mA, and the voltage across the parallel branches is 20 V. Is there an open resistor, and, if so, which one is it?

FIGURE 6–56

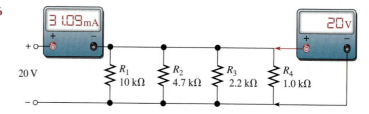

Solution Calculate the current in each branch.

$$I_1 = \frac{V}{R_1} = \frac{20 \text{ V}}{10 \text{ k}\Omega} = 2 \text{ mA}$$

$$I_2 = \frac{V}{R_2} = \frac{20 \text{ V}}{4.7 \text{ k}\Omega} = 4.26 \text{ mA}$$

$$I_3 = \frac{V}{R_3} = \frac{20 \text{ V}}{2.2 \text{ k}\Omega} = 9.09 \text{ mA}$$

$$I_4 = \frac{V}{R_4} = \frac{20 \text{ V}}{1.0 \text{ k}\Omega} = 20 \text{ mA}$$

The total current should be

$$I_T = I_1 + I_2 + I_3 + I_4 = 2 \text{ mA} + 4.26 \text{ mA} + 9.09 \text{ mA} + 20 \text{ mA} = 35.35 \text{ mA}$$

The actual measured current is 31.09 mA, as stated, which is 4.26 mA less than normal, indicating that the branch carrying 4.26 mA is open. Thus, R_2 **must be open.**

Related Problem What is the total current measured in Figure 6–56 if R_4 and not R_2 is open?

Finding an Open Branch by Resistance Measurement

If the parallel circuit to be checked can be disconnected from its voltage source and from any other circuit to which it may be connected, a measurement of the total resistance can be used to locate an open branch.

Conductance, *G*, is the reciprocal of resistance $(1/R)$ and its unit is the siemens (S). Recall that Equation (6–3) stated that the total conductance of a parallel circuit is the sum of the conductances of all the resistors.

$$G_T = G_1 + G_2 + G_3 + \cdots + G_n$$

To locate an open branch, do the following steps:

1. Calculate what the total conductance should be using the individual resistor values.

$$G_{T(calc)} = \frac{1}{R_1} + \frac{1}{R_2} + \frac{1}{R_3} + \cdots + \frac{1}{R_n}$$

2. Measure the total resistance with an ohmmeter and calculate the total measured conductance.

$$G_{T(meas)} = \frac{1}{R_{T(meas)}}$$

3. Subtract the measured total conductance (Step 2) from the calculated total conductance (Step 1). The result is the conductance of the open branch and the resistance is obtained by taking its reciprocal ($R = 1/G$).

$$R_{\text{open}} = \frac{1}{G_{\text{T(calc)}} - G_{\text{T(meas)}}}$$

(6–12)

EXAMPLE 6–23

Check the PC board in Figure 6–57 for open branches.

FIGURE 6–57

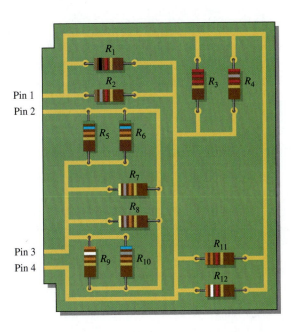

Solution There are two separate parallel circuits on the board. The circuit between pin 1 and pin 4 is checked as follows (we will assume one of the resistors is open):

1. Calculate what the total conductance should be using the individual resistor values.

$$G_{\text{T(calc)}} = \frac{1}{1.0 \text{ k}\Omega} + \frac{1}{1.8 \text{ k}\Omega} + \frac{1}{2.2 \text{ k}\Omega} + \frac{1}{2.7 \text{ k}\Omega} + \frac{1}{3.3 \text{ k}\Omega} + \frac{1}{3.9 \text{ k}\Omega} = 2.94 \text{ mS}$$

2. Measure the total resistance with an ohmmeter and calculate the total measured conductance. Assume that your ohmmeter measures 402 Ω.

$$G_{\text{T(meas)}} = \frac{1}{402 \text{ }\Omega} = 2.49 \text{ mS}$$

3. Subtract the measured total conductance (Step 2) from the calculated total conductance (Step 1). The result is the conductance of the open branch and the resistance is obtained by taking its reciprocal.

$$G_{\text{open}} = G_{\text{T(calc)}} - G_{\text{T(meas)}} = 2.94 \text{ mS} - 2.49 \text{ mS} = 0.45 \text{ mS}$$
$$R_{\text{open}} = \frac{1}{G_{\text{open}}} = \frac{1}{0.45 \text{ mS}} = 2.2 \text{ k}\Omega$$

Resistor R_3 is open and must be replaced.

Related Problem Your ohmmeter indicates 9.6 kΩ between pin 2 and pin 3 on the PC board in Figure 6–57. Determine if this is correct and, if not, which resistor is open.

Shorted Branches

When a branch in a parallel circuit shorts, the current increases to an excessive value, usually causing the resistor to burn open or a fuse or circuit breaker to blow. This results in a difficult troubleshooting problem because it is hard to isolate the shorted branch.

<table>
<tr>
<td>

**SECTION 6–10
REVIEW**

</td>
<td>

1. If a parallel branch opens, what changes can be detected in the circuit's voltage and the currents, assuming that the parallel circuit is across a constant-voltage source?

2. What happens to the total resistance if one branch opens?

3. If several light bulbs are connected in parallel and one of the bulbs opens (burns out), will the others continue to glow?

4. There is 1 A of current in each branch of a parallel circuit. If one branch opens, what is the current in each of the remaining branches?

5. A three-branch circuit normally has the following branch currents: 1 A, 2.5 A, and 1.2 A. If the total current measures 3.5 A, which branch is open?

</td>
</tr>
</table>

6–11 ■ TECHnology Theory Into Practice

A five-range milliammeter has just come off the assembly line, but it has failed the line check. For any current in excess of 1 mA, the needle "pegs" (goes off scale to the right) on all the range settings except 1 mA and 50 mA. In these two ranges, the meter seems to work correctly. As you know, a multiple-range meter circuit is based on shunt resistance placed in parallel with the meter movement to achieve the specified full-scale deflection of the needle. Your task is to troubleshoot the meter and determine what repairs are necessary.

The Meter Circuit

The meter face is shown in Figure 6–58(a). The circuitry is exposed by removing the front of the meter as shown in part (b). The precision resistors are 1% tolerance with a five-

FIGURE 6–58

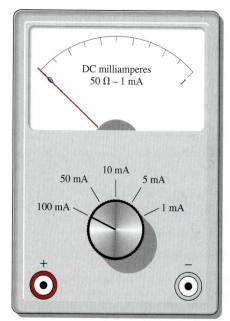

(a)

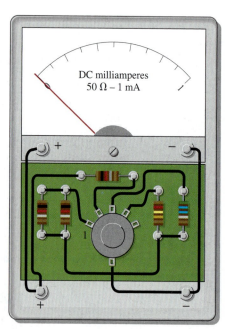

(b)

band color code. The first three bands indicate resistance value. In the fourth band, gold indicates a multiplier of 0.1 and silver a multiplier of 0.01. The brown fifth band indicates 1% tolerance.

The Schematic

■ The meter schematic is shown in Figure 6–59. Carefully check the circuit connections in Figure 6–58(b) to make sure they agree with the schematic. If there is a wiring problem, specify how to repair it. Resistors R_1, R_2, etc. can be identified by the way they are wired in the circuit. The 100 mA switch position is labeled "1". Resistance values are not shown in the schematic.

FIGURE 6–59

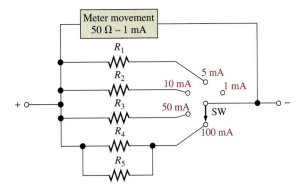

Troubleshooting

There was a wiring problem in the meter circuit which, let's assume, you have located and corrected. Now, assume that when you connect the meter to the test instrument to check for proper operation you find that the meter works properly on the 1 mA, 5 mA, 10 mA, and 50 mA ranges but the needle still "pegs" on the 100 mA range setting for a current of 50 mA or greater.

Since the needle pegs on the 100 mA range, all or most of the current must be going through the meter movement. Recall that a shunt resistor carries most of the current being measured so that the current through the meter movement does not exceed its 1 mA maximum. For this problem to occur, one of the shunt resistors for this range is either not connected, failed open, or has a resistance value that is much too high.

■ Check the circuit in Figure 6–58(b) again for another wiring error and check the color-coded values of R_4 and R_5. For some reason, the schematic does not show the resistor values so you will have to calculate what they should be using your knowledge of Ohm's law and current dividers. Refer to the table of standard resistor values in Appendix A.

SECTION 6–11 REVIEW

1. What is the total resistance between the positive and negative terminals of the milliammeter in Figure 6–58 when the range switch is in the 1 mA position? The 5 mA position? The 10 mA position?

2. When the switch is in the 5 mA position and the needle points to the middle mark on the scale, how much current is being measured?

3. When the meter is on the 5 mA range and is measuring the amount of current determined in Question 2, how much of the total current is through the meter movement and how much through the shunt resistor?

■ SUMMARY

- Resistors in parallel are connected across the same separate points.
- A parallel combination has more than one path for current.
- The number of current paths equals the number of resistors in parallel.
- The total parallel resistance is less than the lowest-value resistor.
- The voltages across all branches of a parallel circuit are the same.
- Current sources in parallel add algebraically.
- One way to state Kirchhoff's current law: The sum of the currents into a junction (total current in) equals the sum of the currents out of the junction (total current out).
- Another way to state Kirchhoff's current law: The algebraic sum of all the currents entering and leaving a junction is equal to zero.
- A parallel circuit is a current divider, so called because the total current entering the junction of parallel branches divides up into each of the branches.
- If all of the branches of a parallel circuit have equal resistance, the currents through all of the branches are equal.
- The total power in a parallel-resistive circuit is the sum of all of the individual powers of the resistors making up the parallel circuit.
- The total power for a parallel circuit can be calculated with the power formulas using values of total current, total resistance, or total voltage.
- If one of the branches of a parallel circuit opens, the total resistance increases, and therefore the total current decreases.
- If a branch of a parallel circuit opens, there is no change in current through the remaining branches.

■ GLOSSARY

These terms are also in the end-of-book glossary.

Branch   One current path in a parallel circuit.

Junction   A point at which two or more components are connected.

Kirchhoff's current law   A law stating that the total current into a junction equals the total current out of the junction.

Parallel   The relationship in electric circuits in which two or more current paths are connected between the same two separate points.

■ FORMULAS

(6–1) $$I_{IN(1)} + I_{IN(2)} + \cdots + I_{IN(n)} = I_{OUT(1)} + I_{OUT(2)} + \cdots + I_{OUT(m)}$$ Kirchhoff's current law

(6–2) $$\frac{1}{R_T} = \frac{1}{R_1} + \frac{1}{R_2} + \frac{1}{R_3} + \cdots + \frac{1}{R_n}$$ Reciprocal for total parallel resistance

(6–3) $$G_T = G_1 + G_2 + G_3 + \cdots + G_n$$ Total conductance

(6–4) $$R_T = \frac{1}{\left(\frac{1}{R_1}\right) + \left(\frac{1}{R_2}\right) + \left(\frac{1}{R_3}\right) + \cdots + \left(\frac{1}{R_n}\right)}$$ Total parallel resistance

(6–5) $$R_T = \frac{R_1 R_2}{R_1 + R_2}$$ Special case for two resistors in parallel

(6–6) $$R_T = \frac{R}{n}$$ Special case for n equal-value resistors in parallel

(6–7) $$R_x = \frac{R_A R_T}{R_A - R_T}$$ Unknown parallel resistor

(6–8) $$I_1 = \left(\frac{R_2}{R_1 + R_2}\right) I_T$$ Two-branch current-divider formula

(6–9) $I_2 = \left(\dfrac{R_1}{R_1 + R_2}\right)I_T$ Two-branch current-divider formula

(6–10) $I_x = \left(\dfrac{R_T}{R_x}\right)I_T$ General current-divider formula

(6–11) $P_T = P_1 + P_2 + P_3 + \cdots + P_n$ Total power

(6–12) $R_{open} = \dfrac{1}{G_{T(calc)} - G_{T(meas)}}$ Open branch resistance

---

▪ SELF-TEST

1. In a parallel circuit, each resistor has
   - (a) the same current
   - (b) the same voltage
   - (c) the same power
   - (d) all of the above

2. When a 1.2 kΩ resistor and a 100 Ω resistor are connected in parallel, the total resistance is
   - (a) greater than 1.2 kΩ
   - (b) greater than 100 Ω but less than 1.2 kΩ
   - (c) less than 100 Ω but greater than 90 Ω
   - (d) less than 90 Ω

3. A 330 Ω resistor, a 270 Ω resistor, and a 68 Ω resistor are all in parallel. The total resistance is approximately
   - (a) 668 Ω   (b) 47 Ω   (c) 68 Ω   (d) 22 Ω

4. Eight resistors are in parallel. The two lowest-value resistors are both 1.0 kΩ. The total resistance
   - (a) is less than 8 kΩ   (b) is greater than 1.0 kΩ
   - (c) is less than 1.0 kΩ   (d) is less than 500 Ω

5. When an additional resistor is connected across an existing parallel circuit, the total resistance
   - (a) decreases   (b) increases
   - (c) remains the same   (d) increases by the value of the added resistor

6. If one of the resistors in a parallel circuit is removed, the total resistance
   - (a) decreases by the value of the removed resistor   (b) remains the same
   - (c) increases   (d) doubles

7. One current into a junction is 5 A and the other current into the same junction is 3 A. The total current out of the junction is
   - (a) 2 A   (b) unknown   (c) 8 A   (d) the larger of the two

8. The following resistors are in parallel across a voltage source: 390 Ω, 560 Ω, and 820 Ω. The resistor with the least current is
   - (a) 390 Ω   (b) 560 Ω
   - (c) 820 Ω   (d) impossible to determine without knowing the voltage

9. A sudden decrease in the total current into a parallel circuit may indicate
   - (a) a short   (b) an open resistor
   - (c) a drop in source voltage   (d) either (b) or (c)

10. In a four-branch parallel circuit, there are 10 mA of current in each branch. If one of the branches opens, the current in each of the other three branches is
    - (a) 13.3 mA   (b) 10 mA   (c) 0 A   (d) 30 mA

11. In a certain three-branch parallel circuit, R_1 has 10 mA through it, R_2 has 15 mA through it, and R_3 has 20 mA through it. After measuring a total current of 35 mA, you can say that
    - (a) R_1 is open   (b) R_2 is open
    - (c) R_3 is open   (d) the circuit is operating properly

12. If there are a total of 100 mA into a parallel circuit consisting of three branches and two of the branch currents are 40 mA and 20 mA, the third branch current is
    - (a) 60 mA   (b) 20 mA   (c) 160 mA   (d) 40 mA

13. A complete short develops across one of five parallel resistors on a PC board. The most likely result is

    (a) the shorted resistor will burn out

    (b) one or more of the other resistors will burn out

    (c) the fuse in the power supply will blow

    (d) the resistance values will be altered

14. The power dissipation in each of four parallel branches is 1 W. The total power dissipation is

    (a) 1 W   **(b)** 4 W   **(c)** 0.25 W   **(d)** 16 W

■ **PROBLEMS**   *More difficult problems are indicated by an asterisk (*).*

SECTION 6–1   Resistors in Parallel

1. Show how to connect the resistors in Figure 6–60(a) in parallel across the battery.

2. Determine whether or not all the resistors in Figure 6–60(b) are connected in parallel on the printed circuit (PC) board.

FIGURE 6–60

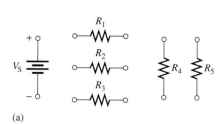

(a)

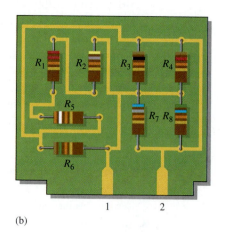

(b)

*3. Identify which groups of resistors are in parallel on the double-sided PC board in Figure 6–61.

FIGURE 6–61

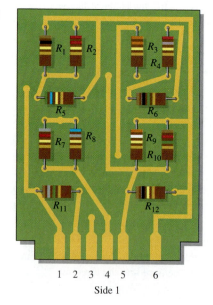

1 2 3 4 5 6

Side 1

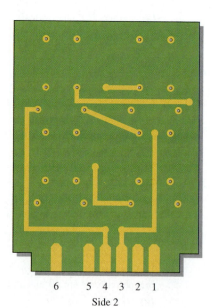

6 5 4 3 2 1

Side 2

SECTION 6–2　Voltage Drop in Parallel Circuits

4. What is the voltage across and the current through each parallel resistor if the total voltage is 12 V and the total resistance is 550 Ω? There are four resistors, all of equal value.

5. The source voltage in Figure 6–62 is 100 V. How much voltage does each of the meters read?

6. What is the voltage across each resistor in Figure 6–63 for each switch position?

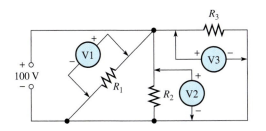

FIGURE 6–62

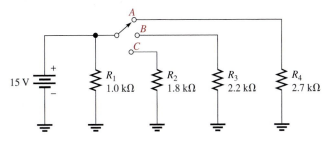

FIGURE 6–63

SECTION 6–3　Kirchhoff's Current Law

7. The following currents are measured in the same direction in a three-branch parallel circuit: 250 mA, 300 mA, and 800 mA. What is the value of the current into the junction of these three branches?

8. There is a total of 500 mA of current into five parallel resistors. The currents through four of the resistors are 50 mA, 150 mA, 25 mA, and 100 mA. What is the current through the fifth resistor?

9. In the circuit of Figure 6–64, determine the resistance R_2, R_3, and R_4.

FIGURE 6–64

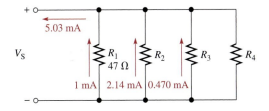

*10. The electrical circuit in a room has a ceiling lamp that draws 1.25 A and four wall outlets. Two table lamps that each draw 0.833 A are plugged into two outlets, and a TV set that draws 1 A is connected to the third outlet. When all of these items are in use, how much current is in the main line serving the room? If the main line is protected by a 5 A circuit breaker, how much current can be drawn from the fourth outlet? Draw a schematic of this wiring.

*11. The total resistance of a parallel circuit is 25 Ω. What is the current through a 220 Ω resistor that makes up part of the parallel circuit if the total current is 100 mA?

SECTION 6–4　Total Parallel Resistance

12. The following resistors are connected in parallel: 1.0 MΩ, 2.2 MΩ, 5.6 MΩ, 12 MΩ, and 22 MΩ. Determine the total resistance.

13. Find the total resistance for each of the following groups of parallel resistors:
(a) 560 Ω and 1000 Ω (b) 47 Ω and 56 Ω
(c) 1.5 kΩ, 2.2 kΩ, 10 kΩ　(d) 1.0 MΩ, 470 kΩ, 1.0 kΩ, 2.7 MΩ

FIGURE 6–65

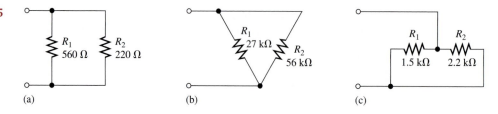

(a)   (b)   (c)

14. Calculate R_T for each circuit in Figure 6–65.
15. What is the total resistance of twelve 6.8 kΩ resistors in parallel?
16. Five 47 Ω, ten 100 Ω, and two 10 Ω resistors are all connected in parallel. What is the total resistance for each of the three groupings?
17. Find the total resistance for the entire parallel circuit in Problem 16.
18. If the total resistance in Figure 6–66 is 389.2 Ω, what is the value of R_2?

FIGURE 6–66

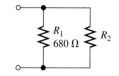

19. What is the total resistance between point A and ground in Figure 6–67 for the following conditions?
    (a) SW1 and SW2 open   (b) SW1 closed, SW2 open
    (c) SW1 open, SW2 closed   (d) SW1 and SW2 closed

FIGURE 6–67

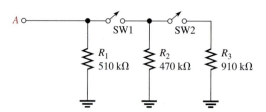

SECTION 6–5 Ohm's Law in Parallel Circuits

20. What is the total current in each circuit of Figure 6–68?

FIGURE 6–68

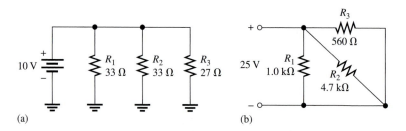

(a)   (b)

21. Three 33 Ω resistors are connected in parallel with a 110 V source. What is the current from the source?
22. Four equal-value resistors are connected in parallel. Five volts are applied across the parallel circuit, and 1.11 mA are measured from the source. What is the value of each resistor?
23. Christmas tree lights are usually connected in parallel. If a set of lights is connected to a 110 V source and the filament of each bulb has a resistance of 2.2 kΩ, what is the current through each bulb? Why is it better to have these bulbs in parallel rather than in series?
24. Find the values of the unspecified labeled quantities in each circuit of Figure 6–69.

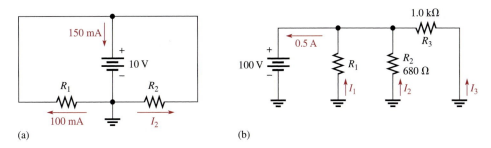

(a) (b)

FIGURE 6–69

25. To what minimum value can the 100 Ω rheostat in Figure 6–70 be adjusted before the 0.5 A fuse blows?

FIGURE 6–70

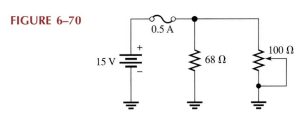

26. Determine the total current from the source and the current through each resistor for each switch position in Figure 6–71.

FIGURE 6–71

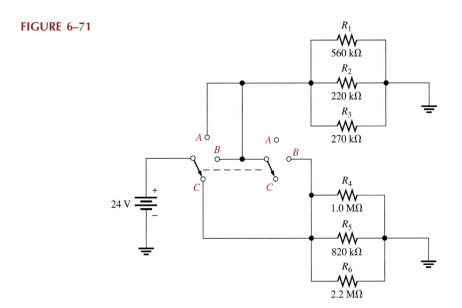

27. Find the values of the unspecified quantities in Figure 6–72.

FIGURE 6–72

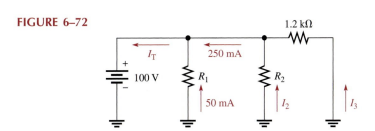

SECTION 6–6 Current Sources in Parallel

28. Determine the current through R_L in each circuit in Figure 6–73.

FIGURE 6–73

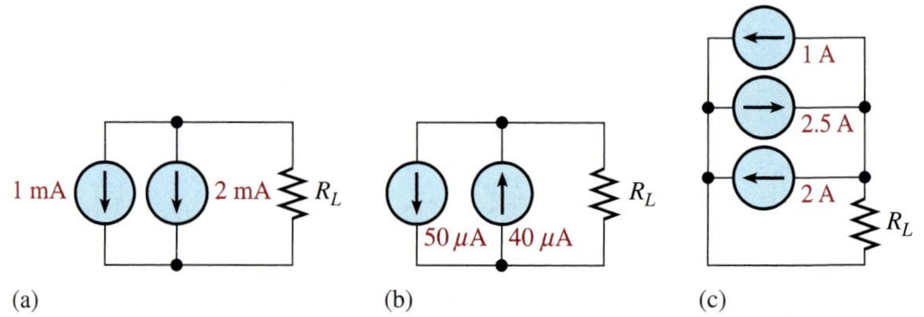

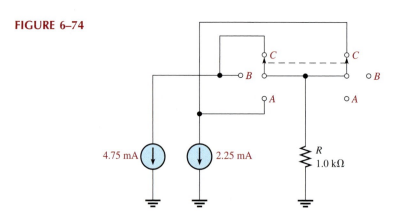

29. Find the current through the resistor for each position of the ganged switch in Figure 6–74.

FIGURE 6–74

SECTION 6–7 Current Dividers

30. How much branch current should each meter in Figure 6–75 indicate?

31. Determine the current in each branch of the current dividers of Figure 6–76.

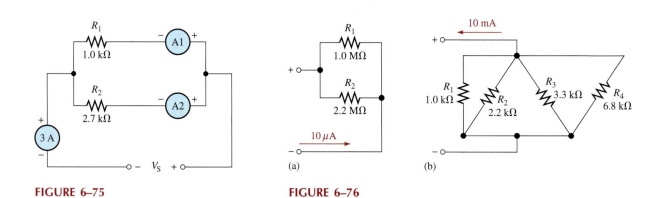

FIGURE 6–75

FIGURE 6–76

32. What is the current through each resistor in Figure 6–77? R is the lowest-value resistor, and all others are multiples of that value as indicated.

33. Determine all of the resistor values in Figure 6–78. $R_T = 773 \ \Omega$.

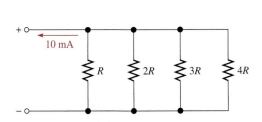

FIGURE 6–77

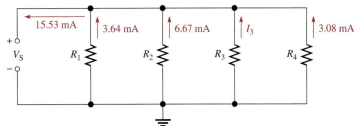

FIGURE 6–78

*34. (a) Determine the required value of the shunt resistor R_{SH1} in the ammeter of Figure 6–49 if the resistance of the meter movement is 50 Ω.

(b) Find the required value for R_{SH2} in the meter circuit of Figure 6–50 ($R_M = 50$ Ω).

*35. Add a fourth range position to the meter in Figure 6–50 so that currents up to 1 A (1000 mA) can be measured. Specify the value of the additional shunt resistor. Assume a 1 mA, 50 Ω meter movement.

SECTION 6–8 Power in Parallel Circuits

36. Five parallel resistors each handle 40 mW. What is the total power?

37. Determine the total power in each circuit of Figure 6–76.

38. Six light bulbs are connected in parallel across 110 V. Each bulb is rated at 75 W. What is the current through each bulb, and what is the total current?

*39. Find the values of the unspecified quantities in Figure 6–79.

FIGURE 6–79

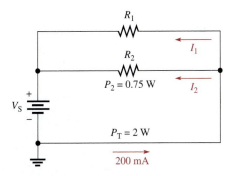

*40. A certain parallel circuit consists of only ½ W resistors. The total resistance is 1.0 kΩ, and the total current is 50 mA. If each resistor is operating at one-half its maximum power level, determine the following:

(a) The number of resistors (b) The value of each resistor

(c) The current in each branch (d) The applied voltage

SECTION 6–10 Troubleshooting

41. If one of the bulbs burns out in Problem 38, how much current will be through each of the remaining bulbs? What will the total current be?

42. In Figure 6–80, the current and voltage measurements are indicated. Has a resistor opened, and, if so, which one?

FIGURE 6–80

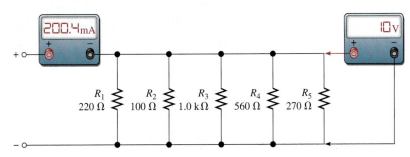

43. What is wrong with the circuit in Figure 6–81?

44. What is wrong with the circuit in Figure 6–81 if the meter reads 5.55 mA?

*45. Develop a test procedure to check the circuit board in Figure 6–82 to make sure that there are no open components. You must do this test without removing a component from the board. List the procedure in a detailed step-by-step format.

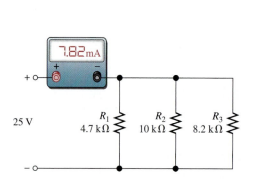

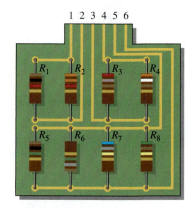

FIGURE 6–81

FIGURE 6–82

*46. For the circuit board shown in Figure 6–83, determine the resistance between the following pins if there is a short between pins 2 and 4:

(a) 1 and 2   (b) 2 and 3   (c) 3 and 4   (d) 1 and 4

*47. For the circuit board shown in Figure 6–83, determine the resistance between the following pins if there is a short between pins 3 and 4:

(a) 1 and 2   (b) 2 and 3   (c) 2 and 4   (d) 1 and 4

FIGURE 6–83

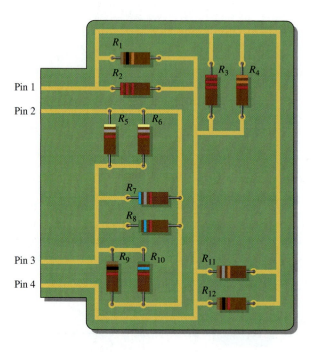

EWB Troubleshooting and Analysis

These problems require your EWB compact disk.

48. Open file PRO06-48.EWB and measure the total parallel resistance.

49. Open file PRO06-49.EWB. Determine by measurement if there is an open resistor and, if so, which one.

50. Open file PRO06-50.EWB and determine the unspecified resistance value.
51. Open file PRO06-51.EWB and determine the unspecified source voltage.
52. Open file PRO06-52.EWB and find the fault if there is one.

■ **ANSWERS TO SECTION REVIEWS**

Section 6–1

1. Parallel resistors are connected between the same two separate points.
2. A parallel circuit has more than one current path between two given points.
3. See Figure 6–84.

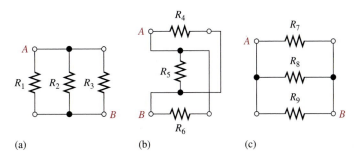

(a)   (b)   (c)

FIGURE 6–84

4. See Figure 6–85.

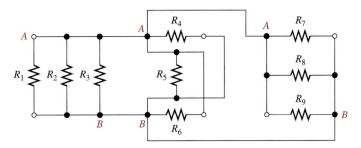

FIGURE 6–85

Section 6–2

1. $V_{10\Omega} = V_{22\Omega} = 5$ V
2. $V_{R2} = 118$ V; $V_S = 118$ V
3. $V_{R1} = 50$ V and $V_{R2} = 50$ V
4. Voltage is the same across all parallel branches.

Section 6–3

1. Kirchhoff's law: The algebraic sum of all the currents at a junction is zero; The sum of the currents entering a junction equals the sum of the currents leaving that junction.
2. $I_1 = I_2 = I_3 = I_T = 2.5$ A
3. $I_{OUT} = 100$ mA $+ 300$ mA $= 400$ mA
4. $I_1 = I_T - I_2 = 3$ μA
5. $I_{IN} = 8$ A $- 1$ A $= 7$ A; $I_{OUT} = 8$ A $- 3$ A $= 5$ A

Section 6–4

1. R_T decreases with more resistors in parallel.
2. The total parallel resistance is less than the smallest branch resistance.

3. $R_T = \dfrac{1}{(1/R_1) + (1/R_2) + \cdots + (1/R_n)}$

4. $R_T = R_1R_2/(R_1 + R_2)$

5. $R_T = R/n$

6. $R_T = (1.0 \text{ k}\Omega)(2.2 \text{ k}\Omega)/3.2 \text{ k}\Omega = 688 \ \Omega$

7. $R_T = 1.0 \text{ k}\Omega/4 = 250 \ \Omega$

8. $R_T = \dfrac{1}{1/47 \ \Omega + 1/150 \ \Omega + 1/100 \ \Omega} = 26.4 \ \Omega$

Section 6–5

1. $I_T = 10 \text{ V}/22.7 \ \Omega = 441 \text{ mA}$

2. $V_S = (2 \text{ A})(222 \ \Omega) = 444 \text{ V}$

3. $I_1 = 444 \text{ V}/680 \ \Omega = 653 \text{ mA}; I_2 = 444 \text{ V}/330 \ \Omega = 1.35 \text{ A}$

4. $R_T = 12 \text{ V}/5.85 \text{ mA} = 2.05 \text{ k}\Omega; R = (2.05 \text{ k}\Omega)(4) = 8.2 \text{ k}\Omega$

5. $V = (100 \text{ mA})(688 \ \Omega) = 68.8 \text{ V}$

Section 6–6

1. $I_T = 4(0.5 \text{ A}) = 2 \text{ A}$

2. Three sources; See Figure 6–86.

3. $I_{R_E} = 10 \text{ mA} + 10 \text{ mA} = 20 \text{ mA}$

FIGURE 6–86

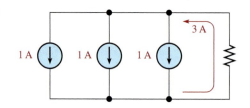

Section 6–7

1. $I_1 = \left(\dfrac{R_2}{R_1 + R_2}\right)I_T \qquad I_2 = \left(\dfrac{R_1}{R_1 + R_2}\right)I_T$

2. $I_x = (R_T/R_x)I_T$

3. The 22 Ω has the most current; the 220 Ω has the least current.

4. $I_1 = (680 \ \Omega/1010 \ \Omega)10 \text{ mA} = 6.73 \text{ mA}; I_2 = (330 \ \Omega/1010 \ \Omega)10 \text{ mA} = 3.27 \text{ mA}$

5. $I_3 = (114 \ \Omega/470 \ \Omega)4 \text{ mA} = 970 \ \mu\text{A}$

Section 6–8

1. Add the power of each resistor to get total power.

2. $P_T = 2.38 \text{ W} + 5.12 \text{ W} + 1.09 \text{ W} + 8.76 \text{ W} = 17.4 \text{ W}$

3. $P_T = (1 \text{ A})^2(615 \ \Omega) = 615 \text{ W}$

Section 6–9

1. $R_{max} = 50 \ \Omega; I_{max} = 1 \text{ mA}$

2. R_{SH} is less than R_M because the shunt resistors must allow currents much greater than the current through the meter movement.

Section 6–10

1. When a branch opens, there is no change in voltage; the total current decreases.

2. If a branch opens, total parallel resistance increases.

3. The remaining bulbs continue to glow.

4. All remaining branch currents are 1 A.

5. The branch with 1.2 A is open.

Section 6–11

1. $R_T = 50\ \Omega$ in 1 mA position; $R_T = 9.94\ \Omega$ in 5 mA position; $R_T = 5.08\ \Omega$ in 10 mA position.

2. $I = 2.5$ mA

3. $I_M = 0.5$ mA; $I_{R1} = 2$ mA

■ **ANSWERS TO RELATED PROBLEMS FOR EXAMPLES**

6–1   See Figure 6–87.

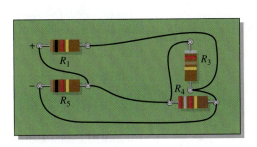

FIGURE 6–87

6–2   Connect pin 1 to pin 2 and pin 3 to pin 4.

6–3   25 V

6–4   20 mA into junction A and out of junction B

6–5 $I_T = 112$ mA, $I_2 = 50$ mA

6–6   2.5 A; 5 A

6–7   9.33 Ω

6–8   Replace Step 9 with "Press $\boxed{+}$." Display shows $100^{-1} + 47^{-1} + 22^{-1} +$.
Replace Step 10 with "Enter 33." Display shows $100^{-1} + 47^{-1} + 22^{-1} + 33$.
Step 11: Press $\boxed{\text{2nd}}$ $\boxed{x^{-1}}$. Display shows $100^{-1} + 47^{-1} + 22^{-1} + 33^{-1}$.
Step 12: Press $\boxed{\text{ENTER}}$. Display shows 0.107034171502.
Step 13: Press $\boxed{\text{2nd}}$ $\boxed{x^{-1}}$ then $\boxed{\text{ENTER}}$. Display shows 9.34281067406.

6–9   111 Ω

6–10 4 Ω

6–11 1044 Ω

6–12 1.83 A; 1 A

6–13 $I_1 = 20$ mA; $I_2 = 9.09$ mA; $I_3 = 35.7$ mA, $I_4 = 22.0$ mA

6–14 1.28 V

6–15 Measure R_T with an ohmmeter and calculate R_1 using $R_1 = \dfrac{1}{(1/R_T) - (1/R_2) - (1/R_3)}$

6–16 30 mA

6–17 $I_1 = 59.4$ mA; $I_2 = 40.6$ mA

6–18 $I_1 = 3.27$ A; $I_2 = 6.73$ A

6–19 178 W

6–20 162 W

6–21 0.0347 μA

6–22 15.4 mA

6–23 Not correct, R_{10} (68 kΩ) must be open.

■ **ANSWERS TO SELF-TEST**

1. (b)   **2.** (c)   **3.** (b)   **4.** (d)   **5.** (a)   **6.** (c)   **7.** (c)   **8.** (c)
9. (d)   **10.** (b)   **11.** (a)   **12.** (d)   **13.** (c)   14. (b)

7

SERIES-PARALLEL CIRCUITS

 Electronics Workbench (EWB) and PSpice Tutorials available at http://www.prenhall.com/floyd

■ INTRODUCTION

In Chapters 5 and 6, series circuits and parallel circuits were studied individually. In this chapter, both series and parallel resistors are combined into series-parallel circuits. In many practical situations, you will have both series and parallel combinations within the same circuit, and the methods you learned for series circuits and for parallel circuits will apply.

Important types of series-parallel circuits are introduced in this chapter. These circuits include the voltage divider with a resistive load, the ladder network, and the Wheatstone bridge.

The analysis of series-parallel circuits requires the use of Ohm's law, Kirchhoff's voltage and current laws, and the methods for finding total resistance and power that you learned in the last two chapters. The topic of loaded voltage dividers is very important because this type of circuit is found in many practical situations. One example is the voltage-divider bias circuit for a transistor amplifier, which you will study in a later course. Ladder networks are important in several areas including a major type of digital-to-analog conversion, which you will study in the digital fundamentals course. The Wheatstone bridge is used in many systems for the measurement of unknown parameters.

In the TECH TIP assignment in Section 7–8, you will evaluate a voltage-divider circuit board used in a portable power supply by applying your knowledge of loaded voltage dividers gained in this chapter as well as skills developed in previous chapters. The voltage divider in this application is designed to provide reference voltages to three different instruments that act as loads on the circuit. You will also troubleshoot the circuit board for various common faults.

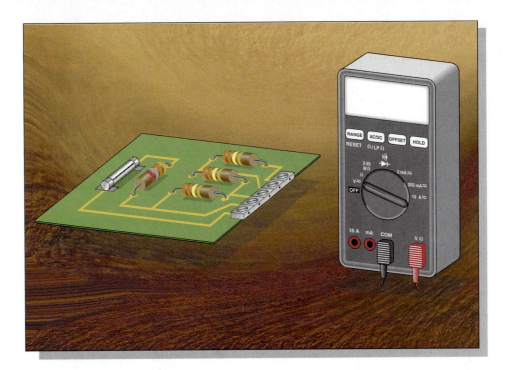

■ TECHnology
Theory
Into
Practice

■ CHAPTER OBJECTIVES

❏ Identify series-parallel relationships
❏ Analyze series-parallel circuits
❏ Analyze loaded voltage dividers
❏ Determine the loading effect of a voltmeter on a circuit

❏ Analyze ladder networks
❏ Analyze a Wheatstone bridge
❏ Troubleshoot series-parallel circuits

7–1 ■ IDENTIFYING SERIES-PARALLEL RELATIONSHIPS

A series-parallel circuit consists of combinations of both series and parallel current paths. It is important to be able to identify how the components in a circuit are arranged in terms of their series and parallel relationships.

After completing this section, you should be able to

■ **Identify series-parallel relationships**
  • Recognize how each resistor in a given circuit is related to the other resistors
  • Determine series and parallel relationships on a PC board

Figure 7–1(a) shows an example of a simple series-parallel combination of resistors. Notice that the resistance from point A to point B is R_1. The resistance from point B to point C is R_2 and R_3 in parallel ($R_2 \| R_3$). The resistance from point A to point C is R_1 in series with the parallel combination of R_2 and R_3, as indicated in Figure 7–1(b).

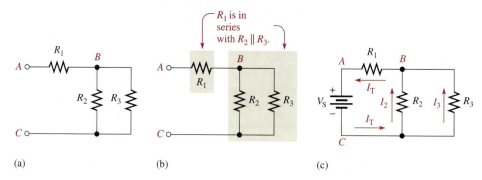

(a)   (b)   (c)

FIGURE 7–1
A simple series-parallel circuit.

When the circuit of Figure 7–1(a) is connected to a voltage source as shown in Figure 7–1(c), the total current is out of the negative source terminal and divides into the two parallel paths. These two branch currents then recombine at point B, and the total current is into the positive source terminal as shown.

Now, to illustrate series-parallel relationships, let's increase the complexity of the circuit in Figure 7–1(a) step-by-step. In Figure 7–2(a), another resistor (R_4) is connected in series with R_1. The resistance between points A and B is now $R_1 + R_4$, and this combination is in series with the parallel combination of R_2 and R_3, as illustrated in Figure 7–2(b).

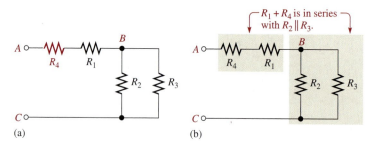

(a)   (b)

FIGURE 7–2
R_4 is added to the circuit in series with R_1.

In Figure 7–3(a), R_5 is connected in series with R_2. The series combination of R_2 and R_5 is in parallel with R_3. This entire series-parallel combination is in series with the $R_1 + R_4$ combination, as illustrated in Figure 7–3(b).

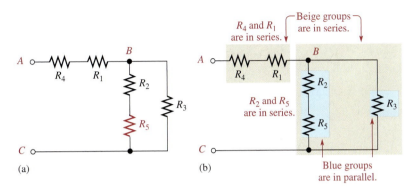

FIGURE 7–3
R_5 is added to the circuit in series with R_2.

In Figure 7–4(a), R_6 is connected in parallel with the series combination of R_1 and R_4. The series-parallel combination of R_1, R_4, and R_6 is in series with the series-parallel combination of R_2, R_3, and R_5, as indicated in Figure 7–4(b).

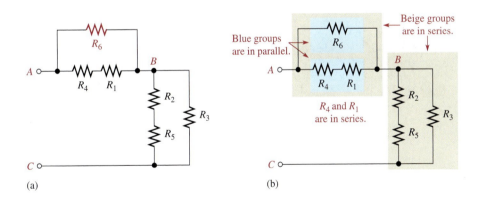

FIGURE 7–4
R_6 is added to the circuit in parallel with the series combination of R_1 and R_4.

EXAMPLE 7–1   Identify the series-parallel relationships in Figure 7–5.

FIGURE 7–5

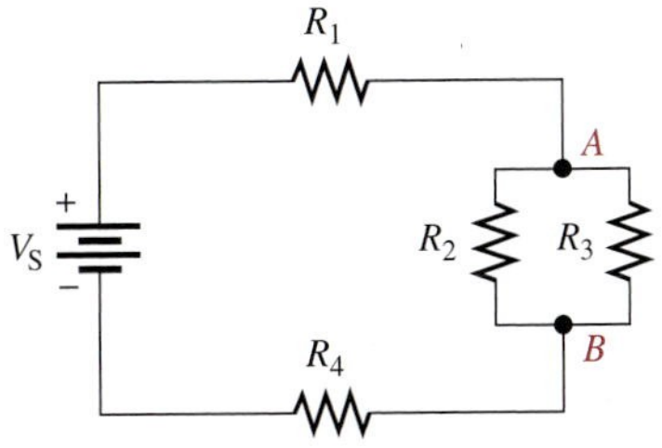

Solution   Starting at the negative terminal of the source, follow the current paths. All of the current produced by the source must go through R_4, which is in series with the rest of the circuit.

The total current takes two paths when it gets to point *B*. Part of it is through R_2, and part of it through R_3. Resistors R_2 and R_3 are in parallel with each other, and this parallel combination is in series with R_4.

At point *A*, the currents through R_2 and R_3 come together again. Thus, the total current is through R_1. Resistor R_1 is in series with R_4 and the parallel combination of R_2 and R_3. The currents are shown in Figure 7–6, where I_T is the total current.

FIGURE 7–6

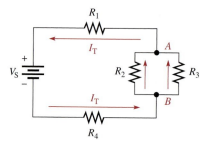

In summary, R_1 and R_4 are in series with the parallel combination of R_2 and R_3 as stated by the following expression:

$$R_1 + R_2 \| R_3 + R_4$$

Related Problem   If another resistor, R_5, is connected from point *A* to the negative side of the source in Figure 7–6, what is its relationship to the other resistors?

EXAMPLE 7–2   Identify the series-parallel relationships in Figure 7–7.

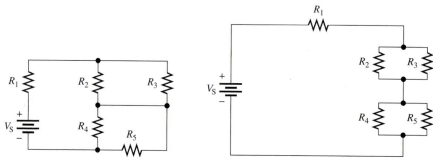

FIGURE 7–7   **FIGURE 7–8**

Solution   Sometimes it is easier to see a particular circuit arrangement if it is drawn in a different way. In this case, the circuit schematic is redrawn in Figure 7–8, which better illustrates the series-parallel relationships. Now you can see that R_2 and R_3 are in parallel with each other and also that R_4 and R_5 are in parallel with each other. Both parallel combinations are in series with each other and with R_1 as stated by the following expression:

$$R_1 + R_2 \| R_3 + R_4 \| R_5$$

Related Problem   If a resistor is connected from the bottom end of R_3 to the top end of R_5 in Figure 7–8, what effect does it have on the circuit?

EXAMPLE 7–3

Describe the series-parallel combination between points A and D in Figure 7–9.

FIGURE 7–9

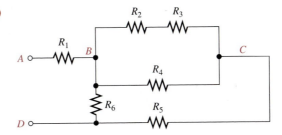

Solution   Between points B and C, there are two parallel paths. The lower path consists of R_4, and the upper path consists of a series combination of R_2 and R_3. This parallel combination is in series with R_5. The R_2, R_3, R_4, R_5 combination is in parallel with R_6. Resistor R_1 is in series with this entire combination as stated by the following expression:

$$R_1 + R_6 \parallel (R_5 + (R_4 \parallel (R_2 + R_3)))$$

Related Problem   If a resistor is connected from point C to point D in Figure 7–9, describe its parallel relationship.

EXAMPLE 7–4

Describe the total resistance between each pair of points in Figure 7–10.

FIGURE 7–10

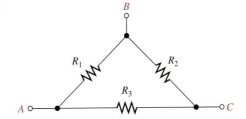

Solution
1. From point A to B: R_1 is in parallel with the series combination of R_2 and R_3.

$$R_1 \parallel (R_2 + R_3)$$

2. From point A to C: R_3 is in parallel with the series combination of R_1 and R_2.

$$R_3 \parallel (R_1 + R_2)$$

3. From point B to C: R_2 is in parallel with the series combination of R_1 and R_3.

$$R_2 \parallel (R_1 + R_3)$$

Related Problem   Describe the total resistance between each point in Figure 7–10 and ground if a resistor, R_4, is connected from point C to ground.

Determining Relationships on a Printed Circuit (PC) Board

Usually, the physical arrangement of components on a PC board bears no resemblance to the actual circuit relationships. By tracing out the circuit on the PC board and rearranging the components on paper into a recognizable form, you can determine the series-parallel relationships. This is illustrated in Example 7–5.

EXAMPLE 7–5   Determine the relationships of the resistors on the PC board in Figure 7–11.

FIGURE 7–11

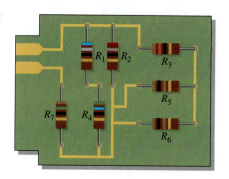

Solution   In Figure 7–12(a), the schematic is drawn in the same arrangement as that of the resistors on the board. In part (b), the resistors are rearranged so that the series-parallel relationships are obvious. Resistors R_1 and R_4 are in series; $R_1 + R_4$ is in parallel with R_2; R_5 and R_6 are in parallel and this combination is in series with R_3. The R_3, R_5, and R_6 series-parallel combination is in parallel with both R_2 and the $R_1 + R_4$ combination. This entire series-parallel combination is in series with R_7, as Figure 7–12(c) illustrates.

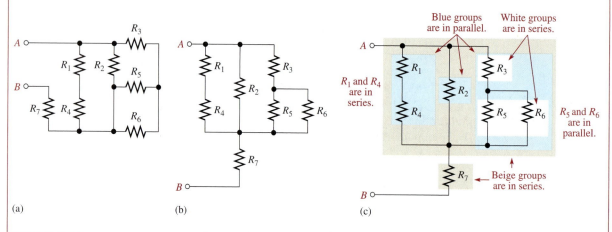

(a)   (b)   (c)

FIGURE 7–12

Related Problem   If R_5 were removed from the circuit, what would be the relationship of R_3 and R_6?

**SECTION 7–1
REVIEW**

1. Define *series-parallel resistive circuit.*
2. A certain series-parallel circuit is described as follows: R_1 and R_2 are in parallel. This parallel combination is in series with another parallel combination of R_3 and R_4. Sketch the circuit.
3. In the circuit of Figure 7–13, describe the series-parallel relationships of the resistors.
4. Which resistors are in parallel in Figure 7–14?

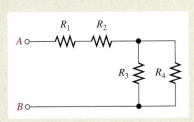

FIGURE 7–13

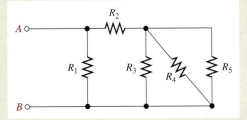

FIGURE 7–14

5. Describe the parallel arrangements in Figure 7–15.
6. Are the parallel combinations in Figure 7–15 in series?

FIGURE 7–15

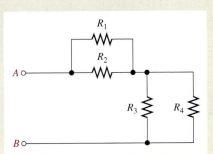

7–2 ■ ANALYSIS OF SERIES-PARALLEL CIRCUITS

Several quantities are important when you have a circuit that is a series-parallel configuration of resistors.

After completing this section, you should be able to

■ **Analyze series-parallel circuits**
  • Determine total resistance
  • Determine all the currents
  • Determine all the voltage drops

Total Resistance

In Chapter 5, you learned how to determine total series resistance. In Chapter 6, you learned how to determine total parallel resistance. To find the total resistance (R_T) of a series-parallel combination, simply define the series and parallel relationships; then perform the calculations that you have previously learned. The following two examples illustrate this general approach.

EXAMPLE 7–6   Determine R_T of the circuit in Figure 7–16 between points A and B.

FIGURE 7–16

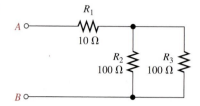

Solution   First, calculate the equivalent parallel resistance of R_2 and R_3. Since R_2 and R_3 are equal in value, you can use Equation (6–6).

$$R_{2-3} = \frac{R}{n} = \frac{100 \ \Omega}{2} = 50 \ \Omega$$

Notice that the term R_{2-3} was used here to designate the total resistance of a portion of a circuit in order to distinguish it from the total resistance, R_T, of the complete circuit.
Now, since R_1 is in series with R_{2-3}, add their values as follows:

$$R_T = R_1 + R_{2-3} = 10 \ \Omega + 50 \ \Omega = \mathbf{60 \ \Omega}$$

Related Problem   Determine R_T in Figure 7–16 if R_3 is changed to 82 Ω.

EXAMPLE 7–7   Find the total resistance between the positive and negative terminals of the battery in Figure 7–17.

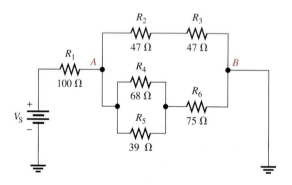

FIGURE 7–17

Solution   In the upper branch, R_2 is in series with R_3. This series combination is designated R_{2-3} and is equal to $R_2 + R_3$.

$$R_{2-3} = R_2 + R_3 = 47 \ \Omega + 47 \ \Omega = 94 \ \Omega$$

In the lower branch, R_4 and R_5 are in parallel with each other. This parallel combination is designated R_{4-5} and is calculated as follows:

$$R_{4-5} = \frac{R_4 R_5}{R_4 + R_5} = \frac{(68 \ \Omega)(39 \ \Omega)}{68 \ \Omega + 39 \ \Omega} = 24.8 \ \Omega$$

Also in the lower branch, the parallel combination of R_4 and R_5 is in series with R_6. This series-parallel combination is designated R_{4-5-6} and is calculated as follows:

$$R_{4-5-6} = R_6 + R_{4-5} = 75 \ \Omega + 24.8 \ \Omega = 99.8 \ \Omega$$

Figure 7–18 shows the original circuit in a simplified equivalent form.

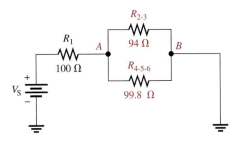

FIGURE 7–18

Now you can find the equivalent resistance between points A and B. It is $R_{2\text{-}3}$ in parallel with $R_{4\text{-}5\text{-}6}$. The equivalent resistance is calculated as follows:

$$R_{AB} = \frac{1}{(1/94\ \Omega) + (1/99.8\ \Omega)} = 48.4\ \Omega$$

Finally, the total resistance is R_1 in series with R_{AB}.

$$R_T = R_1 + R_{AB} = 100\ \Omega + 48.4\ \Omega = \mathbf{148.4\ \Omega}$$

Related Problem   Determine R_T if a 68 Ω resistor is added in parallel from point A to point B in Figure 7–17.

Total Current

Once the total resistance and the source voltage are known, you can find total current in a circuit by applying Ohm's law. Total current is the total source voltage divided by the total resistance.

$$I_T = \frac{V_S}{R_T}$$

For example, assuming that the source voltage is 30 V, the total current in the circuit of Example 7–7 (Figure 7–17) is

$$I_T = \frac{V_S}{R_T} = \frac{30\ \text{V}}{148.4\ \Omega} = 202\ \text{mA}$$

Branch Currents

Using the current-divider formula, Kirchhoff's current law, Ohm's law, or combinations of these, you can find the current in any branch of a series-parallel circuit. In some cases, it may take repeated application of the formula to find a given current. The following two examples will help you understand the procedure. (Notice that the subscripts for the current variables (I) match the R subscripts; for example, current through R_1 is referred to as I_1.)

EXAMPLE 7–8   Find the current through R_2 and the current through R_3 in Figure 7–19.

FIGURE 7–19

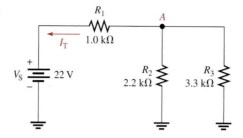

Solution   First, you need to know how much current is out of the junction (point A) of the parallel branches. This is the total circuit current. To find I_T, you need to know R_T.

$$R_T = R_1 + \frac{R_2R_3}{R_2 + R_3} = 1.0 \text{ k}\Omega + \frac{(2.2 \text{ k}\Omega)(3.3 \text{ k}\Omega)}{2.2 \text{ k}\Omega + 3.3 \text{ k}\Omega} = 1.0 \text{ k}\Omega + 1.32 \text{ k}\Omega = 2.32 \text{ k}\Omega$$

$$I_T = \frac{V_S}{R_T} = \frac{22 \text{ V}}{2.32 \text{ k}\Omega} = 9.48 \text{ mA}$$

Use the current-divider rule for two branches as given in Chapter 6 to find the current through R_2.

$$I_2 = \left(\frac{R_3}{R_2 + R_3}\right)I_T = \left(\frac{3.3 \text{ k}\Omega}{5.5 \text{ k}\Omega}\right)9.48 \text{ mA} = \textbf{5.69 mA}$$

Now you can use Kirchhoff's current law to find the current through R_3.

$$I_T = I_2 + I_3$$
$$I_3 = I_T - I_2 = 9.48 \text{ mA} - 5.69 \text{ mA} = \textbf{3.79 mA}$$

Related Problem   A 4.7 kΩ resistor is connected in parallel with R_3 in Figure 7–19. Determine the current through the new resistor.

EXAMPLE 7–9   Determine the current through R_4 in Figure 7–20 if $V_S = 50$ V.

FIGURE 7–20

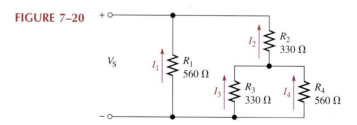

Solution   First, find the current (I_2) out of the junction of R_3 and R_4. Once you know this current, use the current-divider formula to find I_4.

Notice that there are two main branches in the circuit. The left-most branch consists of only R_1. The right-most branch has R_2 in series with the parallel combination of R_3 and R_4. The voltage across both of these main branches is the same and equal to 50 V. Find the current (I_2) out of the junction of R_3 and R_4 by calculating the equivalent resistance (R_{2-3-4}) of the right-most main branch and then applying Ohm's law; I_2 is the total current through this main branch. Thus,

$$R_{2\text{-}3\text{-}4} = R_2 + \frac{R_3 R_4}{R_3 + R_4} = 330\ \Omega + \frac{(330\ \Omega)(560\ \Omega)}{890\ \Omega} = 538\ \Omega$$

$$I_2 = \frac{V_S}{R_{2\text{-}3\text{-}4}} = \frac{50\ \text{V}}{538\ \Omega} = 93\ \text{mA}$$

Use the current-divider formula to calculate I_4.

$$I_4 = \left(\frac{R_3}{R_3 + R_4}\right)I_2 = \left(\frac{330\ \Omega}{890\ \Omega}\right)93\ \text{mA} = \textbf{34.5 mA}$$

Related Problem Determine the current through R_1 and R_3 in Figure 7–20 if $V_S = 20$ V.

Voltage Drops

It is often necessary to find the voltages across certain parts of a series-parallel circuit. You can normally find these voltages by using the voltage-divider formula given in Chapter 5, Kirchhoff's voltage law, Ohm's law, or combinations of each. The following three examples illustrate use of the formulas.

EXAMPLE 7–10   Determine the voltage drop from point A to ground in Figure 7–21. Then find the voltage (V_1) across R_1.

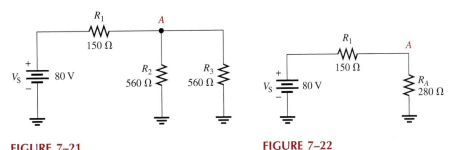

FIGURE 7–21   **FIGURE 7–22**

Solution   Note that R_2 and R_3 are in parallel in this circuit. Since they are equal in value, their equivalent resistance from point A to ground is

$$R_A = \frac{560\ \Omega}{2} = 280\ \Omega$$

In the equivalent circuit shown in Figure 7–22, R_1 is in series with R_A. The total circuit resistance as seen from the source is

$$R_T = R_1 + R_A = 150\ \Omega + 280\ \Omega = 430\ \Omega$$

Use the voltage-divider formula to find the voltage across the parallel combination of Figure 7–21 (between point A and ground).

$$V_A = \left(\frac{R_A}{R_T}\right)V_S = \left(\frac{280\ \Omega}{430\ \Omega}\right)80\ \text{V} = \textbf{52.1 V}$$

Now use Kirchhoff's voltage law to find V_1.

$$V_S = V_1 + V_A$$
$$V_1 = V_S - V_A = 80\ \text{V} - 52.1\ \text{V} = \textbf{27.9 V}$$

Related Problem   Determine V_A and V_1 if R_1 is changed to 220 Ω in Figure 7–21.

EXAMPLE 7–11   Determine the voltage across each resistor in the circuit of Figure 7–23.

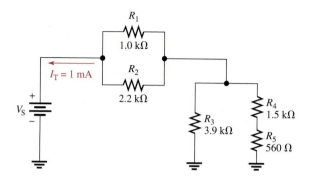

FIGURE 7–23

Solution   The source voltage is not given, but you know the total current from the figure. Since R_1 and R_2 are in parallel, they each have the same voltage. The current through R_1 is

$$I_1 = \left(\frac{R_2}{R_1 + R_2}\right)I_T = \left(\frac{2.2 \text{ k}\Omega}{3.2 \text{ k}\Omega}\right)1 \text{ mA} = 688 \text{ }\mu\text{A}$$

The voltages across R_1 and R_2 are

$$V_1 = I_1R_1 = (688 \text{ }\mu\text{A})(1.0 \text{ k}\Omega) = \textbf{688 mV}$$
$$V_2 = V_1 = \textbf{688 mV}$$

The current through R_3 is found by applying the current-divider formula.

$$I_3 = \left[\frac{R_4 + R_5}{R_3 + (R_4 + R_5)}\right]I_T = \left(\frac{2.06 \text{ k}\Omega}{5.96 \text{ k}\Omega}\right)1 \text{ mA} = 346 \text{ }\mu\text{A}$$

The voltage across R_3 is

$$V_3 = I_3R_3 = (346 \text{ }\mu\text{A})(3.9 \text{ k}\Omega) = \textbf{1.35 V}$$

The currents through R_4 and R_5 are the same because these resistors are in series.

$$I_4 = I_5 = I_T - I_3 = 1 \text{ mA} - 346 \text{ }\mu\text{A} = 654 \text{ }\mu\text{A}$$

The voltages across R_4 and R_5 are calculated as follows:

$$V_4 = I_4R_4 = (654 \text{ }\mu\text{A})(1.5 \text{ k}\Omega) = \textbf{981 mV}$$
$$V_5 = I_5R_5 = (654 \text{ }\mu\text{A})(560 \text{ }\Omega) = \textbf{366 mV}$$

Related Problem   What is the source voltage, V_S, in the circuit of Figure 7–23?

EXAMPLE 7–12   Determine the voltage drop across each resistor in Figure 7–24.

FIGURE 7–24

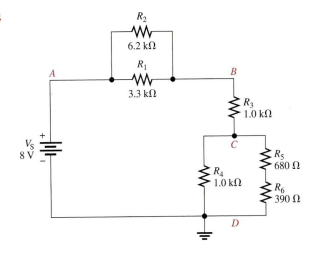

Solution   Because the total voltage is given in the figure, you can solve this problem using the voltage-divider formula.

First, you need to reduce each parallel combination to an equivalent resistance. Since R_1 and R_2 are in parallel between points A and B, combine their values.

$$R_{AB} = \frac{R_1 R_2}{R_1 + R_2} = \frac{(3.3 \text{ k}\Omega)(6.2 \text{ k}\Omega)}{9.5 \text{ k}\Omega} = 2.15 \text{ k}\Omega$$

Since R_4 is in parallel with the series combination of R_5 and R_6 between points C and D, combine these values.

$$R_{CD} = \frac{R_4(R_5 + R_6)}{R_4 + R_5 + R_6} = \frac{(1.0 \text{ k}\Omega)(1.07 \text{ k}\Omega)}{2.07 \text{ k}\Omega} = 517 \text{ }\Omega$$

The equivalent circuit is drawn in Figure 7–25. The total circuit resistance is

$$R_T = R_{AB} + R_3 + R_{CD} = 2.15 \text{ k}\Omega + 1.0 \text{ k}\Omega + 517 \text{ }\Omega = 3.67 \text{ k}\Omega$$

FIGURE 7–25

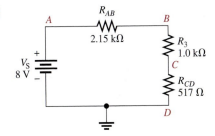

Next, use the voltage-divider formula to determine the voltages in the equivalent circuit.

$$V_{AB} = \left(\frac{R_{AB}}{R_T}\right)V_S = \left(\frac{2.15 \text{ k}\Omega}{3.67 \text{ k}\Omega}\right)8 \text{ V} = 4.69 \text{ V}$$

$$V_{CD} = \left(\frac{R_{CD}}{R_T}\right)V_S = \left(\frac{517 \text{ }\Omega}{3.67 \text{ k}\Omega}\right)8 \text{ V} = 1.13 \text{ V}$$

$$V_3 = \left(\frac{R_3}{R_T}\right)V_S = \left(\frac{1.0 \text{ k}\Omega}{3.67 \text{ k}\Omega}\right)8 \text{ V} = \textbf{2.18 V}$$

Refer to Figure 7–24. V_{AB} equals the voltage across both R_1 and R_2, so

$$V_1 = V_2 = V_{AB} = \textbf{4.69 V}$$

V_{CD} is the voltage across R_4 and across the series combination of R_5 and R_6. Therefore,

$$V_4 = V_{CD} = \textbf{1.13 V}$$

Now apply the voltage-divider formula to the series combination of R_5 and R_6 to get V_5 and V_6.

$$V_5 = \left(\frac{R_5}{R_5 + R_6}\right)V_{CD} = \left(\frac{680\ \Omega}{1070\ \Omega}\right)1.13\ V = \textbf{718 mV}$$

$$V_6 = \left(\frac{R_6}{R_5 + R_6}\right)V_{CD} = \left(\frac{390\ \Omega}{1070\ \Omega}\right)1.13\ V = \textbf{412 mV}$$

Related Problem R_2 is removed from the circuit in Figure 7–24. Calculate V_{AB}, V_{BC}, and V_{CD}.

As you have seen in this section, the analysis of series-parallel circuits can be approached in many ways, depending on what information you need and what circuit values you know. The examples in this section do not represent an exhaustive coverage, but they give you an idea of how to approach series-parallel circuit analysis.

If you know Ohm's law, Kirchhoff's laws, the voltage-divider formula, and the current-divider formula, and if you know how to apply these laws, you can solve most resistive circuit analysis problems. The ability to recognize series and parallel combinations is, of course, essential. A few circuits, such as the unbalanced Wheatstone bridge, do not have basic series and paralled combinations. Other methods are needed for these cases, as we will discuss later.

SECTION 7–2 REVIEW

1. List the circuit laws and formulas that may be necessary in the analysis of series-parallel circuits.
2. Find the total resistance between A and B in the circuit of Figure 7–26.
3. Find the current through R_3 in Figure 7–26.
4. Find the voltage drop across R_2 in Figure 7–26.
5. Determine R_T and I_T in Figure 7–27 as "seen" by the source.

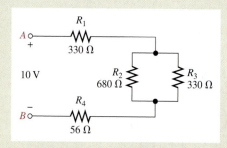

FIGURE 7–26

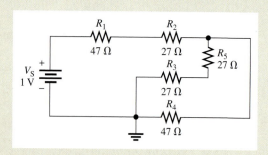

FIGURE 7–27

7–3 ■ VOLTAGE DIVIDERS WITH RESISTIVE LOADS

Voltage dividers were introduced in Chapter 5. In this section, you will learn how resistive loads affect the operation of voltage-divider circuits.

After completing this section, you should be able to

■ **Analyze loaded voltage dividers**
  • Determine the effect of a resistive load on a voltage-divider circuit
  • Define bleeder current

The voltage divider in Figure 7–28(a) produces an output voltage (V_{OUT}) of 5 V because the two resistors are of equal value. This voltage is the *unloaded output voltage.* When a load resistor, R_L, is connected from the output to ground as shown in Figure 7–28(b), the output voltage is reduced by an amount that depends on the value of R_L. The load resistor is in parallel with R_2, reducing the resistance from point A to ground and, as a result, also reducing the voltage across the parallel combination. This is one effect of loading a voltage divider. Another effect of a **load** is that more current is drawn from the source because the total resistance of the circuit is reduced.

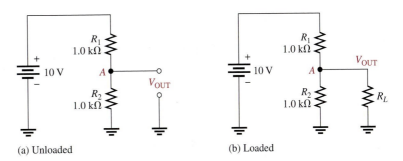

(a) Unloaded   (b) Loaded

FIGURE 7–28
A voltage divider with both unloaded and loaded outputs.

The larger R_L is compared to R_2, the less the output voltage is reduced from its unloaded value, as illustrated in Figure 7–29. When two resistors are connected in parallel and one of the resistors is much greater than the other, the total resistance is close to the value of the smaller resistance.

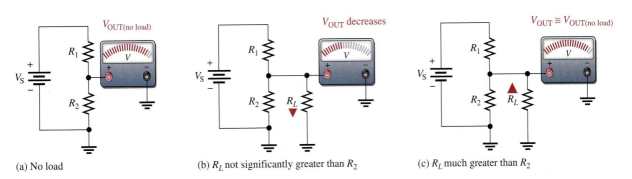

(a) No load   (b) R_L not significantly greater than R_2 (c) R_L much greater than R_2

FIGURE 7–29
The effect of a load resistor.

EXAMPLE 7–13   (a) Determine the unloaded output voltage of the voltage divider in Figure 7–30.
(b) Find the loaded output voltages of the voltage divider in Figure 7–30 for the following two values of load resistance: $R_L = 10 \text{ k}\Omega$ and $R_L = 100 \text{ k}\Omega$.

FIGURE 7–30

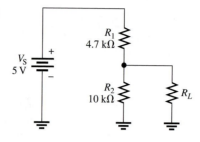

Solution
(a) The unloaded output voltage is

$$V_{OUT(unloaded)} = \left(\frac{R_2}{R_1 + R_2}\right)V_S = \left(\frac{10 \text{ k}\Omega}{14.7 \text{ k}\Omega}\right)5 \text{ V} = \mathbf{3.40 \text{ V}}$$

(b) With the 10 kΩ load resistor connected, R_L is in parallel with R_2, which gives

$$R_2 \| R_L = \frac{R_2 R_L}{R_2 + R_L} = \frac{100 \text{ k}\Omega}{20} = 5 \text{ k}\Omega$$

The equivalent circuit is shown in Figure 7–31(a). The loaded output voltage is

$$V_{OUT(loaded)} = \left(\frac{R_2 \| R_L}{R_1 + R_2 \| R_L}\right)V_S = \left(\frac{5 \text{ k}\Omega}{9.7 \text{ k}\Omega}\right)5 \text{ V} = \mathbf{2.58 \text{ V}}$$

With the 100 kΩ load, the resistance from output to ground is

$$R_2 \| R_L = \frac{R_2 R_L}{R_2 + R_L} = \frac{(10 \text{ k}\Omega)(100 \text{ k}\Omega)}{110 \text{ k}\Omega} = 9.1 \text{ k}\Omega$$

The equivalent circuit is shown in Figure 7–31(b). The loaded output voltage is

$$V_{OUT(loaded)} = \left(\frac{R_2 \| R_L}{R_1 + R_2 \| R_L}\right)V_S = \left(\frac{9.1 \text{ k}\Omega}{13.8 \text{ k}\Omega}\right)5 \text{ V} = \mathbf{3.30 \text{ V}}$$

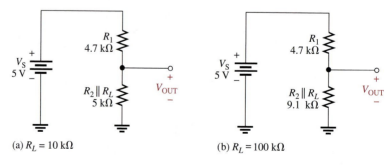

(a) $R_L = 10 \text{ k}\Omega$ (b) $R_L = 100 \text{ k}\Omega$

FIGURE 7–31

The smaller value of R_L causes a greater reduction in V_{OUT} (3.40 V − 2.58 V = 0.82 V) than does the larger value of R_L (3.40 V − 3.30 V = 0.10 V). This illustrates the loading effect of R_L on the voltage divider.

Related Problem   Determine V_{OUT} in Figure 7–30 for a 1.0 MΩ load resistance.

Bleeder Current

Voltage dividers are sometimes useful in obtaining various voltages from a fixed power supply. For example, suppose that you wish to derive 12 V and 6 V from a 24 V supply. To do so requires a voltage divider with two taps, as shown in Figure 7–32. In this example, R_1 must equal $R_2 + R_3$, and R_2 must equal R_3. The actual values of the resistors are set by the amount of current that is to be drawn from the source under unloaded conditions. This current, called the **bleeder current,** represents a continuous drain on the source. With these ideas in mind, in Example 7–14 a voltage divider is designed to meet certain specified requirements.

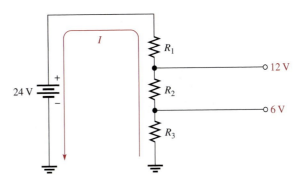

FIGURE 7–32
Voltage divider with two output taps.

EXAMPLE 7–14

A power supply requires 12 V and 6 V from a 24 V battery. The unloaded current drain on this battery is not to exceed 1 mA. Determine the values of the resistors. Also determine the output voltage at the 12 V tap when both outputs are loaded with 100 kΩ each.

Solution A circuit as shown in Figure 7–32 is required. In order to have an unloaded current of 1 mA, the total resistance must be

$$R_T = \frac{V_S}{I} = \frac{24 \text{ V}}{1 \text{ mA}} = 24 \text{ k}\Omega$$

To get exactly 12 V,

$$R_1 = R_2 + R_3 = \textbf{12 k}\Omega$$

To get exactly 6 V,

$$R_2 = R_3 = \textbf{6 k}\Omega$$

The 12 kΩ is a standard value, but the closest standard value to 6 kΩ is 6.04 kΩ in a 1% resistor and 6.2 kΩ in a 5% resistor. We will use **6.2 kΩ** for R_2 and R_3, although this will result in small differences from the desired unloaded output voltages.

$$V_{12V} = \left(\frac{R_2 + R_3}{R_1 + R_2 + R_3}\right)V_S = \left(\frac{12.4 \text{ k}\Omega}{24.4 \text{ k}\Omega}\right)24 \text{ V} = 12.2 \text{ V}$$

$$V_{6V} = \left(\frac{R_3}{R_1 + R_2 + R_3}\right)V_S = \left(\frac{6.2 \text{ k}\Omega}{24.4 \text{ k}\Omega}\right)24 \text{ V} = 6.1 \text{ V}$$

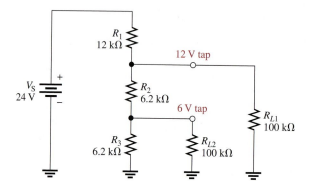

FIGURE 7–33

The 100 kΩ loads are connected to the outputs as shown in Figure 7–33. The loaded output voltage at the 12 V tap is determined as follows. First, determine the equivalent resistance in the circuit. The equivalent resistance from the 12 V tap to ground is the 100 kΩ load resistor, R_{L1}, in parallel with the combination of R_2 in series with the parallel combination of R_3 and R_{L2}. For R_3 in parallel with R_{L2}, the equivalent resistance is

$$R_{EQ1} = \frac{R_3 R_{L2}}{R_3 + R_{L2}} = \frac{(6.2\ \text{k}\Omega)(100\ \text{k}\Omega)}{106.2\ \text{k}\Omega} = 5.84\ \text{k}\Omega$$

For R_2 in series with R_{EQ1}, the equivalent resistance is

$$R_{EQ2} = R_2 + R_{EQ1} = 6.2\ \text{k}\Omega + 5.84\ \text{k}\Omega = 12.0\ \text{k}\Omega$$

For R_{L1} in parallel with R_{EQ2}, the equivalent resistance is

$$R_{EQ3} = \frac{R_{L1} R_{EQ2}}{R_{L1} + R_{EQ2}} = \frac{(100\ \text{k}\Omega)(12.0\ \text{k}\Omega)}{112\ \text{k}\Omega} = 10.7\ \text{k}\Omega$$

R_{EQ3} is the equivalent resistance from the 12 V tap to ground. The equivalent circuit from the 12 V tap to ground is shown in Figure 7–34. Now, using this equivalent circuit, calculate the voltage at the 12 V tap of the loaded voltage divider.

$$V_{12V} = \left(\frac{R_{EQ3}}{R_1 + R_{EQ3}}\right) V_S = \left(\frac{10.7\ \text{k}\Omega}{22.7\ \text{k}\Omega}\right) 24\ \text{V} = \textbf{11.3 V}$$

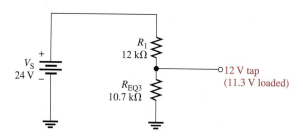

FIGURE 7–34

As you can see, the output voltage at the 12 V tap decreases slightly from its unloaded value when the 100 kΩ loads are connected. Smaller values of load resistance would result in a greater decrease in the output voltage.

Related Problem   Determine the output voltage at the 6 V tap when both outputs are loaded with 100 kΩ each.

**SECTION 7–3
REVIEW**

1. A load resistor is connected to an output tap on a voltage divider. What effect does the load resistor have on the output voltage at this tap?

2. A larger-value load resistor will cause the output voltage to change less than a smaller-value one will.   (T or F)

3. For the voltage divider in Figure 7–35, determine the unloaded output voltage. Also determine the output voltage with a 10 kΩ load resistor connected across the output.

FIGURE 7–35

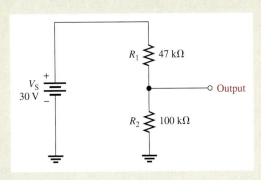

7–4 ■ LOADING EFFECT OF A VOLTMETER

As you have learned, voltmeters must be connected in parallel with a resistor in order to measure the voltage across the resistor. Because of its internal resistance, a voltmeter puts a load on the circuit and will affect, to a certain extent, the voltage that is being measured. Until now, we have ignored the loading effect because the internal resistance of a voltmeter is very high, and normally it has negligible effect on the circuit that is being measured. However, if the internal resistance of the voltmeter is not sufficiently greater than the circuit resistance across which it is connected, the loading effect will cause the measured voltage to be less than its actual value. You should always be aware of this effect.

After completing this section, you should be able to

■ **Determine the loading effect of a voltmeter on a circuit**
  • Explain why a voltmeter can load a circuit
  • Discuss the internal resistance of a voltmeter

Why a Voltmeter Can Load a Circuit

When a voltmeter is connected to a circuit as shown, for example, in Figure 7–36(a), its internal resistance appears in parallel with R_3, as shown in part (b). The resistance from point A to point B is altered by the loading effect of the voltmeter's internal resistance, R_M, and is equal to $R_3 \parallel R_M$, as indicated in part (c).

If R_M is much greater than R_3, the resistance from A to B changes very little, and the meter indicates the actual voltage. If R_M is not sufficiently greater than R_3, the resistance from A to B is reduced significantly, and the voltage across R_3 is altered by the loading effect of the meter. A good rule of thumb is that *if the loading effect is less than 10%, it can usually be neglected, depending on the accuracy required.*

Internal Resistance of a Voltmeter

Two categories of voltmeters are the electromagnetic analog voltmeter (commonly called VOM), whose internal resistance is determined by its **sensitivity factor,** and the digital voltmeter (the most commonly used type and commonly called DMM), whose internal

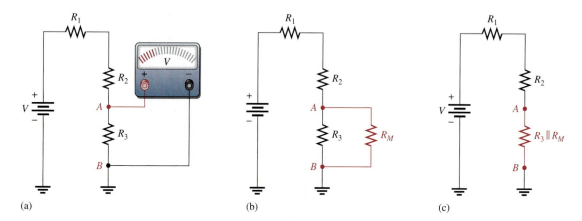

FIGURE 7–36
The loading effect of a voltmeter.

resistance is also typically at least 10 MΩ. The digital voltmeter presents fewer loading problems than the electromagnetic type because the internal resistances of DMMs are much higher.

As mentioned, the internal resistance of an electromagnetic voltmeter (VOM) is specified by the sensitivity factor. A common sensitivity value is 20,000 Ω/V. The internal resistance depends on the dc voltage range switch setting of the meter and is determined by multiplying the sensitivity by the range setting. For example, if the dc voltage range switch is set at 10 V, the internal resistance of the meter is

$$R_M = 20,000 \ \Omega/V \times 10 \ V = 200,000 \ \Omega$$

The lower the range setting, the less the internal resistance and the greater the loading effect of the voltmeter on a circuit. Always use the highest possible range setting that will allow an accurate reading from the meter scale. However, you would not use a 60 V setting to measure 1 V because you could not read 1 V accurately on the 60 V meter scale. The following example shows how the range setting affects the loading.

EXAMPLE 7–15

How much does the electromagnetic voltmeter (VOM) affect the voltage being measured for each range switch setting indicated in Figure 7–37? Assume the meter has a sensitivity factor of 20,000 Ω/V.

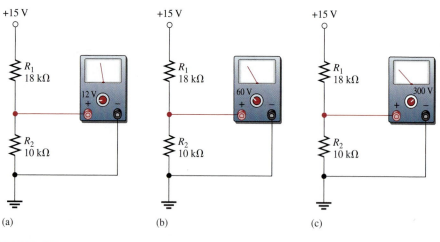

FIGURE 7–37

Solution The unloaded voltage across R_2 in the voltage-divider circuit is

$$V_{R2} = \left(\frac{R_2}{R_1 + R_2}\right)V = \left(\frac{10\ \text{k}\Omega}{28\ \text{k}\Omega}\right)15\ \text{V} = 5.36\ \text{V}$$

Refer to Figure 7–37(a). The internal resistance of the meter is

$$R_M = 20{,}000\ \Omega/\text{V} \times 12\ \text{V} = 240\ \text{k}\Omega$$

The meter's resistance in parallel with R_2 is

$$R_2 \parallel R_M = \left(\frac{R_2 \parallel R_M}{R_2 + R_M}\right) = \frac{(10\ \text{k}\Omega)\parallel(240\ \text{k}\Omega)}{250\ \text{k}\Omega} = 9.6\ \text{k}\Omega$$

The actual voltage measured by the meter is

$$V_{R2} = \left(\frac{R_2 \parallel R_M}{R_1 + R_2 \parallel R_M}\right)V = \left(\frac{9.6\ \text{k}\Omega}{27.6\ \text{k}\Omega}\right)15\ \text{V} = \mathbf{5.22\ V}$$

Refer to Figure 7–37(b). The internal resistance of the meter is

$$R_M = 20{,}000\ \Omega/\text{V} \times 60\ \text{V} = 1.2\ \text{M}\Omega$$

The meter's resistance in parallel with R_2 is

$$R_2 \parallel R_M = \frac{R_2 R_M}{R_2 + R_M} = \frac{(10\ \text{k}\Omega)(1.2\ \text{M}\Omega)}{1.21\ \text{M}\Omega} = 9.92\ \text{k}\Omega$$

The actual voltage measured is

$$V_{R2} = \left(\frac{R_2 \parallel R_M}{R_1 + R_2 \parallel R_M}\right)V = \left(\frac{9.92\ \text{k}\Omega}{27.9\ \text{k}\Omega}\right)15\ \text{V} = \mathbf{5.33\ V}$$

Refer to Figure 7–37(c). The internal resistance of the meter is

$$R_M = 20{,}000\ \Omega/\text{V} \times 300\ \text{V} = 6\ \text{M}\Omega$$

The meter's resistance in parallel with R_2 is

$$R_2 \parallel R_M = \frac{R_2 R_M}{R_2 + R_M} = \frac{(10\ \text{k}\Omega)(6\ \text{M}\Omega)}{6.01\ \text{M}\Omega} = 9.98\ \text{k}\Omega$$

The actual voltage measured is

$$V_{R2} = \left(\frac{R_2 \parallel R_M}{R_1 + R_2 \parallel R_M}\right)V = \left(\frac{9.98\ \text{k}\Omega}{27.98\ \text{k}\Omega}\right)15\ \text{V} = \mathbf{5.35\ V}$$

As you can see, the loading decreases as you increase the range setting on the voltmeter because the measured voltage is closer to the unloaded voltage. However, the 12 V setting is the best choice in this case because, although the loading effect is greater, you can read the voltage much more accurately than you can on the 60 V range. Of course, using the 300 V range is not a good choice in this case.

Related Problem Calculate the voltage across R_2 in Figure 7–37 if the range switch is set on 100 V.

SECTION 7-4 REVIEW

1. What is meant when you say a voltmeter loads a circuit?

2. If a voltmeter with a 10 MΩ internal resistance is measuring the voltage across a 1.0 kΩ resistor, should you normally be concerned about the loading effect?

3. A certain electromagnetic-type voltmeter (VOM) is set on the 12 V range to measure 2.5 V. If you switch it down to the 3 V range, will there be an increase or a decrease in the measured voltage? What is the advantage of using the 3 V range instead of the 12 V range in this situation?

4. What is the internal resistance of a 30,000 Ω/V VOM on its 50 V range setting?

7–5 ■ LADDER NETWORKS

A resistive ladder network is a special type of series-parallel circuit. One form of ladder network is commonly used to scale down voltages to certain weighted values for digital-to-analog conversion, a process that you will study in another course.

After completing this section, you should be able to

■ **Analyze ladder networks**
  • Determine the voltages in a three-step ladder network
  • Analyze an *R/2R* ladder

In this section, we examine basic resistive ladder networks of limited complexity, beginning with the one shown in Figure 7–38. One approach to the analysis of a ladder network is to simplify it one step at a time, starting at the side farthest from the source. In this way, the current in any branch or the voltage at any point can be determined, as illustrated in Example 7–16.

FIGURE 7–38
Basic three-step ladder network.

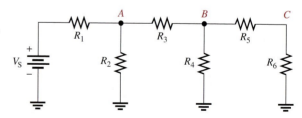

EXAMPLE 7–16

Determine the current through each resistor and the voltage at each labeled point with respect to ground in the ladder network of Figure 7–39.

FIGURE 7–39

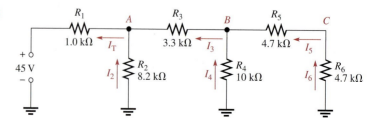

Solution To find the current through each resistor, you must know the total current from the source (I_T). To obtain I_T, you must find the total resistance "seen" by the source.

Determine R_T in a step-by-step process, starting at the right of the circuit diagram. First, notice that R_5 and R_6 are in series across R_4. So the resistance from point B to ground is

$$R_B = \frac{R_4(R_5 + R_6)}{R_4 + (R_5 + R_6)} = \frac{(10 \text{ k}\Omega)(9.4 \text{ k}\Omega)}{19.4 \text{ k}\Omega} = 4.85 \text{ k}\Omega$$

Using R_B (the resistance from point B to ground), you can draw the equivalent circuit as shown in Figure 7–40.

FIGURE 7–40

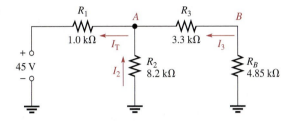

Next, the resistance from point A to ground (R_A) is R_2 in parallel with the series combination of R_3 and R_B. Resistance R_A is calculated as follows:

$$R_A = \frac{R_2(R_3 + R_B)}{R_2 + (R_3 + R_B)} = \frac{(8.2 \text{ k}\Omega)(8.15 \text{ k}\Omega)}{16.35 \text{ k}\Omega} = 4.09 \text{ k}\Omega$$

Using R_A, you can further simplify the equivalent circuit of Figure 7–40 as shown in Figure 7–41.

FIGURE 7–41

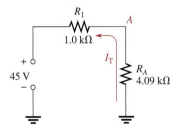

Finally, the total resistance "seen" by the source is R_1 in series with R_A.

$$R_T = R_1 + R_A = 1.0 \text{ k}\Omega + 4.09 \text{ k}\Omega = 5.09 \text{ k}\Omega$$

The total circuit current is

$$I_T = \frac{V_S}{R_T} = \frac{45 \text{ V}}{5.09 \text{ k}\Omega} = \textbf{8.84 mA}$$

As indicated in Figure 7–40, I_T divides between R_2 and the branch containing $R_3 + R_B$. Since the branch resistances are approximately equal in this particular example, half the total current is through R_2 and half through R_3 and R_B. So the currents through R_2 and R_3 are

$$I_2 = \textbf{4.42 mA}$$
$$I_3 = \textbf{4.42 mA}$$

If the branch resistances are not equal, use the current-divider formula. As indicated in Figure 7–39, I_3 is into point B and is divided between R_4 and the branch containing $R_5 + R_6$. Therefore, the currents through R_4, R_5, and R_6 can be calculated.

$$I_4 = \left(\frac{R_5 + R_6}{R_4 + (R_5 + R_6)} \right) I_3 = \left(\frac{9.4 \text{ k}\Omega}{19.4 \text{ k}\Omega} \right) 4.42 \text{ mA} = \mathbf{2.14 \text{ mA}}$$

$$I_5 = I_6 = I_3 - I_4 = 4.42 \text{ mA} - 2.14 \text{ mA} = \mathbf{2.28 \text{ mA}}$$

To determine V_A, V_B, and V_C, apply Ohm's law.

$$V_A = I_2 R_2 = (4.42 \text{ mA})(8.2 \text{ k}\Omega) = \mathbf{36.2 \text{ V}}$$

$$V_B = I_4 R_4 = (2.14 \text{ mA})(10 \text{ k}\Omega) = \mathbf{21.4 \text{ V}}$$

$$V_C = I_6 R_6 = (2.28 \text{ mA})(4.7 \text{ k}\Omega) = \mathbf{10.7 \text{ V}}$$

Related Problem   Recalculate the currents through each resistor and the voltages at each point in Figure 7–39 if R_1 is increased to 2.2 kΩ.

The *R/2R* Ladder Network

A basic *R/2R* ladder network circuit is shown in Figure 7–42. As you can see, the name comes from the relationship of the resistor values (one set of resistors has twice the value of the others). This type of ladder network circuit is used in applications where digital codes are converted to speech, music, or other types of analog signals as found, for example, in the area of digital recording and reproduction. This application area is called *digital-to-analog (D/A) conversion*.

Let's examine the general operation of a basic *R/2R* ladder using the four-step circuit in Figure 7–43. In a later course in digital fundamentals, you will learn specifically how this type of circuit is used in D/A conversion.

The switches are used in this illustration to simulate the digital (two-level) inputs. One switch position is connected to ground (0 V), and the other position is connected to a positive voltage (*V*). The analysis is as follows: Start by assuming that switch SW4 in Figure 7–43 is at the *V* position and the others are at ground so that the inputs are as shown in Figure 7–44(a).

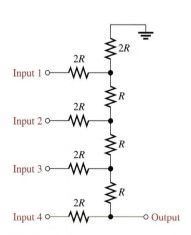

FIGURE 7–42
A basic four-step R/2R ladder network.

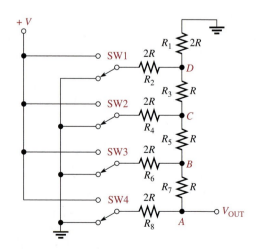

FIGURE 7–43
R/2R ladder with switch inputs to simulate a two-level (digital) code.

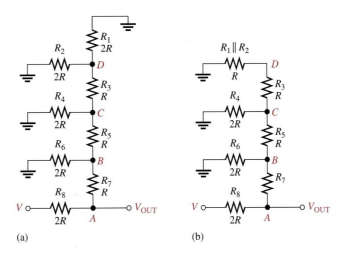

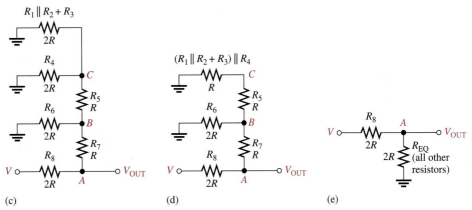

FIGURE 7–44
Simplification of R/2R ladder for analysis.

The total resistance from point A to ground is found by first combining R_1 and R_2 in parallel from point D to ground to simplify the circuit as shown in Figure 7–44(b).

$$R_1 \parallel R_2 = \frac{2R}{2} = R$$

$R_1 \parallel R_2$ is in series with R_3 from point C to ground as illustrated in part (c).

$$R_1 \parallel R_2 + R_3 = R + R = 2R$$

Next, the above combination is in parallel with R_4 from point C to ground as shown in part (d).

$$(R_1 \parallel R_2 + R_3) \parallel R_4 = 2R \parallel 2R = \frac{2R}{2} = R$$

Continuing this simplification process results in the circuit in part (e) in which the output voltage can be expressed using the voltage-divider formula as

$$V_{OUT} = \left(\frac{2R}{4R}\right)V = \frac{V}{2}$$

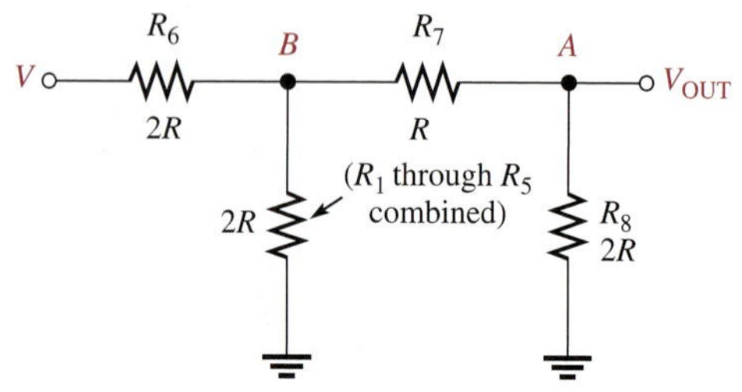

FIGURE 7–45
Simplified ladder with only V input at SW3 in Figure 7–43.

A similar analysis, except with switch SW3 in Figure 7–43 connected to V and the other switches connected to ground, results in the simplified circuit shown in Figure 7–45. The analysis for this case is as follows: The resistance from point B to ground is

$$R_B = (R_7 + R_8) \parallel 2R = 3R \parallel 2R = \frac{6R}{5}$$

Using the voltage-divider formula, we can express the voltage at point B with respect to ground as

$$V_B = \left(\frac{R_B}{R_6 + R_B}\right)V = \left(\frac{6R/5}{2R + 6R/5}\right)V$$

$$= \left(\frac{6R/5}{10R/5 + 6R/5}\right)V = \left(\frac{6R/5}{16R/5}\right)V = \left(\frac{6R}{16R}\right)V = \frac{3V}{8}$$

The output voltage is, therefore,

$$V_{OUT} = \left(\frac{R_8}{R_7 + R_8}\right)V_B = \left(\frac{2R}{3R}\right)\left(\frac{3V}{8}\right) = \frac{V}{4}$$

Notice that the output voltage in this case ($V/4$) is one half the output voltage ($V/2$) for the case where V is connected at switch SW4.

A similar analysis for each of the remaining switch inputs in Figure 7–43 results in output voltages as follows: For SW2 connected to V and the other switches connected to ground,

$$V_{OUT} = \frac{V}{8}$$

For SW1 connected to V and the other switches connected to ground,

$$V_{OUT} = \frac{V}{16}$$

When more than one input at a time are connected to V, the total output is the sum of the individual outputs. These particular relationships among the output voltages for the various levels of inputs are very important in the application of $R/2R$ ladder networks to digital-to-analog conversion.

**SECTION 7–5
REVIEW**

1. Sketch a basic four-step ladder network.
2. Determine the total circuit resistance presented to the source by the ladder network of Figure 7–46.
3. What is the total current in Figure 7–46?
4. What is the current through R_2 in Figure 7–46?
5. What is the voltage at point A with respect to ground in Figure 7–46?

FIGURE 7–46

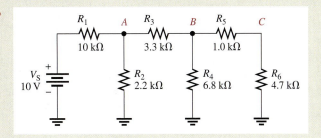

7–6 ■ THE WHEATSTONE BRIDGE

Bridge circuits are widely used in measurement devices and other applications that you will learn later. In this section, you will study the balanced resistive bridge, which can be used to measure unknown resistance values.

After completing this section, you should be able to

■ **Analyze a Wheatstone bridge**
  • Determine when a bridge is balanced
  • Determine an unknown resistance using a balanced bridge
  • Describe how a Wheatstone bridge can be used for temperature measurement

The circuit shown in Figure 7–47(a) is known as a *Wheatstone bridge.* Figure 7–47(b) is the same circuit electrically, but it is drawn in a different way.

A bridge is said to be balanced when the voltage (V_{OUT}) across the output terminals A and B is zero; that is, $V_A = V_B$. In Figure 7–47(b), if V_A equals V_B, then $V_{R1} = V_{R2}$ because the top sides of both R_1 and R_2 connect to the same point. Also $V_{R3} = V_{R4}$ because the bottom sides of both R_3 and R_4 connect to the same point. The voltage ratios can be written as

$$\frac{V_1}{V_3} = \frac{V_2}{V_4}$$

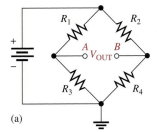
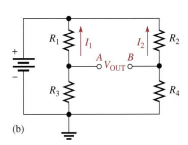

(a) (b)

FIGURE 7–47
Wheatstone bridge.

Substituting by Ohm's law yields

$$\frac{I_1 R_1}{I_1 R_3} = \frac{I_2 R_2}{I_2 R_4}$$

The currents cancel to give

$$\frac{R_1}{R_3} = \frac{R_2}{R_4}$$

Solving for R_1 yields the following formula:

$$R_1 = R_3 \left(\frac{R_2}{R_4} \right)$$

This formula can be used to determine an unknown resistance in a balanced bridge. First, make R_3 a variable resistor and call it R_V. Also, set the ratio R_2/R_4 to a known value. If R_V is adjusted until the bridge is balanced, the product of R_V and the ratio R_2/R_4 is equal to R_1, which is the unknown resistor (R_{UNK}).

$$R_{UNK} = R_V \left(\frac{R_2}{R_4} \right) \tag{7–1}$$

The bridge is balanced when the voltage across the output terminals equals zero ($V_A = V_B$). A *galvanometer* (a meter that measures small currents in either direction and is zero at center scale) is connected between the output terminals. Then R_V is adjusted until the galvanometer shows zero current ($V_A = V_B$), indicating a balanced condition. The setting of R_V multiplied by the ratio R_2/R_4 gives the value of R_{UNK}. Figure 7–48 shows this arrangement. For example, if $R_2/R_4 = \frac{1}{10}$ and $R_V = 680\ \Omega$, then $R_{UNK} = (680\ \Omega)(\frac{1}{10}) = 68\ \Omega$.

FIGURE 7–48
Balanced Wheatstone bridge.

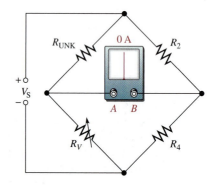

EXAMPLE 7–17   What is R_{UNK} under the balanced bridge conditions shown in Figure 7–49?

FIGURE 7–49

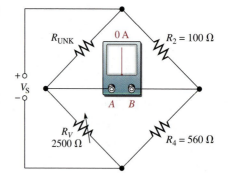

Solution

$$R_{UNK} = R_V\left(\frac{R_2}{R_4}\right) = 2500\ \Omega\left(\frac{100\ \Omega}{560\ \Omega}\right) = \textbf{446 } \boldsymbol{\Omega}$$

Related Problem If R_V must be adjusted to 1.8 kΩ in order to balance the bridge, what is R_{UNK}?

A Bridge Application

Bridge circuits are used for many measurements other than for determining an unknown resistance. One application of the Wheatstone bridge is in accurate temperature measurement. A temperature-sensitive element such as a thermistor is connected in a Wheatstone bridge as shown in Figure 7–50. An amplifier is connected across the output from A to B in order to increase the output voltage from the bridge to a usable value. The bridge is calibrated so that it is balanced at a specified reference temperature. As the temperature changes, the resistance of the sensing element changes proportionately, and the bridge becomes unbalanced. As a result, V_{AB} changes and is amplified (increased) and converted to a form for direct temperature readout on a gauge or a digital-type display.

FIGURE 7–50
A simplified circuit for temperature measurement.

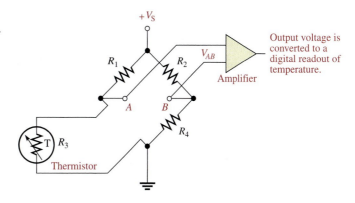

Output voltage is converted to a digital readout of temperature.

SECTION 7–6 REVIEW

1. Sketch a basic Wheatstone bridge circuit.
2. Under what condition is the bridge balanced?
3. What formula is used to determine the value of the unknown resistance when the bridge is balanced?
4. What is the unknown resistance for the values shown in Figure 7–51?

FIGURE 7–51

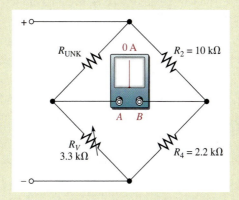

7–7 ■ TROUBLESHOOTING

Troubleshooting is the process of identifying and locating a failure or problem in a circuit. Some troubleshooting techniques have already been discussed in relation to both series circuits and parallel circuits. These methods are now extended to the series-parallel circuits.

After completing this section, you should be able to

■ **Troubleshoot series-parallel circuits**
  • Determine the effects of an open circuit
  • Determine the effects of a short circuit
  • Locate opens and shorts

Opens and shorts are typical problems that occur in electric circuits. As mentioned in Chapter 5, if a resistor burns out, it will normally produce an open circuit. Bad solder connections, broken wires, and poor contacts can also be causes of open paths. Pieces of foreign material, such as solder splashes, broken insulation on wires, and so on, can often lead to shorts in a circuit. A short is a zero resistance path between two points. The following three examples illustrate troubleshooting in series-parallel resistive circuits.

EXAMPLE 7–18

From the indicated voltmeter reading, determine if there is a fault in Figure 7–52. If there is a fault, identify it as either a short or an open.

FIGURE 7–52

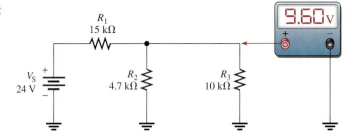

Solution First, determine what the voltmeter should be indicating. Since R_2 and R_3 are in parallel, their equivalent resistance is

$$R_{2\text{-}3} = \frac{R_2 R_3}{R_2 + R_3} = \frac{(4.7 \text{ k}\Omega)(10 \text{ k}\Omega)}{14.7 \text{ k}\Omega} = 3.20 \text{ k}\Omega$$

The voltage across the equivalent parallel combination is determined by the voltage-divider formula.

$$V_{2\text{-}3} = \left(\frac{R_{2\text{-}3}}{R_1 + R_{2\text{-}3}}\right) V_S = \left(\frac{3.20 \text{ k}\Omega}{18.2 \text{ k}\Omega}\right) 24 \text{ V} = 4.22 \text{ V}$$

Thus, 4.22 V is the voltage reading that you should get on the meter. But the meter reads 9.60 V instead. This value is incorrect, and, because it is higher than it should be, R_2 or R_3 is probably open. Why? Because if either of these two resistors is open, the resistance across which the meter is connected is larger than expected. A higher resistance will drop a higher voltage in this circuit, which is, in effect, a voltage divider. Start by assuming that R_2 is open. If it is, the voltage across R_3 is

$$V_3 = \left(\frac{R_3}{R_1 + R_3}\right) V_S = \left(\frac{10 \text{ k}\Omega}{25 \text{ k}\Omega}\right) 24 \text{ V} = 9.6 \text{ V}$$

Since the measured voltage is also 9.6 V, this calculation shows that the path through R_2 **is open.** Replace R_2 with a new resistor.

Related Problem What would be the voltmeter reading if R_3 were open? If R_1 were open?

EXAMPLE 7–19 Suppose that you measure 24 V with the voltmeter in Figure 7–53. Determine if there is a fault, and, if there is, isolate it.

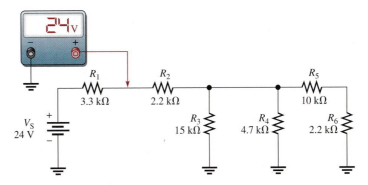

FIGURE 7–53

Solution There is no voltage drop across R_1 because both sides of the resistor are at +24 V. Either there is no current through R_1 from the source, which tells you that the path through R_2 **is open or** R_1 **is shorted.**

If R_1 were open, the meter in Figure 7–53 would read 0 V. The most likely failure is an open path through R_2. If R_2 is open, then there will be no current from the source and thus no voltage is dropped across R_1. To verify this, measure across R_2 with the voltmeter as shown in Figure 7–54. If R_2 is open, the meter will indicate 24 V. The right side of R_2 will be at zero volts because there is no current through any of the other resistors to cause a voltage drop across them.

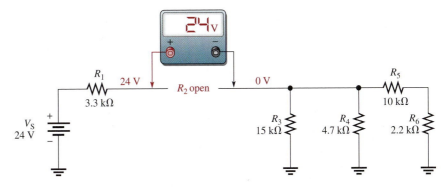

FIGURE 7–54

Related Problem What would be the voltage across an open R_5 in Figure 7–53, assuming no other faults?

EXAMPLE 7–20   The two voltmeters in Figure 7–55 indicate the voltages shown. Determine if there are any opens or shorts in the circuit and, if so, where they are located.

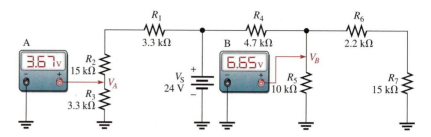

FIGURE 7–55

Solution   First, determine if the voltmeter readings are correct. R_1, R_2, and R_3 act as a voltage divider on the left side of the source. The voltage (V_A) across R_3 is calculated as follows:

$$V_A = \left(\frac{R_3}{R_1 + R_2 + R_3} \right) V_S = \left(\frac{3.3 \text{ k}\Omega}{21.6 \text{ k}\Omega} \right) 24 \text{ V} = 3.67 \text{ V}$$

The voltmeter A reading is correct.

Now see if the voltmeter B reading is correct. The part of the circuit to the right of the source also acts as a voltage divider. The series-parallel combination of R_5, R_6, and R_7 is in series with R_4. The equivalent resistance of the R_5, R_6, and R_7 combination is calculated as

$$R_{5\text{-}6\text{-}7} = \frac{(R_6 + R_7)R_5}{R_5 + R_6 + R_7} = \frac{(17.2 \text{ k}\Omega)(10 \text{ k}\Omega)}{27.2 \text{ k}\Omega} = 6.32 \text{ k}\Omega$$

where R_5 is in parallel with R_6 and R_7 in series. $R_{5\text{-}6\text{-}7}$ and R_4 form a voltage divider. Voltmeter B is measuring the voltage across $R_{5\text{-}6\text{-}7}$. Is it correct? Check as follows:

$$V_B = \left(\frac{R_{5\text{-}6\text{-}7}}{R_4 + R_{5\text{-}6\text{-}7}} \right) V_S = \left(\frac{6.32 \text{ k}\Omega}{11 \text{ k}\Omega} \right) 24 \text{ V} = 13.8 \text{ V}$$

Thus, the actual measured voltage (6.65 V) at this point is incorrect. Some further thought will help to isolate the problem.

Resistor R_4 is not open, because if it were, the meter would read 0 V. If there were a short across it, the meter would read 24 V. Since the actual voltage is much less than it should be, $R_{5\text{-}6\text{-}7}$ must be less than the calculated value of 6.32 kΩ. The most likely problem is a short across R_7. If there is a short from the top of R_7 to ground, R_6 is effectively in parallel with R_5. In this case, $R_{5\text{-}6}$ is

$$R_{5\text{-}6} = \frac{R_5 R_6}{R_5 + R_6} = \frac{(10 \text{ k}\Omega)(2.2 \text{ k}\Omega)}{12.2 \text{ k}\Omega} = 1.80 \text{ k}\Omega$$

Then V_B is

$$V_B = \left(\frac{R_{5\text{-}6}}{R_4 + R_{5\text{-}6}} \right) V_S = \left(\frac{1.80 \text{ k}\Omega}{6.5 \text{ k}\Omega} \right) 24 \text{ V} = 6.65 \text{ V}$$

This value for V_B agrees with the voltmeter B reading. So there is a **short across R_7.** If this were an actual circuit, you would try to find the physical cause of the short.

Related Problem   If R_2 in Figure 7–55 were shorted instead of R_7, what would voltmeter A read? What would voltmeter B read?

SECTION 7–7 REVIEW

1. Name two types of common circuit faults.

2. In Figure 7–56, one of the resistors in the circuit is open. Based on the meter reading, determine which is the open resistor.

FIGURE 7–56

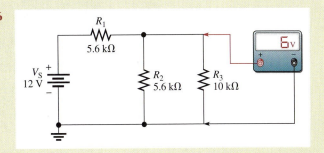

3. For the following faults in Figure 7–57, what voltage would be measured at point A with respect to ground?
   (a) No faults   **(b)** R_1 open   **(c)** Short across R_5 **(d)** R_3 and R_4 open
   (e) R_2 open

FIGURE 7–57

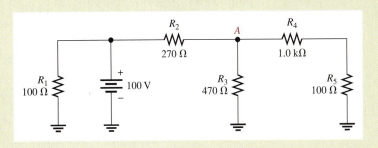

7–8 ■ TECHnology Theory Into Practice

A voltage divider with three output voltages has been designed and constructed on a PC board. The voltage divider is to be used as part of a portable power supply unit for supplying up to three different reference voltages to measuring instruments in the field. The power supply unit contains a battery pack combined with a voltage regulator that produces a constant +12 V to the voltage-divider circuit board. In this assignment, you will apply your knowledge of loaded voltage dividers, Kirchhoff's laws, and Ohm's law to determine the operating parameters of the voltage divider in terms of voltages and currents for all possible load configurations. You will also troubleshoot the circuit for various malfunctions.

The Schematic of the Voltage Divider

■ Draw the schematic and label the resistor values for the circuit board in Figure 7–58.

The 12 V Power Supply

■ Specify how to connect a 12 V power supply to the circuit board so that all resistors are in series and pin 2 has the highest output voltage.

FIGURE 7–58
Voltage-divider circuit board.

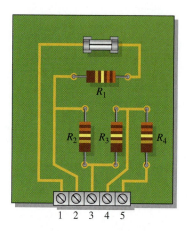

The Unloaded Output Voltages

■ Calculate each of the output voltages with no loads connected. Add these voltage values to a copy of the table in Figure 7–59.

The Loaded Output Voltages

The instruments to be connected to the voltage divider each have a 10 MΩ input resistance. This means that when an instrument is connected to a voltage-divider output there is effectively a 10 MΩ resistor from that output to ground (negative side of source).

■ Determine the output voltage across the load for each of the following load configurations and add these voltage values to a copy of the table in Figure 7–59.

1. A 10 MΩ load connected from pin 2 to ground.
2. A 10 MΩ load connected from pin 3 to ground.

FIGURE 7–59

Table of operating parameters for the power supply voltage divider.

10 MΩ Load	$V_{OUT\,(2)}$	$V_{OUT\,(3)}$	$V_{OUT\,(4)}$	% Deviation	$I_{LOAD\,(2)}$	$I_{LOAD\,(3)}$	$I_{LOAD\,(4)}$
None							
Pin 2 to ground							
Pin 3 to ground							
Pin 4 to ground							
Pin 2 to ground				2			
Pin 3 to ground				3			
Pin 2 to ground				2			
Pin 4 to ground				4			
Pin 3 to ground				3			
Pin 4 to ground				4			
Pin 2 to ground				2			
Pin 3 to ground				3			
Pin 4 to ground				4			

3. A 10 MΩ load connected from pin 4 to ground.

4. A 10 MΩ load connected from pin 2 to ground and another 10 MΩ load from pin 3 to ground.

5. A 10 MΩ load connected from pin 2 to ground and another 10 MΩ load from pin 4 to ground.

6. A 10 MΩ load connected from pin 3 to ground and another 10 MΩ load from pin 4 to ground.

7. A 10 MΩ load connected from pin 2 to ground, another from pin 3 to ground, and a third from pin 4 to ground.

Percent Deviation of the Output Voltages

■ Calculate how much each loaded output voltage deviates from its unloaded value for each of the load configurations listed above and express each as a percentage using the following formula:

$$\text{Percent deviation} = \left(\frac{V_{\text{OUT(unloaded)}} - V_{\text{OUT(loaded)}}}{V_{\text{OUT(unloaded)}}} \right) 100\%$$

Add the values to a copy of the table of Figure 7–59.

The Load Currents

■ Calculate the current to each 10 MΩ load for each of the load configurations listed above. Add these values to a copy of the table in Figure 7–59.

Troubleshooting

The voltage-divider circuit board is connected to a 12 V power supply and to the three instruments to which it provides reference voltages, as shown in Figure 7–60. Voltages at each of the numbered test points are measured with a voltmeter in each of eight different cases.

■ For each case in Figure 7–60, determine the fault indicated by the voltage measurements.

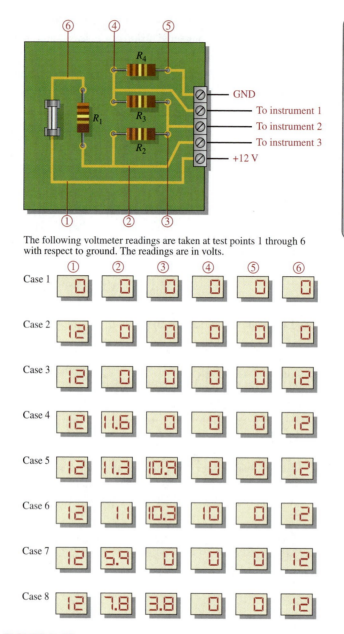

The following voltmeter readings are taken at test points 1 through 6 with respect to ground. The readings are in volts.

	①	②	③	④	⑤	⑥
Case 1	0	0	0	0	0	0
Case 2	12	0	0	0	0	0
Case 3	12	0	0	0	0	12
Case 4	12	11.6	0	0	0	12
Case 5	12	11.3	10.9	0	0	12
Case 6	12	11	10.3	10	0	12
Case 7	12	5.9	0	0	0	12
Case 8	12	7.8	3.8	0	0	12

FIGURE 7–60

SECTION 7–8 REVIEW	**1.** If the portable unit covered in this section is to supply reference voltages to all three instruments, how many days can a 100 mAh battery be used as the power supply?
	2. Can $\frac{1}{8}$ W resistors be used on the voltage-divider board?
	3. If $\frac{1}{8}$ W resistors are used, will an output shorted to ground cause any of the resistors to overheat due to excessive power?

■ **SUMMARY**

- A series-parallel circuit is a combination of both series paths and parallel paths.
- To determine total resistance in a series-parallel circuit, identify the series and parallel relationships, and then apply the formulas for series resistance and parallel resistance from Chapters 5 and 6.
- To find the total current, apply Ohm's law and divide the total voltage by the total resistance.
- To determine branch currents, apply the current-divider formula, Kirchhoff's current law, or Ohm's law. Consider each circuit problem individually to determine the most appropriate method.
- To determine voltage drops across any portion of a series-parallel circuit, use the voltage-divider formula, Kirchhoff's voltage law, or Ohm's law. Consider each circuit problem individually to determine the most appropriate method.
- When a load resistor is connected across a voltage-divider output, the output voltage decreases.
- The load resistor should be large compared to the resistance across which it is connected, in order that the loading effect may be minimized.
- To find total resistance of a ladder network, start at the point farthest from the source and reduce the resistance in steps.
- A Wheatstone bridge can be used to measure an unknown resistance.
- A bridge is balanced when the output voltage is zero. The balanced condition produces zero current through a load connected across the output terminals of the bridge.
- Open circuits and short circuits are typical circuit faults.
- Resistors normally open when they burn out.

■ **GLOSSARY**

These terms are also in the end-of-book glossary.

Bleeder current   The current left after the total load current is subtracted from the total current into the circuit.

Load   An element (resistor or other component) connected across the output terminals of a circuit that draws current from the circuit.

Sensitivity factor   The ohms-per-volt rating of an electromagnetic voltmeter.

■ **FORMULA**

(7–1) $R_{UNK} = R_V \left(\dfrac{R_2}{R_4} \right)$ Unknown resistance in a Wheatstone bridge

■ **SELF-TEST**

1. Which of the following statements are true concerning Figure 7–61?
   (a) R_1 and R_2 are in series with R_3, R_4, and R_5
   (b) R_1 and R_2 are in series
   (c) R_3, R_4, and R_5 are in parallel
   (d) The series combination of R_1 and R_2 is in parallel with the series combination of R_3, R_4, and R_5
   (e) answers (b) and (d)

FIGURE 7–61

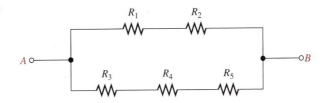

2. The total resistance of Figure 7–61 can be found with which of the following formulas?

   (a) $R_1 + R_2 + R_3 \| R_4 \| R_5$ **(b)** $R_1 \| R_2 + R_3 \| R_4 \| R_5$

   (c) $(R_1 + R_2) \| (R_3 + R_4 + R_5)$ **(d)** none of these answers

3. If all of the resistors in Figure 7–61 have the same value, when voltage is applied across terminals A and B, the current is

   (a) greatest in R_5 **(b)** greatest in R_3, R_4, and R_5

   (c) greatest in R_1 and R_2 **(d)** the same in all the resistors

4. Two 1.0 kΩ resistors are in series and this series combination is in parallel with a 2.2 kΩ resistor. The voltage across one of the 1.0 kΩ resistors is 6 V. The voltage across the 2.2 kΩ resistor is

   (a) 6 V   **(b)** 3 V   **(c)** 12 V   **(d)** 13.2 V

5. The parallel combination of a 330 Ω resistor and a 470 Ω resistor is in series with the parallel combination of four 1.0 kΩ resistors. A 100 V source is connected across the circuit. The resistor with the most current has a value of

   (a) 1.0 kΩ   **(b)** 330 Ω   **(c)** 470 Ω

6. In the circuit described in Question 5, the resistor(s) with the most voltage has (have) a value of

   (a) 1.0 kΩ   **(b)** 470 Ω   **(c)** 330 Ω

7. In the circuit of Question 5, the percentage of the total current through any single 1.0 kΩ resistor is

   (a) 100%   **(b)** 25%   **(c)** 50%   **(d)** 31.3%

8. The output of a certain voltage divider is 9 V with no load. When a load is connected, the output voltage

   (a) increases   **(b)** decreases

   (c) remains the same   **(d)** becomes zero

9. A certain voltage divider consists of two 10 kΩ resistors in series. Which of the following load resistors will have the most effect on the output voltage?

   (a) 1.0 MΩ   **(b)** 20 kΩ   **(c)** 100 kΩ   **(d)** 10 kΩ

10. When a load resistance is connected to the output of a voltage-divider circuit, the current drawn from the source

    (a) decreases   **(b)** increases   **(c)** remains the same   **(d)** is cut off

11. In a ladder network, simplification should begin at

    (a) the source   **(b)** the resistor farthest from the source

    (c) the center   **(d)** the resistor closest to the source

12. In a certain four-step $R/2R$ ladder network, the smallest resistor value is 10 kΩ. The largest value is

    (a) indeterminable   **(b)** 20 kΩ   **(c)** 50 kΩ   **(d)** 100 kΩ

13. The output voltage of a balanced Wheatstone bridge is

    (a) equal to the source voltage

    (b) equal to zero

    (c) dependent on all of the resistor values in the bridge

    (d) dependent on the value of the unknown resistor

14. A certain Wheatstone bridge has the following resistor values: $R_V = 8$ kΩ, $R_2 = 680$ Ω, and $R_4 = 2.2$ kΩ. The unknown resistance is

    (a) 2473 Ω   **(b)** 25.9 kΩ   **(c)** 187 Ω   **(d)** 2890 Ω

15. You are measuring the voltage at a given point in a circuit that has very high resistance values and the measured voltage is a little lower than it should be. This is possibly because of

    (a) one or more of the resistance values being off

    (b) the loading effect of the voltmeter

    (c) the source voltage is too low

    (d) all the above

■ PROBLEMS

More difficult problems are indicated by an asterisk (*).

SECTION 7–1 Identifying Series-Parallel Relationships

1. Visualize and sketch the following series-parallel combinations:
   (a) R_1 in series with the parallel combination of R_2 and R_3
   (b) R_1 in parallel with the series combination of R_2 and R_3
   (c) R_1 in parallel with a branch containing R_2 in series with a parallel combination of four other resistors

2. Visualize and sketch the following series-parallel circuits:
   (a) A parallel combination of three branches, each containing two series resistors
   (b) A series combination of three parallel circuits, each containing two resistors

3. In each circuit of Figure 7–62, identify the series and parallel relationships of the resistors viewed from the source.

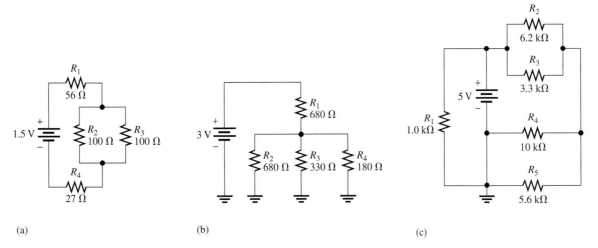

(a)   (b)   (c)

FIGURE 7–62

4. For each circuit in Figure 7–63, identify the series and parallel relationships of the resistors viewed from the source.

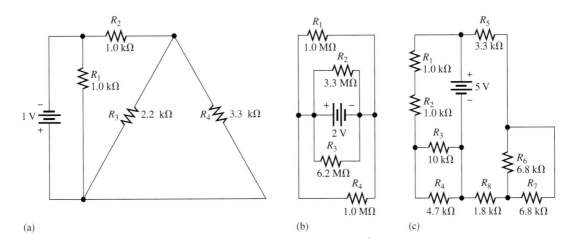

(a)   (b)   (c)

FIGURE 7–63

FIGURE 7–64

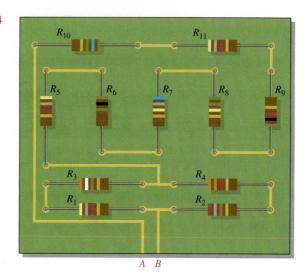

A   B

5. Draw the schematic of the PC board layout in Figure 7–64 showing resistor values and identify the series-parallel relationships.

*6. Develop a schematic for the double-sided PC board in Figure 7–65 and label the resistor values.

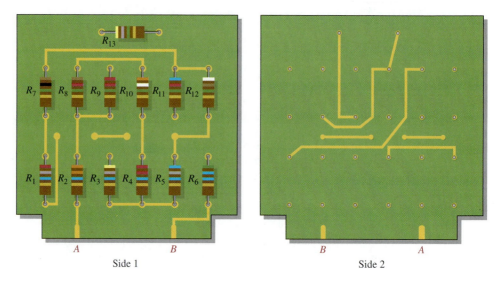

A   B   B   A

Side 1   Side 2

FIGURE 7–65

*7. Lay out a PC board for the circuit in Figure 7–63(c). The battery is to be connected external to the board.

SECTION 7–2   Analysis of Series-Parallel Circuits

8. A certain circuit is composed of two parallel resistors. The total resistance is 667 Ω. One of the resistors is 1.0 kΩ. What is the other resistor?

9. For each circuit in Figure 7–62, determine the total resistance presented to the source.

10. Repeat Problem 9 for each circuit in Figure 7–63.

11. Determine the current through each resistor in each circuit in Figure 7–62; then calculate each voltage drop.

12. Determine the current through each resistor in each circuit in Figure 7–63; then calculate each voltage drop.

13. Find R_T for all combinations of the switches in Figure 7–66.

FIGURE 7–66

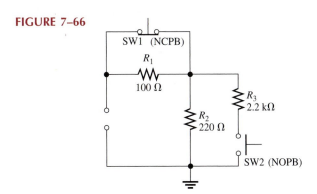

14. Determine the resistance between *A* and *B* in Figure 7–67 with the source removed.
15. Determine the voltage at each point with respect to ground in Figure 7–67.
16. Determine the voltage at each point with respect to ground in Figure 7–68.
17. In Figure 7–68, how would you determine the voltage across R_2 by measuring without connecting a meter directly across the resistor?

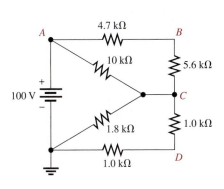

FIGURE 7–67

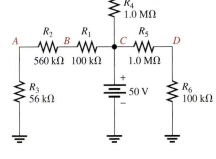

FIGURE 7–68

18. Determine the voltage, V_{AB}, in Figure 7–69.
19. Find the value of R_2 in Figure 7–70.

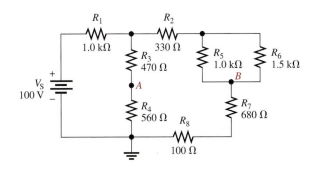

FIGURE 7–69

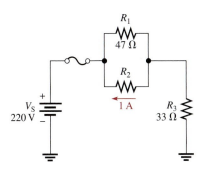

FIGURE 7–70

FIGURE 7–71

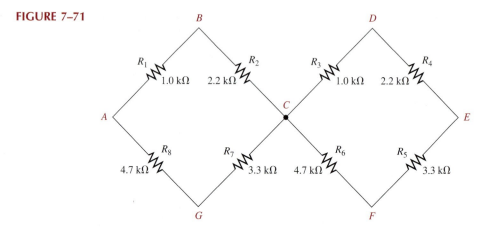

*20. Find the resistance between point A and each of the other points (R_{AB}, R_{AC}, R_{AD}, R_{AE}, R_{AF}, and R_{AG}) in Figure 7–71.

*21. Find the resistance between each of the following sets of points in Figure 7–72: *AB, BC,* and *CD.*

*22. Determine the value of each resistor in Figure 7–73.

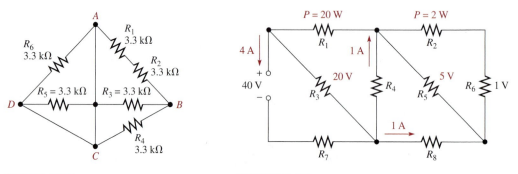

FIGURE 7–72   **FIGURE 7–73**

SECTION 7–3   Voltage Dividers with Resistive Loads

23. A voltage divider consists of two 56 kΩ resistors and a 15 V source. Calculate the unloaded output voltage. What will the output voltage be if a load resistor of 1.0 MΩ is connected to the output?

24. A 12 V battery output is divided down to obtain two output voltages. Three 3.3 kΩ resistors are used to provide the two taps. Determine the output voltages. If a 10 kΩ load is connected to the higher of the two outputs, what will its loaded value be?

25. Which will cause a smaller decrease in output voltage for a given voltage divider, a 10 kΩ load or a 47 kΩ load?

26. In Figure 7–74, determine the continuous current drain on the battery with no load across the output terminals. With a 10 kΩ load, what is the battery current?

FIGURE 7–74

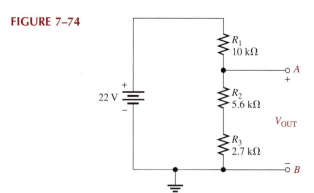

*27. Determine the resistance values for a voltage divider that must meet the following specifications: The current drain under unloaded condition is not to exceed 5 mA. The source voltage is to be 10 V, and the required outputs are to be 5 V and 2.5 V. Sketch the circuit. Determine the effect on the output voltages if a 1.0 kΩ load is connected to each tap one at a time.

28. The voltage divider in Figure 7–75 has a switched load. Determine the voltage at each tap (V_1, V_2, and V_3) for each position of the switch.

FIGURE 7–75

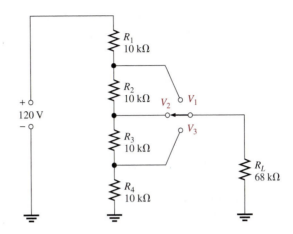

*29. Figure 7–76 shows a dc biasing arrangement for a field-effect transistor amplifier. Biasing is a common method for setting up certain dc voltage levels required for proper amplifier operation. Although you are not expected to be familiar with transistor amplifiers at this point, the dc voltages and currents in the circuit can be determined using methods that you already know.

    (a) Find V_G and V_S **(b)** Determine I_1, I_2, I_D, and I_S **(c)** Find V_{DS} and V_{DG}

FIGURE 7–76

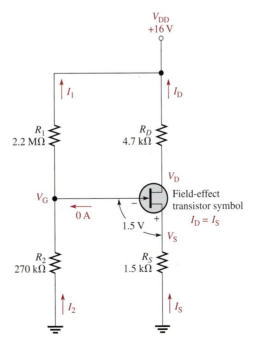

*30. Design a voltage divider to provide a 6 V output with no load and a minimum of 5.5 V across a 1.0 kΩ load. The source voltage is 24 V, and the unloaded current drain is not to exceed 100 mA.

SECTION 7–4 Loading Effect of a Voltmeter

31. On which one of the following voltage range settings will a voltmeter present the minimum load on a circuit?

 (a) 1 V **(b)** 10 V **(c)** 100 V **(d)** 1000 V

32. Determine the internal resistance of a 20,000 Ω/V voltmeter on each of the following range settings.

 (a) 0.5 V **(b)** 1 V **(c)** 5 V **(d)** 50 V **(e)** 100 V **(f)** 1000 V

33. The voltmeter described in Problem 32 is used to measure the voltage across R_4 in Figure 7–62(a).

 (a) What range should be used?

 (b) How much less is the voltage measured by the meter than the actual voltage?

34. Repeat Problem 33 if the voltmeter is used to measure the voltage across R_4 in the circuit of Figure 7–62(b).

SECTION 7–5 Ladder Networks

35. For the circuit shown in Figure 7–77, calculate the following:

 (a) Total resistance across the source **(b)** Total current from the source

 (c) Current through the 910 Ω resistor **(d)** Voltage from point A to point B

36. Determine the total resistance and the voltage at points A, B, and C in the ladder network of Figure 7–78.

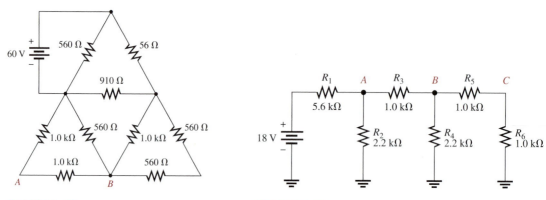

FIGURE 7–77

FIGURE 7–78

*37. Determine the total resistance between terminals A and B of the ladder network in Figure 7–79. Also calculate the current in each branch with 10 V between A and B.

38. What is the voltage across each resistor in Figure 7–79 with 10 V between A and B?

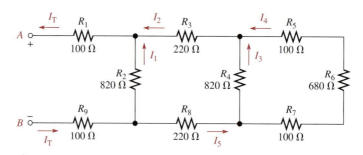

FIGURE 7–79

*39. Find I_T and V_{OUT} in Figure 7–80.

FIGURE 7–80

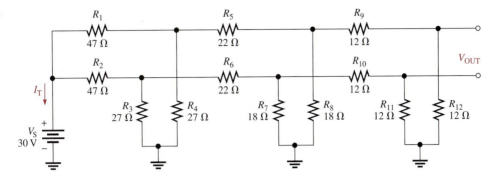

40. Determine V_{OUT} for the $R/2R$ ladder network in Figure 7–81 for the following conditions:
    (a) Switch SW2 connected to +12 V and the others connected to ground
    (b) Switch SW1 connected to +12 V and the others connected to ground

FIGURE 7–81

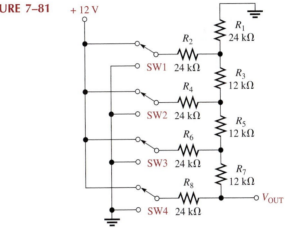

41. Repeat Problem 40 for the following conditions:
    (a) SW3 and SW4 to +12 V, SW1 and SW2 to ground
    (b) SW3 and SW1 to +12 V, SW2 and SW4 to ground
    (c) All switches to +12 V

SECTION 7–6 The Wheatstone Bridge

42. A resistor of unknown value is connected to a Wheatstone bridge circuit. The bridge parameters are set as follows: $R_V = 18$ kΩ and $R_2/R_4 = 0.02$. What is R_{UNK}?

43. A bridge network is shown in Figure 7–82. To what value must R_V be set in order to balance the bridge?

FIGURE 7–82

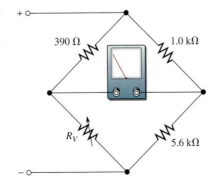

*44. The temperature-sensitive bridge circuit in Figure 7–50 is used to detect when the tempera-ture in a chemical manufacturing process reaches 100°C. The resistance of the thermistor drops from 5 kΩ at a nominal 20°C to 100 Ω at 100°C. If $R_1 = 1.0$ kΩ and $R_2 = 2.2$ kΩ, to what value must R_4 be set to produce a balanced bridge when the temperature reaches 100°C?

SECTION 7–7 Troubleshooting

45. Is the voltmeter reading in Figure 7–83 correct?
46. Are the meter readings in Figure 7–84 correct?

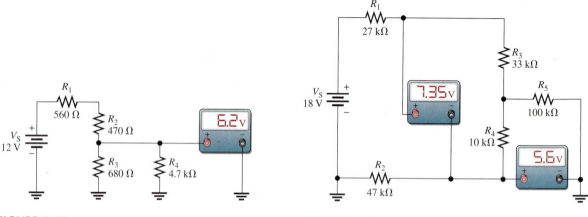

FIGURE 7–83

FIGURE 7–84

47. There is one fault in Figure 7–85. Based on the meter indications, determine what the fault is.
48. Look at the meters in Figure 7–86 and determine if there is a fault in the circuit. If there is a fault, identify it.

FIGURE 7–85

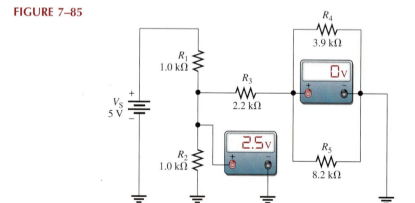

FIGURE 7–86

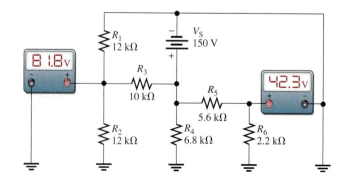

ANSWERS TO SECTION REVIEWS ■ 257

49. Check the meter readings in Figure 7–87 and locate any fault that may exist.

50. If R_2 in Figure 7–88 opens, what voltages will be read at points A, B, and C?

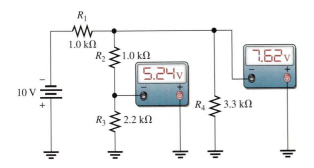

FIGURE 7–87

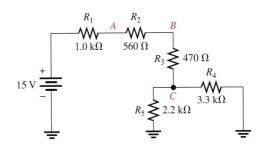

FIGURE 7–88

EWB Troubleshooting and Analysis

These problems require your EWB compact disk.

51. Open file PRO07-51.EWB and measure the total resistance.

52. Open file PRO07-52.EWB. Determine by measurement if there is an open resistor and, if so, which one.

53. Open file PRO07-53.EWB and determine the unspecified resistance value.

54. Open file PRO07-54.EWB and determine how much the load resistance affects each of the resistor voltages.

55. Open file PRO07-55.EWB and find the shorted resistor, if there is one.

56. Open file PRO07-56.EWB and adjust the value of R_x until the bridge is approximately balanced.

■ ANSWERS TO SECTION REVIEWS

Section 7–1

1. A series-parallel resistive circuit is a circuit consisting of both series and parallel connections.

2. See Figure 7–89.

3. Resistors R_1 and R_2 are in series with the parallel combination of R_3 and R_4.

4. R_3, R_4, and R_5 are in parallel. Also the series-parallel combination $R_2 + (R_3 \parallel R_4 \parallel R_5)$ is in parallel with R_1.

5. Resistors R_1 and R_2 are in parallel; R_3 and R_4 are in parallel.

6. Yes, the parallel combinations are in series.

FIGURE 7–89

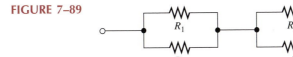

Section 7–2

1. Voltage-divider and current-divider formulas, Kirchhoff's laws, and Ohm's law can be used in series-parallel analysis.

2. $R_T = R_1 + R_2 \parallel R_3 + R_4 = 608\ \Omega$

3. $I_3 = [R_2/(R_2 + R_3)]I_T = 11.1\ \text{mA}$

4. $V_2 = I_2R_2 = 3.65\ \text{V}$

5. $R_T = 47\ \Omega + 27\ \Omega + (27\ \Omega + 27\ \Omega) \parallel 47\ \Omega = 99.1\ \Omega$; $I_T = 1\ \text{V}/99.1\ \Omega = 10.1\ \text{mA}$

Section 7–3

1. The load resistor decreases the output voltage.

2. True

3. $V_{OUT(unloaded)} = (100 \text{ k}\Omega/147 \text{ k}\Omega)30 \text{ V} = 20.4 \text{ V}$; $V_{OUT(loaded)} = (9.1 \text{ k}\Omega/56.1 \text{ k}\Omega)30 \text{ V} = 4.87 \text{ V}$

Section 7–4

1. A voltmeter loads a circuit because the internal resistance of the meter appears in parallel with the circuit resistance across which it is connected, reducing the resistance between those two points of the circuit and drawing current from the circuit.

2. No, because the meter resistance is much larger than 1.0 kΩ.

3. There is a decrease in measured voltage because R_M is smaller. You can read the scale more accurately on the 3 V range.

4. $R_M = (30,000 \ \Omega/\text{V})5 \text{ V} = 1.5 \text{ M}\Omega$

Section 7–5

1. See Figure 7–90.

2. $R_T = 11.6 \text{ k}\Omega$

3. $I_T = 10 \text{ V}/11.6 \text{ k}\Omega = 859 \ \mu\text{A}$

4. $I_2 = 640 \ \mu\text{A}$

5. $V_A = 1.41 \text{ V}$

FIGURE 7–90

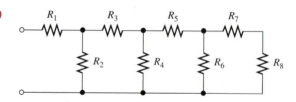

Section 7–6

1. See Figure 7–91.

2. The bridge is balanced when $V_A = V_B$.

3. $R_{UNK} = R_V(R_2/R_4)$

4. $R_{UNK} = 15 \text{ k}\Omega$

FIGURE 7–91

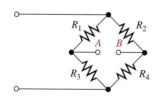

Section 7–7

1. Common circuit faults are opens and shorts.

2. The 10 kΩ resistor (R_3) is open.

3. **(a)** $V_A = 55 \text{ V}$ **(b)** $V_A = 55 \text{ V}$ **(c)** $V_A = 54.2 \text{ V}$ **(d)** $V_A = 100 \text{ V}$ **(e)** $V_A = 0 \text{ V}$

Section 7–8

1. The battery will last 386 days.

2. Yes, $\frac{1}{8}$ W resistors can be used.

3. No, none of the resistors will overheat.

■ **ANSWERS TO RELATED PROBLEMS FOR EXAMPLES**

7–1 The new resistor is in parallel with $R_4 + R_2 \parallel R_3$.

7–2 The resistor has no effect because it is shorted.

7–3 The new resistor is in parallel with R_5.

7–4 A to gnd: $R_T = R_4 + R_3 \parallel (R_1 + R_2)$
B to gnd: $R_T = R_4 + R_2 \parallel (R_1 + R_3)$
C to gnd: $R_T = R_4$

7–5 R_3 and R_6 are in series.

7–6 55.1 Ω

7–7 128.3 Ω

7–8 2.38 mA

7–9 $I_1 = 35.7$ mA; $I_3 = 23.4$ mA

7–10 $V_A = 44.8$ V; $V_1 = 35.2$ V

7–11 2.04 V

7–12 $V_{AB} = 5.48$ V; $V_{BC} = 1.66$ V; $V_{CD} = 0.86$ V

7–13 3.39 V

7–14 5.48 V

7–15 5.34 V

7–16 $I_1 = 7.16$ mA; $I_2 = 3.57$ mA; $I_3 = 3.57$ mA; $I_4 = 1.74$ mA; $I_5 = 1.85$ mA; $I_6 = 1.85$ mA;
$V_A = 29.3$ V; $V_B = 17.4$ V; $V_C = 8.70$ V

7–17 321 Ω

7–18 5.73 V; 0 V

7–19 9.46 V

7–20 $V_A = 12$ V; $V_B = 13.8$ V

■ **ANSWERS TO SELF-TEST**

1. (e) **2.** (c) **3.** (c) **4.** (c) **5.** (b) **6.** (a) **7.** (b) **8.** (b)
9. (d) **10.** (b) **11.** (b) **12.** (b) **13.** (b) **14.** (a) **15.** (d)

8

CIRCUIT THEOREMS AND CONVERSIONS

 Electronics Workbench (EWB) and
PSpice Tutorials available at
http://www.prenhall.com/floyd

■ INTRODUCTION

In previous chapters, you saw how to analyze various types of circuits using Ohm's law and Kirchhoff's laws. Some types of circuits are difficult to analyze using only those basic laws and require additional methods in order to simplify the analysis.

The theorems and conversions in this chapter make analysis easier for certain types of circuits. These methods do not replace Ohm's law and Kirchhoff's laws, but they are normally used in conjunction with the laws in certain situations.

Because all electric circuits are driven by either voltage sources or current sources, it is important to understand how to work with these elements. The superposition theorem will help you to deal with circuits that have multiple sources. Thevenin's and Norton's theorems provide methods for reducing a circuit to a simple equivalent form for ease of analysis. The maximum power transfer theorem is used in applications where it is important for a given circuit to provide maximum power to a load. An example of this is an audio amplifier that provides maximum power to a speaker. Delta-to-wye and wye-to-delta conversions are sometimes useful when analyzing bridge circuits that are commonly found in systems that measure physical parameters such as temperature, pressure, and strain.

In the TECH TIP assignment in Section 8–9, you will be working with a temperature measurement and control circuit that uses a Wheatstone bridge, which you studied in Chapter 7. You will utilize Thevenin's theorem as well as other techniques in the evaluation of this circuit.

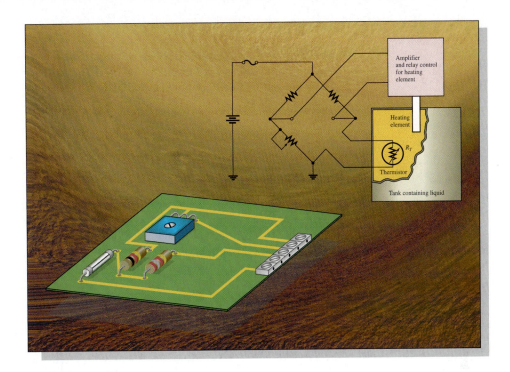

■ TECHnology
   Theory
   Into
   Practice

■ CHAPTER OBJECTIVES

❑ Describe the characteristics of a voltage source

❑ Describe the characteristics of a current source

❑ Perform source conversions

❑ Apply the superposition theorem to circuit analysis

❑ Apply Thevenin's theorem to simplify a circuit for analysis

❑ Apply Norton's theorem to simplify a circuit

❑ Apply the maximum power transfer theorem

❑ Perform Δ-to-Y and Y-to-Δ conversions

HISTORICAL NOTE

Leon Charles Thevenin

1857–1926

Leon Charles Thevenin was born in Paris, France, in 1857. He graduated from the Ecole Polytechnique in 1876 and, in 1878, joined the Corps of Telegraph Engineers where he initially worked on the development of long-distance underground telegraph lines. During his career, Thevenin became increasingly interested in the problems of measurements in electrical circuits. As a result of studying Kirchhoff's laws, which were essentially derived from Ohm's law, he developed his now famous theorem which made calculations involving complex circuits possible.

8–1 ■ THE VOLTAGE SOURCE

The voltage source is the principal type of energy source in electronic applications, so it is important to understand its characteristics. The voltage source ideally provides constant voltage to a load even when the load resistance varies.

After completing this section, you should be able to

■ **Describe the characteristics of a voltage source**
  • Compare a practical voltage source to an ideal source
  • Discuss the effect of loading on a practical voltage source

Figure 8–1(a) is the familiar symbol for an ideal dc **voltage source.** The voltage across its terminals, A and B, remains fixed regardless of the value of load resistance that may be connected across its output. Figure 8–1(b) shows a load resistor, R_L, connected. All of the source voltage, V_S, is dropped across R_L. Ideally, R_L can be changed to any value except zero, and the voltage will remain fixed. The ideal voltage source has an internal resistance of zero.

FIGURE 8–1
Ideal dc voltage source.

(a) Unloaded   (b) Loaded

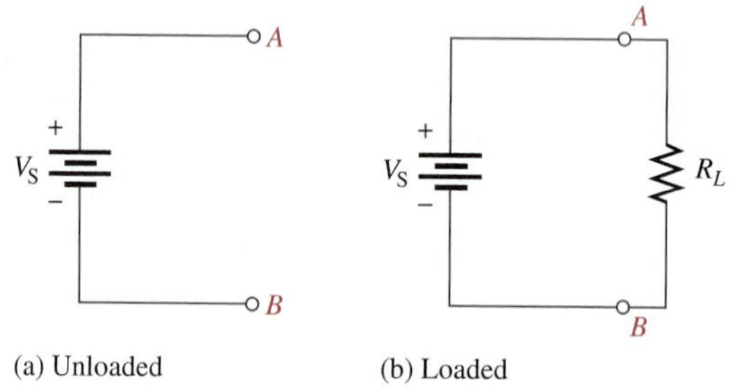

In reality, no voltage source is ideal. That is, all voltage sources have some inherent internal resistance as a result of their physical and/or chemical makeup, which can be represented by a resistor in series with an ideal source, as shown in Figure 8–2(a). R_S is the internal source resistance and V_S is the source voltage. With no load, the output voltage (voltage from A to B) is V_S. This voltage is sometimes called the *open circuit voltage.*

FIGURE 8–2
Practical voltage source.

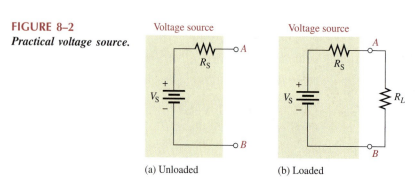

(a) Unloaded   (b) Loaded

Loading of the Voltage Source

When a load resistor is connected across the output terminals, as shown in Figure 8–2(b), all of the source voltage does not appear across R_L. Some of the voltage is dropped across R_S because R_S and R_L are in series.

If R_S is very small compared to R_L, the source approaches ideal because almost all of the source voltage, V_S, appears across the larger resistance, R_L. Very little voltage is dropped across the internal resistance, R_S. If R_L changes, most of the source voltage remains across the output as long as R_L is much larger than R_S. As a result, very little change occurs in the output voltage. The larger R_L is, compared to R_S, the less change there is in the output voltage.

Example 8–1 illustrates the effect of changes in R_L on the output voltage when R_L is much greater than R_S. Example 8–2 shows the effect of smaller load resistances.

EXAMPLE 8–1

Calculate the voltage output of the source in Figure 8–3 for the following values of R_L: 100 Ω, 560 Ω, and 1.0 kΩ.

FIGURE 8–3

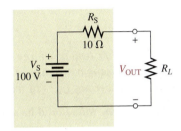

Solution For $R_L = 100$ Ω, the voltage output is

$$V_{OUT} = \left(\frac{R_L}{R_S + R_L} \right) V_S = \left(\frac{100 \ \Omega}{110 \ \Omega} \right) 100 \ V = \textbf{90.9 V}$$

For $R_L = 560$ Ω,

$$V_{OUT} = \left(\frac{560 \ \Omega}{570 \ \Omega} \right) 100 \ V = \textbf{98.2 V}$$

For $R_L = 1.0$ kΩ,

$$V_{OUT} = \left(\frac{1000 \ \Omega}{1010 \ \Omega} \right) 100 \ V = \textbf{99.0 V}$$

Notice that the output voltage is within 10% of the source voltage, V_S, for all three values of R_L because R_L is at least ten times R_S.

Related Problem Determine V_{OUT} in Figure 8–3 if $R_S = 50$ Ω and $R_L = 10$ kΩ.

EXAMPLE 8–2

Determine V_{OUT} for $R_L = 10$ Ω and for $R_L = 1.0$ Ω in Figure 8–3.

Solution For $R_L = 10$ Ω, the voltage output is

$$V_{OUT} = \left(\frac{R_L}{R_S + R_L} \right) V_S = \left(\frac{10 \ \Omega}{20 \ \Omega} \right) 100 \ V = \textbf{50 V}$$

For $R_L = 1.0$ Ω,

$$V_{OUT} = \left(\frac{1.0 \ \Omega}{11 \ \Omega} \right) 100 \ V = \textbf{9.09 V}$$

Related Problem What is V_{OUT} with no load resistor in Figure 8–3?

Notice in Example 8–2 that the output voltage decreases significantly as R_L is made smaller compared to R_S. This example illustrates the requirement that R_L must be much larger than R_S in order to maintain the output voltage near its open circuit value.

SECTION 8–1 REVIEW	**1.** What is the symbol for the ideal voltage source?
	2. Sketch a practical voltage source.
	3. What is the internal resistance of the ideal voltage source?
	4. What effect does the load have on the output voltage of the practical voltage source?

8–2 ■ THE CURRENT SOURCE

The current source is another type of energy source that ideally provides a constant current to a load even when the resistance of the load varies. The concept of the current source is important in certain types of transistor circuits.

After completing this section, you should be able to

■ **Describe the characteristics of a current source**
  • Compare a practical current source to an ideal source
  • Discuss the effect of loading on a practical current source

Figure 8–4(a) shows a symbol for the ideal **current source.** The arrow indicates the direction of current, and I_S is the value of the source current. An ideal current source produces a constant value of current through a load, regardless of the value of the load. This concept is illustrated in Figure 8–4(b), where a load resistor is connected to the current source between terminals A and B. The ideal current source has an infinitely large internal parallel resistance.

FIGURE 8–4
Ideal current source.

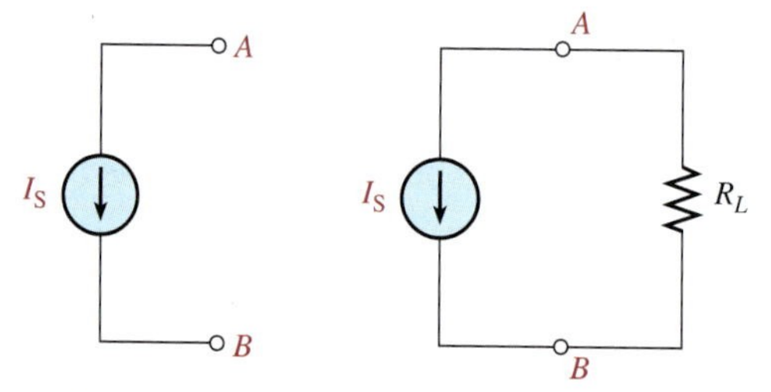

(a) Unloaded   (b) Loaded

Transistors act basically as current sources, and for this reason, knowledge of the current source concept is important. You will find that the equivalent model of a transistor does contain a current source.

Although the ideal current source can be used in most analysis work, no actual device is ideal. A practical current source representation is shown in Figure 8–5. Here the internal resistance appears in parallel with the ideal current source.

If the internal source resistance, R_S, is much larger than a load resistor, the practical source approaches ideal. The reason is illustrated in the practical current source shown in Figure 8–5. Part of the current, I_S, is through R_S, and part is through R_L. Resistors R_S and R_L act as a current divider. If R_S is much larger than R_L, most of the current is through

FIGURE 8–5
Practical current source with load.

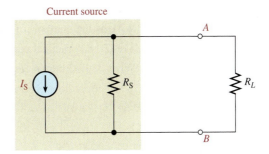

Current source

R_L and very little through R_S. As long as R_L remains much smaller than R_S, the current through it will stay almost constant, no matter how much R_L changes.

If there is a constant-current source, you can normally assume that R_S is so much larger than the load that R_S can be neglected. This simplifies the source to ideal, making the analysis easier.

Example 8–3 illustrates the effect of changes in R_L on the load current when R_L is much smaller than R_S. Generally, R_L should be at least ten times smaller than R_S ($10R_L \leq R_S$).

EXAMPLE 8–3

Calculate the load current (I_L) in Figure 8–6 for the following values of R_L: 100 Ω, 560 Ω, and 1.0 kΩ.

FIGURE 8–6

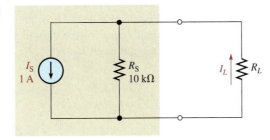

Solution For $R_L = 100$ Ω, the load current is

$$I_L = \left(\frac{R_S}{R_S + R_L}\right)I_S = \left(\frac{10 \text{ k}\Omega}{10.1 \text{ k}\Omega}\right)1 \text{ A} = \textbf{990 mA}$$

For $R_L = 560$ Ω,

$$I_L = \left(\frac{10 \text{ k}\Omega}{10.56 \text{ k}\Omega}\right)1 \text{ A} = \textbf{947 mA}$$

For $R_L = 1.0$ kΩ,

$$I_L = \left(\frac{10 \text{ k}\Omega}{11 \text{ k}\Omega}\right)1 \text{ A} = \textbf{909 mA}$$

Notice that the load current, I_L, is within 10% of the source current for each value of R_L because R_L is at least ten times smaller than R_S.

Related Problem At what value of R_L in Figure 8–6 will the load current equal 750 mA?

SECTION 8–2 REVIEW

1. What is the symbol for an ideal current source?
2. Sketch the practical current source.
3. What is the internal resistance of the ideal current source?
4. What effect does the load have on the load current of the practical current source?

8–3 ■ SOURCE CONVERSIONS

In circuit analysis, it is sometimes useful to convert a voltage source to an equivalent current source, or vice versa.

After completing this section, you should be able to

■ **Perform source conversions**
  • Convert a voltage source to a current source
  • Convert a current source to a voltage source
  • Define *terminal equivalency*

Converting a Voltage Source to a Current Source

The source voltage, V_S, divided by the internal source resistance, R_S, gives the value of the equivalent source current.

$$I_S = \frac{V_S}{R_S}$$

The value of R_S is the same for both the voltage and current sources. As illustrated in Figure 8–7, the directional arrow for the current points from plus to minus. The equivalent current source is in parallel with R_S.

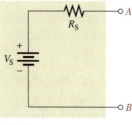
(a) Voltage source

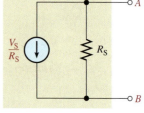
(b) Current source

FIGURE 8–7
Conversion of voltage source to equivalent current source.

Equivalency of two sources means that for any given load resistance connected to the two sources, the same load voltage and load current are produced by both sources. This concept is called **terminal equivalency.**

You can show that the voltage source and the current source in Figure 8–7 are equivalent by connecting a load resistor to each, as shown in Figure 8–8, and then calculating the load current. For the voltage source, the load current is

$$I_L = \frac{V_S}{R_S + R_L}$$

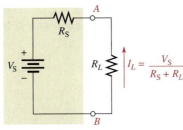

(a) Loaded voltage source

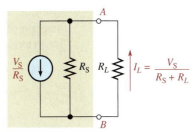

(b) Loaded current source

FIGURE 8–8
Equivalent sources with loads.

For the current source,

$$I_L = \left(\frac{R_S}{R_S + R_L}\right)\frac{V_S}{R_S} = \frac{V_S}{R_S + R_L}$$

As you see, both expressions for I_L are the same. These equations show that the sources are equivalent as far as the load or terminals A and B are concerned.

EXAMPLE 8–4

Convert the voltage source in Figure 8–9 to an equivalent current source and show the equivalent circuit.

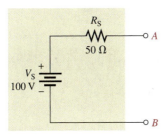

FIGURE 8–9

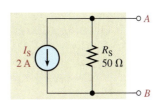

FIGURE 8–10

Solution The value of R_S is the same as with a voltage source. Therefore, the equivalent current source is

$$I_S = \frac{V_S}{R_S} = \frac{100 \text{ V}}{50 \text{ }\Omega} = 2 \text{ A}$$

Figure 8–10 shows the equivalent circuit.

Related Problem Determine I_S and R_S of a current source equivalent to a voltage source with $V_S = 12$ V and $R_S = 10$ Ω.

Converting a Current Source to a Voltage Source

The source current, I_S, multiplied by the internal source resistance, R_S, gives the value of the equivalent source voltage.

$$V_S = I_S R_S$$

Again, R_S remains the same. The polarity of the voltage source is plus to minus in the direction of the current. The equivalent voltage source is the voltage in series with R_S, as illustrated in Figure 8–11.

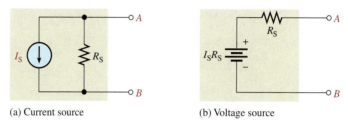

(a) Current source   (b) Voltage source

FIGURE 8–11
Conversion of current source to equivalent voltage source.

EXAMPLE 8–5

Convert the current source in Figure 8–12 to an equivalent voltage source and show the equivalent circuit.

FIGURE 8–12

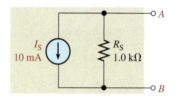

Solution   The value of R_S is the same as with a current source. Therefore, the equivalent voltage source is

$$V_S = I_S R_S = (10 \text{ mA})(1.0 \text{ k}\Omega) = 10 \text{ V}$$

Figure 8–13 shows the equivalent circuit.

FIGURE 8–13

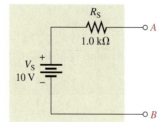

Related Problem   Determine V_S and R_S of a voltage source equivalent to a current source with $I_S = 500$ mA and $R_S = 600$ Ω.

**SECTION 8–3
REVIEW**

1. Write the formula for converting a voltage source to a current source.
2. Write the formula for converting a current source to a voltage source.
3. Convert the voltage source in Figure 8–14 to an equivalent current source.
4. Convert the current source in Figure 8–15 to an equivalent voltage source.

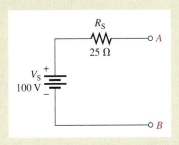

FIGURE 8–14

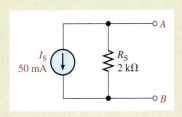

FIGURE 8–15

8–4 ■ THE SUPERPOSITION THEOREM

Some circuits require more than one voltage or current source. For example, most amplifiers operate with two voltage sources: an ac and a dc source. Some amplifiers require both a positive and a negative dc voltage source for proper operation.

After completing this section, you should be able to

■ **Apply the superposition theorem to circuit analysis**
  • State the superposition theorem
  • List the steps in applying the theorem

The superposition method is a way to determine currents and voltages in a circuit that has multiple sources by taking one source at a time. The other sources are replaced by their internal resistances. Recall that the ideal voltage source has a zero internal resistance. In this section, all voltage sources will be treated as ideal in order to simplify the coverage.

A general statement of the **superposition theorem** is as follows:

> **The current in any given branch of a multiple-source circuit can be found by determining the currents in that particular branch produced by each source acting alone, with all other sources replaced by their internal resistances. The total current in the branch is the algebraic sum of the individual source currents in that branch.**

The steps in applying the superposition method are as follows:

Step 1. Take one voltage (or current) source at a time and replace each of the other voltage (or current) sources with either a short for a voltage source or an open for a current source (a short represents zero internal resistance and an open represents infinite internal resistance for ideal sources).

Step 2. Determine the particular current or voltage that you want just as if there were only one source in the circuit.

Step 3. Take the next source in the circuit and repeat Steps 1 and 2. Do this for each source.

Step 4. To find the actual current in a given branch, algebraically sum the currents due to each individual source. (If the currents are in the same direction, they are added. If the currents are in opposite directions, they are subtracted with the direction of the resulting current the same as the larger of the original quantities.) Once the current is found, voltage can be determined.

An example of the approach to superposition is demonstrated in Figure 8–16 for a series-parallel circuit with two voltage sources. Study the steps in this figure. Examples 8–6 through 8–9 will clarify this procedure.

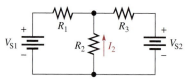

(a) Problem: Find I_2.

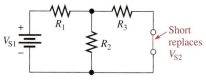

(b) Replace V_{S2} with zero resistance (short).

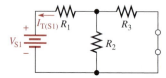

(c) Find R_T and I_T looking from V_{S1}:
$$R_{T(S1)} = R_1 + R_2 \,\|\, R_3$$
$$I_{T(S1)} = V_{S1}/R_{T(S1)}$$

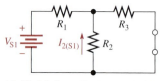

(d) Find I_2 due to V_{S1} (current divider):
$$I_{2(S1)} = \left(\frac{R_3}{R_2 + R_3}\right) I_{T(S1)}$$

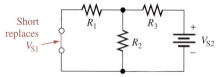

(e) Replace V_{S1} with zero resistance (short).

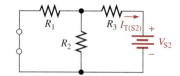

(f) Find R_T and I_T looking from V_{S2}:
$$R_{T(S2)} = R_3 + R_1 \,\|\, R_2$$
$$I_{T(S2)} = V_{S2}/R_{T(S2)}$$

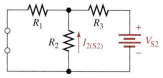

(g) Find I_2 due to V_{S2}:
$$I_{2(S2)} = \left(\frac{R_1}{R_1 + R_2}\right) I_{T(S2)}$$

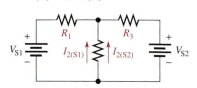

(h) Add $I_{2(S1)}$ and $I_{2(S2)}$ to get the actual I_2 (they are in same direction):
$$I_2 = I_{2(S1)} + I_{2(S2)}$$

FIGURE 8–16
Demonstration of the superposition method.

EXAMPLE 8–6   Find the current in R_2 of Figure 8–17 by using the superposition theorem.

FIGURE 8–17

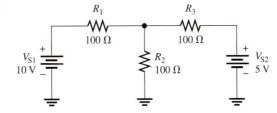

Solution

Step 1.   Replace V_{S2} with a short and find the current in R_2 due to voltage source V_{S1}, as shown in Figure 8–18. To find I_2, use the current-divider formula (Equation 6–10). Looking from V_{S1},

$$R_{T(S1)} = R_1 + \frac{R_3}{2} = 100\ \Omega + 50\ \Omega = 150\ \Omega$$

$$I_{T(S1)} = \frac{V_{S1}}{R_{T(S1)}} = \frac{10\ \text{V}}{150\ \Omega} = 66.7\ \text{mA}$$

The current in R_2 due to V_{S1} is

$$I_{2(S1)} = \left(\frac{R_3}{R_2 + R_3}\right)I_{T(S1)} = \left(\frac{100\ \Omega}{200\ \Omega}\right)66.7\ \text{mA} = 33.3\ \text{mA}$$

Note that this current is upward through R_2.

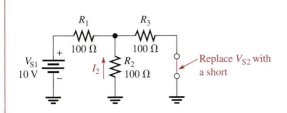

FIGURE 8–18

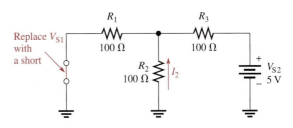

FIGURE 8–19

Step 2.   Find the current in R_2 due to voltage source V_{S2} by replacing V_{S1} with a short, as shown in Figure 8–19. Looking from V_{S2},

$$R_{T(S2)} = R_3 + \frac{R_1}{2} = 100\ \Omega + 50\ \Omega = 150\ \Omega$$

$$I_{T(S2)} = \frac{V_{S2}}{R_{T(S2)}} = \frac{5\ \text{V}}{150\ \Omega} = 33.3\ \text{mA}$$

The current in R_2 due to V_{S2} is

$$I_{2(S2)} = \left(\frac{R_1}{R_1 + R_2}\right)I_{T(S2)} = \left(\frac{100\ \Omega}{200\ \Omega}\right)33.3\ \text{mA} = 16.7\ \text{mA}$$

Note that this current is upward through R_2.

Step 3.   Both component currents are upward through R_2, so they have the same algebraic sign. Therefore, add the values to get the total current through R_2.

$$I_{2(\text{tot})} = I_{2(S1)} + I_{2(S2)} = 33.3\ \text{mA} + 16.7\ \text{mA} = \textbf{50 mA}$$

Related Problem   Determine the total current through R_2 if the polarity of V_{S2} in Figure 8–17 is reversed.

EXAMPLE 8–7   Find the current through R_2 in the circuit of Figure 8–20.

FIGURE 8–20

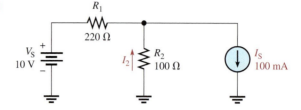

Solution

Step 1. Find the current in R_2 due to V_S by replacing I_S with an open, as shown in Figure 8–21.

FIGURE 8–21

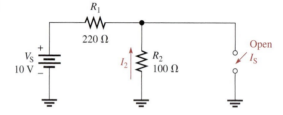

Notice that all of the current produced by V_S is through R_2. Looking from V_S,

$$R_T = R_1 + R_2 = 320 \ \Omega$$

The current through R_2 due to V_S is

$$I_{2(V_s)} = \frac{V_S}{R_T} = \frac{10 \ V}{320 \ \Omega} = 31.2 \ mA$$

Note that this current is upward through R_2.

Step 2. Find the current through R_2 due to I_S by replacing V_S with a short, as shown in Figure 8–22.

FIGURE 8–22

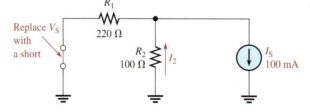

Use the current-divider formula to determine the current through R_2 due to I_S.

$$I_{2(I_s)} = \left(\frac{R_1}{R_1 + R_2} \right) I_S = \left(\frac{220 \ \Omega}{320 \ \Omega} \right) 100 \ mA = 68.8 \ mA$$

Note that this current also is upward through R_2.

Step 3. Both currents are in the same direction through R_2, so add them to get the total.

$$I_{2(tot)} = I_{2(V_s)} + I_{2(I_s)} = 31.2 \ mA + 68.8 \ mA = \mathbf{100 \ mA}$$

Related Problem If the polarity of V_S in Figure 8–20 is reversed, how is the value of I_S affected?

EXAMPLE 8–8   Find the current through the 100 Ω resistor in Figure 8–23.

FIGURE 8–23

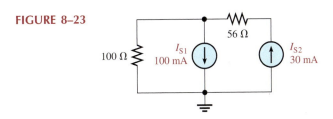

Solution
Step 1. Find the current through the 100 Ω resistor due to current source I_{S1} by replacing source I_{S2} with an open, as shown in Figure 8–24. As you can see, the entire 100 mA from the current source I_{S1} is upward through the 100 Ω resistor.

FIGURE 8–24

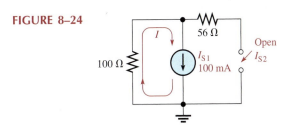

Step 2. Find the current through the 100 Ω resistor due to source I_{S2} by replacing source I_{S1} with an open, as indicated in Figure 8–25. Notice that all of the 30 mA from source I_{S2} is downward through the 100 Ω resistor.

FIGURE 8–25

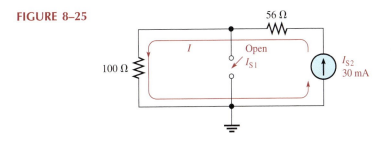

Step 3. To get the total current through the 100 Ω resistor, subtract the smaller current from the larger because they are in opposite directions. The resulting total current is in the direction of the larger current from source I_{S1}.

$$I_{100\Omega(\text{tot})} = I_{100\Omega(I_{S1})} - I_{100\Omega(I_{S2})}$$
$$= 100 \text{ mA} - 30 \text{ mA} = \textbf{70 mA}$$

The resulting current is upward through the resistor.

Related Problem   If the 100 Ω resistor in Figure 8–23 is changed to 68 Ω, what will be the current through it?

EXAMPLE 8–9   Find the total current through R_3 in Figure 8–26.

FIGURE 8–26

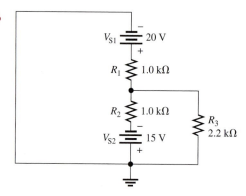

Solution

Step 1.   Find the current through R_3 due to source V_{S1} by replacing source V_{S2} with a short, as shown in Figure 8–27.

FIGURE 8–27

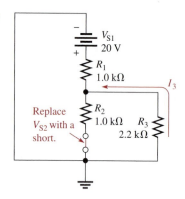

Looking from V_{S1},

$$R_{T(S1)} = R_1 + \frac{R_2 R_3}{R_2 + R_3} = 1.0 \text{ k}\Omega + \frac{(1.0 \text{ k}\Omega)(2.2 \text{ k}\Omega)}{3.2 \text{ k}\Omega} = 1.69 \text{ k}\Omega$$

$$I_{T(S1)} = \frac{V_{S1}}{R_{T(S1)}} = \frac{20 \text{ V}}{1.69 \text{ k}\Omega} = 11.8 \text{ mA}$$

Now apply the current-divider formula to get the current through R_3 due to source V_{S1}.

$$I_{3(S1)} = \left(\frac{R_2}{R_2 + R_3}\right) I_{T(S1)} = \left(\frac{1.0 \text{ k}\Omega}{3.2 \text{ k}\Omega}\right) 11.8 \text{ mA} = 3.69 \text{ mA}$$

Notice that this current is upward through R_3.

Step 2.   Find I_3 due to source V_{S2} by replacing source V_{S1} with a short, as shown in Figure 8–28. Looking from V_{S2},

$$R_{T(S2)} = R_2 + \frac{R_1 R_3}{R_1 + R_3} = 1.0 \text{ k}\Omega + \frac{(1.0 \text{ k}\Omega)(2.2 \text{ k}\Omega)}{3.2 \text{ k}\Omega} = 1.69 \text{ k}\Omega$$

$$I_{T(S2)} = \frac{V_{S2}}{R_{T(S2)}} = \frac{15 \text{ V}}{1.69 \text{ k}\Omega} = 8.88 \text{ mA}$$

FIGURE 8–28

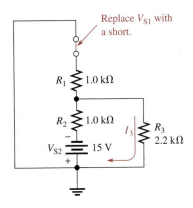

Replace V_{S1} with a short.

Now apply the current-divider formula to find the current through R_3 due to source V_{S2}.

$$I_{3(S2)} = \left(\frac{R_1}{R_1 + R_3}\right)I_{T(S2)} = \left(\frac{1.0 \text{ k}\Omega}{3.2 \text{ k}\Omega}\right)8.88 \text{ mA} = 2.78 \text{ mA}$$

Notice that this current is downward through R_3.

Step 3. Calculate the total current through R_3.

$$I_{3(tot)} = I_{3(S1)} - I_{3(S2)} = 3.69 \text{ mA} - 2.78 \text{ mA} = 0.91 \text{ mA} = \textbf{910 } \pmb{\mu}\textbf{A}$$

This current is upward through R_3.

Related Problem Find the total current through R_3 in Figure 8–26 if V_{S1} is changed to 12 V and its polarity reversed.

SECTION 8–4
REVIEW

1. State the superposition theorem.
2. Why is the superposition theorem useful for analysis of multiple-source linear circuits?
3. Why is an ideal voltage source shorted and an ideal current source opened when the superposition theorem is applied?
4. Using the superposition theorem, find the current through R_1 in Figure 8–29.
5. If, as a result of applying the superposition theorem, two currents are in opposing directions through a branch of a circuit, in which direction is the net current?

FIGURE 8–29

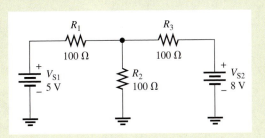

8–5 ■ THEVENIN'S THEOREM

Thevenin's theorem provides a method for simplifying a circuit to a standard equivalent form. In many cases, this theorem can be used to simplify the analysis of complex circuits.

After completing this section, you should be able to

■ **Apply Thevenin's theorem to simplify a circuit for analysis**
  • Describe the form of a Thevenin equivalent circuit
  • Obtain the Thevenin equivalent voltage source
  • Obtain the Thevenin equivalent resistance
  • Explain terminal equivalency in the context of Thevenin's theorem
  • Thevenize a portion of a circuit
  • Thevenize a bridge circuit

The Thevenin equivalent form of any two-terminal resistive circuit consists of an equivalent voltage source (V_{TH}) and an equivalent resistance (R_{TH}), arranged as shown in Figure 8–30. The values of the equivalent voltage and resistance depend on the values in the original circuit. Any resistive circuit can be simplified regardless of its complexity.

FIGURE 8–30

The general form of a Thevenin equivalent circuit is simply a nonideal voltage source. Any resistive circuit can be reduced to this form.

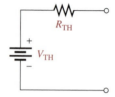

Thevenin's Equivalent Voltage (V_{TH}) and Equivalent Resistance (R_{TH})

The equivalent voltage, V_{TH}, is one part of the complete Thevenin equivalent circuit. The other part is R_{TH}.

> **The Thevenin equivalent voltage (V_{TH}) is the open circuit (no-load) voltage between two terminals in a circuit.**

Any component connected between these two terminals effectively "sees" V_{TH} in series with R_{TH}. As defined by **Thevenin's theorem,**

> **The Thevenin equivalent resistance (R_{TH}) is the total resistance appearing between two terminals in a given circuit with all sources replaced by their internal resistances.**

Terminal Equivalency

Although a Thevenin equivalent circuit is not the same as its original circuit, it acts the same in terms of the output voltage and current. Try the following demonstration as illustrated in Figure 8–31. Place a resistive circuit of any complexity in a box with only the output terminals exposed. Then place the Thevenin equivalent of that circuit in an identical box with, again, only the output terminals exposed. Connect identical load resistors across the output terminals of each box. Next connect a voltmeter and an ammeter to measure the voltage and current for each load as shown in the figure. The measured values will be identical (neglecting tolerance variations), and you will not be able to determine which box contains the original circuit and which contains the Thevenin equivalent. That is, in terms of your observations based on any electrical measurements, both circuits

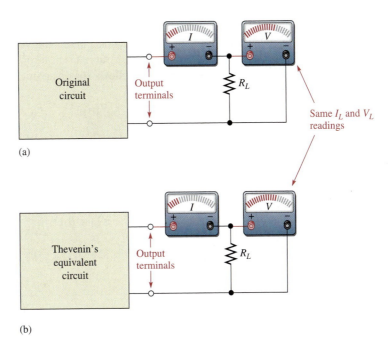

(a)

(b)

FIGURE 8–31
Which box contains the original circuit and which contains the Thevenin equivalent circuit? You cannot tell by observing the meters.

are the same. This condition is sometimes known as *terminal equivalency* because both circuits look the same from the "viewpoint" of the two output terminals.

The Thevenin Equivalent of a Circuit

To find the Thevenin equivalent of any circuit, determine the equivalent voltage, V_{TH}, and the equivalent resistance, R_{TH}, looking from the output terminals. As an example, the Thevenin equivalent for the circuit between terminals A and B is developed in Figure 8–32.

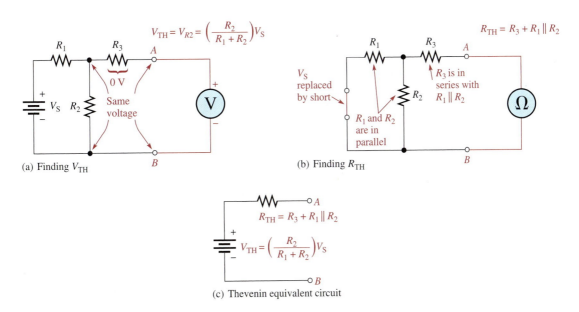

FIGURE 8–32
Example of the simplification of a circuit by Thevenin's theorem.

In Figure 8–32(a), the voltage across the designated points A and B is the Thevenin equivalent voltage. In this particular circuit, the voltage from A to B is the same as the voltage across R_2 because there is no current through R_3 and, therefore, no voltage drop across it. V_{TH} is expressed as follows for this particular example:

$$V_{TH} = \left(\frac{R_2}{R_1 + R_2}\right)V_S$$

In Figure 8–32(b), the resistance between points A and B with the source replaced by a short (zero internal resistance) is the Thevenin equivalent resistance. In this particular circuit, the resistance from A to B is R_3 in series with the parallel combination of R_1 and R_2. Therefore, R_{TH} is expressed as follows:

$$R_{TH} = R_3 + \frac{R_1 R_2}{R_1 + R_2}$$

The Thevenin equivalent circuit is shown in Figure 8–32(c).

EXAMPLE 8–10   Find the Thevenin equivalent between terminals A and B of the circuit in Figure 8–33.

FIGURE 8–33

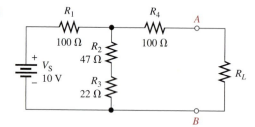

Solution   First, remove R_L. Then V_{TH} equals the voltage across $R_2 + R_3$ as shown in Figure 8–34(a). Use the voltage-divider principle to find V_{TH}.

$$V_{TH} = \left(\frac{R_2 + R_3}{R_1 + R_2 + R_3}\right)V_S = \left(\frac{69\ \Omega}{169\ \Omega}\right)10\ V = \textbf{4.08 V}$$

R_4 is in series with $R_1 \parallel (R_2 + R_3)$.

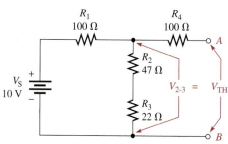

(a) The voltage from A to B is V_{TH} and equals $V_{2\text{-}3}$.

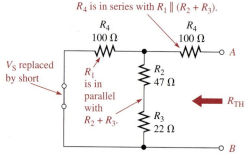

(b) Looking from terminals A and B, R_4 appears in series with the combination of R_1 in parallel with $(R_2 + R_3)$.

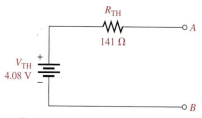

(c) Thevenin equivalent circuit

FIGURE 8–34

THEVENIN'S THEOREM ■ 279

To find R_{TH}, first replace the source with a short to simulate a zero internal resistance. Then R_1 appears in parallel with $R_2 + R_3$, and R_4 is in series with the series-parallel combination of R_1, R_2, and R_3 as indicated in Figure 8–34(b).

$$R_{TH} = R_4 + \frac{R_1(R_2 + R_3)}{R_1 + R_2 + R_3} = 100\ \Omega + \frac{(100\ \Omega)(69\ \Omega)}{169\ \Omega} = \mathbf{141\ \Omega}$$

The resulting Thevenin equivalent circuit is shown in Figure 8–34(c).

Related Problem Determine V_{TH} and R_{TH} if a 56 Ω resistor is connected in parallel across R_2 and R_3.

Thevenin Equivalency Depends on the Viewpoint

The Thevenin equivalent for any circuit depends on the location of the two terminals from between which the circuit is "viewed." In Figure 8–33, you viewed the circuit from between the two terminals labeled A and B. Any given circuit can have more than one Thevenin equivalent, depending on how the viewpoints are designated. For example, if you view the circuit in Figure 8–35 from between terminals A and C, you obtain a completely different result than if you viewed it from between terminals A and B or from between terminals B and C.

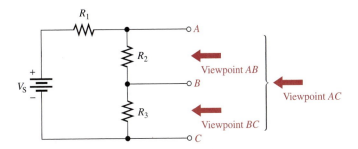

FIGURE 8–35
Thevenin's equivalent depends on viewpoint.

In Figure 8–36(a), when viewed from between terminals A and C, V_{TH} is the voltage across $R_2 + R_3$ and can be expressed using the voltage-divider formula as

$$V_{TH} = \left(\frac{R_2 + R_3}{R_1 + R_2 + R_3}\right)V_S$$

Also, as shown in Figure 8–36(b), the resistance between terminals A and C is $R_2 + R_3$ in parallel with R_1 (the source is replaced by a short) and can be expressed as

$$R_{TH} = \frac{R_1(R_2 + R_3)}{R_1 + R_2 + R_3}$$

The resulting Thevenin equivalent circuit is shown in Figure 8–36(c).

When viewed from between terminals B and C as indicated in Figure 8–36(d), V_{TH} is the voltage across R_3 and can be expressed as

$$V_{TH} = \left(\frac{R_3}{R_1 + R_2 + R_3}\right)V_S$$

As shown in Figure 8–36(e), the resistance between terminals B and C is R_3 in parallel with the series combination of R_1 and R_2.

$$R_{TH} = \frac{R_3(R_1 + R_2)}{R_1 + R_2 + R_3}$$

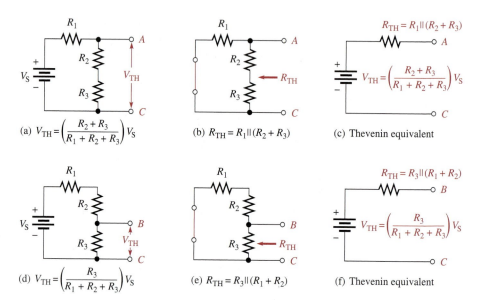

FIGURE 8–36

Example of circuit thevenized from two viewpoints, resulting in two different equivalent circuits. (The V_{TH} and R_{TH} are different.)

The resulting Thevenin equivalent is shown in Figure 8–36(f).

Thevenizing a Portion of a Circuit

In many cases, it helps to thevenize only a portion of a circuit. For example, when you need to know the equivalent circuit as viewed by one particular resistor in the circuit, you can remove the resistor and apply Thevenin's theorem to the remaining part of the circuit as viewed from the points between which that resistor was connected. Figure 8–37 illustrates the thevenizing of part of a circuit.

Using this type of approach, you can easily find the voltage and current for a specified resistor for any number of resistor values using only Ohm's law. This method eliminates the necessity of reanalyzing the original circuit for each different resistance value.

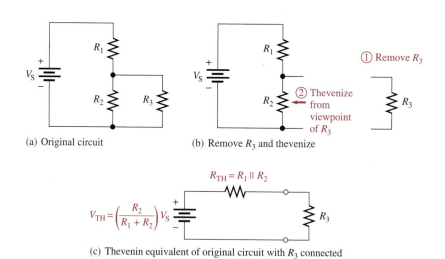

FIGURE 8–37

Example of thevenizing a portion of a circuit. In this case, the circuit is thevenized from the viewpoint of the load resistor, R_3.

Thevenizing a Bridge Circuit

The usefulness of Thevenin's theorem is perhaps best illustrated when it is applied to a Wheatstone bridge circuit. For example, when a load resistor is connected to the output terminals of a Wheatstone bridge, as shown in Figure 8–38, the circuit is very difficult to analyze because it is not a straightforward series-parallel arrangement. There are no resistors that are in series or in parallel with another resistor.

FIGURE 8–38

Wheatstone bridge with load resistor is not a series-parallel circuit.

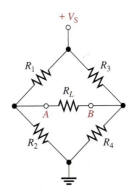

Using Thevenin's theorem, you can simplify the bridge circuit to an equivalent circuit viewed from the load resistor as shown step-by-step in Figure 8–39. Study carefully the steps in this figure. Once the equivalent circuit for the bridge is found, the voltage and current for any value of load resistor can easily be determined.

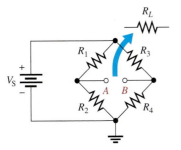

(a) Remove R_L.

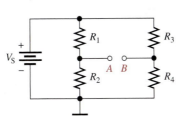

(b) Redraw to find V_{TH}.

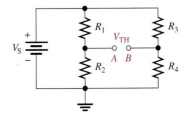

(c) $V_{TH} = V_A - V_B = \left(\dfrac{R_2}{R_1 + R_2} \right) V_S - \left(\dfrac{R_4}{R_3 + R_4} \right) V_S$

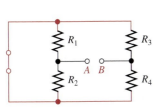

(d) Replace V_S with a short. *Note:* The red lines represent the same electrical point as the red lines in Part (e).

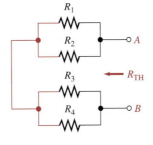

(e) Redraw to find R_{TH}:
$R_{TH} = R_1 \| R_2 + R_3 \| R_4$

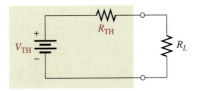

(f) Thevenin's equivalent with R_L reconnected

FIGURE 8–39

Simplifying a Wheatstone bridge with Thevenin's theorem.

EXAMPLE 8–11   Determine the voltage and current for the load resistor, R_L, in the bridge circuit of Figure 8–40.

FIGURE 8–40

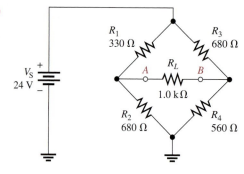

Solution

Step 1. Remove R_L.

Step 2. To thevenize the bridge as viewed from between terminals A and B, as was shown in Figure 8–39, first determine V_{TH}.

$$V_{TH} = V_A - V_B = \left(\frac{R_2}{R_1 + R_2}\right)V_S - \left(\frac{R_4}{R_3 + R_4}\right)V_S$$

$$= \left(\frac{680\ \Omega}{1010\ \Omega}\right)24\ \text{V} - \left(\frac{560\ \Omega}{1240\ \Omega}\right)24\ \text{V} = 16.16\ \text{V} - 10.84\ \text{V} = 5.32\ \text{V}$$

Step 3. Determine R_{TH}.

$$R_{TH} = \frac{R_1 R_2}{R_1 + R_2} + \frac{R_3 R_4}{R_3 + R_4}$$

$$= \frac{(330\ \Omega)(680\ \Omega)}{1010\ \Omega} + \frac{(680\ \Omega)(560\ \Omega)}{1240\ \Omega} = 222\ \Omega + 307\ \Omega = 529\ \Omega$$

Step 4. Place V_{TH} and R_{TH} in series to form the Thevenin equivalent circuit.

Step 5. Connect the load resistor from terminals A and B of the equivalent circuit, and determine the load voltage and current as illustrated in Figure 8–41.

FIGURE 8–41   Thevenin's equivalent for the Wheatstone bridge

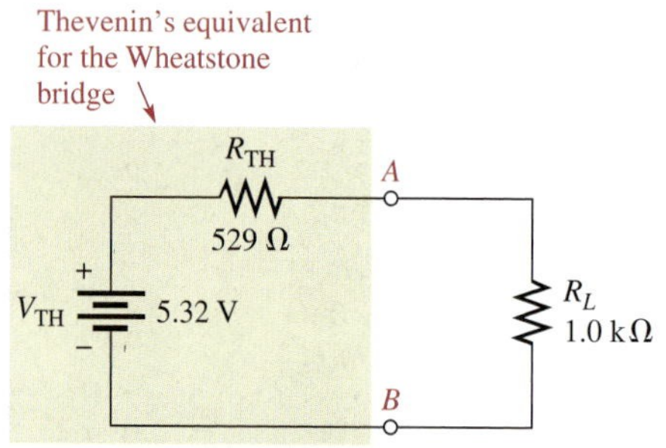

$$V_L = \left(\frac{R_L}{R_L + R_{TH}}\right)V_{TH} = \left(\frac{1.0\ \text{k}\Omega}{1.529\ \text{k}\Omega}\right)5.32\ \text{V} = \textbf{3.48 V}$$

$$I_L = \frac{V_L}{R_L} = \frac{3.48\ \text{V}}{1.0\ \text{k}\Omega} = \textbf{3.48 mA}$$

Related Problem   Calculate I_L for $R_1 = 2.2\ \text{k}\Omega$, $R_2 = 3.3\ \text{k}\Omega$, $R_3 = 3.9\ \text{k}\Omega$, and $R_4 = 2.7\ \text{k}\Omega$.

Summary of Thevenin's Theorem

Remember, the Thevenin equivalent circuit is *always* in the form of an equivalent voltage source in series with an equivalent resistance regardless of the original circuit that it replaces. The significance of Thevenin's theorem is that the equivalent circuit can replace the original circuit as far as any external load is concerned. Any load resistor connected between the terminals of a Thevenin equivalent circuit will have the same current through it and the same voltage across it as if it were connected to the terminals of the original circuit.

A summary of steps for applying Thevenin's theorem is as follows:

Step 1. Open the two terminals (remove any load) between which you want to find the Thevenin equivalent circuit.

Step 2. Determine the voltage (V_{TH}) across the two open terminals.

Step 3. Determine the resistance (R_{TH}) between the two open terminals with all sources replaced with their internal resistances (ideal voltage sources shorted and ideal current sources opened).

Step 4. Connect V_{TH} and R_{TH} in series to produce the complete Thevenin equivalent for the original circuit.

Step 5. Place the load resistor removed in Step 1 across the terminals of the Thevenin equivalent circuit. The load current can now be calculated using only Ohm's law, and it has the same value as the load current in the original circuit.

Determining V_{TH} and R_{TH} by Measurement

Thevenin's theorem is largely an analytical tool that is applied theoretically in order to simplify circuit analysis. However, in many cases, Thevenin's equivalent can be found for an actual circuit by the following general measurement methods. These steps are illustrated in Figure 8–42.

Step 1. Remove any load from the output terminals of the circuit.

Step 2. Measure the open terminal voltage. The voltmeter used must have an internal resistance much greater (at least 10 times greater) than the R_{TH} of the circuit. (V_{TH} is the open terminal voltage.)

Step 3. Connect a variable resistor (rheostat) across the output terminals. Its maximum value must be greater than R_{TH}.

Step 4. Adjust the rheostat and measure the terminal voltage. When the terminal voltage equals $0.5V_{TH}$, the resistance of the rheostat is equal to R_{TH}.

Step 5. Disconnect the rheostat from the terminals and measure its resistance with an ohmmeter. This measured resistance is equal to R_{TH}.

This procedure for determining R_{TH} differs from the theoretical procedure because it is impractical to short voltage sources or open current sources in an actual circuit. Also, when measuring R_{TH}, be certain that the circuit is capable of providing the required current to the variable resistor load and that the variable resistor can handle the required power. These considerations may make the procedure impractical in some cases.

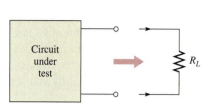

Step 1: Open the output terminals (remove load).

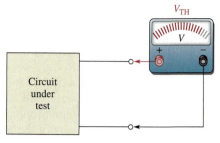

Step 2: Measure V_{TH}.

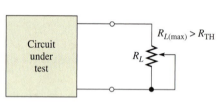

Step 3: Connect variable load resistance across the terminals.

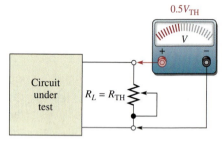

Step 4: Adjust R_L until $V_L = 0.5V_{TH}$.
When $V_L = 0.5V_{TH}$, $R_L = R_{TH}$.

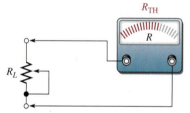

Step 5: Remove R_L and measure its resistance to get R_{TH}.

FIGURE 8–42

Determination of Thevenin's equivalent by measurement.

SECTION 8–5 REVIEW

1. What are the two components of a Thevenin equivalent circuit?
2. Draw the general form of a Thevenin equivalent circuit.
3. How is V_{TH} defined?
4. How is R_{TH} defined?
5. For the original circuit in Figure 8–43, draw the Thevenin equivalent circuit as viewed by R_L.

FIGURE 8–43

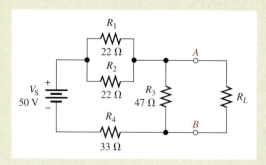

8–6 ■ NORTON'S THEOREM

Like Thevenin's theorem, Norton's theorem provides a method of reducing a more complex circuit to a simpler equivalent form. The basic difference is that Norton's theorem results in an equivalent current source in parallel with an equivalent resistance.

After completing this section, you should be able to

■ **Apply Norton's theorem to simplify a circuit**
  • Describe the form of a Norton equivalent circuit
  • Obtain the Norton equivalent current source
  • Obtain the Norton equivalent resistance

The form of Norton's equivalent circuit is shown in Figure 8–44. Regardless of how complex the original two-terminal circuit is, it can always be reduced to this equivalent form. The equivalent current source is designated I_N, and the equivalent resistance is designated R_N.

FIGURE 8–44
Form of Norton's equivalent circuit.

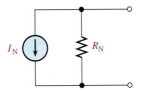

To apply **Norton's theorem,** you must know how to find the two quantities I_N and R_N. Once you know them for a given circuit, simply connect them in parallel to get the complete Norton circuit.

Norton's Equivalent Current (I_N)

As stated, I_N is one part of the complete Norton equivalent circuit; R_N is the other part.

> **Norton's equivalent current (I_N) is the short-circuit current between two terminals in a circuit.**

Any component connected between these two terminals effectively "sees" a current source of value I_N in parallel with R_N.

To illustrate, suppose that a resistive circuit of some kind has a resistor (R_L) connected between two terminals in the circuit, as shown in Figure 8–45(a). You want to find the Norton circuit that is equivalent to the one shown as "seen" by R_L. To find I_N, calculate the current between terminals A and B with these two terminals shorted, as shown in Figure 8–45(b). Example 8–12 demonstrates how to find I_N.

FIGURE 8–45
Determining the Norton equivalent current, I_N.

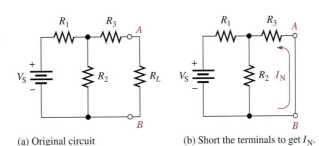

(a) Original circuit   (b) Short the terminals to get I_N.

EXAMPLE 8–12   Determine I_N for the circuit within the beige area in Figure 8–46(a).

FIGURE 8–46

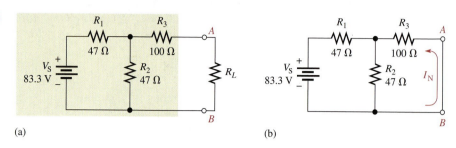

(a)   (b)

Solution   Short terminals A and B as shown in Figure 8–46(b). I_N is the current through the short and is calculated as follows. First, the total resistance seen by the voltage source is

$$R_T = R_1 + \frac{R_2 R_3}{R_2 + R_3} = 47\ \Omega + \frac{(47\ \Omega)(100\ \Omega)}{147\ \Omega} = 79\ \Omega$$

The total current from the source is

$$I_T = \frac{V_S}{R_T} = \frac{83.3\ \text{V}}{79\ \Omega} = 1.05\ \text{A}$$

Now apply the current-divider formula to find I_N (the current through the short).

$$I_N = \left(\frac{R_2}{R_2 + R_3}\right) I_T = \left(\frac{47\ \Omega}{147\ \Omega}\right) 1.05\ \text{A} = \mathbf{336\ mA}$$

This is the value for the equivalent Norton current source.

Related Problem   Determine I_N in Figure 8–46(a) if all the resistor values are doubled.

Norton's Equivalent Resistance (R_N)

Norton's equivalent resistance (R_N) is defined in the same way as R_{TH}.

> **The Norton equivelent resistance, R_N, is the total resistance appearing between two terminals in a given circuit with all sources replaced by their internal resistances.**

Example 8–13 demonstrates how to find R_N.

EXAMPLE 8–13   Find R_N for the circuit within the beige area of Figure 8–46(a) (see Example 8–12).

Solution   First reduce V_S to zero by shorting it, as shown in Figure 8–47. Looking in at terminals A and B, you can see that the parallel combination of R_1 and R_2 is in series with R_3. Thus,

$$R_N = R_3 + \frac{R_1}{2} = 100\ \Omega + \frac{47\ \Omega}{2} = \mathbf{124\ \Omega}$$

FIGURE 8–47

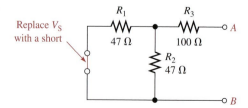

Related Problem   Determine R_N in Figure 8–46(a) if all the resistor values are doubled.

Examples 8–12 and 8–13 showed how to find the two equivalent components of a Norton equivalent circuit, I_N and R_N. Keep in mind that these values can be found for any linear circuit. Once these are known, they must be connected in parallel to form the Norton equivalent circuit, as illustrated in Example 8–14.

EXAMPLE 8–14

Draw the complete Norton equivalent circuit for the original circuit in Figure 8–46(a) (Example 8–12).

Solution In Examples 8–12 and 8–13 you found that I_N = 336 mA and R_N = 124 Ω. The Norton equivalent circuit is shown in Figure 8–48.

FIGURE 8–48

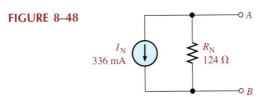

Related Problem Find R_N for the circuit in Figure 8–46(a) if all the resistor values are doubled.

Summary of Norton's Theorem

Any load resistor connected between the output terminals of a Norton equivalent circuit will have the same current through it and the same voltage across it as if it were connected to the output terminals of the original circuit. A summary of steps for theoretically applying Norton's theorem is as follows:

Step 1. Short the two terminals between which you want to find the Norton equivalent circuit.

Step 2. Determine the current (I_N) through the shorted terminals.

Step 3. Determine the resistance (R_N) between the two open terminals with all sources replaced with their internal resistances (ideal voltage sources shorted and ideal current sources opened). $R_N = R_{TH}$.

Step 4. Connect I_N and R_N in parallel to produce the complete Norton equivalent for the original circuit.

Norton's equivalent circuit can also be derived from Thevenin's equivalent circuit by use of the source conversion method discussed in Section 8–3.

SECTION 8–6 REVIEW

1. What are the two components of a Norton equivalent circuit?
2. Draw the general form of a Norton equivalent circuit.
3. How is I_N defined?
4. How is R_N defined?
5. Find the Norton circuit as seen by R_L in Figure 8–49.

FIGURE 8–49

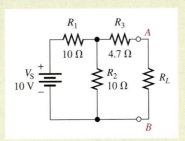

8–7 ■ MAXIMUM POWER TRANSFER THEOREM

The maximum power transfer theorem is important when you need to know the value of the load at which the most power is delivered from the source.

After completing this section, you should be able to

■ **Apply the maximum power transfer theorem**
  • State the theorem
  • Determine the value of load resistance for which maximum power is transferred from a given circuit

The **maximum power transfer** theorem is stated as follows:

> **When a source is connected to a load, maximum power is delivered to the load when the load resistance is equal to the internal source resistance.**

The source resistance, R_S, of a circuit is the equivalent resistance as viewed from the output terminals using Thevenin's theorem. An equivalent circuit with its output resistance and load is shown in Figure 8–50. When $R_L = R_S$, the maximum power possible is transferred from the voltage source to R_L.

FIGURE 8–50

Maximum power is transferred to the load when $R_L = R_S$.

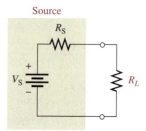

Practical applications of this theorem include audio systems such as stereo, radio, and public address. In these systems the resistance of the speaker is the load. The circuit that drives the speaker is a power amplifier. The systems are typically optimized for maximum power to the speakers. Thus, the resistance of the speaker must equal the internal source resistance of the amplifier.

Example 8–15 shows that maximum power occurs when $R_L = R_S$.

EXAMPLE 8–15

The source in Figure 8–51 has an internal source resistance of 75 Ω. Determine the load power for each of the following values of load resistance:
(a) 25 Ω   **(b)** 50 Ω   **(c)** 75 Ω   **(d)** 100 Ω   **(e)** 125 Ω
Draw a graph showing the load power versus the load resistance.

FIGURE 8–51

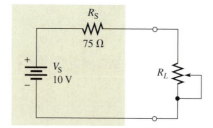

Solution Use Ohm's law ($I = V/R$) and the power formula ($P = I^2R$) to find the load power, P_L, for each value of load resistance.

(a) For $R_L = 25\ \Omega$,

$$I = \frac{V_S}{R_S + R_L} = \frac{10\ \text{V}}{75\ \Omega + 25\ \Omega} = 100\ \text{mA}$$
$$P_L = I^2R_L = (100\ \text{mA})^2(25\ \Omega) = \textbf{250 mW}$$

(b) For $R_L = 50\ \Omega$,

$$I = \frac{V_S}{R_S + R_L} = \frac{10\ \text{V}}{125\ \Omega} = 80\ \text{mA}$$
$$P_L = I^2R_L = (80\ \text{mA})^2(50\ \Omega) = \textbf{320 mW}$$

(c) For $R_L = 75\ \Omega$,

$$I = \frac{V_S}{R_S + R_L} = \frac{10\ \text{V}}{150\ \Omega} = 66.7\ \text{mA}$$
$$P_L = I^2R_L = (66.7\ \text{mA})^2(75\ \Omega) = \textbf{334 mW}$$

(d) For $R_L = 100\ \Omega$,

$$I = \frac{V_S}{R_S + R_L} = \frac{10\ \text{V}}{175\ \Omega} = 57.1\ \text{mA}$$
$$P_L = I^2R_L = (57.1\ \text{mA})^2(100\ \Omega) = \textbf{326 mW}$$

(e) For $R_L = 125\ \Omega$,

$$I = \frac{V_S}{R_S + R_L} = \frac{10\ \text{V}}{200\ \Omega} = 50\ \text{mA}$$
$$P_L = I^2R_L = (50\ \text{mA})^2(125\ \Omega) = \textbf{313 mW}$$

Notice that the load power is greatest when $R_L = 75\ \Omega$, which is the same as the internal source resistance. When the load resistance is less than or greater than this value, the power drops off, as the curve in Figure 8–52 graphically illustrates.

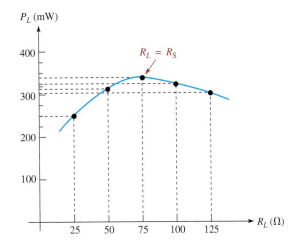

FIGURE 8–52
Curve showing that the load power is maximum when $R_L = R_S$.

Related Problem If the source resistance in Figure 8–51 is 600 Ω, what is the maximum power than can be delivered to a load?

SECTION 8–7
REVIEW

1. State the maximum power transfer theorem.

2. When is maximum power delivered from a source to a load?

3. A given circuit has an internal source resistance of 50 Ω. What will be the value of the load to which the maximum power is delivered?

8–8 ■ DELTA-TO-WYE (Δ-TO-Y) AND WYE-TO-DELTA (Y-TO-Δ) CONVERSIONS

Conversions between delta-type and wye-type network arrangements are useful in certain specialized three-terminal applications. One example is in the analysis of a loaded Wheatstone bridge circuit. In this section, the conversion formulas and rules for remembering them are given.

After completing this section, you should be able to

■ **Perform Δ-to-Y and Y-to-Δ conversions**
  • Apply Δ-to-Y conversion to a bridge circuit

A resistive delta (Δ) network is a three-terminal arrangement as shown in Figure 8–53(a). A wye (Y) network is shown in Figure 8–53(b). Notice that letter subscripts are used to designate resistors in the delta network and that numerical subscripts are used to designate resistors in the wye network.

FIGURE 8–53
Delta and wye networks.

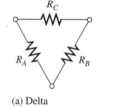

(a) Delta   (b) Wye

Δ-to-Y Conversion

It is convenient to think of the wye positioned within the delta, as shown in Figure 8–54. To convert from delta to wye, you need R_1, R_2, and R_3 in terms of R_A, R_B, and R_C. The conversion rule is as follows:

> **Each resistor in the wye is equal to the product of the resistors in two adjacent delta branches, divided by the sum of all three delta resistors.**

FIGURE 8–54
"Y within Δ" aid for conversion formulas.

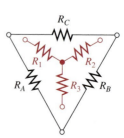

In Figure 8–54, R_A and R_C are adjacent to R_1; therefore,

$$R_1 = \frac{R_A R_C}{R_A + R_B + R_C} \qquad \text{(8–1)}$$

Also, R_B and R_C are adjacent to R_2, so

$$R_2 = \frac{R_B R_C}{R_A + R_B + R_C} \qquad \text{(8–2)}$$

and R_A and R_B are adjacent to R_3, so

$$R_3 = \frac{R_A R_B}{R_A + R_B + R_C} \qquad \text{(8–3)}$$

Y-to-Δ Conversion

To convert from wye to delta, you need R_A, R_B, and R_C in terms of R_1, R_2, and R_3. The conversion rule is as follows:

Each resistor in the delta is equal to the sum of all possible products of wye resistors taken two at a time, divided by the opposite wye resistor.

In Figure 8–54, R_2 is opposite to R_A; therefore,

$$R_A = \frac{R_1 R_2 + R_1 R_3 + R_2 R_3}{R_2} \qquad \text{(8–4)}$$

Also, R_1 is opposite to R_B, so

$$R_B = \frac{R_1 R_2 + R_1 R_3 + R_2 R_3}{R_1} \qquad \text{(8–5)}$$

and R_3 is opposite to R_C, so

$$R_C = \frac{R_1 R_2 + R_1 R_3 + R_2 R_3}{R_3} \qquad \text{(8–6)}$$

The following two examples illustrate conversion between these two forms of networks.

EXAMPLE 8–16   Convert the delta network in Figure 8–55 to a wye network.

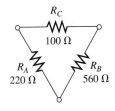

FIGURE 8–55

Solution Use Equations (8–1), (8–2), and (8–3).

$$R_1 = \frac{R_A R_C}{R_A + R_B + R_C} = \frac{(220\ \Omega)(100\ \Omega)}{220\ \Omega + 560\ \Omega + 100\ \Omega} = \mathbf{25\ \Omega}$$

$$R_2 = \frac{R_B R_C}{R_A + R_B + R_C} = \frac{(560\ \Omega)(100\ \Omega)}{880\ \Omega} = \mathbf{63.6\ \Omega}$$

$$R_3 = \frac{R_A R_B}{R_A + R_B + R_C} = \frac{(220\ \Omega)(560\ \Omega)}{880\ \Omega} = \mathbf{140\ \Omega}$$

The resulting wye network is shown in Figure 8–56.

FIGURE 8–56

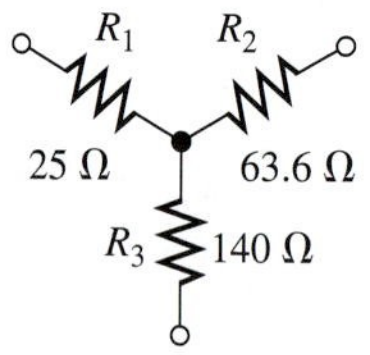

R_1 R_2
25 Ω 63.6 Ω
R_3 140 Ω

Related Problem Convert the delta network to a wye network for R_A = 2.2 kΩ, R_B = 1.0 kΩ, and R_C = 1.8 kΩ.

EXAMPLE 8–17 Convert the wye network in Figure 8–57 to a delta network.

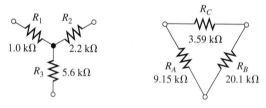

R_1 R_2
1.0 kΩ 2.2 kΩ
R_3 5.6 kΩ

R_C
3.59 kΩ
R_A R_B
9.15 kΩ 20.1 kΩ

FIGURE 8–57   **FIGURE 8–58**

Solution Use Equations (8–4), (8–5), and (8–6).

$$R_A = \frac{R_1 R_2 + R_1 R_3 + R_2 R_3}{R_2}$$

$$= \frac{(1.0\ \text{k}\Omega)(2.2\ \text{k}\Omega) + (1.0\ \text{k}\Omega)(5.6\ \text{k}\Omega) + (2.2\ \text{k}\Omega)(5.6\ \text{k}\Omega)}{2.2\ \text{k}\Omega} = \mathbf{9.15\ k\Omega}$$

$$R_B = \frac{R_1 R_2 + R_1 R_3 + R_2 R_3}{R_1}$$

$$= \frac{(1.0\ \text{k}\Omega)(2.2\ \text{k}\Omega) + (1.0\ \text{k}\Omega)(5.6\ \text{k}\Omega) + (2.2\ \text{k}\Omega)(5.6\ \text{k}\Omega)}{1.0\ \text{k}\Omega} = \mathbf{20.1\ k\Omega}$$

$$R_C = \frac{R_1 R_2 + R_1 R_3 + R_2 R_3}{R_3}$$

$$= \frac{(1.0\ \text{k}\Omega)(2.2\ \text{k}\Omega) + (1.0\ \text{k}\Omega)(5.6\ \text{k}\Omega) + (2.2\ \text{k}\Omega)(5.6\ \text{k}\Omega)}{5.6\ \text{k}\Omega} = \mathbf{3.59\ k\Omega}$$

The resulting delta network is shown in Figure 8–58.

Related Problem Convert the wye network to a delta network for R_1 = 100 Ω, R_2 = 330 Ω, and R_3 = 470 Ω.

Application of Δ-to-Y Conversion to the Simplification of a Bridge Circuit

In Section 8–5 you learned how Thevenin's theorem can be used to simplify a bridge circuit. Now you will see how Δ-to-Y conversion can be used for converting a bridge circuit to a series-parallel form for easier analysis.

Figure 8–59 illustrates how the delta (Δ) formed by R_A, R_B, and R_C can be converted to a wye (Y), thus creating an equivalent series-parallel circuit. Equations (8–1), (8–2), and (8–3) are used in this conversion.

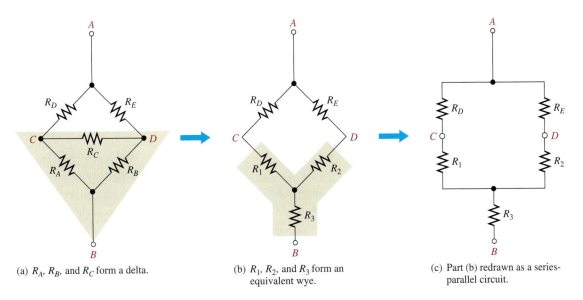

(a) R_A, R_B, and R_C form a delta.

(b) R_1, R_2, and R_3 form an equivalent wye.

(c) Part (b) redrawn as a series-parallel circuit.

FIGURE 8–59
Conversion of a bridge circuit to a series-parallel configuration.

In a bridge circuit, the load is connected across points C and D. In Figure 8–59(a), R_C represents the load resistor. When voltage is applied across points A and B, the voltage from C to D (V_{CD}) can be determined using the equivalent series-parallel circuit in Figure 8–59(c) as follows. The total resistance from point A to point B is

$$R_T = \frac{(R_1 + R_D)(R_2 + R_E)}{(R_1 + R_D) + (R_2 + R_E)} + R_3$$

Then,

$$I_T = \frac{V_{AB}}{R_T}$$

The resistance of the parallel portion of the circuit in Figure 8–59(c) is

$$R_{T(p)} = \frac{(R_1 + R_D)(R_2 + R_E)}{(R_1 + R_D) + (R_2 + R_E)}$$

The current through the left branch is

$$I_{AC} = \left(\frac{R_{T(p)}}{R_1 + R_D}\right) I_T$$

The current through the right branch is

$$I_{AD} = \left(\frac{R_{T(p)}}{R_2 + R_E}\right) I_T$$

The voltage at point C with respect to point A is

$$V_{CA} = V_A - I_{AC}R_D$$

The voltage at point D with respect to point A is

$$V_{DA} = V_A - I_{AD}R_E$$

The voltage from point C to point D is

$$V_{CD} = V_{CA} - V_{DA}$$
$$= (V_A - I_{AC}R_D) - (V_A - I_{AD}R_E) = I_{AD}R_E - I_{AC}R_D$$

V_{CD} is the voltage across the load (R_C) in the bridge circuit of Figure 8–59(a). The load current through R_C can be found by Ohm's law.

$$I_{R_C} = \frac{V_{CD}}{R_C}$$

EXAMPLE 8–18

Determine the voltage across the load resistor and the current through the load resistor in the bridge circuit in Figure 8–60. Notice that the resistors are labeled for convenient conversion using Equations (8–1), (8–2), and (8–3). R_C is the load resistor.

FIGURE 8–60

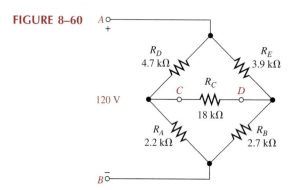

Solution First, convert the delta formed by R_A, R_B, and R_C to a wye.

$$R_1 = \frac{R_A R_C}{R_A + R_B + R_C} = \frac{(2.2\ \text{k}\Omega)(18\ \text{k}\Omega)}{2.2\ \text{k}\Omega + 2.7\ \text{k}\Omega + 18\ \text{k}\Omega} = 1.73\ \text{k}\Omega$$

$$R_2 = \frac{R_B R_C}{R_A + R_B + R_C} = \frac{(2.7\ \text{k}\Omega)(18\ \text{k}\Omega)}{22.9\ \text{k}\Omega} = 2.12\ \text{k}\Omega$$

$$R_3 = \frac{R_A R_B}{R_A + R_B + R_C} = \frac{(2.2\ \text{k}\Omega)(2.7\ \text{k}\Omega)}{22.9\ \text{k}\Omega} = 259\ \Omega$$

The resulting equivalent series-parallel circuit is shown in Figure 8–61. Next, determine R_T and the branch currents in Figure 8–61.

$$R_T = \frac{(R_1 + R_D)(R_2 + R_E)}{(R_1 + R_D) + (R_2 + R_E)} + R_3$$

$$= \frac{(6.43\ \text{k}\Omega)(6.02\ \text{k}\Omega)}{6.43\ \text{k}\Omega + 6.02\ \text{k}\Omega} + 259\ \Omega = 3.11\ \text{k}\Omega + 259\ \Omega = 3.37\ \text{k}\Omega$$

$$I_T = \frac{V_{AB}}{R_T} = \frac{120\ \text{V}}{3.37\ \text{k}\Omega} = 35.6\ \text{mA}$$

FIGURE 8–61

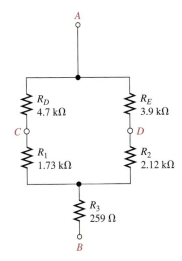

The total resistance of the parallel part of the circuit, $R_{T(p)}$, is 3.11 kΩ.

$$I_{AC} = \left(\frac{R_{T(p)}}{R_1 + R_D}\right)I_T = \left(\frac{3.11\ k\Omega}{1.73\ k\Omega + 4.7\ k\Omega}\right)35.6\ mA = 17.2\ mA$$

$$I_{AD} = \left(\frac{R_{T(p)}}{R_2 + R_E}\right)I_T = \left(\frac{3.11\ k\Omega}{2.12\ k\Omega + 3.9\ k\Omega}\right)35.6\ mA = 18.4\ mA$$

The voltage from point C to point D is

$$V_{CD} = I_{AD}R_E - I_{AC}R_D = (18.4\ mA)(3.9\ k\Omega) - (17.2\ mA)(4.7\ k\Omega)$$
$$= 71.8\ V - 80.8\ V = -9\ V$$

V_{CD} is the voltage across the load (R_C) in the bridge circuit shown in Figure 8–60.
The load current through R_C is

$$I_{R_C} = \frac{V_{CD}}{R_C} = \frac{-9\ V}{18\ k\Omega} = -500\ \mu A$$

Related Problem Determine the load current, I_{R_C}, in Figure 8–60 for the following resistor values: $R_A = 27\ k\Omega$, $R_B = 33\ k\Omega$, $R_D = 39\ k\Omega$, $R_E = 47\ k\Omega$, and $R_C = 100\ k\Omega$.

**SECTION 8–8
REVIEW**

1. Sketch a delta circuit.
2. Sketch a wye circuit.
3. Write the formulas for delta-to-wye conversion.
4. Write the formulas for wye-to-delta conversion.

8–9 ■ TECHnology Theory Into Practice

The Wheatstone bridge circuit was covered in Chapter 7. In this section, you will work with a bridge that is to be used in a temperature-measuring circuit in which a device called a thermistor is the temperature sensor. You will be doing a preliminary analysis of the circuit in which Thevenin's theorem can be used to advantage.

The Wheatstone bridge circuit will be used in a temperature-sensing application where the temperature of a liquid that is used in a certain industrial process is monitored using a thermistor in one leg of the bridge. The **thermistor** used in this application is a temperature-sensing resistor with a negative temperature coefficient in which the resistance decreases as temperature increases.

When a certain preset temperature is reached, the bridge becomes balanced and its output voltage is zero. This zero-voltage condition is detected by a high-gain amplifier circuit that operates a relay to turn off the heating element. As the temperature decreases below the preset value, the bridge again becomes unbalanced causing the amplifier to close the relay and turn the heating element back on. This process maintains the temperature of the liquid in a tank within defined limits.

The amplifier effectively has an internal resistance of 10 kΩ between its input terminals. You do not need to know any additional details of the amplifier circuit in this assignment because you are to concentrate only on the bridge circuit. The study of amplifiers will come in a later course.

The Wheatstone bridge control and temperature-measuring circuit is shown in Figure 8–62. The amplifier and relay circuitry is to be connected across the bridge between terminals A and B as indicated, so there will be a 10 kΩ load between these terminals. The thermistor is connected in one leg of the bridge but is remotely located in the tank and away from the rest of the circuit. The variable resistor, R_2, is used to set the desired temperature at which the liquid in the tank will be maintained. The temperature characteristics of the thermistor, shown in the graph of Figure 8–63, indicates how the resistance of the thermistor changes with temperature.

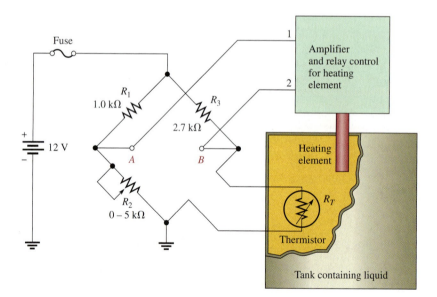

FIGURE 8–62
Wheatstone bridge control and temperature-measuring circuit.

The Wheatstone bridge is built on a PC board as shown in Figure 8–64(a). A probe-type thermistor is inserted through the wall of the tank and into the liquid as indicated in part (b); the circuit is powered by a 12 V battery shown in part (c). The amplifier and relay circuitry is housed in a separate module that is not shown.

The Printed Circuit Board

■ Check the PC board to make sure that it agrees with the schematic in Figure 8–62. Relate each input, output, and component on the board to the schematic.

FIGURE 8–63
Graph of thermistor resistance versus temperature.

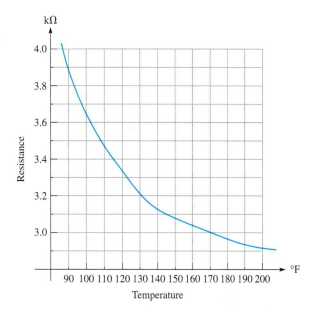

FIGURE 8–64

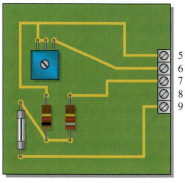

(a) Circuit board

(b) Thermister inserted in the tank

(c) Battery

Wiring List

■ Develop a point-to-point wiring list to properly interconnect the elements in Figure 8–62. Although it is not shown, include the amplifier inputs (call them Amp 1 and Amp 2).

Balancing the Bridge

■ From the graph in Figure 8–63, calculate the resistance value to which R_2 must be set in order to balance the bridge at 170°F.

Analysis

■ Assume that R_2 is adjusted for balance at 170°F. Using Thevenin's theorem, determine the voltage across the thermistor and the current through the thermistor for each of the following temperatures: 90°, 100°, 110°, 120°, 130°, 140°, 150°, 160°, 170°, 180°, 190°, and 200°. These data could be used to evaluate the power dissipation requirements for the thermistor based on a derating formula.

■ In Figure 8–65, determine the approximate temperature in the tank for each of the voltages indicated by the voltmeter. R_2 is set at 1.5 kΩ. Assume the board is completely connected according to the wiring list that you developed although, for simplicity, the wiring is not shown. Also, assume the meter presents no load to the bridge circuit.

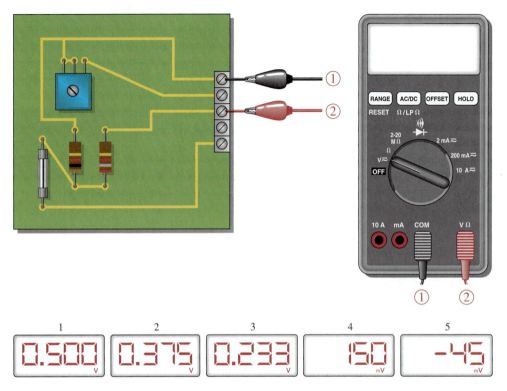

1	2	3	4	5
0.500 V	0.375 V	0.233 V	150 mV	-45 mV

FIGURE 8–65

SECTION 8–9 REVIEW

1. Discuss the purpose of the thermistor.
2. In the system diagram of Figure 8–62, when does the heating element turn on?

■ **SUMMARY**

■ An ideal voltage source has zero internal resistance. It provides a constant voltage across its terminals regardless of the load resistance.

■ A practical voltage source has a nonzero internal resistance.

■ An ideal current source has infinite internal resistance. It provides a constant current regardless of the load resistance.

■ A practical current source has a finite internal resistance.

■ The superposition theorem is useful for multiple-source circuits.

■ Thevenin's theorem provides for the reduction of any two-terminal linear resistive circuit to an equivalent form consisting of an equivalent voltage source in series with an equivalent resistance.

■ The term *equivalency,* as used in Thevenin's and Norton's theorems, means that when a given load resistance is connected to the equivalent circuit, it will have the same voltage across it and the same current through it as when it was connected to the original circuit.

■ Norton's theorem provides for the reduction of any two-terminal linear resistive circuit to an equivalent form consisting of an equivalent current source in parallel with an equivalent resistance.

■ Maximum power is transferred to a load from a source when the load resistance equals the internal source resistance.

■ GLOSSARY

These terms are also in the end-of-book glossary.

Current source   A device that ideally provides a constant value of current regardless of the load.

Maximum power transfer theorem   A theorem that states the maximum power is transferred from a source to a load when the load resistance equals the internal source resistance.

Norton's theorem   A method for simplifying a two-terminal linear circuit to an equivalent circuit with only a current source in parallel with a resistance.

Superposition theorem   A method for the analysis of circuits with more than one source.

Terminal equivalency   The concept that when any given load resistance is connected to two sources, the same load voltage and load current are produced by both sources.

Thermistor   A temperature-sensitive resistor.

Thevenin's theorem   A method for simplifying a two-terminal linear circuit to an equivalent circuit with only a voltage source in series with a resistance.

Voltage source   A device that ideally provides a constant value of voltage regardless of the load.

■ FORMULAS

Δ-to-Y Conversions

(8–1) $$R_1 = \frac{R_A R_C}{R_A + R_B + R_C}$$

(8–2) $$R_2 = \frac{R_B R_C}{R_A + R_B + R_C}$$

(8–3) $$R_3 = \frac{R_A R_B}{R_A + R_B + R_C}$$

Y-to-Δ Conversions

(8–4) $$R_A = \frac{R_1 R_2 + R_1 R_3 + R_2 R_3}{R_2}$$

(8–5) $$R_B = \frac{R_1 R_2 + R_1 R_3 + R_2 R_3}{R_1}$$

(8–6) $$R_C = \frac{R_1 R_2 + R_1 R_3 + R_2 R_3}{R_3}$$

■ SELF-TEST

1. A 100 Ω load is connected across an ideal voltage source with $V_S = 10$ V. The voltage across the load is

   (a) 0 V   (b) 10 V   (c) 100 V

2. A 100 Ω load is connected across a voltage source with $V_S = 10$ V and $R_S = 10$ Ω. The voltage across the load is

   (a) 10 V   (b) 0 V   (c) 9.09 V   (d) 0.909 V

3. A certain voltage source has the values $V_S = 25$ V and $R_S = 5$ Ω. The values for an equivalent current source are

   (a) 5 A, 5 Ω   (b) 25 A, 5 Ω   (c) 5 A, 125 Ω

4. A certain current source has the values $I_S = 3$ μA and $R_S = 1.0$ MΩ. The values for an equivalent voltage source are

   (a) 3 μV, 1.0 MΩ   (b) 3 V, 1.0 MΩ   (c) 1 V, 3.0 MΩ

5. In a two-source circuit, one source acting alone produces 10 mA through a given branch. The other source acting alone produces 8 mA in the opposite direction through the same branch. The actual current through the branch is

   (a) 10 mA   (b) 18 mA   (c) 8 mA   (d) 2 mA

6. Thevenin's theorem converts a circuit to an equivalent form consisting of
   (a) a current source and a series resistance
   (b) a voltage source and a parallel resistance
   (c) a voltage source and a series resistance
   (d) a current source and a parallel resistance

7. The Thevenin equivalent voltage for a given circuit is found by
   (a) shorting the output terminals
   (b) opening the output terminals
   (c) shorting the voltage source
   (d) removing the voltage source and replacing it with a short

8. A certain circuit produces 15 V across its open output terminals, and when a 10 kΩ load is connected across its output terminals, it produces 12 V. The Thevenin equivalent for this circuit is
   (a) 15 V in series with 10 kΩ   (b) 12 V in series with 10 kΩ
   (c) 12 V in series with 2.5 kΩ   (d) 15 V in series with 2.5 kΩ

9. Maximum power is transferred from a source to a load when
   (a) the load resistance is very large
   (b) the load resistance is very small
   (c) the load resistance is twice the source resistance
   (d) the load resistance equals the source resistance

10. For the circuit described in Question 8, maximum power is transferred to a
    (a) 10 kΩ load   (b) 2.5 kΩ load   (c) an infinitely large resistance load

---

■ PROBLEMS

More difficult problems are indicated by an asterisk (*).

SECTION 8–3 Source Conversions

1. A voltage source has the values V_S = 300 V and R_S = 50 Ω. Convert it to an equivalent current source.

2. Convert the practical voltage sources in Figure 8–66 to equivalent current sources.

FIGURE 8–66

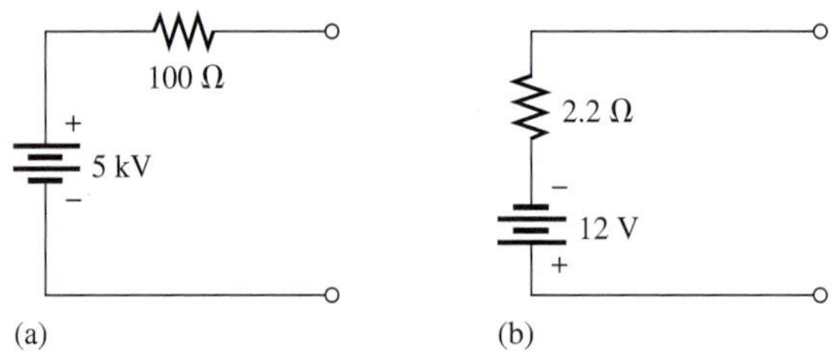

100 Ω

+
5 kV
–

(a)

2.2 Ω

–
12 V
+

(b)

3. A current source has an I_S of 600 mA and an R_S of 1.2 kΩ. Convert it to an equivalent voltage source.

4. Convert the practical current sources in Figure 8–67 to equivalent voltage sources.

FIGURE 8–67

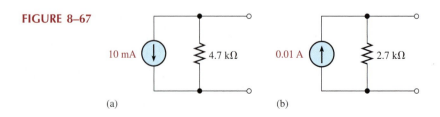

10 mA   4.7 kΩ

(a)

0.01 A   2.7 kΩ

(b)

SECTION 8–4 The Superposition Theorem

5. Using the superposition method, calculate the current through R_5 in Figure 8–68.

6. Use the superposition theorem to find the current in and the voltage across the R_2 branch of Figure 8–68.

FIGURE 8–68

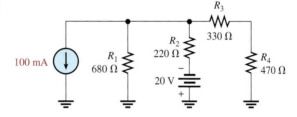

7. Using the superposition theorem, solve for the current through R_3 in Figure 8–69.

FIGURE 8–69

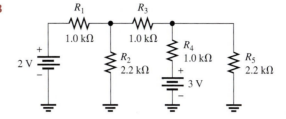

8. Using the superposition theorem, find the load current in each circuit of Figure 8–70.

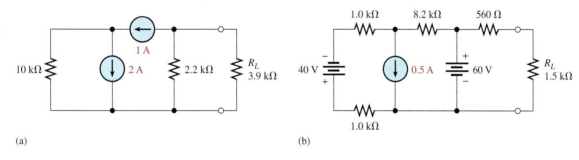

(a)   (b)

FIGURE 8–70

*9. Determine the voltage from point A to point B in Figure 8–71.

FIGURE 8–71

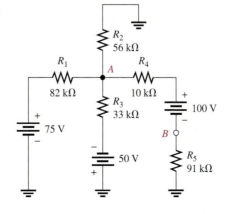

10. The switches in Figure 8–72 are closed in sequence, SW1 first. Find the current through R_4 after each switch closure.

FIGURE 8–72

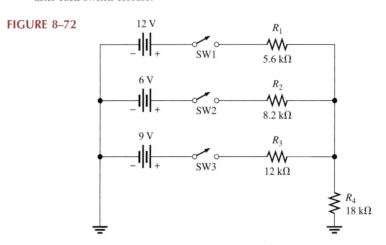

FIGURE 8–72

*11. Figure 8–73 shows two ladder networks. Determine the current provided by each of the batteries when terminals A are connected (A to A) and terminals B are connected (B to B).

FIGURE 8–73

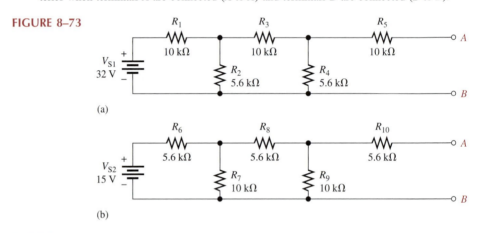

SECTION 8–5 Thevenin's Theorem

12. For each circuit in Figure 8–74, determine the Thevenin equivalent as seen by R_L.

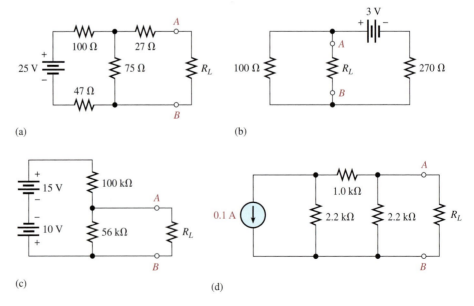

FIGURE 8–74

13. Using Thevenin's theorem, determine the current through the load R_L in Figure 8–75.

FIGURE 8–75

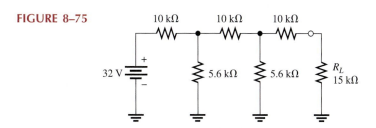

*14. Using Thevenin's theorem, find the voltage across R_4 in Figure 8–76.

FIGURE 8–76

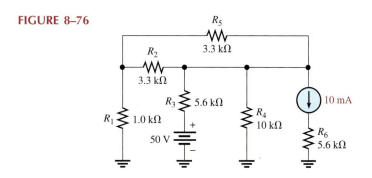

15. Find the Thevenin equivalent for the circuit external to the amplifier in Figure 8–77.

FIGURE 8–77

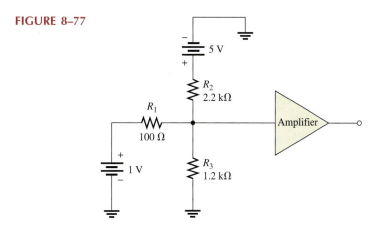

16. Determine the current into point A when R_8 is 1.0 kΩ, 5 kΩ, and 10 kΩ in Figure 8–78.

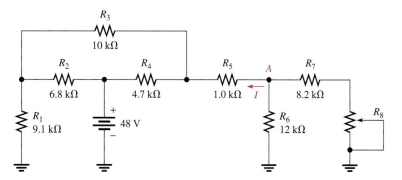

FIGURE 8–78

*17. Find the current through the load resistor in the bridge circuit of Figure 8–79.

18. Determine the Thevenin equivalent looking from terminals A and B for the circuit in Figure 8–80.

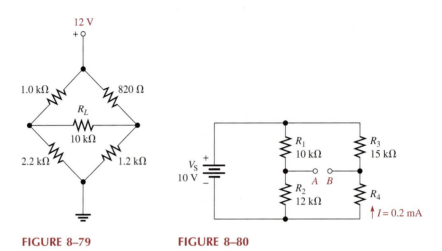

FIGURE 8–79   **FIGURE 8–80**

SECTION 8–6   Norton's Theorem

19. For each circuit in Figure 8–74, determine the Norton equivalent as seen by R_L.

20. Using Norton's theorem, find the current through the load resistor R_L in Figure 8–75.

*21. Using Norton's theorem, find the voltage across R_5 in Figure 8–76.

22. Using Norton's theorem, find the current through R_1 in Figure 8–78 when $R_8 = 8$ kΩ.

23. Determine the Norton equivalent circuit for the bridge in Figure 8–79 with R_L removed.

24. Reduce the circuit between terminals A and B in Figure 8–81 to its Norton equivalent.

FIGURE 8–81

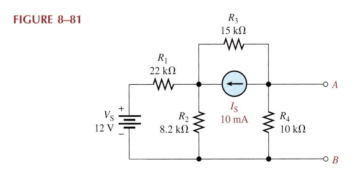

25. Apply Norton's theorem to the circuit of Figure 8–82.

FIGURE 8–82

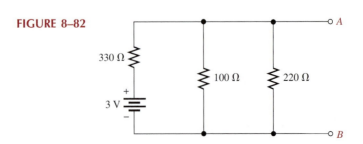

SECTION 8–7   Maximum Power Transfer Theorem

26. For each circuit in Figure 8–83, maximum power is to be transferred to the load R_L. Determine the appropriate value for R_L in each case.

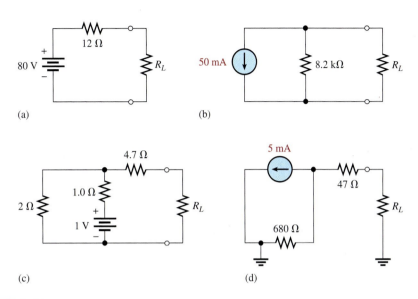

FIGURE 8–83

27. Determine the value of R_L for maximum power in Figure 8–84.

FIGURE 8–84

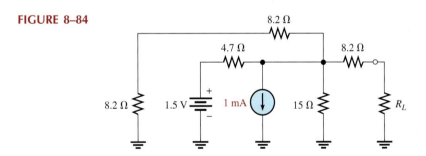

*28. How much power is delivered to the load when R_L is 10% higher than its value for maximum power in Figure 8–84.

*29. What are the values of R_4 and R_{TH} when the maximum power is transferred from the thevenized source to the ladder network in Figure 8–85?

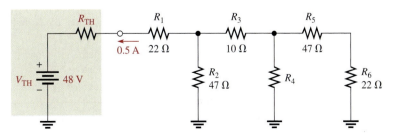

FIGURE 8–85

SECTION 8–8   Delta-to-Wye (Δ-to-Y) and Wye-to-Delta (Y-to-Δ) Conversions

30. In Figure 8–86, convert each delta network to a wye network.

FIGURE 8–86

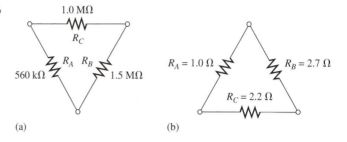

(a)   (b)

31. In Figure 8–87, convert each wye network to a delta network.

FIGURE 8–87

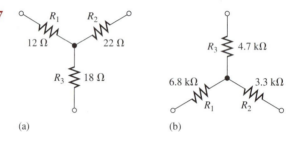

(a)   (b)

*32. Find all currents in the circuit of Figure 8–88.

FIGURE 8–88

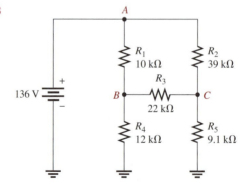

EWB Troubleshooting and Analysis

These problems require your EWB compact disk.

33. Open file PRO08-33.EWB and verify that the current through each resistor is correct and, if not, determine the fault.

34. Open file PRO08-34.EWB. and determine by measurement the Thevenin equivalent for the circuit between terminal *A* and ground.

35. Open file PRO08-35.EWB and determine by measurement the Norton equivalent for the circuit between terminal *A* and ground.

36. Open file PRO08-36.EWB and determine the fault, if any.

37. Open file PRO08-37.EWB and determine the value of a load resistor to be connected between terminals *A* and *B* to achieve maximum power transfer.

■ **ANSWERS**
TO SECTION
REVIEWS

Section 8–1

1. For ideal voltage source, see Figure 8–89.

2. For practical voltage source, see Figure 8–90.

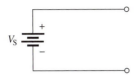

FIGURE 8–89

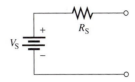

FIGURE 8–90

3. The internal resistance of an ideal voltage source is zero ohms.

4. Output voltage of a voltage source varies directly with load resistance.

Section 8–2

1. For ideal current source, see Figure 8–91.

2. For practical current source, see Figure 8–92.

3. An ideal current source has infinite internal resistance.

4. Load current from a current source varies inversely with load resistance.

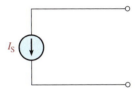

FIGURE 8–91

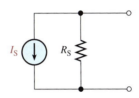

FIGURE 8–92

Section 8–3

1. $I_S = V_S/R_S$

2. $V_S = I_S R_S$

3. See Figure 8–93.

4. See Figure 8–94.

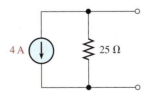

FIGURE 8–93

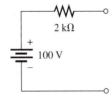

FIGURE 8–94

Section 8–4

1. The superposition theorem states that the total current in any branch of a multiple-source linear circuit is equal to the algebraic sum of the currents due to the individual sources acting alone, with the other sources replaced by their internal resistances.

2. The superposition theorem allows each source to be treated independently.

3. A short simulates the internal resistance of an ideal voltage source; an open simulates the internal resistance of an ideal current source.

4. $I_{R1} = 6.67$ mA

5. The net current is in the direction of the larger current.

Section 8–5

1. A Thevenin equivalent circuit consists of V_{TH} and R_{TH}.

2. See Figure 8–95 for the general form of a Thevenin equivalent circuit.

FIGURE 8–95

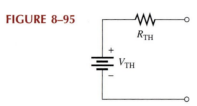

3. V_{TH} is the open circuit voltage between two terminals in a circuit.

4. R_{TH} is the resistance as viewed from two terminals in a circuit, with all sources replaced by their internal resistances.

5. See Figure 8–96.

FIGURE 8–96

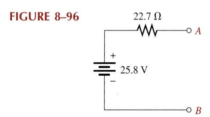

Section 8–6

1. A Norton equivalent circuit consists of I_N and R_N.

2. See Figure 8–97 for the general form of a Norton equivalent circuit.

FIGURE 8–97

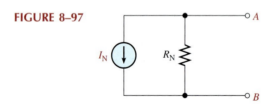

3. I_N is the short circuit current between two terminals in a circuit.

4. R_N is the resistance as viewed from the two open terminals in a circuit.

5. See Figure 8–98.

FIGURE 8–98

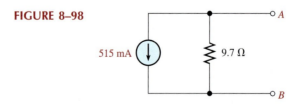

Section 8–7

1. The maximum power transfer theorem states that maximum power is transferred from a source to a load when the load resistance is equal to the internal source resistance.

2. Maximum power is delivered to a load when $R_L = R_S$.

3. $R_L = R_S = 50 \, \Omega$

Section 8–8

1. For a delta circuit see Figure 8–99.

2. For a wye circuit, see Figure 8–100.

FIGURE 8–99   **FIGURE 8–100**

3. The delta-to-wye conversion equations are

$$R_1 = \frac{R_A R_C}{R_A + R_B + R_C} \qquad R_2 = \frac{R_B R_C}{R_A + R_B + R_C} \qquad R_3 = \frac{R_A R_B}{R_A + R_B + R_C}$$

4. The wye-to-delta conversion equations are

$$R_A = \frac{R_1 R_2 + R_1 R_3 + R_2 R_3}{R_2} \qquad R_B = \frac{R_1 R_2 + R_1 R_3 + R_2 R_3}{R_1} \qquad R_C = \frac{R_1 R_2 + R_1 R_3 + R_2 R_3}{R_3}$$

Section 8–9

1. A thermister senses a change in temperature and produces a resulting change in resistance.

2. The heating element turns on when the bridge becomes unbalanced.

■ **ANSWERS TO RELATED PROBLEMS FOR EXAMPLES**

8–1 99.5 V	**8–11** 1.17 mA
8–2 100 V	**8–12** 168 mA
8–3 3.33 kΩ	**8–13** 247 Ω
8–4 1.2 A; 10 Ω	**8–14** $R_N = 247 \, \Omega$
8–5 300 V; 600 Ω	**8–15** 41.7 mW
8–6 16.6 mA	**8–16** $R_1 = 792 \, \Omega, R_2 = 360 \, \Omega, R_3 = 440 \, \Omega$
8–7 I_S is not affected.	**8–17** $R_A = 712 \, \Omega, R_B = 2.35 \, k\Omega, R_C = 500 \, \Omega$
8–8 70 mA	**8–18** 3 μA
8–9 5 mA	
8–10 2.36 V; 124 Ω	

■ **ANSWERS TO SELF-TEST**

1. (b)   **2.** (c)   **3.** (a)   **4.** (b)   **5.** (d)   **6.** (c)   **7.** (b)   **8.** (d)
9. (d)   **10.** (b)

9

BRANCH, MESH, AND NODE ANALYSIS

Electronics Workbench (EWB) and PSpice Tutorials available at http://www.prenhall.com/floyd

■ INTRODUCTION

In the last chapter, you learned about the superposition theorem, Thevenin's theorem, Norton's theorem, maximum power transfer theorem, and several types of conversion methods. These theorems and conversion methods are useful in solving some types of circuit problems.

In this chapter, three more circuit analysis methods are introduced. These methods are based on Ohm's law and Kirchhoff's laws and are particularly useful in the analysis of multiple loop circuits having two or more voltage or current sources. The methods presented here can be used alone or in conjunction with the techniques covered in the previous chapters. With experience, you will learn which method is best for a particular problem or you may develop a preference for one of them.

In the branch current method, Kirchhoff's laws are applied to solve for current in various branches of a multiple-loop circuit. A loop is a complete current path within a circuit. The method of determinants is useful in solving simultaneous equations that occur in multiple-loop analysis. Using a calculator to solve simultaneous equations is also thoroughly covered. In the mesh current method, you will solve for loop currents rather than branch currents. In the node voltage method, the voltages at the independent nodes in a circuit are found. A node is the junction of two or more components.

For this chapter, the TECH TIP assignment in Section 9–6 is to analyze a dual-polarity loaded voltage divider to determine if certain voltage measurements are correct. One of the methods covered in this chapter will be used for the analysis.

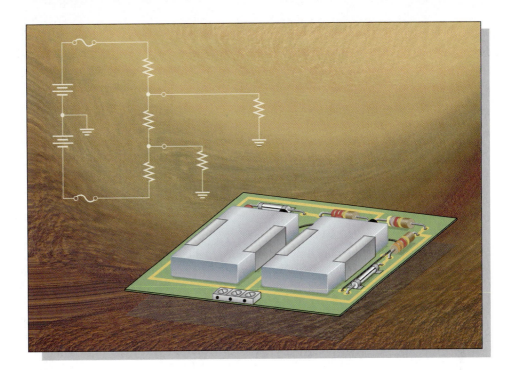

■ CHAPTER OBJECTIVES

❑ Use the branch current method to find unknown
  quantities in a circuit
❑ Use determinants to solve simultaneous equations
❑ Use a calculator to solve simultaneous equations for
  unknown quantities

❑ Use mesh analysis to find unknown quantities in a
  circuit
❑ Use node analysis to find unknown quantities in a
  circuit

9–1 ■ BRANCH CURRENT METHOD

In the branch current method, Kirchhoff's voltage and current laws are used to find the current in each branch of a circuit. Once the branch currents are known, voltages can be determined.

After completing this section, you should be able to

■ **Use the branch current method to find unknown quantities in a circuit**
- Identify loops and nodes in a circuit
- Develop a set of branch current equations
- Solve simultaneous equations by the substitution method

Loops, Nodes, and Branches

Figure 9–1 shows a circuit with two voltage sources and two loops (the arrow directions are arbitrary). This circuit will be used as the basic model throughout the chapter to illustrate each of the three circuit analysis methods. In this circuit, there are only two nonredundant closed loops, as indicated by the arrows. A **loop** is a complete current path within a circuit, and a set of nonredundant closed loops can be viewed as a set of "windowpanes," where each windowpane represents one nonredundant loop. Also, there are four nodes as indicated by the letters *A, B, C,* and *D.* A **node** is a point where two or more components are connected. A **branch** is a path that connects two nodes.

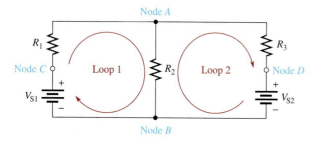

FIGURE 9–1
Two-loop circuit showing loops and nodes.

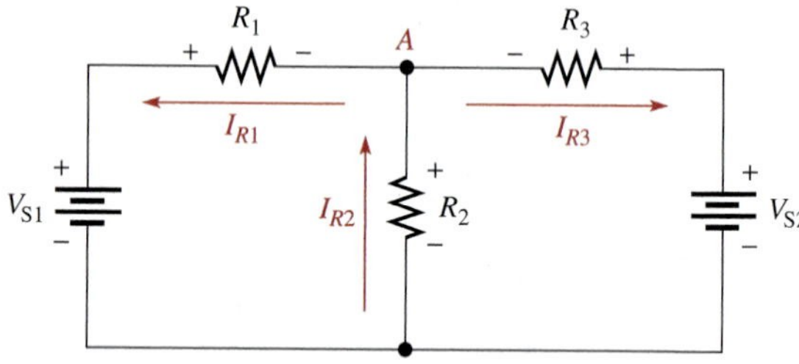

FIGURE 9–2
Circuit for demonstrating branch current analysis.

The following are the general steps used in applying the branch current method. These steps are demonstrated with the aid of Figure 9–2.

Step 1. Assign a current in each circuit branch in an arbitrary direction.

Step 2. Show the polarities of the resistor voltages according to the assigned branch current directions.

Step 3. Apply Kirchhoff's voltage law around each closed loop (algebraic sum of voltages is equal to zero).

Step 4. Apply Kirchhoff's current law at the minimum number of nodes so that all branch currents are included (algebraic sum of currents at a node equals zero).

Step 5. Solve the equations resulting from Steps 3 and 4 for the branch current values.

First, the **branch currents** I_{R1}, I_{R2}, and I_{R3} are assigned in the direction shown in Figure 9–2. Don't worry about the actual current directions at this point.

Second, the polarities of the voltage drops across R_1, R_2, and R_3 are indicated in the figure according to the assigned current directions.

Third, Kirchhoff's voltage law applied to the two loops gives the following equations where the resistance values are the coefficients for the unknown currents:

$$\text{Equation 1:} \quad R_1 I_{R1} + R_2 I_{R2} - V_{S1} = 0 \quad \text{for loop 1}$$

$$\text{Equation 2:} \quad R_2 I_{R2} + R_3 I_{R3} - V_{S2} = 0 \quad \text{for loop 2}$$

Fourth, Kirchhoff's current law is applied to node A, including all branch currents as follows:

$$\text{Equation 3:} \quad I_{R1} - I_{R2} + I_{R3} = 0$$

The negative sign indicates that I_{R2} is out of the junction.

Fifth and last, the three equations must be solved for the three unknown currents, I_{R1}, I_{R2}, and I_{R3}. The three equations in the above steps are called *simultaneous equations* and can be solved in two ways: by substitution or by determinants. Example 9–1 shows how to solve equations by the *substitution* method. In Section 9–2, you will study determinants and how to use them to find branch currents; in the following sections, you will use determinants in two other methods of circuit analysis.

EXAMPLE 9–1

Use the branch current method to find each branch current in Figure 9–3.

FIGURE 9–3

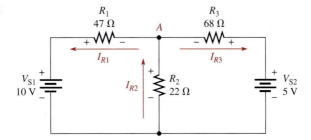

Solution

Step 1. Assign branch currents as shown in Figure 9–3. Keep in mind that you can assume any current direction at this point and that the final solution will have a negative sign if the actual current is opposite to the assigned current.

Step 2. Mark the polarities of the resistor voltage drops in accordance with the assigned current directions as shown in the figure.

Step 3. Applying Kirchhoff's voltage law around the left loop gives

$$47I_{R1} + 22I_{R2} - 10 = 0$$

Around the right loop gives

$$22I_{R2} + 68I_{R3} - 5 = 0$$

where all resistance values are in ohms and voltage values are in volts. For simplicity, the units are not shown.

Step 4. At node A, the current equation is

$$I_{R1} - I_{R2} + I_{R3} = 0$$

Step 5. The equations are solved by substitution as follows. First, find I_{R1} in terms of I_{R2} and I_{R3}.

$$I_{R1} = I_{R2} - I_{R3}$$

Now, substitute $I_{R2} - I_{R3}$ for I_{R1} in the left loop equation.

$$47(I_{R2} - I_{R3}) + 22I_{R2} = 10$$
$$47I_{R2} - 47I_{R3} + 22I_{R2} = 10$$
$$69I_{R2} - 47I_{R3} = 10$$

Next, take the right loop equation and solve for I_{R2} in terms of I_{R3}.

$$22I_{R2} = 5 - 68I_{R3}$$

$$I_{R2} = \frac{5 - 68I_{R3}}{22}$$

Substituting this expression for I_{R2} into $69I_{R2} - 47I_{R3} = 10$ yields

$$69\left(\frac{5 - 68I_{R3}}{22}\right) - 47I_{R3} = 10$$

$$\frac{345 - 4692I_{R3}}{22} - 47I_{R3} = 10$$

$$15.68 - 213.27I_{R3} - 47I_{R3} = 10$$

$$-260.27I_{R3} = -5.68$$

$$I_{R3} = \frac{5.68}{260.27} = 0.0218 \text{ A} = \textbf{21.8 mA}$$

Now, substitute the value of I_{R3} in amps into the right loop equation.

$$22I_{R2} + 68(0.0218) = 5$$

Solve for I_{R2}.

$$I_{R2} = \frac{5 - 68(0.0218)}{22} = \frac{3.52}{22} = 0.16 \text{ A} = \textbf{160 mA}$$

Substituting I_{R2} and I_{R3} values into the current equation at node A yields

$$I_{R1} - 0.16 + 0.0218 = 0$$

$$I_{R1} = 0.16 - 0.0218 = 0.138 \text{ A} = \textbf{138 mA}$$

Related Problem Determine the branch currents in Figure 9–3 with the polarity of the 5 V source reversed.

SECTION 9–1 REVIEW

1. What basic circuit laws are used in the branch current method?
2. When assigning branch currents, you should be careful that the assigned directions match the actual directions.   (T or F)
3. What is a loop?
4. What is a node?

9–2 ■ DETERMINANTS

When several unknown quantities are to be found, such as the three branch currents in Example 9–1, you must have a number of equations equal to the number of unknowns. In this section, you will learn how to solve for two and three unknowns using the systematic method of determinants. This method is an alternate to the substitution method, which you used in the previous section, and will help you appreciate your calculator even more.

After completing this section, you should be able to

■ **Use determinants to solve simultaneous equations**
  • Set up second-order determinants to solve two simultaneous equations
  • Set up third-order determinants to solve three simultaneous equations
  • Evaluate determinants using either the expansion method or the cofactor method

Solving Two Simultaneous Equations for Two Unknowns

To illustrate the method of second-order determinants, let's assume two loop equations as follows:

$$10I_1 + 5I_2 = 15$$
$$2I_1 + 4I_2 = 8$$

We want to find the value of I_1 and I_2. To do so, we form a **determinant** with the coefficients of the unknown currents. A **coefficient** is the number associated with an unknown. For example, 10 is the coefficient for I_1 in the first equation and is a resistance value (units are omitted for simplicity).

The first column in the determinant consists of the coefficients of I_1, and the second column consists of the coefficients of I_2. The resulting determinant appears as follows:

1st column ⟶ ⟵ 2nd column

$$\begin{vmatrix} 10 & 5 \\ 2 & 4 \end{vmatrix}$$

This is called the *characteristic determinant* for the set of equations.

Next, we form another determinant and use it in conjunction with the characteristic determinant to solve for I_1. We form this determinant for our example by replacing the coefficients of I_1 in the first column of the characteristic determinant with the constants (fixed numbers) on the right side of the equations. Doing this, we get the following determinant:

$$\begin{vmatrix} 15 & 5 \\ 8 & 4 \end{vmatrix}$$ Replace coefficients of I_1 with constants from right sides of equations.

We can now solve for I_1 by evaluating both determinants and then dividing by the characteristic determinant. To evaluate the determinants, we cross-multiply and subtract the resulting products. An evaluation of the characteristic determinant in this example is illustrated in the following two steps:

Step 1. Multiply the first number in the left column by the second number in the right column.

$$\begin{vmatrix} 10 & 5 \\ 2 & 4 \end{vmatrix} = 10 \times 4 = 40$$

Step 2. Multiply the second number in the left column by the first number in the right column and subtract from the product in Step 1. This result is the value of the determinant (30 in this case).

$$\begin{vmatrix} 10 & 5 \\ 2 & 4 \end{vmatrix} = 40 - (2 \times 5) = 40 - 10 = 30$$

Repeat the same procedure for the other determinant that was set up for I_1.

$$\begin{vmatrix} 15 & 5 \\ 8 & 4 \end{vmatrix} = 15 \times 4 = 60$$

$$\begin{vmatrix} 15 & 5 \\ 8 & 4 \end{vmatrix} = 60 - (8 \times 5) = 60 - 40 = 20$$

The value of this determinant is 20. Now we can solve for I_1 by dividing the I_1 determinant by the characteristic determinant as follows:

$$I_1 = \frac{\begin{vmatrix} 15 & 5 \\ 8 & 4 \end{vmatrix}}{\begin{vmatrix} 10 & 5 \\ 2 & 4 \end{vmatrix}} = \frac{20}{30} = 0.667 \text{ A}$$

To find I_2, we form another determinant by substituting the constants on the right side of the equations for the coefficients of I_2 in the second column of the characteristic determinant.

$$\begin{vmatrix} 10 & 15 \\ 2 & 8 \end{vmatrix}$$

Replace coefficients of I_2 with constants from right sides of equations.

We solve for I_2 by dividing this determinant by the characteristic determinant already evaluated.

$$I_2 = \frac{\begin{vmatrix} 10 & 15 \\ 2 & 8 \end{vmatrix}}{30} = \frac{(10 \times 8) - (2 \times 15)}{30} = \frac{80 - 30}{30} = \frac{50}{30} = 1.67 \text{ A}$$

EXAMPLE 9–2

Solve the following set of equations for the unknown currents:

$$2I_1 - 5I_2 = 10$$
$$6I_1 + 10I_2 = 20$$

Solution The characteristic determinant is evaluated as follows:

$$\begin{vmatrix} 2 & -5 \\ 6 & 10 \end{vmatrix} = (2)(10) - (-5)(6) = 20 - (-30) = 20 + 30 = 50$$

Solving for I_1 yields

$$I_1 = \frac{\begin{vmatrix} 10 & -5 \\ 20 & 10 \end{vmatrix}}{50} = \frac{(10)(10) - (-5)(20)}{50} = \frac{100 - (-100)}{50} = \frac{200}{50} = \textbf{4 A}$$

Solving for I_2 yields

$$I_2 = \frac{\begin{vmatrix} 2 & 10 \\ 6 & 20 \end{vmatrix}}{50} = \frac{(2)(20) - (6)(10)}{50} = \frac{40 - 60}{50} = \textbf{-0.4 A}$$

In a circuit problem, a result with a negative sign indicates that the direction of actual current is opposite to the assigned direction.

Note that multiplication can be expressed either by the multiplication sign such as 2×10 or by parentheses such as $(2)(10)$.

Related Problem Solve the following set of equations for I_1:

$$5I_1 + 3I_2 = 4$$
$$I_1 + 2I_2 = -6$$

Solving Three Simultaneous Equations for Three Unknowns

Third-order determinants can be evaluated by either the expansion method or the cofactor method. First, we will illustrate the expansion method (which is good only for second and third order) using the following three equations:

$$1I_1 + 3I_2 - 2I_3 = 7$$
$$0I_1 + 4I_2 + 1I_3 = 8$$
$$-5I_1 + 1I_2 + 6I_3 = 9$$

The three-column characteristic determinant for this set of equations is formed in a similar way to that used earlier for the second-order determinant. The first column consists of the coefficients of I_1, the second column consists of the coefficients of I_2, and the third column consists of the coefficients of I_3, as shown below.

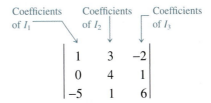

$$\begin{vmatrix} 1 & 3 & -2 \\ 0 & 4 & 1 \\ -5 & 1 & 6 \end{vmatrix}$$

The Expansion Method   This third-order determinant is evaluated by the expansion method as shown in the following steps:

Step 1.   Rewrite the first two columns immediately to the right of the determinant.

$$\begin{vmatrix} 1 & 3 & -2 \\ 0 & 4 & 1 \\ -5 & 1 & 6 \end{vmatrix} \begin{matrix} 1 & 3 \\ 0 & 4 \\ -5 & 1 \end{matrix}$$

Step 2.   Identify the three downward diagonal groups of three coefficients each.

$$\begin{vmatrix} 1 & 3 & -2 \\ 0 & 4 & 1 \\ -5 & 1 & 6 \end{vmatrix} \begin{matrix} 1 & 3 \\ 0 & 4 \\ -5 & 1 \end{matrix}$$

Step 3.   Multiply the numbers in each diagonal and add the products.

$$\begin{vmatrix} 1 & 3 & -2 \\ 0 & 4 & 1 \\ -5 & 1 & 6 \end{vmatrix} \begin{matrix} 1 & 3 \\ 0 & 4 \\ -5 & 1 \end{matrix}$$

$$(1)(4)(6) + (3)(1)(-5) + (-2)(0)(1) = 24 + (-15) + 0 = 9$$

Step 4.   Repeat Steps 2 and 3 for the three upward diagonal groups of three coefficients.

$$\begin{vmatrix} 1 & 3 & -2 \\ 0 & 4 & 1 \\ -5 & 1 & 6 \end{vmatrix} \begin{matrix} 1 & 3 \\ 0 & 4 \\ -5 & 1 \end{matrix}$$

$$(-5)(4)(-2) + (1)(1)(1) + (6)(0)(3) = 40 + 1 + 0 = 41$$

Step 5.   Subtract the result in Step 4 from the result in Step 3 to get the value of the characteristic determinant.

$$9 - 41 = -32$$

To solve for I_1 in the given set of three equations, a determinant is formed by substituting the constants on the right of the equations for the coefficients of I_1 in the characteristic determinant.

$$\begin{vmatrix} 7 & 3 & -2 \\ 8 & 4 & 1 \\ 9 & 1 & 6 \end{vmatrix}$$

This determinant is evaluated using the method described in the previous steps.

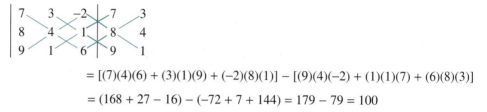

$$= [(7)(4)(6) + (3)(1)(9) + (-2)(8)(1)] - [(9)(4)(-2) + (1)(1)(7) + (6)(8)(3)]$$

$$= (168 + 27 - 16) - (-72 + 7 + 144) = 179 - 79 = 100$$

I_1 is found by dividing this determinant value by the value of the characteristic determinant. The negative results indicates that the actual current is in a direction opposite to the original assumption.

$$I_1 = \frac{\begin{vmatrix} 7 & 3 & -2 \\ 8 & 4 & 1 \\ 9 & 1 & 6 \end{vmatrix}}{\begin{vmatrix} 1 & 3 & -2 \\ 0 & 4 & 1 \\ -5 & 1 & 6 \end{vmatrix}} = \frac{100}{-32} = -3.125 \text{ A}$$

I_2 and I_3 are found in a similar way.

EXAMPLE 9–3

Determine the value of I_2 from the following set of equations:

$$2I_1 + 0.5I_2 + 1I_3 = 0$$
$$0.75I_1 + 0I_2 + 2I_3 = 1.5$$
$$3I_1 + 0.2I_2 + 0I_3 = -1$$

Solution The characteristic determinant is evaluated as follows:

$$\begin{vmatrix} 2 & 0.5 & 1 \\ 0.75 & 0 & 2 \\ 3 & 0.2 & 0 \end{vmatrix} \begin{matrix} 2 & 0.5 \\ 0.75 & 0 \\ 3 & 0.2 \end{matrix}$$

$$= [(2)(0)(0) + (0.5)(2)(3) + (1)(0.75)(0.2)] - [(3)(0)(1) + (0.2)(2)(2) + (0)(0.75)(0.5)]$$
$$= (0 + 3 + 0.15) - (0 + 0.8 + 0) = 3.15 - 0.8 = 2.35$$

The determinant for I_2 is evaluated as follows:

$$\begin{vmatrix} 2 & 0 & 1 \\ 0.75 & 1.5 & 2 \\ 3 & -1 & 0 \end{vmatrix} \begin{matrix} 2 & 0 \\ 0.75 & 1.5 \\ 3 & -1 \end{matrix}$$

$$= [(2)(1.5)(0) + (0)(2)(3) + (1)(0.75)(-1)] - [(3)(1.5)(1) + (-1)(2)(2) + (0)(0.75)(0)]$$
$$= [0 + 0 + (-0.75)] - [4.5 + (-4) + 0] = -0.75 - 0.5 = -1.25$$

Finally,

$$I_2 = \frac{-1.25}{2.35} = -0.532 \text{ A} = -\textbf{532 mA}$$

Related Problem   Determine the value of I_1 in the set of equations used in Example 9–3.

The Cofactor Method   Unlike the expansion method, the cofactor method can be used to evaluate determinants with higher orders than three and is therefore more versatile. We will use a third-order determinant to illustrate the method, keeping in mind that fourth-, fifth-, and higher-order determinants can be evaluated in a similar way. The following specific determinant is used to demonstrate the cofactor method on a step-by-step basis.

$$\begin{vmatrix} 1 & 3 & -2 \\ 4 & 0 & -1 \\ 5 & 1.5 & 6 \end{vmatrix}$$

Step 1.   Select any one column or row in the determinant. Each number in the selected column or row is used as a multiplying factor. For illustration, we will use the first column.

$$\begin{vmatrix} 1 & 3 & -2 \\ 4 & 0 & -1 \\ 5 & 1.5 & 6 \end{vmatrix}$$

Step 2.   Determine the cofactor for each number in the selected column (or row). The cofactor for a given number is the determinant formed by all numbers that are *not* in the same column or row as the given number. This is illustrated as follows:

$$\begin{vmatrix} 1 & 3 & -2 \\ 4 & 0 & -1 \\ 5 & 1.5 & 6 \end{vmatrix} \qquad \begin{vmatrix} 1 & 3 & -2 \\ 4 & 0 & -1 \\ 5 & 1.5 & 6 \end{vmatrix} \qquad \begin{vmatrix} 1 & 3 & -2 \\ 4 & 0 & -1 \\ 5 & 1.5 & 6 \end{vmatrix}$$

Cofactor for 1   Cofactor for 4   Cofactor for 5

Step 3.   Assign the proper sign to each multiplying factor according to the following format (note the alternating pattern):

$$\begin{vmatrix} + & - & + \\ - & + & - \\ + & - & + \end{vmatrix}$$

Step 4.   Sum all of the products of each multiplying factor and its associated cofactor using the appropriate sign.

$$1 \times \begin{vmatrix} 0 & -1 \\ 1.5 & 6 \end{vmatrix} - 4 \times \begin{vmatrix} 3 & -2 \\ 1.5 & 6 \end{vmatrix} + 5 \times \begin{vmatrix} 3 & -2 \\ 0 & -1 \end{vmatrix}$$

$$= 1[(0)(6) - (1.5)(-1)] - 4[(3)(6) + (1.5)(-2)] + 5[(3)(-1) + (0)(-2)]$$

$$= 1(1.5) - 4(15) + 5(-3) = 1.5 - 60 - 15 = -73.5$$

EXAMPLE 9–4   Repeat Example 9–3 using the cofactor method to find I_2. The equations are repeated below.

$$2I_1 + 0.5I_2 + 1I_3 = 0$$
$$0.75I_1 + 0I_2 + 2I_3 = 1.5$$
$$3I_1 + 0.2I_2 + 0I_3 = -1$$

Solution   Evaluate the characteristic determinant as follows:

$$\begin{vmatrix} 2 & 0.5 & 1 \\ 0.75 & 0 & 2 \\ 3 & 0.2 & 0 \end{vmatrix} = 2 \times \begin{vmatrix} 0 & 2 \\ 0.2 & 0 \end{vmatrix} - 0.75 \times \begin{vmatrix} 0.5 & 1 \\ 0.2 & 0 \end{vmatrix} + 3 \times \begin{vmatrix} 0.5 & 1 \\ 0 & 2 \end{vmatrix}$$

$$= 2[(0)(0) - (0.2)(2)] - 0.75[(0.5)(0) - (0.2)(1)] + 3[(0.5)(2) - (0)(1)]$$
$$= 2(-0.4) - 0.75(-0.2) + 3(1) = -0.8 + 0.15 + 3 = 2.35$$

The determinant for I_2 is

$$\begin{vmatrix} 2 & 0 & 1 \\ 0.75 & 1.5 & 2 \\ 3 & -1 & 0 \end{vmatrix} = 2 \times \begin{vmatrix} 1.5 & 2 \\ -1 & 0 \end{vmatrix} - 0.75 \times \begin{vmatrix} 0 & 1 \\ -1 & 0 \end{vmatrix} + 3 \times \begin{vmatrix} 0 & 1 \\ 1.5 & 2 \end{vmatrix}$$

$$= 2[(1.5)(0) - (-1)(2)] - 0.75[(0)(0) - (-1)(1)] + 3[(0)(2) - (1.5)(1)]$$
$$= 2(2) - 0.75(1) + 3(-1.5) = 4 - 0.75 - 4.5 = -1.25$$

Then,

$$I_2 = \frac{-1.25}{2.35} = -0.532 \text{ A} = -532 \text{ mA}$$

Related Problem   Find I_1 using the cofactor method. Use the set of equations in Example 9–4.

SECTION 9–2 REVIEW

1. Evaluate the following determinants:

(a) $\begin{vmatrix} 0 & -1 \\ 4 & 8 \end{vmatrix}$ (b) $\begin{vmatrix} 0.25 & 0.33 \\ -0.5 & 1 \end{vmatrix}$ (c) $\begin{vmatrix} 1 & 3 & 7 \\ 2 & -1 & 7 \\ -4 & 0 & -2 \end{vmatrix}$

2. Set up the characteristic determinant for the following set of simultaneous equations:

$$2I_1 + 3I_2 = 0$$
$$5I_1 + 4I_2 = 1$$

3. Find I_2 in Question 2.

9–3 ■ SOLVING SIMULTANEOUS EQUATIONS USING A CALCULATOR

You have learned two ways to solve simultaneous equations, the substitution method and the determinant method. In this section, you will learn how to use a calculator to solve any number of simultaneous equations up to thirty. Your calculator and the method discussed in this section can be applied whenever simultaneous equations are part of a circuit analysis problem, regardless of method used.

After completing this section, you should be able to

■ **Use a calculator to solve simultaneous equations for unknown quantities**
- Set up the calculator for any number of simultaneous equations up to thirty
- Enter the simultaneous equations
- Determine the values of the unknown variables
- Edit the equations

Entering Simultaneous Equations

The following steps are used to enter simultaneous equations in the TI-85 calculator:

Step 1. Press and then SIMULT; the screen in Figure 9–4 appears.

FIGURE 9–4

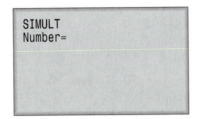

Step 2. Enter the number of simultaneous equations and press (ENTER). The coefficient entry screen for the first equation appears as shown in Figure 9–5(a) for a three-equation example. The coefficient $a1,1$ is the first coefficient in the first equation, $a1,2$ is the second coefficient in the first equation, and so on. The equation is displayed on the top line as $a1,1 \times 1 \ldots a1,3 \times 3 = b1$. Completely written out, this equation would be

$$a1,1 \times 1 + a1,2 \times 2 + a1,3 \times 3 = b1$$

where $\times 1$, $\times 2$, and $\times 3$ are the unknown variables and $b1$ is the constant.

Step 3. Enter the value for each of the coefficients, $a1,1$ through $a1,3$ and for $b1$. Press (ENTER) after each entry. If you press (ENTER) after entering the last coefficient or select NEXT using the (F2) key, the second equation and coefficients are displayed as shown in Figure 9–5(b). Enter the value for each of the coefficients $a2,1$ through $a2,3$ and for $b2$. Repeat the entry process for the third equation, which is displayed as shown in Figure 9–5(c).

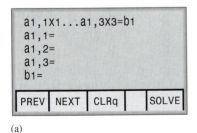

(a)

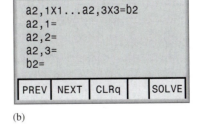

(b)

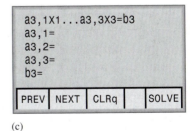

(c)

FIGURE 9–5

Solving the Equations

After entering the coefficients in steps 1 through 3, select SOLVE by pressing (F5). The values for $\times 1$, $\times 2$, and $\times 3$ are displayed.

Editing the Equations

You can change the coefficients of any of the equations by selecting COEFS using the F1 key. This will return you to the first equation entry screen. To get to the next equation entry screen, simply step through the coefficients in the current screen until the next screen comes up.

EXAMPLE 9–5

Use the TI-85 calculator to solve the following three simultaneus equations for the three unknowns.

$$8I_1 + 4I_2 + 1I_3 = 7$$
$$2I_1 - 5I_2 + 6I_3 = 3$$
$$3I_1 + 3I_2 - 2I_3 = -5$$

Solution Press 2nd then SIMULT to enter the number of equations as shown in Figure 9–6.

FIGURE 9–6

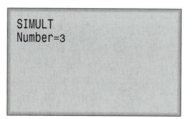

```
SIMULT
Number=3
```

After you enter 3 and press ENTER, the first equation screen comes up. The coefficients 8, 4, 1 and the constant 7 are entered by pressing each number key followed by the ENTER key, which results in the screen shown in Figure 9–7(a). After you enter the last number and press ENTER, the second equation screen appears. Enter the coefficients 2, −5, 6 and the constant 3 as shown in Figure 9–7(b) (A negative value is entered by first pressing the (−) key.). Finally, enter the coefficients of the third equation (3, 3, −2) and the constant −5 as shown in Figure 9–7(c).

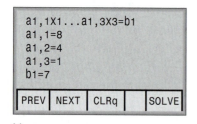

(a)

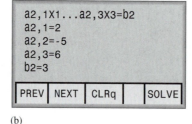

(b)

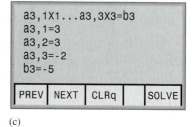

(c)

FIGURE 9–7

Selecting SOLVE, which is F5, produces the results displayed in Figure 9–8. $\times 1$ is I_1, $\times 2$ is I_2, and $\times 3$ is I_3.

FIGURE 9–8

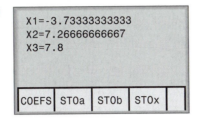

```
X1=-3.73333333333
X2=7.26666666667
X3=7.8



COEFS STOa STOb STOx
```

Related Problem Edit the equations to change a1,2 from 4 to −3, a2,3 from 6 to 2.5, and b3 from −5 to 8 and solve the modified equations.

SECTION 9–3 REVIEW

1. Use your calculator to solve the following set of simultaneous equations for I_1, I_2, I_3, and I_4.

$$100I_1 + 220I_2 + 180I_3 + 330I_4 = 0$$
$$470I_1 + 390I_2 + 100I_3 + 100I_4 = 12$$
$$120I_1 - 270I_2 + 150I_3 - 180I_4 = -9$$
$$560I_1 + 680I_2 - 220I_3 + 390I_4 = 0$$

2. Modify the equations in Question 1 by changing the constant in the first equation to 8.5, the coefficient of I_3 in the second equation to 220, and the coefficient of I_1 in the fourth equation to 330. Solve the new set of equations.

9–4 ■ MESH CURRENT METHOD

In the mesh current method, you will work with loop currents instead of branch currents. A branch current is the actual current through a branch. An ammeter placed in a given branch will measure the branch current. Loop currents are different because they are mathematical quantities that are used to make circuit analysis somewhat easier than with the branch current method. The term mesh comes from the fact that a multiple-loop circuit, when drawn, can be imagined to resemble a wire mesh.

After completing this section, you should be able to

■ **Use mesh analysis to find unknown quantities in a circuit**
  • Assign loop currents
  • Apply Kirchhoff's voltage law around each loop
  • Develop the loop (mesh) equations
  • Solve the loop equations

A systematic method of mesh analysis is given in the following steps and is illustrated in Figure 9–9, which is essentially the same circuit configuration as in Figure 9–1 used in the branch current analysis. It demonstrates the basic principles well.

Step 1. Although direction of an assigned loop current is arbitrary, we will assign a current in the counterclockwise (CCW) direction around each nonredundant closed loop, for consistency. This may not be the actual current direction, but it does not matter. The number of loop-current assignments must be sufficient to include current through all components in the circuit.

FIGURE 9–9
Circuit for mesh analysis.

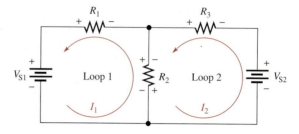

Step 2. Indicate the voltage drop polarities in each loop based on the assigned current directions.

Step 3. Apply Kirchhoff's voltage law around each closed loop. When more than one loop current passes through a component, include its voltage drop. This results in one equation for each loop.

Step 4. Using substitution or determinants, solve the resulting equations for the loop currents.

First, the loop currents I_1 and I_2 are assigned in the CCW direction as shown in Figure 9–9. A loop current could be assigned around the outer perimeter of the circuit, but this would be redundant since I_1 and I_2 already pass through all of the components.

Second, the polarities of the voltage drops across R_1, R_2, and R_3 are shown based on the loop-current directions. Notice that I_1 and I_2 are in opposite directions through R_2 because R_2 is common to both loops. Therefore, two voltage polarities are indicated. In reality, the R_2 current cannot be separated into two parts, but remember that the loop currents are basically mathematical quantities used for analysis purposes. The polarities of the voltage sources are fixed and are not affected by the current assignments.

Third, Kirchhoff's voltage law applied to the two loops results in the following two equations:

$$R_1I_1 + R_2(I_1 - I_2) = V_{S1} \qquad \text{for loop 1}$$
$$R_3I_2 + R_2(I_2 - I_1) = -V_{S2} \qquad \text{for loop 2}$$

Notice that I_1 is positive in loop 1 and I_2 is positive in loop 2.

Fourth, the like terms in the equations are combined and rearranged into a form for convenient solution so that they have the same position in each equation, that is, the I_1 term is first and the I_2 term is second. The equations are rearranged into the following form. Once the loop currents are evaluated, all of the branch currents can be determined.

$$(R_1 + R_2)I_1 - R_2I_2 = V_{S1} \qquad \text{for loop 1}$$
$$-R_2I_1 + (R_2 + R_3)I_2 = -V_{S2} \qquad \text{for loop 2}$$

Notice that in the mesh current method only two equations are required for the same circuit that required three equations in the branch current method. The last two equations (developed in the fourth step) follow a form to make mesh analysis easier. Referring to these last two equations, notice that for loop 1, the total resistance in the loop, $R_1 + R_2$, is multiplied by I_1 (its loop current). Also in the loop 1 equation, the resistance common to both loops, R_2, is multiplied by the other loop current, I_2, and subtracted from the first term. The same form is seen in the loop 2 equation except that the terms have been rearranged. From these observations, a concise rule for applying steps 1 to 4 is as follows:

(Sum of resistors in loop) times (loop current) minus (each common resistor) times (associated adjacent loop current) equals (source voltage in the loop).

Example 9–6 illustrates the application of this rule to the mesh current analysis of a circuit.

EXAMPLE 9–6   Using the mesh current method, find the branch currents in Figure 9–10.

FIGURE 9–10

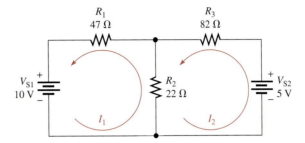

Solution   Assign the loop currents (I_1 and I_2) as shown in Figure 9–10; resistance values are in ohms and voltage values are in volts. Use the rule described to set up the two loop equations.

$$(47 + 22)I_1 - 22I_2 = 10$$
$$69I_1 - 22I_2 = 10 \qquad \text{for loop 1}$$

$$-22I_1 + (22 + 82)I_2 = -5$$
$$-22I_1 + 104I_2 = -5 \qquad \text{for loop 2}$$

Use determinants to find I_1.

$$I_1 = \frac{\begin{vmatrix} 10 & -22 \\ -5 & 104 \end{vmatrix}}{\begin{vmatrix} 69 & -22 \\ -22 & 104 \end{vmatrix}} = \frac{(10)(104) - (-5)(-22)}{(69)(104) - (-22)(-22)} = \frac{1040 - 110}{7176 - 484} = 139 \text{ mA}$$

Solving for I_2 yields

$$I_2 = \frac{\begin{vmatrix} 69 & 10 \\ -22 & -5 \end{vmatrix}}{6692} = \frac{(69)(-5) - (-22)(10)}{6692} = \frac{-345 - (-220)}{6692} = -18.7 \text{ mA}$$

The negative sign on I_2 means that its assigned direction is opposite to the actual current.
Now find the actual branch currents. Since I_1 is the only current through R_1, it is also the branch current I_{R1}.

$$I_{R1} = I_1 = \textbf{139 mA}$$

Since I_2 is the only current through R_3, it is also the branch current I_{R3}.

$$I_{R3} = I_2 = \textbf{--18.7 mA} \qquad \text{(opposite direction of that originally assigned to } I_2\text{)}$$

Both loop currents I_1 and I_2 are through R_2 in the same direction. Remember, the negative I_2 value told you to reverse its assigned direction.

$$I_{R2} = I_1 - I_2 = 139 \text{ mA} - (-18.7 \text{ mA}) = \textbf{158 mA}$$

Keep in mind that once you know the branch currents, you can find the voltages by using Ohm's law.

Related Problem   Solve for the two loop currents using your calculator.

Circuits with More Than Two Loops

The mesh method also can be systematically applied to circuits with any number of loops. Of course, the more loops there are, the more difficult is the solution, but calculators have greatly simplified the problem. However, the basic procedure still applies. For example, for a three-loop circuit, three simultaneous equations are required. Example 9–7 illustrates the analysis of a three-loop circuit.

EXAMPLE 9–7   Find I_3 in Figure 9–11.

FIGURE 9–11

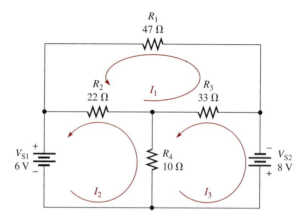

Solution   Assign three CCW loop currents (I_1, I_2, and I_3) as shown in Figure 9–11. Then use the rule to set up each loop equation. The polarity of a voltage source is positive when the assigned mesh current is into the positive terminal. The loop equations are

$$102I_1 - 22I_2 - 33I_3 = 0 \qquad \text{for loop 1}$$
$$-22I_1 + 32I_2 - 10I_3 = 6 \qquad \text{for loop 2}$$
$$-33I_1 - 10I_2 + 43I_3 = 8 \qquad \text{for loop 3}$$

You can solve these three equations for the loop currents by substitution or, more easily, with third-order determinants.

Determine I_3 using determinants as follows. First, evaluate the characteristic determinant.

$$\begin{vmatrix} 102 & -22 & -33 \\ -22 & 32 & -10 \\ -33 & -10 & 43 \end{vmatrix} = 102 \times \begin{vmatrix} 32 & -10 \\ -10 & 43 \end{vmatrix} - (-22) \times \begin{vmatrix} -22 & -33 \\ -10 & 43 \end{vmatrix} + (-33) \times \begin{vmatrix} -22 & -33 \\ 32 & -10 \end{vmatrix}$$

$$= 102[(32)(43) - (-10)(-10)] - (-22)[(-22)(43) - (-10)(-33)] + (-33)[(-22)(-10) - (32)(-33)]$$

$$= 102(1276) + 22(-1276) - 33(1276) = 130,152 - 28,072 - 42,108 = 59,972$$

Next, evaluate the I_3 determinant.

$$\begin{vmatrix} 102 & -22 & 0 \\ -22 & 32 & 6 \\ -33 & -10 & 8 \end{vmatrix} = 102 \times \begin{vmatrix} 32 & 6 \\ -10 & 8 \end{vmatrix} - (-22) \times \begin{vmatrix} -22 & 0 \\ -10 & 8 \end{vmatrix} + (-33) \times \begin{vmatrix} -22 & 0 \\ 32 & 6 \end{vmatrix}$$

$$= 102[(33)(8) - (-10)(6)] + 22[(-22)(8) - (-10)(0)] - 33[(-22)(6) - (32)(0)]$$

$$= 102(316) + 22(-176) - 33(-132) = 32,232 - 3872 + 4356 = 32,716$$

Determine I_3 by dividing the value of the I_3 determinant by the value of the characteristic determinant.

$$I_3 = \frac{32,716}{59,972} = \textbf{546 mA}$$

The other loop currents are found similarly. The actual branch currents and voltages can be determined once you know the loop currents.

Related Problem   Solve for the three loop currents using your calculator.

SECTION 9–4 REVIEW

1. Do the loop currents necessarily represent the actual currents in the branches?
2. When you solve for a loop current and get a negative value, what does it mean?
3. What circuit law is used in the mesh current method?

9–5 ■ NODE VOLTAGE METHOD

Another method of analysis of multiple-loop circuits is called the node voltage method. It is based on finding the voltages at each node in the circuit using Kirchhoff's current law. A node is the junction of two or more components.

After completing this section, you should be able to

■ **Use node analysis to find unknown quantities in a circuit**
  • Select the nodes at which the voltage is unknown and assign currents
  • Apply Kirchhoff's current law at each node
  • Develop the node equations
  • Solve the node equations

The general steps for the node voltage method of circuit analysis are as follows:

Step 1.   Determine the number of nodes.

Step 2.   Select one node as a reference. All voltages will be relative to the reference node. Assign voltage designations to each node where the voltage is unknown.

Step 3.   Assign currents at each node where the voltage is unknown, except at the reference node. The directions are arbitrary.

Step 4.   Apply Kirchhoff's current law to each node where currents are assigned.

Step 5.   Express the current equations in terms of voltages, and solve the equations for the unknown node voltages using Ohm's law.

We will use Figure 9–12 to illustrate the general approach to node voltage analysis. First, establish the nodes. In this case, there are four nodes, as indicated in the figure. Second, let's use node B as the reference. Think of it as the circuit's reference ground. Node voltages C and D are already known to be the source voltages. The voltage at node A is the only unknown; it is designated as V_A. Third, arbitrarily assign the branch currents at node A as indicated in the figure. Fourth, the Kirchhoff current equation at node A is

$$I_{R1} - I_{R2} + I_{R3} = 0$$

FIGURE 9–12
Circuit for node voltage analysis.

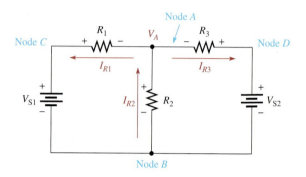

Fifth, express the currents in terms of circuit voltages using Ohm's law.

$$I_{R1} = \frac{V_1}{R_1} = \frac{V_{S1} - V_A}{R_1}$$

$$I_{R2} = \frac{V_2}{R_2} = \frac{V_A}{R_2}$$

$$I_{R3} = \frac{V_3}{R_3} = \frac{V_{S2} - V_A}{R_3}$$

Substituting these terms into the current equation yields

$$\frac{V_{S1} - V_A}{R_1} - \frac{V_A}{R_2} + \frac{V_{S2} - V_A}{R_3} = 0$$

The only unknown is V_A; so solve the single equation by combining and rearranging terms. Once the voltage is known, all branch currents can be calculated. Example 9–8 illustrates this method further.

EXAMPLE 9–8   Find the node voltage V_A in Figure 9–13.

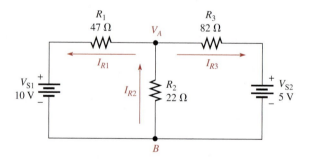

FIGURE 9–13

Solution   The reference node is chosen at *B*. The unknown node voltage is V_A, as indicated in Figure 9–13. This is the only unknown voltage. Branch currents are assigned at node *A* as shown. The current equation is

$$I_{R1} - I_{R2} + I_{R3} = 0$$

Substitution for currents using Ohm's law gives the equation in terms of voltages.

$$\frac{10 - V_A}{47} - \frac{V_A}{22} + \frac{5 - V_A}{82} = 0$$

Rearranging the terms yields

$$\frac{10}{47} - \frac{V_A}{47} - \frac{V_A}{22} + \frac{5}{82} - \frac{V_A}{82} = 0$$

$$-\frac{V_A}{47} - \frac{V_A}{22} - \frac{V_A}{82} = -\frac{10}{47} - \frac{5}{82}$$

To solve for V_A, combine the terms on each side of the equation and find the common denominator.

$$\frac{1804V_A + 3854V_A + 1034V_A}{84,788} = \frac{820 + 235}{3854}$$

$$\frac{6692V_A}{84,788} = \frac{1055}{3854}$$

$$V_A = \frac{(1055)(84,788)}{(6692)(3854)} = \textbf{3.47 V}$$

Related Problem Find V_A in Figure 9–13 if the 5 V source is reversed.

Using the same basic procedure, you can analyze circuits with more than one unknown node voltage. Example 9–9 illustrates this calculation for two unknown node voltages.

EXAMPLE 9–9 Using the node analysis method, calculate V_A and V_B in the circuit of Figure 9–14.

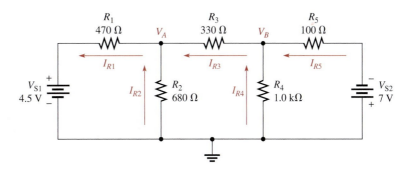

FIGURE 9–14

Solution First, assign the branch currents as shown in Figure 9–14. Next, apply Kirchhoff's current law at each node. At node A,

$$I_{R1} - I_{R2} - I_{R3} = 0$$

Using Ohm's law substitution for the currents yields

$$\left(\frac{4.5 - V_A}{470}\right) - \left(\frac{V_A}{680}\right) - \left(\frac{V_A - V_B}{330}\right) = 0$$

$$\frac{4.5}{470} - \frac{V_A}{470} - \frac{V_A}{680} - \frac{V_A}{330} + \frac{V_B}{330} = 0$$

$$\left(\frac{1}{470} + \frac{1}{680} + \frac{1}{330}\right)V_A - \left(\frac{1}{330}\right)V_B = \frac{4.5}{470}$$

Next, using your calculator, evaluate the coefficients and constant in the last equation. The resulting equation for node A is

$$0.00663V_A - 0.00303V_B = 0.00957$$

At node B,

$$I_{R3} - I_{R4} - I_{R5} = 0$$

Again use Ohm's law substitution.

$$\left(\frac{V_A - V_B}{330}\right) - \left(\frac{V_B}{1000}\right) - \left(\frac{V_B - (-7)}{100}\right) = 0$$

$$\frac{V_A}{330} - \frac{V_B}{330} - \frac{V_B}{1000} - \frac{V_B}{100} - \frac{7}{100} = 0$$

$$\left(\frac{1}{330}\right)V_A - \left(\frac{1}{330} + \frac{1}{1000} + \frac{1}{100}\right)V_B = \frac{7}{100}$$

Evaluate the coefficients and constant. The equation for node B is

$$0.00303V_A - 0.01403V_B = 0.07$$

Next, these two node equations must be solved for V_A and V_B. Use determinants to get the solutions.

$$V_A = \frac{\begin{vmatrix} 0.00957 & -0.00303 \\ 0.07 & -0.01403 \end{vmatrix}}{\begin{vmatrix} 0.00663 & -0.00303 \\ 0.00303 & -0.01403 \end{vmatrix}} = \frac{(0.00957)(-0.01403) - (0.07)(-0.00303)}{(0.00663)(-0.01403) - (0.00303)(-0.00303)} = -928 \text{ mV}$$

$$V_B = \frac{\begin{vmatrix} 0.00663 & 0.00957 \\ 0.00303 & 0.07 \end{vmatrix}}{\begin{vmatrix} 0.00663 & -0.00303 \\ 0.00303 & -0.01403 \end{vmatrix}} = \frac{(0.00663)(0.07) - (0.00303)(0.00957)}{(0.00663)(-0.01403) - (0.00303)(-0.00303)} = -5.19 \text{ V}$$

Related Problem Solve the two node equations for V_A and V_B using your calculator.

**SECTION 9–5
REVIEW**

1. What circuit law is the basis for the node voltage method?
2. What is the reference node?

9–6 ■ TECHnology Theory Into Practice

Analysis of a dual-polarity loaded voltage divider provides an opportunity to apply one of the analysis methods covered in this chapter. The dual-polarity voltage divider circuit in this section operates from two voltage sources. One source is +9 V and the other is −9 V. These two voltage sources supply both positive and negative voltages that are divided down to produce reference voltages for two different devices.

The voltage divider that you will check out in this TECH TIP section will be used to provide reference voltages to two devices using 9 V batteries. One of the devices requires a positive reference voltage and presents a 27 kΩ load to the voltage divider. The other device requires a negative reference voltage and presents a 15 kΩ load to the voltage divider. The schematic of the loaded dual-polarity voltage divider is shown in Figure 9–15.

The self-contained dual-polarity voltage divider is constructed on the PC board shown in Figure 9–16. The two batteries are clip-mounted directly on the board and wired to the printed circuit pads as indicated. The two load devices can be connected to the terminal strip.

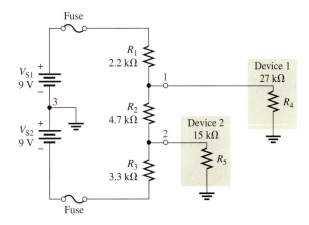

FIGURE 9–15

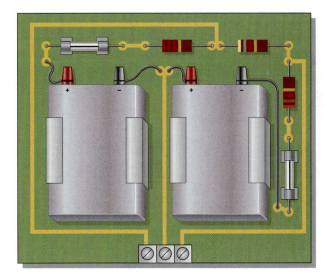

FIGURE 9–16

The Printed Circuit Board and Schematic

■ Check the PC board in Figure 9–16 to make sure that it agrees with the schematic in Figure 9–15. Relate each input, output, and component on the board to the schematic.

Analysis and Troubleshooting

■ Referring to Figure 9–17, determine if the voltmeter readings are correct. The output voltages are measured without the loads connected.

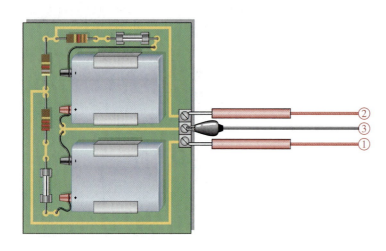

FIGURE 9–17
Circled numbers show corresponding connections.

- Referring to Figure 9–18, apply the node voltage method to determine if the voltmeter readings are correct. You may need to redraw the schematic in a more familiar form. The output voltages are measured with a 27 kΩ load connected from output 1 to ground to simulate one of the devices connected to the voltage divider.

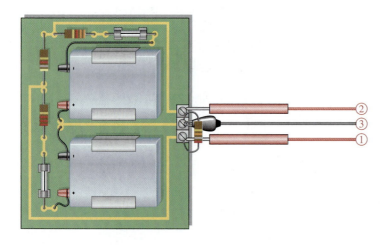

FIGURE 9–18
Circled numbers show corresponding connections.

- Referring to Figure 9–19, apply the node voltage method to determine if the voltmeter readings are correct. You may need to redraw the schematic in a more familiar form. The output voltages are measured with a 27 kΩ load connected from output 1 to ground and a 15 kΩ load from output 2 to ground to simulate both devices connected to the voltage divider.
- If meter 1 reads +7.50 V and meter 2 reads +5.71 V in Figure 9–19, what is the problem?
- If meter 1 reads +8.27 V and meter 2 reads −7.38 V in Figure 9–19, what is the problem?

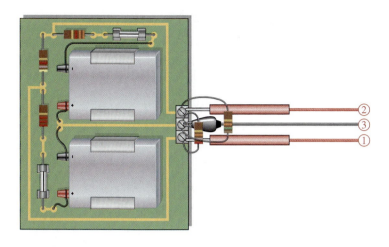

FIGURE 9–19
Circled numbers show corresponding connections.

<table>
<tr>
<td>

SECTION 9–6 REVIEW

</td>
<td>

1. Determine the minimum value for the fuses in the voltage-divider circuit.
2. If the batteries are each rated at 10 Ah, how long will the voltage-divider circuit operate under unloaded conditions?

</td>
</tr>
</table>

■ **SUMMARY**

- The branch current method is based on Kirchhoff's voltage law and Kirchhoff's current law.
- Simultaneous equations can be solved by substitution, by determinants, or by a graphics calculator.
- The number of equations must be equal to the number of unknowns.
- Second-order determinants are evaluated by adding the signed cross-products.
- Third-order determinants are evaluated by the expansion method or by the cofactor method.
- The mesh current method is based on Kirchhoff's voltage law.
- A loop current is not necessarily the actual current in a branch.
- The node voltage method is based on Kirchhoff's current law.

■ **GLOSSARY**

These terms are also in the end-of-book glossary.

Branch   One current path that connects two nodes.

Branch current   The actual current in a branch.

Coefficient   The constant number that appears in front of a variable.

Determinant   An array of coefficients and constants in a given set of simultaneous equations.

Loop   A closed current path in a circuit.

Node   The junction of two or more components.

■ **SELF-TEST**

1. Assuming the voltage source values in Figure 9–1 are known, there is/are
   (a) 3 nonredundant loops   **(b)** 1 unknown node   **(c)** 2 nonredundant loops
   (d) 2 unknown nodes   **(e)** both answers (b) and (c)

2. In assigning the direction of branch currents,
   - (a) the directions are critical
   - (b) they must all be in the same direction
   - (c) they must all point into a node
   - (d) the directions are not critical

3. The branch current method uses
   - (a) Ohm's law and Kirchhoff's voltage law
   - (b) Kirchhoff's voltage and current laws
   - (c) the superposition theorem and Kirchhoff's current law
   - (d) Thevenin's theorem and Kirchhoff's voltage law

4. A characteristic determinant for two simultaneous equations will have
   - (a) 2 rows and 1 column
   - (b) 1 row and 2 columns
   - (c) 2 rows and 2 columns

5. The first row of a certain determinant has the numbers 2 and 4. The second row has the numbers 6 and 1. The value of this determinant is
   - (a) 22
   - (b) 2
   - (c) –22
   - (d) 8

6. The expansion method for evaluating determinants is
   - (a) good only for second-order determinants
   - (b) good only for both second and third-order determinants
   - (c) good for any determinant
   - (d) better than the cofactor method

7. The mesh current method is based on
   - (a) Kirchhoff's current law
   - (b) Ohm's law
   - (c) the superposition theorem
   - (d) Kirchhoff's voltage law

8. The node voltage method is based on
   - (a) Kirchhoff's current law
   - (b) Ohm's law
   - (c) the superposition theorem
   - (d) Kirchhoff's voltage law

9. In the node voltage method,
   - (a) currents are assigned at each node
   - (b) currents are assigned at the reference node
   - (c) the current directions are arbitrary
   - (d) currents are assigned only at the nodes where the voltage is unknown
   - (e) both answers (c) and (d)

10. Generally, the node voltage method results in
    - (a) more equations than the mesh current method
    - (b) fewer equations than the mesh current method
    - (c) the same number of equations as the mesh current method

---

■ PROBLEMS

More difficult problems are indicated by an asterisk (*).

SECTION 9–1   Branch Current Method

1. Identify all possible nonredundant loops in Figure 9–20.

FIGURE 9–20

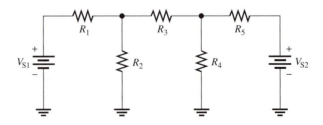

2. Identify all nodes in Figure 9–20. Which ones have a known voltage?

3. Write the Kirchhoff current equation for the current assignment shown at node A in Figure 9–21.

FIGURE 9–21

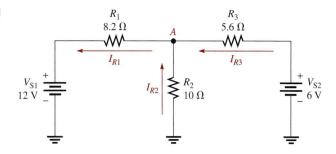

4. Solve for each of the branch currents in Figure 9–21.

5. Find the voltage drop across each resistor in Figure 9–21 and indicate its actual polarity.

6. Using the substitution method, solve the following set of equations for I_{R1} and I_{R2}.

$$100I_{R1} + 50I_{R2} = 30$$
$$75I_{R1} + 90I_{R2} = 15$$

7. Using the substitution method, solve the following set of three equations for all currents:

$$5I_{R1} - 2I_{R2} + 8I_{R3} = 1$$
$$2I_{R1} + 4I_{R2} - 12I_{R3} = 5$$
$$10I_{R1} + 6I_{R2} + 9I_{R3} = 0$$

*8. Find the current through each resistor in Figure 9–22.

FIGURE 9–22

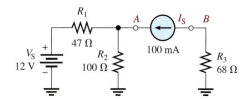

9. In Figure 9–22, determine the voltage across the current source (points A and B).

SECTION 9–2   Determinants

10. Evaluate each determinant:

(a) $\begin{vmatrix} 4 & 6 \\ 2 & 3 \end{vmatrix}$ (b) $\begin{vmatrix} 9 & -1 \\ 0 & 5 \end{vmatrix}$ (c) $\begin{vmatrix} 12 & 15 \\ -2 & -1 \end{vmatrix}$ (d) $\begin{vmatrix} 100 & 50 \\ 30 & -20 \end{vmatrix}$

11. Using determinants, solve the following set of equations for both currents:

$$-I_1 + 2I_2 = 4$$
$$7I_1 + 3I_2 = 6$$

12. Evaluate each of the determinants using the expansion method:

(a) $\begin{vmatrix} 1 & 0 & -2 \\ 5 & 4 & 1 \\ 2 & 10 & 0 \end{vmatrix}$ (b) $\begin{vmatrix} 0.5 & 1 & -0.8 \\ 0.1 & 1.2 & 1.5 \\ -0.1 & -0.3 & 5 \end{vmatrix}$

13. Evaluate each of the determinants using the cofactor method:

(a) $\begin{vmatrix} 25 & 0 & -20 \\ 10 & 12 & 5 \\ -8 & 30 & -16 \end{vmatrix}$ (b) $\begin{vmatrix} 1.08 & 1.75 & 0.55 \\ 0 & 2.12 & -0.98 \\ 1 & 3.49 & -1.05 \end{vmatrix}$

14. Find I_1 and I_3 in Example 9–3.

15. Solve for I_1, I_2, I_3 in the following set of equations:

$$2I_1 - 6I_2 + 10I_3 = 9$$
$$3I_1 + 7I_2 - 8I_3 = 3$$
$$10I_1 + 5I_2 - 12I_3 = 0$$

*16. Find V_1, V_2, V_3, and V_4 from the following set of equations:

$$16V_1 + 10V_2 - 8V_3 - 3V_4 = 15$$
$$2V_1 + 0V_2 + 5V_3 + 2V_4 = 0$$
$$-7V_1 - 12V_2 + 0V_3 + 0V_4 = 9$$
$$-1V_1 + 20V_2 - 18V_3 + 0V_4 = 10$$

SECTION 9–3   Solving Simultaneous Equations Using a Calculator

17. Solve the two simultaneous equations in Problem 6 using your calculator.

18. Solve the three simultaneous equations in Problem 7 using your calculator.

19. Solve the three simultaneous equations in Problem 15 using your calculator.

20. Solve the four simultaneous equations in Problem 16 using your calculator.

SECTION 9–4   Mesh Current Method

21. Using the mesh current method, find the loop currents in Figure 9–23.

22. Find the branch currents in Figure 9–23.

23. Determine the voltages and their proper polarities for each resistor in Figure 9–23.

24. Write the loop equations for the circuit in Figure 9–24.

FIGURE 9–23

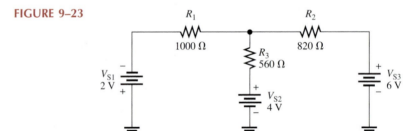

25. Solve for the loop currents in Figure 9–24 using your calculator.

26. Find the current through each resistor in Figure 9–24.

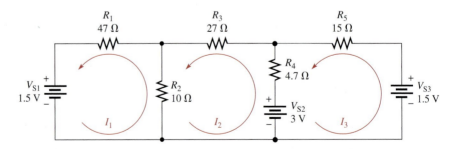

FIGURE 9–24

27. Determine the voltage across the open bridge terminals, A and B, in Figure 9–25.

28. When a 10 Ω resistor is connected from point A to point B in Figure 9–25, what is the current through it?

29. Find the current through R_1 in Figure 9–26.

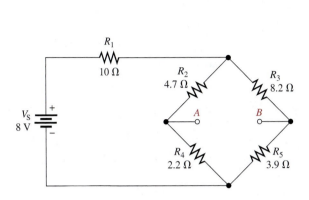

FIGURE 9–25

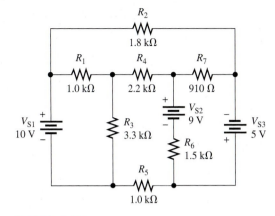

FIGURE 9–26

SECTION 9–5 Node Voltage Method

30. In Figure 9–27, use the node voltage method to find the voltage at point A with respect to ground.

31. What are the branch current values in Figure 9–27? Show the actual direction of current in each branch.

32. Write the node voltage equations for Figure 9–24. Use your calculator to find the node voltages.

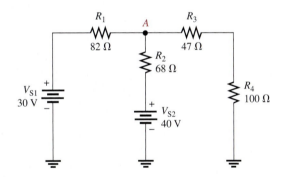

FIGURE 9–27

33. Use node analysis to determine the voltage at points A and B with respect to ground in Figure 9–28.

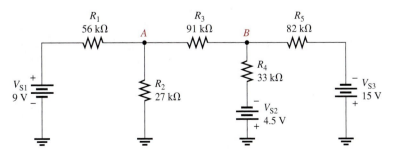

FIGURE 9–28

*34. Find the voltage at points A, B, and C in Figure 9–29.

FIGURE 9–29

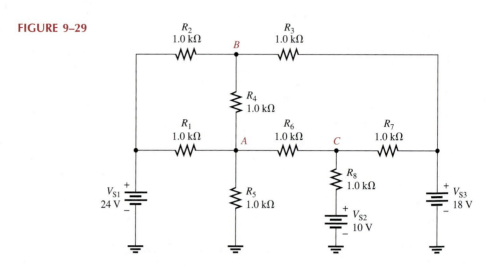

*35. Use node analysis, mesh analysis, or any other procedure to find all currents and the voltages at each unknown node in Figure 9–30.

FIGURE 9–30

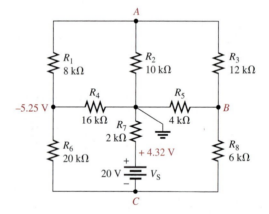

EWB Troubleshooting and Analysis

These problems require your EWB compact disk.

36. Open file PRO09-36.EWB and measure the current through each resistor.

37. Open file PRO09-37.EWB and measure the current through each resistor.

38. Open file PRO09-38.EWB and measure the voltages with respect to ground at nodes A and B.

39. Open file PRO09-39.EWB. Determine if there is a fault and, if so, specify the fault.

40. Open file PRO09-40.EWB and measure the voltages with respect to ground at output terminals 1 and 2.

41. Open file PRO09-41.EWB and determine what the fault is.

42. Open file PRO09-42.EWB and determine what the fault is.

43. Open file PRO09-43.EWB and determine what the fault is.

■ **ANSWERS TO SECTION REVIEWS**

Section 9–1

1. Kirchhoff's voltage law and Kirchhoff's current law are used in the branch current method.
2. False, but write the equations so that they are consistent with your assigned directions.
3. A loop is a closed path within a circuit.
4. A node is a junction of two or more components.

Section 9–2

1. (a) 4   (b) 0.415   (c) −98
2. $\begin{vmatrix} 2 & 3 \\ 5 & 4 \end{vmatrix}$
3. −0.286 A = −286 mA

Section 9–3

1. $I_1 = -.038893513289$
   $I_2 = .084110232475$
   $I_3 = .041925798204$
   $I_4 = -.067156192401$
2. $I_1 = -.056363148617$
   $I_2 = .07218287729$
   $I_3 = .065684612774$
   $I_4 = -.041112571034$

Section 9–4

1. No, loop currents are not necessarily the same as branch currents.
2. A negative value means the direction should be reversed.
3. Kirchhoff's voltage law is used in mesh analysis.

Section 9–5

1. Kirchhoff's current law is the basis for node analysis.
2. A reference node is the junction to which all circuit voltages are referenced.

Section 9–6

1. $I_T = 1.9$ mA; use smallest available fuse with a rating greater than 1.9 mA.
2. 10 Ah/1.76 mA = 5682 h

■ **ANSWERS TO RELATED PROBLEMS FOR EXAMPLES**

9–1 $I_{R1} = 176$ mA; $I_{R2} = 77.8$ mA; $I_{R3} = -98.7$ mA
9–2 3.71 A
9–3 −298 mA
9–4 −298 mA
9–5 $X_1 = -1.76923076923$; $X_2 = -18.5384615385$; $X_3 = -34.4615384615$
9–6 $I_1 = X_1 = .138971906754$ (≈ 139 mA); $I_2 = X_2 = -.018679019725$ (≈ −18.7 mA)
9–7 $I_1 = X_1 = .297872340426$ (≈ 298 mA); $I_2 = X_2 = .562762622557$ (≈ 563 mA);
    $I_3 = X_3 = .545521243247$ (≈ 546 mA)
9–8 1.92 V
9–9 $V_A = X_1 = -.928372575682$ (≈ −928 mV); $V_B = X_2 = -5.18980533887$ (≈ −5.19 V)

■ **ANSWERS TO SELF-TEST**

1. (e)   2. (d)   3. (b)   4. (c)   5. (c)   6. (b)   7. (d)   8. (a)
9. (e)   10. (b)

10

MAGNETISM AND ELECTROMAGNETISM

PSpice Tutorial available at
http://www.prenhall.com/floyd

■ INTRODUCTION

This chapter is somewhat of a departure from the coverage of dc circuits in the previous nine chapters because two totally different concepts are introduced—magnetism and electromagnetism. The operation of many types of devices such as the relay, the solenoid, and the speaker is based partially on magnetic or electromagnetic principles.

The concept of electromagnetic induction is important in an electrical component called an inductor or coil that is covered in Chapter 14. At that time, a review of portions of this chapter may be helpful.

Two types of magnets are the permanent magnet and the electromagnet. The permanent magnet maintains a constant magnetic field between its two poles with no external excitation. The electromagnet produces a magnetic field only when there is current through it. The electromagnet is basically a coil of wire wound around a magnetic core material.

In the TECH TIP assignment in Section 10–7, you will learn how electromagnetic relays can be used in burglar alarm systems, and you will develop a procedure to check out the basic alarm system.

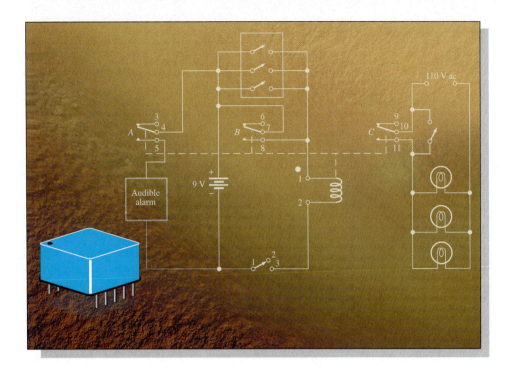

■ CHAPTER OBJECTIVES

❏ Explain the principles of the magnetic field
❏ Explain the principles of electromagnetism
❏ Describe the principle of operation for several types of electromagnetic devices

❏ Explain magnetic hysteresis
❏ Discuss the principle of electromagnetic induction
❏ Describe some applications of electromagnetic induction

HISTORICAL NOTES

Michael Faraday
1791–1867

Michael Faraday was an English physicist and chemist born on September 22, 1791. Faraday is best remembered for his contribution to the understanding of electromagnetism. He discovered that electricity could be produced by moving a magnet inside a coil of wire and was able to build the first electric motor. He later built the first electromagnetic generator and transformer. The statement of the principles of electromagnetic induction is known today as Faraday's law. Also, several words which are commonly used today were coined by Faraday: *ion, electrode, cathode,* and *anode.* Later in life, Faraday became a professor of chemistry at the Royal Institution. His accomplishments were honored when the electrical unit of capacitance, the farad, was named after him. *Photo credit: Library of Congress.*

Heinrich F. E. Lenz
1804–1865

Heinrich F. E. Lenz was born in 1804 in Tartu, Estonia (then Russia). He was a professor at the University of St. Petersburg and carried out many experiments following Faraday's lead. The law of electromagnetism that defines the polarity of the voltage induced in a coil of wire as a result of a change in current is named in Lenz's honor. Very little is known of his early life, but it is thought that he originally studied for the priesthood. *Photo credit: AIP Emilio Segrè Visual Archives, E. Scott Barr Collection.*

10–1 ■ THE MAGNETIC FIELD

A permanent magnet has a magnetic field surrounding it. The magnetic field consists of lines of force that radiate from the north pole to the south pole and back to the north pole through the magnetic material.

After completing this section, you should be able to

■ **Explain the principles of the magnetic field**
- Define *magnetic flux*
- Define *magnetic flux density*
- Discuss how materials are magnetized
- Explain how a magnetic switch works

A permanent magnet, such as the bar magnet shown in Figure 10–1, has a magnetic field surrounding it. You can visualize the magnetic field as consisting of lines of force, or flux lines, that radiate from the north pole (N) to the south pole (S) and back to the north pole through the magnetic material. For clarity, only a few lines of force are shown in the figure. Imagine, however, that many lines surround the magnet in three dimensions. The lines shrink to the smallest possible size and blend together, although they do not touch. This effectively forms a continuous magnetic field surrounding the magnet.

FIGURE 10–1
Magnetic lines of force around a bar magnet.

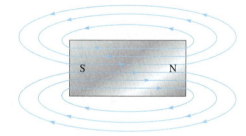

Blue lines represent only a few of the many magnetic lines of force in the magnetic field.

Attraction and Repulsion of Magnetic Poles

When unlike poles of two permanent magnets are placed close together, an attractive force is produced by the magnetic fields, as indicated in Figure 10–2(a). When two like poles are brought close together, they repel each other, as shown in part (b).

Altering a Magnetic Field

When a nonmagnetic material such as paper, glass, wood, or plastic is placed in a magnetic field, the lines of force are unaltered, as shown in Figure 10–3(a). However, when a magnetic material such as iron is placed in the magnetic field, the lines of force tend to change course and pass through the iron rather than through the surrounding air. They do so because the iron provides a magnetic path that is more easily established than that of air. Figure 10–3(b) illustrates this principle.

Magnetic Flux (ϕ)

The group of force lines going from the north pole to the south pole of a magnet is called the **magnetic flux,** symbolized by ϕ (the Greek letter phi). The number of lines of force in a magnetic field determines the value of the flux. The more lines of force, the greater the flux and the stronger the magnetic field.

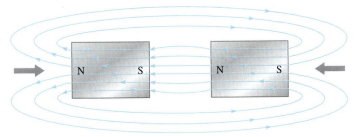

(a) Unlike poles attract.

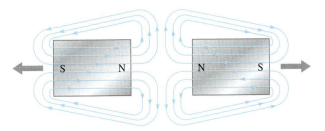

(b) Like poles repel.

FIGURE 10–2
Magnetic attraction and repulsion.

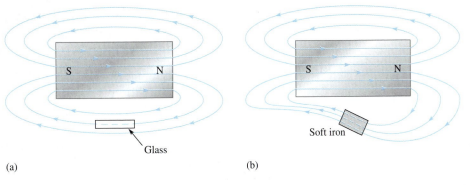

(a)   (b)

FIGURE 10–3
Effect of (a) nonmagnetic and (b) magnetic materials on a magnetic field.

The unit of magnetic flux is the **weber** (Wb). One weber equals 10^8 lines. The weber is a very large unit; thus, in most practical situations, the microweber (μWb) is used. One microweber equals 100 lines of magnetic flux.

Magnetic Flux Density *(B)*

The **magnetic flux density** is the amount of flux per unit area perpendicular to the magnetic field. Its symbol is B, and its SI unit is the **tesla** (T). One tesla equals one weber per square meter (Wb/m^2). The following formula expresses the flux density:

$$B = \frac{\phi}{A}$$

(10–1)

where ϕ is the flux and A is the cross-sectional area in square meters (m^2) of the magnetic field.

EXAMPLE 10–1   Find the flux density in a magnetic field in which the flux in 0.1 m² is 800 μWb.

Solution
$$B = \frac{\phi}{A} = \frac{800 \ \mu\text{Wb}}{0.1 \ \text{m}^2} = \textbf{8000} \ \boldsymbol{\mu}\textbf{T}$$

Related Problem   Calculate ϕ if $B = 4700 \ \mu$T and $A = 0.05$ m².

EXAMPLE 10–2   If the flux density in a certain magnetic material is 2.3 T and the area of the material is 0.38 in.², what is the flux through the material?

Solution   First, 0.38 in.² must be converted to square meters. 39.37 in. = 1 m; therefore,

$$A = 0.38 \ \text{in.}^2[1 \ \text{m}^2/(39.37 \ \text{in.})^2] = 245 \times 10^{-6} \ \text{m}^2$$

The flux through the material is

$$\phi = BA = (2.3 \ \text{T})(245 \times 10^{-6} \ \text{m}^2) = \textbf{564} \ \boldsymbol{\mu}\textbf{Wb}$$

Related Problem   Calculate B if $A = 0.05$ in.² and $\phi = 1000 \ \mu$Wb.

The Gauss   Although the tesla (T) is the SI unit for flux density, another unit called the *gauss,* from the CGS (centimeter-gram-second) system, is sometimes used (10^4 gauss = 1 T). In fact, the instrument used to measure flux density is the gaussmeter.

How Materials Become Magnetized

Ferromagnetic materials such as iron, nickel, and cobalt become magnetized when placed in the magnetic field of a magnet. We have all seen a permanent magnet pick up things like paper clips, nails, and iron filings. In these cases, the object becomes magnetized (that is, it actually becomes a magnet itself) under the influence of the permanent magnetic field and becomes attracted to the magnet. When removed from the magnetic field, the object tends to lose its magnetism.

Ferromagnetic materials have minute magnetic domains created within their atomic structure. These domains can be viewed as very small bar magnets with north and south poles. When the material is not exposed to an external magnetic field, the magnetic domains are randomly oriented, as shown in Figure 10–4(a). When the material is placed in a magnetic field, the domains align themselves as shown in part (b). Thus, the object itself effectively becomes a magnet.

(a) The magnetic domains (N ⬤ S) are randomly oriented in the unmagnetized material.

(b) The magnetic domains become aligned when the material is magnetized.

FIGURE 10–4

Magnetic domains in (a) an unmagnetized and (b) a magnetized material.

An Application

Permanent magnets have numerous applications. The normally closed (NC) magnetic switch is presented here as an illustration. When the magnet is near the switch mechanism as in Figure 10–5(a), the metallic arm is held in its NC position. When the magnet is moved away as in part (b), the spring pulls the arm up, breaking the contact.

FIGURE 10–5
Operation of a magnetic switch.

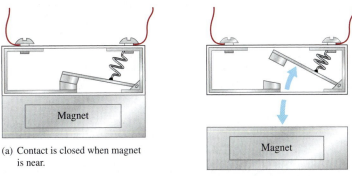

(a) Contact is closed when magnet is near.

(b) Contact opens when magnet is moved away.

Switches of this type are commonly used in perimeter alarm systems to detect entry into a building through windows or doors. As Figure 10–6 shows, several openings can be protected by magnetic switches wired to a common transmitter. When any one of the switches opens, the transmitter is activated and sends a signal to a central receiver and alarm unit.

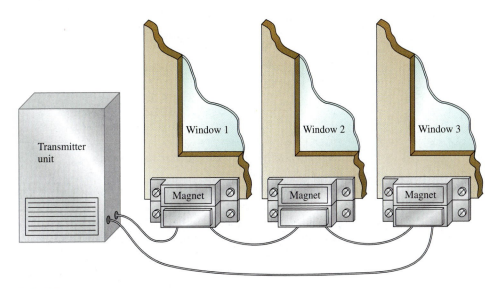

FIGURE 10–6
Connection of a typical perimeter alarm system.

SECTION 10–1 REVIEW

1. When the north poles of two magnets are placed close together, do they repel or attract each other?

2. What is magnetic flux?

3. What is the flux density when $\phi = 4.5$ μWb and $A = 5 \times 10^{-3}$ m^2?

10–2 ■ ELECTROMAGNETISM

Electromagnetism is the production of a magnetic field by current in a conductor. Many types of useful devices such as tape recorders, electric motors, speakers, solenoids, and relays are based on electromagnetism.

After completing this section, you should be able to

■ **Explain the principles of electromagnetism**
  • Determine the direction of the magnetic lines of force
  • Define *permeability*
  • Define *reluctance*
  • Define *magnetomotive force*
  • Describe a basic electromagnet

Current produces a magnetic field, called an **electromagnetic field,** around a conductor, as illustrated in Figure 10–7. The invisible lines of force of the magnetic field form a concentric circular pattern around the conductor and are continuous along its length. Unlike the bar magnet, the magnetic field surrounding a wire does not have a north or south pole.

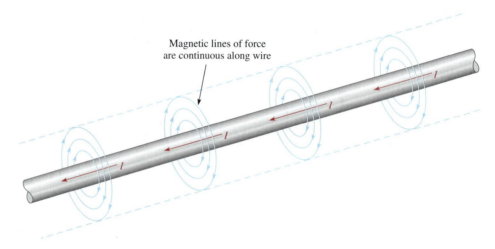

Magnetic lines of force are continuous along wire

FIGURE 10–7
Magnetic field around a current-carrying conductor.

Although the magnetic field cannot be seen, it is capable of producing visible effects. For example, if a current-carrying wire is inserted through a sheet of paper in a perpendicular direction, iron filings placed on the surface of the paper arrange themselves along the magnetic lines of force in concentric rings, as illustrated in Figure 10–8(a). Part (b) of the figure illustrates that the north pole of a compass placed in the electromagnetic field will point in the direction of the lines of force. The field is stronger closer to the conductor and becomes weaker with increasing distance from the conductor.

FIGURE 10–8
Visible effects of an electromagnetic field.

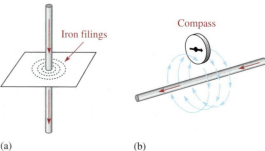

Iron filings

Compass

(a)   (b)

Direction of the Lines of Force

The direction of the lines of force surrounding the conductor is indicated in Figure 10–9. When the direction of current is right to left, as in part (a), the lines are in a clockwise direction. When current is left to right, as in part (b), the lines are in a counterclockwise direction.

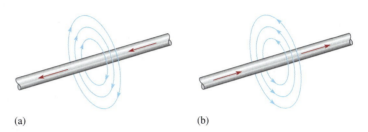

(a)   (b)

FIGURE 10–9
Magnetic lines of force around a current-carrying conductor.

Left-Hand Rule   An aid to remembering the direction of the lines of force is illustrated in Figure 10–10. Imagine that you are grasping the conductor with your left hand, with your thumb pointing in the direction of current. Your fingers point in the direction of the magnetic lines of force.

FIGURE 10–10
Illustration of left-hand rule.

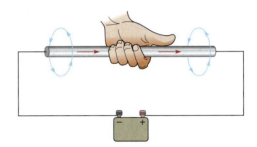

Electromagnetic Properties

Several important properties relating to electromagnetic fields are now discussed.

Permeability (μ)   The ease with which a magnetic field can be established in a given material is measured by the **permeability** of that material. The higher the permeability, the more easily a magnetic field can be established.

The symbol of permeability is μ (the Greek letter mu), and its value varies depending on the type of material. The permeability of a vacuum (μ_0) is $4\pi \times 10^{-7}$ Wb/At·m (weber/ampere-turn·meter) and is used as a reference. Ferromagnetic materials typically have permeabilities hundreds of times larger than that of a vacuum, indicating that a magnetic field can be set up with relative ease in these materials. Ferromagnetic materials include iron, steel, nickel, cobalt, and their alloys.

The *relative permeability* (μ_r) of a material is the ratio of its absolute permeability to the permeability of a vacuum.

$$\mu_r = \frac{\mu}{\mu_0}$$

(10–2)

Reluctance ($\mathcal{R}$)   The opposition to the establishment of a magnetic field in a material is called **reluctance.** The value of reluctance is directly proportional to the length (l) of the magnetic path and inversely proportional to the permeability (μ) and to the cross-sectional area (A) of the material, as expressed by the following equation:

$$\mathcal{R} = \frac{l}{\mu A} \qquad\qquad (10\text{--}3)$$

Reluctance in magnetic circuits is analogous to resistance in electric circuits. The unit of reluctance can be derived using l in meters, A (area) in square meters, and μ in Wb/At·m as follows:

$$\mathcal{R} = \frac{l}{\mu A} = \frac{\cancel{m}}{(\text{Wb/At}\cdot\cancel{m})(\cancel{m^2})} = \frac{\text{At}}{\text{Wb}}$$

At/Wb is ampere-turns/weber.

EXAMPLE 10–3   What is the reluctance of a material that has a length of 0.05 m, a cross-sectional area of 0.012 m², and a permeability of 3500 μWb/At·m?

Solution
$$\mathcal{R} = \frac{l}{\mu A} = \frac{0.05 \text{ m}}{(3500 \times 10^{-6} \text{ Wb/At}\cdot\text{m})(0.012 \text{ m}^2)} = \textbf{1190 At/Wb}$$

Related Problem   What happens to the reluctance of the material in this example if l is doubled and A is halved?

Magnetomotive Force (mmf)   As you have learned, current in a conductor produces a magnetic field. The force that produces the magnetic field is called the **magnetomotive force** (mmf). The unit of mmf, the **ampere-turn** (At), is established on the basis of the current in a single loop (turn) of wire. The formula for mmf is

$$F_m = NI \qquad\qquad (10\text{--}4)$$

where F_m is the magnetomotive force, N is the number of turns of wire, and I is the current in amperes.

Figure 10–11 illustrates that a number of turns of wire carrying a current around a magnetic material creates a force that sets up flux lines through the magnetic path. The amount of flux depends on the magnitude of the mmf and on the reluctance of the material, as expressed by the following equation:

$$\phi = \frac{F_m}{\mathcal{R}} \qquad\qquad (10\text{--}5)$$

Equation (10–5) is known as the *Ohm's law for magnetic circuits* because the flux (ϕ) is analogous to current, the mmf (F_m) is analogous to voltage, and the reluctance ($\mathcal{R}$) is analogous to resistance.

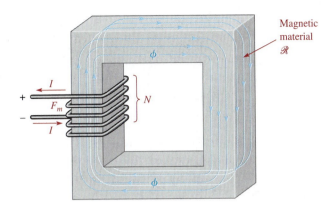

FIGURE 10–11
A basic magnetic circuit.

EXAMPLE 10–4

How much flux is established in the magnetic path of Figure 10–12 if the reluctance of the material is 28×10^3 At/Wb?

FIGURE 10–12

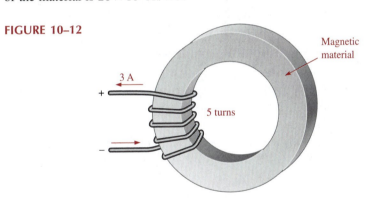

Solution

$$\phi = \frac{F_m}{\mathcal{R}} = \frac{NI}{\mathcal{R}} = \frac{(5 \text{ t})(3 \text{ A})}{28 \times 10^3 \text{ At/Wb}} = \mathbf{536 \ \mu Wb}$$

Related Problem How much flux is established in the magnetic path of Figure 10–12 if the reluctance is 7.5×10^3 At/Wb, the number of turns is 30, and the current is 1.8 A?

EXAMPLE 10–5

There are two amperes of current through a wire with 5 turns.
(a) What is the mmf?
(b) What is the reluctance of the circuit if the flux is 250 μWb?

Solution
(a) $N = 5$ and $I = 2$ A
$$F_m = NI = (5 \text{ t})(2 \text{ A}) = \mathbf{10 \ At}$$
(b) $\mathcal{R} = \dfrac{F_m}{\phi} = \dfrac{10 \text{ At}}{250 \ \mu\text{Wb}} = \mathbf{40 \times 10^3 \ At/Wb}$

Related Problem Rework the example for $I = 850$ mA and $N = 50$. The flux is 500 μWb.

The Electromagnet

An electromagnet is based on the properties that you have just learned. A basic electro-magnet is simply a coil of wire wound around a core material that can be easily magne-tized.

   The shape of the electromagnet can be designed for various applications. For exam-ple, Figure 10–13 shows a U-shaped magnetic core. When the coil of wire is connected to a battery and there is current, as shown in part (a), a magnetic field is established as indicated. If the current is reversed, as shown in part (b), the direction of the magnetic field is also reversed. The closer the north and south poles are brought together, the smaller the air gap between them becomes, and the easier it becomes to establish a mag-netic field because the reluctance is lessened.

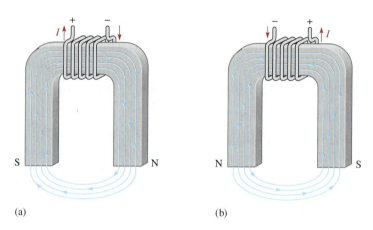

(a)   (b)

FIGURE 10–13
Reversing the current in the coil causes the electromagnetic field to reverse.

Application Examples

Magnetic Disk/Tape Read/Write Head   A simplified diagram of the magnetic disk or tape surface read/write operation is shown in Figure 10–14. A data bit (1 or 0) is written on the magnetic surface by the magnetization of a small segment of the surface as it moves by the write head. The direction of the magnetic flux lines is controlled by the direction of the current pulse in the winding, as shown in Figure 10–14(a). At the air gap in the write head, the magnetic flux takes a path through the surface of the storage device. This magnetizes a small spot on the surface in the direction of the field. A magnetized spot of one polarity represents a binary 1, and one of the opposite polarity represents a binary 0. Once a spot on the surface is magnetized, it remains until written over with an opposite magnetic field.

   When the magnetic surface passes a read head, the magnetized spots produce mag-netic fields in the read head, which induce voltage pulses in the winding. The polarity of these pulses depends on the direction of the magnetized spot and indicates whether the stored bit is a 1 or a 0. This process is illustrated in Figure 10–14(b). Often the read and write heads are combined into a single unit.

The Magneto-Optical Disk   The magneto-optical disk uses an electromagnet and laser beams to read and write (record) data on a magnetic surface. Magneto-optical disks are formatted in tracks and sectors similar to magnetic floppy disks and hard disks. However, because of the ability of a laser beam to be precisely directed to an extremely small spot, magneto-optical disks are capable of storing much more data than standard magnetic hard disks.

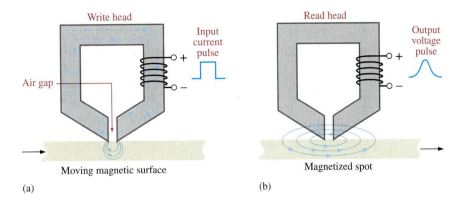

(a)   (b)

FIGURE 10–14

Read/write function on a magnetic surface.

Figure 10–15(a) illustrates a small cross-sectional area of a disk before recording, with an electromagnet positioned above it. Tiny magnetic particles, represented by the arrows, are all magnetized in the same direction.

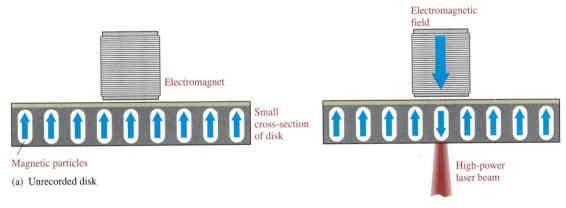

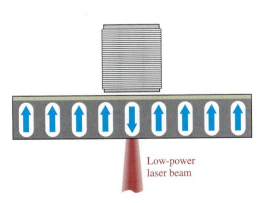

(c) Reading from the disk. Low-power laser beam reflects off of reversed polarity particle and its polarization shifts. If the particle is not reversed, the polarization of the reflected beam is unchanged.

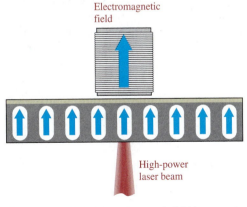

(d) Erasing the disk. External magnetic field is reversed and the high-power laser beam causes the magnetic particle to align with the external beam restoring its original polarity.

FIGURE 10–15

Basic concept of the magneto-optical disk.

Writing (recording) on the disk is accomplished by applying an external magnetic field opposite to the direction of the magnetic particles as indicated in Figure 10–15(b) and then directing a high-power laser beam to heat the disk at a precise point where a binary 1 is to be stored. The disk material, a magneto-optic alloy, is highly resistant to magnetization at room temperature; but at the spot where the laser beam heats the material, the inherent direction of magnetism is reversed by the external magnetic field produced by the electromagnet. At points where binary 0s are to be stored, the laser beam is not applied and the inherent upward direction of the magnetic particle remains.

As illustrated in Figure 10–15(c), reading data from the disk is accomplished by turning off the external magnetic field and directing a low-power laser beam at a spot where a bit is to be read. Basically, if a binary 1 is stored at the spot (reversed magnetization), the laser beam is reflected and its polarization is shifted; but if a binary 0 is stored, the polarization of the reflected laser beam is unchanged. A detector senses the difference in the polarity of the reflected laser beam to determine if the bit being read is a 1 or a 0.

Figure 10–15(d) shows that the disk is erased by restoring the original magnetic direction of each particle by reversing the external magnetic field and applying the high power laser beam.

SECTION 10–2 REVIEW

1. Explain the difference between magnetism and electromagnetism.
2. What happens to the magnetic field in an electromagnet when the current through the coil is reversed?
3. State Ohm's law for a magnetic circuit.
4. Compare each quantity in Question 3 to its electrical counterpart.

10–3 ■ ELECTROMAGNETIC DEVICES

In the last section, you learned that the recording head is a type of electromagnetic device. Now, several other common devices are introduced.

After completing this section, you should be able to

■ **Describe the principle of operation for several types of electromagnetic devices**
  • Discuss how a solenoid works
  • Discuss how a relay works
  • Discuss how a speaker works
  • Discuss the basic analog meter movement

The magnetic disk/tape read/write head and the magneto-optical disk illustrated in the last section are two examples of electromagnetic devices. Several other examples are now presented.

The Solenoid

The **solenoid** is a type of electromagnetic device that has a movable iron core called a *plunger*. The movement of this iron core depends on both an electromagnetic field and a mechanical spring force. A basic structure of a solenoid is shown in Figure 10–16. It consists of a cylindrical coil of wire wound around a nonmagnetic hollow form. A stationary iron core is fixed in position at the end of the shaft and a sliding iron core (plunger) is attached to the stationary core with a spring.

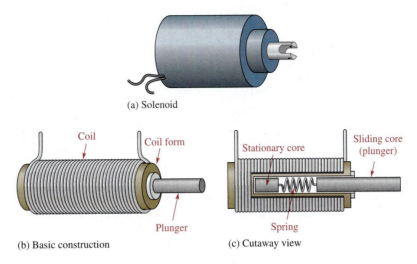

(a) Solenoid

(b) Basic construction

(c) Cutaway view

FIGURE 10–16
Basic solenoid structure.

In the at-rest (or unenergized) state, the plunger is extended. The solenoid is energized by current through the coil, which sets up an electromagnetic field that magnetizes both iron cores. The south pole of the stationary core attracts the north pole of the movable core causing it to slide inward, thus retracting the plunger and compressing the spring. As long as there is coil current, the plunger remains retracted by the attractive force of the magnetic fields. When the current is cut off, the magnetic fields collapse and the force of the compressed spring pushes the plunger back out. This basic solenoid operation is illustrated in Figure 10–17 for the unenergized and the energized conditions. The solenoid is used for applications such as opening and closing valves and automobile door locks.

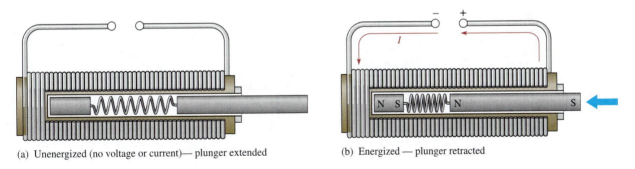

(a) Unenergized (no voltage or current)— plunger extended

(b) Energized — plunger retracted

FIGURE 10–17
Basic solenoid operation.

The Relay

Relays differ from solenoids in that the electromagnetic action is used to open or close electrical contacts rather than to provide mechanical movement. Figure 10–18 shows the basic operation of an *armature-type relay* with one normally open (NO) contact and one normally closed (NC) contact (single pole–double throw). When there is no coil current, the armature is held against the upper contact by the spring, thus providing continuity from terminal 1 to terminal 2, as shown in part (a) of the figure. When energized with coil current, the armature is pulled down by the attractive force of the electromagnetic field and makes connection with the lower contact to provide continuity from terminal 1 to terminal 3, as shown in Figure 10–18(b). The schematic symbol is shown in Figure 10–18(c).

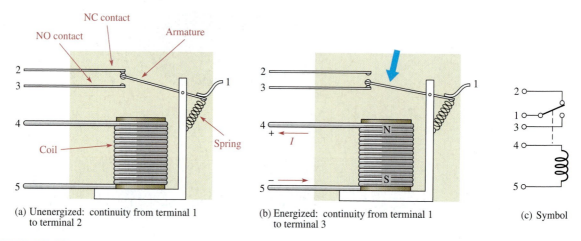

(a) Unenergized: continuity from terminal 1 to terminal 2

(b) Energized: continuity from terminal 1 to terminal 3

(c) Symbol

FIGURE 10–18
Basic structure of a single-pole–double-throw relay.

Another widely used type of relay is the *reed relay,* which is shown in Figure 10–19. The reed relay, like the armature relay uses an electromagnetic coil. The contacts are thin reeds of magnetic material and are usually located inside the coil. When there is no coil current, the reeds are in the open position as shown in part (b). When there is current through the coil, the reeds make contact because they are magnetized and attract each other as shown in part (c).

Reed relays are superior to armature relays in that they are faster, more reliable, and produce less contact arcing. However, they have less current-handling capability than armature relays and are more susceptible to mechanical shock.

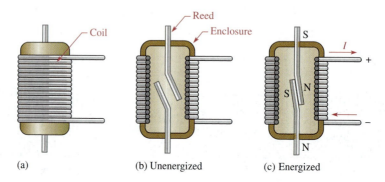

(a)

(b) Unenergized

(c) Energized

FIGURE 10–19
Basic structure of a reed relay.

The Speaker

Permanent-magnet speakers are commonly used in stereos, radios, and TVs, and their operation is based on the principle of electromagnetism. A typical speaker is constructed with both a permanent magnet and an electromagnet, as shown in Figure 10–20(a). The cone of the speaker consists of a paper-like diaphragm to which is attached a hollow cylinder with a coil around it, forming an electromagnet. One of the poles of the permanent magnet is positioned within the cylindrical coil. When there is current through the coil in one direction, the interaction of the permanent magnetic field with the electromagnetic field causes the cylinder to move to the right, as indicated in Figure 10–20(b). Current through the coil in the other direction causes the cylinder to move to the left, as shown in part (c).

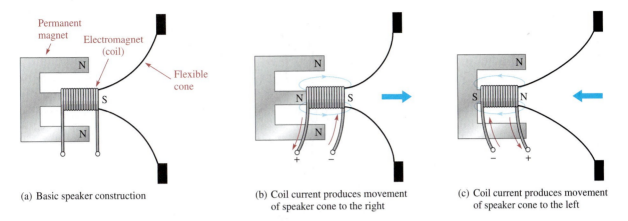

(a) Basic speaker construction

(b) Coil current produces movement of speaker cone to the right

(c) Coil current produces movement of speaker cone to the left

FIGURE 10–20
Basic speaker operation.

The movement of the coil cylinder causes the flexible diaphragm (cone) also to move in or out, depending on the direction of the coil current. The amount of coil current determines the intensity of the magnetic field, which controls the amount that the diaphragm moves.

As shown in Figure 10–21, when an audio signal (voice or music) is applied to the coil, the current varies in both direction and amount. In response, the diaphragm will vibrate in and out by varying amounts and at varying rates corresponding to the audio signal. Vibration in the diaphragm causes the air that is in contact with it to vibrate in the same manner. These air vibrations move through the air as sound waves.

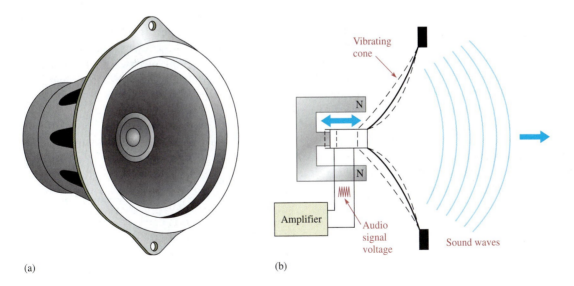

(a)

(b)

FIGURE 10–21
The speaker converts audio signal voltages into sound waves.

Analog Meter Movement

The d'Arsonval meter movement is the most common type used in analog multimeters. In this type of meter movement, the pointer is deflected in proportion to the amount of current through a coil. Figure 10–22 shows a basic d'Arsonval meter movement. It consists of a coil of wire wound on a bearing-mounted assembly that is placed between the poles of a permanent magnet. A pointer is attached to the moving assembly. With no current

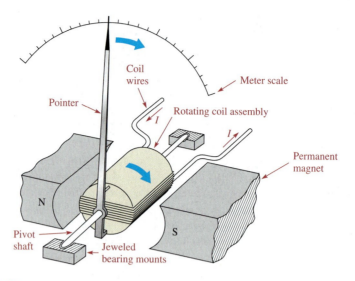

FIGURE 10–22
The basic d'Arsonval meter movement.

through the coil, a spring mechanism keeps the pointer at its left-most (zero) position. When there is current through the coil, electromagnetic forces act on the coil, causing a rotation to the right. The amount of rotation depends on the amount of current.

Figure 10–23 illustrates how the interaction of magnetic fields produces rotation of the coil assembly. The current is inward at the "cross" and outward at the "dot" in the single winding shown. The outward current produces a clockwise electromagnetic field that reinforces the permanent magnetic field above it. The result is a downward force on the right side of the coil as shown. The inward current produces a counterclockwise electromagnetic field that reinforces the permanent magnetic field below it. The result is an upward force on the left side of the coil as shown. These forces produce a clockwise rotation of the coil assembly and are opposed by a spring mechanism. The indicated forces and the spring force are balanced at the value of the current. When current is removed, the spring force returns the pointer to its zero position.

FIGURE 10–23
When the electromagnetic field interacts with the permanent magnetic field, forces are exerted on the rotating coil assembly, causing it to move clockwise and thus deflecting the pointer.

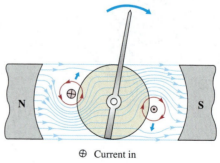

⊕ Current in
⊙ Current out

SECTION 10–3 REVIEW

1. Explain the difference between a solenoid and a relay.
2. What is the movable part of a solenoid called?
3. What is the movable part of a relay called?
4. Upon what basic principle is the d'Arsonval meter movement based?

10–4 ■ MAGNETIC HYSTERESIS

When a magnetizing force is applied to a material, the flux density in the material changes in a certain way, which we will now examine.

After completing this section, you should be able to

■ **Explain magnetic hysteresis**
  • State the formula for magnetizing force
  • Discuss a hysteresis curve
  • Define *retentivity*

Magnetizing Force *(H)*

The **magnetizing force** in a material is defined to be the magnetomotive force (F_m) per unit length (l) of the material, as expressed by the following equation. The unit of magnetizing force (H) is ampere-turns per meter (At/m).

$$H = \frac{F_m}{l} \qquad \textbf{(10–6)}$$

where $F_m = NI$. Note that the magnetizing force depends on the number of turns (N) of the coil of wire, the current (I) through the coil, and the length (l) of the material. It does not depend on the type of material.

Since $\phi = F_m/\mathcal{R}$, as F_m increases, the flux increases. Also, the magnetizing force (H) increases. Recall that the flux density (B) is the flux per unit cross-sectional area ($B = \phi/A$), so B is also proportional to H. The curve showing how these two quantities (B and H) are related is called the *B-H* curve or the hysteresis curve. The parameters that influence both B and H are illustrated in Figure 10–24.

FIGURE 10–24
Parameters that determine the magnetizing force (H) and the flux density (B).

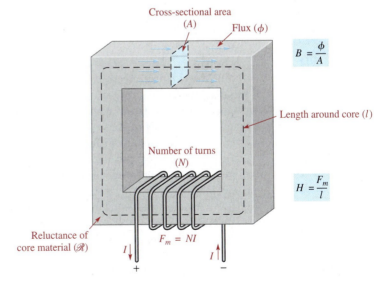

Cross-sectional area (A)
Flux (ϕ)
$B = \dfrac{\phi}{A}$
Length around core (l)
Number of turns (N)
$H = \dfrac{F_m}{l}$
Reluctance of core material ($\mathcal{R}$)
$F_m = NI$

The Hysteresis Curve and Retentivity

Hysteresis is a characteristic of a magnetic material whereby a change in magnetization lags the application of a magnetizing force. The magnetizing force (H) can be readily increased or decreased by varying the current through the coil of wire, and it can be reversed by reversing the voltage polarity across the coil.

Figure 10–25 illustrates the development of the hysteresis curve. Let's start by assuming a magnetic core is unmagnetized so that $B = 0$. As the magnetizing force (H) is increased from zero, the flux density (B) increases proportionally as indicated by the curve in Figure 10–25(a). When H reaches a certain value, B begins to level off. As H continues to increase, B reaches a saturation value (B_{sat}) when H reaches a value (H_{sat}) as illustrated in Figure 10–25(b). Once saturation is reached, a further increase in H will not increase B.

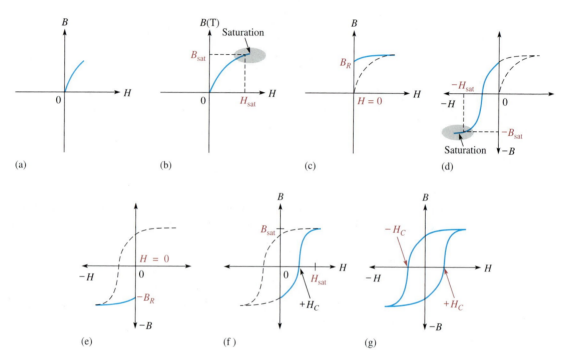

FIGURE 10–25
Development of a magnetic hysteresis curve.

Now, if H is decreased to zero, B will fall back along a different path to a residual value (B_R) as shown in Figure 10–25(c). This indicates that the material continues to be magnetized even with the magnetizing force removed ($H = 0$). The ability of a material to maintain a magnetized state without the presence of a magnetizing force is called **retentivity.** The retentivity of a material represents the maximum flux that can be retained after the material has been magnetized to saturation and is indicated by the ratio of B_R to B_{sat}.

Reversal of the magnetizing force is represented by negative values of H on the curve and is achieved by reversing the current in the coil of wire. An increase in H in the negative direction causes saturation to occur at a value ($-H_{sat}$) where the flux density is at its maximum negative value as indicated in Figure 10–25(d).

When the magnetizing force is removed ($H = 0$), the flux density goes to its negative residual value ($-B_R$) as shown in Figure 10–25(e). From the $-B_R$ value, the flux density follows the curve indicated in part (f) back to its maximum positive value when the magnetizing force equals H_{sat} in the positive direction.

The complete B-H curve is shown in Figure 10–25(g) and is called the *hysteresis curve.* The magnetizing force required to make the flux density zero is called the *coercive force, H_C.*

Materials with a low retentivity do not retain a magnetic field very well, while those with high retentivities exhibit values of B_R very close to the saturation value of B. Depending on the application, retentivity in a magnetic material can be an advantage or a disadvantage. In permanent magnets and magnetic tape, for example, high retentivity is required; while in tape recorder read/write heads, low retentivity is necessary. In ac motors, retentivity is undesirable because the residual magnetic field must be overcome each time the current reverses, thus wasting energy.

SECTION 10–4 REVIEW	**1.** For a given wirewound core, how does an increase in current through the coil affect the flux density? **2.** Define *retentivity*. **3.** Why is low retentivity required for tape recorder read/write heads but high retentivity is required for magnetic tape?

10–5 ■ ELECTROMAGNETIC INDUCTION

When a conductor is moved through a magnetic field, a voltage is produced across the conductor. This principle is known as electromagnetic induction and the resulting voltage is an induced voltage. The principle of electromagnetic induction is what makes transformers, electrical generators, and many other devices possible.

After completing this section, you should be able to

■ **Discuss the principle of electromagnetic induction**
  • Explain how voltage is induced in a conductor in a magnetic field
  • Determine polarity of an induced voltage
  • Discuss forces on a conductor in a magnetic field
  • State Faraday's law
  • State Lenz's law

Relative Motion

When a wire is moved across a magnetic field, there is a relative motion between the wire and the magnetic field. Likewise, when a magnetic field is moved past a stationary wire, there is also relative motion. In either case, this relative motion results in an induced voltage (v_{ind}) in the wire, as Figure 10–26 indicates. The lowercase v stands for instantaneous voltage.

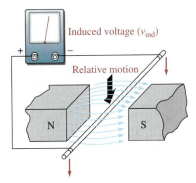

(a) Wire moving downward

(b) Magnetic field moving upward

FIGURE 10–26
Relative motion between a wire and a magnetic field.

The amount of the induced voltage depends on the rate at which the wire and the magnetic field move with respect to each other. The faster the relative speed, the greater the induced voltage.

Polarity of the Induced Voltage

If the conductor in Figure 10–26 is moved first one way and then another in the magnetic field, a reversal of the polarity of the induced voltage will be observed. As the wire is moved downward, a voltage is induced with the polarity indicated in Figure 10–27(a). As the wire is moved upward, the polarity is as indicated in part (b) of the figure.

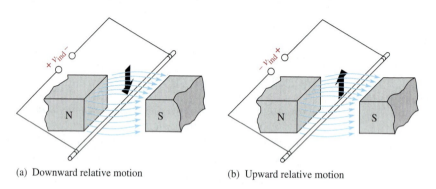

(a) Downward relative motion   (b) Upward relative motion

FIGURE 10–27
Polarity of induced voltage depends on direction of motion.

Induced Current

When a load resistor is connected to the wire in Figure 10–27, the voltage induced by the relative motion in the magnetic field will cause a current in the load, as shown in Figure 10–28. This current is called the induced current (i_{ind}). The lowercase i stands for instantaneous current.

FIGURE 10–28
Induced current in a load as the wire moves through the magnetic field.

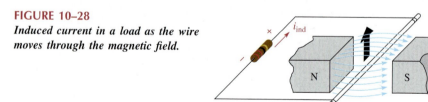

The action of producing a voltage and a resulting current in a load by moving a conductor across a magnetic field is the basis for electrical generators. The concept of a conductor existing in a moving magnetic field is the basis for inductance in an electric circuit.

Forces on a Current-Carrying Conductor in a Magnetic Field (Motor Action)

Figure 10–29(a) shows current inward through a wire in a magnetic field. The electromagnetic field set up by the current interacts with the permanent magnetic field; as a result, the permanent lines of force above the wire tend to be deflected down under the wire, because they are opposite in direction to the electromagnetic lines of force. Therefore, the flux density above is reduced, and the magnetic field is weakened. The flux density below the conductor is increased, and the magnetic field is strengthened. An upward force on the conductor results, and the conductor tends to move toward the weaker magnetic field.

Figure 10–29(b) shows the current outward, resulting in a force on the conductor in the downward direction. This force is the basis for electrical motors.

(a) Upward force: weak field above, strong field below.

(b) Downward force: strong field above, weak field below

⊙ Current out
⊕ Current in

FIGURE 10–29
Forces on a current-carrying conductor in a magnetic field (motor action).

Faraday's Law

Michael Faraday discovered the principle of **electromagnetic induction** in 1831. He found that moving a magnet through a coil of wire induced a voltage across the coil, and that when a complete path was provided, the induced voltage caused an induced current, as you have learned. Faraday's two observations are stated as follows:

1. The amount of voltage induced in a coil is directly proportional to the rate of change of the magnetic field with respect to the coil ($d\phi/dt$).

2. The amount of voltage induced in a coil is directly proportional to the number of turns of wire in the coil (N).

Faraday's first observation is demonstrated in Figure 10–30, where a bar magnet is moved through a coil, thus creating a changing magnetic field. In part (a) of the figure, the magnet is moved at a certain rate, and a certain induced voltage is produced as indicated. In part (b), the magnet is moved at a faster rate through the coil, creating a greater induced voltage.

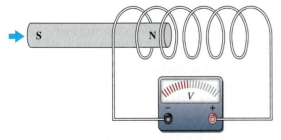

(a) As magnet moves slowly to the right, magnetic field is changing with respect to coil, and a voltage is induced.

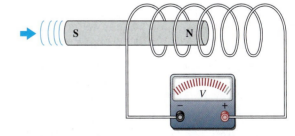

(b) As magnet moves more rapidly to the right, magnetic field is changing more rapidly with respect to coil, and a greater voltage is induced.

FIGURE 10–30
A demonstration of Faraday's first observation: The amount of induced voltage is directly proportional to the rate of change of the magnetic field with respect to the coil.

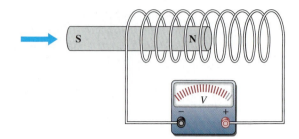

(a) Magnet moves through a coil and induces a voltage.

(b) Magnet moves at same rate through a coil with more turns (loops) and induces a greater voltage.

FIGURE 10–31

A demonstration of Faraday's second observation: The amount of induced voltage is directly proportional to the number of turns in the coil.

Faraday's second observation is demonstrated in Figure 10–31. In part (a), the magnet is moved through the coil and a voltage is induced as shown. In part (b), the magnet is moved at the same speed through a coil that has a greater number of turns. The greater number of turns creates a greater induced voltage.

Faraday's law is stated as follows:

The voltage induced across a coil of wire equals the number of turns in the coil times the rate of change of the magnetic flux.

Faraday's law is expressed in equation form as

$$v_{ind} = N\left(\frac{d\phi}{dt}\right)$$ (10–7)

EXAMPLE 10–6

Apply Faraday's law to find the induced voltage across a coil with 100 turns that is located in a magnetic field that is changing at a rate of 5 Wb/s.

Solution
$$v_{ind} = N\left(\frac{d\phi}{dt}\right) = (100\ t)(5\ \text{Wb/s}) = \textbf{500 V}$$

Related Problem Find the induced voltage across a 250 turn coil in a magnetic field that is changing at 50 μWb/s.

Lenz's Law

You have learned that a changing magnetic field induces a voltage in a coil that is directly proportional to the rate of change of the magnetic field and the number of turns in the coil. Lenz's law defines the polarity or direction of the induced voltage.

When the current through a coil changes, an induced voltage is created as a result of the changing electromagnetic field, and the direction of the induced voltage is such that it always opposes the change in current.

SECTION 10–5 REVIEW

1. What is the induced voltage across a stationary conductor in a stationary magnetic field?

2. When the speed at which a conductor is moved through a magnetic field is increased, does the induced voltage increase, decrease, or remain the same?

3. When there is current through a conductor in a magnetic field, what happens?

10–6 ■ APPLICATIONS OF ELECTROMAGNETIC INDUCTION

In this section, two interesting applications of electromagnetic induction are discussed—an automotive crankshaft position sensor and a dc generator. Although there are many varied applications, these two are representative.

After completing this section, you should be able to

■ **Describe some applications of electromagnetic induction**
  • Explain how a crankshaft position sensor works
  • Explain how a dc generator works

Automotive Crankshaft Position Sensor

An interesting automotive application is a type of engine sensor that detects the crankshaft position directly using electromagnetic induction. The electronic engine controller in many automobiles uses the position of the crankshaft to set ignition timing and, sometimes, to adjust the fuel control system. Figure 10–32 shows the basic concept. A steel disk is attached to the engine's crankshaft by an extension rod; the protruding tabs on the disk represent specific crankshaft positions.

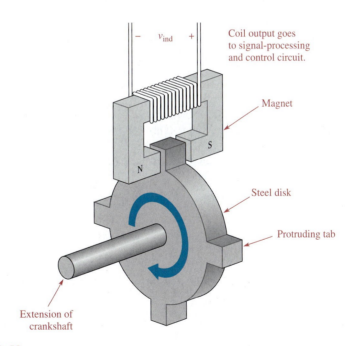

FIGURE 10–32
A crankshaft position sensor that produces a voltage when a tab passes through the air gap of the magnet.

As illustrated in Figure 10–32, as the disk rotates with the crankshaft, the tabs periodically pass through the air gap of the permanent magnet. Since steel has a much lower reluctance than does air (a magnetic field can be established in steel much more easily than in air), the magnetic flux suddenly increases as a tab comes into the air gap, causing a voltage to be induced across the coil. This process is illustrated in Figure 10–33. The electronic engine control circuit uses the induced voltage as an indicator of the crankshaft position.

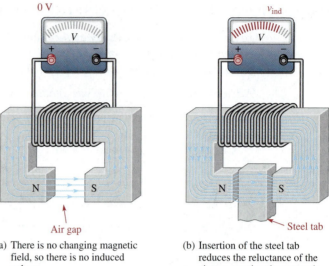

(a) There is no changing magnetic field, so there is no induced voltage.

(b) Insertion of the steel tab reduces the reluctance of the air gap, causing the magnetic flux to increase and thus inducing a voltage.

FIGURE 10–33

As the tab passes through the air gap of the magnet, the coil senses a change in the magnetic field, and a voltage is induced.

DC Generator

Figure 10–34 shows a simplified dc generator consisting of a single loop of wire in a permanent magnetic field. Notice that each end of the wire loop is connected to a split-ring arrangement. This conductive metal ring is called a *commutator.* As the wire loop is rotated in the magnetic field, the split commutator ring also rotates. Each half of the split ring rubs against the fixed contacts, called *brushes,* and connects the wire loop to an external circuit.

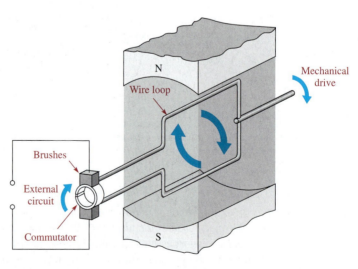

FIGURE 10–34

A simplified dc generator.

As the wire loop rotates through the magnetic field, it cuts through the flux lines at varying angles, as illustrated in Figure 10–35. At position *A* in its rotation, the loop of wire is effectively moving parallel with the magnetic field. Therefore, at this instant, the rate at which it is cutting through the magnetic flux lines is zero. As the loop moves from position *A* to position *B*, it cuts through the flux lines at an increasing rate. At position *B*, it is moving effectively perpendicular to the magnetic field and thus is cutting through a maximum number of lines. As the loop rotates from position *B* to position *C*, the rate at which it cuts the flux lines decreases to minimum (zero) at *C*. From position *C* to position *D*, the rate at which the loop cuts the flux lines increases to a maximum at *D* and then back to a minimum again at *A*.

FIGURE 10–35

End view of wire loop cutting through the magnetic field.

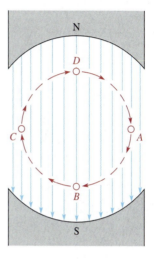

As you have learned, when a wire moves through a magnetic field, a voltage is induced, and by Faraday's law, the amount of induced voltage is proportional to the number of loops (turns) in the wire and the rate at which it is moving with respect to the magnetic field. Now you know that the angle at which the wire moves with respect to the magnetic flux lines determines the amount of induced voltage, because the rate at which the wire cuts through the flux lines depends on the angle of motion.

Figure 10–36 illustrates how a voltage is induced in the external circuit as the single loop rotates in the magnetic field. Assume that the loop is in its instantaneous horizontal position, so the induced voltage is zero. As the loop continues in its rotation, the induced voltage builds up to a maximum at position *B*, as shown in part (a) of the figure. Then, as the loop continues from *B* to *C*, the voltage decreases to zero at position *C*, as shown in part (b).

During the second half of the revolution, shown in Figure 10–36(c) and (d), the brushes switch to opposite commutator sections, so the polarity of the voltage remains the same across the output. Thus, as the loop rotates from position *C* to position *D* and then back to position *A*, the voltage increases from zero at *C* to a maximum at *D* and back to zero at *A*.

Figure 10–37 shows how the induced voltage varies as the loop goes through several rotations (three in this case). This voltage is a dc voltage because its polarities do not change. However, the voltage is pulsating between zero and its maximum value.

When more wire loops are added, the voltages induced across each loop are combined across the output. Since the voltages are offset from each other, they do not reach their maximum or zero values at the same time. A smoother dc voltage results, as shown in Figure 10–38 for two loops. The variations can be further smoothed out by filters to achieve a nearly constant dc voltage. (Filters are covered in Chapter 19.)

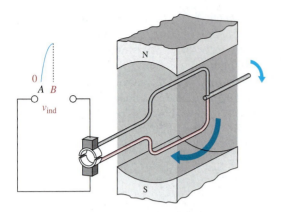

(a) Position *B*: Loop is moving perpendicular to flux lines, and voltage is maximum.

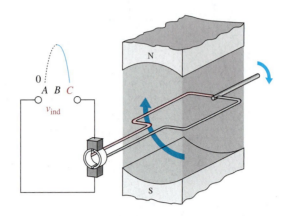

(b) Position *C*: Loop is moving parallel with flux lines, and voltage is zero.

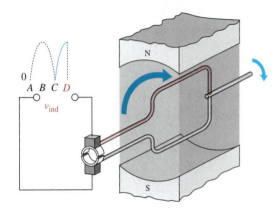

(c) Position *D*: Loop is moving perpendicular to flux lines, and voltage is maximum.

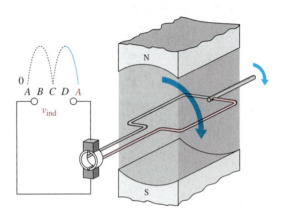

(d) Position *A*: Loop is moving parallel with flux lines, and voltage is zero.

FIGURE 10–36

Operation of a basic dc generator.

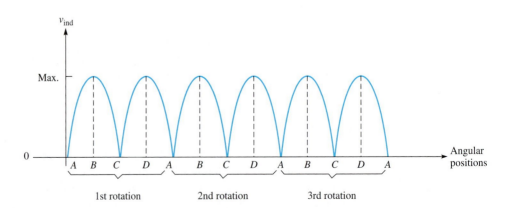

FIGURE 10–37

Induced voltage over three rotations of the loop.

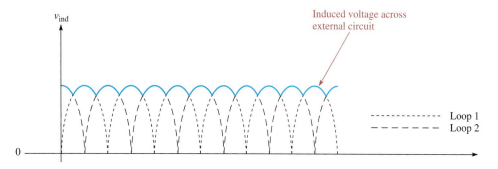

FIGURE 10–38
The induced voltage for a two-loop generator. There is much less variation in the induced voltage.

SECTION 10–6 REVIEW

1. If the steel disk in the crankshaft position sensor has stopped, with a tab in the magnet's air gap, what is the induced voltage?

2. What happens to the induced voltage if the wire loop in the basic dc generator suddenly begins rotating at a faster speed?

10–7 ■ TECHnology Theory Into Practice

The relay is a common type of electromagnetic device that is used in many types of control applications. With a relay, a lower voltage, such as from a battery, can be used to switch a much higher voltage, such as the 110 V from an ac outlet. In this section, you will see how a relay can be used in a basic burglar alarm system.

The schematic in Figure 10–39 shows a basic simplified intrusion alarm system that uses a relay to turn on an audible alarm (siren) and lights. The system operates from a 9 V battery so that even if power to the house is off, the audible alarm will still work.

FIGURE 10–39
Simplified burglar alarm system.

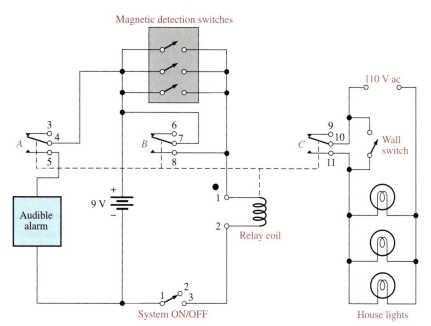

TABLE 10–1

Symbol	Quantity	SI Unit
B	Magnetic flux density	Tesla (T)
ϕ	Magnetic flux	Weber (Wb)
μ	Permeability	Weber/ampere turn · meter (Wb/At · m)
$\mathcal{R}$	Reluctance	At/Wb
F_m	Magnetomotive force (mmf)	Ampere-turn (At)
H	Magnetizing force	At/m

■ **GLOSSARY**

These terms are also in the end-of-book glossary.

Ampere-turn   The unit of magnetomotive force (mmf).

Electromagnetic field   A formation of a group of magnetic lines of force surrounding a conductor created by electrical current in the conductor.

Electromagnetic induction   The phenomenon or process by which a voltage is produced in a conductor when there is relative motion between the conductor and a magnetic or electromagnetic field.

Faraday's law   A law stating that the voltage induced across a coil of wire equals the number of turns in the coil times the rate of change of the magnetic flux.

Hysteresis   A characteristic of a magnetic material whereby a change in magnetization lags the application of a magnetizing force.

Magnetic flux   The lines of force between the north and south poles of a permanent magnet or an electromagnet.

Magnetic flux density   The amount of flux per unit area perpendicular to the magnetic field.

Magnetizing force   The amount of mmf per unit length of magnetic material.

Magnetomotive force   The force that produces the magnetic field.

Permeability   The measure of ease with which a magnetic field can be established in a material.

Relay   An electromagnetically controlled mechanical device in which electrical contacts are opened or closed by a magnetizing current.

Reluctance   The opposition to the establishment of a magnetic field in a material.

Retentivity   The ability of a material, once magnetized, to maintain a magnetized state without the presence of a magnetizing force.

Solenoid   An electromagnetically controlled device in which the mechanical movement of a shaft or plunger is activated by a magnetizing current.

Tesla   The SI unit of flux density.

Weber   The SI unit of magnetic flux.

■ **FORMULAS**

(10–1) $B = \dfrac{\phi}{A}$ Magnetic flux density

(10–2) $\mu_r = \dfrac{\mu}{\mu_0}$ Relative permeability

(10–3) $\mathcal{R} = \dfrac{l}{\mu A}$ Reluctance

(10–4) $F_m = NI$ Magnetomotive force

(10–5) $\phi = \dfrac{F_m}{\mathcal{R}}$ Magnetic flux

(10–6) $H = \dfrac{F_m}{l}$ Magnetizing force

(10–7) $v_{\text{ind}} = N\left(\dfrac{d\phi}{dt}\right)$ Faraday's law

■ SELF-TEST

1. When the south poles of two bar magnets are brought close together, there will be
   - (a) a force of attraction
   - (b) a force of repulsion
   - (c) an upward force
   - (d) no force

2. A magnetic field is made up of
   - (a) positive and negative charges
   - (b) magnetic domains
   - (c) flux lines
   - (d) magnetic poles

3. The direction of a magnetic field is from
   - (a) north pole to south pole
   - (b) south pole to north pole
   - (c) inside to outside the magnet
   - (d) front to back

4. Reluctance in a magnetic circuit is analogous to
   - (a) voltage in an electric circuit
   - (b) current in an electric circuit
   - (c) power in an electric circuit
   - (d) resistance in an electric circuit

5. The unit of magnetic flux is the
   - (a) tesla
   - (b) weber
   - (c) ampere-turn
   - (d) ampere-turn/weber

6. The unit of magnetomotive force is the
   - (a) tesla
   - (b) weber
   - (c) ampere-turn
   - (d) ampere-turn/weber

7. The unit of flux density is the
   - (a) tesla
   - (b) weber
   - (c) ampere-turn
   - (d) electron-volt

8. The electromagnetic activation of a movable shaft is the basis for
   - (a) relays
   - (b) circuit breakers
   - (c) magnetic switches
   - (d) solenoids

9. When there is current through a wire placed in a magnetic field,
   - (a) the wire will overheat
   - (b) the wire will become magnetized
   - (c) a force is exerted on the wire
   - (d) the magnetic field will be cancelled

10. A coil of wire is placed in a changing magnetic field. If the number of turns in the coil is increased, the voltage induced across the coil will
    - (a) remain unchanged
    - (b) decrease
    - (c) increase
    - (d) be excessive

11. If a conductor is moved back and forth at a constant rate in a constant magnetic field, the voltage induced in the conductor will
    - (a) remain constant
    - (b) reverse polarity
    - (c) be reduced
    - (d) be increased

12. In the crankshaft position sensor in Figure 10–32, the induced voltage across the coil is caused by
    - (a) current in the coil
    - (b) rotation of the disk
    - (c) a tab passing through the magnetic field
    - (d) acceleration of the disk's rotational speed

■ PROBLEMS

SECTION 10–1 The Magnetic Field

1. The cross-sectional area of a magnetic field is increased, but the flux remains the same. Does the flux density increase or decrease?

2. In a certain magnetic field the cross-sectional area is 0.5 m² and the flux is 1500 μWb. What is the flux density?

3. What is the flux in a magnetic material when the flux density is 2500×10^{-6} T and the cross-sectional area is 150 cm²?

SECTION 10–2 Electromagnetism

4. What happens to the compass needle in Figure 10–8 when the current through the conductor is reversed?

5. What is the relative permeability of a ferromagnetic material whose absolute permeability is 750×10^{-6} Wb/At · m?

6. Determine the reluctance of a material with a length of 0.28 m and a cross-sectional area of 0.08 m^2 if the absolute permeability is 150×10^{-7} Wb/At · m.

7. What is the magnetomotive force in a 50 turn coil of wire when there are 3 A of current through it?

SECTION 10–3   Electromagnetic Devices

8. Typically, when a solenoid is activated, is the plunger extended or retracted?

9. **(a)** What force moves the plunger when a solenoid is activated?

   (b) What force causes the plunger to return to its at-rest position?

10. Explain the sequence of events in the circuit of Figure 10–42 starting when switch 1 (SW1) is closed.

FIGURE 10–42

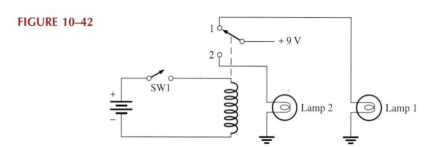

11. What causes the pointer in a d'Arsonval movement to deflect when there is current through the coil?

SECTION 10–4   Magnetic Hysteresis

12. What is the magnetizing force in Problem 7 if the length of the core is 0.2 m?

13. How can the flux density in Figure 10–43 be changed without altering the physical characteristics of the core?

14. In Figure 10–43, determine the following:

   (a) H **(b)** ϕ **(c)** B

FIGURE 10–43

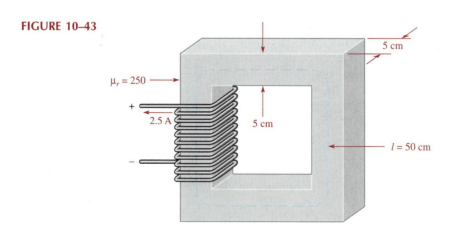

15. Determine from the hysteresis curves in Figure 10–44 which material has the most retentivity.

FIGURE 10–44

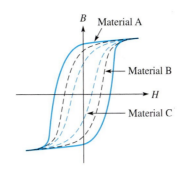

B Material A

Material B

→ H

Material C

SECTION 10–5   Electromagnetic Induction

16. According to Faraday's law, what happens to the induced voltage across a given coil if the rate of change of magnetic flux doubles?

17. The voltage induced across a certain coil is 100 mV. A 100 Ω resistor is connected to the coil terminals. What is the induced current?

18. A magnetic field is changing at a rate of 3500×10^{-3} Wb/s. How much voltage is induced across a 50 turn coil that is placed in the magnetic field?

19. How does Lenz's law complement Faraday's law?

SECTION 10–6   Applications of Electromagnetic Induction

20. In Figure 10–32, why is there no induced voltage when the steel disk is not rotating?

21. Explain the purpose of the commutator and brushes in Figure 10–34.

22. A basic one-loop dc generator is rotated at 60 rev/s. How many times each second does the dc output voltage peak (reach a maximum)?

23. Assume that another loop, 90 degrees from the first loop, is added to the dc generator in Problem 22. Make a graph of voltage versus time to show how the output voltage appears. Let the maximum voltage be 10 V.

■ **ANSWERS TO SECTION REVIEWS**

Section 10–1

1. North poles repel.

2. Magnetic flux is the group of lines of force that make up a magnetic field.

3. $B = \phi/A = 900 \; \mu\text{T}$

Section 10–2

1. Electromagnetism is produced by current through a conductor. An electromagnetic field exists only when there is current. A magnetic field exists independently of current.

2. When current reverses, the direction of the magnetic field also reverses.

3. Flux (ϕ) equals magnetomotive force (F_m) divided by reluctance ($\mathcal{R}$).

4. Flux: current, mmf : voltage, reluctance: resistance.

Section 10–3

1. A solenoid produces a movement only. A relay provides an electrical contact closure.

2. The movable part of a solenoid is the plunger.

3. The movable part of a relay is the armature.

4. The d'Arsonval movement is based on the interaction of magnetic fields.

Section 10–4

1. An increase in current increases the flux density.

2. Retentivity is the ability of a material to remain magnetized after removal of the magnetizing force.

3. Heads should not remain magnetized after magnetic force is removed, but tape should.

Section 10–5

1. Zero voltage is induced.

2. Induced voltage increases.

3. A force is exerted on the conductor when there is current.

Section 10–6

1. Zero voltage is induced in the air gap.

2. A faster rotation increases induced voltage.

Section 10–7

1. The detection switches when closed indicate an intrusion through a window or door.

2. Section B latches the relay and keeps it energized when intrusion is detected.

▪ **ANSWERS TO RELATED PROBLEMS FOR EXAMPLES**

10–1 235 μWb

10–2 31.0 T

10–3 Reluctance increases to 4762 At/Wb.

10–4 7.2 mWb

10–5 **(a)** $F_m = 42.5$ At
    (b) $\mathcal{R} = 85 \times 10^3$ At/Wb

10–6 12.5 mV

▪ **ANSWERS TO SELF-TEST**

1. (b) **2.** (c) **3.** (a) **4.** (d) **5.** (b) **6.** (c) **7.** (a) **8.** (d)
9. (c) **10.** (c) **11.** (b) **12.** (c)

11

INTRODUCTION TO ALTERNATING CURRENT AND VOLTAGE

 Electronics Workbench (EWB) and PSpice Tutorials at http://www.prenhall.com/floyd

■ INTRODUCTION

In the preceding chapters, you have studied resistive circuits with dc currents and voltages.

This chapter provides an introduction to ac circuit analysis in which time-varying electrical signals, particularly the sine wave, are studied. An electrical signal is a voltage or current that changes in some consistent manner with time. In other words, the voltage or current fluctuates according to a certain pattern called a **waveform.**

Special emphasis is given to the sine wave because of its fundamental importance in ac circuit analysis. Other types of waveforms are also introduced, including pulse, triangular, and sawtooth. The use of the oscilloscope for displaying and measuring waveforms is introduced.

An alternating voltage is one that changes polarity at a certain rate, and an alternating current is one that changes direction at a certain rate. The sinusoidal waveform is the most common and fundamental type because all other types of repetitive waveforms can be broken down into composite sine waves. The sine wave is a periodic type of waveform that repeats at fixed intervals. The time for each repetition is the *period* and the repetition rate is the *frequency.*

In the TECH TIP assignment in Section 11–10, you will measure voltage signals in an AM receiver using an oscilloscope.

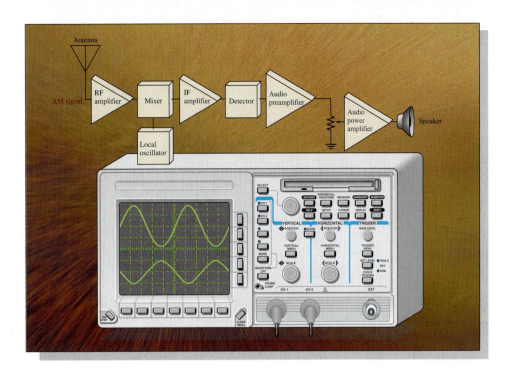

■ CHAPTER OBJECTIVES

- ❑ Identify a sinusoidal waveform and measure its characteristics
- ❑ Describe how sine waves are generated
- ❑ Determine the various voltage and current values of a sine wave
- ❑ Describe angular relationships of sine waves
- ❑ Mathematically analyze a sinusoidal waveform

- ❑ Apply the basic circuit laws to ac resistive circuits
- ❑ Determine total voltages that have both ac and dc components
- ❑ Identify the characteristics of basic nonsinusoidal waveforms
- ❑ Use the oscilloscope to measure waveforms

HISTORICAL NOTE

Heinrich Rudolf Hertz
1857–1894

Heinrich Rudolf Hertz, a German physicist born in 1857, was the first to broadcast and receive electromagnetic (radio) waves. Between 1885 and 1889, then a professor of physics, Hertz produced electromagnetic waves in the laboratory and measured their wavelength and velocity. He proved that the nature of the reflection and refraction of electromagnetic waves was the same as those of light. The unit of frequency is named in his honor. *Photo credit: Deutsches Museum, courtesy AIP Emilio Segrè Visual Archives.*

11–1 ■ THE SINE WAVE

The sine wave is a common type of alternating current (ac) and alternating voltage. It is also referred to as a sinusoidal wave or, simply, sinusoid. The electrical service provided by the power company is in the form of sinusoidal voltage and current. In addition, other types of repetitive waveforms are composites of many individual sine waves called harmonics.

After completing this section, you should be able to

■ **Identify a sinusoidal waveform and measure its characteristics**
  • Determine the period
  • Determine the frequency
  • Relate the period and the frequency

FIGURE 11–1
Symbol for a sinusoidal voltage source.

Sine waves are produced by two types of sources: rotating electrical machines (ac generators) or electronic oscillator circuits, which are used in instruments commonly known as electronic signal generators. Figure 11–1 shows the symbol used to represent either source of sinusoidal voltage.

Figure 11–2 is a graph showing the general shape of a sine wave, which can be either an **alternating current** or an alternating voltage. Voltage (or current) is displayed on the vertical axis and time (*t*) is displayed on the horizontal axis. Notice how the voltage (or current) varies with time. Starting at zero, the voltage (or current) increases to a positive maximum (peak), returns to zero, and then increases to a negative maximum (peak) before returning again to zero, thus completing one full cycle.

FIGURE 11–2
Graph of one cycle of a sine wave.

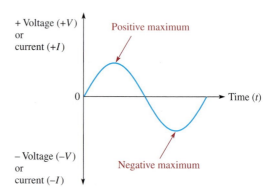

Polarity of a Sine Wave

As you have learned, a sine wave changes polarity at its zero value; that is, it alternates between positive and negative values. When a sinusoidal voltage source (V_s) is applied to a resistive circuit, as in Figure 11–3, an alternating sinusoidal current results. When the voltage changes polarity, the current correspondingly changes direction as indicated.

During the positive alternation of the applied voltage V_s, the current is in the direction shown in Figure 11–3(a). During a negative alternation of the applied voltage, the current is in the opposite direction, as shown in Figure 11–3(b). The combined positive and negative alternations make up one **cycle** of a sine wave.

FIGURE 11–3

Alternating current and voltage.

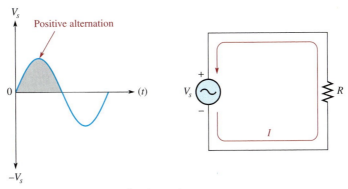

(a) Positive voltage: current direction as shown

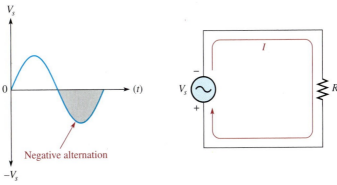

(b) Negative voltage: current reverses direction

Period of a Sine Wave

A sine wave varies with time (*t*) in a definable manner.

The time required for a sine wave to complete one full cycle is called the period (*T*).

Figure 11–4(a) illustrates the **period** of a sine wave. Typically, a sine wave continues to repeat itself in identical cycles, as shown in Figure 11–4(b). Since all cycles of a repetitive sine wave are the same, the period is always a fixed value for a given sine wave. The period of a sine wave does not necessarily have to be measured between the zero crossings at the beginning and end of a cycle; it can be measured between any two corresponding points on the waveform. For example, it can be measured from any peak in a given cycle to the corresponding peak in the next cycle.

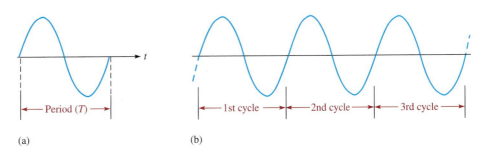

(a)

(b)

FIGURE 11–4

The period of a sine wave is the same for each cycle.

EXAMPLE 11–1   What is the period of the sine wave in Figure 11–5?

FIGURE 11–5

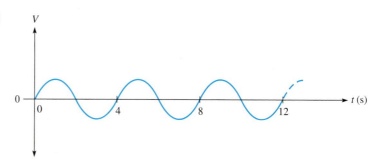

Solution   As shown in Figure 11–5, it takes four seconds (4 s) to complete each cycle. Therefore, the period is 4 s.

$$T = \textbf{4 s}$$

Related Problem   What is the period if the sine wave goes through five cycles in 12 s?

EXAMPLE 11–2   Show three possible ways to measure the period of the sine wave in Figure 11–6. How many cycles are shown?

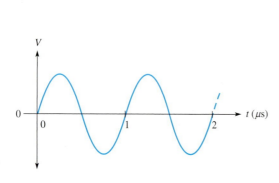

FIGURE 11–6

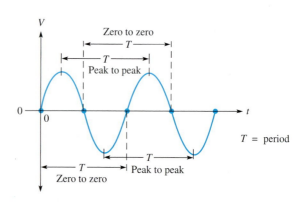

FIGURE 11–7
Measurement of the period of a sine wave.

Solution

Method 1: The period can be measured from one zero crossing to the corresponding zero crossing in the next cycle.

Method 2: The period can be measured from the positive peak in one cycle to the positive peak in the next cycle.

Method 3: The period can be measured from the negative peak in one cycle to the negative peak in the next cycle.

These measurements are indicated in Figure 11–7, where **two cycles of the sine wave** are shown. Keep in mind that you obtain the same value for the period no matter which corresponding points on the waveform you use.

Related Problem   If a positive peak occurs at 1 ms and the next positive peak occurs at 2.5 ms, what is the period?

Frequency of a Sine Wave

Frequency is the number of cycles that a sine wave completes in one second.

The more cycles completed in one second, the higher the frequency. **Frequency** (f) is measured in units of **hertz,** Hz. One hertz is equivalent to one cycle per second; 60 Hz is 60 cycles per second; and so on. Figure 11–8 shows two sine waves. The sine wave in part (a) completes two full cycles in one second. The one in part (b) completes four cycles in one second. Therefore, the sine wave in part (b) has twice the frequency of the one in part (a).

FIGURE 11–8
Illustration of frequency.

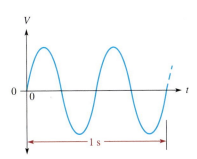

(a) Lower frequency: fewer cycles per second

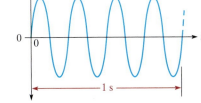

(b) Higher frequency: more cycles per second

Relationship of Frequency and Period

The formulas for the relationship between frequency (f) and period (T) are as follows:

$$f = \frac{1}{T}$$

(11–1)

$$T = \frac{1}{f}$$

(11–2)

There is a reciprocal relationship between f and T. Knowing one, you can calculate the other with the [2nd] [x⁻¹] keys on your calculator. This inverse relationship makes sense because a sine wave with a longer period goes through fewer cycles in one second than one with a shorter period.

EXAMPLE 11–3   Which sine wave in Figure 11–9 has a higher frequency? Determine the period and the frequency of both waveforms.

FIGURE 11–9

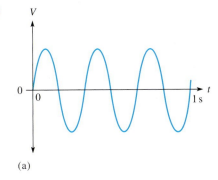

(a)

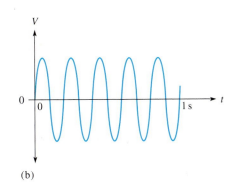

(b)

Solution   The sine wave in Figure 11–9(b) has the higher frequency because it completes more cycles in 1 s than does the sine wave in part (a).

In Figure 11–9(a), three cycles take 1 s. Therefore, one cycle takes 0.333 s (one-third second), and this is the period.

$$T = 0.333 \text{ s} = \textbf{333 ms}$$

The frequency is

$$f = \frac{1}{T} = \frac{1}{333 \text{ ms}} = \textbf{3 Hz}$$

In Figure 11–9(b), five cycles take 1 s. Therefore, one cycle takes 0.2 s (one-fifth second), and this is the period.

$$T = 0.2 \text{ s} = \textbf{200 ms}$$

The frequency is

$$f = \frac{1}{T} = \frac{1}{200 \text{ ms}} = \textbf{5 Hz}$$

Related Problem   If the time between negative peaks of a given sine wave is 50 μs, what is the frequency?

EXAMPLE 11–4

The period of a certain sine wave is 10 ms. What is the frequency?

Solution   Use Equation (11–1).

$$f = \frac{1}{T} = \frac{1}{10 \text{ ms}} = \frac{1}{10 \times 10^{-3} \text{ s}} = \textbf{100 Hz}$$

Related Problem   A certain sine wave goes through four cycles in 20 ms. What is the frequency?

EXAMPLE 11–5

The frequency of a sine wave is 60 Hz. What is the period?

Solution   Use Equation (11–2).

$$T = \frac{1}{f} = \frac{1}{60 \text{ Hz}} = \textbf{16.7 ms}$$

Related Problem   If $T = 15$ μs, what is f?

SECTION 11–1 REVIEW

1. Describe one cycle of a sine wave.
2. At what point does a sine wave change polarity?
3. How many maximum points does a sine wave have during one cycle?
4. How is the period of a sine wave measured?
5. Define *frequency,* and state its unit.
6. Determine f when $T = 5$ μs.
7. Determine T when $f = 120$ Hz.

11–2 ■ SINUSOIDAL VOLTAGE SOURCES

Two basic methods of generating sinusoidal voltages are electromagnetic and electronic. Sine waves are produced electromagnetically by ac generators and electronically by oscillator circuits.

After completing this section, you should be able to

■ **Describe how sine waves are generated**
- Discuss the basic operation of an ac generator
- Discuss factors that affect frequency in ac generators
- Discuss factors that affect voltage in ac generators

An AC Generator

Figure 11–10 shows a greatly simplified ac **generator** consisting of a single loop of wire in a permanent magnetic field. Notice that each end of the wire loop is connected to a separate solid conductive ring called a *slip ring*. As the wire loop rotates in the magnetic field between the north and south poles, the slip rings also rotate and rub against the brushes that connect the loop to an external load. Compare this generator to the basic dc generator in Figure 10–34, and note the difference in the ring and brush arrangements.

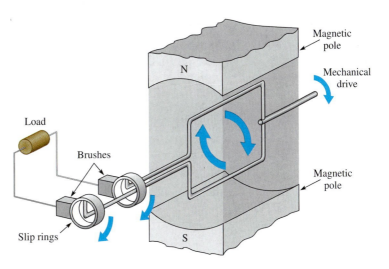

FIGURE 11–10
A simplified ac generator.

As you learned in Chapter 10, when a conductor moves through a magnetic field, a voltage is induced. Figure 11–11 illustrates how a sinusoidal voltage is produced by the basic ac generator as the wire loop rotates. An oscilloscope is used to display the voltage waveform.

To begin, Figure 11–11(a) shows the wire loop rotating through the first quarter of a revolution. It goes from an instantaneous horizontal position, where the induced voltage is zero, to an instantaneous vertical position, where the induced voltage is maximum. At the horizontal position, the loop is instantaneously moving parallel with the flux lines, which exist between the north (N) and south (S) poles of the magnet. Thus, no lines are being cut and the voltage is zero. As the loop rotates through the first quarter-cycle, it cuts through the flux lines at an increasing rate until it is instantaneously moving perpendicular to the flux lines at the vertical position and cutting through them at a maximum rate.

Thus, the induced voltage increases from zero to a peak during the quarter-cycle. As shown on the display in part (a), this part of the rotation produces the first quarter of the sine wave cycle as the voltage builds up from zero to its positive maximum.

Figure 11–11(b) shows the loop completing the first half of a revolution. During this part of the rotation, the voltage decreases from its positive maximum back to zero as the rate at which the loop cuts through the flux lines decreases.

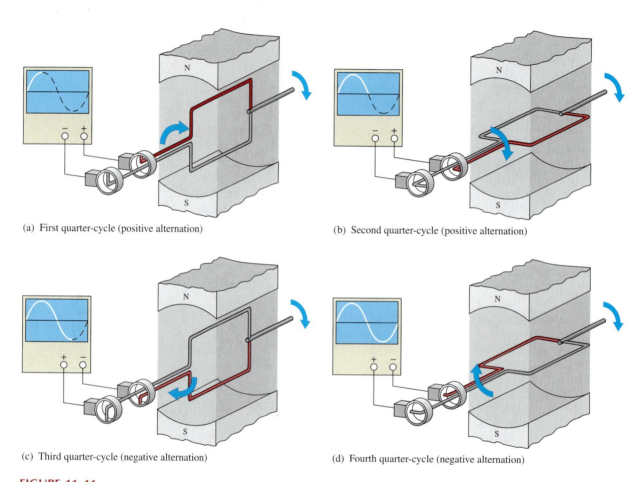

(a) First quarter-cycle (positive alternation)

(b) Second quarter-cycle (positive alternation)

(c) Third quarter-cycle (negative alternation)

(d) Fourth quarter-cycle (negative alternation)

FIGURE 11–11
One revolution of the wire loop generates one cycle of the sinusoidal voltage.

During the second half of the revolution, illustrated in Figures 11–11(c) and 11–11(d), the loop is cutting through the magnetic field in the opposite direction, so the voltage produced has a polarity opposite to that produced during the first half of the revolution. After one complete revolution of the loop, one full cycle of the sinusoidal voltage has been produced. As the wire loop continues to rotate, repetitive cycles of the sine wave are generated.

Frequency You have seen that one revolution of the conductor through the magnetic field in the basic ac generator (also called an *alternator*) produces one cycle of induced sinusoidal voltage. It is obvious that the rate at which the conductor is rotated determines the time for completion of one cycle. For example, if the conductor completes 60 revolutions in one second (rps), the period of the resulting sine wave is 1/60 s, corresponding to a frequency of 60 Hz. Thus, the faster the conductor rotates, the higher the resulting frequency of the induced voltage, as illustrated in Figure 11–12.

FIGURE 11–12
Frequency is directly proportional to the rate of rotation of the wire loop.

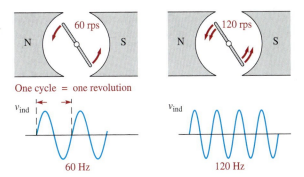

One cycle = one revolution

Another way of achieving a higher frequency is to increase the number of magnetic poles. In the previous discussion, two magnetic poles were used to illustrate the ac generator principle. During one revolution, the conductor passes under a north pole and a south pole, thus producing one cycle of a sine wave. When four magnetic poles are used instead of two, as shown in Figure 11–13, one cycle is generated during one-half a revolution. This doubles the frequency for the same rate of rotation.

An expression for frequency in terms of the number of pole pairs and the number of revolutions per second (rps) is as follows:

$$f = (\text{number of pole pairs})(\text{rps}) \qquad (11\text{–}3)$$

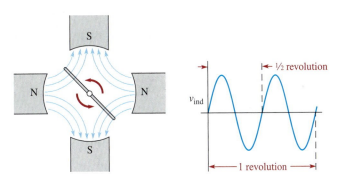

FIGURE 11–13
Four poles achieve a higher frequency than two for the same rps.

EXAMPLE 11–6   A four-pole generator has a rotation speed of 100 rps. Determine the frequency of the output voltage.

Solution $f = (\text{number of pole pairs})(\text{rps}) = 2(100) = \textbf{200 Hz}$

Related Problem   If the frequency of the output of a four-pole generator is 60 Hz, what is the rps?

Voltage Amplitude   Recall from Chapter 10 that the voltage induced in a conductor depends on the number of turns (N) and the rate of change with respect to the magnetic field. Therefore, when the speed of rotation of the conductor is increased, not only the frequency of the induced voltage increases—so also does the amplitude. Since the frequency value normally is fixed, the most practical method of increasing the amount of induced voltage is to increase the number of wire loops.

Electronic Signal Generators

The signal generator is an instrument that electronically produces sine waves for use in testing or controlling electronic circuits and systems. There are a variety of signal generators, ranging from special-purpose instruments that produce only one type of waveform in a limited frequency range, to programmable instruments that produce a wide range of frequencies and a variety of waveforms. Generally, instruments that produce more than one waveform are called function generators. All signal generators consist basically of an **oscillator**, which is an electronic circuit that produces repetitive waves. All generators have controls for adjusting the amplitude and frequency. Typical signal generators are shown in Figure 11–14.

(a)   (b)

FIGURE 11–14
Typical signal generators. Photography courtesy of B&K Precision Corp.

SECTION 11–2 REVIEW

1. What two basic methods are used to generate sinusoidal voltages?
2. How are the speed of rotation and the frequency in an ac generator related?
3. What is an oscillator?

11–3 ■ VOLTAGE AND CURRENT VALUES OF SINE WAVES

There are several ways to express the value of a sine wave in terms of its voltage or its current magnitude. These are instantaneous, peak, peak-to-peak, rms, and average values.

After completing this section, you should be able to

■ **Determine the various voltage and current values of a sine wave**
  • Find the instantaneous value at any point
  • Find the peak value
  • Find the peak-to-peak value
  • Define *rms*
  • Explain why the average value is always zero over a complete cycle
  • Find the half-cycle average value

Instantaneous Value

Figure 11–15 illustrates that at any point in time on a sine wave, the voltage (or current) has an **instantaneous value.** This instantaneous value is different at different points along the curve. Instantaneous values are positive during the positive alternation and negative during the negative alternation. Instantaneous values of voltage and current are symbol-

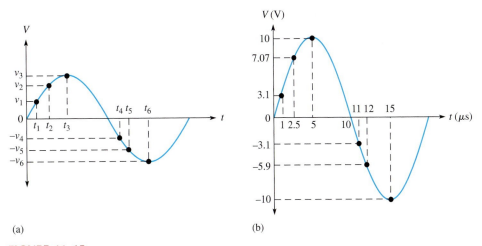

(a)   (b)

FIGURE 11–15
Instantaneous values.

ized by lowercase v and i, respectively, as shown in part (a). The curve is shown for voltage only, but it applies equally for current when the v's are replaced with i's. An example of instantaneous values is shown in part (b) where the instantaneous voltage is 3.1 V at 1 μs, 7.07 V at 2.5 μs, 10 V at 5 μs, 0 V at 10 μs, −3.1 V at 11 μs, and so on.

Peak Value

The **peak value** of a sine wave is the value of voltage (or current) at the positive or the negative maximum (peak) with respect to zero. Since the peaks are equal in **magnitude,** a sine wave is characterized by a single peak value. This is illustrated in Figure 11–16. For a given sine wave, the peak value is constant and is represented by V_p or I_p.

Peak-to-Peak Value

The **peak-to-peak value** of a sine wave, as shown in Figure 11–17, is the voltage or current from the positive peak to the negative peak. It is always twice the peak value as expressed in the following equations. Peak-to-peak voltage or current values are represented by V_{pp} or I_{pp}.

$$V_{pp} = 2V_p \qquad \text{(11–4)}$$

$$I_{pp} = 2I_p \qquad \text{(11–5)}$$

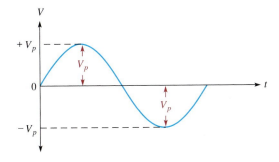

FIGURE 11–16
Peak values.

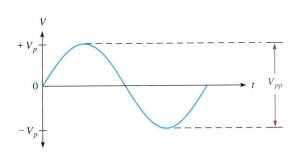

FIGURE 11–17
Peak-to-peak value.

RMS Value

The term *rms* stands for **root mean square.** It refers to the mathematical process by which this value is derived (see Appendix C for the derivation). The rms value is also referred to as the **effective value.** Most ac voltmeters display rms voltage. The 110 volts at your wall outlet is an rms value.

The rms value of a sinusoidal voltage is actually a measure of the heating effect of the sine wave. For example, when a resistor is connected across an ac (sinusoidal) voltage source, as shown in Figure 11–18(a), a certain amount of heat is generated by the power in the resistor. Figure 11–18(b) shows the same resistor connected across a dc voltage source. The value of the dc voltage can be adjusted so that the resistor gives off the same amount of heat as it does when connected to the ac source.

> **The rms value of a sinusoidal voltage is equal to the dc voltage that produces the same amount of heat in a resistance as does the sinusoidal voltage.**

FIGURE 11–18

The meaning of the rms value of a sinusoidal voltage: when the same amount of heat is produced in both setups, the sinusoidal voltage has an rms value equal to the dc voltage.

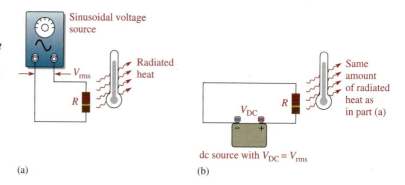

(a)   (b)

The peak value of a sine wave can be converted to the corresponding rms value using the following relationships, derived in Appendix C, for either voltage or current:

$$V_{rms} = 0.707V_p \qquad\qquad \textbf{(11–6)}$$

$$I_{rms} = 0.707I_p \qquad\qquad \textbf{(11–7)}$$

Using these formulas, you can also determine the peak value knowing the rms value.

$$V_p = \frac{V_{rms}}{0.707}$$

$$V_p = 1.414V_{rms} \qquad\qquad \textbf{(11–8)}$$

Similarly,

$$I_p = 1.414I_{rms} \qquad\qquad \textbf{(11–9)}$$

To get the peak-to-peak value, simply double the peak value.

$$V_{pp} = 2.828V_{rms} \qquad\qquad \textbf{(11–10)}$$

and

$$I_{pp} = 2.828I_{rms} \qquad\qquad \textbf{(11–11)}$$

Average Value

The average value of a sine wave taken over one complete cycle is always zero, because the positive values (above the zero crossing) offset the negative values (below the zero crossing).

To be useful for certain purposes such as measuring types of voltages found in power supplies, the average value of a sine wave is defined over a half-cycle rather than over a full cycle. The **average value** is the total area under the half-cycle curve divided by the distance in radians of the curve along the horizontal axis. The result is derived in Appendix C and is expressed in terms of the peak value as follows for both voltage and current sine waves:

$$V_{avg} = \left(\frac{2}{\pi}\right)V_p$$

$$V_{avg} = 0.637V_p \qquad \text{(11–12)}$$

$$I_{avg} = \left(\frac{2}{\pi}\right)I_p$$

$$I_{avg} = 0.637I_p \qquad \text{(11–13)}$$

EXAMPLE 11–7 Determine V_p, V_{pp}, V_{rms}, and the half-cycle V_{avg} for the sine wave in Figure 11–19.

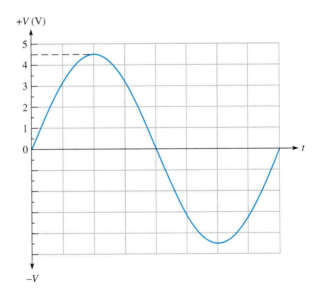

FIGURE 11–19

Solution $V_p = \mathbf{4.5\ V}$ is read directly from the graph. From this, calculate the other values.

$$V_{pp} = 2V_p = 2(4.5\ V) = \mathbf{9\ V}$$
$$V_{rms} = 0.707V_p = 0.707(4.5\ V) = \mathbf{3.18\ V}$$
$$V_{avg} = 0.637V_p = 0.637(4.5\ V) = \mathbf{2.87\ V}$$

Related Problem If $V_p = 25$ V, determine V_{pp}, V_{rms}, and V_{avg} for a voltage sine wave.

SECTION 11–3
REVIEW

1. Determine V_{pp} in each case when
   (a) $V_p = 1$ V   (b) $V_{rms} = 1.414$ V   (c) $V_{avg} = 3$ V
2. Determine V_{rms} in each case when
   (a) $V_p = 2.5$ V   (b) $V_{pp} = 10$ V   (c) $V_{avg} = 1.5$ V
3. Determine the half-cycle V_{avg} in each case when
   (a) $V_p = 10$ V   (b) $V_{rms} = 2.3$ V   (c) $V_{pp} = 60$ V

11–4 ■ ANGULAR MEASUREMENT OF A SINE WAVE

As you have seen, sine waves can be measured along the horizontal axis on a time basis; however, since the time for completion of one full cycle or any portion of a cycle is frequency-dependent, it is often useful to specify points on the sine wave in terms of an angular measurement expressed in degrees or radians.

After completing this section, you should be able to

■ **Describe angular relationships of sine waves**
   • Show how to measure a sine wave in terms of angles
   • Define *radian*
   • Convert radians to degrees
   • Determine the phase angle of a sine wave

A sinusoidal voltage can be produced by an ac generator. As the rotor of the ac generator goes through a full 360° of rotation, the resulting voltage output is one full cycle of a sine wave. Thus, the angular measurement of a sine wave can be related to the angular rotation of a generator, as shown in Figure 11–20.

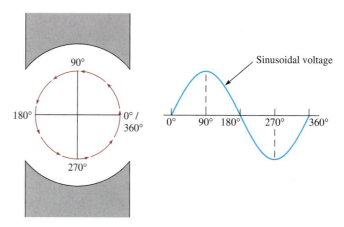

FIGURE 11–20
Relationship of a sine wave to the rotational motion in an ac generator.

Angular Measurement

A **degree** is an angular measurement corresponding to 1/360 of a circle or a complete revolution. A **radian** (rad) is defined as the angular measurement along the circumference of a circle that is equal to the radius of the circle. One radian is equivalent to 57.3°, as illustrated in Figure 11–21. In a 360° revolution, there are 2π radians.

FIGURE 11–21
Angular measurement showing relationship of radian (rad) to degrees (°).

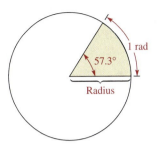

The Greek letter π (pi) represents the ratio of the circumference of any circle to its diameter and has a constant value of approximately 3.1416.

Scientific calculators have a π function so that the actual numerical value does not have to be entered.

Table 11–1 lists several values of degrees and the corresponding radian values. These angular measurements are illustrated in Figure 11–22.

TABLE 11–1

Degrees (°)	Radians (rad)
0	0
45	π/4
90	π/2
135	3π/4
180	π
225	5π/4
270	3π/2
315	7π/4
360	2π

FIGURE 11–22
Angular measurements.

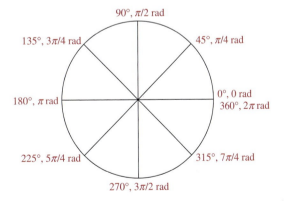

Radian/Degree Conversion

Degrees can be converted to radians using Equation (11–14).

$$rad = \left(\frac{\pi \text{ rad}}{180°}\right) \times degrees \tag{11–14}$$

Similarly, radians can be converted to degrees with Equation (11–15).

$$degrees = \left(\frac{180°}{\pi \text{ rad}}\right) \times rad \tag{11–15}$$

EXAMPLE 11–8   (a) Convert 60° to radians.   (b) Convert π/6 rad to degrees.

Solution

(a) $\text{Rad} = \left(\dfrac{\pi \text{ rad}}{180°}\right)60° = \dfrac{\pi}{3} \textbf{ rad}$ (b) $\text{Degrees} = \left(\dfrac{180°}{\pi \text{ rad}}\right)\left(\dfrac{\pi}{6} \text{ rad}\right) = \textbf{30°}$

Related Problem   (a) Convert 15° to radians.   (b) Convert 2π rad to degrees.

Sine Wave Angles

The angular measurement of a sine wave is based on 360° or 2π rad for a complete cycle. A half-cycle is 180° or π rad; a quarter-cycle is 90° or π/2 rad; and so on. Figure 11–23(a) shows angles in degrees for a full cycle of a sine wave; part (b) shows the same points in radians.

FIGURE 11–23
Sine wave angles.

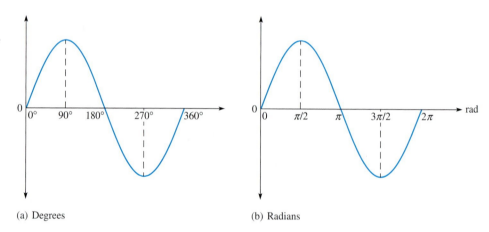

(a) Degrees

(b) Radians

Phase of a Sine Wave

The **phase** of a sine wave is an angular measurement that specifies the position of that sine wave relative to a reference. Figure 11–24 shows one cycle of a sine wave to be used as the reference. Note that the first positive-going crossing of the horizontal axis (zero crossing) is at 0° (0 rad), and the positive peak is at 90° (π/2 rad). The negative-going zero crossing is at 180° (π rad), and the negative peak is at 270° (3π/2 rad). The cycle is completed at 360° (2π rad). When the sine wave is shifted left or right with respect to this reference, there is a phase shift.

FIGURE 11–24
Phase reference.

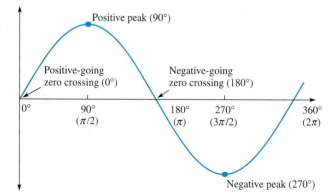

Figure 11–25 illustrates phase shifts of a sine wave. In part (a), sine wave *B* is shifted to the right by 90° (π/2 rad). Thus, there is a phase angle of 90° between sine wave *A* and sine wave *B*. In terms of time, the positive peak of sine wave *B* occurs later than the positive peak of sine wave *A* because time increases to the right along the horizontal axis. In this case, sine wave *B* is said to **lag** sine wave *A* by 90° or π/2 radians. Stated another way, sine wave *A* leads sine wave *B* by 90°.

In Figure 11–25(b), sine wave *B* is shown shifted left by 90°. Thus, again there is a phase angle of 90° between sine wave *A* and sine wave *B*. In this case, the positive peak of sine wave *B* occurs earlier in time than that of sine wave *A*; therefore, sine wave *B* is said to **lead** by 90°. A sine wave shifted 90° to the left with respect to the reference is called a *cosine wave*.

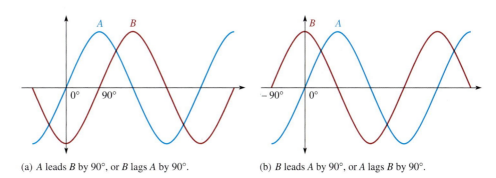

(a) *A* leads *B* by 90°, or *B* lags *A* by 90°.　　　(b) *B* leads *A* by 90°, or *A* lags *B* by 90°.

FIGURE 11–25
Illustration of a phase shift.

EXAMPLE 11–9　　What are the phase angles between the two sine waves in parts (a) and (b) of Figure 11–26?

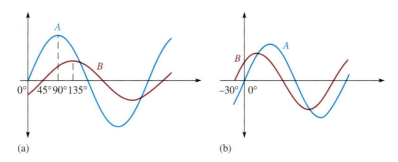

(a)　　　　　　　　　　　　　　　　(b)

FIGURE 11–26

Solution　In Figure 11–26(a) the zero crossing of sine wave *A* is at 0°, and the corresponding zero crossing of sine wave *B* is at 45°. There is a 45° phase angle between the two waveforms with sine wave *B* lagging.

In Figure 11–26(b) the zero crossing of sine wave *B* is at −30°, and the corresponding zero crossing of sine wave *A* is at 0°. There is a 30° phase angle between the two waveforms with sine wave *B* leading.

Related Problem　If the positive-going zero crossing of one sine wave is at 15° and that of the second sine wave is at 23°, what is the phase angle between them?

As a practical matter, when you measure the phase shift between two waveforms on an oscilloscope, you should make them appear to have the same amplitude. This is done by taking one of the oscilloscope channels out of vertical calibration and adjusting the corresponding waveform until its apparent amplitude equals that of the other waveform. This procedure eliminates the error caused if both waveforms are not measured at their exact center.

SECTION 11–4
REVIEW

1. When the positive-going zero crossing of a sine wave occurs at 0°, at what angle does each of the following points occur?
   (a) Positive peak   **(b)** Negative-going zero crossing
   (c) Negative peak   **(d)** End of first complete cycle

2. A half-cycle is completed in _____ degrees or _____ radians.

3. A full cycle is completed in _____ degrees or _____ radians.

4. Determine the phase angle between the two sine waves in Figure 11–27.

FIGURE 11–27

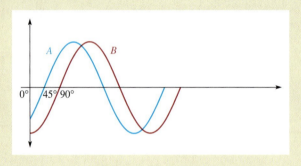

11–5 ▪ THE SINE WAVE FORMULA

A sine wave can be graphically represented by voltage or current values on the vertical axis and by angular measurement (degrees or radians) along the horizontal axis. This graph can be expressed mathematically, as you will see.

After completing this section, you should be able to

▪ **Mathematically analyze a sinusoidal waveform**
   • State the sine wave formula
   • Find instantaneous values using the sine wave formula

A generalized graph of one cycle of a sine wave is shown in Figure 11–28. The **amplitude,** A, is the maximum value of the voltage or current on the vertical axis, and angular values run along the horizontal axis. The variable y is an instantaneous value representing either voltage or current at a given angle, θ.

FIGURE 11–28

One cycle of a generic sine wave showing amplitude and phase.

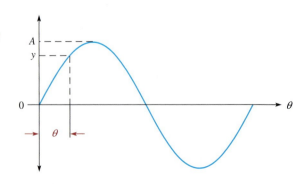

A sine wave curve follows a specific mathematical formula. The general expression for the sine wave curve in Figure 11–28 is

$$y = A \sin \theta \qquad \qquad (11\text{–}16)$$

This expression states that any point on the sine wave, represented by an instantaneous value (y), is equal to the maximum value A times the sine (sin) of the angle θ at that point. For example, a certain voltage sine wave has a peak value of 10 V. The instantaneous voltage at a point 60° along the horizontal axis can be calculated as follows, where $y = v$ and $A = V_p$:

$$v = V_p \sin \theta = 10 \sin 60° = 10(0.866) = 8.66 \text{ V}$$

Figure 11–29 shows this particular instantaneous value of the curve. You can find the sine of any angle on your calculator by first entering the value of the angle and then pressing the ⌊sin⌋ key. Verify that your calculator is in the degree mode. The TI-85 is placed in the degree mode by pressing ⌊2nd⌋ ⌊MODE⌋, using the arrow keys to highlight "Degree" on the screen, and pressing ⌊ENTER⌋.

FIGURE 11–29

Illustration of the instantaneous value of a voltage sine wave at θ = 60°.

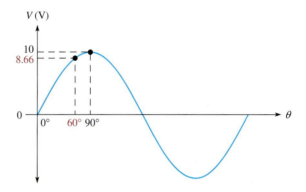

Expressions for Shifted Sine Waves

When a sine wave is shifted to the right of the reference (lagging) by a certain angle, ϕ, as illustrated in Figure 11–30(a) where the reference is the vertical axis, the general expression is

$$y = A \sin(\theta - \phi) \qquad \qquad (11\text{–}17)$$

When a sine wave is shifted to the left of the reference (leading) by a certain angle, ϕ, as shown in Figure 11–30(b), the general expression is

$$y = A \sin(\theta + \phi) \qquad \qquad (11\text{–}18)$$

FIGURE 11–30

Shifted sine waves.

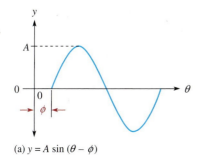

(a) $y = A \sin (\theta - \phi)$

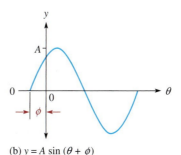

(b) $y = A \sin (\theta + \phi)$

EXAMPLE 11–10   Determine the instantaneous value at the 90° reference point on the horizontal axis for each voltage sine wave in Figure 11–31.

FIGURE 11–31

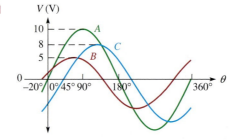

Solution   Sine wave A is the reference. Sine wave B is shifted left by 20° with respect to A, so it leads. Sine wave C is shifted right by 45° with respect to A, so it lags.

$$v_A = V_p\sin\theta$$
$$= 10\sin(90°) = 10(1) = \mathbf{10\ V}$$

$$v_B = V_p\sin(\theta + \phi_B)$$
$$= 5\sin(90° + 20°) = 5\sin(110°) = 5(0.9397) = \mathbf{4.70\ V}$$

$$v_C = V_p\sin(\theta - \phi_C)$$
$$= 8\sin(90° - 45°) = 8\sin(45°) = 8(0.7071) = \mathbf{5.66\ V}$$

Related Problem   A voltage sine wave has a peak value of 20 V. What is its instantaneous value at 65° from its zero crossing?

SECTION 11–5 REVIEW

1. Calculate the instantaneous value at 120° for the sine wave in Figure 11–29.

2. Determine the instantaneous value at the 45° point of a sine wave shifted 10° to the left of the zero reference ($V_p = 10\ V$).

3. Find the instantaneous value of the 90° point of a sine wave shifted 25° to the right from the zero reference ($V_p = 5\ V$).

11–6 ■ OHM'S LAW AND KIRCHHOFF'S LAWS IN AC CIRCUITS

When time-varying ac voltages such as a sinusoidal voltage are applied to a circuit, the circuit laws that you studied earlier still apply. Ohm's law and Kirchhoff's laws apply to ac circuits in the same way that they apply to dc circuits.

After completing this section, you should be able to

■ **Apply the basic circuit laws to ac resistive circuits**
  • Apply Ohm's law to resistive circuits with ac sources
  • Apply Kirchhoff's voltage law and current law to resistive circuits with ac sources

---

If a sinusoidal voltage is applied across a resistor as shown in Figure 11–32, there is a sinusoidal current. The current is zero when the voltage is zero and is maximum when the voltage is maximum. When the voltage changes polarity, the current reverses direction. As a result, the voltage and current are said to be in phase with each other.

FIGURE 11–32

A sinusoidal voltage produces a sinusoidal current.

Sine wave generator

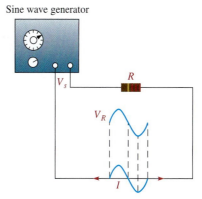

When using Ohm's law in ac circuits, remember that both the voltage and the current must be expressed consistently, that is, both as peak values, both as rms values, both as average values, and so on.

EXAMPLE 11–11   Determine the rms voltage across each resistor and the rms current in Figure 11–33. The source voltage is given as an rms value.

FIGURE 11–33

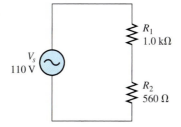

Solution   The total resistance of the circuit is

$$R_T = R_1 + R_2 = 1.0 \text{ k}\Omega + 560 \ \Omega = 1.56 \text{ k}\Omega$$

Use Ohm's law to find the rms current.

$$I_{rms} = \frac{V_{s(rms)}}{R_T} = \frac{110 \text{ V}}{1.56 \text{ k}\Omega} = 70.5 \text{ mA}$$

The rms voltage drop across each resistor is

$$V_{1(rms)} = I_{rms}R_1 = (70.5 \text{ mA})(1.0 \text{ k}\Omega) = \textbf{70.5 V}$$
$$V_{2(rms)} = I_{rms}R_2 = (70.5 \text{ mA})(560 \ \Omega) = \textbf{39.5 V}$$

Related Problem   Repeat this example for a source voltage of 10 V peak.

Kirchhoff's voltage and current laws apply to ac circuits as well as to dc circuits. Figure 11–34 illustrates Kirchhoff's voltage law in a resistive circuit that has a sinusoidal voltage source. As you can see, the source voltage is the sum of all the voltage drops across the resistors, just as in a dc circuit.

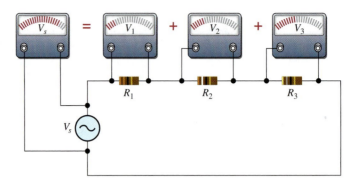

FIGURE 11–34
Illustration of Kirchhoff's voltage law in an ac circuit.

EXAMPLE 11–12   All values in Figure 11–35 are given in rms.
(a) Find the unknown peak voltage drop in Figure 11–35(a).
(b) Find the total rms current in Figure 11–35(b).

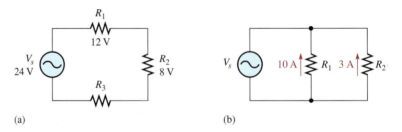

FIGURE 11–35

Solution
(a) Use Kirchhoff's voltage law to find V_3.

$$V_s = V_1 + V_2 + V_3$$

$$V_{3(\text{rms})} = V_{s(\text{rms})} - V_{1(\text{rms})} - V_{2(\text{rms})} = 24\text{ V} - 12\text{ V} - 8\text{ V} = 4\text{ V}$$

Convert rms to peak.

$$V_{3(p)} = 1.414V_{3(\text{rms})} = 1.414(4\text{ V}) = \textbf{5.66 V}$$

(b) Use Kirchhoff's current law to find I_{tot}.

$$I_{tot(\text{rms})} = I_{1(\text{rms})} + I_{2(\text{rms})} = 10\text{ A} + 3\text{ A} = \textbf{13 A}$$

Related Problem   A series circuit has the following voltage drops: $V_{1(\text{rms})} = 3.50$ V, $V_{2(p)} = 4.25$ V, $V_{3(\text{avg})} = 1.70$ V. Determine the peak-to-peak source voltage.

**SECTION 11–6
REVIEW**

1. A sinusoidal voltage with a half-cycle average value of 12.5 V is applied to a circuit with a resistance of 330 Ω. What is the peak current in the circuit?

2. The peak voltage drops in a series resistive circuit are 6.2 V, 11.3 V, and 7.8 V. What is the rms value of the source voltage?

11–7 ■ SUPERIMPOSED DC AND AC VOLTAGES

In many practical circuits, you will find both dc and ac voltages combined. An example of this is in amplifier circuits where ac signal voltages are superimposed on dc operating voltages. This is one of the most common applications of the superposition theorem studied in Chapter 8.

After completing this section, you should be able to

■ **Determine total voltages that have both ac and dc components**

Figure 11–36 shows a dc source and an ac source in series. These two voltages will add algebraically to produce an ac voltage "riding" on a dc level, as measured across the resistor.

FIGURE 11–36
Superimposed dc and ac voltages.

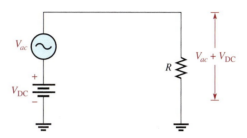

If V_{DC} is greater than the peak value of the sinusoidal voltage, the combined voltage is a sine wave that never reverses polarity and is therefore nonalternating. That is, we have a sine wave riding on a dc level, as shown in Figure 11–37(a). If V_{DC} is less than the peak value of the sine wave, the sine wave will be negative during a portion of its lower half-cycle, as illustrated in Figure 11–37(b), and is therefore alternating. In either case, the sine wave will reach a maximum voltage equal to $V_{DC} + V_p$, and it will reach a minimum voltage equal to $V_{DC} - V_p$.

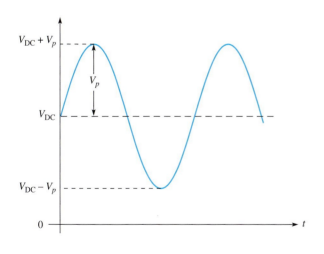

(a) $V_{DC} > V_p$. The sine wave never goes negative.

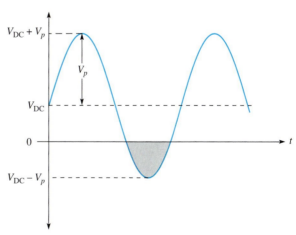

(b) $V_{DC} < V_p$. The sine wave reverses polarity during a portion of its cycle.

FIGURE 11–37
Sine waves with dc levels.

EXAMPLE 11–13   Determine the maximum and minimum voltage across the resistor in each circuit of Figure 11–38.

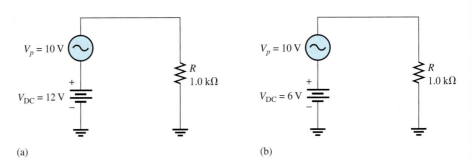

(a)   (b)

FIGURE 11–38

Solution   In Figure 11–38(a), the maximum voltage across R is

$$V_{max} = V_{DC} + V_p = 12 \text{ V} + 10 \text{ V} = \textbf{22 V}$$

The minimum voltage across R is

$$V_{min} = V_{DC} - V_p = 12 \text{ V} - 10 \text{ V} = \textbf{2 V}$$

Therefore, $V_{R(tot)}$ is a nonalternating sine wave that varies from +22 V to + 2 V, as shown in Figure 11–39(a).

In Figure 11–38(b), the maximum voltage across R is

$$V_{max} = V_{DC} + V_p = 6 \text{ V} + 10 \text{ V} = \textbf{16 V}$$

The minimum voltage across R is

$$V_{min} = V_{DC} - V_p = \textbf{−4 V}$$

Therefore, $V_{R(tot)}$ is an alternating sine wave that varies from +16 V to −4 V, as shown in Figure 11–39(b).

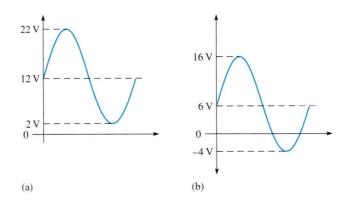

(a)   (b)

FIGURE 11–39

Related Problem   Explain why the waveform in Figure 11–39(a) is nonalternating but the waveform in part (b) is considered to be alternating.

SECTION 11–7 REVIEW

1. What is the maximum positive value of the resulting total voltage when a sine wave with $V_p = 5$ V is added to a dc voltage of +2.5 V?
2. Will the resulting voltage in Question 1 alternate polarity?
3. If the dc voltage in Question 1 is −2.5 V, what is the maximum positive value of the resulting total voltage?

11–8 ■ NONSINUSOIDAL WAVEFORMS

Sine waves are important in electronics, but they are by no means the only type of ac or time-varying waveform. Two other major types of waveforms, the pulse waveform and the triangular waveform, are discussed next.

After completing this section, you should be able to

■ **Identify the characteristics of basic nonsinusoidal waveforms**
  • Discuss the properties of a pulse waveform
  • Define *duty cycle*
  • Discuss the properties of triangular and sawtooth waveforms
  • Discuss the harmonic content of a waveform

Pulse Waveforms

Basically, a **pulse** can be described as a very rapid transition (**leading edge**) from one voltage or current level (**baseline**) to an amplitude level, and then, after an interval of time, a very rapid transition (**trailing edge**) back to the original baseline level. The transitions in level are also called *steps*. An ideal pulse consists of two opposite-going steps of equal amplitude. When the leading or trailing edge is positive-going, it is called a **rising edge.** When the leading or trailing edge is negative-going, it is called a **falling edge.**

Figure 11–40(a) shows an ideal positive-going pulse consisting of two equal but opposite instantaneous steps separated by an interval of time called the **pulse width.** Part (b) of Figure 11–40 shows an ideal negative-going pulse. The height of the pulse measured from the baseline is its voltage (or current) amplitude.

In many applications, analysis is simplified by treating all pulses as ideal (composed of instantaneous steps and perfectly rectangular in shape). Actual pulses, however, are never ideal. All pulses possess certain characteristics that cause them to be different from the ideal.

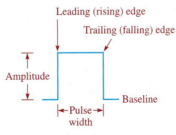

(a) Positive-going pulse

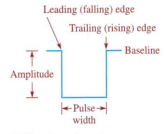

(b) Negative-going pulse

FIGURE 11–40
Ideal pulses.

In practice, pulses cannot change from one level to another instantaneously. Time is always required for a transition (step), as illustrated in Figure 11–41(a). As you can see, there is an interval of time during the rising edge in which the pulse is going from its lower value to its higher value. This interval is called the **rise time, t_r.**

> **Rise time is the time required for the pulse to go from 10% of its full amplitude to 90% of its full amplitude.**

The interval of time during the falling edge in which the pulse is going from its higher value to its lower value is called the **fall time, t_f.**

> **Fall time is the time required for the pulse to go from 90% of its full amplitude to 10% of its full amplitude.**

Pulse width, t_W, also requires a precise definition for the nonideal pulse because the rising and falling edges are not vertical.

> **Pulse width is the time between the point on the rising edge, where the value is 50% of full amplitude, to the point on the falling edge, where the value is 50% of full amplitude.**

Pulse width is shown in Figure 11–41(b).

FIGURE 11–41
Nonideal pulse.

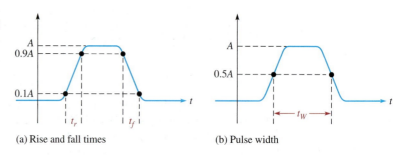

(a) Rise and fall times   (b) Pulse width

Repetitive Pulses

Any waveform that repeats itself at fixed intervals is **periodic.** Some examples of periodic pulse waveforms are shown in Figure 11–42. Notice that, in each case, the pulses repeat at regular intervals. The rate at which the pulses repeat is the **pulse repetition frequency,** which is the fundamental frequency of the waveform. The frequency can be expressed in hertz or in pulses per second. The time from one pulse to the corresponding point on the next pulse is the period, T. The relationship between frequency and period is the same as with the sine wave, $f = 1/T$.

FIGURE 11–42
Repetitive pulse waveforms.

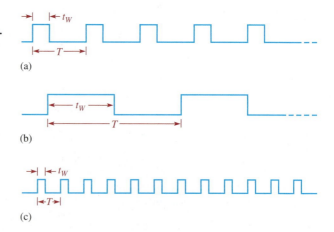

(a)

(b)

(c)

A very important characteristic of repetitive pulse waveforms is the **duty cycle.**

The duty cycle is the ratio of the pulse width (t_W) to the period (T) and is usually expressed as a percentage.

$$\text{percent duty cycle} = \left(\frac{t_W}{T}\right)100\% \qquad\qquad \text{(11–19)}$$

EXAMPLE 11–14   Determine the period, frequency, and duty cycle for the pulse waveform in Figure 11–43.

FIGURE 11–43

Solution

$$T = \textbf{10 } \mu\textbf{s}$$

$$f = \frac{1}{T} = \frac{1}{10 \ \mu s} = \textbf{100 kHz}$$

$$\text{percent duty cycle} = \left(\frac{1 \ \mu s}{10 \ \mu s}\right)100\% = \textbf{10\%}$$

Related Problem   A certain pulse waveform has a frequency of 200 kHz and a pulse width of 0.25 μs. Determine the duty cycle.

Square Waves

A square wave is a pulse waveform with a duty cycle of 50%. Thus, the pulse width is equal to one-half of the period. A square wave is shown in Figure 11–44.

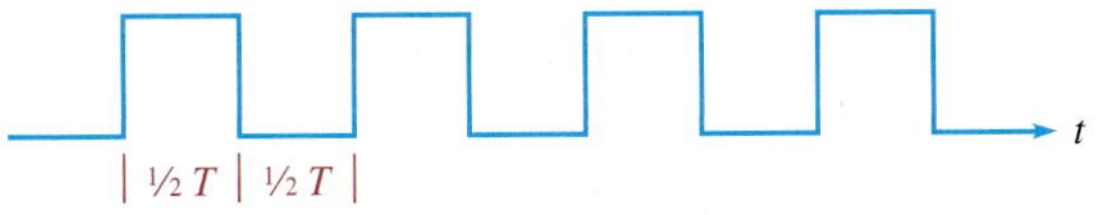

FIGURE 11–44
Square wave.

The Average Value of a Pulse Waveform

The average value (V_{avg}) of a pulse waveform is equal to its baseline value plus its duty cycle times its amplitude. The lower level of a positive-going waveform or the upper level of a negative-going waveform is taken as the baseline. The formula is as follows:

$$V_{avg} = \text{baseline} + (\text{duty cycle})(\text{amplitude}) \qquad\qquad \text{(11–20)}$$

The following example illustrates the calculation of the average value.

EXAMPLE 11–15   Determine the average value of each of the waveforms in Figure 11–45.

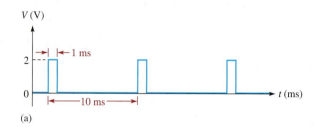

(a)

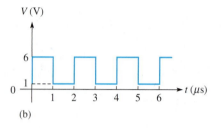

(b)

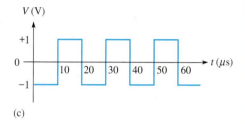

(c)

FIGURE 11–45

Solution   In Figure 11–45(a), the baseline is at 0 V, the amplitude is 2 V, and the duty cycle is 10%. The average value is

$$V_{avg} = \text{baseline} + (\text{duty cycle})(\text{amplitude})$$
$$= 0 \text{ V} + (0.1)(2 \text{ V}) = \textbf{0.2 V}$$

The waveform in Figure 11–45(b) has a baseline of +1 V, an amplitude of 5 V, and a duty cycle of 50%. The average value is

$$V_{avg} = \text{baseline} + (\text{duty cycle})(\text{amplitude})$$
$$= 1 \text{ V} + (0.5)(5 \text{ V}) = 1 \text{ V} + 2.5 \text{ V} = \textbf{3.5 V}$$

Figure 11–45(c) shows a square wave with a baseline of −1 V and an amplitude of 2 V. The average value is

$$V_{avg} = \text{baseline} + (\text{duty cycle})(\text{amplitude})$$
$$= -1 \text{ V} + (0.5)(2 \text{ V}) = -1 \text{ V} + 1 \text{ V} = \textbf{0 V}$$

This is an alternating square wave, and, as with an alternating sine wave, it has an average of zero.

Related Problem   If the baseline of the waveform in Figure 11–45(a) is shifted to 1 V, what is the average value?

Triangular and Sawtooth Waveforms

Triangular and sawtooth waveforms are formed by voltage or current ramps. A **ramp** is a linear increase or decrease in the voltage or current. Figure 11–46 shows both positive- and negative-going ramps. In part (a), the ramp has a positive slope; in part (b), the ramp has a negative slope. The slope of a voltage ramp is $\pm V/t$ and is expressed in units of V/s. The slope of a current ramp is $\pm I/t$ and is expressed in units of A/s.

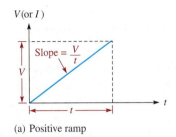
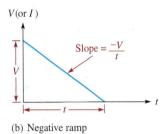

(a) Positive ramp   (b) Negative ramp

FIGURE 11–46
Ramps.

EXAMPLE 11–16   What are the slopes of the voltage ramps in Figure 11–47?

FIGURE 11–47

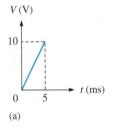
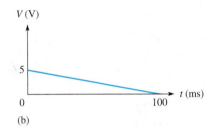

(a)   (b)

Solution   In Figure 11–47(a), the voltage increases from 0 V to +10 V in 5 ms. Thus, $V = 10$ V and $t = 5$ ms. The slope is

$$\frac{V}{t} = \frac{10 \text{ V}}{5 \text{ ms}} = \textbf{2 V/ms} = \textbf{2 kV/s}$$

In Figure 11–47(b), the voltage decreases from +5 V to 0 V in 100 ms. Thus, $V = -5$ V and $t = 100$ ms. The slope is

$$\frac{V}{t} = \frac{-5 \text{ V}}{100 \text{ ms}} = \textbf{-0.05 V/ms} = \textbf{-50 V/s}$$

Related Problem   A certain voltage ramp has a slope of +12 V/μs. If the ramp starts at zero, what is the voltage at 0.01 ms?

Triangular Waveforms   Figure 11–48 shows that a **triangular waveform** is composed of positive-going and negative-going ramps having equal slopes. The period of this waveform is measured from one peak to the next corresponding peak, as illustrated. This particular triangular waveform is alternating and has an average value of zero.

FIGURE 11–48
Alternating triangular waveform with a zero average value.

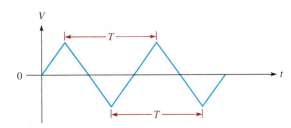

Figure 11–49 depicts a triangular waveform with a nonzero average value. The frequency for triangular waves is determined in the same way as for sine waves, that is, $f = 1/T$.

Sawtooth Waveforms   The **sawtooth waveform** is actually a special case of the triangular wave consisting of two ramps, one of much longer duration than the other. Sawtooth waveforms are used in many electronic systems. For example, the electron beam that sweeps across the screen of your TV receiver, creating the picture, is controlled by sawtooth voltages and currents. One sawtooth wave produces the horizontal beam movement, and the other produces the vertical beam movement. A sawtooth voltage is sometimes called a *sweep voltage*.

Figure 11–50 is an example of a sawtooth wave. Notice that it consists of a positive-going ramp of relatively long duration, followed by a negative-going ramp of relatively short duration.

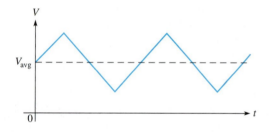

FIGURE 11–49
Nonalternating triangular waveform with a nonzero average value.

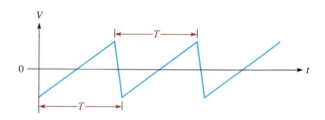

FIGURE 11–50
Alternating sawtooth waveform.

Harmonics

A repetitive nonsinusoidal waveform is composed of a fundamental frequency and harmonic frequencies. The **fundamental frequency** is the repetition rate of the waveform, and the **harmonics** are higher frequency sine waves that are multiples of the fundamental.

Odd Harmonics   *Odd harmonics* are frequencies that are odd multiples of the fundamental frequency of a waveform. For example, a 1 kHz square wave consists of a fundamental of 1 kHz and odd harmonics of 3 kHz, 5 kHz, 7 kHz, and so on. The 3 kHz frequency in this case is called the third harmonic, the 5 kHz frequency is the fifth harmonic, and so on.

Even Harmonics   *Even harmonics* are frequencies that are even multiples of the fundamental frequency. For example, if a certain wave has a fundamental of 200 Hz, the second harmonic is 400 Hz, the fourth harmonic is 800 Hz, the sixth harmonic is 1200 Hz, and so on. These are even harmonics.

Composite Waveform   Any variation from a pure sine wave produces harmonics. A nonsinusoidal wave is a composite of the fundamental and the harmonics. Some types of waveforms have only odd harmonics, some have only even harmonics, and some contain both. The shape of the wave is determined by its harmonic content. Generally, only the fundamental and the first few harmonics are of significant importance in determining the wave shape.

A square wave is an example of a waveform that consists of a fundamental and only odd harmonics. When the instantaneous values of the fundamental and each odd harmonic are added algebraically at each point, the resulting curve will have the shape of a square wave, as illustrated in Figure 11–51. In part (a) of the figure, the fundamental and the third harmonic produce a wave shape that begins to resemble a square wave. In part (b), the fundamental, third, and fifth harmonics produce a closer resemblance. When the seventh harmonic is included, as in part (c), the resulting wave shape becomes even more like a square wave. As more harmonics are included, a periodic square wave is approached.

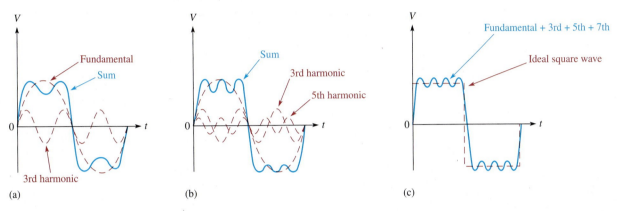

FIGURE 11–51
Odd harmonics produce a square wave.

SECTION 11–8 REVIEW

1. Define the following parameters:
   (a) rise time   (b) fall time   (c) pulse width

2. In a certain repetitive pulse waveform, the pulses occur once every millisecond. What is the frequency of this waveform?

3. Determine the duty cycle, amplitude, and average value of the waveform in Figure 11–52(a).

4. What is the period of the triangular wave in Figure 11–52(b)?

5. What is the frequency of the sawtooth wave in Figure 11–52(c)?

FIGURE 11–52

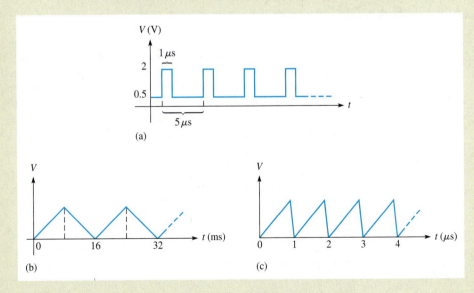

6. Define *fundamental frequency.*

7. What is the second harmonic of a fundamental frequency of 1 kHz?

8. What is the fundamental frequency of a square wave having a period of 10 μs?

11–9 ■ OSCILLOSCOPE MEASUREMENTS

The oscilloscope, or scope for short, is one of the most widely used and versatile test instruments. It displays on a screen the actual shape of a voltage that is changing with time so that waveform measurements can be made.

After completing this section, you should be able to

■ **Use the oscilloscope to measure waveforms**
  • Identify basic oscilloscope controls
  • Explain how to measure amplitude
  • Explain how to measure period and frequency

Figure 11–53 shows two typical oscilloscopes. The one in part (a) is an analog oscilloscope. The one in part (b) is a digital instrument. You can think of the **oscilloscope** as essentially a "graphing machine" that graphs out a voltage and shows how it varies with time. The shape of the sine wave that you have seen throughout this chapter is simply a graph of voltage versus time. Although, oscilloscopes can display any type of waveform, we will use the sine wave to illustrate basic concepts.

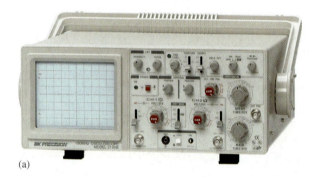
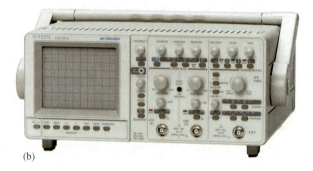

(a)   (b)

FIGURE 11–53
Oscilloscopes (photography courtesy of B&K Precision Corp.).

Analog and digital oscilloscopes are distinguished by the way in which the input signal is processed prior to being displayed on the screen of the cathode ray tube (CRT). The principal front panel controls are functionally the same for both types; however, digital scopes can generally do more automated operations than an analog scope.

An analog scope works by applying the signal voltage being measured to an electron beam that is sweeping across the screen. The measured voltage deflects the beam up and down proportional to the amount of voltage, immediately tracing the waveform on the screen.

A digital scope samples the signal voltage and uses an analog-to-digital converter to convert the voltage being measured into digital information. The digital information is then used to reconstruct the waveform on the screen.

Although there are still some analog scopes being manufactured and many older ones that are still in use, the digital scope is widely used and is becoming the instrument of choice to replace older analog instruments.

Analog Oscilloscope

Figure 11–54 shows a generic front panel view of a typical analog oscilloscope. There are two VOLTS/DIV controls, one for each of the two channels. These controls determine the attenuation or amplification of the signal, and each of the settings on the dial indicates the

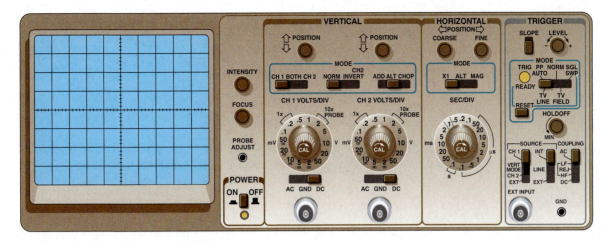

FIGURE 11–54
A typical dual-channel analog oscilloscope.

number of volts (V) or millivolts (mV) represented by each vertical division on the screen. Typically, there are two brackets on the VOLTS/DIV dial, one for a times 10 (×10) voltage probe and one for a times 1 (×1) voltage probe. The most commonly used probe is a ×10, which attenuates the input signal by ten to reduce loading effects on the circuit. When using a ×10 probe, you must read the VOLTS/DIV setting in the ×10 bracket.

The time base or SEC/DIV control sets the number of seconds(s), milliseconds (ms), or microseconds (μs) represented by each horizontal division as indicated by the dial settings. You can measure the period of a waveform on the horizontal scale and then calculate the frequency.

EXAMPLE 11–17   Based on the control dial settings, determine the peak-to-peak amplitude and the period of the waveform on the screen of an analog oscilloscope as shown in Figure 11–55. Calculate the frequency.

FIGURE 11–55

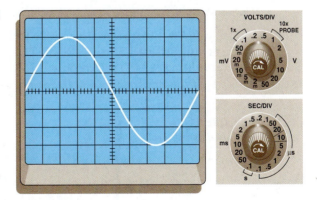

Solution   The VOLTS/DIV setting is 1 V. The sine wave is six divisions high from the negative peak to the positive peak and, since each division represents 1 V, the peak-to-peak value of the sine wave is

$$\text{Amplitude} = (6 \text{ divisions})(1 \text{ V/division}) = \mathbf{6\ V}$$

The SEC/DIV setting is 10 μs. A full cycle of the waveform covers ten divisions; therefore, the period is

$$\text{Period} = (10 \text{ divisions})(10 \ \mu\text{s/division}) = \mathbf{100 \ \mu s}$$

The frequency is calculated as

$$f = \frac{1}{100 \ \mu\text{s}} = \mathbf{10 \ kHz}$$

Related Problem   For a VOLTS/DIV setting of 5 V and a SEC/DIV setting of 2 ms, determine the peak value, period, and frequency of the sine wave shown on the screen in Figure 11–55.

Other Basic Controls   The following descriptions refer to the analog scope in Figure 11–54. However, many of these are also common to digital scopes but with some functions determined by a menu-driven format.

Intensity   The intensity control varies the brightness of the trace on the screen. Caution should be used so that the intensity is not left too high for an extended period of time, especially when the beam forms a motionless dot on the screen.

Focus   This control focuses the beam so that it converges to a tiny point at the screen. An out-of-focus condition results in a fuzzy trace.

Horizontal and vertical positions   These controls are used to move a trace horizontal across the screen and up or down for easier viewing or measurement.

AC-GND-DC switch   This switch allows the input signal to be ac coupled, dc coupled, or grounded. The ac coupling eliminates any dc component on the input signal by inserting a capacitor in series with the signal. The dc coupling permits dc values to be displayed. The ground position disconnects the input and allows a 0 V reference to be established on the screen. *For digital signals, dc coupling should be used.*

Signal inputs   The signal voltages to be displayed are connected into the channel 1 (CH1) and/or channel 2 (CH2). As mentioned previously, these input connections are done with an attenuator probe that minimizes the loading effect of the scope on a circuit being measured. The common type of oscilloscope probe attenuates (reduces) the signal voltage by a factor of ten and is called a *times 10* (×10) probe. Times 1 (×1) probes are also sometimes used when measuring very small voltages but lose accuracy for voltage measurements at higher frequencies. A typical probe is shown in Figure 11–56.

Mode switches   These switches provide for displaying either or both channel input signals, inverting channel 2 signal (INVERT), adding two waveforms (ADD), and selecting between alternate (ALT) and chopped (CHOP) mode of sweep. *As a rule, ALT is selected when the frequency is above 100 Hz; otherwise, CHOP is used.*

FIGURE 11–56
An oscilloscope probe.

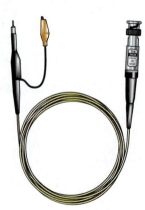

Trigger controls These controls allow the scope to be triggered from various selected sources. Triggering causes the trace to begin its sweep across the screen. Triggering can occur from an internal signal, an external signal, or from the line voltage. Typical trigger modes are *normal, auto, single-sweep,* and *TV.* In the auto mode, sweep occurs in the absence of an adequate trigger signal. In the normal mode, a trigger signal must be present for the sweep to occur. The TV mode allows stable triggering on the TV field or TV line signals by placing a low-pass filter in the triggering circuit. The *slope* switch sets the trigger to occur on either the positive-going or the negative-going slope of the trigger waveform. The *level* control selects the voltage level on the trigger signal at which the triggering occurs. Basically, the *trigger* controls provide for synchronization of the horizontal sweep waveform in the scope and the input signals. As a result, the display of the input signal is stable on the screen, rather than appearing to drift, as shown in Figure 11–57.

FIGURE 11–57
Proper triggering stabilizes a repeating waveform.

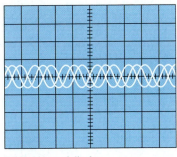

(a) Untriggered display

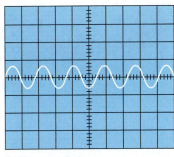

(b) Triggered display

Digital Oscilloscope

A generic front-panel view of a typical digital oscilloscope is shown in Figure 11–58. Notice that the Vertical and the Horizontal sections each consist of a *position control,* a *menu button,* and a *scale control.* Again, it is not necessarily the types of front panel controls but the way that the input signal is processed that distinguishes a digital scope from an analog scope. However, most digital scopes have automated measurements, waveform storage, and other features.

In the vertical section, the controls apply to either channel as determined by channel-selection buttons. The position control lets you move the waveform up or down on the screen. The menu button provides for the selection of several items that appear on the screen, such as coupling (ac, dc, or ground) and waveform inversion. The scale control adjusts the number of volts represented by each vertical division; but in this type of scope, the volts/division setting for a channel is displayed on the screen rather than having to read it from the dial. Probes for digital scopes have a special element that detects whether the probe is a ×1 or an ×10 and automatically adjusts the readouts.

In the horizontal section, the controls apply to both channels. The position control lets you move the waveform horizontally on the screen. The menu button provides for the selection of several items that appear on the screen, such as main or delayed sweep and other parameters. The scale control adjusts the time represented by each horizontal division, but in this type of scope the sec/division is displayed on the screen rather than having to read it from the dial.

In the trigger section, the level control determines where the trigger point occurs. The menu button provides for selection of items that appear on the screen, such as normal mode, auto mode, video mode, trigger source, trigger slope, and other parameters.

Many digital scopes have a diskette drive that allows you to store waveforms for later viewing, analysis, or for importing to desktop publishing or other programs on a computer.

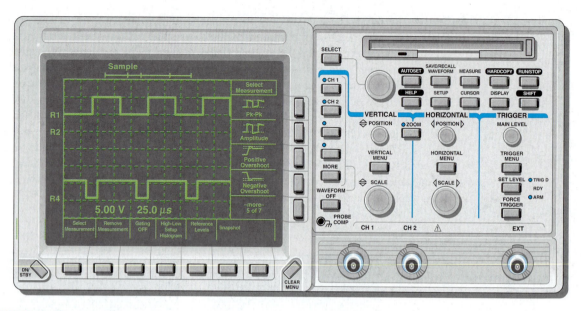

FIGURE 11–58
A typical dual-channel digital oscilloscope.

EXAMPLE 11–18   Determine the peak value and period of each sine wave in Figure 11–59 from the scope displays and the indicated settings for volts/division and sec/division on a digital oscilloscope.

Solution   Looking at the vertical scale in Figure 11–59(a),

$$V_p = 3 \text{ divisions} \times 0.5 \text{ V/division} = \textbf{1.5 V}$$

From the horizontal scale (one cycle covers ten divisions),

$$T = 10 \text{ divisions} \times 2 \text{ ms/division} = \textbf{20 ms}$$

Looking at the vertical scale in Figure 11–59(b),

$$V_p = 2.5 \text{ divisions} \times 50 \text{ mV/division} = \textbf{125 mV}$$

From the horizontal scale (one cycle covers six divisions),

$$T = 6 \text{ divisions} \times 0.1 \text{ ms/division} = 0.6 \text{ ms} = \textbf{600 } \boldsymbol{\mu}\textbf{s}$$

Looking at the vertical scale in Figure 11–59(c),

$$V_p = 3.4 \text{ divisions} \times 2 \text{ V/division} = \textbf{6.8 V}$$

From the horizontal scale (one-half cycle covers ten divisions),

$$T = 20 \text{ divisions} \times 10 \text{ } \mu\text{s/division} = \textbf{200 } \boldsymbol{\mu}\textbf{s}$$

Looking at the vertical scale in Figure 11–59(d),

$$V_p = 2 \text{ divisions} \times 5 \text{ V/division} = \textbf{10 V}$$

From the horizontal scale (one cycle covers two divisions),

$$T = 2 \text{ divisions} \times 2 \text{ } \mu\text{s/division} = \textbf{4 } \boldsymbol{\mu}\textbf{s}$$

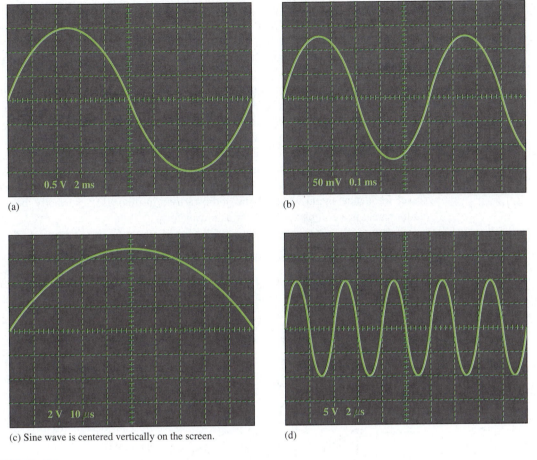

(a)

(b)

(c) Sine wave is centered vertically on the screen.

(d)

FIGURE 11–59

Related Problem   Determine the rms value and the frequency for each waveform displayed in Figure 11–59.

**SECTION 11–9
REVIEW**

1. Explain the primary difference between an analog and a digital oscilloscope.
2. On an oscilloscope, voltage is measured (horizontally, vertically) on the screen and time is measured (horizontally, vertically).
3. What can an oscilloscope do that a multimeter cannot?
4. When should you choose a ×10 probe for making a measurement?

11–10 ■ TECHnology Theory Into Practice

As you learned in this chapter, nonsinusoidal waveforms contain a combination of various harmonic frequencies. Each of these harmonics is a sinusoidal waveform with a certain frequency. Certain sine wave frequencies are audible; that is, they can be heard by the human ear. A single audible frequency, or pure sine wave, is called a tone and generally falls in the frequency range from about 300 Hz to about 15 kHz. When you hear a tone reproduced through a speaker, its loudness, or volume, depends on its voltage amplitude. In this section, you will use your knowledge of sine wave characteristics and the operation of an oscilloscope to measure the frequency and amplitude of signals at various points in a basic radio receiver.

Actual voice or music signals that are picked up by a radio receiver contain many harmonic frequencies with different voltage values. A voice or music signal is continuously changing, so its harmonic content is also changing. However, if a single sinusoidal frequency is transmitted and picked up by the receiver, you will hear a constant tone from the speaker.

Although, at this point you do not have the background to study amplifiers and receiver systems in detail, you can observe the signals at various points in the receiver. A block diagram of a typical AM receiver is shown in Figure 11–60. AM stands for amplitude modulation, a topic which will be covered in another course. For now, all you need to know is what a basic AM signal looks like and this is shown in Figure 11–61. As you can see, the amplitude of the sinusoidal waveform is changing. The higher radio frequency (RF) signal is called the *carrier* and its amplitude is varied or modulated by a lower frequency signal which is the audio (a tone in this case). Normally, however, the audio signal is a complex voice or music waveform.

Oscilloscope Measurements

Signals that are indicated by circled numbers at several test points on the receiver block diagram in Figure 11–60 are measured on the oscilloscope in Figure 11–62 on the

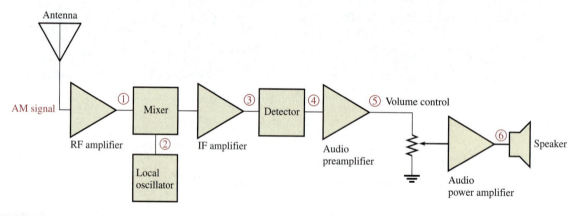

FIGURE 11–60
Simplified block diagram of a basic radio receiver.

FIGURE 11–61
Example of an amplitude modulated (AM) signal.

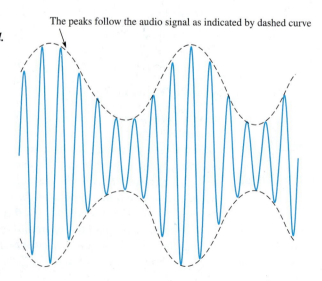

The peaks follow the audio signal as indicated by dashed curve

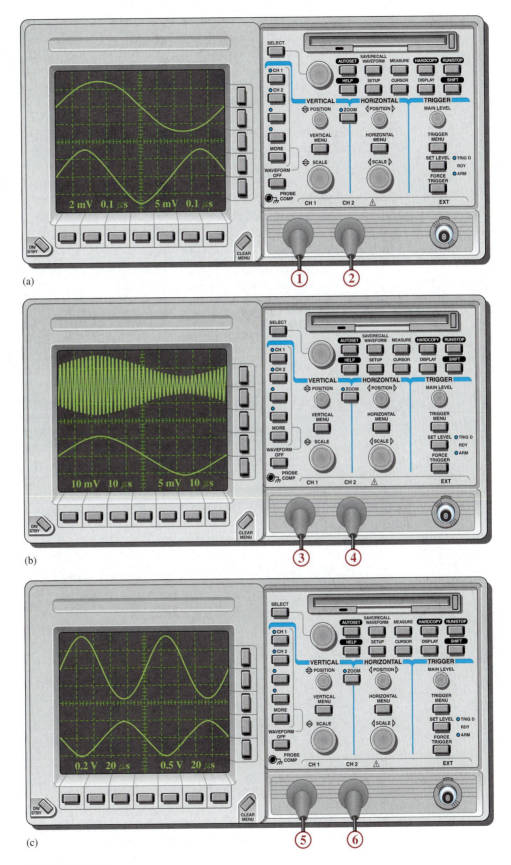

FIGURE 11–62

Circled numbers correspond to the numbered test points in Figure 11–60. The format of the screen is simplified to emphasize waveforms and measurements.

channels with the same corresponding circled numbers. In all cases, the upper waveform on the screen is channel 1 and the lower waveform is channel 2. The readings on the bottom left of the screen are for channel 1 and those on the bottom right are for channel 2.

The signal at point 1 is an AM signal but you can't see the amplitude variation because of the short time base. The waveform is spread out too much to see the modulating audio signal, which causes amplitude variations; so what you see is just one cycle of the carrier. At point 3, the higher carrier frequency is difficult to determine because the time base was selected to allow viewing of one full cycle of the modulating signal. In an AM receiver, this intermediate frequency is 455 kHz. In actual practice, the modulated carrier signal at point 3 cannot easily be viewed on the scope because it contains two frequencies which make it difficult to synchronize in order to obtain a stable pattern. Sometimes external triggering or TV field is used to obtain a stable display. A stable pattern is shown in this case to illustrate what the modulated waveform looks like.

▪ For each waveform in Figure 11–62, except point 3, determine the frequency and rms value. The signal at point 4 is the modulating tone extracted by the detector from the higher intermediate frequency (455 kHz).

Amplifier Analysis

▪ All voltage amplifiers have a characteristic known as voltage gain. The voltage gain is the amount by which the amplitude of the output signal is greater than the amplitude of the input signal. Using this definition and the appropriate scope measurements, determine the gain of the audio preamplifier in this particular receiver.

▪ When an electrical signal is converted to sound by a speaker, the loudness of the sound depends on the amplitude of the signal applied to the speaker. Based on this, explain how the volume control potentiometer is used to adjust the loudness (volume) of the sound and determine the rms amplitude at the speaker.

SECTION 11–10 REVIEW	**1.** What does RF stand for?
	2. What does IF stand for?
	3. Which frequency is higher, the carrier or the audio?
	4. What is the variable in a given AM signal?

▪ SUMMARY

▪ The sine wave is a time-varying, periodic waveform.

▪ Alternating current changes direction in response to changes in the polarity of the source voltage.

▪ One cycle of an alternating sine wave consists of a positive alternation and a negative alternation.

▪ Two common sources of sine waves are the electromagnetic ac generator and the electronic oscillator circuit.

▪ A full cycle of a sine wave is 360°, or 2π radians. A half-cycle is 180°, or π radian. A quarter-cycle is 90°, or $\pi/2$ radians.

▪ A sinusoidal voltage can be generated by a conductor rotating in a magnetic field.

▪ Phase angle is the difference in degrees or radians between a given sine wave and a reference sine wave.

▪ A pulse consists of a transition from a baseline level to an amplitude level, followed by a transition back to the baseline level.

- A triangle or sawtooth wave consists of positive-going and negative-going ramps.
- Harmonic frequencies are odd or even multiples of the repetition rate of a nonsinusoidal waveform.
- Conversions of sine wave values are summarized in Table 11–2.

TABLE 11–2

To Change From	To	Multiply By
Peak	rms	0.707
Peak	Peak-to-peak	2
Peak	Average	0.637
rms	Peak	1.414
Peak-to-peak	Peak	0.5
Average	Peak	1.57

■ GLOSSARY

These terms are also in the end-of-book glossary.

Alternating current (ac)   Current that reverses direction in response to a change in source voltage polarity.

Amplitude   The maximum value of a voltage or current.

Average value   The average of a sine wave over one half-cycle. It is 0.637 times the peak value.

Baseline   The normal level of a pulse waveform; the voltage level in the absence of a pulse.

Cycle   One repetition of a periodic waveform.

Degree   The unit of angular measure corresponding to 1/360 of a complete revolution.

Duty cycle   A characteristic of a pulse waveform that indicates the percentage of time that a pulse is present during a cycle; the ratio of pulse width to period expressed as either a fraction or as a percentage.

Effective value   A measure of the heating effect of a sine wave; also known as the rms (root mean square) value.

Falling edge   The negative-going transition of a pulse.

Fall time (t_f)   The time interval required for a pulse to change from 90% to 10% of its full amplitude.

Frequency   A measure of the rate of change of a periodic function; the number of cycles completed in 1 s. The unit of frequency is the hertz.

Fundamental frequency   The repetition rate of a waveform.

Generator   An energy source that produces electrical signals.

Harmonics   The frequencies contained in a composite waveform, which are integer multiples of the pulse repetition frequency (fundamental).

Hertz (Hz)   The unit of frequency. One hertz equals one cycle per second.

Instantaneous value   The voltage or current value of a waveform at a given instant in time.

Lag   Refers to a condition of the phase or time relationship of waveforms in which one waveform is behind the other in phase or time.

Lead   Refers to a condition of the phase or time relationship of waveforms in which one waveform is ahead of the other in phase or time; also, a wire or cable connection to a device or instrument.

Leading edge   The first step or transition of a pulse.

Magnitude   The value of a quantity, such as the number of volts of voltage or the number of amperes of current.

Oscillator   An electronic circuit that produces a time-varying signal without an external input signal using positive feedback.

Oscilloscope A measurement instrument that displays signal waveforms on a screen.

Peak-to-peak value The voltage or current value of a waveform measured from its minimum to its maximum points.

Peak value The voltage or current value of a waveform at its maximum positive or negative points.

Period (T) The time interval of one complete cycle of a periodic waveform.

Periodic Characterized by a repetition at fixed-time intervals.

Phase The relative angular displacement of a time-varying waveform in terms of its occurrence with respect to a reference.

Pulse A type of waveform that consists of two equal and opposite steps in voltage or current separated by a time interval.

Pulse repetition frequency The fundamental frequency of a repetitive pulse waveform; the rate at which the pulses repeat expressed in either hertz or pulses per second.

Pulse width (t_W) The time interval between the opposite steps of an ideal pulse. For a nonideal pulse, the time between the 50% points on the leading and trailing edges.

Radian A unit of angular measurement. There are 2π radians in one complete 360° revolution. One radian equals 57.3°.

Ramp A type of waveform characterized by a linear increase or decrease in voltage or current.

Rise time (t_r) The time interval required for a pulse to change from 10% to 90% of its amplitude.

Rising edge The positive-going transition of a pulse.

Root mean square (rms) The value of a sinusoidal voltage that indicates its heating effect, also known as the effective value. It is equal to 0.707 times the peak value.

Sawtooth waveform A type of electrical waveform composed of ramps; a special case of a triangular waveform in which one ramp is much shorter than the other.

Trailing edge The second step or transition of a pulse.

Triangular waveform A type of electrical waveform that consists of two ramps.

Trigger The activating signal for some electronic devices or instruments.

Waveform The pattern of variations of a voltage or current showing how the quantity changes with time.

■ FORMULAS

(11–1)	$f = \dfrac{1}{T}$	Frequency
(11–2)	$T = \dfrac{1}{f}$	Period
(11–3)	$f = \text{(number of pole pairs)(rps)}$	Output frequency of a generator
(11–4)	$V_{pp} = 2V_p$	Peak-to-peak voltage (sine wave)
(11–5)	$I_{pp} = 2I_p$	Peak-to-peak current (sine wave)
(11–6)	$V_{rms} = 0.707V_p$	Root-mean-square voltage (sine wave)
(11–7)	$I_{rms} = 0.707I_p$	Root-mean-square current (sine wave)
(11–8)	$V_p = 1.414V_{rms}$	Peak voltage (sine wave)
(11–9)	$I_p = 1.414I_{rms}$	Peak current (sine wave)
(11–10)	$V_{pp} = 2.828V_{rms}$	Peak-to-peak voltage (sine wave)
(11–11)	$I_{pp} = 2.828I_{rms}$	Peak to peak current (sine wave)
(11–12)	$V_{avg} = 0.637V_p$	Half-cycle average voltage (sine wave)
(11–13)	$I_{avg} = 0.637I_p$	Half-cycle average current (sine wave)
(11–14)	$\text{rad} = \left(\dfrac{\pi \text{ rad}}{180°}\right) \times \text{degrees}$	

(11–15) $\text{degrees} = \left(\dfrac{180°}{\pi\ \text{rad}}\right) \times \text{rad}$

(11–16) $y = A \sin \theta$ General formula for a sine wave

(11–17) $y = A \sin(\theta - \phi)$ Sine wave lagging the reference

(11–18) $y = A \sin(\theta + \phi)$ Sine wave leading the reference

(11–19) $\text{percent duty cycle} = \left(\dfrac{t_W}{T}\right)100\%$

(11–20) $V_{avg} = \text{baseline} + (\text{duty cycle})(\text{amplitude})$ Average value of a pulse waveform

■ **SELF-TEST**

1. The difference between alternating current (ac) and direct current (dc) is
   (a) ac changes value and dc does not   (b) ac changes direction and dc does not
   (c) both answers (a) and (b)   (d) neither answer (a) nor (b)

2. During each cycle, a sine wave reaches a peak value
   (a) one time   (b) two times
   (c) four times   (d) a number of times depending on the frequency

3. A sine wave with a frequency of 12 kHz is changing at a faster rate than a sine wave with a frequency of
   (a) 20 kHz   (b) 15,000 Hz   (c) 10,000 Hz   (d) 1.25 MHz

4. A sine wave with a period of 2 ms is changing at a faster rate than a sine wave with a period of
   (a) 1 ms   (b) 0.0025 s   (c) 1.5 ms   (d) 1200 μs

5. When a sine wave has a frequency of 60 Hz, in 10 s it goes through
   (a) 6 cycles   (b) 10 cycles   (c) 1/16 cycle   (d) 600 cycles

6. If the peak value of a sine wave is 10 V, the peak-to-peak value is
   (a) 20 V   (b) 5 V   (c) 100 V   (d) none of these

7. If the peak value of a sine wave is 20 V, the rms value is
   (a) 14.14 V   (b) 6.37 V   (c) 7.07 V   (d) 0.707 V

8. The average value of a 10 V peak sine wave over one complete cycle is
   (a) 0 V   (b) 6.37 V   (c) 7.07 V   (d) 5 V

9. The average half-cycle value of a sine wave with a 20 V peak is
   (a) 0 V   (b) 6.37 V   (c) 12.74 V   (d) 14.14 V

10. One sine wave has a positive-going zero crossing at 10° and another sine wave has a positive-going zero crossing at 45°. The phase angle between the two waveforms is
    (a) 55°   (b) 35°   (c) 0°   (d) none of these

11. The instantaneous value of a 15 A peak sine wave at a point 32° from its positive-going zero crossing is
    (a) 7.95 A   (b) 7.5 A   (c) 2.13 A   (d) 7.95 V

12. If the rms current through a 10 kΩ resistor is 5 mA, the rms voltage drop across the resistor is
    (a) 70.7 V   (b) 7.07 V   (c) 5 V   (d) 50 V

13. Two series resistors are connected to an ac source. If there are 6.5 V rms across one resistor and 3.2 V rms across the other, the peak source voltage is
    (a) 9.7 V   (b) 9.19 V   (c) 13.72 V   (d) 4.53 V

14. A 10 kHz pulse waveform consists of pulses that are 10 μs wide. Its duty cycle is
    (a) 100%   (b) 10%   (c) 1%   (d) not determinable

15. The duty cycle of a square wave
    (a) varies with the frequency   (b) varies with the pulse width
    (c) both answers (a) and (b)   (d) is 50%

■ PROBLEMS

More difficult problems are indicated by an asterisk (*).

SECTION 11–1   The Sine Wave

1. Calculate the frequency for each of the following values of period:
   (a) 1 s   (b) 0.2 s   (c) 50 ms
   (d) 1 ms   (e) 500 μs   (f) 10 μs

2. Calculate the period of each of the following values of frequency:
   (a) 1 Hz   (b) 60 Hz   (c) 500 Hz
   (d) 1 kHz   (e) 200 kHz   (f) 5 MHz

3. A sine wave goes through 5 cycles in 10 μs. What is its period?

4. A sine wave has a frequency of 50 kHz. How many cycles does it complete in 10 ms?

SECTION 11–2   Sinusoidal Voltage Sources

5. The conductive loop on the rotor of a simple two-pole, single-phase generator rotates at a rate of 250 rps. What is the frequency of the induced output voltage?

6. A certain four-pole generator has a speed of rotation of 3600 rpm. What is the frequency of the voltage produced by this generator?

7. At what speed of rotation must a four-pole generator be operated to produce a 400 Hz sinusoidal voltage?

SECTION 11–3   Voltage and Current Values of Sine Waves

8. A sine wave has a peak value of 12 V. Determine the following values:
   (a) rms   (b) peak-to-peak   (c) average

9. A sinusoidal current has an rms value of 5 mA. Determine the following values:
   (a) peak   (b) average   (c) peak-to-peak

10. For the sine wave in Figure 11–63, determine the peak, peak-to-peak, rms, and average values.

FIGURE 11–63

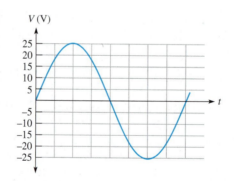

SECTION 11–4   Angular Measurement of a Sine Wave

11. Convert the following angular values from degrees to radians:
    (a) 30°   (b) 45°   (c) 78°
    (d) 135°   (e) 200°   (f) 300°

12. Convert the following angular values from radians to degrees:
    (a) $\pi/8$ rad   (b) $\pi/3$ rad   (c) $\pi/2$ rad
    (d) $3\pi/5$ rad   (e) $6\pi/5$ rad   (f) 1.8π rad

13. Sine wave *A* has a positive-going zero crossing at 30°. Sine wave *B* has a positive-going zero crossing at 45°. Determine the phase angle between the two signals. Which signal leads?

14. One sine wave has a positive peak at 75°, and another has a positive peak at 100°. How much is each sine wave shifted in phase from the 0° reference? What is the phase angle between them?

15. Make a sketch of two sine waves as follows: Sine wave A is the reference, and sine wave B lags A by 90°. Both have equal amplitudes.

SECTION 11–5 The Sine Wave Formula

16. A certain sine wave has a positive-going zero crossing at 0° and an rms value of 20 V. Calculate its instantaneous value at each of the following angles:

   (a) 15°   (b) 33°   (c) 50°   (d) 110°

   (e) 70°   (f) 145°   (g) 250°   (h) 325°

17. For a particular 0° reference sinusoidal current, the peak value is 100 mA. Determine the instantaneous value at each of the following points:

   (a) 35°   (b) 95°   (c) 190°   (d) 215°   (e) 275°   (f) 360°

18. For a 0° reference sine wave with an rms value of 6.37 V, determine its instantaneous value at each of the following points:

   (a) $\pi/8$ rad   (b) $\pi/4$ rad   (c) $\pi/2$ rad   (d) $3\pi/4$ rad

   (e) π rad   (f) $3\pi/2$ rad   (g) 2π rad

19. Sine wave A lags sine wave B by 30°. Both have peak values of 15 V. Sine wave A is the reference with a positive-going crossing at 0°. Determine the instantaneous value of sine wave B at 30°, 45°, 90°, 180°, 200°, and 300°.

20. Repeat Problem 19 for the case when sine wave A leads sine wave B by 30°.

*21. A certain sine wave has a frequency of 2.2 kHz and an rms value of 25 V. Assuming a given cycle begins (zero crossing) at $t = 0$ s, what is the change in voltage from 0.12 ms to 0.2 ms?

SECTION 11–6 Ohm's Law and Kirchhoff's Laws in AC Circuits

22. A sinusoidal voltage is applied to the resistive circuit in Figure 11–64. Determine the following:

   (a) I_{rms} (b) I_{avg} (c) I_p (d) I_{pp} (e) i at the positive peak

FIGURE 11–64

23. Find the half-cycle average values of the voltages across R_1 and R_2 in Figure 11–65. All values shown are rms.

24. Determine the rms voltage across R_3 in Figure 11–66.

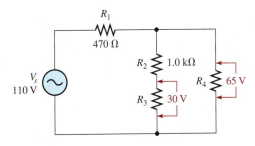

FIGURE 11–65

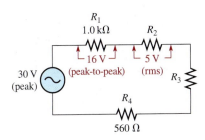

FIGURE 11–66

SECTION 11–7 Superimposed DC and AC Voltages

25. A sine wave with an rms value of 10.6 V is riding on a dc level of 24 V. What are the maximum and minimum values of the resulting waveform?

26. How much dc voltage must be added to a 3 V rms sine wave in order to make the resulting voltage nonalternating (no negative values)?

27. A 6 V peak sine wave is riding on a dc voltage of 8 V. If the dc voltage is lowered to 5 V, how far negative will the sine wave go?

*28. Figure 11–67 shows a sinusoidal voltage source in series with a dc source. Effectively, the two voltages are superimposed. Determine the power dissipation in the load resistor.

FIGURE 11–67

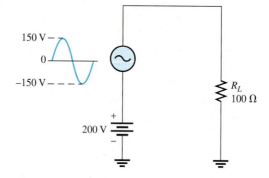

SECTION 11–8 Nonsinusoidal Waveforms

29. From the graph in Figure 11–68, determine the approximate values of t_r, t_f, t_W, and amplitude.

FIGURE 11–68

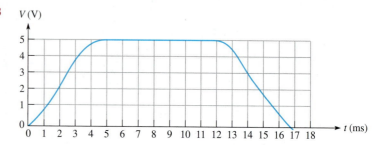

30. The repetition frequency of a pulse waveform is 2 kHz, and the pulse width is 1 μs. What is the percent duty cycle?

31. Calculate the average value of the pulse waveform in Figure 11–69.

FIGURE 11–69

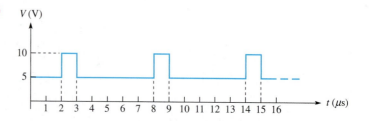

32. Determine the duty cycle for each waveform in Figure 11–70.

33. Find the average value of each pulse waveform in Figure 11–70.

34. What is the frequency of each waveform in Figure 11–70?

FIGURE 11–70

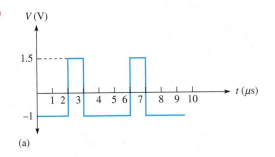 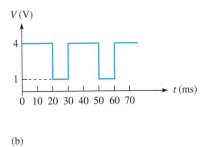

35. What is the frequency of each sawtooth waveform in Figure 11–71?

FIGURE 11–71

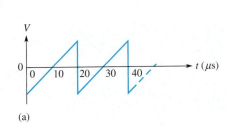 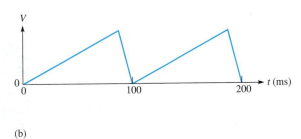

*36. A nonsinusoidal waveform called a *stairstep* is shown in Figure 11–72. Determine its average value.

FIGURE 11–72

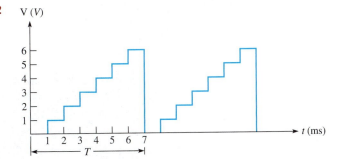

37. A square wave has a period of 40 μs. List the first six odd harmonics.

38. What is the fundamental frequency of the square wave mentioned in Problem 37?

SECTION 11–9   Oscilloscope Measurements

39. Determine the peak value and the period of the sine wave displayed on the scope screen in Figure 11–73.

FIGURE 11–73

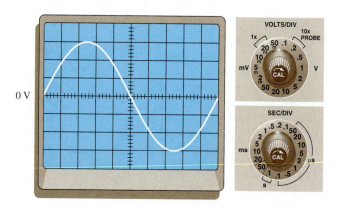

40. Determine the rms value and the frequency of the sine wave displayed on the scope screen in Figure 11–74.

FIGURE 11–74

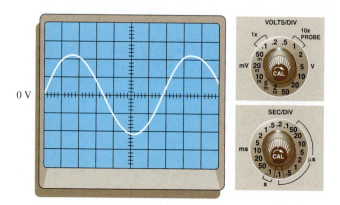

41. Find the amplitude, pulse width, and duty cycle for the pulse waveform displayed on the scope screen in Figure 11–75.

FIGURE 11–75

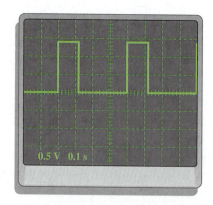

*42. Based on the instrument settings and an examination of the scope display and the circuit board in Figure 11–76, determine the frequency and peak value of the input signal and output signal. The waveform shown is channel 1. Sketch the channel 2 waveform as it would appear on the scope with the indicated settings. The settings on the bottom left of the screen are for channel 1 and those on the bottom right are for channel 2.

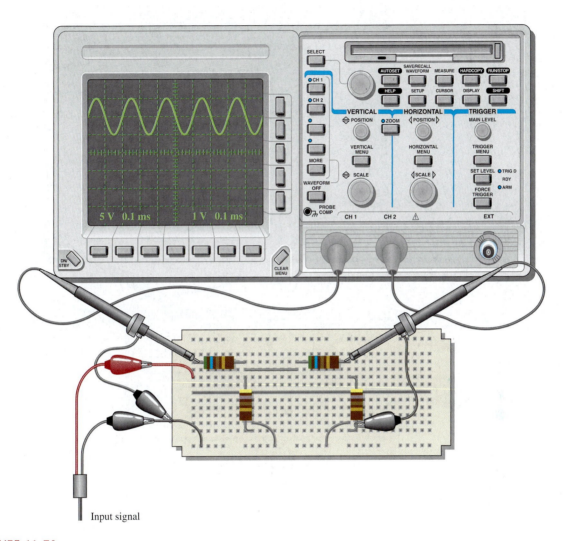

FIGURE 11–76

*43. Examine the circuit board and the oscilloscope display in Figure 11–77 and determine the peak value and the frequency of the unknown input signal.

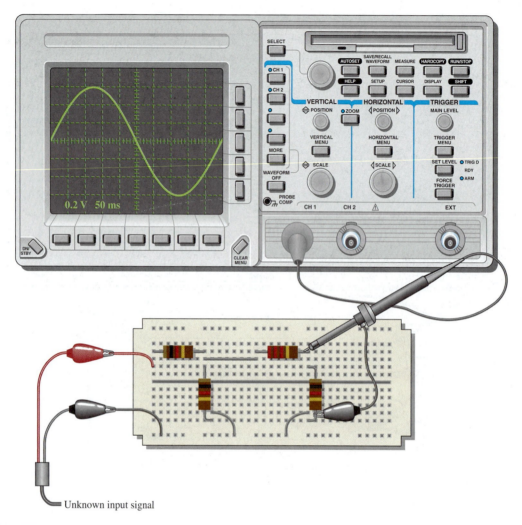

Unknown input signal

FIGURE 11–77

EWB Troubleshooting and Analysis

These problems require your EWB compact disk.

44. Open file PRO11-44.EWB and measure the peak and rms voltage across each of the resistors.

45. Open file PRO11-45.EWB and measure the peak and rms voltage across each of the resistors.

46. Open file PRO11-46.EWB. Determine if there is a fault and, if so, identify the fault.

47. Open file PRO11-47.EWB and measure the rms current in each branch of the circuit.

48. Open file PRO11-48.EWB. Determine if there is a fault and, if so, identify the fault.

49. Open file PRO11-49.EWB and measure the total voltage across the resistor using the oscilloscope.

50. Open file PRO11-50.EWB and measure the total voltage across the resistor using the oscilloscope.

■ **ANSWERS TO SECTION REVIEWS**

Section 11–1

1. One cycle of a sine wave is from the zero crossing through a positive peak, then through zero to a negative peak and back to the zero crossing.

2. A sine wave changes polarity at the zero crossings.

3. A sine wave has two maximum points (peaks) per cycle.

4. The period is from one zero crossing to the next corresponding zero crossing, or from one peak to the next corresponding peak.

5. Frequency is the number of cycles completed in one second; the unit of frequency is the hertz.

6. $f = 1/T = 200$ kHz

7. $T = 1/f = 8.33$ ms

Section 11–2

1. Sine waves are generated by electromagnetic and electronic methods.

2. Speed and frequency are directly proportional.

3. An oscillator is an electronic circuit that produces repetitive waveforms.

Section 11–3

1. (a) $V_{pp} = 2(1 \text{ V}) = 2$ V (b) $V_{pp} = 2(1.414)(1.414 \text{ V}) = 4$ V (c) $V_{pp} = 2(1.57)(3 \text{ V}) = 9.42$ V

2. (a) $V_{rms} = (0.707)(2.5 \text{ V}) = 1.77$ V (b) $V_{rms} = (0.5)(0.707)(10 \text{ V}) = 3.54$ V

  (c) $V_{rms} = (0.707)(1.57)(1.5 \text{ V}) = 1.66$ V

3. (a) $V_{avg} = (0.637)(10 \text{ V}) = 6.37$ V (b) $V_{avg} = (0.637)(1.414)(2.3 \text{ V}) = 2.07$ V

  (c) $V_{avg} = (0.637)(0.5)(60 \text{ V}) = 19.1$ V

Section 11–4

1. (a) Positive peak at 90° (b) Negative-going zero crossing at 180°

  (c) Negative peak at 270° (d) End of cycle at 360°

2. Half-cycle: 180°; π

3. Full cycle: 360°; 2π

4. $90° - 45° = 45°$

Section 11–5

1. $v = 10 \sin(120°) = 8.66$ V

2. $v = 10 \sin(45° + 10°) = 8.19$ V

3. $v = 5 \sin(90° - 25°) = 4.53$ V

Section 11–6

1. $I_p = V_p/R = (1.57)(12.5 \text{ V})/330 \ \Omega = 59.5$ mA

2. $V_{s(rms)} = (0.707)(25.3 \text{ V}) = 17.9$ V

Section 11–7

1. $+V_{max} = 5 \text{ V} + 2.5 \text{ V} = 7.5$ V

2. Yes, it will alternate.

3. $+V_{max} = 5 \text{ V} - 2.5 \text{ V} = 2.5$ V

Section 11–8

1. (a) Rise time is the time interval from 10% to 90% of the rising pulse edge; (b) Fall time is the time interval from 90% to 10% of the falling pulse edge; (c) Pulse width is the time interval from 50% of the leading pulse edge to 50% of the trailing pulse edge.

2. $f = 1/1$ ms $= 1$ kHz

3. d.c. $= (1/5)100\% = 20\%$; Ampl. 1.5 V; $V_{avg} = 0.5 \text{ V} + 0.2(1.5 \text{ V}) = 0.8$ V

4. $T = 16$ ms

5. $f = 1/T = 1/1$ μs $= 1$ MHz

6. Fundamental frequency is the repetition rate of the waveform.

7. 2nd harm.: 2 kHz

8. $f = 1/10$ μs $= 100$ kHz

Section 11–9

1. Analog : Signal drives display directly.
Digital : Signal is converted to digital for processing and then reconstructed for display.

2. Voltage is measured vertically; time is measured horizontally.

3. An oscilloscope can display time-varying quantities.

4. Always, unless you are trying to measure a very small, low-frequency signal.

Section 11–10

1. RF is radio frequency.

2. IF is intermediate frequency.

3. Carrier frequency is higher than audio.

4. The amplitude varies in an AM signal.

■ **ANSWERS TO RELATED PROBLEMS FOR EXAMPLES**

11–1 2.4 s

11–2 1.5 ms

11–3 20 kHz

11–4 200 Hz

11–5 66.7 kHz

11–6 30 rps

11–7 $V_{pp} = 50$ V; $V_{rms} = 17.7$ V; $V_{avg} = 15.9$ V

11–8 (a) $\pi/12$ rad   (b) 360°

11–9 8°

11–10 18.1 V

11–11 $I_{rms} = 4.53$ mA; $V_{1(rms)} = 4.53$ V; $V_{2(rms)} = 2.54$ V

11–12 23.7 V

11–13 The waveform in part (a) never goes negative. The waveform in part (b) goes negative for a portion of its cycle.

11–14 5%

11–15 1.2 V

11–16 120 V

11–17 15 V, 20 ms, 50 Hz

11–18 Part (a) 1.06 V, 50 Hz;
part (b) 88.4 mV, 1.67 kHz
part (c) 4.81 V, 5 kHz;
part (d) 7.07 V, 250 kHz

■ **ANSWERS TO SELF-TEST**

1. (b)	**2.** (b)	**3.** (c)	**4.** (b)	**5.** (d)	**6.** (a)	**7.** (a)	**8.** (a)
9. (c)	**10.** (b)	**11.** (a)	**12.** (d)	**13.** (c)	**14.** (b)	**15.** (d)	

12

PHASORS AND COMPLEX NUMBERS

PSpice Tutorial at
http://www.prenhall.com/floyd

■ INTRODUCTION

In this chapter, two important tools for the analysis of ac circuits are introduced. These are phasors and complex numbers. You will see how phasors are a convenient, graphic way to represent sinusoidal voltages and currents in terms of their magnitude and phase angle. In later chapters, you will see how phasors can also represent other ac circuit quantities.

The complex number system is a means for expressing phasor quantities and for performing mathematical operations with those quantities.

Phasor diagrams are an abstract method of representing quantities that have both magnitude and direction. In the case of sinusoidal voltages and currents, the magnitude is the amplitude of the sine wave and the direction is its phase angle. Phasors provide a way to diagram sine waves and their phase relationships with other sine waves. The complex number system provides a way to mathematically express a phasor quantity and allows phasor quantities to be added, subtracted, multiplied, or divided. Use of a calculator in complex number conversions and arithmetic is covered thoroughly.

The phase relationship of two sine waves can be graphically represented by phasors and it can also be measured on an oscilloscope, as you will see in the TECH TIP in Section 12–5.

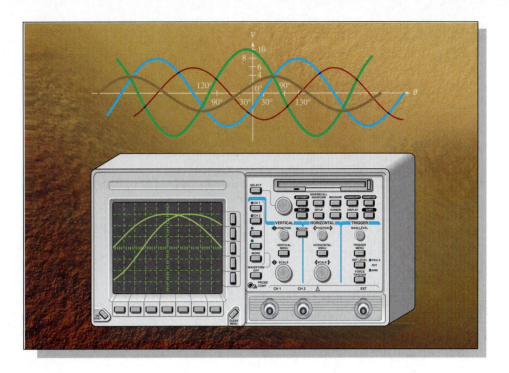

■ CHAPTER OBJECTIVES

❏ Use a phasor to represent a sine wave
❏ Use complex numbers to express phasor quantities
❏ Represent phasors in two complex forms

❏ Do mathematical operations with complex numbers both manually and with a calculator

12–1 ■ INTRODUCTION TO PHASORS

Phasors provide a graphic means for representing quantities that have both magnitude and direction (angular position). Phasors are especially useful for representing sine waves in terms of their magnitude and phase angle and also for analysis of reactive circuits studied in later chapters.

After completing this section, you should be able to

■ **Use a phasor to represent a sine wave**
  • Define *phasor*
  • Explain how phasors are related to the sine wave formula
  • Draw a phasor diagram
  • Discuss angular velocity

You may already be familiar with vectors. In math and science, a vector is any quantity with both magnitude and direction. Examples of vectors are force, velocity, and acceleration. The simplest way to describe a vector is to assign a magnitude and an angle to a quantity.

In electronics, a **phasor** is similar to a vector but generally refers to quantities that vary with time such as sine waves. Examples of phasors are shown in Figure 12–1. The length of the phasor "arrow" represents the magnitude of a quantity. The angle, θ (relative to 0°), represents the angular position, as shown in part (a) for a positive angle. The specific phasor example in part (b) has a magnitude of 2 and a phase angle of 45°. The phasor in part (c) has a magnitude of 3 and a phase angle of 180°. The phasor in part (d) has a magnitude of 1 and a phase angle of −45° (or +315°). Notice that positive angles are measured counterclockwise (CCW) from the reference (0°) and negative angles are measured clockwise (CW) from the reference.

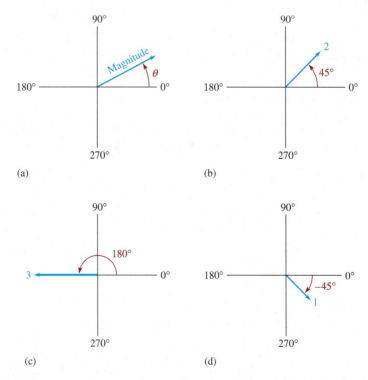

FIGURE 12–1
Examples of phasors.

Phasor Representation of a Sine Wave

A full cycle of a sine wave can be represented by rotation of a phasor through 360 degrees.

> **The instantaneous value of the sine wave at any point is equal to the vertical distance from the tip of the phasor to the horizontal axis.**

Figure 12–2 shows how the phasor traces out the sine wave as it goes from 0° to 360°. You can relate this concept to the rotation in an ac generator (refer to Chapter 11).

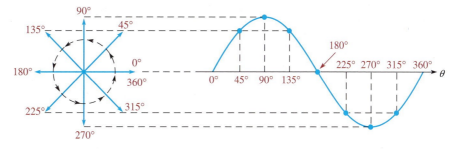

FIGURE 12–2
Sine wave represented by rotational phasor motion.

Notice in Figure 12–2 that the length of the phasor is equal to the peak value of the sine wave (observe the 90° and the 270° points). The angle of the phasor measured from 0° is the corresponding angular point on the sine wave.

Phasors and the Sine Wave Formula

Let's examine a phasor representation at one specific angle. Figure 12–3 shows a voltage phasor at an angular position of 45° and the corresponding point on the sine wave. The instantaneous value of the sine wave at this point is related to both the position and the length of the phasor. As previously mentioned, the vertical distance from the phasor tip down to the horizontal axis represents the instantaneous value of the sine wave at that point.

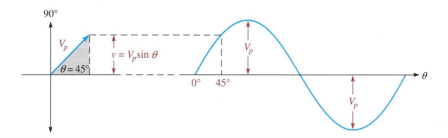

FIGURE 12–3
Right triangle derivation of sine wave formula.

Notice that when a vertical line is drawn from the phasor tip down to the horizontal axis, a right triangle is formed, as shown shaded in Figure 12–3. The length of the phasor is the hypotenuse of the triangle, and the vertical projection is the opposite side. From trigonometry,

> **The opposite side of a right triangle is equal to the hypotenuse times the sine of the angle θ.**

The length of the phasor is the peak value of the sinusoidal voltage, V_p. Thus, the opposite side of the triangle, which is the instantaneous value, can be expressed as

$$v = V_p \sin \theta$$

Recall that this formula is the one stated in Chapter 11 for calculating instantaneous sinusoidal voltage. A similar formula applies to a sinusoidal current.

$$i = I_p \sin \theta$$

Positive and Negative Phasor Angles

The position of a phasor at any instant can be expressed as a positive angle, as you have seen, or as an equivalent negative angle. Positive angles are measured counterclockwise from 0°. Negative angles are measured clockwise from 0°. For a given positive angle θ, the corresponding negative angle is $\theta - 360°$, as illustrated in Figure 12–4(a). In part (b), a specific example is shown. The angle of the phasor in this case can be expressed as +225° or −135°.

FIGURE 12–4
Positive and negative phasor angles.

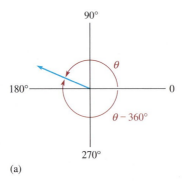

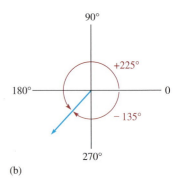

EXAMPLE 12–1   For the phasor in each part of Figure 12–5, determine the instantaneous sine wave value. Also express each positive angle shown as an equivalent negative angle. The length of each phasor represents the peak value of the sine wave.

FIGURE 12–5

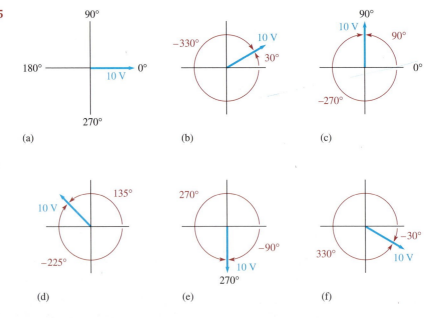

Solution
(a) $v = 10 \sin 0° = 10(0) = \mathbf{0\ V}$
$\theta = \mathbf{0°}$

(b) $v = 10 \sin 30° = 10(0.5) = \mathbf{5\ V}$
$\theta = 30° = \theta - 360° = 30° - 360° = \mathbf{-330°}$

(c) $v = 10 \sin 90° = 10(1) = \mathbf{10\ V}$
$\theta = 90° = \mathbf{-270°}$

(d) $v = 10 \sin 135° = 10(0.707) = \mathbf{7.07\ V}$
$\theta = 135° = \mathbf{-225°}$

(e) $v = 10 \sin 270° = 10(-1) = \mathbf{-10\ V}$
$\theta = 270° = \mathbf{-90°}$

(f) $v = 10 \sin 330° = 10(-0.5) = \mathbf{-5\ V}$
$\theta = 330° = \mathbf{-30°}$

The equivalent negative angles are shown in Figure 12–5.

Related Problem   If a phasor is at 45° and its length represents 15 V, what is the instantaneous sine wave value?

Phasor Diagrams

A phasor diagram can be used to show the relative relationship of two or more sine waves of the same frequency. A phasor in a *fixed position* is used to represent a complete sine wave because once the phase angle between two or more sine waves of the same frequency or between the sine wave and a reference is established, the phase angle remains constant throughout the cycles. For example, the two sine waves in Figure 12–6(a) can be represented by a phasor diagram, as shown in part (b). As you can see, sine wave *B* leads sine wave *A* by 30° and has less amplitude than sine wave *A*, as indicated by the lengths of the phasors.

FIGURE 12–6
Example of a phasor diagram.

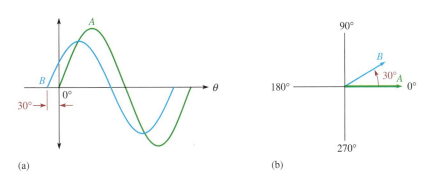

(a)   (b)

EXAMPLE 12–2   Use a phasor diagram to represent the sine waves in Figure 12–7.

FIGURE 12–7

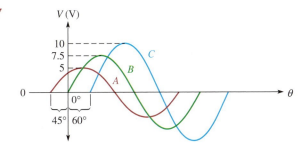

Solution The phasor diagram representing the sine waves is shown in Figure 12–8. The length of each phasor represents the peak value of the sine wave.

FIGURE 12–8

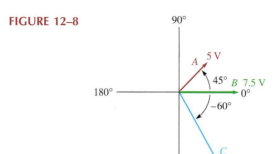

Related Problem Describe a phasor to represent a 5 V peak sine wave that lags sine wave *C* in Figure 12–7 by 25°.

Angular Velocity of a Phasor

As you have seen, one cycle of a sine wave is traced out when a phasor is rotated through 360 degrees. The faster it is rotated, the faster the sine wave cycle is traced out. Thus, the period and frequency are related to the velocity of rotation of the phasor. The velocity of rotation is called the **angular velocity** and is designated ω (the small Greek letter omega).

When a phasor rotates through 360 degrees or 2π radians, one complete cycle is traced out. Therefore, the time required for the phasor to go through 2π radians is the period of the sine wave. Because the phasor rotates through 2π radians in a time equal to the period T, the angular velocity can be expressed as

$$\omega = \frac{2\pi}{T}$$

Since $f = 1/T$,

$$\omega = 2\pi f \tag{12–1}$$

When a phasor is rotated at an angular velocity ω, then ωt is the angle through which the phasor has passed at any instant. Therefore, the following relationship can be stated:

$$\theta = \omega t \tag{12–2}$$

Substituting $2\pi f$ for ω, you get $\theta = 2\pi f t$. With this relationship between angle and time, the equation for the instantaneous value of a sinusoidal voltage, $v = V_p \sin \theta$, can be written as

$$v = V_p \sin 2\pi f t \tag{12–3}$$

The instantaneous value can be calculated at any point in time along the sine wave curve if the frequency and peak value are known. The unit of $2\pi f t$ is the radian.

EXAMPLE 12–3   What is the value of a sinusoidal voltage at 3 μs from the positive-going zero crossing when $V_p = 10$ V and $f = 50$ kHz?

Solution $v = V_p \sin 2\pi f t$
$= 10 \sin[2\pi(50 \text{ kHz})(3 \times 10^{-6} \text{ s})] = \textbf{8.09 V}$

Related Problem   What is the value of a sinusoidal voltage at 12 μs from the positive-going zero crossing when $V_p = 50$ V and $f = 10$ kHz?

SECTION 12–1 REVIEW

1. What is a phasor?
2. What is the angular velocity of a phasor representing a sine wave with a frequency of 1500 Hz?
3. A certain phasor has an angular velocity of 628 rad/s. To what frequency does this correspond?
4. Sketch a phasor diagram to represent the two sine waves in Figure 12–9. Use peak values.

FIGURE 12–9

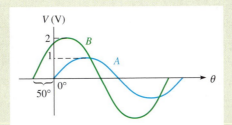

12–2 ■ THE COMPLEX NUMBER SYSTEM

Complex numbers allow mathematical operations with phasor quantities and are useful in analysis of ac circuits. With the complex number system, you can add, subtract, multiply, and divide quantities that have both magnitude and angle, such as sine waves and other ac circuit quantities that will be studied later.

After completing this section, you should be able to

■ **Use complex numbers to express phasor quantities**
  • Describe the complex plane
  • Represent a point on the complex plane
  • Discuss real and imaginary numbers

Positive and Negative Numbers

Positive numbers can be represented by points to the right of the origin on the horizontal axis of a graph, and negative numbers can be represented by points to the left of the origin, as illustrated in Figure 12–10(a). Also, positive numbers can be represented by points on the vertical axis above the origin, and negative numbers can be represented by points below the origin, as shown in Figure 12–10(b).

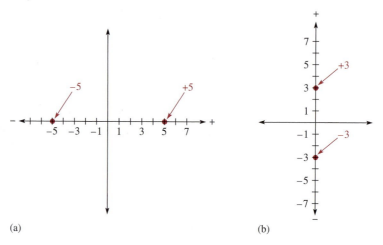

(a)   (b)

FIGURE 12–10
Graphic representation of positive and negative numbers.

The Complex Plane

To distinguish between values on the horizontal axis and values on the vertical axis, a **complex plane** is used. In the complex plane, the horizontal axis is called the *real axis,* and the vertical axis is called the *imaginary axis,* as shown in Figure 12–11.

FIGURE 12–11
The complex plane.

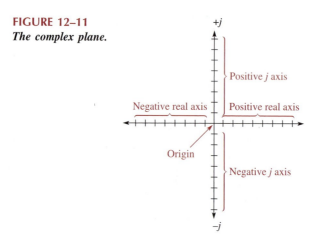

In electrical circuit work, a $\pm j$ prefix is used to designate numbers that lie on the imaginary axis in order to distinguish them from numbers lying on the real axis. This prefix is known as the *j operator.* In mathematics, an *i* is used instead of a *j*, but in electric circuits, the *i* can be confused with instantaneous current, so *j* is used.

Angular Position on the Complex Plane

Angular positions can be represented on the complex plane, as shown in Figure 12–12. The positive real axis represents zero degrees. Proceeding counterclockwise, the $+j$ axis represents 90°, the negative real axis represents 180°, the $-j$ axis is the 270° point, and, after a full rotation of 360°, we are back to the positive real axis. Notice that the plane is sectioned into four quadrants.

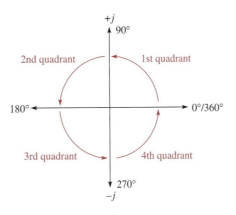

FIGURE 12–12
Angles on the complex plane.

Representing a Point on the Complex Plane

A point located on the complex plane can be classified as real, imaginary ($\pm j$), or a combination of the two. For example, a point located 4 units from the origin on the positive real axis is the positive real number, +4, as shown in Figure 12–13(a). A point 2 units from the origin on the negative real axis is the negative real number, −2, as shown in part (b). A point on the +j axis 6 units from the origin, as in part (c), is the positive **imaginary number,** +j6. Finally, a point 5 units along the −j axis is the negative imaginary number, −j5, as in part (d).

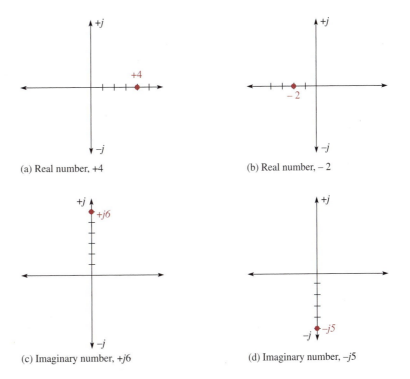

(a) Real number, +4

(b) Real number, − 2

(c) Imaginary number, +j6

(d) Imaginary number, −j5

FIGURE 12–13
Real and imaginary (j) numbers on the complex plane.

When a point lies not on any axis but somewhere in one of the four quadrants, it is a complex number and can be defined by its coordinates. For example, in Figure 12–14, the point located in the first quadrant has a real value of +4 and a j value of $+j4$ and is expressed as +4, +j4. The point located in the second quadrant has coordinates −3 and $+j2$. The point located in the third quadrant has coordinates −3 and $-j5$. The point located in the fourth quadrant has coordinates of +6 and $-j4$.

FIGURE 12–14
Coordinate points on the complex plane.

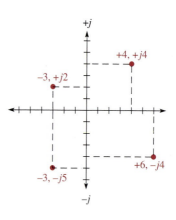

EXAMPLE 12–4

(a) Locate the following points on the complex plane: 7, $j5$; 5, $-j2$; -3.5, $j1$; and -5.5, $-j6.5$.

(b) Determine the coordinates for each point in Figure 12–15.

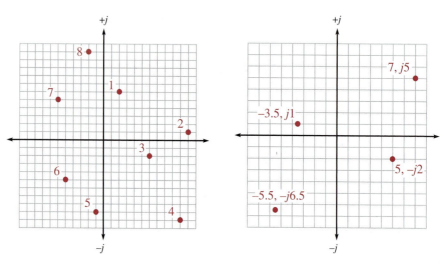

FIGURE 12–15   **FIGURE 12–16**

Solution

(a) See Figure 12–16.

(b) 1: **2, $j6$**   2:**11, $j1$**   3: **6, $-j2$**   4: **10, $-j10$**
     5: **−1, $-j9$**   6: **−5, $-j5$**   7: **−6, $j5$**   8: **−2, $j11$**

Related Problem   In what quadrant is each of the following points located?
(a) +2.5, +j1   (b) 7, $-j5$ (c) −10, $-j5$ (d) −11, +$j6.8$

Value of j

If we multiply the positive real value of +2 by j, the result is $+j2$. This multiplication has effectively moved the +2 through a 90° angle to the $+j$ axis. Similarly, multiplying +2 by $-j$ rotates it −90° to the $-j$ axis. Thus, j is considered a rotational operator.

Mathematically, the j operator has a value of $\sqrt{-1}$. If $+j2$ is multiplied by j, we get

$$j^2 2 = (\sqrt{-1})(\sqrt{-1})(2) = (-1)(2) = -2$$

This calculation effectively places the value on the negative real axis. Therefore, multiplying a positive real number by j^2 converts it to a negative real number, which, in effect, is a rotation of 180° on the complex plane. This operation is illustrated in Figure 12–17.

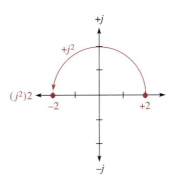

FIGURE 12–17
Effect of the j operator on location of a number on the complex plane.

SECTION 12–2 REVIEW

1. Locate the following points on the complex plane:
   (a) +3   (b) −4   (c) +j1

2. What is the angular difference between the following numbers:
   (a) +4 and +j4   (b) +j6 and −6   (c) +j2 and −j2

12–3 ■ RECTANGULAR AND POLAR FORMS

The rectangular form and the polar form are two forms of complex numbers that are used to represent phasor quantities. Each has certain advantages when used in circuit analysis, depending on the particular application.

After completing this section, you should be able to

■ **Represent phasors in two complex forms**
 • Show how to represent a phasor in rectangular form
 • Show how to represent a phasor in polar form
 • Convert between rectangular and polar forms

As you know, a phasor quantity contains both *magnitude* and angular position or *phase*. In this text, italic letters such as V and I are used to represent magnitude only, and boldface nonitalic letters such as **V** and **I** are used to represent complete phasor quantities. Other circuit quantities that can be expressed in phasor form will be studied in later chapters.

Rectangular Form

A phasor quantity is represented in **rectangular form** by the algebraic sum of the real value (A) of the coordinate and the j value (B) of the coordinate, expressed in the following general form:

$$A + jB$$

An "arrow" drawn from the origin to the coordinate point in the complex plane is used to represent graphically the phasor quantity. Examples of phasor quantities are $1 + j2$, $5 - j3$, $-4 + j4$, and $-2 - j6$, which are shown on the complex plane in Figure 12–18. As you can see, the rectangular coordinates describe the phasor in terms of its values projected onto the real axis and the j axis.

FIGURE 12–18
Examples of phasors specified by rectangular coordinates.

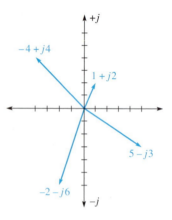

Polar Form

Phasor quantities can also be expressed in **polar form,** which consists of the phasor magnitude (C) and the angular position relative to the positive real axis (θ), expressed in the following general form:

$$C \angle \pm \theta$$

Examples are $2\angle45°$, $5\angle120°$, $4\angle110°$, and $8\angle-30°$. The first number is the magnitude, and the symbol $\angle$ precedes the value of the angle. Figure 12–19 shows these phasors on the complex plane. The length of the phasor, of course, represents the magnitude of the quantity. Keep in mind that for every phasor expressed in polar form, there is also an equivalent expression in rectangular form.

FIGURE 12–19
Examples of phasors specified by polar values.

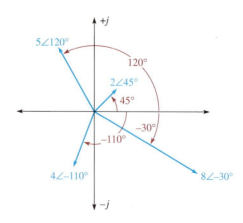

Most scientific calculators have provisions for conversion between rectangular and polar forms. The basic conversion methods are presented first so that you will understand the mathematical procedure, followed by the calculator methods.

Conversion from Rectangular to Polar Form

A phasor can exist in any of the four quadrants of the complex plane, as indicated in Figure 12–20. The phase angle θ in each case is measured relative to the positive real axis (0°) as shown.

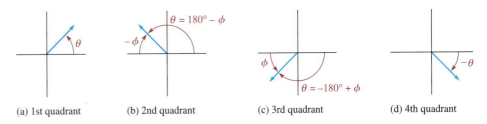

| (a) 1st quadrant | (b) 2nd quadrant | (c) 3rd quadrant | (d) 4th quadrant |

FIGURE 12–20
All possible phasor quadrant locations. θ is the angle of the phasor relative to the positive real axis in each case, and ϕ is the angle in the 2nd and 3rd quadrants relative to the negative real axis.

The first step to convert from rectangular form to polar form is to determine the magnitude of the phasor. A phasor can be visualized as forming a right triangle in the complex plane, as indicated in Figure 12–21, for each quadrant location. The horizontal side of the triangle is the real value, A, and the vertical side is the j value, B. The hypotenuse of the triangle is the length of the phasor, C, representing the magnitude, and can be expressed, using the Pythagorean theorem, as

$$C = \sqrt{A^2 + B^2} \qquad (12\text{–}4)$$

Next, the angle θ indicated in parts (a) and (d) of Figure 12–21 is expressed as an inverse tangent function.

$$\theta = \tan^{-1}\left(\frac{\pm B}{A}\right) \qquad (12\text{–}5)$$

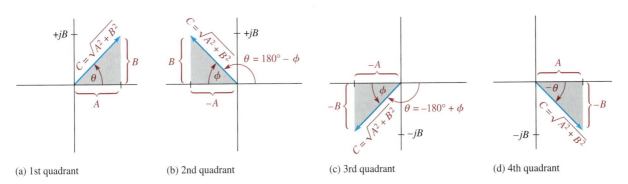

| (a) 1st quadrant | (b) 2nd quadrant | (c) 3rd quadrant | (d) 4th quadrant |

FIGURE 12–21
Right angle relationships in the complex plane.

The angle θ indicated in parts (b) and (c) of Figure 12–21 is

$$\theta = \pm 180° \mp \phi$$

which includes both conditions as indicated by the dual signs.

$$\theta = \pm 180° \mp \tan^{-1}\left(\frac{B}{A}\right) \qquad (12\text{–}6)$$

In each case the appropriate signs must be used in the calculation.

The general formula for converting from rectangular to polar is as follows:

$$\pm A \pm jB = C\angle \pm\theta \qquad (12\text{–}7)$$

Example 12–5 illustrates the conversion procedure.

EXAMPLE 12–5

Convert the following complex numbers from rectangular form to polar form by determining the magnitude and angle:

(a) $8 + j6$ (b) $10 - j5$ (c) $-12 - j18$ (d) $-7 + j10$

Solution

(a) The magnitude of the phasor represented by $8 + j6$ is

$$C = \sqrt{A^2 + B^2} = \sqrt{8^2 + 6^2} = \sqrt{100} = \mathbf{10}$$

Since the phasor is in the first quadrant, use Equation (12–5). The angle is

$$\theta = \tan^{-1}\left(\frac{\pm B}{A}\right) = \tan^{-1}\left(\frac{6}{8}\right) = \mathbf{36.9°}$$

θ is the angle relative to the positive real axis. The complete polar expression for this phasor is

$$\mathbf{C} = 10\angle 36.9°$$

Boldface, nonitalic letters represent phasor quantities.

(b) The magnitude of the phasor represented by $10 - j5$ is

$$C = \sqrt{10^2 + (-5)^2} = \sqrt{125} = \mathbf{11.2}$$

Since the phasor is in the fourth quadrant, use Equation (12–5). The angle is

$$\theta = \tan^{-1}\left(\frac{-5}{10}\right) = \mathbf{-26.6°}$$

θ is the angle relative to the positive real axis. The complete polar expression for this phasor is

$$\mathbf{C} = 11.2\angle{-26.6°}$$

(c) The magnitude of the phasor represented by $-12 - j18$ is

$$C = \sqrt{(-12)^2 + (-18)^2} = \sqrt{468} = \mathbf{21.6}$$

Since the phasor is in the third quadrant, use Equation (12–6). The angle is

$$\theta = -180° + \tan^{-1}\left(\frac{18}{12}\right) = -180° + 56.3° = \mathbf{-123.7°}$$

The complete polar expression for this phasor is

$$\mathbf{C} = 21.6\angle{-123.7°}$$

(d) The magnitude of the phasor represented by $-7 + j10$ is

$$C = \sqrt{(-7)^2 + 10^2} = \sqrt{149} = \mathbf{12.2}$$

Since the angle is in the second quadrant, use Equation (12–6). The angle is

$$\theta = 180° - \tan^{-1}\left(\frac{10}{7}\right) = 180° - 55° = \mathbf{125°}$$

The complete polar expression for this phasor is

$$\mathbf{C} = 12.2\angle 125°$$

Related Problem   Convert $18 + j23$ to polar form.

Conversion from Polar to Rectangular Form

The polar form gives the magnitude and angle of a phasor quantity, as indicated in Figure 12–22.

FIGURE 12–22
Polar components of a phasor.

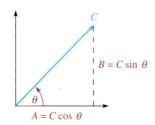

To get the rectangular form, sides A and B of the triangle must be found, using the rules from trigonometry stated below:

$$A = C\cos\theta \tag{12–8}$$

$$B = C\sin\theta \tag{12–9}$$

The polar-to-rectangular conversion formula is as follows:

$$C\angle\theta = C\cos\theta + jC\sin\theta = A + jB \tag{12–10}$$

The following example demonstrates this conversion.

EXAMPLE 12–6

Convert the following polar quantities to rectangular form:
(a) $10\angle 30°$ **(b)** $200\angle -45°$ **(c)** $4\angle 135°$

Solution
(a) The real part of the phasor represented by $10\angle 30°$ is

$$A = C\cos\theta = 10\cos 30° = 10(0.866) = 8.66$$

The j part of this phasor is

$$jB = jC\sin\theta = j10\sin 30° = j10(0.5) = j5$$

The complete rectangular expression is

$$A + jB = \mathbf{8.66 + j5}$$

(b) The real part of the phasor represented by $200\angle-45°$ is

$$A = 200 \cos(-45°) = 200(0.707) = 141$$

The j part is

$$jB = j200 \sin(-45°) = j200(-0.707) = -j141$$

The complete rectangular expression is

$$A + jB = \mathbf{141 - j141}$$

(c) The real part of the phasor represented by $4\angle135°$ is

$$A = 4 \cos 135° = 4(-0.707) = -2.83$$

The j part is

$$jB = j4 \sin 135° = 4(0.707) = 2.83$$

The complete rectangular expression is

$$A + jB = \mathbf{-2.83 + j2.83}$$

Related Problem   Convert $78\angle-26°$ to rectangular form.

Calculator Conversion of Complex Numbers

The following discussion and examples apply to the TI-85 calculator. The procedure on other calculators may differ.

Entering Complex Numbers   All complex numbers must begin and end with parentheses, and each component must be separated by either a comma for rectangular or an angle sign for polar. The angle sign is a secondary function. Complex numbers are entered on the TI-85 as follows. A number in rectangular form is entered in this format:

(real,imaginary)

A number in polar form is entered in this format:

(magnitude∠angle)

EXAMPLE 12–7   Enter the following complex numbers on your calculator:
  (a) $3 + j4$ **(b)** $10 - j8$ **(c)** $4\angle30°$ **(d)** $25\angle-60°$

Solution
  (a) $3 + j4$ is entered as **(3,4)**.
  (b) $10 - j8$ is entered as **(10,−8)**.
  (c) $4\angle30°$ is entered as **(4∠30)**.
  (d) $25\angle-60°$ is entered as **(24∠−60)**.

Related Problem   Enter each of these complex numbers on your calculator: $15 + j18$ and $130\angle45°$.

Form Conversions   To convert one form of complex number to the other, you will first use the MODE key on your calculator to select the form. To get into the mode screen, press the [2nd] key and then the [MODE] key. The mode screen will appear as shown in Figure 12–23. The highlighted (dark) items indicate the default selections. Of course, we are

only interested in the Radian/Degree and the RectC/PolarC selections. Degree is the angular default, and PolarC is the complex form default. To choose a nonselected item, move the flashing highlight box to the desired item using the arrow keys and press ENTER. Press EXIT to exit the mode screen.

FIGURE 12–23
Default mode screen.

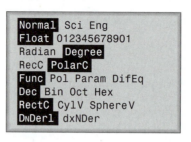

With PolarC highlighted, you can enter a number in rectangular form and convert it to polar form. To do this, simply enter the rectangular number and press the ENTER key.

(real,imaginary)   ENTER ⟶ (magnitude∠angle)

To convert from polar to rectangular, use the directional arrow key and move the flashing highlight box from Normal down to RectC and press ENTER. Exit the mode screen, enter the polar number, and press ENTER.

(magnitude∠angle)   ENTER ⟶ (real,imaginary)

EXAMPLE 12–8

(a) Convert $10 - j5$ to polar form.
(b) Convert $10∠30°$ to rectangular form.

Solution

(a) Select PolarC on the mode screen, exit, enter the retangular number, and press ENTER. The result is shown in Figure 12–24(a). To view the part of the number not originally displayed, press the right arrow key.
(b) Select RectC on the mode screen, exit, enter the polar number, and press ENTER. The result is shown in Figure 12–24(b).

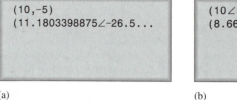

(a)   (b)

FIGURE 12–24

Related Problem   (a) Convert $8 + j6$ to polar form. (b) Convert $200∠-45°$ to rectangular form.

The Complex (CPLX) Mode   Another way of polar-to-rectangular and rectangular-to-polar conversions is the CPLX mode, which is selected by pressing 2nd and CPLX. In this mode you will see the screen in Figure 12–25(a). Press the MORE key and you get the screen in Figure 12–25(b).

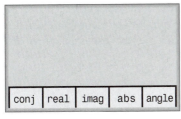

(a) Press 2nd then ENTER.

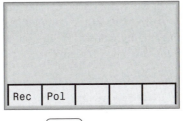

(b) Press MORE.

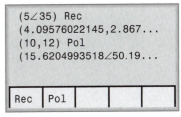

(c) Enter polar number, press F1.

Enter rectangular number, press F2.

FIGURE 12–25
Using the CPLX mode for conversions.

To convert a polar number to rectangular form, enter the number in the proper format (magnitude∠angle) and press F1 then ENTER. To convert a rectangular number to polar form, enter the number in the proper format and press F2 then ENTER. The results are shown for two example numbers in Figure 12–25(c).

SECTION 12–3 REVIEW

1. Name the two parts of a complex number in rectangular form.
2. Name the two parts of a complex number in polar form.
3. Convert $2 + j2$ to polar form. In which quadrant does this phasor lie?
4. Convert $5∠{-45°}$ to rectangular form. In which quadrant does this phasor lie?

12–4 ■ MATHEMATICAL OPERATIONS

Complex numbers can be added, subtracted, multiplied, and divided.

After completing this section, you should be able to

■ **Do mathematical operations with complex numbers**
  • Add complex numbers
  • Subtract complex numbers
  • Multiply complex numbers
  • Divide complex numbers
  • Apply complex numbers to sine waves

Addition

Complex numbers must be in rectangular form in order to add them. The rule is

Add the real parts of each complex number to get the real part of the sum. Then add the j parts of each complex number to get the j part of the sum.

EXAMPLE 12–9

Add the following sets of complex numbers:
(a) $8 + j5$ and $2 + j1$ (b) $20 - j10$ and $12 + j6$

Solution
(a) $(8 + j5) + (2 + j1) = (8 + 2) + j(5 + 1) = \mathbf{10 + j6}$

(b) $(20 - j10) + (12 + j6) = (20 + 12) + j(-10 + 6) = 32 + j(-4) = \mathbf{32 - j4}$

Related Problem Add $5 - j11$ and $-6 + j3$.

Subtraction

As in addition, the numbers must be in rectangular form to be subtracted. The rule is

Subtract the real parts of the numbers to get the real part of the difference. Then subtract the *j* parts of the numbers to get the *j* part of the difference.

EXAMPLE 12–10

Perform the following subtractions:
(a) Subtract $1 + j2$ from $3 + j4$. **(b)** Subtract $10 - j8$ from $15 + j15$.

Solution
(a) $(3 + j4) - (1 + j2) = (3 - 1) + j(4 - 2) = \mathbf{2 + j2}$
(b) $(15 + j15) - (10 - j8) = (15 - 10) + j[15 - (-8)] = \mathbf{5 + j23}$

Related Problem Subtract $3.5 - j4.5$ from $-10 - j9$.

Multiplication

Multiplication of two complex numbers in rectangular form is accomplished by multiplying, in turn, each term in one number by both terms in the other number and then combining the resulting real terms and the resulting *j* terms (recall that $j \times j = -1$). As an example,

$$(5 + j3)(2 - j4) = 10 - j20 + j6 + 12 = 22 - j14$$

Multiplication of two complex numbers is easier when both numbers are in polar form. The rule is

Multiply the magnitudes, and add the angles algebraically.

EXAMPLE 12–11

Perform the following multiplications:
(a) $10\angle45°$ times $5\angle20°$ **(b)** $2\angle60°$ times $4\angle-30°$

Solution
(a) $(10\angle45°)(5\angle20°) = (10)(5)\angle(45° + 20°) = \mathbf{50\angle65°}$
(b) $(2\angle60°)(4\angle-30°) = (2)(4)\angle[60° + (-30°)] = \mathbf{8\angle30°}$

Related Problem Multiply $50\angle10°$ times $30\angle-60°$.

Division

Division of two complex numbers in rectangular form is accomplished by multiplying both the numerator and the denominator by the complex conjugate of the denominator and then combining terms and simplifying. The complex conjugate of a number is found by changing the sign of the *j* term. As an example,

$$\frac{10 + j5}{2 + j4} = \frac{(10 + j5)(2 - j4)}{(2 + j4)(2 - j4)} = \frac{20 - j30 + 20}{4 + 16} = \frac{40 - j30}{20} = 2 - j1.5$$

Like multiplication, division is easier when the numbers are in polar form. The rule is

> **Divide the magnitude of the numerator by the magnitude of the denominator to get the magnitude of the quotient. Then subtract the denominator angle from the numerator angle to get the angle of the quotient.**

EXAMPLE 12–12   Perform the following divisions:
(a) Divide $100\angle50°$ by $25\angle20°$.   (b) Divide $15\angle10°$ by $3\angle-30°$.

Solution

(a) $\dfrac{100\angle50°}{25\angle20°} = \left(\dfrac{100}{25}\right)\angle(50° - 20°) = \mathbf{4\angle30°}$

(b) $\dfrac{15\angle10°}{3\angle-30°} = \left(\dfrac{15}{3}\right)\angle[10° - (-30°)] = \mathbf{5\angle40°}$

Related Problem   Divide $24\angle-30°$ by $6\angle12°$.

Using Complex Numbers with Sine Waves

Since sine waves can be represented by phasors, they can be described in terms of complex numbers either in rectangular or polar form. For example, four series sinusoidal voltage sources all with the same frequency are shown in Figure 12–26. The sine waves are graphed in Figure 12–27(a), and the phasor representation is shown in part (b). The total voltage across the load in Figure 12–26 can be determined by first converting each phasor to rectangular form and then adding as follows:

$$\begin{aligned}
\mathbf{V}_{tot} &= \mathbf{V}_1 + \mathbf{V}_2 + \mathbf{V}_3 + \mathbf{V}_4 \\
&= 10\angle120° \text{ V} + 4\angle30° \text{ V} + 8\angle-30° \text{ V} + 6\angle-130° \text{ V} \\
&= (-5 \text{ V} + j8.66 \text{ V}) + (3.46 \text{ V} + j2 \text{ V}) + (6.93 \text{ V} - j4 \text{ V}) + (-3.86 \text{ V} - j4.60 \text{ V}) \\
&= 1.53 \text{ V} + j2.06 \text{ V} = 2.57\angle53.4° \text{ V}
\end{aligned}$$

The total voltage has a magnitude of 2.57 V and a phase angle of 53.4°.

As you have seen, sine waves can be represented in complex form and can be added, subtracted, multiplied, and divided using the rules that we have discussed. Also, as you will learn later, other electrical quantities, such as capacitive and inductive reactances, impedance, and power, can be described in complex form to ease many circuit analysis problems.

FIGURE 12–26
Superimposed sinusoidal sources.

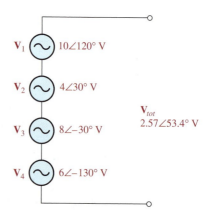

FIGURE 12–27

A phasor diagram representing the four out-of-phase sine waves in Figure 12–26.

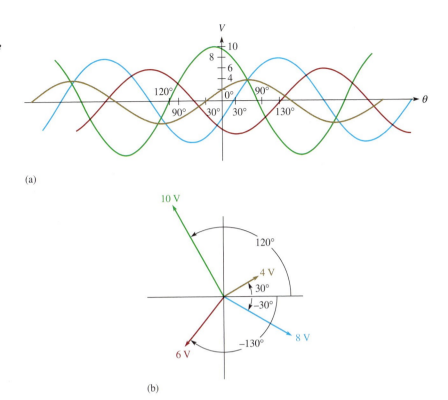

(a)

(b)

Complex Number Operations with the Calculator

Addition, subtraction, multiplication, and division of complex numbers can be easily done with the calculator. All operations are accomplished by simply entering the numbers in the proper format along with the arithmetic sign, just as you would for real numbers. The TI-85 is used to illustrate the procedures.

Addition   To add two or more complex numbers, enter the numbers with the plus sign and press ENTER . All the numbers to be added can be in rectangular format, all in polar format, or there can be a mixture of both formats. The form of the result is determined by the selection on the mode screen.

EXAMPLE 12–13   Add the following sets of complex numbers with the results in rectangular form:
(a) $8 + j5$ and $2 + j1$ **(b)** $5\angle45°$ and $10\angle30°$ **(c)** $12\angle20°$ and $8 + j6$

Solution   For all of these additions, select RectC on the mode screen so that the sums are in rectangular form; then exit the mode screen. The calculator screens should appear as follows in Figure 12–28 after entering the numbers and pressing ENTER .

```
(8,5)+(2,1)

          (10,6)
```

(a)

```
(5∠45)+(10∠30)
(12.1957879438,8.535...
```

(b)

```
(12∠20)+(8,6)
(19.2763114494,10.10...
```

(c)

FIGURE 12–28

Related Problem   Add $100 + j50$ and $75 - j45$ and $35 + j65$. Obtain the sum in polar form.

Subtraction   To subtract complex numbers, enter the numbers with the minus sign and press ENTER , as illustrated in the following example.

EXAMPLE 12–14   Subtract the following sets of complex numbers with the results in rectangular form:
(a) $1 + j2$ from $3 + j4$ (b) $8\angle35°$ from $12\angle10°$ (c) $22\angle60°$ from $100 + j50$

Solution   For all of these subtractions, select RectC on the mode screen so that the differences are in rectangular form; then exit the mode screen. The calculator screens should appear as follows in Figure 12–29 after entering the numbers and pressing ENTER .

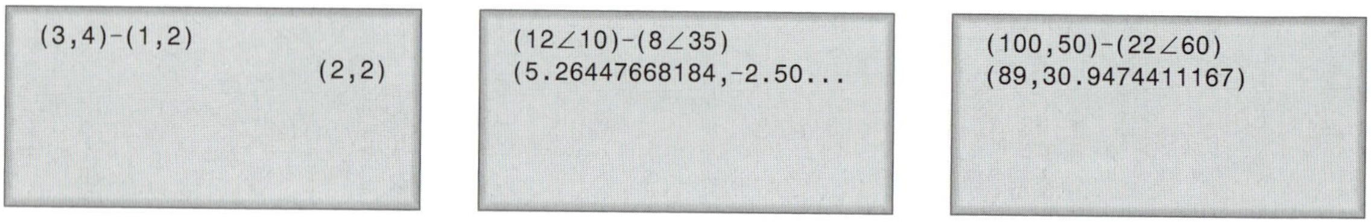

```
(3,4)-(1,2)
            (2,2)
```
(a)

```
(12∠10)-(8∠35)
(5.26447668184,-2.50...
```
(b)

```
(100,50)-(22∠60)
(89,30.9474411167)
```
(c)

FIGURE 12–29

Related Problem   Subtract $10 + j50$ from $25 - j30$. Obtain the difference in polar form.

Multiplication   To multiply complex numbers, enter the numbers with the multiplication sign and press ENTER , as illustrated in the following example.

EXAMPLE 12–15   Multiply the following sets of complex numbers with the results in polar form:
(a) $1 + j2$ and $3 + j4$ (b) $8\angle35°$ and $12\angle10°$ (c) $22\angle60°$ and $100 + j50$

Solution   For all of these multiplications, select PolarC on the mode screen so that the products are in polar form; then exit the mode screen. The calculator screens should appear as follows in Figure 12–30 after entering the numbers and pressing ENTER .

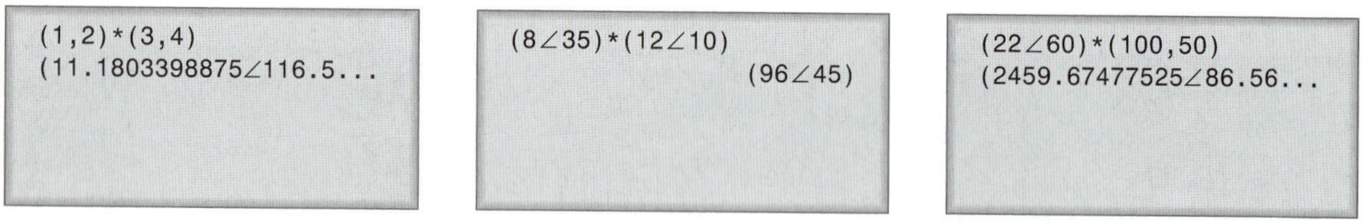

```
(1,2)*(3,4)
(11.1803398875∠116.5...
```
(a)

```
(8∠35)*(12∠10)
            (96∠45)
```
(b)

```
(22∠60)*(100,50)
(2459.67477525∠86.56...
```
(c)

FIGURE 12–30

Related Problem   Multiply $10 + j50$ and $25 - j30$. Obtain the product in rectangular form.

Division   To divide complex numbers, enter the numbers with the division sign and press ENTER , as illustrated in the following example.

EXAMPLE 12–16   Divide the following sets of complex numbers with the results in polar form:
(a) $5 + j2$ by $4 + j4$ (b) $16\angle 45°$ by $10\angle 50°$ (c) $25\angle 50°$ and $85 + j55$

Solution   For all of these divisions, select PolarC on the mode screen so that the quotients are in polar form; then exit the mode screen. The calculator screens should appear as follows in Figure 12–31 after entering the numbers and pressing ENTER .

```
(5,2)/(4,4)
(.951971638233∠-23.1...
```

```
(16∠45)/(10∠50)
           (1.6∠-5)
```

```
(22∠50)/(85,55)
(.552157630374∠30.52...
```

(a)   (b)   (c)

FIGURE 12–31

Related Problem   Divide $15 + j20$ by $15 + j10$. Obtain the quotient in rectangular form.

SECTION 12–4 REVIEW

1. Add $1 + j2$ and $3 - j1$. Verify your result with a calculator.
2. Subtract $12 + j18$ from $15 + j25$. Verify your result with a calculator.
3. Multiply $8\angle 45°$ times $2\angle 65°$. Verify your result with a calculator.
4. Divide $30\angle 75°$ by $6\angle 60°$. Verify your result with a calculator.

12–5 ■ TECHnology Theory Into Practice

Phasors and complex numbers are mathematical concepts that are used for the purpose of ac circuit analysis. Although this Tech TIP does not deal directly with phasors or complex numbers, the angular relationships that are measured can be represented by phasors.

One way to measure the phase angle between two sine waves with the same frequency is to first adjust the amplitude of one waveform on the scope screen so that both waveforms appear equal. Measure the time (Δt) between corresponding points on the waveforms and measure the period. Then, using the relationship $\Delta t/T = \theta/360°$, calculate the phase angle θ as $\theta = (\Delta t/T)360°$. On most digital oscilloscopes, the cursors may be used to determine Δt and T.

Another way to measure the phase angle between two sine waves with the same frequency is to use an analog oscilloscope and convert the horizontal axis into angular divisions. The seconds/division control can be switched off of the calibrated position and varied until there is exactly one half-cycle of the sine wave displayed across the screen as illustrated in Figure 12–32(a). (Generally, the time base of digital oscilloscopes cannot be

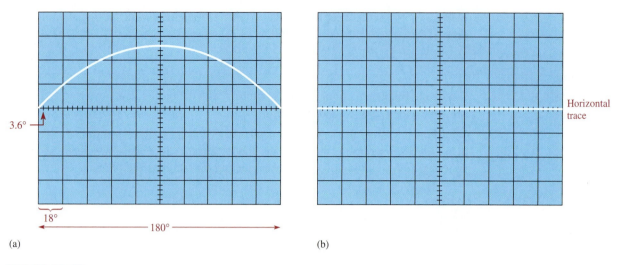

3.6°

18°

180°

(a)

Horizontal
trace

(b)

FIGURE 12–32

decalibrated.) Since a half-cycle contains 180°, each of the ten main horizontal divisions represents 18° and each of the small divisions represents 3.6°, as indicated. A quarter cycle can be used although it is difficult to establish the exact positive peak when the waveform is spread out.

After the phase scale has been established using one of the sine waves, the traces for both oscilloscope channels must be superimposed on each other and aligned along the horizontal axis to prevent any vertical offset of the waveforms. This is done by touching channel 1 probe to ground (0 V) or by switching the channel input coupling switch to the ground (GND) position and adjusting the vertical position to bring it to the center line on the screen, as indicated in Figure 12–32(b). This is repeated for the channel 2 trace.

Next the probes are connected to the two signals and each is ac coupled (channel input switch set to AC) into the scope. The scope should be triggered on the reference channel—do not use composite or vertical-mode triggering. You should set the amplitudes to an approximately equal height by taking the volts/division controls off of the calibrate position and adjusting each one. This is illustrated in Figure 12–33. The phase angle between the two waveforms can be most easily measured from the zero crossings, as shown. In this example, the angle is 36°.

FIGURE 12–33

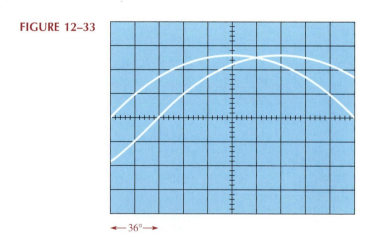

36°

Phase Angle Measurement

■ Determine the phase angle for each of the scope displays in Figure 12–34. A quarter cycle is shown in part (c).

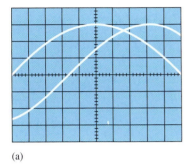

(a)

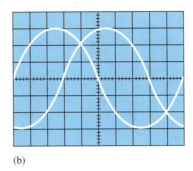

(b)

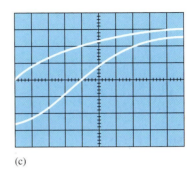

(c)

FIGURE 12–34

SECTION 12–5 REVIEW

1. When measuring the phase angle between two waveforms on an oscilloscope, is the seconds/division setting critical?
2. How do you prevent vertical offset of the waveforms when measuring the phase angle?
3. What triggering method should be selected for a phase shift measurement?

■ **SUMMARY**

- The angular position of a phasor represents the angle of the sine wave with respect to a reference, and the length of a phasor represents the amplitude.
- A complex number represents a phasor quantity.
- Complex numbers can be added, subtracted, multiplied, and divided.
- The rectangular form of a complex number consists of a real part and a j part of the form $A + jB$.
- The polar form of a complex number consists of a magnitude and an angle of the form $C\angle\pm\theta$.

■ **GLOSSARY**

These terms are also in the end-of-book glossary.

Angular velocity   The rotational velocity of a phasor which is related to the frequency of the sine wave that the phasor represents.

Complex plane   An area consisting of four quadrants on which a quantity containing both magnitude and direction can be represented.

Imaginary number   A number that exists on the vertical axis of the complex plane.

Phasor   A representation of a sine wave in terms of its magnitude (amplitude) and direction (phase angle).

Polar form   One form of a complex number made up of a magnitude and an angle.

Rectangular form   One form of a complex number made up of a real part and an imaginary part.

■ **FORMULAS**

(12–1) $\omega = 2\pi f$

(12–2) $\theta = \omega t$

(12–3) $v = V_p\sin 2\pi ft$

$$(12\text{–}4) \qquad C = \sqrt{A^2 + B^2}$$

$$(12\text{–}5) \qquad \theta = \tan^{-1}\left(\frac{\pm B}{A}\right)$$

$$(12\text{–}6) \qquad \theta = \pm 180° \mp \tan^{-1}\left(\frac{B}{A}\right)$$

$$(12\text{–}7) \qquad \pm A \pm jB = C\angle\pm\theta$$

$$(12\text{–}8) \qquad A = C \cos\theta$$

$$(12\text{–}9) \qquad B = C \sin\theta$$

$$(12\text{–}10) \qquad C\angle\theta = C \cos\theta + jC \sin\theta = A + jB$$

■ **SELF-TEST**

1. A phasor represents
   (a) the magnitude of a quantity　　(b) the magnitude and direction of a quantity
   (c) the phase angle　　(d) the length of a quantity

2. A positive angle of 20° is equivalent to a negative angle of
   (a) −160°　　(b) −340°　　(c) −70°　　(d) −20°

3. In the complex plane, the number $3 + j4$ is located in the
   (a) first quadrant　　(b) second quadrant
   (c) third quadrant　　(d) fourth quadrant

4. In the complex plane, $12 − j6$ is located in the
   (a) first quadrant　　(b) second quadrant
   (c) third quadrant　　(d) fourth quadrant

5. The complex number $5 + j5$ is equivalent to
   (a) $5\angle 45°$　　(b) $25\angle 0°$　　(c) $7.07\angle 45°$　　(d) $7.07\angle 135°$

6. The complex number $35\angle 60°$ is equivalent to
   (a) $35 + j35$　　(b) $35 + j60$　　(c) $17.5 + j30.3$　　(d) $30.3 + j17.5$

7. $(4 + j7) + (−2 + j9)$ is equal to
   (a) $2 + j16$　　(b) $11 + j11$　　(c) $−2 + j16$　　(d) $2 − j2$

8. $(16 − j8) − (12 + j5)$ is equal to
   (a) $28 − j13$　　(b) $4 − j13$　　(c) $4 − j3$　　(d) $−4 + j13$

9. $(5\angle 45°)(2\angle 20°)$ is equal to
   (a) $7\angle 65°$　　(b) $10\angle 25°$　　(c) $10\angle 65°$　　(d) $7\angle 25°$

10. $(50\angle 10°) / (25\angle 30°)$ is equal to
    (a) $25\angle 40°$　　(b) $2\angle 40°$　　(c) $25\angle −20°$　　(d) $2\angle −20°$

■ **PROBLEMS**

More difficult problems are indicated by an asterisk (*).

SECTION 12–1　**Introduction to Phasors**

1. Draw a phasor diagram to represent the sine waves in Figure 12–35 with respect to a 0° reference.

2. Sketch the sine waves represented by the phasor diagram in Figure 12–36. The phasor lengths represent peak values.

FIGURE 12–35

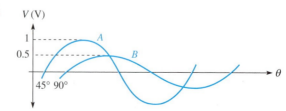

FIGURE 12–36

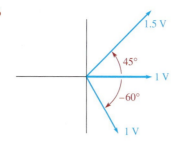

3. Determine the frequency for each angular velocity:

(a) 60 rad/s   (b) 360 rad/s   (c) 2 rad/s   (d) 1256 rad/s

4. Determine the value of sine wave A in Figure 12–35 at each of the following times, measured from the positive-going zero crossing. Assume the frequency is 5 kHz.

(a) 30 μs   (b) 75 μs   (c) 125 μs

*5. In Figure 12–35, how many microseconds after the zero crossing does sine wave A reach 0.8 V? Assume the frequency is 5 kHz.

SECTION 12–2 The Complex Number System

6. Locate the following numbers on the complex plane:

(a) +6   (b) –2   (c) +j3   (d) –j8

7. Locate the points represented by each of the following coordinates on the complex plane:

(a) 3, j5   (b) –7, j1   (c) –10, –j10

*8. Determine the coordinates of each point having the same magnitude but located 180° away from each point in Problem 7.

*9. Determine the coordinates of each point having the same magnitude but located 90° away from those in Problem 7.

SECTION 12–3 Rectangular and Polar Forms

10. Points on the complex plane are described below. Express each point as a complex number in rectangular form:

(a) 3 units to the right of the origin on the real axis, and up 5 units on the j axis.

(b) 2 units to the left of the origin on the real axis, and 1.5 units up on the j axis.

(c) 10 units to the left of the origin on the real axis, and down 14 units on the –j axis.

11. What is the value of the hypotenuse of a right triangle whose sides are 10 and 15?

12. Convert each of the following rectangular numbers to polar form:

(a) $40 - j40$ (b) $50 - j200$ (c) $35 - j20$ (d) $98 + j45$

13. Convert each of the following polar numbers to rectangular form:

(a) $1000\angle-50°$ (b) $15\angle160°$ (c) $25\angle-135°$ (d) $3\angle180°$

14. Express each of the following polar numbers using a negative angle to replace the positive angle:

(a) $10\angle120°$ (b) $32\angle85°$ (c) $5\angle310°$

15. Identify the quadrant in which each of the points in Problem 12 is located.

16. Identify the quadrant in which each point in Problem 14 is located.

17. Write the polar expressions using positive angles for each phasor in Figure 12–37.

FIGURE 12–37

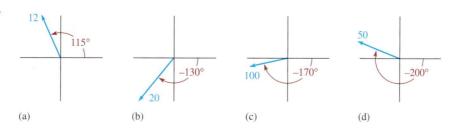

(a)   (b)   (c)   (d)

SECTION 12–4 Mathematical Operations

18. Add the following sets of complex numbers:

    (a) $9 + j3$ and $5 + j8$ **(b)** $3.5 - j4$ and $2.2 + j6$

    (c) $-18 + j23$ and $30 - j15$ **(d)** $12\angle 45°$ and $20\angle 32°$

    (e) $3.8\angle 75°$ and $1 + j1.8$ **(f)** $50 - j39$ and $60\angle -30°$

19. Perform the following subtractions:

    (a) $(2.5 + j1.2) - (1.4 + j0.5)$ **(b)** $(-45 - j23) - (36 + j12)$

    (c) $(8 - j4) - 3\angle 25°$ **(d)** $48\angle 135° - 33\angle -60°$

20. Multiply the following numbers:

    (a) $4.5\angle 48°$ and $3.2\angle 90°$ **(b)** $120\angle -220°$ and $95\angle 200°$

    (c) $-3\angle 150°$ and $4 - j3$ **(d)** $67 + j84$ and $102\angle 40°$

    (e) $15 - j10$ and $-25 - j30$ **(f)** $0.8 + j0.5$ and $1.2 - j1.5$

21. Perform the following divisions:

    (a) $\dfrac{8\angle 50°}{2.5\angle 39°}$ **(b)** $\dfrac{63\angle -91°}{9\angle 10°}$ **(c)** $\dfrac{28\angle 30°}{14 - j12}$ **(d)** $\dfrac{40 - j30}{16 + j8}$

22. Perform the following operations:

    (a) $\dfrac{2.5\angle 65° - 1.8\angle -23°}{1.2\angle 37°}$ **(b)** $\dfrac{(100\angle 15°)(85 - j150)}{25 + j45}$

    (c) $\dfrac{(250\angle 90° + 175\angle 75°)(50 - j100)}{(125 + j90)(35\angle 50°)}$ **(d)** $\dfrac{(1.5)^2(3.8)}{1.1} + j\left(\dfrac{8}{4} - j\dfrac{4}{2}\right)$

*23. Three sinusoidal voltage sources are connected in series as shown in Figure 12–38. Determine the total voltage and current expressed as polar quantities. Resistance always has a zero phase angle as you will learn later, so $R_2 = 2.2\angle 0°$ kΩ.

*24. What is the magnitude and phase of the voltages across each resistor in Figure 12–38?

FIGURE 12–38

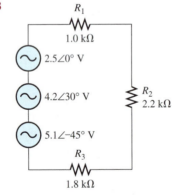

R_1
1.0 kΩ

$2.5\angle 0°$ V

$4.2\angle 30°$ V

R_2
2.2 kΩ

$5.1\angle -45°$ V

R_3
1.8 kΩ

▪ **ANSWERS TO SECTION REVIEWS**

Section 12–1

1. A graphic representation of the magnitude and angular position of a time-varying quantity

2. 9425 rad/s

3. 100 Hz

4. See Figure 12–39.

FIGURE 12–39

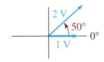

2 V

50°

0°

1 V

Section 12–2

1. **(a)** 3 units right of the origin on real axis   **(b)** 4 units left of the origin on real axis
   (c) 1 unit above origin on j axis
2. **(a)** 90°   **(b)** 90°   **(c)** 180°

Section 12–3

1. Real part and j (imaginary) part
2. Magnitude and angle
3. 2.828∠45°; first
4. 3.54 − j3.54, fourth

Section 12–4

1. 4 + j1
2. 3 + j7
3. 16∠110°
4. 5∠15°

Section 12–5

1. No, the seconds/division setting is not critical.
2. Superimpose the traces by adjusting the vertical deflection (position).
3. Reference channel

■ **ANSWERS TO RELATED PROBLEMS FOR EXAMPLES**

12–1   10.6 V
12–2   5 V at −85°
12–3   34.2 V
12–4   **(a)** 1st   **(b)** 4th   **(c)** 3rd   **(d)** 2nd
12–5   29.2∠52°
12–6   70.1 − j34.2
12–7   (16∠18); (130∠45)
12–8   **(a)** (10∠36.8698976458)   **(b)** (141.421356237, −141.421356237)
12–9   −1 − j8
12–10 −13.5 − j4.5
12–11 1500∠−50°
12–12 4∠−42°
12–13 (221.359436212∠18.4349488229)
12–14 (52.2015325446∠73.300755766)
12–15 (1750,950)
12–16 (1.30769230769, .461538461538)

■ **ANSWERS TO SELF-TEST**

1. (b)   **2.** (b)   **3.** (a)   **4.** (d)   **5.** (c)   **6.** (c)   **7.** (a)   **8.** (b)
9. (c)   **10.** (d)

13

CAPACITORS

Electronics Workbench (EWB) and
PSpice Tutorials at
http://www.prenhall.com/floyd

■ INTRODUCTION

In previous chapters, the resistor has been the only passive electrical component that you have studied. The *capacitor* is the second type of basic passive electrical component.

In this chapter, you will learn about the capacitor and its characteristics. The basic construction and electrical properties are examined, and the effects of connecting capacitors in series and in parallel are analyzed. How a capacitor works in both dc and ac circuits is an important part of this coverage and forms the basis for the study of reactive circuits in terms of both frequency response and time response. You will learn how to check for a faulty capacitor.

The capacitor is an electrical device that can store electrical charge, thereby creating an electric field that, in turn, stores energy. The measure of the energy-storing ability of a capacitor is its capacitance. When a sine wave signal is applied to a capacitor, it reacts in a certain way and produces an opposition to current, which depends on the frequency of the applied signal. This opposition to current is called *capacitive reactance*.

In the TECH TIP assignment in Section 13–9, you will see how a capacitor is used to couple signal voltages to and from an amplifier. You will also troubleshoot the amplifier using oscilloscope waveforms.

■ CHAPTER OBJECTIVES

❑ Describe the basic structure and characteristics of a capacitor
❑ Discuss various types of capacitors
❑ Analyze series capacitors
❑ Analyze parallel capacitors

❑ Analyze capacitive dc switching circuits
❑ Analyze capacitive ac circuits
❑ Discuss some capacitor applications
❑ Test a capacitor

HISTORICAL NOTE

Charles Augustin de Coulomb
1736–1806

Charles Augustin de Coulomb was born in France in 1736. He spent several years as a military engineer in the West Indies. As the French Revolution began, ill health forced him to retire and he began devoting his time to scientific research. Coulomb worked on applied mechanics, but he is best known for his work on electricity and magnetism. He established experimentally the inverse square law for the force between two charges which became the basis for Poisson's mathematical theory of magnetism. The unit of electrical charge is named in his honor. *Photo credit: Courtesy of the Smithsonian Institution. Photo number 52,597.*

13–1 ■ THE BASIC CAPACITOR

In this section, the basic structure and characteristics of capacitors are examined.

After completing this section, you should be able to

■ **Describe the basic structure and characteristics of a capacitor**
  - Explain how a capacitor stores charge
  - Define *capacitance* and state its unit
  - State Coulomb's law
  - Explain how a capacitor stores energy
  - Discuss voltage rating and temperature coefficient
  - Explain capacitor leakage
  - Specify how the physical characteristics affect the capacitance

Basic Construction

In its simplest form, a **capacitor** is an electrical device constructed of two parallel conductive plates separated by an insulating material called the **dielectric.** Connecting leads are attached to the parallel plates. A basic capacitor is shown in Figure 13–1(a), and a schematic symbol is shown in part (b).

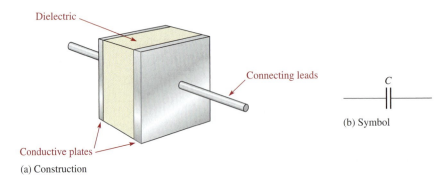

Dielectric

Connecting leads

Conductive plates

(a) Construction

C

(b) Symbol

FIGURE 13–1
The basic capacitor.

How a Capacitor Stores Charge

In the neutral state, both plates of a capacitor have an equal number of free electrons, as indicated in Figure 13–2(a). When the capacitor is connected to a voltage source through a resistor, as shown in part (b), electrons (negative charge) are removed from plate *A*, and an equal number are deposited on plate *B*. As plate *A* loses electrons and plate *B* gains electrons, plate *A* becomes positive with respect to plate *B*. During this charging process, electrons flow only through the connecting leads and the source. No electrons flow through the dielectric of the capacitor because it is an insulator. The movement of electrons ceases when the voltage across the capacitor equals the source voltage, as indicated in Figure 13–2(c). If the capacitor is disconnected from the source, it retains the stored charge for a long period of time (the length of time depends on the type of capacitor) and still has the voltage across it, as shown in Figure 13–2(d). A charged capacitor can act as a temporary battery.

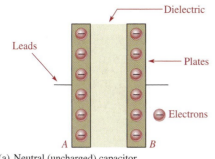

(a) Neutral (uncharged) capacitor
(same charge on both plates)

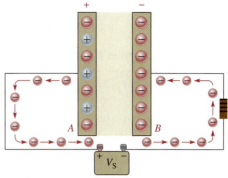

(b) Electrons flow from plate A to plate B as capacitor charges.

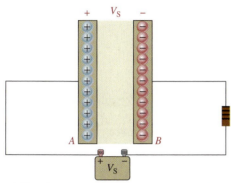

(c) Capacitor charged to V_S. No more electrons flow.

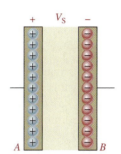

(d) Capacitor retains charge when disconnected
from source.

FIGURE 13–2
Illustration of a capacitor storing charge.

Capacitance

The amount of charge that a capacitor can store per volt across its plates is its **capacitance,** designated C. That is, capacitance is a measure of a capacitor's ability to store charge. The more charge per volt that a capacitor can store, the greater its capacitance, as expressed by the following formula:

$$C = \frac{Q}{V} \qquad \text{(13–1)}$$

where C is capacitance, Q is charge, and V is voltage.

By rearranging Equation (13–1), we obtain two other formulas as follows:

$$Q = CV \qquad \text{(13–2)}$$

$$V = \frac{Q}{C} \qquad \text{(13–3)}$$

The Unit of Capacitance   The **farad (F)** is the basic unit of capacitance, and the **coulomb (C)** is the unit of electrical charge. By definition, one farad is the amount of capacitance when one coulomb (C) of charge is stored with one volt across the plates.

Most capacitors that are used in electronics work have capacitance values that are specified in microfarads (μF) and picofarads (pF). A microfarad is one-millionth of a farad (1 μF = 1×10^{-6} F), and a picofarad is one-trillionth of a farad (1 pF = 1×10^{-12} F).

Conversions for farads, microfarads, and picofarads are given in Table 13–1.

TABLE 13–1

Conversions for farads, microfarads, and picofarads.

To Convert from	To	Move the Decimal Point
Farads	Microfarads	6 places to right ($\times 10^6$)
Farads	Picofarads	12 places to right ($\times 10^{12}$)
Microfarads	Farads	6 places to left ($\times 10^{-6}$)
Microfarads	Picofarads	6 places to right ($\times 10^6$)
Picofarads	Farads	12 places to left ($\times 10^{-12}$)
Picofarads	Microfarads	6 places to left ($\times 10^{-6}$)

EXAMPLE 13–1

(a) A certain capacitor stores 50 microcoulombs (50 μC) with 10 V across its plates. What is its capacitance in units of microfarads?

(b) A 2 μF capacitor has 100 V across its plates. How much charge does it store?

(c) Determine the voltage across a 1000 pF capacitor that is storing 20 microcoulombs (20 μC) of charge.

Solution

(a) $C = \dfrac{Q}{V} = \dfrac{50\ \mu C}{10\ V} = \textbf{5}\ \boldsymbol{\mu}\textbf{F}$

(b) $Q = CV = (2\ \mu F)(100\ V) = \textbf{200}\ \boldsymbol{\mu}\textbf{C}$

(c) $V = \dfrac{Q}{C} = \dfrac{20\ \mu C}{1000\ pF} = \textbf{20 kV}$

Related Problem Determine V if $C = 1000$ pF and $Q = 100\ \mu$C.

EXAMPLE 13–2

Convert the following values to microfarads:
(a) 0.00001 F   (b) 0.005 F   (c) 1000 pF   (d) 200 pF

Solution

(a) $0.00001\ F \times 10^6\ \mu F/F = \textbf{10}\ \boldsymbol{\mu}\textbf{F}$ (b) $0.005\ F \times 10^6\ \mu F/F = \textbf{5000}\ \boldsymbol{\mu}\textbf{F}$

(c) $1000\ pF \times 10^{-6}\ \mu F/pF = \textbf{0.001}\ \boldsymbol{\mu}\textbf{F}$ (d) $200\ pF \times 10^{-6}\ \mu F/pF = \textbf{0.0002}\ \boldsymbol{\mu}\textbf{F}$

Related Problem Convert 50,000 pF to microfarads.

EXAMPLE 13–3

Convert the following values to picofarads:
(a) 0.1×10^{-8} F   (b) 0.000025 F   (c) 0.01 μF   (d) 0.005 μF

Solution

(a) $0.1 \times 10^{-8}\ F \times 10^{12}\ pF/F = \textbf{1000 pF}$

(b) $0.000025\ F \times 10^{12}\ pF/F = \textbf{25} \times \textbf{10}^6\ \textbf{pF}$

(c) $0.01\ \mu F \times 10^6\ pF/\mu F = \textbf{10,000 pF}$

(d) $0.005\ \mu F \times 10^6\ pF/\mu F = \textbf{5000 pF}$

Related Problem Convert 100 μF to picofarads.

How a Capacitor Stores Energy

A capacitor stores energy in the form of an electric field that is established by the opposite charges on the two plates. The electric field is represented by lines of force between the positive and negative charges and concentrated within the dielectric, as shown in Figure 13–3.

FIGURE 13–3
The electric field stores energy in a capacitor.

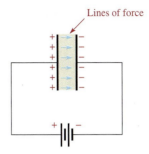

Lines of force

Coulomb's law states

A force exists between two point-source charges that is directly proportional to the product of the two charges and inversely proportional to the square of the distance between the charges.

This relationship is expressed as

$$F = \frac{kQ_1Q_2}{d^2} \tag{13–4}$$

where F is the force in newtons, Q_1 and Q_2 are the charges in coulombs, d is the distance between the charges in meters, and k is a proportionality constant equal to 9×10^9 newton-meter^2/coulomb^2.

Figure 13–4(a) illustrates the line of force between a positive and a negative charge. Figure 13–4(b) shows that many opposite charges on the plates of a capacitor create many lines of force, which form an electric field that stores energy within the dielectric.

FIGURE 13–4
Lines of force are created by opposite charges.

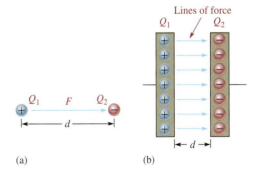

Lines of force

(a)

(b)

The greater the forces between the charges on the plates of a capacitor, the more energy is stored. Therefore, the amount of energy stored is directly proportional to the capacitance because, from Coulomb's law, the more charge stored, the greater the force.

Also, from Equation (13–2), the amount of charge stored is directly related to the voltage as well as to the capacitance. Therefore, the amount of energy stored is also dependent on the square of the voltage across the plates of the capacitor. The formula for the energy stored by a capacitor is

$$W = \frac{1}{2}CV^2 \tag{13–5}$$

When capacitance (C) is in farads and voltage (V) is in volts, energy (W) is in joules.

Voltage Rating

Every capacitor has a limit on the amount of voltage that it can withstand across its plates. The voltage rating specifies the maximum dc voltage that can be applied without risk of damage to the device. If this maximum voltage, commonly called the *breakdown voltage* or *working voltage,* is exceeded, permanent damage to the capacitor can result.

Both the capacitance and the voltage rating must be taken into consideration before a capacitor is used in a circuit application. The choice of capacitance value is based on particular circuit requirements. The voltage rating should always be above the maximum voltage expected in a particular application.

Dielectric Strength The breakdown voltage of a capacitor is determined by the **dielectric strength** of the dielectric material used. The dielectric strength is expressed in V/mil (1 mil = 0.001 in.). Table 13–2 lists typical values for several materials. Exact values vary depending on the specific composition of the material.

TABLE 13–2

Some common dielectric materials and their dielectric strengths.

Material	Dielectric Strength (V/mil)
Air	80
Oil	375
Ceramic	1000
Paper (paraffined)	1200
Teflon®	1500
Mica	1500
Glass	2000

The dielectric strength can best be explained by an example. Assume that a certain capacitor has a plate separation of 1 mil and that the dielectric material is ceramic. This particular capacitor can withstand a maximum voltage of 1000 V because its dielectric strength is 1000 V/mil. If the maximum voltage is exceeded, the dielectric may break down and conduct current, causing permanent damage to the capacitor. Similarly, if the ceramic capacitor has a plate separation of 2 mils, its breakdown voltage is 2000 V.

Temperature Coefficient

The **temperature coefficient** indicates the amount and direction of a change in capacitance value with temperature. A positive temperature coefficient means that the capacitance increases with an increase in temperature or decreases with a decrease in temperature. A negative coefficient means that the capacitance decreases with an increase in temperature or increases with a decrease in temperature.

Temperature coefficients are typically specified in parts per million per Celsius degree (ppm/°C). For example, a negative temperature coefficient of 150 ppm/°C for a 1 μF capacitor means that for every degree rise in temperature, the capacitance decreases by 150 pF (there are one million picofarads in one microfarad).

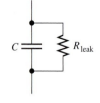

FIGURE 13–5

Equivalent circuit for a nonideal capacitor.

Leakage

No insulating material is perfect. The dielectric of any capacitor will conduct some very small amount of current. Thus, the charge on a capacitor will eventually leak off. Some types of capacitors, such as large electrolytic types, have higher leakages than others. An equivalent circuit for a nonideal capacitor is shown in Figure 13–5. The parallel resistor R_{leak} represents the extremely high resistance (several hundred kΩ or more) of the dielectric material through which there is leakage current.

Physical Characteristics of a Capacitor

The following parameters are important in establishing the capacitance and the voltage rating of a capacitor: plate area, plate separation, and dielectric constant.

Plate Area   Capacitance is directly proportional to the physical size of the plates as determined by the plate area, A. A larger plate area produces a larger capacitance, and a smaller plate area produces a smaller capacitance. Figure 13–6(a) shows that the plate area of a parallel plate capacitor is the area of one of the plates. If the plates are moved in relation to each other, as shown in Figure 13–6(b), the overlapping area determines the effective plate area. This variation in effective plate area is the basis for a certain type of variable capacitor.

FIGURE 13–6
Capacitance is directly proportional to plate area (A).

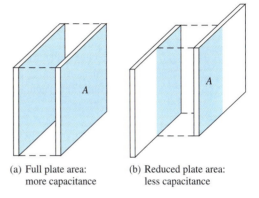

(a) Full plate area:
    more capacitance

(b) Reduced plate area:
    less capacitance

Plate Separation   Capacitance is inversely proportional to the distance between the plates. The plate separation is designated *d,* as shown in Figure 13–7. A greater separation of the plates produces a smaller capacitance, as illustrated in the figure. As previously discussed, the breakdown voltage is directly proportional to the plate separation. The further the plates are separated, the greater the breakdown voltage.

FIGURE 13–7
Capacitance is inversely proportional to the distance between the plates.

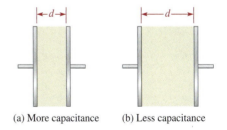

(a) More capacitance   (b) Less capacitance

Dielectric Constant   As you know, the insulating material between the plates of a capacitor is called the *dielectric.* Every dielectric material has the ability to concentrate the lines of force of the electric field existing between the oppositely charged plates of a capacitor and thus increase the capacity for energy storage. The measure of a material's ability to establish an electric field is called the **dielectric constant** or *relative permittivity,* symbolized by ε_r. (ε is the Greek letter epsilon.)

    Capacitance is directly proportional to the dielectric constant. The dielectric constant of a vacuum is defined as 1 and that of air is very close to 1. These values are used as a reference, and all other materials have values of ε_r specified with respect to that of a vacuum or air. For example, a material with $\varepsilon_r = 8$ can result in a capacitance eight times greater than that of air with all other factors being equal.

Table 13–3 lists several common dielectric materials and typical dielectric constants for each. Values can vary because they depend on the specific composition of the material.

TABLE 13–3

Some common dielectric materials and their dielectric constants.

Material	Typical ε_r Values
Air (vacuum)	1.0
Teflon®	2.0
Paper (paraffined)	2.5
Oil	4.0
Mica	5.0
Glass	7.5
Ceramic	1200

The dielectric constant (relative permittivity) is dimensionless because it is a relative measure and is a ratio of the absolute permittivity of a material, ε, to the absolute permittivity of a vacuum, ε_0, as expressed by the following formula:

$$\varepsilon_r = \frac{\varepsilon}{\varepsilon_0} \tag{13–6}$$

The value of ε_0 is 8.85×10^{-12} F/m (farads per meter).

Formula for Capacitance in Terms of Physical Parameters

You have seen how capacitance is directly related to plate area, A, and the dielectric constant, ε_r, and inversely related to plate separation, d. An exact formula for calculating the capacitance in terms of these three quantities is

$$C = \frac{A\varepsilon_r(8.85 \times 10^{-12} \text{ F/m})}{d} \tag{13–7}$$

where A is in square meters (m²), d is in meters (m), and C is in farads (F). Recall that the absolute permittivity of a vacuum, ε_0, is 8.85×10^{-12} F/m and that the absolute permittivity of a dielectric (ε), as derived from Equation (13–6), is $\varepsilon_r(8.85 \times 10^{-12}$ F/m).

EXAMPLE 13–4

Determine the capacitance of a parallel plate capacitor having a plate area of 0.01 m² and a plate separation of 0.02 m. The dielectric is mica, which has a dielectric constant of 5.0.

Solution   Use Equation (13–7).

$$C = \frac{A\varepsilon_r(8.85 \times 10^{-12} \text{ F/m})}{d} = \frac{(0.01 \text{ m}^2)(5.0)(8.85 \times 10^{-12} \text{ F/m})}{0.02 \text{ m}} = \textbf{22.1 pF}$$

The calculator sequence is

[.] [0] [1] [×] [5] [×] [8] [.] [8] [5] [EE] [(−)] [1] [2] [÷] [.] [0] [2] [ENTER]

Related Problem   Determine C where $A = 0.005$ m², $d = 0.008$ m, and ceramic is the dielectric.

**SECTION 13–1
REVIEW**

1. Define *capacitance.*
2. **(a)** How many microfarads in one farad?
   (b) How many picofarads in one farad?
   (c) How many picofarads in one microfarad?
3. Convert 0.0015 μF to picofarads. To farads.
4. How much energy in joules is stored by a 0.01 μF capacitor with 15 V across its plates?
5. **(a)** When the plate area of a capacitor is increased, does the capacitance increase or decrease?
   (b) When the distance between the plates is increased, does the capacitance increase or decrease?
6. The plates of a ceramic capacitor are separated by 10 mils. What is the typical breakdown voltage?
7. A ceramic capacitor has a plate area of 0.2 m^2. The thickness of the dielectric is 0.005 m. What is the capacitance?
8. A capacitor with a value of 2 μF at 25°C has a positive temperature coefficient of 50 ppm/°C. What is the capacitance value when the temperature increases to 125°C?

13–2 ■ TYPES OF CAPACITORS

Capacitors normally are classified according to the type of dielectric material and whether they are polarized or nonpolarized. The most common types of dielectric materials are mica, ceramic, plastic-film, and electrolytic (aluminum oxide and tantalum oxide). In this section, the characteristics and construction of each of these types of capacitors and variable capacitors are examined.

After completing this section, you should be able to

■ **Discuss various types of capacitors**
  • Describe the characteristics of mica, ceramic, plastic-film, and electrolytic capacitors
  • Describe types of variable capacitors
  • Identify capacitor labeling

Fixed Capacitors

Mica Capacitors   Two types of mica capacitors are stacked-foil and silver-mica. The basic construction of the stacked-foil type is shown in Figure 13–8. It consists of alternate layers of metal foil and thin sheets of mica. The metal foil forms the plate, with alternate

FIGURE 13–8
Construction of a typical radial-lead mica capacitor.

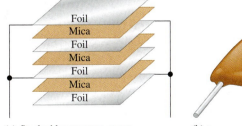

(a) Stacked layer arrangement

(b) Layers are pressed together and encapsulated.

foil sheets connected together to increase the plate area. More layers are used to increase the plate area, thus increasing the capacitance. The mica/foil stack is encapsulated in an insulating material such as Bakelite®, as shown in Figure 13–8(b). The silver-mica capacitor is formed in a similar way by stacking mica sheets with silver electrode material screened on them.

Mica capacitors are available with capacitance values ranging from 1 pF to 0.1 μF and voltage ratings from 100 V dc to 2500 V dc. Common temperature coefficients range from −20 ppm/°C to +100 ppm/°C. Mica has a typical dielectric constant of 5.

Ceramic Capacitors Ceramic dielectrics provide very high dielectric constants (1200 is typical). As a result, comparatively high capacitance values can be achieved in a small physical size. Ceramic capacitors are commonly available in a ceramic disk form, as shown in Figure 13–9, in a multilayer radial-lead configuration, as shown in Figure 13–10, or in a

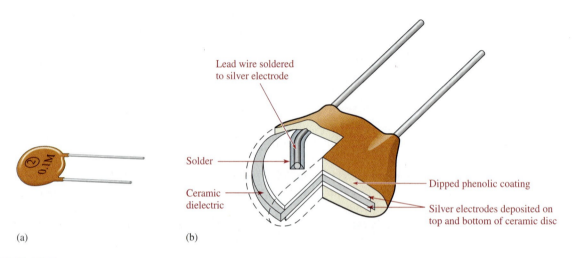

(a)　　　(b)

FIGURE 13–9
A ceramic disk capacitor and its basic construction.

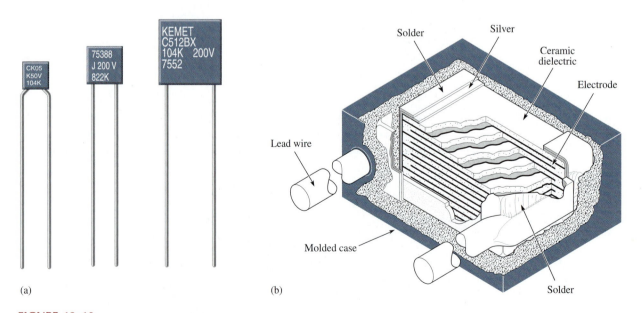

(a)　　　(b)

FIGURE 13–10
(a) Typical ceramic capacitors. (b) Construction view.

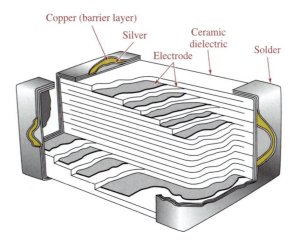

FIGURE 13–11
Construction view of a typical ceramic chip capacitor used for surface mounting on printed circuit boards.

leadless ceramic chip, as shown in Figure 13–11, for surface mounting on printed circuit boards.

Ceramic capacitors typically are available in capacitance values ranging from 1 pF to 2.2 μF with voltage ratings up to 6 kV. A typical temperature coefficient for ceramic capacitors is 200,000 ppm/°C. A special type of disk ceramic has a zero temperature coefficient.

Plastic-Film Capacitors There are several types of plastic-film capacitors. Polycarbonate, propylene, parylene, polyester, polystyrene, polypropylene, and mylar are some of the more common dielectric materials used. Some of these types have capacitance values up to 100 μF.

Figure 13–12 shows a common basic construction used in many plastic-film capacitors. A thin strip of plastic-film dielectric is sandwiched between two thin metal strips that act as plates. One lead is connected to the inner plate and one to the outer plate as indicated. The strips are then rolled in a spiral configuration and encapsulated in a molded case. Thus, a large plate area can be packaged in a relatively small physical size, thereby achieving large capacitance values. Another method uses metal deposited directly on the film dielectric to form the plates.

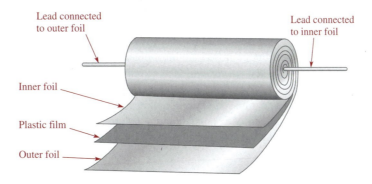

FIGURE 13–12
Basic construction of axial-lead tubular plastic-film dielectric capacitors.

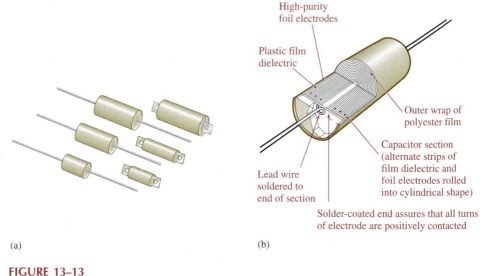

High-purity
foil electrodes

Plastic film
dielectric

Outer wrap of
polyester film

Capacitor section
(alternate strips of
film dielectric and
foil electrodes rolled
into cylindrical shape)

Lead wire
soldered to
end of section

Solder-coated end assures that all turns
of electrode are positively contacted

(a)   (b)

FIGURE 13–13
(a) Several typical capacitors. (b) Construction view of plastic-film capacitor.

Figure 13–13(a) shows typical plastic-film capacitors. Figure 13–13(b) shows a construction view for one type of plastic-film capacitor.

Electrolytic Capacitors   Electrolytic capacitors are polarized so that one plate is positive and the other negative. These capacitors are used for high capacitance values up to over 200,000 μF, but they have relatively low breakdown voltages (350 V is a typical maximum) and high amounts of leakage. In this text, capacitors with values of 1 μF or greater are considered to be polarized.

Electrolytic capacitors offer much higher capacitance values than mica or ceramic capacitors, but their voltage ratings are typically lower. Aluminum electrolytics are probably the most commonly used type. While other capacitors use two similar plates, the electrolytic consists of one plate of aluminum foil and another plate made of a conducting electrolyte applied to a material such as plastic film. These two "plates" are separated by a layer of aluminum oxide that forms on the surface of the aluminum plate. Figure 13–14(a) illustrates the basic construction of a typical aluminum electrolytic capacitor with axial leads. Other electrolytics with radial leads are shown in Figure 13–14(b); the symbol for an electrolytic capacitor is shown in part (c).

Tantalum electrolytics can be in either a tubular configuration similar to Figure 13–14 or "tear drop" shape as shown in Figure 13–15. In the tear drop configuration, the positive plate is actually a pellet of tantalum powder rather than a sheet of foil. Tantalum oxide forms the dielectric and manganese dioxide forms the negative plate.

Because of the process used for the insulating oxide dielectric, the metallic (aluminum or tantalum) plate must be connected so that it is always positive with respect to the electrolyte plate, and, thus all electrolytic capacitors are polarized. The metal plate (positive lead) is usually indicated by a plus sign or some other obvious marking and must always be connected in a dc circuit where the voltage across the capacitor does not change polarity regardless of any ac present. Reversal of the polarity of the voltage will usually result in complete destruction of the capacitor.

FIGURE 13–14
Electrolytic capacitors.

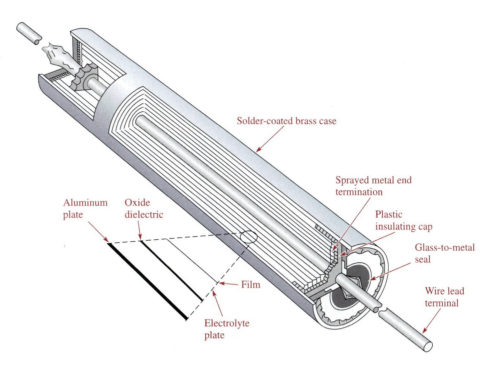

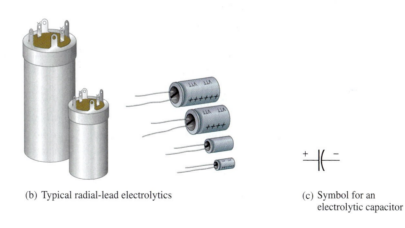

(a) Construction view of an axial-lead electrolytic capacitor

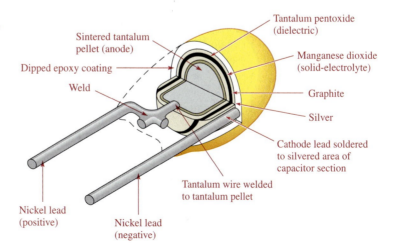

(b) Typical radial-lead electrolytics

(c) Symbol for an electrolytic capacitor

FIGURE 13–15
Construction view of a typical "tear drop" shaped tantalum electrolytic capacitor.

Variable Capacitors

FIGURE 13–16
Schematic symbol for a variable capacitor.

Variable capacitors are used in a circuit when there is a need to adjust the capacitance value either manually or automatically, for example, in radio or TV tuners. The schematic symbol for a variable capacitor is shown in Figure 13–16.

Adjustable capacitors that normally have slotted screw-type adjustments and are used for very fine adjustments in a circuit are called **trimmers.** Ceramic or mica is a common dielectric in these types of capacitors, and the capacitance usually is changed by adjusting the plate separation. Figure 13–17 shows some typical devices.

FIGURE 13–17
Trimmer capacitors.

The varactor is a semiconductor device that exhibits a capacitance characteristic that is varied by changing the voltage across its terminals. This device usually is covered in detail in a course on electronic devices.

Capacitor Labeling

Capacitor values are indicated on the body of the capacitor either by typographical labels or by color codes. Typographical labels consist of letters and numbers that indicate various parameters such as capacitance, voltage rating, and tolerance.

Some capacitors carry no unit designation for capacitance. In these cases, the units are implied by the value indicated and are recognized by experience. For example, a ceramic capacitor marked .001 or .01 has units of microfarads because picofarad values that small are not available. As another example, a ceramic capacitor labeled 50 or 330 has units of picofarads because microfarad units that large normally are not available in this type. In some cases, a 3-digit designation is used. The first two digits are the first two digits of the capacitance value. The third digit is the number of zeros after the second digit. For example, 103 means 10,000 pF. In some instances, the units are labeled as pF or μF; sometimes the microfarad unit is labeled as MF or MFD.

Voltage rating appears on some types of capacitors with WV or WVDC and is omitted on others. When it is omitted, the voltage rating can be determined from information supplied by the manufacturer. The tolerance of the capacitor is usually labeled as a percentage, such as ±10%. The temperature coefficient is indicated by a *parts per million* marking. This type of label consists of a P or N followed by a number. For example, N750 means a negative temperature coefficient of 750 ppm/°C, and P30 means a positive temperature coefficient of 30 ppm/°C. An NP0 designation means that the positive and negative coefficients are zero; thus the capacitance does not change with temperature. Certain types of capacitors are color coded. Refer to Appendix D, for color code information.

SECTION 13–2 REVIEW

1. Name one way capacitors can be classified.
2. What is the difference between a fixed and a variable capacitor?
3. What type of capacitor is polarized?
4. What precautions must be taken when installing a polarized capacitor in a circuit?

13–3 ■ SERIES CAPACITORS

In this section, you will see why the total capacitance of a series connection of capacitors is less than any of the individual capacitances.

After completing this section, you should be able to

■ **Analyze series capacitors**
  • Determine total capacitance
  • Determine capacitor voltages

Total Capacitance

When capacitors are connected in series, the total capacitance is less than the smallest capacitance value because the effective plate separation increases. The calculation of total series capacitance is analogous to the calculation of total resistance of parallel resistors.

Consider the generalized circuit in Figure 13–18(a), which has n capacitors in series with a voltage source and a switch. When the switch is closed, the capacitors charge as current is established through the circuit. Since this is a series circuit, the current must be the same at all points, as illustrated. Since current is the rate of flow of charge, the amount of charge stored by each capacitor is equal to the total charge, expressed as follows:

$$Q_T = Q_1 = Q_2 = Q_3 = \cdots = Q_n \qquad (13\text{–}8)$$

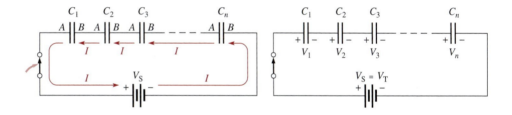

(a) Charging current is same for each capacitor, $I = Q/t$.   (b) All capacitors store same amount of charge and $V = Q/C$.

FIGURE 13–18
Series capacitive circuit.

Next, according to Kirchhoff's voltage law, the sum of the voltages across the charged capacitors must equal the total voltage, V_T, as shown in Figure 13–18(b). This is expressed in equation form as

$$V_T = V_1 + V_2 + V_3 + \cdots + V_n$$

From Equation (13–3), $V = Q/C$. When this relationship is substituted into each term of the voltage equation, the following result is obtained:

$$\frac{Q_T}{C_T} = \frac{Q_1}{C_1} + \frac{Q_2}{C_2} + \frac{Q_3}{C_3} + \cdots + \frac{Q_n}{C_n}$$

Since the charges on all the capacitors are equal, the Q terms can be factored and canceled, resulting in

$$\frac{1}{C_T} = \frac{1}{C_1} + \frac{1}{C_2} + \frac{1}{C_3} + \cdots + \frac{1}{C_n} \qquad (13\text{–}9)$$

Taking the reciprocal of both sides of Equation (13–9) yields the following general formula for total series capacitance:

$$C_T = \cfrac{1}{\cfrac{1}{C_1} + \cfrac{1}{C_2} + \cfrac{1}{C_3} + \cdots + \cfrac{1}{C_n}}$$ (13–10)

Remember,

The total series capacitance is always less than the smallest capacitance.

Two Capacitors in Series When only two capacitors are in series, a special form of Equation (13–9) can be used.

$$\frac{1}{C_T} = \frac{1}{C_1} + \frac{1}{C_2} = \frac{C_1 + C_2}{C_1 C_2}$$

Taking the reciprocal of the left and right terms gives the formula for total capacitance of two capacitors in series.

$$C_T = \frac{C_1 C_2}{C_1 + C_2}$$ (13–11)

Capacitors of Equal Value in Series This special case is another in which a formula can be developed from Equation (13–9). When all capacitor values are the same and equal to C, the formula is

$$\frac{1}{C_T} = \frac{1}{C} + \frac{1}{C} + \frac{1}{C} + \cdots + \frac{1}{C}$$

Adding all the terms on the right yields

$$\frac{1}{C_T} = \frac{n}{C}$$

where n is the number of equal-value capacitors. Taking the reciprocal of both sides yields

$$C_T = \frac{C}{n}$$ (13–12)

The capacitance value of the equal capacitors divided by the number of equal series capacitors gives the total capacitance.

EXAMPLE 13–5

Determine the total capacitance between points A and B in Figure 13–19.

FIGURE 13–19

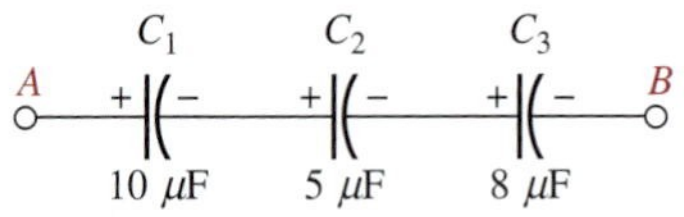

Solution Use Equation (13–10).

$$C_T = \cfrac{1}{\cfrac{1}{C_1} + \cfrac{1}{C_2} + \cfrac{1}{C_3}} = \cfrac{1}{\cfrac{1}{10\ \mu F} + \cfrac{1}{5\ \mu F} + \cfrac{1}{8\ \mu F}} = \cfrac{1}{0.425}\ \mu F = \mathbf{2.35\ \mu F}$$

The calculator sequence is

$\boxed{1}\boxed{0}\boxed{EE}\boxed{(-)}\boxed{6}\boxed{2nd}\boxed{x^{-1}}\boxed{+}\boxed{5}\boxed{EE}\boxed{(-)}\boxed{6}\boxed{2nd}\boxed{x^{-1}}\boxed{+}$
$\boxed{8}\boxed{EE}\boxed{(-)}\boxed{6}\boxed{2nd}\boxed{x^{-1}}\boxed{ENTER}\boxed{2nd}\boxed{x^{-1}}\boxed{ENTER}$

Related Problem If a 4.7 μF capacitor is connected in series with the three existing capacitors in Figure 13–19, what is C_T?

EXAMPLE 13–6   Find the total capacitance, C_T, in Figure 13–20.

FIGURE 13–20

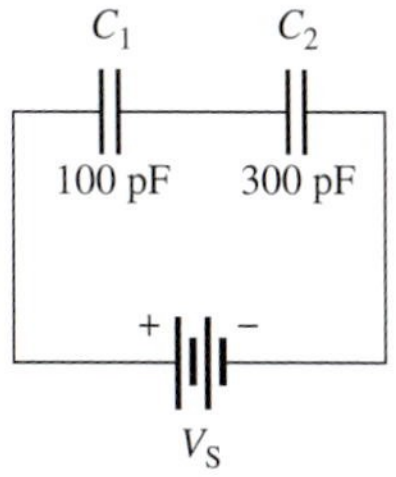

C_1 C_2

100 pF   300 pF

V_S

Solution From Equation (13–11),

$$C_T = \frac{C_1 C_2}{C_1 + C_2} = \frac{(100 \text{ pF})(300 \text{ pF})}{400 \text{ pF}} = \textbf{75 pF}$$

For a calculator solution, use Equation (13–10).

$$C_T = \frac{1}{\dfrac{1}{100 \text{ pF}} + \dfrac{1}{300 \text{ pF}}}$$

$\boxed{1}\boxed{0}\boxed{0}\boxed{EE}\boxed{(-)}\boxed{1}\boxed{2}\boxed{2nd}\boxed{x^{-1}}\boxed{+}\boxed{3}\boxed{0}\boxed{0}\boxed{EE}\boxed{(-)}\boxed{1}\boxed{2}$
$\boxed{2nd}\boxed{x^{-1}}\boxed{ENTER}\boxed{2nd}\boxed{x^{-1}}\boxed{ENTER}$

Related Problem Determine C_T if $C_1 = 470$ pF and $C_2 = 680$ pF in Figure 13–20.

EXAMPLE 13–7   Determine C_T for the series capacitors in Figure 13–21.

FIGURE 13–21

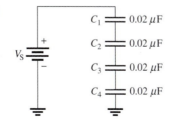

V_S

C_1 0.02 μF
C_2 0.02 μF
C_3 0.02 μF
C_4 0.02 μF

Solution Since $C_1 = C_2 = C_3 = C_4 = C$, use Equation (13–12).

$$C_T = \frac{C}{n} = \frac{0.02 \ \mu\text{F}}{4} = \textbf{0.005} \ \boldsymbol{\mu}\textbf{F}$$

Related Problem Determine C_T if the capacitor values in Figure 13–21 are doubled.

Capacitor Voltages

A series connection of charged capacitors acts as a voltage divider. The voltage across each capacitor in series is inversely proportional to its capacitance value, as shown by the formula $V = Q/C$.

The voltage across any capacitor in series can be calculated as follows:

$$V_x = \left(\frac{C_T}{C_x}\right)V_T \qquad\qquad (13\text{–}13)$$

where C_x is any capacitor in series, such as C_1, C_2, or C_3, and V_x is the voltage across C_x. The derivation is as follows: Since the charge on any capacitor in series is the same as the total charge ($Q_x = Q_T$), and since $Q_x = V_x C_x$ and $Q_T = V_T C_T$, then

$$V_x C_x = V_T C_T$$

Solving for V_x yields

$$V_x = \frac{C_T V_T}{C_x}$$

The largest-value capacitor in series will have the smallest voltage; and the smallest-value capacitor will have the largest voltage.

EXAMPLE 13–8   Find the voltage across each capacitor in Figure 13–22.

FIGURE 13–22

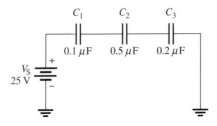

Solution   Calculate the total capacitance.

$$\frac{1}{C_T} = \frac{1}{C_1} + \frac{1}{C_2} + \frac{1}{C_3} = \frac{1}{0.1\ \mu F} + \frac{1}{0.5\ \mu F} + \frac{1}{0.2\ \mu F}$$

$$C_T = \frac{1}{17}\ \mu F = 0.0588\ \mu F$$

From Figure 13–22, $V_S = V_T = 25$ V. Therefore, use Equation (13–13) to calculate the voltage across each capacitor.

$$V_1 = \left(\frac{C_T}{C_1}\right)V_T = \left(\frac{0.0588\ \mu F}{0.1\ \mu F}\right)25\ V = \textbf{14.7 V}$$

$$V_2 = \left(\frac{C_T}{C_2}\right)V_T = \left(\frac{0.0588\ \mu F}{0.5\ \mu F}\right)25\ V = \textbf{2.94 V}$$

$$V_3 = \left(\frac{C_T}{C_3}\right)V_T = \left(\frac{0.0588\ \mu F}{0.2\ \mu F}\right)25\ V = \textbf{7.35 V}$$

Related Problem   A 0.47 μF capacitor is connected in series with the existing capacitors in Figure 13–22. Determine the voltage across the new capacitor.

SECTION 13–3 REVIEW

1. Is the total capacitance of a series connection less than or greater than the value of the smallest capacitor?

2. The following capacitors are in series: 100 pF, 250 pF, and 500 pF. What is the total capacitance?

3. A 0.01 μF and a 0.015 μF capacitor are in series. Determine the total capacitance.

4. Five 100 pF capacitors are connected in series. What is C_T?

5. Determine the voltage across C_1 in Figure 13–23.

FIGURE 13–23

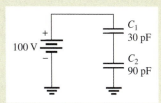

100 V

C_1
30 pF

C_2
90 pF

13–4 ■ PARALLEL CAPACITORS

In this section, you will see why capacitances add when capacitors are connected in parallel.

After completing this section, you should be able to

■ **Analyze parallel capacitors**
  • Determine total capacitance

When capacitors are connected in parallel, the total capacitance is the sum of the individual capacitances because the effective plate area increases. The calculation of total parallel capacitance is analogous to the calculation of total series resistance.

Consider what happens when the switch in Figure 13–24 is closed. The total charging current from the source divides at the junction of the parallel branches. There is a separate charging current through each branch so that a different charge can be stored by each capacitor. By Kirchhoff's current law, the sum of all of the charging currents is equal to the total current. Therefore, the sum of the charges on the capacitors is equal to the total charge. Also, the voltages across all of the parallel branches are equal. These observations are used to develop a formula for total parallel capacitance as follows for the general case of n capacitors in parallel.

$$Q_T = Q_1 + Q_2 + Q_3 + \cdots + Q_n \qquad \text{(13–14)}$$

From Equation (13–2), $Q = CV$. When this relationship is substituted into each term of Equation (13–14), the following result is obtained:

$$C_T V_T = C_1 V_1 + C_2 V_2 + C_3 V_3 + \cdots + C_n V_n$$

FIGURE 13–24
Capacitors in parallel.

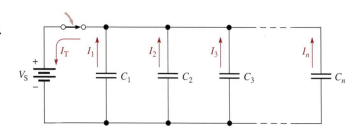

V_S

I_T I_1 I_2 I_3 I_n

C_1 C_2 C_3 C_n

Since $V_T = V_1 = V_2 = V_3 = \cdots = V_n$, the voltages can be factored and canceled, giving

$$C_T = C_1 + C_2 + C_3 + \cdots + C_n \qquad \text{(13–15)}$$

Equation (13–15) is the general formula for total parallel capacitance where n is the number of capacitors. Remember,

The total parallel capacitance is the sum of all the capacitors in parallel.

For the special case when all of the capacitors have the same value, C, multiply the value by the number (n) of capacitors in parallel.

$$C_T = nC \qquad \text{(13–16)}$$

EXAMPLE 13–9   What is the total capacitance in Figure 13–25? What is the voltage across each capacitor?

FIGURE 13–25

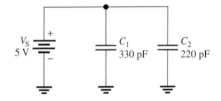

Solution   The total capacitance is

$$C_T = C_1 + C_2 = 330 \text{ pF} + 220 \text{ pF} = \textbf{550 pF}$$

The voltage across each capacitor in parallel is equal to the source voltage.

$$V_S = V_1 = V_2 = \textbf{5 V}$$

Related Problem   What is C_T if a 100 pF capacitor is connected in parallel with C_2 in Figure 13–25?

EXAMPLE 13–10   Determine C_T in Figure 13–26.

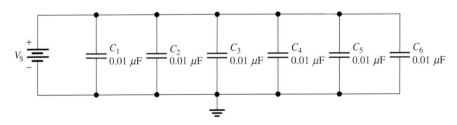

FIGURE 13–26

Solution   There are six equal-value capacitors in parallel, so $n = 6$.

$$C_T = nC = (6)(0.01 \ \mu\text{F}) = \textbf{0.06 } \boldsymbol{\mu}\textbf{F}$$

Related Problem   If three more 0.01 μF capacitors are connected in parallel in Figure 13–26, what is the total capacitance?

SECTION 13–4 REVIEW

1. How is total parallel capacitance determined?

2. In a certain application, you need 0.05 μF. The only values available are 0.01 μF, which are available in large quantities. How can you get the total capacitance that you need?

3. The following capacitors are in parallel: 10 pF, 5 pF, 33 pF, and 50 pF. What is C_T?

13–5 ■ CAPACITORS IN DC CIRCUITS

A capacitor will charge up when it is connected to a dc voltage source. The buildup of charge across the plates occurs in a predictable manner that is dependent on the capacitance and the resistance in a circuit.

After completing this section, you should be able to

■ **Analyze capacitive dc switching circuits**
- Describe the charging and discharging of a capacitor
- Define *time constant*
- Relate the time constant to charging and discharging
- Write equations for the charging and discharging curves
- Explain why a capacitor blocks dc

Charging a Capacitor

A capacitor charges when it is connected to a dc voltage source, as shown in Figure 13–27. The capacitor in part (a) of the figure is uncharged; that is, plate A and plate B have equal numbers of free electrons. When the switch is closed, as shown in part (b), the source moves electrons away from plate A through the circuit to plate B as the arrows indicate. As plate A loses electrons and plate B gains electrons, plate A becomes positive with respect to plate B. As this charging process continues, the voltage across the plates builds up rapidly until it is equal to the applied voltage, V_S, but opposite in polarity, as shown in part (c). When the capacitor is fully charged, there is no current.

A capacitor blocks constant dc.

FIGURE 13–27
Charging a capacitor.

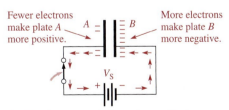

(a) Uncharged

(b) Charging (arrows indicate electron flow)

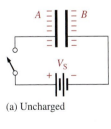

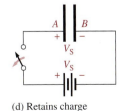

(c) Fully charged

(d) Retains charge

When the charged capacitor is disconnected from the source, as shown in Figure 13–27(d), it remains charged for long periods of time, depending on its leakage resistance, and can cause severe electrical shock. The charge on an electrolytic capacitor generally leaks off more rapidly than in other types of capacitors.

Discharging a Capacitor

When a wire is connected across a charged capacitor, as shown in Figure 13–28, the capacitor will discharge. In this particular case, a very low resistance path (the wire) is connected across the capacitor with a switch. Before the switch is closed, the capacitor is charged to 50 V, as indicated in part (a). When the switch is closed, as shown in part (b), the excess electrons on plate B move through the circuit to plate A (indicated by the arrows); as a result of the current through the low resistance of the wire, the energy stored by the capacitor is dissipated in the wire. The charge is neutralized when the numbers of free electrons on both plates are again equal. At this time, the voltage across the capacitor is zero, and the capacitor is completely discharged, as shown in part (c).

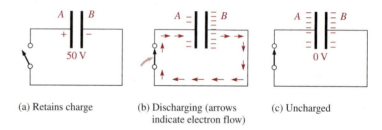

(a) Retains charge   (b) Discharging (arrows   (c) Uncharged
                                indicate electron flow)

FIGURE 13–28
Discharging a capacitor.

Current and Voltage During Charging and Discharging

Notice in Figures 13–27 and 13–28 that the direction of the current during discharge is opposite to that of the charging current. It is important to understand that *there is no current through the dielectric of the capacitor during charging or discharging because the dielectric is an insulating material.* There is current from one plate to the other only through the external circuit.

Figure 13–29(a) shows a capacitor connected in series with a resistor and a switch to a dc voltage source. Initially, the switch is open and the capacitor is uncharged with zero volts across its plates. At the instant the switch is closed, the current jumps to its maximum value and the capacitor begins to charge. The current is maximum initially because the capacitor has zero volts across it and, therefore, effectively acts as a short; thus, the current is limited only by the resistance. As time passes and the capacitor charges, the current decreases and the voltage across the capacitor (V_C) increases. The resistor voltage is proportional to the current during this charging period.

After a certain period of time, the capacitor reaches full charge. At this point, the current is zero and the capacitor voltage is equal to the dc source voltage, as shown in Figure 13–29(b). If the switch were opened now, the capacitor would retain its full charge (neglecting any leakage).

In Figure 13–29(c), the voltage source has been removed. When the switch is closed, the capacitor begins to discharge. Initially, the current jumps to a maximum but in a direction opposite to its direction during charging. As time passes, the current and capacitor voltage decrease. The resistor voltage is always proportional to the current. When the capacitor has fully discharged, the current and the capacitor voltage are zero.

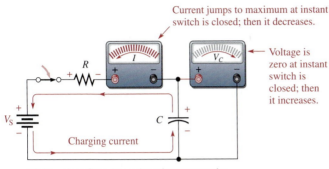

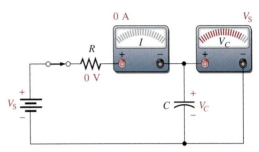

(a) Charging: Capacitor voltage increases as the current and resistor voltage decrease.

(b) Fully charged: Capacitor voltage equals source voltage. The current is zero.

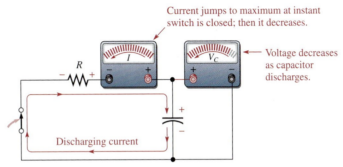

(c) Discharging: Capacitor voltage, resistor voltage, and the current decrease from initial maximums. Note that the discharge current is opposite to the charge current.

FIGURE 13–29
Current and voltage in a charging and discharging capacitor.

Remember the following rules about capacitors in dc circuits:

1. Voltage across a capacitor *cannot* change instantaneously.

2. Ideally, current in a capacitive circuit *can* change instantaneously.

3. A fully charged capacitor appears as an *open* to nonchanging current.

4. An uncharged capacitor appears as a *short* to an instantaneous change in current.

Now let's examine in more detail how the voltage and current change with time in a capacitive circuit.

The *RC* Time Constant

In a practical situation, there cannot be capacitance without some resistance in a circuit. It may simply be the small resistance of a wire, a Thevenin source resistance, or it may be a physical resistor. Because of this, the charging and discharging characteristics of a capacitor must always be considered with the associated resistance. The resistance introduces the element of *time* in the charging and discharging of a capacitor.

When a capacitor charges or discharges through a resistance, a certain time is required for the capacitor to charge fully or discharge fully. The voltage across a capacitor cannot change instantaneously because a finite time is required to move charge from one point to another. The rate at which the capacitor charges or discharges is determined by the **time constant** of the circuit.

The time constant of a series *RC* circuit is a time interval that equals the product of the resistance and the capacitance.

The time constant is expressed in seconds when resistance is in ohms and capacitance is in farads. It is symbolized by τ (Greek letter tau), and the formula is

$$\tau = RC \tag{13-17}$$

where τ is in seconds when resistance is in ohms and capacitance is in farads.

Recall that $I = Q/t$. The current depends on the amount of charge moved in a given time. When the resistance is increased, the charging current is reduced, thus increasing the charging time of the capacitor. When the capacitance is increased, the amount of charge increases; thus, for the same current, more time is required to charge the capacitor.

EXAMPLE 13–11   A series *RC* circuit has a resistance of 1.0 MΩ and a capacitance of 5 μF. What is the time constant?

Solution $\tau = RC = (1.0 \times 10^6 \ \Omega)(5 \times 10^{-6} \ F) = \mathbf{5 \ s}$

Related Problem   A series *RC* circuit has a 270 kΩ resistor and a 3300 pF capacitor. What is the time constant?

During one time-constant interval, the charge on a capacitor changes approximately 63%.

An uncharged capacitor charges to 63% of its fully charged voltage in one time constant. When a capacitor is discharging, its voltage drops to approximately $100\% - 63\% = 37\%$ of its initial value in one time constant, which is a 63% change.

The Charging and Discharging Curves

A capacitor charges and discharges following a nonlinear curve, as shown in Figure 13–30. In these graphs, the approximate percentage of full charge is shown at each time-constant interval. This type of curve follows a precise mathematical formula and is called an *exponential curve*. The charging curve is an increasing exponential, and the discharging curve is a decreasing exponential. It takes five time constants to change the voltage by 99%. This five time-constant interval is accepted as the time to fully charge or discharge a capacitor and is called the *transient time*.

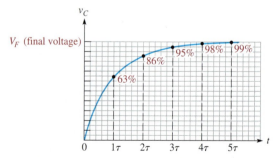
(a) Charging curve with percentages of the final voltage

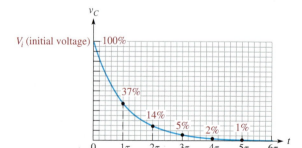
(b) Discharging curve with percentages of the initial voltage

FIGURE 13–30
Charging and discharging exponential curves for an RC circuit.

General Formula   The general expressions for either increasing or decreasing exponential curves are given in the following equations for both instantaneous voltage and instantaneous current.

$$v = V_F + (V_i - V_F)e^{-t/\tau} \tag{13–18}$$

$$i = I_F + (I_i - I_F)e^{-t/\tau} \tag{13–19}$$

where V_F and I_F are the final values of voltage and current, and V_i and I_i are the initial values of voltage and current. v and i are the instantaneous values of the capacitor voltage or current at time t, and e is the base of natural logarithms with a value of 2.71828182846. The e^x function key on your calculator makes it easy to evaluate this exponential term. (e^x may or may not be a secondary function on your calculator.)

Charging from Zero   The formula for the special case in which an increasing exponential voltage curve begins at zero ($V_i = 0$) is given in Equation (13–20). It is developed as follows, starting with the general formula, Equation (13–18).

$$v = V_F + (V_i - V_F)e^{-t/\tau}$$
$$= V_F + (0 - V_F)e^{-t/RC}$$
$$= V_F - V_Fe^{-t/RC}$$

$$v = V_F(1 - e^{-t/RC}) \tag{13–20}$$

Using Equation (13–20), you can calculate the value of the charging voltage of a capacitor at any instant of time if it is initially uncharged. The same is true for an increasing current.

EXAMPLE 13–12   In Figure 13–31, determine the capacitor voltage 50 μs after the switch is closed if the capacitor is initially uncharged. Sketch the charging curve.

FIGURE 13–31

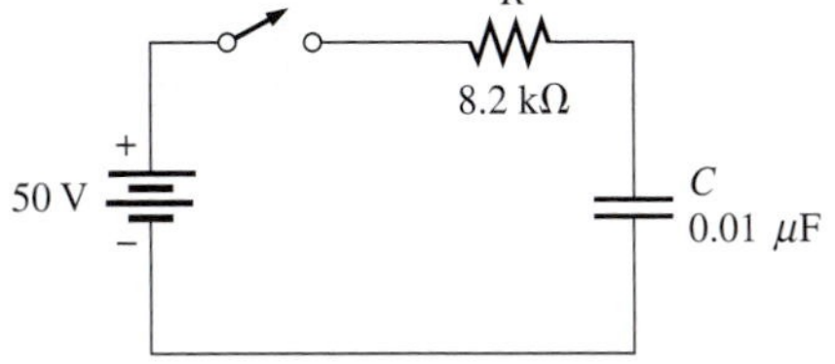

Solution   The time constant is $RC = (8.2\ \text{k}\Omega)(0.01\ \mu\text{F}) = 82\ \mu\text{s}$. The voltage to which the capacitor will fully charge is 50 V (this is V_F). The initial voltage is zero. Notice that 50 μs is less than one time constant; so the capacitor will charge less than 63% of the full voltage in that time.

$$v_C = V_F(1 - e^{-t/RC}) = (50\ \text{V})(1 - e^{-50\mu s/82\mu s})$$
$$= (50\ \text{V})(1 - e^{-0.61}) = (50\ \text{V})(1 - 0.543) = \textbf{22.8 V}$$

The charging curve for the capacitor is shown in Figure 13–32.

FIGURE 13–32

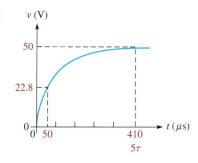

The calculator sequence for v_C is

5 0 (1 − 2nd e^x (−) ((5 0 ÷ 8 2))) ENTER

Related Problem Determine the capacitor voltage 15 μs after switch closure in Figure 13–31.

Discharging to Zero The formula for the special case in which a decreasing exponential voltage curve ends at zero ($V_F = 0$) is derived from the general formula as follows:

$$v = V_F + (V_i - V_F)e^{-t/\tau}$$
$$= 0 + (V_i - 0)e^{-t/RC}$$

$$v = V_i e^{-t/RC} \qquad \text{(13–21)}$$

where V_i is the voltage at the beginning of the discharge as shown in Figure 13–30(b). You can use this formula to calculate the discharging voltage at any instant, as Example 13–13 illustrates.

EXAMPLE 13–13 Determine the capacitor voltage in Figure 13–33 at a point in time 6 ms after the switch is closed. Sketch the discharging curve.

FIGURE 13–33

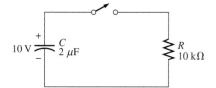

Solution The discharge time constant is $RC = (10\text{ k}\Omega)(2\text{ }\mu\text{F}) = 20$ ms. The initial capacitor voltage is 10 V. Notice that 6 ms is less than one time constant, so the capacitor will discharge less than 63%. Therefore, it will have a voltage greater than 37% of the initial voltage at 6 ms.

$$v_C = V_i e^{-t/RC} = 10e^{-6\text{ms}/20\text{ms}} = 10e^{-0.3} = 10(0.741) = \textbf{7.41 V}$$

Again, the value of v_C can be determined with your calculator as follows:

1 0 × 2nd e^x (−) ((6 ÷ 2 0)) ENTER

The discharging curve for the capacitor is shown in Figure 13–34.

FIGURE 13–34

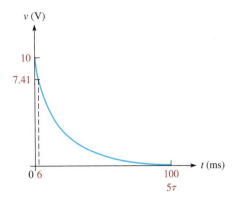

FIGURE 13–34

Related Problem In Figure 13–33, change R to 2.2 kΩ and determine the capacitor voltage 1 ms after the switch is closed.

Graphical Method Using Universal Exponential Curves The universal curves in Figure 13–35 provide a graphic solution of the charge and discharge of capacitors. Example 13–14 illustrates this graphical method.

FIGURE 13–35
Normalized universal exponential curves.

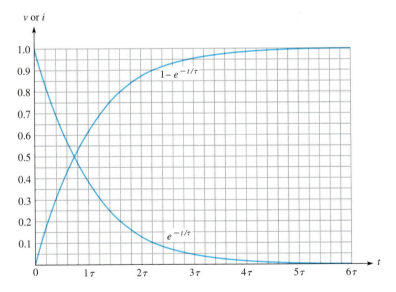

EXAMPLE 13–14 How long will it take the initially uncharged capacitor in Figure 13–36 to charge to 75 V? What is the capacitor voltage 2 ms after the switch is closed? Use the normalized universal exponential curves in Figure 13–35 to determine the answers.

FIGURE 13–36

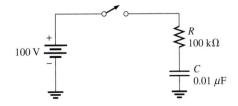

Solution   The full charge voltage is 100 V, which is at the 100% level (1.0) on the normalized vertical scale of the graph. The value 75 V is 75% of maximum, or 0.75 on the graph. You can see that this value occurs at 1.4 time constants. In this circuit, one time constant is 1 ms. Therefore, the capacitor voltage reaches 75 V at 1.4 ms after the switch is closed.

Reading the universal exponential curve, you see that the capacitor is at approximately 86 V (0.86 on the vertical axis) in 2 ms, which is 2 time constants. These graphic solutions are shown in Figure 13–37.

FIGURE 13–37

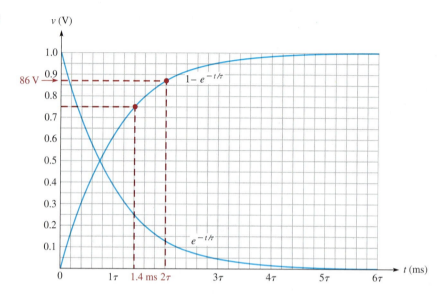

Related Problem   Using the normalized universal exponential curves, determine how long it will take the capacitor in Figure 13–36 to charge to 50 V? What is the capacitor voltage 3 ms after switch closure?

Time-Constant Percentage Tables   The percentages of full charge or discharge at each time-constant interval can be calculated using the exponential formulas, or they can be extracted from the universal exponential curves. The results are summarized in Tables 13–4 and 13–5.

TABLE 13–4
Percentage of final charge after each charging time-constant interval.

Number of Time Constants	% of Final Charge
1	63
2	86
3	95
4	98
5	99 (considered 100%)

TABLE 13–5
Percentage of initial charge after each discharging time-constant interval.

Number of Time Constants	% of Initial Charge
1	37
2	14
3	5
4	2
5	1 (considered 0)

Solving for Time

Occasionally, it is necessary to determine how long it will take a capacitor to charge or discharge to a specified voltage. Equations (13–18) and (13–20) can be solved for t if v is specified. The natural logarithm (abbreviated ln) of $e^{-t/RC}$ is the exponent $-t/RC$. Therefore, taking the natural logarithm of both sides of the equation allows you to solve for time. This procedure is done as follows for the decreasing exponential formula when $V_F = 0$ (Equation 13–21).

$$v = V_i e^{-t/RC}$$

$$\frac{v}{V_i} = e^{-t/RC}$$

$$\ln\left(\frac{v}{V_i}\right) = \ln e^{-t/RC}$$

$$\ln\left(\frac{v}{V_i}\right) = \frac{-t}{RC}$$

$$t = -RC \ln\left(\frac{v}{V_i}\right) \qquad \text{(13–22)}$$

The same procedure can be used for the increasing exponential formula in Equation (13–20) as follows:

$$v = V_F(1 - e^{-t/RC})$$

$$\frac{v}{V_F} = 1 - e^{-t/RC}$$

$$1 - \frac{v}{V_F} = e^{-t/RC}$$

$$\ln\left(1 - \frac{v}{V_F}\right) = \ln e^{-t/RC}$$

$$\ln\left(1 - \frac{v}{V_F}\right) = \frac{-t}{RC}$$

$$t = -RC \ln\left(1 - \frac{v}{V_F}\right) \qquad \text{(13–23)}$$

EXAMPLE 13–15   In Figure 13–38, how long will it take the capacitor to discharge to 25 V when the switch is closed?

FIGURE 13–38

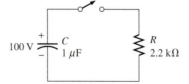

Solution   Use Equation (13–22) to find the discharge time.

$$t = -RC \ln\left(\frac{v}{V_i}\right) = -(2.2 \text{ k}\Omega)(1 \text{ } \mu\text{F})\ln\left(\frac{25 \text{ V}}{100 \text{ V}}\right)$$

$$= -(2.2 \text{ ms})\ln(0.25) = -(2.2 \text{ ms})(-1.39) = \textbf{3.05 ms}$$

You can determine ln(0.25) with your calculator by pressing the LN key, entering 0.25, then pressing ENTER.

Related Problem   How long will it take the capacitor in Figure 13–38 to discharge to 50 V?

SECTION 13-5 REVIEW

1. Determine the time constant when $R = 1.2$ kΩ and $C = 1000$ pF.

2. If the circuit mentioned in Question 1 is charged with a 5 V source, how long will it take the capacitor to reach full charge? At full charge, what is the capacitor voltage?

3. A certain circuit has a time constant of 1 ms. If it is charged with a 10 V battery, what will the capacitor voltage be at each of the following intervals: 2 ms, 3 ms, 4 ms, and 5 ms?

4. A capacitor is charged to 100 V. If it is discharged through a resistor, what is the capacitor voltage at one time constant?

5. In Figure 13–39, determine the voltage across the capacitor at 2.5 time constants after the switch is closed.

6. In Figure 13–39, how long will it take the capacitor to discharge to 15 V?

FIGURE 13–39

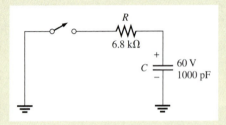

13–6 ■ CAPACITORS IN AC CIRCUITS

As you saw in the last section, a capacitor blocks dc. You will learn in this section that a capacitor passes ac but with an amount of opposition, called capacitive reactance, that depends on the frequency of the ac.

After completing this section, you should be able to

■ **Analyze capacitive ac circuits**
  • Explain why a capacitor causes a phase shift between voltage and current
  • Define *capacitive reactance*
  • Determine the value of capacitive reactance in a given circuit
  • Discuss instantaneous, true, and reactive power in a capacitor

In order to understand fully the action of capacitors in ac circuits, the concept of the derivative must be introduced. *The derivative of a time-varying quantity is the instantaneous rate of change of that quantity.*

Recall that current is the rate of flow of charge (electrons). Therefore, instantaneous current, *i*, can be expressed as the instantaneous rate of change of charge, *q*, with respect to time, *t*.

$$i = \frac{dq}{dt}$$ (13–24)

The term *dq/dt* is the derivative of *q* with respect to time and represents the instantaneous rate of change of *q*. Also, in terms of instantaneous quantities, $q = Cv$. Therefore, from a basic rule of differential calculus, the derivative of q is $dq/dt = C(dv/dt)$. Since $i = dq/dt$, we get the following relationship:

$$i = C\left(\frac{dv}{dt}\right)$$ (13–25)

This equation states

> **The instantaneous capacitor current is equal to the capacitance times the instantaneous rate of change of the voltage across the capacitor.**

From this, you can see that the faster the voltage across a capacitor changes, the greater the current. These calculus terms are introduced here for the limited purpose of explaining the phase relationship between current and voltage in a capacitive circuit. Calculus is not used for circuit analysis in this text.

Phase Relationship of Current and Voltage in a Capacitor

Now consider what happens when a sinusoidal voltage is applied across a capacitor, as shown in Figure 13–40. The voltage waveform has a maximum rate of change ($dv/dt =$ max) at the zero crossings and a zero rate of change ($dv/dt = 0$) at the peaks, as indicated in Figure 13–41.

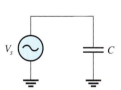

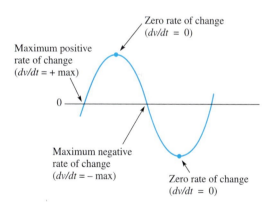

FIGURE 13–40
Sine wave applied to a capacitor.

FIGURE 13–41
The rates of change of a sine wave.

Using Equation (13–25), the **phase** relationship between the current and the voltage for the capacitor can be established. When $dv/dt = 0$, i is also zero because $i = C(dv/dt) = C(0) = 0$. When dv/dt is a positive-going maximum, i is a positive maximum; when dv/dt is a negative-going maximum, i is a negative maximum.

A sinusoidal voltage always produces a sinusoidal current in a capacitive circuit. Therefore, the current can be plotted with respect to the voltage by knowing the points on the voltage curve at which the current is zero and those at which it is maximum. This relationship is shown in Figure 13–42(a). Notice that the current leads the voltage in phase by 90°. This is always true in a purely capacitive circuit. The relationship between the voltage and current phasors is shown in Figure 13–42(b).

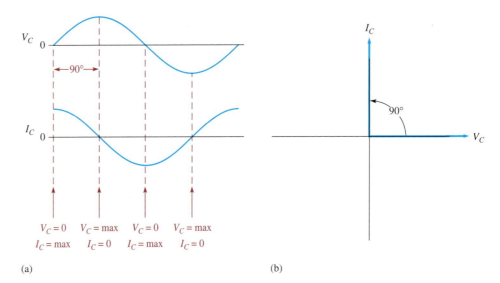

FIGURE 13–42
Phase relation of V_C and I_C in a capacitor. Current always leads the capacitor voltage by 90°.

Capacitive Reactance, X_C

Capacitive reactance is the opposition to sinusoidal current, expressed in ohms. The symbol for capacitive reactance is X_C.

To develop a formula for X_C, we use the relationship $i = C(dv/dt)$ and the curves in Figure 13–43. The rate of change of voltage is directly related to frequency. The faster the voltage changes, the higher the frequency. For example, you can see that in Figure 13–43 the slope of sine wave A at the zero crossings is greater than that of sine wave B. The slope of a curve at a point indicates the rate of change at that point. Sine wave A has a higher frequency than sine wave B, as indicated by a greater maximum rate of change (dv/dt is greater at the zero crossings).

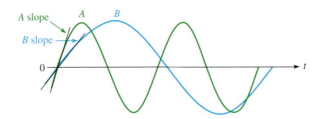

FIGURE 13–43
The higher frequency waveform (A) has a greater slope at its zero crossings, corresponding to a higher rate of change.

When frequency increases, dv/dt increases, and thus i increases. When frequency decreases, dv/dt decreases, and thus i decreases.

$$\uparrow \qquad \uparrow$$
$$i = C(dv/dt) \qquad \text{and} \qquad i = C(dv/dt)$$
$$\downarrow \qquad \downarrow$$

An increase in i means that there is less opposition to current (X_C is less), and a decrease in i means a greater opposition to current (X_C is greater). Therefore, X_C is inversely proportional to i and thus inversely proportional to frequency.

$$X_C \text{ is proportional to } \frac{1}{f}.$$

From the same relationship $i = C(dv/dt)$, you can see that if dv/dt is constant and C is varied, an increase in C produces an increase in i, and a decrease in C produces a decrease in i.

$$\overset{\uparrow}{i} = C(\overset{\uparrow}{dv/dt}) \qquad \text{and} \qquad i = C(dv/dt) \\ \qquad\qquad\qquad\qquad\qquad\qquad \downarrow \quad \downarrow$$

Again, an increase in i means less opposition (X_C is less), and a decrease in i means greater opposition (X_C is greater). Therefore, X_C is inversely proportional to i and thus inversely proportional to capacitance.

The capacitive reactance is inversely proportional to both f and C.

$$X_C \text{ is proportional to } \frac{1}{fC}.$$

Thus far, we have determined a proportional relationship between X_C and $1/fC$. We need a formula that tells us what X_C is equal to so that it can be calculated. This important formula is derived in Appendix C and is stated as follows:

$$X_C = \frac{1}{2\pi fC} \qquad\qquad (13\text{–}26)$$

X_C is in ohms when f is in hertz and C is in farads. Notice that 2π appears in the denominator as a constant of proportionality. This term is derived from the relationship of a sine wave to rotational motion.

EXAMPLE 13–16   A sinusoidal voltage is applied to a capacitor, as shown in Figure 13–44. The frequency of the sine wave is 1 kHz. Determine the capacitive reactance.

FIGURE 13–44

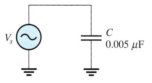

Solution
$$X_C = \frac{1}{2\pi fC} = \frac{1}{2\pi(1 \times 10^3 \text{ Hz})(0.005 \times 10^{-6} \text{ F})} = \mathbf{31.8 \text{ k}\Omega}$$

Related Problem   Determine the frequency required to make the capacitive reactance in Figure 13–44 equal to 10 kΩ.

Analysis of Capacitive AC Circuits

As you have seen, the current leads the voltage by 90° in purely capacitive ac circuits. If the applied voltage is assigned a reference phase angle of zero, it can be expressed in polar form as $V_s\angle0°$. The resulting current can be expressed in polar form as $I\angle90°$ or in rectangular form as jI, as shown in Figure 13–45.

FIGURE 13–45

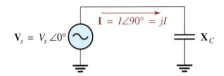

Ohm's law applies to ac circuits containing capacitive reactance with R replaced by $\mathbf{X}_C$ in the Ohm's law formula. Reactance, resistance, voltage, and current are expressed as complex numbers because of the introduction of phase angles, as indicated by their bold-face, nonitalic format. Applying Ohm's law to the circuit in Figure 13–45 gives the following result:

$$\mathbf{X}_C = \frac{V_s \angle 0°}{I \angle 90°} = \left(\frac{V_s}{I}\right)\angle{-90°}$$

This shows that $\mathbf{X}_C$ always has a $-90°$ angle attached to its magnitude and is written as $X_C \angle{-90°}$ or $-jX_C$.

EXAMPLE 13–17   Determine the rms current in Figure 13–46.

FIGURE 13–46

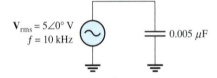

Solution   The magnitude of X_C is

$$X_C = \frac{1}{2\pi f C} = \frac{1}{2\pi(10 \times 10^3 \text{ Hz})(0.005 \times 10^{-6} \text{ F})} = 3.18 \text{ k}\Omega$$

Expressed in polar form, $\mathbf{X}_C$ is

$$\mathbf{X}_C = 3.18\angle{-90°} \text{ k}\Omega$$

Applying Ohm's law,

$$\mathbf{I}_{rms} = \frac{\mathbf{V}_{rms}}{\mathbf{X}_C} = \frac{5\angle 0° \text{ V}}{3.18\angle{-90°} \text{ k}\Omega} = 1.57\angle 90° \text{ mA}$$

Notice that the current expression has a $90°$ phase angle indicating that it leads the voltage by $90°$.

Related Problem   Change the frequency in Figure 13–46 to 25 kHz and determine the rms current.

Power in a Capacitor

As discussed earlier in this chapter, a charged capacitor stores energy in the electric field within the dielectric. An ideal capacitor does not dissipate energy; it only stores it. When an ac voltage is applied to a capacitor, energy is stored by the capacitor during a portion of the voltage cycle; then the stored energy is returned to the source during another portion of the cycle. There is no net energy loss. Figure 13–47 shows the power curve that results from one cycle of capacitor voltage and current.

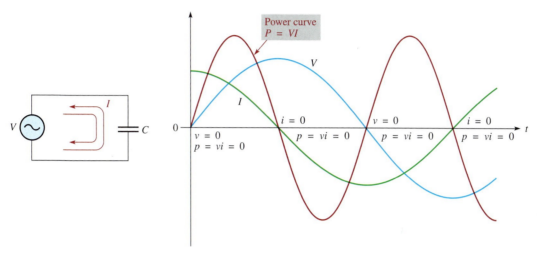

FIGURE 13–47
Power curve.

Instantaneous Power (p) The product of v and i gives instantaneous power, p. At points where v or i is zero, p is also zero. When both v and i are positive, p is also positive. When either v or i is positive and the other is negative, p is negative. When both v and i are negative, p is positive. As you can see, the power follows a sinusoidal-shaped curve. Positive values of power indicate that energy is stored by the capacitor. Negative values of power indicate that energy is returned from the capacitor to the source. Note that the power fluctuates at a frequency twice that of the voltage or current as energy is alternately stored and returned to the source.

True Power (P_{true}) Ideally, all of the energy stored by a capacitor during the positive portion of the power cycle is returned to the source during the negative portion. No net energy is consumed in the capacitor, so the true power is zero. Actually, because of leakage and foil resistance in a practical capacitor, a small percentage of the total power is dissipated in the form of true power.

Reactive Power (P_r) The rate at which a capacitor stores or returns energy is called its **reactive power, P_r**. The reactive power is a nonzero quantity, because at any instant in time, the capacitor is actually taking energy from the source or returning energy to it. Reactive power does not represent an energy loss. The following formulas apply:

$$P_r = V_{rms}I_{rms} \qquad (13\text{–}27)$$

$$P_r = \frac{V_{rms}^2}{X_C} \qquad (13\text{–}28)$$

$$P_r = I_{rms}^2 X_C \qquad (13\text{–}29)$$

Notice that these equations are of the same form as those introduced in Chapter 4 for power in a resistor. The voltage and current are expressed in rms. The unit of reactive power is **volt-ampere reactive (VAR).**

EXAMPLE 13–18   Determine the true power and the reactive power in Figure 13–48.

FIGURE 13–48

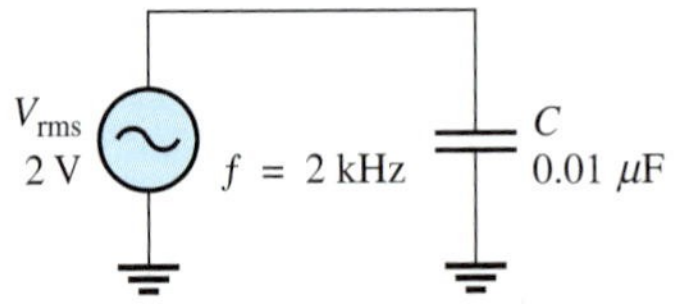

Solution   The true power, P_{true}, is *always* **zero** for an ideal capacitor. The reactive power is determined by first finding the value for the capacitive reactance and then using Equation (13–28).

$$X_C = \frac{1}{2\pi f C} = \frac{1}{2\pi(2 \times 10^3 \text{ Hz})(0.01 \times 10^{-6} \text{ F})} = 7.96 \text{ k}\Omega$$

$$P_r = \frac{V_{rms}^2}{X_C} = \frac{(2 \text{ V})^2}{7.96 \text{ k}\Omega} = 503 \times 10^{-6} \text{ VAR} = \textbf{503 } \boldsymbol{\mu}\textbf{VAR}$$

Related Problem   If the frequency is doubled in Figure 13–48, what are the true power and the reactive power?

SECTION 13–6 REVIEW

1. State the phase relationship between current and voltage in a capacitor.
2. Calculate X_C for $f = 5$ kHz and $C = 50$ pF.
3. At what frequency is the reactance of a 0.1 μF capacitor equal to 2 kΩ?
4. Calculate the rms current in Figure 13–49.
5. A 1 μF capacitor is connected to an ac voltage source of 12 V rms. What is the true power?
6. In Question 5, determine reactive power at a frequency of 500 Hz.

FIGURE 13–49

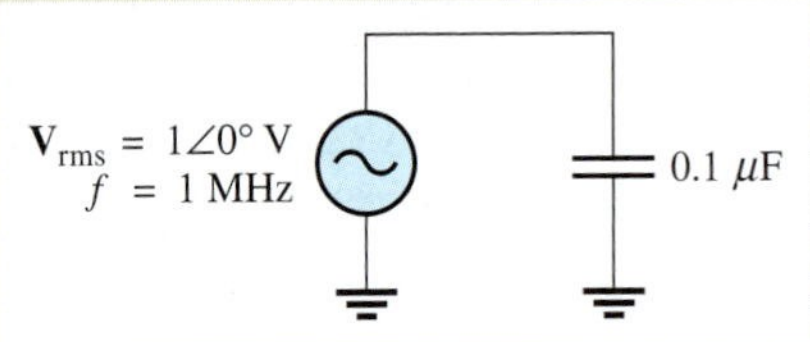

13–7 ■ CAPACITOR APPLICATIONS

Capacitors are widely used in electrical and electronic applications. A few applications are discussed in this section to illustrate the usefulness of this component.

After completing this section, you should be able to

■ **Discuss some capacitor applications**
  • Describe a power supply filter
  • Explain the purpose of coupling and bypass capacitors
  • Discuss the basics of capacitors applied to tuned circuits, timing circuits, and computer memories

If you pick up any circuit board, open any power supply, or look inside any piece of electronic equipment, chances are you will find capacitors of one type or another. These components are used for a variety of reasons in both dc and ac applications.

Electrical Storage

One of the most basic applications of a capacitor is as a backup voltage source for low-power circuits such as certain types of semiconductor memories in computers. This particular application requires a very high capacitance value and negligible leakage.

The storage capacitor is connected between the dc power supply input to the circuit and ground. When the circuit is operating from its normal power supply, the capacitor remains fully charged to the dc power supply voltage. If the normal power source is disrupted, effectively removing the power supply from the circuit, the storage capacitor temporarily becomes the power source for the circuit.

The capacitor provides voltage and current to the circuit as long as its charge remains sufficient. As current is drawn by the circuit, charge is removed from the capacitor and the voltage decreases. For this reason, the storage capacitor can only be used as a temporary power source. The length of time that the capacitor can provide sufficient power to the circuit depends on the capacitance and the amount of current drawn by the circuit. The smaller the current and the higher the capacitance, the longer the time.

Power Supply Filtering

A basic dc power supply consists of a circuit known as a **rectifier** followed by a **filter.** The rectifier converts the 110 V, 60 Hz sinusoidal voltage available at a standard outlet to a pulsating dc voltage that can be either a half-wave rectified voltage or a full-wave rectified voltage, depending on the type of rectifier circuit. As shown in Figure 13–50(a), a half-wave rectifier removes each negative half-cycle of the sinusoidal voltage. As shown in Figure 13–50(b), a full-wave rectifier actually reverses the polarity of the negative portion of each cycle. Both half-wave and full-wave rectified voltages are dc because, even though they are changing, they do not alternate polarity.

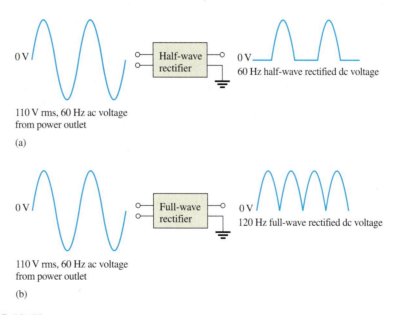

FIGURE 13–50
Half-wave and full-wave rectifier operation.

To be useful for powering electronic circuits, the rectified voltage must be changed to constant dc voltage because all circuits require constant power. The filter eliminates the fluctuations in the rectified voltage and ideally provides a smooth constant-value dc voltage to the load which is the electronic circuit, as indicated by the displays in Figure 13–51.

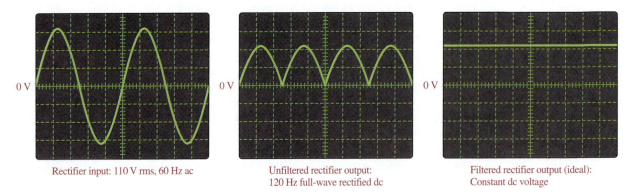

Rectifier input: 110 V rms, 60 Hz ac

Unfiltered rectifier output:
120 Hz full-wave rectified dc

Filtered rectifier output (ideal):
Constant dc voltage

FIGURE 13–51
Basic waveforms showing the operation of a dc power supply.

The Capacitor as a Power Supply Filter Capacitors are used as filters in dc power supplies because of their ability to store electrical charge. Figure 13–52(a) shows a dc power supply with a full-wave rectifier and a capacitor filter. The operation can be described from a charging and discharging point-of-view as follows. Assume the capacitor is initially uncharged. When the power supply is first turned on and the first cycle of the rectified voltage occurs, the capacitor will quickly charge through the low forward resistance of the rectifier. The capacitor voltage will follow the rectified voltage curve up to the peak of the rectified voltage. As the rectified voltage passes the peak and begins to decrease, the capacitor will begin to discharge very slowly through the high resistance of the load circuit, as indicated in Figure 13–52(b). The amount of discharge is typically very small and is exaggerated in the figure for purposes of illustration. The next cycle of the rectified voltage will recharge the capacitor back to the peak value by replenishing the small amount of charge lost since the previous peak. This pattern of a small amount of charging and discharging continues as long as the power is on.

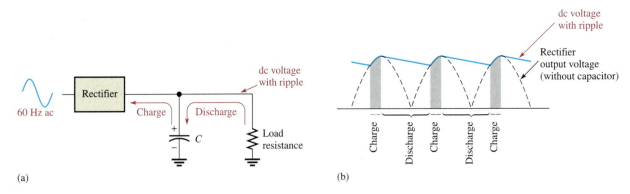

(a)

(b)

FIGURE 13–52
Basic operation of a power supply filter capacitor.

A rectifier is designed so that it allows current only in the direction to charge the capacitor. The capacitor will not discharge back through the rectifier but will only discharge a small amount through the relatively high resistance of the load. The small fluctuation in voltage due to the charging and discharging of the capacitor is called the **ripple voltage.** A good dc power supply has a very small amount of ripple on its dc output. Since the discharge time constant of a power supply filter capacitor depends on its capacitance and the resistance of the load, the higher the capacitance value, the longer the discharge time and therefore, the smaller the ripple voltage.

DC Blocking and AC Coupling

Capacitors are commonly used to block the constant dc voltage in one part of a circuit from getting to another part. As an example of this, a capacitor is connected between two stages of an amplifier to prevent the dc voltage at the output of stage 1 from affecting the dc voltage at the input of stage 2, as illustrated in Figure 13–53. Assume that, for proper operation, the output of stage 1 has a zero dc voltage and the input to stage 2 has a 3 V dc voltage. The capacitor prevents the 3 V dc at stage 2 from getting to the stage 1 output and affecting its zero value, and vice versa.

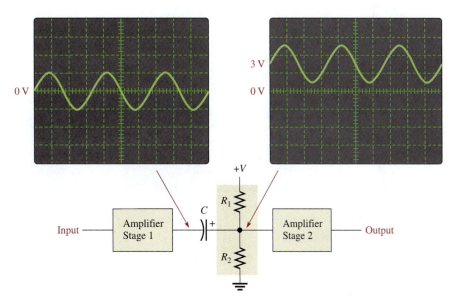

FIGURE 13–53
An application of a capacitor to block dc and couple ac in an amplifier.

If a sinusoidal signal voltage is applied to the input to stage 1, the signal voltage is increased (amplified) and appears on the ouput of stage 1, as shown in Figure 13–53. The amplified signal voltage is then coupled through the capacitor to the input of stage 2 where it is superimposed on the 3 V dc level and then again amplified by stage 2. In order for the signal voltage to be passed through the capacitor without being reduced, the capacitor must be large enough so that its reactance at the frequency of the signal voltage is negligible. In this type of application, the capacitor is known as a *coupling capacitor,* which ideally appears as an open to dc and as a short to ac. As the signal frequency is reduced, the capacitive reactance increases and, at some point, the capacitive reactance becomes large enough to cause a significant reduction in ac voltage between stage 1 and stage 2.

Power Line Decoupling

Capacitors connected from the dc supply voltage line to ground are used on circuit boards to decouple unwanted voltage transients or spikes that occur on the dc supply voltage because of fast switching digital circuits. A voltage transient contains high frequencies that may affect the operation of the circuits. These transients are shorted to ground through the very low reactance of the decoupling capacitors. Several decoupling capacitors are often used at various points along the supply voltage line on a circuit board.

Bypassing

Another capacitor application is in bypassing an ac voltage around a resistor in a circuit without affecting the dc voltage across the resistor. In amplifier circuits, for example, dc voltages called *bias voltages* are required at various points. For the amplifier to operate properly, certain bias voltages must remain constant and, therefore, any ac voltages must be removed. A sufficiently large capacitor connected from a bias point to ground provides a low reactance path to ground for ac voltages, leaving the constant dc bias voltage at the given point. At lower frequencies, the bypass capacitor becomes less effective because of its increased reactance. This bypass application is illustrated in Figure 13–54.

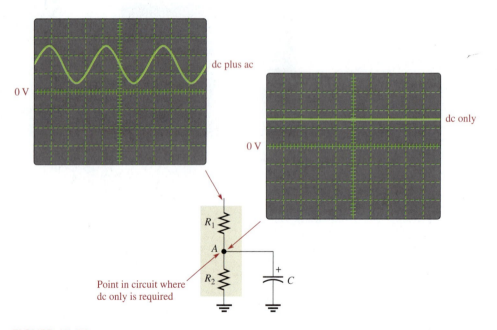

FIGURE 13–54
Example of the operation of a bypass capacitor. Point A is at ac ground due to the low reactance path through the capacitor.

Signal Filters

Capacitors are essential to the operation of a class of circuits called *filters* that are used for selecting one ac signal with a certain specified frequency from a wide range of signals with many different frequencies or for selecting a certain band of frequencies and eliminating all others. A common example of this application is in radio and television receivers where it is necessary to select the signal transmitted from a given station and eliminate or filter out the signals transmitted from all the other stations in the area.

When you tune your radio or TV, you are actually changing the capacitance in the tuner circuit (which is a type of filter) so that only the signal from the station or channel you want passes through to the receiver circuitry. Capacitors are used in conjunction with resistors, inductors (covered in the next chapter), and other components in these types of filters. The topic of filters will be covered in detail in Chapter 19.

The main characteristic of a filter is its frequency selectivity, which is based on the fact that the reactance of a capacitor depends on frequency ($X_C = 1/2\pi fC$).

Timing Circuits

Another important area in which capacitors are used is in timing circuits that generate specified time delays or produce waveforms with specific characteristics. Recall that the time constant of a circuit with resistance and capacitance can be controlled by selecting appropriate values for R and C. The charging time of a capacitor can be used as a basic time delay in various types of circuits. An example is the circuit that controls the turn indicators on your car where the light flashes on and off at regular intervals.

Computer Memories

Dynamic memories in computers use very tiny capacitors as the basic storage element for binary information, which consists of two binary digits, 1 and 0. A charged capacitor can represent a stored 1 and a discharged capacitor can represent a stored 0. Patterns of 1s and 0s that make up binary data are stored in a memory that consists of an array of capacitors with associated circuitry. You will study this topic in a computer or digital fundamentals course.

SECTION 13–7 **REVIEW**	**1.** Explain how half-wave or full-wave rectified dc voltages are smoothed out by a filter capacitor. **2.** Explain the purpose of a coupling capacitor. **3.** How large must a coupling capacitor be? **4.** Explain the purpose of a decoupling capacitor. **5.** Discuss how the relationship of frequency and capacitive reactance is important in frequency-selective circuits such as signal filters. **6.** What characteristic of a capacitor is most important in time-delay applications?

13–8 ■ TESTING CAPACITORS

Capacitors are very reliable devices but their useful life can be extended significantly by operating them well within the voltage rating and at moderate temperatures. In this section, the basic types of failures are discussed and methods for checking for them are introduced.

After completing this section, you should be able to

■ Test a capacitor
  • Perform an ohmmeter check
  • Explain what an *LC* meter is

Capacitor failures can be categorized into two areas—catastrophic and degradation. The catastrophic failures are usually a short circuit caused by dielectric breakdown or an open circuit caused by connection failure. Degradation usually results in a gradual decrease in leakage resistance, hence an increase in leakage current or an increase in equivalent series resistance or dielectric absorption.

Ohmmeter Check

When there is a suspected problem, the capacitor can be removed from the circuit and checked with an analog ohmmeter. First, to be sure that the capacitor is discharged, short its leads, as indicated in Figure 13–55(a). Connect the meter—set on a high ohms range such as ×1M—to the capacitor, as shown in part (b), and observe the needle. It should initially indicate near zero ohms. Then it should begin to move toward the high-resistance end of the scale as the capacitor charges from the ohmmeter's battery, as shown in part (c). When the capacitor is fully charged, the meter will indicate an extremely high resistance as shown in part (d).

(a) Discharge by shorting leads

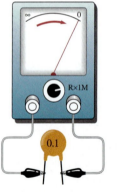

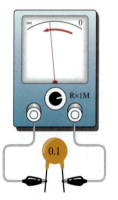

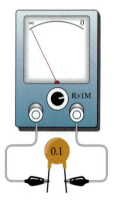

(b) Initially, when the meter is first connected, the pointer jumps immediately to zero.

(c) The needle moves slowly toward infinity as the capacitor charges from the ohmmeter's battery.

(d) When the capacitor is fully charged, the pointer is at infinity.

FIGURE 13–55
Checking a capacitor with an ohmmeter. This check shows a good capacitor.

As mentioned, the capacitor charges from the internal battery of the ohmmeter, and the meter responds to the charging current. The larger the capacitance value, the more slowly the capacitor will charge, as indicated by the needle movement. For very small capacitance values, the meter response may be insufficient to indicate the fast charging action.

If the capacitor is internally shorted, the meter will go to zero and stay there. If it is leaky, the final meter reading will be much less than normal. Most capacitors have a resistance of several hundred megohms. The exception is the electrolytic, which may normally have less than one megohm of leakage resistance. If the capacitor is open, no charging action will be observed, and the meter will indicate an infinite resistance.

Testing for Capacitance Value and Other Parameters with an *LC* Meter

An *LC* meter such as the one shown in Figure 13–56 can be used to check the value of a capacitor. Most capacitors change value over a period of time, some more than others. Ceramic capacitors, for example, often exhibit a 10% to 15% change in value during the first year. Electrolytic capacitors are particularly subject to value change due to drying of the electrolytic solution. In other cases, capacitors may be labeled incorrectly or the wrong value was installed in the circuit. Although a value change represents less than 25% of defective capacitors, a value check can quickly eliminate this as a source of trouble when troubleshooting a circuit.

FIGURE 13–56

A typical LC meter (photography courtesy of B&K Precision Corp.).

Typically, values from 1 pF to 200,000 μF can be measured by simply connecting the capacitor, pushing the appropriate button, and reading the value on the display.

Many *LC* meters can also be used to check for leakage current in capacitors. In order to check for leakage, a sufficient voltage must be applied across the capacitor to simulate operating conditions. This is automatically done by the test instrument. Over 40% of all defective capacitors have excessive leakage current and electrolytics are particularly susceptible to this problem.

The problem of dielectric absorption occurs mostly in electrolytic capacitors when they do not completely discharge during use and retain a residual charge. Approximately 25% of defective capacitors exhibit this condition.

Another defect sometimes found in capacitors is excessive equivalent series resistance. This problem may be caused by a defective lead to plate contacts, resistive leads, or resistive plates and shows up only under ac conditions. This is the least common capacitor defect and occurs in less than 10% of all defects.

SECTION 13–8 REVIEW

1. How can a capacitor be discharged after removal from the circuit?
2. Describe how the needle of an ohmmeter responds when a good capacitor is checked.
3. List four common capacitor defects.

13–9 ■ TECHnology Theory Into Practice

Capacitors are used in certain types of amplifiers to couple the ac signal while blocking the dc voltage. Capacitors are used in many other applications, but in this TECH TIP, you will focus on the coupling capacitors in an amplifier circuit. This topic was introduced in Section 13–7. A knowledge of amplifier circuits is not necessary for this assignment.

All amplifier circuits contain transistors that require dc voltages to establish proper operating conditions for amplifying ac signals. These dc voltages are referred to as bias voltages. As indicated in Figure 13–57(a), a common type of dc bias circuit used in amplifiers is the voltage divider formed by R_1 and R_2, which sets up the proper dc voltage at the input to the amplifier.

When an ac signal voltage is applied to the amplifier, the input coupling capacitor, C_1, prevents the internal resistance of the ac source from changing the dc bias voltage. Without the capacitor, the internal source resistance would appear in parallel with R_2 and drastically change the value of the dc voltage.

The coupling capacitance is chosen so that its reactance (X_C) at the frequency of the ac signal is very small compared to the bias resistor values. The coupling capacitance therefore efficiently couples the ac signal from the source to the input of the amplifier. On the source side of the input coupling capacitor there is only ac but on the amplifier side there is ac plus dc (the signal voltage is riding on the dc bias voltage set by the voltage divider), as indicated in Figure 13–57(a). Capacitor C_2 is the output coupling capacitor, which couples the amplified ac signal to another amplifier stage that would be connected to the output.

You will check three amplifier boards like the one in Figure 13–57(b) for the proper input voltages using an oscilloscope. If the voltages are incorrect, you will determine the most likely fault. For all measurements, assume the amplifier has no dc loading effect on the voltage-divider bias circuit.

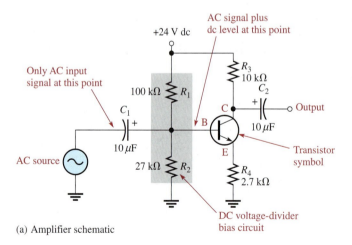

(a) Amplifier schematic

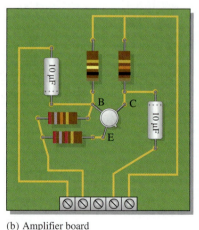

(b) Amplifier board

FIGURE 13–57
Capacitively coupled amplifier.

The Printed Circuit Board and the Schematic

■ Check the printed circuit board in Figure 13–57(b) to make sure it agrees with the amplifier schematic in part (a).

Testing Board 1

The oscilloscope probe is connected from channel 1 to the board as shown in Figure 13–58. The input signal from a sinusoidal voltage source is connected to the board and set to a frequency of 5 kHz with an amplitude of 1 V rms.

■ Determine if the voltage and frequency displayed on the scope are correct. If the scope measurement is incorrect, specify the most likely fault in the circuit.

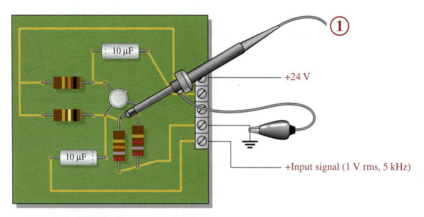

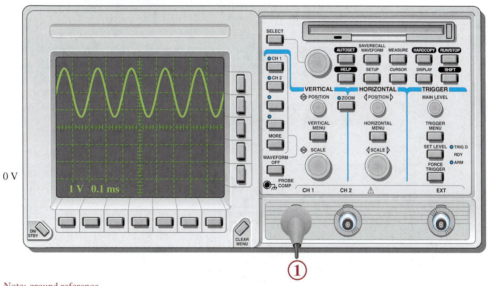

Note: ground reference
has been established at
bottom horizontal line

FIGURE 13–58
Testing board 1.

Testing Board 2

The oscilloscope probe is connected from channel 1 to board 2 the same as was shown in Figure 13–58 for board 1. The input signal from the sinusoidal voltage source is the same as it was for board 1.

■ Determine if the scope display in Figure 13–59 is correct. If the scope measurement is incorrect, specify the most likely fault in the circuit.

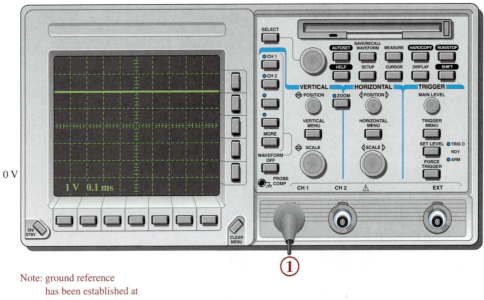

Note: ground reference
has been established at
bottom horizontal line

FIGURE 13–59
Testing board 2.

Testing Board 3

The oscilloscope probe is connected from channel 1 to board 3 the same as was shown in Figure 13–58 for board 1. The input signal from the sinusoidal voltage source is the same as before.

▪ Determine if the scope display in Figure 13–60 is correct. If the scope measurement is incorrect, specify the most likely fault in the circuit.

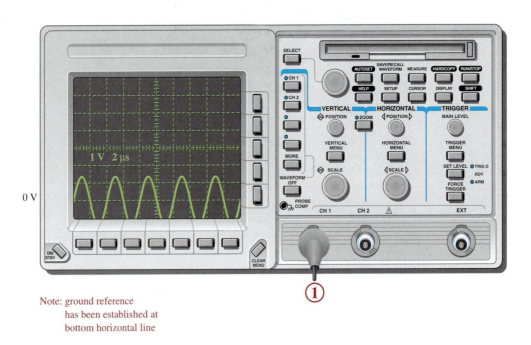

Note: ground reference
has been established at
bottom horizontal line

FIGURE 13–60
Testing board 3.

(13–21)	$v = V_i e^{-t/RC}$	Decreasing exponential voltage ending at zero
(13–22)	$t = -RC \ln\left(\dfrac{v}{V_i}\right)$	Time on decreasing exponential ($V_F = 0$)
(13–23)	$t = -RC \ln\left(1 - \dfrac{v}{V_F}\right)$	Time on increasing exponential ($V_i = 0$)
(13–24)	$i = \dfrac{dq}{dt}$	Instantaneous current using charge derivative
(13–25)	$i = C\left(\dfrac{dv}{dt}\right)$	Instantaneous capacitor current using voltage derivative
(13–26)	$X_C = \dfrac{1}{2\pi f C}$	Capacitive reactance
(13–27)	$P_r = V_{rms} I_{rms}$	Reactive power in a capacitor
(13–28)	$P_r = \dfrac{V_{rms}^2}{X_C}$	Reactive power in a capacitor
(13–29)	$P_r = I_{rms}^2 X_C$	Reactive power in a capacitor

■ **SELF-TEST**

1. The following statement(s) accurately describes a capacitor:
   (a) The plates are conductive.
   (b) The dielectric is an insulator between the plates.
   (c) Constant dc flows through a fully charged capacitor.
   (d) A practical capacitor stores charge indefinitely when disconnected from the source.
   (e) none of the above answers
   (f) all of the above answers
   (g) only answers (a) and (b)

2. Which one of the following statements is true?
   (a) There is current through the dielectric of a charging capacitor.
   (b) When a capacitor is connected to a dc voltage source, it will charge to the value of the source.
   (c) An ideal capacitor can be discharged by disconnecting it from the voltage source.

3. A capacitance of 0.01 μF is larger than
   (a) 0.00001 F   (b) 100,000 pF   (c) 1000 pF   (d) all of the above answers

4. A capacitance of 1000 pF is smaller than
   (a) 0.01 μF   (b) 0.001 μF   (c) 0.00000001 F   (d) both (a) and (c)

5. When the voltage across a capacitor is increased, the stored charge
   (a) increases   (b) decreases   (c) remains constant   (d) fluctuates

6. When the voltage across a capacitor is doubled, the stored charge
   (a) stays the same   (b) is halved
   (c) increases by four   (d) doubles

7. The voltage rating of a capacitor is increased by
   (a) increasing the plate separation   (b) decreasing the plate separation
   (c) increasing the plate area   (d) answers (b) and (c)

8. The capacitance value is increased by
   (a) decreasing the plate area   (b) increasing the plate separation
   (c) decreasing the plate separation   (d) increasing the plate area
   (e) answers (a) and (b)   (f) answers (c) and (d)

9. A 1 μF, a 2.2 μF, and a 0.05 μF capacitor are connected in series. The total capacitance is less than
   (a) 1 μF   (b) 2.2 μF   (c) 0.05 μF   (d) 0.001 μF

10. Four 0.02 μF capacitors are in parallel. The total capacitance is
    (a) 0.02 μF   (b) 0.08 μF   (c) 0.05 μF   (d) 0.04 μF

11. An uncharged capacitor and a resistor are connected in series with a switch and a 12 V battery. At the instant the switch is closed, the voltage across the capacitor is
    (a) 12 V   (b) 6 V   (c) 24 V   (d) 0 V

12. In Question 11, the voltage across the capacitor when it is fully charged is
    (a) 12 V   (b) 6 V   (c) 24 V   (d) −6 V

13. In Question 11, the capacitor will reach full charge in a time equal to approximately
    (a) RC (b) $5RC$ (c) $12RC$ (d) cannot be predicted

14. A sinusoidal voltage is applied across a capacitor. When the frequency of the voltage is increased, the current
    (a) increases   (b) decreases   (c) remains constant   (d) ceases

15. A capacitor and a resistor are connected in series to a sine wave generator. The frequency is set so that the capacitive reactance is equal to the resistance and, thus, an equal amount of voltage appears across each component. If the frequency is decreased,
    (a) $V_R > V_C$ (b) $V_C > V_R$ (c) $V_R = V_C$

16. An ohmmeter is connected across a discharged capacitor and the needle stabilizes at approximately 50 kΩ. The capacitor is
    (a) good   (b) charged   (c) too large   (d) leaky

▪ PROBLEMS

More difficult problems are indicated by an asterisk (*).

SECTION 13–1   The Basic Capacitor

1. (a) Find the capacitance when $Q = 50 \mu$C and $V = 10$ V.
   (b) Find the charge when $C = 0.001 \mu$F and $V = 1$ kV.
   (c) Find the voltage when $Q = 2$ mC and $C = 200 \mu$F.

2. Convert the following values from microfarads to picofarads:
   (a) 0.1 μF   (b) 0.0025 μF   (c) 5 μF

3. Convert the following values from picofarads to microfarads:
   (a) 1000 pF   (b) 3500 pF   (c) 250 pF

4. Convert the following values from farads to microfarads:
   (a) 0.0000001 F   (b) 0.0022 F   (c) 0.0000000015 F

5. Calculate the force of repulsion between two electrons 0.001 m apart.

6. What size capacitor is capable of storing 10 mJ of energy with 100 V across its plates?

7. Calculate the absolute permittivity, ε, for each of the following materials. Refer to Table 13–3 for ε_r values.
   (a) air   (b) oil   (c) glass   (d) Teflon®

8. A mica capacitor has a plate area of 0.04 m² and a dielectric thickness of 0.008 m. What is its capacitance?

9. An air capacitor has 0.1 m square plates. The plates are separated by 0.01 m. Calculate the capacitance.

10. At ambient temperature (25°C), a certain capacitor is specified to be 1000 pF. It has a negative temperature coefficient of 200 ppm/°C. What is its capacitance at 75°C?

11. A 0.001 μF capacitor has a positive temperature coefficient of 500 ppm/°C. How much change in capacitance will a 25°C increase in temperature cause?

SECTION 13–2   Types of Capacitors

12. In the construction of a stacked-foil mica capacitor, how is the plate area increased?

13. What type of capacitor has the highest dielectric constant, mica or ceramic?

FIGURE 13–61

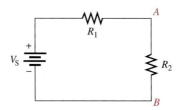

14. Show how to connect an electrolytic capacitor across R_2 between points A and B in Figure 13–61.

15. Name two types of electrolytic capacitors. How do electrolytics differ from other capacitors?

16. Identify the parts of the ceramic disk capacitor shown in the cutaway view of Figure 13–62.

FIGURE 13–62

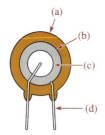

17. Determine the value of the ceramic disk capacitors in Figure 13–63.

FIGURE 13–63

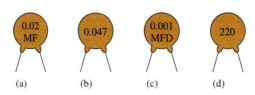

SECTION 13–3   Series Capacitors

18. Five 1000 pF capacitors are in series. What is the total capacitance?

19. Find the total capacitance for each circuit in Figure 13–64.

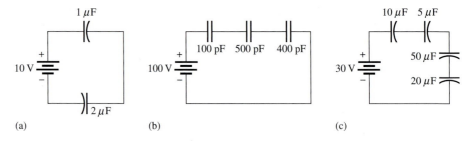

FIGURE 13–64

20. For each circuit in Figure 13–64, determine the voltage across each capacitor.

21. Two series capacitors (one 1 μF, the other of unknown value) are charged from a 12 V source. The 1 μF capacitor is charged to 8 V and the other to 4 V. What is the value of the unknown capacitor?

22. The total charge stored by the series capacitors in Figure 13–65 is 10 μC. Determine the voltage across each of the capacitors.

FIGURE 13–65

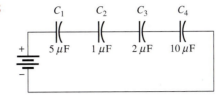

SECTION 13–4 Parallel Capacitors

23. Determine C_T for each circuit in Figure 13–66.

FIGURE 13–66

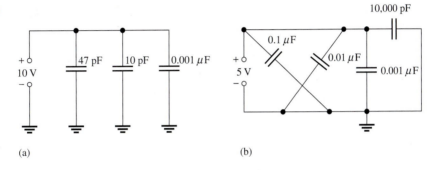

(a)

(b)

24. What is the charge on each capacitor in Figure 13–66?

25. Determine C_T for each circuit in Figure 13–67.

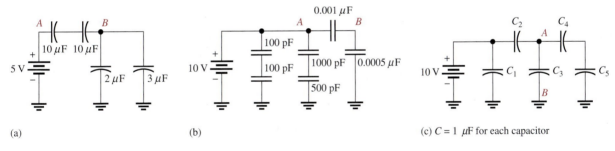

(a)

(b)

(c) $C = 1$ μF for each capacitor

FIGURE 13–67

26. What is the voltage between points A and B in each circuit in Figure 13–67?

*27. How much does the voltage across C_5 and the voltage across C_6 change when the ganged switch is thrown from position 1 to position 2 in Figure 13–68?

FIGURE 13–68

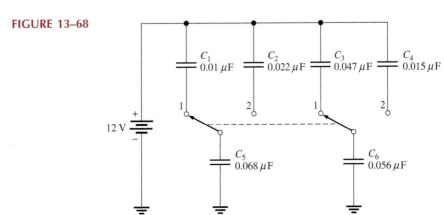

SECTION 13–5 Capacitors in DC Circuits

28. Determine the time constant for each of the following series RC combinations:

    (a) $R = 100\ \Omega,\ C = 1\ \mu F$ **(b)** $R = 10\ M\Omega,\ C = 50\ pF$

    (c) $R = 4.7\ k\Omega,\ C = 0.005\ \mu F$ **(d)** $R = 1.5\ M\Omega,\ C = 0.01\ \mu F$

29. Determine how long it takes the capacitor to reach full charge for each of the following combinations:

    (a) $R = 56\ \Omega,\ C = 50\ \mu F$ **(b)** $R = 3300\ \Omega,\ C = 0.015\ \mu F$

    (c) $R = 22\ k\Omega,\ C = 100\ pF$ **(d)** $R = 5.6\ M\Omega,\ C = 10\ pF$

30. In the circuit of Figure 13–69, the capacitor is initially uncharged. Determine the capacitor voltage at the following times after the switch is closed:

    (a) $10\ \mu s$ **(b)** $20\ \mu s$ **(c)** $30\ \mu s$ **(d)** $40\ \mu s$ **(e)** $50\ \mu s$

FIGURE 13–69

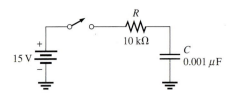

31. In Figure 13–70, the capacitor is charged to 25 V. When the switch is closed, what is the capacitor voltage after the following times?

    (a) 1.5 ms   **(b)** 4.5 ms   **(c)** 6 ms   **(d)** 7.5 ms

FIGURE 13–70

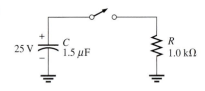

32. Repeat Problem 30 for the following time intervals:

    (a) $2\ \mu s$ **(b)** $5\ \mu s$ **(c)** $15\ \mu s$

33. Repeat Problem 31 for the following times:

    (a) 0.5 ms   **(b)** 1 ms   **(c)** 2 ms

*34. Derive the formula for finding the time at any point on an increasing exponential voltage curve. Use this formula to find the time at which the voltage in Figure 13–71 reaches 6 V after switch closure.

FIGURE 13–71

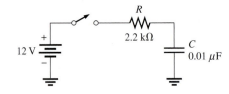

35. How long does it take C to charge to 8 V in Figure 13–69?

36. How long does it take C to discharge to 3 V in Figure 13–70?

37. Determine the time constant for the circuit in Figure 13–72.

FIGURE 13–72

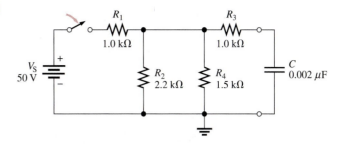

*38. In Figure 13–73, the capacitor is initially uncharged. At $t = 10$ μs after the switch is closed, the instantaneous capacitor voltage is 7.2 V. Determine the value of R.

FIGURE 13–73

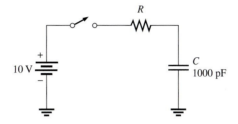

*39. (a) The capacitor in Figure 13–74 is uncharged when the switch is thrown into position 1. The switch remains in position 1 for 10 ms and is then thrown into position 2, where it remains indefinitely. Sketch the complete waveform for the capacitor voltage.

(b) If the switch is thrown back to position 1 after 5 ms in position 2, and then left in position 1, how would the waveform appear?

FIGURE 13–74

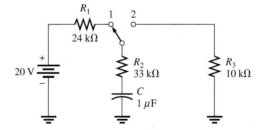

SECTION 13–6 Capacitors in AC Circuits

40. What is the value of the total capacitive reactance in each circuit in Figure 13–75?

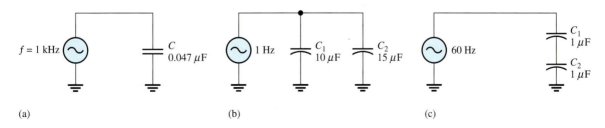

(a)   (b)   (c)

FIGURE 13–75

41. In Figure 13–67, each dc voltage source is replaced by a 10 V rms, 2 kHz ac source. Determine the total reactance in each case.

42. In each circuit of Figure 13–75, what frequency is required to produce an X_C of 100 Ω? An X_C of 1 kΩ?

43. A sinusoidal voltage of 20 V rms produces an rms current of 100 mA when connected to a certain capacitor. What is the reactance?

44. A 10 kHz voltage is applied to a 0.0047 μF capacitor, and 1 mA of rms current is measured. What is the value of the voltage?

45. Determine the true power and the reactive power in Problem 44.

*46. Determine the ac voltage across each capacitor and the current in each branch of the circuit in Figure 13–76. What is the phase angle between the current and the voltage in each case?

FIGURE 13–76

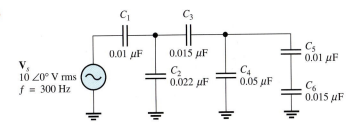

47. Find the value of C_1 in Figure 13–77.

FIGURE 13–77

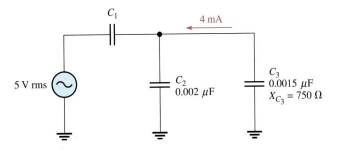

SECTION 13–7 Capacitor Applications

48. If another capacitor is connected in parallel with the existing capacitor in the power supply filter of Figure 13–52, how is the ripple voltage affected?

49. Ideally, what should the reactance of a bypass capacitor be in order to eliminate a 10 kHz ac voltage at a given point in an amplifier circuit?

SECTION 13–8 Testing Capacitors

50. Assume that you are checking a capacitor with an ohmmeter, and when you connect the leads across the capacitor, the pointer does not move from its left-end scale position. What is the problem?

51. In checking a capacitor with the ohmmeter, you find that the pointer goes all the way to the right end of the scale and stays there. What is the problem?

*52. If C_4 in Figure 13–76 opened, determine the voltages that would be measured across the other capacitors.

EWB Troubleshooting and Analysis

These problems require your EWB compact disk.

53. Open file PRO13-53.EWB and measure the voltage across each capacitor.

54. Open file PRO13-54.EWB and measure the voltage across each capacitor.

55. Open file PRO13-55.EWB and measure the current. Decrease the frequency by one-half and measure the current again. Double the original frequency and measure the current again. Explain your observations.

56. Open file PRO13-56.EWB. and find the open capacitor if there is one.

57. Open file PRO13-57.EWB and find the shorted capacitor if there is one.

■ **ANSWERS TO SECTION REVIEWS**

Section 13–1

1. Capacitance is the ability (capacity) to store electrical charge.
2. **(a)** 1,000,000 μF in 1 F   **(b)** 1×10^{12} pF in 1 F   **(c)** 1,000,000 pF in 1 μF
3. 0.0015 μF = 1500 pF; 0.0015 μF = 0.0000000015 F
4. $W = \frac{1}{2}CV^2 = 1.125 \ \mu$J
5. **(a)** C increases.   **(b)** C decreases.
6. (V/mil) mils = 10 kV
7. $C = 0.425 \ \mu$F
8. $C = 2.01 \ \mu$F

Section 13–2

1. Capacitors can be classified by the dielectric material.
2. A fixed capacitor cannot be changed; a variable capacitor can.
3. Electrolytic capacitors are polarized.
4. When connecting a polarized capacitor, make sure the voltage rating is sufficient. Connect the positive end to the positive side of the circuit.

Section 13–3

1. Series C_T is less than smallest C.
2. $C_T = 62.5$ pF
3. $C_T = 0.006 \ \mu$F
4. $C_T = 20$ pF
5. $V_1 = 75$ V

Section 13–4

1. The values of the individual capacitors are added in parallel.
2. Achieve C_T by using five 0.01 μF capacitors in parallel.
3. $C_T = 98$ pF

Section 13–5

1. $\tau = RC = 1.2 \ \mu$s
2. $5\tau = 6 \ \mu$s; $V_F = 4.97$ V
3. $v_{2ms} = 8.65$ V; $v_{3ms} = 9.50$ V; $v_{4ms} = 9.82$ V; $v_{5ms} = 9.93$ V
4. $v_C = 36.8$ V
5. $v_C = 4.93$ V
6. $t = 9.43 \ \mu$s

Section 13–6

1. Current leads voltage by 90° in a capacitor.
2. $X_C = 1/2\pi fC = 637$ kΩ
3. $f = 1/2\pi X_C C = 796$ Hz
4. $I_{rms} = 628\angle 90°$ mA
5. $P_{true} = 0$ W
6. $P_r = 0.453$ VAR

Section 13–7

1. Once the capacitor charges to the peak voltage, it discharges very little before the next peak, thus smoothing the rectified voltage.
2. A coupling capacitor allows ac to pass from one point to another, but blocks constant dc.
3. A coupling capacitor must be large enough to have a negligible reactance at the frequency that is to be passed without opposition.

4. A decoupling capacitor shorts power line voltage transients to ground.

5. X_C is inversely proportional to frequency and so is the filter's ability to pass ac signals.

6. The time constant is used in delay applications.

Section 13–8

1. Discharge a capacitor by shorting its leads.

2. Initially, the needle jumps to zero; then it slowly moves to the high-resistance end of the scale when connected across a good capacitor.

3. Shorted, open, leakage, and dielectric absorption are common capacitor defects.

Section 13–9

1. The coupling capacitor prevents the source from affecting the dc voltage but passes the input signal.

2. An ac voltage riding on a dc voltage is at point C. An ac voltage only at the output.

■ **ANSWERS TO RELATED PROBLEMS FOR EXAMPLES**

13–1 100 kV

13–2 0.05 μF

13–3 100×10^6 pF

13–4 6638 pF

13–5 1.57 μF

13–6 278 pF

13–7 0.01 μF

13–8 2.78 V

13–9 650 pF

13–10 0.09 μF

13–11 891 μs

13–12 8.36 V

13–13 7.97 V

13–14 ≈0.74 ms; 95 V

13–15 1.52 ms

13–16 3.18 kHz

13–17 3.93∠90° mA

13–18 0 W; 1.01 mVAR

■ **ANSWERS TO SELF-TEST**

1. (g)	**2.** (b)	**3.** (c)	**4.** (d)	**5.** (a)	**6.** (d)	**7.** (a)	**8.** (f)
9. (c)	**10.** (b)	**11.** (d)	**12.** (a)	**13.** (b)	**14.** (a)	**15.** (b)	**16.** (d)

14

INDUCTORS

 Electronics Workbench (EWB) and PSpice Tutorials at http://www.prenhall.com/floyd

■ INTRODUCTION

You have already learned about two of the three types of passive electrical components, the resistor and the capacitor. Now you will learn about the *inductor,* the third type of basic passive component.

In this chapter, you will study the inductor and its characteristics. The basic construction and electrical properties are discussed, and the effects of connecting inductors in series and in parallel are analyzed. How an inductor works in both dc and ac circuits is an important part of this coverage and forms the basis for the study of reactive circuits in terms of both frequency response and time response. You will also learn how to check for a faulty inductor.

The inductor, which is basically a coil of wire, is based on the principle of electromagnetic induction, which was studied in Chapter 10.

Inductance is the property of a coil of wire that opposes a change in current. The basis for inductance is the electromagnetic field that surrounds any conductor when there is current through it. The electrical component designed to have the property of inductance is called an *inductor, coil,* or in certain applications a *choke.* All of these terms refer to the same type of device.

In the TECH TIP assignment in Section 14–9, you will determine the inductance of coils by measuring the time constant of a test circuit using oscilloscope waveforms.

■ TECHnology
Theory
Into
Practice

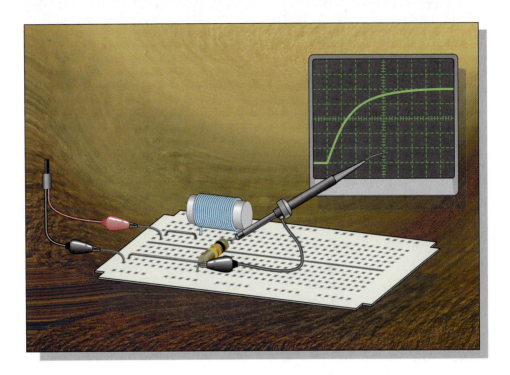

■ CHAPTER OBJECTIVES

❑ Describe the basic structure and characteristics of an inductor

❑ Discuss various types of inductors

❑ Analyze series inductors

❑ Analyze parallel inductors

❑ Analyze inductive dc switching circuits

❑ Analyze inductive ac circuits

❑ Discuss some inductor applications

❑ Test an inductor

HISTORICAL NOTE

Joseph Henry
1797–1878

Joseph Henry was born in 1797. His career began as a professor at a small school in Albany, NY. He was the first American since Franklin to undertake original scientific experiments. Henry was the first to superimpose coils of wire wrapped on an iron core, and it is said that he insulated the wire for one of his electromagnets using a silk dress belonging to his wife. He first observed electromagnetic induction in 1830, a year before Faraday, although he did not publish his findings. He did obtain credit for the discovery of self-induction, however. Later Henry received an appointment at New Jersey College which eventually became Princeton University and, in 1846, became the first director of the Smithsonian Institution. The unit of inductance is named in his honor. *Photo Credit: Courtesy of the Smithsonian Institution. Photo number 52,054.*

14–1 ■ THE BASIC INDUCTOR

In this section, the construction and characteristics of inductors are examined.

After completing this section, you should be able to

■ **Describe the basic structure and characteristics of an inductor**
- Explain how an inductor stores energy
- Define *inductance* and state its unit
- Discuss induced voltage
- Specify how the physical characteristics affect inductance
- Discuss winding resistance and winding capacitance
- State Faraday's law
- State Lenz's law

When a length of wire is formed into a coil, as shown in Figure 14–1, it becomes a basic **inductor.** The terms *coil* and *inductor* are used interchangeably. Current through the coil produces an electromagnetic field, as illustrated. The magnetic lines of force around each loop (turn) in the **winding** of the coil effectively add to the lines of force around the adjoining loops, forming a strong electromagnetic field within and around the coil. The net direction of the total electromagnetic field creates a north and a south pole.

FIGURE 14–1

A coil of wire forms an inductor. When there is current through it, a three-dimensional electromagnetic field is created, surrounding the coil in all directions.

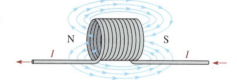

To understand the formation of the total electromagnetic field in a coil, consider the interaction of the electromagnetic fields around two adjacent loops. The magnetic lines of force around adjacent loops are each deflected into a single outer path when the loops are brought close together. This effect occurs because the magnetic lines of force are in opposing directions between adjacent loops and therefore cancel out when the loops are close together, as illustrated in Figure 14–2. The total electromagnetic field for the two loops is depicted in part (b). This effect is additive for many closely adjacent loops in a coil; that is, each additional loop adds to the strength of the electromagnetic field. For simplicity, only single lines of force are shown, although there are many.

FIGURE 14–2

Interaction of magnetic lines of force in two adjacent loops of a coil.

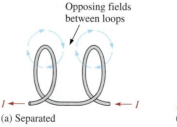

(a) Separated

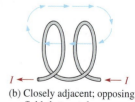

(b) Closely adjacent; opposing fields between loops cancel.

Self-Inductance

When there is current through an inductor, an electromagnetic field is established. When the current changes, the electromagnetic field also changes. An increase in current expands the electromagnetic field, and a decrease in current reduces it. Therefore, a changing current produces a changing electromagnetic field around the inductor. In turn, the changing electromagnetic field causes an **induced voltage** across the coil in a direction to oppose the change in current. This property is called *self-inductance* but is usually referred to as simply **inductance**, symbolized by *L*.

> **Self-inductance is a measure of a coil's ability to establish an induced voltage as a result of a change in its current, and that induced voltage is in a direction to oppose that change in current.**

The Unit of Inductance   The **henry, H,** is the basic unit of inductance. By definition, the inductance is one henry when current through the coil, changing at the rate of one ampere per second, induces one volt across the coil. In many practical applications, millihenries (mH) and microhenries (μH) are the more common units. Figure 14–3 shows a schematic symbol for the inductor.

FIGURE 14–3
Symbol for inductor.

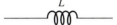

The Induced Voltage Depends on *L* and *di/dt*

The inductance (*L*) of a coil and the time rate of change of the current (*di/dt*) determine the induced voltage (v_{ind}). A change in current causes a change in the electromagnetic field, which, in turn, induces a voltage across the coil, as you know. The induced voltage is directly proportional to *L* and *di/dt,* as stated by the following formula:

$$v_{ind} = L\left(\frac{di}{dt}\right) \tag{14–1}$$

This formula indicates that the greater the inductance, the greater the induced voltage. Also, it means that the faster the coil current changes (greater *di/dt*), the greater the induced voltage. Notice the similarity of Equation (14–1) to Equation (13–25): $i = C(dv/dt)$.

EXAMPLE 14–1

Determine the induced voltage across a 1 henry (1 H) inductor when the current is changing at a rate of 2 A/s.

Solution

$$v_{ind} = L\left(\frac{di}{dt}\right) = (1 \text{ H})(2 \text{ A/s}) = \textbf{2 V}$$

Related Problem   Determine the inductance when a current changing at a rate of 10 A/s causes 50 V to be induced.

Energy Storage

An inductor stores energy in the electromagnetic field created by the current. The energy stored is expressed as follows:

$$W = \frac{1}{2}LI^2 \tag{14–2}$$

As you can see, the energy stored is proportional to the inductance and the square of the current. When current (*I*) is in amperes and inductance (*L*) is in henries, energy (*W*) is in joules.

Physical Characteristics of Inductors

The following parameters are important in establishing the inductance of a coil: permeability of the core material, number of turns of wire, core length, and cross-sectional area of the core.

Core Material   As discussed earlier, an inductor is basically a coil of wire. The material around which the coil is formed is called the **core.** Coils are wound on either nonmagnetic or magnetic materials. Examples of nonmagnetic materials are air, wood, copper, plastic, and glass. The permeabilities of these materials are the same as for a vacuum. Examples of magnetic materials are iron, nickel, steel, cobalt, or alloys. These materials have permeabilities that are hundreds or thousands of times greater than that of a vacuum and are classified as *ferromagnetic.* A ferromagnetic core provides a better path for the magnetic lines of force and thus permits a stronger magnetic field.

As you learned in Chapter 10, the permeability (μ) of the core material determines how easily a magnetic field can be established. *The inductance is directly proportional to the permeability of the core material.*

Physical Parameters   The number of turns of wire, the length, and the cross-sectional area of the core, as indicated in Figure 14–4, are factors in setting the value of inductance. The inductance is inversely proportional to the length of the core and directly proportional to the cross-sectional area. Also, the inductance is directly related to the number of turns squared. This relationship is as follows:

$$L = \frac{N^2 \mu A}{l} \tag{14-3}$$

where L is the inductance in henries, N is the number of turns of wire, μ is the permeability, A is the cross-sectional area in meters squared, and l is the core length in meters.

FIGURE 14–4
Physical parameters of an inductor.

Length, l
Cross-sectional area, A
Core material
Number of turns, N

EXAMPLE 14–2   Determine the inductance of the coil in Figure 14–5. The permeability of the core is 0.25×10^{-3}.

FIGURE 14–5

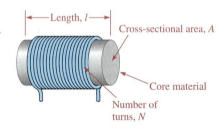

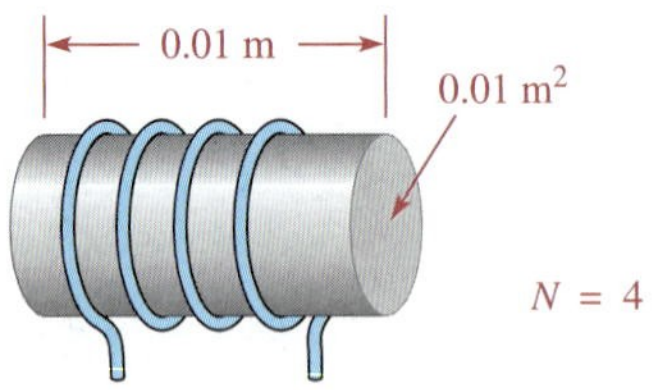

0.01 m
0.01 m^2
$N = 4$

Solution

$$L = \frac{N^2 \mu A}{l} = \frac{(4)^2 (0.25 \times 10^{-3})(0.01)}{0.01} = \textbf{40 mH}$$

The calculator sequence is

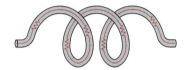

Related Problem Determine the inductance of a coil with 12 turns around a core that is 0.05 m long and has a cross-sectional area of 0.015 m². The permeability is 0.25×10^{-3}.

Winding Resistance

When a coil is made of a certain material, for example, insulated copper wire, that wire has a certain resistance per unit of length. When many turns of wire are used to construct a coil, the total resistance may be significant. This inherent resistance is called the *dc resistance* or the *winding resistance* (R_W). Although this resistance is distributed along the length of the wire, it effectively appears in series with the inductance of the coil, as shown in Figure 14–6. In many applications, the winding resistance may be small enough to be ignored and the coil considered as an ideal inductor. In other cases, the resistance must be considered.

FIGURE 14–6
Winding resistance of a coil.

(a) The wire has resistance
distributed along its length.

(b) Equivalent circuit

Winding Capacitance

When two conductors are placed side by side, there is always some capacitance between them. Thus, when many turns of wire are placed close together in a coil, a certain amount of stray capacitance, called *winding capacitance* (C_W), is a natural side effect. In many applications, this winding capacitance is very small and has no significant effect. In other cases, particularly at high frequencies, it may become quite important.

The equivalent circuit for an inductor with both its winding resistance (R_W) and its winding capacitance (C_W) is shown in Figure 14–7. The capacitance effectively acts in parallel.

FIGURE 14–7
Winding capacitance of a coil.

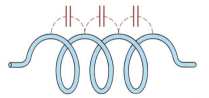

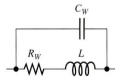

(a) Stray capacitance between each loop appears
as a total parallel capacitance.

(b) Equivalent circuit

Review of Faraday's Law

Faraday's law was introduced in Chapter 10 and is reviewed here because of its importance in the study of inductors. Michael Faraday discovered the principle of electromagnetic induction in 1831. He found that by moving a magnet through a coil of wire, a voltage was induced across the coil and that when a complete path was provided, the induced voltage caused an induced current. Faraday observed that

> **The amount of voltage induced in a coil is directly proportional to the rate of change of the magnetic field with respect to the coil.**

This principle is illustrated in Figure 14–8, where a bar magnet is moved through a coil of wire. An induced voltage is indicated by the voltmeter connected across the coil. The faster the magnet is moved, the greater is the induced voltage.

FIGURE 14–8
Induced voltage created by a changing magnetic field.

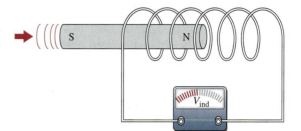

When a wire is formed into a certain number of loops or turns and is exposed to a changing magnetic field, a voltage is induced across the coil. The induced voltage is proportional to the number of turns of wire in the coil, N, and to the rate at which the magnetic field changes. The rate of change of the magnetic field is designated $d\phi/dt$, where ϕ is the magnetic flux. $d\phi/dt$ is expressed in webers/second (Wb/s). Faraday's law states that the induced voltage across a coil is equal to the number of turns (loops) times the rate of flux change and is expressed in concise form as follows:

$$v_{\text{ind}} = N\left(\frac{d\phi}{dt}\right)$$

(14–4)

EXAMPLE 14–3   Apply Faraday's law to find the induced voltage across a coil with 500 turns located in a magnetic field that is changing at a rate of 5 Wb/s.

Solution
$$v_{\text{ind}} = N\left(\frac{d\phi}{dt}\right) = (500 \text{ t})(5 \text{ Wb/s}) = \textbf{2.5 kV}$$

Related Problem   A 1000 turn coil has an induced voltage of 500 V across it. What is the rate of change of the magnetic field?

Lenz's Law

Lenz's law was introduced in Chapter 10 and is restated here.

> **When the current through a coil changes, an induced voltage is created as a result of the changing electromagnetic field, and the direction of the induced voltage is such that it always opposes the change in current.**

Figure 14–9 illustrates Lenz's law. In part (a), the current is constant and is limited by R_1. There is no induced voltage because the electromagnetic field is unchanging. In part (b), the switch suddenly is closed, placing R_2 in parallel with R_1 and thus reducing the resistance. Naturally, the current tries to increase and the electromagnetic field begins to expand, but the induced voltage opposes this attempted increase in current for an instant.

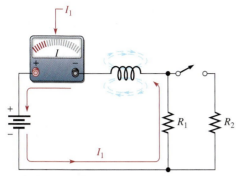

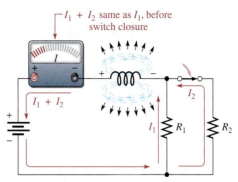

(a) Switch open: Constant current and constant magnetic field; no induced voltage.

(b) At instant of switch closure: Expanding magnetic field induces voltage, which opposes increase in total current. The total current remains the same at this instant.

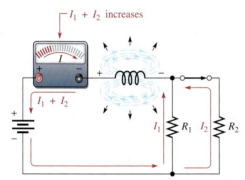

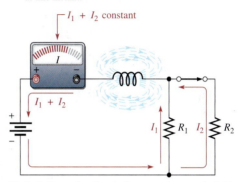

(c) Right after switch closure: The rate of expansion of the magnetic field decreases, allowing the current to increase exponentially as induced voltage decreases.

(d) Switch remains closed: Current and magnetic field reach constant value.

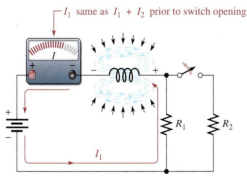

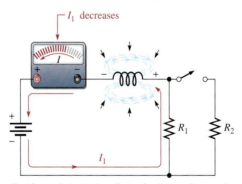

(e) At instant of switch opening: Magnetic field begins to collapse, creating an induced voltage, which opposes decrease in current.

(f) After switch opening: Rate of collapse of magnetic field decreases, allowing current to decrease exponentially back to original value.

FIGURE 14–9

Demonstration of Lenz's law in an inductive circuit: When the current tries to change suddenly, the electromagnetic field changes and induces a voltage in a direction that opposes that change in current.

In Figure 14–9(c), the induced voltage gradually decreases, allowing the current to increase. In part (d), the current has reached a constant value as determined by the parallel resistors, and the induced voltage is zero. In part (e), the switch has been suddenly opened, and, for an instant, the induced voltage prevents any decrease in current, and arcing between the switch contacts results. In part (f), the induced voltage gradually decreases, allowing the current to decrease back to a value determined by R_1. Notice that the induced voltage has a polarity that opposes any current change. The polarity of the induced voltage is opposite that of the battery voltage for an increase in current and aids the battery voltage for a decrease in current.

SECTION 14–1 REVIEW

1. List the parameters that contribute to the inductance of a coil.
2. The current through a 15 mH inductor is changing at the rate of 500 mA/s. What is the induced voltage?
3. Describe what happens to L when
   (a) N is increased
   (b) The core length is increased
   (c) The cross-sectional area of the core is decreased
   (d) A ferromagnetic core is replaced by an air core
4. Explain why inductors have some winding resistance.
5. Explain why inductors have some winding capacitance.

14–2 ■ TYPES OF INDUCTORS

Inductors normally are classified according to the type of core material. In this section, the basic types of inductors are examined.

After completing this section, you should be able to

■ **Discuss various types of inductors**
   • Describe the basic types of fixed inductors
   • Distinguish between fixed and variable inductors

Inductors are made in a variety of shapes and sizes. Basically, they fall into two general categories: fixed and variable. The standard schematic symbols are shown in Figure 14–10.

Both fixed and variable inductors can be classified according to the type of core material. Three common types are the air core, the iron core, and the ferrite core. Each has a unique symbol, as shown in Figure 14–11.

Adjustable (variable) inductors usually have a screw-type adjustment that moves a sliding core in and out, thus changing the inductance. A wide variety of inductors exist, and some are shown in Figure 14–12. Small fixed inductors are frequently encapsulated in a insulating material that protects the fine wire in the coil. Encapsulated inductors have an appearance similar to a resistor.

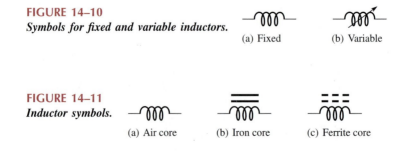

FIGURE 14–10
Symbols for fixed and variable inductors.

(a) Fixed   (b) Variable

FIGURE 14–11
Inductor symbols.

(a) Air core   (b) Iron core   (c) Ferrite core

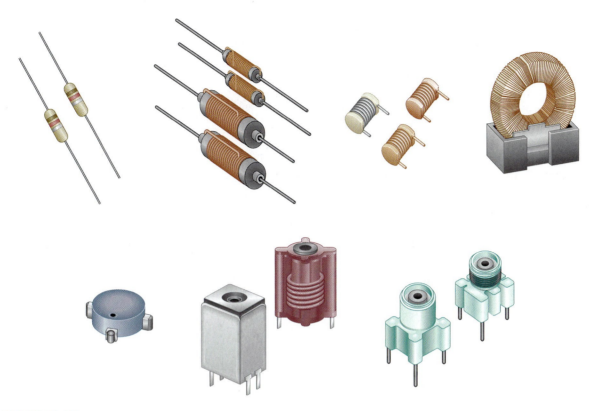

FIGURE 14–12
Typical inductors.

SECTION 14–2 REVIEW	1. Name two general categories of inductors. 2. Identify the inductor symbols in Figure 14–13.

FIGURE 14–13

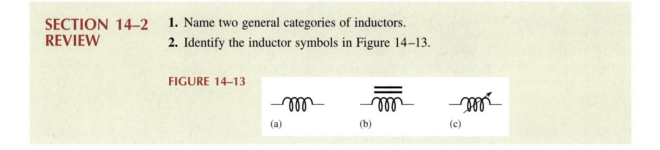

(a)   (b)   (c)

14–3 ■ SERIES INDUCTORS

In this section, you will see that when inductors are connected in series, the total inductance increases.

After completing this section, you should be able to

■ **Analyze series inductors**
  • Determine total inductance

When inductors are connected in series, as in Figure 14–14, the total inductance, L_T, is the sum of the individual inductances. The formula for L_T is expressed in the following equation for the general case of n inductors in series:

$$L_T = L_1 + L_2 + L_3 + \cdots + L_n$$

(14–5)

Notice that the formula for total inductance in series is similar to the formulas for total resistance in series (Chapter 5) and total capacitance in parallel (Chapter 13).

FIGURE 14–14
Inductors in series.

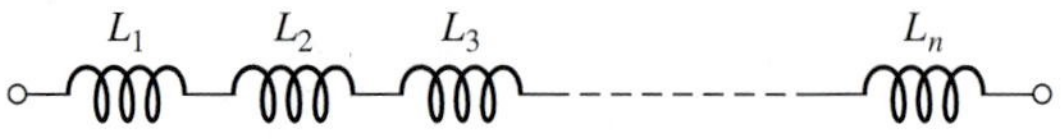

L_1 L_2 L_3 L_n

EXAMPLE 14–4

Determine the total inductance for each of the series connections in Figure 14–15.

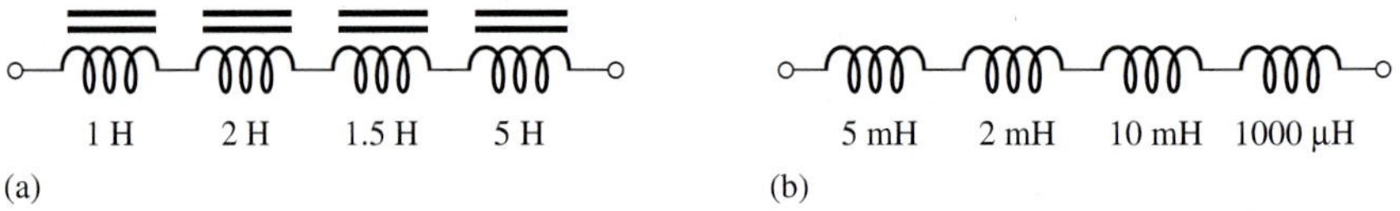

1 H   2 H   1.5 H   5 H

(a)

5 mH   2 mH   10 mH   1000 μH

(b)

FIGURE 14–15

Solution   In Figure 14–15(a),

$$L_T = 1\text{ H} + 2\text{ H} + 1.5\text{ H} + 5\text{ H} = \textbf{9.5 H}$$

In Figure 14–15(b),

$$L_T = 5\text{ mH} + 2\text{ mH} + 10\text{ mH} + 1\text{ mH} = \textbf{18 mH}$$

Note: 1000 μH = 1 mH

Related Problem   What is the total inductance of ten 50 μH inductors in series?

SECTION 14–3 REVIEW

1. State the rule for combining inductors in series.
2. What is L_T for a series connection of 100 μH, 500 μH, and 2 mH?
3. Five 100 mH coils are connected in series. What is the total inductance?

14–4 ■ PARALLEL INDUCTORS

In this section, you will see that when inductors are connected in parallel, total inductance is reduced.

After completing this section, you should be able to

■ **Analyze parallel inductors**
  • Determine total inductance

Total Inductance

When inductors are connected in parallel, as in Figure 14–16, the total inductance is less than the smallest inductance. The formula for total inductance in parallel is similar to the formulas for total parallel resistance (Chapter 6) and total series capacitance (Chapter 13).

$$\frac{1}{L_T} = \frac{1}{L_1} + \frac{1}{L_2} + \frac{1}{L_3} + \cdots + \frac{1}{L_n}$$

(14–6)

This general formula states that the reciprocal of the total inductance is equal to the sum of the reciprocals of the individual inductances. L_T can be found by taking the reciprocal of both sides of Equation (14–6).

$$L_T = \frac{1}{\left(\dfrac{1}{L_1}\right) + \left(\dfrac{1}{L_2}\right) + \left(\dfrac{1}{L_3}\right) + \cdots + \left(\dfrac{1}{L_n}\right)} \qquad \text{(14–7)}$$

FIGURE 14–16
Inductors in parallel.

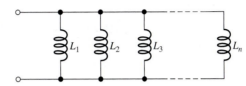

Two Parallel Inductors   When only two inductors are in parallel, a special product over sum form of Equation (14–6) can be used.

$$L_T = \frac{L_1 L_2}{L_1 + L_2} \qquad \text{(14–8)}$$

Equal-Value Parallel Inductors   This is another special case in which a short-cut formula can be used. This formula is also derived from the general Equation (14–6) and is stated as follows for n equal-value inductors in parallel:

$$L_T = \frac{L}{n} \qquad \text{(14–9)}$$

EXAMPLE 14–5   Determine L_T in Figure 14–17.

FIGURE 14–17

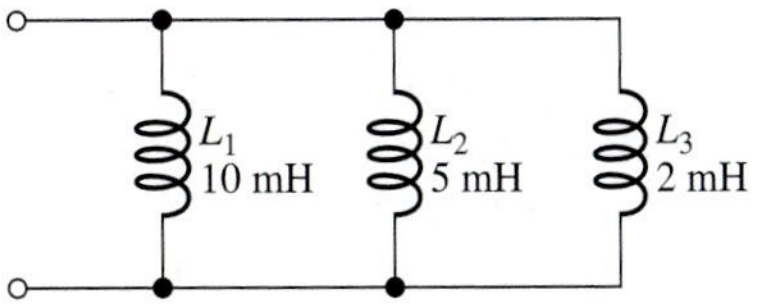

L_1 10 mH L_2 5 mH L_3 2 mH

Solution   Use Equation (14–7) to determine the total inductance.

$$L_T = \frac{1}{\left(\dfrac{1}{L_1}\right) + \left(\dfrac{1}{L_2}\right) + \left(\dfrac{1}{L_3}\right)} = \frac{1}{\dfrac{1}{10\ \text{mH}} + \dfrac{1}{5\ \text{mH}} + \dfrac{1}{2\ \text{mH}}} = \frac{1}{0.8\ \text{mH}} = \textbf{1.25 mH}$$

The calculator sequence is

[1] [0] [EE] [(−)] [3] [2nd] [x^{-1}] [+] [5] [EE] [(−)] [3] [2nd] [x^{-1}] [+]
[2] [EE] [(−)] [3] [2nd] [x^{-1}] [ENTER] [2nd] [x^{-1}]

Related Problem   Determine L_T for a parallel connection of 50 μH, 80 μH, 100 μH, and 150 μH.

EXAMPLE 14-6 Find L_T for both circuits in Figure 14–18.

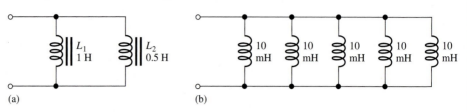

FIGURE 14-18

Solution Use Equation (14–8) for the two parallel inductors in Figure 14–18(a).

$$L_T = \frac{L_1 L_2}{L_1 + L_2} = \frac{(1\ \text{H})(0.5\ \text{H})}{1.5\ \text{H}} = \textbf{333 mH}$$

Use Equation (14–9) for the equal-value parallel inductors in Figure 14–18(b).

$$L_T = \frac{L}{n} = \frac{10\ \text{mH}}{5} = \textbf{2 mH}$$

Related Problem Find L_T for each of the following:
(a) $L_1 = 10\ \mu\text{H}$ and $L_2 = 27\ \mu\text{H}$ in parallel   **(b)** Five $100\ \mu\text{H}$ coils in parallel

SECTION 14–4 REVIEW

1. Compare the total inductance in parallel with the smallest-value individual inductor.
2. The calculation of total parallel inductance is similar to that for parallel resistance. (T or F)
3. Determine L_T for each parallel combination:
   (a) 100 mH, 50 mH, and 10 mH   **(b)** $40\ \mu\text{H}$ and $60\ \mu\text{H}$
   (c) Ten 1 H coils

14–5 ▪ INDUCTORS IN DC CIRCUITS

An inductor will energize when it is connected to a dc voltage source. The buildup of current through the inductor occurs in a predictable manner, which is dependent on the inductance and the resistance in a circuit. In this section, switches are opened and closed simultaneously in illustrations. Although this isn't practical, it illustrates fundamental ideas in transient inductive circuits.

After completing this section, you should be able to

▪ **Analyze inductive dc switching circuits**
  • Describe the energizing and deenergizing of an inductor
  • Define *time constant*
  • Relate the time constant to energizing and deenergizing
  • Describe induced voltage
  • Write the exponential equations for current in an inductor

When there is constant direct current in an inductor, there is no induced voltage. There is, however, a voltage drop due to the winding resistance of the coil. The inductance itself appears as a short to dc. Energy is stored in the electromagnetic field according to the formula previously stated in Equation (14–2), $W = \frac{1}{2}LI^2$. The only energy loss occurs in the winding resistance ($P = I^2 R_W$). This condition is illustrated in Figure 14–19.

FIGURE 14–19
Energy storage and conversion to heat in an inductor in a dc circuit.

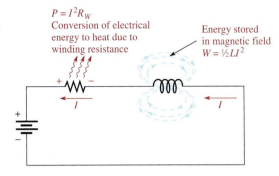

FIGURE 14–19
Energy storage and conversion to heat in an inductor in a dc circuit.

The *RL* Time Constant

Because the inductor's basic action is to oppose a change in its current, it follows that current cannot change instantaneously in an inductor. A certain time is required for the current to make a change from one value to another. The rate at which the current changes is determined by the **time constant.** The time constant for a series *RL* circuit is

$$\tau = \frac{L}{R} \qquad\qquad (14\text{–}10)$$

where τ is in seconds when inductance (L) is in henries and resistance (R) is in ohms.

EXAMPLE 14–7

A series *RL* circuit has a resistance of 1.0 kΩ and an inductance of 1 mH. What is the time constant?

Solution   Calculate the time constant as follows:

$$\tau = \frac{L}{R} = \frac{1\ \text{mH}}{1.0\ \text{k}\Omega} = \frac{1 \times 10^{-3}\ \text{H}}{1 \times 10^{3}\ \Omega} = 1 \times 10^{-6}\ \text{s} = \mathbf{1\ \mu s}$$

Related Problem   Find the time constant for $R = 2.2$ kΩ and $L = 500\ \mu$H.

Energizing Current in an Inductor

In a series *RL* circuit, the current will increase to approximately 63% of its full value in one time-constant interval after the switch is closed. This buildup of current is analogous to the buildup of capacitor voltage during the charging in an *RC* circuit; they both follow an exponential curve and reach the approximate percentages of the final current as indicated in Table 14–1 and as illustrated in Figure 14–20.

TABLE 14–1
Percentage of the final current after each time-constant interval during current buildup.

Number of Time Constants	% Final Current
1	63
2	86
3	95
4	98
5	99 (considered 100%)

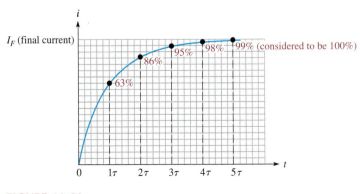

FIGURE 14–20
Energizing current in an inductor.

The change in current over five time-constant intervals is illustrated in Figure 14–21. When the current reaches its final value at approximately 5τ, it ceases to change. At this time, the inductor acts as a short (except for winding resistance) to the constant current. The final value of the current is

$$I_F = \frac{V_S}{R} = \frac{10\ \text{V}}{1.0\ \text{k}\Omega} = 10\ \text{mA}$$

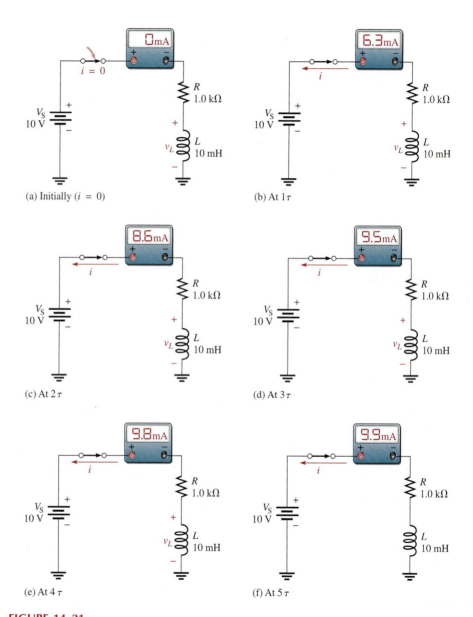

FIGURE 14–21
Current buildup in an inductor.

EXAMPLE 14–8 Calculate the time constant for Figure 14–22. Then determine the current and the time at each time-constant interval, measured from the instant the switch is closed.

Solution The time constant is

$$\tau = \frac{L}{R} = \frac{50 \text{ mH}}{100 \text{ }\Omega} = \textbf{500 } \boldsymbol{\mu}\textbf{s}$$

FIGURE 14–22

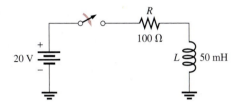

The current at each time-constant interval is a certain percentage of the final current. The final current is

$$I_F = \frac{V_S}{R} = \frac{20 \text{ V}}{100 \text{ }\Omega} = 0.2 \text{ A} = 200 \text{ mA}$$

Using the time-constant percentage values from Table 14–1,

At $1\tau = $ **500 μs:** $i = 0.63(200 \text{ mA}) = $ **126 mA**

At $2\tau = $ **1 ms:** $i = 0.86(200 \text{ mA}) = $ **172 mA**

At $3\tau = $ **1.5 ms:** $i = 0.95(200 \text{ mA}) = $ **190 mA**

At $4\tau = $ **2 ms:** $i = 0.98(200 \text{ mA}) = $ **196 mA**

At $5\tau = $ **2.5 ms:** $i = 0.99(200 \text{ mA}) = 198 \text{ mA} \cong $ **200 mA**

Related Problem Repeat the calculations if R is 680 Ω and L is 100 μH.

Deenergizing Current in an Inductor

Current in an inductor decreases exponentially according to the approximate percentage values in Table 14–2 and in Figure 14–23.

TABLE 14–2

Percentage of initial current after each time-constant interval while current is decreasing.

Number of Time Constants	% of Initial Current
1	37
2	14
3	5
4	2
5	1 (considered 0)

FIGURE 14–23

Deenergizing current in an inductor.

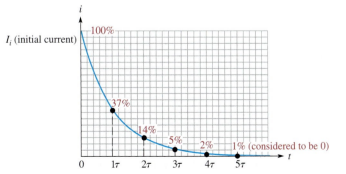

Figure 14–24(a) shows a constant current of 1 A (1000 mA) through an inductor. Switch 1 (SW1) is opened and switch 2 (SW2) is closed simultaneously, and for an instant the induced voltage keeps the 1 A current through the inductor. During the first time-constant interval, the current decreases by 63% down to 370 mA (37% of its initial value), as indicated in Figure 14–24(b). During the second time-constant interval, the current decreases by another 63% to 140 mA (14% of its initial value), as shown in Figure 14–24(c). The continued decrease in the current is illustrated by the remaining parts of Figure 14–24. Part (f) shows that only 1% of the initial current is left at the end of five time constants. Traditionally, this value is accepted as the final value and is approximated as zero current. Notice that until after the five time constants have elapsed, there is an induced voltage across the coil which is trying to maintain the current. This voltage follows a decreasing exponential curve, as will be discussed later.

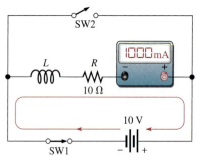

(a) Initially, there is 1 A of constant current. Then SW2 is closed and SW1 opened simultaneously ($t = 0$).

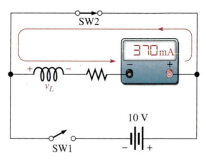

(b) At the end of one time constant ($t = 1\tau$)

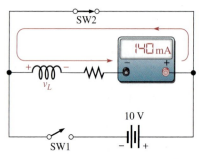

(c) At the end of two time constants ($t = 2\tau$)

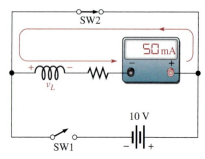

(d) At the end of three time constants ($t = 3\tau$)

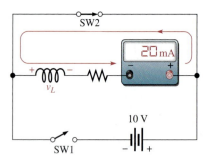

(e) At the end of four time constants ($t = 4\tau$)

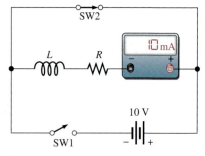

(f) At the end of five time constants ($t = 5\tau$). Since only 1% of the current is left, this value is taken as the final zero value.

FIGURE 14–24

Illustration of the exponential decrease of current in an inductor. The current decreases another 63% during each time constant interval.

EXAMPLE 14–9

In Figure 14–25, SW1 is opened at the instant that SW2 is closed. Assume steady-state current through the coil prior to switch change.
(a) What is the time constant?
(b) What is the initial coil current at the instant of switching?
(c) What is the coil current at 1τ?

FIGURE 14–25

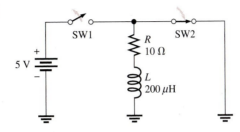

Solution

(a) $\tau = \dfrac{L}{R} = \dfrac{200\ \mu H}{10\ \Omega} = \textbf{20}\ \boldsymbol{\mu}\textbf{s}$

(b) Current cannot change instantaneously in an inductor. Therefore, the current at the instant of the switch change is the same as the steady-state current.

$$I = \frac{5\ V}{10\ \Omega} = \textbf{500 mA}$$

(c) At 1τ, the current has decreased to 37% of its initial value.

$$i = 0.37(500\ mA) = \textbf{185 mA}$$

Related Problem Change R to 47 Ω and L to 1 mH in Figure 14–25 and repeat each calculation.

Induced Voltage in the Series *RL* Circuit

As you know, when current changes in an inductor, a voltage is induced. Let's examine what happens to the voltages across the resistor and the coil in a series circuit when a change in current occurs.

Look at the circuit in Figure 14–26(a). When the switch is open, there is no current, and the resistor voltage and the coil voltage are both zero. At the instant the switch is closed, as indicated in part (b), the instantaneous voltage across the resistor (v_R) is zero and the instantaneous voltage across the inductor (v_L) is 10 V. The reason for this change is that the induced voltage across the coil is equal and opposite to the applied voltage, preventing the current from changing instantaneously. Therefore, *at the instant of switch closure, the inductor effectively acts as an open with all the applied voltage across it.*

During the first five time constants, the current is building up exponentially, and the induced coil voltage is decreasing. The resistor voltage increases with the current, as Figure 14–26(c) illustrates. After five time constants have elapsed, the current has reached its final value, V_S/R. At this time, all of the applied voltage is dropped across the resistor and none across the coil. Thus, the inductor effectively acts as a short to nonchanging current, as Figure 14–26(d) illustrates. Keep in mind that the inductor always reacts to a change in current by creating an induced voltage in order to counteract that change in current.

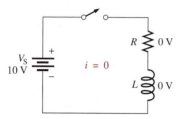

(a) Before switch is closed.

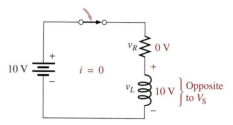

(b) At instant switch is closed, v_L is equal and opposite to V_S.

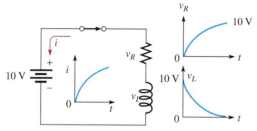

(c) During the first five time constants, v_R increases exponentially with current, and v_L decreases exponentially.

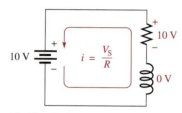

(d) After the first five time constants, $v_R = 10$ V and $v_L \approx 0$ V. The current is at a constant maximum value.

FIGURE 14–26

Voltage in an RL circuit as the inductor energizes. The winding resistance is neglected.

Now let's examine the case illustrated in Figure 14–27, where the steady-state current is switched out, and the inductor discharges through another path. Part (a) shows the steady-state condition, and part (b) illustrates the instant at which the source is removed by opening SW1 and the discharge path is connected with the closure of SW2. There was 1 A through L prior to this. Notice that 10 V are induced in L in the direction to aid the 1 A in an effort to keep it from changing. Then, as shown in part (c), the current decays exponentially, and so do v_R and v_L. After 5τ, as shown in part (d), all of the energy stored in the magnetic field of L is dissipated, and all values are zero.

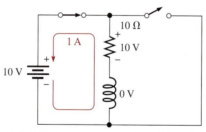

(a) Initially, there is a constant 1 A and the voltage is dropped across R.

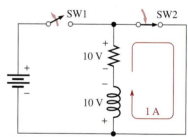

(b) At the instant that SW1 is opened and SW2 closed, 10 V is induced across L.

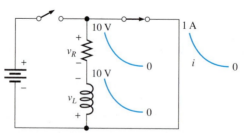

(c) During the five-time-constant interval, v_R and v_L decrease exponentially with the current.

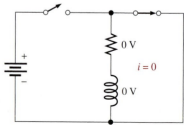

(d) After the five time constants, v_R, v_L, and i are all zero.

FIGURE 14–27

Voltage in an RL circuit as the inductor deenergizes. The winding resistance is neglected.

EXAMPLE 14–10   **(a)** In Figure 14–28(a), what is v_L at the instant SW1 is closed? What is v_L after 5τ?
(b) In Figure 14–28(b), what is v_L at the instant SW1 opens and SW2 closes? What is v_L after 5τ?

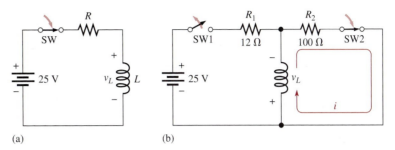

FIGURE 14–28

Solution

(a) At the instant the switch is closed, all of the source voltage is across L. Thus, at the instant SW1 is closed, $v_L =$ **25 V,** with the polarity as shown. After 5τ, L acts as a short, so $v_L =$ **0 V.**

(b) With SW1 closed and SW2 open, the steady-state current is

$$I = \frac{25\ \text{V}}{12\ \Omega} = \textbf{2.08 A}$$

When the switches are thrown, an induced voltage is created across L sufficient to keep this 2.08 A current for an instant. In this case, it takes an induced voltage of

$$v_L = IR_2 = (2.08\ \text{A})(100\ \Omega) = \textbf{208 V}$$

After 5τ, the inductor voltage is **zero.**

Related Problem   Repeat part (a) if the source voltage is 9 V. Repeat part (b) if R_1 is 27 Ω with the source voltage at 25 V.

The Exponential Formulas

The formulas for the exponential current and voltage in an RL circuit are similar to those used in the last chapter for the RC circuit, and the universal exponential curves in Figure 13–35 apply to inductors as well as capacitors. The general formulas for RL circuits are stated as follows:

$$v = V_F + (V_i - V_F)e^{-Rt/L} \tag{14–11}$$

$$i = I_F + (I_i - I_F)e^{-Rt/L} \tag{14–12}$$

where V_F and I_F are the final values of voltage and current, V_i and I_i are the initial values of voltage and current, and v and i are the instantaneous values of the inductor voltage or current at time t.

Increasing Current   The formula for the special case in which an increasing exponential current curve begins at zero ($I_i = 0$) is

$$i = I_F(1 - e^{-Rt/L}) \tag{14–13}$$

Using Equation (14–13), you can calculate the value of the increasing inductor current at any instant of time. The same is true for voltage.

EXAMPLE 14–11   In Figure 14–29, determine the inductor current 30 μs after the switch is closed.

FIGURE 14–29

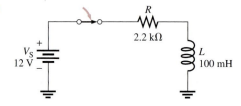

Solution   The time constant is

$$\tau = \frac{L}{R} = \frac{100 \text{ mH}}{2.2 \text{ k}\Omega} = 45.5 \ \mu s$$

The final current is

$$I_F = \frac{V_S}{R} = \frac{12 \text{ V}}{2.2 \text{ k}\Omega} = 5.45 \text{ mA}$$

The initial current is zero. Notice that 30 μs is less than one time constant, so the current will reach less than 63% of its final value in that time.

$$i_L = I_F(1 - e^{-Rt/L}) = 5.45 \text{ mA}(1 - e^{-0.66}) = 5.45 \text{ mA}(1 - 0.517) = \mathbf{2.63 \text{ mA}}$$

The calculator sequence for the entire calculation of i_L is

(1 2 ÷ 2 • 2 EE 3) ((1 − 2nd e^x (−) (2 • 2 EE 3 × 3 0 EE (−) 6
÷ 1 0 0 EE (−) 3))) ENTER

Related Problem   In Figure 14–29, determine the inductor current 55 μs after the switch is closed.

Decreasing Current   The formula for the special case in which a decreasing exponential current has a final value of zero ($I_F = 0$) is

$$i = I_i e^{-Rt/L} \tag{14–14}$$

This formula can be used to calculate the deenergizing current at any instant, as the following example shows.

EXAMPLE 14–12   Determine the inductor current in Figure 14–30 at a point in time 2 ms after the switches are simultaneously thrown (SW1 opened and SW2 closed).

FIGURE 14–30

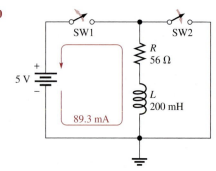

Solution The deenergizing time constant is

$$\tau = \frac{L}{R} = \frac{200 \text{ mH}}{56 \ \Omega} = 3.57 \text{ ms}$$

The initial current in the inductor is 89.3 mA. Notice that 2 ms is less than one time constant, so the current will show a decrease less than 63%. Therefore, the current will be greater than 37% of its initial value at 2 ms after the switches are thrown.

$$i = I_i e^{-Rt/L} = (89.3 \text{ mA})e^{-0.56} = \textbf{51.0 mA}$$

Related Problem Determine the inductor current in Figure 14–30 at a point in time 6 ms after the switches are simultaneously thrown if the source voltage is changed to 10 V.

SECTION 14–5 REVIEW

1. A 15 mH inductor with a winding resistance of 10 Ω has a constant direct current of 10 mA through it. What is the voltage drop across the inductor?

2. A 20 V dc source is connected to a series *RL* circuit with a switch. At the instant of switch closure, what are the values of v_R and v_L?

3. In the same circuit as in Question 2, after a time interval equal to 5τ from switch closure, what are v_R and v_L?

4. In a series *RL* circuit where $R = 1.0$ kΩ and $L = 500$ μH, what is the time constant? Determine the current 0.25 μs after a switch connects 10 V across the circuit.

14–6 ■ INDUCTORS IN AC CIRCUITS

You will learn in this section that an inductor passes ac but with an amount of opposition called inductive reactance that depends on the frequency of the ac.

After completing this section, you should be able to

■ **Analyze inductive ac circuits**
  • Explain why an inductor causes a phase shift between voltage and current
  • Define *inductive reactance*
  • Determine the value of inductive reactance in a given circuit
  • Discuss instantaneous, true, and reactive power in an inductor

The concept of the derivative was introduced in Chapter 13. The expression for induced voltage in an inductor was stated earlier in Equation (14–1). This formula is $v_{ind} = L(di/dt)$.

Phase Relationship of Current and Voltage in an Inductor

From Equation (14–1), the formula for induced voltage, you can see that the faster the current through an inductor changes, the greater the induced voltage will be. For example, if the rate of change of current is zero, the voltage is zero [$v_{ind} = L(di/dt) = L(0) = 0$ V]. When di/dt is a positive-going maximum, v_{ind} is a positive maximum; when di/dt is a negative-going maximum, v_{ind} is a negative maximum.

A sinusoidal current always induces a sinusoidal voltage in inductive circuits. Therefore, the voltage can be plotted with respect to the current by knowing the points on the current curve at which the voltage is zero and those at which it is maximum. This phase relationship is shown in Figure 14–31(a). Notice that the voltage leads the current by 90°. This is always true in a purely inductive circuit. The current and voltage of this relationship is shown by the phasors in Figure 14–31(b).

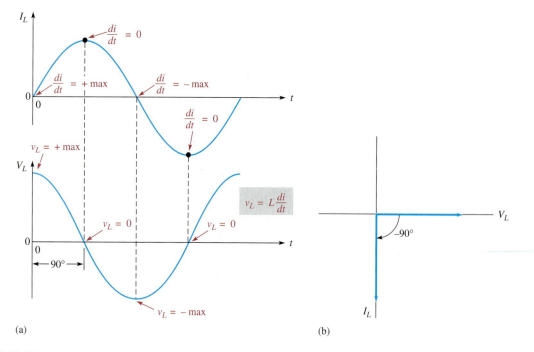

FIGURE 14–31

Phase relation of V_L and I_L in an inductor. Current always lags the inductor voltage by 90°.

Inductive Reactance, X_L

Inductive reactance is the opposition to sinusoidal current, expressed in ohms. The symbol for inductive reactance is X_L.

To develop a formula for X_L, we use the relationship $v_{ind} = L(di/dt)$ and the curves in Figure 14–32. The rate of change of current is directly related to frequency. The faster the current changes, the higher the frequency. For example, you can see that in Figure 14–32, the slope of sine wave A at the zero crossings is greater than that of sine wave B. Recall that the slope of a curve at a point indicates the rate of change at that point. Sine wave A has a higher frequency than sine wave B, as indicated by a greater maximum rate of change (di/dt is greater at the zero crossings).

FIGURE 14–32

Slope indicates rate of change. Sine wave A has a greater rate of change at the zero crossing than B, and thus A has a higher frequency.

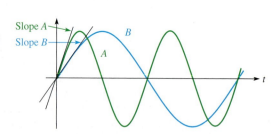

When frequency increases, di/dt increases, and thus v_{ind} increases. When frequency decreases, di/dt decreases, and thus v_{ind} decreases. The induced voltage is directly dependent on frequency.

$$v_{ind} = L(di/dt) \qquad \text{and} \qquad v_{ind} = L(di/dt)$$

An increase in induced voltage means more opposition (X_L is greater). Therefore, X_L is directly proportional to induced voltage and thus directly proportional to frequency.

X_L is proportional to f.

Now, if di/dt is constant and the inductance is varied, an increase in L produces an increase in v_{ind}, and a decrease in L produces a decrease in v_{ind}.

$$v_{ind} = L(di/dt) \qquad \text{and} \qquad v_{ind} = L(di/dt)$$

Again, an increase in v_{ind} means more opposition (greater X_L). Therefore, X_L is directly proportional to induced voltage and thus directly proportional to inductance. The inductive reactance is directly proportional to both f and L.

X_L is proportional to fL.

The complete formula (derived in Appendix C) for inductive reactance, X_L, is

$$X_L = 2\pi f L \qquad\qquad (14\text{--}15)$$

Notice that 2π appears as a constant factor in the equation. This comes from the relationship of a sine wave to rotational motion. X_L is in ohms when f is in hertz and L is in henries.

EXAMPLE 14–13   A sinusoidal voltage is applied to the circuit in Figure 14–33. The frequency is 1 kHz. Determine the inductive reactance.

FIGURE 14–33

Solution   Convert 1 kHz to 1×10^3 Hz and 5 mH to 5×10^{-3} H. Therefore, the inductive reactance is

$$X_L = 2\pi f L = 2\pi(1 \times 10^3 \text{ Hz})(5 \times 10^{-3} \text{ H}) = \textbf{31.4 } \Omega$$

Related Problem   What is X_L in Figure 14–33 if the frequency is increased to 3.5 kHz?

Analysis of Inductive AC Circuits

As you have seen, the current lags the voltage by 90° in inductive ac circuits. If the applied voltage is assigned a reference phase angle of 0°, it can be expressed in polar form as $V_s \angle 0°$. The resulting current can be expressed in polar form as $I \angle -90°$ or in rectangular form as $-jI$, as shown in Figure 14–34.

FIGURE 14–34

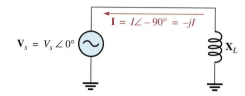

Ohm's law applies to ac circuits with inductive reactance with R replaced by $\mathbf{X}_L$ in the Ohm's law formula. The quantities are expressed as complex numbers because of the introduction of phase angles. Applying Ohm's law to the circuit in Figure 14–34 gives the following result:

$$\mathbf{X}_L = \frac{V_s \angle 0°}{I \angle -90°} = \left(\frac{V_s}{I}\right) \angle 90°$$

This shows that $\mathbf{X}_L$ always has a 90° angle attached to its magnitude and is written as $X_L \angle 90°$ or jX_L.

EXAMPLE 14–14   Determine the rms current in Figure 14–35.

FIGURE 14–35

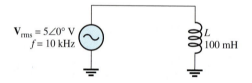

Solution   Convert 10 kHz to 10×10^3 Hz and 100 mH to 100×10^{-3} H. Then calculate the magnitude of X_L.

$$X_L = 2\pi f L = 2\pi (10 \times 10^3 \text{ Hz})(100 \times 10^{-3} \text{ H}) = 6283 \ \Omega$$

Expressed in polar form, X_L is

$$\mathbf{X}_L = 6283 \angle 90° \ \Omega$$

Apply Ohm's law to determine the rms current.

$$\mathbf{I}_{\text{rms}} = \frac{\mathbf{V}_{\text{rms}}}{\mathbf{X}_L} = \frac{5 \angle 0° \text{ V}}{6283 \angle 90° \ \Omega} = \mathbf{796} \angle -\mathbf{90°} \ \mu\mathbf{A}$$

Related Problem   Determine the rms current in Figure 14–35 for the following values: $\mathbf{V}_{\text{rms}} = 12 \angle 0°$ V, $f = 4.9$ kHz, and $L = 680 \ \mu$H.

Power in an Inductor

As discussed earlier, an inductor stores energy in its magnetic field when there is current through it. An ideal inductor (assuming no winding resistance) does not dissipate energy; it only stores it. When an ac voltage is applied to an ideal inductor, energy is stored by the inductor during a portion of the cycle; then the stored energy is returned to the source during another portion of the cycle. There is no net energy loss in an ideal inductor due to conversion to heat. Figure 14–36 shows the power curve that results from one cycle of inductor current and voltage.

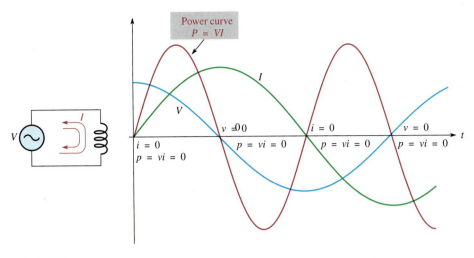

FIGURE 14–36
Power curve.

Instantaneous Power (p) The product of v and i gives instantaneous power, p. At points where v or i is zero, p is also zero. When both v and i are positive, p is also positive. When either v or i is positive and the other negative, p is negative. When both v and i are negative, p is positive. As you can see in Figure 14–36, the power follows a sinusoidal-shaped curve. Positive values of power indicate that energy is stored by the inductor. Negative values of power indicate that energy is returned from the inductor to the source. Note that the power fluctuates at a frequency twice that of the voltage or current as energy is alternately stored and returned to the source.

True Power (P_true) Ideally, all of the energy stored by an inductor during the positive portion of the power cycle is returned to the source during the negative portion. No net energy is consumed in the inductance, so the true power is zero. Actually, because of winding resistance in a practical inductor, some power is always dissipated; and there is a very small amount of true power, which can normally be neglected.

$$P_{\text{true}} = (I_{\text{rms}})^2 R_W \tag{14–16}$$

Reactive Power (P_r) The rate at which an inductor stores or returns energy is called its **reactive power**, P_r, with the unit of VAR (volt-ampere reactive). The reactive power is a nonzero quantity, because at any instant in time, the inductor is actually taking energy from the source or returning energy to it. Reactive power does not represent an energy loss due to conversion to heat. The following formulas apply:

$$P_r = V_{\text{rms}} I_{\text{rms}} \tag{14–17}$$

$$P_r = \frac{V_{\text{rms}}^2}{X_L} \tag{14–18}$$

$$P_r = I_{\text{rms}}^2 X_L \tag{14–19}$$

EXAMPLE 14–15

A 10 V rms signal with a frequency of 1 kHz is applied to a 10 mH coil with a negligible winding resistance. Determine the reactive power (P_r).

Solution First, calculate the inductive reactance and current values.

$$X_L = 2\pi fL = 2\pi(1 \text{ kHz})(10 \text{ mH}) = 62.8 \ \Omega$$

$$I = \frac{V_S}{X_L} = \frac{10 \text{ V}}{62.8 \ \Omega} = 159 \text{ mA}$$

Then, use Equation (14–19).

$$P_r = I^2X_L = (159 \text{ mA})^2(62.8 \ \Omega) = \textbf{1.59 VAR}$$

Related Problem What happens to the reactive power if the frequency increases?

The Quality Factor (Q) of a Coil

The quality factor (Q) is the ratio of the reactive power in the inductor to the true power in the winding resistance of the coil or the resistance in series with the coil. It is a ratio of the power in L to the power in R_W. The quality factor is very important in resonant circuits, which are studied in Chapter 18. A formula for Q is developed as follows:

$$Q = \frac{\text{reactive power}}{\text{true power}} = \frac{I^2X_L}{I^2R_W}$$

In a series circuit, I is the same in L and R; thus, the I^2 terms cancel, leaving

$$Q = \frac{X_L}{R_W} \qquad (14\text{–}20)$$

When the resistance is just the winding resistance of the coil, the circuit Q and the coil Q are the same. Note that Q is a ratio of like units and, therefore, has no unit itself.

SECTION 14–6 REVIEW

1. State the phase relationship between current and voltage in an inductor.
2. Calculate X_L for $f = 5$ kHz and $L = 100$ mH.
3. At what frequency is the reactance of a 50 μH inductor equal to 800 Ω?
4. Calculate the rms current in Figure 14–37.
5. An ideal 50 mH inductor is connected to a 12 V rms source. What is the true power? What is the reactive power at a frequency of 1 kHz?

FIGURE 14–37

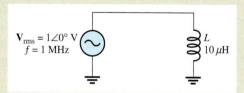

$\mathbf{V}_{rms} = 1\angle0° \text{ V}$
$f = 1 \text{ MHz}$

L
$10 \ \mu H$

14–7 ■ INDUCTOR APPLICATIONS

Inductors are not as versatile as capacitors and tend to be more limited in their applications due, in part, to size and cost factors. However, there are many practical uses for inductors (coils) such as those discussed in Chapter 10. Recall that relay and solenoid coils, recording and pick-up heads, and sensing elements were introduced as electromagnetic applications of coils. In this section, some additional uses of inductors are presented.

After completing this section, you should be able to

■ **Discuss some inductor applications**
  • Describe a power supply filter
  • Explain the purpose of an RF choke
  • Discuss the basics of tuned circuits

Power Supply Filter

In Chapter 13, you saw that a capacitor is used to filter the pulsating dc in a power supply. The final output voltage was a dc voltage with a small amount of ripple. In some types of power supplies, an inductor is used in the filter, as shown in Figure 14–38(a), to smooth out the ripple voltage. The inductor, placed in series with the load as shown, tends to oppose the current fluctuations caused by the ripple voltage, and thus the voltage developed across the load is more constant, as shown in Figure 14–38(b).

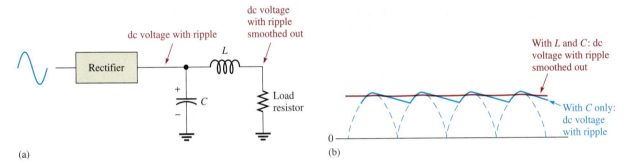

FIGURE 14–38
Basic capacitor power supply filter with a series inductor.

RF Choke

Certain types of inductors called **chokes** are used in applications where radio frequencies (RF) must be prevented from getting into parts of a system, such as the power supply or the audio section of a receiver. In these situations, an inductor is used as a series filter which "chokes" off any unwanted RF signals that may be picked up on a line. This filtering action is based on the fact that the reactance of a coil increases with frequency. When the frequency of the current is sufficiently high, the reactance of the coil becomes extremely large and essentially blocks the current. A basic illustration of an inductor used as an RF choke is shown in Figure 14–39.

FIGURE 14–39
An inductor used as an RF choke to minimize interfering signals on the power supply line.

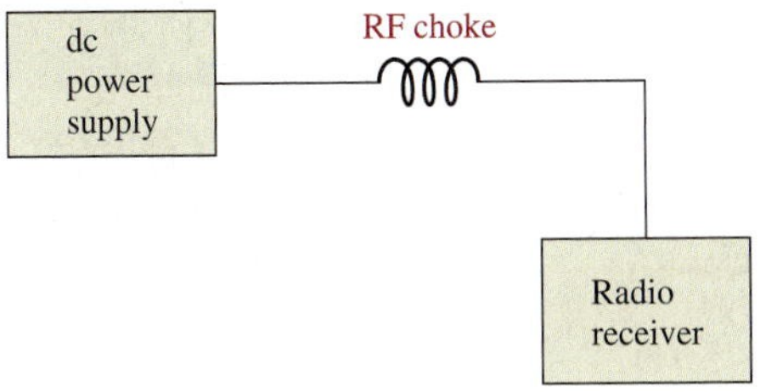

Tuned Circuits

Inductors are used in conjunction with capacitors to provide frequency selection in communications systems. These tuned circuits allow a narrow band of frequencies to be selected while all other frequencies are rejected. The tuners in your TV and radio receivers are based on this principle and permit you to select one channel or station out of the many that are available.

Frequency selectivity is based on the fact that the reactances of both capacitors and inductors depend on the frequency and on the interaction of these two components when connected in series or parallel. Since the capacitor and the inductor produce opposite phase shifts, their combined opposition to current can be used to obtain a desired response at a selected frequency. Tuned *RLC* circuits are covered in Chapter 18.

<table>
<tr><td>

SECTION 14–7 REVIEW

</td><td>

1. Explain how the ripple voltage from a power supply filter can be reduced through use of an inductor.

2. How does an inductor connected in series act as an RF choke?

</td></tr>
</table>

14–8 ■ TESTING INDUCTORS

In this section, two basic types of failures in inductors are discussed and methods for testing inductors are introduced.

After completing this section, you should be able to

■ **Test an inductor**
  • Perform an ohmmeter check for an open winding
  • Perform an ohmmeter check for shorted windings

The most common failure in an inductor is an open. To check for an open, the coil should be removed from the circuit. If there is an open, an ohmmeter check will indicate infinite resistance, as shown in Figure 14–40(a). If the coil is good, the ohmmeter will show the winding resistance. The value of the winding resistance depends on the wire size and length of the coil. It can be anywhere from one ohm to several hundred ohms. Figure 14–40(b) shows a good reading.

(a) Coil open: Meter reads infinity

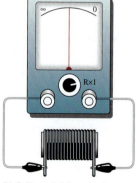

(b) Coil good: Meter reads winding resistance

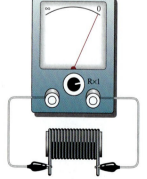

(c) Shorted windings: Meter may read zero or a lower than normal winding resistance depending on the number of turns that are shorted

FIGURE 14–40
Checking a coil by measuring the resistance.

Occasionally, when an inductor is overheated with excessive current, the wire insulation will melt, and two or more turns will short together. This must be tested on an *LC* meter because, with two shorted turns (or even several), an ohmmeter check may show the coil to be perfectly good from a resistance standpoint. Two shorted turns occur more frequently because the turns are adjacent and can easily short across from poor insulation, voltage breakdown, or simple wear if something is rubbing on them. Usually, a few shorted turns will have negligible effect on a circuit.

<table>
<tr><td>SECTION 14–8
REVIEW</td><td>1. When a coil is checked, a reading of infinity on the ohmmeter indicates a partial short. (T or F)

2. An ohmmeter check of a good coil will indicate the value of the inductance. (T or F)</td></tr>
</table>

14–9 ■ TECHnology Theory Into Practice

In this TECH TIP section, you will test coils for their unknown inductance values using a test setup consisting of a square wave generator and an oscilloscope.

You are given two coils for which the inductance values are not known. The coils are to be tested using simple laboratory instruments to determine the inductance values. The method is to place the coil in series with a resistor with a known value and measure the time constant. Knowing the time constant and the resistance value, the value of *L* can be calculated.

The method of determining the time constant is to apply a square wave to the circuit and measure the resulting voltage across the resistor. Each time the square wave input voltage goes high, the inductor is energized and each time the square wave goes back to zero, the inductor is deenergized. The time it takes for the exponential resistor voltage to increase to approximately its final value equals five time constants. This operation is illustrated in Figure 14–41. To make sure that the winding resistance of the coil can be neglected, it must be measured and the value of the resistor used in the circuit must be selected to be considerably larger than the winding resistance.

FIGURE 14–41
Circuit for time-constant measurement.

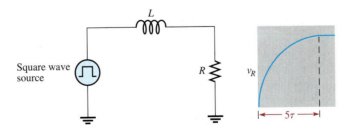

The Winding Resistance

Assume that the winding resistance of the coil in Figure 14–42 has been measured with an ohmmeter and found to be 85 Ω. To make the winding resistance negligible for time constant measurement, a 10 kΩ series resistor is used in the circuit.

■ If 10 V dc is connected with the clip leads as shown, how much current is in the circuit after $t = 5\tau$?

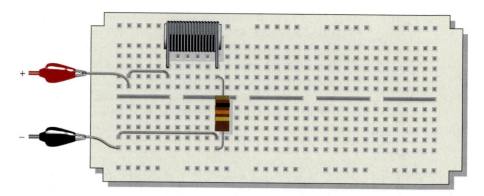

FIGURE 14–42
Breadboard setup for measuring the time constant.

Inductance of Coil 1

Refer to Figure 14–43. To measure the inductance of coil 1, a square wave voltage is applied to the circuit. The amplitude of the square wave is adjusted to 10 V. The frequency is adjusted so that the inductor has time to fully energize during each square wave pulse; the scope is set to view a complete energizing curve as shown.

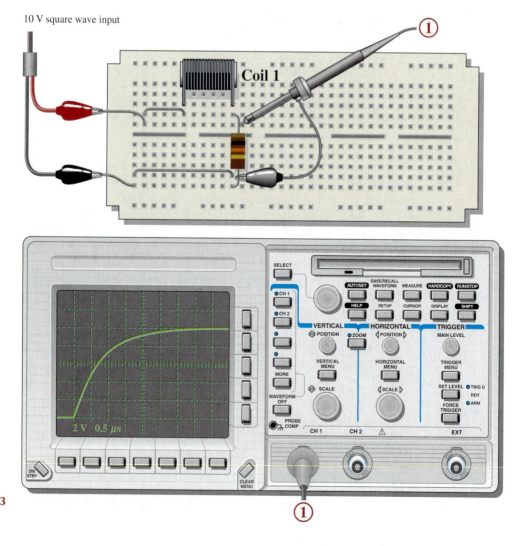

FIGURE 14–43
Testing coil 1.

- Determine the approximate circuit time constant.
- Calculate the inductance of coil 1.

The Inductance of Coil 2

Refer to Figure 14–44 in which coil 2 replaces coil 1. To determine the inductance, a 10 V square wave is applied to the breadboarded circuit. The frequency of the square wave is adjusted so that the inductor has time to fully energize during each square wave pulse; the scope is set to view a complete energizing curve as shown.

- Determine the approximate circuit time constant.
- Calculate the inductance of coil 2.
- Discuss any difficulty in using this method.
- Specify how you can use a sinusoidal input voltage instead of a square wave to determine inductance.

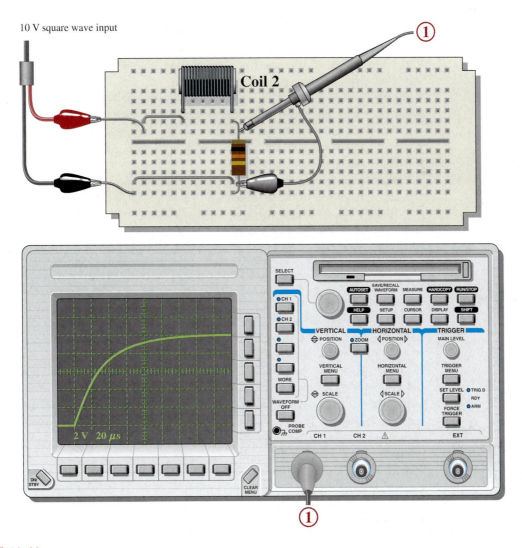

FIGURE 14–44
Testing coil 2.

SECTION 14–9 REVIEW

1. What is the maximum square wave frequency that can be used in Figure 14–43?

2. What is the maximum square wave frequency that can be used in Figure 14–44?

3. What happens if the frequency exceeds the maximum you determined in Questions 1 and 2? Explain how your measurements would be affected.

■ SUMMARY

- Self-inductance is a measure of a coil's ability to establish an induced voltage as a result of a change in its current.
- An inductor opposes a change in its own current.
- Faraday's law states that relative motion between a magnetic field and a coil induces a voltage across the coil.
- The amount of induced voltage is directly proportional to the inductance and to the rate of change in current.
- Lenz's law states that the polarity of induced voltage is such that the resulting induced current is in a direction that opposes the change in the magnetic field that produced it.
- Energy is stored by an inductor in its magnetic field.
- One henry is the amount of inductance when current, changing at the rate of one ampere per second, induces one volt across the inductor.
- Inductance is directly proportional to the square of the number of turns, the permeability, and the cross-sectional area of the core. It is inversely proportional to the length of the core.
- The permeability of a core material is an indication of the ability of the material to establish a magnetic field.
- The time constant for a series RL circuit is the inductance divided by the resistance.
- In an RL circuit, the voltage and current in an energizing or deenergizing inductor make a 63% change during each time-constant interval.
- Energizing and deenergizing follow exponential curves.
- Inductors add in series.
- Total parallel inductance is less than that of the smallest inductor in parallel.
- Voltage leads current by 90° in an inductor.
- X_L is directly proportional to frequency and inductance.
- The true power in an inductor is zero; that is, there is no energy loss in an ideal inductor due to conversion to heat, only in its winding resistance.

■ GLOSSARY

These terms are also in the end-of-book glossary.

Choke A type of inductor used to block or choke off high frequencies.

Core The structure around which the winding of an inductor is formed. The core material influences the electromagnetic characteristics of the inductor.

Henry (H) The unit of inductance.

Induced voltage Voltage produced as a result of a changing magnetic field.

Inductance The property of an inductor that produces an opposition to any change in current.

Inductive reactance The opposition of an inductor to sinusoidal current. The unit is the ohm.

Inductor An electrical device formed by a wire wound around a core having the property of inductance; also known as *coil*.

Lenz's law A physical law that states when the current through a coil changes, an induced voltage is created in a direction to oppose the change in current. The current cannot change instantaneously.

Reactive power (P_r) The rate at which energy is alternately stored and returned to the source by an inductor. The unit is the volt-ampere reactive (VAR).

Time constant A fixed time interval, set by the L and R values, that determines the time response of a circuit.

Winding The loops or turns of wire in an inductor.

■ FORMULAS

(14–1)	$v_{ind} = L\left(\dfrac{di}{dt}\right)$	Induced voltage
(14–2)	$W = \dfrac{1}{2}LI^2$	Energy stored by an inductor
(14–3)	$L = \dfrac{N^2\mu A}{l}$	Inductance in terms of physical parameters
(14–4)	$v_{ind} = N\left(\dfrac{d\phi}{dt}\right)$	Faraday's law
(14–5)	$L_T = L_1 + L_2 + L_3 + \cdots + L_n$	Series inductance
(14–6)	$\dfrac{1}{L_T} = \dfrac{1}{L_1} + \dfrac{1}{L_2} + \dfrac{1}{L_3} + \cdots + \dfrac{1}{L_n}$	Reciprocal of total parallel inductance
(14–7)	$L_T = \dfrac{1}{\left(\dfrac{1}{L_1}\right) + \left(\dfrac{1}{L_2}\right) + \left(\dfrac{1}{L_3}\right) + \cdots + \left(\dfrac{1}{L_n}\right)}$	Total parallel inductance
(14–8)	$L_T = \dfrac{L_1 L_2}{L_1 + L_2}$	Total inductance of two inductors in parallel
(14–9)	$L_T = \dfrac{L}{n}$	Total inductance of equal-value inductors in parallel
(14–10)	$\tau = \dfrac{L}{R}$	Time constant
(14–11)	$v = V_F + (V_i - V_F)e^{-Rt/L}$	Exponential voltage (general)
(14–12)	$i = I_F + (I_i - I_F)e^{-Rt/L}$	Exponential current (general)
(14–13)	$i = I_F(1 - e^{-Rt/L})$	Increasing exponential current beginning at zero
(14–14)	$i = I_i e^{-Rt/L}$	Decreasing exponential current ending at zero
(14–15)	$X_L = 2\pi f L$	Inductive reactance
(14–16)	$P_{true} = (I_{rms})^2 R_W$	True power
(14–17)	$P_r = V_{rms} I_{rms}$	Reactive power
(14–18)	$P_r = \dfrac{V_{rms}^2}{X_L}$	Reactive power
(14–19)	$P_r = I_{rms}^2 X_L$	Reactive power
(14–20)	$Q = \dfrac{X_L}{R_W}$	Quality factor

■ SELF-TEST

1. An inductance of 0.05 μH is larger than
   (a) 0.0000005 H   (b) 0.000005 H   (c) 0.000000008 H   (d) 0.00005 mH

2. An inductance of 0.33 mH is smaller than
   (a) 33 μH   (b) 330 μH   (c) 0.05 mH   (d) 0.0005 H

3. When the current through an inductor increases, the amount of energy stored in the electromagnetic field
   (a) decreases   (b) remains constant   (c) increases   (d) doubles

4. When the current through an inductor doubles, the stored energy
   (a) doubles   (b) quadruples   (c) is halved   (d) does not change

5. The winding resistance of a coil can be decreased by
   (a) reducing the number of turns   (b) using a larger wire
   (c) changing the core material   (d) either answer (a) or (b)

6. The inductance of an iron-core coil increases if
    (a) the number of turns is increased   (b) the iron core is removed
    (c) the length of the core is increased   (d) larger wire is used

7. Four 10 mH inductors are in series. The total inductance is
    (a) 40 mH   (b) 2.5 mH   (c) 40,000 μH   (d) answers (a) and (c)

8. A 1 mH, a 3.3 mH, and a 0.1 mH inductor are connected in parallel. The total inductance is
    (a) 4.4 mH   (b) greater than 3.3 mH
    (c) less than 0.1 mH   (d) answers (a) and (b)

9. An inductor, a resistor, and a switch are connected in series to a 12 V battery. At the instant the switch is closed, the inductor voltage is
    (a) 0 V   (b) 12 V   (c) 6 V   (d) 4 V

10. A sinusoidal voltage is applied across an inductor. When the frequency of the voltage is increased, the current
    (a) decreases   (b) increases
    (c) does not change   (d) momentarily goes to zero

11. An inductor and a resistor are in series with a sinusoidal voltage source. The frequency is set so that the inductive reactance is equal to the resistance. If the frequency is increased, then
    (a) $V_R > V_L$ (b) $V_L < V_R$ (c) $V_L = V_R$ (d) $V_L > V_R$

12. An ohmmeter is connected across an inductor and the pointer indicates an infinite value. The inductor is
    (a) good   (b) open   (c) shorted   (d) resistive

▪ PROBLEMS

More difficult problems are indicated by an asterisk (*).

SECTION 14–1   The Basic Inductor

1. Convert the following to millihenries:
    (a) 1 H   (b) 250 μH   (c) 10 μH   (d) 0.0005 H

2. Convert the following to microhenries:
    (a) 300 mH   (b) 0.08 H   (c) 5 mH   (d) 0.00045 mH

3. What is the voltage across a coil when $di/dt = 10$ mA/μs and $L = 5$ μH?

4. Fifty volts are induced across a 25 mH coil. At what rate is the current changing?

5. The current through a 100 mH coil is changing at a rate of 200 mA/s. How much voltage is induced across the coil?

6. How many turns are required to produce 30 mH with a coil wound on a cylindrical core having a cross-sectional area of 10×10^{-5} m^2 and a length of 0.05 m? The core has a permeability of 1.2×10^{-6}.

7. A 12 V battery is connected across a coil with a winding resistance of 12 Ω. How much current is there in the coil?

8. How much energy is stored by a 100 mH inductor with a current of 1 A?

SECTION 14–3   Series Inductors

9. Five inductors are connected in series. The lowest value is 5 μH. If the value of each inductor is twice that of the preceding one, and if the inductors are connected in order of ascending values, what is the total inductance?

10. Suppose that you require a total inductance of 50 mH. You have available a 10 mH coil and a 22 mH coil. How much additional inductance do you need?

11. Determine the total inductance in Figure 14–45.

12. What is the total inductance between points A and B for each switch position in Figure 14–46?

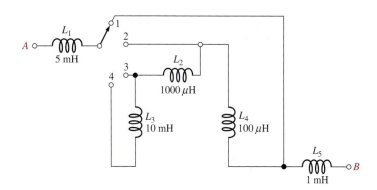

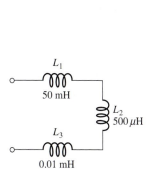

FIGURE 14–45

FIGURE 14–46

SECTION 14–4 Parallel Inductors

13. Determine the total parallel inductance for the following coils in parallel: 75 μH, 50 μH, 25 μH, and 15 μH.

14. You have a 12 mH inductor, and it is your smallest value. You need an inductance of 8 mH. What value can you use in parallel with the 12 mH to obtain 8 mH?

15. Determine the total inductance of each circuit in Figure 14–47.

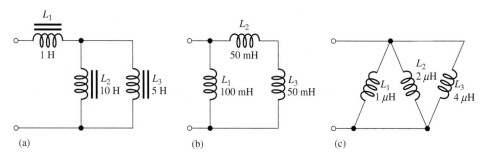

FIGURE 14–47

16. Determine the total inductance of each circuit in Figure 14–48.

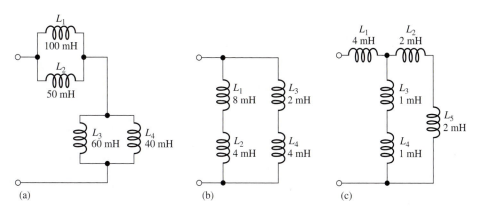

FIGURE 14–48

SECTION 14–5 Inductors in DC Circuits

17. Determine the time constant for each of the following series *RL* combinations:

   (a) $R = 100 \ \Omega$, $L = 100 \ \mu$H   **(b)** $R = 4.7 \ k\Omega$, $L = 10$ mH

   (c) $R = 1.5 \ M\Omega$, $L = 3$ H

18. In a series *RL* circuit, determine how long it takes the current to build up to its full value for each of the following:

   (a) $R = 56\ \Omega$, $L = 50\ \mu H$ (b) $R = 3300\ \Omega$, $L = 15$ mH

   (c) $R = 22$ kΩ, $L = 100$ mH

19. In the circuit of Figure 14–49, there is initially no current. Determine the inductor voltage at the following times after the switch is closed:

   (a) 10 μs   (b) 20 μs   (c) 30 μs   (d) 40 μs   (e) 50 μs

*20. In Figure 14–50, there are 114 mA through the coil. When SW1 is opened and SW2 simultaneously closed, find the inductor voltage at the following times:

   (a) Initially   (b) 1.7 ms   (c) 5.1 ms   (d) 6.8 ms

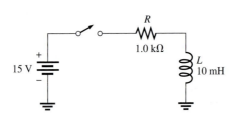

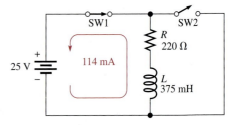

FIGURE 14–49   **FIGURE 14–50**

21. Repeat Problem 19 for the following times:

   (a) 2 μs   (b) 5 μs   (c) 15 μs

*22. Repeat Problem 20 for the following times:

   (a) 0.5 ms   (b) 1 ms   (c) 2 ms

23. In Figure 14–49, at what time after switch closure does the inductor voltage reach 5 V?

24. What is the polarity of the induced voltage in Figure 14–51 when the switch is closed? What is the final value of current if $R_W = 10\ \Omega$?

FIGURE 14–51

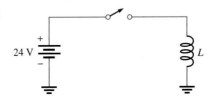

*25. Determine the time constant for the circuit in Figure 14–52.

FIGURE 14–52

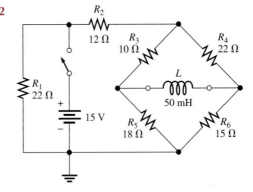

*26. Find the inductor current at 10 μs after the switch is thrown from position 1 to position 2 in Figure 14–53. For simplicity, assume that the switch makes contact with position 2 at the same instant it breaks contact with position 1.

FIGURE 14–53

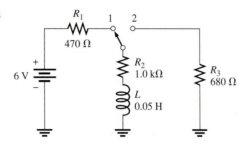

*27. In Figure 14–54, switch 1 is opened and switch 2 is closed at the same instant (t_0). What is the instantaneous voltage across R_2 at t_0?

FIGURE 14–54

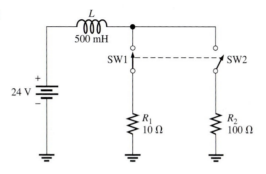

SECTION 14–6   Inductors in AC Circuits

28. Find the total reactance for each circuit in Figure 14–47 when a voltage with a frequency of 5 kHz is applied across the terminals.

29. Find the total reactance for each circuit in Figure 14–48 when a 400 Hz voltage is applied.

30. Determine the total rms current in Figure 14–55. What are the currents through L_2 and L_3? Express all currents in polar form.

FIGURE 14–55

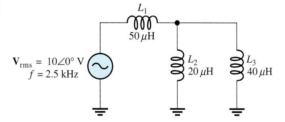

31. What frequency will produce 500 mA total rms current in each circuit of Figure 14–48 with an rms input voltage of 10 V?

32. Determine the reactive power in Figure 14–55.

33. Determine $\mathbf{I}_{L2}$ in Figure 14–56.

FIGURE 14–56

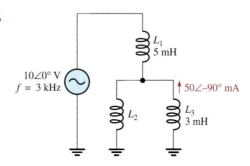

SECTION 14–8 Testing Inductors

34. A certain coil that is supposed to have a 5 Ω winding resistance is measured with an ohm-meter. The meter indicates 2.8 Ω. What is the problem with the coil?

35. What is the indication corresponding to each of the following failures in a coil?

   (a) open   **(b)** completely shorted   **(c)** some windings shorted

EWB Troubleshooting and Analysis

These problems require your EWB compact disk.

36. Open file PRO14-36.EWB and measure the voltage across each inductor.

37. Open file PRO14-37.EWB and measure the voltage across each inductor.

38. Open file PRO14-38.EWB and measure the current. Double the frequency and measure the current again. Reduce the original frequency by one-half and measure the current. Explain your observations.

39. Open file PRO14-39.EWB and determine the fault if there is one.

40. Open file PRO14-40.EWB and find the fault if there is one.

■ **ANSWERS TO SECTION REVIEWS**

Section 14–1

1. Inductance depends on number of turns of wire, permeability, cross-sectional area, and core length.

2. $v_{ind} = 7.5$ mV

3. **(a)** L increases when N increases.   **(b)** L decreases when core length increases.

   (c) L decreases when core cross-sectional area decreases.

   (d) L decreases when ferromagnetic core is replaced by air core.

4. All wire has some resistance, and because inductors are made from turns of wire, there is always resistance.

5. Adjacent turns in a coil act as plates of a capacitor.

Section 14–2

1. Two categories of inductors are fixed and variable.

2. **(a)** air core   **(b)** iron core   **(c)** variable

Section 14–3

1. Inductances are added in series.

2. $L_T = 2.60$ mH

3. $L_T = 5(100$ mH$) = 500$ mH

Section 14–4

1. The total parallel inductance is smaller than that of the smallest-value inductor in parallel.

2. True, calculation of parallel inductance is similar to parallel resistance.

3. **(a)** $L_T = 7.69$ mH   **(b)** $L_T = 24$ μH   **(c)** $L_T = 100$ mH

Section 14–5

1. $V_L = IR_W = 100$ mV

2. $v_R = 0$ V, $v_L = 20$ V

3. $v_R = 20$ V, $v_L = 0$ V

4. $\tau = 500$ ns, $i_L = 3.93$ mA

Section 14–6

1. Voltage leads current by 90 degrees in an inductor.

2. $X_L = 2\pi fL = 3.14$ kΩ

3. $f = X_L/2\pi L = 2.55$ MHz

4. $I_{rms} = 15.9\angle{-90°}$ mA

5. $P_{true} = 0$ W; $P_r = 458$ mVAR

Section 14–7

1. The inductor tends to level out the ripple voltage because of its opposition to changes in current.

2. The inductive reactance is extremely high at radio frequencies, thus blocking signals with these frequencies.

Section 14–8

1. False, a reading of infinity indicates an open.

2. False, it indicates the winding resistance.

Section 14–9

1. $f_{max} = 125$ kHz $(5\tau = 4$ ms$)$

2. $f_{max} = 3.13$ kHz $(5\tau = 160$ μs$)$

3. If $f > f_{max}$, the inductor will not fully energize because $T/2 < 5\tau$.

■ **ANSWERS TO RELATED PROBLEMS FOR EXAMPLES**

14–1	5 H
14–2	10.8 mH
14–3	0.5 Wb/s
14–4	500 μH
14–5	20.3 μH
14–6	**(a)** 7.30 μH
	(b) 20 μH
14–7	227 ns
14–8	$I_F = 29.4$ mA, $\tau = 147$ ns;
	at 1τ, $i = 18.5$ mA;
	at 2τ, $i = 25.3$ mA;
	at 3τ, $i = 27.9$ mA;
	at 4τ, $i = 28.8$ mA;
	at 5τ, $i = 29.1$ mA

14–9	**(a)** 21.3 μs
	(b) 106 mA
	(c) 39.2 mA
14–10	**(a)** 9 V, 0 V
	(b) 92.6 V, 0 V
14–11	3.82 mA
14–12	33.3 mA
14–13	110 Ω
14–14	574 $\angle{-90°}$ mA
14–15	P_r decreases.

■ **ANSWERS TO SELF-TEST**

1. (c)	**2.** (d)	**3.** (c)	**4.** (b)	**5.** (d)	**6.** (a)	**7.** (d)	**8.** (c)
9. (b)	**10.** (a)	**11.** (d)	**12.** (b)				

15

TRANSFORMERS

Electronics Workbench (EWB) and
PSpice Tutorials at
http://www.prenhall.com/floyd

■ INTRODUCTION

In Chapter 14, you learned about self-inductance. In this chapter, you will study mutual inductance, which is the basis for the operation of transformers. Transformers are used in all types of applications such as power supplies, electrical power distribution, and signal coupling in communications systems.

The operation of the transformer is based on the principle of mutual inductance, which occurs when two or more coils are in close proximity. A simple transformer is actually two coils that are electromagnetically coupled by their mutual inductance. Because there is no electrical contact between two magnetically coupled coils, the transfer of energy from one coil to the other can be achieved in a situation of complete electrical isolation. This has many advantages, as you will learn in this chapter.

In the TECH TIP assignment in Section 15–12, you will troubleshoot a power supply transformer.

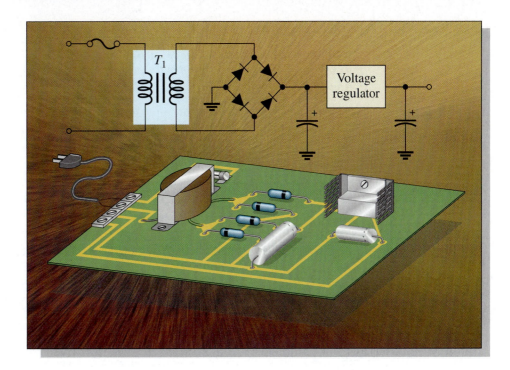

■ CHAPTER OBJECTIVES

❑ Explain mutual inductance
❑ Describe how a transformer is constructed and how it operates
❑ Explain how a step-up transformer works
❑ Explain how a step-down transformer works
❑ Discuss the effect of a resistive load across the secondary winding
❑ Discuss the concept of a reflected load in a transformer

❑ Discuss impedance matching with transformers
❑ Explain how the transformer acts as an isolation device
❑ Describe a practical transformer
❑ Describe several types of transformers
❑ Troubleshoot transformers

15–1 ■ MUTUAL INDUCTANCE

When two coils are placed close to each other, a changing electromagnetic field produced by the current in one coil will cause an induced voltage in the second coil because of the mutual inductance.

After completing this section, you should be able to

■ **Explain mutual inductance**
  • Discuss magnetic coupling
  • Define *electrical isolation*
  • Define *coefficient of coupling*
  • Identify the factors that affect mutual inductance and state the formula

Recall that the electromagnetic field surrounding a coil expands, collapses, and reverses as the current increases, decreases, and reverses.

When a second coil is placed very close to the first coil so that the changing magnetic flux lines cut through the second coil, the coils are magnetically coupled and a voltage is induced, as indicated in Figure 15–1. When two coils are magnetically coupled, they provide **electrical isolation** because there is no electrical connection between them, only a magnetic link. If the current in the first coil is a sine wave, the voltage induced in the second coil is also a sine wave. The amount of voltage induced in the second coil as a result of the current in the first coil is dependent on the **mutual inductance, L_M,** between the two coils. The mutual inductance is established by the inductance of each coil (L_1 and L_2) and by the amount of coupling (k) between the two coils. To maximize coupling, the two coils are wound on a common core.

FIGURE 15–1

A voltage is induced in the second coil as a result of the changing current in the first coil, producing a changing electromagnetic field that links the second coil.

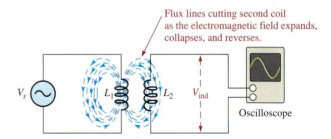

Flux lines cutting second coil as the electromagnetic field expands, collapses, and reverses.

Oscilloscope

Coefficient of Coupling

The **coefficient of coupling, k,** between two coils is the ratio of the lines of force (flux) produced by coil 1 linking coil 2 ($\phi_{1\text{-}2}$) to the total flux produced by coil 1 (ϕ_1).

$$k = \frac{\phi_{1\text{-}2}}{\phi_1}$$

(15–1)

For example, if half of the total flux produced by coil 1 links coil 2, then $k = 0.5$. A greater value of k means that more voltage is induced in coil 2 for a certain rate of change of current in coil 1. Note that k has no units. Recall that the unit of magnetic lines of force (flux) is the weber, abbreviated Wb.

The coefficient of coupling, k, depends on the physical closeness of the coils and the type of core material on which they are wound. Also, the construction and shape of the cores are factors.

Formula for Mutual Inductance

The three factors influencing L_M (k, L_1, and L_2) are shown in Figure 15–2. The formula for mutual inductance is

$$L_M = k\sqrt{L_1 L_2} \tag{15-2}$$

FIGURE 15–2
The mutual inductance of two coils.

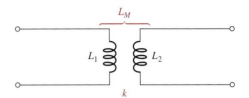

EXAMPLE 15–1

One coil produces a total magnetic flux of 50 μWb, and 20 μWb link coil 2. What is the coefficient of coupling, k?

Solution
$$k = \frac{\phi_{1\text{-}2}}{\phi_1} = \frac{20\ \mu\text{Wb}}{50\ \mu\text{Wb}} = \textbf{0.4}$$

Related Problem Determine k when $\phi_1 = 500\ \mu$Wb and $\phi_{1\text{-}2} = 375\ \mu$Wb.

EXAMPLE 15–2

Two coils are wound on a single core, and the coefficient of coupling is 0.3. The inductance of coil 1 is 10 μH, and the inductance of coil 2 is 15 μH. What is L_M?

Solution $\quad L_M = k\sqrt{L_1 L_2} = 0.3\sqrt{(10\ \mu\text{H})(15\ \mu\text{H})} = \textbf{3.67}\ \boldsymbol{\mu}\textbf{H}$

Related Problem Determine the mutual inductance when $k = 0.5$, $L_1 = 1$ mH, and $L_2 = 600\ \mu$H.

**SECTION 15–1
REVIEW**

1. Define *mutual inductance*.
2. Two 50 mH coils have $k = 0.9$. What is L_M?
3. If k is increased, what happens to the voltage induced in one coil as a result of a current change in the other coil?

15–2 ■ THE BASIC TRANSFORMER

A basic transformer is an electrical device constructed of two coils placed in close proximity to each other so that there is a mutual inductance.

After completing this section, you should be able to

■ **Describe how a transformer is constructed and how it operates**
  • Identify the parts of a basic transformer
  • Discuss the importance of the core material
  • Define *primary winding* and *secondary winding*
  • Define *turns ratio*
  • Discuss how the direction of windings affects voltage polarities

A schematic of a **transformer** is shown in Figure 15–3(a). As shown, one coil is called the **primary winding,** and the other is called the **secondary winding.** The source voltage is applied to the primary winding, and the load is connected to the secondary winding, as shown in Figure 15–3(b). So, the primary winding is the input winding, and the secondary winding is the output winding.

FIGURE 15–3
The basic transformer.

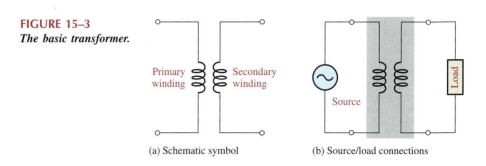

Primary winding   Secondary winding

Source   Load

(a) Schematic symbol   (b) Source/load connections

The windings of a transformer are formed around the **core.** The core provides both a physical structure for placement of the windings and a magnetic path so that the magnetic flux lines are concentrated close to the coils. There are three general categories of core material: air, ferrite, and iron. The schematic symbol for each type is shown in Figure 15–4.

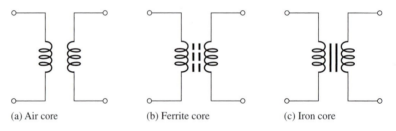

(a) Air core   (b) Ferrite core   (c) Iron core

FIGURE 15–4
Schematic symbols based on type of core.

Air-core and ferrite-core transformers generally are used for high-frequency applications and consist of windings on an insulating shell which is hollow (air) or constructed of ferrite, such as depicted in Figure 15–5. The wire is typically covered by a varnish-type coating to prevent the windings from shorting together. The amount of **magnetic coupling** between the primary winding and the secondary winding is set by the type of core material and by the relative positions of the windings. In Figure 15–5(a), the windings are loosely coupled because they are separated, and in part (b) they are tightly coupled because they are overlapping. The tighter the coupling, the greater the induced voltage in the secondary for a given current in the primary.

Iron-core transformers generally are used for audio frequency (AF) and power applications. These transformers consist of windings on a core constructed from laminated sheets of ferromagnetic material insulated from each other, as shown in Figure 15–6. This construction provides an easy path for the magnetic flux and increases the amount of coupling between the windings. Figure 15–6(a) and 15–6(b) show the basic construction of two major configurations of iron-core transformers. In the core-type construction, shown in part (a), the windings are on separate legs of the laminated core. In the shell-type construction, shown in part (b), both windings are on the same leg. A variety of transformers are shown in Figure 15–7. Each type has certain advantages. Generally, the core type has more room for insulation and can handle higher voltages. The shell type can produce higher magnetic fluxes in the core, resulting in the need for fewer turns.

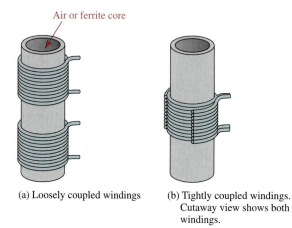

Air or ferrite core

(a) Loosely coupled windings

(b) Tightly coupled windings. Cutaway view shows both windings.

FIGURE 15–5
Transformers with cylindrical-shaped cores.

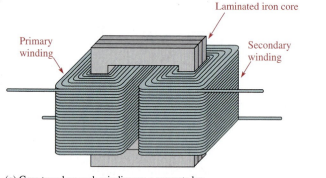

Laminated iron core

Primary winding

Secondary winding

Laminated iron core

(a) Core type has each winding on a separate leg.

(b) Shell type has both windings on the same leg.

FIGURE 15–6
Iron-core transformer construction with multilayer windings.

FIGURE 15–7
Some common types of transformers.

Turns Ratio

A transformer parameter that is very useful in understanding how a transformer operates is the turns ratio. In this text, the **turns ratio (*n*)** is defined as the ratio of the number of turns in the secondary winding (N_{sec}) to the number of turns in the primary winding (N_{pri}).

$$n = \frac{N_{sec}}{N_{pri}} \tag{15-3}$$

Although the definition of turns ratio stated by Equation (15–3) is used in this text, there seems, unfortunately, to be no universal agreement on how the turns ratio is defined. Many sources state that the turns ratio is N_{sec}/N_{pri}, while others use N_{pri}/N_{sec}. Either definition is correct as long as it is clearly stated and used consistently. The turns ratio of a transformer is rarely if ever given as a transformer specification. Generally, the input and output voltages and the power rating are the key specifications. However, the turns ratio is useful in studying the operating principle of a transformer.

EXAMPLE 15–3

A transformer primary winding has 100 turns, and the secondary winding has 400 turns. What is the turns ratio?

Solution $N_{sec} = 400$ and $N_{pri} = 100$; therefore, the turns ratio is

$$n = \frac{N_{sec}}{N_{pri}} = \frac{400}{100} = 4$$

Related Problem A certain transformer has a turns ratio of 10. If $N_{pri} = 500$, what is N_{sec}?

Direction of Windings

Another important transformer parameter is the direction in which the windings are placed around the core. As illustrated in Figure 15–8, the direction of the windings determines the polarity of the voltage across the secondary winding (secondary voltage) with respect to the voltage across the primary winding (primary voltage). Phase dots are used on the schematic symbols to indicate polarities, as shown in Figure 15–9.

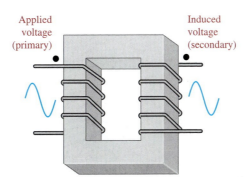
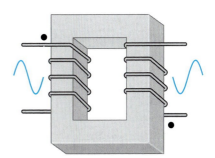

Applied voltage (primary)   Induced voltage (secondary)

(a) The primary and secondary voltages are in phase when the windings are in the same effective direction around the magnetic path.

(b) The primary and secondary voltages are 180° out of phase when the windings are in the opposite direction.

FIGURE 15–8

The direction of the windings determines the relative polarities of the voltages.

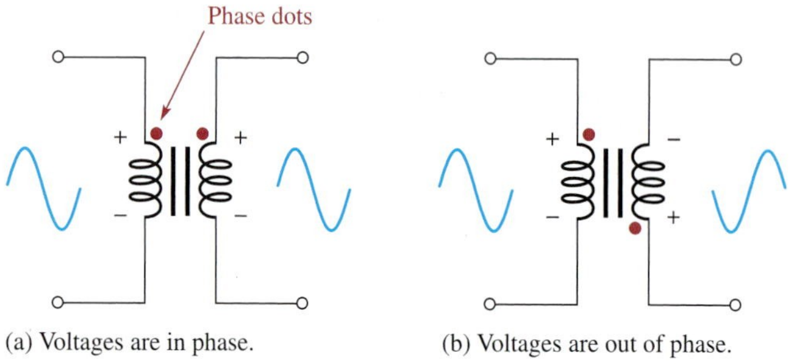

Phase dots

(a) Voltages are in phase. (b) Voltages are out of phase.

FIGURE 15–9
Phase dots indicate relative polarities of primary and secondary voltages.

SECTION 15–2 REVIEW

1. Upon what principle is the operation of a transformer based?
2. Define *turns ratio*.
3. Why are the directions of the windings of a transformer important?
4. A certain transformer has a primary winding with 500 turns and a secondary winding with 250 turns. What is the turns ratio?

15–3 ▪ STEP-UP TRANSFORMERS

A step-up transformer has more turns in its secondary winding than in its primary winding and is used to increase ac voltage.

After completing this section, you should be able to

▪ **Explain how a step-up transformer works**
  • State the relationship between primary and secondary voltages and the number of turns in the primary and secondary windings
  • Identify a step-up transformer by its turns ratio

A transformer in which the secondary voltage is greater than the primary voltage is called a **step-up transformer.** The amount that the voltage is stepped up depends on the turns ratio.

The ratio of secondary voltage (V_{sec}) to primary voltage (V_{pri}) is equal to the ratio of the number of turns in the secondary winding (N_{sec}) to the number of turns in the primary winding (N_{pri}).

$$\frac{V_{sec}}{V_{pri}} = \frac{N_{sec}}{N_{pri}}$$

(15–4)

From this relationship,

$$V_{sec} = \left(\frac{N_{sec}}{N_{pri}}\right) V_{pri}$$

(15–5)

Equation (15–5) shows that the secondary voltage is equal to the turns ratio (or reciprocal of turns ratio if you define it to be N_{pri}/N_{sec}) times the primary voltage. This condition assumes that the coefficient of coupling is 1, and a good iron core transformer approaches this value.

The turns ratio for a step-up transformer is always greater than 1 because the number of turns in the secondary winding (N_{sec}) is always greater than the number of turns in the primary winding (N_{pri}).

EXAMPLE 15–4

The transformer in Figure 15–10 has a 200 turn primary winding and a 600 turn secondary winding. What is the voltage across the secondary winding?

FIGURE 15–10

Solution   The secondary voltage is

$$V_{sec} = \left(\frac{N_{sec}}{N_{pri}}\right)V_{pri} = \left(\frac{600}{200}\right)120\ \text{V} = (3)120\ \text{V} = \mathbf{360\ V}$$

Note that the turns ratio of 3 is indicated on the schematic as 1:3, meaning that there are three secondary turns for each primary turn.

Related Problem   The transformer in Figure 15–10 is changed to one with $N_{pri} = 75$ and $N_{sec} = 300$. Determine V_{sec}.

SECTION 15–3 REVIEW

1. What does a step-up transformer do?
2. If the turns ratio is 5, how much greater is the secondary voltage than the primary voltage?
3. When 240 V ac are applied to the primary winding of a transformer with a turns ratio of 10, what is the secondary voltage?

15–4 ■ STEP-DOWN TRANSFORMERS

A step-down transformer has more turns in its primary winding than in its secondary winding and is used to decrease ac voltage.

After completing this section, you should be able to

■ **Explain how a step-down transformer works**
  • Identify a step-down transformer by its turns ratio

A transformer in which the secondary voltage is less than the primary voltage is called a **step-down transformer.** The amount by which the voltage is stepped down depends on the turns ratio. Equation (15–5) applies also to a step-down transformer.

The turns ratio of a step-down transformer is always less than 1 because the number of turns in the secondary winding is always fewer than the number of turns in the primary winding.

EXAMPLE 15–5   The transformer in Figure 15–11 has 500 turns in the primary winding and 100 turns in the secondary winding. What is the secondary voltage?

FIGURE 15–11

Solution   The secondary voltage is

$$V_{sec} = \left(\frac{N_{sec}}{N_{pri}}\right)V_{pri} = \left(\frac{100}{500}\right)120 \text{ V} = (0.2)120 \text{ V} = \mathbf{24 \text{ V}}$$

Related Problem   The transformer in Figure 15–11 is changed to one with $N_{pri} = 250$ and $N_{sec} = 120$. Determine the secondary voltage.

SECTION 15–4 REVIEW

1. What does a step-down transformer do?
2. A voltage of 120 V ac is applied to the primary winding of a transformer with a turns ratio of 0.5. What is the secondary voltage?
3. A primary voltage of 120 V ac is reduced to 12 V ac. What is the turns ratio?

15–5 ■ LOADING THE SECONDARY WINDING

When a resistive load is connected to the secondary winding of a transformer, the load current depends on both the primary current and the turns ratio.

After completing this section, you should be able to

■ **Discuss the effect of a resistive load across the secondary winding**
  • Determine the secondary current when a step-up transformer is loaded
  • Determine the secondary current when a step-down transformer is loaded
  • Discuss power in a transformer

When a load resistor is connected to the secondary winding, as shown in Figure 15–12, there is current through the resulting secondary circuit because of the voltage induced in the secondary coil. It can be shown that the ratio of the primary current, I_{pri}, to the secondary current, I_{sec}, is equal to the turns ratio, as expressed in the following equation:

$$\frac{I_{pri}}{I_{sec}} = \frac{N_{sec}}{N_{pri}}$$

(15–6)

FIGURE 15–12

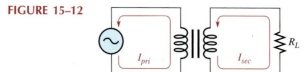

A manipulation of Equation (15–6) gives Equation (15–7), which shows that I_{sec} is equal to I_{pri} times the reciprocal of the turns ratio.

$$I_{sec} = \left(\frac{N_{pri}}{N_{sec}}\right)I_{pri} \tag{15–7}$$

Thus, for a step-up transformer, in which N_{sec}/N_{pri} is greater than 1, the secondary current is less than the primary current. For a step-down transformer, N_{sec}/N_{pri} is less than 1, and I_{sec} is greater than I_{pri}.

EXAMPLE 15–6

The transformers in Figure 15–13(a) and (b) have loaded secondary windings. If the primary current is 100 mA in each case, what is the load current?

FIGURE 15–13

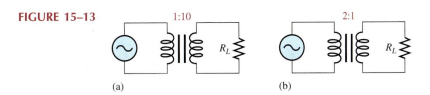

(a)   (b)

Solution   In Figure 15–13(a), the current through the load is

$$I_{sec} = \left(\frac{N_{pri}}{N_{sec}}\right)I_{pri} = (0.1)100 \text{ mA} = \textbf{10 mA}$$

In Figure 15–13(b), the current through the load is

$$I_{sec} = \left(\frac{N_{pri}}{N_{sec}}\right)I_{pri} = (2)100 \text{ mA} = \textbf{200 mA}$$

Related Problem   What is the secondary current in Figure 15–13(a) if the turns ratio is doubled? What is the secondary current in Figure 15–13(b) if the turns ratio is halved? Assume I_{pri} remains the same in both circuits.

Primary Power Equals Load Power

When a load is connected to the secondary winding of a transformer, the power transferred to the load can never be greater than the power in the primary winding. For an ideal transformer, the power delivered to the primary equals the power delivered by the secondary to the load. When losses are considered, some of the power is dissipated in the transformer rather than the load; therefore, the load power is always less than the power delivered to the primary.

Power is dependent on voltage and current, and there can be no increase in power in a transformer. Therefore, if the voltage is stepped up, the current is stepped down and vice versa. In an ideal transformer, the secondary power is equal to the primary power regardless of the turns ratio, as the following equations show. The power delivered to the primary is

$$P_{pri} = V_{pri}I_{pri}$$

and the power delivered to the load is

$$P_{sec} = V_{sec}I_{sec}$$

From Equations (15–7) and (15–5),

$$I_{sec} = \left(\frac{N_{pri}}{N_{sec}}\right)I_{pri} \quad \text{and} \quad V_{sec} = \left(\frac{N_{sec}}{N_{pri}}\right)V_{pri}$$

By substitution,

$$P_{sec} = \left(\frac{\cancel{N}_{pri}}{\cancel{N}_{sec}}\right)\left(\frac{\cancel{N}_{sec}}{\cancel{N}_{pri}}\right)V_{pri}I_{pri}$$

Canceling terms yields

$$P_{sec} = V_{pri}I_{pri} = P_{pri}$$

This result is closely approached in practice by power transformers because of the very high efficiencies.

<table>
<tr>
<td>SECTION 15–5
REVIEW</td>
<td>
1. If the turns ratio of a transformer is 2, is the secondary current greater than or less than the primary current? By how much?

2. A transformer has 1000 turns in its primary winding and 250 turns in its secondary winding, and I_{pri} is 0.5 A. What is the value of I_{sec}?

3. In Problem 2, how much primary current is necessary to produce a secondary load current of 10 A?
</td>
</tr>
</table>

15–6 ■ REFLECTED LOAD

From the viewpoint of the primary circuit, a load connected across the secondary winding of a transformer appears to have a resistance that is not necessarily equal to the actual resistance of the load. The actual load is essentially "reflected" into the primary circuit altered by the turns ratio. This reflected load is what the primary source effectively sees, and it determines the amount of primary current.

After completing this section, you should be able to

■ **Discuss the concept of a reflected load in a transformer**
  • Define *reflected resistance*
  • Explain how the turns ratio affects the reflected resistance
  • Calculate reflected resistance

The concept of the **reflected load** is illustrated in Figure 15–14. The load (R_L) in the secondary circuit of a transformer is reflected into the primary circuit by transformer action. The load appears to the source in the primary circuit to be a resistance (R_{pri}) with a value determined by the turns ratio and the actual value of the load resistance. The resistance R_{pri} is called the **reflected resistance.**

The resistance in the primary circuit of Figure 15–14 is $R_{pri} = V_{pri}/I_{pri}$. The resistance in the secondary circuit is $R_L = V_{sec}/I_{sec}$. From Equations (15–4) and (15–6), you know that $V_{sec}/V_{pri} = N_{sec}/N_{pri}$ and $I_{pri}/I_{sec} = N_{sec}/N_{pri}$. Using these relationships, a formula for R_{pri} in terms of R_L is determined as follows:

$$\frac{R_{pri}}{R_L} = \frac{V_{pri}/I_{pri}}{V_{sec}/I_{sec}} = \left(\frac{V_{pri}}{V_{sec}}\right)\left(\frac{I_{sec}}{I_{pri}}\right) = \left(\frac{N_{pri}}{N_{sec}}\right)\left(\frac{N_{pri}}{N_{sec}}\right) = \frac{N_{pri}^2}{N_{sec}^2} = \left(\frac{N_{pri}}{N_{sec}}\right)^2$$

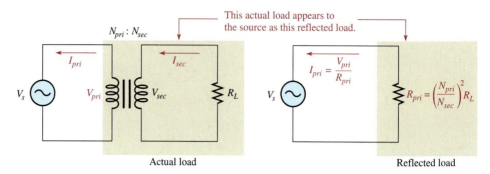

FIGURE 15–14
Reflected load in a transformer circuit.

Solving for R_{pri} yields

$$R_{pri} = \left(\frac{N_{pri}}{N_{sec}}\right)^2 R_L \qquad \text{(15–8)}$$

Equation (15–8) shows that the resistance reflected into the primary circuit is the square of the reciprocal of the turns ratio times the load resistance.

EXAMPLE 15–7

Figure 15–15 shows a source that is transformer-coupled to a load resistor of 100 Ω. The transformer has a turns ratio of 4. What is the reflected resistance seen by the source?

FIGURE 15–15

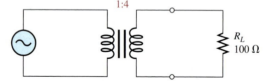

Solution The reflected resistance is determined by Equation (15–8).

$$R_{pri} = \left(\frac{N_{pri}}{N_{sec}}\right)^2 R_L = \left(\frac{1}{4}\right)^2 R_L = \left(\frac{1}{16}\right)100 \ \Omega = \mathbf{6.25 \ \Omega}$$

The source sees a resistance of 6.25 Ω just as if it were connected directly, as shown in the equivalent circuit of Figure 15–16.

FIGURE 15–16

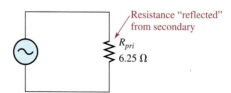

Related Problem If the turns ratio in Figure 15–15 is 10 and R_L is 600 Ω, what is the reflected resistance?

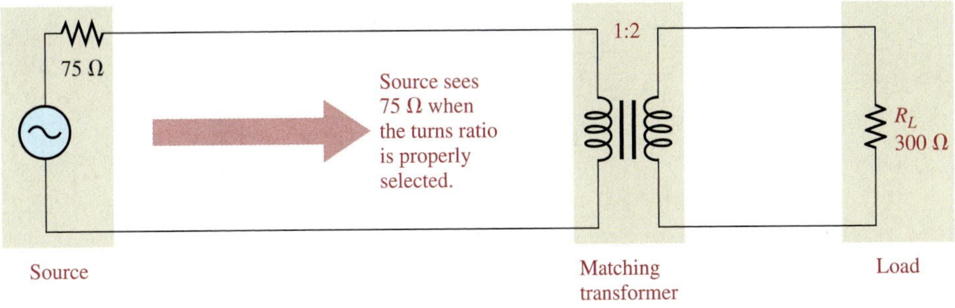

FIGURE 15–19
Example of a load matched to a source by transformer coupling for maximum power transfer.

To match the resistances, that is, to reflect the load resistance (R_L) into the primary circuit so that it appears to have a value equal to the internal source resistance (R_{int}), you must select a proper value of turns ratio (n). You want the 300 Ω load to look like 75 Ω to the source. You can use Equation (15–8) to determine a formula for the turns ratio, N_{sec}/N_{pri}, when you know the values for R_L and R_{pri}, the reflected resistance, as follows:

$$R_{pri} = \left(\frac{N_{pri}}{N_{sec}}\right)^2 R_L$$

Transpose terms and divide both sides by R_L.

$$\left(\frac{N_{pri}}{N_{sec}}\right)^2 = \frac{R_{pri}}{R_L}$$

Take the square root of both sides.

$$\frac{N_{pri}}{N_{sec}} = \sqrt{\frac{R_{pri}}{R_L}}$$

Invert both sides to get the following formula for the turns ratio:

$$n = \frac{N_{sec}}{N_{pri}} = \sqrt{\frac{R_L}{R_{pri}}} \tag{15–9}$$

Finally, solve for this particular turns ratio.

$$n = \frac{N_{sec}}{N_{pri}} = \sqrt{\frac{R_L}{R_{pri}}} = \sqrt{\frac{300\ \Omega}{75\ \Omega}} = \sqrt{4} = 2$$

Therefore, a matching transformer with a turns ratio of 2 must be used in this application.

EXAMPLE 15–9

A certain amplifier has an 800 Ω internal resistance looking from its output. In order to provide maximum power to an 8 Ω speaker, what turns ratio must be used in the coupling transformer?

Solution The reflected resistance must equal 800 Ω. Thus, from Equation (15–9), the turns ratio can be determined.

$$n = \frac{N_{sec}}{N_{pri}} = \sqrt{\frac{R_L}{R_{pri}}} = \sqrt{\frac{8\ \Omega}{800\ \Omega}} = \sqrt{0.01} = \mathbf{0.1}$$

There must be ten primary turns for each secondary turn. The diagram and its equivalent reflected circuit are shown in Figure 15–20.

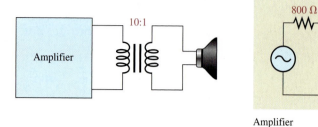

FIGURE 15–20

Related Problem What must be the turns ratio in Figure 15–20 to provide maximum power to two 8 Ω speakers in parallel?

SECTION 15–7 REVIEW

1. What does impedance matching mean?
2. What is the advantage of matching the load resistance to the resistance of a source?
3. A transformer has 100 turns in its primary winding and 50 turns in its secondary winding. What is the reflected resistance with 100 Ω across the secondary winding?

15–8 ■ THE TRANSFORMER AS AN ISOLATION DEVICE

Transformers are useful in providing electrical isolation between the primary circuit and the secondary circuit because there is no electrical connection between the two windings. In a transformer, energy is transferred entirely by magnetic coupling.

After completing this section, you should be able to

■ **Explain how the transformer acts as an isolation device**
  • Discuss dc isolation
  • Discuss power line isolation

DC Isolation

As illustrated in Figure 15–21(a), if there is a direct current in the primary circuit of a transformer, nothing happens in the secondary circuit. The reason is that a changing current in the primary winding is necessary to induce a voltage in the secondary winding, as shown in part(b). Therefore, the transformer isolates the secondary circuit from any dc voltage in the primary circuit.

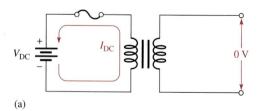

(a)

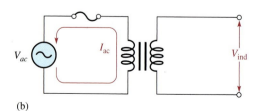

(b)

FIGURE 15–21
DC isolation and ac coupling.

In a typical application, a transformer can be used to keep the dc voltage on the output of an amplifier stage from affecting the dc bias of the next amplifier. Only the ac signal is coupled through the transformer from one stage to the next, as Figure 15–22 illustrates.

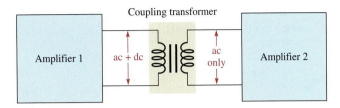

FIGURE 15–22
Amplifier stages with transformer coupling for dc isolation.

Power Line Isolation

Transformers are often used to electrically isolate electronic equipment from the 60 Hz, 110 V ac power line. The reason for using an isolation transformer to couple the 60 Hz ac to an instrument is to prevent a possible shock hazard if the 110 V line is connected to the metal chassis of the equipment. This condition is possible if the line cord plug can be inserted into an outlet either way. Incidentally, to prevent this situation, many plugs have keyed prongs so that they can be plugged in only one way.

Figure 15–23 illustrates how a transformer can prevent the metal chassis from being connected to the 110 V line rather than to neutral (ground), no matter how the cord is plugged into the outlet. When an isolation transformer is used, the secondary circuit is said to be "floating" because it is not referenced to the power line ground. Should a person come in contact with the secondary voltage, there is no complete current path back to ground, and therefore the shock hazard is reduced. There must be current through your body in order for you to receive an electrical shock.

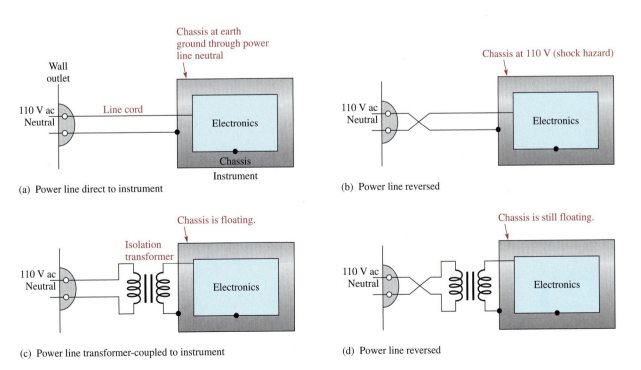

FIGURE 15–23
The use of an isolation transformer to prevent a shock hazard.

SECTION 15–8
REVIEW

1. What does the term *electrical isolation* mean?

2. Can a dc voltage be coupled by a transformer?

15–9 ■ NONIDEAL TRANSFORMER CHARACTERISTICS

Up to this point, transformer operation has been discussed from an ideal point of view, and this approach is valid when you are learning new concepts. However, you should be aware of the nonideal characteristics of practical transformers and how they affect performance.

After completing this section, you should be able to

■ **Describe a practical transformer**
  • List and describe the nonideal characteristics
  • Explain power rating of a transformer
  • Define *efficiency* of a transformer

So far, we have considered the transformer to be an ideal device. That is, the winding resistance, the winding capacitance, and nonideal core characteristics were all neglected and the transformer was treated as if it had an efficiency of 100%. For studying the basic concepts and in many applications, the ideal model is valid. However, the practical transformer has several nonideal characteristics of which you should be aware.

Winding Resistance

Both the primary and the secondary windings of a practical transformer have winding resistance. You learned about the winding resistance of inductors in Chapter 14. The winding resistances of a practical transformer are represented as resistors in series with the windings as shown in Figure 15–24.

FIGURE 15–24
Winding resistances in a practical transformer.

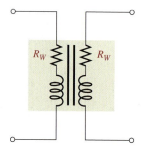

Winding resistance in a practical transformer results in less voltage across a secondary load. Voltage drops due to the winding resistance effectively subtract from the primary and secondary voltages and result in load voltage that is less than that predicted by the relationship $V_{sec} = (N_{sec}/N_{pri})V_{pri}$. In many cases, the effect is relatively small and can be neglected.

Losses in the Core

There is always some energy conversion in the core material of a practical transformer. This conversion is seen as a heating of ferrite and iron cores, but it does not occur in air cores. Part of this energy conversion is because of the continuous reversal of the magnetic field due to the changing direction of the primary current; this component of the energy conversion is called *hysteresis loss*. The rest of the energy conversion to heat is caused by eddy currents produced when voltage is induced in the core material by the changing magnetic flux, according to Faraday's law. The eddy currents occur in circular patterns in the core resistance, thus producing heat. This conversion to heat is greatly reduced by the use of laminated construction of iron cores. The thin layers of ferromagnetic material are insulated from each other to minimize the buildup of eddy currents by confining them to a small area and to keep core losses to a minimum.

Magnetic Flux Leakage

In an ideal transformer, all of the magnetic flux produced by the primary current is assumed to pass through the core to the secondary winding, and vice versa. In a practical transformer, some of the magnetic flux lines break out of the core and pass through the surrounding air back to the other end of the winding, as illustrated in Figure 15–25 for the magnetic field produced by the primary current. Magnetic flux leakage results in a reduced secondary voltage.

FIGURE 15–25

Flux leakage in a practical transformer.

Leakage flux

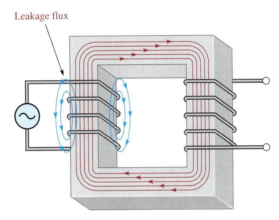

The percentage of magnetic flux that actually reaches the secondary winding determines the coefficient of coupling of the transformer. For example, if nine out of ten flux lines remain inside the core, the coefficient of coupling is 0.90 or 90%. Most iron-core transformers have very high coefficients of coupling (greater than 0.99), while ferrite-core and air-core devices have lower values.

Winding Capacitance

As you learned in Chapter 14, there is always some stray capacitance between adjacent turns of a winding. These stray capacitances result in an effective capacitance in parallel with each winding of a transformer, as indicated in Figure 15–26.

FIGURE 15–26

Winding capacitance in a practical transformer.

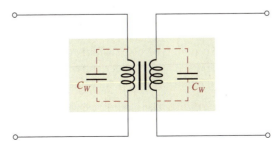

These stray capacitances have very little effect on the transformer's operation at low frequencies (such as power line frequencies) because the reactances (X_C) are very high. However, at higher frequencies, the reactances decrease and begin to produce a bypassing effect across the primary winding and across the secondary load. As a result, less of the total primary current is through the primary winding, and less of the total secondary current is through the load. This effect reduces the load voltage as the frequency goes up.

Transformer Power Rating

A transformer is typically rated in volt-amperes (VA), primary/secondary voltage, and operating frequency. For example, a given transformer rating may be specified as 2 kVA, 500/50, 60 Hz. The 2 kVA value is the **apparent power rating.** The 500 and the 50 can be either secondary or primary voltages. The 60 Hz is the operating frequency.

The transformer rating can be helpful in selecting the proper transformer for a given application. Let's assume, for example, that 50 V is the secondary voltage. In this case the load current is

$$I_L = \frac{P_{sec}}{V_{sec}} = \frac{2 \text{ kVA}}{50 \text{ V}} = 40 \text{ A}$$

On the other hand, if 500 V is the secondary voltage, then

$$I_L = \frac{P_{sec}}{V_{sec}} = \frac{2 \text{ kVA}}{500 \text{ V}} = 4 \text{ A}$$

These are the maximum currents that the secondary can handle in either case.

The reason that the power rating is in volt-amperes (apparent power) rather than in watts (true power) is as follows: If the transformer load is purely capacitive or purely inductive, the true power (watts) delivered to the load is zero. However, the current for $V_{sec} = 500$ V and $X_C = 100 \ \Omega$ at 60 Hz, for example, is 5 A. This current exceeds the maximum that the 2 kVA secondary can handle, and the transformer may be damaged. So it is meaningless to specify power in watts.

Transformer Efficiency

Recall that the power delivered to the load is equal to the power delivered to the primary in an ideal transformer. Because the nonideal characteristics just discussed result in a power loss in the transformer, the secondary (output) power is always less than the primary (input) power. The **efficiency** (η) of a transformer is a measure of the percentage of the input power that is delivered to the output.

$$\eta = \left(\frac{P_{out}}{P_{in}}\right)100\% \qquad \text{(15–10)}$$

Most power transformers have efficiencies in excess of 95% under load.

EXAMPLE 15–10   A certain type of transformer has a primary current of 5 A and a primary voltage of 4800 V. The secondary current is 90 A, and the secondary voltage is 240 V. Determine the efficiency of this transformer.

Solution   The input power is

$$P_{in} = V_{pri}I_{pri} = (4800 \text{ V})(5 \text{ A}) = 24 \text{ kVA}$$

The output power is

$$P_{out} = V_{sec}I_{sec} = (240 \text{ V})(90 \text{ A}) = 21.6 \text{ kVA}$$

The efficiency is

$$\eta = \left(\frac{P_{out}}{P_{in}}\right)100\% = \left(\frac{21.6 \text{ kVA}}{24 \text{ kVA}}\right)100\% = \mathbf{90\%}$$

Related Problem   A transformer has a primary current of 8 A with a primary voltage of 440 V. The secondary current is 30 A and the secondary voltage is 100 V. What is the efficiency?

SECTION 15–9 REVIEW

1. Explain how a practical transformer differs from the ideal model.
2. The coefficient of coupling of a certain transformer is 0.85. What does this mean?
3. A certain transformer has a rating of 10 kVA. If the secondary voltage is 250 V, how much load current can the transformer handle?

15–10 ■ OTHER TYPES OF TRANSFORMERS

There are several important variations of the basic transformer. They include tapped transformers, multiple-winding transformers, and autotransformers.

After completing this section, you should be able to

■ **Describe several types of transformers**
  • Describe center-tapped transformers
  • Describe multiple-winding transformers
  • Describe autotransformers

Tapped Transformers

A schematic of a transformer with a center-tapped secondary winding is shown in Figure 15–27(a). The **center tap (CT)** is equivalent to two secondary windings with half the total voltage across each.

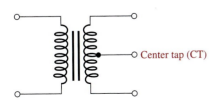

(a) Center-tapped transformer

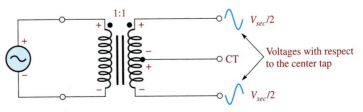

(b) Output voltages with respect to the center tap are 180° out of phase with each other and are one-half the magnitude of the secondary voltage.

FIGURE 15–27
Operation of a center-tapped transformer.

The voltages between either end of the secondary winding and the center tap are, at any instant, equal in magnitude but opposite in polarity, as illustrated in Figure 15–27(b). Here, for example, at some instant on the sinusoidal voltage, the polarity across the entire secondary winding is as shown (top end +, bottom −). At the center tap, the voltage is less positive than the top end but more positive than the bottom end of the secondary. Therefore, measured with respect to the center tap, the top end of the secondary is positive, and the bottom end is negative. This center-tapped feature is used in power supply rectifiers in which the ac voltage is converted to dc, as illustrated in Figure 15–28.

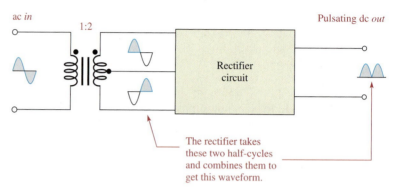

FIGURE 15–28
Application of a center-tapped transformer in ac-to-dc conversion.

Some tapped transformers have taps on the secondary winding at points other than the electrical center. Also, single and multiple primary and secondary taps are sometimes used in certain applications, such as impedance-matching transformers that normally have a center-tapped primary. Examples of these types of transformers are shown in Figure 15–29.

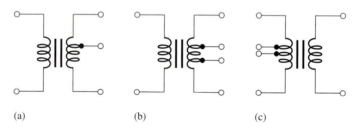

(a)   (b)   (c)

FIGURE 15–29
Tapped transformers.

One example of a transformer with a multiple-tap primary winding and a center-tapped secondary winding is the utility-pole transformer used by power companies to step down the high voltage from the power line to 110 V/220 V service for residential and commercial customers, as shown in Figure 15–30. The multiple taps on the primary winding are used for minor adjustments in the turns ratio in order to overcome line voltages that are slightly too high or too low.

Multiple-Winding Transformers

Some transformers are designed to operate from either 110 V ac or 220 V ac lines. These transformers usually have two primary windings, each of which is designed for 110 V ac. When the two are connected in series, the transformer can be used for 220 V ac operations, as illustrated in Figure 15–31.

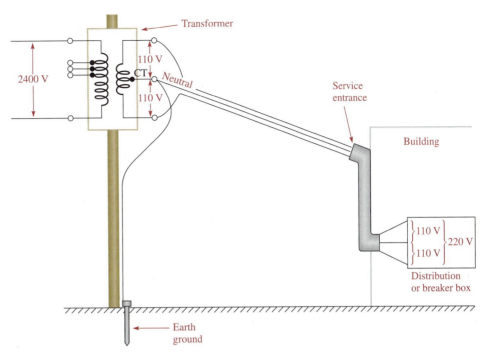

FIGURE 15–30
Utility-pole transformer in a typical power distribution system.

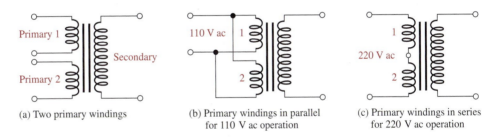

(a) Two primary windings

(b) Primary windings in parallel
for 110 V ac operation

(c) Primary windings in series
for 220 V ac operation

FIGURE 15–31
Multiple-primary transformer.

   More than one secondary can be wound on a common core. Transformers with several secondary windings are often used to achieve several voltages by either stepping up or stepping down the primary voltage. These types are commonly used in power supply applications in which several voltage levels are required for the operation of an electronic instrument.

   A typical schematic of a multiple-secondary transformer is shown in Figure 15–32; this transformer has three secondaries. Sometimes you will find combinations of multiple-primary, multiple-secondary, and tapped transformers all in one unit.

FIGURE 15–32

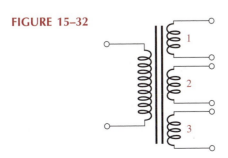

EXAMPLE 15–11 The transformer shown in Figure 15–33 has the numbers of turns indicated. One of the secondaries is also center tapped. If 120 V ac are connected to the primary, determine each secondary voltage and the voltages with respect to the center tap (CT) on the middle secondary.

FIGURE 15–33

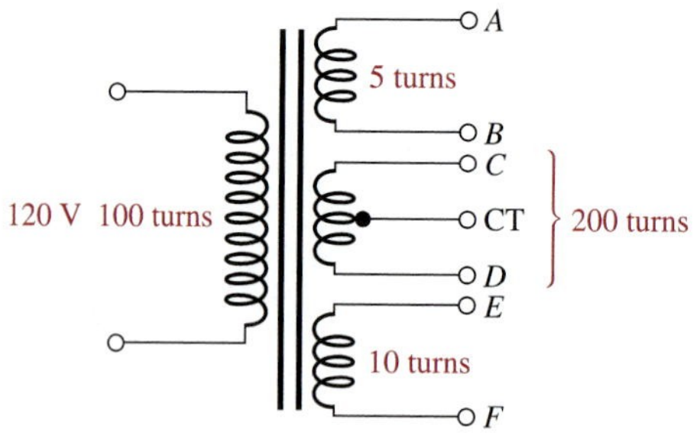

Solution

$$V_{AB} = \left(\frac{N_{sec}}{N_{pri}}\right) V_{pri} = \left(\frac{5}{100}\right) 120 \text{ V} = \textbf{6 V}$$

$$V_{CD} = \left(\frac{200}{100}\right) 120 \text{ V} = \textbf{240 V}$$

$$V_{(CT)C} = V_{(CT)D} = \frac{240 \text{ V}}{2} = \textbf{120 V}$$

$$V_{EF} = \left(\frac{10}{100}\right) 120 \text{ V} = \textbf{12 V}$$

Related Problem   Repeat the calculations for a primary with 50 turns.

Autotransformers

In an **autotransformer,** one winding serves as both the primary and the secondary. The winding is tapped at the proper points to achieve the desired turns ratio for stepping up or stepping down the voltage.

Autotransformers differ from conventional transformers in that there is no electrical isolation between the primary and the secondary because both are on one winding. Autotransformers normally are smaller and lighter than equivalent conventional transformers because they require a much lower kVA rating for a given load. Many autotransformers provide an adjustable tap using a sliding contact mechanism so that the output voltage can be varied (these are often called *variacs*). Figure 15–34 shows schematic symbols for various types of auto transformers.

Example 15–12 illustrates why an autotransformer has a kVA requirement that is less than the input or output kVA.

FIGURE 15–34
The variable autotransformer.

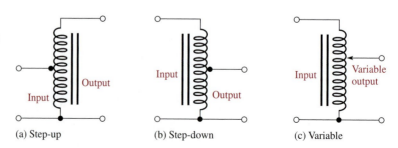

(a) Step-up   (b) Step-down   (c) Variable

EXAMPLE 15–12   A certain autotransformer is used to change a source voltage of 220 V to a load voltage of 160 V across an 8 Ω load resistance. Determine the input and output power in kilovolt-amperes, and show that the actual kVA requirement is less than this value. Assume that this transformer is ideal.

Solution   The circuit is shown in Figure 15–35 with voltages and currents indicated.

FIGURE 15–35

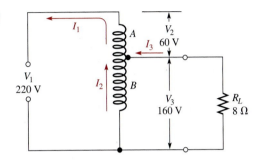

The load current, I_3, is determined as

$$I_3 = \frac{V_3}{R_L} = \frac{160 \text{ V}}{8 \text{ Ω}} = 20 \text{ A}$$

The input power is the total source voltage (V_1) times the total current from the source (I_1).

$$P_{in} = V_1 I_1$$

The output power is the load voltage, V_3, times the load current, I_3.

$$P_{out} = V_3 I_3$$

For an ideal transformer, $P_{in} = P_{out}$; thus,

$$V_1 I_1 = V_3 I_3$$

Solving for I_1 yields

$$I_1 = \frac{V_3 I_3}{V_1} = \frac{(160 \text{ V})(20 \text{ A})}{220 \text{ V}} = 14.55 \text{ A}$$

Applying Kirchhoff's current law at the tap junction,

$$I_1 = I_2 + I_3$$

Solving for I_2, the current through winding B, yields

$$I_2 = I_1 - I_3 = 14.55 \text{ A} - 20 \text{ A} = -5.45 \text{ A}$$

The minus sign can be dropped because the current directions are arbitrary.
    The input and output power are

$$P_{in} = P_{out} = V_3 I_3 = (160 \text{ V})(20 \text{ A}) = \textbf{3.2 kVA}$$

The power in winding A is

$$P_A = V_2 I_1 = (60 \text{ V})(14.55 \text{ A}) = 873 \text{ VA} = 0.873 \text{ kVA}$$

The power in winding B is

$$P_B = V_3 I_2 = (160 \text{ V})(5.45 \text{ A}) = 872 \text{ VA} = 0.872 \text{ kVA}$$

Thus, the power rating required for each winding is less than the power that is delivered to the load. The slight difference in the calculated powers in windings A and B is due to rounding.

Related Problem What happens to the kVA requirement if the load is changed to 4 Ω?

SECTION 15–10 REVIEW

1. A certain transformer has two secondary windings. The turns ratio from the primary winding to the first secondary is 10. The turns ratio from the primary to the other secondary is 0.2. If 240 V ac are applied to the primary, what are the secondary voltages?

2. Name one advantage and one disadvantage of an autotransformer over a conventional transformer.

15–11 ■ TROUBLESHOOTING TRANSFORMERS

Transformers are very simple and reliable devices when they are operated within their specified range. The common failures in transformers are opens in either the primary or the secondary windings. One cause of such failures is the operation of the device under conditions that exceed its ratings. A few transformer failures and the associated symptoms are covered in this section.

After completing this section, you should be able to

■ **Troubleshoot transformers**
   • Find an open primary or secondary winding
   • Find a shorted or partially shorted primary or secondary winding

Open Primary Winding

When there is an open primary winding, there is no primary current and, therefore, no induced voltage or current in the secondary. This condition is illustrated in Figure 15–36(a), and the method of checking with an ohmmeter is shown in part (b).

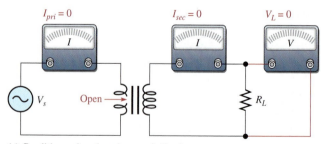

(a) Conditions when the primary winding is open

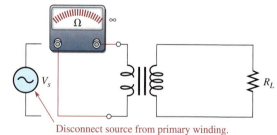

Disconnect source from primary winding.

(b) Checking the primary winding with an ohmmeter

FIGURE 15–36
Open primary winding.

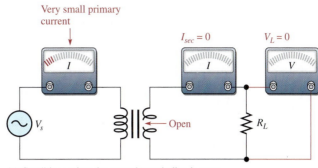

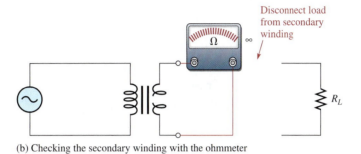

(a) Conditions when the secondary winding is open

(b) Checking the secondary winding with the ohmmeter

FIGURE 15–37
Open secondary winding.

Open Secondary Winding

When there is an open secondary winding, there is no current in the secondary circuit and, as a result, no voltage across the load. Also, an open secondary causes the primary current to be very small (there is only a small magnetizing current). In fact, the primary current may be practically zero. This condition is illustrated in Figure 15–37(a), and the ohmmeter check is shown in part (b).

Shorted or Partially Shorted Primary Winding

Although shorted windings are very unlikely and if they do occur are very difficult to find, a brief discussion follows. A completely shorted primary winding will draw excessive current from the source; and unless there is a breaker or a fuse in the circuit, either the source or the transformer or both will burn out. A partial short in the primary winding can cause higher than normal or even excessive primary current.

Shorted or Partially Shorted Secondary Winding

In the case of a shorted or partially shorted secondary winding, there is an excessive primary current because of the low reflected resistance due to the short. Often, this excessive current will burn out the primary winding and result in an open. The short-circuit current in the secondary winding causes the load current to be zero (full short) or smaller than normal (partial short), as demonstrated in Figure 15–38(a) and 15–38(b). The ohmmeter check for this condition is shown in part (c).

Normally, when a transformer fails, it is very difficult to repair, and therefore the simplest procedure is to replace it.

FIGURE 15–38
Shorted secondary winding.

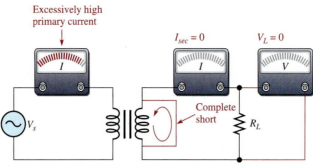

(a) Secondary winding completely shorted

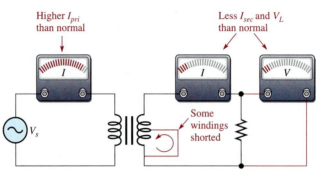

(b) Secondary winding partially shorted

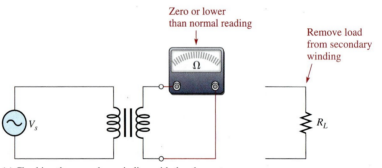

(c) Checking the secondary winding with the ohmmeter

SECTION 15–11
REVIEW

1. Name two possible failures in a transformer and state the most likely one.
2. What is often the cause of transformer failure?

15–12 ■ TECHnology Theory Into Practice

A common application of the transformer is in dc power supplies. The transformer is used to couple the ac line voltage into the power supply circuitry where it is converted to a dc voltage. Your assignment is to troubleshoot four identical transformer-coupled dc power supplies and, based on a series of measurements, determine the fault, if any, in each.

The transformer (T) in the power supply schematic of Figure 15–39 steps the 110 V rms at the ac outlet down to a level that can be converted by the diode bridge rectifier, filtered, and regulated to obtain a 6 V dc output. The diode rectifier changes the ac to a pulsating full-wave dc voltage that is smoothed by the capacitor filter C_1. The voltage regulator is an integrated circuit that takes the filtered voltage and provides a constant 6 V dc over a range of load values and line voltage variations. Additional filtering is provided by capacitor C_2. You will learn about these circuits in a later course. The circled numbers in Figure 15–39 correspond to measurement points on the power supply unit.

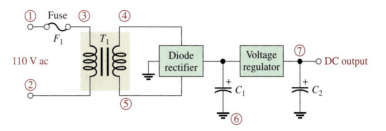

FIGURE 15–39
Basic transformer-coupled dc power supply.

The Power Supply

You have four identical power supply units to troubleshoot like the one shown in Figure 15–40. The power line to the primary winding of transformer T_1 is protected by the fuse. The secondary winding is connected to the circuit board containing the rectifier, filter, and regulator. Measurement points are indicated by the circled numbers.

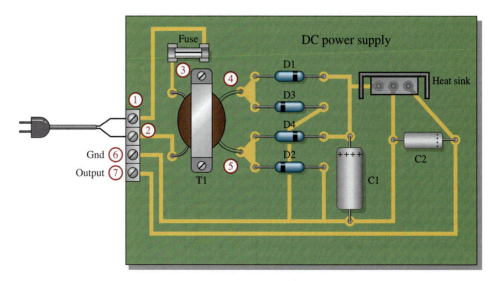

FIGURE 15–40
Power supply unit (top view).

Measuring Voltages on Power Supply Unit 1

After plugging the power supply into a standard wall outlet, an autoranging portable multimeter is used to measure the voltages. In an autoranging meter, the appropriate measurement range is automatically selected instead of being manually selected as in a standard multimeter.

■ Determine from the meter readings in Figure 15–41 whether or not the power supply is operating properly. If it is not, isolate the problem to one of the following: the circuit board containing the rectifier, filter, and regulator; the transformer; the fuse; or the power source. The circled numbers on the meter inputs correspond to the numbered points on the power supply in Figure 15–40.

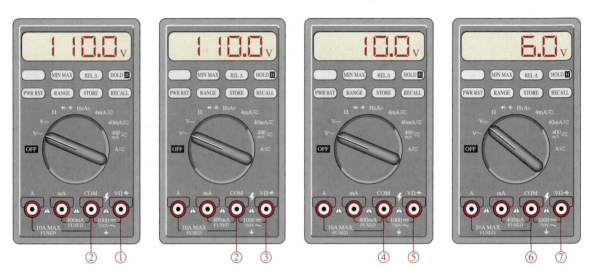

FIGURE 15–41
Voltage measurements on power supply unit 1.

Measuring Voltages on Power Supply Units 2, 3, and 4

■ Determine from the meter readings for units 2, 3, and 4 in Figure 15–42 whether or not each power supply is operating properly. If it is not, isolate the problem to one of the following: the circuit board containing the rectifier, filter, and regulator; the transformer; the fuse; or the power source. Only the meter displays and corresponding measurement points are shown.

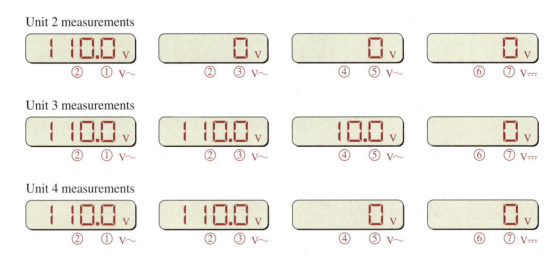

FIGURE 15–42
Measurements for power supply units 2, 3, and 4.

SECTION 15–12 REVIEW
1. In the case where the transformer was found to be faulty, how can you determine the specific fault (open windings or shorted windings)?
2. What type of fault could cause the fuse to blow?

■ SUMMARY

- A normal transformer consists of two or more coils that are magnetically coupled on a common core.
- There is mutual inductance between two magnetically coupled coils.
- When current in one coil changes, voltage is induced in the other coil.
- The primary is the winding connected to the source, and the secondary is the winding connected to the load.
- The number of turns in the primary and the number of turns in the secondary determine the turns ratio.
- The relative polarities of the primary and secondary voltages are determined by the direction of the windings around the core.
- A step-up transformer has a turns ratio greater than 1.
- A step-down transformer has a turns ratio less than 1.
- A transformer cannot increase power.
- In an ideal transformer, the power from the source (input power) is equal to the power delivered to the load (output power).
- If the voltage is stepped up, the current is stepped down, and vice versa.
- A load across the secondary winding of a transformer appears to the source as a reflected load having a value dependent on the reciprocal of the turns ratio squared.
- Certain transformers can match a load resistance to a source resistance to achieve maximum power transfer to the load by selecting the proper turns ratio.
- A typical transformer does not respond to dc.
- Conversion of electrical energy to heat in an actual transformer results from winding resistances, hysteresis loss in the core, eddy currents in the core, and flux leakage.

■ GLOSSARY

These terms are also in the end-of-book glossary.

Apparent power rating   The method of rating transformers in which the power capability is expressed in volt-amperes (VA).

Autotransformer   A transformer in which the primary and secondary are in a single winding.

Center tap (CT)   A connection at the midpoint of a winding in a transformer.

Coefficient of coupling (k)   A constant associated with transformers that is the ratio of secondary magnetic flux to primary magnetic flux. The ideal value of 1 indicates that all the flux in the primary winding is coupled into the secondary winding.

Core   The physical structure around which the windings are placed.

Efficiency (η)   The ratio of output power delivered to a load to input power to a circuit expressed as a percentage.

Electrical isolation   The condition that exists when two coils are magnetically linked but have no electrical connection between them.

Impedance matching   A technique used to match a load resistance to a source resistance in order to achieve maximum transfer of power.

Magnetic coupling   The magnetic connection between two coils as a result of the changing magnetic flux lines of one coil cutting through the second coil.

Mutual inductance (L_M)   The inductance between two separate coils, such as a transformer.

Primary winding   The input winding of a transformer; also called *primary*.

Reflected load   The load as it appears to the source in the primary of a transformer.

Reflected resistance   The resistance in the secondary circuit reflected into the primary circuit.

Secondary winding   The output winding of a transformer; also called *secondary*.

Step-down transformer   A transformer in which the secondary voltage is less than the primary voltage.

Step-up transformer   A transformer in which the secondary voltage is greater than the primary voltage.

Transformer   A device formed by two or more windings that are magnetically coupled to each other and providing a transfer of power electromagnetically from one winding to another.

Turns ratio (*n*)   The ratio of turns in the secondary winding to turns in the primary winding.

■ FORMULAS

(15–1)	$k = \dfrac{\phi_{1\text{-}2}}{\phi_1}$	Coefficient of coupling
(15–2)	$L_M = k\sqrt{L_1 L_2}$	Mutual inductance
(15–3)	$n = \dfrac{N_{sec}}{N_{pri}}$	Turns ratio
(15–4)	$\dfrac{V_{sec}}{V_{pri}} = \dfrac{N_{sec}}{N_{pri}}$	Voltage ratio
(15–5)	$V_{sec} = \left(\dfrac{N_{sec}}{N_{pri}}\right) V_{pri}$	Secondary voltage
(15–6)	$\dfrac{I_{pri}}{I_{sec}} = \dfrac{N_{sec}}{N_{pri}}$	Current ratio
(15–7)	$I_{sec} = \left(\dfrac{N_{pri}}{N_{sec}}\right) I_{pri}$	Secondary current
(15–8)	$R_{pri} = \left(\dfrac{N_{pri}}{N_{sec}}\right)^2 R_L$	Reflected resistance
(15–9)	$n = \dfrac{N_{sec}}{N_{pri}} = \sqrt{\dfrac{R_L}{R_{pri}}}$	Turns ratio for impedance matching
(15–10)	$\eta = \left(\dfrac{P_{out}}{P_{in}}\right) 100\%$	Transformer efficiency

■ SELF-TEST

1. A transformer is used for
   (a) dc voltages   (b) ac voltages   (c) both dc and ac

2. Which one of the following is affected by the turns ratio of a transformer?
   (a) primary voltage   (b) dc voltage
   (c) secondary voltage   (d) none of these

3. If the windings of a certain transformer with a turns ratio of 1 are in opposite directions around the core, the secondary voltage is
   (a) in phase with the primary voltage   (b) less than the primary voltage
   (c) greater than the primary voltage   (d) out of phase with the primary voltage

4. When the turns ratio of a transformer is 10 and the primary ac voltage is 6 V, the secondary voltage is
   (a) 60 V   (b) 0.6 V   (c) 6 V   (d) 36 V

5. When the turns ratio of a transformer is 0.5 and the primary ac voltage is 100 V, the secondary voltage is
   (a) 200 V   (b) 50 V   (c) 10 V   (d) 100 V

6. A certain transformer has 500 turns in the primary winding and 2500 turns in the secondary winding. The turns ratio is
   (a) 0.2   (b) 2.5   (c) 5   (d) 0.5

7. If 10 W of power are applied to the primary of an ideal transformer with a turns ratio of 5, the power delivered to the secondary load is
   (a) 50 W   (b) 0.5 W   (c) 0 W   (d) 10 W

8. In a certain loaded transformer, the secondary voltage is one-third the primary voltage. The secondary current is
   (a) one-third the primary current   (b) three times the primary current
   (c) equal to the primary current   (d) less than the primary current

9. When a 1.0 kΩ load resistor is connected across the secondary winding of a transformer with a turns ratio of 2, the source "sees" a reflected load of
   (a) 250 Ω   (b) 2 kΩ   (c) 4 kΩ   (d) 1.0 kΩ

10. In Question 9, if the turns ratio is 0.5, the source "sees" a reflected load of
    (a) 1.0 kΩ   (b) 2 kΩ   (c) 4 kΩ   (d) 500 Ω

11. The turns required to match a 50 Ω source to a 200 Ω load is
    (a) 0.25   (b) 0.5   (c) 4   (d) 2

12. Maximum power is transferred from a source to a load in a transformer coupled circuit when
    (a) $R_L > R_{int}$ (b) $R_L < R_{int}$ (c) $\left(\dfrac{1}{n}\right)^2 R_L = R_{int}$ (d) $R_L = nR_{int}$

13. When a 12 V battery is connected across the primary of a transformer with a turns ratio of 4, the secondary voltage is
    (a) 0 V   (b) 12 V   (c) 48 V   (d) 3 V

14. A certain transformer has a turns ratio of 1 and a 0.95 coefficient of coupling. When 1 V ac is applied to the primary, the secondary voltage is
    (a) 1 V   (b) 1.95 V   (c) 0.95 V

■ PROBLEMS

More difficult problems are indicated by an asterisk (*).

SECTION 15–1   Mutual Inductance

1. What is the mutual inductance when $k = 0.75$, $L_1 = 1$ μH, and $L_2 = 4$ μH?
2. Determine the coefficient of coupling when $L_M = 1$ μH, $L_1 = 8$ μH, and $L_2 = 2$ μH.

SECTION 15–2   The Basic Transformer

3. What is the turns ratio of a transformer having 250 primary turns and 1000 secondary turns? What is the turns ratio when the primary winding has 400 turns and the secondary winding has 100 turns?
4. A certain transformer has 250 turns in its primary winding. In order to double the voltage, how many turns must be in the secondary winding?
5. For each transformer in Figure 15–43, sketch the secondary voltage showing its relationship to the primary voltage. Also indicate the amplitude.

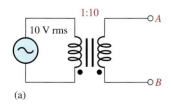

(a)

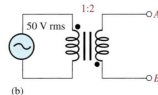

(b)

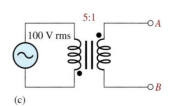

(c)

FIGURE 15–43

SECTION 15–3   Step-Up Transformers

6. To step 240 V ac up to 720 V, what must the turns ratio be?

7. The primary winding of a transformer has 120 V ac across it. What is the secondary voltage if the turns ratio is 5?

8. How many primary volts must be applied to a transformer with a turns ratio of 10 to obtain a secondary voltage of 60 V ac?

SECTION 15–4   Step-Down Transformers

9. To step 120 V down to 30 V, what must the turns ratio be?

10. The primary winding of a transformer has 1200 V across it. What is the secondary voltage if the turns ratio is 0.2?

11. How many primary volts must be applied to a transformer with a turns ratio of 0.1 to obtain a secondary voltage of 6 V ac?

SECTION 15–5   Loading the Secondary Winding

12. Determine I_s in Figure 15–44. What is the value of R_L?

FIGURE 15–44

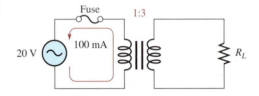

13. Determine the following quantities in Figure 15–45.

    (a) Primary current   **(b)** Secondary current

    (c) Secondary voltage   **(d)** Power in the load

FIGURE 15–45

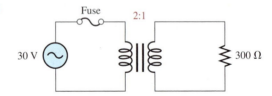

SECTION 15–6   Reflected Load

14. What is the load resistance as seen by the source in Figure 15–46?

FIGURE 15–46

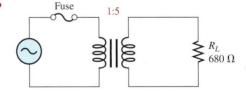

15. What must the turns ratio be in Figure 15–47 in order to reflect 300 Ω into the primary circuit?

FIGURE 15–47

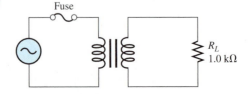

SECTION 15–7 Matching the Load and Source Resistances

16. For the circuit in Figure 15–48, find the turns ratio required to deliver maximum power to the 4 Ω speaker.

17. In Figure 15–48, what is the maximum power that can be delivered to the 4 Ω speaker?

FIGURE 15–48

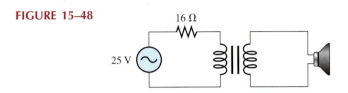

*18. Find the appropriate turns ratio for each switch position in Figure 15–49 in order to transfer the maximum power to each load when the source resistance is 10 Ω. Specify the number of turns for the secondary winding if the primary winding has 1000 turns.

FIGURE 15–49

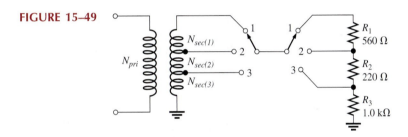

SECTION 15–8 The Transformer as an Isolation Device

19. What is the voltage across the load in each circuit of Figure 15–50?

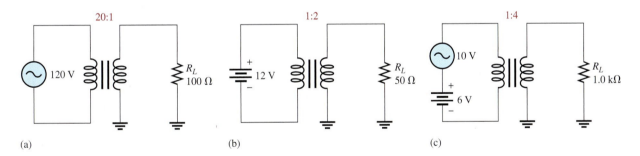

FIGURE 15–50

20. Determine the unspecified meter readings in Figure 15–51.

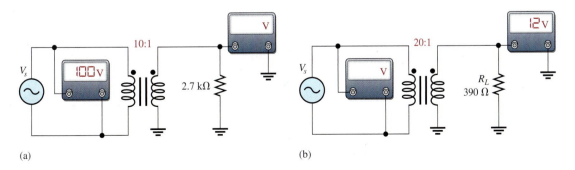

FIGURE 15–51

SECTION 15–9 Nonideal Transformer Characteristics

21. In a certain transformer, the input power to the primary is 100 W. If 5.5 W are lost in the winding resistances, what is the output power to the load, neglecting any other losses?

22. What is the efficiency of the transformer in Problem 21?

23. Determine the coefficient of coupling for a transformer in which 2% of the total flux generated in the primary does not pass through the secondary.

*24. A certain transformer is rated at 1 kVA. It operates on 60 Hz, 120 V ac. The secondary voltage is 600 V.

   (a) What is the maximum load current?

   (b) What is the smallest R_L that you can drive?

   (c) What is the largest capacitor that can be connected as a load?

25. What kVA rating is required for a transformer that must handle a maximum load current of 10 A with a secondary voltage of 2.5 kV?

*26. A certain transformer is rated at 5 kVA, 2400/120 V, at 60 Hz.

   (a) What is the turns ratio if the 120 V is the secondary voltage?

   (b) What is the current rating of the secondary if 2400 V is the primary voltage?

   (c) What is the current rating of the primary winding if 2400 V is the primary voltage?

SECTION 15–10 Other Types of Transformers

27. Determine each unknown voltage indicated in Figure 15–52.

FIGURE 15–52

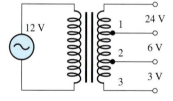

28. Using the indicated secondary voltages in Figure 15–53 determine the turns ratio of the primary winding to each tapped section of the secondary winding.

FIGURE 15–53

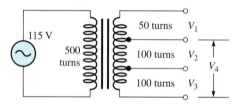

29. Find the secondary voltage for each autotransformer in Figure 15–54.

FIGURE 15–54

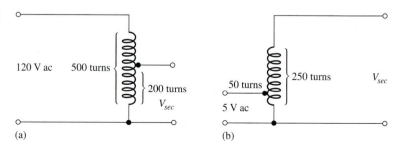

(a)   (b)

30. In Figure 15–55, each primary can accommodate 120 V ac. How should the primaries be connected for 240 V ac operation? Determine each secondary voltage for 240 V operation.

FIGURE 15–55

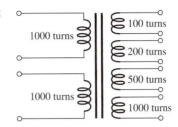

*31. For the loaded, tapped-secondary transformer in Figure 15–56, determine the following:
   (a) All load voltages and currents
   (b) The resistance reflected into the primary

FIGURE 15–56

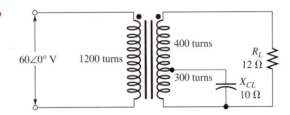

SECTION 15–11   Troubleshooting

32. When you apply 120 V ac across the primary winding of a transformer and check the voltage across the secondary winding, you get 0 V. Further investigation shows no primary or secondary currents. List the possible faults. What is your next step in investigating the problem?

33. What is likely to happen if the primary winding of a transformer shorts?

34. While checking out a transformer, you find that the secondary voltage is less than it should be although it is not zero. What is the most likely fault?

EWB Troubleshooting and Analysis

These problems require your EWB compact disk.

35. Open file PRO15-35.EWB and measure the secondary voltage. Determine the turns ratio.

36. Open file PRO15-36.EWB and determine by measurement if there is an open winding.

37. Open file PRO15-37.EWB and determine if there is a fault in the circuit.

■ **ANSWERS TO SECTION REVIEWS**

Section 15–1

1. Mutual inductance is the inductance between two coils.
2. $L_M = k\sqrt{L_1L_2} = 45$ mH
3. The induced voltage increases if k increases.

Section 15–2

1. Transformer operation is based on mutual inductance.
2. The turns ratio is the ratio of turns in the secondary winding to turns in the primary winding.
3. The directions of the windings determine the relative polarities of the voltages.
4. $n = 250/500 = 0.5$

Section 15–3

1. A step-up transformer produces a secondary voltage that is greater than the primary voltage.
2. V_{sec} is five times greater than V_{pri}.
3. $V_{sec} = (N_{sec}/N_{pri})V_{pri} = 10(240 \text{ V}) = 2400$ V

Section 15–4

1. A step-down transformer produces a secondary voltage that is less than the primary voltage.
2. $V_{sec} = (0.5)120 \text{ V} = 60 \text{ V}$
3. $n = 12 \text{ V}/120 \text{ V} = 0.1$

Section 15–5

1. I_{sec} is less than I_{pri} by half.
2. $I_{sec} = (1000/250)0.5 \text{ A} = 2 \text{ A}$
3. $I_{pri} = (250/1000)10 \text{ A} = 2.5 \text{ A}$

Section 15–6

1. Reflected resistance is the resistance in the secondary circuit, altered by the reciprocal of the turns ratio squared, as it appears to the primary circuit.
2. The turns ratio determines reflected resistance.
3. $R_{pri} = (0.1)^2 50 \text{ }\Omega = 0.5 \text{ }\Omega$
4. $n = 0.1$

Section 15–7

1. Impedance matching makes the load resistance equal the source resistance.
2. Maximum power is delivered to the load when $R_L = R_s$.
3. $R_{pri} = (100/50)^2 100 \text{ }\Omega = 400 \text{ }\Omega$

Section 15–8

1. Electrical isolation means no electrical connection between the primary and secondary.
2. No, transformers do not couple dc.

Section 15–9

1. In a practical transformer, conversion of electrical energy to heat reduces the efficiency. An ideal transformer has an efficiency of 100%.
2. When $k = 0.85$, 85% of the magnetic flux generated in the primary winding passes through the secondary winding.
3. $I_L = 10 \text{ kVA}/250 \text{ V} = 40 \text{ A}$

Section 15–10

1. $V_{sec} = (10)240 \text{ V} = 2400 \text{ V}$, $V_{sec} = (0.2)240 \text{ V} = 48 \text{ V}$
2. An autotransformer is smaller and lighter for the same rating than a conventional one. An autotransformer has no electrical isolation.

Section 15–11

1. Transformer faults: open windings are the most common, shorted windings are much less common.
2. Operating above rated values will cause a failure.

Section 15–12

1. Use an ohmmeter to check for open windings. Shorted windings are indicated by an incorrect secondary voltage.
2. A short will cause the fuse to blow.

■ **ANSWERS TO RELATED PROBLEMS FOR EXAMPLES**

15–1 0.75

15–2 387 μH

15–3 5000 turns

15–4 480 V

15–5 57.6 V

15–6 5 mA; 400 mA

15–7 6 Ω

15–8 0.354

15–9 0.0707 or 14.14:1

15–10 85.2%

15–11 $V_{AB} = 12$ V, $V_{CD} = 480$ V, $V_{(CT)C} = V_{(CT)D} = 240$ V, $V_{EF} = 24$ V

15–12 Increases to 1.75 kVA

■ **ANSWERS TO SELF-TEST**

1. (b) **2.** (c) **3.** (d) **4.** (a) **5.** (b) **6.** (c) **7.** (d) **8.** (b)

9. (a) **10.** (c) **11.** (d) **12.** (c) **13.** (a) **14.** (c)

16

RC CIRCUITS

Electronics Workbench (EWB) and PSpice Tutorials at
http://www.prenhall.com/floyd

■ INTRODUCTION

An *RC* circuit contains both resistance and capacitance. It is one of the basic types of reactive circuits that you will study. In this chapter, basic series and parallel *RC* circuits and their responses to sinusoidal ac voltages are presented. Series-parallel combinations are also analyzed. True, reactive, and apparent power in *RC* circuits are discussed and some basic *RC* applications are introduced. Applications of *RC* circuits include filters, amplifier coupling, oscillators, and wave-shaping circuits. Troubleshooting is also covered in this chapter.

The frequency response of the *RC* input network in an amplifier circuit is similar to the one you worked with in Chapter 13 and is the subject of this chapter's TECH TIP.

■ COVERAGE OPTIONS

This chapter is divided into four parts: Series Reactive Circuits, Parallel Reactive Circuits, Series-Parallel Reactive Circuits, and Special Topics. The purpose of this organization is to facilitate either of two approaches to the coverage of reactive circuits in Chapters 16, 17, and 18.

In the first approach, all *RC* circuits (Chapter 16) are covered first, followed by all *RL* circuits (Chapter 17), and then all *RLC* circuits (Chapter 18). Using this approach, you simply cover Chapters 16, 17, and 18 in sequence.

In the second approach, all *series* reactive circuits are covered first. Then all *parallel* reactive circuits are covered next, followed by *series-parallel* reactive circuits and finally *special topics*. Using this approach, you cover Part 1: Series Reactive Circuits in Chapters 16, 17, and 18; then Part 2: Parallel Reactive Circuits in Chapters 16, 17, and 18; then Part 3: Series-Parallel Reactive Circuits in Chapters 16, 17, and 18. Finally, Part 4: Special Topics can be covered in each of the chapters.

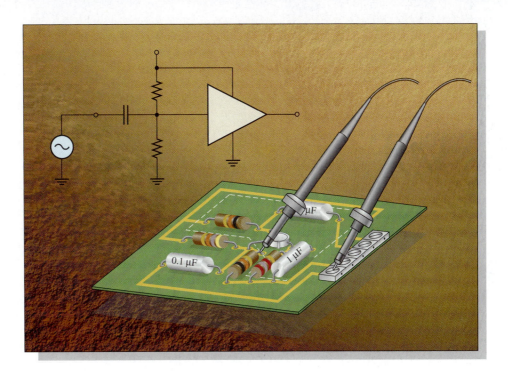

■ **TECH**nology
Theory
Into
Practice

■ **CHAPTER OBJECTIVES**

PART 1: SERIES REACTIVE CIRCUITS
❑ Describe the relationship between current and voltage in an *RC* circuit.
❑ Determine impedance and phase angle in a series *RC* circuit
❑ Analyze a series *RC* circuit

PART 2: PARALLEL REACTIVE CIRCUITS
❑ Determine impedance and phase angle in a parallel *RC* circuit
❑ Analyze a parallel *RC* circuit

PART 3: SERIES-PARALLEL REACTIVE CIRCUITS
❑ Analyze series-parallel *RC* circuits

PART 4: SPECIAL TOPICS
❑ Determine power in *RC* circuits
❑ Discuss some basic *RC* applications
❑ Troubleshoot *RC* circuits

PART 1

SERIES REACTIVE CIRCUITS

16–1 ■ SINUSOIDAL RESPONSE OF *RC* CIRCUITS

When a sinusoidal voltage is applied to any type of RC circuit, each resulting voltage drop and the current in the circuit are also sinusoidal and have the same frequency as the applied voltage. The capacitance causes a phase shift between the voltage and current that depends on the relative values of the resistance and the capacitive reactance.

After completing this section, you should be able to

■ **Describe the relationship between current and voltage in an *RC* circuit**
- Discuss voltage and current waveforms
- Discuss phase shift
- Describe types of signal generators

As shown in Figure 16–1, the resistor voltage (V_R), the capacitor voltage (V_C), and the current (I) are all sine waves with the frequency of the source. Phase shifts are introduced because of the capacitance. As you will learn, the resistor voltage and current **lead** the source voltage, and the capacitor voltage **lags** the source voltage. The phase angle between the current and the capacitor voltage is always 90°. These generalized phase relationships are indicated in Figure 16–1.

FIGURE 16–1

Illustration of sinusoidal response with general phase relationships of V_R, V_C, and I relative to the source voltage. V_R leads V_s, V_C lags V_s, and I leads V_s. V_R and I are in phase while V_R and V_C are 90° out of phase.

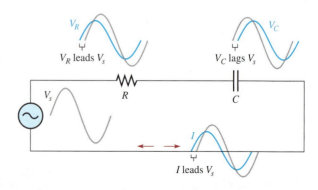

The amplitudes and the phase relationships of the voltages and current depend on the values of the resistance and the capacitive reactance. When a circuit is purely resistive, the phase angle between the applied (source) voltage and the total current is zero. When a circuit is purely capacitive, the phase angle between the applied voltage and the total current is 90°, with the current leading the voltage. When there is a combination of both resistance and capacitive reactance in a circuit, the phase angle between the applied voltage and the total current is somewhere between 0° and 90°, depending on the relative values of the resistance and the reactance.

Signal Generators

When a circuit is hooked up for a laboratory experiment or for troubleshooting, a signal generator similar to those shown in Figure 16–2 is used to provide the source voltage. These instruments, depending on their capability, are classified as sine wave generators, which produce only sine waves; sine/square generators, which produce either sine waves or square waves; or function generators, which produce sine waves, pulse waveforms, or triangular (ramp) waveforms.

(a)

(b)

FIGURE 16–2
Typical signal (function) generators used in circuit testing and troubleshooting. (Photography courtesy of B&K Precision Corp.).

SECTION 16–1 REVIEW	**1.** A 60 Hz sinusoidal voltage is applied to an *RC* circuit. What is the frequency of the capacitor voltage? What is the frequency of the current?
	2. What causes the phase shift between V_s and I in a series *RC* circuit?
	3. When the resistance in an *RC* circuit is greater than the capacitive reactance, is the phase angle between the applied voltage and the total current closer to 0° or to 90°?

16–2 ■ IMPEDANCE AND PHASE ANGLE OF SERIES *RC* CIRCUITS

The impedance of any type of RC circuit is the total opposition to sinusoidal current and its unit is the ohm. The phase angle is the phase difference between the total current and the source voltage.

After completing this section, you should be able to

■ **Determine impedance and phase angle in a series *RC* circuit**
  • Define impedance
  • Express capacitive reactance in complex form
  • Express total impedance in complex form
  • Draw an impedance triangle
  • Calculate impedance magnitude and the phase angle

In a purely capacitive circuit, the **impedance** is equal to the total capacitive reactance. The impedance of a series *RC* circuit is determined by both the resistance and the capacitive reactance. These cases are illustrated in Figure 16–3. The magnitude of the impedance is symbolized by *Z*.

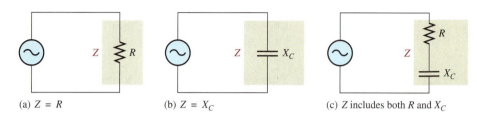

(a) $Z = R$ (b) $Z = X_C$ (c) *Z* includes both *R* and X_C

FIGURE 16–3
Three cases of impedance.

Recall from Chapter 13 that capacitive reactance is expressed as a complex number in rectangular form as

$$\mathbf{X}_C = -jX_C \qquad (16\text{–}1)$$

where boldface $\mathbf{X}_C$ designates a phasor quantity (representing both magnitude and angle) and X_C is just the magnitude.

In the series *RC* circuit of Figure 16–4, the total impedance is the phasor sum of *R* and $-jX_C$ and is expressed as

$$\mathbf{Z} = R - jX_C \qquad (16\text{–}2)$$

FIGURE 16–4
Series RC circuit.

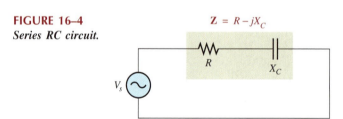

The Impedance Triangle

In ac analysis, both *R* and X_C are treated as phasor quantities, as shown in the phasor diagram of Figure 16–5(a), with X_C appearing at a –90° angle with respect to *R*. This relationship comes from the fact that the capacitor voltage in a series *RC* circuit lags the current,

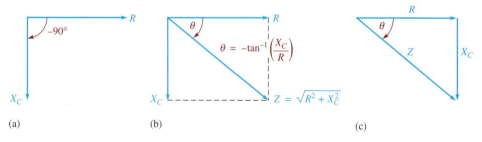

(a)   (b)   (c)

FIGURE 16–5
Development of the impedance triangle for a series RC circuit.

and thus the resistor voltage, by 90°. Since **Z** is the phasor sum of R and $-jX_C$, its phasor representation is shown in Figure 16–5(b). A repositioning of the phasors, as shown in part (c), forms a right triangle. This is called the *impedance triangle*. The length of each phasor represents the magnitude in ohms, and the angle θ is the phase angle of the *RC* circuit and represents the phase difference between the applied voltage and the current.

From right-angle trigonometry (Pythagorean theorem), the magnitude (length) of the impedance can be expressed in terms of the resistance and reactance as

$$Z = \sqrt{R^2 + X_C^2} \tag{16–3}$$

The italic letter Z represents the magnitude of the phasor quantity **Z** and is expressed in ohms.

The phase angle, θ, is expressed as

$$\theta = -\tan^{-1}\left(\frac{X_C}{R}\right) \tag{16–4}$$

The symbol $\tan^{-1}$ stands for inverse tangent and can be found by pressing 2nd , then tan⁻¹ . Combining the magnitude and angle, the phasor expression for impedance in polar form is

$$\mathbf{Z} = \sqrt{R^2 + X_C^2}\angle{-\tan^{-1}\left(\frac{X_C}{R}\right)} \tag{16–5}$$

EXAMPLE 16–1

For each circuit in Figure 16–6, write the phasor expression for the impedance in both rectangular form and polar form.

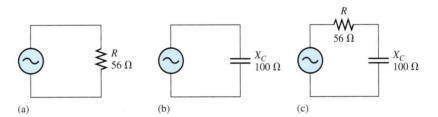

FIGURE 16–6

Solution   For the circuit in Figure 16–6(a), the impedance is

$$\mathbf{Z} = R - j0 = R = \mathbf{56\ \Omega} \quad \text{in rectangular form } (X_C = 0)$$
$$\mathbf{Z} = R\angle 0° = \mathbf{56\angle 0°\ \Omega} \quad \text{in polar form}$$

The impedance is simply the resistance, and the phase angle is zero because pure resistance does not cause a phase shift between the voltage and current.

For the circuit in Figure 16–6(b), the impedance is

$$\mathbf{Z} = 0 - jX_C = \mathbf{-j100\ \Omega} \quad \text{in rectangular form } (R = 0)$$
$$\mathbf{Z} = X_C\angle{-90°} = \mathbf{100\angle{-90°}\ \Omega} \quad \text{in polar form}$$

The impedance is simply the capacitive reactance, and the phase angle is –90° because the capacitance causes the current to lead the voltage by 90°.

For the circuit in Figure 16–6(c), the impedance in rectangular form is

$$\mathbf{Z} = R - jX_C = \mathbf{56\ \Omega} - \mathbf{j100\ \Omega}$$

The impedance in polar form is

$$\mathbf{Z} = \sqrt{R^2 + X_C^2}\angle -\tan^{-1}\!\left(\frac{X_C}{R}\right)$$

$$= \sqrt{(56\ \Omega)^2 + (100\ \Omega)^2}\angle -\tan^{-1}\!\left(\frac{100\ \Omega}{56\ \Omega}\right) = \mathbf{115\angle -60.8°\ \Omega}$$

In this case, the impedance is the phasor sum of the resistance and the capacitive reactance. The phase angle is fixed by the relative values of X_C and R. Rectangular to polar conversion using a calculator was illustrated in Chapter 12 and can be used in problems like this one.

Related Problem   Use your calculator to convert the impedance in Figure 16–6(c) from rectangular to polar form. Draw the impedance phasor diagram.

SECTION 16–2 REVIEW

1. The impedance of a certain *RC* circuit is 150 Ω – *j*220 Ω. What is the value of the resistance? The capacitive reactance?

2. A series *RC* circuit has a total resistance of 33 kΩ and a capacitive reactance of 50 kΩ. Write the phasor expression for the impedance in rectangular form.

3. For the circuit in Question 2, what is the magnitude of the impedance? What is the phase angle?

16–3 ▪ ANALYSIS OF SERIES *RC* CIRCUITS

In the previous section, you learned how to express the impedance of a series RC circuit. Now, Ohm's law and Kirchhoff's voltage law are used in the analysis of RC circuits.

After completing this section, you should be able to

▪ **Analyze a series *RC* circuit**
  • Apply Ohm's law and Kirchhoff's voltage law to series *RC* circuits
  • Express the voltages and current as phasor quantities
  • Show how impedance and phase angle vary with frequency

Ohm's Law

The application of Ohm's law to series *RC* circuits involves the use of the phasor quantities of **Z**, **V**, and **I**. Keep in mind that the use of boldface nonitalic letters indicates phasor quantities where both magnitude and angle are included. The three equivalent forms of Ohm's law are as follows:

$$\mathbf{V} = \mathbf{IZ} \tag{16–6}$$

$$\mathbf{I} = \frac{\mathbf{V}}{\mathbf{Z}} \tag{16–7}$$

$$\mathbf{Z} = \frac{\mathbf{V}}{\mathbf{I}} \tag{16–8}$$

From your study of phasor algebra in Chapter 12, you should recall that multiplication and division are most easily accomplished with the polar forms. Since Ohm's law calculations involve multiplications and divisions, the voltage, current, and impedance should be expressed in polar form. The following two examples show the relationship between the source voltage and source current. In Example 16–2, the current is the reference and in Example 16–3, the voltage is the reference. Notice that the reference is drawn along the *X*-axis in both cases.

EXAMPLE 16–2

If the current in Figure 16–7 is expressed in polar form as $\mathbf{I} = 0.2\angle 0°$ mA, determine the source voltage expressed in polar form, and draw a phasor diagram showing the relation between source voltage and current.

FIGURE 16–7

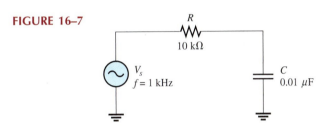

Solution   The magnitude of the capacitive reactance is

$$X_C = \frac{1}{2\pi fC} = \frac{1}{2\pi(1000 \text{ Hz})(0.01 \ \mu F)} = 15.9 \text{ k}\Omega$$

The total impedance in rectangular form is

$$\mathbf{Z} = R - jX_C = 10 \text{ k}\Omega - j15.9 \text{ k}\Omega$$

Converting to polar form yields

$$\mathbf{Z} = \sqrt{R^2 + X_C^2}\angle -\tan^{-1}\left(\frac{X_C}{R}\right)$$

$$= \sqrt{(10 \text{ k}\Omega)^2 + (15.9 \text{ k}\Omega)^2}\angle -\tan^{-1}\left(\frac{15.9 \text{ k}\Omega}{10 \text{ k}\Omega}\right) = 18.8\angle -57.8° \text{ k}\Omega$$

Use Ohm's law to determine the source voltage.

$$\mathbf{V}_s = \mathbf{IZ} = (0.2\angle 0° \text{ mA})(18.8\angle -57.8° \text{ k}\Omega) = \mathbf{3.76\angle -57.8°} \text{ V}$$

The magnitude of the source voltage is 3.76 V at an angle of −57.8° with respect to the current; that is, the voltage lags the current by 57.8°, as shown in the phasor diagram of Figure 16–8.

FIGURE 16–8

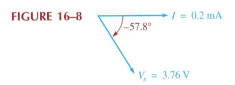

Related Problem   Determine $\mathbf{V}_s$ in Figure 16–7 if $f = 2$ kHz and $\mathbf{I} = 0.2\angle 0°$ A.

EXAMPLE 16–3   Determine the current in the circuit of Figure 16–9, and draw a phasor diagram showing the relation between source voltage and current.

FIGURE 16–9

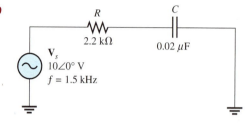

Solution   The magnitude of the capacitive reactance is

$$X_C = \frac{1}{2\pi f C} = \frac{1}{2\pi (1.5 \text{ kHz})(0.02 \text{ } \mu\text{F})} = 5.3 \text{ k}\Omega$$

The total impedance in rectangular form is

$$\mathbf{Z} = R - jX_C = 2.2 \text{ k}\Omega - j5.3 \text{ k}\Omega$$

Converting to polar form yields

$$\mathbf{Z} = \sqrt{R^2 + X_C^2} \angle -\tan^{-1}\left(\frac{X_C}{R}\right)$$

$$= \sqrt{(2.2 \text{ k}\Omega)^2 + (5.3 \text{ k}\Omega)^2} \angle -\tan^{-1}\left(\frac{5.3 \text{ k}\Omega}{2.2 \text{ k}\Omega}\right) = 5.74 \angle -67.5° \text{ k}\Omega$$

Use Ohm's law to determine the current.

$$\mathbf{I} = \frac{\mathbf{V}}{\mathbf{Z}} = \frac{10 \angle 0° \text{ V}}{5.74 \angle -67.5° \text{ k}\Omega} = \mathbf{1.74 \angle 67.5° \text{ mA}}$$

The magnitude of the current is 1.74 mA. The positive phase angle of 67.5° indicates that the current leads the voltage by that amount, as shown in the phasor diagram of Figure 16–10.

FIGURE 16–10

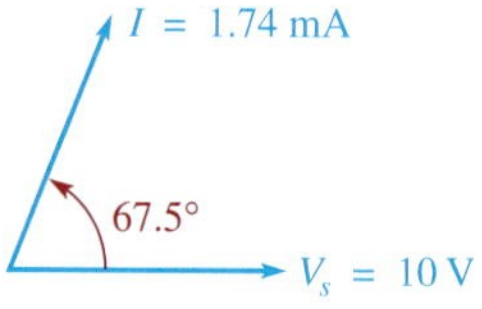

$I = 1.74$ mA

67.5°

$V_s = 10$ V

Related Problem   Determine **I** in Figure 16–9 if the frequency is increased to 5 kHz.

Relationships of the Current and Voltages in a Series *RC* Circuit

In a series circuit, the current is the same through both the resistor and the capacitor. Thus, the resistor voltage is in phase with the current, and the capacitor voltage lags the current by 90°. Therefore, there is a phase difference of 90° between the resistor voltage, V_R, and the capacitor voltage, V_C, as shown in the waveform diagram of Figure 16–11.

FIGURE 16–11

Phase relation of voltages and current in a series RC circuit.

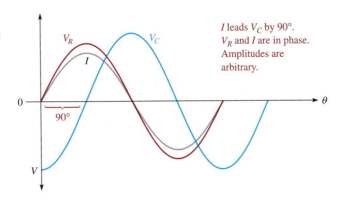

I leads V_C by 90°.
V_R and *I* are in phase.
Amplitudes are arbitrary.

You know from Kirchhoff's voltage law that the sum of the voltage drops must equal the applied voltage. However, since V_R and V_C are not in phase with each other, they must be added as phasor quantities, with V_C lagging V_R by 90°, as shown in Figure 16–12(a). As shown in Figure 16–12(b), $\mathbf{V}_s$ is the phasor sum of V_R and V_C, as expressed in rectangular form in the following equation:

$$\mathbf{V}_s = V_R - jV_C \tag{16–9}$$

This equation can be expressed in polar form as

$$\mathbf{V}_s = \sqrt{V_R^2 + V_C^2}\, \angle -\tan^{-1}\left(\frac{V_C}{V_R}\right) \tag{16–10}$$

where the magnitude of the source voltage is

$$V_s = \sqrt{V_R^2 + V_C^2} \tag{16–11}$$

and the phase angle between the resistor voltage and the source voltage is

$$\theta = -\tan^{-1}\left(\frac{V_C}{V_R}\right) \tag{16–12}$$

Since the resistor voltage and the current are in phase, θ also represents the phase angle between the source voltage and the current. Figure 16–13 shows a complete voltage and current phasor diagram that represents the waveform diagram of Figure 16–11.

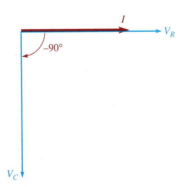

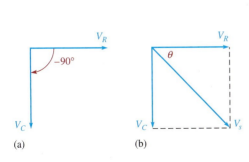

FIGURE 16–12

Voltage phasor diagram for a series RC circuit.

FIGURE 16–13

Voltage and current phasor diagram for the waveforms in Figure 16–11.

Variation of Impedance with Frequency

As you know, capacitive reactance varies inversely with frequency. Since $Z = \sqrt{R^2 + X_C^2}$, you can see that when X_C increases, the entire term under the square root sign increases and thus the magnitude of the total impedance also increases; and when X_C decreases, the magnitude of the total impedance also decreases. Therefore, *in an RC circuit, Z is inversely dependent on frequency.*

Figure 16–14 illustrates how the voltages and current in a series *RC* circuit vary as the frequency increases or decreases, with the source voltage held at a constant value. In part (a), as the frequency is increased, X_C decreases; so less voltage is dropped across the capacitor. Also, *Z* decreases as X_C decreases, causing the current to increase. An increase in the current causes more voltage across *R*.

In Figure 16–14(b), as the frequency is decreased, X_C increases; so more voltage is dropped across the capacitor. Also, *Z* increases as X_C increases, causing the current to decrease. A decrease in the current causes less voltage across *R*.

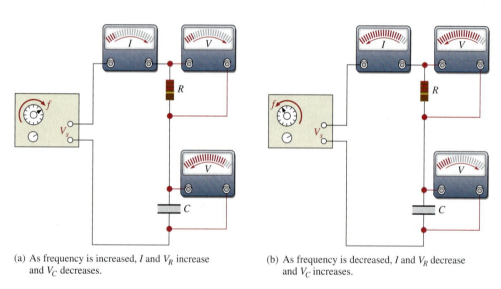

(a) As frequency is increased, *I* and V_R increase and V_C decreases.

(b) As frequency is decreased, *I* and V_R decrease and V_C increases.

FIGURE 16–14

An illustration of how the variation of impedance affects the voltages and current as the source frequency is varied. The source voltage is held at a constant amplitude.

The effect of changes in *Z* and X_C can be observed as shown in Figure 16–15. As the frequency increases, the voltage across *Z* remains constant because V_s is constant. Also, the voltage across *C* decreases. The increasing current indicates that *Z* is decreasing. It does so because of the inverse relationship stated in Ohm's law ($Z = V_Z/I$). The increasing current also indicates that X_C is decreasing ($X_C = V_C/I$). The decrease in V_C corresponds to the decrease in X_C.

Variation of the Phase Angle with Frequency

Since X_C is the factor that introduces the phase angle in a series *RC* circuit, a change in X_C produces a change in the phase angle. As the frequency is increased, X_C becomes smaller, and thus the phase angle decreases. As the frequency is decreased, X_C becomes larger, and thus the phase angle increases. This variation is illustrated in Figure 16–16 where a "phase meter" is connected across the capacitor to illustrate the change in angle between V_s and V_R. This angle is the phase angle of the circuit because *I* is in phase with V_R. By measuring the phase of V_R, you are effectively measuring the phase of *I*. An oscilloscope is normally used to observe the phase angle. The meter is used for convenient illustration of the concept.

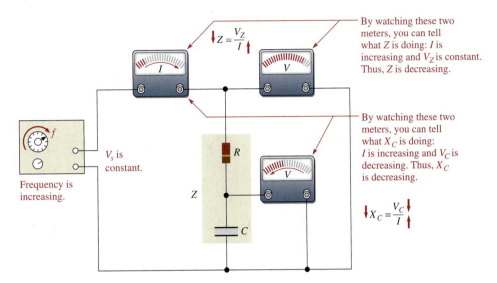

FIGURE 16–15
An illustration of how Z and X_C change with frequency.

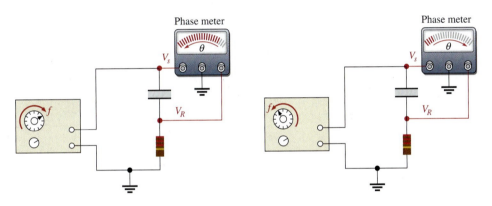

FIGURE 16–16
The "phase meter" shows the effect of frequency on the phase angle of a circuit. The "phase meter" indicates the phase angle change between two voltages, V_s and V_R. Since V_R and I are in phase, this angle is the same as the angle between V_s and I.

Figure 16–17 uses the impedance triangle to illustrate the variations in X_C, Z, and θ as the frequency changes. Of course, R remains constant. The key point is that because X_C varies inversely with the frequency, so also do the magnitude of the total impedance and the phase angle. Example 16–4 illustrates this.

FIGURE 16–17

As the frequency increases, X_C decreases, Z decreases, and θ decreases. Each value of frequency can be visualized as forming a different impedance triangle.

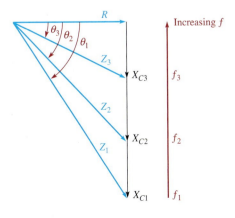

EXAMPLE 16–4

For the series *RC* circuit in Figure 16–18, determine the magnitude of the total impedance and the phase angle for each of the following values of input frequency:
(a) 10 kHz   **(b)** 20 kHz   **(c)** 30 kHz

FIGURE 16–18

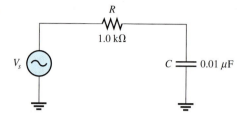

Solution
(a) For $f = 10$ kHz,

$$X_C = \frac{1}{2\pi fC} = \frac{1}{2\pi(10 \text{ kHz})(0.01 \ \mu\text{F})} = 1.59 \text{ k}\Omega$$

$$\mathbf{Z} = \sqrt{R^2 + X_C^2} \angle -\tan^{-1}\left(\frac{X_C}{R}\right)$$

$$= \sqrt{(1.0 \text{ k}\Omega)^2 + (1.59 \text{ k}\Omega)^2} \angle -\tan^{-1}\left(\frac{1.59 \text{ k}\Omega}{1.0 \text{ k}\Omega}\right) = 1.88 \angle -57.9° \text{ k}\Omega$$

Thus, $Z = \mathbf{1.88 \text{ k}\Omega}$ and $\theta = \mathbf{-57.9°}$.
(b) For $f = 20$ kHz,

$$X_C = \frac{1}{2\pi(20 \text{ kHz})(0.01 \ \mu\text{F})} = 796 \ \Omega$$

$$\mathbf{Z} = \sqrt{(1.0 \text{ k}\Omega)^2 + (796 \ \Omega)^2} \angle -\tan^{-1}\left(\frac{796 \ \Omega}{1.0 \text{ k}\Omega}\right) = 1.28 \angle -38.5° \text{ k}\Omega$$

Thus, $Z = \mathbf{1.28 \text{ k}\Omega}$ and $\theta = \mathbf{-38.5°}$.
(c) For $f = 30$ kHz,

$$X_C = \frac{1}{2\pi(30 \text{ kHz})(0.01 \ \mu\text{F})} = 531 \ \Omega$$

$$\mathbf{Z} = \sqrt{(1.0 \text{ k}\Omega)^2 + (531 \ \Omega)^2} \angle -\tan^{-1}\left(\frac{531 \ \Omega}{1.0 \text{ k}\Omega}\right) = 1.13 \angle -28.0° \text{ k}\Omega$$

Thus, $Z = \mathbf{1.13 \text{ k}\Omega}$ and $\theta = \mathbf{-28.0°}$.
Notice that as the frequency increases, X_C, Z, and θ decrease.

Related Problem   Find the magnitude of the total impedance and the phase angle in
Figure 16–18 for $f = 1$ kHz.

**SECTION 16–3
REVIEW**

1. In a certain series *RC* circuit, $V_R = 4$ V, and $V_C = 6$ V. What is the magnitude of the
source voltage?

2. In Question 1, what is the phase angle between the source voltage and the current?

3. What is the phase difference between the capacitor voltage and the resistor voltage
in a series *RC* circuit?

4. When the frequency of the applied voltage in a series *RC* circuit is increased, what
happens to the capacitive reactance? What happens to the magnitude of the total
impedance? What happens to the phase angle?

♦ *Coverage of series reactive circuits continues in Chapter 17, Part 1, on page 664.*

PART 2
PARALLEL REACTIVE CIRCUITS

16–4 ■ IMPEDANCE AND PHASE ANGLE OF PARALLEL *RC* CIRCUITS

In this section, you will learn how to determine the impedance and phase angle of a parallel RC circuit. Also, capacitive susceptance and admittance of a parallel RC circuit are introduced.

After completing this section, you should be able to

■ **Determine impedance and phase angle in a parallel *RC* circuit**
  • Express total impedance in complex form
  • Define and calculate *conductance, capacitive susceptance,* and *admittance*

Figure 16–19 shows a basic parallel *RC* circuit connected to an ac voltage source.

FIGURE 16–19
Basic parallel RC circuit.

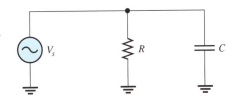

The expression for the total impedance is developed as follows, using the rules of phasor algebra. Since there are only two components, the total impedance can be found from the product-over-sum rule.

$$\mathbf{Z} = \frac{(R\angle 0°)(X_C\angle -90°)}{R - jX_C}$$

By multiplying the magnitudes, adding the angles in the numerator, and converting the denominator to polar form, we get

$$\mathbf{Z} = \frac{RX_C\angle(0° - 90°)}{\sqrt{R^2 + X_C^2}\angle -\tan^{-1}\left(\dfrac{X_C}{R}\right)}$$

Now, dividing the magnitude expression in the numerator by that in the denominator, and by subtracting the angle in the denominator from that in the numerator, we get

$$\mathbf{Z} = \left(\frac{RX_C}{\sqrt{R^2 + X_C^2}}\right)\angle\left(-90° + \tan^{-1}\left(\frac{X_C}{R}\right)\right) \tag{16–13}$$

Equation (16–13) is the expression for the total impedance for a basic parallel *RC* circuit, where the magnitude is

$$Z = \frac{RX_C}{\sqrt{R^2 + X_C^2}} \tag{16–14}$$

and the phase angle between the applied voltage and the total current is

$$\theta = -90° + \tan^{-1}\left(\frac{X_C}{R}\right) \tag{16–15}$$

Equivalently, this expression can be written as

$$\theta = -\tan^{-1}\left(\frac{R}{X_C}\right) \tag{16–16}$$

EXAMPLE 16–5 For each circuit in Figure 16–20, determine the magnitude of the total impedance and the phase angle.

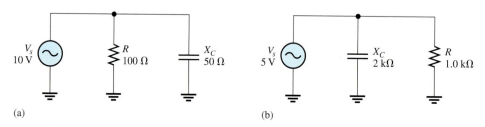

(a)   (b)

FIGURE 16–20

Solution For the circuit in Figure 16–20(a), the total impedance is

$$\mathbf{Z} = \left(\frac{RX_C}{\sqrt{R^2 + X_C^2}}\right)\angle-\tan^{-1}\left(\frac{R}{X_C}\right)$$

$$= \left[\frac{(100\ \Omega)(50\ \Omega)}{\sqrt{(100\ \Omega)^2 + (50\ \Omega)^2}}\right]\angle-\tan^{-1}\left(\frac{100\ \Omega}{50\ \Omega}\right) = 44.7\angle-63.4°\ \Omega$$

Thus, $Z = \mathbf{44.7\ \Omega}$ and $\theta = \mathbf{-63.4°}$.

For the circuit in Figure 16–20(b), the total impedance is

$$\mathbf{Z} = \left[\frac{(1.0\ k\Omega)(2\ k\Omega)}{\sqrt{(1.0\ k\Omega)^2 + (2\ k\Omega)^2}}\right]\angle-\tan^{-1}\left(\frac{1.0\ k\Omega}{2\ k\Omega}\right) = 894\angle-26.6°\ \Omega$$

Thus, $Z = \mathbf{894\ \Omega}$ and $\theta = \mathbf{-26.6°}$.

Related Problem Determine **Z** in Figure 16–20(a) if the frequency is doubled.

Conductance, Susceptance, and Admittance

Recall that **conductance**, G, is the reciprocal of resistance. The phasor expression for conductance is expressed as

$$\mathbf{G} = \frac{1}{R\angle 0°} = G\angle 0° \tag{16–17}$$

Two new terms are now introduced for use in parallel *RC* circuits. **Capacitive susceptance** (B_C) is the reciprocal of capacitive reactance and the phasor expression for capacitive susceptance is

$$\mathbf{B}_C = \frac{1}{X_C\angle -90°} = B_C\angle 90° = +jB_C \tag{16–18}$$

Admittance (Y) is the reciprocal of impedance and the phasor expression for admittance is

$$\mathbf{Y} = \frac{1}{Z\angle \pm\theta} = Y\angle \mp\theta \tag{16–19}$$

The unit of each of these terms is the siemens (S), which is the reciprocal of the ohm.

In working with parallel circuits, it is often easier to use G, B_C, and Y rather than R, X_C, and Z. In a parallel *RC* circuit, as shown in Figure 16–21, the total admittance is simply the phasor sum of the conductance and the capacitive susceptance.

$$\mathbf{Y} = G + jB_C \tag{16–20}$$

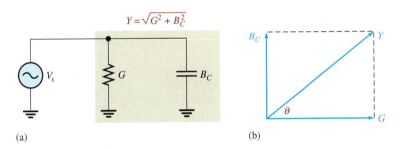

$$Y = \sqrt{G^2 + B_C^2}$$

(a) (b)

FIGURE 16–21
Admittance in a parallel RC circuit.

EXAMPLE 16–6

Determine the total admittance (**Y**) and total impedance (**Z**) in Figure 16–22. Sketch the admittance phasor diagram.

FIGURE 16–22

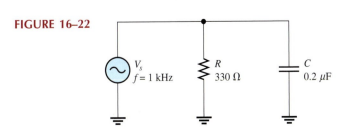

Solution   From Figure 16–22, $R = 330\ \Omega$; thus $G = 1/R = 1/330\ \Omega = 3.03$ mS. The capacitive reactance is

$$X_C = \frac{1}{2\pi fC} = \frac{1}{2\pi(1000\ \text{Hz})(0.2\ \mu\text{F})} = 796\ \Omega$$

The capacitive susceptance magnitude is

$$B_C = \frac{1}{X_C} = \frac{1}{796\ \Omega} = 1.26\ \text{mS}$$

The total admittance is

$$\mathbf{Y}_{tot} = G + jB_C = \mathbf{3.03\ mS + j1.26\ mS}$$

which can be expressed in polar form as

$$\mathbf{Y}_{tot} = \sqrt{G^2 + B_C^2}\angle\tan^{-1}\!\left(\frac{B_C}{G}\right)$$

$$= \sqrt{(3.03\ \text{mS})^2 + (1.26\ \text{mS})^2}\angle\tan^{-1}\!\left(\frac{1.26\ \text{mS}}{3.03\ \text{mS}}\right) = \mathbf{3.28\angle 22.6°\ mS}$$

Total admittance is converted to total impedance as follows:

$$\mathbf{Z}_{tot} = \frac{1}{\mathbf{Y}_{tot}} = \frac{1}{(3.28\angle 22.6°\ \text{mS})} = \mathbf{305\angle -22.6°\ \Omega}$$

The admittance phasor diagram is shown in Figure 16–23.

FIGURE 16–23

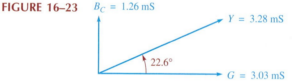

Related Problem   Calculate the total admittance in Figure 16–22 if f is increased to 2.5 kHz.

**SECTION 16–4
REVIEW**

1. Define *conductance, capacitive susceptance,* and *admittance.*
2. If $Z = 100\ \Omega$, what is the value of *Y*?
3. In a certain parallel *RC* circuit, $R = 47\ \Omega$ and $X_C = 75\ \Omega$. Determine **Y**.
4. In Question 3, what is **Z**?

16–5 ■ ANALYSIS OF PARALLEL *RC* CIRCUITS

In the previous section, you learned how to express the impedance of a parallel RC circuit. Now, Ohm's law and Kirchhoff's current law are used in the analysis of RC circuits. Current and voltage relationships in a parallel RC circuit are examined.

After completing this section, you should be able to

■ **Analyze a parallel *RC* circuit**
  • Apply Ohm's law and Kirchhoff's current law to parallel *RC* circuits
  • Express the voltages and currents as phasor quantities

- Show how impedance and phase angle vary with frequency
- Convert from a parallel circuit to an equivalent series circuit

For convenience in the analysis of parallel circuits, the Ohm's law formulas using impedance, previously stated, can be rewritten for admittance using the relation $Y = 1/Z$. Remember, the use of boldface nonitalic letters indicates phasor quantities.

$$\mathbf{V} = \frac{\mathbf{I}}{\mathbf{Y}} \qquad (16\text{–}21)$$

$$\mathbf{I} = \mathbf{V}\mathbf{Y} \qquad (16\text{–}22)$$

$$\mathbf{Y} = \frac{\mathbf{I}}{\mathbf{V}} \qquad (16\text{–}23)$$

EXAMPLE 16–7

Determine the total current and phase angle in Figure 16–24. Draw a phasor diagram showing the relationship of $\mathbf{V}_s$ and $\mathbf{I}_{tot}$.

FIGURE 16–24

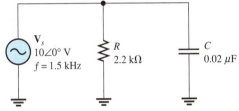

Solution The capacitive reactance is

$$X_C = \frac{1}{2\pi f C} = \frac{1}{2\pi(1.5 \text{ kHz})(0.02 \ \mu\text{F})} = 5.31 \text{ k}\Omega$$

The capacitive susceptance magnitude is

$$B_C = \frac{1}{X_C} = \frac{1}{5.31 \text{ k}\Omega} = 188 \ \mu\text{S}$$

The conductance magnitude is

$$G = \frac{1}{R} = \frac{1}{2.2 \text{ k}\Omega} = 455 \ \mu\text{S}$$

The total admittance is

$$\mathbf{Y}_{tot} = G + jB_C = 455 \ \mu\text{S} + j188 \ \mu\text{S}$$

Converting to polar form yields

$$\mathbf{Y}_{tot} = \sqrt{G^2 + B_C^2} \angle\tan^{-1}\left(\frac{B_C}{G}\right)$$

$$= \sqrt{(455 \ \mu\text{S})^2 + (188 \ \mu\text{S})^2} \angle\tan^{-1}\left(\frac{188 \ \mu\text{S}}{455 \ \mu\text{S}}\right) = 492\angle22.5° \ \mu\text{S}$$

The phase angle is 22.5°.

Use Ohm's law to determine the total current.

$$\mathbf{I}_{tot} = \mathbf{V}_s\mathbf{Y}_{tot} = (10\angle 0°\ \text{V})(492\angle 22.5°\ \mu\text{S}) = \mathbf{4.92\angle 22.5°\ mA}$$

The magnitude of the total current is 4.92 mA, and it leads the applied voltage by **22.5°**, as the phasor diagram in Figure 16–25 indicates.

FIGURE 16–25

$I_{tot} = 4.92\ \text{mA}$

22.5°

$V_s = 10\ \text{V}$

Related Problem What is the total current (in polar form) if *f* is doubled?

Relationships of the Currents and Voltages in a Parallel *RC* Circuit

Figure 16–26(a) shows all the currents in a basic parallel *RC* circuit. The total current, I_{tot}, divides at the junction into the two branch currents, I_R and I_C. The applied voltage, V_s, appears across both the resistive and the capacitive branches, so V_s, V_R, and V_C are all in phase and of the same magnitude.

FIGURE 16–26
Currents in a parallel RC circuit.

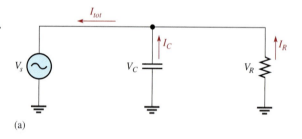 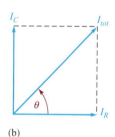

(a)   (b)

The current through the resistor is in phase with the voltage. The current through the capacitor leads the voltage, and thus the resistive current, by 90°. By Kirchhoff's current law, the total current is the phasor sum of the two branch currents, as shown by the phasor diagram in Figure 16–26(b). The total current is expressed as

$$\mathbf{I}_{tot} = I_R + jI_C \tag{16–24}$$

This equation can be expressed in polar form as

$$\mathbf{I}_{tot} = \sqrt{I_R^2 + I_C^2}\angle\tan^{-1}\left(\frac{I_C}{I_R}\right) \tag{16–25}$$

where the magnitude of the total current is

$$I_{tot} = \sqrt{I_R^2 + I_C^2} \tag{16–26}$$

and the phase angle between the resistor current and the total current is

$$\theta = \tan^{-1}\left(\frac{I_C}{I_R}\right) \tag{16–27}$$

Since the resistor current and the applied voltage are in phase, θ also represents the phase angle between the total current and the applied voltage. Figure 16–27 shows a complete current and voltage phasor diagram.

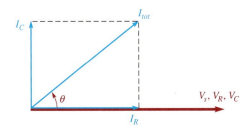

FIGURE 16–27
Current and voltage phasor diagram for a parallel RC circuit (amplitudes are arbitrary).

EXAMPLE 16–8   Determine the value of each current in Figure 16–28, and describe the phase relationship of each with the applied voltage. Draw the current phasor diagram.

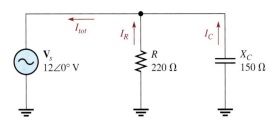

FIGURE 16–28

Solution   The resistor current, the capacitor current, and the total current are expressed as follows:

$$\mathbf{I}_R = \frac{\mathbf{V}_s}{\mathbf{R}} = \frac{12\angle0°\text{ V}}{220\angle0°\text{ }\Omega} = \mathbf{54.5\angle0°}\text{ mA}$$

$$\mathbf{I}_C = \frac{\mathbf{V}_s}{\mathbf{X}_C} = \frac{12\angle0°\text{ V}}{150\angle-90°\text{ }\Omega} = \mathbf{80\angle90°}\text{ mA}$$

$$\mathbf{I}_{tot} = I_R + jI_C = 54.5\text{ mA} + j80\text{ mA}$$

Converting $\mathbf{I}_{tot}$ to polar form yields

$$\mathbf{I}_{tot} = \sqrt{I_R^2 + I_C^2}\angle\tan^{-1}\left(\frac{I_C}{I_R}\right)$$

$$= \sqrt{(54.5\text{ mA})^2 + (80\text{ mA})^2}\angle\tan^{-1}\left(\frac{80\text{ mA}}{54.5\text{ mA}}\right) = \mathbf{96.8\angle55.7°}\text{ mA}$$

As the results show, the resistor current is 54.5 mA and is in phase with the voltage. The capacitor current is 80 mA and leads the voltage by 90°. The total current is 96.8 mA and leads the voltage by 55.7°. The phasor diagram in Figure 16–29 illustrates these relationships.

FIGURE 16–29

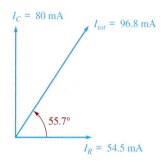

I_C = 80 mA   *I_tot* = 96.8 mA   55.7°   *I_R* = 54.5 mA

Related Problem In a parallel circuit, $\mathbf{I}_R = 100\angle0°$ mA and $\mathbf{I}_C = 60\angle90°$ mA. Determine the total current.

Conversion from Parallel to Series Form

For every parallel *RC* circuit, there is an equivalent series *RC* circuit. Two circuits are considered equivalent when they both present an equal impedance at their terminals; that is, the magnitude of impedance and the phase angle are identical.

To obtain the equivalent series circuit for a given parallel *RC* circuit, first find the impedance and phase angle of the parallel circuit. Then use the values of *Z* and *θ* to construct an impedance triangle shown in Figure 16–30. The vertical and horizontal sides of the triangle represent the equivalent series resistance and capacitive reactance as indicated. These values can be found using the following trigonometric relationships:

$$R_{eq} = Z \cos \theta \qquad (16\text{–}28)$$

$$X_{C(eq)} = Z \sin \theta \qquad (16\text{–}29)$$

FIGURE 16–30
Impedance triangle for the series equivalent of a parallel RC circuit. Z and θ are the known values for the parallel circuit. R_{eq} and $X_{C(eq)}$ are the series equivalent values.

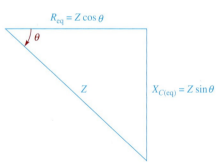

$R_{eq} = Z \cos \theta$ θ Z $X_{C(eq)} = Z \sin \theta$

EXAMPLE 16–9 Convert the parallel circuit in Figure 16–31 to a series form.

FIGURE 16–31

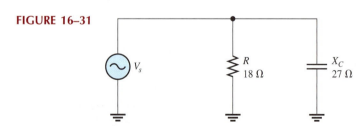

V_s R 18 Ω X_C 27 Ω

Solution   First, find the admittance of the parallel circuit as follows:

$$G = \frac{1}{R} = \frac{1}{18 \ \Omega} = 55.6 \text{ mS}$$

$$B_C = \frac{1}{X_C} = \frac{1}{27 \ \Omega} = 37.0 \text{ mS}$$

$$\mathbf{Y} = G + jB_C = 55.6 \text{ mS} + j37.0 \text{ mS}$$

Converting to polar form yields

$$\mathbf{Y} = \sqrt{G^2 + B_C^2} \angle \tan^{-1}\left(\frac{B_C}{G}\right)$$

$$= \sqrt{(55.6 \text{ mS})^2 + (37.0 \text{ mS})^2} \angle \tan^{-1}\left(\frac{37.0 \text{ mS}}{55.6 \text{ mS}}\right) = 66.8 \angle 33.6° \text{ mS}$$

Then, the total impedance is

$$\mathbf{Z}_{tot} = \frac{1}{\mathbf{Y}} = \frac{1}{66.8 \angle 33.6° \text{ mS}} = 15.0 \angle -33.6° \ \Omega$$

Converting to rectangular form yields

$$\mathbf{Z}_{tot} = Z \cos \theta - jZ \sin \theta = R_{eq} - jX_{C(eq)}$$
$$= 15.0 \cos(-33.6°) - j15.0 \sin(33.6°) = 12.5 \ \Omega - j8.31 \ \Omega$$

The equivalent series *RC* circuit is a 12.5 Ω resistor in series with a capacitive reactance of 8.31 Ω. This is shown in Figure 16–32.

FIGURE 16–32

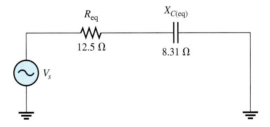

Related Problem   The impedance of a parallel *RC* circuit is $\mathbf{Z} = 10\angle -26° \text{ k}\Omega$. Convert to an equivalent series circuit.

SECTION 16–5 REVIEW

1. The admittance of an *RC* circuit is 3.50 mS, and the applied voltage is 6 V. What is the total current?

2. In a certain parallel *RC* circuit, the resistor current is 10 mA, and the capacitor current is 15 mA. Determine the magnitude and phase angle of the total current. This phase angle is measured with respect to what?

3. What is the phase angle between the capacitor current and the applied voltage in a parallel *RC* circuit?

♦ *Coverage of parallel reactive circuits continues in Chapter 17, Part 2, on page 672.*

PART 3

SERIES-PARALLEL REACTIVE CIRCUITS

16–6 ■ SERIES-PARALLEL *RC* CIRCUITS

In this section, the concepts studied with respect to series and parallel circuits are used to analyze circuits with combinations of both series and parallel R and C elements.

After completing this section, you should be able to

■ **Analyze series-parallel *RC* circuits**
  • Determine total impedance
  • Calculate currents and voltages
  • Measure impedance and phase angle

Series-parallel circuits consist of arrangements of both series and parallel elements. The following two examples demonstrate how to approach the analysis of series-parallel *RC* networks.

EXAMPLE 16–10   In the circuit of Figure 16–33, determine the following:
(a) total impedance   (b) total current   (c) phase angle by which I_{tot} leads V_s

FIGURE 16–33

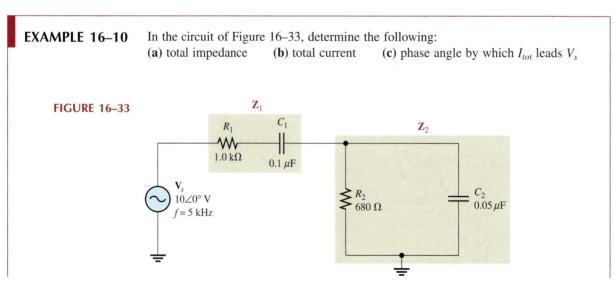

Solution

(a) First, calculate the magnitudes of capacitive reactance.

$$X_{C1} = \frac{1}{2\pi fC} = \frac{1}{2\pi(5\text{ kHz})(0.1\ \mu\text{F})} = 318\ \Omega$$

$$X_{C2} = \frac{1}{2\pi fC} = \frac{1}{2\pi(5\text{ kHz})(0.05\ \mu\text{F})} = 637\ \Omega$$

One approach is to find the impedance of the series portion and the impedance of the parallel portion and combine them to get the total impedance. The impedance of the series combination of R_1 and C_1 is

$$\mathbf{Z}_1 = R_1 - jX_{C1} = 1.0\text{ k}\Omega - j318\ \Omega$$

To determine the impedance of the parallel portion, first determine the admittance of the parallel combination of R_2 and C_2.

$$G_2 = \frac{1}{R_2} = \frac{1}{680\ \Omega} = 1.47\text{ mS}$$

$$B_{C2} = \frac{1}{X_{C2}} = \frac{1}{637\ \Omega} = 1.57\text{ mS}$$

$$\mathbf{Y}_2 = G_2 + jB_{C2} = 1.47\text{ mS} + j1.57\text{ mS}$$

Converting to polar form yields

$$\mathbf{Y}_2 = \sqrt{G_2^2 + B_{C2}^2}\angle\tan^{-1}\left(\frac{B_{C2}}{G_2}\right)$$

$$= \sqrt{(1.47\text{ mS})^2 + (1.57\text{ mS})^2}\angle\tan^{-1}\left(\frac{1.57\text{ mS}}{1.47\text{ mS}}\right) = 2.15\angle46.9°\text{ mS}$$

Then, the impedance of the parallel portion is

$$\mathbf{Z}_2 = \frac{1}{\mathbf{Y}_2} = \frac{1}{2.15\angle46.9°\text{ mS}} = 465\angle-46.9°\ \Omega$$

Converting to rectangular form yields

$$\mathbf{Z}_2 = Z_2\cos\theta - jZ_2\sin\theta$$
$$= (465\ \Omega)\cos(-46.9°) - j(465\ \Omega)\sin(-46.9°) = 318\ \Omega - j339\ \Omega$$

The series portion and the parallel portion are in series with each other. Combine $\mathbf{Z}_1$ and $\mathbf{Z}_2$ to get the total impedance.

$$\mathbf{Z}_{tot} = \mathbf{Z}_1 + \mathbf{Z}_2$$
$$= (1.0\text{ k}\Omega - j318\ \Omega) + (318\ \Omega - j339\ \Omega) = 1318\ \Omega - j657\ \Omega$$

Expressing $\mathbf{Z}_{tot}$ in polar form yields

$$\mathbf{Z}_{tot} = \sqrt{Z_1^2 + Z_2^2}\angle-\tan^{-1}\left(\frac{Z_2}{Z_1}\right)$$

$$= \sqrt{(1318\ \Omega)^2 + (657\ \Omega)^2}\angle-\tan^{-1}\left(\frac{657\ \Omega}{1318\ \Omega}\right) = \mathbf{1.47\angle-26.5°\text{ k}\Omega}$$

(b) Use Ohm's law to determine the total current.

$$\mathbf{I}_{tot} = \frac{\mathbf{V}_s}{\mathbf{Z}_{tot}} = \frac{10\angle0°\text{ V}}{1.47\angle-26.5°\text{ k}\Omega} = \mathbf{6.80\angle26.5°\text{ mA}}$$

(c) The total current leads the applied voltage by **26.5°**.

Related Problem Determine the voltages across $\mathbf{Z}_1$ and $\mathbf{Z}_2$ in Figure 16–33 and express in polar form.

EXAMPLE 16–11   Determine all currents in Figure 16–34. Sketch a current phasor diagram.

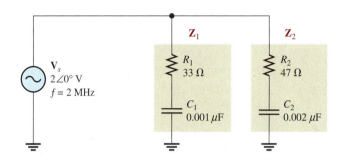

FIGURE 16–34

Solution   First, calculate X_{C1} and X_{C2}.

$$X_{C1} = \frac{1}{2\pi fC} = \frac{1}{2\pi(2 \text{ MHz})(0.001 \ \mu\text{F})} = 79.6 \ \Omega$$

$$X_{C2} = \frac{1}{2\pi fC} = \frac{1}{2\pi(2 \text{ MHz})(0.002 \ \mu\text{F})} = 39.8 \ \Omega$$

Next, determine the impedance of each of the two parallel branches.

$$\mathbf{Z}_1 = R_1 - jX_{C1} = 33 \ \Omega - j79.6 \ \Omega$$
$$\mathbf{Z}_2 = R_2 - jX_{C2} = 47 \ \Omega - j39.8 \ \Omega$$

Convert these impedances to polar form.

$$\mathbf{Z}_1 = \sqrt{R_1^2 + X_{C1}^2}\angle -\tan^{-1}\left(\frac{X_{C1}}{R_1}\right)$$

$$= \sqrt{(33 \ \Omega)^2 + (79.6 \ \Omega)^2}\angle -\tan^{-1}\left(\frac{79.6 \ \Omega}{33 \ \Omega}\right) = 86.2\angle -67.5° \ \Omega$$

$$\mathbf{Z}_2 = \sqrt{R_2^2 + X_{C2}^2}\angle -\tan^{-1}\left(\frac{X_{C2}}{R_2}\right)$$

$$= \sqrt{(47 \ \Omega)^2 + (39.8 \ \Omega)^2}\angle -\tan^{-1}\left(\frac{39.8 \ \Omega}{47 \ \Omega}\right) = 61.6\angle -40.3° \ \Omega$$

Calculate each branch current.

$$\mathbf{I}_1 = \frac{\mathbf{V}_s}{\mathbf{Z}_1} = \frac{2\angle 0° \text{ V}}{86.2\angle -67.5° \ \Omega} = \mathbf{23.2}\angle \mathbf{67.5° \text{ mA}}$$

$$\mathbf{I}_2 = \frac{\mathbf{V}_s}{\mathbf{Z}_2} = \frac{2\angle 0° \text{ V}}{61.6\angle -40.3° \ \Omega} = \mathbf{32.5}\angle \mathbf{40.3° \text{ mA}}$$

To get the total current, express each branch current in rectangular form so that they can be added.

$$\mathbf{I}_1 = 8.89 \text{ mA} + j21.4 \text{ mA}$$
$$\mathbf{I}_2 = 24.8 \text{ mA} + j21.0 \text{ mA}$$

The total current is

$$\mathbf{I}_{tot} = \mathbf{I}_1 + \mathbf{I}_2$$
$$= (8.89 \text{ mA} + j21.4 \text{ mA}) + (24.8 \text{ mA} + j21.0 \text{ mA}) = 33.7 \text{ mA} + j42.4 \text{ mA}$$

Converting $\mathbf{I}_{tot}$ to polar form yields

$$\mathbf{I}_{tot} = \sqrt{(33.7 \text{ mA})^2 + (42.4 \text{ mA})^2} \angle \tan^{-1}\left(\frac{42.4 \ \Omega}{33.7 \ \Omega}\right) = \mathbf{54.2 \angle 51.6° \ mA}$$

The current phasor diagram is shown in Figure 16–35.

FIGURE 16–35

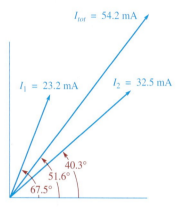

Related Problem Determine the voltages across each component in Figure 16–34 and sketch a voltage phasor diagram.

Measurement of Z_{tot} and θ

Now, let's see how the values of Z_{tot} and θ for the circuit in Example 16–10 can be determined by measurement. First, the total impedance is measured as outlined in the following steps and as illustrated in Figure 16–36 (other ways are also possible):

Step 1. Using a sine wave generator, set the source voltage to a known value (10 V) and the frequency to 5 kHz. If your generator is not accurate, then it is advisable to check the voltage with an ac voltmeter and the frequency with a frequency counter rather than relying on the marked values on the generator controls.

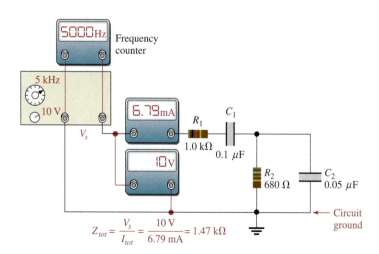

FIGURE 16–36
Determining Z_{tot} by measurement of V_s and I_{tot}.

Step 2. Connect an ac ammeter as shown in Figure 16–36, and measure the total current.

Step 3. Calculate the total impedance by using Ohm's law.

To measure the phase angle, an analog oscilloscope is used in this illustration. The basic method of measuring a phase angle on an analog oscilloscope was introduced in the TECH TIP in Chapter 12. We will use that method here in an *RC* circuit.

To measure the phase angle, the source voltage and the total current must be displayed on the screen in the proper time relationship. Two basic types of scope probes are available to measure the quantities with an oscilloscope: the voltage probe and the current probe. Although the current probe is a convenient device, it is often not as readily available or as practical to use as a voltage probe. For this reason, we will confine our phase measurement technique to the use of voltage probes in conjunction with the oscilloscope. A typical oscilloscope voltage probe has two points, the probe tip and the ground lead, that are connected to the circuit. Thus, all voltage measurements must be referenced to ground.

Since only voltage probes are to be used, the total current cannot be measured directly. However, for phase measurement, the voltage across R_1 is in phase with the total current and can be used to establish the phase angle.

Before proceeding with the actual phase measurement, note that there is a problem with displaying V_{R1}. If the scope probe is connected across the resistor, as indicated in Figure 16–37(a), the ground lead of the scope will short point B to ground, thus bypassing the rest of the components and effectively removing them from the circuit electrically, as illustrated in Figure 16–37(b) (assuming that the scope is not isolated from power line ground).

To avoid this problem, you can switch the generator output terminals so that one end of R_1 is connected to ground, as shown in Figure 16–38(a). This connection does not alter

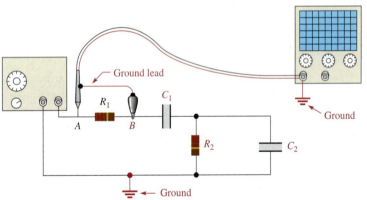

(a) Ground lead on scope probe grounds point *B*.

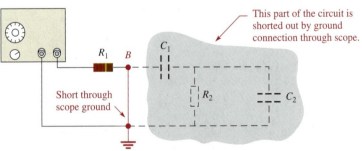

(b) The effect of grounding point *B* is to short out the rest of the circuit.

FIGURE 16–37

Undesirable effects of measuring directly across a component when the instrument and the circuit are grounded.

the circuit electrically because R_1 still has the same series relationship with the rest of the circuit. Now the scope can be connected across it to display V_{R1}, as indicated in part (b) of the figure. The other probe is connected across the voltage source to display V_s as indicated. Now channel 1 of the scope has V_{R1} as an input, and channel 2 has V_s. The trigger source switch on the scope should be on internal so that each trace on the screen will be triggered by one of the inputs and the other will then be shown in the proper time relationship to it. Since amplitudes are not important, the volts/div settings are arbitrary. The sec/div settings should be adjusted so that one half-cycle of the waveforms appears on the screen.

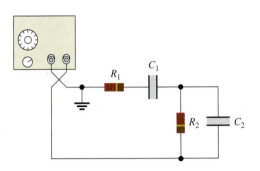

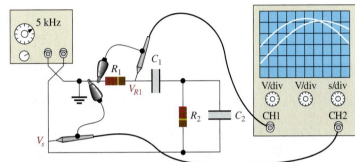

(a) Ground repositioned so that one end of R_1 is grounded.

(b) The scope displays a half-cycle of V_{R1} and V_s. V_{R1} represents the phase of the total current. Decalibrate both channels to make both voltages appear to have the same amplitude.

FIGURE 16–38

Repositioning ground so that a direct voltage measurement can be made with respect to ground without shorting out part of the circuit.

Before connecting the probes to the circuit in Figure 16–38, you must align the two horizontal lines (traces) so that they appear as a single line across the center of the screen. To do so, ground the probe tips and adjust the vertical position knobs to move the traces toward the center line of the screen until they are superimposed. This procedure ensures that both waveforms have the same zero crossing so that an accurate phase measurement can be made.

The resulting oscilloscope display is shown in Figure 16–39. Since there are 180° in one half-cycle, each of the ten horizontal divisions across the screen represents 18°. Thus, the horizontal distance between the corresponding points of the two waveforms is the phase angle in degrees as indicated.

FIGURE 16–39

Measurement of the phase angle on the oscilloscope.

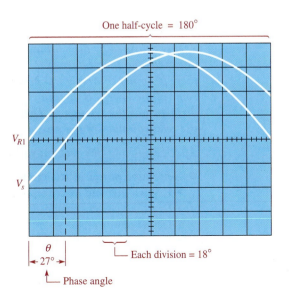

**SECTION 16–6
REVIEW**

1. What is the equivalent series *RC* circuit for the series-parallel circuit in Figure 16–33?
2. What is the total impedance in polar form of the circuit in Figure 16–34?

♦ *Coverage of series-parallel reactive circuits continues in Chapter 17, Part 3, on page 679.*

PART 4
SPECIAL TOPICS

16–7 ■ POWER IN *RC* CIRCUITS

In a purely resistive ac circuit, all of the energy delivered by the source is dissipated in the form of heat by the resistance. In a purely capacitive ac circuit, all of the energy delivered by the source is stored by the capacitor during a portion of the voltage cycle and then returned to the source during another portion of the cycle so that there is no net conversion to heat. When there is both resistance and capacitance, some of the energy is alternately stored and returned by the capacitance and some is dissipated by the resistance. The amount of energy converted to heat is determined by the relative values of the resistance and the capacitive reactance.

After completing this section, you should be able to

■ **Determine power in *RC* circuits**
  • Explain true and reactive power
  • Draw the power triangle
  • Define *power factor*
  • Explain apparent power
  • Calculate power in an *RC* circuit

It is reasonable to assume that when the resistance is greater than the capacitive reactance, more of the total energy delivered by the source is converted to heat by the resistance than is stored by the capacitance. Likewise, when the reactance is greater than the resistance, more of the total energy is stored and returned than is converted to heat.

The formulas for power in a resistor, sometimes called *true power* (P_{true}), and the power in a capacitor, called *reactive power* (P_r), are restated here. The unit of true power is the watt, and the unit of reactive power is the VAR (volt-ampere reactive).

$$P_{\text{true}} = I^2R \tag{16–30}$$

$$P_r = I^2X_C \tag{16–31}$$

The Power Triangle for *RC* Circuits

The generalized impedance phasor diagram is shown in Figure 16–40(a). A phasor relationship for the powers can also be represented by a similar diagram because the respective magnitudes of the powers, P_{true} and P_r, differ from R and X_C by a factor of I^2. This is shown in Figure 16–40(b).

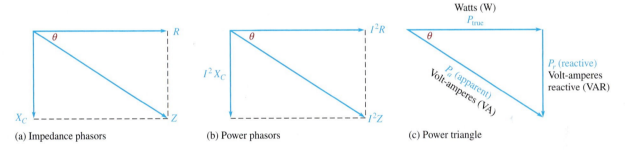

(a) Impedance phasors   (b) Power phasors   (c) Power triangle

FIGURE 16–40
Development of the power triangle for an RC circuit.

The resultant power phasor, I^2Z, represents the **apparent power**, P_a. At any instant in time P_a is the total power that appears to be transferred between the source and the *RC* circuit. The unit of apparent power is the volt-ampere, VA. The expression for apparent power is

$$P_a = I^2Z \tag{16–32}$$

The power phasor diagram in Figure 16–40(b) can be rearranged in the form of a right triangle, as shown in Figure 16–40(c). This is called the *power triangle*. Using the rules of trigonometry, P_{true} can be expressed as

$$P_{\text{true}} = P_a\cos\theta \tag{16–33}$$

Since P_a equals I^2Z or VI, the equation for the true power dissipation in an *RC* circuit can be written as

$$P_{\text{true}} = VI\cos\theta \tag{16–34}$$

where V is the applied voltage and I is the total current.

For the case of a purely resistive current, $\theta = 0°$ and $\cos 0° = 1$, so P_{true} equals VI. For the case of a purely capacitive circuit, $\theta = 90°$ and $\cos 90° = 0$, so P_{true} is zero. As you already know, there is no power dissipation in an ideal capacitor.

The Power Factor

The term $\cos \theta$ is called the **power factor** and is stated as

$$PF = \cos \theta \qquad \text{(16–35)}$$

As the phase angle between applied voltage and total current increases, the power factor decreases, indicating an increasingly reactive circuit. The smaller the power factor, the smaller the power dissipation.

The power factor can vary from 0 for a purely reactive circuit to 1 for a purely resistive circuit. In an RC circuit, the power factor is referred to as a leading power factor because the current leads the voltage.

EXAMPLE 16–12 Determine the power factor and the true power in the circuit of Figure 16–41.

FIGURE 16–41

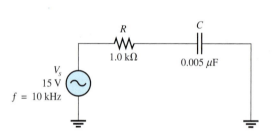

Solution The capacitive reactance is

$$X_C = \frac{1}{2\pi f C} = \frac{1}{2\pi (10 \text{ kHz})(0.005 \ \mu F)} = 3.18 \text{ k}\Omega$$

The total impedance of the circuit in rectangular form is

$$\mathbf{Z} = R - jX_C = 1.0 \text{ k}\Omega - j3.18 \text{ k}\Omega$$

Converting to polar form yields

$$\mathbf{Z} = \sqrt{R^2 + X_C^2} \angle -\tan^{-1}\left(\frac{X_C}{R}\right)$$

$$= \sqrt{(1.0 \text{ k}\Omega)^2 + (3.18 \text{ k}\Omega^2)} \angle -\tan^{-1}\left(\frac{3.18 \text{ k}\Omega}{1.0 \text{ k}\Omega}\right) = 3.33 \angle -72.5° \text{ k}\Omega$$

The angle associated with the impedance is θ, the angle between the applied voltage and the total current; therefore, the power factor is

$$PF = \cos \theta = \cos(-72.5°) = \mathbf{0.301}$$

The current magnitude is

$$I = \frac{V_s}{Z} = \frac{15 \text{ V}}{3.33 \text{ k}\Omega} = 4.50 \text{ mA}$$

The true power is

$$P_{true} = V_s I \cos \theta = (15 \text{ V})(4.50 \text{ mA})(0.301) = \mathbf{20.3 \ mW}$$

Related Problem What is the power factor if f is reduced by half in Figure 16–41?

The Significance of Apparent Power

As mentioned, apparent power is the power that appears to be transferred between the source and the load, and it consists of two components—a true power component and a reactive power component.

In all electrical and electronic systems, it is the true power that does the work. The reactive power is simply shuttled back and forth between the source and load. Ideally, in terms of performing useful work, all of the power transferred to the load should be true power and none of it reactive power. However, in most practical situations the load has some reactance associated with it, and therefore you must deal with both power components.

In Chapter 15, we discussed the use of apparent power in relation to transformers. For any reactive load, there are two components of the total current: the resistive component and the reactive component. If you consider only the true power (watts) in a load, you are dealing with only a portion of the total current that the load demands from a source. In order to have a realistic picture of the actual current that a load will draw, you must consider apparent power (VA).

A source such as an ac generator can provide current to a load up to some maximum value. If the load draws more than this maximum value, the source can be damaged. Figure 16–42(a) shows a 120 V generator that can deliver a maximum current of 5 A to a load. Assume that the generator is rated at 600 W and is connected to a purely resistive load of 24 Ω (power factor of 1). The ammeter shows that the current is 5 A, and the wattmeter indicates that the power is 600 W. The generator has no problem under these conditions, although it is operating at maximum current and power.

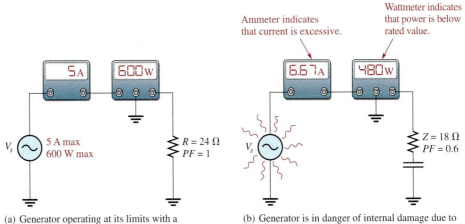

(a) Generator operating at its limits with a resistive load.

(b) Generator is in danger of internal damage due to excess current, even though the wattmeter indicates that the power is below the maximum wattage rating.

FIGURE 16–42

Wattage rating of a source is inappropriate when the load is reactive. The rating should be in VA rather than in watts.

Now, consider what happens if the load is changed to a reactive one with an impedance of 18 Ω and a power factor of 0.6, as indicated in Figure 16–42(b). The current is 120 V/18 Ω = 6.67 A, which *exceeds* the maximum. Even though the wattmeter reads 480 W, which is less than the power rating of the generator, the excessive current probably will cause damage. This illustration shows that a true power rating can be deceiving and is inappropriate for ac sources. The ac generator should be rated at 600 VA, a rating that manufacturers generally use, rather than 600 W.

EXAMPLE 16–13   For the circuit in Figure 16–43, find the true power, the reactive power, and the apparent power.

FIGURE 16–43

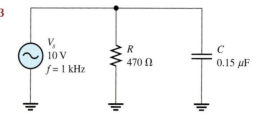

Solution From Figure 16–43, $R = 470\ \Omega$; thus $G = 1/R = 1/470\ \Omega = 2.13$ mS. The capacitive reactance is

$$X_C = \frac{1}{2\pi fC} = \frac{1}{2\pi(1000\ \text{Hz})(0.15\ \mu\text{F})} = 1061\ \Omega$$

$$I_R = \frac{V_s}{R} = \frac{10\ \text{V}}{470\ \Omega} = 21.3\ \text{mA}$$

$$I_C = \frac{V_s}{X_C} = \frac{10\ \text{V}}{1061\ \Omega} = 9.43\ \text{mA}$$

The true power is

$$P_{\text{true}} = I_R^2 R = (21.3\ \text{mA})^2(470\ \Omega) = \textbf{213 mW}$$

The reactive power is

$$P_r = I_C^2 X_C = (9.43\ \text{mA})^2(1061\ \Omega) = \textbf{94.3 mVAR}$$

The apparent power is

$$P_a = \sqrt{P_{\text{true}}^2 + P_r^2} = \sqrt{(213\ \text{mW})^2 + (94.3\ \text{mVAR})^2} = \textbf{233 mVA}$$

Related Problem What is the true power in Figure 16–43 if the frequency is changed to 2 kHz?

SECTION 16–7
REVIEW

1. To which component in an RC circuit is the power dissipation due?
2. The phase angle, θ, is 45°. What is the power factor?
3. A certain series RC circuit has the following parameter values: $R = 330\ \Omega$, $X_C = 460\ \Omega$, and $I = 2$ A. Determine the true power, the reactive power, and the apparent power.

16–8 ■ BASIC APPLICATIONS

RC circuits are found in a variety of applications, often as part of a more complex circuit. Two major applications, phase shift networks and frequency-selective networks (filters), are covered in this section.

After completing this section, you should be able to

■ **Discuss some basic RC applications**
  • Discuss and analyze the RC lag network
  • Discuss and analyze the RC lead network
  • Discuss how the RC circuit operates as a filter

The *RC* Lag Network

The *RC* lag network is a phase shift circuit in which the output voltage lags the input voltage by a specified amount. Figure 16–44(a) shows a series *RC* circuit with the output voltage taken across the capacitor. The source voltage is the input, V_{in}. As you know, θ, the phase angle between the current and the input voltage, is also the phase angle between the resistor voltage and the input voltage because V_R and I are in phase with each other.

FIGURE 16–44

RC lag network ($V_{out} = V_C$).

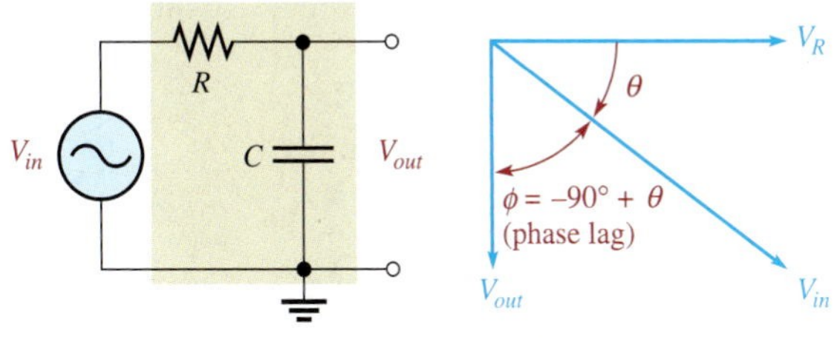

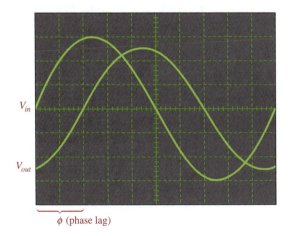

(a) A basic *RC* lag network

(b) Phasor voltage diagram showing the phase lag between V_{in} and V_{out}

Since V_C lags V_R by 90°, the phase angle between the capacitor voltage and the input voltage is the difference between −90° and θ, as shown in Figure 16–44(b). The capacitor voltage is the output, and it lags the input, thus creating a basic lag network.

When the input and output voltage waveforms of the lag network are displayed on an oscilloscope, a relationship similar to that in Figure 16–45 is observed. The amount of phase difference, designated ϕ, between the input and the output is dependent on the relative sizes of the capacitive reactance and the resistance, as is the magnitude of the output voltage.

V_{in}

V_{out}

ϕ (phase lag)

FIGURE 16–45

Oscilloscope display of the input and output voltage waveforms of a lag network (V_{out} lags V_{in}). The angle shown is arbitrary.

Phase Difference Between Input and Output As already established, θ is the phase angle between I and V_{in}. The angle between V_{out} and V_{in} is designated ϕ (phi) and is developed as follows.

The polar expressions for the input voltage and the current are $V_{in}\angle 0°$ and $I\angle\theta$, respectively. The output voltage is

$$\mathbf{V}_{out} = (I\angle\theta)(X_C\angle{-90°}) = IX_C\angle(-90° + \theta)$$

The preceding equation states that the output voltage is at an angle of $-90° + \theta$ with respect to the input voltage. Since $\theta = -\tan^{-1}(X_C/R)$, the angle between the input and output is

$$\phi = -90° + \tan^{-1}\left(\frac{X_C}{R}\right) \tag{16–36}$$

This angle is always negative, indicating that the output voltage lags the input voltage, as shown in Figure 16–46.

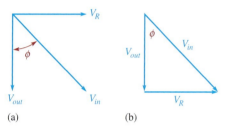

(a)   (b)

FIGURE 16–46

EXAMPLE 16–14   Determine the amount of phase lag from input to output in each lag network in Figure 16–47.

FIGURE 16–47

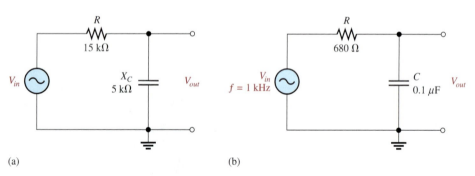

(a)   (b)

Solution   For the lag network in Figure 16–47(a),

$$\phi = -90° + \tan^{-1}\left(\frac{X_C}{R}\right) = -90° + \tan^{-1}\left(\frac{5 \text{ k}\Omega}{15 \text{ k}\Omega}\right) = -90° + 18.4° = \mathbf{-71.6°}$$

The output lags the input by 71.6°.
   For the lag network in Figure 16–47(b), first determine the capacitive reactance.

$$X_C = \frac{1}{2\pi fC} = \frac{1}{2\pi(1 \text{ kHz})(0.1 \text{ } \mu\text{F})} = 1.59 \text{ k}\Omega$$

$$\phi = -90° + \tan^{-1}\left(\frac{X_C}{R}\right) = -90° + \tan^{-1}\left(\frac{1.59 \text{ k}\Omega}{680 \text{ }\Omega}\right) = \mathbf{-23.2°}$$

The output lags the input by 23.2°.

Related Problem   In a lag network, what happens to the phase lag if the frequency increases?

Magnitude of the Output Voltage   To evaluate the output voltage in terms of its magnitude, visualize the *RC* lag network as a voltage divider. A portion of the total input voltage is dropped across the resistor and a portion across the capacitor. Because the output voltage is the voltage across the capacitor, it can be calculated as

$$V_{out} = \left(\frac{X_C}{\sqrt{R^2 + X_C^2}} \right) V_{in} \qquad \text{(16–37)}$$

Or it can be calculated using Ohm's law as

$$V_{out} = IX_C \qquad \text{(16–38)}$$

The total phasor expression for the output voltage of an *RC* lag network is

$$\mathbf{V}_{out} = V_{out} \angle \phi \qquad \text{(16–39)}$$

EXAMPLE 16–15

For the lag network in Figure 16–47(b) (Example 16–14), determine the output voltage in phasor form when the input voltage has an rms value of 10 V. Sketch the input and output voltage waveforms showing the proper phase relationship. X_C (1.59 kΩ) and ϕ (−23.2°) were found in Example 16–14.

Solution   The output voltage in phasor form is

$$\mathbf{V}_{out} = \left(\frac{X_C}{\sqrt{R^2 + X_C^2}} \right) V_{in} \angle \phi$$

$$= \left(\frac{1.59 \text{ k}\Omega}{\sqrt{(680 \ \Omega)^2 + (1.59 \text{ k}\Omega)^2}} \right) 10 \angle -23.2° \text{ V} = \mathbf{9.20 \angle -23.2° \text{ V rms}}$$

The waveforms are shown in Figure 16–48.

FIGURE 16–48

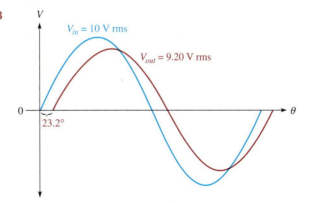

Related Problem   In a lag network, what happens to the output voltage if the frequency increases?

The *RC* Lead Network

The *RC* lead network is a phase shift circuit in which the output voltage leads the input voltage by a specified amount. When the output of a series *RC* circuit is taken across the resistor rather than across the capacitor, as shown in Figure 16–49(a), it becomes a lead network.

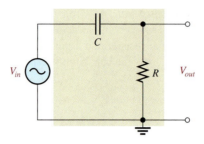
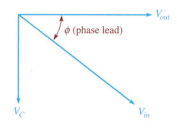

(a) A basic *RC* lead network

(b) Phasor voltage diagram showing
the phase lead between V_{in} and V_{out}

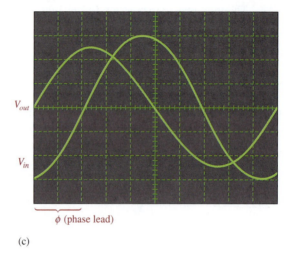

(c)

FIGURE 16–49
RC lead network ($V_{out} = V_R$).

Phase Difference Between Input and Output In a series *RC* circuit, the current leads
the input voltage. Also, as you know, the resistor voltage is in phase with the current.
Since the output voltage is taken across the resistor, the output leads the input, as indicated by the phasor diagram in Figure 16–49(b). A typical oscilloscope display of the
waveforms is shown in Figure 16–49(c).

As in the lag network, the amount of phase difference between the input and output
and also the magnitude of the output voltage in the lead network is dependent on the relative values of the resistance and the capacitive reactance. When the input voltage is
assigned a reference angle of 0°, the angle of the output voltage is the same as θ (the
angle between total current and applied voltage) because the resistor voltage (output) and
the current are in phase with each other. Therefore, since $\phi = \theta$ in this case, the expression is

$$\phi = \tan^{-1}\left(\frac{X_C}{R}\right)$$

(16–40)

This angle is positive because the output leads the input. The following example illustrates the computation of phase angles for lead networks.

EXAMPLE 16–16   Calculate the output phase angle for each circuit in Figure 16–50.

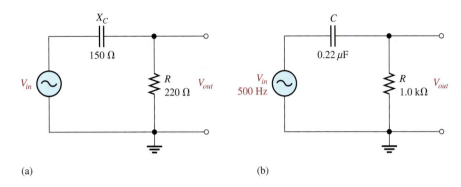

(a)   (b)

FIGURE 16–50

Solution   For the lead network in Figure 16–50(a),

$$\phi = \tan^{-1}\left(\frac{X_C}{R}\right) = \tan^{-1}\left(\frac{150\ \Omega}{220\ \Omega}\right) = \mathbf{34.3°}$$

The output leads the input by 34.3°.
    For the lead network in Figure 16–50(b), first determine the capacitive reactance.

$$X_C = \frac{1}{2\pi f C} = \frac{1}{2\pi(500\ \text{Hz})(0.22\ \mu\text{F})} = 1.45\ \text{k}\Omega$$

$$\phi = \tan^{-1}\left(\frac{X_C}{R}\right) = \tan^{-1}\left(\frac{1.45\ \text{k}\Omega}{1.0\ \text{k}\Omega}\right) = \mathbf{55.4°}$$

The output leads the input by 55.4°.

Related Problem   In a lead network, what happens to the phase lead if the frequency increases?

Magnitude of the Output Voltage   Since the output voltage of an *RC* lead network is taken across the resistor, the magnitude can be calculated using either the voltage-divider formula or Ohm's law.

$$V_{out} = \left(\frac{R}{\sqrt{R^2 + X_C^2}}\right)V_{in} \qquad \qquad \textbf{(16–41)}$$

$$V_{out} = IR \qquad \qquad \textbf{(16–42)}$$

The expression for the output voltage in phasor form is

$$\mathbf{V}_{out} = V_{out}\angle\phi \qquad \qquad \textbf{(16–43)}$$

EXAMPLE 16–17   The input voltage in Figure 16–50(b) (Example 16–16) has an rms value of 10 V. Determine the phasor expression for the output voltage. Sketch the waveform relationships for the input and output voltages showing peak values. The phase angle (55.4°) and X_C (1.45 kΩ) were found in Example 16–16.

Solution   The phasor expression for the output voltage is

$$\mathbf{V}_{out} = \left(\frac{R}{\sqrt{R^2 + X_C^2}}\right) V_{in} \angle \phi = \left(\frac{1.0\ \text{k}\Omega}{1.76\ \text{k}\Omega}\right) 10 \angle 55.4° \text{ V} = \mathbf{5.68 \angle 55.4°\ V\ rms}$$

The peak value of the input voltage is

$$V_{in(p)} = 1.414 V_{in(rms)} = 1.414(10\ \text{V}) = 14.14\ \text{V}$$

The peak value of the output voltage is

$$V_{out(p)} = 1.414 V_{out(rms)} = 1.414(5.68\ \text{V}) = 8.03\ \text{V}$$

The waveforms are shown in Figure 16–51.

FIGURE 16–51

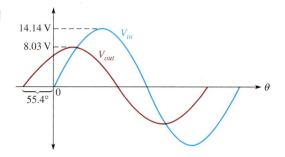

Related Problem   In a lead network, what happens to the output voltage if the frequency is reduced?

The *RC* Circuit as a Filter

Filters are frequency-selective circuits that permit signals of certain frequencies to pass from the input to the output while blocking all others. That is, all frequencies but the selected ones are filtered out. Filters are covered in greater depth in Chapter 19 but are introduced here as an application example.

Series *RC* circuits exhibit a frequency-selective characteristic and therefore act as basic filters. There are two types. The first one that we examine, called a **low-pass filter**, is realized by taking the output across the capacitor, just as in a lag network. The second type, called a **high-pass filter**, is implemented by taking the output across the resistor, as in a lead network.

Low-Pass Filter   You have already seen what happens to the output magnitude and phase angle in the lag network. In terms of its filtering action, we are interested primarily in the variation of the output magnitude with frequency.

Figure 16–52 shows the filtering action of a series *RC* circuit using specific values for illustration. In part (a) of the figure, the input is zero frequency (dc). Since the capacitor blocks constant direct current, the output voltage equals the full value of the input voltage because there is no voltage dropped across *R*. Therefore, the circuit passes all of the input voltage to the output (10 V in, 10 V out).

In Figure 16–52(b), the frequency of the input voltage has been increased to 1 kHz, causing the capacitive reactance to decrease to 159 Ω. For an input voltage of 10 V rms,

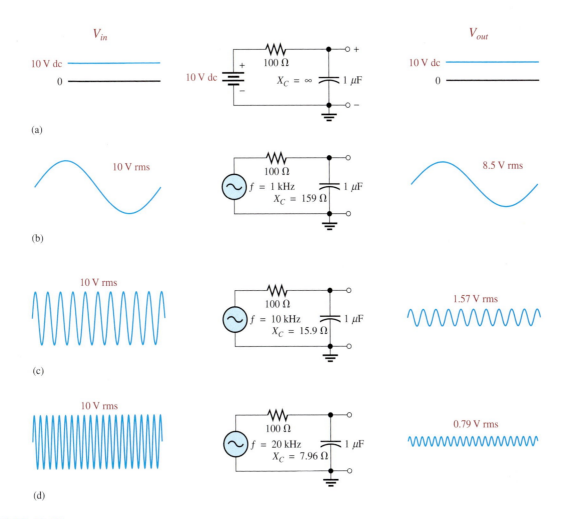

FIGURE 16–52
Low-pass filter action (phase shifts are not indicated).

the output voltage is approximately 8.5 V rms, which can be calculated using the voltage-divider approach or Ohm's law.

In Figure 16–52(c), the input frequency has been increased to 10 kHz, causing the capacitive reactance to decrease further to 15.9 Ω. For a constant input voltage of 10 V rms, the output voltage is now 1.57 V rms.

As the input frequency is increased further, the output voltage continues to decrease and approaches zero as the frequency becomes very high, as shown in Figure 16–52(d).

A description of the circuit action is as follows: As the frequency of the input increases, the capacitive reactance decreases. Because the resistance is constant and the capacitive reactance decreases, the voltage across the capacitor (output voltage) also decreases according to the voltage-divider principle. The input frequency can be increased until it reaches a value at which the reactance is so small compared to the resistance that the output voltage can be neglected because it is very small compared to the input voltage. At this value of frequency, the circuit is essentially completely blocking the input signal.

As shown in Figure 16–52, the circuit passes dc (zero frequency) completely. As the frequency of the input increases, less of the input voltage is passed through to the output; that is, the output voltage decreases as the frequency increases. It is apparent that the lower frequencies pass through the circuit much better than the higher frequencies. This *RC* circuit is therefore a very basic form of low-pass filter.

The **frequency response** of the low-pass filter circuit in Figure 16–52 is shown in Figure 16–53 with a graph of output voltage magnitude versus frequency. This graph, called a *response curve,* indicates that the output decreases as the frequency increases.

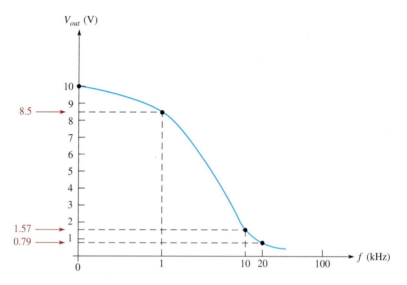

FIGURE 16–53
Frequency response curve for the low-pass filter in Figure 16–52.

High-Pass Filter High-pass filter action is illustrated in Figure 16–54, where the output is taken across the resistor, just as in a lead network. When the input voltage is dc (zero frequency) in part (a), the output is zero volts because the capacitor blocks direct current; therefore, no voltage is developed across R.

In Figure 16–54(b), the frequency of the input signal has been increased to 100 Hz with an rms value of 10 V. The output voltage is 0.63 V rms. Thus, only a small percentage of the input voltage appears on the output at this frequency.

In Figure 16–54(c), the input frequency is increased further to 1 kHz, causing more voltage to be developed across the resistor because of the further decrease in the capacitive reactance. The output voltage at this frequency is 5.32 V rms. As you can see, the output voltage increases as the frequency increases. A value of frequency is reached at which the reactance is negligible compared to the resistance, and most of the input voltage appears across the resistor, as shown in Figure 16–54(d).

As illustrated, this circuit tends to prevent lower frequencies from appearing on the output but allows higher frequencies to pass through from input to output. Therefore, this *RC* circuit is a very basic form of high-pass filter.

The frequency response of the high-pass filter circuit in Figure 16–54 is shown in Figure 16–55 with a graph of output voltage magnitude versus frequency. This response curve shows that the output increases as the frequency increases and then levels off and approaches the value of the input voltage.

The Cutoff Frequency and the Bandwidth of a Filter The frequency at which the capacitive reactance equals the resistance in a low-pass or high-pass *RC* filter is called the **cutoff frequency** and is designated f_c. This condition is expressed as $1/(2\pi f_c C) = R$. Solving for f_c results in the following formula:

$$f_c = \frac{1}{2\pi RC} \tag{16–44}$$

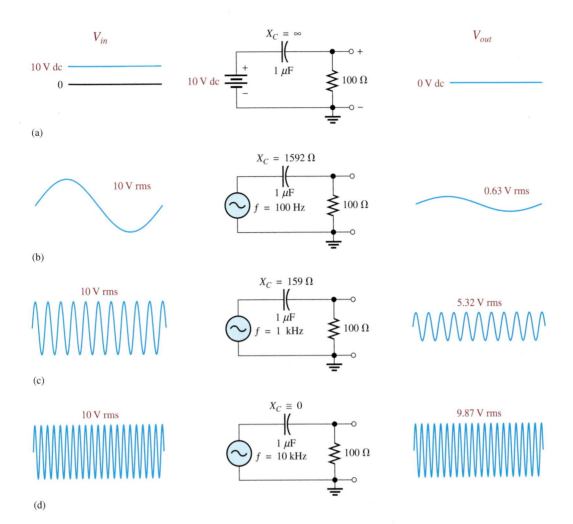

FIGURE 16–54

High-pass filter action (phase shifts are not indicated).

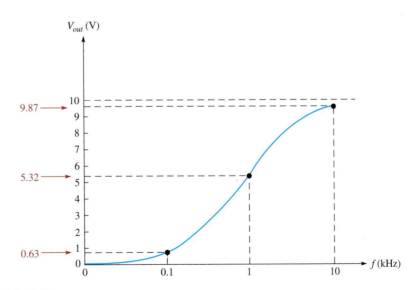

FIGURE 16–55

Frequency response curve for the high-pass filter in Figure 16–54.

At f_c, the output voltage of the filter is 70.7% of its maximum value. It is standard practice to consider the cutoff frequency as the limit of a filter's performance in terms of passing or rejecting frequencies. For example, in a high-pass filter, all frequencies above f_c are considered to be passed by the filter, and all those below f_c are considered to be rejected. The reverse is true for a low-pass filter.

The range of frequencies that is considered to be passed by a filter is called the **bandwidth**. Figure 16–56 illustrates the bandwidth and the cutoff frequency for a low-pass filter.

FIGURE 16–56

Normalized general response curve of a low-pass filter showing the cutoff frequency and the bandwidth.

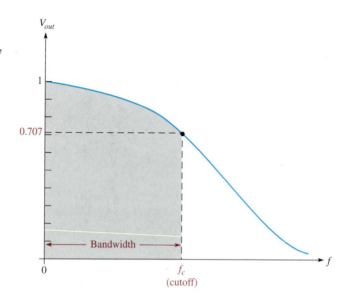

Coupling an AC Signal into a DC Bias Network

Figure 16–57 shows an *RC* network that is used to create a dc voltage level with an ac voltage superimposed on it. This type of circuit is commonly found in amplifiers in which the dc voltage is required to **bias** the amplifier to the proper operating point and the signal voltage to be amplified is coupled through a capacitor and superimposed on the dc level. The capacitor prevents the low internal resistance of the signal source from affecting the dc bias voltage.

FIGURE 16–57

Amplifier bias and signal-coupling circuit.

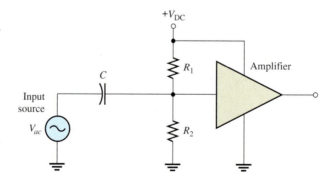

In this type of application, a relatively high value of capacitance is selected so that for the frequencies to be amplified, the reactance is very small compared to the resistance of the bias network. When the reactance is very small (ideally zero), there is practically no phase shift or signal voltage dropped across the capacitor. Therefore, all of the signal voltage passes from the source to the input of the amplifier.

Figure 16–58 illustrates the application of the superposition principle to the circuit in Figure 16–57. In part (a), the ac source has been effectively removed from the circuit and replaced with a short to represent its ideal internal resistance (actual generators typically have 50 Ω or 600 Ω of internal resistance). Since C is open to dc, the voltage at point A is determined by the voltage-divider action of R_1 and R_2 and the dc voltage source.

In Figure 16–58(b), the dc source has been effectively removed from the circuit and replaced with a short to represent its ideal internal resistance. Since C appears as a short at the frequency of the ac, the signal voltage is coupled directly to point A and appears across the parallel combination of R_1 and R_2. Figure 16–58(c) illustrates that the combined effect of the superposition of the dc and the ac voltages results in the signal voltage "riding" on the dc level.

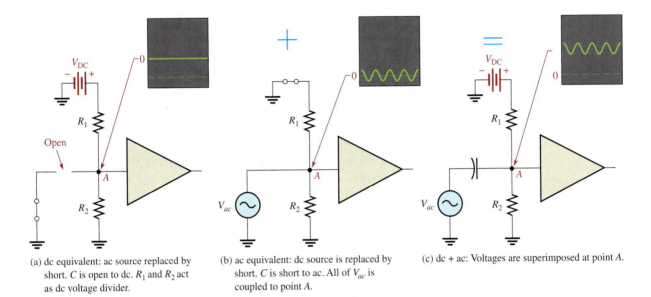

(a) dc equivalent: ac source replaced by short. C is open to dc. R_1 and R_2 act as dc voltage divider.

(b) ac equivalent: dc source is replaced by short. C is short to ac. All of V_{ac} is coupled to point A.

(c) dc + ac: Voltages are superimposed at point A.

FIGURE 16–58

The superposition of dc and ac voltages in an RC bias and coupling circuit.

SECTION 16–8 REVIEW

1. A certain *RC* lag network consists of a 4.7 kΩ resistor and a 0.022 μF capacitor. Determine the phase shift between input and output at a frequency of 3 kHz.

2. An *RC* lead network has the same component values as the lag network in Question 1. What is the magnitude of the output voltage at 3 kHz when the input is 10 V rms?

3. When an *RC* circuit is used as a low-pass filter, across which component is the output taken?

16–9 ■ TROUBLESHOOTING

In this section, the effects that typical component failures or degradation have on the response of basic RC circuits are considered.

After completing this section, you should be able to

■ **Troubleshoot *RC* circuits**
  • Find an open resistor or open capacitor
  • Find a shorted capacitor
  • Find a leaky capacitor

Effect of an Open Resistor

It is easy to see how an open resistor affects the operation of a basic series *RC* circuit, as shown in Figure 16–59. Obviously, there is no path for current, so the capacitor voltage remains at zero; thus, the total voltage, V_s, appears across the open resistor.

FIGURE 16–59
Effect of an open resistor.

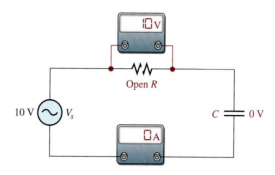

Effect of an Open Capacitor

When the capacitor is open, there is no current; thus, the resistor voltage remains at zero. The total source voltage is across the open capacitor, as shown in Figure 16–60.

FIGURE 16–60
Effect of an open capacitor.

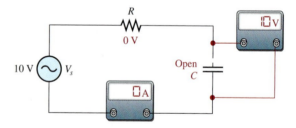

Effect of a Shorted Capacitor

Capacitors rarely short; but when a capacitor does short out, the voltage across it is zero, the current equals V_s/R, and the total voltage appears across the resistor, as shown in Figure 16–61.

FIGURE 16–61
Effect of a shorted capacitor.

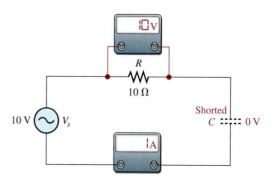

Effect of a Leaky Capacitor

When a large electrolytic capacitor exhibits a high leakage current, the leakage resistance effectively appears in parallel with the capacitor, as shown in Figure 16–62(a). When the leakage resistance is comparable in value to the circuit resistance, R, the circuit response is drastically affected. The circuit, looking from the capacitor toward the source, can be thevenized, as shown in Figure 16–62(b). The Thevenin equivalent resistance is R in parallel with R_{leak} (the source appears as a short), and the Thevenin equivalent voltage is determined by the voltage-divider action of R and R_{leak}.

$$R_{th} = R \parallel R_{leak}$$

$$R_{th} = \frac{RR_{leak}}{R + R_{leak}} \tag{16–45}$$

$$V_{th} = \left(\frac{R_{leak}}{R + R_{leak}}\right)V_s \tag{16–46}$$

As you can see, the voltage across the capacitor is reduced since $V_{th} < V_s$. Also, the circuit time constant is reduced, and the current is increased. The Thevenin equivalent circuit is shown in Figure 16–62(c).

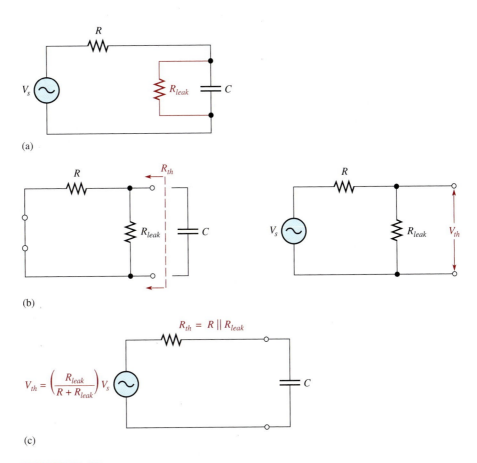

(a)

(b)

(c)

FIGURE 16–62
Effect of a leaky capacitor.

EXAMPLE 16–18   Assume that the capacitor in Figure 16–63 is degraded to a point where its leakage resistance is 10 kΩ. Determine the output voltage under the degraded condition.

FIGURE 16–63

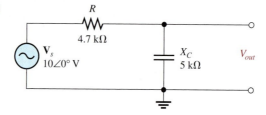

Solution   The effective circuit resistance is

$$R_{th} = \frac{RR_{leak}}{R + R_{leak}} = \frac{(4.7 \text{ k}\Omega)(10 \text{ k}\Omega)}{14.7 \text{ k}\Omega} = 3.20 \text{ k}\Omega$$

To determine the output voltage, find the Thevenin equivalent voltage.

$$V_{th} = \left(\frac{R_{leak}}{R + R_{leak}}\right)V_s = \left(\frac{10 \text{ k}\Omega}{14.7 \text{ k}\Omega}\right)10 \text{ V} = 6.80 \text{ V}$$

Then,

$$V_{out} = \left(\frac{X_C}{\sqrt{R_{th}^2 + X_C^2}}\right)V_{th} = \left(\frac{5 \text{ k}\Omega}{\sqrt{(3.2 \text{ k}\Omega)^2 + (5 \text{ k}\Omega)^2}}\right)6.80 \text{ V} = \textbf{5.73 V}$$

Related Problem   What would the output voltage be if the capacitor were not leaky?

SECTION 16–9 REVIEW

1. Describe the effect of a leaky capacitor on the response of an *RC* circuit.
2. In a series *RC* circuit, if all of the applied voltage appears across the capacitor, what is the problem?
3. What faults can cause 0 V across a capacitor in a parallel *RC* circuit if the source is functioning properly?

16–10 ▪ TECHnology Theory Into Practice

In Chapter 13, you worked with the capacitively coupled input to an amplifier with voltage-divider bias. In this TECH TIP, you will check the output voltage and phase lag of a similar amplifier's input circuit to determine how they change with frequency. If too much voltage is dropped across the coupling capacitor, the overall performance of the amplifier is adversely affected. You should review the TECH TIP in Chapter 13 before proceeding.

As you learned in Chapter 13, the coupling capacitor (C_1) in Figure 16–64 passes the input signal voltage to the input of the amplifier (point *A* to point *B*) without affecting the dc level at point *B* produced by the resistive voltage divider (R_1 and R_2). If the input frequency is high enough so that the reactance of the coupling capacitor is negligibly small, essentially no ac signal voltage is dropped across the capacitor. As the signal frequency is

FIGURE 16–64

A capacitively coupled amplifier.

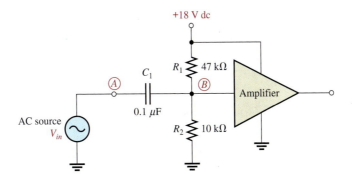

reduced, the capacitive reactance increases and more of the signal voltage is dropped across the capacitor. This lowers the overall voltage gain of the amplifier and thus degrades its performance.

The amount of signal voltage that is coupled from the input source (point A) to the amplifier input (point B) is determined by the values of the capacitor and the dc bias resistors (assuming the amplifier has no loading effect) in Figure 16–64. These components actually form a high-pass RC filter, as shown in Figure 16–65. The voltage-divider bias resistors are effectively in parallel with each other as far as the ac source is concerned because the power supply has zero internal resistance. The lower end of R_2 goes to ground and the upper end of R_1 goes to the dc supply voltage as shown in Figure 16–65(a). Since there is no ac voltage at the +18 V dc terminal, the upper end of R_1 is at 0 V ac which is referred to as *ac ground.* The development of the circuit into an effective high-pass RC filter is shown in parts (b) and (c).

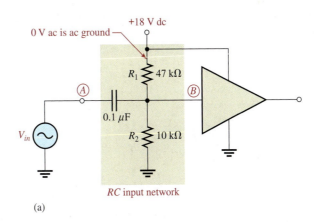

(a)

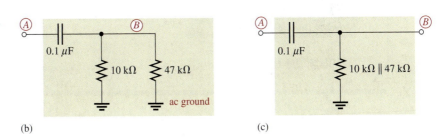

(b) (c)

FIGURE 16–65

The RC input circuit acts effectively like a high-pass RC filter.

The Amplifier Input Circuit

▪ Determine the value of the equivalent resistance of the input circuit. Assume the amplifier (shown inside the white dashed lines in Figure 16–66) has no loading effect on the input circuit.

The Response at Frequency f_1

Refer to Figure 16–66. The input signal voltage is applied to the amplifier circuit board and displayed on channel 1 of the oscilloscope, and channel 2 is connected to a point on the circuit board.

▪ Determine to what point on the circuit the channel 2 probe is connected, the frequency, and the voltage that should be displayed.

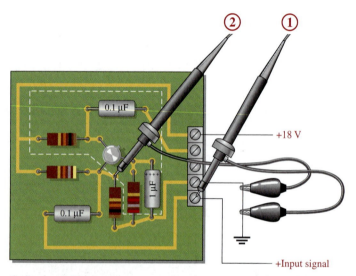

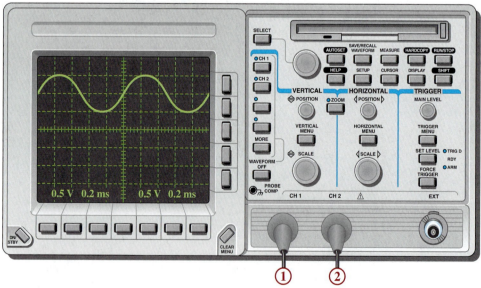

FIGURE 16–66

Measuring the input circuit response at frequency f_1. Circled numbers relate scope inputs to the probes. The channel 1 waveform is shown. Channel 1 settings are on bottom left, and Channel 2 settings are on bottom right.

The Response at Frequency f_2

Refer to Figure 16–67 and the circuit board in Figure 16–66. The input signal voltage displayed on channel 1 of the oscilloscope is applied to the amplifier circuit board.

- Determine the frequency and the voltage that should be displayed on channel 2.
- State the difference between the channel 2 waveforms determined for f_1 and f_2. Explain the reason for the difference.

FIGURE 16–67

Measuring the input circuit response at frequency f_2. The channel 1 waveform is shown.

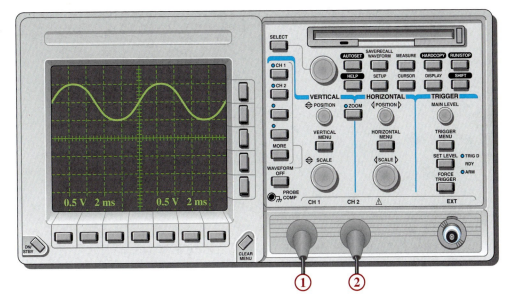

The Response at Frequency f_3

Refer to Figure 16–68 and the circuit board in Figure 16–66. The input signal voltage displayed on channel 1 of the oscilloscope is applied to the amplifier circuit board.

- Determine the frequency and the voltage that should be displayed on channel 2.
- State the difference between the channel 2 waveforms determined for f_2 and f_3. Explain the reason for the difference.

FIGURE 16–68

Measuring the input circuit response at frequency f_3. The channel 1 waveform is shown.

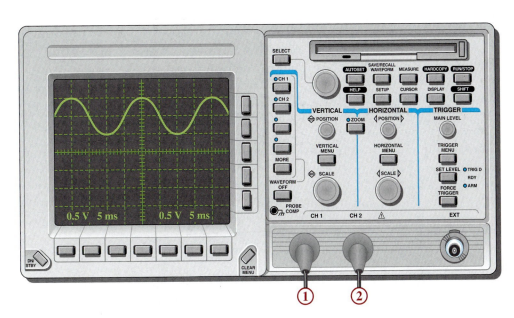

Response Curve for the Amplifier Input Circuit

- Determine the frequency at which the signal voltage at point *B* in Figure 16–64 is 70.7% of its maximum value.
- Plot the response curve using this voltage value and the values at frequencies f_1, f_2, and f_3.
- How does this curve show that the input circuit acts as a high-pass filter?
- What can you do to the circuit to lower the frequency at which the voltage is 70.7% of maximum without affecting the dc bias voltage?

SECTION 16–10 REVIEW

1. Explain the effect on the response of the amplifier input circuit of reducing the value of the coupling capacitor.
2. What is the voltage at point *B* in Figure 16–64 if the coupling capacitor opens when the ac input signal is 10 mV rms?
3. What is the voltage at point *B* in Figure 16–64 if resistor R_1 is open when the ac input signal is 10 mV rms?

◆ *Coverage of special topics continues in Chapter 17, Part 4, on page 683.*

■ SUMMARY

- When a sinusoidal voltage is applied to an *RC* circuit, the current and all the voltage drops are also sine waves.
- Total current in an *RC* circuit always leads the source voltage.
- The resistor voltage is always in phase with the current.
- The capacitor voltage always lags the current by 90°.
- In an *RC* circuit, the impedance is determined by both the resistance and the capacitive reactance combined.
- Impedance is expressed in units of ohms.
- The circuit phase angle is the angle between the total current and the applied (source) voltage.
- The impedance of a series *RC* circuit varies inversely with frequency.
- The phase angle (θ) of a series *RC* circuit varies inversely with frequency.
- For each parallel *RC* circuit, there is an equivalent series circuit for any given frequency.
- For each series *RC* circuit, there is an equivalent parallel circuit for any given frequency.
- The impedance of a circuit can be determined by measuring the applied voltage and the total current and then applying Ohm's law.
- In an *RC* circuit, part of the power is resistive and part reactive.
- The phasor combination of resistive power (true power) and reactive power is called *apparent power*.
- Apparent power is expressed in volt-amperes (VA).
- The power factor (*PF*) indicates how much of the apparent power is true power.
- A power factor of 1 indicates a purely resistive circuit, and a power factor of 0 indicates a purely reactive circuit.
- In a lag network, the output voltage lags the input voltage in phase.
- In a lead network, the output voltage leads the input voltage.
- A filter passes certain frequencies and rejects others.

■ GLOSSARY

These terms are also in the end-of-book glossary.

Admittance   A measure of the ability of a reactive circuit to permit current; the reciprocal of impedance. The unit is the siemens (S).

Apparent power   The phasor combination of resistive power (true power) and reactive power. The unit is the volt-ampere (VA).

Bandwidth   The range of frequencies that is considered to be passed by a filter.

Bias   The application of a dc voltage to an electronic device to produce a desired mode of operation.

Capacitive susceptance   The ability of a capacitor to permit current: the reciprocal of capacitive reactance. The unit is the siemens (S).

Conductance   The reciprocal of resistance. The unit is the siemens (S).

Cutoff frequency   The frequency at which the output voltage of a filter is 70.7% of the maximum output voltage.

Filter   A type of circuit that passes certain frequencies and rejects all others.

Frequency response   In electric circuits, the variation in the output voltage (or current) over a specified range of frequencies.

High-pass filter   A certain type of filter whereby higher frequencies are passed and lower frequencies are rejected.

Impedance   The total opposition to sinusoidal current expressed in ohms.

Lag   Refers to a condition of the phase or time relationship of waveforms in which one waveform is behind the other in phase or time.

Lead   Refers to a condition of the phase or time relationship of waveforms in which one waveform is ahead of the other in phase or time.

Low-pass filter   A certain type of filter whereby lower frequencies are passed and higher frequencies are rejected.

Power factor   The relationship between volt-amperes and true power or watts. Volt-amperes multiplied by the power factor equals true power.

■ FORMULAS

Series *RC* Circuits

(16–1) $\mathbf{X}_C = -jX_C$

(16–2) $\mathbf{Z} = R - jX_C$

(16–3) $Z = \sqrt{R^2 + X_C^2}$

(16–4) $\theta = -\tan^{-1}\left(\dfrac{X_C}{R}\right)$

(16–5) $\mathbf{Z} = \sqrt{R^2 + X_C^2}\angle -\tan^{-1}\left(\dfrac{X_C}{R}\right)$

(16–6) $\mathbf{V} = \mathbf{IZ}$

(16–7) $\mathbf{I} = \dfrac{\mathbf{V}}{\mathbf{Z}}$

(16–8) $\mathbf{Z} = \dfrac{\mathbf{V}}{\mathbf{I}}$

(16–9) $\mathbf{V}_s = V_R - jV_C$

(16–10) $\mathbf{V}_s = \sqrt{V_R^2 + V_C^2}\angle -\tan^{-1}\left(\dfrac{V_C}{V_R}\right)$

(16–11) $V_s = \sqrt{V_R^2 + V_C^2}$

(16–12) $\theta = -\tan^{-1}\left(\dfrac{V_C}{V_R}\right)$

Parallel *RC* Circuits

$$\textbf{(16–13)} \qquad \mathbf{Z} = \left(\frac{RX_C}{\sqrt{R^2 + X_C^2}} \right) \angle \left(-90° + \tan^{-1}\left(\frac{X_C}{R} \right) \right)$$

$$\textbf{(16–14)} \qquad Z = \frac{RX_C}{\sqrt{R^2 + X_C^2}}$$

$$\textbf{(16–15)} \qquad \theta = -90° + \tan^{-1}\left(\frac{X_C}{R} \right)$$

$$\textbf{(16–16)} \qquad \theta = -\tan^{-1}\left(\frac{R}{X_C} \right)$$

$$\textbf{(16–17)} \qquad \mathbf{G} = \frac{1}{R\angle 0°} = G\angle 0°$$

$$\textbf{(16–18)} \qquad \mathbf{B}_C = \frac{1}{X_C\angle -90°} = B_C\angle 90° = +jB_C$$

$$\textbf{(16–19)} \qquad \mathbf{Y} = \frac{1}{Z\angle \pm\theta} = Y\angle \mp\theta$$

$$\textbf{(16–20)} \qquad \mathbf{Y} = G + jB_C$$

$$\textbf{(16–21)} \qquad \mathbf{V} = \frac{\mathbf{I}}{\mathbf{Y}}$$

$$\textbf{(16–22)} \qquad \mathbf{I} = \mathbf{V}\mathbf{Y}$$

$$\textbf{(16–23)} \qquad \mathbf{Y} = \frac{\mathbf{I}}{\mathbf{V}}$$

$$\textbf{(16–24)} \qquad \mathbf{I}_{tot} = I_R + jI_C$$

$$\textbf{(16–25)} \qquad \mathbf{I}_{tot} = \sqrt{I_R^2 + I_C^2}\angle \tan^{-1}\left(\frac{I_C}{I_R} \right)$$

$$\textbf{(16–26)} \qquad I_{tot} = \sqrt{I_R^2 + I_C^2}$$

$$\textbf{(16–27)} \qquad \theta = \tan^{-1}\left(\frac{I_C}{I_R} \right)$$

$$\textbf{(16–28)} \qquad R_{eq} = Z \cos \theta$$

$$\textbf{(16–29)} \qquad X_{C(eq)} = Z \sin \theta$$

Power in *RC* Circuits

$$\textbf{(16–30)} \qquad P_{true} = I^2 R$$

$$\textbf{(16–31)} \qquad P_r = I^2 X_C$$

$$\textbf{(16–32)} \qquad P_a = I^2 Z$$

$$\textbf{(16–33)} \qquad P_{true} = P_a \cos \theta$$

$$\textbf{(16–34)} \qquad P_{true} = VI \cos \theta$$

$$\textbf{(16–35)} \qquad PF = \cos \theta$$

Lag Network

$$\textbf{(16–36)} \qquad \phi = -90° + \tan^{-1}\left(\frac{X_C}{R} \right)$$

$$\textbf{(16–37)} \qquad V_{out} = \left(\frac{X_C}{\sqrt{R^2 + X_C^2}} \right) V_{in}$$

$$\textbf{(16–38)} \qquad V_{out} = IX_C$$

$$\textbf{(16–39)} \qquad \mathbf{V}_{out} = V_{out}\angle \phi$$

Lead Network

$$(16\text{–}40) \qquad \phi = \tan^{-1}\!\left(\frac{X_C}{R}\right)$$

$$(16\text{–}41) \qquad V_{out} = \left(\frac{R}{\sqrt{R^2 + X_C^2}}\right) V_{in}$$

$$(16\text{–}42) \qquad V_{out} = IR$$

$$(16\text{–}43) \qquad \mathbf{V}_{out} = V_{out} \angle \phi$$

$$(16\text{–}44) \qquad f_c = \frac{1}{2\pi RC}$$

Troubleshooting

$$(16\text{–}45) \qquad R_{th} = \frac{R R_{leak}}{R + R_{leak}}$$

$$(16\text{–}46) \qquad V_{th} = \left(\frac{R_{leak}}{R + R_{leak}}\right) V_s$$

■ SELF-TEST

1. In a series RC circuit, the voltage across the resistance is
   - (a) in phase with the source voltage
   - (b) lagging the source voltage by 90°
   - (c) in phase with the current
   - (d) lagging the current by 90°

2. In a series RC circuit, the voltage across the capacitor is
   - (a) in phase with the source voltage
   - (b) lagging the resistor voltage by 90°
   - (c) in phase with the current
   - (d) lagging the source voltage by 90°

3. When the frequency of the voltage applied to a series RC circuit is increased, the impedance
   - (a) increases
   - (b) decreases
   - (c) remains the same
   - (d) doubles

4. When the frequency of the voltage applied to a series RC circuit is decreased, the phase angle
   - (a) increases
   - (b) decreases
   - (c) remains the same
   - (d) becomes erratic

5. In a series RC circuit when the frequency and the resistance are doubled, the impedance
   - (a) doubles
   - (b) is halved
   - (c) is quadrupled
   - (d) cannot be determined without values

6. In a series RC circuit, 10 V rms is measured across the resistor and 10 V rms is also measured across the capacitor. The rms source voltage is
   - (a) 20 V
   - (b) 14.14 V
   - (c) 28.28 V
   - (d) 10 V

7. The voltages in Question 6 are measured at a certain frequency. To make the resistor voltage greater than the capacitor voltage, the frequency
   - (a) must be increased
   - (b) must be decreased
   - (c) is held constant
   - (d) has no effect

8. When $R = X_C$, the phase angle is
   - (a) 0°
   - (b) +90°
   - (c) −90°
   - (d) 45°

9. To decrease the phase angle below 45°, the following condition must exist:
   - (a) $R = X_C$
   - (b) $R < X_C$
   - (c) $R > X_C$
   - (d) $R = 10 X_C$

10. When the frequency of the source voltage is increased, the impedance of a parallel RC circuit
   - (a) increases
   - (b) decreases
   - (c) does not change

11. In a parallel RC circuit, there is 1 A rms through the resistive branch and 1 A rms through the capacitive branch. The total rms current is
   - (a) 1 A
   - (b) 2 A
   - (c) 2.28 A
   - (d) 1.414 A

12. A power factor of 1 indicates that the circuit phase angle is
   - (a) 90°
   - (b) 45°
   - (c) 180°
   - (d) 0°

13. For a certain load, the true power is 100 W and the reactive power is 100 VAR. The apparent power is

   (a) 200 VA   (b) 100 VA   (c) 141.4 VA   (d) 141.4 W

14. Energy sources are normally rated in

   (a) watts   (b) volt-amperes   (c) volt-amperes reactive   (d) none of these

---

▪ PROBLEMS

More difficult problems are indicated by an asterisk (*).

PART 1: SERIES REACTIVE CIRCUITS

SECTION 16–1   Sinusoidal Response of *RC* Circuits

1. An 8 kHz sinusoidal voltage is applied to a series *RC* circuit. What is the frequency of the voltage across the resistor? Across the capacitor?

2. What is the wave shape of the current in the circuit of Problem 1?

SECTION 16–2   Impedance and Phase Angle of Series *RC* Circuits

3. Express the total impedance of each circuit in Figure 16–69 in both polar and rectangular forms.

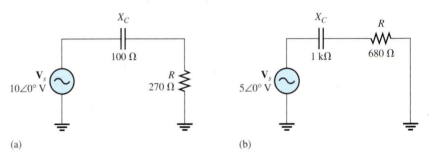

(a)   (b)

FIGURE 16–69

4. Determine the impedance magnitude and phase angle in each circuit in Figure 16–70.

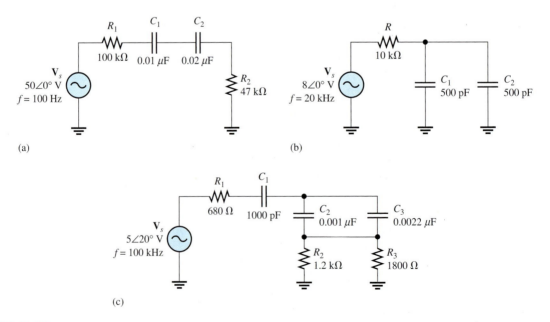

(a)   (b)

(c)

FIGURE 16–70

5. For the circuit of Figure 16–71, determine the impedance expressed in rectangular form for each of the following frequencies:
   (a) 100 Hz   (b) 500 Hz   (c) 1 kHz   (d) 2.5 kHz

FIGURE 16–71

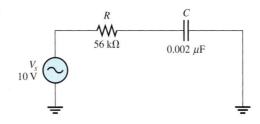

6. Repeat Problem 5 for $C = 0.005 \, \mu F$.
7. Determine the values of R and X_C in a series RC circuit for the following values of total impedance:
   (a) $\mathbf{Z} = 33 \, \Omega - j50 \, \Omega$ (b) $\mathbf{Z} = 300\angle{-25°} \, \Omega$
   (c) $\mathbf{Z} = 1.8\angle{-67.2°} \, k\Omega$ (d) $\mathbf{Z} = 789\angle{-45°} \, \Omega$

SECTION 16–3 Analysis of Series *RC* Circuits

8. Express the current in polar form for each circuit of Figure 16–69.
9. Calculate the total current in each circuit of Figure 16–70 and express in polar form.
10. Determine the phase angle between the applied voltage and the current for each circuit in Figure 16–70.
11. Repeat Problem 10 for the circuit in Figure 16–71, using $f = 5$ kHz.
12. For the circuit in Figure 16–72, draw the phasor diagram showing all voltages and the total current. Indicate the phase angles.

FIGURE 16–72

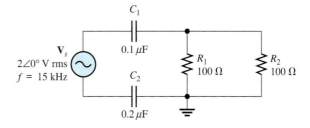

13. For the circuit in Figure 16–73, determine the following in polar form:
    (a) **Z**   (b) $\mathbf{I}_{tot}$ (c) $\mathbf{V}_R$ (d) $\mathbf{V}_C$

FIGURE 16–73

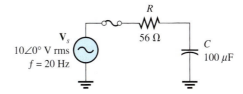

*14. To what value must the rheostat be set in Figure 16–74 to make the total current 10 mA? What is the resulting angle?

FIGURE 16–74

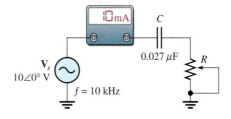

*15. Determine the series element or elements that must be installed in the block of Figure 16–75 to meet the following requirements: $P_{true} = 400$ W and there is a leading power factor (I_{tot} leads V_s).

FIGURE 16–75

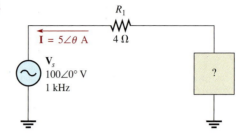

PART 2: PARALLEL REACTIVE CIRCUITS

SECTION 16–4 Impedance and Phase Angle of Parallel *RC* Circuits

16. Determine the impedance and express it in polar form for the circuit in Figure 16–76.

FIGURE 16–76

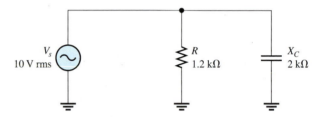

17. Determine the impedance magnitude and phase angle in Figure 16–77.

18. Repeat Problem 17 for the following frequencies:

(**a**) 1.5 kHz   (**b**) 3 kHz   (**c**) 5 kHz   (**d**) 10 kHz

FIGURE 16–77

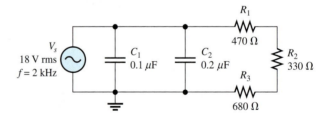

SECTION 16–5 Analysis of Parallel *RC* Circuits

19. For the circuit in Figure 16–78, find all the currents and voltages in polar form.

20. For the parallel circuit in Figure 16–79, find the magnitude of each branch current and the total current. What is the phase angle between the applied voltage and the total current?

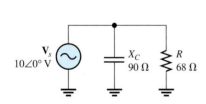

FIGURE 16–78

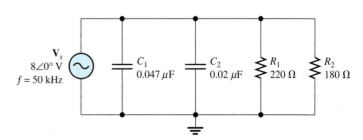

FIGURE 16–79

21. For the circuit in Figure 16–80, determine the following:

(a) **Z**   (b) $\mathbf{I}_R$ (c) $\mathbf{I}_{C(tot)}$ (d) $\mathbf{I}_{tot}$ (e) θ

FIGURE 16–80

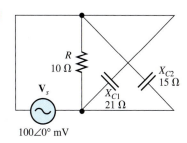

R $10\ \Omega$

X_{C2} $15\ \Omega$

X_{C1} $21\ \Omega$

$\mathbf{V}_s$

$100\angle0°$ mV

22. Repeat Problem 21 for $R = 5.6$ kΩ, $C_1 = 0.05\ \mu$F, $C_2 = 0.022\ \mu$F, and $f = 500$ Hz.

***23.** Convert the circuit in Figure 16–81 to an equivalent series form.

FIGURE 16–81

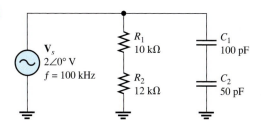

$\mathbf{V}_s$ $2\angle0°$ V $f = 100$ kHz

R_1 10 kΩ

R_2 12 kΩ

C_1 100 pF

C_2 50 pF

***24.** Determine the value to which R_1 must be adjusted to get a phase angle of 30° between the source voltage and the total current in Figure 16–82.

FIGURE 16–82

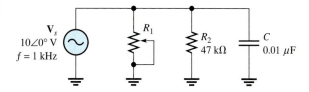

$\mathbf{V}_s$ $10\angle0°$ V $f = 1$ kHz

R_1

R_2 47 kΩ

C $0.01\ \mu$F

PART 3: SERIES-PARALLEL REACTIVE CIRCUITS

SECTION 16–6 Series-Parallel *RC* Circuits

25. Determine the voltages in polar form across each element in Figure 16–83. Sketch the voltage phasor diagram.

26. Is the circuit in Figure 16–83 predominantly resistive or predominantly capacitive?

27. Find the current through each branch and the total current in Figure 16–83. Express the currents in polar form. Sketch the current phasor diagram.

FIGURE 16–83

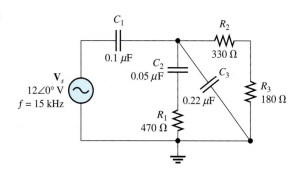

C_1 $0.1\ \mu$F

C_2 $0.05\ \mu$F

R_2 $330\ \Omega$

C_3 $0.22\ \mu$F

R_3 $180\ \Omega$

$\mathbf{V}_s$ $12\angle0°$ V $f = 15$ kHz

R_1 $470\ \Omega$

28. For the circuit in Figure 16–84, determine the following:

(a) $\mathbf{I}_{tot}$ (b) θ (c) $\mathbf{V}_{R1}$ (d) $\mathbf{V}_{R2}$ (e) $\mathbf{V}_{R3}$ (f) $\mathbf{V}_C$

FIGURE 16–84

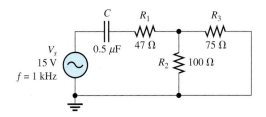

*29. Determine the value of C_2 in Figure 16–85 when $V_A = V_B$.

FIGURE 16–85

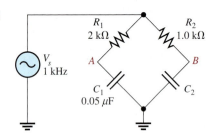

*30. Determine the voltage and its phase angle at each point labeled in Figure 16–86.

31. Find the current through each component in Figure 16–86.

32. Sketch the voltage and current phasor diagram for Figure 16–86.

FIGURE 16–86

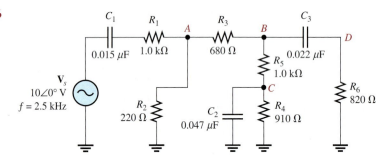

PART 4: SPECIAL TOPICS

SECTION 16–7 Power in *RC* Circuits

33. In a certain series *RC* circuit, the true power is 2 W, and the reactive power is 3.5 VAR. Determine the apparent power.

34. In Figure 16–73, what is the true power and the reactive power?

35. What is the power factor for the circuit of Figure 16–81?

36. Determine P_{true}, P_r, P_a, and *PF* for the circuit in Figure 16–84. Sketch the power triangle.

*37. A single 240 V, 60 Hz source drives two loads. Load *A* has an impedance of 50 Ω and a power factor of 0.85. Load *B* has an impedance of 72 Ω and a power factor of 0.95.

(a) How much current does each load draw?

(b) What is the reactive power in each load?

(c) What is the true power in each load?

(d) What is the apparent power in each load?

(e) Which load has more voltage drop along the lines connecting it to the source?

SECTION 16–8   Basic Applications

38. For the lag network in Figure 16–87, determine the phase shift between the input voltage and the output voltage for each of the following frequencies:

    (a) 1 Hz   **(b)** 100 Hz   **(c)** 1 kHz   **(d)** 10 kHz

FIGURE 16–87

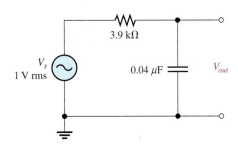

39. The lag network in Figure 16–87 also acts as a low-pass filter. Draw a response curve for this circuit by plotting the output voltage versus frequency for 0 Hz to 10 kHz in 1 kHz increments.

40. Repeat Problem 38 for the lead network in Figure 16–88.

FIGURE 16–88

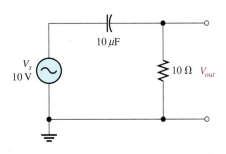

41. Plot the frequency response curve of the output amplitude for the lead network in Figure 16–88 for a frequency range of 0 Hz to 10 kHz in 1 kHz increments.

42. Draw the voltage phasor diagram for each circuit in Figures 16–87 and 16–88 for a frequency of 5 kHz with $V_s = 1$ V rms.

*43. What value of coupling capacitor is required in Figure 16–89 so that the signal voltage at the input of amplifier 2 is at least 70.7% of the signal voltage at the output of amplifier 1 when the frequency is 20 Hz?

FIGURE 16–89

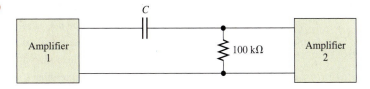

44. The rms value of the signal voltage out of amplifier A in Figure 16–90 is 50 mV. If the input resistance to amplifier B is 10 kΩ, how much of the signal is lost due to the coupling capacitor when the frequency is 3 kHz?

FIGURE 16–90

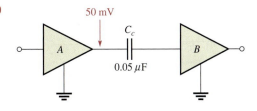

SECTION 16–9 Troubleshooting

45. Assume that the capacitor in Figure 16–91 is excessively leaky. Show how this degradation affects the output voltage and phase angle, assuming that the leakage resistance is 5 kΩ and the frequency is 10 Hz.

FIGURE 16–91

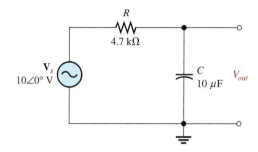

*46. Each of the capacitors in Figure 16–92 has developed a leakage resistance of 2 kΩ. Determine the output voltages under this condition for each circuit.

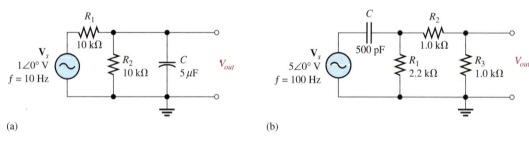

(a)   (b)

FIGURE 16–92

47. Determine the output voltage for the circuit in Figure 16–92(a) for each of the following failure modes, and compare it to the correct output:

    (a) R_1 open   **(b)** R_2 open   **(c)** *C* open   **(d)** *C* shorted

48. Determine the output voltage for the circuit in Figure 16–92(b) for each of the following failure modes, and compare it to the correct output:

    (a) *C* open   **(b)** *C* shorted   **(c)** R_1 open   **(d)** R_2 open   **(e)** R_3 open

EWB Troubleshooting and Analysis

These problems require your EWB compact disk.

49. Open file PRO16-49.EWB and determine if there is a fault. If so, find the fault.

50. Open file PRO16-50.EWB and determine if there is a fault. If so, find the fault.

51. Open file PRO16-51.EWB and determine if there is a fault. If so, find the fault.

52. Open file PRO16-52.EWB and determine if there is a fault. If so, find the fault.

53. Open file PRO16-53.EWB and determine if there is a fault. If so, find the fault.

54. Open file PRO16-54.EWB and determine if there is a fault. If so, find the fault.

55. Open file PRO16-55.EWB and determine the frequency response for the filter.

56. Open file PRO16-56.EWB and determine the frequency response for the filter.

■ **ANSWERS TO SECTION REVIEWS**

Section 16–1

1. The voltage frequency is 60 Hz. The current frequency is 60 Hz.

2. The capacitive reactance causes the phase shift.

3. The phase angle is closer to 0°.

Section 16–2

1. $R = 150\ \Omega$; $X_C = 220\ \Omega$
2. $\mathbf{Z} = 33\ k\Omega - j50\ k\Omega$
3. $Z = \sqrt{R^2 + X_C^2} = 59.9\ k\Omega$; $\theta = -\tan^{-1}(X_C/R) = -56.6°$

Section 16–3

1. $V_s = \sqrt{V_R^2 + V_C^2} = 7.21\ V$
2. $\theta = -\tan^{-1}(X_C/R) = -56.3°$
3. $\theta = 90°$
4. When f increases, X_C decreases, Z decreases, and θ decreases.

Section 16–4

1. Conductance is the reciprocal of resistance, capacitive susceptance is the reciprocal of capacitive reactance, and admittance is the reciprocal of impedance.
2. $Y = 1/Z = 1/\sqrt{R^2 + X_C^2} = 10\ mS$
3. $\mathbf{Y} = 1/\mathbf{Z} = 25.1\angle 32.1°\ mS$
4. $\mathbf{Z} = 39.8\angle -32.1°\ \Omega$

Section 16–5

1. $I_{tot} = V_s Y = 21\ mA$
2. $I_{tot} = \sqrt{I_R^2 + I_C^2} = 18\ mA$; $\theta = \tan^{-1}(I_C/I_R) = 56.3°$; θ is with respect to applied voltage.
3. $\theta = 90°$

Section 16–6

1. See Figure 16–93.
2. $\mathbf{Z}_{tot} = \mathbf{V}_s/\mathbf{I}_{tot} = 36.9\angle -51.6°\ \Omega$

FIGURE 16–93

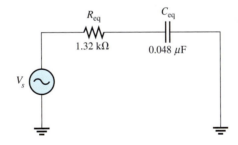

Section 16–7

1. Power dissipation is due to resistance.
2. $PF = \cos\theta = 0.707$
3. $P_{true} = I^2R = 1.32\ kW$; $P_r = I^2X_C = 1.84\ kVAR$; $P_a = I^2Z = 2.26\ kVA$

Section 16–8

1. $\phi = -90° + \tan^{-1}(X_C/R) = -62.8°$
2. $V_{out} = \left(R/\sqrt{R^2 + X_C^2}\right)V_{in} = 8.90\ V$ rms
3. The output is across the capacitor.

Section 16–9

1. The leakage resistance acts in parallel with C, which alters the circuit time constant.
2. The capacitor is open.
3. Any shorted parallel component can cause 0 V across the capacitor.

Section 16–10

1. A lower value coupling capacitor will increase the frequency at which a significant drop in voltage occurs.
2. V_B = 3.16 V dc
3. V_B = 10 mV rms

■ **ANSWERS TO RELATED PROBLEMS FOR EXAMPLES**

16–1 Select polar on mode screen:

(5 6 , (–) 1 0 0)) ENTER (114.612390255∠–60.75. . .).
See Figure 16–94.

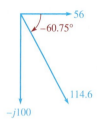

FIGURE 16–94

16–2 V_s = 2.56∠–38.5° V
16–3 **I** = 3.68∠35.9° mA
16–4 Z = 15.9 kΩ, θ = –86.4°
16–5 **Z** = 24.3∠–76.0° Ω
16–6 **Y** = 4.36∠46.0° mS
16–7 **I** = 5.91∠39.6° mA
16–8 I_{tot} = 117∠31.0° mA
16–9 R_{eq} = 8.99 kΩ, $X_{C(eq)}$ = 4.38 kΩ
16–10 V_1 = 7.14∠8.9° V, V_2 = 3.16∠–20.4° V
16–11 V_{R1} = 760∠67.5° mV; V_{C1} = 1.85∠–22.5° V; V_{R2} = 1.53∠40.3° V; V_{C2} = 1.29∠–49.7° V; See Figure 16–95.

FIGURE 16–95

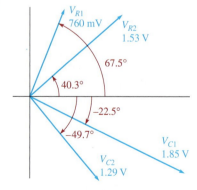

16–12 $PF = 0.155$

16–13 $P_{\text{true}} = 213$ mW

16–14 The phase lag increases.

16–15 The output voltage decreases.

16–16 The phase lead decreases.

16–17 The output voltage increases.

16–18 $V_{out} = 7.29$ V

■ **ANSWERS TO SELF-TEST**

1. (c)   **2.** (b)   **3.** (b)   **4.** (a)   **5.** (d)   **6.** (b)   **7.** (a)   **8.** (d)

9. (c)   **10.** (b)   **11.** (d)   **12.** (d)   **13.** (c)   **14.** (b)

17

RL CIRCUITS

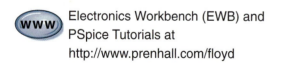

Electronics Workbench (EWB) and PSpice Tutorials at
http://www.prenhall.com/floyd

■ INTRODUCTION

In this chapter you will study series and parallel *RL* circuits. The analyses of *RL* and *RC* circuits are similar. The major difference is that the phase responses are opposite; inductive reactance increases with frequency, while capacitive reactance decreases with frequency.

An *RL* circuit contains both resistance and inductance. It is one of the basic types of reactive circuits that you will study. In this chapter, basic series and parallel *RL* circuits and their responses to sinusoidal ac voltages are presented. Series-parallel combinations are also analyzed. True, reactive, and apparent power in *RL* circuits are discussed and some basic *RL* applications are introduced. Applications of *RL* circuits include filters and phase shift networks. Troubleshooting is also covered in this chapter.

In the TECH TIP assignment in Section 17–10, you will use your knowledge of *RL* circuits to determine, based on parameter measurements, the type of filter circuits and their component values that are encapsulated in sealed modules.

■ COVERAGE OPTIONS

If you chose to cover all of Chapter 16 on *RC* circuits, then all of this chapter should be covered next.

If you chose to cover reactive circuits beginning in Chapter 16 on the basis of the four major parts, then the appropriate part of this chapter should be covered next, followed by the corresponding part in Chapter 18.

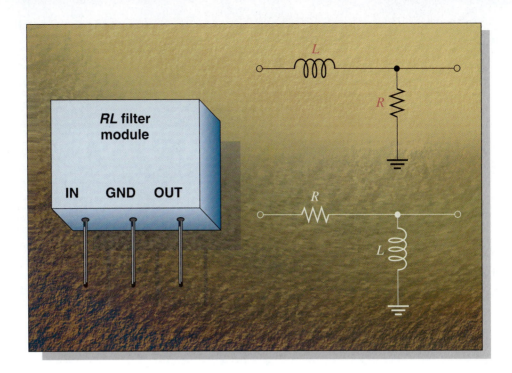

RL filter module

IN   GND   OUT

L

R

R

L

■ CHAPTER OBJECTIVES

PART 1: SERIES REACTIVE CIRCUITS

❑ Describe the relationship between current and voltage in an *RL* circuit

❑ Determine impedance and phase angle in a series *RL* circuit

❑ Analyze series-parallel *RL* circuits

PART 2: PARALLEL REACTIVE CIRCUITS

❑ Determine impedance and phase angle in a parallel *RL* circuit

❑ Analyze a parallel *RL* circuit

PART 3: SERIES-PARALLEL REACTIVE CIRCUITS

❑ Analyze series-parallel *RL* circuits

PART 4: SPECIAL TOPICS

❑ Determine power in *RL* circuits

❑ Discuss some basic *RL* applications

❑ Troubleshoot *RL* circuits

PART 1
SERIES REACTIVE CIRCUITS

17–1 ■ SINUSOIDAL RESPONSE OF *RL* CIRCUITS

As with the RC circuit, all currents and voltages in any type of RL circuit are sinusoidal when the input voltage is sinusoidal. The inductance causes a phase shift between the voltage and the current that depends on the relative values of the resistance and the inductive reactance.

After completing this section, you should be able to

■ **Describe the relationship between current and voltage in an *RL* circuit**
- Discuss voltage and current waveforms
- Discuss phase shift

As you will learn, the resistor voltage and the current lag the source voltage. The inductor voltage leads the source voltage. The phase angle between the current and the inductor voltage is always 90°. These generalized phase relationships are indicated in Figure 17–1. Notice that they are opposite from those of the *RC* circuit, as discussed in Chapter 16.

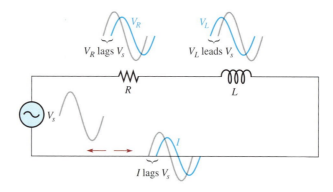

FIGURE 17–1

Illustration of sinusoidal response with general phase relationships of V_R, V_L, and I relative to the source voltage. V_R lags V_s, V_L leads V_s, and I lags V_s. V_R and I are in phase, while V_R and V_L are 90° out of phase with each other.

The amplitudes and the phase relationships of the voltages and current depend on the values of the resistance and the **inductive reactance.** When a circuit is purely inductive, the phase angle between the applied voltage and the total current is 90°, with the current lagging the voltage. When there is a combination of both resistance and inductive reactance in a circuit, the phase angle is somewhere between 0° and 90°, depending on the relative values of the resistance and the reactance.

Recall that practical inductors have winding resistance, capacitance between windings, and other factors that prevent an inductor from behaving as an ideal component. In practical circuits, these effects can be significant; however, for the purpose of isolating the inductive effects, we will treat inductors in this chapter as ideal (except in the TECHTIP).

**SECTION 17–1
REVIEW**

1. A 1 kHz sinusoidal voltage is applied to an *RL* circuit. What is the frequency of the resulting current?

2. When the resistance in an *RL* circuit is greater than the inductive reactance, is the phase angle between the applied voltage and the total current closer to 0° or to 90°?

17–2 ■ IMPEDANCE AND PHASE ANGLE OF SERIES *RL* CIRCUITS

The impedance of any type of RL circuit is the total opposition to sinusoidal current and its unit is the ohm. The phase angle is the phase difference between the total current and the source voltage.

After completing this section, you should be able to

■ **Determine impedance and phase angle in a series *RL* circuit**
  • Express inductive reactance in complex form
  • Express total impedance in complex form
  • Calculate impedance magnitude and the phase angle

The impedance of a series *RL* circuit is determined by the resistance and the inductive reactance. Recall from Chapter 14 that inductive reactance is expressed as a phasor quantity in rectangular form as

$$\mathbf{X}_L = jX_L \qquad (17\text{–}1)$$

In the series *RL* circuit of Figure 17–2, the total impedance is the phasor sum of R and jX_L and is expressed as

$$\mathbf{Z} = R + jX_L \qquad (17\text{–}2)$$

FIGURE 17–2
Series RL circuit.

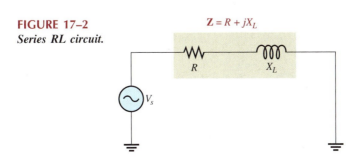

$$\mathbf{Z} = R + jX_L$$

The Impedance Triangle

In ac analysis, both R and X_L are treated as phasor quantities, as shown in the phasor diagram of Figure 17–3(a), with X_L appearing at a $+90°$ angle with respect to R. This relationship comes from the fact that the inductor voltage leads the current, and thus the resistor voltage, by $90°$. Since $\mathbf{Z}$ is the phasor sum of R and jX_L, its phasor representation is shown in Figure 17–3(b). A repositioning of the phasors, as shown in part (c), forms a right triangle. This is called the *impedance triangle*. The length of each phasor represents the magnitude of the quantity, and θ is the phase angle between the applied voltage and the current in the *RL* circuit.

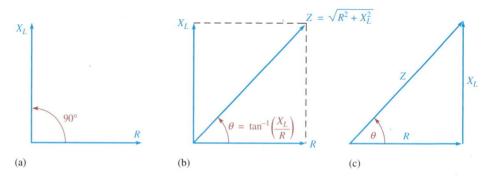

(a)   (b)   (c)

FIGURE 17–3
Development of the impedance triangle for a series RL circuit.

The impedance magnitude of the series *RL* circuit can be expressed in terms of the resistance and reactance as

$$Z = \sqrt{R^2 + X_L^2} \tag{17–3}$$

The magnitude of the impedance is expressed in ohms.
The phase angle, θ, is expressed as

$$\theta = \tan^{-1}\left(\frac{X_L}{R}\right) \tag{17–4}$$

Combining the magnitude and the angle, the impedance can be expressed in polar form as

$$\mathbf{Z} = \sqrt{R^2 + X_L^2}\angle\tan^{-1}\left(\frac{X_L}{R}\right) \tag{17–5}$$

EXAMPLE 17–1   For each circuit in Figure 17–4, write the phasor expression for the impedance in both rectangular and polar forms.

FIGURE 17–4

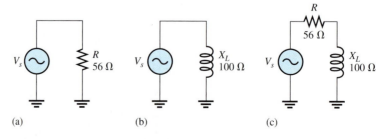

(a)   (b)   (c)

Solution For the circuit in Figure 17–4(a), the impedance is

$$\mathbf{Z} = R + j0 = R = 56\ \Omega \qquad \text{in rectangular form } (X_L = 0)$$

$$\mathbf{Z} = R\angle 0° = 56\angle 0°\ \Omega \qquad \text{in polar form}$$

The impedance is simply equal to the resistance, and the phase angle is zero because pure resistance does not introduce a phase shift.

For the circuit in Figure 17–4(b), the impedance is

$$\mathbf{Z} = 0 + jX_L = j100\ \Omega \qquad \text{in rectangular form } (R = 0)$$

$$\mathbf{Z} = X_L\angle 90° = 100\angle 90°\ \Omega \qquad \text{in polar form}$$

The impedance equals the inductive reactance in this case, and the phase angle is $+90°$ because the inductance causes the current to lag the voltage by $90°$.

For the circuit in Figure 17–4(c), the impedance in rectangular form is

$$\mathbf{Z} = R + jX_L = 56\ \Omega + j100\ \Omega$$

The impedance in polar form is

$$\mathbf{Z} = \sqrt{R^2 + X_L^2}\ \angle \tan^{-1}\!\left(\frac{X_L}{R}\right)$$

$$= \sqrt{(56\ \Omega)^2 + (100\ \Omega)^2}\ \angle \tan^{-1}\!\left(\frac{100\ \Omega}{56\ \Omega}\right) = 115\angle 60.8°\ \Omega$$

In this case, the impedance is the phasor sum of the resistance and the inductive reactance. The phase angle is fixed by the relative values of X_L and R.

Related Problem In a series *RL* circuit, $R = 1.8\ \text{k}\Omega$ and $X_L = 950\ \Omega$. Express the impedance in both rectangular and polar forms.

SECTION 17–2 REVIEW

1. The impedance of a certain *RL* circuit is $150\ \Omega + j220\ \Omega$. What is the value of the resistance? The inductive reactance?

2. A series *RL* circuit has a total resistance of $33\ \text{k}\Omega$ and an inductive reactance of $50\ \text{k}\Omega$. Write the phasor expression for the impedance in rectangular form. Convert the impedance to polar form.

17–3 ■ ANALYSIS OF SERIES *RL* CIRCUITS

In the previous section, you learned how to express the impedance of a series RL circuit. Now, Ohm's law and Kirchhoff's voltage law are used in the analysis of RL circuits.

After completing this section, you should be able to

■ **Analyze a series *RL* circuit**
 • Apply Ohm's law and Kirchhoff's voltage law to series *RL* circuits
 • Express the voltages and current as phasor quantities
 • Show how impedance and phase angle vary with frequency

Ohm's Law

The application of Ohm's law to series *RL* circuits involves the use of the phasor quantities of **Z**, **V**, and **I**. The three equivalent forms of Ohm's law were stated in Chapter 16 for *RC* circuits. They apply also to *RL* circuits and are restated here:

$$\mathbf{V} = \mathbf{IZ} \qquad \mathbf{I} = \frac{\mathbf{V}}{\mathbf{Z}} \qquad \mathbf{Z} = \frac{\mathbf{V}}{\mathbf{I}}$$

Recall that since Ohm's law calculations involve multiplication and division operations, the voltage, current, and impedance should be expressed in polar form.

EXAMPLE 17–2

The current in Figure 17–5 is expressed in polar form as $\mathbf{I} = 0.2\angle0°$ mA. Determine the source voltage expressed in polar form, and draw a phasor diagram showing the relationship between the source voltage and the current.

FIGURE 17–5

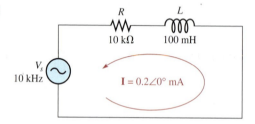

Solution   The inductive reactance is

$$X_L = 2\pi f L = 2\pi(10 \text{ kHz})(100 \text{ mH}) = 6.28 \text{ k}\Omega$$

The impedance in rectangular form is

$$\mathbf{Z} = R + jX_L = 10 \text{ k}\Omega + j6.28 \text{ k}\Omega$$

Converting to polar form yields

$$\mathbf{Z} = \sqrt{R^2 + X_L^2}\angle\tan^{-1}\left(\frac{X_L}{R}\right)$$

$$= \sqrt{(10 \text{ k}\Omega)^2 + (6.28 \text{ k}\Omega)^2}\angle\tan^{-1}\left(\frac{6.28 \text{ k}\Omega}{10 \text{ k}\Omega}\right) = \mathbf{11.8\angle32.1° \text{ k}\Omega}$$

Use Ohm's law to determine the source voltage.

$$\mathbf{V}_s = \mathbf{IZ} = (0.2\angle0° \text{ mA})(11.8\angle32.1° \text{ k}\Omega) = \mathbf{2.36\angle32.1° \text{ V}}$$

The magnitude of the source voltage is 2.36 V at an angle of 32.1° with respect to the current; that is, the voltage leads the current by 32.1°, as shown in the phasor diagram of Figure 17–6.

FIGURE 17–6

Related Problem   If the source voltage in Figure 17–5 were $5\angle0°$ V, what would be the current expressed in polar form?

Relationships of the Current and Voltages in a Series *RL* Circuit

In a series *RL* circuit, the current is the same through both the resistor and the inductor. Thus, the resistor voltage is in phase with the current, and the inductor voltage leads the current by 90°. Therefore, there is a phase difference of 90° between the resistor voltage, V_R, and the inductor voltage, V_L, as shown in the waveform diagram of Figure 17–7.

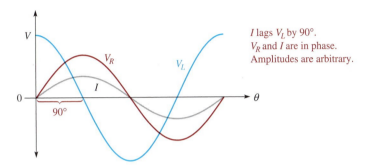

FIGURE 17–7
Phase relation of voltages and current in a series RL circuit.

From Kirchhoff's voltage law, the sum of the voltage drops must equal the applied voltage. However, since V_R and V_L are not in phase with each other, they must be added as phasor quantities with V_L leading V_R by 90°, as shown in Figure 17–8(a). As shown in part (b), $\mathbf{V}_s$ is the phasor sum of V_R and V_L.

$$\mathbf{V}_s = V_R + jV_L \tag{17–6}$$

This equation can be expressed in polar form as

$$\mathbf{V}_s = \sqrt{V_R^2 + V_L^2} \angle \tan^{-1}\left(\frac{V_L}{V_R}\right) \tag{17–7}$$

where the magnitude of the source voltage is

$$V_s = \sqrt{V_R^2 + V_L^2} \tag{17–8}$$

and the phase angle between the resistor voltage and the source voltage is

$$\theta = \tan^{-1}\left(\frac{V_L}{V_R}\right) \tag{17–9}$$

FIGURE 17–8
Voltage phasor diagram for a series RL circuit.

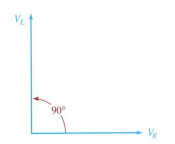

(a)

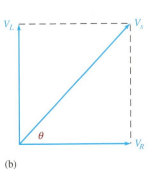

(b)

Since the resistor voltage and the current are in phase, θ is also the phase angle between the source voltage and the current. Figure 17–9 shows a voltage and current phasor diagram that represents the waveform diagram of Figure 17–7.

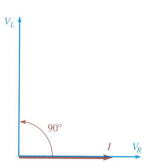

FIGURE 17–9

Voltage and current phasor diagram for the waveforms in Figure 17–7.

Variation of Impedance and Phase Angle with Frequency

The impedance triangle is useful in visualizing how the frequency of the applied voltage affects the *RL* circuit response. As you know, inductive reactance varies directly with frequency. When X_L increases, the magnitude of the total impedance also increases; and when X_L decreases, the magnitude of the total impedance decreases. Thus, Z is directly dependent on frequency. The phase angle θ also varies directly with frequency because $\theta = \tan^{-1}(X_L/R)$. As X_L increases with frequency, so does θ, and vice versa.

The impedance triangle is used in Figure 17–10 to illustrate the variations in X_L, Z, and θ as the frequency changes. Of course, R remains constant. The main point is that because X_L varies directly as the frequency, so also do the magnitude of the total impedance and the phase angle. Example 17–3 illustrates this.

FIGURE 17–10

As the frequency increases, X_L increases, Z increases, and θ increases. Each value of frequency can be visualized as forming a different impedance triangle.

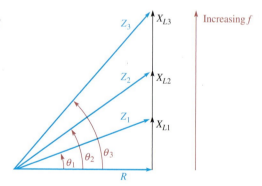

EXAMPLE 17–3   For the series *RL* circuit in Figure 17–11, determine the magnitude of the total impedance and the phase angle for each of the following frequencies:

(a) 10 kHz   **(b)** 20 kHz   **(c)** 30 kHz

FIGURE 17–11

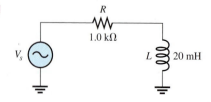

Solution

(a) For $f = 10$ kHz,

$$X_L = 2\pi fL = 2\pi(10 \text{ kHz})(20 \text{ mH}) = 1.26 \text{ k}\Omega$$

$$\mathbf{Z} = \sqrt{R^2 + X_L^2}\angle\tan^{-1}\left(\frac{X_L}{R}\right)$$

$$= \sqrt{(1.0 \text{ k}\Omega)^2 + (1.26 \text{ k}\Omega)^2}\angle\tan^{-1}\left(\frac{1.26 \text{ k}\Omega}{1.0 \text{ k}\Omega}\right) = 1.61\angle 51.6° \text{ k}\Omega$$

Thus, $Z = \mathbf{1.61 \text{ k}\Omega}$ and $\theta = \mathbf{51.6°}$.

(b) For $f = 20$ kHz,

$$X_L = 2\pi(20 \text{ kHz})(20 \text{ mH}) = 2.51 \text{ k}\Omega$$

$$\mathbf{Z} = \sqrt{(1.0 \text{ k}\Omega)^2 + (2.51 \text{ k}\Omega)^2}\angle\tan^{-1}\left(\frac{2.51 \text{ k}\Omega}{1.0 \text{ k}\Omega}\right) = 2.70\angle 68.3° \text{ k}\Omega$$

Thus, $Z = \mathbf{2.70 \text{ k}\Omega}$ and $\theta = \mathbf{68.3°}$.

(c) For $f = 30$ kHz,

$$X_L = 2\pi(30 \text{ kHz})(20 \text{ mH}) = 3.77 \text{ k}\Omega$$

$$\mathbf{Z} = \sqrt{(1.0 \text{ k}\Omega)^2 + (3.77 \text{ k}\Omega)^2}\angle\tan^{-1}\left(\frac{3.77 \text{ k}\Omega}{1.0 \text{ k}\Omega}\right) = \mathbf{3.90\angle 75.1° \text{ k}\Omega}$$

Thus, $Z = \mathbf{3.90 \text{ k}\Omega}$ and $\theta = \mathbf{75.1°}$.

Notice that as the frequency increases, X_L, Z, and θ also increase.

Related Problem Determine Z and θ in Figure 17–11 if f is 100 kHz.

SECTION 17–3 REVIEW

1. In a certain series *RL* circuit, $V_R = 2$ V and $V_L = 3$ V. What is the magnitude of the source voltage?

2. In Question 1, what is the phase angle between the source voltage and the current?

3. When the frequency of the applied voltage in a series *RL* circuit is increased, what happens to the inductive reactance? What happens to the magnitude of the total impedance? What happens to the phase angle?

♦ *Coverage of series reactive circuits continues in Chapter 18, Part 1, on page 710.*

PART 2
PARALLEL REACTIVE CIRCUITS

17–4 ■ IMPEDANCE AND PHASE ANGLE OF PARALLEL *RL* CIRCUITS

In this section, you will learn how to determine the impedance and phase angle of a parallel RL circuit. Also, inductive susceptance and admittance of a parallel RL circuit are introduced.

After completing this section, you should be able to

■ **Determine impedance and phase angle in a parallel *RL* circuit**
  • Express total impedance in complex form
  • Define and calculate *inductive susceptance* and *admittance*

Figure 17–12 shows a basic parallel *RL* circuit connected to an ac voltage source.

FIGURE 17–12
Parallel RL circuit.

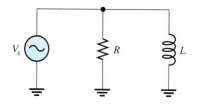

The expression for the total impedance of a two-component parallel *RL* circuit is developed as follows, using the product-over-sum rule.

$$\mathbf{Z} = \frac{(R\angle 0°)(X_L \angle 90°)}{R + jX_L} = \frac{RX_L \angle(0° + 90°)}{\sqrt{R^2 + X_L^2}\,\angle \tan^{-1}\left(\dfrac{X_L}{R}\right)}$$

$$\mathbf{Z} = \left(\frac{RX_L}{\sqrt{R^2 + X_L^2}}\right)\angle\left(90° - \tan^{-1}\left(\frac{X_L}{R}\right)\right) \qquad \textbf{(17–10)}$$

Equation (17–10) is the expression for the total parallel impedance where the magnitude is

$$Z = \frac{RX_L}{\sqrt{R^2 + X_L^2}}$$

(17–11)

and the phase angle between the applied voltage and the total current is

$$\theta = 90° - \tan^{-1}\left(\frac{X_L}{R}\right)$$

(17–12)

This equation can also be expressed equivalently as

$$\theta = \tan^{-1}\left(\frac{R}{X_L}\right)$$

(17–13)

EXAMPLE 17–4

For each circuit in Figure 17–13, determine the magnitude of the total impedance and the phase angle.

FIGURE 17–13

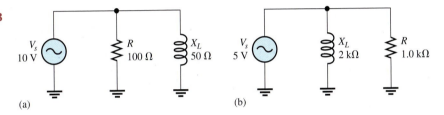

(a)   (b)

Solution   For the circuit in Figure 17–13(a), the total impedance is

$$\mathbf{Z} = \left(\frac{RX_L}{\sqrt{R^2 + X_L^2}}\right)\angle\tan^{-1}\left(\frac{R}{X_L}\right)$$

$$= \left[\frac{(100\ \Omega)(50\ \Omega)}{\sqrt{(100\,\Omega)^2 + (50\ \Omega)^2}}\right]\angle\tan^{-1}\left(\frac{100\ \Omega}{50\ \Omega}\right) = 44.7\angle 63.4°\ \Omega$$

Thus, $Z = \mathbf{44.7\ \Omega}$ and $\theta = \mathbf{63.4°}$.
   For the circuit in Figure 17–13(b), the total impedance is

$$\mathbf{Z} = \left[\frac{(1.0\ k\Omega)(2\ k\Omega)}{\sqrt{(1.0\ k\Omega)^2 + (2\ k\Omega)^2}}\right]\angle\tan^{-1}\left(\frac{1.0\ k\Omega}{2\ k\Omega}\right) = 894\angle 26.6°\ \Omega$$

Thus, $Z = \mathbf{894\ \Omega}$ and $\theta = \mathbf{26.6°}$.
   Notice that the positive angle indicates that the voltage leads the current, as opposed to the *RC* case where the voltage lags the current.

Related Problem   In a parallel circuit, $R = 10\ k\Omega$ and $X_L = 14\ k\Omega$. Determine the total impedance in polar form.

Conductance, Susceptance, and Admittance

As you know from the previous chapter, conductance (*G*) is the reciprocal of resistance, susceptance (*B*) is the reciprocal of reactance, and admittance (*Y*) is the reciprocal of impedance.

For parallel *RL* circuits, the phasor expression for **inductive susceptance (B_L)** is

$$\mathbf{B}_L = \frac{1}{X_L\angle 90° = B_L\angle -90° = -jB_L}$$

(17–14)

and the phasor expression for **admittance** is

$$\mathbf{Y} = \frac{1}{Z\angle \pm\theta} = Y\angle \mp\theta$$

(17–15)

In the basic parallel *RL* circuit shown in Figure 17–14, the total admittance is the phasor sum of the conductance and the inductive susceptance.

$$\mathbf{Y} = G - jB_L$$

(17–16)

As with the *RC* circuit, the unit for *G*, B_L, and *Y* is the siemens (S).

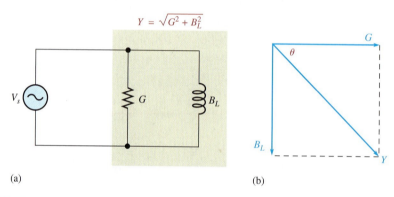

FIGURE 17–14
Admittance in a parallel RL circuit.

EXAMPLE 17–5

Determine the total admittance and total impedance in Figure 17–15. Draw the admittance phasor diagram.

FIGURE 17–15

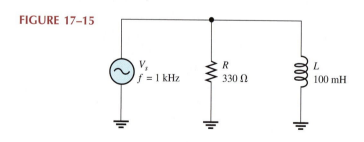

Solution First, determine the conductance magnitude. $R = 330\ \Omega$; thus,

$$G = \frac{1}{R} = \frac{1}{330\ \Omega} = 3.03\ \text{mS}$$

Then, determine the inductive reactance.

$$X_L = 2\pi fL = 2\pi(1000\ \text{Hz})(100\ \text{mH}) = 628\ \Omega$$

The inductive susceptance magnitude is

$$B_L = \frac{1}{X_L} = \frac{1}{628 \ \Omega} = 1.59 \text{ mS}$$

The total admittance is

$$\mathbf{Y}_{tot} = G - jB_L = 3.03 \text{ mS} - j1.59 \text{ mS}$$

which can be expressed in polar form as

$$\mathbf{Y}_{tot} = \sqrt{G^2 + B_L^2}\angle-\tan^{-1}\!\left(\frac{B_L}{G}\right)$$

$$= \sqrt{(3.03 \text{ mS})^2 + (1.59 \text{ mS})^2}\angle-\tan^{-1}\!\left(\frac{1.59 \text{ mS}}{3.03 \text{ mS}}\right) = \mathbf{3.42\angle-27.7° \text{ mS}}$$

Total admittance is converted to total impedance as follows:

$$\mathbf{Z}_{tot} = \frac{1}{\mathbf{Y}_{tot}} = \frac{1}{3.42\angle-27.7° \text{ mS}} = \mathbf{292\angle27.7° \ \Omega}$$

Again, the positive phase angle in the impedance expression indicates that the voltage leads the current. The admittance phasor diagram is shown in Figure 17–16.

FIGURE 17–16

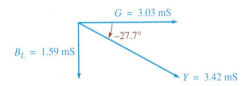

Related Problem   What is the total admittance of the circuit in Figure 17–15 if *f* is increased to 2 kHz?

SECTION 17–4 REVIEW

1. If $Z = 500 \ \Omega$, what is the value of Y?
2. In a certain parallel *RL* circuit, $R = 47 \ \Omega$ and $X_L = 75 \ \Omega$. Determine the magnitude of the admittance.
3. In the circuit of Question 2, does the total current lead or lag the applied voltage? By what phase angle?

17–5 ■ ANALYSIS OF PARALLEL *RL* CIRCUITS

In the previous section, you learned how to express the impedance of a parallel RL circuit. Now, Ohm's law and Kirchhoff's current law are used in the analysis of RL circuits. Current and voltage relationships in a parallel RL circuit are examined.

After completing this section, you should be able to

■ **Analyze a parallel *RL* circuit**
  • Apply Ohm's law and Kirchhoff's current law to parallel *RL* circuits
  • Express the voltages and currents as phasor quantities

The following example applies Ohm's law to the analysis of a parallel *RL* circuit.

EXAMPLE 17–6

Determine the total current and the phase angle in the circuit of Figure 17–17. Draw a phasor diagram showing the relationship of $\mathbf{V}_s$ and $\mathbf{I}_{tot}$.

FIGURE 17–17

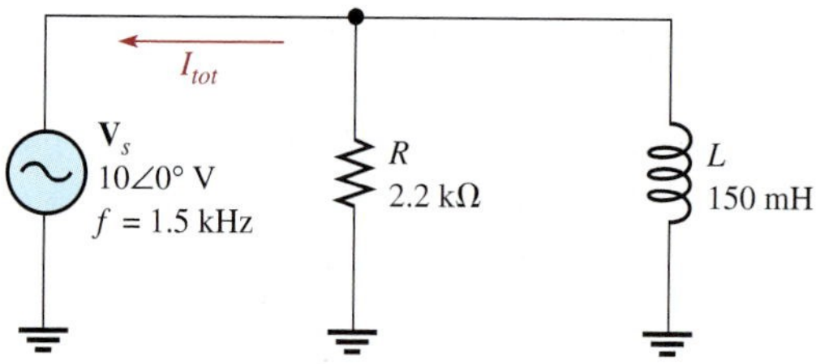

I_{tot}

$\mathbf{V}_s$
$10\angle 0°$ V
$f = 1.5$ kHz

R
2.2 kΩ

L
150 mH

Solution The inductive reactance is

$$X_L = 2\pi f L = 2\pi(1.5 \text{ kHz})(150 \text{ mH}) = 1.41 \text{ k}\Omega$$

The inductive susceptance magnitude is

$$B_L = \frac{1}{X_L} = \frac{1}{1.41 \text{ k}\Omega} = 709 \ \mu\text{S}$$

The conductance magnitude is

$$G = \frac{1}{R} = \frac{1}{2.2 \text{ k}\Omega} = 455 \ \mu\text{S}$$

The total admittance is

$$\mathbf{Y}_{tot} = G - jB_L = 455 \ \mu\text{S} - j709 \ \mu\text{S}$$

Converting to polar form yields

$$\mathbf{Y}_{tot} = \sqrt{G^2 + B_L^2} \angle -\tan^{-1}\left(\frac{B_L}{G}\right)$$

$$= \sqrt{(455 \ \mu\text{S})^2 + (709 \ \mu\text{S})^2} \angle -\tan^{-1}\left(\frac{709 \ \mu\text{S}}{455 \ \mu\text{S}}\right) = 842\angle -57.3° \ \mu\text{S}$$

The phase angle is −57.3°.
Use Ohm's law to determine the total current.

$$\mathbf{I}_{tot} = \mathbf{V}_s\mathbf{Y}_{tot} = (10\angle 0° \text{ V})(842\angle -57.3° \ \mu\text{S}) = \mathbf{8.42\angle -57.3° \text{ mA}}$$

The magnitude of the total current is 8.42 mA, and it lags the applied voltage by **57.3°**, as indicated by the negative angle associated with it. The phasor diagram in Figure 17–18 shows the voltage–total current relationship.

FIGURE 17–18

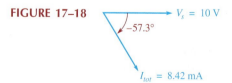

$V_s = 10$ V

$-57.3°$

$I_{tot} = 8.42$ mA

Related Problem Determine the current in polar form if f is reduced to 800 Hz in Figure 17–17.

Relationships of the Currents and Voltages in a Parallel *RL* Circuit

Figure 17–19(a) shows all the currents in a basic parallel *RL* circuit. The total current, I_{tot}, divides at the junction into the two branch currents, I_R and I_L. The applied voltage, V_s, appears across both the resistive and the inductive branches, so V_s, V_R, and V_L are all in phase and of the same magnitude.

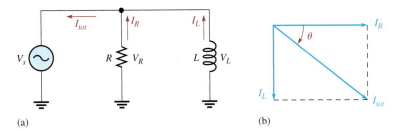

(a)   (b)

FIGURE 17–19
Currents in a parallel RL circuit.

The current through the resistor is in phase with the voltage. The current through the inductor lags the voltage and the resistor current by 90°. By Kirchhoff's current law, the total current is the phasor sum of the two branch currents, as shown by the phasor diagram in Figure 17–19(b). The total current is expressed as

$$\mathbf{I}_{tot} = I_R - jI_L \tag{17–17}$$

This equation can be expressed in polar form as

$$\mathbf{I}_{tot} = \sqrt{I_R^2 + I_L^2}\angle-\tan^{-1}\left(\frac{I_L}{I_R}\right) \tag{17–18}$$

where the magnitude of the total current is

$$\mathbf{I}_{tot} = \sqrt{I_R^2 + I_L^2} \tag{17–19}$$

and the phase angle between the resistor current and the total current is

$$\theta = -\tan^{-1}\left(\frac{I_L}{I_R}\right) \tag{17–20}$$

Since the resistor current and the applied voltage are in phase, θ also represents the phase angle between the total current and the applied voltage. Figure 17–20 shows a complete current and voltage phasor diagram.

FIGURE 17–20
Current and voltage phasor diagram for a parallel RL circuit (amplitudes are arbitrary).

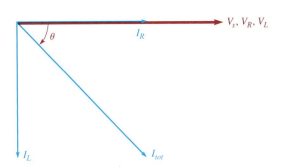

EXAMPLE 17–7   Determine the value of each current in Figure 17–21, and describe the phase relationship of each with the applied voltage. Draw the current phasor diagram.

FIGURE 17–21

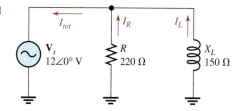

Solution   The resistor current, the inductor current, and the total current are expressed as follows:

$$\mathbf{I}_R = \frac{\mathbf{V}_s}{\mathbf{R}} = \frac{12\angle 0° \text{ V}}{220\angle 0° \ \Omega} = \mathbf{54.5\angle 0° \ mA}$$

$$\mathbf{I}_L = \frac{\mathbf{V}_s}{\mathbf{X}_L} = \frac{12\angle 0° \text{ V}}{150\angle 90° \ \Omega} = \mathbf{80\angle -90° \ mA}$$

$$\mathbf{I}_{tot} = I_R - jI_L = 54.5 \text{ mA} - j80 \text{ mA}$$

Converting $\mathbf{I}_{tot}$ to polar form yields

$$\mathbf{I}_{tot} = \sqrt{I_R^2 + I_L^2}\angle -\tan^{-1}\left(\frac{I_L}{I_R}\right)$$

$$= \sqrt{(54.5 \text{ mA})^2 + (80 \text{ mA})^2}\angle -\tan^{-1}\left(\frac{80 \text{ mA}}{54.5 \text{ mA}}\right) = \mathbf{96.8\angle -55.7° \ mA}$$

As the results show, the resistor current is 54.5 mA and is in phase with the applied voltage. The inductor current is 80 mA and lags the applied voltage by 90°. The total current is 96.8 mA and lags the voltage by 55.7°. The phasor diagram in Figure 17–22 shows these relationships.

FIGURE 17–22

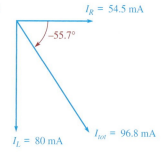

Related Problem   Find the magnitude of $\mathbf{I}_{tot}$ and the circuit phase angle if $X_L = 300 \ \Omega$ in Figure 17–21.

SECTION 17–5 REVIEW

1. The admittance of an *RL* circuit is 4 mS, and the applied voltage is 8 V. What is the total current?

2. In a certain parallel *RL* circuit, the resistor current is 12 mA, and the inductor current is 20 mA. Determine the magnitude and phase angle of the total current. This phase angle is measured with respect to what?

3. What is the phase angle between the inductor current and the applied voltage in a parallel *RL* circuit?

♦ *Coverage of parallel reactive circuits continues in Chapter 18, Part 2, on page 723.*

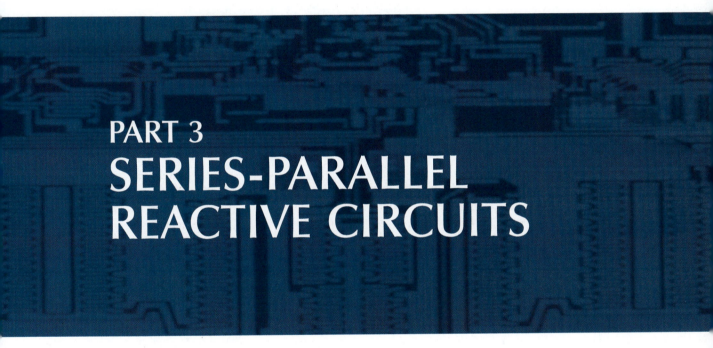

PART 3
SERIES-PARALLEL REACTIVE CIRCUITS

17–6 ■ SERIES-PARALLEL *RL* CIRCUITS

In this section, the concepts studied with respect to series and parallel circuits are used to analyze circuits with combinations of both series and parallel R and L elements.

After completing this section, you should be able to

■ **Analyze series-parallel *RL* circuits**
  • Determine total impedance
  • Calculate currents and voltages

The following two examples demonstrate how to approach the analysis of series-parallel *RL* networks, by combining approaches that you have previously learned.

EXAMPLE 17–8   In the circuit of Figure 17–23, determine the following values:
(a) $\mathbf{Z}_{tot}$ (b) $\mathbf{I}_{tot}$ (c) θ

FIGURE 17–23

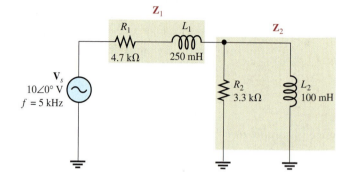

Solution

(a) First, calculate the magnitudes of inductive reactance.

$$X_{L1} = 2\pi f L_1 = 2\pi(5 \text{ kHz})(250 \text{ mH}) = 7.85 \text{ k}\Omega$$

$$X_{L2} = 2\pi f L_2 = 2\pi(5 \text{ kHz})(100 \text{ mH}) = 3.14 \text{ k}\Omega$$

One approach is to find the impedance of the series portion and the impedance of the parallel portion and combine them to get the total impedance. The impedance of the series combination of R_1 and L_1 is

$$\mathbf{Z}_1 = R_1 + jX_{L1} = 4.7 \text{ k}\Omega + j7.85 \text{ k}\Omega$$

To determine the impedance of the parallel portion, first determine the admittance of the parallel combination of R_2 and L_2.

$$G_2 = \frac{1}{R_2} = \frac{1}{3.3 \text{ k}\Omega} = 303 \ \mu S$$

$$B_{L2} = \frac{1}{X_{L2}} = \frac{1}{3.14 \text{ k}\Omega} = 318 \ \mu S$$

$$\mathbf{Y}_2 = G_2 - jB_L = 303 \ \mu S - j318 \ \mu S$$

Converting to polar form yields

$$\mathbf{Y}_2 = \sqrt{G_2^2 + B_L^2} \angle -\tan^{-1}\left(\frac{B_L}{G_2}\right)$$

$$= \sqrt{(303 \ \mu S)^2 + (318 \ \mu S)^2} \angle -\tan^{-1}\left(\frac{318 \ \mu S}{303 \ \mu S}\right) = 439 \angle -46.4° \ \mu S$$

Then, the impedance of the parallel portion is

$$\mathbf{Z}_2 = \frac{1}{\mathbf{Y}_2} = \frac{1}{439 \angle -46.4° \ \mu S} = 2.28 \angle 46.4° \text{ k}\Omega$$

Converting to rectangular form yields

$$\mathbf{Z}_2 = Z_2 \cos \theta + jZ_2 \sin \theta$$
$$= (2.28 \text{ k}\Omega)\cos(46.4°) + j(2.28 \text{ k}\Omega)\sin(46.4°) = 1.57 \text{ k}\Omega + j1.65 \text{ k}\Omega$$

The series portion and the parallel portion are in series with each other. Combine $\mathbf{Z}_1$ and $\mathbf{Z}_2$ to get the total impedance.

$$\mathbf{Z}_{tot} = \mathbf{Z}_1 + \mathbf{Z}_2$$
$$= (4.7 \text{ k}\Omega + j7.85 \text{ k}\Omega) + (1.57 \text{ k}\Omega + j1.65 \text{ k}\Omega) = 6.27 \text{ k}\Omega + j9.50 \text{ k}\Omega$$

Expressing $\mathbf{Z}_{tot}$ in polar form yields

$$\mathbf{Z}_{tot} = \sqrt{Z_1^2 + Z_2^2} \angle \tan^{-1}\left(\frac{Z_2}{Z_1}\right)$$

$$= \sqrt{(6.27 \text{ k}\Omega)^2 + (9.50 \text{ k}\Omega)^2} \angle \tan^{-1}\left(\frac{9.50 \text{ k}\Omega}{6.27 \text{ k}\Omega}\right) = \mathbf{11.4 \angle 56.6° \text{ k}\Omega}$$

(b) Use Ohm's law to find the total current.

$$\mathbf{I}_{tot} = \frac{\mathbf{V}_s}{\mathbf{Z}_{tot}} = \frac{10\angle 0° \text{ V}}{11.4 \angle 56.6° \text{ k}\Omega} = \mathbf{877 \angle -56.6° \text{ } \mu A}$$

(c) The total current lags the applied voltage by **56.6°**.

Related Problem
(a) Determine the voltage across the series part of the circuit in Figure 17–23.
(b) Determine the voltage across the parallel part of the circuit.

EXAMPLE 17–9   Determine the voltage across each element in Figure 17–24. Sketch a voltage phasor diagram and a current phasor diagram.

FIGURE 17–24

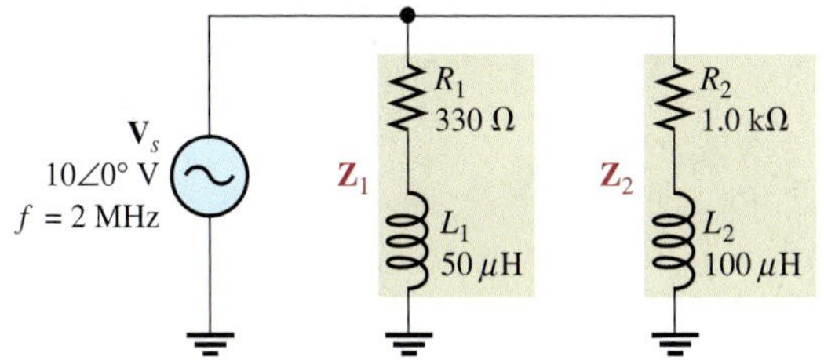

Solution   First, calculate X_{L1} and X_{L2}.

$$X_{L1} = 2\pi f L_1 = 2\pi(2 \text{ MHz})(50 \text{ } \mu H) = 628 \text{ } \Omega$$
$$X_{L2} = 2\pi f L_2 = 2\pi(2 \text{ MHz})(100 \text{ } \mu H) = 1.26 \text{ } \Omega$$

Next, determine the impedance of each branch.

$$\mathbf{Z}_1 = R_1 + jX_{L1} = 330 \text{ } \Omega + j628 \text{ } \Omega$$
$$\mathbf{Z}_2 = R_2 + jX_{L2} = 1.0 \text{ k}\Omega + j1.26 \text{ k}\Omega$$

Convert these impedances to polar form.

$$\mathbf{Z}_1 = \sqrt{R_1^2 + X_{L1}^2} \angle \tan^{-1}\left(\frac{X_{L1}}{R_1}\right)$$

$$= \sqrt{(330 \text{ } \Omega)^2 + (628 \text{ } \Omega)^2} \angle \tan^{-1}\left(\frac{628 \text{ } \Omega}{330 \text{ } \Omega}\right) = 709\angle 62.3° \text{ } \Omega$$

$$\mathbf{Z}_2 = \sqrt{R_2^2 + X_{L2}^2} \angle \tan^{-1}\left(\frac{X_{L2}}{R_2}\right)$$

$$= \sqrt{(1.0 \text{ k}\Omega)^2 + (1.26 \text{ k}\Omega)^2} \angle \tan^{-1}\left(\frac{1.26 \text{ k}\Omega}{1.0 \text{ k}\Omega}\right) = 1.61\angle 51.6° \text{ k}\Omega$$

Calculate each branch current.

$$\mathbf{I_1} = \frac{\mathbf{V}_s}{\mathbf{Z_1}} = \frac{10\angle 0° \text{ V}}{709\angle 62.3° \text{ } \Omega} = 14.1\angle -62.3° \text{ mA}$$

$$\mathbf{I_2} = \frac{\mathbf{V}_s}{\mathbf{Z_2}} = \frac{10\angle 0° \text{ V}}{1.61\angle 51.6° \text{ k}\Omega} = 6.21\angle -51.6° \text{ mA}$$

Now, use Ohm's law to get the voltage across each element.

$$\mathbf{V}_{R1} = \mathbf{I_1}\mathbf{R_1} = (14.1\angle -62.3° \text{ mA})(330\angle 0° \text{ }\Omega) = \mathbf{4.65\angle -62.3° \text{ V}}$$

$$\mathbf{V}_{L1} = \mathbf{I_1}\mathbf{X}_{L1} = (14.1\angle -62.3° \text{ mA})(628\angle 90° \text{ }\Omega) = \mathbf{8.85\angle 27.7° \text{ V}}$$

$$\mathbf{V}_{R2} = \mathbf{I_2}\mathbf{R_2} = (6.21\angle -51.6° \text{ mA})(1\angle 0° \text{ k}\Omega) = \mathbf{6.21\angle -51.6° \text{ V}}$$

$$\mathbf{V}_{L2} = \mathbf{I_2}\mathbf{X}_{L2} = (6.21\angle -51.6° \text{ mA})(1.26\angle 90° \text{ k}\Omega) = \mathbf{7.82\angle 38.4° \text{ V}}$$

The voltage phasor diagram is shown in Figure 17–25, and the current phasor diagram is shown in Figure 17–26.

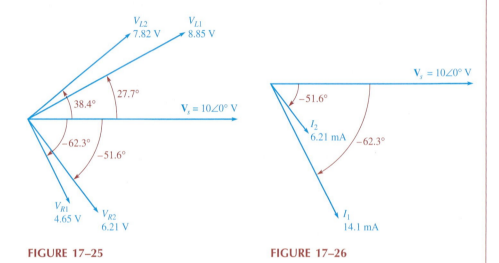

FIGURE 17–25   **FIGURE 17–26**

Related Problem   What is the total current in polar form in Figure 17–24?

SECTION 17–6 REVIEW

1. What is the total impedance in polar form of the circuit in Figure 17–24?
2. Determine the total current in rectangular form for the circuit in Figure 17–24.

◆ *Coverage of series-parallel reactive circuits continues in Chapter 18, Part 3, on page 732.*

17–7 ■ POWER IN *RL* CIRCUITS

In a purely resistive ac circuit, all of the energy delivered by the source is dissipated in the form of heat by the resistance. In a purely inductive ac circuit, all of the energy delivered by the source is stored by the inductor in its magnetic field during a portion of the voltage cycle and then returned to the source during another portion of the cycle so that there is no net energy conversion to heat. When there is both resistance and inductance, some of the energy is alternately stored and returned by the inductance and some is dissipated by the resistance. The amount of energy converted to heat is determined by the relative values of the resistance and the inductive reactance.

After completing this section, you should be able to

■ **Determine power in *RL* circuits**
  • Explain true and reactive power
  • Draw the power triangle
  • Define *power factor*
  • Explain power factor correction

When the resistance is greater than the inductive reactance, more of the total energy delivered by the source is converted to heat by the resistance than is stored by the inductor; and when the reactance is greater than the resistance, more of the total energy is stored and returned than is converted to heat.

As you know, the power dissipation in a resistance is called the *true power*. The power in an inductor is reactive power and is expressed as

$$P_r = I^2 X_L \tag{17–21}$$

The Power Triangle for *RL* Circuits

The generalized power triangle for the *RL* circuit is shown in Figure 17–27. The **apparent power**, P_a, is the resultant of the average power, P_{true}, and the reactive power, P_r.

FIGURE 17–27
Power triangle for an RL circuit.

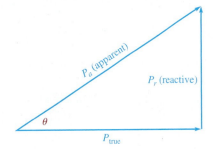

Recall that the power factor equals the cosine of θ ($PF = \cos \theta$). As the phase angle between the applied voltage and the total current increases, the power factor decreases, indicating an increasingly reactive circuit. The smaller the power factor, the smaller the true power is compared to the reactive power.

EXAMPLE 17–10   Determine the power factor, the true power, the reactive power, and the apparent power in Figure 17–28.

FIGURE 17–28

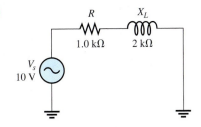

Solution   The total impedance of the circuit in rectangular form is

$$\mathbf{Z} = R + jX_L = 1.0 \text{ k}\Omega + j2 \text{ k}\Omega$$

Converting to polar form yields

$$\mathbf{Z} = \sqrt{R_2^2 + X_L^2}\angle\tan^{-1}\left(\frac{X_L}{R}\right)$$

$$= \sqrt{(1.0 \text{ k}\Omega)^2 + (2 \text{ k}\Omega)^2}\angle\tan^{-1}\left(\frac{2 \text{ k}\Omega}{1.0 \text{ k}\Omega}\right) = 2.24\angle63.4° \text{ k}\Omega$$

The current magnitude is

$$I = \frac{V_s}{Z} = \frac{10 \text{ V}}{2.24 \text{ k}\Omega} = 4.46 \text{ mA}$$

The phase angle, indicated in the expression for **Z**, is

$$\theta = 63.4°$$

The power factor is, therefore,

$$PF = \cos \theta = \cos(63.4°) = \mathbf{0.448}$$

The true power is

$$P_{\text{true}} = V_sI \cos \theta = (10 \text{ V})(4.46 \text{ mA})(0.448) = \mathbf{20 \text{ mW}}$$

The reactive power is

$$P_r = I^2 X_L = (4.46 \text{ mA})^2(2 \text{ k}\Omega) = \textbf{39.8 mVAR}$$

The apparent power is

$$P_a = I^2 Z = (4.46 \text{ mA})^2(2.24 \text{ k}\Omega) = \textbf{44.6 mVA}$$

Related Problem If the frequency in Figure 17–28 is increased, what happens to P_{true}, P_r, and P_a?

Significance of the Power Factor

As you learned in Chapter 16, the **power factor** (*PF*) is important in determining how much useful power (true power) is transferred to a load. The highest power factor is 1, which indicates that all of the current to a load is in phase with the voltage (resistive). When the power factor is 0, all of the current to a load is 90° out of phase with the voltage (reactive).

Generally, a power factor as close to 1 as possible is desirable because then most of the power transferred from the source to the load is the useful or true power. True power goes only one way—from source to load—and performs work on the load in terms of energy dissipation. Reactive power simply goes back and forth between the source and the load with no net work being done. Energy must be used in order for work to be done.

Many practical loads have inductance as a result of their particular function, and it is essential for their proper operation. Examples are transformers, electric motors, and speakers, to name a few. Therefore, inductive (and capacitive) loads are important considerations.

To see the effect of the power factor on system requirements, refer to Figure 17–29. This figure shows a representation of a typical inductive load consisting effectively of inductance and resistance in parallel. Part (a) shows a load with a relatively low power factor (0.75), and part (b) shows a load with a relatively high power factor (0.95). Both loads dissipate equal amounts of power as indicated by the wattmeters. Thus, an equal amount of work is done on both loads.

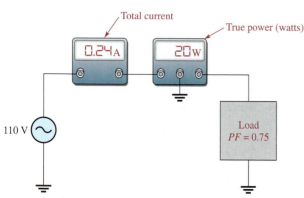

(a) A lower power factor means more total current for a given power dissipation (watts). A larger source VA rating is required to deliver the true power (watts).

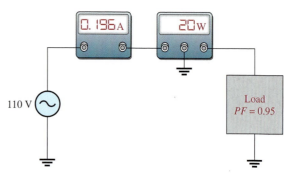

(b) A higher power factor means less total current for a given power dissipation. A smaller source can deliver the same true power (watts).

FIGURE 17–29

Illustration of the effect of the power factor on system requirements such as source rating (VA) and conductor size.

Although both loads are equivalent in terms of the amount of work done (true power), the low power factor load in Figure 17–29(a) draws more current from the source than does the high power factor load in Figure 17–29(b), as indicated by the ammeters. Therefore, the source in part (a) must have a higher VA rating than the one in part (b). Also, the lines connecting the source to the load in part (a) must be a larger wire gage than those in part (b), a condition that becomes significant when very long transmission lines are required, such as in power distribution.

Figure 17–29 has demonstrated that a higher power factor is an advantage in delivering power more efficiently to a load.

Power Factor Correction

The power factor of an inductive load can be increased by the addition of a capacitor in parallel, as shown in Figure 17–30. The capacitor compensates for the phase lag of the total current by creating a capacitive component of current that is 180° out of phase with the inductive component. This has a canceling effect and reduces the phase angle (and power factor) as well as the total current, as illustrated in the figure.

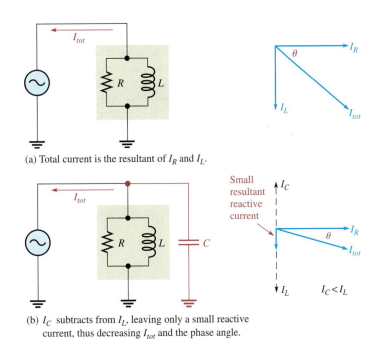

(a) Total current is the resultant of I_R and I_L.

(b) I_C subtracts from I_L, leaving only a small reactive current, thus decreasing I_{tot} and the phase angle.

FIGURE 17–30
Example of how the power factor can be increased by the addition of a compensating capacitor.

<table>
<tr><td>**SECTION 17–7 REVIEW**</td><td>

1. To which component in an *RL* circuit is the power dissipation due?

2. Calculate the power factor when $\theta = 50°$.

3. A certain *RL* circuit consists of a 470 Ω resistor and an inductive reactance of 620 Ω at the operating frequency. Determine P_{true}, P_r, and P_a when $I = 100$ mA.
</td></tr>
</table>

17–8 ■ BASIC APPLICATIONS

Two basic applications, phase shift networks and frequency-selective networks (filters), are covered in this section.

After completing this section, you should be able to

■ **Discuss some basic *RL* applications**
- Discuss and analyze the *RL* lead network
- Discuss and analyze the *RL* lag network
- Discuss how the *RL* circuit operates as a filter

The *RL* Lead Network

The *RL* lead network is a phase shift circuit in which the output voltage leads the input voltage by a specified amount. Figure 17–31(a) shows a series *RL* circuit with the output voltage taken across the inductor. Note that in the *RC* lead network, the output was taken across the resistor. The source voltage is the input, V_{in}. As you know, θ is the angle between the current and the input voltage; it is also the angle between the resistor voltage and the input voltage, because V_R and I are in phase.

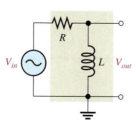

(a) A basic *RL* lead network

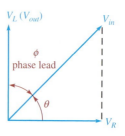

(b) Phasor voltage diagram showing V_{out} leading V_{in}

FIGURE 17–31
The RL lead network ($V_{out} = V_L$).

Since V_L leads V_R by 90°, the phase angle between the inductor voltage and the input voltage is the difference between 90° and θ, as shown in Figure 17–31(b). The inductor voltage is the output; it leads the input, thus creating a basic lead network.

When the input and output voltage waveforms of the lead network are displayed on an oscilloscope, a relationship similar to that in Figure 17–32 is observed. The amount of phase difference, designated ϕ, between the input and the output is dependent on the relative values of the inductive reactance and the resistance, as is the magnitude of the output voltage.

FIGURE 17–32
Input and output voltage waveforms.

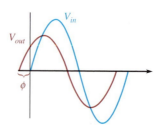

Phase Difference Between Input and Output The angle between V_{out} and V_{in} is designated ϕ (phi) and is developed as follows. The polar expressions for the input voltage and the current are $V_{in}\angle 0°$ and $I\angle -\theta$, respectively. The output voltage in polar form is

$$\mathbf{V}_{out} = (I\angle -\theta)(X_L\angle 90°) = IX_L\angle(90° - \theta)$$

This expression shows that the output voltage is at an angle of $90° - \theta$ with respect to the input voltage. Since $\theta = \tan^{-1}(X_L/R)$, the angle ϕ between the input and output is

$$\phi = 90° - \tan^{-1}\left(\frac{X_L}{R}\right) \tag{17–22}$$

This angle can equivalently be expressed as

$$\phi = \tan^{-1}\left(\frac{R}{X_L}\right) \tag{17–23}$$

The angle ϕ between the output and input is always positive, indicating that the output voltage leads the input voltage, as indicated in Figure 17–33.

FIGURE 17–33

EXAMPLE 17–11

Determine the amount of phase lead from input to output in each lead network in Figure 17–34.

FIGURE 17–34

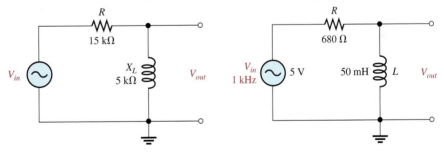

Solution For the lead network in Figure 17–34(a),

$$\phi = 90° - \tan^{-1}\left(\frac{X_L}{R}\right) = 90° - \tan^{-1}\left(\frac{5\text{ k}\Omega}{15\text{ k}\Omega}\right) = 90° - 18.4° = \mathbf{71.6°}$$

The output leads the input by 71.6°.
  For the lead network in Figure 17–34(b), first determine the inductive reactance.

$$X_L = 2\pi fL = 2\pi(1\text{ kHz})(50\text{ mH}) = 314\ \Omega$$

$$\phi = 90° - \tan^{-1}\left(\frac{X_L}{R}\right) = 90° - \tan^{-1}\left(\frac{314\ \Omega}{680\ \Omega}\right) = \mathbf{65.2°}$$

The output leads the input by 65.2°.

Related Problem In a certain lead network, $R = 2.2\text{ k}\Omega$ and $X_L = 1\text{ k}\Omega$. What is the phase lead?

Magnitude of the Output Voltage   To evaluate the output voltage in terms of its magnitude, visualize the *RL* lead network as a voltage divider. A portion of the total input voltage is dropped across the resistor and a portion across the inductor. Because the output voltage is the voltage across the inductor, it can be calculated as

$$V_{out} = \left(\frac{X_L}{\sqrt{R^2 + X_L^2}} \right) V_{in}$$
(17–24)

The output voltage can also be found using Ohm's law as

$$V_{out} = IX_L$$
(17–25)

The total phasor expression for the output voltage of an *RL* lead network is

$$\mathbf{V}_{out} = V_{out}\angle\phi$$
(17–26)

EXAMPLE 17–12   For the lead network in Figure 17–34(b) (Example 17–11), determine the output voltage in phasor form when the input voltage has an rms value of 5 V. Sketch the input and output voltage waveforms showing the proper relationships. X_L (314 Ω) and ϕ (65.2°) were found in Example 17–11.

Solution   The output voltage in phasor form is

$$\mathbf{V}_{out} = \left(\frac{X_L}{\sqrt{R^2 + X_L^2}} \right) V_{in}\angle\phi$$

$$= \left[\frac{314\ \Omega}{\sqrt{(680\ \Omega)^2 + (314\ \Omega)^2}} \right] 5\angle 65.2°\ \text{V} = \mathbf{2.10}\angle\mathbf{65.2}°\ \mathbf{V}$$

The waveforms with their peak values are shown in Figure 17–35. Notice that the output voltage leads the input voltage by 65.2°.

FIGURE 17–35

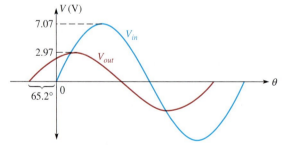

Related Problem   In a lead network, does the output voltage increase or decrease when the frequency increases?

The *RL* Lag Network

The *RL* lag network is a phase shift circuit in which the output voltage lags the input voltage by a specified amount. When the output of a series *RL* circuit is taken across the resistor rather than the inductor, as shown in Figure 17–36(a), it becomes a lag network.

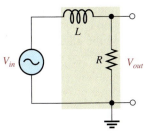

(a) A basic *RL* lag network

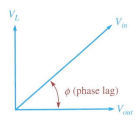

(b) Phasor voltage diagram
showing phase lag between
V_{in} and V_{out}

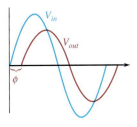

(c) Input and output waveforms

FIGURE 17–36
The RL lag network ($V_{out} = V_R$).

Phase Difference Between Input and Output In a series *RL* circuit, the current lags the input voltage. Since the output voltage is taken across the resistor, the output lags the input, as indicated by the phasor diagram in Figure 17–36(b). The waveforms are shown in Figure 17–36(c).

As in the lead network, the amount of phase difference between the input and output and the magnitude of the output voltage are dependent on the relative values of the resistance and the inductive reactance. When the input voltage is assigned a reference angle of 0°, the angle of the output voltage (ϕ) with respect to the input voltage equals θ, because the resistor voltage (output) and the current are in phase with each other. The expression for the angle between the input voltage and the output voltage is

$$\phi = -\tan^{-1}\left(\frac{X_L}{R}\right) \tag{17-27}$$

This angle is negative because the output lags the input.

EXAMPLE 17–13 Calculate the output phase angle for each circuit in Figure 17–37.

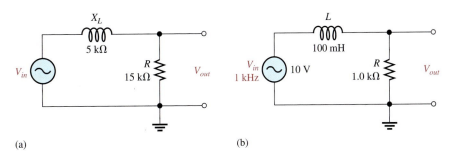

(a) (b)

FIGURE 17–37

Solution For the lag network in Figure 17–37(a).

$$\phi = -\tan^{-1}\left(\frac{X_L}{R}\right) = -\tan^{-1}\left(\frac{5\ k\Omega}{15\ k\Omega}\right) = \mathbf{-18.4°}$$

The output lags the input by 18.4°.

For the lag network in Figure 17–37(b), first determine the inductive reactance.

$$X_L = 2\pi f L = 2\pi(1 \text{ kHz})(100 \text{ mH}) = 628 \ \Omega$$

$$\phi = -\tan^{-1}\left(\frac{X_L}{R}\right) = -\tan^{-1}\left(\frac{628 \ \Omega}{1.0 \text{ k}\Omega}\right) = -32.1°$$

The output lags the input by 32.1°.

Related Problem In a certain lag network, $R = 5.6$ kΩ and $X_L = 3.5$ kΩ. Determine the phase angle.

Magnitude of the Output Voltage Since the output voltage of an *RL* lag network is taken across the resistor, the magnitude can be calculated using either the voltage-divider approach or Ohm's law.

$$V_{out} = \left(\frac{R}{\sqrt{R^2 + X_L^2}}\right)V_{in} \qquad (17\text{–}28)$$

$$V_{out} = IR \qquad (17\text{–}29)$$

The expression for the output voltage in phasor form is

$$\mathbf{V}_{out} = V_{out}\angle{-\phi} \qquad (17\text{–}30)$$

EXAMPLE 17–14 The input voltage in Figure 17–37(b) (Example 17–13) has an rms value of 10 V. Determine the phasor expression for the output voltage. Sketch the waveform relationships for the input and output voltages. The phase angle (−32.1°) and X_L (628 Ω) were found in Example 17–13.

Solution The phasor expression for the output voltage is

$$\mathbf{V}_{out} = \left(\frac{R}{\sqrt{R^2 + X_L^2}}\right)V_{in}\angle\phi = \left(\frac{1.0 \text{ k}\Omega}{1181 \ \Omega}\right)10\angle{-32.1°} \text{ V} = \mathbf{8.47}\angle{-32.1°} \text{ V rms}$$

The waveforms are shown in Figure 17–38.

FIGURE 17–38

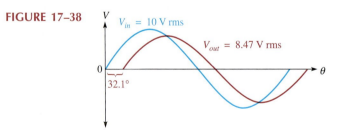

Related Problem In a lag network, $R = 4.7$ kΩ and $X_L = 6$ kΩ. If the rms input voltage is 20 V, what is the output voltage?

The *RL* Circuit as a Filter

As with *RC* circuits, series *RL* circuits also exhibit a frequency-selective characteristic and therefore act as basic filters. Filters are introduced here as an application example and will be covered in depth in Chapter 19.

Low-Pass Filter You have seen what happens to the output magnitude and phase angle in the lag network. In terms of the filtering action, the variation of the magnitude of the output voltage as a function of frequency is important.

Figure 17–39 shows the filtering action of a series *RL* circuit using specific values for purposes of illustration. In part (a) of the figure, the input is zero frequency (dc). Since the inductor ideally acts as a short to constant direct current, the output voltage equals the full value of the input voltage (neglecting the winding resistance). Therefore, the circuit passes all of the input voltage to the output (10 V in, 10 V out).

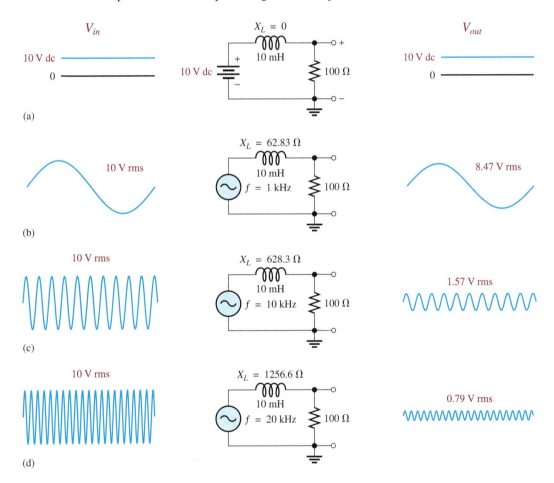

FIGURE 17–39

Low-pass filter action of an RL circuit (phase shift from input to output is not indicated).

In Figure 17–39(b), the frequency of the input voltage has been increased to 1 kHz, causing the inductive reactance to increase to 62.83 Ω. For an input voltage of 10 V rms, the output voltage is approximately 8.47 V rms, which can be calculated using the voltage divider approach or Ohm's law.

In Figure 17–39(c), the input frequency has been increased to 10 kHz, causing the inductive reactance to increase further to 628.3 Ω. For a constant input voltage of 10 V rms, the output voltage is now 1.57 V rms.

As the input frequency is increased further, the output voltage continues to decrease and approaches zero as the frequency becomes very high, as shown in Figure 17–39(d) for $f = 20$ kHz.

A description of the circuit action is as follows: As the frequency of the input increases, the inductive reactance increases. Because the resistance is constant and the inductive reactance increases, the voltage across the inductor increases, and that across the resistor (output voltage) decreases. The input frequency can be increased until it reaches a value at which the reactance is so large compared to the resistance that the output voltage can be neglected because it becomes very small compared to the input voltage.

As shown in Figure 17–39, the circuit passes dc (zero frequency) completely. As the frequency of the input increases, less of the input voltage is passed through to the output. That is, the output voltage decreases as the frequency increases. It is apparent that the lower frequencies pass through the circuit much better than the higher frequencies. This *RL* circuit is therefore a very basic form of low-pass filter.

Figure 17–40 shows a response curve for a low-pass filter.

FIGURE 17–40

Low-pass filter response curve.

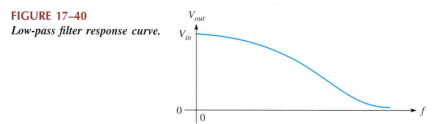

High-Pass Filter Figure 17–41 illustrates high-pass filter action, where the output is taken across the inductor. When the input voltage is dc (zero frequency) in part (a), the output is zero volts because the inductor ideally appears as a short across the output.

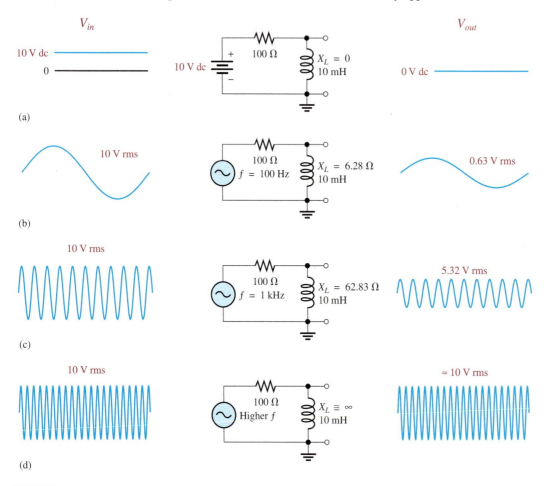

(a)

(b)

(c)

(d)

FIGURE 17–41

High-pass filter action of an RL circuit (phase shift from input to output is not indicated).

In Figure 17–41(b), the frequency of the input signal has been increased to 100 Hz with an rms value of 10 V. The output voltage is 0.63 V rms. Thus, only a small percentage of the input voltage appears at the output at this frequency.

In Figure 17–41(c), the input frequency is increased further to 1 kHz, causing more voltage to be developed as a result of the increase in the inductive reactance. The output voltage at this frequency is 5.32 V rms. As you can see, the output voltage increases as the frequency increases. A value of frequency is reached at which the reactance is very large compared to the resistance and most of the input voltage appears across the inductor, as shown in Figure 17–41(d).

This circuit tends to prevent lower frequency signals from appearing on the output but permits higher frequency signals to pass through from input to output; thus, it is a very basic form of high-pass filter.

The response curve in Figure 17–42 shows that the output voltage increases and then levels off as it approaches the value of the input voltage as the frequency increases.

FIGURE 17–42

High-pass filter response curve.

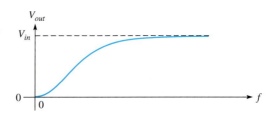

**SECTION 17–8
REVIEW**

1. A certain *RL* lead network consists of a 3.3 kΩ resistor and a 15 mH inductor. Determine the phase shift between input and output at a frequency of 5 kHz.

2. An *RL* lag network has the same component values as the lead network in Question 1. What is the magnitude of the output voltage at 5 kHz when the input is 10 V rms?

3. When an *RL* circuit is used as a low-pass filter, across which component is the output taken?

17–9 ■ TROUBLESHOOTING

In this section, the effects that typical component failures have on the response of basic RL circuits are considered.

After completing this section, you should be able to

■ **Troubleshoot *RL* circuits**
   • Find an open inductor
   • Find an open resistor
   • Find an open in a parallel circuit

Effect of an Open Inductor

The most common failure mode for inductors occurs when the winding opens as a result of excessive current or a mechanical contact failure. It is easy to see how an open coil affects the operation of a basic series *RL* circuit, as shown in Figure 17–43. Obviously, there is no current path; therefore, the resistor voltage is zero, and the total applied voltage appears across the inductor. If you suspect an open coil, remove one or both leads from the circuit and check continuity with an ohmmeter.

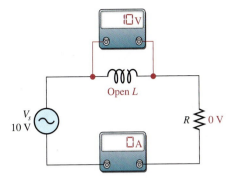

FIGURE 17–43
Effect of an open coil.

Effect of an Open Resistor

When the resistor is open, there is no current and the inductor voltage is zero. The total input voltage is across the open resistor, as shown in Figure 17–44.

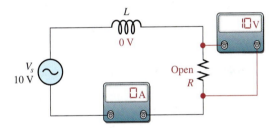

FIGURE 17–44
Effect of an open resistor.

Open Components in Parallel Circuits

In a parallel *RL* circuit, an open resistor or inductor will cause the total current to decrease because the total impedance will increase. Obviously, the branch with the open component will have zero current. Figure 17–45 illustrates these conditions.

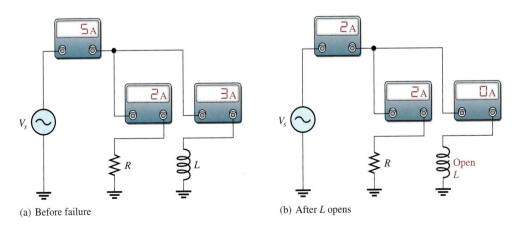

(a) Before failure   (b) After *L* opens

FIGURE 17–45
Effect of an open component in a parallel circuit with V_s constant.

Effect of an Inductor with Shorted Windings

Although a very rare occurrence, it is possible for some of the windings of coils to short together as a result of damaged insulation. This failure mode is much less likely than the open coil and is difficult to detect. Shorted windings result in a reduction in inductance because the inductance of a coil is proportional to the square of the number of turns. A short between windings effectively reduces the number of turns, which may or may not have an adverse effect on the circuit.

SECTION 17–9 REVIEW

1. Describe the effect of an inductor with shorted windings on the response of a series *RL* circuit.

2. In the circuit of Figure 17–46, indicate whether I_{tot}, V_{R1}, and V_{R2} increase or decrease as a result of *L* opening.

FIGURE 17–46

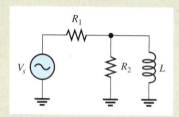

17–10 ■ TECHnology Theory Into Practice

You are given two sealed modules that have been removed from a communications system that is being modified. Each module has three terminals and is labeled as an RL filter, but no specifications are given. Your supervisor asks you to test the modules to determine the type of filters and the component values.

The sealed modules have three terminals labeled IN, GND, and OUT as shown in Figure 17–47. You will apply your knowledge of series *RL* circuits and some basic measurements to determine the internal circuit configuration and the component values.

FIGURE 17–47
Ohmmeter measurements of module 1.

Ohmmeter Measurement of Module 1

- Determine the arrangement of the two components and the values of the resistor and winding resistance for module 1 indicated by the meter readings in Figure 17–47.

AC Measurement of Module 1

- Determine the inductance value for module 1 indicated by the test setup in Figure 17–48.

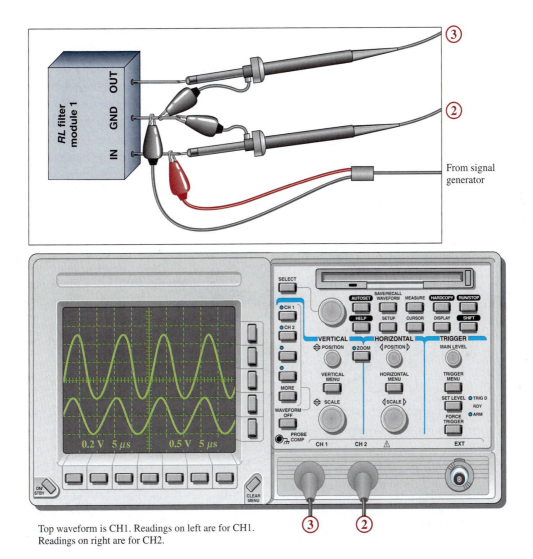

Top waveform is CH1. Readings on left are for CH1.
Readings on right are for CH2.

FIGURE 17–48
AC measurements for module 1.

Ohmmeter Measurement of Module 2

- Determine the arrangement of the two components and the values of the resistor and the winding resistance for module 2 indicated by the meter readings in Figure 17–49.

AC Measurement of Module 2

- Determine the inductance value for module 2 indicated by the test setup in Figure 17–50.

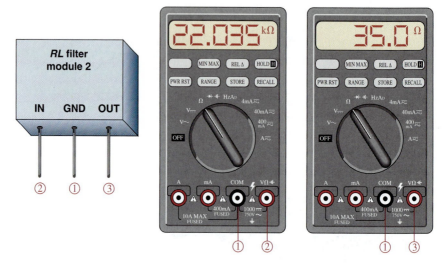

FIGURE 17–49
Ohmmeter measurements of module 2.

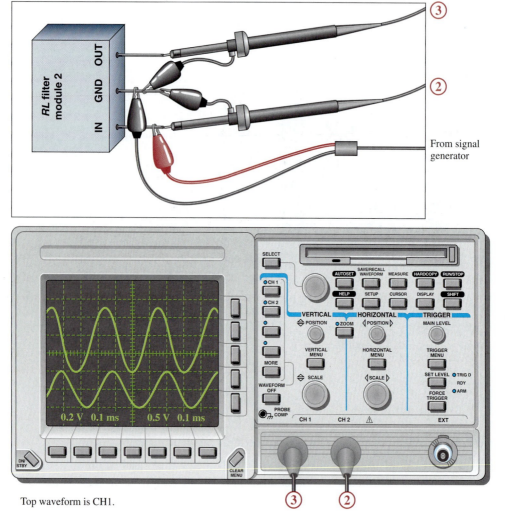

Top waveform is CH1.

FIGURE 17–50
AC measurements for module 2.

SECTION 17–10 REVIEW

1. If the inductor in module 1 were open, what would you measure on the output with the test setup of Figure 17–48?
2. If the inductor in module 2 were open, what would you measure on the output with the test setup of Figure 17–50?

♦ *Coverage of special topics continues in Chapter 18, Part 4, on page 740.*

■ SUMMARY

- When a sinusoidal voltage is applied to an *RL* circuit, the current and all the voltage drops are also sine waves.
- Total current in an *RL* circuit always lags the source voltage.
- The resistor voltage is always in phase with the current.
- In an ideal inductor, the voltage always leads the current by 90°.
- In an *RL* circuit, the impedance is determined by both the resistance and the inductive reactance combined.
- Impedance is expressed in units of ohms.
- The impedance of an *RL* circuit varies directly with frequency.
- The phase angle (θ) of a series *RL* circuit varies directly with frequency.
- You can determine the impedance of a circuit by measuring the applied voltage and the total current and then applying Ohm's law.
- In an *RL* circuit, part of the power is resistive and part reactive.
- The power factor indicates how much of the apparent power is true power.
- A power factor of 1 indicates a purely resistive circuit, and a power factor of 0 indicates a purely reactive circuit.
- In a lag network, the output voltage lags the input voltage in phase.
- In a lead network, the output voltage leads the input voltage in phase.
- A filter passes certain frequencies and rejects others.

■ GLOSSARY

These terms are also in the end-of-book glossary.

Admittance   A measure of the ability of a reactive circuit to permit current; the reciprocal of impedance. The unit is the siemens (S).

Apparent power   The phasor combination of resistive power (true power) and reactive power. The unit is the volt-ampere (VA).

Inductive reactance   The opposition of an inductor to sinusoidal current. The unit is the ohm.

Inductive susceptance   The reciprocal of inductive reactance. The unit is the siemens (S).

Power factor   The relationship between volt-amperes and true power or watts. Volt-amperes multiplied by the power factor equals true power.

■ FORMULAS

Series *RL* Circuits

(17–1) $\mathbf{X}_L = jX_L$

(17–2) $\mathbf{Z} = R + jX_L$

(17–3) $Z = \sqrt{R^2 + X_L^2}$

(17–4) $\theta = \tan^{-1}\left(\dfrac{X_L}{R}\right)$

(17–5) $\mathbf{Z} = \sqrt{R^2 + X_L^2} \angle \tan^{-1}\left(\dfrac{X_L}{R}\right)$

(17–6) $\mathbf{V}_s = V_R + jV_L$

(17–7) $\mathbf{V}_s = \sqrt{V_R^2 + V_L^2} \angle \tan^{-1}\left(\dfrac{V_L}{V_R}\right)$

(17–8) $V_s = \sqrt{V_R^2 + V_L^2}$

(17–9) $\theta = \tan^{-1}\left(\dfrac{V_L}{V_R}\right)$

Parallel *RL* Circuits

(17–10) $\mathbf{Z} = \left(\dfrac{RX_L}{\sqrt{R^2 + X_L^2}}\right) \angle \left(90° - \tan^{-1}\left(\dfrac{X_L}{R}\right)\right)$

(17–11) $Z = \dfrac{RX_L}{\sqrt{R^2 + X_L^2}}$

(17–12) $\theta = 90° - \tan^{-1}\left(\dfrac{X_L}{R}\right)$

(17–13) $\theta = \tan^{-1}\left(\dfrac{R}{X_L}\right)$

(17–14) $\mathbf{B}_L = \dfrac{1}{X_L \angle 90°} = B_L \angle -90° = -jB_L$

(17–15) $\mathbf{Y} = \dfrac{1}{Z \angle \pm \theta} = Y \angle \pm\mp\, \theta$

(17–16) $\mathbf{Y} = G - jB_L$

(17–17) $\mathbf{I}_{tot} = I_R - jI_L$

(17–18) $\mathbf{I}_{tot} = \sqrt{I_R^2 + I_L^2} \angle -\tan^{-1}\left(\dfrac{I_L}{I_R}\right)$

(17–19) $\mathbf{I}_{tot} = \sqrt{I_R^2 + I_L^2}$

(17–20) $\theta = -\tan^{-1}\left(\dfrac{I_L}{I_R}\right)$

Power in *RL* Circuits

(17–21) $P_r = I^2 X_L$

Lead Network

(17–22) $\phi = 90° - \tan^{-1}\left(\dfrac{X_L}{R}\right)$

(17–23) $\phi = \tan^{-1}\left(\dfrac{R}{X_L}\right)$

(17–24) $V_{out} = \left(\dfrac{X_L}{\sqrt{R^2 + X_L^2}}\right) V_{in}$

(17–25) $V_{out} = IX_L$

(17–26) $\mathbf{V}_{out} = V_{out} \angle \phi$

Lag Network

(17–27) $\phi = -\tan^{-1}\left(\dfrac{X_L}{R}\right)$

$$(17\text{–}28) \qquad V_{out} = \left(\frac{R}{\sqrt{R^2 + X_L^2}}\right) V_{in}$$

$$(17\text{–}29) \qquad V_{out} = IR$$

$$(17\text{–}30) \qquad \mathbf{V}_{out} = V_{out}\angle{-\phi}$$

■ **SELF-TEST**

1. In a series *RL* circuit, the resistor voltage
   (a) leads the applied voltage   (b) lags the applied voltage
   (c) is in phase with the applied voltage   (d) is in phase with the current
   (e) answers (a) and (d)   (f) answers (b) and (d)

2. When the frequency of the voltage applied to a series *RL* circuit is increased, the impedance
   (a) decreases   (b) increases   (c) does not change

3. When the frequency of the voltage applied to a series *RL* circuit is decreased, the phase angle
   (a) decreases   (b) increases   (c) does not change

4. If the frequency is doubled and the resistance is halved, the impedance of a series *RL* circuit
   (a) doubles   (b) halves
   (c) remains constant   (d) cannot be determined without values

5. To reduce the current in a series *RL* circuit, the frequency should be
   (a) increased   (b) decreased   (c) constant

6. In a series *RL* circuit, 10 V rms is measured across the resistor, and 10 V rms is measured across the inductor. The peak value of the source voltage is
   (a) 14.14 V   (b) 28.28 V   (c) 10 V   (d) 20 V

7. The voltages in Problem 6 are measured at a certain frequency. To make the resistor voltage greater than the inductor voltage, the frequency is
   (a) increased   (b) decreased   (c) doubled   (d) not a factor

8. When the resistor voltage in a series *RL* circuit becomes greater than the inductor voltage, the phase angle
   (a) increases   (b) decreases   (c) is not affected

9. When the frequency of the source voltage is increased, the impedance of a parallel *RL* circuit
   (a) increases   (b) decreases   (c) remains constant

10. In a parallel *RL* circuit, there are 2 A rms in the resistive branch and 2 A rms in the inductive branch. The total rms current is
    (a) 4 A   (b) 5.656 A   (c) 2 A   (d) 2.828 A

11. You are observing two voltage waveforms on an analog oscilloscope. The time base (time/division) of the scope is adjusted so that one-half cycle of the waveforms covers the ten horizontal divisions. The positive-going zero crossing of one waveform is at the leftmost division, and the positive-going zero crossing of the other is three divisions to the right. The phase angle between these two waveforms is
    (a) 18°   (b) 36°   (c) 54°   (d) 180°

12. Which of the following power factors results in less energy being converted to heat in an *RL* circuit?
    (a) 1   (b) 0.9   (c) 0.5   (d) 0.1

13. If a load is purely inductive and the reactive power is 10 VAR, the apparent power is
    (a) 0 VA   (b) 10 VA   (c) 14.14 VA   (d) 3.16 VA

14. For a certain load, the true power is 10 W and the reactive power is 10 VAR. The apparent power is
    (a) 5 VA   (b) 20 VA   (c) 14.14 VA   (d) 100 VA

■ PROBLEMS

More difficult problems are indicated by an asterisk (*).

PART 1: SERIES REACTIVE CIRCUITS

SECTION 17–1 Sinusoidal Response of *RL* Circuits

1. A 15 kHz sinusoidal voltage is applied to a series *RL* circuit. What is the frequency of *I*, V_R, and V_L?

2. What are the wave shapes of *I*, V_R, and V_L in Problem 1?

SECTION 17–2 Impedance and Phase Angle of Series *RL* Circuits

3. Express the total impedance of each circuit in Figure 17–51 in both polar and rectangular forms.

FIGURE 17–51

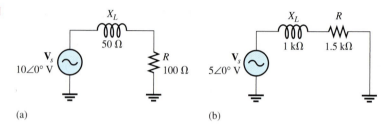

(a)   (b)

4. Determine the impedance magnitude and phase angle in each circuit in Figure 17–52. Sketch the impedance diagrams.

FIGURE 17–52

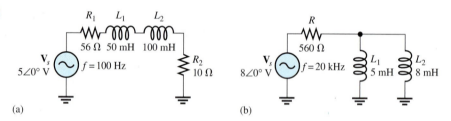

(a)   (b)

5. In Figure 17–53, determine the impedance at each of the following frequencies:
   (a) 100 Hz   (b) 500 Hz   (c) 1 kHz   (d) 2 kHz

6. Determine the values of *R* and X_L in a series *RL* circuit for the following values of total impedance:
   (a) $\mathbf{Z} = 20\ \Omega + j45\ \Omega$ (b) $\mathbf{Z} = 500\angle 35°\ \Omega$
   (c) $\mathbf{Z} = 2.5\angle 72.5°\ k\Omega$ (d) $\mathbf{Z} = 998\angle 45°\ \Omega$

7. Reduce the circuit in Figure 17–54 to a single resistance and inductance in series.

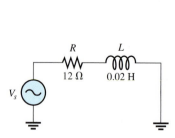

FIGURE 17–53

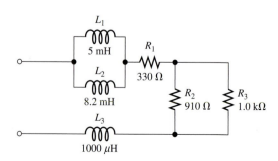

FIGURE 17–54

SECTION 17–3   Analysis of Series *RL* Circuits

8. Express the current in polar form for each circuit of Figure 17–51.

9. Calculate the total current in each circuit of Figure 17–52 and express in polar form.

10. Determine θ for the circuit in Figure 17–55.

11. If the inductance in Figure 17–55 is doubled, does θ increase or decrease, and by how many degrees?

FIGURE 17–55

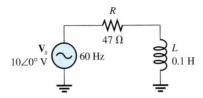

12. Sketch the waveforms for $\mathbf{V}_s$, $\mathbf{V}_R$, and $\mathbf{V}_L$ in Figure 17–55. Show the proper phase relationships.

13. For the circuit in Figure 17–56, find $\mathbf{V}_R$ and $\mathbf{V}_L$ for each of the following frequencies:
   (a) 60 Hz   **(b)** 200 Hz   **(c)** 500 Hz   **(d)** 1 kHz

14. Determine the magnitude and phase angle of the source voltage in Figure 17–57.

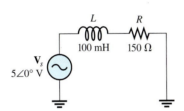

FIGURE 17–56

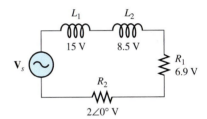

FIGURE 17–57

PART 2: PARALLEL REACTIVE CIRCUITS

SECTION 17–4   Impedance and Phase Angle of Parallel *RL* Circuits

15. What is the impedance expressed in polar form for the circuit in Figure 17–58?

16. Repeat Problem 15 for the following frequencies:
   (a) 1.5 kHz   **(b)** 3 kHz   **(c)** 5 kHz   **(d)** 10 kHz

17. At what frequency does X_L equal R in Figure 17–58?

SECTION 17–5   Analysis of Parallel *RL* Circuits

18. Find the total current and each branch current in Figure 17–59.

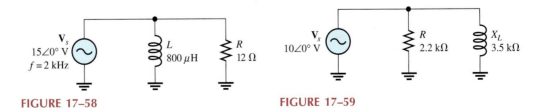

FIGURE 17–58

FIGURE 17–59

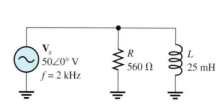

FIGURE 17–60

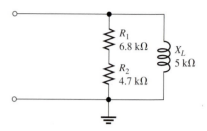

FIGURE 17–61

19. Determine the following quantities in Figure 17–60:

    (a) Z   **(b) $\mathbf{I}_R$**   **(c) $\mathbf{I}_L$**   **(d) $\mathbf{I}_{tot}$**   **(e) θ**

20. Repeat Problem 19 for $R = 56\ \Omega$ and $L = 330\ \mu$H.

21. Convert the circuit in Figure 17–61 to an equivalent series form.

22. Find the magnitude and phase angle of the total current in Figure 17–62.

FIGURE 17–62

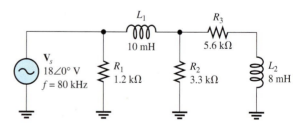

PART 3: SERIES-PARALLEL REACTIVE CIRCUITS

SECTION 17–6 Series-Parallel *RL* Circuits

23. Determine the voltages in polar form across each element in Figure 17–63. Sketch the voltage phasor diagram.

24. Is the circuit in Figure 17–63 predominantly resistive or predominantly inductive?

25. Find the current in each branch and the total current in Figure 17–63. Express the currents in polar form. Sketch the current phasor diagram.

26. For the circuit in Figure 17–64, determine the following:

    (a) $\mathbf{I}_{tot}$ **(b) θ**   **(c) $\mathbf{V}_{R1}$**   **(d) $\mathbf{V}_{R2}$**   **(e) $\mathbf{V}_{R3}$**   **(f) $\mathbf{V}_{L1}$**   **(g) $\mathbf{V}_{L2}$**

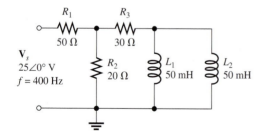

FIGURE 17–63

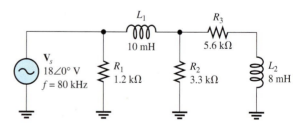

FIGURE 17–64

*27. For the circuit in Figure 17–65, determine the following:

    (a) $\mathbf{I}_{tot}$ **(b) $\mathbf{V}_{L1}$**   **(c) $\mathbf{V}_{AB}$**

*28. Draw the phasor diagram of all voltages and currents in Figure 17–65.

29. Determine the phase shift and attenuation (ratio of V_{out} to V_{in}) from the input to the output for the network in Figure 17–66.

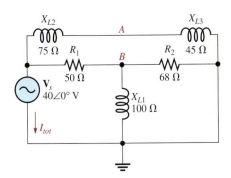

FIGURE 17–65

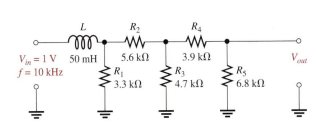

FIGURE 17–66

*30. Determine the phase shift and attenuation from the input to the output for the ladder network in Figure 17–67.

FIGURE 17–67

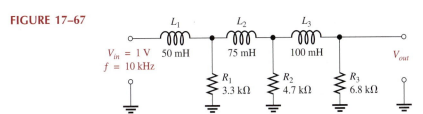

31. Design an ideal inductive switching circuit that will provide a momentary voltage of 2.5 kV from a 12 V dc source when a switch is thrown instantaneously from one position to another. The drain on the source must not exceed 1 A.

PART 4: SPECIAL TOPICS

SECTION 17–7   Power in *RL* Circuits

32. In a certain *RL* circuit, the true power is 100 mW, and the reactive power is 340 mVAR. What is the apparent power?

33. Determine the true power and the reactive power in Figure 17–55.

34. What is the power factor in Figure 17–59?

35. Determine P_{true}, P_r, P_a, and *PF* for the circuit in Figure 17–64. Sketch the power triangle.

*36. Find the true power for the circuit in Figure 17–65.

SECTION 17–8   Basic Applications

37. For the lag network in Figure 17–68, determine the phase lag of the output voltage with respect to the input for the following frequencies:

    (a) 1 Hz   **(b)** 100 Hz   **(c)** 1 kHz   **(d)** 10 kHz

38. Draw the response curve for the circuit in Figure 17–68. Show the output voltage versus frequency in 1 kHz increments from 0 Hz to 5 kHz.

39. Repeat Problem 37 for the lead network to find the phase lead in Figure 17–69.

40. Using the same procedure as in Problem 38, draw the response curve for Figure 17–69.

41. Sketch the voltage phasor diagram for each circuit in Figures 17–68 and 17–69 for a frequency of 8 kHz.

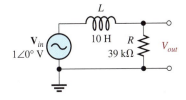

FIGURE 17–68

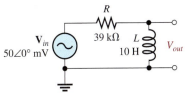

FIGURE 17–69

SECTION 17–9 Troubleshooting

42. Determine the voltage across each element in Figure 17–64 if L_1 is open.

43. Determine the output voltage in Figure 17–70 for each of the following failure modes:

    (a) L_1 open   **(b)** L_2 open   **(c)** R_1 open   **(d)** a short across R_2

FIGURE 17–70

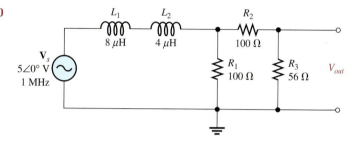

EWB Troubleshooting and Analysis

These problems require your EWB compact disk.

44. Open file PRO17-44.EWB and determine if there is a fault. If so, find the fault.

45. Open file PRO17-45.EWB and determine if there is a fault. If so, find the fault.

46. Open file PRO17-46.EWB and determine if there is a fault. If so, find the fault.

47. Open file PRO17-47.EWB and determine if there is a fault. If so, find the fault.

48. Open file PRO17-48.EWB and determine if there is a fault. If so, find the fault.

49. Open file PRO17-49.EWB and determine if there is a fault. If so, find the fault.

50. Open file PRO17-50.EWB and determine the frequency response for the filter.

51. Open file PRO17-51.EWB and determine the frequency response for the filter.

■ ANSWERS TO SECTION REVIEWS

Section 17–1

1. The current frequency is 1 kHz.

2. The phase angle is closer to 0°.

Section 17–2

1. $R = 150\ \Omega$; $X_L = 220\ \Omega$

2. $\mathbf{Z} = R + jX_L = 33\ \text{k}\Omega + j50\ \text{k}\Omega$; $\mathbf{Z} = \sqrt{R^2 + X_L^2}\ \angle\tan^{-1}(X_L/R) = 59.9\angle56.6°\ \text{k}\Omega$

Section 17–3

1. $V_s = \sqrt{V_R^2 + V_L^2} = 3.61\ \text{V}$

2. $\theta = \tan^{-1}(V_L/V_R) = 56.3°$

3. When f increases, X_L increases, Z increases, and θ increases.

Section 17–4

1. $Y = \dfrac{1}{Z} = \dfrac{1}{\sqrt{R^2 + X_L^2}} = 2\ \text{mS}$

2. $Y = \dfrac{1}{Z} = 25.1\ \text{mS}$

3. $\mathbf{I}$ lags V_s; $\theta = 32.1°$

Section 17–5

1. $I_{tot} = 32\ \text{mA}$

2. $\mathbf{I}_{tot} = 23.3\angle-59.0°\ \text{mA}$; θ is with respect to the input voltage.

3. $\theta = -90°$

Section 17–6

1. $\mathbf{Z} = 494\angle 59.0° \ \Omega$
2. $I_{tot} = 10.4 \text{ mA} - j17.3 \text{ mA}$

Section 17–7

1. Power dissipation is due to resistance.
2. $PF = 0.643$
3. $P_{\text{true}} = 4.7 \text{ W}; \ P_r = 6.2 \text{ VAR}; \ P_a = 7.78 \text{ VA}$

Section 17–8

1. $\phi = 81.9°$
2. $V_{out} = 9.90 \text{ V}$
3. The output is across the resistor.

Section 17–9

1. Shorted windings reduce L and thereby reduce X_L at any given frequency.
2. I_{tot} decreases, V_{R1} decreases, V_{R2} increases.

Section 17–10

1. $V_{out} = 0 \text{ V}$
2. $V_{out} = V_{in}$

■ **ANSWERS TO RELATED PROBLEMS FOR EXAMPLES**

17–1 $\mathbf{Z} = 1.8 \text{ k}\Omega + j950 \ \Omega; \ \mathbf{Z} = 2.04\angle 27.8° \text{ k}\Omega$
17–2 $\mathbf{I} = 423\angle -32.1° \ \mu\text{A}$
17–3 $Z = 12.6 \text{ k}\Omega; \ \theta = 85.5°$
17–4 $\mathbf{Z} = 8.14\angle 35.5° \text{ k}\Omega$
17–5 $\mathbf{Y} = 3.03 \text{ mS} - j0.796 \text{ mS}$
17–6 $\mathbf{I} = 14.0\angle -71.1° \text{ mA}$
17–7 $I_{tot} = 67.6 \text{ mA}; \ \theta = 36.3°$
17–8 (a) $\mathbf{V}_1 = 8.04\angle 2.52° \text{ V}$
      (b) $\mathbf{V}_2 = 2.00\angle -10.2° \text{ V}$
17–9 $\mathbf{I}_{tot} = 20.2\angle -59.0° \text{ mA}$
17–10 P_{true}, P_r, and P_a decrease.
17–11 $\phi = 65.6°$
17–12 V_{out} increases.
17–13 $\phi = -32°$
17–14 $V_{out} = 12.3 \text{ V rms}$

■ **ANSWERS TO SELF-TEST**

1. (f)   2. (b)   3. (a)   4. (d)   5. (a)   6. (d)   7. (b)   8. (b)
9. (a)   10. (d)   11. (c)   12. (d)   13. (b)   14. (c)

18

RLC CIRCUITS AND RESONANCE

 Electronics Workbench (EWB) and PSpice Tutorials at
http://www.prenhall.com/floyd

■ INTRODUCTION

In this chapter, the analysis methods learned in Chapters 16 and 17 are extended to the coverage of circuits with combinations of resistive, inductive, and capacitive elements. Series and parallel *RLC* circuits, plus series-parallel combinations, are studied.

Circuits with both inductance and capacitance can exhibit the property of resonance, which is important in many types of applications. Resonance is the basis for frequency selectivity in communication systems. For example, the ability of a radio or television receiver to select a certain frequency that is transmitted by a particular station and, at the same time, to eliminate frequencies from other stations is based on the principle of resonance. The conditions in *RLC* circuits that produce resonance and the characteristics of resonant circuits are covered in this chapter.

In the TECH TIP assignment in Section 18–10, you will work with the resonant tuning circuit in the RF amplifier of an AM radio receiver. The tuning circuit is used to select any desired frequency within the AM band so that a desired station can be tuned in.

■ COVERAGE OPTIONS

If you chose to cover all of Chapter 16 and all of Chapter 17, then all of this chapter should be covered next.

If you chose to cover reactive circuits in Chapters 16 and 17 on the basis of the four major parts, then the appropriate part of this chapter should be covered next, followed by the next part in Chapter 16, if applicable.

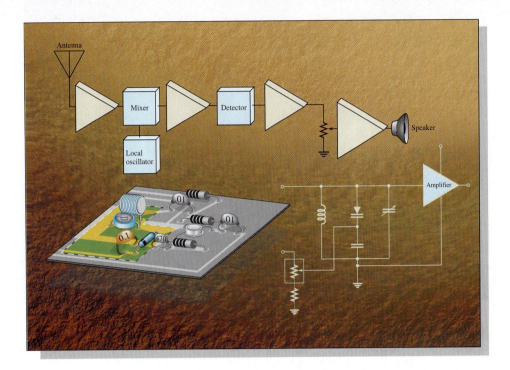

■ CHAPTER OBJECTIVES

PART 1: SERIES REACTIVE CIRCUITS
❑ Determine the impedance of a series *RLC* circuit
❑ Analyze series *RLC* circuits
❑ Analyze a circuit for resonance

PART 2: PARALLEL REACTIVE CIRCUITS
❑ Determine the impedance of a parallel resonant circuit
❑ Analyze parallel *RLC* circuits
❑ Analyze a circuit for parallel resonance

PART 3: SERIES-PARALLEL REACTIVE CIRCUITS
❑ Analyze series-parallel *RLC* circuits

PART 4: SPECIAL TOPICS
❑ Determine the bandwidth of resonant circuits
❑ Discuss some applications of resonant circuits

■ **TECH**nology
Theory
Into
Practice

PART 1

SERIES REACTIVE CIRCUITS

18–1 ■ IMPEDANCE OF SERIES *RLC* CIRCUITS

A series RLC circuit contains both inductance and capacitance. Since inductive reactance and capacitive reactance have opposite effects on the circuit phase angle, the total reactance is less than either individual reactance.

After completing this section, you should be able to

■ **Determine the impedance of a series *RLC* circuit**
  • Calculate total reactance
  • Determine whether a circuit is predominately inductive or capacitive

A series *RLC* circuit is shown in Figure 18–1. It contains resistance, inductance, and capacitance.

FIGURE 18–1
Series RLC circuit.

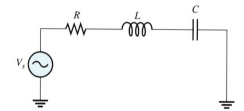

As you know, inductive reactance ($\mathbf{X}_L$) causes the total current to lag the applied voltage. Capacitive reactance ($\mathbf{X}_C$) has the opposite effect: It causes the current to lead the voltage. Thus $\mathbf{X}_L$ and $\mathbf{X}_C$ tend to offset each other. When they are equal, they cancel, and the total reactance is zero. In any case, the magnitude of the total reactance in the series circuit is

$$X_{tot} = |X_L - X_C| \qquad (18–1)$$

The term $|X_L - X_C|$ means the absolute value of the difference of the two reactances. That is, the sign of the result is considered positive no matter which reactance is greater. For example, $3 - 7 = -4$, but the absolute value is

$$|3 - 7| = 4$$

When $X_L > X_C$, the circuit is predominantly inductive, and when $X_C > X_L$, the circuit is predominantly capacitive.

The total impedance for the series *RLC* circuit is stated in rectangular form in Equation (18–2) and in polar form in Equation (18–3).

$$\mathbf{Z} = R + jX_L - jX_C \tag{18–2}$$

$$\mathbf{Z} = \sqrt{R^2 + (X_L - X_C)^2} \angle \tan^{-1}\left(\frac{X_{tot}}{R}\right) \tag{18–3}$$

In Equation (18–3), $\sqrt{R^2 + (X_L - X_C)^2}$ is the magnitude and $\tan^{-1}(X_{tot}/R)$ is the phase angle between the total current and the applied voltage.

EXAMPLE 18–1   Determine the total impedance in Figure 18–2. Express it in both rectangular and polar forms.

FIGURE 18–2

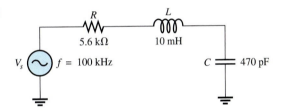

Solution   First, find X_C and X_L.

$$X_C = \frac{1}{2\pi f C} = \frac{1}{2\pi(100 \text{ kHz})(470 \text{ pF})} = 3.39 \text{ k}\Omega$$

$$X_L = 2\pi f L = 2\pi(100 \text{ kHz})(10 \text{ mH}) = 6.28 \text{ k}\Omega$$

In this case, X_L is greater than X_C, and thus the circuit is more inductive than capacitive. The magnitude of the total reactance is

$$X_{tot} = |X_L - X_C| = |6.28 \text{ k}\Omega - 3.39 \text{ k}\Omega| = 2.89 \text{ k}\Omega \qquad \text{inductive}$$

The impedance in rectangular form is

$$\mathbf{Z} = R + (jX_L - jX_C) = 5.6 \text{ k}\Omega + (j6.28 \text{ k}\Omega - j3.39 \text{ k}\Omega) = \mathbf{5.6 \text{ k}\Omega + j2.89 \text{ k}\Omega}$$

The impedance in polar form is

$$\mathbf{Z} = \sqrt{R^2 + X_{tot}^2} \angle \tan^{-1}\left(\frac{X_{tot}}{R}\right)$$

$$= \sqrt{(5.6 \text{ k}\Omega)^2 + (2.89 \text{ k}\Omega)^2} \angle \tan^{-1}\left(\frac{2.89 \text{ k}\Omega}{5.6 \text{ k}\Omega}\right) = \mathbf{6.30\angle 27.3° \text{ k}\Omega}$$

The calculator sequence for conversion from the rectangular to the polar form is to first select polar on the MODE screen, then

(5 • 6 EE 3 , 2 • 8 9 EE 3) ENTER

Related Problem   Determine **Z** in polar form if *f* is increased to 200 kHz.

As you have seen, when the inductive reactance is greater than the capacitive reactance, the circuit appears inductive; so the current lags the applied voltage. When the capacitive reactance is greater, the circuit appears capacitive, and the current leads the applied voltage.

SECTION 18–1 REVIEW

1. In a given series *RLC* circuit, X_C is 150 Ω and X_L is 80 Ω. What is the total reactance in ohms? Is it inductive or capacitive?

2. Determine the impedance in polar form for the circuit in Question 1 when $R = 47$ Ω. What is the magnitude of the impedance? What is the phase angle? Is the current leading or lagging the applied voltage?

18–2 ■ ANALYSIS OF SERIES *RLC* CIRCUITS

Recall that capacitive reactance varies inversely with frequency and that inductive reactance varies directly with frequency. In this section, the combined effects of the reactances as a function of frequency are examined.

After completing this section, you should be able to

■ **Analyze series *RLC* circuits**
  • Determine current in a series *RLC* circuit
  • Determine the voltages in a series *RLC* circuit
  • Determine the phase angle

Figure 18–3 shows that for a typical series *RLC* circuit the total reactance behaves as follows: Starting at a very low frequency, X_C is high, and X_L is low, and the circuit is predominantly capacitive. As the frequency is increased, X_C decreases and X_L increases until a value is reached where $X_C = X_L$ and the two reactances cancel, making the circuit purely resistive. This condition is **series resonance** and will be studied in Section 18–3. As the frequency is increased further, X_L becomes greater than X_C, and the circuit is predominantly inductive. Example 18–2 illustrates how the impedance and phase angle change as the source frequency is varied.

FIGURE 18–3

How X_C and X_L vary with frequency.

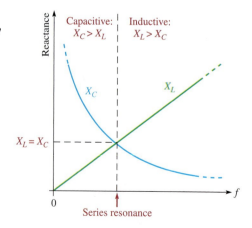

EXAMPLE 18–2

For each of the following input frequencies, find the impedance in polar form for the circuit in Figure 18–4. Note the change in magnitude and phase angle with frequency.

(a) $f = 1$ kHz   (b) $f = 2$ kHz   (c) $f = 3.5$ kHz   (d) $f = 5$ kHz

FIGURE 18–4

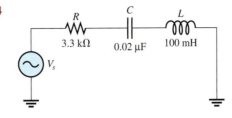

Solution

(a) At $f = 1$ kHz,

$$X_C = \frac{1}{2\pi f C} = \frac{1}{2\pi(1 \text{ kHz})(0.02 \ \mu\text{F})} = 7.96 \text{ k}\Omega$$

$$X_L = 2\pi f L = 2\pi(1 \text{ kHz})(100 \text{ mH}) = 628 \ \Omega$$

The circuit is clearly capacitive, and the impedance is

$$\mathbf{Z} = \sqrt{R^2 + (X_L - X_C)^2} \angle -\tan^{-1}\left(\frac{X_{tot}}{R}\right)$$

$$= \sqrt{(3.3 \text{ k}\Omega)^2 + (628 \ \Omega - 7.96 \text{ k}\Omega)^2} \angle -\tan^{-1}\left(\frac{7.33 \text{ k}\Omega}{3.3 \text{ k}\Omega}\right) = \mathbf{8.04 \angle -65.8° \text{ k}\Omega}$$

(b) At $f = 2$ kHz,

$$X_C = \frac{1}{2\pi(2 \text{ kHz})(0.02 \ \mu\text{F})} = 3.98 \text{ k}\Omega$$

$$X_L = 2\pi(2 \text{ kHz})(100 \text{ mH}) = 1.26 \text{ k}\Omega$$

The circuit is still capacitive, and the impedance is

$$\mathbf{Z} = \sqrt{(3.3 \text{ k}\Omega)^2 + (1.26 \text{ k}\Omega - 3.98 \text{ k}\Omega)^2} \angle -\tan^{-1}\left(\frac{2.72 \text{ k}\Omega}{3.3 \text{ k}\Omega}\right)$$

$$= \mathbf{4.28 \angle -39.5° \text{ k}\Omega}$$

(c) At $f = 3.5$ kHz,

$$X_C = \frac{1}{2\pi(3.5 \text{ kHz})(0.02 \ \mu\text{F})} = 2.27 \text{ k}\Omega$$

$$X_L = 2\pi(3.5 \text{ kHz})(100 \text{ mH}) = 2.20 \text{ k}\Omega$$

The circuit is very close to being purely resistive because X_C and X_L are nearly equal, but is still slightly capacitive. The impedance is

$$\mathbf{Z} = \sqrt{(3.3 \text{ k}\Omega)^2 + (2.20 \text{ k}\Omega - 2.27 \text{ k}\Omega)^2} \angle -\tan^{-1}\left(\frac{0.07 \text{ k}\Omega}{3.3 \text{ k}\Omega}\right)$$

$$= \mathbf{3.3 \angle -1.22° \text{ k}\Omega}$$

(d) At $f = 5$ kHz,

$$X_C = \frac{1}{2\pi(5 \text{ kHz})(0.02 \ \mu\text{F})} = 1.59 \text{ k}\Omega$$

$$X_L = 2\pi(5 \text{ kHz})(100 \text{ mH}) = 3.14 \text{ k}\Omega$$

The circuit is now predominantly inductive. The impedance is

$$\mathbf{Z} = \sqrt{(3.3 \text{ k}\Omega)^2 + (3.14 \text{ k}\Omega - 1.59 \text{ k}\Omega)^2} \angle \tan^{-1}\left(\frac{1.55 \text{ k}\Omega}{3.3 \text{ k}\Omega}\right)$$

$$= 3.65 \angle 25.2° \text{ k}\Omega$$

Notice how the circuit changed from capacitive to inductive as the frequency increased. The phase condition changed from the current leading to the current lagging as indicated by the sign of the angle. It is interesting to note that the impedance magnitude decreased to a minimum approximately equal to the resistance and then began increasing again.

Related Problem   Determine **Z** in polar form for $f = 7$ kHz and sketch a graph of impedance vs. frequency using the values in this example.

In a series *RLC* circuit, the capacitor voltage and the inductor voltage are always 180° out of phase with each other. For this reason, V_C and V_L subtract from each other, and thus the voltage across L and C combined is always less than the larger individual voltage across either element, as illustrated in Figure 18–5 and in the waveform diagram of Figure 18–6.

FIGURE 18–5

The voltage across the series combination of C and L is always less than the larger individual voltage.

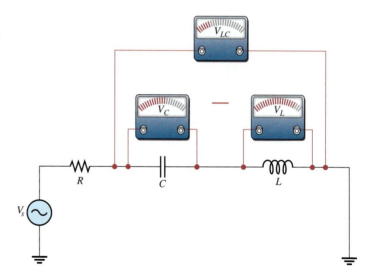

FIGURE 18–6

V_{CL} is the algebraic sum of V_L and V_C. Because of the phase relationship, V_L and V_C effectively subtract.

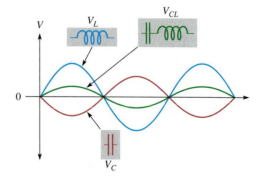

In the next example, Ohm's law is used to find the current and voltages in the series *RLC* circuit.

EXAMPLE 18–3   Find the current and the voltages across each element in Figure 18–7. Express each quantity in polar form, and draw a complete voltage phasor diagram.

FIGURE 18–7

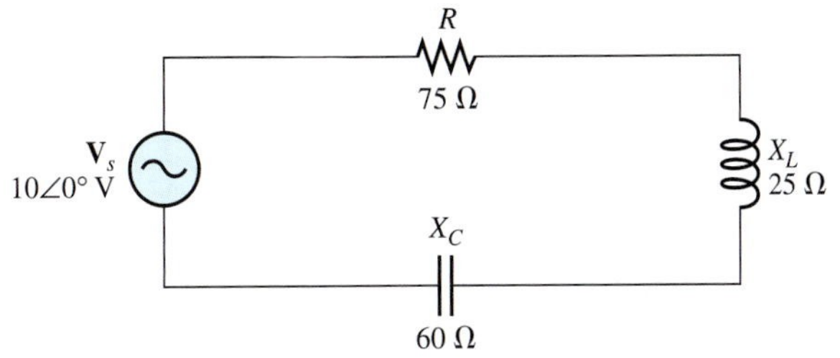

V_s
$10\angle0°$ V

R
75 Ω

X_L
25 Ω

X_C
60 Ω

Solution   First, find the total impedance.

$$\mathbf{Z} = R + jX_L - jX_C = 75\ \Omega + j25\ \Omega - j60\ \Omega = 75\ \Omega - j35\ \Omega$$

Convert to polar form for convenience in applying Ohm's law.

$$\mathbf{Z} = \sqrt{R^2 + X_{tot}^2}\angle{-\tan^{-1}\left(\frac{X_{tot}}{R}\right)}$$

$$= \sqrt{(75\ \Omega)^2 + (35\ \Omega)^2}\angle{-\tan^{-1}\left(\frac{35\ \Omega}{75\ \Omega}\right)} = 82.8\angle{-25°}\ \Omega$$

Apply Ohm's law to find the current.

$$\mathbf{I} = \frac{\mathbf{V}_s}{\mathbf{Z}} = \frac{10\angle0°\ \text{V}}{82.8\angle{-25°}\ \Omega} = \mathbf{121\angle25.0°\ mA}$$

Now, apply Ohm's law to find the voltages across *R, L,* and *C*.

$$\mathbf{V}_R = \mathbf{IR} = (121\angle25.0°\ \text{mA})(75\angle0°\ \Omega) = \mathbf{9.08\angle25.0°\ V}$$
$$\mathbf{V}_L = \mathbf{IX}_L = (121\angle25.0°\ \text{mA})(25\angle90°\ \Omega) = \mathbf{3.03\angle115°\ V}$$
$$\mathbf{V}_C = \mathbf{IX}_C = (121\angle25.0°\ \text{mA})(60\angle{-90°}\ \Omega) = \mathbf{7.26\angle{-65.0°}\ V}$$

The phasor diagram is shown in Figure 18–8. The magnitudes represent rms values. Notice that $\mathbf{V}_L$ is leading $\mathbf{V}_R$ by 90°, and $\mathbf{V}_C$ is lagging $\mathbf{V}_R$ by 90°. Also, there is a 180° phase difference between $\mathbf{V}_L$ and $\mathbf{V}_C$. If the current phasor were shown, it would be at the same angle as $\mathbf{V}_R$. The current is leading $\mathbf{V}_s$, the source voltage, by 25°, indicating a capacitive circuit ($X_C > X_L$). The phasor diagram is rotated 25° from its usual position because the reference is the source voltage, V_s, which is oriented along the *x*-axis.

FIGURE 18–8

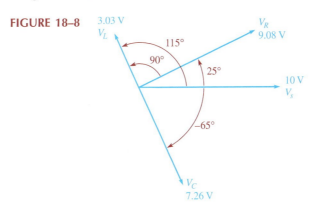

Related Problem   What will happen to the current if the frequency in Figure 18–7 is increased?

SECTION 18–2
REVIEW
1. The following voltages occur in a certain series *RLC* circuit. Determine the source voltage: $\mathbf{V}_R = 24\angle 30°$ V, $\mathbf{V}_L = 15\angle 120°$ V, and $\mathbf{V}_C = 45\angle -60°$ V.
2. When $R = 1.0$ kΩ, $X_C = 1.8$ kΩ, and $X_L = 1.2$ kΩ, does the current lead or lag the applied voltage?
3. Determine the total reactance in Question 2.

18–3 ■ SERIES RESONANCE

In a series RLC circuit, series resonance occurs when $X_C = X_L$. The frequency at which resonance occurs is called the resonant frequency and is designated f_r.

After completing this section, you should be able to

■ **Analyze a circuit for resonance**
  • Define *resonance*
  • Determine the impedance at resonance
  • Explain why the reactances cancel at resonance
  • Determine the series resonant frequency
  • Calculate the current, voltages, and phase angle at resonance

Figure 18–9 illustrates the series resonant condition.

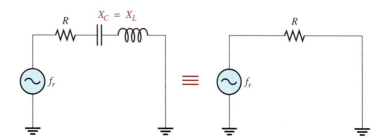

FIGURE 18–9
Series resonance. X_C and X_L cancel each other resulting in a purely resistive circuit.

Resonance is a condition in a series *RLC* circuit in which the capacitive and inductive reactances are equal in magnitude; thus, they cancel each other and result in a purely resistive impedance. In a series *RLC* circuit, the total impedance was given in Equation (18–2) as

$$\mathbf{Z}_r = R + jX_L - jX_C$$

At resonance, $X_L = X_C$ and the j terms cancel; thus, the impedance is purely resistive. These resonant conditions are stated in the following equations:

$$X_L = X_C \qquad\qquad \text{(18–4)}$$

$$Z_r = R \qquad\qquad \text{(18–5)}$$

EXAMPLE 18–4   For the series *RLC* circuit in Figure 18–10, determine X_C and $\mathbf{Z}$ at resonance.

FIGURE 18–10

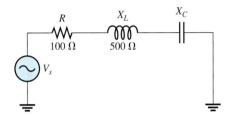

Solution $X_L = X_C$ at the resonant frequency. Thus, $X_C = X_L = 500\ \Omega$. The impedance at resonance is

$$\mathbf{Z}_r = R + jX_L - jX_C = 100\ \Omega + j500\ \Omega - j500\ \Omega = 100\angle 0°\ \Omega$$

The impedance is equal to the resistance because the reactances are equal in magnitude and therefore cancel.

Related Problem   Just below the resonant frequency, is the circuit more inductive or more capacitive?

X_L and X_C Effectively Cancel at Resonance

At the series **resonant frequency,** the voltages across *C* and *L* are equal in magnitude because the reactances are equal and because the same current is through both since they are in series $(IX_C = IX_L)$. Also, V_L and V_C are always 180° out of phase with each other.

   During any given cycle, the polarities of the voltages across *C* and *L* are opposite, as shown in parts (a) and (b) of Figure 18–11. The equal and opposite voltages across *C* and *L* cancel, leaving zero volts from point *A* to point *B* as shown. Since there is no voltage drop from *A* to *B* but there is still current, the total reactance must be zero, as indicated in part (c). Also, the voltage phasor diagram in part (d) shows that V_C and V_L are equal in magnitude and 180° out of phase with each other.

FIGURE 18–11

At the resonant frequency, f_r, the voltages across C and L are equal in magnitude. Since they are 180° out of phase with each other, they cancel, leaving 0 V across the LC combination (point A to point B). The section of the circuit from A to B effectively looks like a short at resonance.

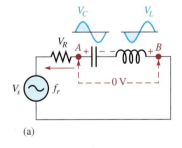

(a)

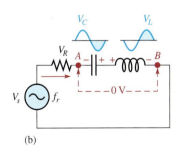

(b)

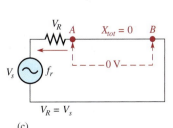

(c)

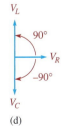

(d)

Series Resonant Frequency

For a given series *RLC* circuit, resonance happens at only one specific frequency. A formula for this resonant frequency is developed as follows:

$$X_L = X_C$$

Substitute the reactance formulas.

$$2\pi f_r L = \frac{1}{2\pi f_r C}$$

Then,

$$f_r^2 = \frac{1}{4\pi^2 LC}$$

Take the square root of both sides. The formula for series resonant frequency is

$$f_r = \frac{1}{2\pi\sqrt{LC}} \qquad\qquad \textbf{(18–6)}$$

EXAMPLE 18–5   Find the series resonant frequency for the circuit in Figure 18–12.

FIGURE 18–12

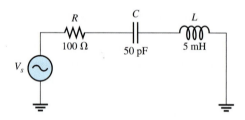

Solution   The resonant frequency is

$$f_r = \frac{1}{2\pi\sqrt{LC}} = \frac{1}{2\pi\sqrt{(5\ \text{mH})(50\ \text{pF})}} = \textbf{318 kHz}$$

Related Problem   If $C = 0.01\ \mu F$ in Figure 18–12, what is the resonant frequency?

Series *RLC* Impedance

At frequencies below f_r, $X_C > X_L$; thus, the circuit is capacitive. At the resonant frequency, $X_C = X_L$, so the circuit is purely resistive. At frequencies above f_r, $X_L > X_C$; thus, the circuit is inductive.

The impedance magnitude is minimum at resonance ($Z = R$) and increases in value above and below the resonant point. The graph in Figure 18–13 illustrates how impedance changes with frequency. At zero frequency, both X_C and Z are infinitely large and X_L is zero because the capacitor looks like an open at 0 Hz and the inductor looks like a short. As the frequency increases, X_C decreases and X_L increases. Since X_C is larger than X_L at frequencies below f_r, Z decreases along with X_C. At f_r, $X_C = X_L$ and $Z = R$. At frequencies above f_r, X_L becomes increasingly larger than X_C, causing Z to increase.

FIGURE 18–13
Series RLC impedance as a function of frequency.

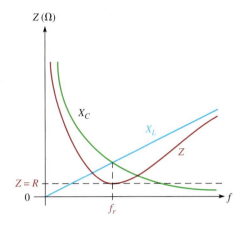

EXAMPLE 18–6

For the circuit in Figure 18–14, determine the impedance magnitude at the following frequencies:

(a) f_r **(b)** 1000 Hz below f_r **(c)** 1000 Hz above f_r

FIGURE 18–14

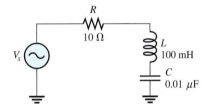

Solution

(a) At f_r, the impedance is equal to R.

$$Z = R = \textbf{10 } \boldsymbol{\Omega}$$

To determine the impedance above and below f_r, first calculate the resonant frequency.

$$f_r = \frac{1}{2\pi\sqrt{LC}} = \frac{1}{2\pi\sqrt{(100 \text{ mH})(0.01 \text{ }\mu\text{F})}} = 5.03 \text{ kHz}$$

(b) At 1000 Hz below f_r, the frequency and reactances are as follows:

$$f = f_r - 1 \text{ kHz} = 5.03 \text{ kHz} - 1 \text{ kHz} = 4.03 \text{ kHz}$$

$$X_C = \frac{1}{2\pi f C} = \frac{1}{2\pi(4.03 \text{ kHz})(0.01 \text{ }\mu\text{F})} = 3.95 \text{ k}\Omega$$

$$X_L = 2\pi f L = 2\pi(4.03 \text{ kHz})(100 \text{ mH}) = 2.53 \text{ k}\Omega$$

Therefore, the impedance at $f_r - 1$ kHz is

$$Z = \sqrt{R^2 + (X_L - X_C)^2} = \sqrt{(10 \text{ }\Omega)^2 + (2.53 \text{ k}\Omega - 3.95 \text{ k}\Omega)^2} = \textbf{1.42 k}\boldsymbol{\Omega}$$

(c) At 1000 Hz above f_r,

$$f = 5.03 \text{ kHz} + 1 \text{ kHz} = 6.03 \text{ kHz}$$

$$X_C = \frac{1}{2\pi(6.03 \text{ kHz})(0.01 \text{ }\mu\text{F})} = 2.64 \text{ k}\Omega$$

$$X_L = 2\pi(6.03 \text{ kHz})(100 \text{ mH}) = 3.79 \text{ k}\Omega$$

Therefore, the impedance at $f_r + 1$ kHz is

$$Z = \sqrt{(10 \text{ }\Omega)^2 + (3.79 \text{ k}\Omega - 2.64 \text{ k}\Omega)^2} = \textbf{1.15 k}\boldsymbol{\Omega}$$

In part (b) Z is capacitive, and in part (c) Z is inductive.

Related Problem What happens to the impedance magnitude if f is decreased below 4.03 kHz? Above 6.03 kHz?

Current and Voltages in a Series *RLC* Circuit

At the series resonant frequency, the current is maximum ($I_{max} = V_s/R$). Above and below resonance, the current decreases because the impedance increases. A response curve showing the plot of current versus frequency is shown in Figure 18–15(a).

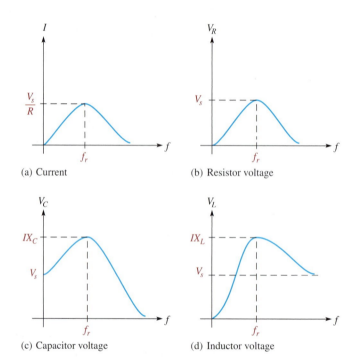

(a) Current

(b) Resistor voltage

(c) Capacitor voltage

(d) Inductor voltage

FIGURE 18–15

Current and voltage magnitudes as a function of frequency in a series RLC circuit. V_C and V_L can be much larger than the source voltage.

The resistor voltage, V_R, follows the current and is maximum (equal to V_s) at resonance and zero at $f = 0$ and at $f = \infty$, as shown in Figure 18–15(b). The general shapes of the V_C and V_L curves are indicated in Figure 18–15(c) and (d). Notice that $V_C = V_s$ when $f = 0$, because the capacitor appears open. Also notice that V_L approaches V_s as f approaches infinity, because the inductor appears open.

The voltages are maximum at resonance but drop off above and below f_r. The voltages across L and C at resonance are exactly equal in magnitude but 180° out of phase; so they cancel. Thus, the total voltage across both L and C is zero, and $V_R = V_s$ at resonance, as indicated in Figure 18–16. Individually, V_L and V_C can be much greater than the source voltage, as you will see later. Keep in mind that V_L and V_C are always opposite in polarity regardless of the frequency, but only at resonance are their magnitudes equal.

FIGURE 18–16

Series RLC circuit at resonance.

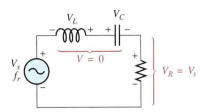

EXAMPLE 18–7

Find I, V_R, V_L, and V_C at resonance in Figure 18–17. The resonant values of X_L and X_C are shown.

FIGURE 18–17

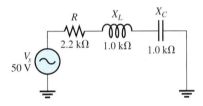

Solution   At resonance, I is maximum and equal to V_s/R.

$$I = \frac{V_s}{R} = \frac{50 \text{ V}}{2.2 \text{ k}\Omega} = \textbf{22.7 mA}$$

Apply Ohm's law to obtain the following voltage magnitudes:

$$V_R = IR = (22.7 \text{ mA})(2.2 \text{ k}\Omega) = \textbf{50 V}$$
$$V_L = IX_L = (22.7 \text{ mA})(1.0 \text{ k}\Omega) = \textbf{22.7 V}$$
$$V_C = IX_C = (22.7 \text{ mA})(1.0 \text{ k}\Omega) = \textbf{22.7 V}$$

Notice that all of the source voltage is dropped across the resistor. Also, of course, V_L and V_C are equal in magnitude but opposite in phase. This causes these voltages to cancel, making the total reactive voltage zero.

Related Problem   What is the current at resonance in Figure 18–17 if $X_L = X_C = 1.0 \text{ k}\Omega$?

The Phase Angle of a Series *RLC* Circuit

At frequencies below resonance, $X_C > X_L$, and the current leads the source voltage, as indicated in Figure 18–18(a). The phase angle decreases as the frequency approaches the resonant value and is 0° at resonance, as indicated in part (b). At frequencies above resonance, $X_L > X_C$, and the current lags the source voltage, as indicated in part (c). As the frequency goes higher, the phase angle approaches 90°. A plot of phase angle versus frequency is shown in part (d) of the figure.

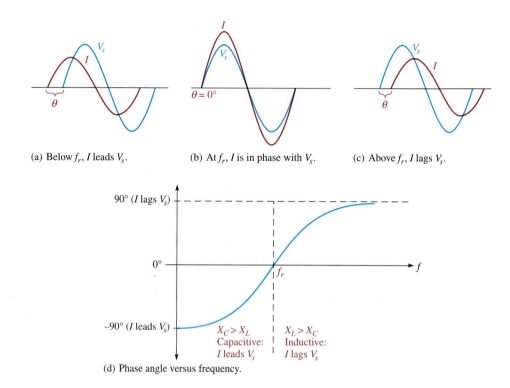

(a) Below f_r, I leads V_s.   (b) At f_r, I is in phase with V_s.   (c) Above f_r, I lags V_s.

(d) Phase angle versus frequency.

FIGURE 18–18
The phase angle as a function of frequency in a series RLC circuit.

**SECTION 18–3
REVIEW**

1. What is the condition for series resonance?
2. Why is the current maximum at the resonant frequency?
3. Calculate the resonant frequency for $C = 1000$ pF and $L = 1000$ μH.
4. In Question 3, is the circuit inductive or capacitive at 50 kHz?

♦ *Coverage of parallel reactive circuits begins in Chapter 16, Part 2, on page 611.*

PART 2
PARALLEL REACTIVE CIRCUITS

18–4 ■ IMPEDANCE OF PARALLEL *RLC* CIRCUITS

In this section, you will learn how to determine the impedance and phase angle of a parallel RLC circuit. Also, conductance, susceptance, and admittance of a parallel RLC circuit are covered.

After completing this section, you should be able to

■ **Determine the impedance of a parallel resonant circuit**
  • Calculate the conductance, susceptance, and admittance
  • Determine whether a circuit is predominately inductive or capacitive

Figure 18–19 shows a parallel *RLC* circuit. The total impedance can be calculated using the reciprocal of the sum-of-reciprocals method, just as was done for circuits with resistors in parallel.

$$\frac{1}{\mathbf{Z}} = \frac{1}{R \angle 0°} + \frac{1}{X_L \angle 90°} + \frac{1}{X_C \angle -90°}$$

or

$$\mathbf{Z} = \frac{1}{\dfrac{1}{R \angle 0°} + \dfrac{1}{X_L \angle 90°} + \dfrac{1}{X_C \angle -90°}} \qquad (18\text{–}7)$$

FIGURE 18–19
Parallel RLC circuit.

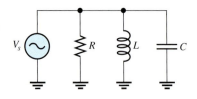

EXAMPLE 18–8   Find **Z** in polar form in Figure 18–20.

FIGURE 18–20

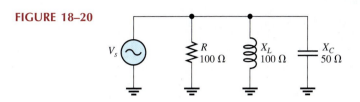

Solution   Use the sum-of-reciprocals formula.

$$\frac{1}{\mathbf{Z}} = \frac{1}{R\angle 0°} + \frac{1}{X_L\angle 90°} + \frac{1}{X_C\angle -90°} = \frac{1}{100\angle 0°\ \Omega} + \frac{1}{100\angle 90°\ \Omega} + \frac{1}{50\angle -90°\ \Omega}$$

Apply the rule for division of polar numbers.

$$\frac{1}{\mathbf{Z}} = 10\angle 0°\ \text{mS} + 10\angle -90°\ \text{mS} + 20\angle 90°\ \text{mS}$$

Recall that the sign of the denominator angle changes when dividing.
Next, convert each term to its rectangular equivalent and combine.

$$\frac{1}{\mathbf{Z}} = 10\ \text{mS} - j10\ \text{mS} + j20\ \text{mS} = 10\ \text{mS} + j10\ \text{mS}$$

Take the reciprocal to obtain **Z** and then convert to polar form.

$$\mathbf{Z} = \frac{1}{10\ \text{mS} + j10\ \text{mS}} = \frac{1}{\sqrt{(10\ \text{mS})^2 + (10\ \text{mS})^2}\angle \tan^{-1}\left(\dfrac{10\ \text{mS}}{10\ \text{mS}}\right)}$$

$$= \frac{1}{14.14\angle 45°\ \text{mS}} = \mathbf{70.7\angle -45°\ \Omega}$$

The negative angle shows that the circuit is capacitive. This may surprise you, since $X_L > X_C$. However, in a parallel circuit, the smaller quantity has the greater effect on the total current. Similar to the case of resistances in parallel, the smaller reactance draws more current and has the greater effect on the total *Z*.
   In this circuit, the total current leads the total voltage by a phase angle of 45°.

Related Problem   If the frequency in Figure 18–20 increases, does the impedance increase or decrease?

Conductance, Susceptance, and Admittance

The concepts of conductance (*G*), capacitive susceptance (B_C), inductive susceptance (B_L) and admittance (*Y*) were discussed in Chapters 16 and 17. The phasor formulas are restated here.

$$\mathbf{G} = \frac{1}{R\angle 0°} = G\angle 0° \tag{18–8}$$

$$\mathbf{B}_C = \frac{1}{X_C\angle -90°} = B_C\angle 90° = jB_C \tag{18–9}$$

$$\mathbf{B}_L = \frac{1}{X_L \angle 90°} = B_L \angle -90° = -jB_L \qquad (18\text{–}10)$$

$$\mathbf{Y} = \frac{1}{Z \angle \pm \theta} = Y \angle \pm \theta = G + jB_C - jB_L \qquad (18\text{–}11)$$

As you know, the unit of each of these quantities is the siemens (S).

EXAMPLE 18–9

Determine the conductance, capacitive susceptance, inductive susceptance, and total admittance in Figure 18–21. Also, determine the impedance.

FIGURE 18–21

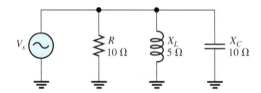

Solution

$$G = \frac{1}{R \angle 0°} = \frac{1}{10 \angle 0° \ \Omega} = 100 \angle 0° \ \text{mS}$$

$$\mathbf{B}_C = \frac{1}{X_C \angle -90°} = \frac{1}{10 \angle -90° \ \Omega} = 100 \angle 90° \ \text{mS}$$

$$\mathbf{B}_L = \frac{1}{X_L \angle 90°} = \frac{1}{5 \angle 90° \ \Omega} = 200 \angle -90° \ \text{mS}$$

$$\mathbf{Y}_{tot} = G + jB_C - jB_L = 100 \ \text{mS} + j100 \ \text{mS} - j200 \ \text{mS}$$
$$= 100 \ \text{mS} - j100 \ \text{mS} = 141.4 \angle -45° \ \text{mS}$$

From $\mathbf{Y}_{tot}$, you can determine $\mathbf{Z}_{tot}$.

$$\mathbf{Z}_{tot} = \frac{1}{\mathbf{Y}_{tot}} = \frac{1}{141.4 \angle -45° \ \text{mS}} = 7.07 \angle 45° \ \Omega$$

Related Problem Is the circuit in Figure 18–21 predominately inductive or predominately capacitive?

SECTION 18–4 REVIEW

1. In a certain parallel *RLC* circuit, the capacitive reactance is 60 Ω, and the inductive reactance is 100 Ω. Is the circuit predominantly capacitive or inductive?

2. Determine the admittance of a parallel circuit in which $R = 1.0 \ \text{k}\Omega$, $X_C = 500 \ \Omega$, and $X_L = 1.2 \ \text{k}\Omega$.

3. In Question 2, what is the impedance?

18–5 ■ ANALYSIS OF PARALLEL *RLC* CIRCUITS

As you have seen, the smaller reactance in a parallel circuit dominates because it results in the larger branch current. In this section, you will examine current relationships in parallel circuits.

After completing this section, you should be able to

■ **Analyze parallel *RLC* circuits**
  • Explain how the currents are related in terms of phase
  • Calculate impedance, currents, and voltages

Recall that capacitive reactance varies inversely with frequency and that inductive reactance varies directly with frequency. In a parallel *RLC* circuit at low frequencies, the inductive reactance is less than the capacitive reactance; therefore, the circuit is inductive. As the frequency is increased, X_L increases and X_C decreases until a value is reached where $X_L = X_C$. This is the point of **parallel resonance.** As the frequency is increased further, X_C becomes smaller than X_L, and the circuit becomes capacitive.

Current Relationships

In a parallel *RLC* circuit, the current in the capacitive branch and the current in the inductive branch are *always* 180° out of phase with each other (neglecting any coil resistance). Because I_C and I_L add algebraically, the total current is actually the difference in their magnitudes. Thus, the total current into the parallel branches of L and C is always less than the largest individual branch current, as illustrated in Figure 18–22 and in the waveform diagram of Figure 18–23. Of course, the current in the resistive branch is always 90° out of phase with both reactive currents, as shown in the current phasor diagram of Figure 18–24.

FIGURE 18–22

The total current into the parallel combination of C and L is the difference of the two branch currents.

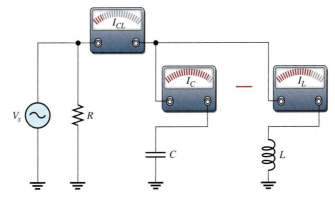

FIGURE 18–23

I_C and I_L effectively subtract.

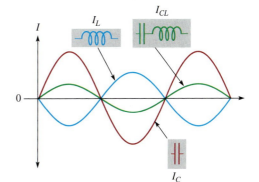

FIGURE 18–24
Typical current phasor diagram for a parallel RLC circuit.

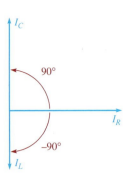

The total current can be expressed as

$$\mathbf{I}_{tot} = \sqrt{I_R^2 + (I_C - I_L)^2} \angle \tan^{-1}\left(\frac{I_{CL}}{I_R}\right) \qquad (18\text{–}12)$$

where I_{CL} is $I_C - I_L$, the total current into the *L* and *C* branches.

EXAMPLE 18–10   Find each branch current and the total current in Figure 18–25.

FIGURE 18–25

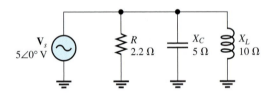

Solution   Use Ohm's law to find each branch current in phasor form.

$$\mathbf{I}_R = \frac{\mathbf{V}_s}{\mathbf{R}} = \frac{5\angle 0° \text{ V}}{2.2\angle 0° \text{ } \Omega} = 2.27\angle 0° \text{ A}$$

$$\mathbf{I}_C = \frac{\mathbf{V}_s}{\mathbf{X}_C} = \frac{5\angle 0° \text{ V}}{5\angle -90° \text{ } \Omega} = 1\angle 90° \text{ A}$$

$$\mathbf{I}_L = \frac{\mathbf{V}_s}{\mathbf{X}_L} = \frac{5\angle 0° \text{ V}}{10\angle 90° \text{ } \Omega} = 0.5\angle -90° \text{ A}$$

The total current is the phasor sum of the branch currents. By Kirchhoff's law,

$$\mathbf{I}_{tot} = \mathbf{I}_R + \mathbf{I}_C + \mathbf{I}_L$$
$$= 2.27\angle 0° \text{ A} + 1\angle 90° \text{ A} + 0.5\angle -90° \text{ A}$$
$$= 2.27 \text{ A} + j1 \text{ A} - j0.5 \text{ A} = 2.27 \text{ A} + j0.5 \text{ A}$$

Converting to polar form yields

$$\mathbf{I}_{tot} = \sqrt{I_R^2 + (I_C - I_L)^2} \angle \tan^{-1}\left(\frac{I_{CL}}{I_R}\right)$$

$$= \sqrt{(2.27 \text{ A})^2 + (0.5 \text{ A})^2} \angle \tan^{-1}\left(\frac{0.5 \text{ A}}{2.27 \text{ A}}\right) = 2.32\angle 12.4° \text{ A}$$

The total current is 2.32 A leading V_s by 12.4°. Figure 18–26 is the current phasor diagram for the circuit.

FIGURE 18–26

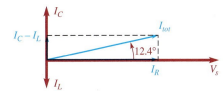

Related Problem Will total current increase or decrease if the frequency in Figure 18–25 is increased?

1. In a three-branch parallel circuit, $R = 150\ \Omega$, $X_C = 100\ \Omega$, and $X_L = 50\ \Omega$. Determine the current in each branch when $V_s = 12$ V.

2. The impedance of a parallel *RLC* circuit is $2.8\angle{-}38.9°$ kΩ. Is the circuit capacitive or inductive?

18–6 ■ PARALLEL RESONANCE

In this section, we will first look at the resonant condition in an ideal parallel LC circuit. Then, we will examine the more realistic case where the resistance of the coil is taken into account.

After completing this section, you should be able to

■ **Analyze a circuit for parallel resonance**
  • Describe parallel resonance in an ideal circuit
  • Describe parallel resonance in a nonideal circuit
  • Explain how impedance varies with frequency
  • Determine current and phase angle at resonance
  • Determine parallel resonant frequency

Condition for Ideal Parallel Resonance

Ideally, parallel resonance occurs when $X_C = X_L$. The frequency at which resonance occurs is called the *resonant frequency,* just as in the series case. When $X_C = X_L$, the two branch currents, I_C and I_L, are equal in magnitude, and, of course, they are always 180° out of phase with each other. Thus, the two currents cancel and the total current is zero, as shown in Figure 18–27.

Since the total current is zero, the impedance of the parallel *LC* circuit is infinitely large (∞). These ideal resonant conditions are stated as follows:

$$X_L = X_C$$
$$Z_r = \infty$$

The Ideal Parallel Resonant Frequency

For an ideal (no resistance) parallel resonant circuit, the frequency at which resonance occurs is determined by the same formula as in series resonant circuits; that is,

$$f_r = \frac{1}{2\pi\sqrt{LC}}$$

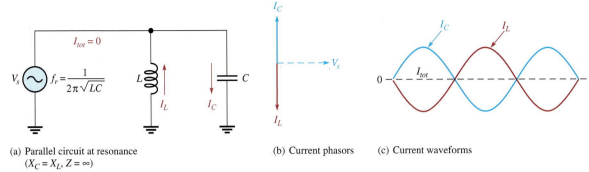

(a) Parallel circuit at resonance $(X_C = X_L, Z = \infty)$

(b) Current phasors

(c) Current waveforms

FIGURE 18–27
An ideal parallel LC circuit at resonance.

Tank Circuit

The parallel resonant *LC* circuit is often called a **tank circuit.** The term *tank circuit* refers to the fact that the parallel resonant circuit stores energy in the magnetic field of the coil and in the electric field of the capacitor. The stored energy is transferred back and forth between the capacitor and the coil on alternate half-cycles as the current goes first one way and then the other when the inductor deenergizes and the capacitor charges, and vice versa. This concept is illustrated in Figure 18–28.

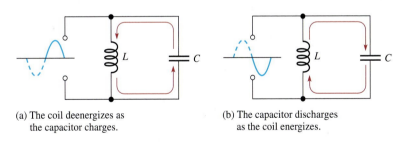

(a) The coil deenergizes as the capacitor charges.

(b) The capacitor discharges as the coil energizes.

FIGURE 18–28
Energy storage in an ideal parallel resonant tank circuit.

Variation of the Impedance with Frequency

Ideally, the impedance of a parallel resonant circuit is infinite. In practice, the impedance is maximum at the resonant frequency and decreases at lower and higher frequencies, as indicated by the curve in Figure 18–29.

At very low frequencies, X_L is very small and X_C is very high, so the total impedance is essentially equal to that of the inductive branch. As the frequency goes up, the impedance also increases, and the inductive reactance dominates (because it is less than X_C) until the resonant frequency is reached. At this point, of course, $X_L \cong X_C$ (for $Q > 10$) and the impedance is at its maximum. As the frequency goes above resonance, the capacitive reactance dominates (because it is less than X_L) and the impedance decreases.

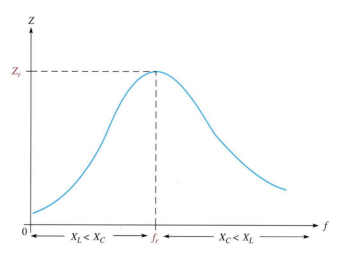

FIGURE 18–29
Generalized impedance curve for a parallel resonant circuit. The circuit is inductive below f_r, resistive at f_r, and capacitive above f_r.

Current and Phase Angle at Resonance

In the ideal tank circuit, the total current from the source at resonance is zero because the impedance is infinite. In the nonideal case when the coil resistance is considered, there is some total current at the resonant frequency, and it is determined by the impedance at resonance.

$$I_{tot} = \frac{V_s}{Z_r} \qquad \text{(18–13)}$$

The phase angle of the parallel resonant circuit is $0°$ because the impedance is purely resistive at the resonant frequency.

Effect of Coil Resistance on the Parallel Resonant Frequency

When the coil resistance is considered, the resonant condition can be expressed as

$$2\pi f_r L \left(\frac{Q^2 + 1}{Q^2} \right) = \frac{1}{2\pi f_r C}$$

where Q is the **quality factor** of the coil, X_L/R_W. Solving for f_r in terms of Q yields

$$f_r = \frac{1}{2\pi\sqrt{LC}} \sqrt{\frac{Q^2}{Q^2 + 1}} \qquad \text{(18–14)}$$

When $Q \geq 10$, the term with the Q factors is approximately 1.

$$\sqrt{\frac{Q^2}{Q^2 + 1}} = \sqrt{\frac{100}{101}} = 0.995 \cong 1$$

Therefore, the parallel resonant frequency is approximately the same as the series resonant frequency as long as Q is equal to or greater than 10.

$$f_r \cong \frac{1}{2\pi\sqrt{LC}} \qquad \text{for } Q \geq 10$$

A precise expression for f_r in terms of the circuit component values is

$$f_r = \frac{\sqrt{1 - (R_W^2 \, C/L)}}{2\pi\sqrt{LC}} \qquad (18\text{--}15)$$

This precise formula is seldom necessary and the simpler equation $f_r = 1/2\pi\sqrt{LC}$ is sufficient for most practical situations. A derivation of Equation (18–15) is given in Appendix C.

EXAMPLE 18–11   Find the precise frequency and the value of Q at resonance for the circuit in Figure 18–30.

FIGURE 18–30

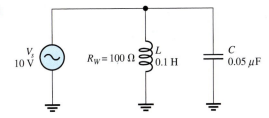

Solution   Use Equation (18–15) to find the frequency.

$$f_r = \frac{\sqrt{1 - (R_W^2 \, C/L)}}{2\pi\sqrt{LC}} = \frac{\sqrt{1 - [(100\ \Omega)^2(0.05\ \mu F)/0.1\ H]}}{2\pi\sqrt{(0.05\ \mu F)(0.1\ H)}} = \textbf{2.25 kHz}$$

To calculate the quality factor, Q, first find X_L.

$$X_L = 2\pi f_r L = 2\pi(2.25\ \text{kHz})(0.1\ \text{H}) = 1.41\ \text{k}\Omega$$

$$Q = \frac{X_L}{R_W} = \frac{1.41\ \text{k}\Omega}{100\ \Omega} = \textbf{14.1}$$

Note that since $Q > 10$, the approximate formula, $f_r \cong 1/2\pi\sqrt{LC}$, can be used.

Related Problem   For a smaller R_W, will f_r be less than or greater than 2.25 kHz?

SECTION 18–6 REVIEW

1. Is the impedance minimum or maximum at parallel resonance?
2. Is the current minimum or maximum at parallel resonance?
3. For ideal parallel resonance, assume $X_L = 1500\ \Omega$. What is X_C?
4. A parallel tank circuit has the following values: $R_W = 4\ \Omega$, $L = 50$ mH, and $C = 10$ pF. Calculate f_r.
5. If $Q = 25$, $L = 50$ mH, and $C = 1000$ pF, what is f_r?
6. In Question 5, if $Q = 2.5$, what is f_r?

♦ *Coverage of series-parallel reactive circuits begins in Chapter 16, Part 3, on page 620.*

PART 3

SERIES-PARALLEL REACTIVE CIRCUITS

18–7 ■ ANALYSIS OF SERIES-PARALLEL *RLC* CIRCUITS

In this section, series and parallel combinations of R, L, and C elements are analyzed in specific examples. Also, conversion of a series-parallel circuit to an equivalent parallel circuit is covered and resonance in a nonideal parallel circuit is considered.

After completing this section, you should be able to

■ Analyze series-parallel *RLC* circuits
  • Determine currents and voltages
  • Convert a series-parallel circuit to an equivalent parallel form
  • Analyze nonideal (with coil resistance) parallel circuits for parallel resonance
  • Examine the effect of a resistive load on a tank circuit

The following two examples illustrate an approach to the analysis of circuits with both series and parallel combinations of resistance, inductance, and capacitance.

EXAMPLE 18–12   In Figure 18–31, find the voltage across the capacitor in polar form. Is this circuit predominantly inductive or capacitive?

FIGURE 18–31

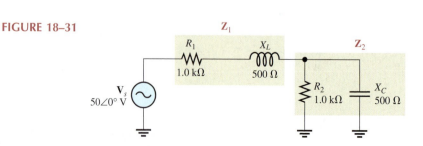

Solution Use the voltage-divider formula in this analysis. The impedance of the series combination of R_1 and X_L is called $\mathbf{Z}_1$. In rectangular form,

$$\mathbf{Z}_1 = R_1 + jX_L = 1000 \ \Omega + j500 \ \Omega$$

Converting to polar form yields

$$\mathbf{Z}_1 = \sqrt{R_1^2 + X_L^2}\angle\tan^{-1}\left(\frac{X_L}{R_1}\right)$$

$$= \sqrt{(1000 \ \Omega)^2 + (500 \ \Omega)^2}\angle\tan^{-1}\left(\frac{500 \ \Omega}{1000 \ \Omega}\right) = 1118\angle 26.6° \ \Omega$$

The impedance of the parallel combination of R_2 and X_C is called $\mathbf{Z}_2$. In polar form,

$$\mathbf{Z}_2 = \left(\frac{R_2 X_C}{\sqrt{R_2^2 + X_C^2}}\right)\angle -\tan^{-1}\left(\frac{R_2}{X_C}\right)$$

$$= \left[\frac{(1000 \ \Omega)(500 \ \Omega)}{\sqrt{(1000 \ \Omega)^2 + (500 \ \Omega)^2}}\right]\angle -\tan^{-1}\left(\frac{1000 \ \Omega}{500 \ \Omega}\right) = 447\angle -63.4° \ \Omega$$

Converting to rectangular form yields

$$\mathbf{Z}_2 = Z_2\cos\theta + jZ_2\sin\theta$$
$$= 447\cos(-63.4°) + j447\sin(-63.4°) = 200 \ \Omega - j400 \ \Omega$$

The total impedance $\mathbf{Z}_{tot}$ in rectangular form is

$$\mathbf{Z}_{tot} = \mathbf{Z}_1 + \mathbf{Z}_2 = (1000 \ \Omega + j500 \ \Omega) + (200 \ \Omega - j400 \ \Omega) = 1200 \ \Omega + j100 \ \Omega$$

Converting to polar form yields

$$\mathbf{Z}_{tot} = \sqrt{(1200 \ \Omega)^2 + (100 \ \Omega)^2}\angle\tan^{-1}\left(\frac{100 \ \Omega}{1200 \ \Omega}\right) = 1204\angle 4.76° \ \Omega$$

Now apply the voltage-divider formula to get $\mathbf{V}_C$.

$$\mathbf{V}_C = \left(\frac{\mathbf{Z}_2}{\mathbf{Z}_{tot}}\right)\mathbf{V}_s = \left(\frac{447\angle -63.4° \ \Omega}{1204\angle 4.76° \ \Omega}\right)50\angle 0° \ \text{V} = \mathbf{18.6\angle -68.2° \ V}$$

Therefore, V_C is 18.6 V and lags V_s by 68.2°.

The $+j$ term in $\mathbf{Z}_{tot}$, or the positive angle in its polar form, indicates that the circuit is more inductive than capacitive. However, it is just slightly more inductive, because the angle is small. This result may surprise you, because $X_C = X_L = 500 \ \Omega$. However, the capacitor is in parallel with a resistor, so the capacitor actually has less effect on the total impedance than does the inductor. Figure 18–32 shows the phasor relationship of $\mathbf{V}_C$ and $\mathbf{V}_s$. Although $X_C = X_L$, this circuit is not at resonance, because the j term of the total impedance is not zero due to the parallel combination of R_2 and X_C. You can see this by noting that the phase angle associated with $\mathbf{Z}_{tot}$ is 4.76° and not zero.

FIGURE 18–32

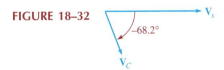

Related Problem Determine the voltage across the capacitor in polar form if R_1 is increased to 2.2 kΩ.

EXAMPLE 18–13   For the reactive circuit in Figure 18–33, find the voltage at point *B* with respect to ground.

FIGURE 18–33

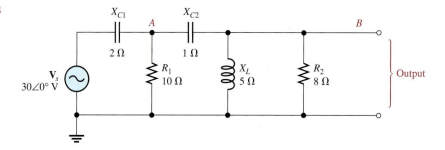

Solution   The voltage ($\mathbf{V}_B$) at point *B* is the voltage across the open output terminals. Use the voltage-divider approach. To do so, you must know the voltage ($\mathbf{V}_A$) at point *A* first; so you need to find the impedance from point *A* to ground as a starting point.

The parallel combination of X_L and R_2 is in series with X_{C2}. This combination is in parallel with R_1. Call this impedance from point *A* to ground, $\mathbf{Z}_A$. To find $\mathbf{Z}_A$, take the following steps. The impedance of the parallel combination of R_2 and X_L is called $\mathbf{Z}_1$.

$$\mathbf{Z}_1 = \left(\frac{R_2 X_L}{\sqrt{R_2^2 + X_L^2}}\right)\angle\tan^{-1}\left(\frac{R_2}{X_L}\right)$$

$$= \left(\frac{(8\ \Omega)(5\ \Omega)}{\sqrt{(8\ \Omega)^2 + (5\ \Omega)^2}}\right)\angle\tan^{-1}\left(\frac{8\ \Omega}{5\ \Omega}\right) = 4.24\angle 58.0°\ \Omega$$

Next, combine $\mathbf{Z}_1$ in series with $\mathbf{X}_{C2}$ to get an impedance $\mathbf{Z}_2$.

$$\begin{aligned}
\mathbf{Z}_2 &= \mathbf{X}_{C2} + \mathbf{Z}_1 \\
&= 1\angle{-90°}\ \Omega + 4.24\angle 58°\ \Omega = -j1\ \Omega + 2.25\ \Omega + j3.6\ \Omega \\
&= 2.25\ \Omega + j2.6\ \Omega
\end{aligned}$$

Converting to polar form yields

$$\mathbf{Z}_2 = \sqrt{(2.25\ \Omega)^2 + (2.6\ \Omega)^2}\angle\tan^{-1}\left(\frac{2.6\ \Omega}{2.25\ \Omega}\right) = 3.44\angle 49.1°\ \Omega$$

Finally, combine $\mathbf{Z}_2$ and $\mathbf{R}_1$ in parallel to get $\mathbf{Z}_A$.

$$\mathbf{Z}_A = \frac{\mathbf{R}_1\mathbf{Z}_2}{\mathbf{R}_1 + \mathbf{Z}_2} = \frac{(10\angle 0°)(3.44\angle 49.1°)}{10 + 2.25 + j2.6}$$

$$= \frac{34.4\angle 49.1°}{12.25 + j2.6} = \frac{34.4\angle 49.1°}{12.5\angle 12.0°} = 2.75\angle 37.1°\ \Omega$$

The simplified circuit is shown in Figure 18–34.

FIGURE 18–34

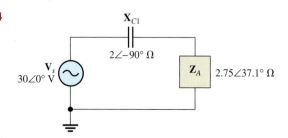

Next, use the voltage-divider principle to find the voltage ($\mathbf{V}_A$) at point A in Figure 18–33. The total impedance is

$$\mathbf{Z}_{tot} = \mathbf{X}_{C1} + \mathbf{Z}_A$$
$$= 2\angle{-90°}\ \Omega + 2.75\angle{37.1°}\ \Omega = -j2\ \Omega + 2.19\ \Omega + j1.66\ \Omega$$
$$= 2.19\ \Omega - j0.340\ \Omega$$

Converting to polar form yields

$$\mathbf{Z}_{tot} = \sqrt{(2.19\ \Omega)^2 + (0.340\ \Omega)^2}\angle{-\tan^{-1}\left(\frac{0.340\ \Omega}{2.19\ \Omega}\right)} = 2.22\angle{-8.82°}\ \Omega$$

The voltage at point A is

$$\mathbf{V}_A = \left(\frac{\mathbf{Z}_A}{\mathbf{Z}_{tot}}\right)\mathbf{V}_s = \left(\frac{2.75\angle{37.1°}\ \Omega}{2.22\angle{-8.82°}\ \Omega}\right)30\angle{0°}\ \text{V} = 37.2\angle{45.9°}\ \text{V}$$

Next, find the voltage ($\mathbf{V}_B$) at point B by dividing $\mathbf{V}_A$ down, as indicated in Figure 18–35. $\mathbf{V}_B$ is the open terminal output voltage.

$$\mathbf{V}_B = \left(\frac{\mathbf{Z}_1}{\mathbf{Z}_2}\right)\mathbf{V}_A = \left(\frac{4.24\angle{58°}\ \Omega}{3.44\angle{49.1°}\ \Omega}\right)37.2\angle{45.9°}\ \text{V} = \mathbf{45.9\angle{54.8°}\ V}$$

Surprisingly, V_A is greater than V_s, and V_B is greater than V_A! This result is possible because of the out-of-phase relationship of the reactive voltages. Remember that X_C and X_L tend to cancel each other.

FIGURE 18–35

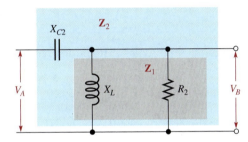

Related Problem What is the voltage in polar form across C_1 in Figure 18–33?

Conversion of Series-Parallel to Parallel

The particular series-parallel configuration shown in Figure 18–36 is important because it represents a circuit having parallel L and C branches, with the winding resistance of the coil taken into account as a series resistance in the L branch.

It is helpful to view the series-parallel circuit in Figure 18–36 in an equivalent parallel form, as indicated in Figure 18–37.

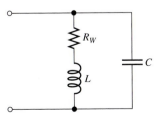

FIGURE 18–36
A series-parallel RLC circuit
($Q = X_L/R_W$).

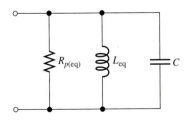

FIGURE 18–37
Parallel equivalent form of the
circuit in Figure 18–36.

The equivalent inductance, L_{eq}, and the equivalent parallel resistance, $R_{p(eq)}$, are given by the following formulas:

$$L_{eq} = L\left(\frac{Q^2 + 1}{Q^2}\right) \tag{18-16}$$

$$R_{p(eq)} = R_W(Q^2 + 1) \tag{18-17}$$

where Q is the quality factor of the coil, X_L/R_W. Derivations of these formulas are quite involved and thus are not given here. Notice in the equations that for a $Q \geq 10$, the value of L_{eq} is approximately the same as the original value of L. For example, if $L = 10$ mH, then

$$L_{eq} = 10 \text{ mH}\left(\frac{10^2 + 1}{10^2}\right) = 10 \text{ mH}(1.01) = 10.1 \text{ mH}$$

The equivalency of the two circuits means that at a given frequency, when the same value of voltage is applied to both circuits, the same total current is in both circuits and the phase angles are the same. Basically, an equivalent circuit simply makes circuit analysis more convenient.

EXAMPLE 18–14   Convert the series-parallel circuit in Figure 18–38 to an equivalent parallel form at the given frequency.

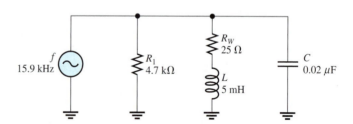

FIGURE 18–38

Solution   Determine the inductive reactance.

$$X_L = 2\pi fL = 2\pi(15.9 \text{ kHz})(5 \text{ mH}) = 500 \ \Omega$$

The Q of the coil is

$$Q = \frac{X_L}{R_W} = \frac{500 \ \Omega}{25 \ \Omega} = 20$$

Since $Q > 10$, then $L_{eq} \cong L = 5$ mH.
The equivalent parallel resistance is

$$R_{p(eq)} = R_W(Q^2 + 1) = (25 \ \Omega)(20^2 + 1) = 10.0 \text{ k}\Omega$$

This equivalent resistance appears in parallel with R_1 as shown in Figure 18–39(a). When combined, they give a total parallel resistance ($R_{p(tot)}$) of 3.2 kΩ, as indicated in Figure 18–39(b).

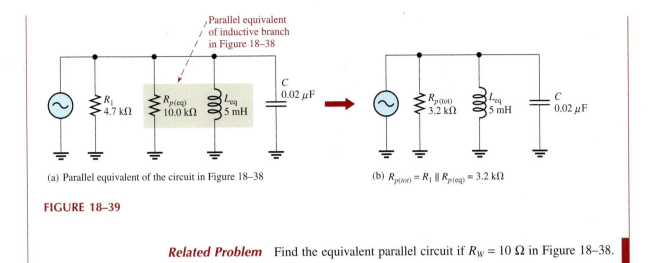

(a) Parallel equivalent of the circuit in Figure 18–38

(b) $R_{p(tot)} = R_1 \| R_{p(eq)} = 3.2$ kΩ

FIGURE 18–39

Related Problem Find the equivalent parallel circuit if $R_W = 10$ Ω in Figure 18–38.

Parallel Resonant Conditions in a Nonideal Circuit

The resonance of an ideal parallel *LC* circuit was examined in Section 18–6. Now, let's consider resonance in a tank circuit with the resistance of the coil taken into account. Figure 18–40 shows a nonideal tank circuit and its parallel *RLC* equivalent.

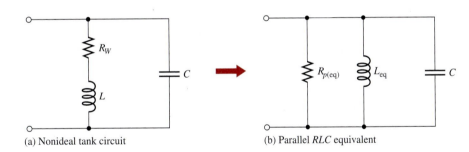

(a) Nonideal tank circuit

(b) Parallel *RLC* equivalent

FIGURE 18–40
A practical treatment of parallel resonant circuits must include the coil resistance.

Recall that the quality factor, *Q,* of the circuit at resonance is simply the *Q* of the coil.

$$Q = \frac{X_L}{R_W}$$

The expressions for the equivalent inductance and the equivalent parallel resistance were given in Equations (18–16) and (18–17) as

$$L_{eq} = L\left(\frac{Q^2 + 1}{Q^2}\right)$$

$$R_{p(eq)} = R_W(Q^2 + 1)$$

For $Q \geq 10$, $L_{eq} \cong L$.

At parallel resonance,

$$X_{L(eq)} = X_C$$

In the parallel equivalent circuit, $R_{p(eq)}$ is in parallel with an ideal coil and a capacitor, so the *L* and *C* branches act as an ideal tank circuit which has an infinite impedance at resonance as shown in Figure 18–41. Therefore, the total impedance of the nonideal tank circuit at resonance can be expressed as simply the equivalent parallel resistance.

$$Z_r = R_W(Q^2 + 1) \tag{18–18}$$

A derivation of Equation (18–18) is given in Appendix C.

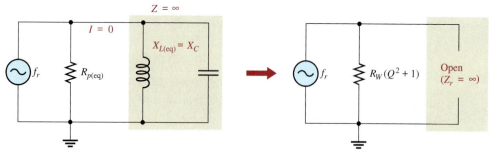

FIGURE 18–41
At resonance, the parallel LC portion appears open and the source sees only $R_{p(eq)}$.

EXAMPLE 18–15   Determine the impedance of the circuit in Figure 18–42 at the resonant frequency ($f_r \cong$ 17,794 Hz).

FIGURE 18–42

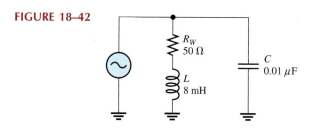

Solution   Before you can calculate the impedance using Equation (18–18), you must find the quality factor. To get *Q*, first find the inductive reactance.

$$X_L = 2\pi f_r L = 2\pi(17,794 \text{ Hz})(8 \text{ mH}) = 894 \text{ } \Omega$$

$$Q = \frac{X_L}{R_W} = \frac{894 \text{ } \Omega}{50 \text{ } \Omega} = 17.9$$

$$Z_r = R_W(Q^2 + 1) = 50 \text{ } \Omega(17.9^2 + 1) = \textbf{16.1 k}\Omega$$

Related Problem   Determine Z_r for $R_W = 10 \text{ } \Omega$.

An External Parallel Load Resistance Affects a Tank Circuit

There are many practical situations in which an external load resistance appears in parallel with a tank circuit as shown in Figure 18–43(a). Obviously, the external resistor (R_L) will dissipate a portion of the power delivered by the source and thus will lower the overall Q of the circuit. The external resistor effectively appears in parallel with the equivalent parallel resistance of the coil, $R_{p(eq)}$, and both are combined to determine a total parallel resistance, $R_{p(tot)}$, as indicated in Figure 18–43(b).

$$R_{p(tot)} = R_L \parallel R_{p(eq)}$$

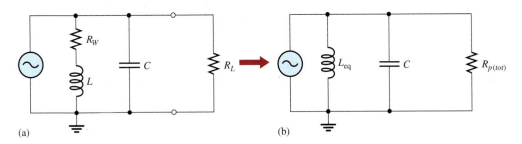

FIGURE 18–43
Tank circuit with a parallel load resistor and its equivalent circuit.

The overall Q, designated Q_O, for a parallel *RLC* circuit is expressed differently from the Q of a series circuit.

$$Q_O = \frac{R_{p(tot)}}{X_{L(eq)}} \qquad \text{(18–19)}$$

As you can see, the effect of loading the tank circuit is to reduce its overall Q (which is equal to the coil Q when unloaded).

SECTION 18–7 REVIEW

1. A certain resonant circuit has a 10 μH inductor with a 20 Ω winding resistance in parallel with a 0.22 μF capacitor. If $Q = 8$, determine the parallel equivalent of this circuit.

2. Find the equivalent parallel inductance and resistance for a 20 mH coil with a winding resistance of 10 Ω at a frequency of 1 kHz.

♦ *Coverage of special topics begins in Chapter 16, Part 4, on page 626.*

18–8 ■ BANDWIDTH OF RESONANT CIRCUITS

As you have learned, the current in a series RLC is maximum at the resonant frequency because the reactances cancel and the current in a parallel RLC is minimum at the resonant frequency because the inductive and capacitive currents cancel. In this section, you will see how this circuit behavior relates to a characteristic called bandwidth.

After completing this section, you should be able to

■ **Determine the bandwidth of resonant circuits**
  • Discuss the bandwidth of series and parallel resonant circuits
  • State the formula for bandwidth
  • Define *half-power frequency*
  • Define *selectivity*
  • Explain how the Q affects the bandwidth

Series Resonant Circuits

The current in a series RLC circuit is maximum at the resonant frequency (also known as *center frequency*) and drops off on either side of this frequency. Bandwidth, sometimes abbreviated *BW,* is an important characteristic of a resonant circuit. The bandwidth is the range of frequencies for which the current is equal to or greater than 70.7% of its resonant value.

Figure 18–44 illustrates bandwidth on the response curve of a series RLC circuit. Notice that the frequency f_1 below f_r is the point at which the current is $0.707I_{max}$ and is

FIGURE 18–44
Bandwidth on series resonant response curve for I.

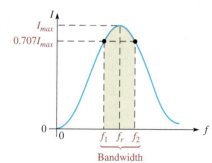

commonly called the *lower critical frequency*. The frequency f_2 above f_r, where the current is again $0.707I_{max}$, is the *upper critical frequency*. Other names for f_1 and f_2 are *−3 dB frequencies, cutoff frequencies,* and *half-power frequencies.* The significance of the latter term is discussed later in the chapter.

EXAMPLE 18–16   A certain series resonant circuit has a maximum current of 100 mA at the resonant frequency. What is the value of the current at the critical frequencies?

Solution   Current at the critical frequencies is 70.7% of maximum.

$$I_{f1} = I_{f2} = 0.707I_{max} = 0.707(100 \text{ mA}) = \textbf{70.7 mA}$$

Related Problem   A certain series resonant circuit has a current of 25 mA at the critical frequencies. What is the current at resonance?

Parallel Resonant Circuits

For a parallel resonant circuit, the impedance is maximum at the resonant frequency; so the total current is minimum. The bandwidth can be defined in relation to the impedance curve in the same manner that the current curve was used in the series circuit. Of course, f_r is the frequency at which Z is maximum; f_1 is the lower critical frequency at which $Z = 0.707Z_{max}$; and f_2 is the upper critical frequency at which again $Z = 0.707Z_{max}$. The bandwidth is the range of frequencies between f_1 and f_2, as shown in Figure 18–45.

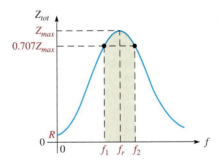

FIGURE 18–45
Bandwidth of the parallel resonant response curve for Z_{tot}.

Formula for Bandwidth

The bandwidth for either series or parallel resonant circuits is the range of frequencies between the critical frequencies for which the response curve (I or Z) is 0.707 of the maximum value. Thus, the bandwidth is actually the difference between f_2 and f_1.

$$BW = f_2 - f_1 \tag{18–20}$$

Ideally, f_r is the center frequency and can be calculated as follows:

$$f_r = \frac{f_1 + f_2}{2} \tag{18–21}$$

EXAMPLE 18–17   A resonant circuit has a lower critical frequency of 8 kHz and an upper critical frequency of 12 kHz. Determine the bandwidth and center (resonant) frequency.

Solution $BW = f_2 - f_1 = 12 \text{ kHz} - 8 \text{ kHz} = \textbf{4 kHz}$

$$f_r = \frac{f_1 + f_2}{2} = \frac{12 \text{ kHz} + 8 \text{ kHz}}{2} = \textbf{10 kHz}$$

Related Problem   If the bandwidth of a resonant circuit is 2.5 kHz and its center frequency is 8 kHz, what are the lower and upper critical frequencies?

Half-Power Frequencies

As previously mentioned, the upper and lower critical frequencies are sometimes called the **half-power frequencies.** This term is derived from the fact that the power from the source at these frequencies is one-half the power delivered at the resonant frequency. The following steps show that this is true for a series circuit. The same end result also applies to a parallel circuit. At resonance,

$$P_{max} = I_{max}^2 R$$

The power at f_1 or f_2 is

$$P_{f1} = I_{f1}^2 R = (0.707 I_{max})^2 R = (0.707)^2 I_{max}^2 R = 0.5 I_{max}^2 R = 0.5 P_{max}$$

Selectivity

The response curves in Figures 18–44 and 18–45 are also called *selectivity curves.* **Selectivity** defines how well a resonant circuit responds to a certain frequency and discriminates against all others. *The narrower the bandwidth, the greater the selectivity.*

We normally assume that a resonant circuit accepts frequencies within its bandwidth and completely eliminates frequencies outside the bandwidth. Such is not actually the case, however, because signals with frequencies outside the bandwidth are not completely eliminated. Their magnitudes, however, are greatly reduced. The further the frequencies are from the critical frequencies, the greater is the reduction, as illustrated in Figure 18–46(a). An ideal selectivity curve is shown in Figure 18–46(b).

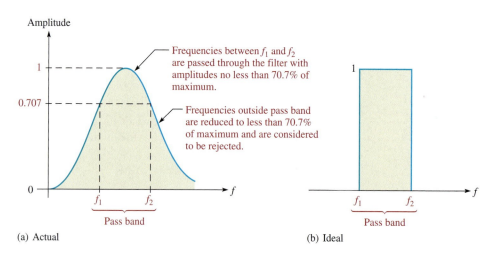

(a) Actual

(b) Ideal

FIGURE 18–46

Generalized selectivity curve of a band-pass filter.

As you can see in Figure 18–46, another factor that influences selectivity is the sharpness of the slopes of the curve. The faster the curve drops off at the critical frequencies, the more selective the circuit is because it responds only to the frequencies within the bandwidth. Figure 18–47 shows a general comparison of three response curves with varying degrees of selectivity.

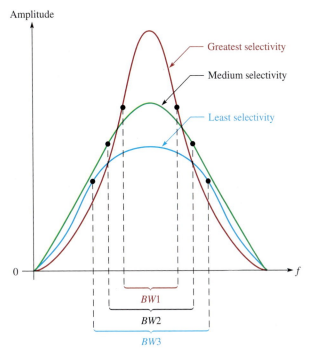

FIGURE 18–47
Comparative selectivity curves.

Q Affects Bandwidth

A higher value of circuit Q results in a narrower bandwidth. A lower value of Q causes a wider bandwidth. A formula for the bandwidth of a resonant circuit in terms of Q is stated in the following equation:

$$BW = \frac{f_r}{Q} \qquad \qquad (18–22)$$

EXAMPLE 18–18   What is the bandwidth of each circuit in Figure 18–48?

FIGURE 18–48

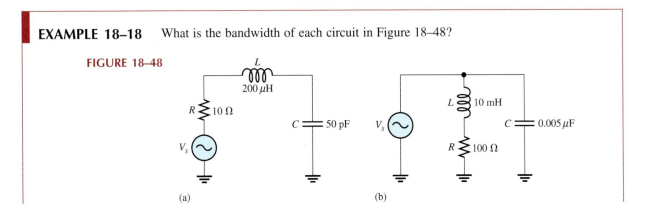

Solution For the circuit in Figure 18–48(a), the bandwidth is found as follows:

$$f_r = \frac{1}{2\pi\sqrt{LC}} = \frac{1}{2\pi\sqrt{(200 \ \mu H)(50 \ pF)}} = 1.59 \ \text{MHz}$$

$$Q = \frac{X_L}{R} = \frac{2 \ k\Omega}{10 \ \Omega} = 200$$

$$BW = \frac{f_r}{Q} = \frac{1.59 \ \text{MHz}}{200} = \textbf{7.95 kHz}$$

For the circuit in Figure 18–48(b),

$$f_r = \frac{\sqrt{1 - (R_W^2 \ C/L)}}{2\pi\sqrt{LC}} \cong \frac{1}{2\pi\sqrt{LC}} = \frac{1}{2\pi\sqrt{(10 \ \text{mH})(0.005 \ \mu F)}} = 22.5 \ \text{kHz}$$

$$Q = \frac{X_L}{R} = \frac{1.41 \ k\Omega}{100 \ \Omega} = 14.1$$

$$BW = \frac{f_r}{Q} = \frac{22.5 \ \text{kHz}}{14.1} = \textbf{1.60 kHz}$$

Related Problem Change C in Figure 18–48(a) to 1000 pF and determine the bandwidth.

**SECTION 18–8
REVIEW**

1. What is the bandwidth when $f_2 = 2.2$ MHz and $f_1 = 1.8$ MHz?
2. For a resonant circuit with the critical frequencies in Question 1, what is the center frequency?
3. The power at resonance is 1.8 W. What is the power at the upper critical frequency?
4. Does a larger Q mean a narrower or a wider bandwidth?

18–9 ■ APPLICATIONS

Resonant circuits are used in a wide variety of applications, particularly in communication systems. In this section, we will look briefly at a few common communication systems applications. The purpose in this section is not to explain how the systems work, but to illustrate the importance of resonant circuits in electronic communication.

After completing this section, you should be able to

■ **Discuss some applications of resonant circuits**
  • Describe a tuned amplifier application
  • Describe antenna coupling
  • Describe tuned amplifiers
  • Describe signal separation in a receiver
  • Describe a radio receiver

Tuned Amplifiers

A *tuned amplifier* is a circuit that amplifies signals within a specified band. Typically, a parallel resonant circuit is used in conjunction with an amplifier to achieve the selectivity. In terms of the general operation, input signals with frequencies that range over a wide band are accepted on the amplifier's input and are amplified. The function of the resonant circuit is to allow only a relatively narrow band of those frequencies to be passed on. The variable capacitor allows tuning over the range of input frequencies so that a desired frequency can be selected, as indicated in Figure 18–49.

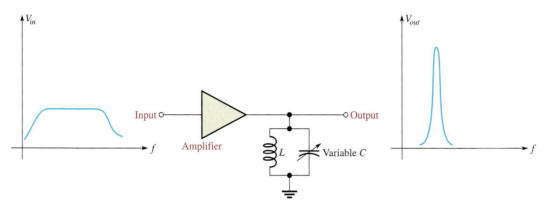

FIGURE 18–49
A basic tuned band-pass amplifier.

Antenna Input to a Receiver

Radio signals are sent out from a transmitter via electromagnetic waves that propagate through the atmosphere. When the electromagnetic waves cut across the receiving antenna, small voltages are induced. Out of all the wide range of electromagnetic frequencies, only one frequency or a limited band of frequencies must be extracted. Figure 18–50 shows a typical arrangement of an antenna coupled to the receiver input by a transformer. A variable capacitor is connected across the transformer secondary to form a parallel resonant circuit.

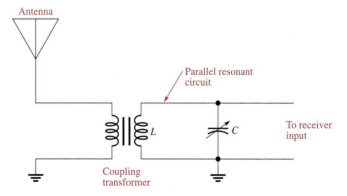

FIGURE 18–50
Resonant coupling from an antenna.

Double-Tuned Transformer Coupling in a Receiver

In some types of communication receivers, tuned amplifiers are transformer-coupled together to increase the amplification. Capacitors can be placed in parallel with the primary and secondary windings of the transformer, effectively creating two parallel resonant band-pass filters that are coupled together. This technique, illustrated in Figure 18–51, can result in a wider bandwidth and steeper slopes on the response curve, thus increasing the selectivity for a desired band of frequencies.

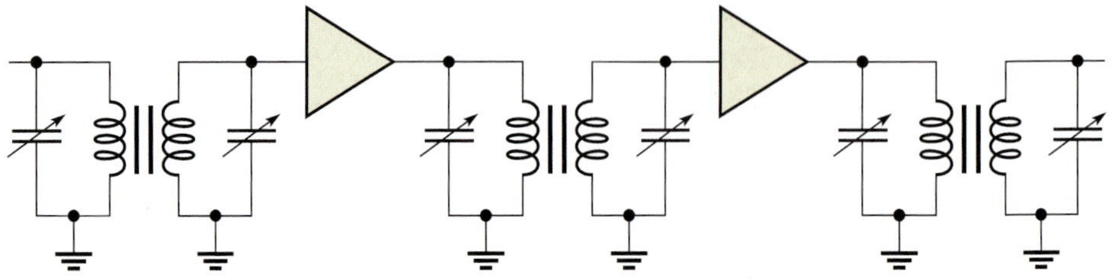

FIGURE 18–51
Double-tuned amplifiers.

Signal Reception and Separation in a TV Receiver

A television receiver must handle both video (picture) signals and audio (sound) signals. Each TV transmitting station is allotted a 6 MHz bandwidth. Channel 2 is allotted a band from 54 MHz through 59 MHz, channel 3 is allotted a band from 60 MHz through 65 MHz, on up to channel 13 which has a band from 210 MHz through 215 MHz. You can tune the front end of the TV receiver to select any one of these channels by using tuned amplifiers. The signal output of the front end of the receiver has a bandwidth from 41 MHz through 46 MHz, regardless of the channel that is tuned in. This band, called the *intermediate frequency* (IF) band, contains both video and audio. Amplifiers tuned to the IF band boost the signal and feed it to the video amplifier.

Before the output of the video amplifier is applied to the picture tube, the audio signal is removed by a 4.5 MHz band-stop filter (called a *wave trap*), as shown in Figure 18–52. This trap keeps the sound signal from interfering with the picture. The video amplifier output is also applied to band-pass circuits that are tuned to the sound carrier frequency of 4.5 MHz. The sound signal is then processed and applied to the speaker as indicated in Figure 18–52.

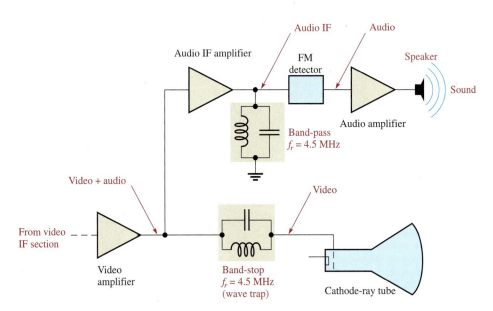

FIGURE 18–52
A simplified portion of a TV receiver showing filter usage.

Superheterodyne Receiver

Another good example of filter applications is in the common AM (amplitude modulation) receiver. The AM broadcast band ranges from 535 kHz to 1605 kHz. Each AM station is assigned a certain narrow bandwidth within that range. A simplified block diagram of a superheterodyne AM receiver is shown in Figure 18–53.

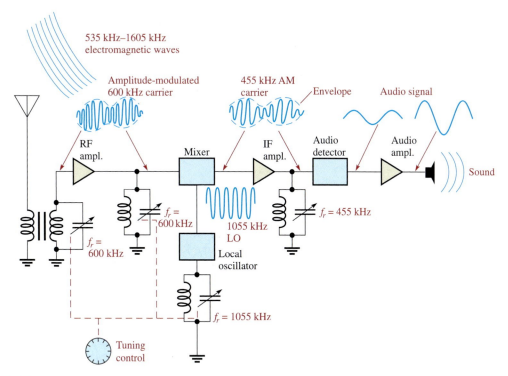

FIGURE 18–53

A simplified diagram of a superheterodyne AM radio broadcast receiver showing an example of the application of tuned resonant circuits.

In this system, there are basically three parallel resonant band-pass filters in the front end of the receiver. Each of these filters is gang-tuned by capacitors; that is, the capacitors are mechanically or electronically linked together so that they change together as the tuning knob is turned. The front end is tuned to receive a desired station, for example, one that transmits at 600 kHz. The input filter from the antenna and the RF (radio frequency) amplifier filter select only a frequency of 600 kHz out of all the frequencies crossing the antenna. The actual audio (sound) signal is carried by the 600 kHz carrier frequency by modulating the amplitude of the carrier so that it follows the audio signal as indicated. The variation in the amplitude of the carrier corresponding to the audio signal is called the *envelope*. The 600 kHz is then applied to a circuit called the *mixer*. The *local oscillator* (LO) is tuned to a frequency that is 455 kHz above the selected frequency (1055 kHz, in this case). By a process called *heterodyning* or *beating*, the AM signal and the local oscillator signal are mixed together, and the 600 kHz AM signal is converted to a 455 kHz AM signal (1055 kHz − 600 kHz = 455 kHz). The 455 kHz is the intermediate frequency (IF) for standard AM receivers. No matter which station within the broadcast band is selected, its frequency is always converted to the 455 kHz IF. The amplitude-modulated IF is applied to an *audio detector* which removes the IF, leaving only the envelope or audio signal. The audio signal is then amplified and applied to the speaker.

SECTION 18–9 REVIEW	**1.** Generally, why is a tuned filter necessary when a signal is coupled from an antenna to the input of a receiver?
	2. What is a wave trap?
	3. What is meant by *ganged tuning*?

18–10 ■ TECHnology Theory Into Practice

In the Chapter 11 TECH TIP, you worked with a receiver system to learn basic ac measurements. In this chapter, the receiver is again used to illustrate one application of resonant circuits. We will focus on a part of the "front end" of the receiver system that contains resonant circuits. Generally, the front end includes the RF amplifier, the local oscillator, and the mixer. In this TECH TIP, the RF amplifier is the focus. A knowledge of amplifier circuits is not necessary at this time.

A basic block diagram of an AM radio receiver is shown in Figure 18–54. In this particular system, the "front end" includes the circuitry used for tuning in a desired broadcasting station by frequency selection and then converting that selected frequency to a standard intermediate frequency (IF). AM radio stations transmit in the frequency range from 535 kHz to 1605 kHz. The purpose of the RF amplifier, which is the focus of this TECH TIP, is to take the signals picked up by the antenna, reject all but the signal from the desired station, and amplify it to a higher level.

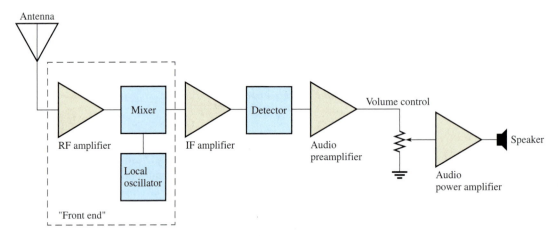

FIGURE 18–54
Simplified block diagram of a basic radio receiver.

A schematic of the RF amplifier is shown in Figure 18–55. The parallel resonant tuning circuit consists of L, C_1 and C_2. This particular RF amplifier does not have a resonant circuit on the output. C_1 is a varactor, which is a semiconductor device that you will learn more about in a later course. All that you need to know at this point is that the varactor is basically a variable capacitor whose capacitance is varied by changing the dc voltage across it. In this circuit, the dc voltage comes from the wiper of the potentiometer used for tuning the receiver.

The voltage from the potentiometer can be varied from +1 V to +9 V. The particular varactor used in this circuit can be varied from 200 pF at 1 V to 5 pF at 9 V. The capacitor C_2 is a trimmer capacitor that is used for initially adjusting the resonant circuit. Once it is preset, it is left at that value. C_1 and C_2 are in parallel and their capacitances add to produce the total capacitance for the resonant circuit. C_3 has a minimal effect on the resonant circuit and can be ignored. The purpose of C_3 is to allow the dc voltage to be applied to the varactor while providing an ac ground.

In this TECH TIP, you will work with the RF amplifier circuit board in Figure 18–56. Although all of the amplifier components are on the board, the part that you are to focus on is the resonant circuit indicated by the highlighted area.

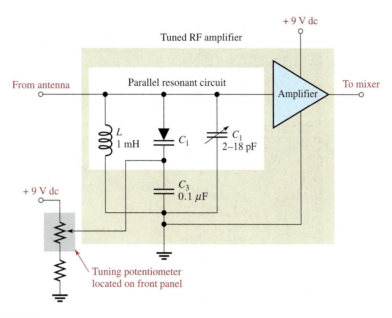

Tuned RF amplifier

+9 V dc

Parallel resonant circuit

From antenna

To mixer

Amplifier

L
1 mH

C_1

C_1
2–18 pF

C_3
0.1 μF

+9 V dc

Tuning potentiometer
located on front panel

FIGURE 18–55
Partial schematic of the RF amplifier showing the resonant tuning circuit.

FIGURE 18–56
RF amplifier circuit board.

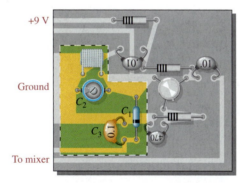

+9 V

Ground

C_2

C_1

C_3

To mixer

Capacitance in the Resonant Circuit

■ Calculate a capacitance setting for C_2 that will ensure a complete coverage of the AM frequency band as the varactor is varied over its capacitance range. C_3 can be ignored. The full range of resonant frequencies for the tuning circuit should more than cover the AM band, so that at the maximum varactor capacitance, the resonant frequency will be less than 535 kHz and at the minimum varactor capacitance, the resonant frequency will be greater than 1605 kHz.

■ Using the value of C_2 that you have calculated, determine the values of the varactor capacitance that will produce a resonant frequency of 535 kHz and 1605 kHz, respectively.

Testing the Resonant Circuit

■ Suggest a procedure for testing the resonant circuit using the instruments in the Test Bench setup of Figure 18–57. Develop a test setup by creating a point-to-point hookup of the board and the instruments.

■ Using the graph in Figure 18–58 that shows the variation in varactor capacitance versus varactor voltage, determine the resonant frequency for each indicated setting from the B outputs of the dc power supply (rightmost output terminals). The B output of the power supply is used to simulate the potentiometer voltage.

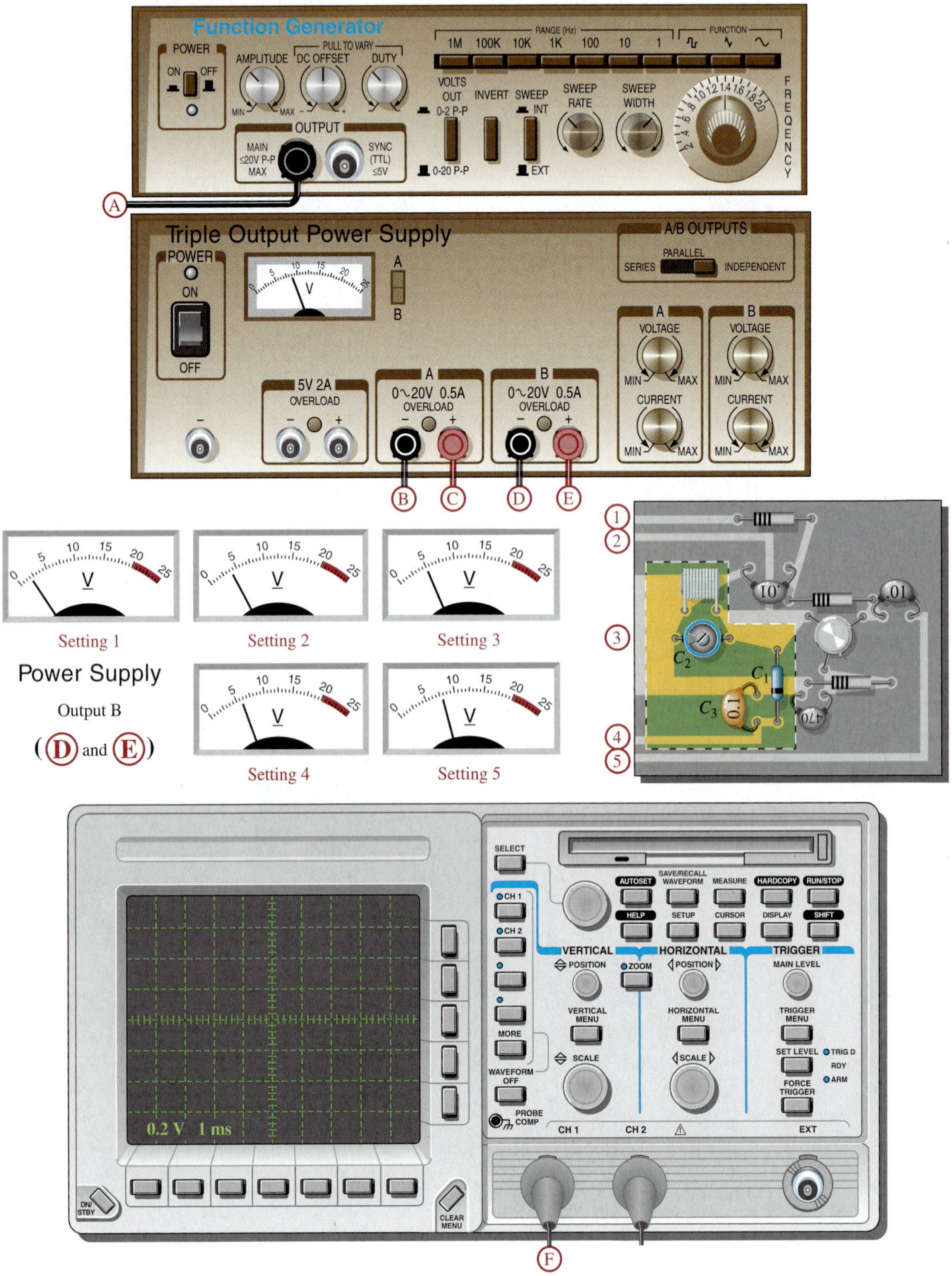

FIGURE 18–57
Test bench setup.

FIGURE 18–58
Varactor capacitance versus voltage.

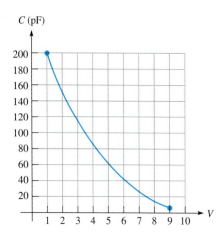

SECTION 18–10 REVIEW

1. What is the AM frequency range?
2. State the purpose of the RF amplifier.
3. How is a particular frequency in the AM band selected?

■ **SUMMARY**

- X_L and X_C have opposing effects in an *RLC* circuit.
- In a series *RLC* circuit, the larger reactance determines the net reactance of the circuit.
- At series resonance, the inductive and capacitive reactances are equal.
- The impedance of a series *RLC* circuit is purely resistive at resonance.
- In a series *RLC* circuit, the current is maximum at resonance.
- The reactive voltages V_L and V_C cancel at resonance in a series *RLC* circuit because they are equal in magnitude and 180° out of phase.
- In a parallel *RLC* circuit, the smaller reactance determines the net reactance of the circuit.
- In a parallel resonant circuit, the impedance is maximum at the resonant frequency.
- A parallel resonant circuit is commonly called a *tank circuit*.
- The impedance of a parallel *RLC* circuit is purely resistive at resonance.
- The bandwidth of a series resonant circuit is the range of frequencies for which the current is $0.707I_{max}$ or greater.
- The bandwidth of a parallel resonant circuit is the range of frequencies for which the impedance is $0.707Z_{max}$ or greater.
- The critical frequencies are the frequencies above and below resonance where the circuit response is 70.7% of the maximum response.
- A higher Q produces a narrower bandwidth.

■ **GLOSSARY**

These terms are also in the end-of-book glossary.

Half-power frequency   The frequency at which the output power of a filter is 50% of the maximum (the output voltage is 70.7% of maximum); another name for *critical* or *cutoff frequency*.

Parallel resonance   A condition in a parallel *RLC* circuit in which the reactances ideally cancel and the impedance is maximum.

Quality factor (Q)   The ratio of true power to reactive power in a resonant circuit or the ratio of inductive reactance to winding resistance in a coil.

Resonance   A condition in a series *RLC* circuit in which the capacitive and inductive reactances are equal in magnitude; thus, they cancel each other and result in a purely resistive impedance.

Resonant frequency   The frequency at which resonance occurs; also known as the *center frequency.*

Selectivity   A measure of how effectively a filter passes certain desired frequencies and rejects all others. Generally, the narrower the bandwidth, the greater the selectivity.

Series resonance   A condition in a series *RLC* circuit in which the reactances cancel and the impedance is minimum.

Tank circuit   A parallel resonant circuit.

■ **FORMULAS**

Series *RLC* Circuits

(18–1) $X_{tot} = |X_L - X_C|$

(18–2) $\mathbf{Z} = R + jX_L - jX_C$

(18–3) $\mathbf{Z} = \sqrt{R^2 + (X_L - X_C)^2}\angle\tan^{-1}\left(\dfrac{X_{tot}}{R}\right)$

Series Resonance

(18–4) $X_L = X_C$

(18–5) $Z_r = R$

(18–6) $f_r = \dfrac{1}{2\pi\sqrt{LC}}$

Parallel *RLC* Circuits

(18–7) $\mathbf{Z} = \dfrac{1}{\dfrac{1}{R\angle 0°} + \dfrac{1}{X_L\angle 90°} + \dfrac{1}{X_C\angle -90°}}$

(18–8) $\mathbf{G} = \dfrac{1}{R\angle 0°} = G\angle 0°$

(18–9) $\mathbf{B}_C = \dfrac{1}{X_C\angle -90°} = B_C\angle 90° = jB_C$

(18–10) $\mathbf{B}_L = \dfrac{1}{X_L\angle 90°} = B_L\angle -90° = -jB_L$

(18–11) $\mathbf{Y} = \dfrac{1}{Z\angle\pm\theta} = Y\angle\pm\theta = G + jB_C - jB_L$

(18–12) $\mathbf{I}_{tot} = \sqrt{I_R^2 + (I_C - I_L)^2}\angle\tan^{-1}\left(\dfrac{I_{CL}}{I_R}\right)$

Parallel Resonance

(18–13) $I_{tot} = \dfrac{V_s}{Z_r}$

(18–14) $f_r = \dfrac{1}{2\pi\sqrt{LC}}\sqrt{\dfrac{Q^2}{Q^2 + 1}}$

(18–15) $f_r = \dfrac{\sqrt{1 - (R_W^2\, C/L)}}{2\pi\sqrt{LC}}$

(18–16) $L_{eq} = L\left(\dfrac{Q^2 + 1}{Q^2}\right)$

(18–17) $R_{p(eq)} = R_W(Q^2 + 1)$

$$\text{(18–18)} \qquad Z_r = R_W(Q^2 + 1)$$

$$\text{(18–19)} \qquad Q_O = \frac{R_{p(tot)}}{X_{L(eq)}}$$

$$\text{(18–20)} \qquad BW = f_2 - f_1$$

$$\text{(18–21)} \qquad f_r = \frac{f_1 + f_2}{2}$$

$$\text{(18–22)} \qquad BW = \frac{f_r}{Q}$$

■ SELF-TEST

1. The total reactance of a series *RLC* circuit at resonance is
   (a) zero   (b) equal to the resistance   (c) infinity   (d) capacitive

2. The phase angle between the source voltage and current of a series *RLC* circuit at resonance is
   (a) −90°   (b) +90°   (c) 0°   (d) dependent on the reactance

3. The impedance at the resonant frequency of a series *RLC* circuit with $L = 15$ mH, $C = 0.015$ μF, and $R_W = 80$ Ω is
   (a) 15 kΩ (b) 80 Ω (c) 30 Ω (d) 0 Ω

4. In a series *RLC* circuit that is operating below the resonant frequency, the current
   (a) is in phase with the applied voltage   (b) lags the applied voltage
   (c) leads the applied voltage

5. If the value of *C* in a series *RLC* circuit is increased, the resonant frequency
   (a) is not affected   (b) increases   (c) remains the same   (d) decreases

6. In a certain series resonant circuit, $V_C = 150$ V, $V_L = 150$ V, and $V_R = 50$ V. The value of the source voltage is
   (a) 150 V   (b) 300 V   (c) 50 V   (d) 350 V

7. A certain series resonant circuit has a bandwidth of 1 kHz. If the existing coil is replaced with one having a lower value of *Q*, the bandwidth will
   (a) increase   (b) decrease   (c) remain the same   (d) be more selective

8. At frequencies below resonance in a parallel *RLC* circuit, the current
   (a) leads the source voltages   (b) lags the source voltage
   (c) is in phase with the source voltage

9. The total current into the *L* and *C* branches of a parallel circuit at resonance is ideally
   (a) maximum   (b) low   (c) high   (d) zero

10. To tune a parallel resonant circuit to a lower frequency, the capacitance should be
    (a) increased   (b) decreased   (c) left alone   (d) replaced with inductance

11. The resonant frequency of a parallel circuit is approximately the same as a series circuit when
    (a) the *Q* is very low   (b) the *Q* is very high
    (c) there is no resistance   (d) either answer (b) or (c)

12. If the resistance in parallel with a parallel resonant circuit is reduced, the bandwidth
    (a) disappears   (b) decreases   (c) becomes sharper   (d) increases

■ PROBLEMS

More difficult problems are indicated by an asterisk.

PART 1: SERIES REACTIVE CIRCUITS

SECTION 18–1   Impedance of Series *RLC* Circuits

1. A certain series *RLC* circuit has the following values: $R = 10$ Ω, $C = 0.05$ μF, and $L = 5$ mH. Determine the impedance in polar form. What is the net reactance? The source frequency is 5 kHz.

2. Find the impedance in Figure 18–59, and express it in polar form.
3. If the frequency of the source voltage in Figure 18–59 is doubled from the value that produces the indicated reactances, how does the magnitude of the impedance change?

FIGURE 18–59

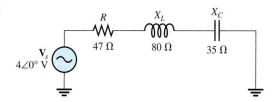

4. For the circuit of Figure 18–59, determine the net reactance that will make the impedance magnitude equal to 100 Ω.

SECTION 18–2 Analysis of Series *RLC* Circuits

5. For the circuit in Figure 18–59, find I_{tot}, V_R, V_L, and V_C in polar form.
6. Sketch the voltage phasor diagram for the circuit in Figure 18–59.
7. Analyze the circuit in Figure 18–60 for the following ($f = 25$ kHz):
   (a) I_{tot} (b) P_{true} (c) P_r (d) P_a

FIGURE 18–60

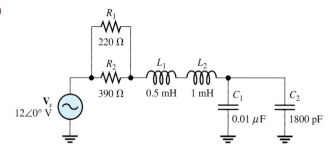

SECTION 18–3 Series Resonance

8. Find X_L, X_C, Z and I at the resonant frequency in Figure 18–61.
9. A certain series resonant circuit has a maximum current of 50 mA and a V_L of 100 V. The applied voltage is 10 V. What is Z? What are X_L and X_C?

FIGURE 18–61

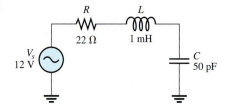

10. For the *RLC* circuit in Figure 18–62, determine the resonant frequency.

FIGURE 18–62

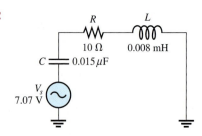

11. What is the value of the current at the half-power points in Figure 18–62?

12. Determine the phase angle between the applied voltage and the current at the critical frequencies in Figure 18–62. What is the phase angle at resonance?

*13. Design a circuit in which the following series resonant frequencies are switch-selectable:

(a) 500 kHz   (b) 1000 kHz   (c) 1500 kHz   (d) 2000 kHz

PART 2: PARALLEL REACTIVE CIRCUITS

SECTION 18–4   Impedance of Parallel *RLC* Circuits

14. Express the impedance of the circuit in Figure 18–63 in polar form.

FIGURE 18–63

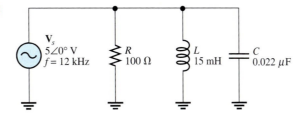

15. Is the circuit in Figure 18–63 capacitive or inductive? Explain.

16. At what frequency does the circuit in Figure 18–63 change its reactive characteristic (from inductive to capacitive or vice versa)?

SECTION 18–5   Analysis of Parallel *RLC* Circuits

17. For the circuit in Figure 18–63, find all the currents and voltages in polar form.

18. Find the total impedance of the circuit in Figure 18–63 at 50 kHz.

19. Change the frequency to 100 kHz in Figure 18–63 and repeat Problem 17.

SECTION 18–6   Parallel Resonance

20. What is the impedance of an ideal parallel resonant circuit (no resistance in either branch)?

21. Find Z at resonance and f_r for the tank circuit in Figure 18–64.

FIGURE 18–64

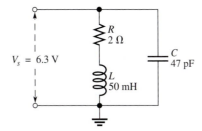

22. How much current is drawn from the source in Figure 18–64 at resonance? What are the inductive current and the capacitive current at the resonant frequency?

23. Find P_{true}, P_r, and P_a in the circuit of Figure 18–64 at resonance.

PART 3: SERIES-PARALLEL REACTIVE CIRCUITS

SECTION 18–7 Analysis of Series-Parallel *RLC* Circuits

24. Find the total impedance for each circuit in Figure 18–65.

FIGURE 18–65

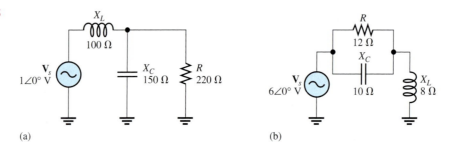

(a)   (b)

25. For each circuit in Figure 18–65, determine the phase angle between the source voltage and the total current.

26. Determine the voltage across each element in Figure 18–66, and express each in polar form.

27. Convert the circuit in Figure 18–66 to an equivalent series form.

FIGURE 18–66

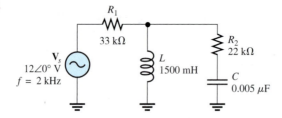

28. What is the current through R_2 in Figure 18–67?

FIGURE 18–67

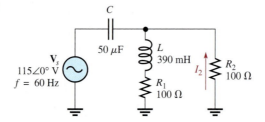

29. In Figure 18–67, what is the phase angle between I_2 and the source voltage?

*30. Determine the total resistance and the total reactance in Figure 18–68.

FIGURE 18–68

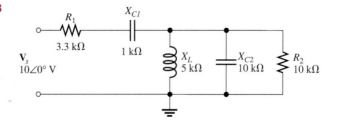

*31. Find the current through each component in Figure 18–68. Find the voltage across each component.

32. Determine if there is a value of C that will make $V_{ab} = 0$ V in Figure 18–69. If not, explain.

*33. If the value of C is 0.2 μF, what is the current through a 100 Ω resistor connected from a to b in Figure 18–69?

FIGURE 18–69

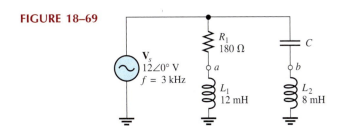

*34. How many resonant frquencies are there in the circuit of Figure 18–70? Why?

*35. Determine the resonant frquencies and the output voltage at each frequency in Figure 18–70.

FIGURE 18–70

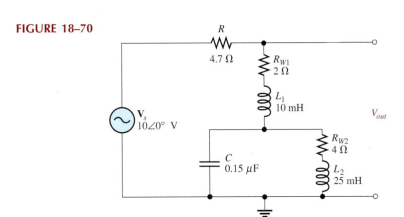

*36. Design a parallel-resonant network using a single coil and switch-selectable capacitors to produce the following resonant frequencies: 8 MHz, 9 MHz, 10 MHz, and 11 MHz. Assume a 10 μH coil with a winding resistance of 5 Ω.

PART 4: SPECIAL TOPICS

SECTION 18–8 Bandwidth of Resonant Circuits

37. At resonance, $X_L = 2$ kΩ and $R_W = 25$ Ω in a parallel RLC circuit. The resonant frequency is 5 kHz. Determine the bandwidth.

38. If the lower critical frequency is 2400 Hz and the upper critical frequency is 2800 Hz, what is the bandwidth? What is the resonant frequency?

39. In a certain RLC circuit, the power at resonance is 2.75 W. What is the power at the lower critical frequency?

*40. What values of L and C should be used in a tank circuit to obtain a resonant frequency of 8 kHz? The bandwidth must be 800 Hz. The winding resistance of the coil is 10 Ω.

41. A parallel resonant circuit has a Q of 50 and a BW of 400 Hz. If Q is doubled, what is the bandwidth for the same f_r?

EWB Troubleshooting and Analysis

These problems require your EWB compact disk.

42. Open file PRO18-42.EWB and determine if there is a fault. If so, find the fault.
43. Open file PRO18-43.EWB and determine if there is a fault. If so, find the fault.
44. Open file PRO18-44.EWB and determine if there is a fault. If so, find the fault.
45. Open file PRO18-45.EWB and determine if there is a fault. If so, find the fault.
46. Open file PRO18-46.EWB and determine if there is a fault. If so, find the fault.
47. Open file PRO18-47.EWB and determine if there is a fault. If so, find the fault.
48. Open file PRO18-48.EWB and determine the resonant frequency of the circuit.
49. Open file PRO18-49.EWB and determine the resonant frequency of the circuit.

■ ANSWERS TO SECTION REVIEWS

Section 18–1

1. $X_{tot} = 70\ \Omega$; capacitive
2. $\mathbf{Z} = 84.3\angle{-56.1}°\ \Omega$; $Z = 84.3\ \Omega$; $\theta = -56.1°$; current is leading V_s.

Section 18–2

1. $\mathbf{V}_s = 38.4\angle{-21.3}°\ V$
2. Current leads the voltage.
3. $X_{tot} = 6\ \Omega$

Section 18–3

1. For series resonance, $X_L = X_C$.
2. The current is maximum because the impedance is minimum.
3. $f_r = 159$ kHz
4. The circuit is capacitive.

Section 18–4

1. The circuit is capacitive.
2. $\mathbf{Y} = 1.54\angle{49.4}°$ mS
3. $\mathbf{Z} = 651\angle{-49.4}°\ \Omega$

Section 18–5

1. $I_R = 80$ mA, $I_C = 120$ mA, $I_L = 240$ mA
2. The circuit is capacitive.

Section 18–6

1. Impedance is maximum at parallel resonance.
2. The current is minimum.
3. $X_C = 1500\ \Omega$
4. $f_r = 225$ kHz
5. $f_r = 22.5$ kHz
6. $f_r = 20.9$ kHz

Section 18–7

1. $R_{p(eq)} = 1300\ \Omega$, $L_{eq} = 10.16\ \mu H$, $C = 0.22\ \mu F$
2. $L_{(eq)} = 20.1$ mH, $R_{p(eq)} = 1.59$ kΩ

Section 18–8

1. $BW = f_2 - f_1 = 400$ kHz
2. $f_r = 2$ MHz
3. $P_{f2} = 0.9$ W
4. Larger Q means narrower BW.

Section 18–9

1. A tuned filter is used to select a narrow band of frequencies.

2. A wave trap is a band-stop filter.

3. Ganged tuning is done with several capacitors (or inductors) whose values can be varied simultaneously with a common control.

Section 18–10

1. The AM frequency range is 535 kHz to 1605 kHz.

2. The RF amplifier rejects all signals but the one from the desired station. It then amplifies the selected signal.

3. A particular AM frequency is selected by varying the varactor capacitance with a dc voltage.

■ **ANSWERS TO RELATED PROBLEMS FOR EXAMPLES**

18–1 $\mathbf{Z} = 12.7\angle 82.3° \ k\Omega$

18–2 $\mathbf{Z} = 4.64\angle 44.7° \ k\Omega$. See Figure 18–71.

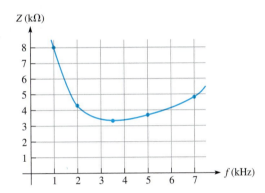

FIGURE 18–71

18–3 Current will increase with frequency to a certain point and then it will decrease.

18–4 The circuit is more capacitive.

18–5 $f_r = 22.5$ kHz

18–6 Z increases; Z increases.

18–7 $I = 22.7$ mA

18–8 Z decreases.

18–9 Inductive

18–10 I_{tot} increases.

18–11 Greater

18–12 $\mathbf{V}_C = 9.30\angle -65.8° \ V$

18–13 $\mathbf{V}_{C1} = 27.1\angle -81.1° \ V$

18–14 $R_{p(eq)} = 25 \ k\Omega$, $L_{eq} = 5$ mH; $C = 0.02 \ \mu F$

18–15 $Z_r = 79.9 \ k\Omega$

18–16 $I = 35.4$ mA

18–17 $f_1 = 6.75$ kHz; $f_2 = 9.25$ kHz

18–18 $BW = 7.96$ kHz

■ **ANSWERS TO SELF-TEST**

1. (a) **2.** (c) **3.** (b) **4.** (c) **5.** (d) **6.** (c) **7.** (a) **8.** (b)
9. (d) **10.** (a) **11.** (b) **12.** (d)

19

BASIC FILTERS

Electronics Workbench (EWB) and
PSpice Tutorials at
http://www.prenhall.com/floyd

■ INTRODUCTION

The concept of filters was introduced in Chapters 16, 17, and 18 to illustrate applications of *RC, RL,* and *RLC* circuits. This chapter is essentially an extension of the earlier material and provides additional coverage of the important topic of filters.

Passive filters are discussed in this chapter. Passive filters use various combinations of resistors, capacitors, and inductors. In a later course, you will study active filters which use passive components combined with amplifiers. You have already seen how basic *RC, RL,* and *RLC* circuits can be used as filters. Now, you will learn that passive filters can be placed in four general categories according to their response characteristics: low-pass, high-pass, band-pass, and band-stop. Within each category, there are several common types that will be examined.

In the TECH TIP assignment in Section 19–5, you will plot the frequency responses of filters based on oscilloscope measurements and identify the types of filters.

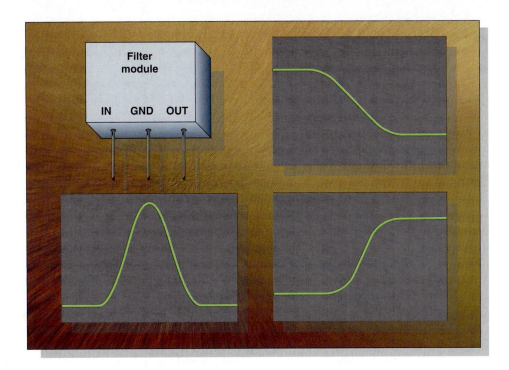

■ CHAPTER OBJECTIVES

- ❏ Analyze the operation of *RC* and *RL* low-pass filters
- ❏ Analyze the operation of *RC* and *RL* high-pass filters
- ❏ Analyze the operation of band-pass filters
- ❏ Analyze the operation of band-stop filters

19–1 ■ LOW-PASS FILTERS

A low-pass filter allows signals with lower frequencies to pass from input to output while rejecting higher frequencies.

After completing this section, you should be able to

■ **Analyze the operation of *RC* and *RL* low-pass filters**
  • Express the voltage and power ratios of a filter in decibels
  • Determine the critical frequency of a low-pass filter
  • Explain the difference between actual and ideal low-pass response curves
  • Define *roll-off*
  • Generate a Bode plot for a low-pass filter
  • Discuss phase shift in a low-pass filter

Figure 19–1 shows a block diagram and a general response curve for a low-pass filter. The range of low frequencies passed by a low-pass filter within a specified limit is called the **passband** of the filter. The point considered to be the upper end of the passband is at the critical frequency, f_c, as illustrated in Figure 19–1(b). The **critical frequency** is the frequency at which the filter's output voltage is 70.7% of the maximum. The filter's critical frequency is also called the *cutoff frequency, break frequency,* or *−3 dB frequency* because the output voltage is down 3 dB from its maximum at this frequency. The term *dB (decibel)* is a commonly used one that you should understand because the decibel unit is used in filter measurements.

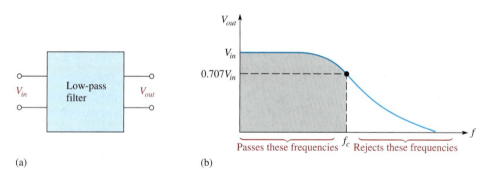

(a) (b)

FIGURE 19–1
Low-pass filter block diagram and general response curve.

Decibels

The basis for the decibel unit stems from the logarithmic response of the human ear to the intensity of sound. The **decibel** is a logarithmic measurement of the ratio of one power to another or one voltage to another, which can be used to express the input-to-output relationship of a filter. The following equation expresses a power ratio in decibels:

$$dB = 10 \log\left(\frac{P_{out}}{P_{in}}\right)$$ (19–1)

From the properties of logarithms, the following decibel formula for a voltage ratio is derived. This formula is correct only when both voltages are measured in the same impedance.

$$dB = 20 \log\left(\frac{V_{out}}{V_{in}}\right)$$ (19–2)

EXAMPLE 19–1
At a certain frequency, the output voltage of a filter is 5 V and the input is 10 V. Express the voltage ratio in decibels.

Solution
$$20 \log\left(\frac{V_{out}}{V_{in}}\right) = 20 \log\left(\frac{5\text{ V}}{10\text{ V}}\right) = 20 \log(0.5) = \mathbf{-6.02\text{ dB}}$$

Related Problem Express the ratio $V_{out}/V_{in} = 0.85$ in decibels.

RC Low-Pass Filter

A basic *RC* low-pass filter is shown in Figure 19–2. Notice that the output voltage is taken across the capacitor.

FIGURE 19–2

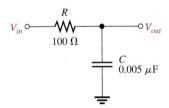

When the input is dc (0 Hz), the output voltage equals the input voltage because X_C is infinitely large. As the input frequency is increased, X_C decreases and, as a result, V_{out} gradually decreases until a frequency is reached where $X_C = R$. This is the critical frequency, f_c, of the filter.

$$X_C = R$$

$$\frac{1}{2\pi f_c C} = R$$

$$f_c = \frac{1}{2\pi RC} \qquad (19\text{–}3)$$

At any frequency, the output voltage magnitude is

$$V_{out} = \left(\frac{X_C}{\sqrt{R^2 + X_C^2}}\right)V_{in}$$

by application of the voltage-divider formula. Since $X_C = R$ at f_c, the output voltage at the critical frequency can be expressed as

$$V_{out} = \left(\frac{R}{\sqrt{R^2 + R^2}}\right)V_{in} = \left(\frac{R}{\sqrt{2R^2}}\right)V_{in} = \left(\frac{R}{R\sqrt{2}}\right)V_{in} = \left(\frac{1}{\sqrt{2}}\right)V_{in} = 0.707V_{in}$$

These calculations show that the output is 70.7% of the input when $X_C = R$. The frequency at which this occurs is, by definition, the critical frequency.

The ratio of output voltage to input voltage at the critical frequency can be expressed in decibels as follows:

$$V_{out} = 0.707V_{in}$$

$$\frac{V_{out}}{V_{in}} = 0.707$$

$$20 \log\left(\frac{V_{out}}{V_{in}}\right) = 20 \log(0.707) = -3\text{ dB}$$

EXAMPLE 19–2   Determine the critical frequency for the low-pass RC filter in Figure 19–2.

Solution

$$f_c = \frac{1}{2\pi RC} = \frac{1}{2\pi(100\ \Omega)(0.005\ \mu\text{F})} = \textbf{318 kHz}$$

The output voltage is 3 dB below V_{in} at this frequency (V_{out} has a maximum value of V_{in}).

Related Problem   A certain low-pass RC filter has $R = 1.0\ \text{k}\Omega$ and $C = 0.022\ \mu\text{F}$. Determine its critical frequency.

"Roll-Off" of the Response Curve

The blue line in Figure 19–3 shows an actual response curve for a low-pass filter. The maximum output is defined to be 0 dB as a reference. Zero decibels corresponds to $V_{out} = V_{in}$, because $20 \log(V_{out}/V_{in}) = 20 \log 1 = 0$ dB. The output drops from 0 dB to -3 dB at the critical frequency and then continues to decrease at a fixed rate. This pattern of decrease is called the **roll-off** of the frequency response. The red line shows an ideal output response that is considered to be "flat" out to f_c. The output then decreases at the fixed rate.

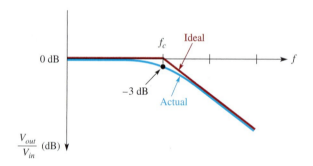

FIGURE 19–3
Actual and ideal response curves for a low-pass filter.

As you have seen, the output voltage of a low-pass filter decreases by 3 dB when the frequency is increased to the critical value f_c. As the frequency continues to increase above f_c, the output voltage continues to decrease. In fact, for each tenfold increase in frequency above f_c, there is a 20 dB reduction in the output, as shown in the following steps.

Let's take a frequency that is ten times the critical frequency ($f = 10f_c$). Since $R = X_C$ at f_c, then $R = 10X_C$ at $10f_c$ because of the inverse relationship of X_C and f.

The **attenuation** of the RC circuit is the ratio V_{out}/V_{in} and is developed as follows:

$$\frac{V_{out}}{V_{in}} = \frac{X_C}{\sqrt{R^2 + X_C^2}} = \frac{X_C}{\sqrt{(10X_C)^2 + X_C^2}}$$

$$= \frac{X_C}{\sqrt{100X_C^2 + X_C^2}} = \frac{X_C}{\sqrt{X_C^2(100+1)}} = \frac{X_C}{\sqrt{X_C^2 101}} = \frac{1}{\sqrt{101}} \cong \frac{1}{10} = 0.1$$

The dB attenuation is

$$20 \log\left(\frac{V_{out}}{V_{in}}\right) = 20 \log(0.1) = -20 \text{ dB}$$

A tenfold change in frequency is called a **decade.** So, for the *RC* circuit, the output voltage is reduced by 20 dB for each decade increase in frequency. A similar result can be derived for the high-pass circuit. The roll-off is a constant −20 dB/decade for a basic *RC* or *RL* filter. Figure 19–4 shows the ideal frequency response plot on a semilog scale, where each interval on the horizontal axis represents a tenfold increase in frequency. This response curve is called a **Bode plot.**

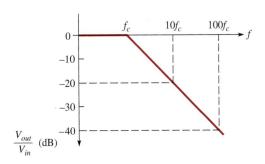

FIGURE 19–4
Frequency roll-off for a low-pass RC filter (Bode plot).

EXAMPLE 19–3   Make a Bode plot for the filter in Figure 19–5 for three decades of frequency. Use semilog graph paper.

FIGURE 19–5

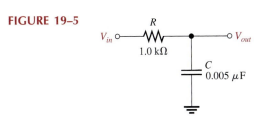

Solution   The critical frequency for this low-pass filter is

$$f_c = \frac{1}{2\pi RC} = \frac{1}{2\pi(1.0 \text{ k}\Omega)(0.005 \text{ }\mu\text{F})} = 31.8 \text{ kHz}$$

The idealized Bode plot is shown with the red line on the semilog graph in Figure 19–6. The approximate actual response curve is shown with the blue line. Notice first that the horizontal scale is logarithmic and the vertical scale is linear. The frequency is on the logarithmic scale, and the filter output in decibels is on the vertical.

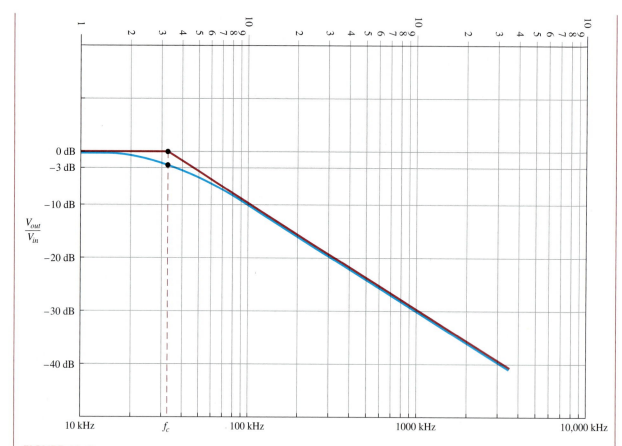

FIGURE 19–6

Bode plot for Figure 19–5. The red line represents the ideal response curve and the blue line represents the actual response.

The output is flat below f_c (31.8 kHz). As the frequency is increased above f_c, the output drops at a −20 dB/decade rate. Thus, for the ideal curve, every time the frequency is increased by ten, the output is reduced by 20 dB. A slight variation from this occurs in actual practice. The output is actually at −3 dB rather than 0 dB at the critical frequency.

Related Problem What happens to the critical frequency and roll-off rate if C is reduced to 0.001 μF in Figure 19–5?

RL Low-Pass Filter

A basic *RL* low-pass filter is shown in Figure 19–7. Notice that the output voltage is taken across the resistor.

FIGURE 19–7
RL low-pass filter.

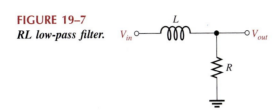

When the input is dc (0 Hz), the output voltage ideally equals the input voltage because X_L is a short (if R_W is neglected). As the input frequency is increased, X_L increases and, as a result, V_{out} gradually decreases until the critical frequency is reached. At this point, $X_L = R$ and the frequency is

$$2\pi f_c L = R$$

$$f_c = \frac{R}{2\pi L}$$

$$f_c = \frac{1}{2\pi(L/R)} \qquad (19\text{–}4)$$

Just as in the *RC* low-pass filter, $V_{out} = 0.707 V_{in}$ and, thus, the output voltage is −3 dB below the input voltage at the critical frequency.

EXAMPLE 19–4

Make a Bode plot for the filter in Figure 19–8 for three decades of frequency. Use semilog graph paper.

FIGURE 19–8

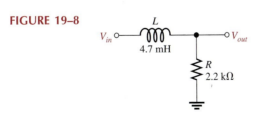

Solution The critical frequency for this low-pass filter is

$$f_c = \frac{1}{2\pi(L/R)} = \frac{1}{2\pi(4.7 \text{ mH}/2.2 \text{ k}\Omega)} = 74.5 \text{ kHz}$$

The idealized Bode plot is shown with the red line on the semilog graph in Figure 19–9. The approximate actual response curve is shown with the blue line. Notice first that the horizontal scale is logarithmic and the vertical scale is linear. The frequency is on the logarithmic scale, and the filter output in decibels is on the vertical.

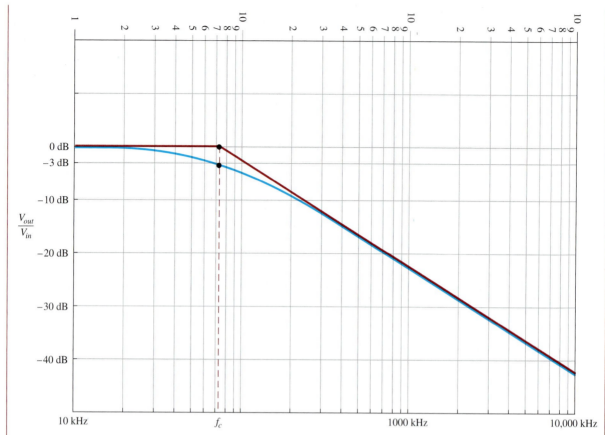

FIGURE 19–9

Bode plot for Figure 19–8. The red line is the ideal response curve and the blue line is the actual response curve.

The output is flat below f_c (74.5 kHz). As the frequency is increased above f_c, the output drops at a −20 dB/decade rate. Thus, for the ideal curve, every time the frequency is increased by ten, the output is reduced by 20 dB. A slight variation from this occurs in actual practice. The output is actually at −3 dB rather than 0 dB at the critical frequency.

Related Problem What happens to the critical frequency and roll-off rate if L is reduced to 1 mH in Figure 19–8?

Phase Shift in a Low-Pass Filter

The *RC* low-pass filter acts as a lag network. Recall from Chapter 16 that the phase shift from input to output is expressed as

$$\phi = -90° + \tan^{-1}\left(\frac{X_C}{R}\right)$$

At the critical frequency, $X_C = R$ and, therefore, $\phi = -45°$. As the input frequency is reduced, ϕ decreases and approaches 0° when the frequency approaches zero. Figure 19–10, illustrates this phase characteristic.

FIGURE 19–10

Phase characteristic of a low-pass filter.

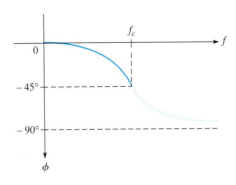

The *RL* low-pass filter also acts as a lag network. Recall from Chapter 17 that the phase shift is expressed as

$$\phi = -\tan^{-1}\left(\frac{X_L}{R}\right)$$

As in the *RC* filter, the phase shift from input to output is −45° at the critical frequency and decreases for frequencies below f_c.

SECTION 19–1 REVIEW

1. In a certain low-pass filter, $f_c = 2.5$ kHz. What is its passband?
2. In a certain low-pass filter, $R = 100 \ \Omega$ and $X_C = 2 \ \Omega$ at a frequency, f_1. Determine $\mathbf{V}_{out}$ at f_1 when $\mathbf{V}_{in} = 5\angle 0° $ V rms.
3. $V_{out} = 400$ mV, and $V_{in} = 1.2$ V. Express the ratio V_{out}/V_{in} in dB.

19–2 ■ HIGH-PASS FILTERS

A high-pass filter allows signals with higher frequencies to pass from input to output while rejecting lower frequencies.

After completing this section, you should be able to

■ **Analyze the operation of *RC* and *RL* high-pass filters**
   • Determine the critical frequency of a high-pass filter
   • Explain the difference between actual and ideal response curves
   • Generate a Bode plot for a high-pass filter
   • Discuss phase shift in a high-pass filter

Figure 19–11 shows a block diagram and a general response curve for a high-pass filter. The frequency considered to be the lower end of the passband is called the *critical frequency*. Just as in the low-pass filter, it is the frequency at which the output is 70.7% of the maximum, as indicated in the figure.

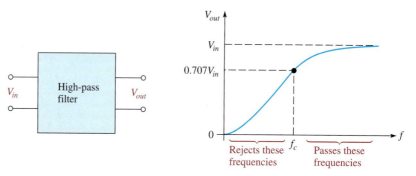

FIGURE 19–11
High-pass filter block diagram and response curve.

RC High-Pass Filter

A basic *RC* high-pass filter is shown in Figure 19–12. Notice that the output voltage is taken across the resistor.

FIGURE 19–12
RC high-pass filter.

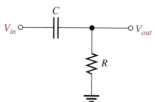

When the input frequency is at its critical value, $X_C = R$ and the output voltage is $0.707V_{in}$, just as in the case of the low-pass filter. As the input frequency increases above f_c, X_C decreases and, as a result, the output voltage increases and approaches a value equal to V_{in}. The expression for the critical frequency of the high-pass filter is the same as for the low-pass filter.

$$f_c = \frac{1}{2\pi RC}$$

Below f_c, the output voltage decreases (rolls off) at a rate of −20 dB/decade. Figure 19–13 shows an actual and an ideal response curve for a high-pass filter.

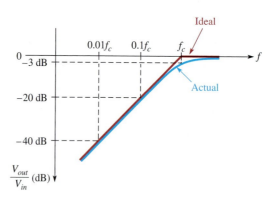

FIGURE 19–13
Actual and ideal response curves for a high-pass filter.

EXAMPLE 19–5   Make a Bode plot for the filter in Figure 19–14 for three decades of frequency. Use semilog graph paper.

FIGURE 19–14

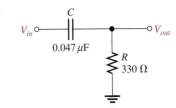

Solution   The critical frequency for this high-pass filter is

$$f_c = \frac{1}{2\pi RC} = \frac{1}{2\pi(330\ \Omega)(0.047\ \mu F)} = 10.3\ \text{kHz} \cong 10\ \text{kHz}$$

The idealized Bode plot is shown with the red line on the semilog graph in Figure 19–15. The approximate actual response curve is shown with the blue line. Notice first that the horizontal scale is logarithmic and the vertical scale is linear. The frequency is on the logarithmic scale, and the filter output in decibels is on the vertical.

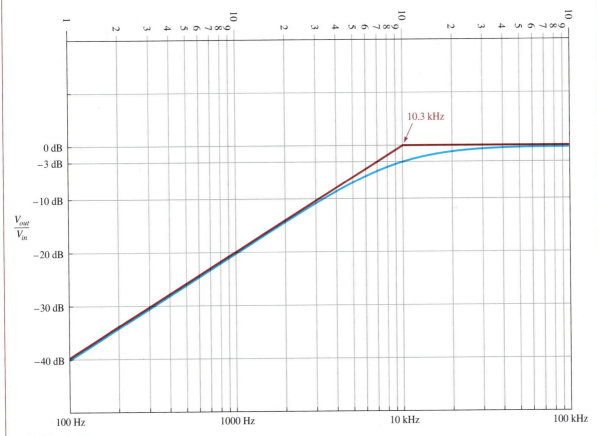

FIGURE 19–15
Bode plot for Figure 19–14. The red line is the ideal response curve and the blue line is the actual response curve.

The output is flat beyond f_c (approximately 10 kHz). As the frequency is reduced below f_c, the output drops at a −20 dB/decade rate. Thus, for the ideal curve, every time the frequency is reduced by ten, the output is reduced by 20 dB. A slight variation from this occurs in actual practice. The output is actually at −3 dB rather than 0 dB at the critical frequency.

Related Problem   If the frequency for the high-pass filter is decreased to 10 Hz, what is the output to input ratio in decibels?

RL High-Pass Filter

A basic *RL* high-pass filter is shown in Figure 19–16. Notice that the output is taken across the inductor.

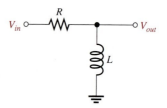

FIGURE 19–16
RL high-pass filter.

When the input frequency is at its critical value, $X_L = R$, and the output voltage is $0.707V_{in}$. As the frequency increases above f_c, X_L increases and, as a result, the output voltage increases until it equals V_{in}. The expression for the critical frequency of the high-pass filter is the same as for the low-pass filter.

$$f_c = \frac{1}{2\pi(L/R)}$$

Phase Shift in a High-Pass Filter

Both the *RC* and the *RL* high-pass filters act as lead networks. Recall from Chapters 16 and 17 that the phase shift from input to output for the *RC* lead network is

$$\phi = \tan^{-1}\left(\frac{X_C}{R}\right)$$

and for the *RL* lead network is

$$\phi = 90° - \tan^{-1}\left(\frac{X_L}{R}\right)$$

At the critical frequency, $X_L = R$ and, therefore, $\phi = 45°$. As the frequency is increased, ϕ decreases toward $0°$, as shown in Figure 19–17.

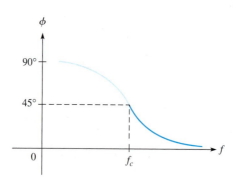

FIGURE 19–17
Phase characteristic of a high-pass filter.

EXAMPLE 19–6

(a) In Figure 19–18, find the value of C so that X_C is ten times less than R at an input frequency of 10 kHz.

(b) If a 5 V sine wave with a dc level of 10 V is applied, what are the output voltage magnitude and the phase shift?

FIGURE 19–18

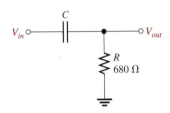

Solution

(a) The value of C is determined as follows:

$$X_C = 0.1R = 0.1(680 \ \Omega) = 68 \ \Omega$$

$$C = \frac{1}{2\pi f X_C} = \frac{1}{2\pi(10 \ \text{kHz})(68 \ \Omega)} = \textbf{0.234} \ \boldsymbol{\mu}\textbf{F}$$

The nearest standard value of C is 0.22 μF.

(b) The magnitude of the sine wave output is determined as follows:

$$V_{out} = \left(\frac{R}{\sqrt{R_2 + X_C^2}}\right) V_{in} = \left(\frac{680 \ \Omega}{\sqrt{(680 \ \Omega)^2 + (68 \ \Omega)^2}}\right) 5 \ \text{V} = \textbf{4.98 V}$$

The phase shift is

$$\phi = \tan^{-1}\left(\frac{X_C}{R}\right) = \tan^{-1}\left(\frac{68 \ \Omega}{680 \ \Omega}\right) = \textbf{5.7}°$$

At $f = 10$ kHz, which is a decade above the critical frequency, the sinusoidal output is almost equal to the input in magnitude, and the phase shift is very small. The 10 V dc level has been filtered out and does not appear at the output.

Related Problem Repeat parts (a) and (b) of the example if R is changed to 220 Ω.

SECTION 19–2 REVIEW

1. The input voltage of a high-pass filter is 1 V. What is V_{out} at the critical frequency?
2. In a certain high-pass filter, $\mathbf{V}_{in} = 10\angle0°$ V, $R = 1.0$ kΩ, and $X_L = 15$ kΩ. Determine $\mathbf{V}_{out}$.

19–3 ▪ BAND-PASS FILTERS

A band-pass filter allows a certain band of frequencies to pass and attenuates or rejects all frequencies below and above the passband.

After completing this section, you should be able to

▪ **Analyze the operation of band-pass filters**
   • Show how a band-pass filter is implemented with low-pass and high-pass filters
   • Define *bandwidth*

- Explain the series-resonant band-pass filter
- Explain the parallel-resonant band-pass filter
- Calculate the bandwidth and output voltage of a band-pass filter

Figure 19–19 shows a typical band-pass response curve.

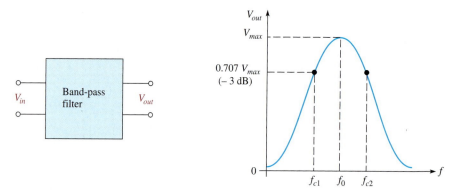

FIGURE 19–19
Typical band-pass response curve.

Low-Pass/High-Pass Filter

A combination of a low-pass and a high-pass filter can be used to form a **band-pass filter,** as illustrated in Figure 19–20. The loading effect of the second filter on the first must be taken into account.

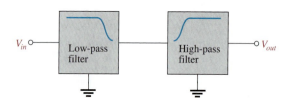

FIGURE 19–20
Low-pass and high-pass filters used to form a band-pass filter.

If the critical frequency, $f_{c(l)}$, of the low-pass filter is higher than the critical frequency, $f_{c(h)}$, of the high-pass filter, the responses overlap. Thus, all frequencies except those between $f_{c(h)}$ and $f_{c(l)}$ are eliminated, as shown in Figure 19–21.

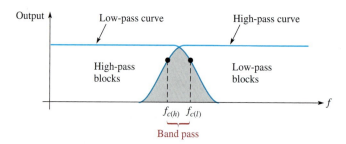

FIGURE 19–21
Overlapping response curves of a high-pass/low-pass filter.

The bandwidth of a band-pass filter is the range of frequencies for which the current, and therefore the output voltage, is equal to or greater than 70.7% of its value at the resonant frequency.

As you know, bandwidth is often abbreviated *BW*.

EXAMPLE 19–7

A high-pass filter with $f_c = 2$ kHz and a low-pass filter with $f_c = 2.5$ kHz are used to construct a band-pass filter. Assuming no loading effect, what is the bandwidth of the passband?

Solution $BW = f_{c(l)} - f_{c(h)} = 2.5 \text{ kHz} - 2 \text{ kHz} = \textbf{500 Hz}$

Related Problem If $f_{c(l)} = 9$ kHz and the bandwidth is 1.5 kHz, what is $f_{c(h)}$?

Series Resonant Band-Pass Filter

A type of series resonant band-pass filter is shown in Figure 19–22. As you learned in Chapter 18, a series resonant circuit has minimum impedance and maximum current at the resonant frequency, f_r. Thus, most of the input voltage is dropped across the resistor at the resonant frequency. Therefore, the output across R has a band-pass characteristic with a maximum output at the frequency of resonance. The resonant frequency is called the **center frequency, f_0.** The bandwidth is determined by the quality factor, Q, of the circuit and the resonant frequency, as was discussed in Chapter 18. Recall that $Q = X_L/R$.

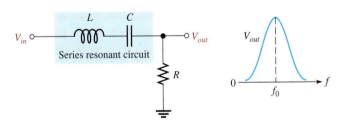

FIGURE 19–22
Series resonant band-pass filter.

A higher value of Q results in a smaller bandwidth. A lower value of Q causes a larger bandwidth. A formula for the bandwidth of a resonant circuit in terms of Q is stated in the following equation:

$$BW = \frac{f_0}{Q} \qquad\qquad (19\text{–}5)$$

EXAMPLE 19–8   Determine the output voltage magnitude at the center frequency (f_0) and the bandwidth for the filter in Figure 19–23.

FIGURE 19–23

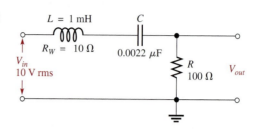

Solution   At f_0, the impedance of the resonant circuit is equal to the winding resistance, R_W. By the voltage-divider formula,

$$V_{out} = \left(\frac{R}{R + R_W}\right)V_{in} = \left(\frac{100 \ \Omega}{110 \ \Omega}\right)10 \ V = \textbf{9.09 V}$$

The center frequency is

$$f_0 = \frac{1}{2\pi\sqrt{LC}} = \frac{1}{2\pi\sqrt{(1 \ mH)(0.0022 \ \mu F)}} = 107 \ kHz$$

At f_0, the inductive reactance is

$$X_L = 2\pi fL = 2\pi(107 \ kHz)(1 \ mH) = 672 \ \Omega$$

and the total resistance is

$$R_{tot} = R + R_W = 100 \ \Omega + 10 \ \Omega = 110 \ \Omega$$

Therefore, the circuit Q is

$$Q = \frac{X_L}{R_{tot}} = \frac{672 \ \Omega}{110 \ \Omega} = 6.11$$

The bandwidth is

$$BW = \frac{f_0}{Q} = \frac{107 \ kHz}{6.11} = \textbf{17.5 kHz}$$

Related Problem   If a 1 mH coil with a winding resistance of 18 Ω replaces the existing coil in Figure 19–23, how is the bandwidth affected?

Parallel Resonant Band-Pass Filter

A type of band-pass filter using a parallel resonant circuit is shown in Figure 19–24. Recall that a parallel resonant circuit has maximum impedance at resonance. The circuit in Figure 19–24 acts as a voltage divider. At resonance, the impedance of the tank is much greater than the resistance. Thus, most of the input voltage is across the tank, producing a maximum output voltage at the resonant (center) frequency.

FIGURE 19–24
Parallel resonant band-pass filter.

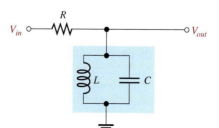

For frequencies above or below resonance, the tank impedance drops off, and more of the input voltage is across R. As a result, the output voltage across the tank drops off, creating a band-pass characteristic.

EXAMPLE 19–9

What is the center frequency of the filter in Figure 19–25? Assume $R_W = 0 \, \Omega$.

FIGURE 19–25

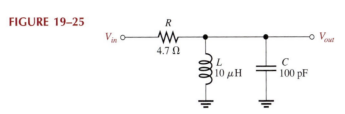

Solution   The center frequency of the filter is its resonant frequency.

$$f_0 = \frac{1}{2\pi\sqrt{LC}} = \frac{1}{2\pi\sqrt{(10 \ \mu H)(100 \ pF)}} = \textbf{5.03 MHz}$$

Related Problem   Determine f_0 in Figure 19–25 if C is changed to 1000 pF.

EXAMPLE 19–10

Determine the center frequency and bandwidth for the band-pass filter in Figure 19–26 if the inductor has a winding resistance of 15 Ω.

FIGURE 19–26

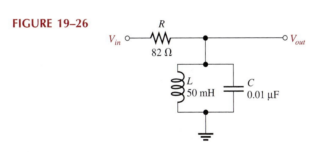

Solution   Recall from Chapter 18 (Eq. 18–15) that the resonant (center) frequency of a nonideal tank circuit is

$$f_0 = \frac{\sqrt{1 - (R_W^2 C/L)}}{2\pi\sqrt{LC}} = \frac{\sqrt{1 - (15 \ \Omega)^2 (0.01 \ \mu F)/50 \ mH}}{2\pi\sqrt{(50 \ mH)(0.01 \ \mu F}} = \textbf{7.12 kHz}$$

The Q of the coil at resonance is

$$Q = \frac{X_L}{R_W} = \frac{2\pi f_0 L}{R_W} = \frac{2\pi(7.12 \ kHz)(50 \ mH)}{15 \ \Omega} = 149$$

The bandwidth of the filter is

$$BW = \frac{f_0}{Q} = \frac{7.12 \ kHz}{149} = \textbf{47.8 Hz}$$

Note that since $Q > 10$, the simpler formula (Eq. 18–6) could have been used to calculate f_0.

Related Problem   Knowing the value of Q, recalculate f_0 using the simpler formula.

SECTION 19–3 REVIEW	**1.** For a band-pass filter, $f_{c(h)} = 29.8$ kHz and $f_{c(l)} = 30.2$ kHz. What is the bandwidth?
	2. A parallel resonant band-pass filter has the following values: $R_W = 15\ \Omega$, $L = 50\ \mu H$, and $C = 470$ pF. Determine the approximate center frequency.

19–4 ■ BAND-STOP FILTERS

A band-stop filter is essentially the opposite of a band-pass filter in terms of the responses. A band-stop filter allows all frequencies to pass except those lying within a certain stopband.

After completing this section, you should be able to

■ **Analyze the operation of band-stop filters**
  • Show how a band-stop filter is implemented with low-pass and high-pass filters
  • Explain the series-resonant band-stop filter
  • Explain the parallel-resonant band-stop filter
  • Calculate the bandwidth and output voltage of a band-stop filter

Figure 19–27 shows a general band-stop response curve.

FIGURE 19–27
General band-stop response curve.

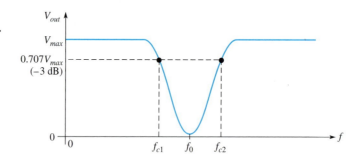

Low-Pass/High-Pass Filter

A **band-stop filter** can be formed from a low-pass and a high-pass filter, as shown in Figure 19–28.

FIGURE 19–28
Low-pass and high-pass filters used to form a band-stop filter.

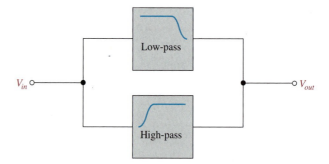

If the low-pass critical frequency, $f_{c(l)}$, is set lower than the high-pass critical frequency, $f_{c(h)}$, a band-stop characteristic is formed as illustrated in Figure 19–29.

FIGURE 19–29
Band-stop response curve.

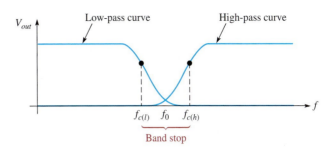

Series Resonant Band-Stop Filter

A series resonant circuit used in a band-stop configuration is shown in Figure 19–30. Basically, it works as follows: At the resonant frequency, the impedance is minimum, and therefore the output voltage is minimum. Most of the input voltage is dropped across R. At frequencies above and below resonance, the impedance increases, causing more voltage across the output.

FIGURE 19–30
Series resonant band-stop filter.

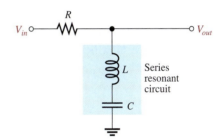

EXAMPLE 19–11

Find the output voltage magnitude at f_0 and the bandwidth in Figure 19–31.

FIGURE 19–31

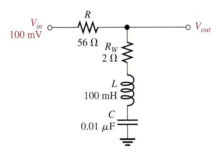

Solution   Since $X_L = X_C$ at resonance, the output voltage is

$$V_{out} = \left(\frac{R_W}{R + R_W}\right)V_{in} = \left(\frac{2\ \Omega}{58\ \Omega}\right)100\ \text{mV} = \textbf{3.45 mV}$$

To determine the bandwidth, calculate the center frequency and Q of the coil.

$$f_0 = \frac{1}{2\pi\sqrt{LC}} = \frac{1}{2\pi\sqrt{(100\ \text{mH})(0.01\ \mu\text{F})}} = 5.03\ \text{kHz}$$

$$Q = \frac{X_L}{R} = \frac{2\pi f L}{R} = \frac{2\pi(5.03\ \text{kHz})(100\ \text{mH})}{58\ \Omega} = \frac{3.16\ \text{k}\Omega}{58\ \Omega} = 54.5$$

$$BW = \frac{f_0}{Q} = \frac{5.03\ \text{kHz}}{54.5} = \textbf{92.3 Hz}$$

Related Problem   Assume $R_W = 10\ \Omega$ in Figure 19–31. Determine V_{out} and the bandwidth.

Parallel Resonant Band-Stop Filter

A parallel resonant circuit used in a band-stop configuration is shown in Figure 19–32. At the resonant frequency, the tank impedance is maximum, and so most of the input voltage appears across it. Very little voltage is across R at resonance. As the tank impedance decreases above and below resonance, the output voltage increases.

FIGURE 19–32
Parallel resonant band-stop filter.

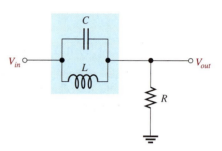

EXAMPLE 19–12   Find the center frequency of the filter in Figure 19–33. Sketch the output response curve showing the minimum and maximum voltages.

FIGURE 19–33

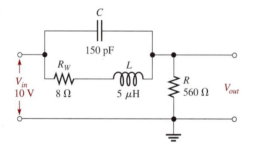

Solution The center frequency is

$$f_0 = \frac{\sqrt{1 - R_W^2 C/L}}{2\pi\sqrt{LC}} = \frac{\sqrt{1 - (8\ \Omega)^2(150\ \text{pF})/5\ \mu\text{H}}}{2\pi\sqrt{(5\ \mu\text{H})(150\ \text{pF})}} = \textbf{5.79 MHz}$$

At the center (resonant) frequency,

$$X_L = 2\pi f_0 L = 2\pi(5.79\ \text{MHz})(5\ \mu\text{H}) = 182\ \Omega$$

$$Q = \frac{X_L}{R_W} = \frac{182\ \Omega}{8\ \Omega} = 22.8$$

$$Z_r = R_W(Q^2 + 1) = 8\ \Omega(22.8^2 + 1) = 4.17\ \text{k}\Omega \quad \text{(purely resistive)}$$

Next, use the voltage-divider formula to find the minimum output voltage magnitude.

$$V_{out(min)} = \left(\frac{R}{R + Z_r}\right)V_{in} = \left(\frac{560\ \Omega}{4.73\ \text{k}\Omega}\right)10\ \text{V} = 1.18\ \text{V}$$

At zero frequency, the impedance of the tank is R_W because $X_C = \infty$ and $X_L = 0\ \Omega$. Therefore, the maximum output voltage below resonance is

$$V_{out(max)} = \left(\frac{R}{R + R_W}\right)V_{in} = \left(\frac{560\ \Omega}{568\ \Omega}\right)10\ \text{V} = 9.86\ \text{V}$$

As the frequency increases much higher than f_0, X_C approaches $0\ \Omega$, and V_{out} approaches V_{in} (10 V). Figure 19–34 shows the response curve.

FIGURE 19–34

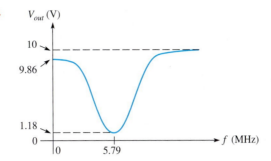

Related Problem What is the minimum output voltage if $R = 1.0 \text{ k}\Omega$ in Figure 19–33?

SECTION 19–4 REVIEW

1. How does a band-stop filter differ from a band-pass filter?
2. Name three basic ways to construct a band-stop filter.

19–5 ■ TECHnology Theory Into Practice

In this TECH TIP, you will plot the frequency responses of two types of filters based on a series of oscilloscope measurements and identify the type of filter in each case.

The filters are contained in sealed modules as shown in Figure 19–35. You are concerned only with determining the filter response characteristics and not the types of internal components.

FIGURE 19–35
Filter modules.

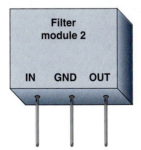

Filter Measurement and Analysis

■ Refer to Figure 19–36. Based on the series of four oscilloscope measurements, create a Bode plot for the filter under test, specify applicable frequencies, and identify the type of filter.

■ Refer to Figure 19–37. Based on the series of six oscilloscope measurements, create a Bode plot for the filter under test, specify applicable frequencies, and identify the type of filter.

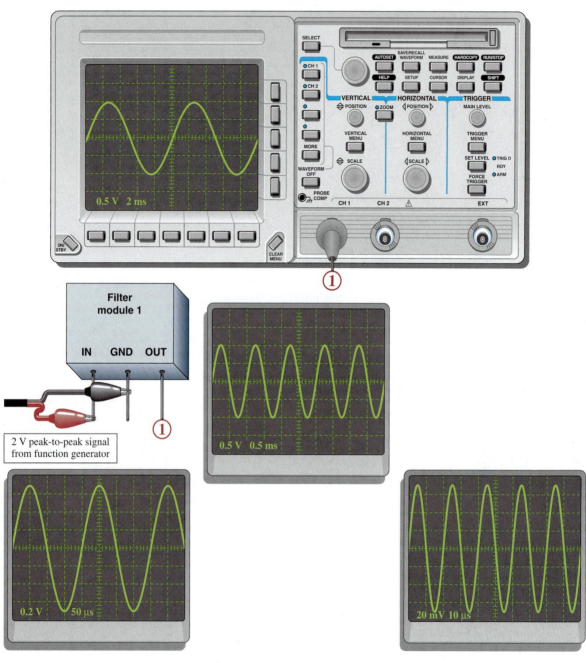

FIGURE 19–36

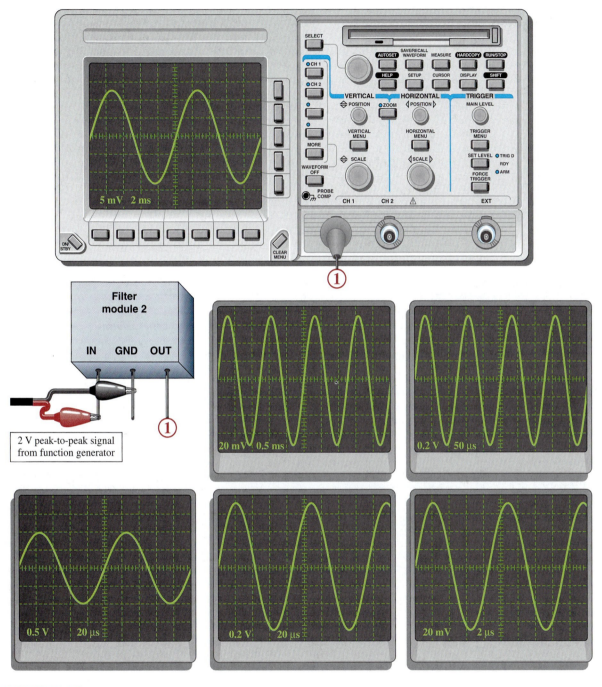

FIGURE 19–37

SECTION 19–5 REVIEW

1. Explain how the waveforms in Figure 19–36 indicate the type of filter.
2. Explain how the waveforms in Figure 19–37 indicate the type of filter.

▪ SUMMARY

- In an *RC* low-pass filter, the output voltage is taken across the capacitor and the output lags the input.
- In an *RL* low-pass filter, the output voltage is taken across the resistor and the output lags the input.
- In an *RC* high-pass filter, the output is taken across the resistor and the output leads the input.
- In an *RL* high-pass filter, the output is taken across the inductor and the output leads the input.
- The roll-off rate of a basic *RC* or *RL* filter is −20 dB per decade.
- A band-pass filter passes frequencies between the lower and upper critical frequencies and rejects all others.
- A band-stop filter rejects frequencies between its lower and upper critical frequencies and passes all others.
- The bandwidth of a resonant filter is determined by the quality factor (*Q*) of the circuit and the resonant frequency.
- Critical frequencies are also called −3 dB frequencies.
- The output voltage is 70.7% of its maximum at the critical frequencies.

▪ GLOSSARY

These terms are also in the end-of-book glossary.

Attenuation   A reduction of the output signal compared to the input signal, resulting in a ratio with a value of less than 1 for the output voltage to the input voltage of a circuit.

Band-pass filter   A filter that passes a range of frequencies lying between two critical frequencies and rejects frequencies above and below that range.

Band-stop filter   A filter that rejects a range of frequencies lying between two critical frequencies and passes frequencies above and below that range.

Bode plot   The graph of a filter's frequency response showing the change in the output voltage to input voltage ratio expressed in dB as a function of frequency for a constant input voltage.

Center frequency (f_0)   The resonant frequency of a band-pass or band-stop filter.

Critical frequency   The frequency at which a filter's output voltage is 70.7% of the maximum.

Decade   A tenfold change in frequency or other parameter.

Decibel   A logarithmic measurement of the ratio of one power to another or one voltage to another, which can be used to express the input-to-output relationship of a filter.

Passband   The range of frequencies passed by a filter.

Roll-off   The rate of decrease of a filter's frequency response.

▪ FORMULAS

(19–1) $dB = 10 \log \left(\dfrac{P_{out}}{P_{in}} \right)$ Power ratio in decibels

(19–2) $dB = 20 \log \left(\dfrac{V_{out}}{V_{in}} \right)$ Voltage ratio in decibels

(19–3) $f_c = \dfrac{1}{2\pi RC}$ Critical frequency

(19–4) $f_c = \dfrac{1}{2\pi(L/R)}$ Critical frequency

(19–5) $BW = \dfrac{f_0}{Q}$ Bandwidth

▪ **SELF-TEST**

1. The maximum output voltage of a certain low-pass filter is 10 V. The output voltage at the critical frequency is
   (a) 10 V   (b) 0 V   (c) 7.07 V   (d) 1.414 V

2. A sinusoidal voltage with a peak-to-peak value of 15 V is applied to an RC low-pass filter. If the reactance at the input frequency is zero, the output voltage is
   (a) 15 V peak-to-peak   (b) zero
   (c) 10.6 V peak-to-peak   (d) 7.5 V peak-to-peak

3. The same signal in Question 2 is applied to an RC high-pass filter. If the reactance is zero at the input frequency, the output voltage is
   (a) 15 V peak-to-peak   (b) zero
   (c) 10.6 V peak-to-peak   (d) 7.5 V peak-to-peak

4. At the critical frequency, the output of a filter is down from its maximum by
   (a) 0 dB   (b) −3 dB   (c) −20 dB   (d) −6 dB

5. If the output of a low-pass RC filter is 12 dB below its maximum at $f = 1$ kHz, then at $f = 10$ kHz, the output is below its maximum by
   (a) 3 dB   (b) 10 dB   (c) 20 dB   (d) 32 dB

6. In a passive filter, the ratio V_{out}/V_{in} is called
   (a) roll-off   (b) gain   (c) attenuation   (d) critical reduction

7. For each decade increase in frequency above the critical frequency, the output of a low-pass filter decreases by
   (a) 20 dB   (b) 3 dB   (c) 10 dB   (d) 0 dB

8. At the critical frequency, the phase shift through a high-pass filter is
   (a) 90°   (b) 0°   (c) 45°   (d) dependent on the reactance

9. In a series resonant band-pass filter, a higher value of Q results in
   (a) a higher resonant frequency   (b) a smaller bandwidth
   (c) a higher impedance   (d) a larger bandwidth

10. At series resonance,
    (a) $X_C = X_L$ (b) $X_C > X_L$ (c) $X_C < X_L$

11. In a certain parallel resonant band-pass filter the resonant frequency is 10 kHz. If the bandwidth is 2 kHz, the lower critical frequency is
    (a) 5 kHz   (b) 12 kHz   (c) 9 kHz   (d) not determinable

12. In a band-pass filter, the output voltage at the resonant frequency is
    (a) minimum   (b) maximum
    (c) 70.7% of maximum   (d) 70.7% of minimum

13. In a band-stop filter, the output voltage at the critical frequencies is
    (a) minimum   (b) maximum
    (c) 70.7% of maximum   (d) 70.7% of minimum

14. At a sufficiently high value of Q, the resonant frequency for a parallel resonant filter is ideally
    (a) much greater than the resonant frequency of a series resonant filter
    (b) much less than the resonant frequency of a series resonant filter
    (c) equal to the resonant frequency of a series resonant filter

▪ **PROBLEMS**

More difficult problems are indicated by an asterisk (*).

SECTION 19–1   Low-Pass Filters

1. In a certain low-pass filter, $X_C = 500\ \Omega$ and $R = 2.2\ \text{k}\Omega$. What is the output voltage (V_{out}) when the input is 10 V rms?

2. A certain low-pass filter has a critical frequency of 3 kHz. Determine which of the following frequencies are passed and which are rejected:
   (a) 100 Hz   (b) 1 kHz   (c) 2 kHz   (d) 3 kHz   (e) 5 kHz

3. Determine the output voltage ($\mathbf{V}_{out}$) of each filter in Figure 19–38 at the specified frequency when $V_{in} = 10$ V.

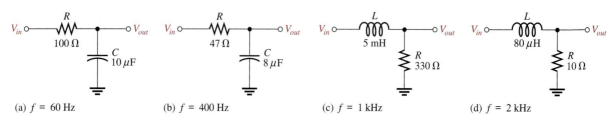

(a) f = 60 Hz   (b) f = 400 Hz   (c) f = 1 kHz   (d) f = 2 kHz

FIGURE 19–38

4. What is f_c for each filter in Figure 19–38? Determine the output voltage at f_c in each case when $V_{in} = 5$ V.
5. For the filter in Figure 19–39, calculate the value of C required for each of the following critical frequencies:

   (a) 60 Hz   **(b)** 500 Hz   **(c)** 1 kHz   **(d)** 5 kHz

FIGURE 19–39

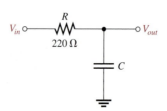

6. Determine the critical frequency for each switch position on the switched filter network of Figure 19–40.

FIGURE 19–40

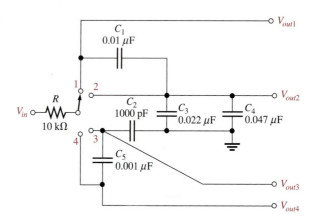

7. Sketch a Bode plot for each part of Problem 5.
8. For each following case, express the voltage ratio in dB:

   (a) $V_{in} = 1$ V, $V_{out} = 1$ V   **(b)** $V_{in} = 5$ V, $V_{out} = 3$ V

   (c) $V_{in} = 10$ V, $V_{out} = 7.07$ V   **(d)** $V_{in} = 25$ V, $V_{out} = 5$ V

9. The input voltage to a low-pass RC filter is 8 V rms. Find the output voltage at the following dB levels:

   (a) −1 dB   **(b)** −3 dB   **(c)** −6 dB   **(d)** −20 dB

10. For a basic RC low-pass filter, find the output voltage in dB relative to a 0 dB input for the following frequencies ($f_c = 1$ kHz):

    (a) 10 kHz   **(b)** 100 kHz   **(c)** 1 MHz

SECTION 19–2 High-Pass Filters

11. In a high-pass filter, $X_C = 500\ \Omega$ and $R = 2.2\ k\Omega$. What is the output voltage ($\mathbf{V}_{out}$) when $V_{in} = 10\ V$ rms?

12. A high-pass filter has a critical frequency of 50 Hz. Determine which of the following frequencies are passed and which are rejected:

   (a) 1 Hz (b) 20 Hz (c) 50 Hz (d) 60 Hz (e) 30 kHz

13. Determine the output voltage of each filter in Figure 19–41 at the specified frequency when $V_{in} = 10\ V$.

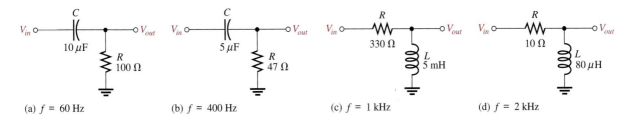

(a) f = 60 Hz (b) f = 400 Hz (c) f = 1 kHz (d) f = 2 kHz

FIGURE 19–41

14. What is f_c for each filter in Figure 19–41? Determine the output voltage at f_c in each case ($V_{in} = 10\ V$).

15. Sketch the Bode plot for each filter in Figure 19–41.

*16. Determine f_c for each switch position in Figure 19–42.

FIGURE 19–42

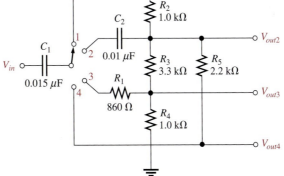

SECTION 19–3 Band-Pass Filters

17. Determine the center frequency for each filter in Figure 19–43.

FIGURE 19–43

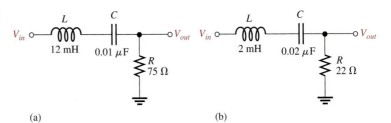

(a) (b)

18. Assuming that the coils in Figure 19–43 have a winding resistance of 10 Ω, find the band-width for each filter.

19. What are the upper and lower critical frequencies for each filter in Figure 19–43? Assume the response is symmetrical about f_0.

20. For each filter in Figure 19–44, find the center frequency of the passband. Neglect R_W.

FIGURE 19–44

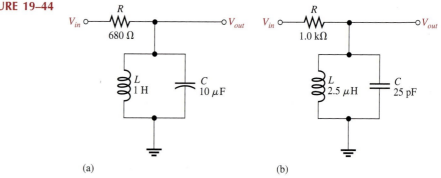

(a)   (b)

21. If the coils in Figure 19–44 have a winding resistance of 4 Ω, what is the output voltage at resonance when $V_{in} = 120$ V?

*22. Determine the separation of center frequencies for all switch positions in Figure 19–45. Do any of the responses overlap? Assume $R_W = 0$ Ω for each coil.

FIGURE 19–45

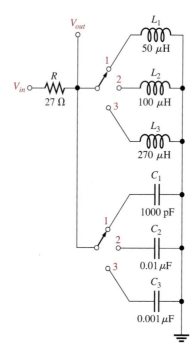

*23. Design a band-pass filter using a parallel resonant circuit to meet all of the following specifi-cations: $BW = 500$ Hz; $Q = 40$; and $I_{C(max)} = 20$ mA, $V_{C(max)} = 2.5$ V.

SECTION 19–4 Band-Stop Filters

24. Determine the center frequency for each filter in Figure 19–46.

FIGURE 19–46

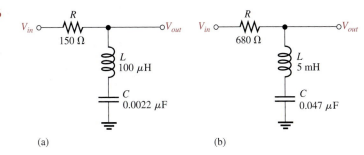

(a)   (b)

25. For each filter in Figure 19–47, find the center frequency of the stopband.
26. If the coils in Figure 19–47 have a winding resistance of 8 Ω, what is the output voltage at resonance when $V_{in} = 50$ V?

FIGURE 19–47

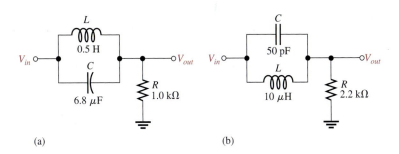

(a)   (b)

*27. Determine the values of L_1 and L_2 in Figure 19–48 to pass a signal with a frequency of 1200 kHz and stop (reject) a signal with a frequency of 456 kHz.

FIGURE 19–48

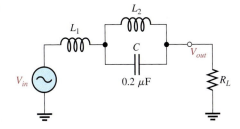

EWB Troubleshooting and Analysis

These problems require your EWB compact disk.

28. Open file PRO19-28.EWB and determine if there is a fault. If so, find the fault.
29. Open file PRO19-29.EWB and determine if there is a fault. If so, find the fault.
30. Open file PRO19-30.EWB and determine if there is a fault. If so, find the fault.
31. Open file PRO19-31.EWB and determine if there is a fault. If so, find the fault.
32. Open file PRO19-32.EWB and determine if there is a fault. If so, find the fault.
33. Open file PRO19-33.EWB and determine if there is a fault. If so, find the fault.
34. Open file PRO19-34.EWB and determine the center frequency of the circuit.
35. Open file PRO19-35.EWB and determine the bandwidth of the circuit.

■ **ANSWERS TO SECTION REVIEWS**

Section 19–1

1. The passband is 0 Hz to 2.5 kHz.
2. $V_{out} = 100\angle-88.9°$ mV rms
3. $20 \log(V_{out}/V_{in}) = -9.54$ dB

Section 19–2

1. $V_{out} = 0.707$ V
2. $V_{out} = 9.98\angle3.81°$ V

Section 19–3

1. $BW = 30.2$ kHz $- 29.8$ kHz $= 400$ Hz
2. $f_0 \cong 1.04$ MHz

Section 19–4

1. A band-stop filter rejects, rather than passes, a certain band of frequencies.
2. High-pass/low-pass combination, series resonant circuit, and parallel resonant circuit

Section 19–5

1. The waveforms indicate that the output amplitude decreases with an increase in frequency as in a low-pass filter.
2. The waveforms indicate that the output amplitude is maximum at 10 kHz and drops off above and below as in a band-pass filter.

■ **ANSWERS TO RELATED PROBLEMS FOR EXAMPLES**

19–1 -1.41 dB
19–2 7.23 kHz
19–3 f_c increases to 159 kHz. Roll-off rate remains -20 dB/decade.
19–4 f_c increases to 350 kHz. Roll-off rate remains -20 dB/decade.
19–5 -60 dB
19–6 $C = 0.723$ μF; $V_{out} = 4.98$ V; $\phi = 5.7°$
19–7 10.5 kHz
19–8 BW increases to 18.8 kHz.
19–9 1.59 MHz
19–10 7.12 kHz (no significant difference)
19–11 $V_{out} = 15.2$ mV; $BW = 105$ Hz
19–12 1.94 V

■ **ANSWERS TO SELF-TEST**

1. (c)	**2.** (b)	**3.** (a)	**4.** (b)	**5.** (d)	**6.** (c)	**7.** (a)	**8.** (c)
9. (b)	**10.** (a)	**11.** (c)	**12.** (b)	**13.** (c)	**14.** (c)		

20

CIRCUIT THEOREMS IN AC ANALYSIS

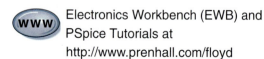

Electronics Workbench (EWB) and PSpice Tutorials at
http://www.prenhall.com/floyd

■ INTRODUCTION

Several important theorems were covered in Chapter 8 with emphasis on their applications in the analysis of dc circuits. This chapter is a continuation of that coverage with emphasis on applications in the analysis of ac circuits with reactive elements.

The theorems in this chapter make analysis easier for certain types of circuits. These methods do not replace Ohm's law and Kirchhoff's laws, but they are normally used in conjunction with those laws in certain situations.

Although you are already familiar with the theorems covered in this chapter, a restatement of their purposes may be helpful. The superposition theorem will help you to deal with circuits that have multiple sources. Thevenin's and Norton's theorems provide methods for reducing a circuit to a simple equivalent form for easier analysis. The maximum power transfer theorem is used in applications where it is important for a given circuit to provide maximum power to a load.

In the TECH TIP assignment in Section 20–5, you will evaluate a band-pass filter module to determine its internal component values, and you will apply Thevenin's theorem to determine an optimum load impedance for maximum power transfer.

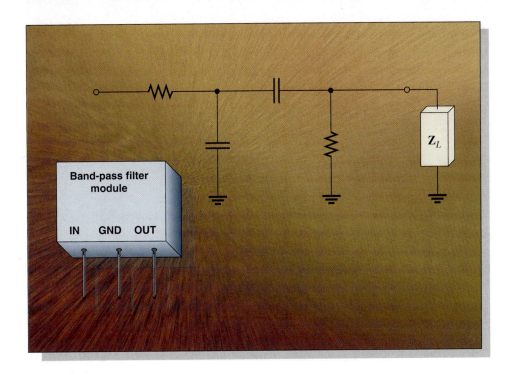

■ **CHAPTER OBJECTIVES**

❑ Apply the superposition theorem to ac circuit analysis

❑ Apply Thevenin's theorem to simplify reactive ac circuits for analysis

❑ Apply Norton's theorem to simplify reactive ac circuits

❑ Apply the maximum power transfer theorem

20–1 ■ THE SUPERPOSITION THEOREM

The superposition theorem was introduced in Chapter 8 for use in dc circuit analysis. In this section, the superposition theorem is applied to circuits with ac sources and reactive elements.

After completing this section, you should be able to

■ **Apply the superposition theorem to ac circuit analysis**
  • State the superposition theorem
  • List the steps in applying the theorem

The **superposition theorem** can be stated as follows:

> **The current in any given branch of a multiple-source circuit can be found by determining the currents in that particular branch produced by each source acting alone, with all other sources replaced by their internal impedances. The total current in the given branch is the phasor sum of the individual source currents in that branch.**

The procedure for the application of the superposition theorem is as follows:

Step 1. Leave one of the sources in the circuit, and replace all others with their internal impedance. For ideal voltage sources, the internal impedance is zero. For ideal current sources, the internal impedance is infinite. We will call this procedure *zeroing* the source.

Step 2. Find the current in the branch of interest produced by the one remaining source.

Step 3. Repeat Steps 1 and 2 for each source in turn. When complete, you will have a number of current values equal to the number of sources in the circuit.

Step 4. Add the individual current values as phasor quantities.

The following three examples illustrate this procedure.

EXAMPLE 20–1

Find the current in R of Figure 20–1 using the superposition theorem. Assume the internal source impedances are zero.

FIGURE 20–1

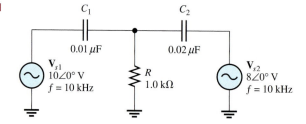

Solution

Step 1. Replace V_{s2} with its internal impedance (zero), and find the current in R due to V_{s1}, as indicated in Figure 20–2.

FIGURE 20–2

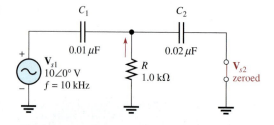

$$X_{C1} = \frac{1}{2\pi f C_1} = \frac{1}{2\pi(10 \text{ kHz})(0.01 \ \mu\text{F})} = 1.59 \text{ k}\Omega$$

$$X_{C2} = \frac{1}{2\pi f C_2} = \frac{1}{2\pi(10 \text{ kHz})(0.02 \ \mu\text{F})} = 796 \ \Omega$$

Looking from V_{s1}, the impedance is

$$\mathbf{Z} = \mathbf{X}_{C1} + \frac{\mathbf{R}\mathbf{X}_{C2}}{\mathbf{R} + \mathbf{X}_{C2}} = 1.59\angle{-90°} \text{ k}\Omega + \frac{(1.0\angle0° \text{ k}\Omega)(796\angle{-90°} \ \Omega)}{1.0 \text{ k}\Omega - j796 \ \Omega}$$

$$= 1.59\angle{-90°} \text{ k}\Omega + 622\angle{-51.5°} \ \Omega$$

$$= -j1.59 \text{ k}\Omega + 387 \ \Omega - j487 \ \Omega = 387 \ \Omega - j2.08 \text{ k}\Omega$$

Converting to polar form yields

$$\mathbf{Z} = 2.12\angle{-79.5°} \text{ k}\Omega$$

The total current from source 1 is

$$\mathbf{I}_{s1} = \frac{\mathbf{V}_{s1}}{\mathbf{Z}} = \frac{10\angle0° \text{ V}}{2.12\angle{-79.5°} \text{ k}\Omega} = 4.72\angle79.5° \text{ mA}$$

Use the current-divider formula. The current through R due to V_{s1} is

$$\mathbf{I}_{R1} = \left(\frac{\mathbf{X}_{C2}\angle{-90°}}{\mathbf{R} - j\mathbf{X}_{C2}}\right)\mathbf{I}_{s1} = \left(\frac{796\angle{-90°} \ \Omega}{1.0 \text{ k}\Omega - j796 \ \Omega}\right)4.72\angle79.5° \text{ mA}$$

$$= (0.623\angle{-51.5°} \ \Omega)(4.72\angle79.5° \text{ mA}) = 2.94\angle28.0° \text{ mA}$$

Step 2. Find the current in R due to source V_{s2} by replacing V_{s1} with its internal impedance (zero), as shown in Figure 20–3.

FIGURE 20–3

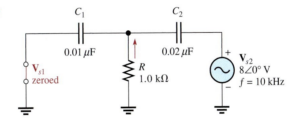

Looking from V_{s2}, the impedance is

$$\mathbf{Z} = \mathbf{X}_{C2} + \frac{\mathbf{R}\mathbf{X}_{C1}}{\mathbf{R} + \mathbf{X}_{C1}} = \frac{796\angle{-90°} \ \Omega + (1.0\angle0° \text{ k}\Omega)(1.59\angle{-90°} \text{ k}\Omega)}{1.0 \text{ k}\Omega - j1.59 \text{ k}\Omega}$$

$$= 796\angle{-90°} \ \Omega + 847\angle{-32.2°} \ \Omega$$

$$= -j796 \ \Omega + 717 \ \Omega - j451 \ \Omega = 717 \ \Omega - j1247 \ \Omega$$

Converting to polar form yields

$$\mathbf{Z} = 1438\angle{-60.1°} \ \Omega$$

The total current from source 2 is

$$\mathbf{I}_{s2} = \frac{\mathbf{V}_{s2}}{\mathbf{Z}} = \frac{8\angle0° \text{ V}}{1438\angle{-60.1°} \ \Omega} = 5.56\angle60.1° \text{ mA}$$

Use the current-divider formula. The current through R due to V_{s2} is

$$\mathbf{I}_{R2} = \left(\frac{\mathbf{X}_{C1}\angle{-90°}}{\mathbf{R} - j\mathbf{X}_{C1}}\right)\mathbf{I}_{s2}$$

$$= \left(\frac{1.59\angle{-90°} \text{ k}\Omega}{1.0 \text{ k}\Omega - j1.59 \text{ k}\Omega}\right)5.56\angle60.1° \text{ mA} = 4.70\angle27.9° \text{ mA}$$

Step 3. Convert the two individual resistor currents to rectangular form and add to get the total current through R.

$$I_{R1} = 2.94\angle 28.0° \text{ mA} = 2.60 \text{ mA} + j1.38 \text{ mA}$$
$$I_{R2} = 4.70\angle 27.9° \text{ mA} = 4.15 \text{ mA} + j2.20 \text{ mA}$$
$$I_R = I_{R1} + I_{R2} = 6.75 \text{ mA} + j3.58 \text{ mA} = \textbf{7.64}\angle \textbf{27.9° mA}$$

Related Problem Determine I_R if $V_{s2} = 8\angle 180°$ V in Figure 20–1.

EXAMPLE 20–2   Find the coil current in Figure 20–4. Assume the sources are ideal.

FIGURE 20–4

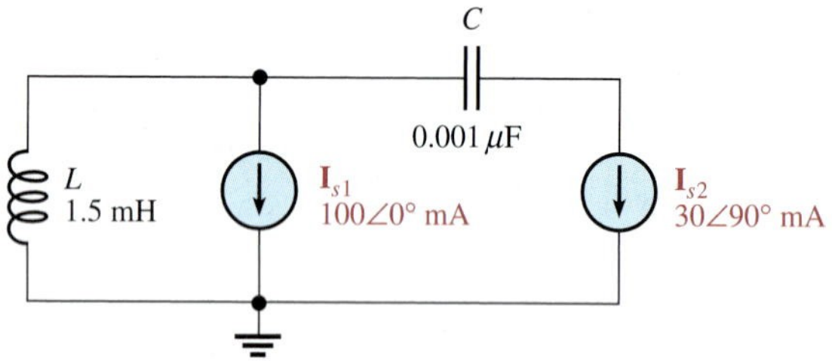

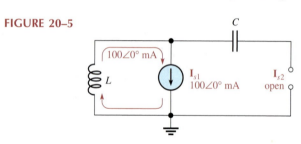

Solution
Step 1. Find the current through the inductor due to current source I_{s1} by replacing source I_{s2} with an open, as shown in Figure 20–5. As you can see, the entire 100 mA from the current source I_{s1} is through the coil.

FIGURE 20–5

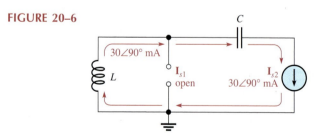

Step 2. Find the current through the inductor due to current source I_{s2} by replacing source I_{s1} with an open, as indicated in Figure 20–6. Notice that all of the 30 mA from source I_{s2} is through the coil.

FIGURE 20–6

Step 3. To get the total inductor current, superimpose the two individual currents and add as phasor quantities.

$$I_L = I_{L1} + I_{L2}$$
$$= 100\angle 0° \text{ mA} + 30\angle 90° \text{ mA} = 100 \text{ mA} + j30 \text{ mA}$$
$$= \textbf{104}\angle \textbf{16.7° mA}$$

Related Problem Find the current through the capacitor in Figure 20–4.

EXAMPLE 20–3   Find the total current in the resistor R_L in Figure 20–7. Assume the sources are ideal.

FIGURE 20–7

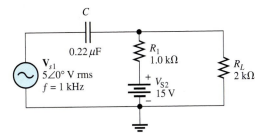

Solution

Step 1.   Find the current through R_L due to source V_{s1} by zeroing (replacing with its internal impedance) the dc source V_{S2}, as shown in Figure 20–8. Looking from V_{s1}, the impedance is

$$\mathbf{Z} = \mathbf{X}_C + \frac{\mathbf{R}_1\mathbf{R}_L}{\mathbf{R}_1 + \mathbf{R}_L}$$

$$X_C = \frac{1}{2\pi(1.0 \text{ kHz})(0.22 \ \mu\text{F})} = 723 \ \Omega$$

$$\mathbf{Z} = 723\angle{-90°} \ \Omega + \frac{(1.0\angle0° \text{ k}\Omega)(2\angle0° \text{ k}\Omega)}{3\angle0° \text{ k}\Omega}$$

$$= -j723 \ \Omega + 667 \ \Omega = 984\angle{-47.3°} \ \Omega$$

The total current from source 1 is

$$\mathbf{I}_{Rs1} = \frac{\mathbf{V}_{s1}}{\mathbf{Z}} = \frac{5\angle0° \text{ V}}{984\angle{-47.3°} \ \Omega} = 5.08\angle47.3° \text{ mA}$$

Use the current-divider approach. The current in R_L due to V_{s1} is

$$\mathbf{I}_{RL(s1)} = \left(\frac{R_1}{R_1 + R_L}\right)\mathbf{I}_{s1} = \left(\frac{1.0 \text{ k}\Omega}{3 \text{ k}\Omega}\right)5.08\angle47.3° \text{ mA} = 1.69\angle47.3° \text{ mA}$$

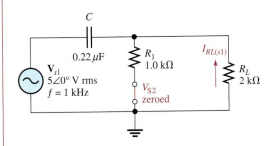

FIGURE 20–8

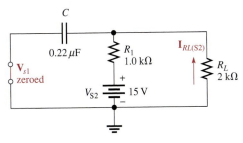

FIGURE 20–9

Step 2.   Find the current in R_L due to the dc source V_{S2} by zeroing V_{s1} (replacing with its internal impedance) , as shown in Figure 20–9. The impedance magnitude as seen by V_{S2} is

$$Z = R_1 + R_L = 3 \text{ k}\Omega$$

The current produced by V_{S2} is

$$I_{RL(S2)} = \frac{V_{S2}}{Z} = \frac{15 \text{ V}}{3 \text{ k}\Omega} = 5 \text{ mA dc}$$

Step 3. By superposition, the total current in R_L is $1.69\angle47.3°$ mA riding on a dc level of 5 mA, as indicated in Figure 20–10.

FIGURE 20–10

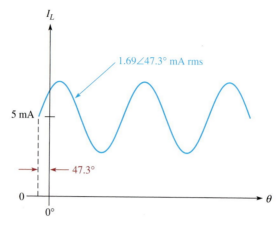

Related Problem Determine the current through R_L if V_{S2} is changed to 9 V.

SECTION 20–1 REVIEW

1. If two equal currents are in opposing directions at any instant of time in a given branch of a circuit, what is the net current at that instant?

2. Why is the superposition theorem useful in the analysis of multiple-source circuits?

3. Using the superposition theorem, find the magnitude of the current through R in Figure 20–11.

FIGURE 20–11

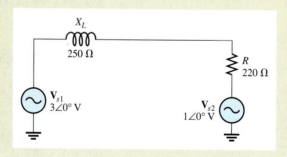

20–2 ■ THEVENIN'S THEOREM

Thevenin's theorem, as applied to ac circuits, provides a method for reducing any circuit to an equivalent form that consists of an equivalent ac voltage source in series with an equivalent impedance.

After completing this section, you should be able to

■ **Apply Thevenin's theorem to simplify reactive ac circuits for analysis**
  • Describe the form of a Thevenin equivalent circuit
  • Obtain the Thevenin equivalent ac voltage source
  • Obtain the Thevenin equivalent impedance
  • List the steps in applying Thevenin's theorem to an ac circuit

The form of Thevenin's **equivalent circuit** is shown in Figure 20–12. Regardless of how complex the original circuit is, it can always be reduced to this equivalent form. The equivalent voltage source is designated $\mathbf{V}_{th}$; the equivalent impedance is designated $\mathbf{Z}_{th}$ (lowercase italic subscript denotes ac quantity). Notice that the impedance is represented by a block in the circuit diagram. This is because the equivalent impedance can be of several forms: purely resistive, purely capacitive, purely inductive, or a combination of a resistance and a reactance.

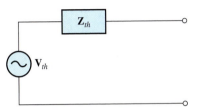

FIGURE 20–12
Thevenin's equivalent circuit.

Equivalency

Figure 20–13(a) shows a block diagram that represents an ac circuit of any given complexity. This circuit has two output terminals, A and B. A load impedance, $\mathbf{Z}_L$, is connected to the terminals. The circuit produces a certain voltage, $\mathbf{V}_L$, and a certain current, $\mathbf{I}_L$, as illustrated.

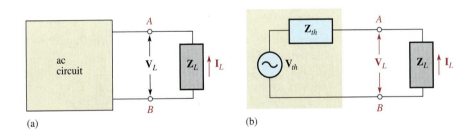

(a)   (b)

FIGURE 20–13
An ac circuit of any complexity can be reduced to a Thevenin equivalent for analysis purposes.

By **Thevenin's theorem,** the circuit in the block can be reduced to an equivalent form, as indicated in the beige area of Figure 20–13(b). The term *equivalent* means that when the same value of load is connected to both the original circuit and Thevenin's equivalent circuit, the load voltages and currents are equal for both. Therefore, as far as the load is concerned, there is no difference between the original circuit and Thevenin's equivalent circuit. The load "sees" the same current and voltage regardless of whether it is connected to the original circuit or to the Thevenin equivalent. For ac circuits, the equivalent circuit is for one particular frequency. When the frequency is changed, the equivalent circuit must be recalculated.

Thevenin's Equivalent Voltage (V_{th})

As you have seen, the equivalent voltage, $\mathbf{V}_{th}$, is one part of the complete Thevenin equivalent circuit.

> **Thevenin's equivalent voltage is defined as the open circuit voltage between two specified terminals in a circuit.**

To illustrate, let's assume that an ac circuit of some type has a resistor connected between two specified terminals, A and B, as shown in Figure 20–14(a). We wish to find the Thevenin equivalent circuit for the circuit as "seen" by R. $\mathbf{V}_{th}$ is the voltage across terminals A and B, with R removed, as shown in part (b) of the figure. The circuit is viewed from the open across terminals A and B, and R is considered external to the circuit for which the Thevenin equivalent is to be found. The following three examples show how to find $\mathbf{V}_{th}$.

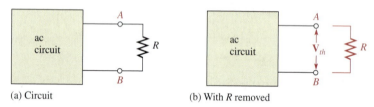

(a) Circuit   (b) With R removed

FIGURE 20–14
How $\mathbf{V}_{th}$ is determined.

EXAMPLE 20–4   Determine $\mathbf{V}_{th}$ for the circuit external to R_L in Figure 20–15. The beige area identifies the portion of the circuit to be thevenized.

FIGURE 20–15

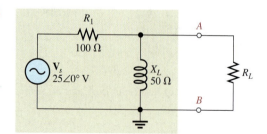

Solution   Remove R_L and determine the voltage from A to B ($\mathbf{V}_{th}$). In this case, the voltage from A to B is the same as the voltage across X_L. This is determined using the voltage-divider method.

$$\mathbf{V}_L = \left(\frac{X_L \angle 90°}{R_1 + jX_L}\right)\mathbf{V}_s = \left(\frac{50 \angle 90° \ \Omega}{112 \angle 26.6° \ \Omega}\right) 25 \angle 0° \text{ V} = 11.2 \angle 63.4° \text{ V}$$

$$\mathbf{V}_{th} = \mathbf{V}_{AB} = \mathbf{V}_L = \mathbf{11.2 \angle 63.4° \text{ V}}$$

Related Problem   Determine $\mathbf{V}_{th}$ if R_1 is changed to 47 Ω in Figure 20–15.

EXAMPLE 20–5

For the circuit in Figure 20–16, determine the Thevenin voltage as seen by R_L.

FIGURE 20–16

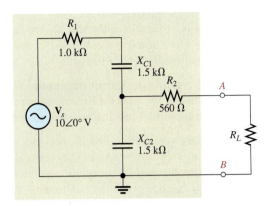

Solution   Thevenin's voltage for the circuit between terminals A and B is the voltage that appears across A and B with R_L removed from the circuit.

There is no voltage drop across R_2 because the open across terminals A and B prevents current through it. Thus, $\mathbf{V}_{AB}$ is the same as $\mathbf{V}_{C2}$ and can be found by the voltage-divider formula.

$$\mathbf{V}_{AB} = \mathbf{V}_{C2} = \left(\frac{X_{C2}\angle{-90°}}{R_1 - jX_{C1} - jX_{C2}}\right)\mathbf{V}_s = \left(\frac{1.5\angle{-90°}\ \text{k}\Omega}{1.0\ \text{k}\Omega - j3\ \text{k}\Omega}\right)10\angle{0°}\ \text{V}$$

$$= \left(\frac{1.5\angle{-90°}\ \text{k}\Omega}{3.16\angle{-71.6°}\ \text{k}\Omega}\right)10\angle{0°}\ \text{V} = 4.75\angle{-18.4°}\ \text{V}$$

$$\mathbf{V}_{th} = \mathbf{V}_{AB} = \mathbf{4.75\angle{-18.4°}\ V}$$

Related Problem   Determine $\mathbf{V}_{th}$ if R_1 is changed to 2.2 kΩ in Figure 20–16.

EXAMPLE 20–6

For Figure 20–17, find $\mathbf{V}_{th}$ for the circuit external to R_L.

FIGURE 20–17

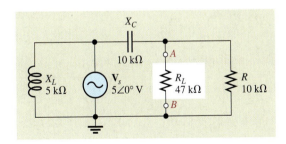

Solution   First remove R_L and determine the voltage across the resulting open terminals, which is $\mathbf{V}_{th}$. Find $\mathbf{V}_{th}$ by applying the voltage-divider formula to X_C and R.

$$\mathbf{V}_{th} = \mathbf{V}_R = \left(\frac{R\angle{0°}}{R - jX_C}\right)\mathbf{V}_s = \left(\frac{10\angle{0°}\ \text{k}\Omega}{10\ \text{k}\Omega - j10\ \text{k}\Omega}\right)5\angle{0°}\ \text{V}$$

$$= \left(\frac{10\angle{0°}\ \text{k}\Omega}{14.14\angle{-45°}\ \text{k}\Omega}\right)5\angle{0°}\ \text{V} = \mathbf{3.54\angle{45°}\ V}$$

Notice the L has no effect on the result, since the 5 V source appears across C and R in combination.

Related Problem   Find $\mathbf{V}_{th}$ if R is 22 kΩ and R_L is 39 kΩ in Figure 20–17.

Thevenin's Equivalent Impedance (Z_{th})

The previous examples illustrated how to find only one part of a Thevenin equivalent circuit. Now, let's turn our attention to determining the Thevenin equivalent impedance, Z_{th}. As defined by Thevenin's theorem,

> **Thevenin's equivalent impedance is the total impedance appearing between two specified terminals in a given circuit with all sources replaced by their internal impedances.**

Thus, when you wish to find Z_{th} between any two terminals in a circuit, all the voltage sources are replaced by a short (any internal impedance remains in series). All the current sources are replaced by an open (any internal impedance remains in parallel). Then the total impedance between the two terminals is determined. The following three examples illustrate how to find Z_{th}.

EXAMPLE 20–7

Find Z_{th} for the part of the circuit in Figure 20–18 that is external to R_L. This is the same circuit used in Example 20–4.

FIGURE 20–18

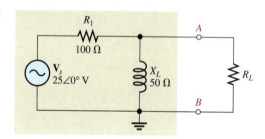

Solution   First, replace V_s with its internal impedance (zero), as shown in Figure 20–19.

FIGURE 20–19

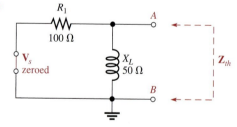

Looking in between terminals A and B, R and X_L are in parallel. Thus,

$$Z_{th} = \frac{(R_1\angle 0°)(X_L\angle 90°)}{R_1 + jX_L} = \frac{(100\angle 0°\ \Omega)(50\angle 90°\ \Omega)}{100\ \Omega + j50\ \Omega}$$

$$= \frac{(100\angle 0°\ \Omega)(50\angle 90°\ \Omega)}{112\angle 26.6°\ \Omega} = \mathbf{44.6\angle 63.4°\ \Omega}$$

Related Problem   Change R_1 to 47 Ω and determine Z_{th}.

EXAMPLE 20–8

For the circuit in Figure 20–20, determine $\mathbf{Z}_{th}$ as seen by R_L. This is the same circuit used in Example 20–5.

FIGURE 20–20

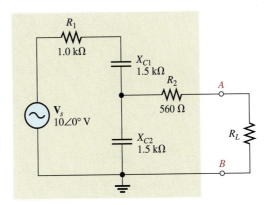

Solution First, replace the voltage source with its internal impedance (zero), as shown in Figure 20–21.

FIGURE 20–21

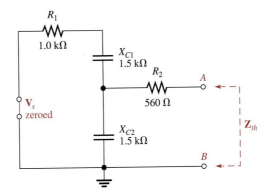

Looking from terminals A and B, C_2 appears in parallel with the series combination of R_1 and C_1. This entire combination is in series with R_2. The calculation for $\mathbf{Z}_{th}$ is as follows:

$$\mathbf{Z}_{th} = R_2\angle 0° + \frac{(X_{C2}\angle -90°)(R_1 - jX_{C1})}{R_1 - jX_{C1} - jX_{C2}}$$

$$= 560\angle 0° \ \Omega + \frac{(1.5\angle -90° \ \text{k}\Omega)(1.0 \ \text{k}\Omega - j1.5 \ \text{k}\Omega)}{1.0 \ \text{k}\Omega - j3 \ \text{k}\Omega}$$

$$= 560\angle 0° \ \Omega + \frac{(1.5\angle -90° \ \text{k}\Omega)(1.8\angle -56.3° \ \text{k}\Omega)}{3.16\angle -71.6° \ \text{k}\Omega}$$

$$= 560\angle 0° \ \Omega + 854\angle -74.7° \ \Omega = 560 \ \Omega + 225 \ \Omega - j824 \ \Omega$$

$$= 785 \ \Omega - j824 \ \Omega = \mathbf{1138\angle -46.4° \ \Omega}$$

Related Problem Determine $\mathbf{Z}_{th}$ if R_1 is changed to 2.2 kΩ in Figure 20–20.

EXAMPLE 20–9

For the circuit in Figure 20–22, determine $\mathbf{Z}_{th}$ for the portion of the circuit external to R_L. This is the same circuit as in Example 20–6.

FIGURE 20–22

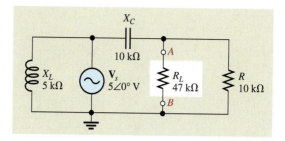

Solution   With the voltage source replaced by its internal impedence (zero), X_L is effectively out of the circuit. R and C appear in parallel when viewed from the open terminals, as indicated in Figure 20–23. $\mathbf{Z}_{th}$ is calculated as follows:

$$\mathbf{Z}_{th} = \frac{(R\angle 0°)(X_C \angle -90°)}{R - jX_C} = \frac{(10\angle 0° \text{ k}\Omega)(10\angle -90° \text{ k}\Omega)}{14.1\angle -45° \text{ k}\Omega} = 7.07\angle -45° \text{ k}\Omega$$

FIGURE 20–23

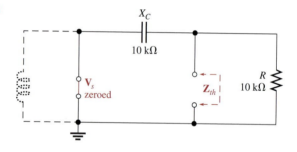

Related Problem   Find $\mathbf{Z}_{th}$ if R is 22 kΩ and R_L is 39 kΩ in Figure 20–22.

EXAMPLE 20–10

Draw the Thevenin equivalent circuit for the circuit in Figure 20–24 that is external to R_L. This is the circuit used in Examples 20–4 and 20–7.

FIGURE 20–24

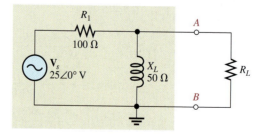

Solution   From Examples 20–4 and 20–7, respectively, $\mathbf{V}_{th} = 11.2\angle 63.4°$ V and $\mathbf{Z}_{th} = 44.6\angle 63.4°$ Ω. In rectangular form, the impedance is

$$\mathbf{Z}_{th} = 20 \text{ } \Omega + j40 \text{ } \Omega$$

This form indicates that the impedance is a 20 Ω resistor in series with a 40 Ω inductive reactance. The Thevenin equivalent circuit is shown in Figure 20–25.

FIGURE 20–25

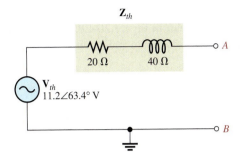

Related Problem Draw the Thevenin equivalent circuit for Figure 20–24 with $R_1 = 47\ \Omega$.

EXAMPLE 20–11 For the circuit in Figure 20–26, sketch the Thevenin equivalent circuit external to R_L. This is the circuit used in Examples 20–5 and 20–8.

FIGURE 20–26

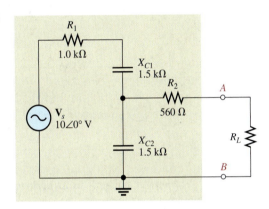

Solution From Examples 20–5 and 20–8, respectively, $\mathbf{V}_{th} = 4.75\angle{-18.4°}$ V and $\mathbf{Z}_{th} = 1138\angle{-46.4°}\ \Omega$. In rectangular form, the impedance is

$$\mathbf{Z}_{th} = 785\ \Omega - j824\ \Omega$$

The Thevenin equivalent circuit is shown in Figure 20–27.

FIGURE 20–27

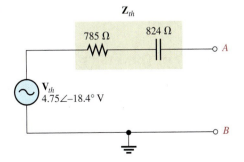

Related Problem Sketch the Thevenin equivalent for the circuit in Figure 20–26 with $R_1 = 2.2\ \mathrm{k}\Omega$.

EXAMPLE 20–12   For the circuit in Figure 20–28, determine the Thevenin equivalent circuit as seen by R_L. This is the circuit in Examples 20–6 and 20–9.

FIGURE 20–28

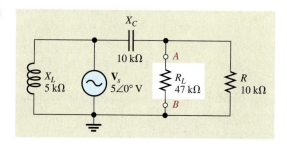

Solution   From Examples 20–6 and 20–9, respectively, $\mathbf{V}_{th} = 3.54\angle 45°$, and $\mathbf{Z}_{th} = 7.07\angle{-45°}$ kΩ. The impedance in rectangular form is

$$\mathbf{Z}_{th} = 5 \text{ k}\Omega - j5 \text{ k}\Omega$$

Thus, the Thevenin equivalent circuit is as shown in Figure 20–29.

FIGURE 20–29

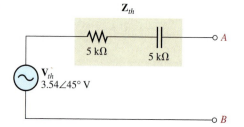

Related Problem   Change R to 22 kΩ and R_L to 39 kΩ in Figure 20–28 and sketch the Thevenin equivalent circuit.

Thevenin's Equivalent Circuit

The previous examples have shown how to find the two equivalent components of a Thevenin circuit, $\mathbf{V}_{th}$ and $\mathbf{Z}_{th}$. Keep in mind that $\mathbf{V}_{th}$ and $\mathbf{Z}_{th}$ can be found for any circuit. Once these equivalent values are determined, they must be connected in series to form the Thevenin equivalent circuit. The following examples use the previous examples to illustrate this final step.

Summary of Thevenin's Theorem

Remember that the Thevenin equivalent circuit is always a voltage source in series with a resistance regardless of the original circuit that it replaces. The significance of Thevenin's theorem is that the equivalent circuit can replace the original circuit as far as any external load is concerned. Any load connected between the terminals of a Thevenin equivalent circuit experiences the same current and voltage as if it were connected to the terminals of the original circuit.

A summary of steps for applying Thevenin's theorem follows.

Step 1.   Open the two terminals between which you want to find the Thevenin circuit. This is done by removing the component from which the circuit is to be viewed.

Step 2. Determine the voltage across the two open terminals.

Step 3. Determine the impedance viewed from the two open terminals with ideal voltage sources replaced with shorts and ideal current sources replaced with opens (zeroed).

Step 4. Connect $\mathbf{V}_{th}$ and $\mathbf{Z}_{th}$ in series to produce the complete Thevenin equivalent circuit.

SECTION 20–2 REVIEW

1. What are the two basic components of a Thevenin equivalent ac circuit?
2. For a certain circuit, $\mathbf{Z}_{th} = 25\ \Omega - j50\ \Omega$, and $\mathbf{V}_{th} = 5\angle 0°$ V. Sketch the Thevenin equivalent circuit.
3. For the circuit in Figure 20–30, find the Thevenin equivalent looking from terminals A and B.

FIGURE 20–30

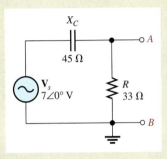

20–3 ■ NORTON'S THEOREM

Like Thevenin's theorem, Norton's theorem provides a method of reducing a more complex circuit to a simpler, more manageable form for analysis. The basic difference is that Norton's theorem gives an equivalent current source (rather than a voltage source) in parallel (rather than in series) with an equivalent impedance.

After completing this section, you should be able to

■ **Apply Norton's theorem to simplify reactive ac circuits**
  • Describe the form of a Norton equivalent circuit
  • Obtain the Norton equivalent ac current source
  • Obtain the Norton equivalent impedance

The form of Norton's equivalent circuit is shown in Figure 20–31. Regardless of how complex the original circuit is, it can be reduced to this equivalent form. The equivalent current source is designated $\mathbf{I}_n$, and the equivalent impedance is $\mathbf{Z}_n$ (lowercase italic subscript denotes ac quantity).

Norton's theorem shows you how to find $\mathbf{I}_n$ and $\mathbf{Z}_n$. Once they are known, simply connect them in parallel to get the complete Norton equivalent circuit.

FIGURE 20–31
Norton equivalent circuit.

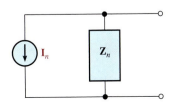

Norton's Equivalent Current Source ($\mathbf{I}_n$)

$\mathbf{I}_n$ is one part of the Norton equivalent circuit; $\mathbf{Z}_n$ is the other part.

Norton's equivalent current is defined as the short-circuit current between two specified terminals in a given circuit.

Any load connected between these two terminals effectively "sees" a current source $\mathbf{I}_n$ in parallel with $\mathbf{Z}_n$.

To illustrate, let's suppose that the circuit shown in Figure 20–32 has a load resistor connected to terminals A and B, as indicated in part (a). We wish to find the Norton equivalent for the circuit external to R_L. To find $\mathbf{I}_n$, calculate the current between terminals A and B with those terminals shorted, as shown in part (b). Example 20–13 shows how to find $\mathbf{I}_n$.

FIGURE 20–32
How $\mathbf{I}_n$ is determined.

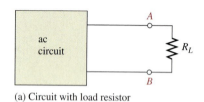

(a) Circuit with load resistor

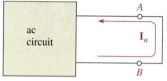

(b) Load is replaced by short and short circuit current is $\mathbf{I}_n$.

EXAMPLE 20–13   In Figure 20–33, determine $\mathbf{I}_n$ for the circuit as "seen" by the load resistor. The beige area identifies the portion of the circuit to be nortonized.

FIGURE 20–33

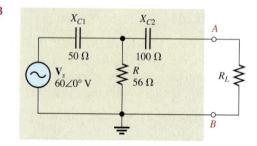

Solution   Short the terminals A and B, as shown in Figure 20–34.

FIGURE 20–34

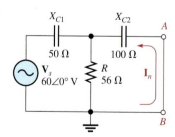

$\mathbf{I}_n$ is the current through the short and is calculated as follows. First, the total impedance viewed from the source is

$$\mathbf{Z} = \mathbf{X}_{C1} + \frac{\mathbf{R}\mathbf{X}_{C2}}{\mathbf{R} + \mathbf{X}_{C2}} = 50\angle{-90°}\ \Omega + \frac{(56\angle{0°}\ \Omega)(100\angle{-90°}\ \Omega)}{56\ \Omega - j100\ \Omega}$$

$$= 50\angle{-90°}\ \Omega + 48.9\angle{-29.3°}\ \Omega$$

$$= -j50\ \Omega + 42.6\ \Omega - j23.9\ \Omega = 42.6\ \Omega - j73.9\ \Omega$$

Converting to polar form yields

$$\mathbf{Z} = 85.3\angle{-60.0°}\ \Omega$$

Next, the total current from the source is

$$\mathbf{I}_s = \frac{\mathbf{V}_s}{\mathbf{Z}} = \frac{60\angle 0°\ \text{V}}{85.3\angle{-60.0°}\ \Omega} = 703\angle 60.0°\ \text{mA}$$

Finally, apply the current-divider formula to get $\mathbf{I}_n$ (the current through the short between terminals A and B).

$$\mathbf{I}_n = \left(\frac{\mathbf{R}}{\mathbf{R} + \mathbf{X}_{C2}}\right)\mathbf{I}_s = \left(\frac{56\angle 0°\ \Omega}{56\ \Omega - j100\ \Omega}\right)703\angle 60.0°\ \text{mA} = \mathbf{344\angle 121°\ mA}$$

This is the value for the equivalent Norton current source.

Related Problem Determine $\mathbf{I}_n$ if $\mathbf{V}_s$ is changed to $25\angle 0°$ V and R is changed to 33 Ω in Figure 20–33.

Norton's Equivalent Impedance (Z_n)

$\mathbf{Z}_n$ is defined the same as $\mathbf{Z}_{th}$: It is the total impedance appearing between two specified terminals of a given circuit viewed from the open terminals with all sources replaced by their internal impedances.

EXAMPLE 20–14   Find $\mathbf{Z}_n$ for the circuit in Figure 20–33 (Example 20–13) viewed from the open across terminals A and B.

Solution   First, replace $\mathbf{V}_s$ with its internal impedance (zero), as indicated in Figure 20–35.

FIGURE 20–35

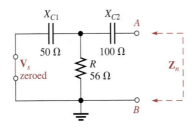

Looking in between terminals A and B, C_2 is in series with the parallel combination of R and C_1. Thus,

$$\mathbf{Z}_n = \mathbf{X}_{C2} + \frac{\mathbf{R}\mathbf{X}_{C1}}{\mathbf{R} + \mathbf{X}_{C1}} = 100\angle{-90°}\ \Omega + \frac{(56\angle 0°\ \Omega)(50\angle{-90°}\ \Omega)}{56\ \Omega - j50\ \Omega}$$

$$= 100\angle{-90°}\ \Omega + 37.3\angle{-48.2°}\ \Omega$$

$$= -j100\ \Omega + 24.8\ \Omega - j27.8\ \Omega = \mathbf{24.8\ \Omega - j128\ \Omega}$$

The Norton equivalent impedance is a 24.8 Ω resistance in series with a 128 Ω capacitive reactance.

Related Problem   Find $\mathbf{Z}_n$ in Figure 20–33 if $\mathbf{V}_s = 25\angle 0°$ V and $R = 33$ Ω.

The previous two examples have shown how to find the two equivalent components of a Norton equivalent circuit. Keep in mind that these values can be found for any given ac circuit. Once these values are known, they are connected in parallel to form the Norton equivalent circuit, as the following example illustrates.

EXAMPLE 20–15

Show the complete Norton equivalent circuit for the circuit in Figure 20–33 (Example 20–13).

Solution From Examples 20–13 and 20–14, respectively, $\mathbf{I}_n = 344\angle121°$ mA and $\mathbf{Z}_n = 24.8 \ \Omega - j128 \ \Omega$. The Norton equivalent circuit is shown in Figure 20–36.

FIGURE 20–36

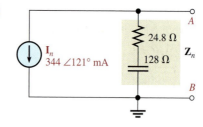

Related Problem Show the Norton equivalent for the circuit in Figure 20–33 if $\mathbf{V}_s = 25\angle0°$ V and $R = 33 \ \Omega$.

Summary of Norton's Theorem

Any load connected between the terminals of a Norton equivalent circuit will have the same current through it and the same voltage across it as it would when connected to the terminals of the original circuit. A summary of steps for theoretically applying Norton's theorem is as follows:

Step 1. Replace the load connected to the two terminals between which the Norton circuit is to be determined with a short.

Step 2. Determine the current through the short. This is $\mathbf{I}_n$.

Step 3. Open the terminals and determine the impedance between the two open terminals with all sources replaced with their internal impedances. This is $\mathbf{Z}_n$.

Step 4. Connect $\mathbf{I}_n$ and $\mathbf{Z}_n$ in parallel.

SECTION 20–3 REVIEW

1. For a given circuit, $\mathbf{I}_n = 5\angle0°$ mA, and $\mathbf{Z}_n = 150 \ \Omega + j100 \ \Omega$. Draw the Norton equivalent circuit.

2. Find the Norton circuit as seen by R_L in Figure 20–37.

FIGURE 20–37

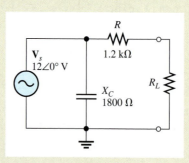

20–4 ■ MAXIMUM POWER TRANSFER THEOREM

When a load is connected to a circuit, maximum power is transferred to the load when the load impedance is the complex conjugate of the circuit's output impedance.

After completing this section, you should be able to

■ **Apply the maximum power transfer theorem**
  • Explain the theorem
  • Determine the value of load impedance for which maximum power is transferred from a given circuit

The **complex conjugate** of $R - jX_C$ is $R + jX_L$, where the resistances and the reactances are equal in magnitude. The output impedance is effectively Thevenin's equivalent impedance viewed from the output terminals. When $\mathbf{Z}_L$ is the complex conjugate of $\mathbf{Z}_{out}$, maximum power is transferred from the circuit to the load with a power factor of 1. An equivalent circuit with its output impedance and load is shown in Figure 20–38.

FIGURE 20–38
Equivalent circuit with load.

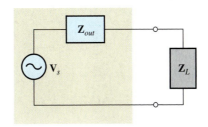

Example 20–16 shows that maximum power occurs when the impedances are conjugately matched.

EXAMPLE 20–16   The circuit to the left of terminals A and B in Figure 20–39 provides power to the load $\mathbf{Z}_L$. This can be viewed as simulating a power amplifier delivering power to a complex load. It is the Thevenin equivalent of a more complex circuit. Calculate and plot a graph of the power delivered to the load for each of the following frequencies: 10 kHz, 30 kHz, 50 kHz, 80 kHz, and 100 kHz.

FIGURE 20–39

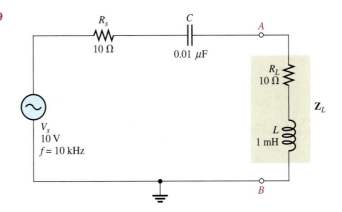

Solution For $f = 10$ kHz,

$$X_C = \frac{1}{2\pi fC} = \frac{1}{2\pi(10 \text{ kHz})(0.01 \ \mu\text{F})} = 1.59 \text{ k}\Omega$$

$$X_L = 2\pi fL = 2\pi(10 \text{ kHz})(1 \text{ mH}) = 62.8 \ \Omega$$

The magnitude of the total impedance is

$$Z_{tot} = \sqrt{(R_s + R_L)^2 + (X_L - X_C)^2} = \sqrt{(20 \ \Omega)^2 + (1.53 \text{ k}\Omega)^2} = 1.53 \text{ k}\Omega$$

The current is

$$I = \frac{V_s}{Z_{tot}} = \frac{10 \text{ V}}{1.53 \text{ k}\Omega} = 6.54 \text{ mA}$$

The load power is

$$P_L = I^2 R_L = (6.54 \text{ mA})^2(10 \ \Omega) = \mathbf{428 \ \mu W}$$

For $f = 30$ kHz,

$$X_C = \frac{1}{2\pi(30 \text{ kHz})(0.01 \ \mu\text{F})} = 531 \ \Omega$$

$$X_L = 2\pi(30 \text{ kHz})(1 \text{ mH}) = 189 \ \Omega$$

$$Z_{tot} = \sqrt{(20 \ \Omega)^2 + (342 \ \Omega)^2} = 343 \ \Omega$$

$$I = \frac{V_s}{Z_{tot}} = \frac{10 \text{ V}}{343 \ \Omega} = 29.2 \text{ mA}$$

$$P_L = I^2 R_L = (29.2 \text{ mA})^2(10 \ \Omega) = \mathbf{8.53 \ mW}$$

For $f = 50$ kHz,

$$X_C = \frac{1}{2\pi(50 \text{ kHz})(0.01 \ \mu\text{F})} = 318 \ \Omega$$

$$X_L = 2\pi(50 \text{ kHz})(1 \text{ mH}) = 314 \ \Omega$$

Note that X_C and X_L are very close to being equal which makes the impedances approximately complex conjugates. The exact frequency at which $X_L = X_C$ is 50.3 kHz.

$$Z_{tot} = \sqrt{(20 \ \Omega)^2 + (4 \ \Omega)^2} = 20.4 \ \Omega$$

$$I = \frac{V_s}{Z_{tot}} = \frac{10 \text{ V}}{20.4 \ \Omega} = 490 \text{ mA}$$

$$P_L = I^2 R_L = (490 \text{ mA})^2(10 \ \Omega) = \mathbf{2.40 \ W}$$

For $f = 80$ kHz,

$$X_C = \frac{1}{2\pi(80 \text{ kHz})(0.01 \ \mu\text{F})} = 199 \ \Omega$$

$$X_L = 2\pi(80 \text{ kHz})(1 \text{ mH}) = 503 \ \Omega$$

$$Z_{tot} = \sqrt{(20 \ \Omega)^2 + (304 \ \Omega)^2} = 305 \ \Omega$$

$$I = \frac{V_s}{Z_{tot}} = \frac{10 \text{ V}}{305 \ \Omega} = 32.8 \text{ mA}$$

$$P_L = I^2 R_L = (32.8 \text{ mA})^2(10 \ \Omega) = \mathbf{10.8 \ mW}$$

For $f = 100$ kHz,

$$X_C = \frac{1}{2\pi(100 \text{ kHz})(0.01 \ \mu\text{F})} = 159 \ \Omega$$

$$X_L = 2\pi(100 \text{ kHz})(1 \text{ mH}) = 628 \ \Omega$$

$$Z_{tot} = \sqrt{(20 \ \Omega)^2 + (469 \ \Omega)^2} = 469 \ \Omega$$

$$I = \frac{V_s}{Z_{tot}} = \frac{10 \text{ V}}{469 \text{ }\Omega} = 21.3 \text{ mA}$$

$$P_L = I^2 R_L = (21.3 \text{ mA})^2 (10 \text{ }\Omega) = \textbf{4.54 mW}$$

As you can see from the results, the power to the load peaks at the frequency (50 kHz) for which the load impedance is the complex conjugate of the output impedance (when the reactances are equal in magnitude). A graph of the load power versus frequency is shown in Figure 20–40. Since the maximum power is so much larger than the other values, an accurate plot is difficult to achieve without intermediate values.

FIGURE 20–40

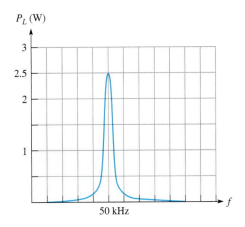

P_L (W)

Related Problem If $R = 47 \text{ }\Omega$ and $C = 0.022 \text{ }\mu\text{F}$ in a series RC circuit, what is the complex conjugate of the impedance at 100 kHz?

EXAMPLE 20–17

(a) Determine the frequency at which maximum power is transferred from the amplifier to the speaker in Figure 20–41(a). The amplifier and coupling capacitor are the source, and the speaker is the load, as shown in the equivalent circuit of Figure 20–41(b).

(b) How many watts of power are delivered to the speaker at this frequency if $V_s = 3.8$ V rms?

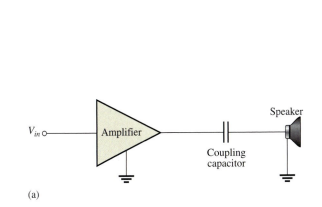

(a)

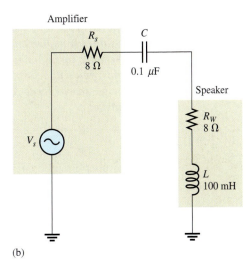

(b)

FIGURE 20–41

Solution

(a) When the power to the speaker is maximum, the source impedance $(R_s - jX_C)$ and the load impedance $(R_W + jX_L)$ are complex conjugates, so

$$X_C = X_L$$

$$\frac{1}{2\pi fC} = 2\pi fL$$

Solving for f,

$$f^2 = \frac{1}{4\pi^2 LC}$$

$$f = \frac{1}{2\pi\sqrt{LC}} = \frac{1}{2\pi\sqrt{(100 \text{ mH})(0.1 \text{ } \mu\text{F})}} \cong \textbf{1.59 kHz}$$

(b) The power to the speaker is calculated as follows:

$$Z_{tot} = R_s + R_W = 8 \text{ } \Omega + 8 \text{ } \Omega = 16 \text{ } \Omega$$

$$I = \frac{V_s}{Z_{tot}} = \frac{3.8 \text{ V}}{16 \text{ } \Omega} = 238 \text{ mA}$$

$$P_{max} = I^2 R_W = (238 \text{ mA})^2 (8 \text{ } \Omega) = \textbf{453 mW}$$

Related Problem Determine the frequency at which maximum power is transferred from the amplifier to the speaker in Figure 20–41 if the coupling capacitor is 1 μF.

SECTION 20–4 REVIEW

1. If the output impedance of a certain driving circuit is 50 $\Omega - j10$ Ω, what value of load impedance will result in the maximum power to the load?

2. For the circuit in Question 1, how much power is delivered to the load when the load impedance is the complex conjugate of the output impedance and when the load current is 2 A?

20–5 ■ TECHnology Theory Into Practice

In this TECH TIP, you are given a sealed band-pass filter module that has been removed from a system and two schematics. Both schematics indicate that the band-pass filter is implemented with a low-pass/high-pass combination. It is uncertain which schematic corresponds to the filter module, but one of them does. By certain measurements, you will determine which schematic represents the filter so that the filter circuit can be reproduced. Also, you will determine the proper load for maximum power transfer.

The filter circuit contained in a sealed module and two schematics, one of which corresponds to the filter circuit, are shown in Figure 20–42.

Filter Measurement and Analysis

■ Based on the oscilloscope measurement of the filter output shown in Figure 20–43, determine which schematic in Figure 20–42 represents the component values of the filter circuit in the module. A 10 V peak-to-peak voltage is applied to the input.

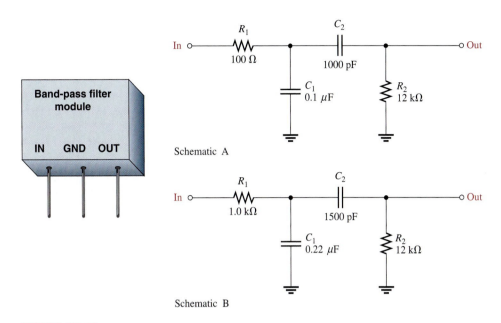

Schematic A

Schematic B

FIGURE 20–42
Filter module and schematics.

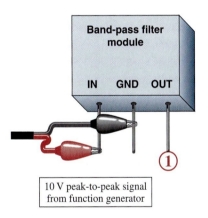

10 V peak-to-peak signal
from function generator

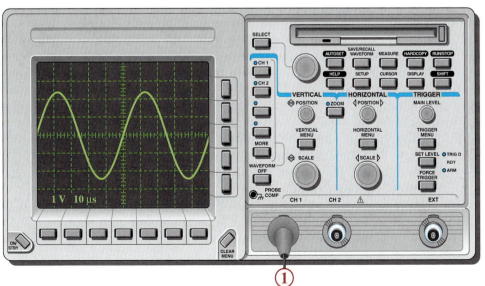

FIGURE 20–43

■ Based on the oscilloscope measurement in Figure 20–43, determine if the filter is operating at its approximate center frequency.

■ Using Thevenin's theorem, determine the load impedance that will provide for maximum power transfer at the center frequency when connected to the output of the filter. Assume the source impedance is zero.

SECTION 20–5 REVIEW

1. Determine the peak-to-peak output voltage at the frequency shown in Figure 20–43 of the circuit in Figure 20–42 that was determined not to be in the module.

2. Find the center frequency of the circuit in Figure 20–42 that was determined not to be in the module.

■ SUMMARY

■ The superposition theorem is useful for the analysis of both ac and dc multiple-source circuits.

■ Thevenin's theorem provides a method for the reduction of any ac circuit to an equivalent form consisting of an equivalent voltage source in series with an equivalent impedance.

■ The term *equivalency,* as used in Thevenin's and Norton's theorems, means that when a given load impedance is connected to the equivalent circuit, it will have the same voltage across it and the same current through it as when it is connected to the original circuit.

■ Norton's theorem provides a method for the reduction of any ac circuit to an equivalent form consisting of an equivalent current source in parallel with an equivalent impedance.

■ Maximum power is transferred to a load when the load impedance is the complex conjugate of the impedance of the driving circuit.

■ GLOSSARY

These terms are also in the end-of-book glossary.

Complex conjugate   An impedance containing the same resistance and a reactance opposite in phase but equal in magnitude to that of a given impedance.

Equivalent circuit   A circuit that produces the same voltage and current to a given load as the original circuit that it replaces.

Norton's theorem   A method for simplifying a two-terminal circuit to an equivalent circuit with only a current source in parallel with an impedance.

Superposition theorem   A method for the analysis of circuits with more than one source.

Thevenin's theorem   A method for simplifying a two-terminal circuit to an equivalent circuit with only a voltage source in series with an impedance.

■ SELF-TEST

1. In applying the superposition theorem,
    (a) all sources are considered simultaneously
    (b) all voltage sources are considered simultaneously
    (c) the sources are considered one at a time with all others replaced by a short
    (d) the sources are considered one at a time with all others replaced by their internal impedances

2. A Thevenin ac equivalent circuit always consists of an equivalent ac voltage source
    (a) and an equivalent capacitance
    (b) and an equivalent inductive reactance
    (c) and an equivalent impedance
    (d) in series with an equivalent capacitive reactance

3. One circuit is equivalent to another when
   (a) the same load has the same voltage and current when connected to either circuit
   (b) different loads have the same voltage and current when connected to either circuit
   (c) the circuits have equal voltage sources and equal series impedances
   (d) the circuits produce the same output voltage

4. The Thevenin equivalent voltage is
   (a) the open circuit voltage   (b) the short circuit voltage
   (c) the voltage across an equivalent load   (d) none of the above

5. The Thevenin equivalent impedance is the impedance looking from
   (a) the source with the output shorted
   (b) the source with the output open
   (c) any two specified open terminals with all sources replaced by their internal impedances
   (d) any two specified open terminals with all sources replaced by a short

6. A Norton ac equivalent circuit always consists of
   (a) an equivalent ac current source in series with an equivalent impedance
   (b) an equivalent ac current source in parallel with an equivalent reactance
   (c) an equivalent ac current source in parallel with an equivalent impedance
   (d) an equivalent ac voltage source in parallel with an equivalent impedance

7. The Norton equivalent current is
   (a) the total current from the source   (b) the short circuit current
   (c) the current to an equivalent load   (d) none of the above

8. The complex conjugate of $50 \, \Omega + j100 \, \Omega$ is
   (a) $50 \, \Omega - j50 \, \Omega$ (b) $100 \, \Omega + j50 \, \Omega$
   (c) $100 \, \Omega - j50 \, \Omega$ (d) $50 \, \Omega - j100 \, \Omega$

9. In order to get maximum power transfer from a capacitive source, the load must
   (a) have a capacitance equal to the source capacitance
   (b) have an impedance equal in magnitude to the source impedance
   (c) be inductive
   (d) have an impedance that is the complex conjugate of the source impedance
   (e) answers (a) and (d)

■ **PROBLEMS**   *More difficult problems are indicated by an asterisk (*).*

SECTION 20–1   The Superposition Theorem

1. Using the superposition method, calculate the current through R_3 in Figure 20–44.
2. Use the superposition theorem to find the current in and the voltage across the R_2 branch of Figure 20–44.

FIGURE 20–44

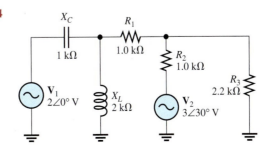

FIGURE 20–45

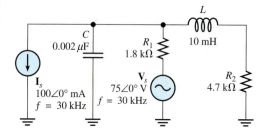

3. Using the superposition theorem, solve for the current through R_1 in Figure 20–45.

4. Using the superposition theorem, find the current through R_L in each circuit of Figure 20–46.

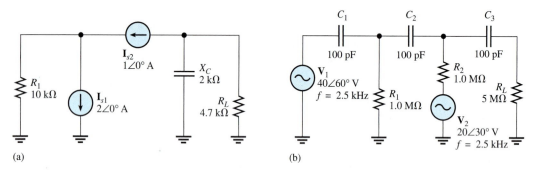

(a)   (b)

FIGURE 20–46

*5. Determine the voltage at each point (A, B, C, D) in Figure 20–47. Assume $X_C = 0$ for all capacitors. Sketch the voltage waveforms at each of the points.

FIGURE 20–47

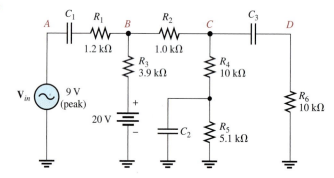

*6. Use the superposition theorem to find the capacitor current in Figure 20–48.

FIGURE 20–48

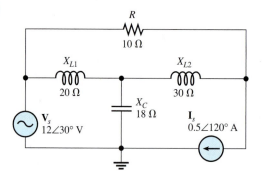

SECTION 20–2 Thevenin's Theorem

7. For each circuit in Figure 20–49, determine the Thevenin equivalent circuit for the portion of the circuit viewed by R_L.

FIGURE 20–49

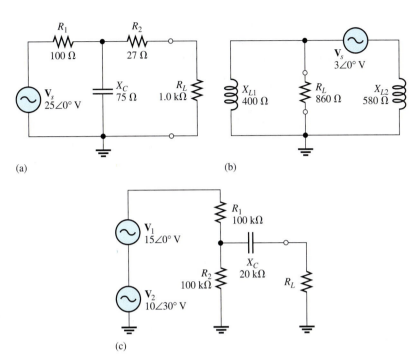

(a)

(b)

(c)

8. Using Thevenin's theorem, determine the current through the load R_L in Figure 20–50.

FIGURE 20–50

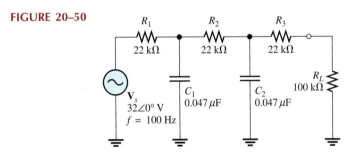

*9. Using Thevenin's theorem, find the voltage across R_4 in Figure 20–51.

FIGURE 20–51

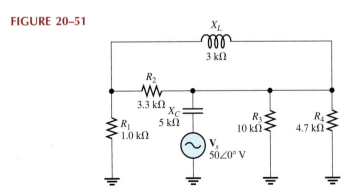

*10. Simplify the circuit external to R_3 in Figure 20–52 to its Thevenin equivalent.

FIGURE 20–52

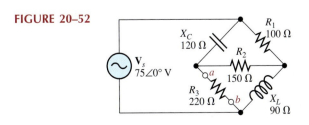

SECTION 20–3 Norton's Theorem

11. For each circuit in Figure 20–49, determine the Norton equivalent as seen by R_L.

12. Using Norton's theorem, find the current through the load resistor R_L in Figure 20–50.

*13. Using Norton's theorem, find the voltage across R_4 in Figure 20–51.

SECTION 20–4 Maximum Power Transfer Theorem

14. For each circuit in Figure 20–53, maximum power is to be transferred to the load R_L. Determine the appropriate value for the load impedance in each case.

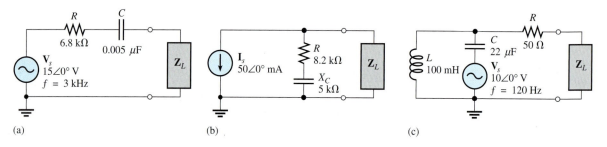

FIGURE 20–53

*15. Determine $\mathbf{Z}_L$ for maximum power in Figure 20–54.

FIGURE 20–54

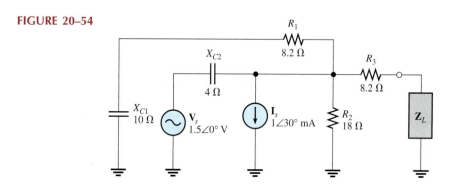

*16. Find the load impedance required for maximum power transfer to $\mathbf{Z}_L$ in Figure 20–55. Determine the maximum true power.

FIGURE 20–55

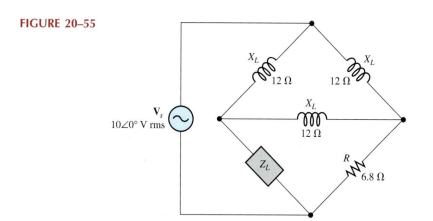

*17. A load is to be connected in the place of R_2 in Figure 20–52 to achieve maximum power transfer. Determine the type of load, and express it in rectangular form.

EWB Troubleshooting and Analysis

These problems require your EWB compact disk.

18. Open file PRO20-18.EWB and determine if there is a fault. If so, find the fault.

19. Open file PRO20-19.EWB and determine if there is a fault. If so, find the fault.

20. Open file PRO20-20.EWB and determine if there is a fault. If so, find the fault.

21. Open file PRO20-21.EWB and determine if there is a fault. If so, find the fault.

22. Open file PRO20-22.EWB and determine the Thevenin equivalent circuit by measurement looking from Point *A*.

23. Open file PRO20-23.EWB and determine the Norton equivalent circuit by measurement looking from Point *A*.

■ ANSWERS TO SECTION REVIEWS

Section 20–1

1. The net current is zero.

2. The circuit can be analyzed one source at a time using superposition.

3. $I_R = 12$ mA

Section 20–2

1. The components of a Thevenin equivalent ac circuit are equivalent voltage source and equivalent series impedance.

2. See Figure 20–56.

FIGURE 20–56

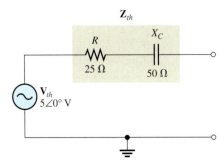

3. $\mathbf{Z}_{th} = 21.5\ \Omega - j15.7\ \Omega;\ \mathbf{V}_{th} = 4.14\angle53.8°$ V

Section 20–3

1. See Figure 20–57.

FIGURE 20–57

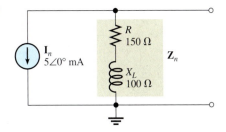

2. $\mathbf{Z}_n = R\angle0° = 1.2\angle0°$ kΩ; $\mathbf{I}_n = 10\angle0°$ mA

Section 20–4

1. $\mathbf{Z}_L = 50\ \Omega + j10\ \Omega$

2. $P_L = 200$ W

Section 20–5

1. $\mathbf{V}_{out} = 166\angle-66.1°$ mV pp

2. $f_0 = 4.76$ kHz

■ **ANSWERS TO RELATED PROBLEMS FOR EXAMPLES**

20–1 $1.77\angle-152°$ mA

20–2 $30\angle90°$ mA

20–3 $1.69\angle47.3°$ mA riding on a dc level of 3 mA

20–4 $18.2\angle43.2°$ V

20–5 $4.03\angle-36.3°$ V

20–6 $4.55\angle24.4°$ V

20–7 $34.3\angle43.2°$ Ω

20–8 $1.37\angle-47.8°$ kΩ

20–9 $9.10\angle-65.6°$ kΩ

20–10 See Figure 20–58.

FIGURE 20–58

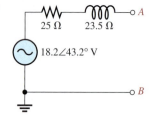

25 Ω   23.5 Ω   A

18.2∠43.2° V

B

20–11 See Figure 20–59.

FIGURE 20–59

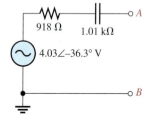

918 Ω   1.01 kΩ   A

4.03∠−36.3° V

B

20–12 See Figure 20–60.

FIGURE 20–60

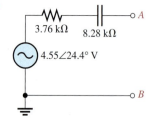

3.76 kΩ   8.28 kΩ   A

4.55∠24.4° V

B

20–13 $117\angle135°$ mA

20–14 $117\angle-78.7°$ Ω

20–15 See Figure 20–61.

FIGURE 20–61

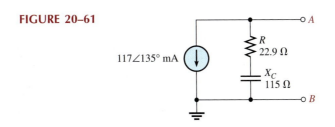

$117\angle 135°$ mA

R
$22.9 \ \Omega$

X_C
$115 \ \Omega$

A

B

20–16 $47 \ \Omega + j72.3 \ \Omega$

20–17 503 Hz

■ **ANSWERS TO SELF-TEST**

1. (d) **2.** (c) **3.** (a) **4.** (a) **5.** (c) **6.** (c) **7.** (b) **8.** (d)

9. (d)

21

PULSE RESPONSE OF REACTIVE CIRCUITS

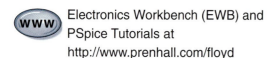

Electronics Workbench (EWB) and PSpice Tutorials at
http://www.prenhall.com/floyd

■ INTRODUCTION

In Chapters 16 and 17, the frequency response of *RC* and *RL* circuits was covered. In this chapter, the response of *RC* and *RL* circuits to pulse inputs is examined. Before starting this chapter, you should review the material in Sections 13–5 and 14–5. Understanding exponential changes in voltages and currents in capacitors and inductors is crucial to the study of pulse response. Throughout this chapter, exponential formulas that were given in Chapters 13 and 14 are used.

With pulse waveform inputs, the time responses of circuits are important. In the areas of pulse and digital circuits, technicians are often concerned with how a circuit responds over an interval of time to rapid changes in voltages or current. The relationship of the circuit time constant to the input pulse characteristics, such as pulse width and period, determines the wave shapes of voltages in the circuit. *Integrator* and *differentiator,* terms used throughout this chapter, refer to mathematical functions that are approximated by these circuits under certain conditions. Mathematical integration is an averaging process, and mathematical differentiation is a process for establishing an instantaneous rate of change of a quantity.

In the TECH TIP in Section 21–10, you will have to specify the circuit wiring. You will also determine component values to meet certain specifications and then determine instrument settings to properly test the circuit.

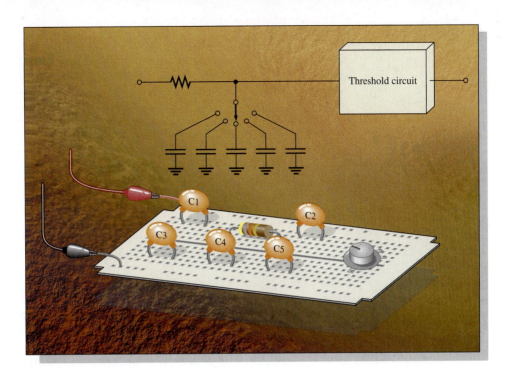

Threshold circuit

■ CHAPTER OBJECTIVES

❑ Explain the operation of an *RC* integrator
❑ Analyze an *RC* integrator with a single input pulse
❑ Analyze an *RC* integrator with repetitive input pulses
❑ Analyze an *RC* differentiator with a single input pulse
❑ Analyze an *RC* differentiator with repetitive input pulses

❑ Analyze the operation of an *RL* integrator
❑ Analyze the operation of an *RL* differentiator
❑ Explain the relationship of time response to frequency response
❑ Troubleshoot *RC* integrators and *RC* differentiators

21–1 ■ THE *RC* INTEGRATOR

In terms of pulse response, a series RC circuit in which the output voltage is taken across the capacitor is known as an integrator. Recall that in terms of frequency response, it is a low-pass filter. The term, integrator, is derived from a mathematical function which this type of circuit approximates under certain conditions.

After completing this section, you should be able to

■ **Explain the operation of an *RC* integrator**
 • Describe how a capacitor charges and discharges
 • Explain how a capacitor reacts to an instantaneous change in voltage or current
 • Describe the basic output voltage waveform

How a Capacitor Charges and Discharges with a Pulse Input

When a pulse generator is connected to the input of an *RC* **integrator,** as shown in Figure 21–1, the capacitor will charge and discharge in response to the pulses. When the input goes from its low level to its high level, the capacitor charges toward the high level of the pulse through the resistor. This charging action is analogous to connecting a battery through a closed switch to the *RC* circuit, as illustrated in Figure 21–2(a). When the pulse goes from its high level back to its low level, the capacitor discharges back through the source. The resistance of the source is assumed to be negligible compared to *R*. This discharging action is analogous to replacing the source with a closed switch, as illustrated in Figure 21–2(b).

FIGURE 21–1

An RC integrating circuit.

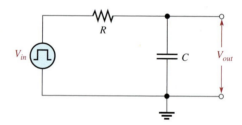

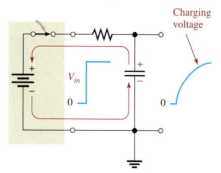

(a) When the input pulse goes HIGH, the source effectively acts as a battery in series with a closed switch, thereby charging the capacitor.

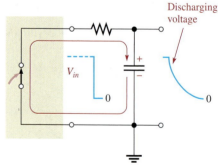

(b) When the input pulse goes back LOW, the source effectively acts as a closed switch, providing a discharge path for the capacitor.

FIGURE 21–2

The equivalent action when a pulse source charges and discharges the capacitor.

As you learned in Chapter 13, a capacitor will charge and discharge following an exponential curve. Its rate of charging and discharging, of course, depends on the *RC* **time constant** ($\tau = RC$).

For an ideal pulse, both edges are considered to be instantaneous. Two basic rules of capacitor behavior help in understanding the **pulse response** of *RC* circuits.

1. The capacitor appears as a short to an instantaneous change in current and as an open to dc.

2. The voltage across the capacitor cannot change instantaneously—it can change only exponentially.

Capacitor Voltage

In an *RC* integrator, the output is the capacitor voltage. The capacitor charges during the time that the pulse is high. If the pulse is at its high level long enough, the capacitor will fully charge to the voltage amplitude of the pulse, as illustrated in Figure 21–3. The capacitor discharges during the time that the pulse is low. If the low time between pulses is long enough, the capacitor will fully discharge to zero, as shown in the figure. Then when the next pulse occurs, it will charge again.

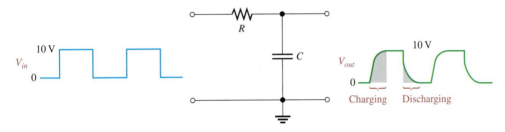

FIGURE 21–3
Illustration of a capacitor fully charging and discharging in response to a pulse input.

SECTION 21–1 REVIEW	**1.** Define the term *integrator* in relation to an *RC* circuit.
	2. What causes the capacitor in an *RC* circuit to charge and discharge?

21–2 ■ SINGLE-PULSE RESPONSE OF *RC* INTEGRATORS

From the previous section, you have a general idea of how an RC integrator responds to a pulse input. In this section, the response to a single pulse is examined in detail.

After completing this section, you should be able to

■ **Analyze an *RC* integrator with a single input pulse**
 • Discuss the importance of the circuit time constant
 • Define *transient time*
 • Determine the response when the pulse width is equal to or greater than five time constants
 • Determine the response when the pulse width is less than five time constants

Two conditions of pulse response must be considered:

1. When the input pulse width (t_W) is equal to or greater than five time constants ($t_W \geq 5\tau$)

2. When the input pulse width is less than five time constants ($t_W < 5\tau$)

Recall that five time constants is accepted as the time for a capacitor to fully charge or fully discharge; this time is often called the **transient time.**

When the Pulse Width Is Equal to or Greater Than Five Time Constants

A capacitor will fully charge if the pulse width is equal to or greater than five time constants (5τ). This condition is expressed as $t_W \geq 5\tau$. At the end of the pulse, the capacitor fully discharges back through the source.

Figure 21–4 illustrates the output waveforms for various RC time constants and a fixed input pulse width. Notice that the shape of the output pulse approaches that of the input as the transient time is made small compared to the pulse width. In each case, the output reaches the full amplitude of the input.

FIGURE 21–4

Variation of an integrator's output pulse shape with time constant. The shaded areas indicate when the capacitor is charging and discharging.

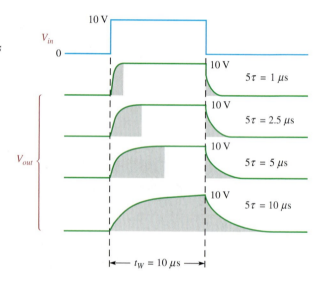

Figure 21–5 shows how a fixed time constant and a variable input pulse width affect the integrator output. Notice that as the pulse width is increased, the shape of the output pulse approaches that of the input. Again, this means that the transient time is short compared to the pulse width.

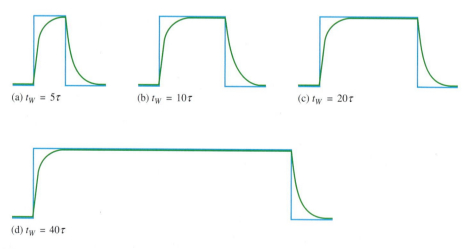

(a) $t_W = 5\tau$

(b) $t_W = 10\tau$

(c) $t_W = 20\tau$

(d) $t_W = 40\tau$

FIGURE 21–5

Variation of an integrator's output pulse shape with input pulse width (the time constant is fixed). Blue is input and green is output.

When the Pulse Width Is Less Than Five Time Constants

Now let's examine the case in which the width of the input pulse is less than five time constants of the integrator. This condition is expressed as $t_W < 5\tau$.

As you know, the capacitor charges for the duration of the pulse. However, because the pulse width is less than the time it takes the capacitor to fully charge (5τ), the output voltage will *not* reach the full input voltage before the end of the pulse. The capacitor only partially charges, as illustrated in Figure 21–6 for several values of *RC* time constants. Notice that for longer time constants, the output reaches a lower voltage because the capacitor cannot charge as much. Of course, in the examples with a single pulse input, the capacitor fully discharges after the pulse ends.

FIGURE 21–6

Capacitor voltage for various time constants that are longer than the input pulse width. Blue is input and green is output.

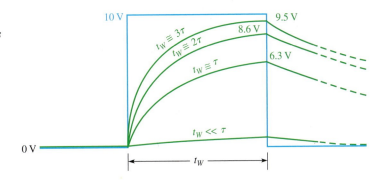

When the time constant is much greater than the input pulse width, the capacitor charges very little, and, as a result, the output voltage becomes almost negligible, as indicated in Figure 21–6.

Figure 21–7 illustrates the effect of reducing the input pulse width for a fixed time constant value. As the width is reduced, the output voltage becomes smaller because the capacitor has less time to charge. However, it takes the capacitor approximtately the same length of time (5τ) to discharge back to zero for each condition after the pulse is removed.

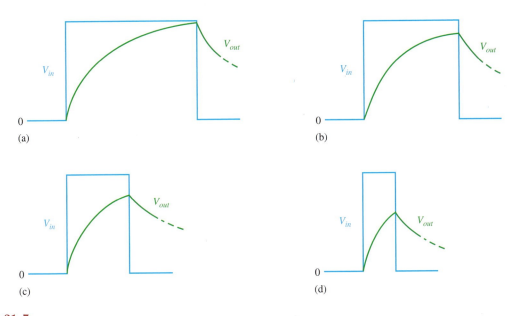

FIGURE 21–7

The capacitor charges less and less as the input pulse width is reduced. The time constant is fixed.

EXAMPLE 21–1

A single 10 V pulse with a width of 100 μs is applied to the integrator in Figure 21–8.
(a) To what voltage will the capacitor charge?
(b) How long will it take the capacitor to discharge if the internal resistance of the pulse source is 50 Ω?
(c) Sketch the output voltage.

FIGURE 21–8

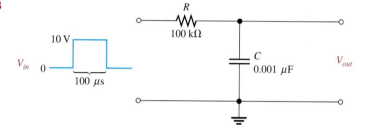

Solution
(a) The circuit time constant is

$$\tau = RC = (100 \text{ k}\Omega)(0.001 \ \mu F) = 100 \ \mu s$$

Notice that the pulse width is exactly equal to the time constant. Thus, the capacitor will charge approximately 63% of the full input amplitude in one time constant, so the output will reach a maximum voltage of

$$V_{out} = (0.63)10 \text{ V} = \mathbf{6.3 \text{ V}}$$

(b) The capacitor discharges back through the source when the pulse ends. You can neglect the 50 Ω source resistance in series with 100 kΩ. The total approximate discharge time, therefore, is

$$5\tau = 5(100 \ \mu s) = \mathbf{500 \ \mu s}$$

(c) The output charging and discharging curve is shown in Figure 21–9.

FIGURE 21–9

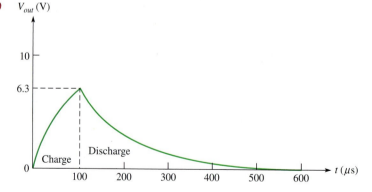

Related Problem If the input pulse width in Figure 21–8 is increased to 200 μs, to what voltage will the capacitor charge?

EXAMPLE 21–2   Determine how much the capacitor in Figure 21–10 will charge when the single pulse is applied to the input.

FIGURE 21–10

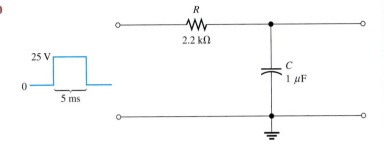

Solution   Calculate the time constant.

$$\tau = RC = (2.2 \text{ k}\Omega)(1 \text{ } \mu\text{F}) = 2.2 \text{ ms}$$

Because the pulse width is 5 ms, the capacitor charges for 2.27 time constants (5 ms/2.2 ms = 2.27). Use the exponential formula from Chapter 13 (Eq. 13–20) to find the voltage to which the capacitor will charge. With $V_F = 25$ V and $t = 5$ ms, the calculation is as follows:

$$v = V_F(1 - e^{-t/RC})$$
$$= (25 \text{ V})(1 - e^{-5ms/2.2ms}) = (25 \text{ V})(1 - e^{-2.27})$$
$$= (25 \text{ V})(1 - 0.103) = (25 \text{ V})(0.897) = \textbf{22.4 V}$$

These calculations show that the capacitor charges to 22.4 V during the 5 ms duration of the input pulse. It will discharge back to zero when the pulse goes back to zero.

Related Problem   Determine how much C will charge if the pulse width is increased to 10 ms.

SECTION 21–2 REVIEW

1. When an input pulse is applied to an RC integrator, what condition must exist in order for the output voltage to reach full amplitude?

2. For the circuit in Figure 21–11, which has a single input pulse, find the maximum output voltage and determine how long the capacitor will discharge.

3. For Figure 21–11, sketch the approximate shape of the output voltage with respect to the input pulse.

4. If an integrator time constant equals the input pulse width, will the capacitor fully charge?

5. Describe the condition under which the output voltage has the approximate shape of a rectangular input pulse.

FIGURE 21–11

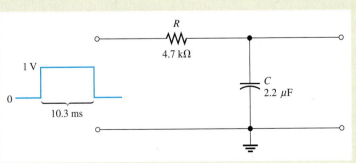

21–3 ■ REPETITIVE-PULSE RESPONSE OF *RC* INTEGRATORS

In the last section, you learned how an RC integrator responds to a single-pulse input. These basic ideas are extended in this section to include the integrator response to repetitive pulses. In electronic systems, you will encounter repetitive-pulse waveforms much more often than single pulses. However, an understanding of the integrator's response to single pulses is necessary in order to understand how these circuits respond to repeated pulses.

After completing this section, you should be able to

■ **Analyze an *RC* integrator with repetitive input pulses**
  • Determine the response when the capacitor does not fully charge or discharge
  • Define *steady state*
  • Describe the effect of an increase in time constant on circuit response

If a **periodic** pulse waveform is applied to an *RC* integrator, as shown in Figure 21–12, *the output waveshape depends on the relationship of the circuit time constant and the frequency (period) of the input pulses.* The capacitor, of course, charges and discharges in response to a pulse input. The amount of charge and discharge of the capacitor depends both on the circuit time constant and on the input frequency, as mentioned.

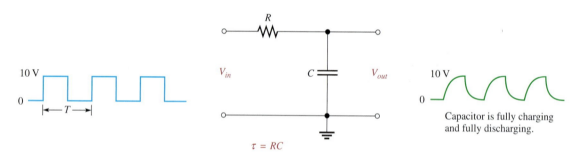

$\tau = RC$

FIGURE 21–12
RC integrator with a repetitive pulse waveform input (T = 10τ).

If the pulse width and the time between pulses are each equal to or greater than five time constants, the capacitor will fully charge and fully discharge during each period of the input waveform. This case is shown in Figure 21–12.

When a Capacitor Does Not Fully Charge and Discharge

When the pulse width and the time between pulses are shorter than five time constants, as illustrated in Figure 21–13 for a square wave, the capacitor will *not* completely charge or discharge. We will now examine the effects of this situation on the output voltage of the *RC* integrator.

For illustration, let's use an *RC* integrator with a charging and discharging time constant equal to the pulse width of a 10 V square wave input, as shown in Figure 21–14. This choice will simplify the analysis and will demonstrate the basic action of the integrator under these conditions. At this point, we really do not care what the exact time constant value is because we know from Chapter 13 that an *RC* circuit charges approximately 63% during one time constant interval.

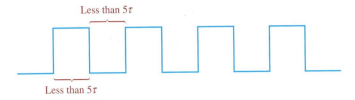

FIGURE 21–13

Input waveform that does not allow full charge or discharge of the capacitor in an RC integrator.

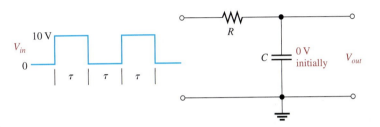

FIGURE 21–14

Integrator with a square wave input having a period equal to two time constants ($T = 2\tau$).

Let's assume that the capacitor in Figure 21–14 begins initially uncharged and examine the output voltage on a pulse-by-pulse basis. The results of this analysis are shown in Figure 21–15.

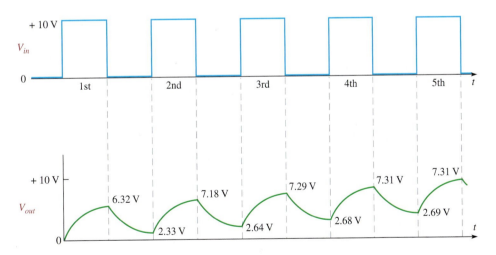

FIGURE 21–15

Input and output for the initially uncharged integrator in Figure 21–14.

First pulse   During the first pulse, the capacitor charges. The output voltage reaches 6.32 V (63.2% of 10 V), as shown in Figure 21–15.

Between first and second pulses   The capacitor discharges, and the voltage decreases to 36.8% of the voltage at the beginning of this interval: 0.368(6.32 V) = 2.33 V.

Second pulse   The capacitor voltage begins at 2.33 V and increases 63.2% of the way to 10 V. This calculation is as follows: The total charging range is 10 V − 2.33 V = 7.67 V. The capacitor voltage will increase an additional 63.2% of 7.67 V, which is 4.85 V. Thus, at the end of the second pulse, the output voltage is 2.33 V + 4.85 V = 7.18 V, as shown in Figure 21–15. Notice that the average is building up.

Between second and third pulses   The capacitor discharges during this time, and therefore the voltage decreases to 36.8% of the initial voltage by the end of the second pulse: 0.368(7.18 V) = 2.64 V.

Third pulse   At the start of the third pulse, the capacitor voltage begins at 2.64 V. The capacitor charges 63.2% of the way from 2.64 V to 10 V: 0.632(10 V − 2.64 V) = 4.65 V. Therefore, the voltage at the end of the third pulse is 2.64 V + 4.65 V = 7.29 V.

Between third and fourth pulses   The voltage during this interval decreases due to capacitor discharge. It will decrease to 36.8% of its value by the end of the third pulse. The final voltage in this interval is 0.368(7.29 V) = 2.68 V.

Fourth pulse   At the start of the fourth pulse, the capacitor voltage is 2.68 V. The voltage increases by 0.632(10 V − 2.68 V) = 4.63 V. Therefore, at the end of the fourth pulse, the capacitor voltage is 2.68 V + 4.63 V = 7.31 V. Notice that the values are leveling off as the pulses continue.

Between fourth and fifth pulses   Between these pulses, the capacitor voltage drops to 0.368(7.31 V) = 2.69 V.

Fifth pulse   During the fifth pulse, the capacitor charges 0.632(10 V − 2.69 V) = 4.62 V. Since it started at 2.69 V, the voltage at the end of the pulse is 2.69 V + 4.62 V = 7.31 V.

Steady-State Response

In the preceding discussion, the output voltage gradually built up and then began leveling off. It takes approximately 5τ for the output voltage to build up to a constant average value. This interval is the transient time of the circuit. Once the output voltage reaches the average value of the input voltage, a **steady-state** condition is reached which continues as long as the periodic input continues. This condition is illustrated in Figure 21–16 based on the values obtained in the preceding discussion.

The transient time for our example circuit is the time from the beginning of the first pulse to the end of the third pulse. The reason for this interval is that the capacitor voltage at the end of the third pulse is 7.29 V, which is about 99% of the final voltage.

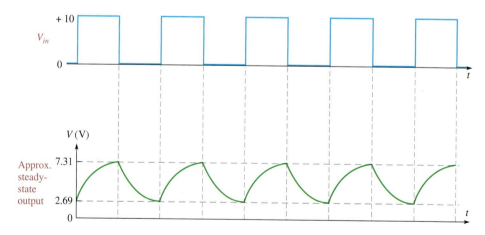

FIGURE 21–16
Output reaches steady state after 5τ.

The Effect of an Increase in Time Constant

What happens to the output voltage if the RC time constant of the integrator is increased with a variable resistor, as indicated in Figure 21–17? As the time constant is increased, the capacitor charges less during a pulse and discharges less between pulses. The result is

FIGURE 21–17
Integrator with a variable time constant.

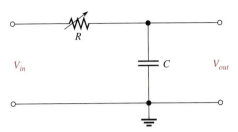

a smaller fluctuation in the output voltage for increasing values of time constant, as shown in Figure 21–18.

As the time constant becomes extremely long compared to the pulse width, the output voltage approaches a constant dc voltage, as shown in Figure 21–18(c). This value is the average value of the input. For a square wave, it is one-half the amplitude.

FIGURE 21–18

Effect of longer time constants on the output of an integrator ($\tau_3 > \tau_2 > \tau_1$).

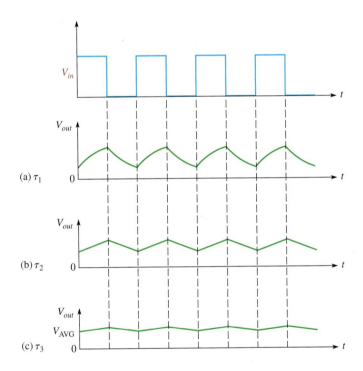

EXAMPLE 21–3   Determine the output voltage waveform for the first two pulses applied to the integrator in Figure 21–19. Assume that the capacitor is initially uncharged and the rheostat is set to 5 kΩ.

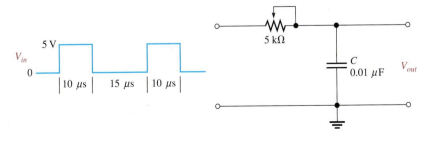

FIGURE 21–19

Solution First, calculate the circuit time constant.

$$\tau = RC = (5 \text{ k}\Omega)(0.01 \ \mu\text{F}) = 50 \ \mu\text{s}$$

Obviously, the time constant is much longer than the input pulse width or the interval between pulses (notice that the input is not a square wave). Thus, in this case, the exponential formulas must be applied, and the analysis is relatively difficult. Follow the solution carefully.

1. *Calculation for first pulse:* Use the equation for an increasing exponential because C is charging. Note that V_F is 5 V, and t equals the pulse width of 10 μs. Therefore,

$$v_C = V_F(1 - e^{-t/RC}) = (5 \text{ V})(1 - e^{-10\mu s/50\mu s})$$
$$= (5 \text{ V})(1 - 0.819) = \textbf{906 mV}$$

This result is plotted in Figure 21–20(a).

FIGURE 21–20

(a)

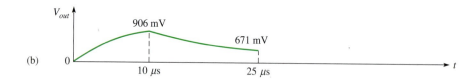

(b)

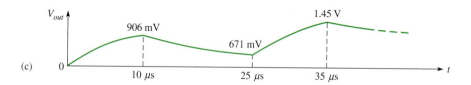

(c)

2. *Calculation for interval between first and second pulse:* Use the equation for a decreasing exponential because C is discharging. Note that V_i is 906 mV because C begins to discharge from this value at the end of the first pulse. The discharge time is 15 μs. Therefore,

$$v_C = V_i e^{-t/RC} = (906 \text{ mV})e^{-15\mu s/50\mu s}$$
$$= (906 \text{ mV})(0.741) = \textbf{671 mV}$$

This result is shown in Figure 21–20(b).

3. *Calculation for second pulse:* At the beginning of the second pulse, the output voltage is 671 mV. During the second pulse, the capacitor will again charge. In this case, it does not begin at zero volts. It already has 671 mV from the previous charge and discharge. To handle this situation, you must use the general exponential formula.

$$v = V_F + (V_i - V_F)e^{-t/\tau}$$

Using this equation, you can calculate the voltage across the capacitor at the end of the second pulse as follows:

$$v_C = V_F + (V_i - V_F)e^{-t/RC}$$
$$= 5 \text{ V} + (671 \text{ mV} - 5 \text{ V})e^{-10\mu s/50\mu s}$$
$$= 5 \text{ V} + (-4.33 \text{ V})(0.819) = 5 \text{ V} - 3.55 \text{ V} = \textbf{1.45 V}$$

This result is shown in Figure 21–20(c).

Notice that the output waveform builds up on successive input pulses. After approximately 5τ, it will reach its steady state and will fluctuate between a constant maximum and a constant minimum, with an average equal to the average value of the input. You can see this pattern by carrying the analysis in this example further.

Related Problem Determine V_{out} at the beginning of the third pulse.

SECTION 21–3 REVIEW

1. What conditions allow an *RC* integrator capacitor to fully charge and discharge when a periodic pulse waveform is applied to the input?

2. What will the output waveform look like if the circuit time constant is extremely small compared to the pulse width of a square wave input?

3. When 5τ is greater than the pulse width of an input square wave, the time required for the output voltage to build up to a constant average value is called _____.

4. Define *steady-state response*.

5. What does the average value of the output voltage of an integrator equal during steady state?

21–4 ■ SINGLE-PULSE RESPONSE OF *RC* DIFFERENTIATORS

In terms of pulse response, a series RC circuit in which the output voltage is taken across the resistor is known as a differentiator. Recall that in terms of frequency response, it is a high-pass filter. The term, differentiator, is derived from a mathematical function which this type of circuit approximates under certain conditions.

After completing this section, you should be able to

■ **Analyze an *RC* differentiator with a single input pulse**
  • Describe the response at the rising edge of the input pulse
  • Determine the response during and at the end of a pulse for various pulse width–time constant relationships

Figure 21–21 shows an *RC* **differentiator** with a pulse input. The same action occurs in a differentiator as in an integrator, except the output voltage is taken across the resistor rather than the capacitor. The capacitor charges exponentially at a rate depending on the *RC* time constant. The shape of the differentiator's resistor voltage is determined by the charging and discharging action of the capacitor.

FIGURE 21–21
An RC differentiating circuit.

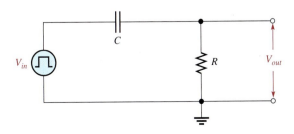

Pulse Response

To understand how the output voltage is shaped by a differentiator, you must consider the following:

1. The response to the rising pulse edge

2. The response between the rising and falling edges

3. The response to the falling pulse edge

Response to the Rising Edge of the Input Pulse Let's assume that the capacitor is initially uncharged prior to the rising pulse edge. Prior to the pulse, the input is zero volts. Thus, there are zero volts across the capacitor and also zero volts across the resistor, as indicated in Figure 21–22(a).

(a) Before pulse is applied

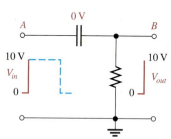

(b) At rising edge of input pulse

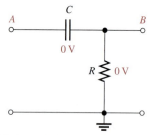

(c) During level part of pulse when $t_W \geq 5\tau$

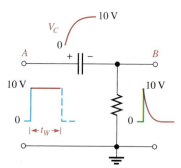

(d) At falling edge of pulse when $t_W \geq 5\tau$

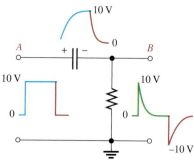

(e) During level part of pulse when $t_W < 5\tau$

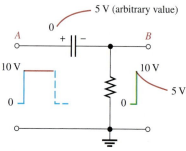

(f) At falling edge of pulse when $t_W < 5\tau$

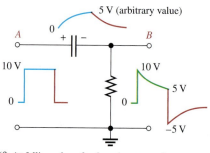

FIGURE 21–22

Examples of the response of a differentiator to a single input pulse under two conditions: $t_W \geq 5\tau$ *and* $t_W < 5\tau$.

Let's also assume that a 10 V pulse is applied to the input. When the rising edge occurs, point *A* goes to +10 V. Recall that the voltage across a capacitor cannot change instantaneously, and thus the capacitor appears instantaneously as a short. Therefore, if point *A* goes instantly to +10 V, then point *B* *must* also go instantly to +10 V, keeping the capacitor voltage zero for the instant of the rising edge. The capacitor voltage is the voltage from point *A* to point *B*.

The voltage at point *B* with respect to ground is the voltage across the resistor (and the output voltage). Thus, the output voltage suddenly goes to +10 V in response to the rising pulse edge, as indicated in Figure 21–22(b).

Response During Pulse When $t_W \geq 5\tau$ While the pulse is at its high level between the rising edge and the falling edge, the capacitor is charging. When the pulse width is equal to or greater than five time constants ($t_W \geq 5\tau$), the capacitor has time to fully charge.

As the voltage across the capacitor builds up exponentially, the voltage across the resistor decreases exponentially until it reaches zero volts at the time the capacitor reaches full charge (+10 V in this case). This decrease in the resistor voltage occurs because the sum of the capacitor voltage and the resistor voltage at any instant must be equal to the applied voltage, in compliance with Kirchhoff's voltage law ($v_C + v_R = v_{in}$). This part of the response is illustrated in Figure 21–22(c).

Response to Falling Edge When $t_W \geq 5\tau$ Let's examine the case in which the capacitor is fully charged at the end of the pulse ($t_W \geq 5\tau$). Refer to Figure 21–22(d). On the falling edge, the input pulse suddenly goes from +10 V back to zero. An instant before the falling edge, the capacitor is charged to 10 V, so point *A* is +10 V and point *B* is 0 V. The voltage across a capacitor cannot change instantaneously, so when point *A* makes a transition from +10 V to zero on the falling edge, point *B* *must* also make a 10 V transition from zero to −10 V. This keeps the voltage across the capacitor at 10 V for the instant of the falling edge.

The capacitor now begins to discharge exponentially. As a result, the resistor voltage goes from −10 V to zero in an exponential curve, as indicated in Figure 21–22(d).

Response During Pulse When $t_W < 5\tau$ When the pulse width is less than five time constants ($t_W < 5\tau$), the capacitor does not have time to fully charge. Its partial charge depends on the relation of the time constant and the pulse width.

Because the capacitor does not reach the full +10 V, the resistor voltage will not reach zero volts by the end of the pulse. For example, if the capacitor charges to +5 V during the pulse interval, the resistor voltage will decrease to +5 V, as illustrated in Figure 21–22(e).

Response to Falling Edge When $t_W < 5\tau$ Now, let's examine the case in which the capacitor is only partially charged at the end of the pulse ($t_W < 5\tau$). For example, if the capacitor charges to +5 V, the resistor voltage at the instant before the falling edge is also +5 V because the capacitor voltage plus the resistor voltage must add up to +10 V, as illustrated in Figure 21–22(e).

When the falling edge occurs, point *A* goes from +10 V to zero. As a result, point *B* goes from +5 V to −5 V, as illustrated in Figure 21–22(f). This decrease occurs, of course, because the capacitor voltage cannot change at the instant of the falling edge. Immediately after the falling edge, the capacitor begins to discharge to zero. As a result, the resistor voltage goes from −5 V to zero, as shown.

Summary of Differentiator Response to a Single Pulse

A good way to summarize this section is to look at the general output waveforms of a differentiator as the time constant is varied from one extreme, when 5τ is much less than the pulse width, to the other extreme, when 5τ is much greater than the pulse width. These situations are illustrated in Figure 21–23. In part (a) of the figure, the output consists of narrow positive and negative "spikes." In part (f), the output approaches the shape of the input. Various conditions between these extremes are illustrated in parts (b) through (e).

You may have observed a pulse that looks similar to Figure 21–23(f) when you ac couple a pulse to an oscilloscope. In this case the capacitor in the oscilloscope coupling circuit can act as an unwanted differentiating circuit, causing the pulse to droop. To avoid this, you can dc couple the scope and check the probe compensation.

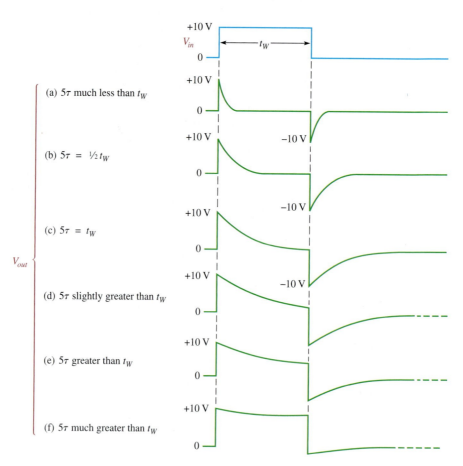

FIGURE 21–23
Effects of a change in time constant on the shape of the output voltage of a differentiator.

EXAMPLE 21–4   Sketch the output voltage for the circuit in Figure 21–24.

FIGURE 21–24

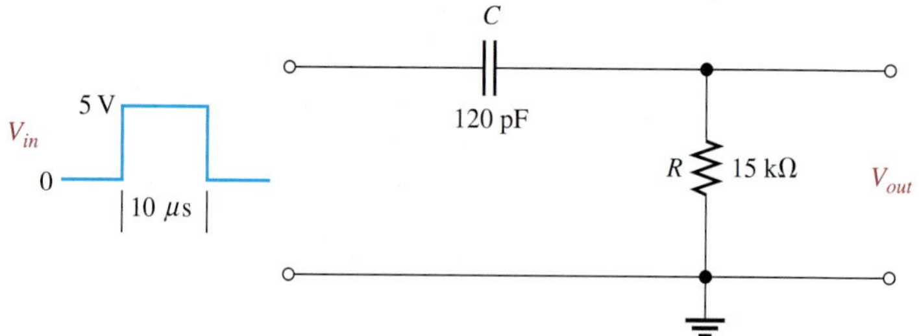

Solution   First, calculate the time constant.

$$\tau = RC = (15\ k\Omega)(120\ pF) = 1.8\ \mu s$$

In this case, $t_W > 5\tau$, so the capacitor reaches full charge before the end of the pulse.

On the rising edge, the resistor voltage jumps to +5 V and then decreases expo-nentially to zero by the end of the pulse. On the falling edge, the resistor voltage jumps to −5 V and then goes back to zero exponentially. The resistor voltage is, of course, the output, and its shape is shown in Figure 21–25.

FIGURE 21–25

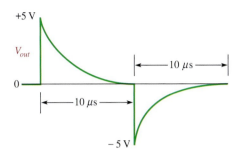

Related Problem Sketch the output voltage if *C* is changed to 12 pF in Figure 21–24.

EXAMPLE 21–5

Determine the output voltage waveform for the differentiator in Figure 21–26 with the rheostat set so that the total resistance is 2 kΩ.

FIGURE 21–26

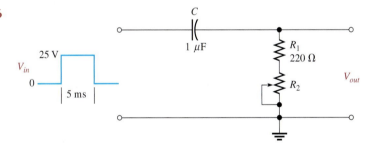

Solution First, calculate the time constant.

$$\tau = (2\ \text{k}\Omega)(1\ \mu\text{F}) = 2\ \text{ms}$$

On the rising edge, the resistor voltage immediately jumps to +25 V. Because the pulse width is 5 ms, the capacitor charges for 2.5 time constants and therefore does not reach full charge. Thus, you must use the formula for a decreasing exponential in order to calculate to what voltage the output decreases by the end of the pulse.

$$v_{out} = V_i e^{-t/RC} = 25e^{-5\text{ms}/2\text{ms}} = 25(0.082) = 2.05\ \text{V}$$

where $V_i = 25$ V and $t = 5$ ms. This calculation gives the resistor voltage (v_{out}) at the end of the 5 ms pulse width interval.

On the falling edge, the resistor voltage immediately jumps from +2.05 V down to −22.95 V (a 25 V transition). The resulting waveform of the output voltage is shown in Figure 21–27.

FIGURE 21–27

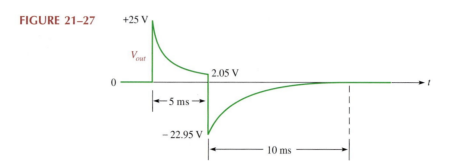

Related Problem Determine the voltage at the end of the pulse in Figure 21–26 if the rheostat is set so that the total resistance is 1.5 kΩ.

SECTION 21–4
REVIEW

1. Sketch the output of a differentiator for a 10 V input pulse when $5\tau = 0.5t_W$.
2. Under what condition does the output pulse shape most closely resemble the input pulse for a differentiator?
3. What does the differentiator output look like when 5τ is much less than the pulse width of the input?
4. If the resistor voltage in a differentiating circuit is down to +5 V at the end of a 15 V input pulse, to what negative value will the resistor voltage go in response to the falling edge of the input?

21–5 ■ REPETITIVE-PULSE RESPONSE OF *RC* DIFFERENTIATORS

The RC differentiator response to a single pulse, covered in the last section, is extended in this section to repetitive pulses.

After completing this section, you should be able to

■ **Analyze an *RC* differentiator with repetitive input pulses**
  • Determine the response when the pulse width is less than five time constants

If a periodic pulse waveform is applied to an *RC* differentiating circuit, two conditions again are possible: $t_W \geq 5\tau$ or $t_W < 5\tau$. Figure 21–28 shows the output when $t_W = 5\tau$. As the time constant is reduced, both the positive and the negative portions of the output become narrower. Notice that the average value of the output is zero.

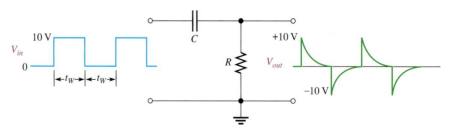

FIGURE 21–28
Example of differentiator response when $t_W = 5\tau$.

Figure 21–29 shows the steady-state output when $t_W < 5\tau$. As the time constant is increased, the positively and negatively sloping portions become flatter. For a very long time constant, the output approaches the shape of the input, but with an average value of zero. An average value of zero means that the waveform has equal positive and negative portions. The average value of a waveform is its **dc component.** Because a capacitor blocks dc, the dc component of the input is prevented from passing through to the output.

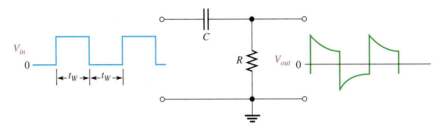

FIGURE 21–29
Example of differentiator response when $t_W < 5\tau$.

Like the integrator, the differentiator output takes time (5τ) to reach steady state. To illustrate the response, let's take an example in which the time constant equals the input pulse width.

Analysis of a Repetitive Waveform

At this point, we do not care what the circuit time constant is because we know that the resistor voltage will decrease to approximately 37% of its maximum value during one pulse (1τ). Let's assume that the capacitor in Figure 21–30 begins initially uncharged and then examine the output voltage on a pulse-by-pulse basis. The results of the analysis that follows are shown in Figure 21–31.

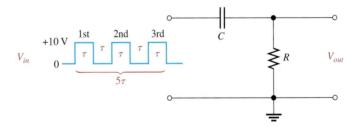

FIGURE 21–30
RC differentiator with $\tau = t_W$.

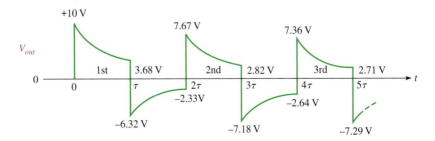

FIGURE 21–31
Differentiator output waveform during transient time for the circuit in Figure 21–30.

First pulse   On the rising edge, the output instantaneously jumps to +10 V. Then the capacitor partially charges to 63.2% of 10 V, which is 6.32 V. Thus, the output voltage must decrease to 3.68 V, as shown in Figure 21–31.

On the falling edge, the output instantaneously makes a negative-going 10 V transition to −6.32 V (−10 V + 3.68 V = −6.32 V).

Between first and second pulses   The capacitor discharges to 36.8% of 6.32 V, which is 2.33 V. Thus, the resistor voltage, which starts at −6.32 V, must increase to −2.33 V. Why? Because at the instant prior to the next pulse, the input voltage is zero. Therefore, the sum of v_C and v_R must be zero (2.33 V − 2.33 V = 0). Remember that $v_C + v_R = v_{in}$ at all times, in accordance with Kirchhoff's voltage law.

Second pulse   On the rising edge, the output makes an instantaneous, positive-going, 10 V transition from −2.33 V to 7.67 V. Then by the end of the pulse the capacitor charges $0.632 \times (10 \text{ V} − 2.33 \text{ V}) = 4.85$ V. Thus, the capacitor voltage increases from 2.33 V to 2.33 V + 4.85 V = 7.18 V. The output voltage drops to 0.368×7.67 V = 2.82 V.

On the falling edge, the output instantaneously makes a negative-going transition from 2.82 V to −7.18 V, as shown in Figure 21–31.

Between second and third pulses   The capacitor discharges to 36.8% of 7.18 V, which is 2.64 V. Thus, the output voltage starts at −7.18 V and increases to −2.64 V because the capacitor voltage and the resistor voltage must add up to zero at the instant prior to the third pulse (the input is zero).

Third pulse   On the rising edge, the output makes an instantaneous 10 V transition from −2.64 V to +7.36 V. Then the capacitor charges $0.632 \times (10 \text{ V} − 2.64 \text{ V}) = 4.65$ V to 2.64 V + 4.65 V = 7.29 V. As a result, the output voltage drops to 0.368×7.36 V = 2.71 V. On the falling edge, the output instantly goes from +2.71 V down to −7.29 V.

After the third pulse, five time constants have elapsed, and the output voltage is close to its steady state. Thus, it will continue to vary from a positive maximum of about +7.3 V to a negative maximum of about −7.3 V, with an average value of zero.

SECTION 21–5 REVIEW

1. What conditions allow an *RC* differentiator to fully charge and discharge when a periodic pulse waveform is applied to the input?

2. What will the output waveform look like if the circuit time constant is extremely small compared to the pulse width of a square wave input?

3. What does the average value of the differentiator output voltage equal during steady state?

21–6 ■ PULSE RESPONSE OF *RL* INTEGRATORS

A series RL circuit in which the output voltage is taken across the resistor is known as an integrator in terms of pulse response.

After completing this section, you should be able to

■ **Analyze the operation of an *RL* integrator**
  • Determine the response to a single input pulse

Figure 21–32 shows an *RL* integrator. The output waveform is taken across the resistor and, under equivalent conditions, is the same shape as that for the *RC* integrator. Recall that in the *RC* case, the output was across the capacitor.

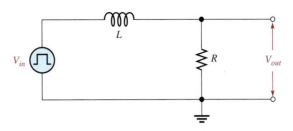

FIGURE 21–32

An RL integrating circuit.

As you know, each edge of an ideal pulse is considered to be instantaneous. Two basic rules for inductor behavior will aid in analyzing *RL* circuit responses to pulse inputs:

1. The inductor appears as an open to an instantaneous change in current and as a short (ideally) to dc.

2. The current in an inductor cannot change instantaneously—it can change only exponentially.

Response of the Integrator to a Single Pulse

When a pulse generator is connected to the input of the integrator and the voltage pulse goes from its low level to its high level, the inductor prevents a sudden change in current. As a result, the inductor acts as an open, and all of the input voltage is across it at the instant of the rising pulse edge. This situation is indicated in Figure 21–33(a).

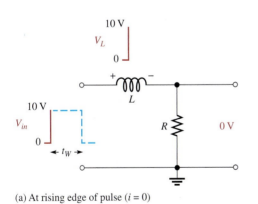

(a) At rising edge of pulse (*i* = 0)

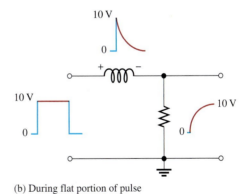

(b) During flat portion of pulse

(c) At falling edge of pulse and after

FIGURE 21–33

Illustration of the pulse response of an RL integrator (t_W > 5τ).

After the rising edge, the current builds up, and the output voltage follows the current as it increases exponentially, as shown in Figure 21–33(b). The current can reach a maximum of V_p/R if the transient time is shorter than the pulse width ($V_p = 10$ V in this example).

When the pulse goes from its high level to its low level, an induced voltage with reversed polarity is created across the coil in an effort to keep the current equal to V_p/R. The output voltage begins to decrease exponentially, as shown in Figure 21–33(c).

The exact shape of the output depends on the L/R time constant as summarized in Figure 21–34 for various relationships between the time constant and the pulse width. You should note that the response of this RL circuit in terms of the shape of the output is identical to that of the RC integrator. The relationship of the L/R time constant to the input pulse width has the same effect as the RC time constant that we discussed earlier in this chapter. For example, when $t_W < 5\tau$, the output voltage will not reach its maximum possible value.

FIGURE 21–34

Illustration of the variation in integrator output pulse shape with time constant.

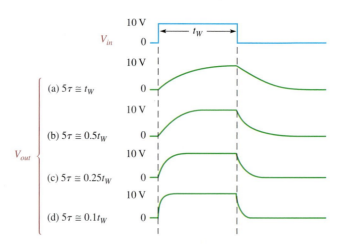

EXAMPLE 21–6

Determine the maximum output voltage for the integrator in Figure 21–35 when a single pulse is applied as shown. The rheostat is set so that the total resistance is 50 Ω.

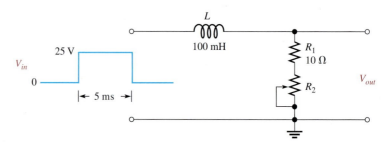

FIGURE 21–35

Solution   Calculate the time constant.

$$\tau = \frac{L}{R} = \frac{100 \text{ mH}}{50 \text{ }\Omega} = 2 \text{ ms}$$

Because the pulse width is 5 ms, the inductor charges for 2.5τ. Use the exponential formula to calculate the voltage.

$$v_{out(max)} = V_F(1 - e^{-t/\tau}) = 25(1 - e^{-5\text{ms}/2\text{ms}})$$
$$= 25(1 - e^{-2.5}) = 25(1 - 0.082) = 25(0.918) = \mathbf{22.9 \text{ V}}$$

Related Problem   To what resistance must the rheostat, R_2, be set for the output voltage to reach 25 V by the end of the pulse in Figure 21–35?

EXAMPLE 21–7

A pulse is applied to the *RL* integrator circuit in Figure 21–36. Determine the complete waveshapes and the values for I, V_R, and V_L.

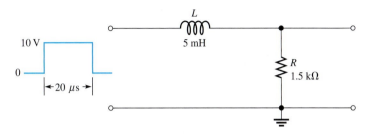

FIGURE 21–36

Solution   The circuit time constant is

$$\tau = \frac{L}{R} = \frac{5 \text{ mH}}{1.5 \text{ k}\Omega} = 3.33 \ \mu s$$

Since $5\tau = 16.7 \ \mu s$ is less than t_W, the current will reach its maximum value and remain there until the end of the pulse.

At the rising edge of the pulse,

$$i = 0 \text{ A}$$
$$v_R = 0 \text{ V}$$
$$v_L = 10 \text{ V}$$

The inductor initially appears as an open, so all of the input voltage appears across L.

During the pulse,

$$i \text{ increases exponentially to } \frac{V_p}{R} = \frac{10 \text{ V}}{1.5 \text{ k}\Omega} = 6.67 \text{ mA in } 16.7 \ \mu s$$

v_R increases exponentially to 10 V in 16.7 μs

v_L decreases exponentially to zero in 16.7 μs

At the falling edge of the pulse,

$$i = 6.67 \text{ mA}$$
$$v_R = 10 \text{ V}$$
$$v_L = -10 \text{ V}$$

After the pulse,

i decreases exponentially to zero in 16.7 μs

v_R decreases exponentially to zero in 16.7 μs

v_L decreases exponentially to zero in 16.7 μs

The waveforms are shown in Figure 21–37.

FIGURE 21–37

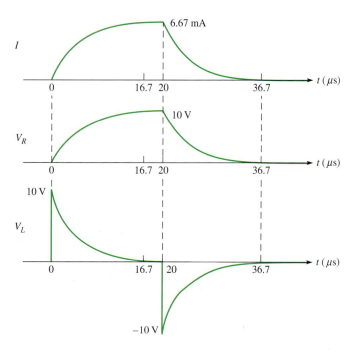

Related Problem What will be the maximum output voltage if the amplitude of the input pulse is increased to 20 V in Figure 21–36?

EXAMPLE 21–8

A 10 V pulse with a width of 1 ms is applied to the integrator in Figure 21–38. Determine the voltage level that the output will reach during the pulse. If the source has an internal resistance of 30 Ω, how long will it take the output to decay to zero? Sketch the output voltage waveform.

FIGURE 21–38

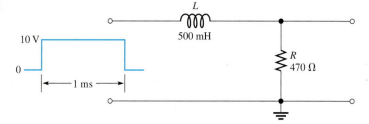

Solution The coil charges through the 30 Ω source resistance plus the 470 Ω external resistor. The time constant is

$$\tau = \frac{L}{R_{tot}} = \frac{500 \text{ mH}}{470 \text{ Ω} + 30 \text{ Ω}} = \frac{500 \text{ mH}}{500 \text{ Ω}} = 1 \text{ ms}$$

Notice that in this case the pulse width is exactly equal to τ. Thus, the output V_R will reach approximately 63% of the full input amplitude in 1τ. Therefore, the output voltage gets to **6.3 V** at the end of the pulse.

After the pulse is gone, the inductor discharges back through the 30 Ω source and the 470 Ω resistor. The source takes **5τ** to completely discharge.

$$5\tau = 5(1 \text{ ms}) = 5 \text{ ms}$$

The output voltage is shown in Figure 21–39.

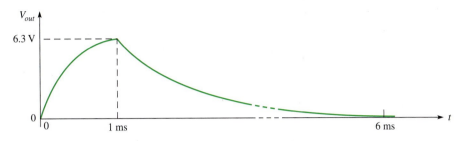

FIGURE 21–39

Related Problem   To what value must *R* be changed to allow the output voltage to reach the input level during the pulse?

SECTION 21–6 REVIEW

1. In an *RL* integrator, across which component is the output voltage taken?
2. When a pulse is applied to an *RL* integrator, what condition must exist in order for the output voltage to reach the amplitude of the input?
3. Under what condition will the output voltage have the approximate shape of the input pulse?

21–7 ▪ PULSE RESPONSE OF *RL* DIFFERENTIATORS

A series RL circuit in which the output voltage is taken across the inductor is known as a differentiator.

After completing this section, you should be able to

▪ **Analyze the operation of an *RL* differentiator**
  • Determine the response to a single input pulse

Response of the Differentiator to a Single Pulse

Figure 21–40 shows an *RL* differentiator with a pulse generator connected to the input. Initially, before the pulse, there is no current in the circuit. When the input pulse goes from its low level to its high level, the inductor prevents a sudden change in current. It does so, as you know, with an induced voltage equal and opposite to the input. As a result, *L* looks like an open, and all of the input voltage appears across it at the instant of the rising edge, as shown in Figure 21–41(a) with a 10 V pulse.

FIGURE 21–40
An RL differentiating circuit.

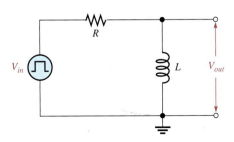

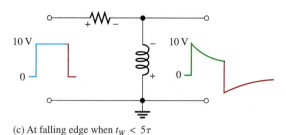

(a) At rising edge of pulse

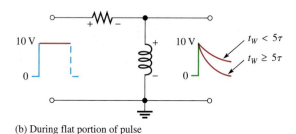

(b) During flat portion of pulse

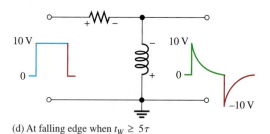

(c) At falling edge when $t_W < 5\tau$

(d) At falling edge when $t_W \geq 5\tau$

FIGURE 21–41

Illustration of the response of an RL differentiator for both time constant conditions.

During the pulse, the current exponentially builds up. As a result, the inductor voltage decreases, as shown in Figure 21–41(b). The rate of decrease, as you know, depends on the L/R time constant. When the falling edge of the input appears, the inductor reacts to keep the current as is, by creating an induced voltage in a direction as indicated in Figure 21–41(c). This reaction is seen as a sudden negative-going transition of the inductor voltage, as indicated in Figure 21–41(c) and (d).

Two conditions are possible, as indicated in Figure 21–41(c) and (d). In part (c), 5τ is greater than the input pulse width, and the output voltage does not have time to decay to zero. In part (d), 5τ is less than or equal to the pulse width, and so the output decays to zero before the end of the pulse. In this case a full, negative, 10 V transition occurs at the trailing edge.

Keep in mind that as far as the input and output waveforms are concerned, the RL integrator and differentiator perform the same as their RC counterparts.

A summary of the RL differentiator response for relationships of various time constants and pulse widths is shown in Figure 21–42.

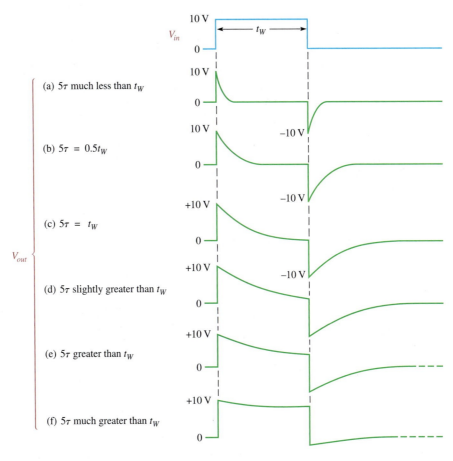

(a) 5τ much less than t_W

(b) $5\tau = 0.5t_W$

(c) $5\tau = t_W$

V_{out}

(d) 5τ slightly greater than t_W

(e) 5τ greater than t_W

(f) 5τ much greater than t_W

FIGURE 21–42

Illustration of the variation in output pulse shape with the time constant.

EXAMPLE 21–9   Sketch the output voltage for the circuit in Figure 21–43.

FIGURE 21–43

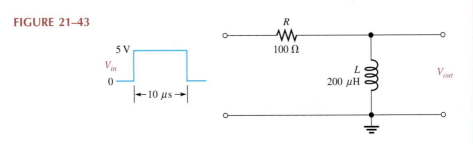

Solution   First, calculate the time constant.

$$\tau = \frac{L}{R} = \frac{200\ \mu H}{100\ \Omega} = 2\ \mu s$$

In this case, $t_W = 5\tau$, so the output will decay to zero at the end of the pulse.

On the rising edge, the inductor voltage jumps to +5 V and then decays exponentially to zero. It reaches approximately zero at the instant of the falling edge. On the falling edge of the input, the inductor voltage jumps to −5 V and then goes back to zero. The output waveform is shown in Figure 21–44.

FIGURE 21–44

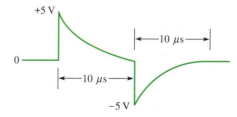

Related Problem Sketch the output voltage if the pulse width is reduced to 5 μs in Figure 21–43.

EXAMPLE 21–10 Determine the output voltage waveform for the differentiator in Figure 21–45.

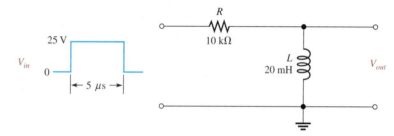

FIGURE 21–45

Solution First, calculate the time constant.

$$\tau = \frac{L}{R} = \frac{20 \text{ mH}}{10 \text{ k}\Omega} = 2 \text{ } \mu s$$

On the rising edge, the inductor voltage immediately jumps to +25 V. Because the pulse width is 5 μs, the inductor charges for only 2.5τ, so you must use the formula for a decreasing exponential.

$$v_L = V_i e^{-t/\tau} = 25 e^{-5\mu s/2\mu s} = 25 e^{-2.5} = 25(0.082) = 2.05 \text{ V}$$

This result is the inductor voltage at the end of the 5 μs input pulse.

On the falling edge, the output immediately jumps from +2.05 V down to −22.95 V (a 25 V negative-going transition). The complete output waveform is sketched in Figure 21–46.

FIGURE 21–46

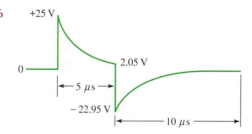

Related Problem What must be the value of R for the output voltage to reach zero by the end of the pulse in Figure 21–45?

SECTION 21–7
REVIEW

1. In an *RL* differentiator, across which component is the output taken?

2. Under what condition does the output pulse shape most closely resemble the input pulse?

3. If the inductor voltage in an *RL* differentiator is down to +2 V at the end of a +10 V input pulse, to what negative voltage will the output go in response to the falling edge of the input?

21–8 ■ RELATIONSHIP OF TIME (PULSE) RESPONSE TO FREQUENCY RESPONSE

A definite relationship exists between time (pulse) response and frequency response. The fast rising and falling edges of a pulse waveform contain the higher frequency components. The flatter portions of the pulse waveform, which are the tops of the pulses, represent slow changes or lower frequency components. The average value of the pulse waveform is its dc component.

After completing this section, you should be able to

■ **Explain the relationship of time response to frequency response**
  • Describe a pulse waveform in terms of its frequency components
  • Explain how *RC* and *RL* integrators act as filters
  • Explain how *RC* and *RL* differentiators act as filters
  • State the formulas that relate rise and fall times to frequency

The relationships of pulse characteristics and frequency content of pulse waveforms are indicated in Figure 21–47.

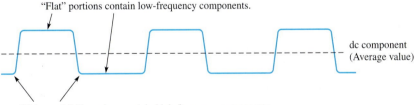

"Flat" portions contain low-frequency components.

dc component
(Average value)

Rising and falling edges contain high-frequency components.

FIGURE 21–47
General relationship of a pulse waveform to frequency content.

The *RC* Integrator Acts as a Low-Pass Filter

As you learned, the integrator tends to exponentially "round off" the edges of the applied pulses. This rounding off occurs to varying degrees, depending on the relationship of the time constant to the pulse width and period. The rounding off of the edges indicates that the integrator tends to reduce the higher frequency components of the pulse waveform, as illustrated in Figure 21–48.

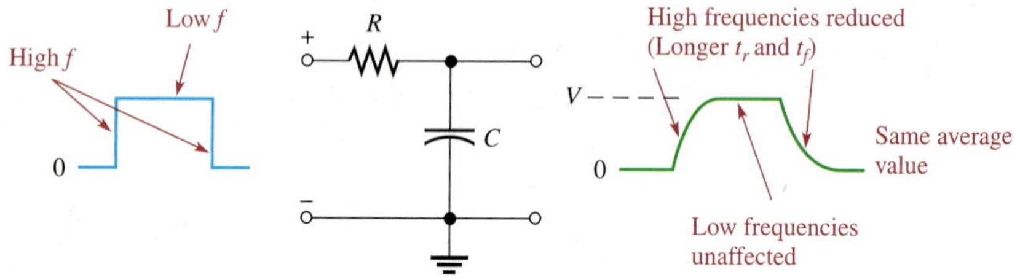

FIGURE 21–48

Time and frequency response relationship in an integrator (one pulse in a repetitive waveform shown).

The *RL* Integrator Acts as a Low-Pass Filter

Like the *RC* integrator, the *RL* integrator also acts as a basic low-pass filter, because *L* is in series between the input and output. X_L is small for low frequencies and offers little opposition. It increases with frequency, so at higher frequencies most of the total voltage is dropped across *L* and very little across *R*, the output. If the input is dc, *L* is like a short ($X_L = 0$). At high frequencies, *L* becomes like an open, as illustrated in Figure 21–49.

FIGURE 21–49

Low-pass filter action.

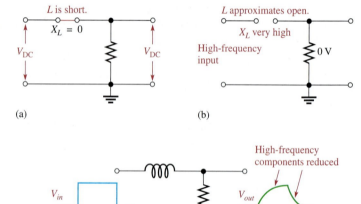

The *RC* Differentiator Acts as a High-Pass Filter

As you know, the differentiator tends to introduce tilt to the flat portion of a pulse. That is, it tends to reduce the lower frequency components of a pulse waveform. Also, it completely eliminates the dc component of the input and produces a zero average-value output. This action is illustrated in Figure 21–50.

FIGURE 21–50

Time and frequency response relationship in a differentiator (one pulse in a repetitive waveform shown).

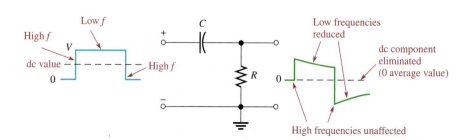

The *RL* Differentiator Acts as a High-Pass Filter

Again like the *RC* differentiator, the *RL* differentiator also acts as a basic high-pass filter. Because *L* is connected across the output, less voltage is developed across it at lower frequencies than at higher ones. There are zero volts across the output for dc (ignoring windng resistance). For high frequencies, most of the input voltage is dropped across the output coil ($X_L = 0$ for dc; $X_L \cong$ open for high frequencies). Figure 21–51 shows high-pass filter action.

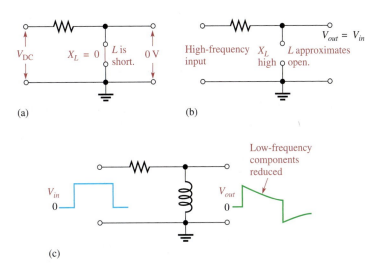

FIGURE 21–51
High-pass filter action.

Formula Relating Rise Time and Fall Time to Frequency

It can be shown that the fast transitions of a pulse (rise time, t_r, and fall time, t_f) are related to the highest frequency component, f_h, in that pulse by the following formula:

$$t_r = \frac{0.35}{f_h} \qquad \text{(21–1)}$$

This formula also applies to fall time, and the fastest transition determines the highest frequency in the pulse waveform.

Equation (21–1) can be rearranged to give the highest frequency as follows:

$$f_h = \frac{0.35}{t_r} \qquad \text{(21–2)}$$

or

$$f_h = \frac{0.35}{t_f} \qquad \text{(21–3)}$$

EXAMPLE 21–11   What is the highest frequency contained in a pulse that has rise and fall times equal to 10 nanoseconds (10 ns)?

Solution
$$f_h = \frac{0.35}{t_r} = \frac{0.35}{10 \times 10^{-9} \text{ s}} = 0.035 \times 10^9 \text{ Hz}$$
$$= 35 \times 10^6 \text{ Hz} = \textbf{35 MHz}$$

Related Problem   What is the highest frequency in a pulse with $t_r = 20$ ns and $t_f = 15$ ns?

SECTION 21–8 REVIEW

1. What type of filter is an integrator?
2. What type of filter is a differentiator?
3. What is the highest frequency component in a pulse waveform having t_r and t_f equal to 1 μs?

21–9 ■ TROUBLESHOOTING

In this section, RC circuits with pulse inputs are used to demonstrate the effects of common component failures in selected cases. The concepts can then be easily related to RL circuits.

After completing this section, you should be able to

■ Troubleshoot *RC* integrators and *RC* differentiators
  • Recognize the effect of an open capacitor
  • Recognize the effect of a leaky capacitor
  • Recognize the effect of a shorted capacitor
  • Recognize the effect of an open resistor

Open Capacitors

If the capacitor in an *RC* integrator opens, the output has the same waveshape as the input, as shown in Figure 21–52(a). If the capacitor in a differentiator opens, the output is zero because it is held at ground through the resistor, as illustrated in part (b).

Leaky Capacitor

If the capacitor in an *RC* integrator becomes leaky, three things happen: (a) the time constant will be effectively reduced by the leakage resistance (when thevenized, looking from *C* it appears in parallel with *R*); (b) the waveshape of the output voltage (across *C*) is altered from normal by a shorter charging time; and (c) the amplitude of the output is reduced because *R* and R_{leak} effectively act as a voltage divider. These effects are illustrated in Figure 21–53(a).

If the capacitor in a differentiator becomes leaky, the time constant is reduced, just as in the integrator (they are both simply series *RC* circuits). When the capacitor reaches full charge, the output voltage (across *R*) is set by the effective voltage-divider action of *R* and R_{leak}, as shown in Figure 21–53(b).

FIGURE 21–52

Examples of the effect of an open capacitor.

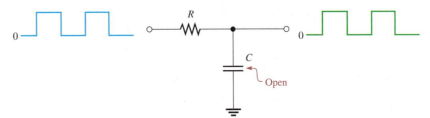

(a) Integrator

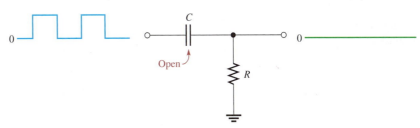

(b) Differentiator

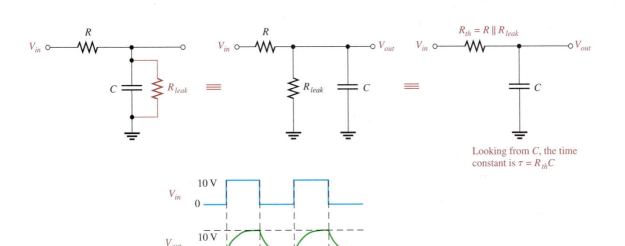

(a)

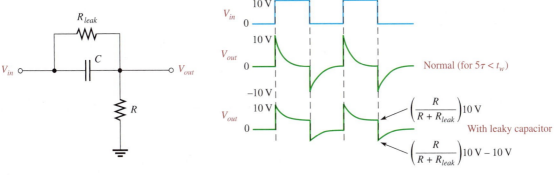

(b)

FIGURE 21–53

Examples of the effect of a leaky capacitor.

Shorted Capacitor

If the capacitor in an *RC* integrator shorts, the output is at ground as shown in Figure 21–54(a). If the capacitor in a differentiator shorts, the output is the same as the input, as shown in part (b).

FIGURE 21–54

Examples of the effect of a shorted capacitor.

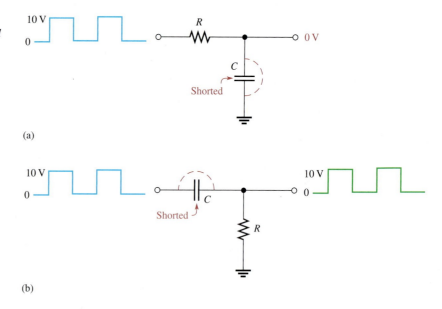

Open Resistor

If the resistor in an *RC* integrator opens, the capacitor has no discharge path, and, ideally, it will hold its charge. In an actual situation, the charge will gradually leak off or the capacitor will discharge slowly through a measuring instrument connected to the output. This is illustrated in Figure 21–55(a).

FIGURE 21–55

Examples of the effects of an open resistor.

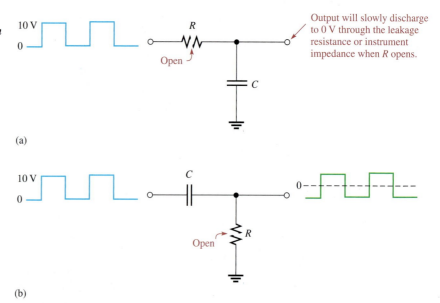

If the resistor in a differentiator opens, the output looks like the input except for the dc level because the capacitor now must charge and discharge through the extremely high resistance of the oscilloscope, as shown in Figure 21–55(b).

SECTION 21–9 REVIEW

1. An *RC* integrator has a zero output with a square wave input. What are the possible causes of this problem?

2. If the capacitor in a differentiator is shorted, what is the output for a square wave input?

21–10 ■ TECHnology Theory Into Practice

In this TECH TIP section, you are asked to build and test a time-delay circuit that will provide five switch-selectable delay times. An RC integrator is selected for this application. The input is a 5 V pulse of long duration, and the output goes to a threshold trigger circuit that is used to turn the power on to a portion of a system at any of the five selected time intervals after the occurrence of the original pulse.

A schematic of the selectable time-delay integrator circuit is shown in Figure 21–56. The *RC* integrator is driven by a pulse input; and the output is an exponentially increasing voltage that is used to trigger a threshold circuit at the 3.5 V level, which then turns power on to part of a system. The basic concept is shown in Figure 21–57. In this application, the delay time of the integrator is specified to be the time from the rising edge of the input pulse to the point where the output voltage reaches 3.5 V. The specified delay times are as listed in Table 21–1.

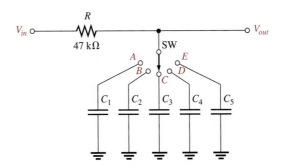

FIGURE 21–56
Integrator delay circuit.

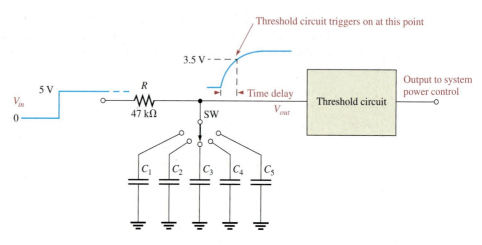

FIGURE 21–57
Illustration of the time-delay application.

TABLE 21–1

Switch Position	Delay Time
A	10 ms
B	25 ms
C	40 ms
D	65 ms
E	85 ms

Capacitor Values

■ Determine a value for each capacitor that will provide the specified delay times within 10%. Select from the following list of standard values (all are in μF): 0.1, 0.12, 0.15, 0.18, 0.22, 0.27, 0.33, 0.39, 0.47, 0.56, 0.68, 0.82, 1.0, 1.2, 1.5, 1.8, 2.2, 2.7, 3.3, 3.9, 4.7, 5.6, 6.8, 8.2.

Circuit Connections

Refer to Figure 21–58. The components for the *RC* integrator in Figure 21–56 are assembled, but not interconnected, on the circuit board.

■ Using the circled numbers, develop a point-to-point wiring list to properly connect the circuit on the board.
■ Indicate, using the appropriate circled numbers, how you would connect the instruments to test the circuit.

Test Procedure

■ Specify the function, amplitude, and minimum frequency settings for the function generator in order to test all output delay times in Figure 21–58.
■ Specify the minimum oscilloscope settings for measuring each of the specified delay times in Figure 21–58.

FIGURE 21–58

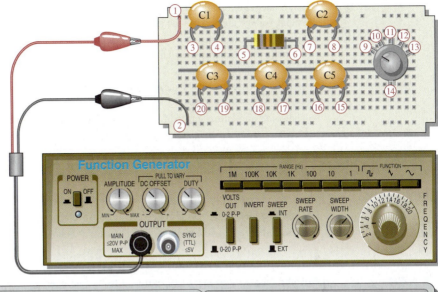

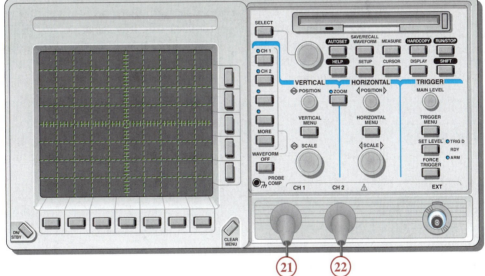

SECTION 21–10 REVIEW

1. To add an additional time delay to the circuit of Figure 21–57, what changes must be made?

2. An additional time delay of 100 ms is required for the time-delay circuit. Determine the capacitor value that should be added.

■ **SUMMARY**

■ In an *RC* integrating circuit, the output voltage is taken across the capacitor.

■ In an *RC* differentiating circuit, the output voltage is taken across the resistor.

■ In an *RL* integrating circuit, the output voltage is taken across the resistor.

■ In an *RL* differentiating circuit, the output voltage is taken across the inductor.

■ In an integrator, when the pulse width (t_W) of the input is much less than the transient time, the output voltage approaches a constant level equal to the average value of the input.

■ In an integrator, when the pulse width of the input is much greater than the transient time, the output voltage approaches the shape of the input.

■ In a differentiator, when the pulse width of the input is much less than the transient time, the output voltage approaches the shape of the input but with an average value of zero.

■ In an differentiator, when the pulse width of the input is much greater than the transient time, the output voltage consists of narrow, positive-going and negative-going spikes occurring on the leading and trailing edges of the input pulses.

■ The rising and falling edges of a pulse waveform contain the higher frequency components.

■ The flat portion of the pulse contains the lower frequency components.

■ GLOSSARY

These terms are also in the end-of-book glossary.

DC component   The average value of a pulse waveform.

Differentiator   A circuit producing an output that approaches the mathematical derivative of the input.

Integrator   A circuit producing an output that approaches the mathematical integral of the input.

Periodic   Characterized by a repetition at fixed-time intervals.

Pulse response   In electric circuits, the reaction of a circuit to a given pulse input.

Steady state   The equilibrium condition of a circuit that occurs after an initial transient time.

Time constant   A fixed-time interval, set by R and C, or R and L values, that determines the time response of a circuit.

Transient time   An interval equal to approximately five time constants.

■ FORMULAS

(21–1)	$t_r = \dfrac{0.35}{f_h}$	Rise time
(21–2)	$f_h = \dfrac{0.35}{t_r}$	Highest frequency in relation to rise time
(21–3)	$f_h = \dfrac{0.35}{t_f}$	Highest frequency in relation to fall time

■ SELF-TEST

1. The output of an RC integrator is taken across the
   (a) resistor   (b) capacitor   (c) source   (d) coil

2. When a 10 V input pulse with a width equal to one time constant is applied to an RC integrator, the capacitor charges to
   (a) 10 V   (b) 5 V   (c) 6.3 V   (d) 3.7 V

3. When a 10 V pulse with a width equal to one time constant is applied to an RC differentiator, the capacitor charges to
   (a) 6.3 V   (b) 10 V   (c) 0 V   (d) 3.7 V

4. In an RC integrator, the output pulse closely resembles the input pulse when
   (a) τ is much larger than the pulse width   (b) τ is equal to the pulse width
   (c) τ is less than the pulse width   (d) τ is much less than the pulse width

5. In an RC differentiator, the output pulse closely resembles the input pulse when
   (a) τ is much larger than the pulse width   (b) τ is equal to the pulse width
   (c) τ is less than the pulse width   (d) τ is much less than the pulse width

6. The positive and negative portions of a differentiator's output voltage are equal when
   (a) $5\tau < t_W$ (b) $5\tau > t_W$
   (c) $5\tau = t_W$ (d) $5\tau > 0$
   (e) both (a) and (c)   (f) both (b) and (d)

7. The output of an RL integrator is taken across the

   (a) resistor   (b) coil   (c) source   (d) capacitor

8. The maximum possible current in an RL integrator is

   (a) $I = V_p/X_L$ (b) $I = V_p/Z$ (c) $I = V_p/R$

9. The current in an RL differentiator reaches its maximum possible value when

   (a) $5\tau = t_W$ (b) $5\tau < t_W$ (c) $5\tau > t_W$ (d) $\tau = 0.5t_W$

10. If you have an RC and an RL differentiator with equal time constants sitting side-by-side and you apply the same input pulse to both,

   (a) the RC has the widest output pulse

   (b) the RL has the most narrow spikes on the output

   (c) the output of one is an increasing exponential and the output of the other is a decreasing exponential

   (d) you can't tell the difference by observing the output waveforms

---

■ PROBLEMS

SECTION 21–1 The RC Integrator

1. An integrating circuit has $R = 2.2$ kΩ in series with $C = 0.05$ μF. What is the time constant?

2. Determine how long it takes the capacitor in an integrating circuit to reach full charge for each of the following series RC combinations:

   (a) $R = 56$ Ω, $C = 50$ μF   (b) $R = 3300$ Ω, $C = 0.015$ μF

   (c) $R = 22$ kΩ, $C = 100$ pF   (d) $R = 5.6$ MΩ, $C = 10$ pF

SECTION 21–2 Single-Pulse Response of RC Integrators

3. A 20 V pulse is applied to an RC integrator. The pulse width equals one time constant. To what voltage does the capacitor charge during the pulse? Assume that it is initially uncharged.

4. Repeat Problem 3 for the following values of t_W:

   (a) 2τ (b) 3τ (c) 4τ (d) 5τ

5. Sketch the approximate shape of an integrator output voltage where 5τ is much less than the pulse width of a 10 V square-wave input. Repeat for the case in which 5τ is much larger than the pulse width.

6. Determine the output voltage for an integrator with a single input pulse, as shown in Figure 21–59. For repetitive pulses, how long will it take this circuit to reach steady state?

FIGURE 21–59

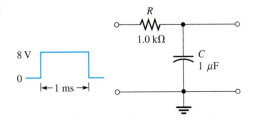

7. (a) What is τ in Figure 21–60?   (b) Sketch the output voltage.

FIGURE 21–60

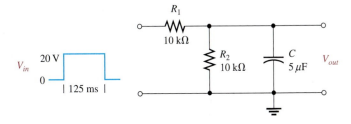

SECTION 21–3   Repetitive-Pulse Response of *RC* Integrators

8. Sketch the integrator in Figure 21–61, showing maximum voltages.

FIGURE 21–61

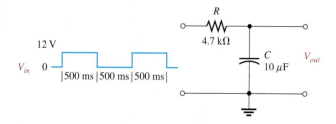

9. A 1 V, 10 kHz pulse waveform with a duty cycle of 25% is applied to an integrator with $\tau = 25 \mu s$. Graph the output voltage for three initial pulses. *C* is initially uncharged.

10. What is the steady-state output voltage of the integrator with a square-wave input shown in Figure 21–62?

FIGURE 21–62

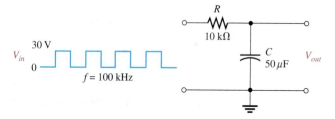

SECTION 21–4   Single-Pulse Response of *RC* Differentiators

11. Repeat Problem 5 for an *RC* differentiator.

12. Redraw the circuit in Figure 21–60 to make it a differentiator, and repeat Problem 6.

13. **(a)** What is τ in Figure 21–63?   **(b)** Sketch the output voltage.

FIGURE 21–63

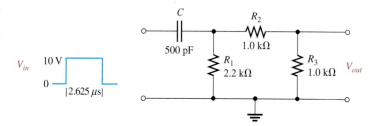

SECTION 21–5   Repetitive-Pulse Response of *RC* Differentiators

14. Sketch the differentiator output in Figure 21–64, showing maximum voltages.

FIGURE 21–64

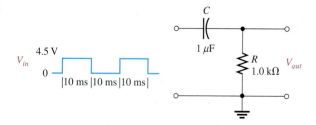

15. What is the steady-state output voltage of the differentiator with the square-wave input shown in Figure 21–65?

FIGURE 21–65

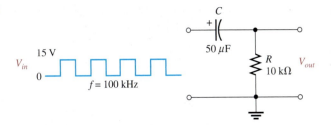

SECTION 21–6 Pulse Response of *RL* Integrators

16. Determine the output voltage for the circuit in Figure 21–66. A single input pulse is applied as shown.

FIGURE 21–66

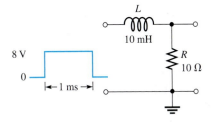

17. Sketch the integrator in Figure 21–67, showing maximum voltages.

FIGURE 21–67

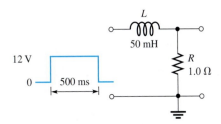

18. Determine the time constant in Figure 21–68. Is this circuit an integrator or a differentiator?

FIGURE 21–68

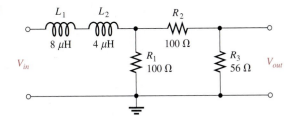

SECTION 21–7 Pulse Response of *RL* Differentiators

19. (a) What is τ in Figure 21–69?   (b) Sketch the output voltage.

20. Draw the output waveform if a periodic pulse waveform with $t_W = 25$ μs and $T = 60$ μs is applied to the circuit in Figure 21–69.

FIGURE 21–69

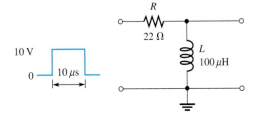

SECTION 21–8   Relationship of Time (Pulse) Response to Frequency Response

21. What is the highest frequency component in the output of an integrator with $\tau = 10$ μs? Assume that $5\tau < t_W$.

22. A certain pulse waveform has a rise time of 55 ns and a fall time of 42 ns. What is the highest frequency component in the waveform?

SECTION 21–9   Troubleshooting

23. Determine the most likely fault(s), in the circuit of Figure 21–70(a) for each set of waveforms in parts (b) through (d). V_{in} is a square wave with a period of 8 ms.

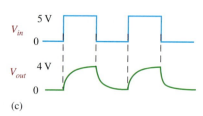

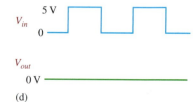

(a)

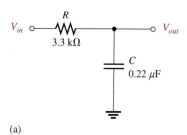

(b)

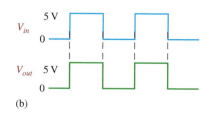

(c)

(d)

FIGURE 21–70

24. Determine the most likely fault(s), if any, in the circuit of Figure 21–71(a) for each set of waveforms in parts (b) through (d). V_{in} is a square wave with a period of 8 ms.

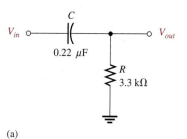

(a)

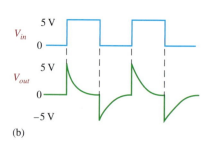

(b)

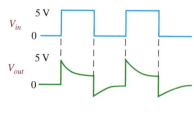

(c)

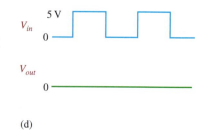

(d)

FIGURE 21–71

EWB Troubleshooting and Analysis

These problems require your EWB compact disk.

25. Open file PRO21-25.EWB and determine if there is a fault. If so, find the fault.

26. Open file PRO21-26.EWB and determine if there is a fault. If so, find the fault.

27. Open file PRO21-27.EWB and determine if there is a fault. If so, find the fault.

28. Open file PRO21-28.EWB and determine if there is a fault. If so, find the fault.

■ **ANSWERS TO SECTION REVIEWS**

Section 21–1

1. An integrator is a series RC circuit in which the output is across the capacitor.

2. A voltage applied to the input causes the capacitor to charge. A short across the input causes the capacitor to discharge.

Section 21–2

1. For the output of an integrator to reach amplitude, $5\tau \le t_W$.

2. $V_{out(max)} = 630$ mV; $t_{disch} = 51.7$ ms

3. See Figure 21–72.

FIGURE 21–72

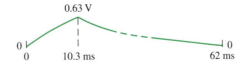

0.63 V

0   10.3 ms   62 ms

4. No, C will not fully charge.

5. The output has approximately the shape of the input when $5\tau \ll t_W$ (5τ much less than t_W).

Section 21–3

1. C will fully charge and discharge when $5\tau \le t_W$ and $5\tau \le$ time between pulses.

2. When $\tau \ll t_W$, the output is approximately like the input.

3. Transient time

4. Steady-state response is the response after the transient time has passed.

5. The average value of the output equals the average value of the input voltage.

Section 21–4

1. See Figure 21–73.

FIGURE 21–73

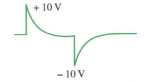

+ 10 V

– 10 V

2. The output resembles the input when $5\tau \gg t_W$.

3. The output appears to be positive and negative spikes.

4. V_R will go to -10 V.

Section 21–5

1. C will fully charge and discharge when $5\tau \le t_W$ and $5\tau \le$ time between pulses.

2. The output appears to be positive and negative spikes.

3. The average value is 0 V.

Section 21–6

1. The output is taken across the resistor.
2. The output reaches the input amplitude when $5\tau \leq t_W$.
3. The output has the approximate shape of the input when $5\tau \ll t_W$.

Section 21–7

1. The output is taken across the inductor.
2. The output has the approximate shape of the input when $5\tau \gg t_W$.
3. V_L will go to −8 V.

Section 21–8

1. An integrator is a low-pass filter.
2. A differentiator is a high-pass filter.
3. $f_{max} = 350$ kHz

Section 21–9

1. A 0 V output may be caused by an open resistor or shorted capacitor.
2. If C is shorted, the output is the same as the input.

Section 21–10

1. A capacitor must be added and the switch changed to one with six positions.
2. $C_6 = 100$ ms/[(1.204)(47 kΩ)] = 1.77 μF (use 1.8 μF)

■ **ANSWERS TO RELATED PROBLEMS FOR EXAMPLES**

21–1 8.65 V

21–2 24.7 V

21–3 1.08 V

21–4 See Figure 21–74.

FIGURE 21–74

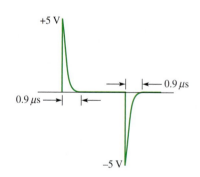

21–5 892 mV

21–6 Impossible with a 50 Ω rheostat

21–7 20 V

21–8 2.5 kΩ

21–9 See Figure 21–75.

FIGURE 21–75

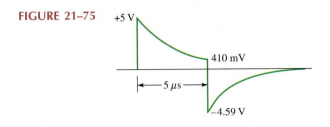

21–10 20 kΩ
21–11 23.3 MHz

■ **ANSWERS TO SELF-TEST**

1. (b) **2.** (c) **3.** (a) **4.** (d) **5.** (a) **6.** (e) **7.** (a) **8.** (c)
9. (b) **10.** (d)

22

POLYPHASE SYSTEMS IN POWER APPLICATIONS

PSpice Tutorial at
http://www.prenhall.com/floyd

■ INTRODUCTION

In the coverage of ac analysis in previous chapters, only single-phase sinusoidal sources have been considered. In Chapter 11, you learned how a sinusoidal voltage can be generated by the rotation of a conductor at a constant velocity in a magnetic field, and the basic concepts of ac generators were introduced.

In this chapter, the basic generation of polyphase sinusoidal waveforms is examined. The advantages of polyphase systems in power applications are covered, and various types of three-phase connections and power measurement are introduced.

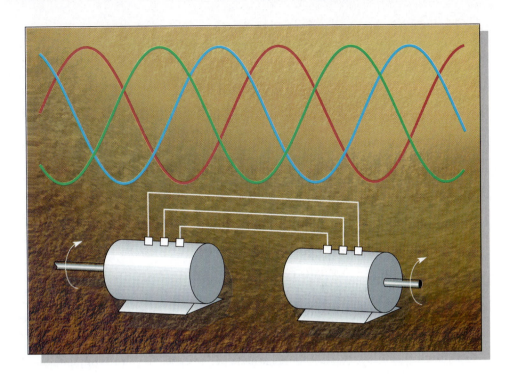

■ TECHnology
  Theory
  Into
  Practice

■ **CHAPTER OBJECTIVES**

❑ Describe a basic polyphase machine
❑ Discuss the advantages of polyphase generators in power applications
❑ Analyze three-phase generator configurations

❑ Analyze three-phase generators with three-phase loads
❑ Discuss power measurements in three-phase systems

22–1 ■ BASIC POLYPHASE MACHINES

Polyphase generators simultaneously produce multiple sinusoidal voltages that are separated by certain constant phase angles. This polyphase generation is accomplished by multiple windings rotating through a magnetic field. Similarly, polyphase motors operate with multiple-phase sinusoidal inputs.

After completing this section, you should be able to

■ **Describe a basic polyphase machine**
  • Discuss a basic two-phase generator
  • Discuss a basic three-phase generator
  • Describe the construction of a three-phase generator
  • Describe a basic three-phase induction motor

A Basic Two-Phase Generator

Figure 22–1(a) shows a second separate conductor winding added to a basic single-phase generator with the two windings separated by 90°. Both windings are mounted on the same **rotor** and therefore rotate at the same speed. Winding *A* is 90° ahead of winding *B* in the direction of rotation. As they rotate, two induced sinusoidal voltages are produced that are 90° apart in phase, as shown in part (b) of the figure.

FIGURE 22–1
Basic two-phase generator.

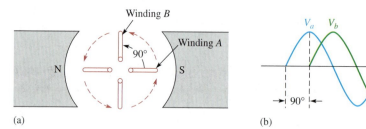

(a)   (b)

A Basic Three-Phase Generator

Figure 22–2(a) shows a **polyphase** generator with three separate conductor windings placed at 120° intervals around the rotor. This configuration generates three sinusoidal voltages that are separated from each other by phase angles of 120°, as shown in part (b).

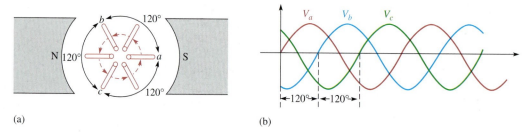

(a)   (b)

FIGURE 22–2
Basic three-phase generator.

A Practical Three-Phase Generator

The purpose of using the simple ac generators (**alternators**) presented up to this point was to illustrate the basic concept of the generation of sinusoidal voltages from the rotation of a conductor in a magnetic field. Many ac generators produce three-phase ac using a configuration that is somewhat different from that previously discussed. The basic principle, however, is the same.

A basic two-pole, three-phase generator is shown in Figure 22–3. Most practical generators are of this basic form. Rather than using a permanent magnet in a fixed position, a rotating electromagnet is used. The electromagnet is created by passing direct current (I_F) through a winding around the rotor, as shown. This winding is called the **field winding.** The direct current is applied through a brush and slip ring assembly. The stationary outer portion of the generator is called the **stator.** Three separate windings are placed 120° apart around the stator; three-phase voltages are induced in these windings as the magnetic field rotates, as indicated in Figure 22–2(b).

FIGURE 22–3
Basic two-pole, three-phase generator.

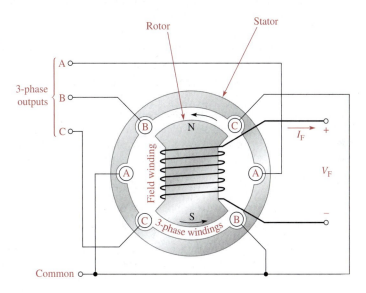

A Basic Three-Phase Motor

The most common type of ac motor is the three-phase induction motor. Basically, it consists of a stator with stator windings and a rotor assembly constructed as a cylindrical frame of metal bars arranged in a **squirrel-cage** type configuration. A basic end-view diagram is shown in Figure 22–4.

When the three-phase voltages are applied to the stator windings, a rotating magnetic field is established. As the magnetic field rotates, currents are induced in the conductors of the squirrel-cage rotor. The interaction of the induced currents and the magnetic field produces forces that cause the rotor to also rotate.

FIGURE 22–4
Basic three-phase induction motor.

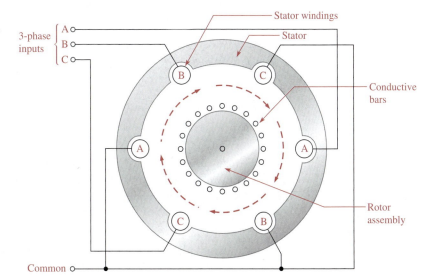

SECTION 22–1 REVIEW

1. Describe the basic principle used in ac generators.

2. A two-pole, single-phase generator rotates at 400 rps. What frequency is produced?

3. How many separate armature windings are required in a three-phase alternator?

22–2 ■ POLYPHASE GENERATORS IN POWER APPLICATIONS

There are several advantages of using polyphase generators to deliver power to a load over using a single-phase machine. These advantages are discussed in this section.

After completing this section, you should be able to

■ **Discuss the advantages of polyphase generators in power applications**
  • Explain the copper advantage
  • Compare single-phase, two-phase, and three-phase systems in terms of the copper advantage
  • Explain the advantage of constant power
  • Explain the advantage of a constant rotating magnetic field

The Copper Advantage

The size of the copper wire required to carry current from a generator to a load can be reduced when a polyphase rather than a single-phase generator is used.

A Single-Phase System Figure 22–5 is a simplified representation of a single-phase generator connected to a resistive load. The coil symbol represents the generator winding.

FIGURE 22–5
Simplified representation of a single-phase generator connected to a resistive load.

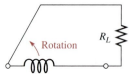

For example, a single-phase sinusoidal voltage is induced in the winding and applied to a 60 Ω load, as indicated in Figure 22–6. The resulting load current is

$$\mathbf{I}_{RL} = \frac{120\angle 0° \text{ V}}{60\angle 0° \text{ Ω}} = 2\angle 0° \text{ A}$$

FIGURE 22–6
Single-phase example.

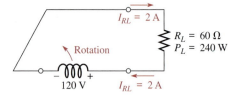

The total current that must be delivered by the generator to the load is $2\angle 0°$ A. This means that the two conductors carrying current to and from the load must each be capable of handling 2 A; thus, the total copper cross section must handle 4 A. (The copper cross section is a measure of the total amount of wire required based on its physical size as related to its diameter.) The total load power is

$$P_{L(tot)} = I_{RL}^2 R_L = 240 \text{ W}$$

A Two-Phase System Figure 22–7 shows a simplified representation of a two-phase generator connected to two 120 Ω load resistors. The coils drawn at a 90° angle represent the armature windings spaced 90° apart. An equivalent single-phase system would be required to feed two 120 Ω resistors in parallel, thus creating a 60 Ω load.

FIGURE 22–7
Simplified representation of a two-phase generator with each phase connected to a 120 Ω load.

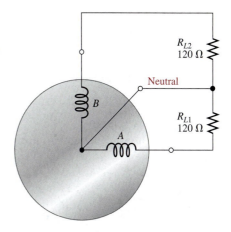

The voltage across load R_{L1} is $120\angle0°$ V, and the voltage across load R_{L2} is $120\angle90°$ V, as indicated in Figure 22–8(a). The current in R_{L1} is

$$\mathbf{I}_{RL1} = \frac{120\angle0° \text{ V}}{120\angle0° \text{ Ω}} = 1\angle0° \text{ A}$$

and the current in R_{L2} is

$$\mathbf{I}_{RL2} = \frac{120\angle90° \text{ V}}{120\angle0° \text{ Ω}} = 1\angle90° \text{ A}$$

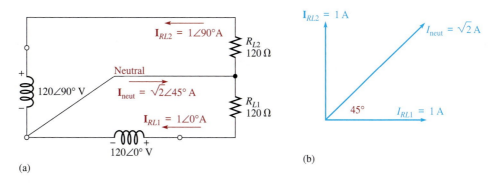

(a)

(b)

FIGURE 22–8
Two-phase example.

Notice that the two load resistors are connected to a common or neutral conductor, which provides a return path for the currents. Since the two load currents are 90° out of phase with each other, the current in the neutral conductor (I_{neut}) is the phasor sum of the load currents.

$$I_{\text{neut}} = \sqrt{I_{RL1}^2 + I_{RL2}^2} = \sqrt{2} \text{ A} = 1.414 \text{ A}$$

Figure 22–8(b) shows the phasor diagram for the currents in the two-phase system.

Three conductors are required in this system to carry current to and from the loads. Two of the conductors must be capable of handling 1 A each, and the neutral conductor must handle 1.414 A. The total copper cross section must handle 1 A + 1 A + 1.414 A = 3.414 A. This is a smaller copper cross section than was required in the single-phase system to deliver the same amount of total load power.

$$P_{L(tot)} = P_{RL1} + P_{RL2} = I^2_{RL1}R_{L1} = I^2_{RL2}R_{L2} = 120 \text{ W} + 120 \text{ W} = 240 \text{ W}$$

A Three-Phase System   Figure 22–9 shows a simplified representation of a three-phase generator connected to three 180 Ω resistive loads. An equivalent single-phase system would be required to feed three 180 Ω resistors in parallel, thus creating an effective load resistance of 60 Ω. The coils represent the generator windings separated by 120°.

FIGURE 22–9

A simplified representation of a three-phase generator with each phase connected to a 180 Ω load.

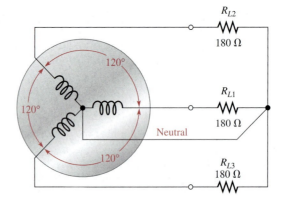

The voltage across R_{L1} is 120∠0° V, the voltage across R_{L2} is 120∠120° V, and the voltage across R_{L3} is 120∠–120° V, as indicated in Figure 22–10(a). The current from each winding to its respective load is as follows:

$$\mathbf{I}_{RL1} = \frac{120\angle 0° \text{ V}}{180\angle 0° \text{ }\Omega} = 667\angle 0° \text{ mA}$$

$$\mathbf{I}_{RL2} = \frac{120\angle 120° \text{ V}}{180\angle 0° \text{ }\Omega} = 667\angle 120° \text{ mA}$$

$$\mathbf{I}_{RL3} = \frac{120\angle -120° \text{ V}}{180\angle 0° \text{ }\Omega} = 667\angle -120° \text{ mA}$$

The total load power is

$$P_{L(tot)} = I^2_{RL1}R_{L1} + I^2_{RL2}R_{L2} + I^2_{RL3}R_{L3} = 240 \text{ W}$$

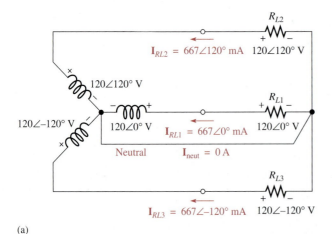

(a)

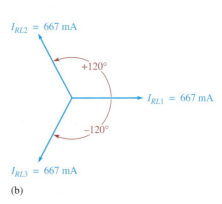

(b)

FIGURE 22–10

Three-phase example.

This is the same total load power as delivered by both the single-phase and the two-phase systems previously discussed.

Notice that four conductors, including the neutral, are required to carry the currents to and from the loads. The current in each of the three conductors is 667 mA, as indicated in Figure 22–10(a). The current in the neutral conductor is the phasor sum of the three load currents and is equal to zero, as shown in the following equation, with reference to the phasor diagram in Figure 22–10(b).

$$\mathbf{I}_{RL1} + \mathbf{I}_{RL2} + \mathbf{I}_{RL3} = 667\angle 0° \text{ mA} + 667\angle 120° \text{ mA} + 667\angle{-120°} \text{ mA}$$
$$= 667 \text{ mA} - 333.5 \text{ mA} + j578 \text{ mA} - 333.5 \text{ mA} - j578 \text{ mA}$$
$$= 667 \text{ mA} - 667 \text{ mA} = 0 \text{ A}$$

This condition, where all load currents are equal and the neutral current is zero, is called a **balanced load** condition.

The total copper cross section must handle 667 mA + 667 mA + 667 mA + 0 mA = 2 A. This result shows that considerably less copper is required to deliver the same load power with a three-phase system than is required for either the single-phase or the two-phase systems. The amount of copper is an important consideration in power distribution systems.

EXAMPLE 22–1

Compare the total copper cross sections in terms of current-carrying capacity for single-phase and three-phase 120 V systems with effective load resistances of 12 Ω.

Solution
Single-phase system: The load current is

$$I_{RL} = \frac{120 \text{ V}}{12 \text{ Ω}} = 10 \text{ A}$$

The conductor to the load must carry 10 A, and the conductor from the load must also carry 10 A.

The total copper cross section, therefore, must be sufficient to handle 2×10 A = 20 A.

Three-phase system: For an effective load resistance of 12 Ω, the three-phase generator feeds three load resistors of 36 Ω each. The current in each load resistor is

$$I_{RL} = \frac{120 \text{ V}}{36 \text{ Ω}} = 3.33 \text{ A}$$

Each of the three conductors feeding the balanced load must carry 3.33 A, and the neutral current is zero.

Therefore, the total copper cross section must be sufficient to handle 3×3.33 A ≅ 10 A. This is significantly less than for the single-phase system with an equivalent load.

Related Problem Compare the total copper cross sections in terms of current-carrying capacity for single-phase and three-phase 240 V systems with effective load resistances of 100 Ω.

The Advantage of Constant Power

A second advantage of polyphase systems over single-phase is that polyphase systems produce a constant amount of power in the load.

A Single-Phase System As shown in Figure 22–11, the load power fluctuates as the square of the sinusoidal voltage divided by the resistance. It changes from a maximum of $V_{RL(max)}^2/R_L$ to a minimum of zero at a frequency equal to twice that of the voltage.

FIGURE 22–11
Single-phase load power (sin² curve).

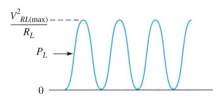

A Polyphase System   The power waveform across one of the load resistors in a two-phase system is 90° out of phase with the power waveform across the other, as shown in Figure 22–12. When the instantaneous power to one load is maximum, the other is minimum. In between the maximum and minimum points, one power is increasing while the other is decreasing. Careful examination of the power waveforms shows that when two instantaneous values are added, the sum is always constant and equal to $V_{RL(max)}^2/R_L$.

FIGURE 22–12
Two-phase power ($P_L = V_{RL(max)}^2/R_L$).

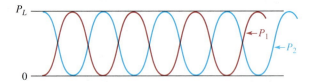

In a three-phase system, the total power delivered to the load resistors is also constant for the same basic reason as for the two-phase system. The sum of the instantaneous voltages is always the same; therefore, the power has a constant value. A constant load power means a uniform conversion of mechanical to electrical energy, which is an important consideration in many power applications.

The Advantage of a Constant, Rotating Magnetic Field

In many applications, ac generators are used to drive ac motors for conversion of electrical energy to mechanical energy in the form of shaft rotation in the motor. The original energy for operation of the generator can come from any of several sources such as hydroelectric or steam. Figure 22–13 illustrates the basic concept.

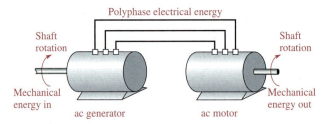

FIGURE 22–13
Simple example of mechanical-to-electrical-to-mechanical energy conversion.

When a polyphase generator is connected to the motor windings as depicted in Figure 22–14, where a two-phase system is used for purposes of illustration, a magnetic field is created within the motor that has a constant flux density and that rotates at the frequency of the two-phase sine wave. The motor's rotor is pulled around at a constant rotational velocity by the rotating magnetic field, producing a constant shaft rotation.

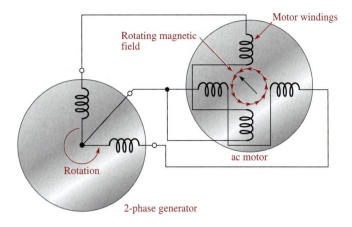

FIGURE 22–14
A two-phase generator producing a constant rotating magnetic field in an ac motor.

A three-phase system, of course, has the same advantage as a two-phase system. A single-phase system is unsuitable for many applications because it produces a magnetic field that fluctuates in flux density and reverses direction during each cycle without providing the advantage of constant rotation.

SECTION 22–2 REVIEW

1. List three advantages of polyphase systems over single-phase systems.
2. Which advantage(s) is/are most important in mechanical-to-electrical energy conversions?
3. Which advantage(s) is/are most important in electrical-to-mechanical energy conversions?

22–3 ■ THREE-PHASE GENERATORS

In the previous sections, the Y-connection was used for illustration. In this section, the Y-connection is examined further and a second type, the Δ-configuration, is introduced.

After completing this section, you should be able to

■ **Analyze three-phase generator configurations**
  • Analyze the Y-connected generator
  • Analyze the Δ-connected generator

The Y-Connected Generator

A Y-connected system can be either a three-wire or, when the neutral is used, a four-wire system, as shown in Figure 22–15, connected to a generalized load represented by the block. Recall that when the loads are perfectly balanced, the neutral current is zero; therefore, the neutral conductor is unnecessary. However, in cases where the loads are not equal (unbalanced), a neutral wire is essential to provide a return current path, because the neutral current has a nonzero value.

FIGURE 22–15
Y-connected generator.

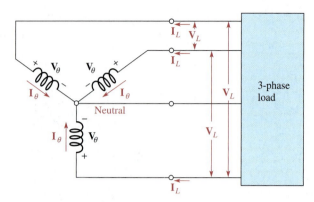

The voltages across the generator windings are called **phase voltages** (V_θ), and the currents through the windings are called **phase currents** (I_θ). Also, the currents in the lines connecting the generator windings to the load are called **line currents** (I_L), and the voltages across the lines are called the **line voltages** (V_L). Note that the magnitude of each line current is equal to the corresponding phase current in the Y-connected circuit.

$$I_L = I_\theta \tag{22–1}$$

In Figure 22–16, the line terminations of the windings are designated *a, b,* and *c,* and the neutral point is designated *n.* These letters are added as subscripts to the phase and line currents to indicate the phase with which each is associated. The phase voltages are also designated in the same manner. Notice that the phase voltages are always positive at the terminal end of the winding and are negative at the neutral point. The line voltages are from one winding terminal to another, as indicated by the double-letter subscripts. For example, $\mathbf{V}_{L(ba)}$ is the line voltage from *b* to *a.*

FIGURE 22–16
*Phase voltages and line voltages
in a Y-connected system.*

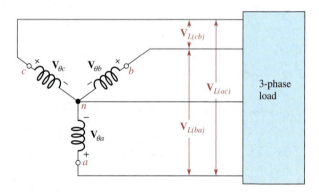

Figure 22–17(a) shows a phasor diagram for the phase voltages. By rotation of the phasors, as shown in part (b), $V_{\theta a}$ is given a reference angle of zero, and the polar expressions for the phasor voltages are as follows:

$$\mathbf{V}_{\theta a} = V_{\theta a}\angle 0°$$
$$\mathbf{V}_{\theta b} = V_{\theta b}\angle 120°$$
$$\mathbf{V}_{\theta c} = V_{\theta c}\angle -120°$$

There are three line voltages: one between *a* and *b,* one between *a* and *c,* and another between *b* and *c.* It can be shown that the magnitude of each line voltage is equal to $\sqrt{3}$ times the magnitude of the phase voltage and that there is a phase angle of 30° between each line voltage and the nearest phase voltage.

$$V_L = \sqrt{3}V_\theta \tag{22–2}$$

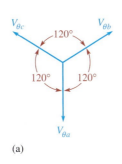
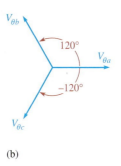

(a)   (b)

FIGURE 22–17
Phase voltage diagram.

Since all phase voltages are equal in magnitude,

$$\mathbf{V}_{L(ba)} = \sqrt{3}V_\theta \angle 150°$$
$$\mathbf{V}_{L(ac)} = \sqrt{3}V_\theta \angle 30°$$
$$\mathbf{V}_{L(cb)} = \sqrt{3}V_\theta \angle -90°$$

The line voltage phasor diagram is shown in Figure 22–18 superimposed on the phasor diagram for the phase voltages. Notice that there is a phase angle of 30° between each line voltage and the nearest phase voltage and that the line voltages are 120° apart.

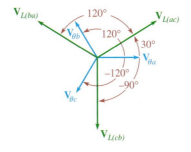

FIGURE 22–18
Phase diagram for the phase voltages and line voltages in a Y-connected, three-phase system.

EXAMPLE 22–2

The instantaneous position of a certain Y-connected ac generator is shown in Figure 22–19. If each phase voltage has a magnitude of 120 V rms, determine the magnitude of each line voltage, and sketch the phasor diagram.

FIGURE 22–19

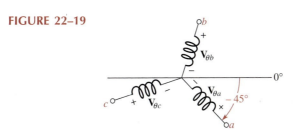

Solution   The magnitude of each line voltage is

$$V_L = \sqrt{3}V_\theta = \sqrt{3}(120 \text{ V}) = \mathbf{208 \text{ V}}$$

FIGURE 22–20

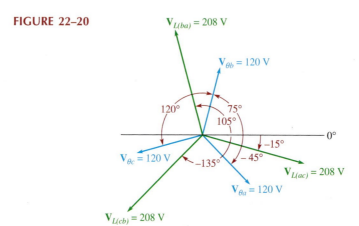

The phasor diagram for the given instantaneous generator position is shown in Figure 22–20.

Related Problem Determine the line voltage magnitude if the generator position indicated in Figure 22–19 is rotated another 45° clockwise.

The Δ-Connected Generator

In the Y-connected generator, two voltage magnitudes are available at the terminals in the four-wire system: the phase voltage and the line voltage. Also, in the Y-connected generator, the line current is equal to the phase current. Keep these characteristics in mind as you examine the Δ-connected generator.

The windings of a three-phase generator can be rearranged to form a Δ-connected generator, as shown in Figure 22–21. By examination of this diagram, it is apparent that the magnitudes of the line voltages and phase voltages are equal, but the line currents do not equal the phase currents.

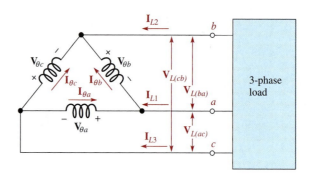

FIGURE 22–21
Δ-connected generator.

Since this is a three-wire system, only a single voltage magnitude is available, expressed as

$$V_L = V_\theta$$

(22–3)

All of the phase voltages are equal in magnitude; thus, the line voltages are expressed in polar form as follows:

$$\mathbf{V}_{L(ac)} = V_\theta \angle 0°$$
$$\mathbf{V}_{L(ba)} = V_\theta \angle 120°$$
$$\mathbf{V}_{L(cb)} = V_\theta \angle -120°$$

The phasor diagram for the phase currents is shown in Figure 22–22, and the polar expressions for each current are as follows:

$$\mathbf{I}_{\theta a} = I_{\theta a} \angle 0°$$
$$\mathbf{I}_{\theta b} = I_{\theta b} \angle 120°$$
$$\mathbf{I}_{\theta c} = I_{\theta c} \angle -120°$$

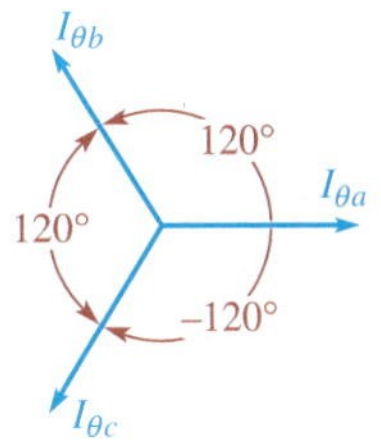

FIGURE 22–22
Phase current diagram for the Δ-connected system.

It can be shown that the magnitude of each line current is equal to $\sqrt{3}$ times the magnitude of the phase current and that there is a phase angle of 30° between each line current and the nearest phase current.

$$I_L = \sqrt{3}I_\theta \qquad\qquad (22\text{–}4)$$

Since all phase currents are equal in magnitude,

$$\mathbf{I}_{L1} = \sqrt{3}I_\theta \angle -30°$$
$$\mathbf{I}_{L2} = \sqrt{3}I_\theta \angle 90°$$
$$\mathbf{I}_{L3} = \sqrt{3}I_\theta \angle -150°$$

The current phasor diagram is shown in Figure 22–23.

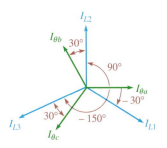

FIGURE 22–23
Phasor diagram of phase currents and line currents.

EXAMPLE 22–3

The three-phase Δ-connected generator represented in Figure 22–24 is driving a balanced load such that each phase current is 10 A in magnitude. When $\mathbf{I}_{\theta a} = 10\angle30°$ A, determine the following:

(a) The polar expressions for the other phase currents
(b) The polar expressions for each of the line currents
(c) The complete current phasor diagram

FIGURE 22–24

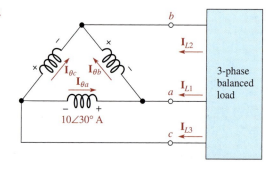

Solution

(a) The phase currents are separated by 120°; therefore,

$$\mathbf{I}_{\theta b} = 10\angle(30° + 120°) = \mathbf{10\angle150°}\ \mathbf{A}$$
$$\mathbf{I}_{\theta c} = 10\angle(30° - 120°) = \mathbf{10\angle{-90°}}\ \mathbf{A}$$

(b) The line currents are separated from the nearest phase current by 30°; therefore,

$$\mathbf{I}_{L1} = \sqrt{3}I_{\theta a}\angle(30° - 30°) = \mathbf{17.3\angle0°}\ \mathbf{A}$$
$$\mathbf{I}_{L2} = \sqrt{3}I_{\theta b}\angle(150° - 30°) = \mathbf{17.3\angle120°}\ \mathbf{A}$$
$$\mathbf{I}_{L3} = \sqrt{3}I_{\theta c}\angle(-90° - 30°) = \mathbf{17.3\angle{-120°}}\ \mathbf{A}$$

(c) The phasor diagram is shown in Figure 22–25.

FIGURE 22–25

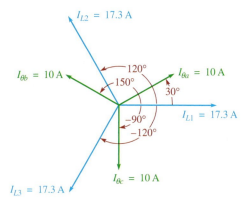

Related Problem Repeat parts (a) and (b) of the example if $\mathbf{I}_{\theta a} = 8\angle60°$ A.

SECTION 22–3
REVIEW

1. In a certain three-wire, Y-connected generator, the phase voltages are 1 kV. Determine the magnitude of the line voltages.

2. In the Y-connected generator mentioned in Question 1, all the phase currents are 5 A. What are the line current magnitudes?

3. In a Δ-connected generator, the phase voltages are 240 V. What are the line voltages?

4. In a Δ-connected generator, a phase current is 2 A. Determine the magnitude of the line current.

22–4 ■ THREE-PHASE SOURCE/LOAD ANALYSIS

In this section, we look at four basic types of source/load configurations. As with the generator connections, a load can be either a Y or a Δ configuration.

After completing this section, you should be able to

■ **Analyze three-phase generators with three-phase loads**
   • Analyze the Y-Y source/load configuration
   • Analyze the Y-Δ source/load configuration
   • Analyze the Δ-Y source/load configuration
   • Analyze the Δ-Δ source/load configuration

A Y-connected load is shown in Figure 22–26(a), and a Δ-connected load is shown in part (b). The blocks Z_a, Z_b, and Z_c represent the load impedances, which can be resistive, reactive, or both.

FIGURE 22–26
Three-phase loads.

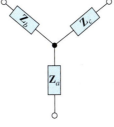

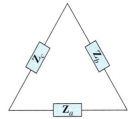

(a) Y-connected load   (b) Δ-connected load

In this section, four source/load configurations are examined: a Y-connected source driving a Y-connected load (Y-Y system), a Y-connected source driving a Δ-connected load (Y-Δ system), a Δ-connected source driving a Y-connected load (Δ-Y system), and a Δ-connected source driving a Δ-connected load (Δ-Δ system).

The Y-Y System

Figure 22–27 shows a Y-connected source driving a Y-connected load. The load can be a balanced load, such as a three-phase motor where $Z_a = Z_b = Z_c$, or it can be three independent single-phase loads where, for example, Z_a is a lighting circuit, Z_b is a heater, and Z_c is an air-conditioning compressor.

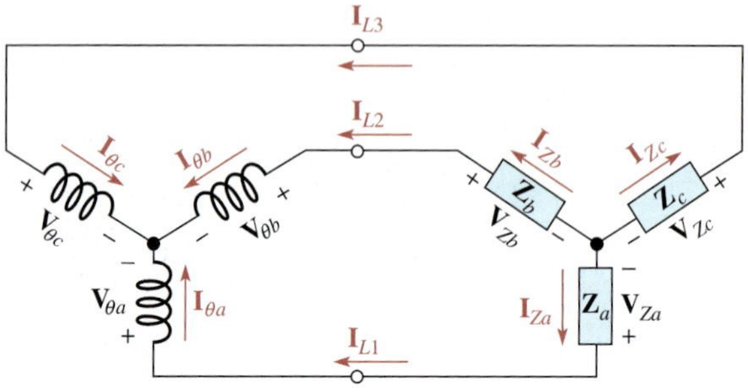

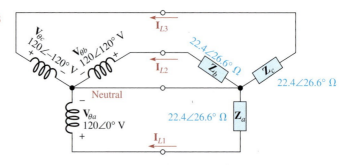

FIGURE 22–27
A Y-connected source feeding a Y-connected load.

An important feature of a Y-connected source is that two different values of three-phase voltage are available: the phase voltage and the line voltage. For example, in the standard power distribution system, a three-phase transformer can be considered a source of three-phase voltage supplying 120 V and 208 V. In order to utilize a phase voltage of 120 V, the loads are connected in the Y configuration. A Δ-connected load is used for the 208 V line voltages.

Notice in the Y-Y system in Figure 22–27 that the phase current, the line current, and the load current are all equal in each phase. Also, each load voltage equals the corresponding phase voltage. These relationships are expressed as follows and are true for either a balanced or an unbalanced load.

$$I_\theta = I_L = I_Z \tag{22–5}$$

$$V_\theta = V_Z \tag{22–6}$$

where V_Z and I_Z are the load voltage and current.

For a balanced load, all the phase currents are equal, and the neutral current is zero. For an unbalanced load, each phase current is different, and the neutral current is, therefore, nonzero.

EXAMPLE 22–4

In the Y-Y system of Figure 22–28, determine the following:
(a) Each load current   **(b)** Each line current   **(c)** Each phase current
(d) Neutral current   **(e)** Each load voltage

FIGURE 22–28

Solution This system has a balanced load. $\mathbf{Z}_a = \mathbf{Z}_b = \mathbf{Z}_c = 22.4\angle26.6°\ \Omega$.

(a) The load currents are

$$\mathbf{I}_{Za} = \frac{\mathbf{V}_{\theta a}}{\mathbf{Z}_a} = \frac{120\angle0°\ \text{V}}{22.4\angle26.6°\ \Omega} = 5.36\angle-26.6°\ \text{A}$$

$$\mathbf{I}_{Zb} = \frac{\mathbf{V}_{\theta b}}{\mathbf{Z}_b} = \frac{120\angle120°\ \text{V}}{22.4\angle26.6°\ \Omega} = 5.36\angle93.4°\ \text{A}$$

$$\mathbf{I}_{Zc} = \frac{\mathbf{V}_{\theta c}}{\mathbf{Z}_c} = \frac{120\angle-120°\ \text{V}}{22.4\angle26.6°\ \Omega} = 5.36\angle-147°\ \text{A}$$

(b) The line currents are

$$\mathbf{I}_{L1} = 5.36\angle-26.6°\ \text{A}$$
$$\mathbf{I}_{L2} = 5.36\angle93.4°\ \text{A}$$
$$\mathbf{I}_{L3} = 5.36\angle-147°\ \text{A}$$

(c) The phase currents are

$$\mathbf{I}_{\theta a} = 5.36\angle-26.6°\ \text{A}$$
$$\mathbf{I}_{\theta b} = 5.36\angle93.4°\ \text{A}$$
$$\mathbf{I}_{\theta c} = 5.36\angle-147°\ \text{A}$$

(d) $\mathbf{I}_{\text{neut}} = \mathbf{I}_{Za} + \mathbf{I}_{Zb} + \mathbf{I}_{Zc}$
$\quad\quad = 5.36\angle-26.6°\ \text{A} + 5.36\angle93.4°\ \text{A} + 5.36\angle-147°\ \text{A}$
$\quad\quad = (4.80\ \text{A} - j2.40\ \text{A}) + (-0.33\ \text{A} + j5.35\ \text{A}) + (-4.47\ \text{A} - j2.95\ \text{A}) = \mathbf{0\ A}$

If the load impedances were not equal (balanced load), the neutral current would have a nonzero value.

(e) The load voltages are equal to the corresponding source phase voltages.

$$\mathbf{V}_{Za} = 120\angle0°\ \text{V}$$
$$\mathbf{V}_{Zb} = 120\angle120°\ \text{V}$$
$$\mathbf{V}_{Zc} = 120\angle-120°\ \text{V}$$

Related Problem Determine the neutral current if $\mathbf{Z}_a$ and $\mathbf{Z}_b$ are the same as in Figure 22–28, but $\mathbf{Z}_c = 50\angle26.6°\ \Omega$.

The Y-Δ System

Figure 22–29 shows a Y-connected source feeding a Δ-connected load. An important feature of this configuration is that each phase of the load has the full line voltage across it.

$$V_Z = V_L \tag{22–7}$$

FIGURE 22–29

A Y-connected source feeding a Δ-connected load.

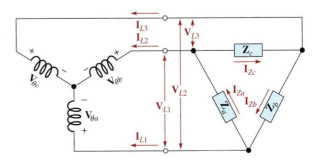

The line currents equal the corresponding phase currents, and each line current divides into two load currents, as indicated. For a balanced load ($Z_a = Z_b = Z_c$), the expression for the current in each load is

$$I_L = \sqrt{3}I_Z \tag{22–8}$$

EXAMPLE 22–5

Determine the load voltages and load currents in Figure 22–30, and show their relationship in a phasor diagram.

FIGURE 22–30

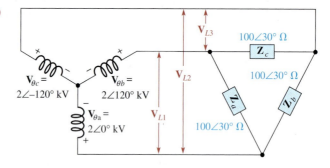

Solution The load voltages are

$$\mathbf{V}_{Za} = \mathbf{V}_{L1} = 2\sqrt{3}\angle150°\text{ kV} = \mathbf{3.46\angle150°\text{ kV}}$$
$$\mathbf{V}_{Zb} = \mathbf{V}_{L2} = 2\sqrt{3}\angle30°\text{ kV} = \mathbf{3.46\angle30°\text{ kV}}$$
$$\mathbf{V}_{Zc} = \mathbf{V}_{L3} = 2\sqrt{3}\angle-90°\text{ kV} = \mathbf{3.46\angle-90°\text{ kV}}$$

The load currents are

$$\mathbf{I}_{Za} = \frac{\mathbf{V}_{Za}}{\mathbf{Z}_a} = \frac{3.46\angle150°\text{ kV}}{100\angle30°\text{ }\Omega} = \mathbf{34.6\angle120°\text{ A}}$$

$$\mathbf{I}_{Zb} = \frac{\mathbf{V}_{Zb}}{\mathbf{Z}_b} = \frac{3.46\angle30°\text{ kV}}{100\angle30°\text{ }\Omega} = \mathbf{34.6\angle0°\text{ A}}$$

$$\mathbf{I}_{Zc} = \frac{\mathbf{V}_{Zc}}{\mathbf{Z}_c} = \frac{3.46\angle-90°\text{ kV}}{100\angle30°\text{ }\Omega} = \mathbf{34.6\angle-120°\text{ A}}$$

The phasor diagram is shown in Figure 22–31.

FIGURE 22–31

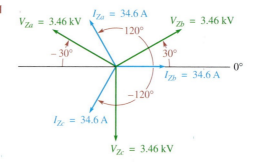

Related Problem Determine the load currents in Figure 22–30 if the phase voltages have a magnitude of 240 V.

The Δ-Y System

Figure 22–32 shows a Δ-connected source feeding a Y-connected balanced load. By examination of the figure, you can see that the line voltages are equal to the corresponding phase voltages of the source. Also, each phase voltage equals the difference of the corresponding load voltages, as you can see by the polarities.

FIGURE 22–32

A Δ-connected source feeding a Y-connected load.

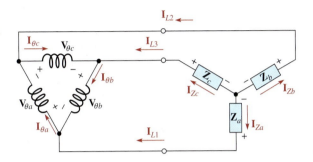

Each load current equals the corresponding line current. The sum of the load currents is zero because the load is balanced; thus, there is no need for a neutral return.

The relationship between the load voltages and the corresponding phase voltages (and line voltages) is

$$V_\theta = \sqrt{3}V_Z \tag{22–9}$$

The line currents and corresponding load currents are equal, and for a balanced load, the sum of the load currents is zero.

$$\mathbf{I}_L = \mathbf{I}_Z \tag{22–10}$$

As you can see in Figure 22–32, each line current is the difference of two phase currents.

$$\mathbf{I}_{L1} = \mathbf{I}_{\theta a} - \mathbf{I}_{\theta b}$$
$$\mathbf{I}_{L2} = \mathbf{I}_{\theta c} - \mathbf{I}_{\theta a}$$
$$\mathbf{I}_{L3} = \mathbf{I}_{\theta b} - \mathbf{I}_{\theta c}$$

EXAMPLE 22–6

Determine the currents and voltages in the balanced load and the magnitude of the line voltages in Figure 22–33.

FIGURE 22–33

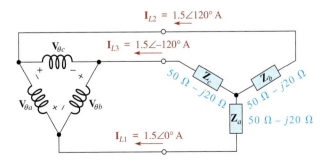

Solution The load currents equal the specified line currents.

$$I_{Za} = I_{L1} = 1.5\angle 0° \text{ A}$$
$$I_{Zb} = I_{L2} = 1.5\angle 120° \text{ A}$$
$$I_{Zc} = I_{L3} = 1.5\angle -120° \text{ A}$$

The load voltages are

$$\mathbf{V}_{Za} = \mathbf{I}_{Za}\mathbf{Z}_a$$
$$= (1.5\angle 0° \text{ A})(50 \text{ Ω} - j20 \text{ Ω})$$
$$= (1.5\angle 0° \text{ A})(53.9\angle -21.8° \text{ Ω}) = \mathbf{80.9\angle -21.8° \text{ V}}$$
$$\mathbf{V}_{Zb} = \mathbf{I}_{Zb}\mathbf{Z}_b$$
$$= (1.5\angle 120° \text{ A})(53.9\angle -21.8° \text{ Ω}) = \mathbf{80.9\angle 98.2° \text{ V}}$$
$$\mathbf{V}_{Zc} = \mathbf{I}_{Zc}\mathbf{Z}_c$$
$$= (1.5\angle -120° \text{ A})(53.9\angle -21.8° \text{ Ω}) = \mathbf{80.9\angle -142° \text{ V}}$$

The magnitude of the line voltages is

$$V_L = V_\theta = \sqrt{3}V_Z = \sqrt{3}(80.9 \text{ V}) = \mathbf{140 \text{ V}}$$

Related Problem If the magnitudes of the line currents are 1 A, what are the load currents?

The Δ-Δ System

Figure 22–34 shows a Δ-connected source driving a Δ-connected load. Notice that the load voltage, line voltage, and source phase voltage are all equal for a given phase.

$$V_{\theta a} = V_{L1} = V_{Za}$$
$$V_{\theta b} = V_{L2} = V_{Zb}$$
$$V_{\theta c} = V_{L3} = V_{Zc}$$

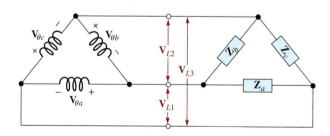

FIGURE 22–34
A Δ-connected source feeding a Δ-connected load.

Of course, when the load is balanced, all the voltages are equal, and a general expression can be written

$$V_\theta = V_L = V_Z \qquad \qquad \textbf{(22–11)}$$

For a balanced load and equal source phase voltages, it can be shown that

$$I_L = \sqrt{3}I_Z \qquad \qquad \textbf{(22–12)}$$

EXAMPLE 22–7

Determine the magnitude of the load currents and the line currents in Figure 22–35.

FIGURE 22–35

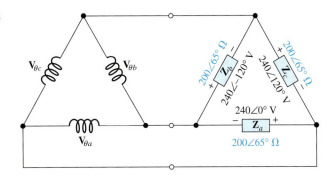

Solution

$$V_{Za} = V_{Zb} = V_{Zc} = 240 \text{ V}$$

The magnitude of the load currents is

$$I_{Za} = I_{Zb} = I_{Zc} = \frac{V_{Za}}{Z_a} = \frac{240 \text{ V}}{200 \ \Omega} = \mathbf{1.20 \text{ A}}$$

The magnitude of the line currents is

$$I_L = \sqrt{3}I_Z = \sqrt{3}(1.20 \text{ A}) = \mathbf{2.08 \text{ A}}$$

Related Problem   Determine the magnitude of the load and line currents in Figure 22–35 if the magnitude of the load voltages is 120 V and the impedances are 600 Ω.

SECTION 22–4 REVIEW

1. List the four types of three-phase source/load configurations.
2. In a certain Y-Y system, the source phase currents each have a magnitude of 3.5 A. What is the magnitude of each load current for a balanced load condition?
3. In a given Y-Δ system, $V_L = 220$ V. Determine V_Z.
4. Determine the line voltages in a balanced Δ-Y system when the magnitude of the source phase voltages is 60 V.
5. Determine the magnitude of the load currents in a balanced Δ-Δ system having a line current magnitude of 3.2 A.

22–5 ■ THREE-PHASE POWER

In this section, power in three-phase systems is studied and methods of power measurement are introduced.

After completing this section, you should be able to

■ **Discuss power measurements in three-phase systems**
  • Describe the three-wattmeter method
  • Describe the two-wattmeter method

Each phase of a balanced three-phase load has an equal amount of power. Therefore, the total true load power is three times the power in each phase of the load.

$$P_{L(tot)} = 3V_Z I_Z \cos \theta \qquad (22\text{–}13)$$

where V_Z and I_Z are the voltage and current associated with each phase of the load, and $\cos \theta$ is the power factor.

Recall that in a balanced Y-connected system, the line voltage and line current were

$$V_L = \sqrt{3}V_Z \qquad \text{and} \qquad I_L = I_Z$$

and in a balanced Δ-connected system, the line voltage and line current were

$$V_L = V_Z \qquad \text{and} \qquad I_L = \sqrt{3}I_Z$$

When either of these relationships is substituted into Equation (22–13), the total true power for both Y- and Δ-connected systems is

$$P_{L(tot)} = \sqrt{3}V_L I_L \cos \theta \qquad (22\text{–}14)$$

EXAMPLE 22–8

In a certain Δ-connected balanced load, the line voltages are 250 V and the impedances are $50\angle 30°\ \Omega$. Determine the total load power.

Solution   In a Δ-connected system, $V_Z = V_L$ and $I_L = \sqrt{3}I_Z$. The load current magnitudes are

$$I_Z = \frac{V_Z}{Z} = \frac{250\ \text{V}}{50\ \Omega} = 5\ \text{A}$$

and

$$I_L = \sqrt{3}I_Z = \sqrt{3}(5\ \text{A}) = 8.66\ \text{A}$$

The power factor is

$$\cos \theta = \cos 30° = 0.866$$

The total load power is

$$P_{L(tot)} = \sqrt{3}V_L I_L \cos \theta = \sqrt{3}(250\ \text{V})(8.66\ \text{A})(0.866) = \mathbf{3.25\ kW}$$

Related Problem   Determine the total load power if $V_L = 120$ V and $\mathbf{Z} = 100\angle 30°\ \Omega$.

Power Measurement

Power is measured in three-phase systems using wattmeters. The wattmeter uses a basic electrodynamometer-type movement consisting of two coils. One coil is used to measure the current, and the other is used to measure the voltage. The needle of the meter is deflected proportionally to the current through a load and the voltage across the load, thus indicating power. Figure 22–36 shows a basic wattmeter symbol and the connections for measuring power in a load. The resistor in series with the voltage coil limits the current through the coil to a small amount proportional to the voltage across the coil.

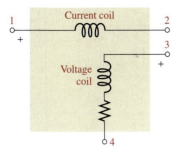 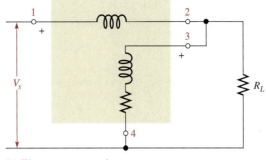

(a) Wattmeter schematic

(b) Wattmeter connected to measure load power

FIGURE 22–36

Three-Wattmeter Method Power can be measured easily in a balanced or unbalanced three-phase load of either the Y or the Δ type by using three wattmeters connected as shown in Figure 22–37. This is sometimes known as the *three-wattmeter method.*

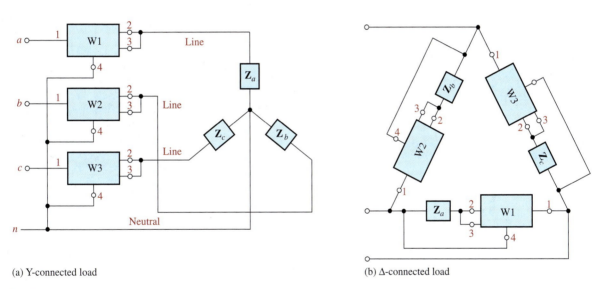

(a) Y-connected load

(b) Δ-connected load

FIGURE 22–37
Three-wattmeter method of power measurement.

The total power is determined by summing the three wattmeter readings.

$$P_{tot} = P_1 + P_2 + P_3 \qquad (22\text{--}15)$$

If the load is balanced, the total power is simply three times the reading on any one wattmeter.

In many three-phase loads, particularly the Δ configuration, it is difficult to connect a wattmeter such that the voltage coil is across the load or such that the current coil is in series with the load because of inaccessibility of points within the load.

Two-Wattmeter Method Another method of three-phase power measurement uses only two wattmeters. The connections for this two-wattmeter method are shown in Figure 22–38. Notice that the voltage coil of each wattmeter is connected across a line voltage

FIGURE 22–38
Two-wattmeter method.

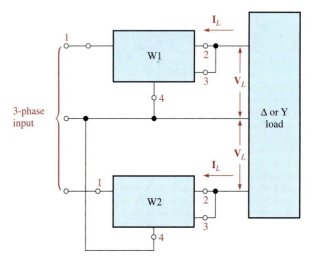

and that the current coil has a line current through it. It can be shown that the algebraic sum of the two wattmeter readings equals the total power in the Y- or Δ-connected load.

$$P_{tot} = P_1 \pm P_2 \qquad\qquad (22\text{–}16)$$

SECTION 22–5 REVIEW

1. $V_L = 30$ V, $I_L = 1.2$ A, and the power factor is 0.257. What is the total power in a balanced Y-connected load? In a balanced Δ-connected load?

2. Three wattmeters connected to measure the power in a certain balanced load indicate a total of 2678 W. How much power does each meter measure?

■ **SUMMARY**

- A simple two-phase generator consists of two conductive loops of wire, separated by 90°, rotating in a magnetic field.
- A simple three-phase generator consists of three conductive loops separated by 120°.
- Three advantages of polyphase systems over single-phase systems are a smaller copper cross section for the same power delivered to the load, constant power delivered to the load, and a constant, rotating magnetic field.
- In a Y-connected generator, $I_L = I_\theta$ and $V_L = \sqrt{3}V_\theta$.
- In a Y-connected generator, there is a 30° difference between each line voltage and the nearest phase voltage.
- In a Δ-connected generator, $V_L = V_\theta$ and $I_L = \sqrt{3}I_\theta$.
- In a Δ-connected generator, there is a 30° difference between each line current and the nearest phase current.
- A balanced load is one in which all the impedances are equal.
- Power is measured in a three-phase load using either the three-wattmeter method or the two-wattmeter method.

■ **GLOSSARY**

These terms are also in the end-of-book glossary.

Alternator   An electromechanical ac generator.

Balanced load   A condition where all the load currents are equal and the neutral current is zero.

Field winding   The winding on the rotor of an ac generator.

Line current (I_L)   The current through a line feeding a load.

Line voltage (V_L)   The voltage between lines feeding a load.

Phase current (I_θ)   The current through a generator winding.

Phase voltage (V_θ) The voltage across a generator winding.

Polyphase Characterized by two or more sinusoidal voltages, each having a different phase angle.

Rotor The rotating assembly in a generator or motor.

Squirrel-cage A type of ac induction motor.

Stator The stationary outer part of a generator or motor.

■ **FORMULAS**

Y Generator

(22–1) $I_L = I_\theta$

(22–2) $V_L = \sqrt{3} V_\theta$

Δ Generator

(22–3) $V_L = V_\theta$

(22–4) $I_L = \sqrt{3} I_\theta$

Y-Y System

(22–5) $I_\theta = I_L = I_Z$

(22–6) $V_\theta = V_Z$

Y-Δ System

(22–7) $V_Z = V_L$

(22–8) $I_L = \sqrt{3} I_Z$

Δ-Y System

(22–9) $V_\theta = \sqrt{3} V_Z$

(22–10) $\mathbf{I}_L = \mathbf{I}_Z$

Δ-Δ SYSTEM

(22–11) $V_\theta = V_L = V_Z$

(22–12) $I_L = \sqrt{3} I_Z$

Three-Phase Power

(22–13) $P_{L(tot)} = 3V_Z I_Z \cos \theta$

(22–14) $P_{L(tot)} = \sqrt{3} V_L I_L \cos \theta$

Three-Wattmeter Method

(22–15) $P_{tot} = P_1 + P_2 + P_3$

Two-Wattmeter Method

(22–16) $P_{tot} = P_1 \pm P_2$

■ **SELF-TEST**

1. In a three-phase system, the voltages are separated by
   (a) 90°   (b) 30°   (c) 180°   (d) 120°

2. The term *squirrel-cage* applies to a type of
   (a) three-phase ac generator   (b) single-phase ac generator
   (c) a three-phase ac motor   (d) a dc motor

3. An alternator is a
   (a) three-phase ac generator   (b) single-phase ac generator
   (c) three-phase ac motor   (d) dc generator

4. Two major parts of an ac generator are
   (a) rotor and stator   (b) rotor and stabilizer
   (c) regulator and slip-ring   (d) magnets and brushes

5. Advantages of a three-phase system over a single-phase system are
   (a) smaller cross-sectional area for the copper conductors
   (b) slower rotor speed
   (c) constant power
   (d) smaller chance of overheating
   (e) both (a) and (c)
   (f) both (b) and (c)

6. The phase current produced by a certain 240 V, Y-connected generator is 12 A. The corresponding line current is
   (a) 36 A   (b) 4 A   (c) 12 A   (d) 6 A

7. A certain Δ-connected generator produces phase voltages of 30 V. The magnitude of the line voltages are
   (a) 10 V   (b) 30 V   (c) 90 V   (d) none of these

8. A certain Δ-Δ system produces phase currents of 5 A. The line currents are
   (a) 5 A   (b) 15 A   (c) 8.66 A   (d) 2.87 A

9. A certain Y-Y system produces phase currents of 15 A. Each line and load current is
   (a) 26 A   (b) 8.66 A   (c) 5 A   (d) 15 A

10. If the source phase voltages of a Δ-Y system are 220 V, the magnitude of the load voltages is
    (a) 220 V   (b) 381 V   (c) 127 V   (d) 73.3 V

■ PROBLEMS

More difficult problems are indicated by an asterisk (*).

SECTION 22–1   Basic Polyphase Machines

1. The output of an ac generator has a maximum value of 250 V. At what angle is the instantaneous value equal to 75 V?

2. A certain two-pole single-phase generator has a speed of rotation of 3600 rpm. What is the frequency of the voltage produced by this generator?

SECTION 22–2   Polyphase Generators in Power Applications

3. A single-phase generator feeds a load consisting of a 200 Ω resistor and a capacitor with a reactance of 175 Ω. The generator produces a voltage of 100 V. Determine the magnitude of the load current and its phase relation to the generator voltage.

4. In a two-phase system, the two currents through the lines connecting the generator to the load are 3.8 A. Determine the current in the neutral line.

5. A certain three-phase unbalanced load in a four-wire system has currents of $2\angle20°$ A, $3\angle140°$ A, and $1.5\angle-100°$ A. Determine the current in the neutral line.

SECTION 22–3   Three-Phase Generators

6. Determine the line voltages in Figure 22–39.

FIGURE 22–39

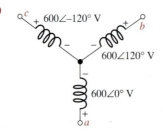

7. Determine the line currents in Figure 22–40.

8. Develop a complete current phasor diagram for Figure 22–40.

FIGURE 22–40

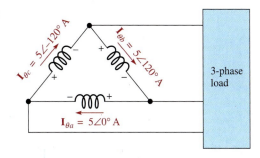

SECTION 22–4 Three-Phase Source/Load Analysis

9. Determine the following quantities for the Y-Y system in Figure 22–41:

   (a) Line voltages   **(b)** Phase currents   **(c)** Line currents

   (d) Load currents   **(e)** Load voltages

FIGURE 22–41

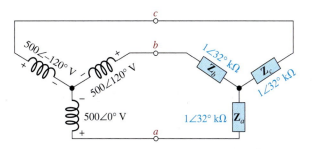

10. Repeat Problem 9 for the system in Figure 22–42, and also find the neutral current.

FIGURE 22–42

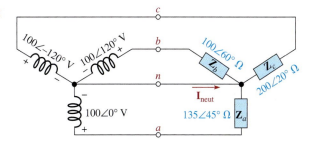

11. Repeat Problem 9 for the system in Figure 22–43.

FIGURE 22–43

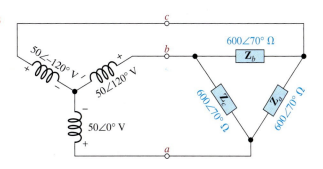

12. Repeat Problem 9 for the system in Figure 22–44.

FIGURE 22–44

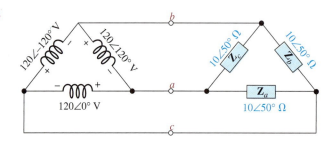

13. Determine the line voltages and load currents for the system in Figure 22–45.

FIGURE 22–45

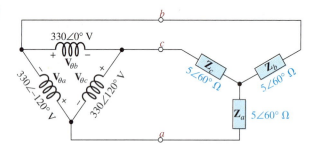

SECTION 22–5 Three-Phase Power

14. The power in each phase of a balanced three-phase system is 1200 W. What is the total power?

15. Determine the load power in Figures 22–41 through 22–45.

16. Find the total load power in Figure 22–46.

FIGURE 22–46

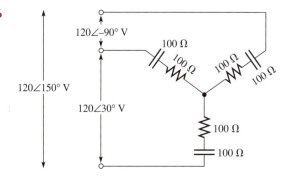

*17. Using the three-wattmeter method for the system in Figure 22–46, how much power does each wattmeter indicate?

*18. Repeat Problem 17 using the two-wattmeter method.

■ **ANSWERS TO SECTION REVIEWS**

Section 22–1

1. In ac generators, a sinusoidal voltage is induced when a conductive loop is rotated in a magnetic field at a constant speed.

2. $f = 400$ Hz

3. Three armature windings

Section 22–2

1. The advantages of polyphase systems are less copper cross section to conduct current; constant power to load; and constant, rotating magnetic field.
2. Constant power
3. Constant magnetic field

Section 22–3

1. $V_L = 1.73$ kV
2. $I_L = 5$ A
3. $V_L = 240$ V
4. $I_L = 3.46$ A

Section 22–4

1. The source/load configurations are Y-Y, Y-Δ, Δ-Y, and Δ-Δ.
2. $I_L = 3.5$ A
3. $V_Z = 220$ V
4. $V_L = 60$ V
5. $I_Z = 1.85$ A

Section 22–5

1. $P_Y = 16.0$ W; $P_\Delta = 16.0$ W
2. $P = 893$ W

■ **ANSWERS TO RELATED PROBLEMS FOR EXAMPLES**

22–1 4.8 A total for single phase; 2.4 A total for three-phase

22–2 208 V

22–3 (a) $\mathbf{I}_{\theta b} = 8\angle 180°$ A, $\mathbf{I}_{\theta c} = 8\angle -60°$ A
(b) $\mathbf{I}_{L1} = 13.9\angle 30°$ A, $\mathbf{I}_{L2} = 13.9\angle 150°$ A, $\mathbf{I}_{L3} = 13.9\angle -90°$ A

22–4 $2.96\angle 33.4°$ A

22–5 $\mathbf{I}_{Za} = 4.16\angle 120°$ A, $\mathbf{I}_{Zb} = 4.16\angle 0°$ A, $\mathbf{I}_{Zc} = 4.16\angle -120°$ A

22–6 $\mathbf{I}_{L1} = \mathbf{I}_{Za} = 1\angle 0°$ A, $\mathbf{I}_{L2} = \mathbf{I}_{Zb} = 1\angle 120°$ A, $\mathbf{I}_{L3} = \mathbf{I}_{Zc} = 1\angle -120°$ A

22–7 $I_Z = 200$ mA, $I_L = 346$ mA

22–8 374 W

■ **ANSWERS TO SELF-TEST**

1. (d) 2. (c) 3. (a) 4. (a) 5. (e) 6. (c) 7. (b) 8. (c)
9. (d) 10. (c)

A TABLE OF STANDARD RESISTOR VALUES

Resistance Tolerance (±%)

0.1% / 0.25% / 0.5%	1%	2% / 5%	10%	0.1% / 0.25% / 0.5%	1%	2% / 5%	10%	0.1% / 0.25% / 0.5%	1%	2% / 5%	10%	0.1% / 0.25% / 0.5%	1%	2% / 5%	10%	0.1% / 0.25% / 0.5%	1%	2% / 5%	10%	0.1% / 0.25% / 0.5%	1%	2% / 5%	10%
10.0	10.0	10	10	14.7	14.7	—	—	21.5	21.5	—	—	31.6	31.6	—	—	46.4	46.4	—	—	68.1	68.1	68	68
10.1	—	—		14.9	—	—		21.8	—	—		32.0	—	—		47.0	—	47	47	69.0	—	—	
10.2	10.2	—		15.0	15.0	15	15	22.1	22.1	22	22	32.4	32.4	—		47.5	47.5	—		69.8	69.8	—	
10.4	—	—		15.2	—	—		22.3	—	—		32.8	—	—		48.1	—	—		70.6	—	—	
10.5	10.5	—		15.4	15.4	—		22.6	22.6	—		33.2	33.2	33	33	48.7	48.7	—		71.5	71.5	—	
10.6	—	—		15.6	—	—		22.9	—	—		33.6	—	—		49.3	—	—		72.3	—	—	
10.7	10.7	—		15.8	15.8	—		23.2	23.2	—		34.0	34.0	—		49.9	49.9	—		73.2	73.2	—	
10.9	—	—		16.0	—	16		23.4	—	—		34.4	—	—		50.5	—	—		74.1	—	—	
11.0	11.0	11		16.2	16.2	—		23.7	23.7	—		34.8	34.8	—		51.1	51.1	51		75.0	75.0	75	
11.1	—	—		16.4	—	—		24.0	—	24		35.2	—	—		51.7	—	—		75.9	—	—	
11.3	11.3	—		16.5	16.5	—		24.3	24.3	—		35.7	35.7	—		52.3	52.3	—		76.8	76.8	—	
11.4	—	—		16.7	—	—		24.6	—	—		36.1	—	36		53.0	—	—		77.7	—	—	
11.5	11.5	—		16.9	16.9	—		24.9	24.9	—		36.5	36.5	—		53.6	53.6	—		78.7	78.7	—	
11.7	—	—		17.2	—	—		25.2	—	—		37.0	—	—		54.2	—	—		79.6	—	—	
11.8	11.8	—		17.4	17.4	—		25.5	25.5	—		37.4	37.4	—		54.9	54.9	—		80.6	80.6	—	
12.0	—	12	12	17.6	—	—		25.8	—	—		37.9	—	—		56.2	—	—		81.6	—	—	
12.1	12.1	—		17.8	17.8	—		26.1	26.1	—		38.3	38.3	—		56.6	56.6	56	56	82.5	82.5	82	82
12.3	—	—		18.0	—	18	18	26.4	—	—		38.8	—	—		56.9	—	—		83.5	—	—	
12.4	12.4	—		18.2	18.2	—		26.7	26.7	—		39.2	39.2	39	39	57.6	57.6	—		84.5	84.5	—	
12.6	—	—		18.4	—	—		27.1	—	27	27	39.7	—	—		58.3	—	—		85.6	—	—	
12.7	12.7	—		18.7	18.7	—		27.4	27.4	—		40.2	40.2	—		59.0	59.0	—		86.6	86.6	—	
12.9	—	—		18.9	—	—		27.7	—	—		40.7	—	—		59.7	—	—		87.6	—	—	
13.0	13.0	13		19.1	19.1	—		28.0	28.0	—		41.2	41.2	—		60.4	60.4	—		88.7	88.7	—	
13.2	—	—		19.3	—	—		28.4	—	—		41.7	—	—		61.2	—	—		89.8	—	—	
13.3	13.3	—		19.6	19.6	—		28.7	28.7	—		42.2	42.2	—		61.9	61.9	62		90.9	90.9	91	
13.5	—	—		19.8	—	—		29.1	—	—		42.7	—	—		62.6	—	—		92.0	—	—	
13.7	13.7	—		20.0	20.0	20		29.4	29.4	—		43.2	43.2	43		63.4	63.4	—		93.1	93.1	—	
13.8	—			20.3	—	—		29.8	—	—		43.7	—	—		64.2	—	—		94.2	—	—	
14.0	14.0	—		20.5	20.5	—		30.1	30.1	30		44.2	44.2	—		64.9	64.9	—		95.3	95.3	—	
14.2	—			20.8	—	—		30.5	—	—		44.8	—	—		65.7	—	—		96.5	—	—	
14.3	14.3	—		21.0	21.0	—		30.9	30.9	—		45.3	45.3	—		66.5	66.5	—		97.6	97.6	—	
14.5	—	—		21.3	—	—		31.2	—	—		45.9	—	—		67.3	—	—		98.8	—	—	

Note: These values are generally available in multiples of 0.1, 1, 10, 100, 1k, and 1M.

B

BATTERIES

Batteries are an important source of dc voltage. They are available in two basic categories: the wet cell and the dry cell. A battery generally is made up of several individual cells.

A cell consists basically of two electrodes immersed in an electrolyte. A voltage is developed between the electrodes as a result of the chemical action between the electrodes and the electrolyte. The electrodes typically are two dissimilar metals, and the electrolyte is a chemical solution.

Simple Wet Cell

Figure B–1 shows a simple copper-zinc (Cu-Zn) chemical cell. One electrode is made of copper, the other of zinc. These electrodes are immersed in a solution of water and hydrochloric acid (HCl), which is the electrolyte.

FIGURE B–1
Simple chemical cell.

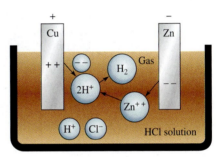

Positive hydrogen ions (H^+) and negative chlorine ions (Cl^-) are formed when the HCl ionizes in the water. Since zinc is more active than hydrogen, zinc atoms leave the zinc electrode and form zinc ions (Zn^{++}) in the solution. When a zinc ion is formed, two excess electrons are left on the zinc electrode, and two hydrogen ions are displaced from the solution. These two hydrogen ions will migrate to the copper electrode, take two electrons from the copper, and form a molecule of hydrogen gas (H_2). As a result of this reaction, a negative charge develops on the zinc electrode, and a positive charge develops on the copper electrode, creating a potential difference or voltage between the two electrodes.

In this copper-zinc cell, the hydrogen gas given off at the copper electrode tends to form a layer of bubbles around the electrodes, insulating the copper from the electrolyte. This effect, called *polarization,* results in a reduction in the voltage produced by the cell. Polarization can be remedied by the addition of an agent to the electrolyte to remove hydrogen gas or by the use of an electrolyte that does not form hydrogen gas.

Lead-Acid Cell   The positive electrode of a lead-acid cell is lead peroxide (PbO_2), and the negative electrode is spongy lead (Pb). The electrolyte is sulfuric acid (H_2SO_4) in water. Thus, the lead-acid cell is classified as a wet cell.

Two positive hydrogen ions ($2H^+$) and one negative sulfate ion (SO_4^{--}) are formed when the sulfuric acid ionizes in the water. Lead ions (Pb^{++}) from both electrodes displace the hydrogen ions in the electrolyte solution. When the lead ion from the spongy lead electrode enters the solution, it combines with a sulfate ion (SO_4^{--}) to form lead sulfate ($PbSO_4$), and it leaves two excess electrons on the electrode.

When a lead ion from the lead peroxide electrode enters the solution, it also leaves two excess electrons on the electrode and forms lead sulfate in the solution. However, because this electrode is lead peroxide, two free oxygen atoms are created when a lead atom leaves and enters the solution as a lead ion. These two oxygen atoms take four electrons from the lead peroxide electrode and become oxygen ions (O^{--}). This process creates a deficiency of two electrons on this electrode (there were initially two excess electrons).

The two oxygen ions ($2O^{--}$) combine in the solution with four hydrogen ions ($4H^+$) to produce two molecules of water ($2H_2O$). This process dilutes the electrolyte over a period of time. Also, there is a buildup of lead sulfate on the electrodes. These two factors result in a reduction in the voltage produced by the cell and necessitate periodic recharging.

As you have seen, for each departing lead ion, there is an excess of two electrons on the spongy lead electrode, and there is a deficiency of two electrons on the lead peroxide electrode. Therefore, the lead peroxide electrode is positive, and the spongy lead electrode is negative. This chemical reaction is pictured in Figure B–2.

FIGURE B–2
Chemical reaction in a discharging lead-acid cell.

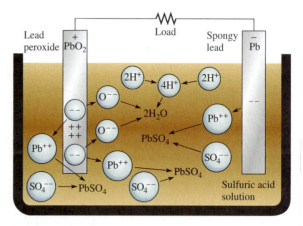

As mentioned, the dilution of the electrolyte by the formation of water and lead sulfate requires that the lead-acid cell be recharged to reverse the chemical process. A chemical cell that can be recharged is called a *secondary cell.* One that cannot be recharged is called a *primary cell.*

The cell is recharged by the connection of an external voltage source to the electrodes, as shown in Figure B–3. The formula for the chemical reaction in a lead-acid cell is

$$Pb + PbO_2 + 2H_2SO_4 \rightarrow 2PbSO_4 + 2H_2O$$

FIGURE B–3
Recharging a lead-acid cell.

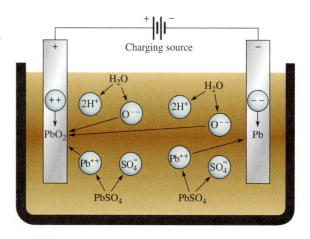

Dry Cell

In a dry cell, some of the disadvantages of a liquid electrolyte are overcome. Actually, the electrolyte in a typical dry cell is not dry but rather is in the form of a moist paste. This electrolyte is a combination of granulated carbon, powdered manganese dioxide, and ammonium chloride solution.

A typical carbon-zinc dry cell is illustrated in Figure B–4. The zinc container or can is dissolved by the electrolyte. As a result of this reaction, an excess of electrons accumulates on the container, making it the negative electrode.

FIGURE B–4

Simplified construction of a dry cell.

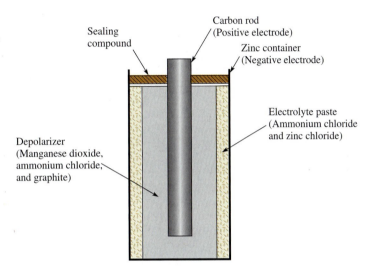

The hydrogen ions in the electrolyte take electrons from the carbon rod, making it the positive electrode. Hydrogen gas is formed near the carbon electrode, but this gas is eliminated by reaction with manganese dioxide (called a *depolarizing agent*). This depolarization prevents bursting of the container due to gas formation. Because the chemical reaction is not reversible, the carbon-zinc cell is a primary cell.

Types of Chemical Cells

Although only two common types of battery cells have been discussed, there are several types, listed in Table B–1.

TABLE B–1

Types of battery cells.

Type	+ electrode	– electrode	Electrolyte	Volts	Comments
Carbon-zinc	Carbon	Zinc	Ammonium and zinc chloride	1.5	Dry, primary
Lead-acid	Lead peroxide	Spongy lead	Sulfuric acid	2.0	Wet, secondary
Manganese-alkaline	Manganese dioxide	Zinc	Potassium hydroxide	1.5	Dry, primary or secondary
Mercury	Zinc	Mercuric oxide	Potassium hydroxide	1.3	Dry, primary
Nickel-cadmium	Nickel	Cadmium hydroxide	Potassium hydroxide	1.25	Dry, secondary
Nickel-iron (Edison cell)	Nickel oxide	Iron	Potassium hydroxide	1.36	Wet, secondary

C DERIVATIONS

Equation (11–6)   RMS (Effective) Value of a Sine Wave

The abbreviation "rms" stands for the root mean square process by which this value is derived. In the process, we first square the equation of a sine wave.

$$v^2 = V_p^2 \sin^2\theta$$

Next, we obtain the mean or average value of v^2 by dividing the area under a half-cycle of the curve by π (see Figure C–1). The area is found by integration and trigonometric identities.

$$V_{avg}^2 = \frac{\text{area}}{\pi} = \frac{1}{\pi} \int_0^\pi V_p^2 \sin^2\theta \, d\theta$$

$$= \frac{V_p^2}{2\pi} \int_0^\pi (1 - \cos 2\theta)d\theta = \frac{V_p^2}{2\pi} \int_0^\pi 1 \, d\theta - \frac{V_p^2}{2\pi} \int_0^\pi (-\cos 2\theta) \, d\theta$$

$$= \frac{V_p^2}{2\pi} (\theta - \tfrac{1}{2} \sin 2\theta)_0^\pi = \frac{V_p^2}{2\pi} (\pi - 0) = \frac{V_p^2}{2}$$

Finally, the square root of V_{avg}^2 is V_{rms}.

$$V_{rms} = \sqrt{V_{avg}^2} = \sqrt{V_p^2/2} = \frac{V_p}{\sqrt{2}} = 0.707V_p$$

FIGURE C–1

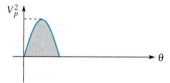

Equation (11–12)   Average Value of a Half-Cycle Sine Wave

The average value of a sine wave is determined for a half-cycle because the average over a full cycle is zero.

The equation for a sine wave is

$$v = V_p \sin \theta$$

The average value of the half-cycle is the area under the curve divided by the distance of the curve along the horizontal axis (see Figure C–2).

$$V_{avg} = \frac{\text{area}}{\pi}$$

FIGURE C–2

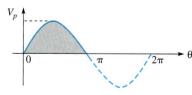

To find the area, we use integral calculus.

$$V_{avg} = \frac{1}{\pi} \int_0^\pi V_p \sin \theta \; d\theta = \frac{V_p}{\pi} (-\cos \theta) \Big|_0^\pi$$

$$= \frac{V_p}{\pi}[-\cos \pi - (-\cos 0)] = \frac{V_p}{\pi}[-(-1) - (-1)]$$

$$= \frac{V_p}{\pi}(2) = \frac{2}{\pi} V_p = 0.637 V_p$$

Equations (13–26) and (14–15) Reactance Derivations

Derivation of Capacitive Reactance

$$\theta = 2\pi f t = \omega t$$

$$i = C\frac{dv}{dt} = C\frac{d(V_p \sin \theta)}{dt} = C\frac{d(V_p \sin \omega t)}{dt} = \omega C(V_p \cos \omega t)$$

$$I_{rms} = \omega C V_{rms}$$

$$X_C = \frac{V_{rms}}{I_{rms}} = \frac{V_{rms}}{\omega C V_{rms}} = \frac{1}{\omega C} = \frac{1}{2\pi f C}$$

Derivation of Inductive Reactance

$$v = L\frac{di}{dt} = L\frac{d(I_p \sin \omega t)}{dt} = \omega L(I_p \cos \omega t)$$

$$V_{rms} = \omega L I_{rms}$$

$$X_L = \frac{V_{rms}}{I_{rms}} = \frac{\omega L I_{rms}}{I_{rms}} = \omega L = 2\pi f L$$

Equation (18–15) Resonant Frequency for a Nonideal Parallel Resonant Circuit

$$\frac{1}{\mathbf{Z}} = \frac{1}{-jX_C} + \frac{1}{R_W + jX_L}$$

$$= j\left(\frac{1}{X_C}\right) + \frac{R_W - jX_L}{(R_W + jX_L)(R_W - jX_L)} = j\left(\frac{1}{X_C}\right) + \frac{R_W - jX_L}{R_W^2 + X_L^2}$$

The first term plus splitting the numerator of the second term yields

$$\frac{1}{\mathbf{Z}} = j\left(\frac{1}{X_C}\right) - j\left(\frac{X_L}{R_W^2 + X_L^2}\right) + \frac{R_W}{R_W^2 + X_L^2}$$

The *j* terms are equal.

$$\frac{1}{X_C} = \frac{X_L}{R_W^2 + X_L^2}$$

Thus,

$$R_W^2 = X_L^2 = X_L X_C$$

$$R_W^2 + (2\pi f_r L)^2 = \frac{2\pi f_r L}{2\pi f_r C}$$

$$R_W^2 + 4\pi^2 f_r^2 L^2 = \frac{L}{C}$$

$$4\pi^2 f_r^2 L^2 = \frac{L}{C} - R_W^2$$

Solving for f_r^2,

$$f_r^2 = \frac{\left(\dfrac{L}{C}\right) - R_W^2}{4\pi^2 L^2}$$

Multiply both numerator and denominator by C,

$$f_r^2 = \frac{L - R_W^2 C}{4\pi^2 L^2 C} = \frac{L - R_W^2 C}{L(4\pi^2 LC)}$$

Factoring an L out of the numerator and canceling gives

$$f_r^2 = \frac{1 - (R_W^2 C/L)}{4\pi^2 LC}$$

Taking the square root of both sides yields f_r,

$$f_r = \frac{\sqrt{1 - (R_W^2 C/L)}}{2\pi\sqrt{LC}}$$

Equation (18–18)   Impedance of Nonideal Tank Circuit at Resonance

Begin with the following expression for $1/\mathbf{Z}$ that was developed in the derivation for Equation (18–15).

$$\frac{1}{\mathbf{Z}} = j\left(\frac{1}{X_C}\right) - j\left(\frac{X_L}{R_W^2 + X_L^2}\right) + \frac{R_W}{R_W^2 + X_L^2}$$

At resonance, $\mathbf{Z}$ is purely resistive; so it has no j part (the j terms in the last expression cancel). Thus, only the real part is left, as stated in the following equation for Z at resonance:

$$Z_r = \frac{R_W^2 + X_L^2}{R_W}$$

Splitting the denominator, we get

$$Z_r = \frac{R_W^2}{R_W} + \frac{X_L^2}{R_W} = R_W + \frac{X_L^2}{R_W}$$

Factoring out R_W gives

$$Z_r = R_W\left(1 + \frac{X_L^2}{R_W^2}\right)$$

Since $X_L^2/R_W^2 = Q^2$, then

$$Z_r = R_W(Q^2 + 1)$$

D CAPACITOR COLOR CODING

Some capacitors have color-coded designations. The color code used for capacitors is basically the same as that used for resistors. Some variations occur in tolerance designation. The basic color codes are shown in Table D–1, and some typical color-coded capacitors are illustrated in Figure D–1.

TABLE D–1

Typical composite color codes for capacitors (picofarads).

Color	Digit	Multiplier	Tolerance
Black	0	1	20%
Brown	1	10	1%
Red	2	100	2%
Orange	3	1000	3%
Yellow	4	10000	
Green	5	100000	5% (EIA)
Blue	6	1000000	
Violet	7		
Gray	8		
White	9		
Gold		0.1	5% (JAN)
Silver		0.01	10%
No color			20%

NOTE: EIA stands for Electronic Industries Association, and JAN stands for Joint Army-Navy, a military standard.

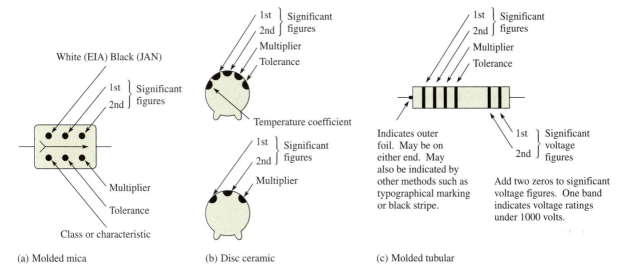

(a) Molded mica   (b) Disc ceramic   (c) Molded tubular

FIGURE D–1

Typical color-coded capacitors.

ANSWERS TO SELECTED ODD-NUMBERED PROBLEMS

Chapter One

1. **(a)** 3×10^3 **(b)** 7.5×10^4 **(c)** 2×10^6
3. **(a)** $8.4 \times 10^3 = 0.84 \times 10^4 = 0.084 \times 10^5$
   (b) $99 \times 10^3 = 9.9 \times 10^4 = 0.99 \times 10^5$
   (c) $200 \times 10^3 = 20 \times 10^4 = 2 \times 10^5$
5. **(a)** 0.0000025   **(b)** 5000   **(c)** 0.39
7. **(a)** 126×10^6 **(b)** 855×10^{-3} **(c)** 606×10^{-8}
9. **(a)** 20×10^8 **(b)** 36×10^{14} **(c)** 15.4×10^{-15}
11. **(a)** 2370×10^{-6} **(b)** 18.56×10^{-6}
    (c) $0.00574389 \times 10^{-6}$ **(d)** $100{,}000{,}000{,}000 \times 10^{-6}$
13. **(a)** 12.25×10^{14} **(b)** 5×10^3
    (c) 10.575×10^{-6} **(d)** 2×10^{10}
15. **(a)** 3 μF   **(b)** 3.3 MΩ **(c)** 350 nA or 0.35 μA
17. **(a)** 24 μA   **(b)** 9.7 MΩ **(c)** 3 pW
19. **(a)** 82 μW   **(b)** 450 W
21. **(a)** 1000   **(b)** 50,000   **(c)** 2×10^{-5}
    (d) 1.55×10^{-4}

Chapter Two

1. 80×10^{12} C
3. **(a)** 10 V   **(b)** 2.5 V   **(c)** 4 V
5. 20 V
7. 33.3 V
9. 0.2 A
11. 0.15 C
13. **(a)** 27 k$\Omega \pm 5\%$ **(b)** 1.8 k$\Omega \pm 10\%$
15. 330 Ω: orange, orange, brown
    2.2 kΩ: red, red, red
    56 kΩ: green, blue, orange

100 kΩ: brown, black, yellow
39 kΩ: orange, white, orange
17. **(a)** 200 mS   **(b)** 40 mS   **(c)** 10 mS
19. AWG #27
21. Through lamp 2
23. Circuit (b)
25. See Figure P–1.

FIGURE P–1

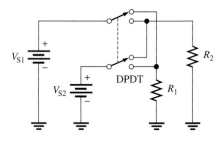

27. See Figure P–2.

FIGURE P–2

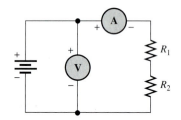

29. Position 1: V1 = 0 V, V2 = V_S
    Position 2: V1 = V_S, V2 = 0 V
31. See Figure P–3.

FIGURE P–3

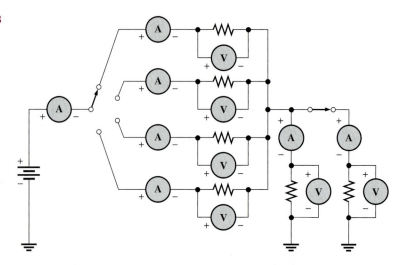

33. (a) 0.25 V   **(b)** 250 V

35. (a) 20 Ω   **(b)** 1.50 MΩ   **(c)** 4500 Ω

37. See Figure P–4.

29. See Figure P–5.

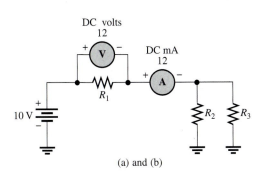

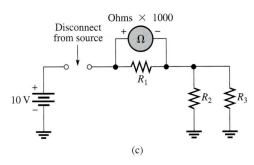

(a) and (b)

(c)

FIGURE P–4

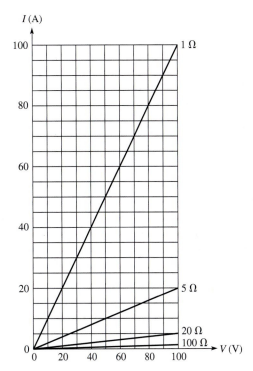

FIGURE P–5

Chapter Three

1. (a) Current triples.   **(b)** Current is reduced 75%.
   (c) Current is halved.   **(d)** Current increases 54%.
   (e) Current quadruples.   **(f)** Current is unchanged.

3. $V = IR$

5. (a) 5 A   **(b)** 1.5 A   **(c)** 500 mA
   (d) 2 mA   **(e)** 44.6 μA

7. 1.2 A

9. 532 μA

11. (a) 36 V   **(b)** 280 V   **(c)** 1700 V
   (d) 28.2 V   **(e)** 56 V

13. 81 V

15. (a) 59.9 mA   **(b)** 5.99 V   **(c)** 4.61 mV

17. (a) 2 kΩ   **(b)** 3.5 kΩ   **(c)** 2 kΩ
   (d) 100 kΩ   **(e)** 1.0 MΩ

19. 150 Ω

21. 133 Ω; 100 Ω; the source can be shorted if the rheostat is set to 0 Ω.

23. The graph is a straight line, indicating a linear relationship between V and I.

25. $R_1 = 0.5$ Ω, $R_2 = 1.0$ Ω, $R_3 = 2$ Ω

27. The voltage decreased by 4 V (from 10 V to 6 V).

Chapter Four

1. 350 W

3. 20 kW

5. (a) 1 MW   **(b)** 3 MW
   (c) 150 MW   **(d)** 8.7 MW

7. (a) 2,000,000 μW   **(b)** 500 μW
   (c) 250 μW   **(d)** 6.67 μW

9. 8640 J

11. 2.02 kW/day

13. 0.00186 kWh

15. 37.5 Ω

17. 360 W

19. 100 μW

21. 40.2 mW

23. (a) 0.480 Wh   **(b)** Equal

25. At least 12 W, to allow a safety margin

27. 7.07 V

29. 8 A

31. 100 mW, 80%

33. 0.032 kWh

FIGURE P–6

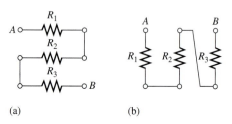 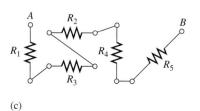

(a)   (b)   (c)

Chapter Five

1. See Figure P–6.

3. R_1, R_7, R_8, R_{10}
R_2, R_4, R_6, R_{11}
R_3, R_5, R_9, R_{12}

5. 5 mA

7. See Figure P–7.

FIGURE P–7

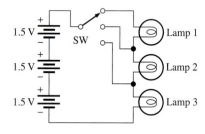

9. (a) 1560 Ω   **(b)** 103 Ω
(c) 13.7 kΩ   **(d)** 3.671 MΩ

11. 67.2 kΩ

13. 3.9 kΩ

15. 17.8 MΩ

17. (a) 625 μA   **(b)** 4.26 μA

19. 355 mA

21. $R_1 = 330$ Ω, $R_2 = 220$ Ω, $R_3 = 100$ Ω, $R_4 = 470$ Ω

23. Position *A:* 5.45 mA
Position *B:* 6.06 mA
Position *C:* 7.95 mA
Position *D:* 12 mA

25. 14 V

27. (a) 23 V   **(b)** 35 V   **(c)** 0 V

29. 4 V

31. 22 Ω

33. Position *A:* 4.0 V
Position *B:* 4.5 V
Position *C:* 5.4 V
Position *D:* 7.2 V

35. 4.82%

37. $V_R = 6$ V, $V_{2R} = 12$ V, $V_{3R} = 18$ V,
$V_{4R} = 24$ V, $V_{5R} = 30$ V

39. $V_2 = 1.79$ V, $V_3 = 1$ V, $V_4 = 17.9$ V

41. See Figure P–8.

FIGURE P–8

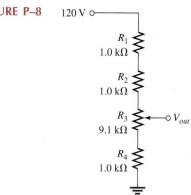

120 V

R_1 1.0 kΩ

R_2 1.0 kΩ

R_3 9.1 kΩ ○ V_{out}

R_4 1.0 kΩ

43. 54.9 mW

45. 12.5 MΩ

47. $V_A = 100$ V, $V_B = 57.7$ V,
$V_C = 15.2$ V, $V_D = 7.58$ V

49. $V_A = 14.82$ V, $V_B = 12.97$ V,
$V_C = 12.64$ V, $V_D = 9.34$ V

51. (a) R_4 is open.
(b) Short from *A* to *B*

53. Table 5–1 is correct.

55. Yes. There is a short between pin 4 and the upper side of
R_{11}.

Chapter Six

1. See Figure P–9.

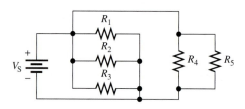

FIGURE P–9

3. $R_1, R_2, R_5, R_9, R_{10}, R_{12}$
R_4, R_6, R_7, R_8
R_3, R_{11}

5. 100 V

7. 1.35 A

9. $R_2 = 22$ Ω, $R_3 = 100$ Ω, $R_4 = 33$ Ω

11. 11.4 mA

13. (a) 359 Ω   (b) 25.6 Ω
  (c) 819 Ω   (d) 997 Ω

15. 567 Ω

17. 2.46 Ω

19. (a) 510 kΩ   (b) 245 kΩ
  (c) 510 kΩ   (d) 193 kΩ

21. 10 A

23. 50 mA; When one bulb burns out the others remain on.

25. 53.7 Ω

27. $I_2 = 167$ mA, $I_3 = 83.3$ mA, $I_T = 300$ mA,
  $R_1 = 2$ kΩ, $R_2 = 600$ Ω

29. Position A: 2.25 mA
  Position B: 4.75 mA
  Position C: 7 mA

31. (a) $I_1 = 6.88$ μA, $I_2 = 3.12$ μA,
  (b) $I_1 = 5.25$ mA, $I_2 = 2.39$ mA,
    $I_3 = 1.59$ mA, $I_4 = 772$ μA

33. $R_1 = 3.3$ kΩ, $R_2 = 1.8$ kΩ, $R_3 = 5.6$ kΩ,
  $R_4 = 3.9$ kΩ

35. 0.05 Ω

37. (a) 68.8 μW   (b) 52.5 mW

39. $P_1 = 1.25$ W, $I_2 = 75$ mA, $I_1 = 125$ mA,
  $V_S = 10$ V, $R_1 = 80$ Ω, $R_2 = 133$ Ω

41. 682 mA, 3.41 A

43. The 8.2 kΩ resistor is open.

45. Connect ohmmeter between the following pins:
Pins 1-2
  Correct reading: $R = 1.0$ kΩ ‖ 3.3 kΩ = 767 Ω
  R_1 open: $R = 3.3$ kΩ
  R_2 open: $R = 1.0$ kΩ
Pins 3-4
  Correct reading: $R = 270$ Ω ‖ 390 Ω = 159.5 Ω
  R_3 open: $R = 390$ Ω
  R_4 open: $R = 270$ Ω
Pins 5-6
  Correct reading:
  $R = 1.0$ MΩ ‖ 1.8 MΩ ‖ 680 kΩ ‖ 510 kΩ = 201 kΩ
  R_5 open: $R = 1.8$ MΩ ‖ 680 kΩ ‖ 510 kΩ = 251 kΩ
  R_6 open: $R = 1.0$ MΩ ‖ 680 kΩ ‖ 510 kΩ = 226 kΩ
  R_7 open: $R = 1.0$ MΩ ‖ 1.8 MΩ ‖ 510 kΩ = 284 kΩ
  R_8 open: $R = 1.0$ MΩ ‖ 1.8 MΩ ‖ 680 kΩ = 330 kΩ

47. Short between pins 3 and 4:
  (a) $R_{1-2} = (R_1 \| R_2 \| R_3 \| R_4 \| R_{11} \| R_{12})$
      $+ (R_5 \| R_6 \| R_7 \| R_8 \| R_9 \| R_{10}) = 940$ Ω
  (b) $R_{2-3} = R_5 \| R_6 \| R_7 \| R_8 \| R_9 \| R_{10} = 518$ Ω
  (c) $R_{2-4} = R_5 \| R_6 \| R_7 \| R_8 \| R_9 \| R_{10} = 518$ Ω
  (d) $R_{1-4} = R_1 \| R_2 \| R_3 \| R_4 \| R_{11} \| R_{12} = 422$ Ω

Chapter Seven

1. See Figure P–10.

3. (a) R_1 and R_4 are in series with the parallel combination
    of R_2 and R_3.

FIGURE P–10

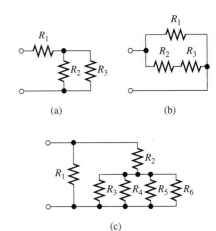

(a)   (b)

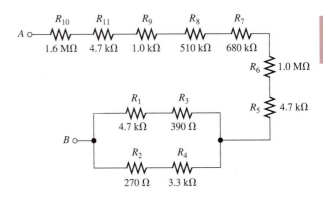

(c)

  (b) R_1 is in series with the parallel combination of R_2, R_3,
    and R_4.
  (c) The parallel combination of R_2 and R_3 is in series
    with the parallel combination of R_4 and R_5. This is all
    in parallel with R_1.

5. See Figure P–11.

FIGURE P–11

7. See Figure P–12.

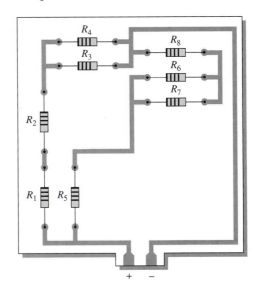

FIGURE P–12

9. (a) 133 Ω **(b)** 779 Ω **(c)** 852 Ω

11. (a) $I_1 = I_4 = 11.3$ mA, $I_2 = I_3 = 5.64$ mA,
   $V_1 = 633$ mV, $V_2 = V_3 = 564$ mV,
   $V_4 = 305$ mV
   (b) $I_1 = 3.85$ mA, $I_2 = 563$ μA,
   $I_3 = 1.16$ mA, $I_4 = 2.13$ mA, $V_1 = 2.62$ V,
   $V_2 = V_3 = V_4 = 383$ mV
   (c) $I_1 = 5$ mA, $I_2 = 303$ μA,
   $I_3 = 568$ μA, $I_4 = 313$ μA,
   $I_5 = 558$ μA, $V_1 = 5$ V,
   $V_2 = V_3 = 1.88$ V, $V_4 = V_5 = 3.13$ V

13. SW1 closed, SW2 open: 220 Ω
   SW1 closed, SW2 closed: 200 Ω
   SW1 open, SW2 open: 320 Ω
   SW1 open, SW2 closed: 300 Ω

15. $V_A = 100$ V, $V_B = 61.5$ V, $V_C = 15.7$ V,
   $V_D = 7.87$ V

17. Measure the voltage at A with respect to ground and the voltage at B with respect to ground. The difference is V_{R2}.

19. 110 Ω

21. $R_{AB} = 1.32$ kΩ
   $R_{BC} = 1.32$ kΩ
   $R_{CD} = 0$ Ω

23. 7.5 V unloaded, 7.29 V loaded

25. 47 kΩ

27. $R_1 = 1000$ Ω; $R_2 = R_3 = 500$ Ω;
   lower tap loaded: $V_{lower} = 1.82$ V, $V_{upper} = 4.55$ V
   upper tap loaded: $V_{lower} = 1.67$ V, $V_{upper} = 3.33$ V

29. (a) $V_G = 1.75$ V, $V_S = 3.25$ V
   (b) $I_1 = I_2 = 6.48$ μA, $I_D = I_S = 2.17$ mA
   (c) $V_{DS} = 2.55$ V, $V_{DG} = 4.05$ V

31. 1000 V

33. (a) 0.5 V range   **(b)** Approximately 1 mV

35. (a) 271 Ω **(b)** 221 mA
   (c) 58.7 mA   **(d)** 12 V

37. 621 Ω, $I_1 = I_9 = 16.1$ mA, $I_2 = 8.27$ mA,
   $I_3 = I_8 = 7.84$ mA, $I_4 = 4.06$ mA,
   $I_5 = I_6 = I_7 = 3.78$ mA

39. 971 mA

41. (a) 9 V   **(b)** 3.75 V   **(c)** 11.25 V

43. 2184 Ω

45. No, it should be 4.39 V.

47. The 2.2 kΩ resistor (R_3) is open.

49. The 3.3 kΩ resistor (R_4) is open.

Chapter Eight

1. $I_S = 6$ A, $R_S = 50$ Ω

3. $V_S = 720$ V, $R_S = 1.2$ kΩ

5. 845 μA

7. 1.6 mA

9. 90.7 V

11. $I_{S1} = 2.28$ mA, $I_{S2} = 1.35$ mA

13. 116 μA

15. $R_{TH} = 88.6$ Ω, $V_{TH} = 1.09$ V

17. 100 μA

19. (a) $I_N = 110$ mA, $R_N = 76.7$ Ω
   (b) $I_N = 11.1$ mA, $R_N = 73$ Ω
   (c) $I_N = 50$ μA, $R_N = 35.9$ kΩ
   (d) $I_N = 68.8$ mA, $R_N = 1.3$ kΩ

21. 17.9 V

23. $I_N = 953$ μA, $R_N = 1175$ Ω

25. $I_N = 48.2$ mA, $R_N = 56.9$ Ω

27. 11.1 Ω

29. $R_{TH} = 48$ Ω, $R_4 = 160$ Ω

31. (a) $R_A = 39.8$ Ω, $R_B = 73$ Ω, $R_C = 48.7$ Ω
   (b) $R_A = 21.2$ kΩ, $R_B = 10.3$ kΩ,
   $R_C = 14.9$ kΩ

Chapter Nine

1. Six possible loops

3. $I_{R1} - I_{R2} - I_{R3} = 0$

5. $V_1 = 5.66$ V, $V_2 = 6.33$ V,
   $V_3 = 325$ mV

7. $I_{R1} = 738$ mA, $I_{R2} = -527$ mA,
   $I_{R3} = -469$ mA

9. -1.84 V

11. $I_1 = 0$ A, $I_2 = 2$ A

13. (a) $-16{,}470$ **(b)** -1.59

15. $I_1 = 1.24$ A, $I_2 = 2.05$ A, $I_3 = 1.89$ A

17. X1 = .371428571429 ($I_1 = 371$ mA)
   X2 = $-$.142857142857 ($I_2 = -143$ mA)

19. X1 = 1.23529411765 ($I_1 = 1.24$ A)
   X2 = 2.05347593583 ($I_2 = 2.05$ A)
   X3 = 1.88502673797 ($I_3 = 1.89$ A)

21. $I_1 = -5.11$ mA, $I_2 = -3.52$ mA

23. $V_1 = 5.11$ V, $V_3 = 890$ mV
   $V_2 = 2.89$ V

25. $I_1 = 15.6$ mA, $I_2 = -61.3$ mA, $I_3 = 61.5$ mA

27. -11.2 mV

29. 2.7 mA

31. $I_{R1} = 20.6$ mA, $I_{R3} = 193$ mA, $I_{R2} = -172$ mA

33. $V_A = 1.5$ V, $V_B = -5.65$ V

35. $I_{R1} = 193$ μA, $I_{R2} = 370$ μA, $I_{R3} = 179$ μA,
   $I_{R4} = 328$ μA, $I_{R5} = 1.46$ mA, $I_{R6} = 522$ μA,
   $I_{R7} = 2.16$ mA, $I_{R8} = 1.64$ mA, $V_A = -3.70$ V,
   $V_B = -5.85$ V, $V_C = -15.7$ V

Chapter Ten

1. Decreases

3. 37.5 μWb

5. 597

7. 150 At

9. (a) Electromagnetic field   **(b)** Spring

11. Forces produced by the interaction of the electromagnetic field and the permanent magnetic field

13. Change the current.

15. Material A

17. 1 mA

19. Lenz's law defines the polarity of the induced voltage.

21. The commutator and brush arrangement electrically connect the loop to the external circuit.

23. Figure P–13.

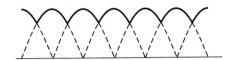

FIGURE P–13

Chapter Eleven

1. (a) 1 Hz   **(b)** 5 Hz
   (c) 20 Hz   **(d)** 1 kHz
   (e) 2 kHz   **(f)** 100 kHz

3. 2 μs

5. 250 Hz

7. 200 rps

9. (a) 7.07 mA   **(b)** 0 A (full cycle), 4.5 mA (half-cycle)   **(c)** 14.14 mA

11. (a) 0.524 or $\pi/6$ rad   **(b)** 0.785 or $\pi/4$ rad
   (c) 1.361 or $39\pi/90$ rad   **(d)** 2.356 or $3\pi/4$ rad
   (e) 3.491 or $10\pi/9$ rad   **(f)** 5.236 or $5\pi/3$ rad

13. 15°, A leading

15. See Figure P–14.

FIGURE P–14

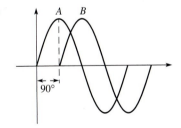

17. (a) 57.4 mA   **(b)** 99.6 mA
   (c) −17.4 mA   **(d)** −57.4 mA
   (e) −99.6 mA   **(f)** 0 mA

19. 30°: 13.0 V
     45°: 14.5 V
     90°: 13.0 V
     180°: −7.5 V
     200°: −11.5 V
     300°: −7.5 V

21. 22.1 V

23. $V_{R1(avg)}$ = 40.5 V, $V_{R2(avg)}$ = 31.5 V

25. V_{max} = 39 V, V_{min} = 9 V

27. −1 V

29. $t_r \cong$ 3.5 ms, $t_f \cong$ 3.5 ms, $t_W \cong$ 12.5 ms, Ampl. $\cong$ 5 V

31. 5.84 V

33. (a) −0.375 V   **(b)** 3.01 V

35. (a) 50 kHz   **(b)** 10 Hz

37. 75 kHz, 125 kHz, 175 kHz, 225 kHz, 275 kHz, 325 kHz

39. V_p = 600 mV, T = 500 ms

41. Ampl = 1.4 V, t_W = 120 ms, T = 400 ms, %dc = 30%

43. $V_{p(in)}$ = 4.44 V, f_{in} = 2 Hz

Chapter Twelve

1. See Figure P–15.

FIGURE P–15

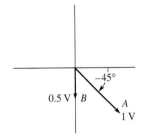

3. (a) 9.55 Hz   **(b)** 57.3 Hz
   (c) 0.318 Hz   **(d)** 200 Hz

5. 54.5 μs

7. See Figure P–16.

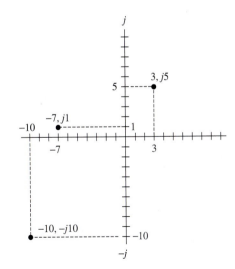

FIGURE P–16

9. (a) −5, +j3 and 5, −j3
   (b) −1, −j7 and 1, +j7
   (c) −10, +j10 and 10, −j10

11. 18.0

13. (a) $643 - j766$ (b) $-14.1 + j5.13$
    (c) $-17.7 - j17.7$ (d) $-3 + j0$

15. (a) Fourth   (b) Fourth   (c) Fourth   (d) First

17. (a) $12\angle115°$ (b) $20\angle230°$
    (c) $100\angle190°$ (d) $50\angle160°$

19. (a) $1.1 + j0.7$ (b) $-81 - j35$
    (c) $5.28 - j5.27$ (d) $-50.4 + j62.5$

21. (a) $3.2\angle11°$ (b) $7\angle-101°$
    (c) $1.52\angle70.6°$ (d) $2.79\angle-63.5°$

23. $9.87\angle-8.80°$ V, $1.97\angle-8.80°$ mA

Chapter Thirteen

1. (a) $5\ \mu F$ (b) $1\ \mu C$ (c) 10 V

3. (a) $0.001\ \mu F$ (b) $0.0035\ \mu F$
    (c) $0.00025\ \mu F$

5. 2.3×10^{-22} newton

7. (a) 8.85×10^{-12} F/m
    (b) 35.4×10^{-12} F/m
    (c) 66.4×10^{-12} F/m
    (d) 17.7×10^{-12} F/m

9. 8.85 pF

11. 12.5 pF increase

13. Ceramic

15. Aluminum, tantalum; they are polarized.

17. (a) $0.02\ \mu F$ (b) $0.047\ \mu F$
    (c) $0.001\ \mu F$ (d) 220 pF

19. (a) $0.667\ \mu F$ (b) 69.0 pF   (c) $2.70\ \mu F$

21. $2\ \mu F$

23. (a) 1057 pF   (b) $0.121\ \mu F$

25. (a) $2.5\ \mu F$ (b) 717 pF   (c) $1.6\ \mu F$

27. $\Delta V_5 = +1.39$ V, $\Delta V_6 = -2.96$ V

29. (a) 14 ms   (b) $247.5\ \mu s$
    (c) $11\ \mu s$ (d) $280\ \mu s$

31. (a) 9.20 V   (b) 1.24 V
    (c) 0.458 V   (d) 0.168 V

33. (a) 17.9 V   (b) 12.8 V   (c) 6.59 V

35. $7.62\ \mu s$

37. $2.94\ \mu s$

39. See Figure P–17.

41. (a) $31.8\ \Omega$ (b) $111\ k\Omega$ (c) $49.7\ \Omega$

43. $200\ \Omega$

45. 0 W, 3.39 mVAR

47. $0.00525\ \mu F$

49. X_C of the bypass capacitor should ideally be $0\ \Omega$.

51. The capacitor is shorted.

Chapter Fourteen

1. (a) 1000 mH   (b) 0.25 mH
    (c) 0.01 mH   (d) 0.5 mH

3. 50 mV

5. 20 mV

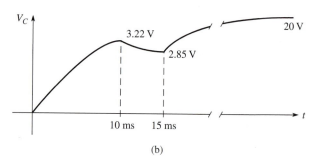

FIGURE P–17

7. 1 A

9. $155\ \mu H$

11. 50.51 mH

13. $7.14\ \mu H$

15. (a) 4.33 H   (b) 50 mH   (c) $0.571\ \mu H$

17. (a) $1\ \mu s$ (b) $2.13\ \mu s$ (c) $2\ \mu s$

19. (a) 5.52 V   (b) 2.03 V   (c) 747 mV
    (d) 275 mV   (e) 101 mV

21. (a) 12.3 V   (b) 9.10 V   (c) 3.35 V

23. $11.0\ \mu s$

25. 3.18 ms

27. 240 V

29. (a) $144\ \Omega$ (b) $10.1\ \Omega$ (c) $13.4\ \Omega$

31. (a) 55.5 Hz   (b) 796 Hz   (c) 597 Hz

33. $26.1\angle-90°$ mA

35. (a) Infinite resistance   (b) Zero resistance
    (c) Lower R_W

Chapter Fifteen

1. $1.5\ \mu H$

3. 4; 0.25

5. (a) 100 V rms; in phase
    (b) 100 V rms; out of phase
    (c) 20 V rms; out of phase

7. 600 V

9. 0.25 (4:1)

11. 60 V

13. (a) 25 mA   (b) 50 mA
    (c) 15 V   (d) 750 mW

15. 1.83

17. 9.76 W

19. (a) 6 V   **(b)** 0 V   **(c)** 40 V

21. 94.5 W

23. 0.98

25. 25 kVA

27. $V_1 = 11.5$ V, $V_2 = 23.0$ V, $V_3 = 23.0$ V, $V_4 = 46.0$ V

29. (a) 48 V   **(b)** 25 V

31. (a) $\mathbf{V}_{RL} = 35\angle 0°$ V, $\mathbf{I}_{RL} = 2.92\angle 0°$ A,
    $\mathbf{V}_C = 15\angle 0°$ V, $\mathbf{I}_C = 1.5\angle 90°$ A
   (b) $34.4\angle -12.5°$ Ω

33. Excessive primary current is drawn, potentially burning out the source and/or the transformer unless the primary is protected by a fuse.

Chapter Sixteen

1. 8 kHz, 8 kHz

3. (a) $270\ \Omega - j100\ \Omega$, $288\angle -20.3°\ \Omega$
   (b) $680\ \Omega - j1000\ \Omega$, $1.21\angle -55.8°\ k\Omega$

5. (a) $56\ k\Omega - j796\ k\Omega$
   (b) $56\ k\Omega - j159\ k\Omega$
   (c) $56\ k\Omega - j79.6\ k\Omega$
   (d) $56\ k\Omega - j31.8\ k\Omega$

7. (a) $R = 33\ \Omega$, $X_C = 50\ \Omega$
   (b) $R = 272\ \Omega$, $X_C = 127\ \Omega$
   (c) $R = 698\ \Omega$, $X_C = 1.66\ k\Omega$
   (d) $R = 558\ \Omega$, $X_C = 558\ \Omega$

9. (a) $179\angle 58.2°\ \mu A$ **(b)** $625\angle 38.5°\ \mu A$
   (c) $1.98\angle 76.2°\ mA$

11. $-15.9°$

13. (a) $97.3\angle -54.9°\ \Omega$ **(b)** $103\angle 54.9°\ mA$
   (c) $5.76\angle 54.9°\ V$ **(d)** $8.18\angle -35.1°\ V$

15. $R_X = 12\ \Omega$, $C_X = 13.3\ \mu F$ in series.

17. $261\ \Omega$, $-79.8°$

19. $\mathbf{V}_C = \mathbf{V}_R = 10\angle 0°$ V
   $\mathbf{I}_{tot} = 184\angle 37.1°\ mA$
   $\mathbf{I}_R = 147\angle 0°\ mA$
   $\mathbf{I}_C = 111\angle 90°\ mA$

21. (a) $6.58\angle -48.8°\ \Omega$ **(b)** $10\angle 0°\ mA$
   (c) $11.4\angle 90°\ mA$ **(d)** $15.2\angle 48.8°\ mA$
   (e) $-48.8°$ (I_{tot} leading V_s)

23. 18.2 kΩ resistor in series with 190 pF capacitor.

25. $\mathbf{V}_{C1} = 8.42\angle -3.0°$ V, $\mathbf{V}_{C2} = 1.50\angle -58.9°$ V
   $\mathbf{V}_{C3} = 3.65\angle 6.8°$ V, $\mathbf{V}_{R1} = 3.32\angle 31.1°$ V
   $\mathbf{V}_{R2} = 2.36\angle 6.8°$ V, $\mathbf{V}_{R3} = 1.29\angle 6.8°$ V

27. $\mathbf{I}_{tot} = 79.5\angle 87°\ mA$, $\mathbf{I}_{C2R1} = 7.07\angle 31.1°\ mA$
   $\mathbf{I}_{C3} = 75.7\angle 96.8°\ mA$, $\mathbf{I}_{R2R3} = 7.16\angle 6.8°\ mA$

29. 0.1 μF

31. $\mathbf{I}_{C1} = \mathbf{I}_{R1} = 2.27\angle 74.5°\ mA$
   $\mathbf{I}_{R2} = 2.04\angle 72.0°\ mA$
   $\mathbf{I}_{R3} = 246\angle 84.3°\ \mu A$
   $\mathbf{I}_{R4} = 149\angle 41.2°\ \mu A$
   $\mathbf{I}_{R5} = 180\angle 75.1°\ \mu A$
   $\mathbf{I}_{R6} = \mathbf{I}_{C3} = 101\angle 135°\ \mu A$
   $\mathbf{I}_{C2} = 101\angle 131°\ \mu A$

33. 4.03 VA

35. 0.909

37. (a) $I_{LA} = 4.8$ A, $I_{LB} = 3.33$ A
   (b) $P_{rA} = 606$ VAR, $P_{rB} = 250$ VAR
   (c) $P_{trueA} = 979$ W, $P_{trueB} = 759$ W
   (d) $P_{aA} = 1151$ VA, $P_{aB} = 799$ VA
   (e) Load A

39. 0 Hz   1 V
   1 kHz   706 mV
   2 kHz   445 mV
   3 kHz   315 mV
   4 kHz   242 mV
   5 kHz   195 mV
   6 kHz   164 mV
   7 kHz   141 mV
   8 kHz   123 mV
   9 kHz   110 mV
  10 kHz   99.0 mV

41. 0 Hz   0 V
   1 kHz   5.32 V
   2 kHz   7.82 V
   3 kHz   8.83 V
   4 kHz   9.29 V
   5 kHz   9.53 V
   6 kHz   9.66 V
   7 kHz   9.76 V
   8 kHz   9.80 V
   9 kHz   9.84 V
  10 kHz   9.87 V

43. 0.0796 μF

45. Reduces V_{out} to 2.83 V and θ to $-56.7°$

47. (a) No output voltage
   (b) $303\angle -72.3°\ mV$
   (c) $500\angle 0°\ mV$
   (d) 0 V

Chapter Seventeen

1. 15 kHz

3. (a) $100\ \Omega + j50\ \Omega$;
    $112\angle 26.6°\ \Omega$
   (b) $1.5\ k\Omega + j1\ k\Omega$;
    $1.80\angle 33.7°\ k\Omega$

5. (a) $17.4\angle 46.4°\ \Omega$
   (b) $64.0\angle 79.2°\ \Omega$
   (c) $127\angle 84.6°\ \Omega$
   (d) $251\angle 87.3°\ \Omega$

7. 806 Ω, 4.11 mH

9. (a) $43.5\angle -55°\ mA$
   (b) $11.8\angle -34.6°\ mA$

11. θ increases from 38.7° to 58.1°.

13. (a) $\mathbf{V}_R = 4.85\angle -14.1°$ V
    $\mathbf{V}_L = 1.22\angle 75.9°$ V

(b) $\mathbf{V}_R = 3.83\angle{-40.0°}$ V
$\mathbf{V}_L = 3.21\angle{50.0°}$ V
(c) $\mathbf{V}_R = 2.16\angle{-64.5°}$ V
$\mathbf{V}_L = 4.51\angle{25.5°}$ V
(d) $\mathbf{V}_R = 1.16\angle{-76.6°}$ V
$\mathbf{V}_L = 4.86\angle{13.4°}$ V

15. $7.75\angle{49.9°}$ Ω

17. 2.39 kHz

19. **(a)** $274\angle{60.7°}$ Ω
(b) $89.3\angle{0°}$ mA
(c) $159\angle{-90°}$ mA
(d) $182\angle{-60.7°}$ mA
(e) $60.7°$ (I_{tot} lagging V_s)

21. 1.83 kΩ resistor in series with 4.21 kΩ inductive reactance

23. $\mathbf{V}_{R1} = 18.6\angle{-3.39°}$ V
$\mathbf{V}_{R2} = 6.52\angle{9.71°}$ V
$\mathbf{V}_{R3} = 2.81\angle{-54.8°}$ V
$\mathbf{V}_{L1} = \mathbf{V}_{L2} = 5.88\angle{35.2°}$ V

25. $\mathbf{I}_{R1} = 372\angle{-3.39°}$ mA
$\mathbf{I}_{R2} = 326\angle{9.71°}$ mA
$\mathbf{I}_{R3} = 93.7\angle{-54.8°}$ mA
$\mathbf{I}_{L1} = \mathbf{I}_{L2} = 46.8\angle{-54.8°}$ mA

27. **(a)** $588\angle{-50.5°}$ mA   **(b)** $22.0\angle{16.1°}$ V
(c) $8.63\angle{-135°}$ V

29. $\theta = 52.5°$ (V_{out} lags V_{in}), 0.143

31. See Figure P–18.

FIGURE P–18

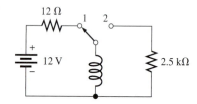

33. 1.29 W, 1.04 VAR

35. $P_{\text{true}} = 290$ mW; $P_r = 50.8$ mVAR;
$P_a = 296$ mVA; $PF = 0.985$

37. **(a)** $-0.0923°$ **(b)** $-9.15°$
(c) $-58.2°$ **(d)** $-86.4°$

39. **(a)** $89.9°$ **(b)** $80.9°$
(c) $31.8°$ **(d)** $3.60°$

41. See Figure P–19.

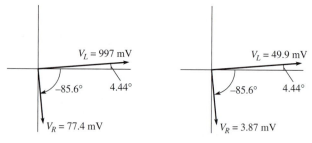

$V_L = 997$ mV $-85.6°$ $4.44°$ $V_R = 77.4$ mV

$V_L = 49.9$ mV $-85.6°$ $4.44°$ $V_R = 3.87$ mV

FIGURE P–19

43. **(a)** 0 V   **(b)** 0 V   **(c)** $1.62\angle{-25.8°}$ V
(d) $2.15\angle{-64.5°}$ V

Chapter Eighteen

1. $480\angle{-88.8°}$ Ω; 480 Ω capacitive

3. Impedance increases to 150 Ω

5. $\mathbf{I}_{tot} = 61.4\angle{-43.8°}$ mA
$\mathbf{V}_R = 2.89\angle{-43.8°}$ V
$\mathbf{V}_L = 4.91\angle{46.2°}$ V
$\mathbf{V}_C = 2.15\angle{-134°}$ V

7. **(a)** $35.8\angle{65.1°}$ mA   **(b)** 181 mW
(c) 390 mVAR   **(d)** 430 mVA

9. $Z = 200$ Ω, $X_C = X_L = 2$ kΩ

11. 500 mA

13. See Figure P–20.

FIGURE P–20

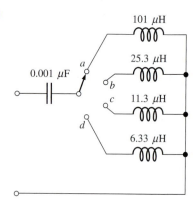

15. The phase angle of $-4.43°$ indicates a slightly capacitive circuit.

17. $\mathbf{I}_R = 50\angle{0°}$ mA
$\mathbf{I}_L = 4.42\angle{-90°}$ mA
$\mathbf{I}_C = 8.29\angle{90°}$ mA
$\mathbf{I}_{tot} = 50.2\angle{4.43°}$ mA
$\mathbf{V}_R = \mathbf{V}_L = \mathbf{V}_C = 5\angle{0°}$ V

19. $\mathbf{I}_R = 50\angle{0°}$ mA, $\mathbf{I}_L = 531\angle{-90°}$ μA,
$\mathbf{I}_C = 69.1\angle{90°}$ mA, $\mathbf{I}_{tot} = 84.9\angle{53.9°}$ mA

21. 531 MΩ, 104 kHz

23. $P_r = 0$ VAR, $P_a = 73.9$ nVA, $P_{\text{true}} = 73.7$ nW

25. **(a)** $-1.97°$ (V_s lags I_{tot})
(b) $23.0°$ (V_s leads I_{tot})

27. 49.0 kΩ resistor in series with 1.33 H inductor

29. $42.8°$ (I_2 leads V_s)

31. $\mathbf{I}_{R1} = \mathbf{I}_{C1} = 1.09\angle{-25.7°}$ mA
$\mathbf{I}_{R2} = 767\angle{19.3°}$ μA
$\mathbf{I}_{C2} = 767\angle{109.3°}$ μA
$\mathbf{I}_L = 1.53\angle{-70.7°}$ mA
$\mathbf{V}_{R2} = \mathbf{V}_{C2} = \mathbf{V}_L = 7.67\angle{19.3°}$ V
$\mathbf{V}_{R1} = 3.60\angle{-25.7°}$ V
$\mathbf{V}_{C1} = 1.09\angle{-116°}$ V

33. $48.9\angle{131°}$ mA

35. $f_{r(series)}$ = 4.1 kHz
$\mathbf{V}_{out}$ = 9.97∠−1.55° V
$f_{r(parallel)}$ = 2.6 kHz
$\mathbf{V}_{out}$ ≅ 10∠0° V

37. 62.5 Hz

39. 1.38 W

41. 200 Hz

Chapter Nineteen

1. 2.22∠−77.2° V rms

3. (a) 9.36∠−20.7° V   (b) 7.29∠−43.2° V
(c) 9.96∠−5.44° V   (d) 9.95∠−5.74° V

5. (a) 12.1 μF   (b) 1.45 μF
(c) 0.723 μF   (d) 0.144 μF

9. (a) 7.13 V   (b) 5.67 V
(c) 4.01 V   (d) 0.800 V

11. 9.75∠12.8° V

13. (a) 3.53 V   (b) 5.08 V
(c) 947 mV   (d) 995 mV

17. (a) 14.5 kHz   (b) 25.2 kHz

19. (a) 15.06 kHz, 13.94 kHz
(b) 26.48 kHz, 23.93 kHz

21. (a) 117 V   (b) 115 V

23. C = 0.064 μF, L = 989 μH, f_r = 20 kHz

25. (a) 86.3 Hz   (b) 7.12 MHz

27. L_1 = 0.088 μH, L_2 = 0.609 μH

Chapter Twenty

1. 1.22∠28.6° mA

3. 80.5∠−11.3° mA

5. $V_{A(dc)}$ = 0 V, $V_{B(dc)}$ = 16.1 V, $V_{C(dc)}$ = 15.1 V,
$V_{D(dc)}$ = 0 V, $V_{A(peak)}$ = 9 V, $V_{B(peak)}$ = 5.96 V,
$V_{C(peak)}$ = $V_{D(peak)}$ = 4.96 V

7. (a) $\mathbf{V}_{th}$ = 15∠−53.1° V
$\mathbf{Z}_{th}$ = 63 Ω − j48 Ω
(b) $\mathbf{V}_{th}$ = 1.22∠0° V
$\mathbf{Z}_{th}$ = j237 Ω
(c) $\mathbf{V}_{th}$ = 12.1∠11.9° V
$\mathbf{Z}_{th}$ = 50 kΩ − j20 kΩ

9. 16.9∠88.2° V

11. (a) $\mathbf{I}_n$ = 189∠−15.8° mA
$\mathbf{Z}_n$ = 63 Ω − j48 Ω
(b) $\mathbf{I}_n$ = 5.15∠−90° mA
$\mathbf{Z}_n$ = j237 Ω
(c) $\mathbf{I}_n$ = 224∠33.7° μA
$\mathbf{Z}_n$ = 50 kΩ − j20 kΩ

13. 16.8∠88.5° V

15. 9.18 Ω + j2.90 Ω

17. 95.2 Ω + j42.7 Ω

Chapter Twenty-One

1. 110 μs

3. 12.6 V

5. See Figure P–21.

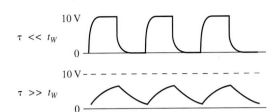

FIGURE P–21

7. (a) 25 ms
(b) See Figure P–22.

FIGURE P–22

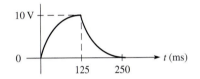

9. See Figure P–23.

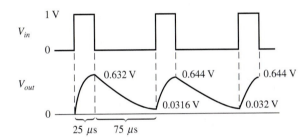

FIGURE P–23

11. See Figure P–24.

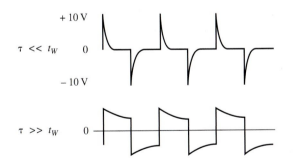

FIGURE P–24

13. (a) 525 ns
(b) See Figure P–25.

FIGURE P–25

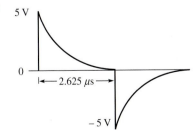

15. An approximate square wave with an average value of zero.

17. See Figure P–26.

FIGURE P–26

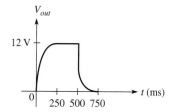

19. (a) 4.55 μs

(b) See Figure P–27.

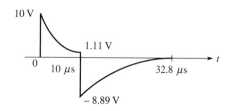

FIGURE P–27

21. 15.9 kHz

23. (b) Capacitor open

(c) C leaky or $R > 3.3$ kΩ or $C > 0.22$ μF

(d) Resistor open or capacitor shorted

Chapter Twenty-Two

1. 17.5°

3. 376∠41.2° mA

5. 1.32∠121° A

7. $\mathbf{I}_{La} = 8.66∠–30°$ A

$\mathbf{I}_{Lb} = 8.66∠90°$ A

$\mathbf{I}_{Le} = 8.66∠–150°$ A

9. (a) $\mathbf{V}_{L(ab)} = 866∠–30°$ V

$\mathbf{V}_{L(ca)} = 866∠–150°$ V

$\mathbf{V}_{L(bc)} = 866∠90°$ V

(b) $\mathbf{I}_{\theta a} = 500∠–32°$ mA

$\mathbf{I}_{\theta b} = 500∠88°$ mA

$\mathbf{I}_{\theta c} = 500∠–152°$ mA

(c) $\mathbf{I}_{La} = 500∠–32°$ mA

$\mathbf{I}_{Lb} = 500∠88°$ mA

$\mathbf{I}_{Lc} = 500∠–152°$ mA

(d) $\mathbf{I}_{Za} = 500∠–32°$ mA

$\mathbf{I}_{Zb} = 500∠88°$ mA

$\mathbf{I}_{Zc} = 500∠–152°$ mA

(e) $\mathbf{V}_{Za} = 500∠0°$ V

$\mathbf{V}_{Zb} = 500∠120°$ V

$\mathbf{V}_{Zc} = 500∠–120°$ V

11. (a) $\mathbf{V}_{L(ab)} = 86.6∠–30°$ V

$\mathbf{V}_{L(ca)} = 86.6∠–150°$ V

$\mathbf{V}_{L(bc)} = 86.6∠90°$ V

(b) $\mathbf{I}_{\theta a} = 250∠110°$ mA

$\mathbf{I}_{\theta b} = 250∠–130°$ mA

$\mathbf{I}_{\theta c} = 250∠–10°$ mA

(c) $\mathbf{I}_{La} = 250∠110°$ mA

$\mathbf{I}_{Lb} = 250∠–130°$ mA

$\mathbf{I}_{Lc} = 250∠–10°$ mA

(d) $\mathbf{I}_{Za} = 144∠140°$ mA

$\mathbf{I}_{Zb} = 144∠20°$ mA

$\mathbf{I}_{Zc} = 144∠–100°$ mA

(e) $\mathbf{V}_{Za} = 86.6∠–150°$ V

$\mathbf{V}_{Zb} = 86.6∠90°$ V

$\mathbf{V}_{Zc} = 86.6∠–30°$ V

13. $\mathbf{V}_{L(ab)} = 330∠–120°$ V

$\mathbf{V}_{L(ca)} = 330∠120°$ V

$\mathbf{V}_{L(bc)} = 330∠0°$ V

$\mathbf{I}_{Za} = 38.2∠–150°$ A

$\mathbf{I}_{Zb} = 38.2∠–30°$ A

$\mathbf{I}_{Zc} = 38.2∠90°$ A

15. Figure 22–41: 636 W

Figure 22–42: 149 W

Figure 22–43: 12.8 W

Figure 22–44: 2.78 kW

Figure 22–45: 10.9 kW

17. 24 W

GLOSSARY

Admittance A measure of the ability of a reactive circuit to permit current; the reciprocal of impedance. The unit is the siemens (S).

Alternating current (ac) Current that reverses direction in response to a change in source voltage polarity.

Alternator An electromechanical ac generator.

American wire gage (AWG) A standardization based on wire diameter.

Ammeter An electrical instrument used to measure current.

Ampere (A) The unit of electrical current.

Ampere-hour rating A number given in ampere-hours (Ah) determined by multiplying the current (A) times the length of time (h) a battery can deliver that current to a load.

Ampere-turn The unit of magnetomotive force (mmf).

Amplitude The maximum value of a voltage or current.

Angular velocity The rotational velocity of a phasor which is related to the frequency of the sine wave that the phasor represents.

Apparent power The phasor combination of resistive power (true power) and reactive power. The unit is the volt-ampere (VA).

Apparent power rating The method of rating transformers in which the power capability is expressed in volt-amperes (VA).

Atom The smallest particle of an element possessing the unique characteristics of that element.

Atomic number The number of protons in a nucleus.

Attenuation A reduction of the output signal compared to the input signal, resulting in a ratio with a value of less than 1 for the output voltage to the input voltage of a circuit.

Autotransformer A transformer in which the primary and secondary are in a single winding.

Average value The average of a sine wave over one half-cycle. It is 0.637 times the peak value.

Balanced load A condition where all the load currents are equal and the neutral current is zero.

Band-pass filter A filter that passes a range of frequencies lying between two critical frequencies and rejects frequencies above and below that range.

Band-stop filter A filter that rejects a range of frequencies lying between two critical frequencies and passes frequencies above and below that range.

Bandwidth The range of frequencies for which the current (or output voltage) is equal to or greater than 70.7% of its value at the resonant frequency that is considered to be passed by a filter.

Baseline The normal level of a pulse waveform; the voltage level in the absence of a pulse.

Battery An energy source that uses a chemical reaction to convert chemical energy into electrical energy.

Bias The application of a dc voltage to an electronic device to produce a desired mode of operation.

Bleeder current The current left after the total load current is subtracted from the total current into the circuit.

Bode plot The graph of a filter's frequency response showing the change in the output voltage to input voltage ratio expressed in dB as a function of frequency for a constant input voltage.

Branch One current path in a parallel circuit; a current path that connects two nodes.

Branch current The actual current in a branch.

Capacitance The ability of a capacitor to store electrical charge.

Capacitive reactance The opposition of a capacitor to sinusoidal current. The unit is the ohm (Ω).

Capacitive susceptance The ability of a capacitor to permit current; the reciprocal of capacitive reactance. The unit is the siemens (S).

Capacitor An electrical device consisting of two conductive plates separated by an insulating material and possessing the property of capacitance.

Center frequency (f_0) The resonant frequency of a band-pass or band-stop filter.

Center tap (CT) A connection at the midpoint of a winding in a transformer.

Charge An electrical property of matter that exists because of an excess or a deficiency of electrons. Charge can be either positive or negative.

Choke A type of inductor used to block or choke off high frequencies.

Circuit An interconnection of electrical components designed to produce a desired result. A basic circuit consists of a source, a load, and an interconnecting current path.

Circuit breaker A resettable protective device used for interrupting excessive current in an electric circuit.

Circuit ground A method of grounding whereby a large conducive area on a printed circuit board or the metal chassis that houses the assembly is used as the common or reference point; also called *chassis ground.*

Circular mil (CM)   A unit of the cross-sectional area of a wire.

Closed circuit   A circuit with a complete current path.

Coefficient   The constant number that appears in front of a variable.

Coefficient of coupling (*k*)   A constant associated with transformers that is the ratio of secondary magnetic flux to primary magnetic flux. The ideal value of 1 indicates that all the flux in the primary winding is coupled into the secondary winding.

Complex conjugate   An impedance containing the same resistance and a reactance opposite in phase but equal in magnitude to that of a given impedance.

Complex plane   An area consisting of four quadrants on which a quantity containing both magnitude and direction can be represented.

Conductance   The ability of a circuit to allow current; the reciprocal of resistance. The unit is the siemens (S).

Conductor   A material in which electric current is easily established. An example is copper.

Core   The physical structure around which the winding of an inductor is formed. The core material influences the electromagnetic characteristics of the inductor.

Coulomb (C)   The unit of electrical charge.

Coulomb's law   A physical law that states a force exists between two charged bodies that is directly proportional to the product of the two charges and inversely proportional to the square of the distance between them.

Critical frequency   The frequency at which a filter's output voltage is 70.7% of the maximum.

Current   The rate of flow of charge (electrons).

Current source   A device that ideally provides a constant value of current regardless of the load.

Cutoff frequency (*f_c*)   The frequency at which the output voltage of a filter is 70.7% of the maximum output voltage; another term for critical frequency.

Cycle   One repetition of a periodic waveform.

DC component   The average value of a pulse waveform.

Decade   A tenfold change in frequency or other parameter.

Decibel   A logarithmic measurement of the ratio of one power to another or one voltage to another, which can be used to express the input-to-output relationship of a filter.

Degree   The unit of angular measure corresponding to 1/360 of a complete revolution.

Determinant   An array of coefficients and constants in a given set of simultaneous equations.

Dielectric   The insulating material between the plates of a capacitor.

Dielectric constant   A measure of the ability of a dielectric material to establish an electric field.

Dielectric strength   A measure of the ability of a dielectric material to withstand voltage without breaking down.

Differentiator   A circuit producing an output that approaches the mathematical derivative of the input.

Duty cycle   A characteristic of a pulse waveform that indicates the percentage of time that a pulse is present during a cycle; the ratio of pulse width to period, expressed as either a fraction or as a percentage.

Effective value   A measure of the heating effect of a sine wave; also known as the rms (root mean square) value.

Efficiency   The ratio of the output power delivered to a load to input power to a circuit expressed as a percentage.

Electrical   Related to the use of electrical voltage and current to achieve desired results.

Electrical isolation   The condition that exists when two coils are magnetically linked but have no electrical connection between them.

Electromagnetic field   A formation of a group of magnetic lines of force surrounding a conductor created by electrical current in the conductor.

Electromagnetic induction   The phenomenon or process by which a voltage is produced in a conductor when there is relative motion between the conductor and a magnetic or electromagnetic field.

Electron   The basic particle of electrical charge in matter. The electron possesses negative charge.

Electronic   Related to the movement and control of free electrons in semiconductors or vacuum devices.

Element   One of the unique substances that make up the known universe. Each element is characterized by a unique atomic structure.

Energy   The ability to do work.

Equivalent circuit   A circuit that produces the same voltage and current to a given load as the original circuit that it replaces.

Falling edge   The negative-going transition of a pulse.

Fall time   The time interval required for a pulse to change from 90% to 10% of its full amplitude.

Farad (F)   The unit of capacitance.

Faraday's law   A law stating that the voltage induced across a coil of wire equals the number of turns in the coil times the rate of change of the magnetic flux.

Field winding   The winding on the rotor of an ac generator.

Filter   A type of circuit that passes certain frequencies and rejects all others.

Free electron   A valence electron that has broken away from its parent atom and is free to move from atom to atom within the atomic structure of a material.

Frequency   A measure of the rate of change of a periodic function; the number of cycles completed in 1 s. The unit of frequency is the hertz.

Frequency response   In electric circuits, the variation in the output voltage (or current) over a specified range of frequencies.

Fundamental frequency   The repetition rate of a waveform.

Fuse   A protective device that burns open when there is excessive current in a circuit.

Generator   An energy source that produces electrical signals.

Ground   In electric circuits, the common or reference point.

Half-power frequency   The frequency at which the output power of a filter is 50% of the maximum (the output voltage is 70.7% of maximum); another name for critical or cutoff frequency.

Harmonics   The frequencies contained in a composite waveform, which are integer multiples of the repetition frequency (fundamental).

Henry (H)   The unit of inductance.

Hertz (Hz)   The unit of frequency. One hertz equals one cycle per second.

High-pass filter   A certain type of filter whereby higher frequencies are passed and lower frequencies are rejected.

Hysteresis   A characteristic of a magnetic material whereby a change in magnetization lags the application of a magnetizing force.

Imaginary number   A number that exists on the vertical axis of the complex plane.

Impedance   The total opposition to sinusoidal current expressed in ohms.

Impedance matching   A technique used to match a load resistance to a source resistance in order to achieve maximum transfer of power.

Induced voltage   Voltage produced as a result of a changing magnetic field.

Inductance   The property of an inductor whereby a change in current causes the inductor to produce a voltage that opposes the change in current.

Inductive reactance   The opposition of an inductor to sinusoidal current. The unit is the ohm (Ω).

Inductive susceptance   The reciprocal of inductive reactance. The unit is the siemens (S).

Inductor   An electrical device formed by a wire wound around a core having the property of inductance; also known as *coil*.

Instantaneous value   The voltage or current value of a waveform at a given instant in time.

Insulator   A material that does not allow current under normal conditions.

Integrator   A circuit producing an output that approaches the mathematical integral of the input.

Ionization   The removal or addition of an electron from or to a neutral atom so that the resulting atom (called an ion) has a net positive or negative charge.

Joule (J)   The unit of energy.

Junction   A point at which two or more components are connected.

Kilowatt-hour (kWh)   A common unit of energy used mainly by utility companies.

Kirchhoff's current law   A law stating that the total current into a junction equals the total current out of the junction.

Kirchhoff's voltage law   A law stating that (1) the sum of the voltage drops around a closed loop equals the source voltage or (2) the algebraic sum of all the voltages (drops and sources) around a closed loop is zero.

Lag   Refers to a condition of the phase or time relationship of waveforms in which one waveform is behind the other in phase or time.

Lead   Refers to a condition of the phase or time relationship of waveforms in which one waveform is ahead of the other in phase or time; also, a wire or cable connection to a device or instrument.

Leading edge   The first step or transition of a pulse.

Lenz's law   A physical law that states when the current through a coil changes, an induced voltage is created in a direction to oppose the change in current. The current cannot change instantaneously.

Linear   Characterized by a straight-line relationship.

Line current   The current through a line feeding a load.

Line voltage   The voltage between lines feeding a load.

Load   An element (resistor or other component) connected across the output terminals of a circuit that draws current from the circuit; the device in a circuit upon which work is done.

Loop   A closed current path in a circuit.

Low-pass filter   A certain type of filter whereby lower frequencies are passed and higher frequencies are rejected.

Magnetic coupling   The magnetic connection between two coils as a result of the changing magnetic flux lines of one coil cutting through the second coil.

Magnetic flux   The lines of force between the north and south poles of a permanent magnet or an electromagnet.

Magnetic flux density   The amount of flux per unit area perpendicular to the magnetic field.

Magnetizing force   The amount of mmf per unit length of magnetic material.

Magnetomotive force (mmf)   The force that produces the magnetic field.

Magnitude   The value of a quantity, such as the number of volts of voltage or the number of amperes of current.

Maximum power transfer theorem   A theorem that states the maximum power is transferred from a source to a load when the load resistance equals the internal source resistance.

Multimeter   An instrument that measures voltage, current, and resistance.

Mutual inductance   The inductance between two separate coils, such as a transformer.

Neutron   An atomic particle having no electrical charge.

Node   A unique point in a circuit where two or more components are connected.

Norton's theorem A method for simplifying a two-terminal linear circuit to an equivalent circuit with only a current source in parallel with a resistance or impedance.

Nucleus The central part of an atom containing protons and neutrons.

Ohm (Ω) The unit of resistance.

Ohmmeter An instrument for measuring resistance.

Ohm's law A law stating that current is directly proportional to voltage and inversely proportional to resistance.

Open circuit A circuit in which there is not a complete current path.

Oscillator An electronic circuit that produces a time-varying signal without an external input signal using positive feedback.

Oscilloscope A measurement instrument that displays signal waveforms on a screen.

Parallel The relationship in electric circuits in which two or more current paths are connected between the same two points.

Parallel resonance A condition in a parallel *RLC* circuit in which the reactances ideally cancel and the impedance is maximum.

Passband The range of frequencies passed by a filter.

Peak-to-peak value The voltage or current value of a waveform measured from its minimum to its maximum points.

Peak value The voltage or current value of a waveform at its maximum positive or negative points.

Period (T) The time interval of one complete cycle of a periodic waveform.

Periodic Characterized by a repetition at fixed-time intervals.

Permeability The measure of ease with which a magnetic field can be established in a material.

Phase The relative angular displacement of a time-varying quantity with respect to a given reference.

Phase current The current through a generator winding.

Phase voltage The voltage across a generator winding.

Phasor A representation of a sine wave in terms of its magnitude (amplitude) and direction (phase angle).

Photoconductive cell A type of variable resistor that is light-sensitive.

Polar form One form of a complex number made up of a magnitude and an angle.

Polyphase Characterized by two or more sinusoidal voltages, each having a different phase angle.

Potentiometer A three-terminal variable resistor.

Power The rate of energy usage.

Power factor The relationship between volt-amperes and true power or watts. Volt-amperes multiplied by the power factor equals true power.

Power rating The maximum amount of power that a resistor can dissipate without being damaged by excessive heat buildup.

Power supply An electronic instrument that produces voltage, current and power from the ac power line or batteries in the form suitable for use in powering electronic equipment.

Primary winding The input winding of a transformer; also called *primary*.

Proton A positively charged atomic particle.

Pulse A type of waveform that consists of two equal and opposite steps in voltage or current separated by a time interval.

Pulse repetition frequency The fundamental frequency of a repetitive pulse waveform; the rate at which the pulses repeat expressed in either hertz or pulses per second.

Pulse response In electric circuits, the reaction of a circuit to a given pulse input.

Pulse width The time interval between the opposite steps of an ideal pulse. For a nonideal pulse, the time between the 50% points of the leading and trailing edges.

Quality factor (Q) The ratio of true power to reactive power in a resonant circuit or the ratio of inductive reactance to winding resistance in a coil.

Radian A unit of angular measurement. There are 2π radians in one complete 360° revolution. One radian equals 57.3°.

Ramp A type of waveform characterized by a linear increase or decrease in voltage or current.

Reactive power The rate at which energy is alternately stored and returned to the source by a capacitor. The unit is the VAR.

Rectangular form One form of a complex number made up of a real part and an imaginary part.

Rectifier An electronic circuit that converts ac into pulsating dc; one part of a power supply.

Reflected load The load as it appears to the source in the primary of a transformer.

Reflected resistance The resistance in the secondary circuit reflected into the primary circuit.

Relay An electromagnetically controlled mechanical device in which electrical contacts are opened or closed by a magnetizing current.

Reluctance The opposition to the establishment of a magnetic field in a material.

Resistance Opposition to current. The unit is the ohm (Ω).

Resistor An electrical component designed specifically to provide resistance.

Resonance A condition in a series *RLC* circuit in which the capacitive and inductive reactances are equal in magnitude; thus, they cancel each other and result in a purely resistive impedance.

Resonant frequency The frequency at which resonance occurs; also known as *center frequency*.

Retentivity The ability of a material, once magnetized, to maintain a magnetized state without the presence of a magnetizing force.

Rheostat A two-terminal variable resistor.

Ripple voltage   The variation in the dc voltage on the output of a filtered rectifier caused by the slight charging and discharging action of the filter capacitor.

Rise time   The time interval required for a pulse to change from 10% to 90% of its amplitude.

Rising edge   The positive-going transition of a pulse.

Roll-off   The rate of decrease of a filter's frequency response.

Root mean square (rms)   The value of a sinusoidal voltage that indicates its heating effect, also known as the effective value. It is equal to 0.707 times the peak value.

Rotor   The rotating assembly in a generator or motor.

Sawtooth waveform   A type of electrical waveform composed of ramps; a special case of a triangular waveform in which one ramp is much shorter than the other.

Schematic   A symbolized diagram of an electrical or electronic circuit.

Secondary winding   The output winding of a transformer; also called *secondary*.

Selectivity   A measure of how effectively a filter passes certain desired frequencies and rejects all others. Generally, the narrower the bandwidth, the greater the selectivity.

Semiconductor   A material that has a conductance value between that of a conductor and an insulator. Silicon and germanium are examples.

Sensitivity factor   The ohms-per-volt rating of an electromagnetic voltmeter.

Series   In an electric circuit, a relationship of components in which the components are connected such that they provide a single current path between two points.

Series resonance   A condition in a series *RLC* circuit in which the reactances cancel and the impedance is minimum.

Shell   The orbit in which an electron revolves.

Short circuit   A circuit in which there is a zero or abnormally low resistance path between two points; usually an inadvertent condition.

Siemens (S)   The unit of conductance.

Solenoid   An electromagnetically controlled device in which the mechanical movement of a shaft or plunger is activated by a magnetizing current.

Source   A device that produces electrical energy.

Squirrel-cage   A type of ac induction motor.

Stator   The stationary outer part of a generator or motor.

Steady state   The equilibrium condition of a circuit that occurs after an initial transient time.

Step-down transformer   A transformer in which the secondary voltage is less than the primary voltage.

Step-up transformer   A transformer in which the secondary voltage is greater than the primary voltage.

Superposition theorem   A method for the analysis of circuits with more than one source.

Switch   An electrical device for opening and closing a current path.

Tank circuit   A parallel resonant circuit.

Tapered   Nonlinear, such as a tapered potentiometer.

Temperature coefficient   A constant specifying the amount of change in the value of a quantity for a given change in temperature.

Terminal equivalency   The concept that when any given load resistance is connected to two sources, the same load voltage and load current are produced by both sources.

Tesla   The *SI* unit of flux density.

Thermistor   A temperature-sensitive resistor.

Thevenin's theorem   A method for simplifying a two-terminal linear circuit to an equivalent circuit with only a voltage source in series with a resistance or impedance.

Time constant   A fixed-time interval, set by *R* and *C*, or *R* and *L* values, that determines the time response of a circuit.

Tolerance   The limits of variation in the value of a component.

Trailing edge   The second step of transition of a pulse.

Transformer   A device formed by two or more windings that are magnetically coupled to each other and provide a transfer of power electromagnetically from one winding to another.

Transient time   An interval equal to approximately five time constants.

Triangular waveform   A type of electrical waveform that consists of two ramps.

Trigger   The activating signal for some electronic devices or instruments.

Trimmer   A small variable capacitor.

Turns ratio (*n*)   The ratio of turns in the secondary winding to turns in the primary winding.

Valance   Related to the outer shell or orbit of an atom.

Valence electron   An electron that is present in the outermost shell of an atom.

Volt-ampere reactive (VAR)   The unit of reactive power.

Volt   The unit of voltage or electromotive force.

Voltage   The amount of energy per charge available to move electrons from one point to another in an electric circuit.

Voltage drop   The drop in energy level through a resistor.

Voltage source   A device that ideally provides a constant value of voltage regardless of the load.

Voltmeter   An instrument used to measure voltage.

Watt (W)   The unit of power.

Watt's law   A law that states the relationships of power to current, voltage, and resistance.

Waveform   The pattern of variations of a voltage or current showing how the quantity changes with time.

Weber   The unit of magnetic flux.

Winding   The loops or turns of wire in an inductor.

Wiper   The sliding contact in a potentiometer.

INDEX

construction of film study through this journal, through theories which asserted rather than demonstrated the ways in which texts (might) work to make meaning. Alternative hypotheses concerning the likely sources of pedagogic influence, especially beyond the examinations streams, also deserve to be explored.

Many teachers in the field would have been influenced by their exposure to social science at first degree level or in teacher training courses; such exposure would have provided an introduction to the major traditions of social science enquiry, including: the orthodox positivist approach of the 'media effects' school of social psychological research; the empirically oriented 'political economy' approach (exemplified by Golding and Murdock's contribution to the 1973 edition of *Socialist Register*) which developed from 1960s neo-Marxism; and the new cultural studies. During the 1970s and 1980s media research began to flourish in the UK at university level, largely within faculties of social sciences, spear-headed by the Universities of Leicester, Westminster, Glasgow, the Open University (whose course, *Mass Communications and Society* was published in 1977) among others. Within the panorama of higher education media journals, *Screen Education* was but one of many, and not a specially significant source.

The clash of political economy (social science) and cultural studies (language and literature) traditions is manifested from time to time in the media education literature – Master-man (1980), for example, clashing with Alvarado (1981) on the merits or otherwise of teaching media industry. Masterman, who at that time had wanted to restrict media educa-tion to television on the grounds that this was all that most children had experience of, argued that teaching about media industries was too difficult to make interesting. Alvarado retorted that this was simply a question of appropriate pedagogy. Supporters of both cultural studies and political economy agreed that media education was principally about the study of ideology, but came at it from different directions and with different intellectual traditions and tools. In addition to the influence of these approaches to media study at higher education, teachers were probably influenced by many other sources: including enthusiasm for amateur photography and film-making, drama, religion and civic concern. In many parts of the world, for example, the Roman Catholic Church took a keen interest in media education; in Latin America, the church supported media teaching for pupils and parents outside of formal education as part of a movement of resistance to American cultural imperialism.

One odd outcome of the excitement generated by theory, and by the focus on the ideo-logical work of the media, was the slightly disparaging place allocated to practice and media creativity. While some researchers claimed that participation in media production helped to develop a range of general literacy, oracy and social skills (Lorac and Weiss, 1981), the media education theorists (e.g. Ferguson, 1981; Masterman, 1980) fretted lest too much practice would be at the expense of critical textual deconstruction, encouraging children to aspire to commercial models of production, in comparison with which their own efforts would seem pitiful, serving only to confirm as self-evidently natural the established hierarchies of access to media technologies and mass markets. They also worried lest practical work would lead to excessive interest in technology, or, on the contrary, become too creatively self-indulgent (see Stafford, 1990, for a summary of such concerns). At best, they believed that practice should illustrate or exemplify theory. Such an outlook undermined teachers who wanted to improve the (continuing) low level of technical resourcing for media education.

This uneasy relationship between theory and practice in a field whose main 'customers' were the less academically inclined, signalled that media education was moving diametrically against the *Zeitgeist* of the long conservative epoch that began in 1979 and helps to explain subsequent political distrust. One of the very few and most celebrated attempts to evaluate the application of media education theory to practice (Williamson, 1981) is a wretchedly small-scale and personal reflection, a tiny oasis of empirical test in a desert of theory and speculation. Williamson, doubting that her male pupils truly assimilated the implications of her deconstruction of gender in texts into their personal value system and behaviour, did not consider that attitude and behaviour-change were anything other than a desirable goal: a revival of the inoculation approach to media education.

A helpful route out of the impasse in relating theory and practice was offered by Buckingham (1987), who differentiated between practical work as self-expression, as a method of learning or as deconstruction. In each case, he argued, the process of learning was more important than the product, was thought to benefit from the presence of an audience, and could be used to illustrate but not do without theory.

As theorised, media studies was radical in a number of ways. First of all, it drew on neo-Marxist structuralist studies of ideology, and was hostile to 'monopoly capitalism'. Second, it was a new subject in an overcrowded curriculum, which could only find a pragmatic home within a discipline which, for much of the time, was deeply hostile to media texts. The home was 'pragmatic' because many if not most teachers of this new area had themselves been trained within English. It was a discipline, furthermore, associated with the anti-educational forces of society, in a society where the claims of teachers to a key role in the packaging and transmission of knowledge and values were subject to attack as never before by journalism and entertainment media. It wanted to take as its proper subject for study the kind of texts which most of society derided as trivial, at the expense, possibly, of introducing children to the revered classics. Some (see Donald, 1977) noted parallels between critical deconstruction of media texts, and the potential for deconstruction of many other forms of text, including the texts of formal education itself with its socially regulated conventions for the labelling, packaging and distribution of knowledge, that were equally open to critical appraisal. Given the novelty of the subject, the nature of its content, the youth of its proponents and the nature of its clients, media studies could too easily be associated by the political right with the worst excesses of permissive or progressive education.

There has been considerable controversy as to the proper range of media education. Masterman's (1980) focus on television on the grounds that television was the one medium with which most children would have any day-to-day familiarity – a position from which he had retreated by 1986 – now seems only eccentric, and even at the time it hardly squared with the by-now popular semiotic insight that social 'texts' are not limited to 'media' texts, yet can be accessed by much the same intellectual tools. Only towards the end of the 1980s and into the 1990s is there a developing awareness not simply of the full range of the conventional mass media but of the need to link this range back to classical print, and forward to the new electronic media.

THE BFI FRAMEWORK

The BFI developed a framework (see Bazalgette, 1992) within which it would be possible to locate all the questions and issues which people typically raise concerning the media. The framework consists of six 'key aspects', each representing a cluster of concepts:

1 agency
2 category
3 technology
4 language
5 audience
6 representation.

The boundaries between the clusters are not intended to be watertight. Nor does the BFI insist that there should be six – it is possible to collapse them into three. But they have a broad heuristic value. It is not suggested that media education in practice should work from category to category. Rather, the idea is that in any media activity it is generally possible to explore issues, engage in practice, that touch on each of these key aspects. The key aspects represent a core source of guidance and inspiration as to the full range of learning potential that exists in any given teaching context. A critical limitation of the key aspects is that they tend to be somewhat 'media-centric', and arguably do not focus sufficiently on the general social, cultural, political and economic contexts within which the media are situated. A second limitation is that the aspects do not of themselves constitute a pedagogy, even though they may facilitate pedagogical thinking.

In the remainder of this section I shall elaborate on the six key aspects, as these are valuable in delineating the broad compass of media education as it is generally encountered in the UK in the 1990s.

Agency

This aspect is concerned with the people, whether singly or in teams, working within or outside of institutions, who produce media texts. The producers of media texts (oral, print, still and moving image, computer-generated communication) typically undergo a lengthy and sometimes rigorous process of learning and training, whether formal or informal, and acquire 'professional' knowledge to help them function effectively in production teams and to develop texts which suit the format of the media for which they work and which are considered likely to be popular with their intended audience(s).

The multi-authored character typical of mass communication texts entails an array of distinct specialist roles and specialist knowledge, whether technical (relating to technical equipment), directive (relating to the management and organisation of creative human talent), allocative (relating to the management of non-human financial and material resources), or performative (writing, editing, reporting, drawing, filming, photographing, acting, dancing, 'hosting', composing, playing, singing, etc.).

Agents are typically concerned that media products should make a profit or that they should contribute to the overall competitive health and viability of the institutions within which or for which they work. By extension, therefore, questions of agency also include issues of distribution and scheduling, media ownership and control, financing, industrial concentration and the relationship of media organisations to political, legal, regulatory and similar environmental influences upon media operations. Such factors can often be situated at a range of different levels from local, through national to international or global.

Category

Media texts can generally be identified as belonging to one or more different categories of text. The concept of 'genre' is one such category, and film and television studies routinely make use of genre categorisations such as 'horror', 'western', 'musical', 'news', 'soap opera', 'situation comedy', 'quiz or game shows', 'chat shows', 'sport'. There may be less consensus as to how to refer to programmes that could be described as 'hospital drama' or 'crime drama', although a case could certainly be made for constructing such groups. Genre categories can also be useful in newspapers ('hard news', 'foreign news', 'editorial', 'op-ed' articles, 'women's features', 'fashion', 'motoring', etc.), in magazines ('women's interest', 'men's interest', 'soft porn', 'hobbies'), in books ('romance', 'murder mystery', 'horror', 'science fiction') and in radio ('call-in programmes', 'record requests').

Some genres, as the above lists indicate, can clearly work across media. But not all media products can easily be identified in terms of genre. Some programmes or products represent more than one genre (e.g. the 'drama-documentary', the 'comedy-western'). There may be similarities between programmes of different genres which are more significant than their genre differences. The genre identification of programmes may vary between different people, according to their relative experience of media texts, their interests and expectations. Furthermore, genre conventions change and develop over time. Even more fundamentally, the aspect of 'category' draws our attention to the expectations we bring to different kinds of texts and to our assumptions about how different kinds of text can be used.

Although there are idiosyncratic features in the ways in which individuals categorise media, categories also have a cultural and sociological reality in that they form the basis, for example, of explicit production, promotional and scheduling practices, even of training programmes and career structures: many journalists spend substantial periods of their entire careers identified as specialist 'sports' journalists, say, or 'crime correspondents', while television producers may specialise in news, current affairs, consumer, sports or drama programme-making. The sociological reality of media categories also has implications for 'reading' practices, in that viewers or readers who have relatively little experience of the conventions of certain categories may experience more 'difficulty' with such texts than more experienced readers, perhaps finding that they cannot position themselves in relation to a text in a way that affords them the pleasure which the producers of the text had hoped to achieve.

Technology

The technologies of any given system of media production and delivery may seem to be just another way of categorising media. Technology has to do with the tools and materials that are used for the creation of meaning. Elevation of 'technology' as a key aspect of the study of mass communications has the heuristic value of concentrating attention on the extent to which media communications reflect technological choices, both at an infrastructural level (design of telephone systems for point-to-point rather than for large audience communication; replacement of valve radio by the transistor), as well as at the level of individual programmes or messages (choice of black-and-white photography, depth-of-field, wide-angle lens, position of microphone). It also highlights the implications of technology choice for the range of meanings that are possible, for the development of communication conventions that accrue to particular technologies and the importance of technology in determining the relative costs and necessary skills of particular forms of media expression. Technologies both define significant differences between the media (radio as opposed to television technology) while also undermining those differences (note the convergences between television, cable, computing, CD-ROM and telecommunications – through the development of 'binary' computer language as the common 'linguistic currency' into which messages can be 'translated' for delivery through a variety of different delivery systems).

Language

The media constitute important contexts for the use, experience and decoding of spoken and written, or printed, languages. There is an immense range of issues that touch upon the choice of languages and language styles in the media, to do with the different language 'registers' or 'patterns of discourse' which are associated with different media or different genres. What may be called the 'socio-linguistics' of media is interested in such issues as the political implications of language choice for media in multilingual societies; the extent to which media language is restricted to standardised and official language categories; relative degrees of formality and informality of language use; how language use varies according to genre, to the kind of relationships that exist between participants within media programmes and to producer perceptions of their audience; particularities of the language structure of media texts; the significance of uses of 'oral' mode in printed media and of 'literary' mode in audio-visual media.

Increasingly, the study of media texts is influenced by post-modernist approaches that stress the interrelationships between given texts and their implicit and explicit borrowings from and representation of existing discourses in society. These discourses may consist of clusters of ideas and associations which are shared by members of a social, occupational, gender, social class or other grouping (sometimes referred to as 'interpretative communities'). The 'repertoires' of discourses available to particular groups, whether through media or non-media sources, is constrained by wider structural features of society which influence the distribution of resources and skills that people need in order to generate and appropriate meanings. In this view, texts do not have single authors; if a production team is responsible for, say, a given film, it need not actually constitute the 'author' for that film.

Rather, a text is multi-layered, it contains echoes of all manner of previous texts and of the broader social discourses from which those texts have drawn.

The media do not generate meaning only through spoken and written language; just as language has 'paralinguistic' features, including tone, inflection, posture and gesture, which constitute related but distinctive semiotic (sign) systems, so too the media represent complexes of interdependent semiotic systems of visual, aural, even tactile communication. Some of these, like the 'languages' of bodily proximity, architecture, dress and food preparation, are found in the everyday world; others are peculiar to the media – like the conventions governing the use of different styles and sizes of type, page layout, the relationships between visual and verbal communication on the printed page, camera positions and movements, juxtapositions of shots, continuity editing, framing, lighting and montage.

Audience

Studies of audiences were at one time mainly concerned with the 'effects' of media on audience beliefs, attitudes and behaviour, and with how such 'effects' were differentially distributed according to the social positioning of audience members, especially in terms of their social class, education and occupation. Audience studies are now as likely to be concerned with the ways in which members of audiences use the media in their day-to-day lives, how their different cultures appropriate media contents and the range of different meanings, interpretations and pleasures that audience members take from the media, as well as with how media use varies according to age, culture, gender, social class and other influences which shape 'personal' identity. Audience studies may still be informed by institutional (and advertiser) interest in the popularity of particular programmes, political interest in the 'effectiveness' of political or other campaigns, the interest of psychologists, criminologists and others in the implications of exposure to programmes containing scenes of violence, or the interest of educationalists in the potential of the media for education. But social anthropologists are interested in the ways in which people use, experience, relate to, live around and take meaning from the media, and how these factors are contextualised by particular cultures, communities, family structures and ideologies.

A key feature of many contemporary audience studies is their rejection of the view that the 'meaning' of a text can be accessed merely through detailed analysis of the text itself, in favour of a view that audiences make meaning, and that to understand the meanings of media texts it is therefore necessary to study, observe and talk to audience members. An unqualified focus on individual difference, however, may simply reflect a liberal theory of the world premised on an assumption of the supremacy of individual choice as sufficient explanation for variations in behaviour. Alternative theories look for systematic patterns or clusters among the differences, and then seek to explain these regularities.

Post-modernism has broadened the concept of audience to include those who participate, as audience, in media programmes (e.g. studio audiences), the audiences which given producers may have particularly in mind when they produce (e.g. influential peers), as well as imagined audiences of their 'average' viewers or readers (the 'Kansas City milkman' of Associated Press folklore). Some audiences are directly addressed in a programme, while others are merely 'listeners-in'. A text can contain echoes of previous audiences for the older texts that it embodies.

Representation

With representation we move back to the texts for an understanding not of their codes and conventions, nor of the languages which they manipulate to construct their meanings, but of their content, and in particular of how they portray, reflect, filter and negotiate the 'real' world. Such concerns are often expressed through the use of terms such as 'ideology' or 'bias'. Today it is commonly appreciated that the media do not simply mirror reality, even when that is their stated aim. Every form of representation involves selection, exclusion and inclusion, from the stage of initial perception through to decisions about what aspects to focus on and from whose point of view, and the kinds of evidence that will be used, using what kind of language(s) and subject to constraints of time, resources, money and imagination. In this respect the media are merely dramatic examples of the ways in which our own everyday, 'non-mediated' representations of 'reality' are subject to similar processes of selection and interpretation. This does not reduce the importance of studying how the media represent the world, whether it be that of political events in news bulletins, the 'news-geography' of news agency 'wires', or gender relations in soap operas.

We can form judgements about such representations in the light of a range of evidence, including other media texts, alternative sources of information, perspectives and evaluations. We shall be left at the end of the day with a judgement – perhaps a more reasoned, convincing judgement than that which informed the original media representation, but none the less a judgement – rather than a 'true' picture of 'how it *really* is'.

ACTION RESEARCH

The BFI framework secures a structure for the subject which is broadly applicable across every phase of education. In that sense it is ingenuously catholic. But in itself the framework does not offer a pedagogy. The BFI has contributed to pedagogy mainly through the provision of case studies of practice, exemplified, for example, in its primary and secondary 'Curriculum Statements' (Bazalgette, 1989; Bowker, 1991), and in the course which it co-produced with the Open University (1992), *Media Education: An Introduction.*

The BFI/Open University course was designed for teachers of media education in primary, secondary and tertiary education, no matter in what part of the formal curriculum they were located. The course was innovative in a number of important respects. It was produced in the period 1990–1992. By this time the BFI had already made a commitment to mainstream education in its attempts to reach a compromise with the government in securing (unsuccessfully) a curriculum niche for media education. Media education had begun to abandon its single-minded focus on ideology and deconstruction. Throughout the 1980s, media research, especially ethnographic research within reception studies, critiqued the older certainties of 1970s political economy and cultural studies' focus on 'hegemony'. Not only was it clear that people read off many different things from the 'same' media message, but that there were many other interesting questions to ask about media as well as about their ideological role.

The course was cross-phase in its scope, and was structured around the BFI framework. It promoted a pedagogy that began with the assumption that teachers and children bring to the subject a great deal of experience and knowledge of the media, and that such knowledge and experience could be articulated with the aid of the key concepts. The course incorporated many examples of practice, through print, audio and video case studies, at primary, secondary and tertiary levels. It offered examples of different kinds of audio, still and moving image text, some of which were accompanied by comment and analysis to illustrate how they might be useful in the classroom and with the aid of the key aspects, and it also provided resource materials for teachers.

The case studies incorporated within the course are themselves problematic in as much as they are not informed by the systematic procedures of self-evaluation known as 'action research' in British education. Significantly, however, the course reader does contain a chapter on action research by Peter Scrimshaw (Scrimshaw, 1992). Equally significant is a chapter by Neil Mercer (Mercer, 1992) on the influence of Vygotsky in education, and his theory of how learning is achieved – is 'scaffolded' – through talk between learners and their 'more competent peers' or teachers. In effect, the course acknowledges that virtually nothing is known about the extent of children's media knowledge or about the nature of learning about media through media education, and that the only way in which such knowledge could be acquired would be through the collaboration of teachers on the course, and the assessment of their work. This approach matched well with the course's use of recordings of children's talk about media as a resource material for interrogating the role of such talk in classroom relationships. It paralleled the work of Buckingham, Moss and others who in their research had begun to examine how children make sense of their media experiences through talk – talk which in turn is influenced by the social dynamics of their interactions with each other, with teachers and with researchers.

The course signifies a more flexible and open-minded approach to media education, in marked contrast, say, with the certainties of the 1970s. It is an approach that lays great store on recognising that children come to the classroom with relevant knowledge, and that their knowledge deserves to be respected and used as a basis for 'scaffolding'. What is to be built has to be informed by the 'key aspects', but may be primarily cognitive or practical in content.

CRITERIA OF EXCELLENCE

Learmonth and Sayer's survey (1996) identifies features of both successful and less successful media education, based on the schools which they observed and which tended to be those where media education was relatively well established. Successful media education, in their judgement, generally evinces the following features:

- it has a clear conceptual framework;
- it encompasses a range of tasks reflecting the different contexts in which the conceptual framework might be encountered and applied;

- it provides an opportunity to develop work over an extended period of time;
- it values highly pupils' personal responses;
- it gives opportunity to work in a variety of situations: independently, in pairs, as groups, as a class;
- it offers the right balance of support and challenge;
- its high expectations and rigorous standards do not affect the pleasure which pupils derive from media work;
- its pupils sense continuity and progression in their media work, which gives them fresh motivation and commitment;
- its teachers take account of the fact that pupils often know as much as, if not more than, their teachers about the media;

Learmonth and Sayer noted the following overall strengths in media education teaching in the schools which they observed:

- a clear and consistent relating of the work done to a set of explicit theoretical concepts;
- an approach by schools or groups of teachers that showed evidence of a common understanding, joint planning and a concern for continuity and progression within the media education curriculum;
- skilled and flexible class management, particularly in relation to group work in practical lessons;
- a teaching approach that was sensitive to the accessibility of media material but which reflected high expectations in both analytical and creative work.

They also observed the following weaknesses:

- a lack of awareness in teachers of the theoretical basis of media education;
- an inability sufficiently to disseminate within the school the good practice of one or two skilled practitioners, with the result that pupils' experience of media education over time is often arbitrary and fragmentary;
- teaching that exploited the pleasures and accessibility of much media material without insisting on high standards of analytical and creative work;
- a lack of confidence in teachers based either in uncertainty about media education's subject matter or in anxiety about their competence to do and manage practical work, or in both of these areas.

CONCLUSION

Teaching media in UK schools has developed significantly over recent decades. This development has been accompanied by considerable contestation between different academic and pedagogical theorists. The national curriculum of England and Wales tends to inscribe media education within English, which can only represent a small part of the field of media education as it has increasingly come to be defined by institutions such as the British Film Institute. A significant feature in recent years is the growing realisation of the benefits of case study and action research, which can contribute significantly to our understanding of the children's knowledge and experience of media, and of how such learning progresses with age, and the potential contribution to such learning of systematic curriculum design and pedagogical principles.

An important challenge to the future of media education is presented by the pace of media and multimedia development. Older assumptions about the separability of magazines, film, radio, television, from video, Internet, CD-ROM and computer graphics, etc. will be increasingly untenable. Just as the technologies themselves become more complex and flexible in their applications, accessibility to them and to the possibility of producing texts through them is improving, even if access to mass markets will always be out of reach for the majority. Traditional media education was developed by a generation of teachers for whom technology was rare, expensive, inaccessible and mysterious. The new environment of multimedia complexity, flexibility and availability may require a revision of old attitudes and assumptions. If children one day have as much instruction, opportunity and time to create audio-visual images and narratives as they traditionally have had for the production of written texts, for example, it is possible that their audio-visual achievements will carry as least as much conviction, comparatively, as their written achievements. This, in turn, will invite a much less 'precious' anxiety about practice, and will invite new perspectives on the relationships between theory and practice.

NOTE

1 This article was originally prepared in 1996. It pertains mainly to the compulsory sector of education in England and Wales to the mid-1990s. It does not include reference to the impact of communications curricula devised for the GNVQ, which at the time of writing were still in the process of development or early implementation. There are grounds for thinking that the GNVQ has succeeded in introducing innovative new thinking to the design of communications curricula which has gone some way towards integrating the practical and the theoretical, and that it has inspired the publication of significant new, pedagogically challenging textbooks. This omission should be held in mind within the context of the system evaluation.

REFERENCES

Alvarado, Manuel (1981) 'Television studies and pedagogy', *Screen Education*, 38, Spring, 64–66.

Bazalgette, Cary (1989) *Primary Media Education: A Curriculum Statement*, London: British Film Institute.

Bazalgette, Cary (1992) 'Key aspects of media education', in M. Alvarado and O. Boyd-Barrett (eds) *Media Education: An Introduction*, London: BFI Publishing in association with the Open University, 199–219.

Bowker, Julian (1991), *Secondary Media Education: A Curriculum Statement*, London: British Film Institute.

British Film Institute/Open University (1992), *Media Education: An Introduction (E555)*, London: Open University Press in association with the British Film Institute.

Buckingham, David (1987) 'Media education', Unit 27 of *Communication and Education* (EH207), Milton Keynes: Open University Press.

Buckingham, David (1990) 'English and media studies: making the difference', *The English Magazine*, 8–12.

Buckingham, David (1992) 'Media education: From pedagogy to practice', in M. Alvarado and O. Boyd-Barrett (eds) *Media Education: An Introduction*, London: British Film Institute.

Buckingham, David (1997) 'Media education', Unit 48 of *MA in Mass Communications*, Leicester: Centre for Mass Communications Research, University of Leicester.

Dickson, Peter (1994) *A Survey of Media Education*, London: British Film Institute.

Donald, James (1977) *Media Studies: Possibilities and Limitations*, London: BFI Occasional Paper.

Ferguson, B. (1981) 'Practical work as pedagogy', *Screen Education*, 38, 42–55.

Learmonth, James and Sayer, Mollie (1996) *A Review of Good Practice in Media Education*, London: British Film Institute.

Lorac, Carol and Weiss, Michael (1981) *Communication and Social Skills*, Exeter: Wheaton.

Masterman, Len (1980) *Teaching about Television*, London: Macmillan.

Mercer, Neil (1992) 'Teaching, talk and learning about the media', in M. Alvarado and O. Boyd-Barrett (eds) *Media Education: an Introduction*, London: BFI Publishing in association with the Open University, 235–241.

Murdock, Graham and Golding, Peter (1973) 'For a political economy of mass communications', in R. Milibrand and J. Saville (eds) *The Socialist Register*, London: Merlin Press.

Murdock, Graham and Phelps, Guy (1973) *Mass Media and the Secondary School*, London: Macmillan/Schools Council.

Open University (1997) *Mass Communications and Society*, Buckingham: Open University Press.

Scrimshaw, Peter (1992) 'Evaluating media education through action research', in M. Alvarado and O. Boyd-Barrett (eds) *Media Education: An Introduction*, London: BFI Publishing in association with the Open University, 242–252.

Stafford, Roy (1990) 'Redefining creativity: Extended project work in GCSE Media Studies', in D. Buckingham (ed.) *Watching Media Learning*, Brighton: Falmer Press, 81–97.

Williamson, Judith (1981), 'How does girl number twenty understand ideology?', *Screen Education*, 40, Winter, 83–84.

31

HEALTH EDUCATION AND THE HEALTH-PROMOTING SCHOOL

Addressing the drugs issue

Keith Tones and Jackie Green

THE HEALTH-PROMOTING SCHOOL

THE SABRE-TOOTHED CURRICULUM

In 1939, using the sobriquet J. A. Peddiwell, Harold Benjamin wrote some particularly penetrating observations on the curriculum. His allegorical observations were set in the Stone Age and described how 'New Fist', the first great educational theorist and practitioner, developed a formal system of schooling designed to cater for his social group's most pressing needs. This resulted in the development of three major curriculum modules:

1.1 Fish-grabbing-with-the-bare-hands
1.2 Woolly-horse-clubbing
1.3 Sabre-tooth-tiger-scaring-with-fire

Naturally 'New Fist' had to overcome the resistance of conservative backwoodsmen (or their Stone Age equivalents) but his political skills gradually overcame resistance and the new curriculum became firmly established and, in Benjamin's words: 'in due time everybody who was anybody in the community knew that the heart of good education lay in the three subjects of fish-grabbing, horse-clubbing, and tiger-scaring.' (Benjamin, 1971, p. 10)

Eventually, with the approach of a new ice age, the situation changed. The streams became muddy and the fish more agile and intelligent; the stupid woolly horses evolved into creatures more fleet of foot who moved into the plains and were replaced by little antelopes. As for the sabre-toothed tigers – they succumbed to a virulent form of tiger pneumonia and died out. They were replaced by a new threat to society – an invasion of ferocious bears. Clearly, the curriculum had become outmoded and totally irrelevant to the conditions prevailing in Stone Age life. In the meantime, practical techniques had been devised to catch fish in nets, snare the antelopes and meet the bear menace by digging anti-bear pits.

And yet, the three long-established and venerated curriculum modules were still taught in the schools.

However, a few daring innovators began to question the relevance of the traditional curriculum and to ask why the new activities of net-making, snare-setting and pit-digging could not be taught in schools. The wise old men who controlled the schools smiled indulgently at these revolutionary notions and pointed out that teaching these new activities would not be *education*. It would be mere training. Moreover, there was even evidence that the three standard cultural subjects of the Stone Age curriculum were not being taught with the rigour of ancient times. There was a need to get back to basics: young people needed a more thorough grounding in these fundamentals. They noted that:

> Even the graduates of the secondary schools don't know the art of fish-grabbing in any complete sense nowadays, they swing their horse clubs awkwardly too, and as for the old science of tiger-scaring – well, even the teachers seem to lack the real flair for the subject which we oldsters got in our teens and never forgot.
>
> (Benjamin, 1971, p. 14)

When challenged about the utility of the curriculum, the wise old men pointed out in patronising fashion that:

> We don't teach fish-grabbing to grab fish; we teach it to develop a generalized agility which can never be developed by mere training. We don't teach horse-clubbing to club horses; we teach it to develop a generalized strength in the learner which he can never get from so prosaic and special-ized a thing as antelope-snare-setting. We don't teach tiger-scaring to scare tigers; we teach it for the purpose of giving that noble courage which carries over into all the affairs of life and which can never come from so base an activity as bear-killing.
>
> (Benjamin, 1971, p. 15)

Benjamin's palaeolithic parable is, of course, still peculiarly relevant today – especially to the development and implementation of health education curricula. Not only does it underline the fact that school curricula are socially constructed and often irrelevant to contemporary concerns, but it also reminds us of the existence of partisan pressures to gain access to a captive population of young people at a formative stage of their development. More importantly, perhaps, we see reflected in the radical challenge to the Stone Age curriculum the ideological competition between pragmatists and idealists; between right and left; between conservatives and radicals. However, whereas Benjamin's satire centred on the inherent tendency for the forces of inertia and conservatism to cause curricula to outlive their original purpose, we shall be concerned in this chapter to examine the potential for compromise between competing ideologies. We shall also assert the importance of identify-ing broad-based '*horizontal*' programmes: 'New Fist's' curriculum consisted of three specific '*vertical*' subjects which would inevitably become irrelevant and subject to radical challenge. Our contention will be that a health-promoting school should be rooted in a broad-based foundation of personal and social education having maximum transfer capability rather than focusing on whatever specific, *vertical* health topics (such as drugs) might be the flavour of the month.

THE SCHOOL AS AN AGENCY OF SOCIALISATION

Socialisation is the process by which individuals acquire the norms associated with a particular culture or social group. These norms incorporate the values and beliefs considered to be particularly useful or important to the nation, community or group. It is, therefore, useful for the purpose of this essay to consider the school as an important agency of secondary socialisation. Since it is impossible to teach everything in schools, selection is inevitable. Moreover with the knowledge explosion of recent decades, globalisation and the increasingly multicultural nature of many countries, the task of selection becomes even more difficult and competition for access to young students more frenetic.

Certainly, in England and Wales, a wide variety of provision prevailed before the implementation of the national curriculum. Much of the impetus for the development of health education curricula had derived from projects funded by bodies such as the Schools Council for Curriculum and Examinations, the Health Education Council, and the Teachers Advisory Centre for Alcohol and Drugs Education (TACADE). Some local education authorities were also very active and, in more committed parts of the country, advisors and inspectors worked with health authorities on curriculum development and provided guidance and training for teachers. There was, however, no uniformity of provision. The implementation of the national curriculum provided an opportunity to remedy this situation, with the risk that it might well inhibit local initiatives. Indeed, the situation in health education nicely reflects general debate about the costs and benefits of central control versus local autonomy. On the one hand, it is possible by means of central control to establish good quality educational entitlement for *all* pupils. On the other hand, central control may reduce a school's responsiveness to the peculiar needs of its local community.

In relation to health education in England, detailed guidance has been provided (National Curriculum Council, 1990). However, the entitlement of all pupils could not be guaranteed since it was not included as a core or foundation subject. DES (1987) suggested that, as a designated cross-curricular theme, it could be taught through the core and foundation subjects to avoid 'crowding out the essential subjects' – a recommendation which provides some insight into the importance attached to health education! Unsurprisingly, this lack of enthusiasm generated concerns about marginalisation of the subject. Furthermore, at a time when there was increasing recognition of the affective component of health education and, at the same time, an acknowledgement of the importance of establishing alliances with personal and social education (PSE), there were real concerns that health education would regress to a former state and be incorporated into a curriculum solely concerned with the acquisition of factual information and driven by a rather simplistic testing imperative (Burrage, 1990). At the time of writing, the pattern of provision continues to vary from school to school in relation to both curriculum content and how and where it is located in the timetable.

Returning to our discussion of the school as an agency of socialisation, we might say that the curriculum of any school encapsulates those aspects of culture that are most valued by society – or, more accurately, that represent the dominant ideology of that society. Before examining key elements of the process of curriculum design, it is worth recalling that the notion of curriculum incorporates much more than what is formally taught to pupils. This assumption was succinctly expressed by Inspectors of Schools' 'View of the Curriculum' in England and Wales (DES, 1980):

> The curriculum in its full sense comprises all the opportunities for learning provided by a school. It includes the formal programme of lessons in the timetable; the so-called 'extra curricula' and 'out of school' activities deliberately promoted or supported by the school; and the climate of relationships, attitudes, styles of behaviour and the general quality of life established in the school community as a whole. Whatever formal programme is adopted, account has to be taken of the other less formal and seemingly less structured programme and of the interactions between the two.

This holistic conceptualisation is, as we shall see later, entirely consistent with more recent notions of the health-promoting school.

Lawton's (1975) model of curriculum planning provides an elegantly simple analysis of the interaction between culturally derived ideological influences and the more technical aspects of designing a curriculum. Figure 31.1 below is adapted from this model.

The curriculum is, then, influenced by two separate but related selections from culture. The first of these reflects broad, universal issues which are the central concern of educational philosophy. They are concerned with the very purpose of education – such as Hirst's (1969, p. 142) emphasis on 'rationality': 'If once the central objectives of rationality are submerged, or are given up so that . . . other pursuits take over, then I suggest that the school has betrayed its educational trust.'

The second influence derives from considerations of more specific cultural issues such as the demands of society for a skilled workforce or a need to inculcate particular religious or moral values or, at a more specific level, to respond to the perceived threat of HIV/AIDS or

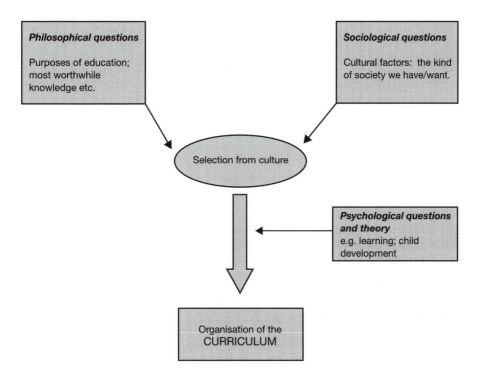

Figure 31.1 The curriculum
Source: Lawton, 1975

drugs. Not surprisingly, there has frequently been conflict between the views of the phil-osophers about what should constitute the essential purpose of schools and the expectations of pragmatists about the kinds of contribution which schools ought to make to society. The result of the various ideological and political debates which constitute these selections from culture are then subjected to technical scrutiny in the form of psychological and pedagogical theory. They are then translated into curriculum content and method. For instance, theories about child development or learning might determine the sequencing of curriculum content, specify the conditions needed for learning different concepts and skills, and recommend particular pedagogical and instructional techniques and methods.

It would, however, be misguided to imagine that this mode of analysis is purely technical and not contaminated by ideological and political imperatives. For instance, at the present time, there is frequently confrontation between those who espouse so-called 'child-centred', 'progressive' approaches to teaching and those who argue for 'traditional' didactic methods. What is superficially a methodological issue is inextricably linked with what is currently described as a 'back-to-basics' movement. This represents a nostalgic journey back to a golden age when children were taught a conventional form of morality and acquired deeply engrained skills in reading, writing, spelling and arithmetical calculation. This 'wholesome mixture' has been rediscovered as the panacea for contemporary social ills and a means for the nation to achieve economic success in the international trading arena. The fact that this curriculum plan is based on dubious morality and even more discredited learning theory does not reduce the fervour with which it is advocated.

Many, if not all, of these ideological and methodological issues have an important and direct relevance to health education and the health-promoting school. Before looking more closely at its curriculum, we shall outline briefly certain key features of health promotion.

HEALTH PROMOTION: ESSENTIAL FEATURES

Even 12 years after its launch by WHO, any discussion of the still essentially contested notion of health promotion must be prefaced by some definition. In short, health promotion is firmly grounded in certain ideological principles. The pursuit of equity and its associated attempts to tackle the inequalities which underlie and characterise health status within and between nations is perhaps the central driving force. This goal is to be achieved by the creation of healthy public policy designed to influence the socio-structural and environ-mental causes of health and illness. Furthermore, in accordance with the Ottawa Charter (WHO, 1986), an integral principle of health promotion is the development of active empowered individuals and communities. Following the Alma Ata (WHO, 1978) review of primary health care, it has been increasingly acknowledged that a wide range of services – other than medical services – have a highly significant contribution to make to the promo-tion of health. Clearly, the education service must have a centrally important part to play.

Logistically speaking, if many and varied services have a potential contribution to make to health, then tactics must be developed first to alert these services to aspects of their health promotion role which are compatible with their primary purpose (i.e. *education* in the context of the present discussion) and, second, to foster inter-sectoral collaboration and establish healthy alliances between partners.

534

The contribution of health education to the broader health promotion goal has provoked some debate (Tones, 1987a); indeed, for some people health education would appear to be synonymous with health promotion. After the ringing endorsement provided by Alma Ata, health education was not always accorded the prominence it merits – although the Ottawa Charter did make reference to the importance of people developing personal skills that could only be provided by the educational process. Although doubtlessly simplistic, the 'formula' adopted here places health education centre-stage. In short, health promotion is viewed as a synergistic interaction between education and health and social policy (Tones, 1997):

Health Promotion = Health Education × Healthy Public Policy

MODELS OF HEALTH EDUCATION

At a 'technical' level, the definition of health education is not problematic. Just as education (or, at any rate, teaching) could be regarded as a deliberate and, hopefully, efficient strategy for promoting learning, *health* education consists of a systematic and planned set of procedures designed to promote health- (and illness-) related learning, i.e.

> some relatively permanent change in an individual's capability or disposition. Effective health education may, thus, produce changes in knowledge and understanding or ways of thinking; it may influence or clarify values; it may bring about some shift in belief or attitude; it may facilitate the acquisition of skills; it may even effect changes in behaviour or lifestyle.
>
> (Tones and Tilford, 1994, p. 11)

However, just as education is more than teaching, health education is more than health teaching or, as the elders of New Fist's tribe declared, 'mere training'. Education – as Peters (1966) observed – has an intrinsic ideology. For example, its purpose must be morally acceptable and voluntaristic. Learners must be fully aware of the nature of the educational enterprise in which they are engaged: understandings should result in freedom of choice – subject only to the twin conditions of paternalism and utilitarianism (i.e. the learner must be capable of exercising choice and that choice should not interfere with the right of others to make their own choices or otherwise harm the public good). In short, the purpose of education is congruent with health promotion's emphasis on client and community participation; on co-operation rather than compliance. The term health education has, however, been applied to a number of activities that would, according to the strictures mentioned above, not be truly 'educational'. Indeed, various 'models' of health education have been identified to define different purposes and philosophies:

- preventive model
- educational model
- empowerment model.

The preventive model

The identification of health education as part of the armamentarium for the prevention of disease is central to the 'preventive model'. This approach derives from the so-called 'medical model' which is considered to have the following main features:

- It views health in terms of the absence of disease.
- Its explanation of the disease process is primarily mechanistic and its focus is on micro causality.
- The body is viewed as a machine whose component parts are subject to attack from microbes or other pathogens.
- The prime function of medicine is to repair the machine when it malfunctions and – a rather less glamorous preventive function – to keep it in good running order.

This less glamorous preventive function of medicine has acquired greater significance in recent decades. The ascendancy of prevention has resulted from the recognition that the capacity of medicine to cure the major diseases afflicting modern civilisations is severely limited. Moreover, despite its limited success, the amount of money spent on curative medicine escalates year by year. Accordingly, in an attempt to curb this accelerating expenditure, politicians – and to a lesser extent the medical profession itself – have increasingly turned to the prevention of the diseases which medicine seems unable to cure. Since human behaviour is typically implicated in the aetiology of those diseases, health education has been viewed as an important device for modifying unhealthy lifestyles and for encouraging people to utilise medical services in an appropriate way. Since it makes sense to try to influence people's behaviours at an early stage – before the 'bad habits' have become engrained – it is not surprising that the medical profession has been one of the major stakeholders seeking to gain access to the 'secret garden' of the curriculum. The rationale for this preventive model is nicely illustrated in the following dramatic justification by the Leverhulme Health Education Project (1978) for encouraging schools to incorporate health education in the curriculum. It explains the likely fate of children in a secondary school of 1,000 pupils:

> Thirty-five of the children, more than one whole class, will die before they reach the age of forty-five; two hundred more, nearly seven whole classes, will be dead before they reach the age of sixty-five, that is before they have time to enjoy retirement. Of those who die before they reach sixty-five, ten will be killed in road accidents – not to mention another hundred who will be seriously injured – sixteen will die from cancer, mainly from lung cancer . . . Approximately two hundred will have none of their own teeth when they reach their fortieth birthday. More than a hundred (nearly four whole classes) will seek treatment for a venereal disease within five years of leaving school. More than a hundred will, for a prolonged period of their adult life, consult their doctor concerning their mental health. Rather more than one in every four of the thousand will abandon, or be deserted by, or become separated from, their wives and husbands, or – what is perhaps worse – will become separated from their children.

The broad trends to which reference is made above remain of current relevance, although some of these threats to the public health have waned in importance while new ones have come on the scene. Most notable of these is, of course, the challenge of AIDS which, in turn, has had its impact in relation to demands for the introduction of more effective sex education in schools in order to prevent HIV infection – and the inclusion of harm minimisation strategies in drug education programmes.

Rather interestingly, the deliberately dramatic use of epidemiological data by the Leverhulme Project represents an early example of what is now known as creative epidemiology. This latter term is probably more usually associated with media advocacy, i.e. the striking use of mass media images to raise public outrage by portraying various social ills – such as the cynical exploitation of the public by the tobacco industry. As such, the techniques relate to the critical consciousness-raising role of the empowerment model to which we refer below.

At all events, although some parents and teachers might be well disposed to the use of the school as a kind of offshoot of the health service, there are problems associated with the adoption of this preventive model of health education – for instance, teachers may, with some justification, view the medical model as equivalent to indoctrination and consequently inconsistent with the true goals of education (although quite clearly teachers regularly attempt to shape behaviours – for instance in the interests of good order and discipline – and in more reflective moments may acknowledge that the very structure and organisation of the school can influence pupil attitudes). Moreover, it is also the case that the medical model is in many ways incompatible with the broader, more holistic goals of health promotion. For example, apart from the reductionist approach illustrated above, the medical model is associated with a propensity to lay claim to ever larger areas of human experience. This process of medicalisation, it is argued, results in doctors and – by a process of diffusion – other medical professionals acquiring disproportionate authority in relation to patients and people in general. Medicine as traditionally practised is consequently intrinsically depowering for the laity.

Apart from the fact that the overriding goal of health promotion is empowerment, the medical model can influence school health education in some rather paradoxical ways. First, even if teachers are not necessarily committed to the dogma of *true* education, they might well have doubts about moving beyond the provision of knowledge and trying to influence behaviour, because this would be tantamount to usurping the parents' role and responsibilities. Second, even though they might have no compunction about acting *in loco parentis* on health matters, they could be the indirect victims of the medicalisation process. For instance, even though they believe that health education should occupy a place in the curriculum, they may consider that anything remotely medical will be so problematic or demand such esoteric knowledge that they lack the necessary skills to teach the subject. They may thus either refuse to teach it or look for someone having at least some association with medicine – such as a school nurse – to undertake the delicate and sensitive task of educating about health. Needless to say, in our view, such an approach is fundamentally misguided.

An educational model

If the prevention of disease is not viewed as the prime purpose of school health education – for the reasons stated above – teachers may fall back on what is often defined as an educational model. In its simplest form, the model is based on the credo that the teacher's duty is merely to present the student with information about health matters. As we have seen, the basis for this point of view may be that the task is inappropriate for the true educator or alternatively problematic and best left to others – such as parents or doctors. On the other hand, it might be ingenuously assumed that presenting information in a sufficiently expert manner will lead to rational decision-making. Although fundamentally wrong, this assumption is not uncommon and in the light of comments made below about the importance of empowerment, we should at this juncture give some thought to the psycho-social and environmental factors which determine healthy – or unhealthy – choices.

DETERMINANTS OF HEALTH CHOICES

The naïve notion that providing people with knowledge will lead inexorably to rational decision-making has long been discredited as it became apparent that knowledge alone would not result in behaviour change. Accordingly the so-called 'K-A-P' formula acquired some currency. If knowledge (K) did not of itself result in positive attitudes (A) then suitable attitude-change techniques should be used to achieve the adoption of desirable practices (P). However, this formulation is itself decidedly suspect on two accounts: (a) it assumes that attitude change is a desirable goal for education and (b) it simplifies to the point of caricature the complex processes involved in the adoption and maintenance of health-related behaviours. Figure 31.2 below provides a simplified overview of these processes.

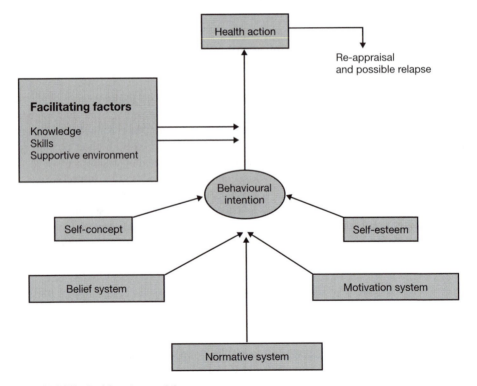

Figure 31.2 The health action model
Source: Tones and Tilford, 1994

Three broad categories of influence contribute to an individual's intention to adopt any given action, namely the Belief System, the Motivation System and the Normative System.

The *Belief System* reminds us that it is not so much knowledge that influences our behaviour but rather whether or not we accept the truth of what is embodied in that knowledge. For example, young people might well have been informed that a variety of dire consequences will result from using drugs. However, their first-hand experience of drug use and drug users may result in their refusing to believe the information given. Again, even if they accept the truth of teachers' assertions that smoking will damage their health, they may well believe that the benefits of smoking outweigh the possibilities of negative consequences (which they understand will only emerge – if at all – in some 40 years' time).

The *Motivation System* emphasises the prime importance of feelings and emotions. Attitudes to the actions which health educators are recommending will depend on a complex interplay of values, drives and emotions. For example, the moral value which might otherwise deter a young person from sexual intercourse might be overridden by the sex drive! Again, lessons designed to alert students to risky behaviours of all kinds will fail miserably if the gratifications which those risky behaviours generate are ignored. There is little merit in pointing out to young people the dangers of fast driving or other hazardous pursuits if sensation-seeking and exposure to danger are the very reasons why the actions were undertaken in the first place.

The *Normative System* alerts the curriculum planner to the need to take account of social pressures. The general and rather diffuse effects of mass media often reinforce unhealthy behaviours by portraying them as normal and acceptable. Soap operas, for instance, frequently present images of alcohol which at once show characters apparently spending inordinate amounts of time in a public bar without, at the same time, demonstrating the negative effects of alcohol misuse (Hansen, 1986).

Educators do not need to be reminded of the potentially powerful influence of significant individuals and the peer group in general. We should, however, insert a note of caution: it would be highly misleading to assume that children are constantly subjected to powerful pressure from their peers to do what they don't want to do. While peer pressure can undoubtedly be powerful, the members of the peer group are typically quite happy to conform to the peer group norms, since the values and gratifications incorporated in these are probably the reason why the young people in question have become members of the peer group in the first place.

Figure 31.2 above places particular emphasis on the potential gap between behavioural intentions, which result from the combined effects of the systems of beliefs, motivations and social influences, and the actions that are supposed to result from those intentions. In short, intentions cannot usually be translated into practice without the existence of additional knowledge and/or a number of particular skills – and, of course, a favourable environment. If, for example, the health teaching in a school has resulted in students forming a reasonably firm intention not to take harmful substances when offered, it would be inefficient, not to say unethical, not to supplement this teaching with assertiveness training so that the young people have the capabilities and the confidence to refuse the offer without loss of face – or friends. Again, high self-esteem is generally considered to be an antidote to pressure and, as we will see, a health-promoting school would try to ensure that the health teaching is supported by a school environment that enhances the self-esteem of all pupils – not just those who might be least likely to make unhealthy choices.

We might also note in passing that once a 'healthy' course of action has been adopted, there is no guarantee it will be sustained. Relapse in many instances is not only possible but highly likely when the action selected does not produce the promised gains and has various negative results – such as loss of gratification or exposure to ridicule. The health educator must then anticipate such negative outcomes and try to offer anticipatory guidance and substitute gratifications – not an easy thing to do! It would, of course, be unreasonable to expect teachers alone to manage such a complex task. This is why the health-promoting school seeks to achieve not only a consistent and co-ordinated approach within the school but also to gain the support and commitment of parents, family and the wider community.

An empowerment model

The third model mentioned here pursues the goals of empowerment. The approaches which are embodied in the model are entirely consistent with the major purpose of WHO and the health promotion movement. In short, it accepts some of the contentions of an educational model that schools should not slavishly act as surrogate agencies for preventing disease. However, it does assert that schools have a responsibility to promote the health of their students and the communities in which they live. Its philosophy is essentially voluntaristic – within the limits imposed by a general concern for other people's rights and well-being. It does not, however, commit the 'victim blaming' error of assuming that knowledge alone is sufficient for empowerment and acknowledges the complex interplay of influences identified in Figure 31.2 above. It would, though, place particular emphasis on some of these influences in the pursuit of *empowerment*. For instance, *Beliefs about Self* and *Self-esteem* are separately identified in the health action model because of their centrality to the empowerment process.

THE EMPOWERMENT PROCESS

It is generally accepted that empowered people have greater control over their lives. On the other hand many individuals are 'depowered'. This 'unhealthy' state may be the result of damaging social and economic circumstances – possibly compounded by poor child-rearing which offers minimal independence training, inconsistent discipline and generally reflects the 'learned helplessness' experienced by severely disadvantaged families.

A belief that positive (and negative) experiences are due to one's own efforts – rather than the result of chance, fate or the overwhelming influence of 'powerful others' – is healthy in its own right and, furthermore, enhances capacity for 'healthy' action. Again, 'self-efficacy' beliefs – individuals' convictions that they are capable of carrying out a particular action – is an essential prerequisite for translating intention into practice. Students who have been convinced that they should not consume so much alcohol might make no attempt to carry out this preferred action if they lack the confidence to challenge the prevailing peer norm.

Beliefs about being in control and, even more importantly, the *actual* exercise of power contribute to self-esteem. It is generally accepted that people with relatively high self-esteem will be more likely to respond positively to appeals to look after themselves than those who do not have such a degree of self-respect. Moreover, individuals with high self-esteem are more likely to have the courage of their convictions – and will pursue courses of action which *they* feel are right and important even in the face of opposition or derision from others. Clearly self-esteem (as we shall see later) is due to factors other than perceived control – for instance respect and love from significant others – including school staff.

Not surprisingly then, health promotion is concerned to empower people through modifying their beliefs about self and enhancing self-esteem and self-respect. Two broad strategies are possible: the first of these emphasises the provision of various 'life-skills' or 'action competences' – for example, by providing assertiveness training. The second strategy derives from a recognition that confidence cannot be created nor can control be exerted in a generally depowering environment. Although life-skills can help increase potential for overcoming adverse circumstances, it would be unrealistic to expect much success when these physical, social or economic circumstances are uniformly oppressive (see, for example, Galbraith's [1992] discussion of 'underclass'). Accordingly, advocacy and action by those who already have power is necessary if the root causes of depowerment and helplessness are to be seriously addressed. Although the health-promoting school cannot be expected to change society, it might well make some contribution to improving the social circumstances outside the school through community liaison.

A full analysis of the dynamics of empowerment is not possible here and has been more completely discussed elsewhere (Tones and Tilford, 1994). However, Figure 31.3 below summarises certain key features of the empowerment process.

In short, empowerment involves:

1 increasing individuals' confidence and self-esteem by providing life-skills and experience of success;

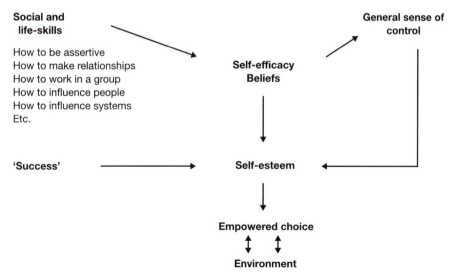

Figure 31.3 Dynamics of empowerment

2 creating concern about social issues and a determination to contribute to an active participating community in order to gain control over the determinants of health;

3 providing supportive environments to achieve 1 and 2 above.

THE SETTINGS APPROACH: EMERGENCE OF THE HEALTH-PROMOTING SCHOOL

Following the translation of the concept and principles of health promotion into the Ottawa Charter (*Health Promotion*, 1988), two important conferences – in Adelaide and in Sundsvall (Pettersson and Tillgren, 1992) – emphasised the importance of healthy public policy and supportive environments. Subsequently, WHO attempted to apply the Ottawa Charter principles to a variety of settings – starting with the 'Healthy City'. At a somewhat later stage, guidelines were developed for a holistic approach to health promotion in a number of different institutions which might contribute to the overriding goals of the Healthy Cities movement – such as, for instance, the 'Health-promoting Hospital'. Since the foundations had already been laid in several countries for the health-promoting school, it is not surprising that schools were soon recruited to the general movement.

The key feature of the settings approach in general, and the health-promoting school in particular, is the imperative to ensure that all of the activities within the setting and its general ethos contribute synergistically to empowerment for health. Moreover, each setting should be 'outward looking': those working in the setting should collaborate with the community at large and with other settings in the pursuit of health promotion goals.

The notion of a 'parallel curriculum' is not new: the relevance of the home and family to the child's progress – and the importance of enlisting family support for the educational endeavour – is a pedagogical truism. Health education, however, provided additional emphasis in four main ways:

1 Health educators viewed primary socialisation (and thus the modelling and shaping function of the family) as critically important in establishing key health habits such as nutrition or smoking;

2 They identified the potentially reciprocal relationship between school and home. More particularly, they identified the possibility of enlisting the support of parents in complementing the educational efforts of the school – for instance in reinforcing education about smoking – and also considered the potential of the 'pester factor' in having children act as informal 'counsellors' to help parents quit smoking!

3 Health education acknowledged the pervasive 'norm sending' influence of mass media (e.g. in relation to cigarette advertising).

4 Health education has for many years been involved in a partnership with local health services in providing training and curriculum resources for teachers. More adventurous and outward-looking schools might even seek greater integration with their local communities with pupils working as local health activists!

A direct concern for the physical, social and mental well-being of children has also, traditionally, been a key part of the wider school curriculum: for instance the school health service and the pastoral care system have been explicitly concerned with the mental and physical health status of pupils. Moreover, certain traditional activities – both curricular and extra curricular – have made a direct contribution to the health and fitness of pupils. Physical education is, of course, a prime example.

The hidden curriculum – the indirect effects of ethos – has also been familiar to educationists for some time – as the following quotation from an inspector's report on religious education in England and Wales confirms:

> If the school itself is a caring community and expresses that care internally in the quality of the relationships and externally through service to the local community, then pupils will be given deeper understanding of concepts like love and service and of what these may demand in personal terms of humane concern.
>
> (DES, 1977, p. 43)

Rennie *et al.* (1974) make a similar point:

> The way the school is organised, streamed or not streamed, the role of examinations in the school, the way the teachers speak to the children, the way children treat each other, the prefect system, the house system, all these tell children something about their place in the school and what the school stands for.

As these various principles were adopted by health education practitioners, it became increasingly clear that the methods, approaches and even the educational philosophy they espoused were entirely consistent with the goals of PSE (Personal and Social Education) and, indeed, in many instances a joint strategy might be adopted in schools under the rubric of Personal, Social and Health Education (PSHE).

WHO's approach to the definition of the health-promoting school has provided an added dimension to the concept of the hidden curriculum by arguing for the need to establish clear policy goals to create and, where necessary, change social and environmental factors to support healthy decision-making. In other words, what might have been hidden should now be made open and subject to scrutiny prior to implementing organisational change. Figure 31.4 presents diagrammatically the WHO conceptualisation and encapsulates the curricular influences discussed above into three complementary contexts:

- teaching in the classroom;
- the school environment and milieu;
- links with family and community – including health services.

By 1998, some 38 countries in Europe were part of the European Network of Health-Promoting Schools and other WHO regions have more recently adopted the concept (WHO, 1996a). The resolution of the Halkidiki Conference (ENHPS, 1997) was that 'Every child and young person in Europe has the right, and should have the opportunity, to be educated in a health-promoting school.' It proposed a set of common principles which 'provide the basis for investing in education, health and democracy for generations to come'. The European Network of Health-Promoting Schools subscribes to 12 common criteria which may be adapted to suit the particular cultural, organisational and political contexts of participating countries. The English Project, for example, lists them in relation to the three broad areas depicted in Figure 31.4, namely: Ethos and Environment; Curriculum; Family and Community. These are presented in more detail below (Health Education Authority, 1996):

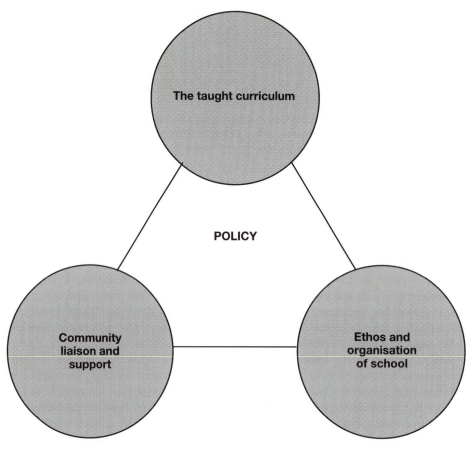

Figure 31.4 The health-promoting school

Ethos and environment

- Provides a safe, secure and stimulating school environment which encourages pupils to be health- and safety-conscious both in and out of school.
- Actively promotes opportunities which develop pupils' self-esteem and self-confidence, enabling them to take initiatives, make choices and exercise responsibility for their own and others' health.
- Fosters a whole-school understanding and sharing of the school's aims for health education and the contribution that individuals can make through their respective skills and personal qualities.
- Creates a school climate in which good relationships, respect and consideration for others flourish.
- Promotes the health and well-being of all staff and pupils and considers the role of staff as an exemplar of a healthy lifestyle.

544

Curriculum

- Formulates a range of health-related policies which are in accord with the school's aims – for example those concerned with nutrition, physical activity, substance misuse and bullying.
- Implements health-related policies and monitors any changes in pupils' knowledge, skills, attitudes and behaviour.
- Plans and implements a coherent health education curriculum which complies with statutory requirements and is accessible to all pupils.
- Ensures that teaching is informed, of a consistently high quality, and is based upon a positive approach which recognises the importance of starting with pupils' existing levels of understanding and experience of health matters.
- Provides stimulating challenges for all pupils through a wide range of physical, academic, social and community activities.

Family and community

- Develops good liaison with other schools, pupils' parents/guardians and the community on a range of health-promoting initiatives.
- Makes effective use of outside agencies and specialist services to advise, support and contribute to the promotion of health, either directly or through the curriculum (Health Education Authority, 1996).

The social environment of the school

The following examples from the WHO's Western Pacific Region's list of checkpoints for the health-promoting school (WHO, 1996b) illustrate the particular importance of the *social* environment in empowering pupils and creating a sense of concern which is central to a healthy school life.

The school ethos is supportive of the mental health and social needs of students and staff.

- Teachers do not use harsh discipline and are supportive of and respectful towards students.
- Students are encouraged to participate in school decision-making processes.

The school creates an environment of care, trust and friendliness which encourages student attendance and involvement.

- The school actively discourages physical and verbal violence, both among students and by staff towards students.

The school provides a fully inclusive environment in which all students are valued and differences are respected.

545

- The school provides opportunities to celebrate cultural, religious and tribal diversity, e.g. through food, costume, dance, craft, displays, festivals and exhibitions.

(WHO, 1996b)

Liaison with the community

We commented earlier that the health-promoting school added extra emphasis to the conventional wisdom of involving family – the primary socialising influence on children – and the local community in the pursuit of health goals. The support and encouragement of parents have always been recognised as prime determinants of children's success at school. However, the health-promoting school is charged with being more proactive in involving parents maximally in school matters and in seeking to influence parental health status by using the often quite substantial influence of the child. For instance, parents might be asked to volunteer to become involved in the development of school nutrition policies; they might be encouraged to help children adopt a more balanced diet and, in the process, introduce changes to family eating practices. The health-promoting school should not only seek and expect community support but might also have an impact on community norms and practices. It might also expect support from community health services. Both aspects are illustrated by the West Pacific Region initiative (WHO, 1996b).

- The school informs the local community of its health initiatives, e.g. through the use of local media, school open days, students providing 'healthy school' displays at community functions.
- Counselling and support services are available for socially and emotionally distressed students and those with medical problems.
- Health service agencies are active in approaching schools with offers of support to them in their work on health promotion.

THE HEALTH-PROMOTING SCHOOL: APPROACHES TO THE TAUGHT CURRICULUM

We have already discussed the importance of ensuring complementarity between school ethos, its links with the community and what is actually taught. We shall now briefly revisit this taught component.

Figure 31.5 below provides a model of the taught curriculum of the health-promoting school and seeks to show how this relates to the policy requirement for the provision of a supportive environment. It also shows how pupils might influence and be influenced by its community – and contribute, in the short or long term, to its empowerment.

Figure 31.5 does not pretend to provide an organisational model for the curriculum: it merely presents a schematic representation of the key elements. Clearly, teaching may be organised in a variety of ways in accordance with the preferences of staff, the dictats of local or national government, or traditional practice and custom. It may appear as a regular timetabled 'slot' or in the context of other subjects (such as biology, home economics, art or

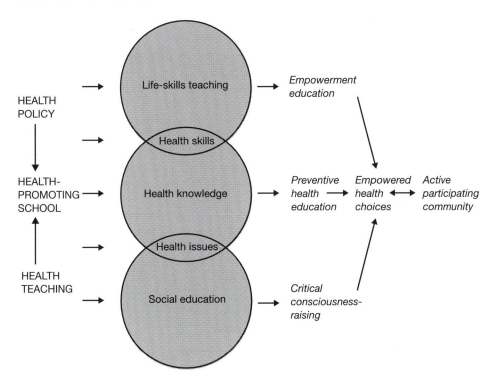

Figure 31.5 The empowering curriculum

literature); it may appear in the pastoral curriculum; it may be included through health projects or topics. It may appear as all of these. What is important, however, is that it be planned and co-ordinated. Ideally, for maximum effect, it would be co-ordinated *across* the curriculum and, utilising the notion of a spiral curriculum, form part of a health career approach from primary to secondary schooling.

Health education as a subversive activity

A recurring theme in this chapter is that, although health education has its peculiar concerns, it shares many key issues with education generally. One of these centres on the extent to which education should be primarily a conservative socialising force or a radical movement for social change. As we have previously observed, one of the main purposes of education – and a central concern of health education – is to empower people. We have also noted how the ethos and organisation of the school can either foster or militate against empowerment. In order to complement the empowering effects of a supportive environment, the taught curriculum should not merely provide the knowledge needed to take empowered decisions or help pupils clarify their values, but it should also provide the skills needed to act and achieve success and help them cope with and act as change agents within a society facing a chronic state of 'future shock' (Toffler, 1970).

547

We noted earlier that health promotion must – almost by definition – adopt a radical stance which centres on empowerment and choice rather than compliance and coercion. *The Sundsvall Handbook* (Haglund *et al.*, 1992) supported a life-skills orientation and remarked that schools have two major goals: 'To educate students in academic or cognitive skills and knowledge; and to help students develop the individual and social skills required for employment and socio-political involvement in society'. However, they also claimed that health education should 'provide people with an opportunity to rise above the limitations of the social group in which they were born' (ibid., p. 62).

Logically, the position adopted by WHO requires health education to adopt a subversive approach. It should thus follow the general educational philosophy exemplified by the rather inelegant but, none the less, graphic words of Postman and Weingartner (1981). In short, education should help students to 'develop built-in, shock-proof crap detectors as basic equipment in their survival kits' (p. 16). Or, following Freire (1972), one of education's prime radical functions should be one of critical conciousness-raising leading to 'praxis' – the application of critical reflection to practical (and political) action.

The term 'social education' is used in Figure 31.5 above to describe this consciousness-raising function of the health-promoting school. Whereas 'life-skills teaching' might provide competences designed to contribute to *individual* empowerment, the consciousness-raising function of social education would address broader social issues, seeking *inter alia* to alert pupils to social injustices and to generate indignation.

Health education and prevention

Figure 31.5 also incorporates health education's traditional function of providing health-related knowledge and understanding. Clearly, the health-promoting school should not lose sight of the preventive goals espoused by the medical model. Indeed, perhaps paradoxically, an empowerment approach is more rather than less likely to facilitate the achievement of those preventive goals while emphasising its prime concern with enhancing feelings of control, facilitating choice and contributing to the development of active, participating communities. The development of both social education and life-skills teaching will, there-fore, complement the teaching of health- and illness-related knowledge and not only help make the healthy choice the easy choice but also contribute to the achievement of those preventive goals associated with public health. For instance, health-skills teaching borrows from the repertoire of general life-skills and applies these to solving specific 'medical prob-lems' – for example, by helping students resist pressure to have unwanted sex or to refuse an offer of drugs. The potential of health and life-skills for making a contribution to both disease prevention and more holistic, positive aspects of health is illustrated by WHO's (1993) mental health programme which identified the following important life-skills:

- decision-making
- problem-solving
- creative thinking
- critical thinking
- effective communication

- interpersonal relationships
- self-awareness empathy
- coping with emotions
- coping with stress.

In the same way, social education would not only be concerned with general issues such as poverty and disadvantage but would also address more specific health issues related to these – for instance the influence of social class on illness experience.

DRUGS AS AN ISSUE FOR SCHOOLS

There is widespread international concern about the use of drugs, including alcohol and tobacco, by young people. The World Health Organisation (1996c) estimates that worldwide some 15 million people are putting their health significantly at risk by using psychoactive substances. The economic impact and the further risks of social and family disruption combine with the direct threat to health to make drug misuse a significant public health problem. Recent surveys conducted in the United Kingdom reveal that a substantial proportion of 15 and 16 year old pupils have used both legal and illegal psychoactive substances. In relation to illegal substances, Miller and Plant (1996) found that 40.6% of this age-group had used cannabis; 20.4% glues and solvents; 14.4% LSD; and 7.3% girls and 9.2% boys ecstasy. They also noted that higher levels of drug use were associated with poorer school performance. Health Education Authority/British Market Research Bureau (1996) identified the period from 14 to 16 as the age at which drug use increases dramatically, with more than 60% of this age-group having been offered a drug and 30% having taken drugs at least once. Although comparison between studies can be problematic because of methodological differences, trends over time indicate increased levels of experimentation: a reduction in the age of first use of drugs and an increase in the number of deaths attributable to drug use.

The school's role as an agency of secondary socialisation has already been discussed and in this context schools are frequently charged with the task of solving problems identified by society. The call to strengthen school health education in the Resolution of the European Council and Ministers of Education (1988) was, in part, a response to the increase in drug abuse, including tobacco and alcohol. In spite of the radical view that experimentation with drugs is an integral part of youth culture, the current level of drug misuse and its effect on individuals, families and communities clearly creates concern. Schools can, and indeed do, play a key part in responding to the problem by providing education about drugs. The aetiology of drug use and misuse is, however, complex and the subject of much debate. An array of often contradictory factors has been associated with the use of drugs. These include

- general environmental factors such as unemployment, deprivation, affluence, cultural background;
- more specific environmental factors such as the availability, acceptability and price of drugs;
- social factors such as norms about drug use and peer pressure;

- personal factors such as curiosity, rebelliousness, life events (including family problems) and psychological predisposition.

Clearly, schools alone cannot address all these factors and any serious attempt to tackle drug misuse will involve different agencies and sectors working collaboratively at all levels from national to local. (See, for example, the English strategy in the White Paper *Tackling Drugs to Build a Better Britain* [HMSO, 1998], which recognises the importance of partnerships and identifies the following essential components: education to reduce the demand for drugs; law enforcement to reduce the supply; treatment and support for drug misusers; and protection for communities from drug-related crime.) The importance of establishing links with the community has been identified as an essential component of the health-promoting school since, typically, parents are also frequently concerned about drug use and unsure about what to do. Information about the school's strategy and opportunities for more active involvement may increase parents' confidence and help to ensure that what is taught at school is reinforced in the home.

WHAT DO WE MEAN BY DRUG EDUCATION?

The term 'drug' is generally used to refer to illegal substances. Whilst there are specific issues associated with legality, there are broad areas of overlap in relation to both the harmful effects and the factors associated with the use and misuse of other substances such as alcohol, tobacco and volatile substances. In addition, there may be an association between the use of legal and illegal substances. Miller and Plant (1996) found a strong relationship between smoking tobacco and the use of cannabis. HEA/BMRB (1996) also reported links between smoking or drinking alcohol and the recent use of illegal drugs. It is, therefore, now generally accepted that education about drugs is better placed within the general context of substance use and within the broader framework of personal, social and health education rather than being dealt with as an isolated issue. As we have argued earlier in discussing the relative merits of horizontal and vertical programmes, those attributes required to make and implement a 'healthy' choice in relation to drugs are essentially the same as those underpinning a whole range of health behaviours.

AIMS OF DRUG EDUCATION

Prevention in the context of substance misuse is conventionally categorised into primary and secondary levels. Primary prevention is concerned with reducing experimentation with and use of drugs, whereas secondary prevention provides treatment and rehabilitation for those who are misusing drugs. It also includes attempts to reduce the negative consequences of drug use (including the spread of HIV and other communicable diseases). This latter, so-called *harm minimisation* approach is somewhat controversial in the school context, where it might be construed as actively promoting drug use and even teaching pupils how best to do it.

A whole spectrum of views about the purpose of school drug education exists. At one end are those who see any drug use as deviant; who feel that drug education should be concerned solely with primary prevention and that harm minimisation strategies encourage drug use. At the opposite end of the spectrum are those who recognise drug use as part of youth culture and feel that the focus of drug education should be on reducing harm. Somewhere between these two poles is the view that drug education should be concerned with the promotion of informed choice and empowerment. This is consistent with notions of voluntarism (Tones, 1987b) and is based on the premise that empowered individuals are less likely to use drugs but, if they do, they are more likely to take action to reduce the probability of harm. Some would also emphasise the fact that accepting that young people use drugs is not necessarily the same as condoning their use. There is clearly room for debate about where the main emphasis should lie. Burgess (1996), however, in arguing for a stronger steer towards primary prevention, draws attention to the effects of deprivation and social inequality which may make decisions about drug use more difficult for some groups than others. He also suggests that although drug use occurs at all levels in society, the harmful consequences, particularly the social and economic consequences, may be greatest for those who are initially most socially disadvantaged.

APPROACHES TO DRUG EDUCATION

The precise nature of drug education remains both sensitive and controversial. Stenhouse (1969) described a controversial issue as involving 'a problem about which different individuals and groups urge conflicting courses of action. It is an issue for which society has not found a solution that can be universally or almost universally accepted.' Schools may avoid this potential maelstrom of competing values by focusing on the delivery of factual information. Whilst the possession of accurate information and realistic beliefs about drugs is an essential basis for sound decision-making and risk appraisal, there is a growing consensus that a substance focus alone is inappropriate and may even be counter-productive by heightening interest. It may also be cynically rejected by young people as an attempt to manipulate their behaviour by presenting as 'fact' what has yet to be proved or which conflicts with their own experience. Such tensions will clearly be exacerbated by didactic approaches. In contrast, experiential methods, which are integral to many contemporary drug education programmes, engage pupils in the process of researching information and distinguishing fact from propaganda for themselves. Credibility can be further enhanced by providing the opportunity to relate what has been learned in the classroom to experience in the world outside.

Trends in drug education have changed over the course of time from didactic to experiential, pupil-centred approaches. There has been a shift from an exclusive focus on drugs towards personal and social development and recognition of the situations in which drugs are likely to be encountered. Information-giving approaches incorporating fear appeals have given way to a whole range of strategies – values clarification, decision-making, development of refusal skills, situational education, life-skills and empowerment. It is generally accepted that shock horror approaches do not work, especially when they are at odds with direct personal experience or awareness of the experience of friends and acquaintances. However, knowing about the negative consequences of substance use, which should include personal and social consequences as well as bio-medical ones (Burgess, 1996), is integral to the notion of informed choice. There is also a potential point of contact here between primary prevention and harm minimisation strategies in that accurate information is required both for making decisions about whether to use drugs and taking action to reduce the risk of associated harm.

The health action model, referred to earlier, provides a useful framework for planning education on drugs. It allows identification of the various components that need to be included and the relationship between them (see Figure 31.2). We can see that knowledge, beliefs, values and attitudes and perceptions of normative influences, not least of which would be 'youth culture', all impact on decision-making. Furthermore, making decisions and translating them into action requires a whole repertoire of skills. Drawing on explanatory models of behaviour such as HAM establishes a priori that, if it is to be effective, drug education needs to be wide-ranging and, as we shall show, there is some empirical evidence to support the use of such comprehensive programmes. Some of the various elements required will be concerned directly with drugs but some will be of a more general and 'empowering' nature such as self-esteem, a sense of being in control, assertiveness and so on (Tones, 1994). As noted earlier, it could be further argued that by contributing to general levels of empowerment, life-skills programmes enhance 'health' *per se*.

The notion of peer group pressure underpins approaches based on developing general life-skills or, more specifically, refusal skills typified by the 'Just Say No' style of programme. This type of approach is, however, predicated on the assumption that young people want to say no in the first place. Simple interpretations of peer influence, which see those who use drugs as somehow more susceptible to pressure and less assertive, have recently been subjected to critical scrutiny (Coggans and McKellar, 1994; Coggans and Watson, 1995; May, 1993; Michell, 1997). A more complex model is required to incorporate the concept of peer selection (which recognises that individuals seek out like-minded friends) together with a more sophisticated and discriminating analysis of the composition of peer groups. Furthermore, although some young people are offered drugs or encouraged to use them by their peers, this is not universally the case. Group norms and peer pressure can equally be an important factor in reinforcing non-use (Shiner and Newburn, 1996) or regulating use. Peer education programmes consciously attempt to harness these more positive aspects of peer influence.

Effectiveness

A recent report (OFSTED, 1997, p. 4) observes that: 'Schools are not taking *monitoring* and *evaluation* of drug education programmes, particularly the quality of the teaching, sufficiently seriously.' It also concedes that: 'Evaluation of the long-term effects of drug education on the *behaviour* of individuals lies beyond the resources of an individual school or local education authorities.'

The paucity of rigorous programme evaluations is clearly problematic in terms of recommending appropriate strategies (White and Pitts, 1997). What evidence is there of the relative effectiveness of different approaches? Isolating the direct effect of school-based interventions from other contextual factors can be difficult. Not least of these would be the process of implementation. A significant finding of the School Health Education Evaluation

(Connell, *et al.*, 1985) was that the impact increased when programmes were fully and faithfully implemented. The provision of training and support materials was found to contribute positively to programme fidelity and hence to potential to achieve goals. All too often, evaluation is restricted to measuring the short-term impact on knowledge or behavioural intention rather than long-term effects on actual behaviour. The complexity of evaluating outcomes is recognised in a report by the Advisory Council on the Misuse of Drugs (1993) which identifies a range of possible behavioural effects. These include 'discourage ever use, delay onset of use, decrease the quantity or frequency of use, discourage particularly harmful forms of use or encourage cessation of use and/or seeking help'. Programmes may have a differential effect on each of these outcomes or indeed with respect to different substances.

A review of the effectiveness of drug education for the International Union for Health Promotion and Education (Kröger, 1994) concludes that the most successful school programmes were comprehensive, drawing on a range of methods, including 'social and life-skills training, role play, promoting social competency and resistance to peer influence'. It recommends that programmes aimed at primary prevention should focus on basic cognitive, social and life-skills; should start before the onset of drug use; and, should take place over several years. Clearly, high quality programmes are more likely to be effective.

These findings support those of an earlier study by Hansen (1992), who also noted that comprehensive and social influence programmes were most effective in preventing the onset of substance abuse. The fact that many evaluated programmes use multiple strategies creates some difficulty in determining whether success is due to experience of the whole programme or to key essential elements. Hansen identified social influence programmes which covered social and peer pressure and the development of resistance skills as the single component which offered most promise.

Support for life-skills approaches also emerges from a brief review of studies in the report of the Advisory Council on the Misuse of Drugs (1993). This also draws attention to the fact that some studies have short-term behavioural effects but that, in the absence of reinforcement, these may decay over time. Coggans and Watson (1995) caution against undue reliance on any single approach and conclude that combinations of strategies (comprehensive approaches) are more likely to be effective, especially within a 'community-wide' context. They also recognise the contribution of providing 'substitute gratification' and behavioural alternatives to drug use and a social context that is supportive of healthy lifestyles. White and Pitts (1997) suggest that (a) there should be more precise targeting of programmes to meet the identified needs of pupils and (b) that schools should take account of the stage of drug use reached by individuals together with other social and cultural factors. They reiterate the value of incorporating a mix of approaches and also point out that a reasonable amount of time (minimum 15 hours) is needed to have any effect and that the impact may be enhanced by 'booster' sessions.

DRUG EDUCATION IN THE HEALTH-PROMOTING SCHOOL

As already noted, there is a strong argument for education about drugs to start in the primary school, when ideas about drugs are beginning to develop and it is less likely that pupils will have actually used drugs themselves (Williams *et al.*, 1989). Clearly, the subject will need to be revisited in accordance with the classic principles of the spiral curriculum. Drug education is, therefore, an issue for all tiers of education, ideally with good co-ordination between tiers.

The identification of clear aims and objectives is a prerequisite for the selection of appropriate approaches or strategies. Developing a school consensus on this is also an essential first stage in the development of a whole-school approach characteristic of the health-promoting school. An agreed policy on the school's response both to teaching about drugs and to dealing with drug-related incidents serves to provide a sense of direction and a co-ordinating framework. Indeed, Blackmann (1996) identified a coherent policy as one of the key factors in shaping the response to drugs. In English and Welsh schools, policies and practices as regards drugs are monitored in the regular programme of inspection conducted by the Office for Standards in Education.

In the health-promoting school, the contribution of the three dimensions identified earlier, i.e. the curriculum, the ethos and environment and links with the community, will all need to be considered. The precise location of drug education within the formal curriculum is arguably of less relevance to achieving desired goals than having a well-planned and co-ordinated teaching programme delivered by committed staff. As the recent report of Her Majesty's Chief Inspector of Schools notes:

> Both primary and secondary schools often opt to teach drug education across the curriculum. However, insufficient co-ordination of the contributions of different subject areas frequently reduces the overall coherence of the drug education programme.
>
> (OFSTED, 1997, p. 3)

In some countries, of course, statutory educational requirements may exert an influence. In England and Wales, for example, the national curriculum statutory orders for science include some aspects of drug education (Department for Education, 1995a). This may be regarded as an absolute minimum provision. The type of comprehensive programme referred to earlier would require the involvement of other subject areas and/or personal, social and health education. Indeed, the general development of personal and social skills could be said to be a whole-school responsibility. The role of the school ethos and environment in supporting this development should not be ignored.

In addition to providing drug education in its broadest sense, it has become increasingly important for schools to give some consideration to the way they handle drug-related incidents. Such incidents may range from the discovery of needles and syringes on school premises through to suspecting or finding pupils in possession of drugs, dealing in drugs, showing signs of being under the influence of drugs or even the effects of acute intoxication. Whilst ensuring the health and safety of pupils (and indeed of all members of the school community) is of paramount importance, any response will also need to take account of the legal position. It is interesting to note in this context that, in England, there is no statutory requirement to inform the police if illegal substances are found on a pupil or in the school, although there is an expectation that schools will do so (Department for Education, 1995b, para. 49). However, liaison with the local police will be helpful in establishing procedural guidelines which staff can feel confident about implementing.

Our earlier discussion of the health-promoting school emphasised the importance of a whole-school approach. It is axiomatic that approaches to dealing with drug-related incidents are consistent with what is taught in the classroom. There are also implications for the pastoral system, which may be required to provide counselling and support for pupils who are using illegal substances. Many schools are not in a position to offer the level of support available from specialised agencies but they can be instrumental in raising awareness of the range of services available and even in mobilising support.

To sum up, a whole range of services can contribute either directly or indirectly to drug education and both primary and secondary prevention. Strong links with these services and the community as a whole were identified earlier as integral to the notion of the health-promoting school. These links provide the school with access to advice and support. Moreover, the community may reinforce messages received at school. The effect of supportive community action in enhancing the impact of school health education programmes has been observed in the North Karelia Youth Project in relation to smoking (Vartiainen *et al.*, 1990) and to food habits (Puska *et al.*, 1982).

Benjamin's Stone Age allegory illustrates the danger of curricula becoming irrelevant. This warning is particularly apt in relation to the rapidly changing 'drug scene' in contemporary society. Critical reflection and ongoing evaluation are therefore essential if programmes are to evolve to meet these changing demands. Above all, programmes must be seen as relevant by young people themselves and must respond directly to their own perceived needs.

We have so far emphasised the importance of 'horizontal' approaches to health education. Logically, therefore, we must question the value of specific drugs-focused programmes. A major advantage of the health-promoting school, as we have demonstrated, is the way in which it provides a context for addressing both specific issues such as drugs and the wider determinants of health-related behaviour. To conclude on a visionary note, empowerment and critical consciousness-raising might even prompt some to challenge the social and environmental causes of ill health, not least the reasons why so many young people feel the need to use mind-altering substances!

REFERENCES

Advisory Council on the Misuse of Drugs (1993) *Drug Education in Schools.* London: HMSO.

Allensworth, D. D. (1994) 'The research base for innovative practices in school health education at the secondary level'. *Journal of School Health*, 46 (5), 180–187.

Benjamin, H. (1971) 'The saber-tooth curriculum', in R. Hooper, (ed.) *The Curriculum: Context, Design and Development.* Edinburgh/Open University Press: Oliver & Boyd.

Blackman, S. (1996) *Drugs Education and the National Curriculum: an Evaluation of 'Drug Studies: a resource for the National Curriculum'.* London: Central Drugs Prevention Unit, Home Office.

Burgess, R. (1996) 'Drugs prevention: Watershed or threshold?' *Health Education Journal*, 55 (4), 345–353.

Burrage, H. (1990) 'Health education: education for health', in B. Dufour (ed.) *The New Social Curriculum: A Guide to Cross-Curricular Issues.* Cambridge, UK: Cambridge University Press.

Coggans, N. and McKellar, S. (1994) 'Drug use amongst peers: peer pressure or peer preference?' *Drugs: Education, Prevention and Policy*, 1 (1), 15–26.

Coggans, N. and Watson, J. (1995) 'Drug education: Approaches, effectiveness and delivery'. *Drugs: Education, Prevention and Policy*, 2 (3), 211–223.

Connell, D. B., Turner, R. R. and Mason, E. F. (1985) 'Summary of findings of the School Health Education Evaluation: Health promotion effectiveness, implementation and costs'. *Journal of School Health*, 55 (8), 316–321.

DES (1977) *Health Education in Schools*. London: HMSO.

DES (1980) *A View of the Curriculum*. London: HMSO.

DES (1987) *The National Curriculum: A Consultative Document*. London: HMSO.

Department for Education (1995a) *The National Curriculum*. London: HMSO.

Department for Education (1995b) Circular 4195, *Drug Prevention and Schools*. London: HMSO.

ENHPS (1997) *The Health Promoting School – an Investment in Education, Health and Democracy*. First Conference of the European Network of Health Promoting Schools. Thessalonika, Halkidiki, Greece, 1–5 May, 1997. WHO European Region: Copenhagen.

Freire, P. (1972) *Pedagogy of the Oppressed*. Harmondsworth: Penguin.

Galbraith, J. K (1992) *The Culture of Contentment*. Harmondsworth: Penguin.

Green, J., Tones, B. K. and Manderscheid, J-C. (1996) 'Efficacité et utilité de l'éducation à la santé à l'école'. *Revue Française de Pedagogie*, 114 (Jan./Feb./March), 103–120.

Haglund, B., Pettersson, B., Finer, D. and Tillgren, P. (1992) *The Sundsvall Handbook: 'We Can Do It!'* Sweden: Karolinska Institute.

Hansen, A. (1986) 'The portrayal of alcohol on television'. *Health Education Journal*, 45 (3), 127–131.

Hansen, W. B. (1992) 'School-based substance abuse prevention: A review of the state of the art in curriculum, 1980–1990'. *Health Education Research*, 7 (3), 403–430.

Health Education Authority (1996) *European Network of Health Promoting Schools*. London: HEA.

Health Education Authority/British Market Research Bureau (HEA/BRMB) (1996) *Drug Realities: National Drugs Campaign Survey*. London: HEA.

Health Promotion (1986), 1 (4). Whole issue on the Ottawa Charter.

Hirst, P. (1969) 'The logic of the curriculum'. *Journal of Curriculum Studies*, 1, 142–158.

HMSO (1998) *Tackling Drugs to Build a Better Britain*. London: HMSO.

Kröger, C. (1994) *Drug Abuse: A Review of the Effectiveness of Health Education and Promotion*. Woerden, The Netherlands: Dutch Centre for Health Promotion and Health Education IUHPE/EURO.

Lawton, D. (1975) *Class, Culture and the Curriculum*. London: Routledge & Kegan Paul.

Leverhulme Health Education Project (1978) 'Health promotion, affective education and the personal-social development of young people', in K. David and T. Williams (eds) *Health Education in Schools*. London: Harper.

Lima, L. (1996) personal communication.

May, C. (1993) 'Resistance to peer group pressure: an inadequate basis for alcohol education'. *Health Education Research*, 12 (1), 1–14.

McDonald, G., Veen, C. and Tones, K. (1996) 'Evidence for success in health promotion: suggestions for improvement'. *Health Education Research*, 11 (3), 367–376.

Michell, L. (1997) 'Loud, sad or bad: Young people's perceptions of peer groups and smoking'. *Health Education Research*, 12 (1), 1–14.

Miller, P. M. and Plant, M. (1996) 'Drinking, smoking and illicit drug use among 15 and 16 year olds in the United Kingdom'. *British Medical Journal*, 313, 394–397.

National Curriculum Council (1990) *Guidance 5: Health Education*. York: National Curriculum Council.

OFSTED (1997) *Drug Education in Schools*. London: HMSO.

Parlett, M. and Hamilton, D. (1978) 'Evaluation as illumination: A new approach to the study of innovatory progammes', in D. Hamilton *et al.* (eds) *Beyond the Numbers Game*. London: Macmillan.

Peters, R. S. (1966) *Ethics and Education*. London: Allen & Unwin.

Pettersson, B. and Tillgren, P. (eds) (1992) *Playing for Time . . . Creating Supportive Environments for Health*. Report on the 3rd International Conference on Health Promotion, Sundsvall, Sweden, 9–15 June. Västerrnorrland, Sundsvall: People's Health.

Postman, N. and Weingartner, C. (1981) *Teaching as a Subversive Activity*. Harmondsworth: Penguin.

Puska, P., Vartiainen, E. and Pallonen, U. (1982) 'The North Karelia Project: Evaluation of two years of intervention on health behaviour and CVD risk factors among 13 to 15 year old children'. *Preventive Medicine*, 11, 550–570.

Rennie, J., Lunzer, G. A. and Williams, W. T. (1974) *Social Education: An Experiment in Four Secondary Schools*. Schools Council Working Paper 51. London: Evans/Methuen.

Resolution of the European Council and of Ministers of Education (1988) *Official Journal of the European Communities* (89/C3/01).

Shiner, M. and Newburn, T. (1996) *Young People, Drugs and Peer Education*. Central Drugs Prevention Unit, Home Office. London: HMSO.

Stenhouse, L. (1969) 'Handling controversial issues in the classroom'. *Education Canada*. December.

Tackling Drugs Together: A Strategy for England 1995–1998. London: HMSO.

Toffler, A. (1970) *Future Shock*. London: Bodley Head.

Tones, B. K (1987a) 'Promoting health: the contribution of education', in D. O'Byrne (ed.) *Education for Health in Europe: A Report on a WHO Consultation, 11–12 June*. Edinburgh: Scottish Health Education Group.

Tones, B. K (1987b) 'Health education, PSE and the question of voluntarism'. *Journal Institute of Education*, 25 (2), 41–52.

Tones, B. K (1994) 'Health promotion, empowerment and action competence', in B. B. Jensen and K. Schnack, *Action and Action Competences as Key Concepts in Critical Pedagogy*. Copenhagen: Royal Danish School of Educational Studies.

Tones, B. K. (1997) 'Health education, behaviour change, and the public health', in R. Dettels and J. McEwen (eds) *Oxford Textbook of Public Health*, Vol. 2. Oxford: Oxford University Press.

Tones, B. K. and Tilford, S. (1994) *Health Education: Effectiveness, Efficiency and Equity*. London: Chapman and Hall.

Vartiainen, E., Pallonen, U., McAlister, A. L., Puska, P. (1990) 'Eight year follow-up results of an adolescent smoking prevention programme: the North Karelia Project'. *American Journal of Public Health*, 80 (1), 78–79.

White, D. and Pitts, M. (1997) *Health Promotion with Young People for the Prevention of Substance Misuse*. London: Health Education Authority.

WHO (1978) *Report on the International Conference on Primary Health Care, Alma Ata, 6–12 September*. Geneva: WHO.

WHO (1984) *Health Promotion: A Discussion Document on the Concept and Principles*. Copenhagen: WHO.

WHO (1986) *Ottawa Charter for Health Promotion*. Copenhagen: WHO.

WHO (1988) 'The Adelaide Recommendations; Healthy public policy'. *Health Promotion*, 6 (4), 297–300.

WHO (1993) *Mental Health Programmes in Schools*. Geneva: WHO.

WHO (1996a) *Network News; The European Network of Health Promoting Schools* (2nd edn.) Copenhagen: WHO.

WHO (1996b) *School Health Promotion – Series 5: Regional Guidelines: Development of Health Promoting Schools: A Framework for Action*. Manila: WHO.

WHO (1996c) *Trends in Substance Use and Associated Health Problems*. Factsheet No. 127, Geneva: WHO.

Williams, T., Wetton, N. and Moon, A. (1989) *A Way In: Five Key Areas of Health Education* (Chapter 7: Children's Perceptions of Drugs). London: Health Education Authority.

32

COMPUTERS IN CLASSROOMS
Learners and teachers in new roles

Anna Chronaki

INTRODUCTION

The computer, during the last three decades, has become a symbol of technological innovation and the source of complex social changes in work and leisure. Information technology has taken a prominent place in industry and in varied sectors of the economy by influencing development and growth, and it has changed dramatically the ways of working and communicating in areas such as research, development, management and financial services, media, communications and publishing. As a result, it has been rightly claimed that the computer's entry into our lives has constituted a 'second industrial revolution' and a basis for the emergence of a 'post-industrial' or 'information' society (Bell, 1980 cited in Ruthven, 1993, p. 187).

Plomp *et al.* (1996) have also pointed out that the rapid implementation of computers in schools currently plays a paramount role in shaping policies and curricula in the educational systems cross-nationally. However, it has been noted that the effects on teachers and their enacted pedagogies have been largely unaffected (see Ruthven, 1993; Sutton, 1991; Watson, 1993). Balacheff and Kaput (1996) argue that whilst the potential learning gains seem to be many (provided that the learner's engagement with computers in specific subject areas is active), a full integration of computers in school teaching practices has not yet been achieved. This chapter aims to provide an overview of computer use in classrooms by considering the various modes of incorporating computers in the curriculum and by discussing the new roles which potentially teachers and learners undertake.

MODES OF COMPUTER USE IN THE CURRICULUM

Looking back into the varied modes of computer use in classrooms during the last three decades and the associated visions for their integration in the school curriculum, Kontogiannopoulou-Polydorides (1996, p. 59) cites Anderson who has classified four different models for computer use in educational practice over the last few decades:

- introductory teaching of programming;
- computer literacy;
- use of the computer as a tool;
- the transparent computer infusion.

The first two models represent the main modes of computer use during early 1980s. The teaching of programming (e.g. Basic, Logo) was initially regarded as the most appropriate way for introducing students to new technology and had largely replaced drill and practice activities (see Sutton, 1991, p. 481), whilst computer literacy was regarded as the necessary knowledge about computers and their generic use (e.g. technicalities, file management, software use). The last two models emerged mainly during the 1980s and are related with wider availability of software applications and educational software packages. The use of the computer as a tool was focusing essentially on the effective use of software (e.g. word processing, graphic tools, databases) in classroom activities and was associated with a trend away from abstract programming and towards an integration of computer use in curriculum activities (McCarthy, 1988). Transparent computer infusion emphasises the integration of computer use in specific subject areas. Here the teaching and learning of basic computer-related skills is not entailed in a separate new course in the school timetable, but it becomes part of the pupils' experience of using software across a number of curriculum subject areas (see Kontogiannopoulou-Polydorides and Makrakis, 1994). One needs to mention that, with flexible curriculum timetables, the above modes can be used simultaneously. For example, Logo, a programming language especially devised for use by young children (Papert, 1980), can be used as a programming language, as a tool for cross-curricular activities and can also be transparently infused in the school timetable for teaching mathematics. It has been identified that children can work in 'microworlds' based on the metaphor of 'turtle', where by exploring its structural properties they can learn to 'talk' with computers (i.e. via programming in Logo language) and at the same time they can learn and more importantly talk about mathematics.

Recently, the linking of computer technology with telecommunications has resulted in what is often called the 'information superhighway', which offers a wide variety of information, communication channels and services. From this, the term ICT (information communication technology) has emerged, embracing the Internet, the World Wide Web (WWW), video-conferencing tools, video and digital television. The range of services can be broadly divided into two categories: (a) communication (e.g. e-mail, usenet newsgroups, talk and Internet Relay Chat, virtual classrooms and colleges) and (b) access to information, resources, materials and databases (see Chronaki and Bourdakis, 1996). ICT or new technologies promise fast access to information and a new way of communicating, networking, teaching, learning and researching (Negroponte, 1995; Windschitl, 1998).

Scrimshaw (1997) has classified different types of software according to their educational characteristics (i.e. view of the learner, suggested group relations and type of knowledge embodied). He refers to a wide range such as word processors, desktop publishing packages, presentation packages, spreadsheets, graphic packages, composition of music, ideas processors, database packages, modelling packages, programming languages, e-mail, computer conferencing, remote databases, filled read-only tools, text disclosure, simulations, adventure games, instructional hypertexts, encyclopedias, talking books, intelligent tutors, video games, data logging and drill and practice programmes. It is interesting to note that learners engaged in data logging and drill and practice programmes are characterised merely as 'receivers' of information whilst in other categories they can potentially be 'creators' or 'explorers'. Further, most software types seem to be oriented around individualised learning (unless otherwise specified by teacher intervention programmes), whilst collaborative or group work is mainly required by types of software that incorporate e-mail and computer conferencing tools.

A different categorisation relates educational software to the intended view of the learners, as has been described across the two distinctive traditions of 'objectivism' and 'constructivism'. Alessi and Trollip (1985) explain that an objectivistic approach is consistent with educational software such as programmed instruction, tutorials, and drill and practice programmes which view learning as a process of repeated practice and rehearsal. The constructivist tradition emphasises the developing of computer-based environments in which the learner is an active organiser of his/her own acquisition of knowledge. Examples of software include hypertext environments, concept mapping environments, simulations and modelling environments (De Jong and Van Joolingen, 1998).

COMPUTERS AS LEARNING ENVIRONMENTS

The pupils' experience of learning, due to their interaction with computers, cannot be seen merely as a relationship between humans and machines. It needs to be understood as an interactive partnership between humans, machines, available software and the broader educational context in which curricular activities take place. The new learning strategies embodied in such partnerships are often described as active, reflective, mindful, self-organising and socially oriented. The effect of the employment of these strategies is that content learning increases significantly. Davis *et al.* (1997) explain that quality in learning can indeed be enhanced when information technology is approached and utilised as an intellectual 'multi-tool' adaptable to learners' needs and supportive of their attempts for conceptual abstracting and for engaging in increasingly decontextualised learning. Somekh (1997) also argues through the experience of the PALM project (Pupil Autonomy in Learning with Microcomputers) about the potential for pupils' active and autonomous learning in computer-based learning environments. In short, the learner is no longer seen as a passive recipient of information (or the consumer of prescriptive guidelines) but has the potential actively to interact with information technology tools and peers and to construct meaning via exploration, discovery, trial and error and social engagement.

Balacheff and Kaput (1996), reviewing seminal projects involved with the development of computer-based environments for mathematics learning, coined the terms 'epistemological penetration' and 'computational transposition' to describe the effect of technology on learning. They argue:

> While technology's impact on daily practice has yet to match expectations from two or three decades ago, its epistemological impact is deeper than expected. This impact is based on a reification of mathematical objects and relations that students can use to act more directly on these objects and relations than ever before. This new mathematical realism, when coupled with the fact that the computer becomes a new partner in the didactical contract, forces us to extend the

didactical transposition of mathematics to a computational transposition. This new realism also drives ever deeper changes in the curriculum, and it challenges widely held assumptions about what mathematics is learnable by which students and when they may learn it.

(Balacheff and Kaput, 1996, p. 469)

Computer-based learning environments are often built around conceptual metaphors (e.g. the 'turtle movement' in Logo as a way to think over geometry; the 'speech bubble' in hypercard as a way to think about informal and formal language) which help to introduce the epistemological features of the learning content. Another integral feature of their construction is the employment of instructional structures (e.g. in the form of tutoring systems) which can be especially engineered to co-ordinate free exploration, didactic intervention and provision of feedback. Exemplars of computer-based environments that view learning in such powerful ways as argued above (i.e. active, reflective and mindful endeavours) will be discussed below, in order to illustrate the vision for the potential new role of the learner.

Cabri and Logo for constructing mathematical meanings

Cabri-Geometre and Logo are generic software environments (in the sense that the users can construct an unlimited number of activities) which enable pupils to construct mathematical understandings of geometry and algebra in ways significantly different to conventional means (see Hillel and Kieran, 1987; Hoyles and Sutherland, 1989; Laborde, 1993; Papert, 1980). Logo is a programme language based on the metaphor of 'turtle movements', and is especially devised so that young children can learn to construct and talk about mathematical concepts whilst learning to programme with Logo. Geometric and algebraic concepts such as length and angle embodied in turtle displacement and turn, and the algebraic variables and functions embodied in their programming equivalents can be constructed. The mathematical potential (and at the same time the epistemological innovation) of this environment is the explicit relation (in both visual and text forms) of geometrical and algebraic notions. Other conceptual processes involve problem-solving strategies such as decomposing a complex problem, instantiated by the use of sub-procedures, and analysing an imperfect solution, instantiated by the process of debugging. A current development of this work is YoYo; a kid-friendly programming language which can be used by very young children as a way to talk and to command physical objects in a virtual environment. One application of this is the Pet Park; a graphical virtual community where kids can interact with virtual pets and teach them to dance, to greet visitors and talk informally (see *http://www.media.mit.edu/projects/petpark/*).

Cabri-Geometre incorporates a set of primitive objects (e.g. point, segment) offered in the system and on which elementary operations (e.g. construction of parallel lines) can be applied to construct geometrical drawings. These drawings are 'dynamic' in the sense that their position and metric properties can be altered by dragging the image on the screen. Thus, the learner is enabled to express rules and descriptions about the ways these operations can be performed and associated (Laborde, 1993). Although both Cabri and Logo integrate visual images of drawings with conceptual understandings of mathematical concepts, the nature of the user's interaction with the drawings is different. In Logo, drawings are 'static' in the sense that one can draw and redraw them by modifying the Logo programming code that has produced them using a process that involves enumeration and generation with functions defined on numbered segments. Drawings on Cabri consist of a representation of what can be produced by means of ruler and compass and their nature is 'dynamic' in the sense that the user can directly manipulate geometrical objects on the surface of the computer screen (Bellemain and Capponi, 1992).

Hypercard and CSILE for constructing understandings for language

McMahon and O'Neill (1989, 1990) have developed a 'hypertext' type of software, called AppleHyperCard, for the construction, categorisation and storing of sets of texts (stacks and cards) which has been especially designed for use in language learning activities in both primary and secondary schools. A specific characteristic of this software is the use of pictorial sequences in the form of cartoons which contain speech bubbles. These 'speech bubbles' can be filled in by the teacher or left empty for the pupils to complete. The bubbles can also be seen as 'thought bubbles', encouraging pupils to suggest what they think a character may be saying and how it relates to another character in the story. The 'bubble dialogue' metaphor is used as a means for helping the learner to explore aspects of language use such as writing and reading skills and building bridges between oral and literary uses of language. Another advantage is that teachers can customise this learning environment by constructing activities based on selected pictorial sequences and texts and can arrange these according to individual needs and rates of progress (e.g. choose between offering ready-made sequences with clear stories to which children are asked to add text or ask pupils to generate their original pictures, stories and texts).

Another type of software oriented for language learning and conceptual development is the CSILE (Computer Supported Intentional Learning Environment), which emphasises the network-based collaboration of learners and enquiry in local school environments and currently in the web. The central component of this software is the idea of a community-shared database that contains graphics, text and links to other media. The learners are encouraged to develop their skills in questioning, exploring concepts in depth, and learning to manage and to edit information (Scardamalia and Bereiter, 1996). For example, users connected to this network can read from elements called 'notes', they can also use certain rules for editing the notes, and finally those notes can be linked to an organisational framework so as to produce an interconnection of notes on a particular topic or issue.

EarthLab as a role play for children as scientists

EarthLab is a computer environment based on the vision of 'children acting as scientists' in their learning of scientific notions. Its central aim is to simulate conditions for children to carry through scientific communication and enable children to take on dialogic roles in the process of scientific reasoning (Newman and Goldman, 1987). It is constructed for use in a local (school-based) network in which children can use computers and play the role of scientific researchers. For example, the learners can collect data, analyse them individually and collectively, and then communicate publicly their findings. Collaborative structures are built into activities, so that, for example, databases are created by different sets of children in a class providing elements which contribute to the 'jigsaw' picture of the object of enquiry.

The WWW as a forum for collaborative projects

The WWW, in particular, has opened up avenues for collaboration in varied styles as compared to more conventional types of computer use or typical classroom resources. Information can be available in web pages only minutes after the events have taken place (e.g. the Shoemaker-Levy comet's impact on Jupiter; the devastating earthquake in Kobe, Japan), and authentic databases provided by governmental and research agencies can be accessed by students (Windschitl, 1998). Recently, the WWW has become the platform for developing projects and collaborative activities between schools and classrooms cross-nationally. An example of this is the Parade scenario (a team game played within a vehicle-simulation system) where a combination of the Internet and independent software components are used and become operable in game-like and role play activities (Kaput, 1993). Children can collaborate and interact at a distance. For example, in this project children in Grenoble, France and Boston, US operate a simulation of car driving and have to solve specific problems related to the estimation of optimum distances, velocities and positions.

Well-documented studies about computer environments that consist of learning activities of the nature described above, have argued that learners can potentially have deep conceptual gains, provided that they undertake specific new learning roles which include becoming more *active, reflective* and *socially oriented*. These new roles entail opportunities for pupils to be involved in more complex and intellectually challenging learning situations (i.e. generalisation or relational thinking, formulating hypotheses and designing experiments in science, drawing inferences from a map, graphical and photographic hypotheses in geography and aspects of content and coherence in pupils' writing of English). Apart from the evidence provided by research focusing on specific computer environments, the above argument has also been supported by empirical studies in projects such as IMPACT, [1] INTENT[2] and PALM, [3] which have explored effects of computer use on learners in various subject areas and software use. In particular, the IMPACT study (see Watson, 1993) has identified that computers were good motivators for pupils' interest and enjoyment and that they also aided concentration by focusing attention on the work at hand. As a result, some pupils and teachers believed that the standard of work produced was of a higher quality than it would have been otherwise. For example, information technology tools assisted in constructing learning environments such as communicating ideas and information, handling information, modelling, as well as measuring and controlling particular situations (see also INTENT, 1993).

However, one needs to keep in mind that learning situations for pupils of the quality described above are the outcome of a number of converging factors that envisage aims for this 'quality learning' at their core. Amongst these one needs to mention the quality of the relevant software and the pupils' attitudes towards learning. Schofield (1995) agrees with Cole *et al.* (1990) who claim that there is a shortage of educational software that promotes learning in the terms described above and that the majority of this is of the drill and practice type. Means *et al.* (1993) explain that such software presents information in a linear mode with no emphasis on interdisciplinary links. The learner is viewed as receiving and assimilating 'information' and 'knowledge', learning input is based on simple responses, mode of work is often individualised, and assessment is based on right and wrong answers. As far as the learner is concerned, Watson (1993) explains that quality learning was prevented by pupils' difficulty in utilising particular software at initial steps, inability to work effectively in a collaborative environment, and lack of true engagement in the activity. To these one needs to add issues of the broader educational context such as: pupil access and opportunity in computer use, teacher characteristics and abilities, as well as school support. Sutton (1991), reviewing empirical studies of computer use during the last decade, identified a lack of equity in terms of race, gender and class when exploring pupils' access to computer facilities and tools at the school level. She explains that despite the rapid growth of computer infrastructure in schools, the increase in the number of machines in classrooms is disproportionate in terms of equity in access for pupils of minority groups.

In relation to the use of the WWW, Wallace and Kupperman (1997) identified that pupils' learning can be naïve and superficial when 'surfing' web pages. In a particular web-based ecology project, sixth graders were not found to be reflective or critical but instead they seemed mainly to take online information at face value without evaluating the source. Salomon *et al.* (1991) argued that the potential for cognitive processing and intellectual performance depends largely on the individual's mindful engagement with the technology at hand. They point out that apart from the product (that is, the effects of technology, in the sense that participants have subsequent cognitive spin-off effects when working away from machines), the process of the learner working with the technology needs to be studied more analytically as it will provide information about the human potential and the kind of mental activities involved. As far as the web-based environments are concerned, Windschitl (1998) argues that with very few exceptions, most evidence about pupils' quality learning is based on gathering 'anecdotal information' that views the web as an extension of existing multimedia and praises uncritically this new learning avenue. The need for exploring critically the nature and effectiveness of the underlying pedagogical structure, the affected human interactions and the true opportunities for the learners in accessing and using search and communicative processes unique for the web has been identified (see Windschitl, 1998).

COMPUTERS, PEDAGOGY AND TEACHERS

A well-supported argument is that the construction of content knowledge in specific subject areas does not emerge spontaneously from interactions between learners and computers. As explained above, it is necessary for the learners to be active, reflective and socially engaged within a complex system that encompasses not only appropriate software but also relevant instructional interventions and a supportive pedagogical context. Alongside, it has been argued that the teachers' influence is paramount for orienting learners towards the new features of their learning role, and as a result, the teacher needs also to adopt new ways in viewing the subject area, learners and pedagogy. For example, Harel (1991), comparing the studying of Logo and fractions arithmetic in a more didactic versus a more constructivist approach, identified that the latter resulted in much deeper mastery and understanding of

Logo and fractions. As a result, pupils' cognitions were largely affected not only by the software but also by the use of software in a culturally and pedagogically goal-setting environment where the teacher's role is a central feature.

Different avenues influencing pedagogy in classroom use of computers

Pedagogy often describes the broader philosophy and visions of a particular educational system in which teaching practices and learning are embedded and embodied (Bruner, 1996). The teacher's new role can be understood in varied dimensions which embrace not only an overall educational vision for using computers in schools and classrooms but also specific teaching strategies employed by teachers whilst interacting with pupils. One then needs to encounter not only the broader educational culture of a system but also the micro-culture of a classroom. Based on the above and considering the potential ways teachers use computers in their classrooms, four different 'avenues' may be suggested which influence the nature of pedagogy when computers are utilised in classrooms:

- the *pedagogical orientation* of the educational system (on a macro-level) in which the computer implementation takes place;
- the *pedagogical structure* embedded within the computer system (i.e. the software);
- the *pedagogical organisation* of lessons;
- the *pedagogical support* provided by teachers during their interventions in pupils' activities.

Concerning the *pedagogical orientation* of the educational system as a whole, Kontogiannopoulou-Polydorides (1996) argues that the 'educational paradigms' of certain educational systems (national cultures, pedagogical philosophies, educational policies and models of practice) not only shape the process of computer implementation in classrooms (in the sense that transnational pedagogical differences are often attributed to cultural differences on a national level) but are also shaped themselves by policy attempts to implement computer use in the curriculum. This influence can be realised not only in the predominant norms in programmes of teacher training, education and support but also in established teachers' views, levels of their confidence, and choices in daily interactions with pupils (see Plomp *et al.*, 1996).

The *pedagogical structure* of the software includes the instructional principles built within it. It contains the 'didactically central features' of the computer system (to use Bellemain and Capponi's [1992] wording) and provides implicit or explicit suggestions for further steps in open or closed ways of interaction and provision of feedback. The nature of the pedagogical structure of the software can be distinguished amongst: *open environments* (see Logo, Cabri) that enable users to explore the content free from guidance, carefully engineered *tutoring systems* (or closed environments) that prescribe certain performances for the user and provide immediate feedback (e.g. *The Geometry Tutor*, Anderson *et al.*, 1985) and *guided discovery environments* that attempt to balance the previous two (see Elsom-Cook, 1990). Bellemain and Capponi (1992) argue that teachers need to be aware of the instructional features of the computer-based environments and, more importantly, they need to be aware that pupils themselves do not have the ability to interpret unassisted the didactical content which at most times appears to be hidden within the structure.

The *pedagogical organisation* of lessons is another avenue for infusing pedagogy in the learning system and refers to the selection of appropriate software, its customisation into specific learning tasks and activities (e.g. in the form of worksheets) and the structuring of lessons in terms of pupils' mode of work. Examples are: constructing lessons where learners can use time of activity away from the computer; working collaboratively in groups; or setting up interdisciplinary projects. A classic case of software customisation is the construction of microworlds for exploratory software (Balacheff and Kaput, 1996).

Lastly, teachers' *pedagogical support* can be realised in teacher–pupil classroom inter-actions and consists of a main avenue for infusing pedagogy since it is based on communicat-ing and intervening with pupils (e.g. in the form of teaching strategies and roles enacted in the classroom). The nature of teachers' pedagogical support will be examined further below.

The nature of teachers' pedagogical support whilst interacting with children

The nature of the support teachers provide to pupils is mainly identified and discussed through observational case studies which often describe varied categories of 'teaching strat-egies' or 'roles' in which teachers position themselves. The changing (or new) role of the teacher has been broadly described by a proportional shift towards a less didactic and open style of teaching and pedagogical vision and approach. The role model of a teacher as a transmitter of information and controller of knowledge is becoming redundant and is being replaced by that of a co-worker, co-learner, facilitator or supporter to pupils' learning. Schofield has described the teacher's changing role as encompassing four main shifts:

> a) from teacher-directed work to student exploration that builds on students' existing knowledge, b) from didactic teaching to interactive modes of instruction that actively involve students in learning, c) from brief class periods devoted to single subjects to longer blocks of time devoted to multidisciplinary work on tasks that have some obvious connection to the world outside of school and d) from individual work to collaborative work.
>
> (Schofield, 1995, p. 218)

The teacher now is more often found to 'stand back' in order to allow time and space for pupils to develop their own ideas (Fraser *et al.*, 1988; Hoyles and Sutherland, 1989; Somekh, 1997). Schofield (1995) also explains that teachers in her study argued that in computer lessons they had more quality time with individual children and groups in terms of provid-ing immediate feedback, co-exploring in tasks and resolving pupils' problems. Descriptions emphasise the increased managerial and organisational features, as well as the new epistemo-logical and pedagogical conceptions that teachers need to develop for their subject area and the human interactions required in classrooms (including virtual classroom interactions).

A classification of teaching strategies has been provided by Hoyles and Sutherland (1989) based on evidence gathered from the LogoMaths project. Concerning the quality of teachers' interventions, Hoyles and Sutherland have developed three categories named *motivational*, *reflection* and *directional*. Motivational interventions consisted of comments aimed towards reinforcement and encouragement of learners. The category of reflection includes actions related to looking forward (encouraging pupils to reflect on and predict the process as well as the ultimate goal of the activity) and looking back (encouraging pupils to reflect back on problem-solving procedures and encouraging pupils to reflect on their goal). The directional intervention aimed to influence or to change the focus of pupils' attention and to include the suggestion or provision of methods, factual information when necessary, introduction of new ideas and enabling pupils to recall past processes or information. De Jong and Van Joolingen (1998) have studied the potential combinations between the simulation type of software for science and instructional support. They explain that support is mainly provided for learners to enable direct access to domain information and to facilitate specific discovery processes. These include teachers' support directed for particular learning processes relevant to simulation and experimental situations, such as hypothesis generation, design of experiments, making predictions, and regulating the learning process.

The types of pedagogical support described above consist of very delicate moves and require both epistemological awareness and pedagogical sensitivity from teachers which will then drive them towards making the right interactions at the right moment for the right pupil. The strength of this research line is that it has enabled us to problematise the nature of teacher–pupil interactions in significant depth, whereby a central (albeit open) question concerning the degree of teachers' intervention for pupils' autonomous learning can be addressed. Some argue in favour of an open and exploratory teaching or a non-interventionist approach, where the teacher 'stands back' and pupils are allowed to try their own ideas and 'mess around'. Papert (1980) in particular believes that the use of exploratory software (e.g. Logo) needs to be treated not as another subject mastered in a didactic manner but instead it needs to encourage pupils' self-directive learning with as little input from teachers as possible. Somekh (1997) also questions the value of 'structuring' lessons and suggests that an increasingly 'non-interventionist' role of the teacher will promote pupils' autonomy and self-organisation in developing their own learning. She claims that support needs to be offered as and when it is needed. Hoyles and Sutherland (1989), reflecting on their own research study on LogoMaths, explain that although teachers adopted initially a 'non-interventionist', 'standing back' approach to allow pupils to express their own ideas, they had to use a mixture of non-intervention and teacher-directed tasks so as to challenge and 'stretch' pupils' cognitive growth.

However, one needs to bear in mind that interactions of such quality are often the result of a close relation between researchers and teachers or teachers who take the role of an action researcher (Hoyles and Sutherland, 1989; Somekh, 1993). In these cases, the researcher works closely with teachers and often support is provided in the form of 'mentoring' or 'scaffolding', which creates the 'mental space' for teachers to develop and practise their ideas. Andrews (1997) finds that teachers are, in most cases, unprepared to use software to its full potential in subject areas and Bigum (1997) has identified that teachers struggle to understand what is required of them and to come to terms with the increased complexity and responsibility of their role. Furthermore, the under-participation of schools in electronic networks has been pointed out by a recent report from the European Union, which suggests that we are still short of feasible pedagogical strategies that can be largely espoused by schools and teachers. It explains that although experimental projects indicate fruitful dimensions for using ICT in learning activities and networking (i.e. experimental schools who are networked electronically at regional or local level and produce thematic databases, practical comparative work and joint projects incorporating text and images), the number of schools who actively participate in existing networks is still small and by mid-1996 less than 5 per cent of European schools were incorporated. The situation varies greatly from one country to the next. For example, two-thirds of schools are connected in Finland and in Sweden but only 15 per cent of schools in the UK and less than 5 per cent in France and Germany (European Commission, 1996).

Fraser *et al.* (1988) studied teachers of varied styles using computers and they described this 'changing role' as comprising a major shift of the 'locus of control' in teachers' managerial and organisational responsibilities. They identified teachers adopting roles such as counsellors and fellow pupils or simply classroom resources for pupils to come and voice particular queries. This is particularly evident in classroom interactions where peer interaction, group work and collaboration (due to the computer presence or the utilisation of particular software based on local or remote networks) between pupils become a central feature in structuring lessons (Webb, 1987). Mercer (1996) and Edwards and Mercer (1987) examined the quality of pupils' discussions in group settings when the pupils were working in computer-based activities. They maintained that at most times 'collaboration' fails because pupils do not share similar views (or ground rules) about the expected behaviours of participants in groups. Chronaki (1998) has also reported that teachers themselves rarely possess coherent understanding about pupils' collaboration or viable strategies that could enable pupils to work in groups. As a result they rely mainly on personal 'survival' strategies which focus more on disciplining pupils rather than fostering a true collaborative pattern of group work. Thus, the increased need for group work and collaboration between pupils in certain computer environments, raises new challenges for teachers' roles in classrooms, since they need to change their patterns of interaction with pupils. Computer use seems to require more active interaction of teachers with individuals and groups, in which teachers are more often faced with facilitating pupils' working relationships and remedying possible false understandings.

Moreover, it is anticipated that the rapid development and provision of environments such as virtual classrooms or customised teacher intervention at a distance will create conditions where pedagogical support (of the type described above) and human interactions geared towards high-order conceptual understandings need to be re-assessed. For example, TeleCabri is a new software medium that represents real-time teaching at a distance. The whole idea is that the teacher interacts with individual students in real time, often supported by a video channel allowing tele-presence. The pupils are working on a geometrical task with Cabri and when the communication is established between the student and the teacher, the latter sees the current screen of Cabri-Geometre and must make sense of what the student has constructed and why. S/he then must decide what action to take and what adequate feedback to provide for the user pupils. A two-way messaging text window may provide more information about the drawing and its construction and perhaps some aspects of what the student has previously tried (see Balacheff and Kaput, 1996). In this type of situation, compared to traditional classrooms, the teacher needs to sustain a substantial dialogue with the pupils. As a result, certain negotiations about pupils' current understandings, the content in curriculum areas, and the provision of feedback cannot be avoided and must be articulated in different forms and discourses.

CONCLUSION

The availability of computers in classrooms has resulted in restructuring classroom contexts, not only in terms of physical rearrangements, but mainly in social terms closely associated with an envisaged 'new role' for both learners and teachers. This vision is shared with educationists who believe that computer use and development of innovative software entail a central goal for transforming experiences of learning and pedagogy (Leach and Moon, 1999; Salomon *et al.*, 1991; Schofield, 1995; Simon, 1993). These new roles are being characterised by a major shift away from the traditional pattern of the learner as passive recipient of knowledge and the teacher as transmitter of information to the adoption of an active, reflective, mindful and socially aware role. Learning and teaching then become contextualised in environments which represent and simulate real-life phenomena, authentic situations and subject-related content on the computer screen. In such environments, learners are asked to perform by taking an active part in problem-solving and exploring novel situations. The teacher's role is seen as 'orchestrating' learners' activity by selecting tasks, monitoring, facilitating and supporting their learning. Overall, an increasingly interactive role between teachers, learners, machines and information is being envisaged.

Although the 'new' roles of learners and teachers are described in very attractive terms, it has been identified that schools, classrooms and teachers in the vast majority, resist changing traditional patterns of working. Obstacles to learning and teaching in the terms described above can be a lack of equity in access to computer use (Sutton, 1991) and the non-availability of educational software to encourage learning environments of the above type (Cole *et al.*, 1990). Schofield (1995) argues that another potential obstacle is that teachers (and school systems) may not espouse the same educational purposes and pedagogical visions for the 'transformative roles' that computer use brings along and are therefore unable to put them into practice. In a similar vein, Leach and Moon (1999) discussing current concerns about learning in multiple contexts and arenas (i.e. classrooms, homes, workshops, electronic forums, institutions) address the need for reconceptualising 'pedagogy' in ways that would inform the rapid global and local changes of our teaching and learning habits. They argue:

> New forms of pedagogy will be in a constant process of renewal taking evidence and ideas from all available sources, driven inevitably with controversy but always forward looking. A more intellectualised pedagogy should provide the cornerstone to legitimating teaching as a professional activity drawing on a wide variety of perspectives.

(Leach and Moon, 1999, p. 462)

In other words, the survival and fostering of these new learning and teaching roles seem to depend on a complex systemic frame. In this, it is necessary to encounter provision not only for adequate infrastructure in terms of computer machines and relevant educational software, but also for channels that would enable communication and the sharing of pedagogical visions which embrace and promote these new roles.

NOTES

1 The IMPACT (An evaluation of the impact of information technology on children's achievements in primary and secondary schools) project has been funded by DfE and focused on accessing the pupils' achievement when using information technology in the subjects of mathematics, science, geography and English and covered a range of ages (8–10, 12–14 and 14–16).
2 The INTENT (Initial Teacher Education and New Technology) project, funded mainly by the NCET (now BECTA), had as aims the developing of quality in teaching and learning with IT, providing support to tutors for integrating IT across the curriculum for initial teacher education, developing management strategies and monitoring the process of institutional change.
3 The PALM (Pupil Autonomy in Learning with Microcomputers) project was also funded by NCET and aimed at working in partnership with teachers and researching the role of IT in developing pupil autonomy in learning.

REFERENCES

Alessi, S. M. and Trollip, S. R. (1985) *Computer-Based Instruction, Methods and Development.* Englewood Cliffs, NY: Prentice-Hall.

Anderson, J., Boyle, C. and Yost, G. (1985) *The Geometry Tutor.* Proceedings of the International Joint Conference on Artificial Intelligence, Los Angeles.

Andrews, P. (1997) 'Information Technology in the Mathematics Classroom'. *British Journal of Educational Technology* 28 (4), 244–255.

Balacheff, N. and Kaput, J. (1996) 'Computer-based learning environments in mathematics'. In A. Bishop, K. Clements, C. Keitel, J. Kilpatrick and C. Laborde (eds) *International Handbook of Mathematics Education.* Dordrecht: Kluwer Academic Publishers, 469–501.

Bell, D. (1980) 'The social framework of the information society'. In T. Forester (ed.) *The Microelectronics Revolution.* Oxford: Basil Blackwell, 500–549.

Bellemain, F. and Capponi, B. (1992) 'Spécificité de l'organisation d'une séquence d'enseignement lors de l'utilisation de l'ordinateur'. *Educational Studies in Mathematics* 23 (1), 59–97.

Bigum, C. (1997) 'Teachers and computers: in control or being controlled?' *Australian Journal of Education*, 41 (3), 247–61.

Bruner, J. (1996) *The Culture of Education.* Cambridge, MA: Harvard University Press.

Chronaki, A. (1998) *Accessing and Interpreting Teachers' Views on Pupils' Social Interaction in Group Settings.* Slovenia: ECER (European Conference on Educational Research).

Chronaki, A. and Bourdakis, B. (1996) 'The Internet: Reality or myth for researchers?' *EERA Bulletin* 2 (2), 12–16.

Cole, M. and Laboratory of Comparative Human Cognition (1990) 'Computers and the organisation of new forms of educational activity: A socio-historical perspective'. *Golem* 2, 6–13.

Davis, N., Desforges, C., Jessel, J., Somekh, B. and Vaughan, G. (1997) 'Can quality in learning be enhanced through the use of IT?' In B. Somekh and N. Davis (eds), *Using Information Technology Effectively in Teaching and Learning.* London and New York: Routledge.

De Jong, T. and Van Joolingen, W. R. (1998). 'Scientific discovery learning with computer simulations of conceptual domains'. *Review of Educational Research* 68 (2), 179–201.

Edwards, M. and Mercer, N. (1987) *Common Knowledge: The Development of Understanding in the Classroom.* London: Methuen.

Elsom-Cook, M. (1990) *Guided Discovery Tutoring.* London: Paul Chapman Publishing.

European Commission (1996) *Learning in the Information Society: Action Plan for a European Initiative (1996–1998)* Brussels: European Commission.

Fraser, R., Burkhardt, H., Coupland, J., Philips, R., Pimm, D. and Ridgway, J. (1988) 'Learning activities and classroom roles with and without the microcomputer'. In A. Jones and P. Scrimshaw (eds) *Computers in Education 5–13.* Milton Keynes: The Open University Press.

Harel, I. (ed.) (1991) *Constructionist Learning*. Cambridge, MA: Media Laboratory, MIT Press.

Hillel, J. and Kieran, K. (1987) 'Schema used by 12 year olds in solving selected turtle geometry tasks'. *Recherches en Didactique des Mathématiques* 8 (1/2), 61–102.

Hoyles, C. and Sutherland, R. (1989) *Logo Mathematics in the Classroom*. London: Routledge.

INTENT (1993) *Strategy Cards: A Series of Five Discussion Documents*. Coventry: National Council for Educational Technology.

Kaput, J. (1993) MathCars (Computer animation video available from the author). Dartmouth: University of Massachusetts.

Kontogiannopoulou-Polydorides, G. (1996). 'Educational paradigms and models of computer use: Does technology change educational practice?' In T. Plomp, R. Anderson and G. Kontogiannopoulou-Polydorides (eds), *Cross National Policies and Practices on Computers in Education*. Dordrecht: Kluwer Academic Press, 49–83.

Kontogiannopoulou-Polydorides, G. and Makrakis, B. (1994) *Computers in Education: A Critical Review*. Athens: Ethniko Idryma Ereynon [National Research Institution].

Laborde, C. (1993) 'The computer as part of the learning environment: The case of geometry'. In C. Keitel and K. Ruthven (eds) *Learning from Computers: Mathematics Education and Technology*. NATO ASI Series, London and Berlin: Springer-Verlag, 48–60.

Leach, J. and Moon, B. (1999) 'Recreating pedagogy'. In J. Leach and B. Moon (eds) *Learners and Pedagogy*. London and New York: Routledge.

McCarthy, R. (1988) 'Educational software: How it stacks up?' *Electronic Learning* 7, 26–30.

McMahon, H. and O'Neill, W. (1989) '*Language hypermedia*'. Coleraine: University of Ulster, Faculty of Education.

McMahon, H. and O'Neill, W. (1990) 'Capturing Dialogue in Learning'. Occasional paper InTER/18/90, Lancaster, ESRC-InTER programme.

Means, B., Blando, J., Olson, K., Middleton, T., Morocco, C., Remz, A. and Zorfass, J. (1993) *Using Technology to Support Education Reform*. Washington, DC: US Government Printing Office.

Mercer, N. (1996) 'The quality of talk in children's collaborative activity in the classroom'. *Learning and Instruction* 6 (4), 359–377.

Negroponte, N. (1995) *Being Digital*. London: Coronet Books.

Newman, D. and Goldman, S. (1987) 'Earth Lab: a local network for collaborative classroom and science'. *Journal of Educational Technology Systems* 15 (3), 237–247.

Papert, S. (1980) *Mindstorms: Children, Computers and Powerful Ideas*. Brighton: Harvester Press.

Plomp, T., Anderson, R., Kontogiannopoulou-Polydorides, G. (eds) (1996) *Cross National Policies and Practices on Computers in Education*. Dordrecht: Kluwer Academic Publishers.

Ruthven, K. (1993) 'Technology and the rationalisation of teaching'. In C. Keitel and K. Ruthven (eds) *Learning from Computers: Mathematics Education and Technology*. NATO ASI Series, Berlin and London: Springer-Verlag, 187–202.

Salomon, G., Perkins, D. and Globerson, T. (1991). *Educational Researcher* 20 (3), 2–9.

Scardamalia, M. and Bereiter, C. (1996) 'Engaging students in a knowledge society'. *Educational Leadership* 54 (3), 6–10.

Schofield, J. W. (1995) *Computers and Classroom Culture*. Cambridge, UK: Cambridge University Press.

Scrimshaw, P. (1997) 'Computers and the teacher's role'. In B. Somekh and N. Davis (eds) *Using Information Technology Effectively in Teaching and Learning*. London and New York: Routledge, 100–114.

Simon, M. (1993) 'The impact of constructivism on mathematics teacher education'. Unpublished manuscript. University Park, PA, Penn State University.

Somekh, B. (1993) *Project INTENT. 1990–92: Final Report*. Coventry: National Council for Educational Technology.

Somekh, B. (1997) 'Classroom investigations: Exploring and evaluating how IT can support learning'. In B. Somekh and N. Davis (eds) *Using Information Technology Effectively in Teaching and Learning*. London and New York: Routledge.

Somekh, B. and Davis, N. (eds) (1997) *Using Information Technology Effectively in Teaching and Learning*. London and New York: Routledge.

571

Sutton, R. (1991) 'Equity and computers in the schools: A decade of research'. *Review of Educational Research* 61 (4), 475–503.

Wallace, R. and Kupperman, J. (1997) *Online searches in science classrooms: Benefits and possibilities*. Chicago: AERA (American Educational Research Association).

Watson, D. (ed.) (1993) *The Impact Report: An Evaluation of the Impact of Information Technology on Children's Achievements in Primary and Secondary Schools*. London: Department for Education and Kings College London, Centre for Educational Studies.

Webb, N. (1987) 'Peer interaction and learning with computers in small groups'. *Computer in Human Behavior* 3, 193–209.

Windschitl, M. (1998) 'The WWW and classroom research: What path should we take?' *Educational Researcher* 27 (1), 28–33.

Part IV

SECTORS

33

EARLY CHILDHOOD EDUCATION THROUGHOUT THE WORLD

Patricia P. Olmsted

In some countries, systematic early childhood education has been in existence for thousands of years, while in others, the idea of educating preschool-aged children is relatively new.[1] In some countries, early childhood programmes serve children 3 to 6 years old, and in others, they serve a much narrower age-range (e.g. only 5 year olds). In some countries, early childhood education is available for nearly all preschool-aged children, while in others, it is available to very few or none at all. Some countries' early childhood education programmes have developed because of a belief that early education is important, while other countries' programmes have developed to provide care (and perhaps also education) for children whose parents participate in the labour force.

From the information just presented, it is clear that any picture of early childhood education programmes around the world is by nature a complicated one. One purpose of this chapter is to present the most complete picture possible by synthesising information from many sources. Following this general discussion, the chapter presents brief sketches of three ongoing cross-national activities related to early childhood education. The first two activities are efforts to assist governments and agencies in expanding and sustaining early childhood programmes. The third activity is the IEA Preprimary Project, a 15-nation early childhood research study examining the nature, quality and effects of children's participation in early childhood programmes.

EARLY CHILDHOOD EDUCATION PROGRAMMES: GENERAL INFORMATION

History

An example of a nation with a long history of providing early childhood education is China. Professor Shi Hui Zhong of the Central Institute of Educational Research in Beijing has noted the following:

Recorded history reveals that early childhood education began to receive widespread attention in the 11th century BC in the Chinese West Zhou Dynasty. A curriculum for young children called Six Arts Education appeared at that time. According to this curriculum, young children were taught to use their right hands as soon as they were able to serve themselves at table; they were taught to recognize spatial orientations and to read at age 6 and taught courtesy at age 7.

(Shi, 1989, p. 241)

Though implementation of the Six Arts Education occurred within the family, and not in a school setting, few other countries in the world can trace this idea of a formalised early childhood curriculum as far back as China can. Several other Asian countries/territories (e.g. Hong Kong, the Philippines, Thailand) began to provide early childhood education services during the late nineteenth and early twentieth centuries (Opper, 1989; Palattao-Corpus, 1989; Passornsiri *et al.*, 1989).

Among European countries, Spain reports the provision of early childhood education services as early as 1677 (Palacios, 1989), while many other countries (e.g. France, Italy, Hungary) date the beginning of early childhood education programmes to the early 1800s (Le Normand, 1992; Pistillo, 1989; Vari, 1989). In many North and South American countries, early education services began to be offered in the mid- to late-1800s, while the comparable dates for many African nations are early and mid-1900s (e.g. Onibokun, 1989; Riak *et al.*, 1989).

During the past several decades, in country after country around the world, social, economic and demographic changes have produced an accelerating demand for early childhood education and care services. One of these changes, improvement in infant survival rates, has meant that a number of nations can now turn their attention from infant survival to child development in the early years. Many of these countries have developed early childhood programmes that have multiple components dealing with not just education but also health, nutrition and parenting (Myers, 1995).

Other global changes are the increasing incidence of one-parent families and the increasing participation of women in the labour force (United Nations, 1966, 1976, 1986, 1996). Matters are further complicated by the increasing urbanisation of developing countries and the high degree of family mobility in some developed countries – two conditions that make childcare by extended family members an increasingly rare option for parents.

Finally, a small but growing body of research is demonstrating the long-term benefits of high-quality early childhood education programmes and thus creating widespread awareness of the importance of the early years in a child's life. Examples of these studies emanate from the United States (Schweinhart *et al.*, 1993), Turkey (Kagitcibasi *et al.*, 1987), Nigeria (Olatuni, 1986; Onibokun, 1980) and India (Lal and Wati, 1986).

The combined effect of these social, economic, demographic and research-knowledge changes is an increase in the provision of early childhood services in countries around the world. Let us now look at the current availability of these early education programmes in various nations.

Availability

Each year UNESCO publishes information about the percentage of preschool-aged children who attend education programmes in nations throughout the world. These figures, included in the *World Education Report*, provide a picture of programme availability. A recent report (1995) provides the data for 1992 and indicates that worldwide, 28 per cent of eligible children are enrolled in early childhood education programmes. The percentage for the developing countries alone is 21 per cent, while that for developed countries alone is 64 per cent. Based on the *World Education Report* figures, Table 33.1 presents the percentages of children enrolled in early education programmes for selected countries from each region of the world. For each region, the table includes overall coverage information and lists the countries with the two highest enrolment percentages and those with the two lowest enrolment percentages. In addition, the table includes, for each region, a few countries with moderate enrolment percentages (i.e. the countries in the middle of an ordered listing).

It is clear from Table 33.1 that, in general, European countries have the highest percentages of children enrolled in early childhood education programmes, while African countries have the lowest percentages. However, every region's countries show a range of enrolment percentages with at least a few countries having the majority of children enrolled in preprimary programmes. Four of the six regions have countries in which fewer than 10 per cent of young children attend such programmes. Only Europe has countries with 100 per cent enrolment.

The table also contains information about the age-range for which early childhood programmes are provided in the various countries. An example of an interpretation of an age-range in Table 33.1 is as follows: [3–5] means that 3, 4, and 5 year olds are included in the early childhood age-range. Of the 56 countries in the table, four countries (Israel, New Zealand, Uruguay, and Spain) include 2 year olds in their early childhood age-ranges. While most countries have age 5 as an upper limit, there are 15 countries where the upper limit is age 6. In general, most countries' programmes serve a 2-year or 3-year age-range.

It is important to note that Table 33.1 includes figures for children enrolled in what the *World Education Report* calls early childhood *education* programmes. It is unclear whether or not individual countries, in reporting data, may have included children in childcare centres, in home-based, parent–child education programmes, and so forth. When looking at programmes for young children, it is difficult, if not impossible, to separate care from education. In fact, some preliminary data from an ongoing cross-national observation study in early childhood settings show that in at least one Asian country, the 'educational' settings and the 'care' settings provide children with about equal amounts of 'pre-academic' activity (e.g. reading, mathematics) (Olmsted, 1996). Thus, if Table 33.1 data were to include children attending *all* types of early childhood settings (i.e. centre-based, home-based, educational, care) the percentages for some countries would be larger than those given in the *World Education Report*. Likewise, if the data were to include *only* educational settings, the percentages for some countries would be lower than those given.

At some levels of education and in some content areas (e.g. science), the percentage of participating males is sometimes higher than the percentage of participating females. In the *World Education Report*, UNESCO includes separate enrolment percentages for males and

Table 33.1 Percentages of children attending early childhood education programmes in selected countries and regions

Region	Overall coverage by country	Countries with:		
		2 highest percentages	2 moderate percentages	2 lowest percentages
Africa N = 24	0% serve 76% or more 8% serve 51–75% 13% serve 26–50% 79% serve 0–25%	Morocco [5–6]* 62% Angola [5–5] 53%	Tunisia [3–5] 9% C.A.R. [4–5] 7% Egypt [4–5] 7%	Mali [5–7] 2% Nigeria [5–6] 2% Senegal [4–6] 2% Ivory Coast [5–6] 1% Djibouti [5–5] 1% Ethiopia [4–6] 1% Zaire [3–5] 1%
America–North N = 16	6% serve 76% or more 38% serve 51–75% 18% serve 26–50% 38% serve 0–25%	Cuba [5–5] 94% Jamaica [3–5] 73%	Haiti [3–5] 41% Guatemala [5–6] 31%	Trinidad/Tobago [3–4] 9% Bahamas [3–4] 7%
America–South N = 11	18% serve 76% or more 0% serve 51–75% 64% serve 26–50% 18% serve 0–25%	Chile [5–5] 86% Guyana [4–5] 79%	Brazil [4–6] 36% Peru [3–5] 34% Uruguay [2–5] 34%	Ecuador [4–5] 23% Colombia [3–5] 20%
Asia N = 31	6% serve 76% or more 13% serve 51–75% 32% serve 26–50% 49% serve 0–25%	Hong Kong [3–5] 81% Israel [2–5] 81% Lebanon [3–5] 68%	Qatar [4–5] 28% Vietnam [3–5] 28% Azerbaijan [3–6] 24% China [3–6] 26%	Turkey [4–5] 5% India [4–5] 3% Oman [4–5] 3%
Europe N = 37	43% serve 76% or more 33% serve 51–75% 16% serve 26–50% 8% serve 0–25%	Belgium [3–5] 100% Germany [3–5] 100% Hungary [3–5] 100% Ireland [4–5] 100% Malta [3–4] 100% Norway [4–6] 100% Denmark [6–6] 98% Netherlands [4–5] 98%	Sweden [3–6] 67% Spain [2–5] 65%	Croatia [3–6] 23% Macedonia [3–6] 21%
Oceania N = 4	Number of countries reporting information is too small for inclusion in this part of the table.	New Zealand [2–4] 81% Australia [5–5] 71%	Fiji [3–5] 15%	Papua New Guinea [5–6] 0%

Source: Data from UNESCO (1995), World Education Report. Oxford: Oxford University Press.

Notes: Africa: 53 countries, 24 with data available; America–North: 25 countries, 16 with data available; America–South: 12 countries, 11 with data available; Asia: 50 countries, 31 with data available; Europe: 41 countries, 37 with data available; Oceania: 10 countries, 4 with data available.

Numbers in brackets denote ages served by early childhood programmes in a country.

* Numbers in brackets denote ages served by early childhood programmes in a country.

females. Of the 131 countries reporting data, in only three countries (Morocco, Angola and Cuba) do the percentages for male enrolment exceed those for female enrolment by more than 15 per cent.

Final comment about preprimary programme availability should point to recent happenings in some Eastern European countries. As might be expected, in many countries around the world, preprimary services have increased in response to the increasing demands noticed earlier. However, in several Eastern European countries, instead of increasing, the percentage of children attending early childhood programmes has decreased in recent years. This change seems to be related to the shift to a market economy in these countries. Specific information about early childhood education programme enrolment during this economic-shift period for four countries (Bulgaria, Hungary, Poland and Romania) is reported by Evans *et al.* (1995) (in Bulgaria, Hungary, and Romania, the programmes serve children 3–6 years of age, while in Poland, they serve 3 to 5 year olds). The 1980 attendance percentages were used as baseline figures and were: Bulgaria 100%, Hungary 96%, Poland 55% and Romania 83% (ibid., p. 19). The (1992) enrolment figures are: Bulgaria 60%, Hungary 87%, Poland 43% and Romania 54%. Thus, between 1980 and 1992, there has been an enrolment decrease of 40% in Bulgaria, 30% in Romania, and approximately 10% in Hungary and Poland. Evans *et al.* state:

> These declines can be explained in terms of supply and demand. On the supply side, one reason for the diminishing supply is the shift from centralized control of and support for social services to local authorities, with an attendant reduction in financial resources available for these services. . . . On the demand side, demand has been affected by women's unemployment (if they are not working in the formal sector they are available to take care of their children themselves) and the introduction of fees.
>
> (Evans *et al.*, pp. 19–20)

Major characteristics of early childhood education settings

This section of the chapter presents summary information about key characteristics of early childhood education settings – sponsorship, curriculum models, patterns of operation, staffing ratios and staff training. Within each topic, information from specific countries is included for illustrative purposes.

Sponsorship/funding

In most countries, the formal education system is sponsored and funded by the government, and parents pay no fees for their children to attend. Although cross-nationally the formal systems may vary in some respects (such as the number of years children spend in different levels of schooling), there are more similarities than differences from nation to nation. The same cannot be said, however, for early childhood education programmes across nations.

There are, for example, major differences among countries regarding the sponsorship and funding of preprimary programmes. In fact, nearly every country has a unique pattern. In some nations, just like formal education programmes, early childhood programmes are under the aegis of the Ministry of Education. Belgium provides an example of this pattern of sponsorship. However, within what appears to be a simple early childhood system, Belgium has three types of preschool networks:

1 preschools sponsored by the state (central government) and completely funded by the Ministry of Education,
2 preschools funded partly by the state and partly by local or provincial authorities,
3 preschools funded partly by the state and partly by private institutions (mainly Roman Catholic schools).

However, regardless of the type of preschool, there is no charge for a child to attend (Delhaxhe, 1989).

A very different sponsorship/funding situation is found in Hong Kong, where nearly all preschool-aged children attend early childhood programmes, as they do in Belgium (Delhaxhe 1989; Opper, 1989). In Hong Kong the government sponsors only a small number of preschools. Most programmes are sponsored and partially supported by religious, voluntary or private organisations, and programmes charge fees for participation (Opper, 1989).

In addition to the two extreme situations found in Belgium (all programmes at least partly government-sponsored/funded, with no parent fees) and Hong Kong (most programmes not government-sponsored/funded, with parent fees), there are many other patterns of sponsorship/funding. For example, in Canada preschools are under the jurisdiction of provincial ministries of social services or human resources. Programmes are supported by federal funds, provincial funds and local funds. Even with the funding from multiple government levels, a fee is charged for children to attend (Biemiller et al., 1992).

Some countries are creative in finding financial support for early childhood education programmes. For example, Godia describes the funding solution found in Kenya as follows:

> The main source of financial support for preschool programmes is the Ministry of Education. However, this is not sufficient. In an attempt to deal with this problem, the Ministry has established a policy of partnership. The Ministry is responsible for the overall administration, provision of policy and professional guidance, provision of grants for training, provision of programme staff at all levels. . . . Bilateral partners include the Bernard Van Leer Foundation, UNICEF, and the Aga Khan Foundation. The principal assistance from UNICEF and Aga Khan Foundation is in the form of grants to support the in-service course for teachers. . . . District partners include parent associations, welfare organizations, and private individuals. They are responsible for establishing and maintaining preschool institutions, and for programs concerned with children's health, nutrition, and care. They also provide salaries of the teachers in the schools they sponsor.
>
> (Godia, 1992, p. 335)

In some nations (e.g. China, Turkey), employers sponsor early childhood programmes for the children of employees. Also, in some countries there are preprimary programmes sponsored by the military (as in China and the United States) or by private individuals (as in Liberia and the United States) (Gormuyor, 1992; Kagitcibasi et al., 1987; Onibokun and Olmsted, 1994). As can be seen from the information provided in this section, unlike formal education systems that are for the most part similarly sponsored and funded from country to country, the organisation of early children education programmes varies from country to country.

Curriculum models and objectives

In the nineteenth and early twentieth centuries, the work of Friedrich Froebel and Maria Montessori strongly influenced early childhood curricula in European countries. During the next several decades, their work spread to preprimary programmes in countries on several other continents (e.g. Brazil, Hong Kong, New Zealand and the United States) (Olmsted, 1989; Opper, 1989; Smith, 1992; Vilarinho, 1992). In fact, many preprimary programmes in these and other countries identified themselves as Froebelian kindergartens or Montessori programmes.

Although, at present, Froebelian and Montessori programmes still exist in countries around the world, their number has decreased somewhat. As the number of early childhood education programmes increased in many countries, their supervision was assumed by a government agency (such as the Ministry of Education or the Ministry of Social Welfare), and in many countries, this agency developed an eclectic curriculum approach that may have included, among other things, components of Montessori and Froebel in addition to ideas from the formal primary education system. Terms sometimes used to describe these various curriculum approaches include *learning-through-play, child-centred, traditional,* or *cognitive-developmental.*

Two descriptions of national curriculum approaches are presented here as examples of 'current formulations'. The first description, from Australia, reads as follows.

> most curriculum goals reflect concerns about children being physically, socially, and cognitively independent, and acting cooperatively in group situations. Emphasis is placed on children creatively expressing their thoughts and feelings, and in extending their understandings about self and the world. Developing oral language skills and related social competencies also figure in goal statements.
>
> (McLean *et al.*, 1992, p. 59)

Nigeria provides this second example:

> The purposes of preprimary education should be
>
> - Effecting a smooth transition from the home to the school
> - Preparing the child for the primary level of education
> - Providing adequate care and supervision for children while their parents are at work (on the farms, in the markets, in offices, and so on)
> - Inculcating social norms
> - Inculcating in the child the spirit of enquiry and creativity through the exploration of nature and the local environment, through playing with toys, through artistic and musical activities, and so on
> - Teaching cooperation and team spirit
> - Teaching the rudiments of numbers, letters, colours, shapes, forms, and so on, through play
> - Teaching good habits, especially good health habits.
>
> (Onibokun, 1989, pp. 225–226)

In the Nigerian example, it is interesting to note the inclusion of 'care and supervision while their parents are at work' as a purpose of preprimary education.

At present, early childhood education programmes in the United States seem to cite the use of specific curriculum models more than programmes in other countries do. This phenomenon may be related to the development of the Head Start programme (a federally funded, comprehensive early childhood programme for children from low-income families) and the subsequent introduction of specific curriculum approaches into Head Start class-rooms. Curriculum models used in Head Start programmes included, among others, the Bank Street model, the High/Scope model, and the Direct Instruction model. These curriculum models and others (e.g. the Reggio Emilio model) continue to be implemented in early childhood programmes around the United States (Epstein *et al.*, 1996).

Patterns of operation

'Patterns of operation' refer to the days and hours whereby early childhood education settings provide services to young children. In some Asian countries (such as China), settings are generally open six days a week (Monday through Saturday), while in most other countries, they are open five days a week (Monday through Friday).

There are basically three patterns of hourly operation across the various nations. The first pattern includes countries in which most services are provided for part of the day. These part-day programmes in some countries operate for 2½ to 3 hours, whereas in others, they operate for 4 to 4½ hours. Examples of countries with part-day programmes include Indonesia and Swaziland (Harianti, 1996; Rollnick, 1992).

The second pattern includes countries in which most services are full-day. Countries following this pattern of operation include Italy, Poland and Thailand (Karwowska-Struczyk, 1996; Passornsiri, 1996; Pistillo, 1989). In some cases these full-day schedules are designed to fit the needs of families. For example, Poland's children generally attend kindergarten for 8 hours a day, five days a week (Karwowska-Struczyk, 1996). But Polish kindergartens are generally open from 6.00 am to 4.00 pm to allow parents to drop off their children before they go to work and to pick up their children after completing their work.

The third pattern is a combination of part-day and full-day services. Some countries offer one type of setting but give families the choice of a part-day or a full-day programme. Argentina and Finland are examples of this service pattern (Hurtado, 1992; Ojala, 1989). Other nations may offer services with two names, one offered part-day and one offered full-day. Often, the part-day service will be labelled as an educational programme (e.g. kindergarten), while the full-day service will be labelled as a childcare programme (observation in the two types of settings, however, may reveal that the two programmes offered are quite similar). Countries offering part-day services under one programme name and full-day services under a different name include Greece and Hong Kong (Frangos, 1996; Opper, 1996).

An even wider variety in patterns of operation can be seen in this final example, from China. In a description of that country's early childhood programmes, Shi Hui Zhong (1989) noted,

> There are four types of kindergarten service offered: daytime service (usually from 7 am to 6 pm); boarding service (except for Sunday, children spend the whole week, day and night, at kindergarten); half-day service; and temporary service (for example, covering just the busiest seasons, for workers in rural areas, or covering just several hours, according to the needs of various kinds of workers).
>
> (Shi, 1989, pp. 250–251).

For people unfamiliar with China's early childhood education system, it is often difficult to believe that preschool-aged children (i.e. 4 year olds) attend a boarding school and are thus separated for extended periods from their families. However, this is not uncommon, especially in urban areas with families in which both parents are employed and have no relatives living nearby.

Staffing ratios

Knowing the staffing ratio of an early childhood education programme provides two types of information. First, the teacher–child ratio provides information about the financial resources available for a preprimary programme since personnel expenditures are one of the largest costs of programme provision. The teacher–child ratio is related to such resource issues as the amount of funding available for teacher salaries, the actual salaries paid (e.g. whether they are comparable to salaries of elementary teachers), and the amount that must be spent on teacher training (i.e. how easy it is to enlarge the pool of trained teachers). Second, the teacher–child ratio indicates, on average, how many children a teacher typically works with. Having a small number of children to work with is a necessary but not sufficient condition for giving a moderate amount of attention to the individual child's development and learning.

The recent *World Education Report* (UNESCO, 1995) includes information about the teacher–child ratios in early childhood education programmes in 1992 for nations around the world. Table 33.2 presents, for each world region, the percentage of countries falling into each of five categories of teacher–child ratio. Examining the findings in the table reveals that for three of the five regions, the category of 1 teacher/21–30 children contains the highest percentages (Africa, 50%; North America, 38%; South America, 64%). In Europe, the category of 1 teacher/11–20 children contains the highest percentage (52%), while in Asia, there are nearly equal percentages in the two categories 1 teacher/11–20 children and 1 teacher/21–30 children. As reported in the table, there are at most 30

Table 33.2 Percentages of early childhood settings with different numbers of children per teacher in various regions of the world

| Region | N | Number of children | | | | |
		10 or less	*11–20*	*21–30*	*31–40*	*40 or more*
Africa	26	8%	11%	50%	23%	8%
America–North	16	12%	25%	38%	19%	6%
America–South	11	0%	27%	64%	0%	9%
Asia	26	4%	46%	42%	4%	4%
Europe	35	34%	52%	14%	0%	0%
Oceania*	2	–	–	–	–	–

Notes: *Number of countries reporting information is too small for inclusion in the table.

Africa: 53 countries, 26 with data available; America–North: 25 countries, 16 with data available; America–South: 12 countries, 11 with data available; Asia: 50 countries, 26 with data available; Europe: 41 countries, 35 with data available: Oceania: 10 countries, 2 with data available.

children per teacher for all settings in European countries while small numbers of settings in four regions (Africa, North America, South America and Asia) have more than 40 children per teacher.

The *World Education Report* provides staffing ratios at the national level, and it is feasible to assume that the figures are related either to enrolment or to reported attendance at early childhood settings in each country. As one component of an ongoing cross-national early childhood study (the IEA Preprimary Project) (discussed more fully later in this chapter), researchers gathered information on staffing ratios in various types of early childhood programmes in 15 countries across four regions of the world (Africa, North America, Asia and Europe). The remainder of this section will consist of a comparison of preliminary findings from the research study with figures reported in the *World Education Report* for two countries.

The *World Education Report* notes that the teacher–child ratio for Chinese preprimary programmes in 1992 was 1 teacher/30 children. During that same period, researchers conducted observations in urban and rural kindergartens in China and reported, among other things, the number of children and adults present in the settings (Xiang, 1996). In urban kindergartens there were, on average, 2 teachers and 30 children, yielding a ratio of 1 teacher/15 children. In rural kindergartens, observers noted, on average, 1 teacher and 30 children, yielding a ratio of 1 teacher/30 children. Since China has a largely rural population, it is easy to reconcile the staffing ratios obtained from the IEA study with those reported in the *World Education Report*. However, the urban–rural differences in staffing ratios are worthy of note.

For Ireland, the *World Education Report* indicates that the staffing ratio is 1 teacher/27 children. Ireland, a participant in the IEA Preprimary Project, has gathered data on two types of preprimary programmes (Hayes, 1996). One type of programme, called a *preschool*, operates independently, while the second type of programme, called a *national school*, operates within the formal school system. The research study findings indicated that in preschools the staffing ratio was, on average, 1 teacher/7 children, and in the national schools the teacher/child ratio was, on average, 1 teacher/25 children. This set of findings from Ireland shows that more specific information can be obtained from data collection for subcategories of early childhood education settings within a country.

Characteristics of teachers

This section includes information about the gender, age, experience and training of early childhood teachers in countries around the world. In most countries, most preprimary teachers are female, either by plan or for other reasons. Of the nations for which information was available, two noted that by regulation only females were employed as teachers in early childhood settings (Ajjawi, 1992; Al-Barwani, 1992). However, even without such a regulation, across many countries, researchers have found that in general, 95 per cent or more of preprimary teachers are women (Pusci and Olmsted, 1999).

Preliminary findings from the 15-nation IEA Preprimary Project indicate that early childhood teachers in many countries are, on average, between 27 and 40 years old. In looking at minimum and maximum ages of preprimary teachers among the countries participating in the IEA Project, we find that (a) some teachers in China were as young as 17 and 18 years of age, and (b) some teachers in several countries were 60 years of age or older (Pusci and Olmsted, 1999).

The IEA Preprimary Project also collected information about the number of years that teachers had worked with 3 to 5 year old children. Across the 15 countries in the study, the average number of years working with preprimary-aged children ranged from 4 years (in China) to 20 years (in Romania). In 12 of the 15 countries, some teachers had worked with children of this age for as many as 30 years (Pusci and Olmsted, 1999).

The final characteristic to be discussed in this section is the type of training that early childhood teachers in various nations receive. There seem to be three major approaches to the training of early childhood teachers. One system consists of three or more years of study at a university, with or without a field experience. Examples of countries using this type of early childhood-teacher training system include Australia and Belgium (Delhaxhe, 1989; McLean et al., 1992). A second system, which involves students attending junior or vocational colleges for 2-4 years, is one system used by countries such as Hong Kong and Taiwan (Opper, 1992; Pan, 1992). In a third system used in some countries, prospective teachers receive their early childhood training at the secondary school level. Albania and Taiwan offer this training path for preprimary teachers (Dedja, 1992; Pan, 1992).

Some countries have had to be creative in designing early childhood teacher-training programmes to meet the needs of prospective teachers and of existing preprimary programmes. An example of this is provided by Kenya.

> [S]ince 1985 the Ministry of Education has operated a two-year, in-service programme for untrained preprimary schoolteachers. The course takes place during the school holidays and is conducted by staff from the district centers for early childhood education using a curriculum developed by the Kenya Institute of Education. The teacher trainees are examined and awarded teacher's certificates by the Ministry of Education.
>
> (Godia, 1992, p. 334)

Current concerns

As the 1990s draw to a close, there are several early childhood education issues of concern in various nations. These issues include such matters as increasing the number of children participating in early childhood programmes, increasing the supply of trained preschool teachers, and developing high-quality programmes. This section presents brief discussions of several of these key issues.

Increased preschool coverage

One major issue identified by both Canada and Bahrain in a recent discussion of their early childhood services was increasing the number of children participating in early childhood programmes (Biemiller et al., 1992; Shirawi, 1992). Regarding Bahrain, Shirawi noted: 'all forms of preschool education, including day care facilities, should be systematically expanded as a means of increasing educational opportunities for younger children' (Shirawi,

1992, p. 90). Along with expanding services to serve more preschool-aged children, Shirawi calls for improved teacher training and involvement of the Ministry of Education and other agencies in the administration of early childhood programmes.

Providing more services to specific groups of children is a concern in some countries (Hurtado, 1992; Wolf, 1992). For example, Hurtado noted:

> In Argentina the problems inherent in providing preschool education are felt most acutely in the poorer rural areas. . . . The people are unevenly dispersed and children must travel long distances to reach the schools. Poverty is widespread and severe among peasant households, social services are almost nonexistent, and lines of communication are inadequate.
>
> (Hurtado, 1992, p. 43)

While most of the discussion of early childhood programmes in this chapter has been about centres or group settings, other types of programmes may need to be considered for special situations such as this. Argentina, like other countries with sparsely populated areas, is designing and operating some innovative models of early childhood education programmes.

Early childhood teacher training

At present, many countries (e.g. Finland, Hong Kong and Thailand) are working to increase the number of trained early childhood teachers and to improve the quality of the training (Ojala, 1989; Opper, 1989, 1992; Passornsiri et al., 1989). For example, in Hong Kong there are proposals to increase the number of teachers who attend teacher-training programmes, to increase the amount of training received, and to modify the content of training. In Thailand, the following proposals have been put forward:

> To improve the training of personnel, the pre-service degree programmes of colleges and universities should put greater emphasis on practical training. At the same time, various types of resources should be employed for in-service training, so that personnel already engaged in prepri-mary education can improve their skills. Educational radio and television programmes by some universities and government agencies could be useful for training personnel who work in remote areas.
>
> (Passornsiri et al., 1989, p. 362)

Early childhood teacher status

In many countries, especially ones in which early childhood teachers receive minimal or only moderate amounts of training, the status of early childhood teachers, as indicated by salary levels, benefits and working conditions, is low. In some countries (e.g. Australia, Great Britain and others in which preschool training may be generally equivalent to that for teachers at other levels of education), preprimary teachers receive the same salary and have equal status with teachers in primary and secondary education (Curtis, 1992; McLean et al., 1992). However, the situation is very different in many other countries. For example, teachers in Hong Kong have low status (Opper, 1989), while in a description of preschool programmes in Swaziland, Rollnick made the following comment: 'In the rural areas about one-quarter of the teaching staff are working for a salary considered below the legal minimum salary in Swaziland. The salaries are so low in some cases that teachers can be considered [to be] doing voluntary work' (Rollnick, 1992, p. 465).

Needs of families

As noted earlier in this chapter, recent global changes include an increasing incidence of one-parent families and increasing participation of women in the labour force. However, in many countries (e.g. Belgium and Canada) the early childhood programme typically operates only part-day, leaving families to find care and supervision for their children for the remainder of the day. In some cases (e.g. for some families in Belgium) extended childcare services may be available in the same setting where the educational programme is held. However, frequently, these extended services are provided by a different agency or person and are of lower quality than the early childhood programme (e.g. staff may lack qualifications) (Delhaxhe, 1989). In other cases (e.g. for some families in Canada), families may need to move the child to a different setting (another centre, childcare home, a relative's home), and this requires the parent to leave work to transport the child from one setting to another (Biemiller *et al.*, 1992).

Early childhood programme quality

Early childhood professionals in several countries have voiced their desire to improve the quality of existing programmes. Australia, China, Finland and the United States are among the countries with this concern (Laing and Pang, 1992; McLean *et al.*, 1992; Ojala and Kuikka, 1992; Olmsted, 1989). Even though programme quality should be considered from the beginning of programme development, sometimes serious discussion occurs only after the physical problems of establishing an early childhood education system have been solved (i.e. obtaining buildings, equipment and materials).

The issue of programme quality has been widely discussed during the past few years. In a recent comprehensive article on quality, Evans noted:

> There is a push from researchers and programme planners, and from practitioners and parents, to define the factors that constitute a high quality programme, to determine what constitutes 'success' in a programme, and to identify those aspects of an intervention that make a difference in the development of young children.
>
> (Evans, 1996, p. 1)

In general, there have been two standard ways to assess programme quality. The first has been to establish guidelines or regulations about the structural characteristics of a programme and then to assume that if these are adhered to, the result will be a high-quality, early childhood programme. Some structural characteristics receiving attention have been staffing ratio, minimum space per child and teacher training. While these characteristics may be important, it is questionable whether or not merely meeting guidelines in these areas produces a high-quality, early childhood programme. Early childhood professionals who have observed preprimary programmes in settings with minimal space, with only the most primitive materials, and with teachers with little training, have sometimes still seen a high level of interest and excitement in the setting, with the children involved in activities (often with locally produced materials) and interacting with each other and with the teacher. To the experienced professional, it is clear that children are developing language skills, cognitive skills and social skills in such a setting, regardless of the structural characteristics.

The second way to assess programme quality has been to examine the long-term impacts of early childhood education programmes. Landmark studies of this nature have been carried out in the United States and have involved following two groups of children (one group attending a preprimary programme and one group not attending such a programme) for many years. For example, a recent High/Scope Perry Preschool study found that adults born in poverty who attended a high-quality, active-learning preschool programme at ages 3 and 4 had half as many criminal arrests, enjoyed higher earnings and property wealth, and a greater commitment to marriage than members of their peer group who did not attend a preschool programme. Also, the study noted that over participants' lifetimes, the public was receiving an estimated $7.61 for every dollar invested (Schweinhart *et al.*, 1993).

The findings of longitudinal follow-up studies often lead early childhood professionals and policy-makers to ask 'Will participation in *any* early childhood programme produce similar significant effects, or are there critical elements of an early childhood programme that must be present in order to show these significant effects?' Also, early childhood educators in countries other than the United States ask whether the findings of these American studies can be generalised.

An answer to the first question is provided by a curriculum comparison study also completed by researchers at High/Scope. This group of researchers conducted a longitudinal study of children attending three different types of preschools and found at age 23 that compared with the Direct Instruction group, the High/Scope and Nursery School groups had significantly fewer felony arrests of various kinds, fewer years of special education for emotional impairment, and more members doing volunteer work (Schweinhart and Weikart, 1997).

In a 1996 article, Sylva and Nabuco attempted to answer both of these questions by conducting a short-term longitudinal study in Portugal. In the first phase of the research, three groups of children attended preschool programmes using curricula similar to the ones reported by the High/Scope study described above. In addition, Sylva and Nabuco included a group of children who did not attend a preschool programme. The study included 15 preschools, 3 curricula, and 219 children. Sylva and Nabuco's findings are in 'complete agreement' (p. 3) with those of the High/Scope researchers. The authors state:

> [A]t primary school, children from the High/Scope nurseries showed significantly higher educational attainment (reading and writing), higher self-esteem (Harter Assessment of Perceived Competence and Acceptance) and lower anxiety than the matched control children. Children from the Formal Skills nurseries were significantly more anxious than the other two groups and had lower self-esteem than the High/Scope children. When compared to the children in the Traditional Nursery, the High/Scope children showed better outcomes, although their superiority was comparatively less than in comparison with the Formal Skills group.
>
> (Sylva and Nabuco, 1996, pp. 3–4)

The authors noted, '[This paper] has attempted to show under what conditions generalisations can be made from research in one country to another' (ibid., p. 5). The Sylva and Nabuco study adds new information to the knowledge base developed from research studies about high-quality early childhood education. Countries around the world will continue to explore the quality issue for many years. Research studies such as those by High/Scope researchers and Sylva and Nabuco provide some information for early childhood professionals and policy-makers to consider; other considerations are also important, such as the culture and the available resources in a given country.

CURRENT CROSS-NATIONAL EARLY CHILDHOOD EFFORTS

As mentioned earlier in this chapter, provision of early childhood education has been growing in countries around the world. At the same time, we are seeing a growing amount of assistance provided to governments and agencies undertaking early childhood efforts and an increase in the number of cross-national early childhood research projects. This portion of the chapter will briefly describe three current cross-national early childhood efforts.

The World Bank

The World Bank, often in conjunction with other agencies, provides financial and technical assistance to developing countries in such areas as agriculture, economics, education, technology and social services. A recent World Bank brochure (n.d., p. 2) noted 'The Bank is the largest single source of external funding for health and education in developing countries.' During the early and mid-1990s, World Bank funding began to be directed more and more towards programmes for young children, whom the World Bank brochure calls 'the human capital of the future' (ibid., p. 2). In a speech in April 1996, Armeane Choksi, Vice President, Human Capital Development, World Bank, stated: 'We are lending about 1 billion dollars a year to various children's programmes. This breaks down to about 650 million for primary education, 350 for health and nutrition and 50 million for early childhood development.' (Choksi, 1996, p. 16) And, the level of the World Bank's financial support for early childhood development programmes has increased for 1997 (M. E. Young, personal communication, December 6, 1996).

In a recent World Bank (1996) description of their Investment in Early Childhood Development programme, the reasons for investing were given as follows:

- Interventions designed to benefit young children can benefit the whole community and allow mothers to pursue earning and education goals.
- Investments in early child development can modify inequalities rooted in poverty and social and gender discrimination.
- Improvements in nutritional, health, and psycho-social well-being increase school enrolment, decrease repetition and drop out, and enhance school performance.
- Early child investments can reduce costs and improve the efficiency of primary schooling.
- Children who reach their full physical and mental potential will be more productive citizens.

The World Bank Human Development Department personnel carry out reviews of recent research studies, most of which are conducted in developed countries and most of which are concerned with centre-based programmes. However, they see the programmes studied 'not so much as models to be imitated but as examples of "best practice" with much to offer anyone interested in helping young children learn' (Young, 1996, p. 4). Using early childhood research along with research in health, nutrition and other areas, World Bank staff work co-operatively with programme planners and participants to examine various programme strategies (i.e. early childhood centres, family childcare homes, parent education) to design a programme that will best serve children and families.

Either alone or in conjunction with other agencies (e.g. UNICEF, UNESCO, USAID), the World Bank is currently investing in early childhood development programmes in developing countries around the world. Brief descriptions of three current programmes follow (Young, 1996).

National dissemination of the Early Enrichment Project in Turkey

During the 1980s Kagitcibasi and her associates conducted an early childhood research study that compared the effectiveness of home-based and centre-based custodial and educational day care services for 3 to 5 year old children (Kagitcibasi *et al.*, 1987). This well-conducted study, along with a follow-up study of the children and families, indicated that the home-based educational programme produced long-term effects in both the children and mothers who participated. Presently,

> [I]n an effort organised by the Mother-Child Foundation and the Adult Education Division of the Ministry of Education and supported by a World Bank loan, the education methods devised and tested by Turkey's Early Enrichment Project are now being disseminated on a national scale.
>
> (Young, 1996, p. 58)

Training caregivers in Kenya

'In Kenya today, roughly half the country's 6 million preschool-age children live in poverty, a third of households are headed by women, and more and more women are entering the workforce' (ibid., p. 65). With assistance from external foundations and agencies, and support at the district and community level, Kenya has developed a large number of community-based preprimary programmes. However, the programmes vary widely in quality. With World Bank support, Kenya is planning

> to train 15,000 preschool teachers and 5,000 community representatives on how to run and monitor enriched childcare programmes. . . . The project will introduce new ways for communities to finance teachers' salaries, subsidize fees for the poorest children, . . . purchase school supplies, provide health and education materials, and improve facilities.
>
> (Ibid., p. 66)

Experimenting with various early childhood service models in Chile

With assistance from the World Bank, Chile is reforming its primary education system to include preprimary services and is testing two different service models of rural preprimary education.

> The project is hiring supervisors, teachers, and paraprofessionals; training parents in how to stimulate the minds of their young children; constructing 100 classrooms to provide roughly 4,500 preschool places; refurbishing 75 rural facilities donated by the communities; providing daily food for the children; providing teaching materials; instituting a mass media campaign to encourage parental participation; and conducting studies to ascertain the cost-effectiveness of each preschool model tried.
>
> (Ibid., p. 83)

The Consultative Group on Early Childhood Care and Development

'The Consultative Group on Early Childhood Care and Development (CG) is an international, interagency group dedicated to improving the condition of young children at risk' (Consultative Group brochure, n.d., p. 2). Initiated in 1984, The CG facilitates communication among international donor agencies, national funders, researchers, practitioners and parents 'with the goal of strengthening programmes benefitting young children and their families' (p. 3).

The CG (n.d., p. 2) lists its goals as follows.

- *To increase the knowledge base:* The CG gathers, synthesises and disseminates information on children's development drawing from field experiences, traditional wisdom and scientific research.
- *To serve as a catalyst:* The CG works to increase awareness of issues affecting children, developing materials and strategies to help move communities, organisations and governments from rhetoric to practice, from policy to programming.
- *To build bridges:* The CG fosters networking among those with common concerns and interests, working across sectoral divisions, putting people in touch with the work of others by organising meetings, by disseminating information through publications, and serving as a communications point.
- *To serve as a sounding board:* The CG engages in dialogue with funders and decision-makers about developments in the field, providing the base for policy formulation, planning, programming and implementation.

The CG is composed of donor agencies who support the activities of the group financially and through participation. Recent donor agencies participating in the group have included the Bernard van Leer Foundation, the Organization of American States, Save The Children USA, and the World Health Organization. Co-ordination of CG activities is handled by a secretariat located in the Bernard van Leu.

Perhaps a good way to understand the CG is to describe its major activities during a typical year. The following list, taken from the 1993–1994 Annual Report, describes the group's activities for that year (Consultative Group, 1994).

591

- Participated in the Education for All Forum in Jomtien, Thailand (September 1993) and accepted the responsibility for organising two follow-up meetings focused on early childhood care and development (1) New York, November 1993, and (2) Paris, April 1994.
- Continued the co-ordination of the Child Status Profile Project, a major early childhood study being conducted in Colombia, Jamaica, Jordan and Kenya. [See description below.]
- With another agency, co-ordinated a meeting in Santa Marta, Colombia, for approximately 20 agencies to discuss activities related to early childhood care and development in Latin America.
- Authored a paper documenting the situation of young children in seven Latin American countries.
- Participated in a conference on child-rearing practices and beliefs, held in Windhoek, Namibia.
- Continued the co-ordination of the Eastern European Child Care Project, a study being conducted in Bulgaria, Hungary, Poland and Romania. [See description below.]
- Developed a project to collect information about early childhood programmes that have been financed in innovative ways.

Two recent cross-national early childhood research projects co-ordinated by the CG are set out below:

Child Status Profile Project

The purpose of this four-nation (Colombia, Jamaica, Jordan and Kenya) project is to develop child developmental status measures to be used with children as they enter school. Over the years, these measures could serve as evaluation measures for early intervention programmes and as baseline measures for the status of children as they enter school. Researchers in each of the four countries have reviewed existing instruments available in their respective countries and have developed pilot-test versions of measures for this study. Through the co-ordination of the CG, the researchers from the four countries are sharing information and preliminary findings as the project progresses (Consultative Group, 1994).

Eastern European Child Care Project

As Eastern European countries have undergone major changes in political and economic systems in recent years, there has been concern about the provision of early childhood care and education. This study was initiated to gain a picture of the current situation for young children in Bulgaria, Hungary, Poland and Romania.

> The specific objectives of this study were to: (a) provide a systematic assessment of the changing childcare situation for young children, in terms of who is caring for the children and the quality of that care; and (b) make recommendations regarding future programming for children and their families, given shifts to a market economy.
>
> (Evans et al., 1995, p. i)

The CG is a unique organisation that serves as a resource for early childhood information; as an agency fostering networking among international, national and community early childhood groups; and as a co-ordinator of cross-national early childhood studies. The CG's continued support by international and national donor organisations is an indication of the usefulness of these services.

IEA Preprimary Project

The final cross-national activity to be discussed is the IEA Preprimary Project, a groundbreaking, comprehensive comparative research study of early childhood services in nations on four continents. The IEA Preprimary Project is being conducted under the sponsorship of the International Association for the Evaluation of Educational Achievement (IEA), an independent international co-operative of research institutions in more than 60 countries which, in order to enhance learning, conducts comparative studies focusing on educational policies and practices. IEA is well known for its 25 years of comparative studies in science, mathematics, written composition and other academic areas, primarily at middle-school and secondary levels of education. The IEA Preprimary Project is the co-operative's first study at the preschool level.

The IEA Preprimary Project is composed of the following three interrelated phases:

- Phase 1: This phase consisted of a household survey with a representative sample of families in 11 countries to explore their use of early childhood services. The findings are reported in Olmsted and Weikart (1994).
- Phase 2: The primary purpose of this phase is to observe the quality of children's experiences in the various care/education settings identified in Phase 1. Extensive observational and interview data are collected to examine the structural and process characteristics of early childhood settings and to explore the impact of these characteristics on children's developmental status at age 4.
- Phase 3: This phase is an age-7 follow-up study of the children observed in Phase 2, including an assessment of their developmental status and their progress since the end of their preprimary experience.

At the request of IEA, the High/Scope Educational Research Foundation in Ypsilanti, Michigan (United States) serves as the International Coordinating Center for the Preprimary Project. David P. Weikart, PhD, serves as the International Co-ordinator of the study. The countries currently participating in the project include Belgium, China (PRC), Finland, Greece, Hong Kong, Indonesia, Ireland, Italy, Nigeria, Poland, Romania, Slovenia, Spain, Thailand and the United States (Olmsted and Weikart, 1996). The study is directed by an international steering committee composed of the following persons, each of whom is an experienced early childhood researcher: Cigdem Kagitcibasi, PhD (Turkey), Lilian Katz, PhD (United States), Sylvia Opper, PhD (Hong Kong) and David P. Weikart, PhD (International Co-ordinator).

A strength of the study is that it is conducted with the significant co-operation and contributions of early childhood researchers in the participating countries. Each participating country sets up its own co-ordinating centre for the study, usually within a university or government agency. This co-ordinating centre, under the direction of a National Research Co-ordinator, locates resources and supervises the study in the country. Consequently, in each country the project is directed by a person familiar with the local provision of early childhood services, with the organisational aspects of local early childhood agencies/ professionals, and with the country's major cultural/ethnicity features.

Another strength of the IEA Preprimary Project is the involvement of the National Research Co-ordinators in all stages of the development and implementation of the cross-national study. The national co-ordinators and the project's steering committee developed the study's conceptual framework, and the co-ordinator group discussed the advantages and disadvantages of different sampling strategies with the project's international sampling referee. Most important, all co-ordinators participated actively in the development of all IEA Preprimary Project instruments. Thus, this is a *co-operative* project, not a study developed by researchers in one country and then conducted in several countries.

The remainder of this section of the essay describes a set of observation instruments and a set of child developmental status measures developed by the IEA Preprimary Project participants. For each set of instruments, following a brief description of the development process, some preliminary findings are presented. The section closes with a brief discussion of the potential uses of the IEA Preprimary Project research.

Observation measures

In preparation for the development of the observation systems, the national co-ordinators prepared videotapes of a typical morning in each type of early childhood setting they planned to include in the study (e.g. kindergarten, childcare centre). The group of co-ordinators then viewed these videotapes and discussed the types of activities in which children were engaged, the adult behaviours exhibited, and the various patterns of activities that occurred during the morning.

The co-ordinators worked hard to have systems that would not be primarily related to the developmental stage of a country or to the socio–economic level of children attending the settings. Also the group agreed that in order to make descriptive comparisons across various types of settings, the final observation systems should be equally appropriate for all types of early childhood settings (e.g. for a preschool programme in urban Belgium, a childcare centre in a Hong Kong high-rise, or an informal group of children with a caregiver in rural Thailand).

Consequently, the co-ordinators decided to focus on the *processes* that occur in an early childhood setting rather than on the physical characteristics of the setting. They selected the following areas for observation:

1 adult's management of children's time,
2 children's activities and interactions with other children and adults, and
3 adult's behaviour and interactions with children.

The group developed draft versions of each of the three instruments and during the next year pilot-tested the observation systems in a small number of settings. Then the group met, reviewed the pilot-test findings and revised the instruments. During the next year the co-ordinators conducted a final round of pilot-testing and a review of those data resulting in a small number of final revisions to the measures.

The final observation systems were titled:

1 Management-of-Time (MOT) Observation System,
2 Child Activities (CA) Observation System, and
3 Adult Behaviours (AB) Observation System.

The MOT system is used continuously during two nonconsecutive mornings and records the activities proposed by the teacher, the duration of each activity and the proposed group-structure for the activity. The CA and AB observation systems are completed during various 10-minute periods of the two nonconsecutive mornings. Over the two observation days, the observer collects a total of 40 minutes of observation data for the teacher/adult and a total of 40 minutes of observation data for *each* child selected. For most settings, the observer gathers a total of 6 to 7 hours of MOT observation, 40 minutes of AB observation, and 160 minutes of CA observation (i.e. for four children in a setting).

The 15 countries participating in the IEA Preprimary Project have collected and coded the data from the three observation systems. Table 33.3 presents preliminary CA findings on the kinds of child activities observed in various types of settings. Since the findings presented here are preliminary, neither the countries nor the specific types of settings observed in each country are identified by name. All four countries conducted CA observations in two different types of settings, but Setting 1 and Setting 2 were not of the same type across the four nations.

As the findings in Table 33.3 indicate, the pattern of percentages varies from country to country – indicating that the CA observation instrument is sufficiently sensitive to produce different patterns of findings. For example, in Country A, in both types of settings,

Table 33.3 Percentage of observations in selected child activity categories by type of setting in four countries

Setting	Activity (%)						
	Motor/ physical	Expressive	Pre-academic	Personal/ social	Transitional	No active engagement	Other
Country A							
Setting 1	23	14	11	26	10	11	5
Setting 2	24	12	13	22	8	15	6
Country B							
Setting 1	9	18	25	15	5	17	11
Setting 2	15	9	19	20	6	25	6
Country C							
Setting 1	24	18	18	18	8	8	6
Setting 2	26	18	20	16	7	7	6
Country D							
Setting 1	11	20	16	28	1	13	11
Setting 2	11	24	15	24	2	14	10

approximately one quarter of the CA observations were in the *motor/physical* category and 12% to 14% were in the *expressive* category (e.g. dramatic play, music). In contrast, in Country D, the percentages of observations in these two categories are nearly the reverse of those in Country A.

Table 33.3 shows that in each of Countries A, C and D, the percentages across Setting 1 and Setting 2 rarely differ by even 4 percentage points. Only in Country B are the percentages for several of the CA categories considerably different across the country's two types of settings. These findings suggest that although children in a country may attend different types of settings, observations reveal that, regardless of the type of setting they attend, children engage in basically similar activities.

Child developmental status measures

Working with measures currently used in individual countries as well as research measures, the national co-ordinators developed a set of child developmental status (CDS) measures. On each measure, the co-ordinators worked to include items with these characteristics:

1 they were cross-nationally appropriate,
2 they were developmentally appropriate,
3 they needed few materials,
4 they were suitable for administration by persons with little or moderate levels of training, and
5 they would be enjoyable for a young child.

Using these criteria, the group developed pilot-test versions of CDS measures in the following areas: cognitive development, language development, fine-motor skills development, social skills and pre-academic skills.

During the next year, each co-ordinator pilot-tested the CDS measures with a small number of children and submitted the results for analysis. Then, during a meeting, the group reviewed the pilot-test results and revised the CDS measures. During the following year, a second pilot-test was conducted in each country and, based on the results, a few revisions were made to the measures.

At present, the CDS findings are being analysed. However, preliminary findings are very promising from an instrument-development perspective. The score distributions for the various instruments in the few countries analysed are generally normal-shaped, and the range of scores is sufficiently wide to permit the use of the CDS findings in an examination of the relationships between the child measures and other variables in the study. The preliminary findings would suggest that, by involving researchers from various nations and following a careful development process, it is possible to develop common measures of child developmental status that are useful in different nations.

Potential applications of the IEA Preprimary Project Research

The information, instruments and strategies resulting from the IEA Preprimary Project have many potential uses. Nations participating in the project, as well as nations that did not participate, stand to benefit from the research. Several of the study's participating countries are already using their own national findings to give early childhood policy-makers and professionals precise, detailed information to use in improving the current services available to young children and their families. In countries not participating in the study, early childhood care/education agencies will be able to use the study's instruments and method-ology to develop their own research-based findings concerning the characteristics and outcomes of various types of early childhood settings.

Predictions for the future of early childhood education

- As policy-makers and parents become more aware of the importance of children's early years to their total development and learning, and as more research findings about the long-term effects of high-quality early childhood education become available, there is likely to be an increased availability of early childhood services in many countries around the world. This increased provision of services will also assist in meeting the needs of families, particularly those in which all adults participate in the labour force.
- In many countries there will be a merging of early childhood education programmes and childcare programmes. The resulting programmes will be placed under one ministry/agency, and a single teacher-training system will be developed.
- Many countries will revise their teacher-training programmes by increasing the amount of training and expanding the content to include such topics as child development and the distinctive nature of early childhood teaching approaches.
- Finally, policy-makers and professionals will do more critical thinking about the quality of their early childhood programmes. For example, they will discuss adult characteristics that are favoured in their countries, such as inventiveness, aggressiveness, compliance and so forth. Then they will begin to think about the types of experiences and inter-actions that might be precursors of these characteristics and incorporate them into an early childhood programme or seek a curriculum model that proposes to develop such characteristics.

NOTE

1 Early childhood programmes go by many different names in countries around the world. Some of the names most frequently used are *preschool, kindergarten, preprimary programme* and *nursery school.* Although a given country may reserve a particular term for a programme aimed at a specific age-range (e.g. in the United States, kindergartens serve primarily 5 year olds), in general, most of the names given above are used for programmes that serve children between age 3 and the age of formal school entry. This chapter uses the various early childhood programme names interchangeably, depending on usage in the particular country or countries being discussed.

REFERENCES

Ajjawi, M. (1992) 'Primary education in the United Arab Emirates'. In G. A. Woodill, J. Bernhard and L. Prochner (eds), *International Handbook of Early Childhood Education*. New York: Garland, 491–501.

Al-Barwani, T. (1992) 'Early childhood education in the Sultanate of Oman'. In G. A. Woodill, J. Bernhard and L. Prochner (eds), *International Handbook of Early Childhood Education*. New York: Garland, 407–416.

Biemiller, A., Regan, E. and Lero, D. (1992) 'Early childhood education in Canada'. In G. A. Woodill, J. Bernhard and L. Prochner (eds), *International Handbook of Early Childhood Education*. New York: Garland, 147–154.

Choksi, A. (1996) 'Early child development: Never too early, but often too late'. Opening speech presented at the conference, Early Child Development: Investing in the Future, held in April 1996 at the Carter Presidential Center, Atlanta, GA.

Consultative Group on Early Childhood Care and Development (1994). *Report to the Consultative Group on Early Childhood Care and Development: Activities for the Secretariat, April 1993–May 1994* (Annual report). Haydenville, MA: Consultative Group in ECCD.

Consultative Group on Early Childhood Care and Development (n.d.). *The Consultative Group on Early Childhood Care and Development: An International Resource* [Brochure]. Haydenville, MA: Consultative Group in ECCD.

Curtis, A. (1992) 'Early childhood education in Great Britain'. In G. A. Woodill, J. Bernhard and L. Prochner (eds), *International Handbook of Early Childhood Education*. New York: Garland, 231–248.

Dedja, B. (1992) 'The development of preschool and primary education in the People's Socialist Republic of Albania'. In G. A. Woodill, J. Bernhard and L. Prochner (eds), *International Handbook of Early Childhood Education*. New York: Garland, 21–30.

Delhaxhe, A. (1989) 'Early childhood care and education in Belgium'. In P. P. Olmsted and D. P. Weikart (eds), *How Nations Serve Young Children: Profiles of Child Care and Education in 14 Countries*. Ypsilanti, MI: High/Scope Press, 13–37.

Epstein, A. S., Schweinhart, L. S. and McAdoo, L. (1996) *Models of Early Childhood Education*. Ypsilanti, MI: High/Scope Press.

Evans, J. (1996) 'Quality in ECCD: Everyone's concern'. *Coordinators' Notebook*, 18, 1–26. Haydenville, MA: The Consultative Group on ECCD.

Evans, J., Karwowska-Struczyk, M., Korintus, M., Herseni, I. and Kornazheva, B. (1995) *Who Is Caring for the Children? An Exploratory Survey Conducted in Hungary, Poland, Bulgaria and Romania* (Part I: Main report). Haydenville, MA: Consultative Group on ECCD.

Frangos, C. (1996) *IEA Preprimary Project Phase 2 Findings: Greece*. Thessaloniki: Aristotelian University of Thessaloniki.

Godia, G. (1992) 'Preschool and primary education in Kenya'. In G. A. Woodill, J. Bernhard and L. Prochner (eds), *International Handbook of Early Childhood Education*. New York: Garland, 327–336.

Gormuyor, J. (1992) 'Early childhood education in Liberia'. In G. A. Woodill, J. Bernhard and L. Prochner (eds), *International Handbook of Early Childhood Education*. New York: Garland, 337–341.

Harianti, D. (1996) *IEA Preprimary Project Phase 2 Findings: Indonesia*. Jakarta: Ministry of Education and Culture.

Hayes, N. (1996) *IEA Preprimary Project Phase 2 Findings: Ireland*. Dublin: Dublin Institute of Technology.

Hurtado, C. (1992) 'Preschool education in Argentina'. In G. A. Woodill, J. Bernhard and L. Prochner (eds), *International Handbook of Early Childhood Education*. New York: Garland, 39–47.

Kagitcibasi, C., Sunar, D. and Bekman, S. (1987) *Comprehensive Preschool Education Project* (final report). Istanbul, Turkey: Bogazici University. A report prepared for the International Development Research Centre.

Karwowska-Struczyk, M. (1996) *IEA Preprimary Project Phase 2 Findings: Poland*. Warsaw: Institute for Educational Research.

Laing, Z. and Pang, L. (1992) 'Early childhood education in the People's Republic of China'. In G. A. Woodill, J. Bernhard and L. Prochner (eds), *International Handbook of Early Childhood Education*. New York: Garland, 169–174.

Lal, S. and Wati, R. (1986) 'Non-formal preschool education – an effort to enhance school enrolment'. Paper presented at the National Conference on Research on ICDS, New Delhi.

Le Normand, M. (1992) 'Early childhood education in France'. In G. A. Woodill, J. Bernhard and L. Prochner (eds), *International Handbook of Early Childhood Education*. New York: Garland, 205–216.

McLean, S., Piscitelli, B., Halliwell, G. and Ashby, G. (1992) 'Australian early childhood education'. In G. A. Woodill, J. Bernhard and L. Prochner (eds), *International Handbook of Early Childhood Education*. New York: Garland, 49–73.

Myers, R. (1988) 'Effects of early childhood intervention on primary school progress and performance in the developing countries: An update'. Paper presented at the meeting on The Importance of Nutrition and Early Stimulation for the Education of Children in the Third World, Stockholm, April.

Myers, R. (1995) *The Twelve Who Survive: Strengthening Programmes of Early Childhood Development in the Third World* (2nd edn). Ypsilanti, MI: High/Scope Press.

Ojala, M. (1989) 'Early childhood training, care, and education in Finland'. In P. P. Olmsted and D. P. Weikart (eds), *How Nations Serve Young Children: Profiles of Child Care and Education in 14 Countries*. Ypsilanti, MI: High/Scope Press, 87–118.

Ojala, M. and Kuikka, M. (1992) 'Early childhood education in Finland'. In G. A. Woodill, J. Bernhard and L. Prochner (eds), *International Handbook of Early Childhood Education*. New York: Garland, 193–203.

Olatuni, K. M. (1986) 'A comparative study of the academic performance of Nigerian primary school pupils, with and without preschool education'. Unpublished doctoral dissertation, University of Ibadan, Nigeria.

Olmsted, P. (1989) 'Early childhood care and education in the United States'. In P. P. Olmsted and D. P. Weikart (eds), *How Nations Serve Young Children: Profiles of Child Care and Education in 14 Countries*. Ypsilanti, MI: High/Scope Press, 365–400.

Olmsted, P. (1996) *IEA Preprimary Project Phase 2 Cross-national Findings*. Ypsilanti, MI: High/Scope Educational Research Foundation.

Olmsted, P. and Weikart, D. (eds) (1994) *Families Speak: Early Childhood Care and Education in 11 Countries*. Ypsilanti, MI: High/Scope Press.

Olmsted, P. and Weikart, D. (eds) (1996) *IEA Preprimary Project Phase 2 General Information*. Ypsilanti, MI: High/Scope Educational Research Foundation.

Onibokun, O. M. (1980) 'The effectiveness of McCarthy scales of children's abilities as a prediction of primary one achievement'. Unpublished doctoral dissertation, University of Ibadan, Nigeria.

Onibokun, O. M. (1989) 'Early childhood care and education in Nigeria'. In P. P. Olmsted and D. P. Weikart (eds), *How Nations Serve Young Children: Profiles of Child Care and Education in 14 Countries*. Ypsilanti, MI: High/Scope Press, 219–240.

Onibokun, O. M. and Olmsted, P. (1994) 'Study findings: Families' weekly use of early childhood services'. In P. P. Olmsted and D. P. Weikart (eds), *Families Speak: Early Childhood Care and Education in 11 Countries*. Ypsilanti, MI: High/Scope Press, 108–140.

Opper, S. (1989) 'Child care and early education in Hong Kong'. In P. P. Olmsted and D. P. Weikart (eds), *How Nations Serve Young Children: Profiles of Child Care and Education in 14 Countries*. Ypsilanti, MI: High/Scope Press, 119–142.

Opper, S. (1992) 'Preschool education and care in Hong Kong'. In G. A. Woodill, J. Bernhard and L. Prochner (eds), *International Handbook of Early Childhood Education*. New York: Garland, 249–258.

Opper, S. (1996) *IEA Preprimary Project Phase 2 Findings: Hong Kong*. Hong Kong: Institute of Education.

Palacios, J. (1989) 'Child care and early education in Spain'. In P. P. Olmsted and D. P. Weikart (eds),

How Nations Serve Young Children: Profiles of Child Care and Education in 14 Countries. Ypsilanti, MI: High/Scope Press, 303–341.

Palattao-Corpus, L. (1989) 'Philippine care and education for children aged 3 to 6'. In P. P. Olmsted and D. P. Weikart (eds), *How Nations Serve Young Children: Profiles of Child Care and Education in 14 Countries*. Ypsilanti, MI: High/Scope Press, 255–271.

Pan, H. (1992) 'Early childhood education in Taiwan'. In G. A. Woodill, J. Bernhard and L. Prochner (eds), *International Handbook of Early Childhood Education*. New York: Garland, 471–479.

Passornsiri, N. (1996) *IEA Preprimary Project Phase 2 Findings: Thailand*. Nonthuburi: Sukhothai Thammathirat Open University.

Passornsiri, N., Kutintara, P. and Suwannapal, A. (1989) 'Child care and early education in Thailand'. In P. P. Olmsted and D. P. Weikart (eds), *How Nations Serve Young Children: Profiles of Child Care and Education in 14 Countries*. Ypsilanti, MI: High/Scope Press, 343–363.

Pistillo, F. (1989) 'Preprimary education and care in Italy'. In P. P. Olmsted and D. P. Weikart (eds), *How Nations Serve Young Children: Profiles of Child Care and Education in 14 Countries*. Ypsilanti, MI: High/Scope Press, 151–202.

Pusci, L. and Olmsted, P. (1999) 'Characteristics of the teacher and parent samples'. In D. P. Weikart (ed.), *What Should Young Children Learn? Teacher and Parent Views in 15 Countries*. Ypsilanti, MI: High/Scope Press.

Riak, P., Rono, R., Kiragu, F. and Nyakuri, M. (1989) 'Early childhood care and education in Kenya'. In P. P. Olmsted and D. P. Weikart (eds), *How Nations Serve Young Children: Profiles of Child Care and Education in 14 Countries*. Ypsilanti, MI: High/Scope Press, 203–218.

Rollnick, M. (1992) 'Early childhood education in Swaziland'. In G. A. Woodill, J. Bernhard and L. Prochner (eds), *International Handbook of Early Childhood Education*. New York: Garland, 461–470.

Schweinhart, L. and Weikart, D. (1997) *Lasting Differences: The High/Scope Preschool Curriculum Comparison Study* (Monographs of the High/Scope Educational Research Foundation, 12). Ypsilanti, MI: High/Scope Press.

Schweinhart, L., Barnes, H. and Weikart, D. (1993) *Significant Benefits: The High/Scope Perry Preschool Study through Age 2–7* (Monographs of the High/Scope Educational Research Foundation, 10). Ypsilanti, MI: High/Scope Press.

Shi, H. Z. (1989) 'Young children's care and education in the People's Republic of China'. In P. P. Olmsted and D. P. Weikart (eds), *How Nations Serve Young Children: Profiles of Child Care and Education in 14 Countries*. Ypsilanti, MI: High/Scope Press, 241–254.

Shirawi, M. (1992) 'Early childhood education in Bahrain'. In G. A. Woodill, J. Bernhard and L. Prochner (eds), *International Handbook of Early Childhood Education*. New York: Garland, 85–91.

Smith, A. (1992) 'Early childhood education in New Zealand: The winds of change'. In G. A. Woodill, J. Bernhard and L. Prochner (eds), *International Handbook of Early Childhood Education*. New York: Garland, 383–398.

Sylva, K. and Nabuco, M. (1996) 'Research on quality in the curriculum'. In *OMEP International Journal of Early Childhood*, 28 (2), 1–6.

UNESCO (1995) *World Education Report*. Oxford: Oxford University Press.

United Nations (1966) *Demographic Yearbook: 1965*. New York: United Nations Department of International Economic and Social Affairs, Statistical Office.

United Nations (1976) *Demographic Yearbook: 1975*. New York: United Nations Department of International Economic and Social Affairs, Statistical Office.

United Nations (1986) *Demographic Yearbook: 1984*. New York: United Nations Department of International Economic and Social Affairs, Statistical Office.

United Nations (1996) *Demographic Yearbook: 1994*. New York: United Nations Department for Economic and Social Information and Policy Analysis.

Vari, P. (1989) 'Care and education in Hungary for 3 to 6 year olds'. In P. P. Olmsted and D. P. Weikart (eds), *How Nations Serve Young Children: Profiles of Child Care and Education in 14 Countries*. Ypsilanti, MI: High/Scope Press, 143–149.

Vilarinho, L. (1992) 'Preschool education in Brazil: Historical and critical perspectives'. In G. A.

Woodill, J. Bernhard and L. Prochner (eds), *International Handbook of Early Childhood Education*. New York: Garland, 129–134.

Wolf, W. (1992) 'Early childhood education in Austria'. In G. A. Woodill, J. Bernhard and L. Prochner (eds), *International Handbook of Early Childhood Education*. New York: Garland, 75–84.

World Bank (Human Development Department) (1996) *Investing in Early Childhood Development: A Global Affirmation* [Brochure]. Washington, DC: World Bank.

World Bank (Population, Health and Nutrition Department) (n.d.) *Early Childhood Development: The World Bank's Agenda* [Brochure], Washington, DC: World Bank.

Xiang, Z. P. (1996) *IEA Preprimary Project Phase 2 Findings: China*. Beijing: China Central Institute of Educational Research.

Young, M. (1996) *Early Child Development: Investing in the Future*. Washington, DC: The World Bank.

34

PRIMARY EDUCATION

Jill Bourne

'PRIMARY' EDUCATION, 'BASIC' EDUCATION AND 'ELEMENTARY' EDUCATION

It is important to delineate the field of 'primary' education with care, distinguishing it from 'elementary' education, from which it has evolved and with which, in many countries, it often remains conflated. *The Oxford Encyclopedic English Dictionary* contains a number of definitions of 'primary', each of which can apply to education in different contexts. One definition is 'fundamental, basic'. This would appear to be the sort of elementary education which is seen as a matter of introducing the basic skills and rudimentary facts to the 'masses'. 'Basic' education is not age specific and can imply a separate educational pathway in itself.

In one sense, 'elementary' education has the same meaning as 'basic' education. However, it is important to note that 'elementary' has at least two distinct meanings. 'Elementary' is defined in the dictionary as 'dealing with the simplest facts of a subject; rudimentary, introductory'. But it is also defined as 'a school in which elementary subjects are taught to young children'. The conflation of 'basic' education with the education of young children has obvious implications for the academic status, expectations and training of elementary school staff in comparison to 'secondary' teachers. Elementary education as a basic education system in itself, with limited expectations of progression for pupils, running parallel to but not necessarily leading on to secondary or further education, lives on in a number of countries as a form of education for those not able to purchase a richer education, as well as being part of the history of the development of education systems in most parts of the world, as we shall explore further below.

Another definition of 'primary' is given as 'earliest, first'. This definition applies to most uses of primary education – referring to a first school experience, with the implication that further schooling is expected and planned to follow. However, this definition contains within it other seeds of tension and dispute, raising questions of whether primary schooling should be seen mainly as preparation for the secondary schooling to follow, as well as by implication denying and downgrading the educative importance of nursery and other forms of early years provision, which for many children are the first or primary experiences.

A fourth definition of 'primary' is given as 'of the first importance'. Certainly, for many primary education professionals, this would be the definition they themselves would prefer – seeing primary education as having aims intrinsic to the age-phase and a specialised curriculum for the age-phase, designed not only to lay the groundwork for a secure and responsible future, but for the present, for the needs of a happy and fulfilled childhood itself, from which children can progress with learning skills, motivation, a sensitivity to others and self-esteem.

From this fourth perspective, influential in the profession, the knowledge, training and status of primary teachers needs to be rigorous, in order to manage effectively the huge demands made on them for understanding and monitoring the different stages of children's development and socialisation. Only with a high level of skills and understanding can teachers plan how to meet children's changing and emerging needs, as well as to challenge and extend them. From the utilitarian teaching of the 'basic skills' of the 3Rs through the attempt to teach cultural values through personal, social and moral education, and on to widening children's horizons and developing critical questioners and aesthetic sensitivities, primary teachers from this perspective face an academically demanding role.

FOR WHOM IS PRIMARY EDUCATION?

The age-phase covered by the primary/elementary schools differs from country to country. In elementary schools offering a basic education, children may attend up until 13–15 years or longer. Where the primary school is seen as a first school, however, the leaving age is usually around 11–12 years. There is more variance in the starting age, and in the separation or inclusion of 'early years' education into the primary school.

In England, the compulsory age for starting full-time school is 5 years old. However, this age has been pushed back and back by schools anxious to maintain their numbers, with parents regularly finding they need to enrol their children in nursery classes in the primary school by 4 years old or earlier in order to gain a guaranteed place in a popular school. In Japan, primary schooling lasts from 6 years to 12 years in *shogakko*. Kindergarten experience, although with a national course of study, is often available, but non-compulsory (Sugimine and Yamamoto, 1998). In Texas, USA, most children attend elementary school kindergartens at age 5, with first grade starting at age 6, and elementary school lasting until 10 or 11 years (De Voogd, 1998). Children in Hong Kong begin school at age 6, but many have already received three years of kindergarten education (Adamson and Morris, 1998). In Sweden (Ball and Larsson, 1989), children do not begin school until as late as 7 years old, but again nursery education is widely available.

In South African primary schools the situation is more complex. The first year of primary schooling in schools with historically black and 'coloured' pupils in the Northern Transvaal, for instance, is reported to include children ranging from below 6 years to over 10 years old (Pell, 1998). Primary school-leaving ages range from under 12 years to over 17 years – partly as a result of the political upheavals of the apartheid years. This wide age-range, combined with large classes of over 70 pupils, together with minimal resources, make for a very different picture of primary education from that of most schools in Western Europe.

In most countries, population mobility means that many children will not complete their primary schooling within the same school; furthermore, diversity in the cultural and linguistic background of children is increasingly becoming the norm rather than the exception, especially in urban areas. Primary school routines and primary curricula are increasingly challenged by the need to adapt to the demands of diversity. This may show itself in innovation and flexibility, or in denial, a defensive retreat to formal and traditional procedures and practices.

PRIMARY CURRICULA IN DIFFERENT CONTEXTS

According to a number of researchers (Cortazzi, 1998; Lockheed and Verspoor, 1991), most official primary curricula around the world contain the same subjects and accord them the same relative importance. There is usually an emphasis on learning to read and write the national language, the teaching of numeracy, as well as moral and social education. Primary schools in Japan cover three fields of study: subjects, moral education and special activities. Subjects include Japanese language, arithmetic, life studies (grades 1, 2) or science (grades 3–6); music; arts and handicrafts; PE; social studies (for grades 3–6 only) and homemaking (grades 5–6). Special activities include clubs, student councils, school events as well as classroom activities (Sugimine and Yamamoto, 1998).

In China, not only moral education but also academic attainment has a collective orientation. Cortazzi (1998, p. 210) claims that:

> Where British teachers are highly conscious of individual child development, meeting individual needs and individualising work, Chinese teachers are more aware of the collective goals, meeting social and moral responsibilities, and classwork. . . . The collective standard is formed by individual achievement and all children are believed to have the right, and potential, to achieve a high standard.

The Chinese curriculum has five aspects: moral, intellectual, physical health, artistic and physical labour, all but the last familiar in many other contexts. As in many curricula, these aspects are linked, so that while children are cleaning the school (physical labour), this is also seen as moral education through labour (Cortazzi, 1998). The Chinese curriculum is seen as ideally a unified fusion between 'Red' aspects (political, moral and social elements) and 'Expert' aspects (knowledge, skills, facts). The aim of all study is to 'serve the people', and this is reflected in the choice of children's storybooks throughout the curriculum.

In the USA, De Voogd (1998) perceives the control of the primary curriculum to be a battleground, with contradictory advice from state government, school district authorities, influential publishers' textbooks and teaching schemes and recommendations from professional organisations and parental groups. In some states, teachers are required to follow specific set schemes and programmes, keeping closely to the teachers' handbook; in others teachers have rather more freedom to make professional decisions about materials and methods. Texas teachers, according to De Voogd, find the lack of autonomy in tension with their initial teacher education programmes, which tend to suggest teachers consider a range of different philosophies of education, and which themselves tend to favour a constructivist approach to learning. Teacher education in the US is accredited by a national organisation which does not necessarily, or even perhaps usually, match the educational philosophies of state governments.

THE AIMS OF PRIMARY EDUCATION

The tension between a primary or an elementary (basic) education and the attempt to meet children's immediate needs and society's demands and financial constraints, has a long history. Benavot *et al.* (1991) argue that the one thing that elementary and primary schools across the globe share is an emphasis on the basics of reading, writing and number. To suggest otherwise is to set up a 'straw man'. Yet there are other elements which create differences in the two forms of education which need to be explored further in order to understand primary education, and to explain some disconcerting attitudes towards teacher training and the status of teachers of the primary years.

In contemporary society one fundamental policy question is whether to teach the 'masses' basic skills and citizenship explicitly directed at workforce requirements to create a disciplined service class to replace the industrial workers of the past, or to prepare all children for a rapidly and unpredictably changing future, where new jobs will require adaptability, lifelong learning, social responsibility and self-reliance. Different aims and societal goals for different groups of children will have different outcomes in the way schooling is implemented and in the way it is experienced by children.

The way childhood is perceived and defined in different education systems varies between that of a time of preparation for adulthood or a stage with intrinsic needs in itself. These contrasting views are often revealed in the metaphors found in educational rhetoric, in the types of metaphors selected to describe educational aims and strategies. Progressive or 'child-centred' educationalists tend to use horticultural metaphors, such as growth; those taking a preparation for adulthood approach use industrial and management metaphors (e.g. audits, targets, investment).

The social mores and values that children are required to take on as they move towards adulthood (and therefore which primary schools are required to transmit) vary, as a comparison of the stated aims of education systems in different countries at particular moments shows. For example, Dearden (1968) analysed the central aims of progressive primary education in England as: unhindered natural growth and development, learning through experience, play, self-expression and moral education. The focus was on the individual and on individual self-realisation.

In contrast, in the old USSR, the goal of education as stated in the Basic Law on Education 1974 was: 'the preparation of highly educated, well-rounded, physically healthy and active builders of communist society' (Grant, 1979). Here social and economic needs are fundamentally implicated in the approach to the individual. Education is explicitly presented as a political task: indeed, Lenin argued that unless political goals are stated explicitly, any education policy must consist of 'hypocrisy and lies' (Grant, 1979, p. 26).

In Korea, individual and collective aims are seen as mutually reinforcing: 'The primary goal of education is to instil a right character and assist in self-realisation which eventually leads to the realisation of national aspirations' (Korean Education Development Institute,

1983, p. 39). The same policy document defines intelligence as 'rationality, control of emotions, critical thinking, adaptability' (p. 85), a faculty to be developed through schooling. This differs markedly from the prevailing definition in the West, which sees intelligence as an innate, fixed ability, with consequent implications for teachers' belief in their ability to teach and extend children.

Most recently, the *Review of the National Curriculum in England* (QCA/DfEE, 1999) presented what it called 'A more explicit rationale for the school curriculum'; presumably both 'more explicit' than the progressive policies of earlier years, as well as more explicit about aims than earlier, controversial changes brought in by the 1998 Education Act. These centralised and changed the curriculum without stating its aims, other than its intention to set out a clear and full statutory entitlement for children. The 1999 QCA revision document stated:

> Education must enable all pupils to respond positively to the opportunities and challenges of the rapidly changing world in which we live and work. In particular, they need to be prepared to respond as individuals, parents, workers and citizens to the rapid expansion of communications technologies, changing modes of employment, and new work and leisure patterns resulting from economic migration and the continued globalisation of the economy and society.
>
> (QCA, 1999, p. 3).

These aims of preparation for new social futures are reflected in the primary curriculum and primary teacher training curriculum in England, with their emphasis on skills in information and communications technology across subject areas, on interactive, whole-class teaching in basic skills combined with a stress on independent group and individual learning, inclusion, citizenship and intercultural education.

Perhaps most importantly, the aims set out above are the same across the primary/secondary divide, with both stages seen as integral to a longer programme of lifelong opportunities for learning. There are no definitions of a specific form of education for the 5–11 year olds, no specific 'childhood' form of education. Instead there is a series of instructional steps directed towards specific attainment targets and expected outcomes. These progress from the very early years of nursery education, through primary and into secondary schooling, and are proposed to lead on to general and vocational qualifications in further and higher education. For many primary educators in England, this rhetoric is new and sits uncomfortably with the rhetoric of their past training, in which the study of child development and of aiming to identify and meet each child's individual needs was dominant.

EFFECTS OF CONTEXT ON TYPES OF PRIMARY SCHOOLING

Views on children's schooling are tied to society's views on children and childhood, and what we want children to be. Together, these determine (De Voogd, 1998) how children are thought to learn, and this in turn determines the kind of experiences and information to which children are given access. This then impacts on the way teachers and teaching are looked at, and whether teachers are seen as professionals, substantially determining the curriculum, or as technicians, delivering 'teacher-proof' materials developed elsewhere.

In Hong Kong, for example, the influence of Confucian philosophy is such that attainment is seen as the result of effort rather than of ability, and the written text is seen as holding authority. The effects of this are likely to be wide-reaching in their implications for classroom practice. In contrast, in UK schools there has been a tendency to see attainment as an in-built ability, which schools can nurture but not alter, and to place more importance on direct experience, or learning by doing, than on texts. Each of these perspectives has implications for the type of education children receive and for the different values each culture places on different kinds of activities and achievements.

Other contextual issues, such as language, also influence the type of primary education on offer in different parts of the world. In Hong Kong, Cantonese, which is the local Chinese dialect, is the medium of the curriculum in the majority of primary schools. Adamson and Morris (1998) point out that the written form of this language in Hong Kong is classical Chinese, which differs from standard spoken Chinese in terms of both structure and vocabulary. The links between Cantonese and the classical written form of the language are even less accessible. With the change in sovereignty, there is an increased need for children to learn to speak and write putonghua, the standard Chinese of mainland China, with a simplified Chinese script, unlike that of classical written Chinese. In this context, the primary curriculum is heavily weighted towards Chinese. Pupils are expected to have learnt at least 2,500 characters by the end of primary school, with these characters having few or no phonemic links to the spoken language, as Chinese is an ideogrammatic language. So children are required to spend a great deal of time memorising and practising the written characters, activities that are dismissed as 'rote learning' and not valued by the dominant educational ideologies of the West.

THE EVOLUTION OF ELEMENTARY INTO PRIMARY EDUCATION

The contrast between what we have defined as 'elementary' education and 'primary' education can be illustrated by a brief examination of the development of education in a number of countries. In France the Revolution brought about one of the earliest systems of public education: 'a public system of education, common to all citizens, free for those parts of education indispensable to all men' (Halls, 1976). However, universal education in fact was not fully implemented across the country. Despite the influence of Rousseau's *Émile* (1762) on early revolutionary thought, and on the tutoring of wealthy families, elementary schools were tightly controlled and focused on the teaching of French as a national language, thought necessary for a unified republic.

With Napoleon the focus shifted from the elementary school system to the development of a separate system of education for the elite in the lycées. From then, elementary and secondary education formed two separate educational channels, not consecutive levels, right up to 1959. Children were enrolled either for the lycée through its feeder schools, or for the elementary school, where they received a very basic education. At the same time, while teacher training was considered of importance from early in the nineteenth century in France, there was a clear difference in status between teachers in the lycée and those working in elementary schools.

Although entrance examinations to the lycées were abolished in 1959, in France different paths through the education system are still established early in the secondary years. Calls for a common education system or 'école unique' have long been opposed in France, on the grounds that this would lead to the 'primarisation' of the school system (an interesting use of 'primary' as a derogatory term), with the clear implication that this would mean the lowering of standards (Halls, 1976).

In the nineteenth century in England, elementary education was provided by the churches and other charitable agencies, with some government funding. However, in 1862, the government established a curriculum for elementary schools, dividing the period into six standards, with a syllabus for reading, writing and arithmetic (with needlework for girls) for each standard or stage. Daily reading of the scriptures was also required. The stated objective was to 'promote the education of children belonging to the classes who support themselves with manual labour'.

Untrained and often themselves poorly educated, schoolteachers were supported by their older pupils, some of whom later became apprentice teachers and then teachers themselves, modelling their practice on their own experience. Lacking in training, elementary school-teachers concentrated largely on the drilling of basic skills. Assessment of teachers' competence was carried out annually by visiting inspectors who examined their pupils, and on the result of this examination depended the size of the salary paid to teachers and the grant payable to the school. One inspector, Edmond Holmes, writing in 1911, despaired of a system in which teachers 'had drilled themselves into passivity and helplessness' attempting to meet the inspection demands (Richards, 1998, p. 58).

However, the curriculum in England has always been contested by different interests and philosophies, and a wider range of subjects was gradually introduced to the school, along with increasing influences from educational philosophers such as Froebel, who appears to have been responsible for the introduction of nature study, painting and local studies into the first years of elementary school. Blyth (1965, p. 40) maintains that Dewey's views on elementary practice, filtering from the USA, were 'undeniable' too. Projects, co-operative activities and the elimination of subject divisions began to figure in the best and most fortunate elementary schools.

However, these progressive overseas influences were strongest in the infant schools or departments (age-phase 5–7 years), where the pressures of examination were less. For most children, elementary schools still meant a focus on the basic skills of reading, writing and arithmetic, and the ideas of Froebel, Dewey, Pestalozzi, Montessori and, more recently, Piaget, influenced theory and rhetoric far more than they influenced practice.

The development of schooling in the UK during the first years of the twentieth century had a major impact on the history of education, both in the UK and in the model it exported to other areas of the globe during the years of British imperialist expansion. In the English model, secondary education was defined as fee-paying and extending over a number of years. It thus became the territory of the middle classes. Elementary education, on the other hand, was where the majority of English children spent their childhood up to the age of 14, following a limited curriculum and being 'inculcated with habits of industry, self control, truthfulness and loyalty' (Vlaeminke, 1998, p. 20). Although there was an opportunity from 1907 for children to take a scholarship examination to move to secondary school at around the age of 11 years, there were not enough places even for those children who succeeded in passing it. Simon (1974, p. 232) has called it 'selection by elimination' masquerading as 'selection by ability'. The basic division was between elementary education for the many and secondary education for a select few.

This tradition remained strong in the UK until well after the Second World War. Although primary schools for the 5-11 age-group were recommended by the Hadow Report as early as 1926, primary education only came into being following the 1944 Education Act, with older children being moved into either grammar or vocational/technical schools. The curriculum for the primary schools was not prescribed, but left to the control of local education authorities and the schools themselves. One result of the selection examinations for secondary schooling, however, was that the junior years (8-11) became examination-driven, as schools attempted to prepare children to pass the tests, including preparation for so-called intelligence tests.

However, in an increasing number of schools, experiments in 'learning by activity' and 'discovery learning' were taking place, and these were legitimated in the Plowden Report (DES, 1967), which created (according to Richards, 1998) the 'myth' of an English progressive form of primary education which provided a model for the rest of the world, a 'myth' because rhetoric was not matched by widespread practice.

Further developments in progressive approaches to primary education were made possible by the ending of selection tests for secondary school at age 11, and the introduction of 'comprehensive' schools intended for children across all levels of attainment from 11 to 16 or 18 years. While there were outstanding examples of creative teaching in some primary schools, the reality in most schools was rather different as the traditions of the elementary school continued to predominate (see Galton et al., 1980). Schools varied considerably and children received very different experiences depending on the particular school they attended.

EDUCATION AND TRAINING AND THE STATUS OF PRIMARY TEACHERS

Alongside these changes in the rhetoric and policy base for primary education, there were significant changes in primary teacher training. Primary teachers in many countries moved from receiving no higher education, to pre-service training based in higher education colleges with low entry requirements, and then to university level courses, attaining degree status. Post-graduate teacher education courses drew subject graduates into primary teaching. Increasingly, primary teachers took up opportunities for Masters level and doctoral studies, with some taught courses developed specifically with the focus on teaching and learning in the primary sector.

In Hong Kong there were no pre-service courses designed specifically for primary teachers until as recently as 1993. Primary teachers were either unqualified or had undertaken a 2-3 year general teacher's certificate. This has been addressed with the establishment of a teacher education programme aiming to bring 35 per cent of primary teachers to first degree level by 2007, when it will also be a requirement for all school principals to hold a degree (Adamson and Morris, 1998)

In South Africa, the situation post-apartheid is one of transforming an overwhelmingly unqualified primary teacher force operating in rural areas, in contrast with a largely 'underqualified' teacher force in urban areas. ('Underqualified' here means having had less than the approved length of professional training of one year for a graduate, and three years for a non-graduate'.) In 1991, of the total number of African primary teachers operating in non-urban areas, only 9 per cent were qualified; 70 per cent had begun but not completed their teacher training, and 21 per cent were unqualified school-leavers (EduSource, 1994, quoted by Pell, 1998). In this context, combined with large classes, often including a wide age-range and with minimal resources, teachers have tended to focus on teaching directly from a set textbook. Ngobeni (1995) suggests that qualified teachers, especially those who are graduates, will tend to be senior teachers, often with administrative roles. Classroom teachers tend to be isolated and are rarely involved in curriculum development; they are treated as 'workers' rather than professionals. The major black South African teacher union has called for greater teacher participation in curriculum development, and the new government is attempting to set up parent–teacher–pupil associations to initiate democratic curriculum development processes.

De Voogd (1998) considers the nature of the primary teacher's role from a US perspective, contrasting views of teaching as a profession with perspectives of the role as technical in nature. Primary teachers in the US are poorly paid by comparison to other graduate professions. He claims that low status and salaries combined with a loss of autonomy brought about by a centralist curriculum and centrally determined materials confirm the dominance of a predominantly technical view of the nature of teaching at the present time in the US.

In contrast, the number of examinations which form the gateway into teaching suggest entry into a profession. In Texas, for example, De Voogd cites a general elementary certificate, bilingual and early childhood certificates, tests of student teachers' knowledge of English, university entrance examinations, and exit examinations at graduate and Master's levels. However, once qualified, De Voogd suggests that many US teachers are required to follow programmes that are scripted and prescribed almost minute by minute, to follow as if merely technicians rather than being able to design and plan lessons to meet the needs of the children. Teachers are required to follow state-set objectives and assessments, and follow state-prescribed commercial textbooks.

Technician or professional, there does seem to be increasingly greater equality in status developing between primary and secondary teachers, although this is still not marked in pay structures: differences in pupil per capita funding between primary and secondary schools remain, favouring secondary provision. Thus implicit and sometimes explicit status differences are maintained in many places. Indeed, many primary teachers from South Asia who completed degree level studies in the UK to improve their primary teacher education, found on their return that they had been 'promoted' to the secondary sector, for which they had not received training.

At one point during the 1990s, however, the increasing professionalisation of primary teachers was almost reversed in England, as UK government policy intensified a move towards a 'free market' approach to education. This involved maintaining a basic education for all children, with wider and more enriched forms of education available on the open market; that is, for parents willing to pay fees for schooling their children. As part of this move, there was increasing pressure for teacher training to be removed from the universities and to be based in schools, with teachers assessed by the school staff against national criteria. There was even the more radical suggestion that entrants into primary teaching would not be required to hold graduate level qualifications at all; this led to an outcry in the profession about the introduction of a 'mum's army' teaching the 5-8 age range in primary schools. While currently the requirement in the UK for teachers to reach graduate level before gaining qualified teacher status remains, the pressure for school-based rather than university-based primary teacher training continues.

Each nation's education system has a unique history; however, similar patterns emerge at different times in different places, often as simultaneous and conflicting currents. So it is that while England appears to be moving teacher education out of the universities, in France the trend appears to be the opposite, with teacher training colleges making way for university-based teacher education and training.

Similarly, while England moves further towards a focus on whole-class teaching and a concentration on the basic skills in primary schools, Korea and Japan (which have been presented as a model to UK primary professionals) are moving towards an increased use of group work, independent learning and the encouragement of 'creativity'.

In Australia, the federal government has sponsored the development, with business involvement, of key competences for effective participation in work (Mayer, 1992). These competences include the ability to collect, analyse and organise information; to communicate ideas and information; to plan and organise one's own activities; to work effectively with others and in teams; to use mathematical ideas and techniques; to solve problems; and to use technology. Despite being employment related, when compared to basic skills-focused primary curricula, these key competences are in line with what are often called 'progressive' approaches to teaching children and unlikely to narrow down the primary curriculum.

PRIMARY SCHOOLING AS FUNDAMENTALLY AN INSTRUMENT OF SOCIAL SELECTION

Bernstein (1990) has reminded us that we need to ask of every change, what has *not* changed? And in that unchanged context, we need to ask whose interests does the change serve, in effect? A massive amount of sociological research has interpreted the history of schooling, despite all the explicitly positive policy aims, as 'primarily a sorting, classifying, selective mechanism' (Galton *et al.*, 1980). In nineteenth-century England, while philanthropist educationists such as Thomas Paine and Thomas Crabbe and various groups of freethinkers attempted to educate the children of the poor, others set up schooling as an attempt to socially control the children of the working classes, who were then congregated in large numbers in the cities and less easily controlled than the rural poor.

While social reform was seen by some to lie in a vernacular elementary education (a form of lifelong learning), so for others elementary education was seen as a tool of social control through the disciplining of young children's bodies and minds. Events like the Chartist riots convinced the rulers that the populace needed the control of elementary education to instil obedience. Reformists recorded how elementary schools had to show through their syllabus their focus on discipline and basic skills, and display a lack of interest in introducing children to wider readings and the thinking of the time. Education was welcomed as social control, but access to ideas through literacy was seen as dangerous and to be deflected. To get funding from wealthy sponsors, schools had to 'avow and plead how little it was that they pretended or presumed to teach' (Foster, J. [1839] *An Essay in the Evils of Popular Ignorance*, Section VI, p. 259, quoted in Birchenough, 1914).

Rose (1984) has examined how, for example, language education was used at the turn of the century in England as a social regulatory device to mark out social groups. The curricula of the different education systems of the time offered 'Classics' for the wealthy in preparatory schools, English literature for the middle classes, often privately tutored, and clear pronunciation and expression for the poor in elementary schools. The poet and reformer Crabbe wrote ironically:

> For every class we have a school assign'd,
> Rules for all ranks and food for every mind.
>   (Cited in Birchenough, 1914, p. 5)

Darwinist and eugenic explanations earlier in this century explained differences in the types of school and schooling offered to different social groups of children in terms of the social success of the 'fittest', the inherited evolutionary characteristics of different social classes. As the century progressed, the idea of 'natural selection' was replaced in England by the concept of the scientific measurement of fixed and innate ability: the IQ or 'intelligence quotient'. Generally, in English primary education, children were not believed to achieve academically through hard work or good teaching, but developed their fixed and innate abilities to their own predetermined levels. This was close to a counsel of despair for teachers. As Simon (1971) argued, 'the school system appeared to be (as indeed it was) run on the assumption that no child could ever rise above himself, that his level of achievement was fatally determined by an IQ' (quoted in Bourne and Moon, 1994, p. 29).

Children were selected and graded at the end of the primary school for different forms of education according to their IQ and academic achievement in a series of tests. Schools quickly adapted to the tests, and began to stream children in accordance with what was believed to be their 'ability', in order to prepare the 'top' classes for the test. Teacher expectations, as might be expected, played a large part in this streaming process, and it is not surprising, therefore, that research (Jackson, 1964) found that the children of low-income parents were disproportionately clustered in the 'low' streams. These children, as a consequence, were not prepared for the tests at age 11, and inevitably went on to less ambitious secondary curricula, and into the lower echelons of the society. Low self-esteem became endemic, as children had been taught from the age of 11, or even younger in streamed primary schools, that they were 'not very bright' and could expect little in their future. This ideology naturalised differences in occupation, remuneration and prosperity by suggesting that wealth was the result of natural and inherited ability.

The influential English progressive educationalist Clegg (1972), in his description of a working-class primary school when he started teaching in the early 1930s in England, writes of children treated as 'animals to be tamed', with public canings and childen expected to stay silent in class. In the first class he was asked to teach, 60 children sat in rows, '[f]or the most part ill-clad and undernourished, bootless and unkempt . . . many of them had been running the streets until they were seven or eight as there was insufficient school accommodation available'. (Clegg, 1972, p. 26). Termly tests were carried out, 'regardless of whether the examinees could read or write'.

He contrasts this authoritarian transmission of basic facts approach of 'elementary' schooling with the 'child-centred', post-Plowden Report education of the 1970s, when both selection examinations and the streaming of children into separate classes by 'ability' had been discouraged. He describes children working independently in primary classrooms and overflowing into school corridors, which were full of books, plants, paintings and displays, making the environment 'attractive and relaxing'. There were carpeted bays set aside for independent reading, filled with books. Other bays were set aside and attractively equipped for writing and music, with art areas complete with sinks and running water. Cupboards covered in the pupils' handiwork of tie-and-dye fabrics had interesting objects displayed on them: 'collections of tree barks, an old apothecary's balance, some mathematical instruments, a display of grasses and dried stems of hogweed' (Clegg 1972, p. 40). Of course, this utopian classroom, its description familiar to many English educationalists even today, emerged at a time of unprecedented public spending in the UK, and was dependent on strong financial support for its facilities and equipment. As a model it remained an impossible dream for many schools in the developing world, to whom these educational ideals and teaching methods were exported by teacher trainers from the 1970s onwards.

In fact, the education legitimated in the Plowden Report (1967) as 'child-centred education' with its demand for teachers to attempt to meet the needs and interests of each individual child, also appeared to be an impossible task for the majority of primary teachers in England, however well they managed the physical trappings of the environment described by Clegg. In a large-scale study, Galton et al. (1980) found that practice rarely matched the child-centred rhetoric, and that most teachers worked within established routines in large classes in which the identification of individual learners' needs and interests was limited, and opportunities for individual learners to plan and carry out their own programmes of study according to their interests, as suggested by the Plowden Report, were rarely observed. Primary curriculum plans reflected a generalised concept of socially acceptable childhood interests and of the appropriateness of different topics to different age-groups.

While the child-centred pedagogy may have been rare in practice, by contrast, its rhetoric was influential and widespread among teachers. Implicit within this so-called 'child-centred' rhetoric, critics concerned with social justice and equality of opportunity have argued, was an implicit device of social selection, replacing that of the explicit selection tests which had preceded it (Bernstein, 1990; Sharp and Green, 1975; Walkerdine, 1984). Although the concept and measurement of IQ was discredited in the 1970s and 1980s, the underlying ideology of fixed individual differences, which could be nurtured but not altered, remained not only in the policy statement rhetoric of 'child-centred' education, but materially in the layout and resources of the classroom and in the methods of recording and assessing achievement.

A typical primary school booklet for parents dated 1985 states, for example, that each pupil is to receive an individual programme of work which recognises that 'each child is an individual who learns at different rates' and has 'special talents and interests to be nurtured' (see Bourne, 1992). Bernstein (1973) has described such 'nurturing' classrooms which naturalise attainment as 'development' as places of covert evaluation, which produce learners at different levels of competence, and there are a number of case studies which provide evidence to support this (for example, Bourne, 1992; King, 1978; Sharp and Green, 1975; Walkerdine, 1984.

King (1978) remains an important study of how a primary ideology impacts directly upon primary classroom practice, even where teachers may not articulate it explicitly. King's task was, drawing on the work of Schutz and Weber, to describe the world of the 'infant' classroom (age 5–7 years) of the time, and to consider how social structures impacted on the local situation through the everyday construction of society by its members, in this case primary teachers. King argued from his three-year study of three infant schools that in contrast to the explanations given by the teachers, in which children's interests determined the curriculum, the 'realities' of the classroom were in fact constructed for the child by the teacher: 'Most of the things that happened in the classrooms were arranged to happen or were allowed to happen by the teacher' (King, 1978, p. 10). Whilst this might not be surprising in a transmission or formal classroom, the teachers he studied saw themselves as progressive or child-centred teachers. This included established views on the nature of children and the nature of learning, especially as enshrined in the Plowden Report (1967). The central features were developmentalism, individualism, learning through play and 'childhood innocence' (ibid., p. 11). King argues that these ideas were accepted unquestioningly and institutionalised in 'recipes': agreed sets of ways of doing things. These recipes not only structured the way in which teachers organised and controlled events in the classroom, but how they assessed children themselves. Regulation of learning activities and of social control was exercised by the teacher, who in effect chose which children would undertake which activities, at which levels, and how much teacher input each would be given in supporting these activities.

Sharp and Green (1975) focused in particular on the construction in primary schools of new entrants into different categories of pupils. They concluded that there was a large gap between the consciously held teaching ideologies expressed outside the classroom by teachers and teachers' actual practices within it. They suggested that the vocabulary of explanation teachers call upon to describe their teaching serves as a 'badge of commitment' to the dominant ideology of the time, rather than an attempt to describe the rationale for their practice. This is a warning that however radical changes in education policy may be, there may be few or no implications for classroom practice unless teacher education tackles fundamental ideologies such as the hegemonic concept of a fixed 'ability', and the exploration of the difficult notion of 'diversity', and the implicit cultural norms of the school and classroom. Sharp and Green (1975, p. 224) concluded that the 'rise of progressivism and the institutional support it receives are a function of its greater effectiveness for social control and structuring aspirations compared with more traditional ideologies whose legitimacy was already being questioned'. Control was achieved through the differentiation of children into a social hierarchy, not only by academic attainment, but by commenting on a wider range of children's attributes observed across a wide range of activities, since all of these reflected their 'development'. This social hierarchy, Sharp and Green argued, reflected the wider social structure.

A more recent study of an ethnically linguistically diverse inner-city primary classroom observed similar differentiation taking place. Here the children, on the basis of very little evidence, were constructed as 'bright' or 'needing support'. They then received different types of input and support which acted to confirm the teacher's assessments (Bourne, 1992).

Bernstein (1990) described 'child-centred' primary education as a 'masked pedagogy', regardless of the good intentions of its originators. Learners are exposed to a range of experiences and learning options, but in fact these experiences are differentially valued, and ultimately children are assessed against a set of norms or standards that are never made explicit to them or to their parents. Yet children's life chances are heavily dependent on these assessments.

In contrast to the utopian myth of the nurturing classroom, primary schools have continually 'broken in' children and institutionalised their expectations. Many children have been convinced that the best they can hope for is to be 'good' and obedient, not to achieve academically like the teacher's own children or the kids in 'the celestial primary school in leafier suburban streets', as Steedman (1982) has put it.

Diversity in children's background and global mobility have created another challenge for primary educators, bringing into contact different traditions and perspectives on primary education as teachers and parents increasingly come from different ethnic backgrounds within the same schools. The Plowden Report wrote of the 'educational problems' of 'children of immigrants':

> Many children are intelligent and eager to learn. Indeed this eagerness sometimes proves an embarrassment when it is for the disciplined book learning and formal instruction of their own culture, and when the language barrier prevents the school explaining fully to parents the different way we go about education in England.
>
> (DES 1967, para. 183)

Stuart Hall (1983) has called on society to reject the myth of a natural way of learning, which

> has never been good enough for the ruling classes but is somehow OK for the ruled. There is no such thing. In fact, every curriculum is constituted through a set of emphases and exclusions and every one is shot through and predicated on certain values. The question is, which values? What emphases? Whose exclusions? There is no escape into nature from the tough and difficult business of designing a curriculum for a specific set of social purposes.

Any form of primary curriculum carries, either explicitly or implicitly, a specific selection from culture. That selection will depend on what is considered to be the purpose of education by those controlling the curriculum. There is no escape into nature.

A NEW PRIMARY PEDAGOGY

Primary pedagogy remains a political battleground. Progressive or child-centred primary pedagogy has been attacked by both the political right and the political left. Its perceived importance and influence in the construction and moulding of future generations mean that few governments leave primary education policy and curricula in the hands of educationalists alone.

For example, in the UK in the late 1990s, the government launched in primary schools first a National Literacy Strategy (DfEE, 1998) and a year later, a National Numeracy Strategy (DfEE, 1999). The explicit aim of these strategies was to improve educational outcomes for all pupils and do away with the long tail of underachievement which has dogged the English education system, by setting out to raise the standards of literacy in primary schools over five years. These strategies are highly centralised and interventionist programmes for schools, with schools inspected against their delivery of the programmes. They focus exclusively upon the basic skills of reading, writing and number, with the effect that wider concerns such as environmental and ecological issues (so notable in, for example, Swedish primary schools) have given way to teacher anxieties about managing the basic curriculum entitlements subject area by subject area.

In a similar way to some of the state primary curriculum programmes in the USA, the Literacy and Numeracy Strategies in England provide a framework of primary school teaching objectives term by term for each year of schooling for children from 5–11 years. As well as teaching objectives, the frameworks provide a firm structure of recommended times and class management procedures, giving details both of what should be taught and the means by which it should be taught.

In contrast to the implicit curriculum of child-centred or progressive primary education, the new pedagogy set out in the strategies is a highly visible pedagogy, with the focus on transmission and the teacher's role in ensuring that learning takes place. It offers a challenge to the concept of the primary teacher's essential role being that of provider of resources, the organiser of the environment, the monitor of learning. Indeed, one central platform of the strategies is that the teacher's role must be 100 per cent teaching.

In its prescribed central curriculum, classroom organisation and teaching methods, its requirement for the setting out of termly and weekly plans to an approved method, and its stipulation that the 'corrrect' techniques be taught in initial teacher training, and be reinforced in schools by inspectors, the new curriculum in English primary schools is less like a return to the eighteenth-century system of teacher payments by results, and more reminiscent of the highly controlled Soviet elementary education system of the 1970s (Grant, 1979).

In a further change in the culture of primary education in the UK, and again with echoes of old Soviet practice, a range of different agencies across the broad spectrum of child and youth work has been brought into play, along with a variety of central government departments. This makes the primary schools one facet of a broader National Childcare Strategy, which is focused on developing local partnerships to plan provision across the board for children from 0–14 years.

These partnerships are bringing teachers into useful working groups with social workers, childcare workers, youth workers, foster carers, librarians, housing department officials and health visitors, in order to thrash out integrated approaches. 'Ring-fenced' funding has been set aside to meet successful bids for local programmes which implement government-backed initiatives – such as homework clubs, summer study centres, literacy projects involving parents and children together, to name a few. In this context, primary schooling must also be seen in the context of wider government strategies linked to welfare reform and to combating social exclusion. There are possibilities within this multi-agency approach, with a variety of different agencies brought together through the early years partnerships, to begin to move the education of young children out into a multiplicity of different sites, not restricting it to the school building, in a forerunner of plans for developing lifelong learning. The challenge is to create networks of opportunity for learning which all children can access.

The big difference between the centralised curricula of the former Soviet Union and that of England today, is there was no separate and parallel path of privately funded primary education in the Soviet Union.

THE IMPLICATIONS OF CHANGES IN PRIMARY EDUCATION FOR THE NEXT MILLENNIUM

In this section I want to consider the possible future for primary education within the context of lifelong learning, within a 'market economy' where the underlying hegemonic concept of children having a natural and fixed level of 'ability' remains strong. The persistence of the concept of fixed and innate abilities in the West is remarkable, and as an ideological construct it seems to have fatally flawed earlier major attempts to improve early childhood educational practice for the many. It was the continuity of the concept of fixed levels of ability carried over from the days of selective schooling and 'intelligence' testing which seems to have subverted progressivist pedagogy, rather than many of the pedagogic approaches themselves (see Bourne, 1988).

Recently there have been renewed efforts (for example, Herrnstein and Murray, 1994) to reconstruct and reinforce the concept of genetically determined fixed abilities, a concept that biologises the underachievement of certain groups and thus attempts to mask and explain as 'natural' the unequal distribution to them of material resources and life chances. As Oakley (1981, p. 62) argues: 'In situations of social change, biological explanations . . . provide easily understood arguments about the undesirability of change by fuelling a retreatist emphasis on the immutability of the natural world.'

In early observations of what is happening in English primary schools with the introduction of the National Literacy Strategy, there is an underlying continuity with earlier educational approaches which explain differential outcomes by appealing to the concept of a fixed intelligence and of differential ability. For example, there has been an increase in the grouping (or 'setting') of children by 'ability' in literacy and numeracy from the time they start school at 5 years old, providing different groups from then on with differential access to a richer curriculum. The introduction of setting is already being reinforced by the move to whole-class teaching as part of the Literacy and Numeracy Strategies, as teachers struggle with inadequate training to improve their repertoire of strategies for involving the whole class.

Of course, as children are differentially grouped, so they tend to be given access to very different models of literacy through the different approaches to teaching taken by class teachers, special needs teachers, English as an additional language teachers, and, in the worst cases, untrained classroom learning support assistants. Instead of the much talked of South Asian model of interactive primary class teaching involving the whole class, giving every child access to valued forms of literacy and numeracy practices and bringing all the children up to the required standard through modelling and collaborative learning, 'differentiation' remains the buzzword in English primary schools and in inspection documents.

Few schools show children moving between groupings, once allocated to a group, although the whole point of 'withdrawal' is supposedly to target teaching so as to bring children up to the level of their peers. Thus the gap between the 'ability' groups is likely to widen rather than draw closer as children grow older. Test results then confirm fixed 'ability' groupings, thus constructing different levels of ability through the different curricula and ways of reading and writing being taught to each group.

Bernstein (1990) has warned of the dangers of trapping some children in a curriculum of facts and skills, subject to a regime of discipline by schooling, while others are introduced to ways of accessing, interpreting and questioning knowledge, learning to control and produce the symbolic order. He argues that for the advantaged, primary education would lead to the sort of teaching which helps children to understand relationships, processes, connections. Meanwhile, disadvantaged children, coming into school without the primary skills and understandings taught by middle-class parents to prepare their children, would be caught up in a 'remedial' system, offered 'a lexical pedagogic code where one-word answers, or short sentences, relaying individual facts/skills/operations may be typical' (Bernstein, 1990, p. 79).

The worst scenario, then, is that state primary schooling for most children could become a narrow entitlement of basic skills leading to secondary training in 'employability'. In this scenario, a richer and wider primary education would not be a right, but would need to be bought from a free market of educational agencies.

Bernstein (1990) prophesies that in the near future, with increasing disparity in public resources, those who succeed in the early years of primary school (that is, mainly children from wealthier, education-oriented families) would be moved on quickly to the freedom of open and distance learning, including independent learning through free access to the Internet. Less privileged children, and thus those usually less immediately successful on entry to school, would, in contrast, move into more highly regulated forms of cheap basic skills training, followed by 'apprenticeships' in production or (more likely given unemployment figures) to places in basic further education. This controlled, low-level schooling would constitute a form of disciplining of the masses, with their attendance monitored and regulated, and their learning assessed and audited in detail on a daily basis, in contrast to those more advantaged learners following the independent learning and relative freedom of self-directed study available in different locations, including the home, using the Internet.

Contrast this scenario with another envisaged for the millennium by Korean policy-makers (Korean Education Development Institute, 1983). This depicts a future where rote learning will disappear as computers take over low-level processing work, and education strategies involve discussion, group learning and independent study, using media and instructional materials; where teachers have autonomy and are involved in education decision-making; and where children and adults share lifelong learning opportunities in and out of school sites, celebrating the fact that 'where learners meet people willing to teach, education takes place in one form or another' (ibid., p. 94).

Since 1989, in contrast to changes in the US and UK, Japanese educational changes at primary level have also focused on changing 'transmission' styles and learning from text-books and introducing an emphasis on independent learning through doing, observation, enquiry, play and self-expression. However, unlike Western child-centred education, the aim appears to be preparation for adapting to a changing society and flexible, self-directed, lifelong learning. Success in school examinations remains of enormous significance socially and for children's life chances, and in 1993 attendance at after-school classes [*juku*] stood at 42 per cent of primary age children.

Child-centred primary pedagogy, wherever it appears, is firmly based in the culture of consumption: choice, individual differences, individual needs, discovery and play. It creates both the pleasure-seeking consumer and the self-regulated worker in a world of economic expansion, with jobs for all. It can be seen, transformed, in imaginings of new types of Internet-based, multimedia forms of self-directed, lifelong learning. However, with recession and fierce competition for work, and an increasingly differentiated society, there appears to be a need for alternative, more explicit frameworks for primary schooling for controlling and regulating the less advantaged, and lessening competition for socially prized careers.

Primary professionals need to be aware how pedagogical outcomes can be used to provide justifications for differential social positioning and how these offer differential opportunities according to scales of attainment which rank and order children, thus 'naturalising' inequalities. Each policy change contains both the seeds of exclusion alongside the seeds of inclusion, especially where there remains the hegemony of the concept of fixed ability. Teaching, perhaps especially at primary level, is always and necessarily a political act – which can be directed either towards exclusion or towards inclusion.

Envisaging the future forms of primary education for the new millennium is a challenge:

> to debate what sorts of children we want to become the citizens of the future, to consider what sort of lives we want them to lead, in childhood and in adulthood, to investigate the conception of the 'good life' for children, and for the society in which they learn. The rigour and creativity of the thinking we engage in, the openness with which we explore difference and dissent, the energy with which we collaborate in the task – all these will affect the quality of the primary education of the future.
>
> (Drummond, 1998, p. 106)

REFERENCES

Adamson, B. and Morris, P. (1998) 'Primary schooling in Hong Kong' in J. Moyles and L. Hargreaves (eds), *The Primary Curriculum: Learning from International Perspectives*. London: Routledge.

Ball, S. and Larsson, S. (1989) *The Struggle for Democratic Education: Equality and Participation in Sweden*. London: Falmer Press.

Benavot, A., Cha, Y-K., Kames, D., Meyer, J. and Wong, S-Y. (1991) 'Knowledge for the masses: World models and national curricula, 1920-86', *American Sociological Review*, 56.

Bernstein, B. (1973) 'On the classification and framing of educational knowledge' in B. Bernstein, *Towards a Theory of Educational Transmissions: Class, Codes and Control*, vol. 3. London: Routledge & Kegan Paul.

Bernstein, B. (1990) *The Structuring of Pedagogic Discourse: Class, Codes and Control*, vol. 4. London: Routledge.

Birchenough, C. (1914) *History of Elementary Education in England and Wales*. London: University Tutorial Press.

Blyth, W. (1965) *English Primary Education*, vol. 2. London: Routledge & Kegan Paul.

Bourne, J. (1988) 'Natural acquisition' and a 'masked pedagogy', *Applied Linguistics*, 9 (1), 83–99.

Bourne, J. (1992) 'Inside a multilingual primary classroom: a teacher, children and theories at work'. Unpublished PhD thesis, University of Southampton.

Bourne, J. and Moon, B. (1994) 'A question of ability?' in B. Moon and A. Shelton-Mayes (eds) *Teaching in the Secondary School*. London: Routledge.

Clegg, A. (1972) *The Changing Primary School*. London: Chatto & Windus.

Cortazzi, M. (1998). 'Curricula across cultures: Contexts and connections' in J. Moyles and L. Hargreaves (1998) (eds) *The Primary Curriculum: Learning from International Perspectives*. London: Routledge.

De Voogd, G. (1998) 'Relationships and tensions in the primary curriculum of the United States' in J. Moyles and L. Hargreaves (eds) *The Primary Curriculum: Learning from International Perspectives*. London: Routledge.

Dearden, R. (1968) *The Philosophy of Primary Education*. London: Routledge & Kegan Paul.

DES (1926) *Report of the Consultative Committee on the Primary School* (The Hadow Report). London: HMSO.

619

DES (1967) *Children and Their Primary Schools* (The Plowden Report). London: HMSO.

DfEE (1998)*The National Literacy Strategy: Framework for Teaching.* London: DfEE.

DfEE (1999) *The National Numeracy Strategy: Framework for Teaching.* London: DfEE.

Drummond, M. (1998) 'Children yesterday, today and tomorrow' in C. Richards, and P. Taylor (eds) *How Shall We School Our Children? Primary Education and Its Future.* London: Falmer Press.

Galton, M., Simon, B. and Croll, P. (1980) *Inside the Primary Classroom.* London: Routledge & Kegan Paul.

Grant, N. (1979) *Soviet Education.* London: Pelican.

Hall, S. (1983) 'Education in crisis' in A. Wolpe and J. Donald (eds) *Is There Anyone Here from Education?* London: Pluto Press.

Halls, W. (1976) *Education, Culture and Politics in Modern France.* Oxford: Pergamon.

Hawkins, J. and Allen, R. (eds) (1991) *The Oxford Encyclopedic English Dictionary.* Oxford: Oxford University Press.

Herrnstein, R. and Murray, C. (1994) *The Bell Curve: Intelligence and Class Structure in American Life.* New York: The Free Press.

Jackson, B. (1964) *Streaming: An Education System in Miniature.* London: Routledge & Kegan Paul.

King, R. (1978) *All Things Bright and Beautiful.* J. Wiley & Sons.

Korean Education Development Institute (KEDI) (1983) *Korean Education 2000.* Korea: KEDI.

Lockheed, M. and Verspoor, A. (1991) *Improving Primary Education in Developing Countries.* Oxford: OUP World Bank.

Mayer, E. (1992) *Employment-related Key Competencies.* Report commissioned by the Australian Education Council. Canberra: Australian Government Publishing Service.

Moyles, J. and Hargreaves, L. (eds) (1998) *The Primary Curriculum: Learning from International Perspectives.* London: Routledge.

Ngobeni, P. (1995) 'Inservice education for primary schools in South Africa'. Unpublished MA dissertation, University of London Institute of Education.

Oakley, A. (1981) *Subject Women.* London: Fontana.

Pell, A. (1998) 'Primary education for the rural black South African child' in J. Moyles and L. Hargreaves (eds) *The Primary Curriculum: Learning from International Perspectives.* London: Routledge.

Qualifications and Curriculum Authority (QCA) (1999) *The Review of the National Curriculum in England: The Consultation Materials.* London: Department for Education and Employment (DfEE).

Richards, C. (1998) 'Changing primary/elementary school curricula' in J. Moyles and L. Hargreaves (eds) *The Primary Curriculum: Learning from International Perspectives.* London: Routledge.

Richards, C. and Taylor, P. (eds) (1998) *How Shall We School Our Children? Primary Education and Its Future.* London: Falmer Press.

Rose, J. (1984) *The Case of 'Peter Pan' or the Impossibility of Children's Fiction.* London: MacMillan.

Sharp, R. and Green, A. (1975) *Education and Social Control.* London: Routledge & Kegan Paul.

Simon, B. (1971) *Intelligence, Psychology, Education.* London: Lawrence & Wishart.

Simon, B. (1974) *The Politics of Educational Reform 1920–1940.* London: Lawrence & Wishart.

Simon, B. (1981) 'The primary school revolution: myth or reality?' in B. Simon, and J. Wilcocks (eds) *Research and Practice in the Primary School.* London: Routledge & Kegan Paul.

Steedman, C. (1982) *The Tidy House: Little Girls Writing.* London: Virago Press.

Sugimine, H. and Yamamoto, K. (1998) 'Primary curriculum: two perspectives from Japan' in J. Moyles and L. Hargreaves (eds) *The Primary Curriculum: Learning from International Perspectives.* London: Routledge.

Vlaeminke, M. (1998) 'Historical and philosophical influences on the primary curriculum' in J. Moyles and L. Hargreaves (eds) *The Primary Curriculum: Learning from International Perspectives.* London: Routledge.

Walkerdine, V. (1984) 'Developmental psychology and the child-centred pedagogy' in J. Henriques, W. Holloway, C. Urwin, C. Venn and V. Walkerdine (eds) *Changing the Subject.* London: Methuen.

35

SECONDARY SCHOOL
A tense stasis in function and form

Anna Ershler Richert, Kristin Donaldson Geiser
and David M. Donahue

What should all graduates of secondary school know and be able to do? How will secondary schools support students to develop such knowledge and skill? We might expect that the answers to these questions would vary significantly from culture to culture, community to community. We might also expect that such answers would alter over time in response to political, economic and social changes within a particular society or community. Each unique response would shape different purposes, structures, curricula and staffing needs. Therefore, we might expect secondary schools to look radically different in different contexts.

It is curious, indeed, that secondary schools in many contexts – around the world and also over time – are more alike than they are different. On the surface, secondary schools in the Czech Republic look much like secondary schools in Israel, India or China: students and teachers gather at the same time of the day, do many of the same tasks in the same order, and leave at the same appointed hour. What makes these similarities even more interesting is that in many countries, the US being the one we know best, there is a consistent effort to change secondary schools to meet more closely the needs of the changing populations of students who reside in them. In looking closely at the reform efforts for secondary schools in the US, however, we find that even when schools do change, they do so in superficial or cosmetic ways; little seems to change with regards to the core of educational practice.[1] In our review of secondary schools we have become acutely aware that changing the relationships, processes, habits and experiences of the adults and children within schools is extremely difficult to accomplish. Beneath a level of 'structural' similarity, there are even deeper consistencies in how teachers teach, what teachers expect of students and, in many instances, what students learn (see Cuban, 1984; Goodlad, 1984; Sizer, 1984). Such consistencies have evolved to become 'regularities' of secondary schooling – practices and processes that are commonly expected, well known and deeply valued (Grossman, 1996).

The regularities of secondary school life are the subject of much discussion and debate in the education literature. Seymour Sarason's book *The Culture of School and the Problem of Change*, published first in 1975 and revised in 1997, provides insight about the regularities of secondary schools by identifying how some of the fundamental regularities we witness in

621

secondary school settings function as barriers to change. Sarason describes various patterns of schools (e.g. 'population regularities' such as students and adults meeting together in periods of five consecutive days, separated by two days of no interaction; 'arithmetic-mathematics programmatic regularities' of drilling students in the use of numbers from the first day of school until graduation) and suggests that such patterns not only reveal the way schools 'are', but, to the great extent to which they remain unquestioned, they function to dictate the way schools 'should be'. He suggests that the regularities of schooling create the 'culture' of schools. The culture of schools is both protected and perpetuated by ideas and structures designed to keep things as they are.

Sarason proposes that further examination and questioning of school regularities may lead us to adjust and transform them, so that they effectively promote our intended object-ives of schooling. In other words, by understanding the way things are, we are challenged to consider *if* this is the way things should be, rather than assuming that things naturally *are* as they should be. Therefore, if the regularities of schooling are not changed – if the culture of schooling is not transformed – then 'change' in secondary schooling is limited to minor adjustments to a system that is firmly in place rather than deeper adjustments that might result in a different form of schooling altogether. The resistance to change that seems to be characteristic of secondary schooling is problematic when one considers the rapidly changing world secondary schools are intended to serve.

A powerful example of the problematic nature of change in secondary schools can be found in the recently sustained effort in the United States to integrate students of diverse backgrounds. Since the mid-1950s, when the courts barred segregation and insisted on equal educational opportunity for all students, integration has been an exceedingly import-ant goal in US education. In recent decades, furthermore, the challenge successfully to integrate has been heightened owing to the high rise in immigration and the growing number of students of diverse cultural and language backgrounds. Drawing on the frame-work for understanding change offered by Sarason, we note that many of the initial efforts to accomplish the goal of integration have been technical in nature – busing students from one neighbourhood to another, creating magnet schools, insisting on language regulations that provide non-English-speaking students with access to the standard curriculum, offer-ing 'remedial' programmes of instruction for students who arrive in American schools with no prior schooling, etc. In reviewing the results of those efforts, we see that creating tech-nical changes in the structure of schools, unless they are accompanied by changes in beliefs and values regarding students' abilities or potential, will not result in the deeper changes for which many believe they were intended. Similarly, technical changes do not necessarily alter the ways students interact with one another, with the teacher, or with the curriculum. Deeper changes in secondary schools require that we question the 'givens' of schooling and challenge assumptions about children, knowledge and access to learning. Therefore, the desired change of integration (and ultimately improved student achievement) requires much more than putting diverse students together into the same building; it requires changes in the fundamental regularities of school.

A central focus in this chapter on secondary schools is the issue of change. We have chosen this focus because of what is revealed as we work to understand where in the domain of secondary schooling the struggle to change occurs, and what deeper issues about second-ary schools come into play as the struggle ensues. Our focus will revolve around four rather conventional domains or commonplaces of secondary schooling in both the US and else-where: purpose, structure, curriculum and personnel. For each commonplace we identified a set of metaphors that are commonly used to describe it. We note that over time, as attempts at change are made in each of these domains of secondary schooling, the metaphor used to describe it changes as well. In this way the changing metaphors we describe below reveal the consistent attempts at change in secondary schooling.

Furthermore, we note that the metaphor shifts that we describe indicate that the struggle for change is often directly connected to the struggle for equitable educational opportun-ities. The questions raised by our analysis cause us to examine a number of critical issues concerning equity and change as they relate to secondary schooling: Who is being served by secondary schools? Who is excluded from secondary schooling? How are resources distrib-uted? Who is labelled as a 'high achiever'? Who is labelled as a 'low achiever'? How are labels that are assigned in secondary schools used to determine opportunities beyond secondary school?

These questions of equity create one lens through which we can look to see some of the characteristics of secondary schooling. This lens also invites us to link our thinking of secondary schooling to the human stories that are the essential – yet often silent – focus of a discussion of schooling. It is our intention that we open a conversation about what second-ary school is and what it might become. To this end, we both describe and question some of the regularities of secondary education. Curiously, while the mechanism we employ to understand the world of secondary school is the shifting metaphor, our analysis considers how the disequilibrium suggested by such shifts results, nevertheless, in a pattern of stasis rather than change in secondary schooling. Let us begin, then, by considering the purpose of secondary school.

THE PURPOSE OF SECONDARY SCHOOLING: FROM SYSTEMATIC INEQUALITY TO IMPROVED OUTCOMES FOR ALL

Tension over the purpose of secondary schools has long endured because societies hold multiple, often conflicting values about why schools exist and what they should accomplish. What would it look like if a secondary school were 'successful' or 'effective'? Who defines what is meant by successful or effective? For whom is secondary school designed to be – or supposed to be – successful or effective? Different responses to these questions reveal diverse notions of the purposes of secondary schools.

The political context of purposes and outcomes of secondary school

Since the purposes of school differ from country to country, we will rely for much of our analysis on the United States and the purpose of secondary school in that setting. At the same time, however, we shall draw on the US experience to consider this issue of purpose as it affects secondary schooling in other countries as well. As we shall see, the initial metaphor of 'systematic inequality' has applied worldwide to secondary schooling at different times in history.

One of the most important values related to the secondary school in the US today is improving outcomes for all students. That is, ensuring that all students leave secondary school with a particular body of knowledge and a particular set of skills. Certainly, secondary schools have not always been viewed as the means for preparing students for opportunities with social, political or economic distinctions based often on race, gender, class or disability. In fact, systems of intentionally unequal schools have been used in many countries to maintain the power of one race, gender or class over another. For example, in South Africa high schools have traditionally perpetuated racial inequality though currently they are moving away from such practices. Most high schools in the United States continue to perpetuate inequities, particularly along lines of socio-economic class. In some parts of Afghanistan following the Taliban takeover, many girls' secondary schools were closed, thus drastically limiting opportunities for girls and young women in that country. In too many nations, students with physical and mental disabilities, if they are educated at all, have been and continue to be segregated in different school systems where secondary education offers only a portion of the education afforded to other students.

In countries where mass secondary education is the norm, however, disparities still remain. In most of Europe and North America, secondary schools segregate students based on their academic potential, ability and preferences. In Germany, students are separated into different types of secondary schools; those wanting academic preparation for university attend the *Gymnasium*, while those preparing for trades attend *Realschule*. Similar differences in types of secondary schools are found in France and Russia; secondary schooling is available to all, but the purpose varies according to the school itself.

Opportunity to go to secondary school

While it is true that various forms of inequality define secondary schooling in some parts of the world, it is also true that in much of the world there is a question as to whether or not all students have equal opportunity to receive secondary education in the first place. Almost all of the world's nations make available some secondary education; however, providing access to secondary education does not ensure that all children receive a quality secondary education. About 55 per cent of the world's children of secondary school age are enrolled in schools. In Europe, North America and Australia, enrolments are in the 80 to 100 per cent range. By contrast, enrolments are more typically 20 to 70 per cent in Africa, South America and parts of Asia, though the percentage of children in secondary schools has risen greatly (US Department of Education, National Center for Education Statistics, 1996).

Even where secondary schools are accessible, free and open to all, poverty requires many children to work rather than seek an education. In other parts of the world, girls' secondary education is seen as inappropriate for religious and cultural reasons. Clearly, the provision of secondary schools is different from ensuring that all children are able to receive a secondary education, or ensuring that they will be able to use that education once they have done the work to receive it.

The structure of opportunity within secondary schools: the US case example

Access to secondary education is one way to consider the issue of equity that focuses our discussion of purpose thus far. However, beyond access to school in the first place, we must also consider the issue of access as it applies to the experience of school once students enter the buildings where they are to learn. In the case of the United States, separate schools with different academic purposes are less common than 'comprehensive' high schools, which bring together many 'tracks' of different students all within one school building.

In a comprehensive high school, students are identified according to the type of education they are to receive and then they move through their high school experience in the 'track' to which they are assigned. These track assignments are determined by such factors as standardised tests, teacher recommendations and parent requests. In this system 'honours' and 'college-bound' students study in classrooms next to vocational, special education and 'general track' students. Typically, students from these different tracks meet only occasionally during the school day in such places as the lunch room or physical education classes. Students whose first language is not English, or others who do not perform well on standardised tests, or those whose parents are not familiar with the tracking system and its requirements, often find themselves isolated from many of the higher track advantages of American secondary schools; furthermore, once tracked, these students are often unable to move into those more advantageous positions even over time.

Critics of differential systems of secondary schooling and tracking note the disproportionate numbers of students from dominant racial, economic and linguistic groups in high-status schools and tracks. By contrast, most of the students in low-status schools and tracks are from groups that have been historically oppressed. Doing away with the differential schools and tracks does not solve the problem, a point we shall develop further in our discussion of how secondary schools are organised and what they teach. Because the content of schooling and the means of teaching remain so unchanging, the same students who have historically been ill-served, often continue to be ill-served whether or not they are in tracks.

Many nations in the world are struggling with educational problems related to providing equity in secondary education to racial, ethnic or language minorities. Once again we shall use the example of race and schools in the United States to illustrate the metaphor shift from systematic inequality to equal opportunity we are describing in this section. As mentioned earlier, until less than 50 years ago, many US school systems enforced racial inequality through segregation. Since the 1954 Supreme Court decision that ended school segregation, efforts at integration have sought to provide equal access to the same public secondary education for students, regardless of race. In reality, however, segregated schools continue to exist in the United States. Parents whose children might attend integrated schools sometimes elect to place them in private or religious schools. Similarly, parents often choose to live in settings characterised by homogeneity, so that their children can attend schools with other children more like themselves. In spite of attempts to integrate schools in the United States, a *de facto* segregation results when parents choose to live in homogeneous settings or to place their children in such settings for school. In sum, the change in access to schools over these past 50 years represents the tension between secondary schools as tools for changing the values of the larger society and secondary schools upholding and reinforcing the values of the larger society.

The continuing racial disparities in public secondary school achievement and graduation rates that result have led many educators to a shift in their focus from educational *opportunity* toward educational *outcomes*. This shift has opened many new considerations about secondary school, including what constitutes viable and equitable outcomes for secondary school students, for example: Are all outcomes equal? Should all students work towards standard outcome measures? An example of the outcome discussion that is illustrative of the equity issue we are considering concerns the curriculum that leads to particular outcomes. The argument proceeds like this: One way to improve outcomes for 'minority' students is to create a curriculum that is relevant to their lives rather than drawn on the history and life experiences of peoples different from themselves. With a curriculum tailored towards them, students from particular cultural groups will be more engaged in school; the outcomes we might expect from their studying their own culture in ways that they find familiar as learners will therefore be improved. One of many examples of this in the US today is reflected in the work of some African American educators who advocate 'immersion schools' (with an Afro-centric curriculum) for African American students to better support their academic success (Leake and Leake, 1992).

Concern for equality also extends to gender. In 1972, Title IX of the US Education Code prohibited sexual discrimination in schools receiving federal funds. At the same time, some secondary schools established special, separate science and maths programmes for girls to close the gender gap in achievement in those subjects and to encourage more girls to pursue science and maths-related careers. By contrast, advocates of equal and improved education for students with disabilities argued for a dismantling of separate schools based on disability and demanded mainstreaming and full inclusion of all students with physical and mental disabilities (Wang and Reynolds, 1996). These variations in approaches to the goal of equality illustrate not only the value-laden nature of secondary schooling but also the way in which the value of equality operates in tension with the value of recognising group and individual differences.

Quality and equality: the persistent dilemma of secondary schooling

Tensions around equality – how to define it, and the best ways to achieve it – are but one example of how the purposes of secondary schools are compound, complex and sometimes contradictory. One urban high school in the San Francisco Bay Area where we live describes its dual mission.

> First, we are determined to create an academically rigorous high school. Second, we are committed to the principle of equity and will do everything we can to insure that a quality education is accessible to all of our students regardless of their prior school experiences.

This mission statement raises another tension in the conventional wisdom about the purpose of secondary education: the tension between equality and excellence. This school is committing itself to both. Indeed, such a commitment is in keeping with both the metaphor of equal opportunity for all students, and the more recent one that describes how schooling in the US is conceived: 'improved outcomes for all students'. This latter metaphor represents a shift that suggests a broad and inclusive goal of excellence rather than excellence for

626

only an elite group of students who mirror the racial, class and gender characteristics of privilege in society at large. Unfortunately, for most of this century, equality and excellence have been defined as competing rather than complementary purposes of secondary schools.

Over the last 100 years, demands for greater equality in secondary education, whether equal access or equal outcomes, have been met by fears of diminishing educational excellence from those who already enjoyed access to and were well served by schools. In the United States, concerns for equality and excellence in school policy have followed on the heels of each other with regularity. During the 1930s and 1940s, secondary education for most teenagers became the norm and schools were charged with meeting the needs of children who in previous decades would not have been in high school.

By the 1950s, school policy was moving away from concerns for equality and focusing on excellence as the nation sought to meet the military and economic challenges of the Cold War with the Soviet Union. Consequently, the purpose of schools was to provide stepped-up instruction in maths, science and foreign languages. Schools were seen as 'sorting machines' identifying the brightest talent who would go on to receive state-of-the-art instruction at universities. Concerns for equity were not entirely overlooked because schools had to sort talent from the widest possible sample, but the talk about school policy was far from establishing equal outcomes for groups who historically had been excluded from secondary education, even as those groups began to win court battles for school integration.

Only during the 1960s and 1970s did policy attention turn towards providing greater equality in secondary education. When concerns for excellence in secondary education were again raised in the 1980s, the motivation was global economic competition from nations like Germany and Japan. School policy focused first and foremost on increasing graduation requirements and raising standards, supplanting concerns about equity as a primary focus.

The tensions around the purpose of secondary schools described in this section bring up further questions about the schools. Should all students be treated alike or individually? How can schools that value both equality and individuality achieve these competing goals? These questions become even harder to answer as schools serve more diverse populations of students (racially, economically and linguistically) and provide an ever wider scope of services (educational, physical and mental health, legal and social services). In the next sections we address these questions.

THE STRUCTURE OF SECONDARY SCHOOL: FROM FACTORIES TO SHOPPING MALLS TO COMMUNITIES OF LEARNERS

In light of the dilemmas that emerge regarding the purpose of secondary schooling, it is not surprising that the very structure of a secondary school – the way in which the school itself is organised to accomplish divergent goals – is subject to persistent attention and adjustment. Again, an equity lens permits us to see how an organisation's purpose directs its structure and actions. For example, in one secondary school it would be considered equitable if all students received the same books for the same course; in another school, students might receive different books for the same course depending on their capabilities and/or prior experience with the subject matter. In this example, different assumptions regarding equity determine a different arrangement for school book distribution.

Two important resources of secondary school are knowledge and experiences. Providing access (and denying access) to each of these is accomplished, in part, through a school's organisational structure. Though every school organises itself to provide access to these resources in some ways that are different and unique, there remain many patterns and organisational structures that persist from one setting to another over time and across regions. Three structural forms that have been used to describe schools with regard to how they distribute knowledge and experience are: *factories*, *shopping malls*, and most recently, *communities*. Let us examine each.

Sorting differences: schools as factories

Many design principles of secondary schools are grounded in the 'factory model' of education, which represents an effort to make schools efficient managers and producers of students. In this model all students are treated the same – they pass through the system with more or less the same set of experiences, the same opportunities for learning, the same books, the same assignments, the same order of experiences, and so forth. One assumption driving this model is that given that each student receives the same set of experiences and opportunities to learn, if there are differences in outcome or their capabilities at the end of the process, these differences must be caused by differences in their capabilities at the outset. This assumption supports school structures that serve as a 'conveyor belt', moving students through a set of experiences with little adjustment or response to students' unique attributes. The quality of the student who completes the system – the graduate, in other words – is determined by the quality of the child who enters the school in the first place.

Importantly, the factory model of schooling gained great momentum during the Industrial Revolution in the United States. As such, it provides a compelling example that is true both in the US and elsewhere, which is that school structures typically reflect operative economic structures at any particular moment in history. Not only did the factory idea correspond with a prevailing set of notions regarding mass production, but schools that were organised according to this model provided products that corresponded to the current needs of society – a few people to assume high status, high-paying jobs, and great numbers of people (for whom the factory system of education did not yield success) to fill the many unskilled labour positions that industry produced. If factory model schools produced some successes and many who were not, then they were supporting the economic structure that was in place at that time.

Within the factory model, certain people, ideas, capabilities and talents fall by the wayside. Efforts to maximise the success of some students have the potential to factor out the interests of others. Many questions that appeared then persist today: Who gets to be successful in school? Whose interests are factored out? Looking at the factory model, the answer appears clear: success is relegated to those students who can perform well in a system designed by and for the dominant culture; students whose experiences and habits are neither reflected nor valued in school are those whose interests are factored out. Since factories are built primarily upon white, middle-class values and knowledge, furthermore, poor students and students of colour are disproportionately perceived to be 'other' than the school culture. Consequently, these students are most often denied access to the experiences and knowledge most valued by the community and the larger society.

The tension around issues of equity that persist in motivating change in schools emerged as the number of 'other' (or non-successful students in the factory model) increased. New models for secondary schools were introduced that sought to provide students with more opportunities for success. One strategy is to create a school with 'something for everyone' – a structural design often described as the 'shopping mall high school'.

Accommodating differences: shopping mall high schools

One model for a secondary school structure that followed from the factory approach was the shopping mall. The attempt was to provide students with more opportunities for acquiring knowledge and experience than the one 'conveyor-belt' option they had in the factory model just described. By adjusting the structures to provide more course offerings, schools sought (and still seek, because there are many 'shopping mall' high schools worldwide today) to accommodate student differences by providing students with multiple opportunities for learning. This 'shopping mall' structure 'enables [the school] to satisfy any particular criticism by opening up a new speciality shop' (McDonald, 1995).

An assumption underlying the shopping mall model is that 'more is better'; the student who enters the shopping mall high school is not confined to one path. He or she can choose from a wide variety of courses and school experiences and can construct as wide and diverse a path as he or she desires. Rather than one route to success, students can be successful in a number of ways by taking a number of different courses and/or choosing a number of unique options for growth. The problems with such a system, however, are many. While it appears that there are many paths to success that draw on students' unique interests and individual talents, the reality is that not all paths are equally good, nor equally valued by the community outside the school. Similarly, when schools create multiple opportunities within a system that depends upon linear and sequential completion of courses (which may not necessarily correspond to mastery of certain knowledge or skills), the options available to a student are deceivingly slim.

An example will make this clear. While many American high schools offer physics and calculus, those courses are only available to students who have the prerequisite courses and adequate language skills. A student who enters the school as a recent immigrant and who does not understand the sequencing of mathematics in American schools may automatically be placed in a remedial maths class because of her English skills. Upon earning an 'A' in this remedial class, she may be placed in the 'next' class – perhaps an algebra or pre-algebra class. After progressing through this 'track', the student has still not completed the courses required to enrol in calculus. Therefore, while the student may have had the intellectual capacity to master calculus, she may never have the 'choice', for she has been placed in a track for recent immigrants rather than 'college-bound' students. To complicate matters further, the same student may not be allowed to enrol in physics until she has completed a certain level of maths. If she does not have the option to take the prerequisite maths class, not only does she miss out on the maths learning, but she is denied access to physics. In this way the path, or track, cuts across other subject areas.

629

Likewise, if a student in the 'shopping mall' high school chooses to take a class on 'family living', 'cooking', or 'child development', he may realise later that this option interfered with his eligibility for admission to many post-secondary institutions of higher education. This consequence is created by the structure of the shopping mall high school. Not only does the time spent in such courses replace the time that the student may have spent in courses required for college admission, but schools often schedule non-college preparatory courses at the very same time of day as traditional college preparatory courses. Therefore, even if a student is willing and able to arrive early or stay late in order to take advantage of the options provided by the shopping mall structure, he is often forced to decide between 'child development' and 'algebra'. Furthermore, the student will likely be counselled into one option or the other, based upon a counsellor or teacher's assumptions of his post-secondary potential. It is as if the mall has several levels or 'floors'; upon entering the mall, students are escorted to a particular floor and their 'choice' is limited to the options available on that floor. Stairs to the levels above and below are difficult to find, and heavily guarded by the structures and regularities of secondary schools.

In this way, each track within the shopping mall school ultimately serves to perpetuate the disparate outcomes of the factory model: a few students have access to the track that provides access to the knowledge and skills valued by the community and society, while others are denied such access and opportunity. However, the school's function of sorting students is often obscured by the appearance of student 'choice'.

The notion of 'choice' is further confounded when we look at students over a long period of time: different opportunities within the shopping mall high school have been linked to advantages and disadvantages beyond high school. Therefore, in an effort to negotiate efficiency and responsiveness to individual differences, the practices of labelling, sorting and selecting students may ultimately provide some individuals with a competitive advantage. This presents a fundamental dilemma within an institution that, in the US, is designed to provide equal access for all students. Without careful attention to who is getting what opportunities, what often happens is that the goal of 'a common education available to all' is redefined as 'an equal opportunity to take differentiated courses to prepare for differentiated adult roles' (Oakes *et al.*, 1992, p. 581). Such a critique of the shopping mall high school has led to yet another metaphor for secondary schools: communities of learners.

Reconceptualising differences: schools as communities of learners

Shifting dramatically from factories and shopping malls, the notion of 'community' suggests that in order to meet the needs of all students, educators need to focus on issues of inclusion, solidarity, caring, capacity building, and the prevention of alienation and isolation. Communitarian notions of isolation suggest that individuals who become inappropriately disconnected from their community are likely to experience feelings of meaninglessness that ultimately affect their ability to function within that environment. In the context of schooling, isolation becomes even more problematic, given current learning theory which suggests that knowledge is socially constructed, and that people learn best in conversation and association with one another. Several scholars have found that student isolation is often a root cause of poor student achievement (Gilligan, 1982; Noblit, 1993; Noddings, 1984; Rose, 1989). Consequently, 'good' schools are increasingly seen as those that bring people into a community in which everyone – students, teachers, administrators, parents and even the school itself – learns and grows together.

A secondary school that reflects a community structure is not only committed to knowing its students and their families, but to including them in the work of the school. Within this structure, we may see students sharing their work and facilitating a discussion about their progress with their teachers and parents. We may also see parents and students as voting members of the school's governing body. A community structure may also support add-itional members of the community (e.g. businesses, students from other schools, artists, health care providers) to become active on-campus partners in the school's work, including its 'core' work of instructing and assessing students.

If schools embrace the challenge of creating a community of learners, they are commit-ting to a complex process – a process that invokes an ethic of care. This process involves getting to know students better – what their individual strengths and limitations are – in order more effectively to respond to their needs and create a learning environment that will encourage their growth (Gilligan, 1982; Mayeroff, 1971). The ethic of care within a com-munity of learners challenges schools to create the organisational conditions that facilitate the relationships between teachers and students. Furthermore, educators are called to exam-ine the ways in which school structures facilitate relationships that support learning by drawing people into meaningful conversations with one another about subject matter and other matters of interest. For example, schools with an underlying philosophy that all children can learn and belong in the school community, 'do not focus on how to help any particular category of students . . . instead, the focus is on how to operate classrooms and schools as supportive communities that include and meet the needs of everyone' (Stainback and Stainback, 1992, p. 34). Depending upon how a particular community defines 'meeting the needs of everyone', a school that is operating like a community of learners may or may not look very different from a factory model school.

Many experts suggest that the ability to achieve educational goals throughout the world is largely dependent upon the ability to educate and prepare more students for more opportunities to become active, engaged and productive citizens. Emerging democracies in other countries are called to respond to this charge as well. Over time and spanning geo-graphic regions, communities have made subtle changes in the structure of schooling, often in the name of responding to students' needs. Responses to such needs impact upon the very way in which secondary schools are organised: the factory model permitted schools to utilise the 'cookie cutter' approach to 'producing' students. The structure of some schools has been modified to provide students with a multitude of choices, resulting in 'shopping mall' schools. Schools are currently moving towards yet another human structure – that of communities – bringing people together in ways that support individual and collective growth and development. Yet these are merely structural elements. How are such designs connected to, or perhaps reflective of, tensions regarding curriculum and instruction?

SECONDARY SCHOOL CURRICULUM: FROM THE ONE BEST WAY TO LIFE-LONG LEARNING

The one best way: teaching students to 'see'

Educators around the world often struggle to develop the 'one best way' to educate all students.[2] Profits earned by companies producing curriculum 'kits' or packages are evidence that secondary schools continue to look for the one best way or one set curriculum that is appropriate for all secondary students. In the US, public debates that simplify curriculum issues into discrete and opposing options (e.g. investigative vs. algorithmic learning in mathematics or thematic vs. chronological approaches to social studies) reveal our society's allegiance to the belief that there is *one* best way.

Referring back to Sarason's advice about the paralysing effects of a school culture that does not reflect on its 'givens', we are compelled to question such regularities. When we look for the one best way, what are we looking for? The best subject matter for everyone? The best way to teach? The best way to learn? For whom is secondary school curricula the 'best'? In the midst of expensive and well-publicised marketing campaigns and debates over curricula, these questions are rarely asked.

The assumption that there is a 'best' way for teachers to teach and for all students to learn assumes that all students need to know a common set of ideas, and be able to perform a common set of tasks. The notion of a 'best' way further assumes that there is a predetermined curriculum that will equip students with such knowledge and skills. In this way, students are expected to absorb what they encounter; 'see' what they are shown. The emphasis is on coverage of a predetermined and fixed body of information that constitutes the curriculum.

This metaphor of 'one best' way assumes that students arrive both intellectually and culturally prepared to see what we see, and to learn what those who are in charge of secondary education deem is important. These assumptions are challenged by theories that assume a deeper connection between who the students are and how they come to know. They suggest that what is taught and how, affects each student differently – a stance which again holds great significance when we view educational outcomes through the lens of equity. Critics of the 'one best system' idea in the US point out many examples of differential effects of curriculum along lines of race, class and gender. Furthermore, they argue that the situation is worsened for these students when they are addressed by remediating curriculum content and teaching strategies to compensate for the students' 'deficits'. Rose (1989, p. 235) characterises this approach as an example of 'how the student's personal history recedes as the what of the classroom is valorized over the how'. The fundamental assumption of this remediation strategy has been critiqued for locating the source of enduring educational problems in the student and assuming that the learning difficulty can be resolved with a short-term 'fix', while the curriculum remains constant.

Based upon their in-depth accounts of students struggling to survive, much less succeed in schools, some scholars go one step further to suggest that many strategies designed and implemented in the name of improving education for at-risk students actually perpetuate the differences and make it more difficult for those very students to succeed (e.g. Fine, 1991;

Rose, 1989). For example, many programmes that are designed to accommodate students' diverse language needs do not provide students with an opportunity to develop the concepts, habits and skills that other students are learning. The assumption that a new language must be developed prior to successful engagement with ideas or skills rather than at the same time or even after (both of which have been shown to be successful in many settings) ensures that some students will never have the opportunity to master concepts of skills that are valued by a particular society or community.

There is sufficient evidence to suggest that this path of identifying and attempting to fix the students who are not served by the 'best' way is an inadequate and inappropriate route in this particular journey. Many individuals over time and in various parts of the world continue to pursue an alternative route: teaching students to 'look' rather than to 'see' in their journey to learn.

Life-long learning: teaching students to 'look'

Mike Rose of the University of California at Los Angeles, has contributed to our understanding of what a preferable route might entail:

> We need an orientation to instruction that provides guidance on how to determine and honor the beliefs and stories, enthusiasms, and apprehensions that students reveal. How to build on them, and when they clash with our curriculum ... how to encourage a discussion that will lead to reflection on what students bring and what they're currently confronting.
>
> (Rose, 1989, p. 236)

Curriculum and instruction can facilitate 'looking' by inviting student enquiry, questioning and exploration of content. The content becomes a means rather than an ends. The enquiry process enables students to look at the content through a filter of their individual experiences. The curriculum becomes more inclusive, therefore, as diverse students are challenged to draw on what they know in the service of what they do not know.

If schools are in the business of preparing students to be 'life-long learners', they are necessarily engaged in rethinking their work in multiple areas. For example, they are required to rethink how content is 'covered' (e.g. integrated curriculum that incorporates concepts and facts from two or more 'subject' areas). They must also revisit their expectations of students and the tools that they employ to measure student learning. Related to the measurement of student learning, schools must revise how they report student learning to their various constituencies (e.g. universities, employers, the public) so that it more accurately aligns student learning with indicators of 'achievement'.

The process of embarking upon a different path, however, requires passage through territory dangerously positioned at the crossroads of social and political tensions around curriculum and control. Many authors posit that disagreement regarding the best curricula reflects each society's competing ideologies pertaining to the purpose of schools (see Oakes, 1985). Linda McNeil (1986) characterises this as the contradiction between educational goals (knowledge) and social efficiency goals (control). Schools and classrooms operate within this unique dynamic. Therefore, any educational practice or process that is connected to the selection of and strategies for sharing knowledge cannot be understood apart from this larger context.

In order to get beyond changes in language and metaphor and actually to accomplish changes in teaching and learning, many scholars (e.g. McNeil 1986; Rose 1989; Sarason 1972) suggest that societies and communities need to be encouraged and supported to reach a better understanding of culture and the function of culture in shaping the curricula of secondary schools. The individuals closest to the work – the professional staff within secondary schools – are central to any effort to rethink and reform the regularities of teaching and learning. The following section examines the shifting roles of these individuals, and how they are prepared to do their work.

THE PROFESSIONAL STAFF OF SECONDARY SCHOOL

As we can see from our discussion thus far, while the purposes of school change over time, the structures designed to address them must change as well. Similarly, the personnel assigned to carry out the work of schools must change and the manner in which they are prepared for and supported to do this work must also develop in new directions. The persistent tension of secondary schooling addressed in this section is that of properly and powerfully staffing the secondary school to meet its goals, preparing this staff to do their complex and changing work, and supporting them as they proceed in doing so. Who should do the work of secondary school teaching is a question that follows the earlier question of what work needs to be done in the first place. This, then, is followed by subsequent sets of questions regarding the preparation and ongoing support of school personnel. It is these latter concerns – initial preparation and ongoing preparation/support – that focus the last of the four persistent tensions discussed in this chapter. We have chosen the metaphor shift 'from training to building capacity' to capture the tension we perceive.

Staffing the secondary school

Before we consider the preparation issues embedded in this metaphor shift, let us consider briefly the personnel requirements for modern secondary schools. The expanded array of purposes and programmes that have characterised secondary schools in recent decades requires that schools employ a broadly prepared staff of professional school personnel. Teachers who are well prepared in the subject matters they teach, and prepared in pedagogy as well, still form the working core of secondary schools; our analysis will focus primarily on them. It is important to note, however, that teachers make up only one part of the secondary school staff. In addition, secondary schools employ administrators who may or may not be teachers, as well as other support providers such as nurses, counsellors, psychologists, coaches for sports and other activities and so forth. The changing purposes of school, and even more the changing populations that schools serve, establish the need for a more diverse group of professional educators to meet the diverse needs of the secondary school student population. Additionally, large secondary schools require a management level of personnel, some of which is housed on secondary school campuses. In short, the number and diversity of adults on many high school campuses have increased according to the numbers of functions the school performs and the diversity of the student population the school serves.

With that growing diversity come changing requirements for governance, support and preparation.

Preparing the personnel

The metaphor shift that characterises the persistent tension we see with regard to school personnel – from training to building capacity – captures a struggle that seems inherent at the intersection between the professions associated with the work of schooling and the institution where that work takes place. By definition, a training model for preparing and supporting teachers and other personnel who work in schools implies a top-down, hierarchical structure in which school workers are the passive recipients of information which they then apply to predictable problems in a predetermined and somewhat fixed manner. The training model corresponds well with the 'one best way' model of curriculum and instruction discussed in the previous section of the chapter. In this model knowledge is seen as something to be acquired; the passive acquisition of the 'one best package' of non-changing facts and processes which one can then apply at the appropriate moments captures the essence of what is expected here. So, too, it captures the essence of school governance because those with the knowledge to choose the best system in the first place have the power to determine intended outcomes and to govern towards their accomplishment. The way that professionals are supported in such a system involves providing them with more information and better skills training so that they can carry out the work of others.

'Building capacity' in the secondary school staff

The capacity-building model for preparing, governing and supporting school personnel is based on a different set of assumptions about the nature of knowledge, the professional work of teaching, and the evolving lives of schools and those who inhabit them (see Darling-Hammond, 1993; Sykes, 1996). In this model, teachers, like students (and like all people who are part of the school community), are seen as active learners who construct rather than receive knowledge. The school itself is seen as a learning organisation in which both the school and those who inhabit it are involved in continual growth and renewal (O'Neil, 1995). The notion of the secondary school being a learning community, as was discussed earlier, applies here. Let us consider as an example the preparation, support and governance of teachers in the capacity-building model. How would teachers be prepared, and what assumptions would guide that process?

Building capacity for secondary school teaching requires, at least, building capacity for dealing with change. Rather than training teachers to acquire a preset body of knowledge, teachers must be able to draw on a variety of different knowledge bases (knowledge of subject matter; cultural knowledge of the students being taught; knowledge of learning; knowledge of context; knowledge of change forces, etc.) to meet the changing requirements of their work in schools. The current challenge for teachers is to teach changing groups of children subject matters which themselves are changing; they must necessarily assume a learning stance towards their work. What at one time was considered to be a persistent regularity of secondary schooling – the system by which teachers were trained with a set body of subject matter knowledge – is now perceived to be one of change. Not only are the subject matters changing in many ways that are important for secondary teaching, but also knowledge about learning and learners is changing. For example, in the US where the student population in secondary schools can present upwards of 70 different languages being spoken as first languages, teachers must draw on a relatively new body of growing information about concept acquisition for second language learners in order to create a curriculum that will meet the needs of their diverse groups of students. For this reason, different forms of both professional preparation and support are needed as part of the challenge for building capacity for secondary schools.

The idea of building capacity also recognises the limited ability of teachers and other school personnel to be fully rational under all circumstances at all times. It is no longer possible (and undoubtedly never was) for teachers to know everything they need to know to teach well in every given circumstance. Given the multiplicity of demands placed on them, the changing populations with whom they work, the growing bodies of knowledge they must know in order to teach, and the uncertainty that characterises life in schools in our society characterised by rapid technological growth, teachers are necessarily bounded in their rationality (Schon, 1983). For this reason, they must learn to work with others. Rather than working in isolation, as is typically the case in secondary school settings, teachers must work jointly with other professionals to serve their communities and students well (Lieberman and Miller, 1992; Little, 1992, 1993a, 1993b; Rosenholtz 1991).

However important it is that they do so, working with colleagues is extraordinarily difficult in the context of secondary schools. Most schools are not organised in ways to facilitate working with colleagues. Rather, secondary teachers are typically isolated from one another by subject matter departments that seldom integrate across disciplines, a heavy teaching load, a demanding set of extra-curricular responsibilities, and a changing knowledge base that requires considerable out-of-school time for preparation. Similarly, teachers have scant opportunity to learn how to work effectively with colleagues. Only recently have we coupled our understanding of the extraordinarily high cognitive demands of teaching with the inherent limitations of one's ability to know enough to teach well (Shulman and Carey, 1984). This knowledge has provided the impetus for preparing teachers with the *capacity* to work with others.

The need for collaborative work among the professional staff of schools is further underscored by our growing understanding of knowledge and learning. As we come to view learning as 'making meaning', and to recognise the role of others in this process of knowledge construction, we have begun to shift our conception of learning for teaching (and for other professional preparation for school personnel) from training to building capacity for this demanding and complex work (Grossman and Richert, 1997).

Part of the capacity that teachers and other school personnel must have is the capacity to participate fully in the governance of schools and in the determination of the new directions those schools could potentially take. It is within this capacity-building model that we in the US reclaim democracy as the central goal of education. The transition from a hierarchical, factory systems model to one that more closely approximates a non-hierarchical living system where building capacity is a central goal, requires our recognising the need for shared leadership (Lambert *et al.*, 1996). The system of professional education and support must adequately prepare teachers to do this expanded work and to sustain one another in the process. In such a living system, the organism grows and changes as the component parts respond to changing circumstances in self-directed and collaborative ways. Teachers are prepared to develop new directions for school practice, while simultaneously teaching children and engaging in ongoing enquiry. The current challenge of professional development for secondary schools is to build the capacity of its professional staff to accomplish these complex and demanding tasks, and at the same time establish schools where this work is supported and sustained.

While the literature cited at the outset of this chapter argues convincingly that secondary schools have a long way to go before they function in ways remotely like the living-systems model suggested here, it is our belief that the current shift away from training to capacity building in the preparation and support of school personnel could ultimately undo some of the universal regularities that have served to paralyse the progress of secondary schools in the United States and elsewhere.

CONCLUDING THOUGHTS

An interesting paradox occurred to us as we began to review the world of secondary schooling in preparation for this chapter. On the one hand, secondary schools appear to be characterised by certain regularities across time and distance. They are common in their form and regular in their function in ways that seem to belie the rapidly changing worlds that surround them. At the same time, we found that secondary schools rest in a context of continuous conversation about what they are for, and how they might best go about accomplishing their multiple and shifting goals. Interestingly, one of the regularities we found most powerful within these conversations about secondary schooling was the persistence of struggle about their purpose and consequent form. The metaphors used to describe the purposes of secondary school over time, for example, and those used to describe the working processes of life in secondary schools, provide access to changing conceptions about the work of secondary schools. And though these metaphors reveal shifts in conception that would suggest considerable change over time (how secondary schools look, how they are organised, how teachers teach, what teachers teach, what children are expected to do, what routines are in place, who is in charge and what systems indicate governance, and so forth), we found that secondary schools have remained and continue to look remarkably the same with regard to many or most of these factors.

A question that perplexes us now is whether or not (and in what ways) schools might continue to look fairly much the same, but be, in fact, importantly different. At the same time, we wonder if those ways in which they begin to look different, for example, in their structural form (as with the magnet schools in the US, or the 'restructured' schools), are but superficial changes that do not alter the core activities of teaching and learning and who gets taught in the first place. Another question we are left with at the end of the chapter is whether or not the metaphors we employ to describe secondary school practice and changes in that practice might be more accurate in revealing changing ideology about secondary schooling than they are at revealing changed practice. Perhaps the very language we use allows us to think that we are making important changes when, in fact, life in school remains fairly much as it always has been.

A look at secondary school policy raises a similar set of questions. The idea of school policy changing and schools remaining the same is discussed widely by educational historians. They point out that legislatures can pass laws and courts can set mandates, but ultimately, authority for shaping classroom practice rests with the teachers. Regardless of policy and mandates, if teachers do not want to change, the core of educational practice – curriculum, instruction, assessment and so forth – will not change. The sword is double-edged, of course. There are times when it is entirely appropriate for teachers, who know their students and community, to resist or adapt a mandated change. There are other times, however, when teachers may be operating from a different position; their resistance may be an attempt to protect usual routines or accustomed methods, even when those routines or methods no longer make sense.

We framed our consideration of secondary schools to stretch across the four common areas of secondary schooling: purpose, structure, curriculum and personnel. In the journey we encountered repeatedly several interrelated themes that correspond with the current reform conversation about secondary schooling in the US. Let us conclude with a brief discussion of those themes, and a consideration of what they contribute to our review of the secondary school.

The first of these themes is *access* – who has access to secondary school. The access theme is a generative one because the question of who has access to secondary school influences the purposes of school and how the work that goes on there is determined. In the United States there has been considerable change in who has access to secondary school. In many ways the changing school population has modified the secondary school agenda considerably. Where the school agenda has not altered in response to changing demographics, schools fall short of their goal of preparing students to participate productively in work and community.

In this way access and *equity*, the second theme of this chapter, are linked. The issue of access raises the issue of equity because greater access, in theory, results in greater equity; as larger numbers of youth have access to the secondary school experience, they will have a more equitable opportunity to participate fully in society. As we discussed in the purposes section of the chapter, however, having access to secondary school does not ensure equity.

The tension between access and equity comes when different groups of youths receive a different quality of education within the context of school. In the United States the issue of differential quality is exacerbated by the issue of diversity. The already-complex world of secondary schooling is rendered even more complex by the multiple and changing populations of children who arrive at the schoolhouse door. We have learned over time that in order for children to experience success in school, the programme has to take into account who they are, what they know, what they care about, how they learn, and so forth. Different students often need to know different things. Sometimes they learn in different ways. Always they raise new concerns for their teachers to consider.

This raises the third theme of our chapter, *quality* as it concerns the goal of excellence in secondary schooling. We opened our argument with a statement concerning the regularities of secondary school and a lament that secondary schools are slow to change and therefore slow to achieve a level of excellence we want to posit as a goal of secondary schooling worldwide. The questions raised by the issue of quality are many, however: What does quality actually mean for secondary schools? What do secondary school students need to know and be able to do? Is quality the same for all students? Is there a common body of knowledge that all citizens should share and therefore towards which all schools should be directed? Might quality be more powerfully connected with educational processes than it is with outcomes?

Our strategy of employing the metaphor shift as a mechanism for examining secondary schools has reminded us that, in spite of their resistance to change, secondary schools are in many ways dynamic places, housed with eager people who are actively working towards both individual and community goals. While we found that at any particular time one metaphor dominated to describe each of the four aspects of high school we considered in our review, the metaphor never existed in absence of a tense relationship with another that was beckoning to take its place. The 'factory' metaphor to describe the structure of school, for example, was replaced by a more complex model that would better respond to changing demographics and a changing world. Those changing demographics and that changing world, incidentally, created just the tension that is revealed in the metaphor shift from 'systematic inequality' to 'equal opportunity' when it comes to describing the purpose of secondary school. The equity ideal that was aimed for as the purpose of secondary school shifted, resulted in the factory structure to accommodate that changing educational goal. The tension that exists between what is and what is next to come, is as ubiquitous in the education world as are the connections between the purposes, practices and consequences which generate those tensions in the first place.

Our method of examining shifting metaphors as a means of understanding secondary schools leads to a conclusion that holds both caution and hope. The metaphors that we found descriptive of the world of secondary school, reveal an 'either/or' tendency that can, and sometimes has, paralysed educational thought and practice. This need not be, however; we are encouraged to find that current thinking in the world of secondary schools is moving away from dichotomies. The discussion of the purposes of secondary school provides an example. Embedded within the purposes discussion is the persistent tension between equal access or opportunity in schooling, on the one hand, and academic excellence on the other. The question of how to provide equal access to all and maintain academic excellence at the same time suggests that we think not about accomplishing one or the other of these important outcomes, but that we strive to accomplish both simultaneously.

It is with the image of secondary schools as accomplishing both excellence and equity that we choose to end our chapter. We are looking towards a future where secondary schools worldwide define their purposes, create their structures, develop their curricula, and prepare and support their personnel fully to meet the changing educational needs of the changing populations of secondary students, and the changing world, that they are designed to serve.

NOTES

1 'Educational core' is a term used by Richard Elmore (1996) of Harvard University. Elmore explains the core of educational practice to include 'how teachers understand the nature of knowledge and the student's role in learning, and how these ideas about knowledge and learning are manifested in

teaching and classwork. The "core" also includes structural arrangements of schools, such as the physical layout of classrooms, students grouping practices, teachers' responsibilities for groups of students, and relations among teachers in their work with students, as well as processes for assessing student learning and communicating it to students, teachers, parents, administrators, and other interested parties' (p. 2).

2 We borrow this phrase from David Tyack, *The One Best System: A History of American Urban Education*, Cambridge, MA: Harvard University Press, 1974.

REFERENCES

Apple, M. (1990) *Ideology and Curriculum* (2nd edn). London and New York: Routledge.

Apple, Michael W. (1982) *Education and Power*. Boston: Routledge & Kegan Paul.

Bowles, Samuel and Gintis, Herbert (1976) *Schooling in Capitalist America*. New York: Basic Books.

Cuban, L. (1984) *How Teachers Taught: Constancy and Change in American Classrooms: 1890–1980*. New York: Longman.

Cuban, L. (1990) 'Reforming again, again, and again'. *Educational Researcher*, 19, 3–13.

Darling-Hammond, L. (1993) 'Reframing the school reform agenda: Developing capacity for school transformation'. *Phi Delta Kappan*, 74 (10), 752–761.

Elmore, Richard F. (1996) 'Getting to scale with good educational practice'. *Harvard Educational Review*, 66 (2), 1–26.

Fine, M. (1991) *Framing Dropouts*. Albany, NY: State University of New York.

Flinders, D. J. (1988) 'Teacher isolation and the new reform'. *Journal of Curriculum and Supervision*, 4 (1), 17–29.

Gilligan, C. (1982) *In a Different Voice*. Cambridge, MA: Harvard University Press.

Goodlad, J. (1984) *A Place Called School*. New York: McGraw-Hill.

Grossman, P. L. (1996) 'Of regularities and reform: Navigating the subject-specific territory of high schools'. In M. W. McLaughlin and I. Oberman (eds) *Teacher Learning: New Policies, New Practices*. New York: Teachers College Press.

Grossman, P. L. and Richert, A. E. (1997) 'Building capacity and commitment for leadership in pre-service teacher education'. *Journal of School Leadership* 6 (2), 202–210.

Gutierrez, K. (1992) 'The social contexts of literacy instruction for Latino children'. Paper presented at the Annual Meeting of the American Educational Research Association, San Francisco, April 1992.

Gutierrez, K. (1993) 'Scripts, counterscripts, and multiple scripts'. Paper presented at the Annual Meeting of the American Educational Research Association, Atlanta, GA, April 1993.

Lambert, L., Collay, M., Dietz, M. E., Kent, K. and Richert, A. E. (1996) *Who Will Save Our Schools? Teachers as Constructivist Leaders*. Thousand Oaks, CA: Corwin Press.

Leake, Donald O. and Leake, Brenda L. (1992) 'Islands of hope: Milwaukee's first African American immersion schools'. *Journal of Negro Education* 61 (1), 24–29.

Lieberman, A. and Miller, L. (1992) *Teachers, Their World and Their Work: Implications for School Improvement*. New York: Teachers College Press.

Little, J. W. (1992) 'Norms of collegiality and experimentation: Workplace conditions of school success'. *American Educational Research Journal*, 19, 32–340.

Little, J. W. (1993a) 'Professional community in comprehensive high schools: The two worlds of academic and vocational teachers'. In J. W. Little and M. W. McLaughlin (eds) *Teachers' Work: Individuals, Colleagues, and Contexts*. New York: Teachers College Press, 137–163.

Little, J. W. (1993b) 'Teachers' professional development in a climate of educational reform'. *Educational Evaluation and Policy Analysis*, 15 (3), 129–151.

McDonald, J. (1995) 'Humanizing the "shopping mall" high school'. *Education Week*, 14 (28).

McNeil, L. M. (1986) *Contradictions of Control*. London and New York: Routledge.

Mayeroff, M. (1971) *On Caring*. New York: Harper and Row.

Noblit, G. W. (1993) 'Power and caring'. *American Educational Research Journal*, 30 (1), 23–38.

Noddings, N. (1984) *Caring: A Feminine Approach to Ethics and Moral Education*. Berkeley, CA: University of California Press.

Oakes, J. (1985). *Keeping Track: How Schools Structure Inequality*. New Haven: Yale University Press.

Oakes, J., Gamoran, A. and Page, R. N. (1992) 'Curriculum differentiation: Opportunities, outcomes, and meanings'. In P. W. Jackson (ed), *Handbook of Research on Curriculum*. New York: Macmillan, 570–608.

Oldenquist, A. (1991) 'Community and de-alienation'. In A. Oldenquist and M. Rosner (eds), *Alienation, Community, and Work*. New York: Greenwood Press, 91–108.

O'Neil, John (1995) 'On schools as learning organisations: A conversation with Peter Senge'. *Educational Leadership*, April, 20–23.

Rose, M. (1989) *Lives on the Boundary*. New York: Free Press.

Rosenholtz, S. (1991) *Teachers' Workplace: The Social Organization of Schools*. New York: Teachers College Press.

Sarason, S. (1972) *The Creation of Settings and the Future Societies*. San Francisco: Jossey-Bass.

Sarason, S. (1990) *The Predictable Failure of Educational Reform*. San Francisco, CA: Jossey Bass.

Sarason, S. (1997) *Revisiting 'The Culture of School' and the Problem of Reform*. New York: Teachers College Press.

Schaps, E. and Solomon, D. (1990) 'Schools and classrooms as caring communities'. *Educational Leadership*, 48 (3), 38–41.

Schon, Donald A. (1983) *The Reflective Practitioner*. New York: Basic Books.

Seemen, M. (1995) 'On the meaning of alienation'. *American Sociological Review*, 24, 783–791.

Shulman, L. S. and Carey, N. B. (1984) 'Psychology and the limitations of individual rationality: Implications for the study of reasoning and civility'. *Review of Educational Research*, 54, Winter, 501–524.

Siskin, L. S. (1994) *Realms of Knowledge: Academic Departments in Secondary Schools*. New York: Falmer Press.

Sizer, T. R. (1984) *Horace's Compromise: The Dilemma of the American High School*. Boston: Houghton Mifflin.

Sizer, T. R. (1992) *Horace's School: Redesigning the American High School*. Boston: Houghton Mifflin.

Stainback, S. and Stainback, W. (1992) 'Controversial issues confronting special education: Divergent perspectives'. Boston: Allyn and Bacon.

Sykes, G. (1996) 'Reform of and as professional development'. *Phi Delta Kappan*, 78, 465–476.

Tyack, D. B. (1976) 'Ways of seeing: An essay of the history of compulsory schooling'. *Harvard Educational Review*, 46 (3), 355–389.

Tyack, D. and Cuban, L. (1995) *Tinkering towards Utopia: Reflections on a Century of Public School Reform*. Cambridge, MA: Harvard University Press.

Tyack, D. and Tobin, W. (1994) 'The "grammar" of schooling: Why has it been so hard to change? *American Educational Research Journal*, 43 (1), 453–479.

US Department of Education National Center for Education Statistics (1996) Digest of Educational Statistics 1996, NCES 96–133. Washington, DC: US Department of Education.

Wang, Margaret C. and Reynolds, Maynard C. (1996) 'Progressive inclusion: Meeting new challenges in special education'. *Theory into Practice*, 35 (1), 20–25.

36

NEW PERSPECTIVES ON THE EVOLUTION OF SECONDARY SCHOOL EDUCATION IN THE UK

Roy Lowe

LEGAL STRUCTURE

The most recent legal definition of secondary education in the United Kingdom is contained in the 1996 Education Act. This defines secondary education thus:

> full time education suitable to the requirements of pupils of compulsory school age who are either senior pupils or junior pupils of 10 years 6 months and over whom it is expedient to educate with them; and full time education for pupils over compulsory school age but ordinarily under 19, which is suitable for, and provided at, a school.

Mercifully, this is also a fairly apt description of what passes as secondary education in the United Kingdom at the present time. It takes place in schools; it is full time; for the majority of pupils it terminates at the age of 16; but for a significant minority it extends to the age of 18 or 19. Those who continue to pursue work at sixth form level within Further Education establishments are considered to have left secondary education behind them. Ninety-three per cent of secondary pupils are educated in schools provided and maintained by the state while 7 per cent are educated in private institutions, the most prestigious of which are called 'public schools'. However, recent changes mean that the distinction between state and private education is by no means as clear-cut as was the case earlier in the twentieth century.

The law identifies three agencies which, between them, have responsibility to ensure that this secondary education is provided efficiently. First, it is the responsibility of parents to ensure that, through regular attendance at school or otherwise, each child receives 'efficient full time education suitable to his age, ability and aptitude and to any special educational needs he may have'. The word 'otherwise' in this legislation effectively grants to parents the power to see that secondary education is provided for their children through agencies other than schools. Thus, a small number of adolescents are educated informally outside the school system. Second, the schools and their governing bodies have a responsibility to ensure that education is available in the form specified by the legislation. Thus, for example, schools have the responsibility to ensure they are offering the national curriculum, that they are specifying clearly the times and days which are prescribed for pupils to be at school, and that the various requirements for religious, personal, social and moral education are all in place. Third, it falls to the local education authority (LEA) to ensure that the education provided by the schools for which they are responsible is 'efficient' and 'suitable'. The local authority's responsibility is one of enforcement in this respect. The efficiency of Independent Schools is determined by the Secretary of State. All schools, whether state or private, have to be registered under the 1996 Act, but the fact that they are registered does not constitute evidence that they are providing efficient and suitable education as defined by the law. Interestingly, both the Secretary of State and the LEAs are required to 'have regard to the general principle that pupils are to be educated in accordance with the wishes of their parents, so far as that is compatible with the provision of efficient instruction and training and the avoidance of unreasonable public expenditure'.

In order to ensure that each of these agencies is fulfilling its obligations, there are a variety of constraints in place. Parents are liable to prosecution if they fall to fulfil their part of the bargain. The Secretary of State is given power to publish guidance for schools and local authorities on the interpretation of existing legislation and may use Circulars to advise or explain. Whilst these Circulars do not have the power of legislation, their specification of the views of the Secretary of State leave the secondary schools with a clear indication of their responsibilities. So, secondary schools and local authorities that fail to follow the advice given in Circulars may be held to be unreasonable. Similarly, local education authorities are subject to redress by central government if they fail to oversee the provision of efficient secondary education within their areas.

There are further legal complications to this already complex situation. Two of the most significant are that, first, local education authorities may provide for pupils living within their geographical area of responsibility by either purchasing school places in neighbouring authorities or by purchasing places in boarding schools at greater distance. Most LEAs use these arrangements to greater or lesser degree to ensure the efficient provision of secondary education. Second, there exists within England a Funding Agency for Schools which takes direct responsibility for Grant Maintained Schools. These schools are not subject to the oversight of their local education authority but are answerable directly to central government. There are also a significant number of middle schools which may be deemed secondary if the majority of their pupils are above the age of 11.

HISTORY AND EVOLUTION

This complex legal structure is fully comprehensible only in the light of the history and evolution of secondary schools in the United Kingdom. Before 1902 the state took no direct responsibility for the provision of secondary education in the United Kingdom, although there was already a thriving and well-established system of secondary schools for boys. During the sixteenth century grammar schools appeared in many towns and villages, most of them funded by the monies raised from the dissolution of the chantries in 1553. These grammar schools enjoyed varied fortunes, but most survived. With industrialisation in the nineteenth century came the growth of towns and cities and the expansion of the middle classes, their income based on commerce and the growing tertiary sector of the economy, with aspirations that their sons, in particular, would receive some kind of secondary education. The swift growth of secondary education in the nineteenth century began with the appearance of the British public (i.e. private) schools in their modern form. Both the landed aristocracy and newly enriched industrialists wished to send their sons away for a gentlemanly education in boarding schools which, by preference, were located at some distance from the hazards and health dangers that were associated with the growing towns. The coming of the railways made these schools economically viable, and during the second half of the nineteenth century numerous well-established London schools relocated in rural situations in the south of England. By the end of the century there were over 100 of these 'public schools' offering an education focused on the classics, the study of literature, mathematics and history, and with a strong emphasis on the increasingly popular team games, especially rugby, cricket and soccer. During this period also, a smaller number of public schools for girls were established.

Those members of the urban middle class who could not afford to send their sons away to these public schools clamoured for more efficient local secondary schools. Their cry was answered by the Endowed Schools Commission (1868), which provided a template for the modernisation of the town grammar schools. During the following 30 years, under the terms of the 1869 Endowed Schools Act, commissioners visited over 1,000 schools across England and Wales, leaving behind precise instructions for the modernisation of the curriculum and classifying schools as first, second or third grade. Many of these schools received financial support from the Department of Science and Art (the first government agency to give any direct financial support to secondary schools in Britain) and by 1914 these schools were preparing a growing number of their pupils for entry to Oxford and Cambridge, to the growing number of civic universities, to employment in commerce or to professions in their local townships.

However, even these reforms did not enable the existing schools to come close to meeting the growing demand for secondary education. Significant administrative reforms at the turn of the century made possible the further expansion of the secondary sector and ensured that it would come increasingly under the influence and control of central government. First, the Board of Education was established in 1899, bringing together three pre-existing departments. The 1902 Education Act established local education authorities for the first time, and these were given the power to open their own municipal secondary schools alongside the existing endowed grammar schools. Many of these new LEAs used this as an opportunity to open municipal girls' secondary schools, with the result that the Edwardian period saw a swift increase in the opportunities for girls to pursue a secondary school education in Britain. The result was that by the end of the First World War there were very few towns of any size in Britain that did not have some kind of provision for secondary education. These arrangements enabled a steady drift towards universal secondary education during the first half of the twentieth century.

This evolutionary nature of the growth of secondary education in Britain enabled several peculiarities which have persisted until the present time. Secondary schools were founded by numerous differing agencies, in some cases merchant companies, in some cases private trusts, in some cases religious organisations. The 1902 Act allowed pre-existing secondary schools to receive some kind of support from the local education authority, although by no means all chose to do so. The result was an administrative hotch-potch, some schools remaining completely outside of the state system, some receiving support from the local authorities but not coming fully within the state system, some refusing to co-operate with the new local education authorities and receiving their funding direct from central government (Direct Grant Schools) and others directly under the control of the LEAs. Beyond this, there were the schools actually founded and run by the LEAs. Thus it is that, down to the present day, there are voluntary aided and voluntary controlled schools under the direction of local education authorities as well as the LEA schools. Each of these categories of school operates under a slightly different set of regulations. The vested interests involved have proved so great that at no time has it proved possible to devise legislation which brings to an end all of these anomalies in the provision of secondary education. It should be remembered too, to complicate the situation further, that for the first half of the twentieth century, many working-class pupils remained throughout their school career in elementary schools, continuing there to the age of 14.

However, there were increasingly strenuous efforts to distinguish clearly between elementary and secondary education. The Board of Education under R. L. Morant, during its early years sought to distinguish clearly the type of curriculum which was appropriate for secondary schools as distinct from elementary. In 1904 a model secondary school curriculum was issued which any school in receipt of a government grant was obliged to follow. Although this curriculum was in force for only three years, it provided a template that led to considerable uniformity of secondary school curricula in Britain, and many commentators have remarked on the similarities between the 1904 curriculum and the national curriculum which was specified in the 1988 Education Act. Furthermore the 1926 Hadow Report, *The Education of the Adolescent*, called for a clear progression from elementary to secondary education. It identified 'a tide rising in the veins of youth' which justified the transfer of pupils from one school to another of different type at the age of 11. The Hadow Report coincided with the growth of the science of educational psychology and the publicising of intelligence tests as a viable tool for classifying pupils. A 1924 Board of Education report on *The Use of Psychological Tests* appeared to give credence to this new science, and during the following 20 years a growing number of local education authorities sought to ensure that pupils transferred at the age of 11 from elementary to either secondary or senior schools, using intelligence tests as a device to discriminate between pupils.

The 1907 Free Place Regulations insisted that every school in receipt of financial support from the government must offer at least one quarter of its places to non-fee-paying pupils. This led to a significant upturn in opportunities for working-class children to aspire to secondary education, although the secondary schools remained predominantly middle-class in recruitment. The ending of the Free Place Regulations at the height of the economic depression in 1931 meant the denial of this opportunity to less well-off families, and led to growing pressure from within the Labour Party for secondary education to be made available to all, as advocated by R. H. Tawney in 1922. Beyond this, there was a growing number within the Labour Party (especially the National Association of Labour Teachers, which was particularly strong in London) who were arguing that all pupils, whatever their ability, should go to a single secondary school, even though they conceded that it might be appropriate for there to be separate tracks provided within that secondary school.

This drift towards universal secondary schooling was confirmed by the 1944 Education Act, the only significant piece of social legislation during the Second World War. This specified that education should be separated into discrete stages, with pupils transferring at the age of 11 from primary to secondary schools. It also made secondary schooling universal, in the first instance to the age of 15+, but to the age of 16+ as soon as provision could be made. In the event, this was not achieved until 1972. This legislation was permissive on questions of the curriculum (the word 'curriculum' was in fact not used at any point in the Act). However, the general assumption was, under the influence of the educational psychologists who remained a powerful lobby, that children would receive different forms of secondary education. Therefore, the majority of local education authorities implemented the 1944 Act by opening secondary modern and, in many cases, technical secondary schools alongside the pre-existing grammar schools. It became pretty well universal in the immediate postwar period for pupils to be selected for these different secondary schools through the use of intelligence tests, so that the 11+ examination became a feature of British education.

Dissatisfaction with this device, which was focused particularly within the Labour Party, led a growing number of LEAs during the 1950s and 1960s to re-structure their systems of secondary education, abandoning the 11+ examination and introducing comprehensive schools. Many existing secondary schools were converted into comprehensives, whilst a significant number of new, purpose-built comprehensive schools were opened. This process was accelerated, although not made mandatory, by Circular 10/65, by which Harold Wilson's Labour government invited all local authorities to set out their plans for comprehensive reorganisation. Although Ted Heath's 1970 government very quickly rescinded this Circular, confirming that local education authorities would be left to make their own judgements on the most appropriate secondary schooling within their areas, the drift towards comprehensive schooling was inexorable. By the end of that decade, over 80 per cent of pupils in secondary schools in Britain were being educated in a comprehensive. Perhaps the most significant element in this reorganisation was that it led to the collapse of single-sex secondary education as a phenomenon in modern Britain, and resulted in the majority of pupils going into mixed secondary schools by the end of the twentieth century.

Throughout this period the private sector remained largely inviolate, with these major changes having little impact beyond the appearance of a growing number of female pupils in the public schools, often initially at sixth form level but increasingly throughout the school. Schemes proposed in 1944 to encourage the LEAs to sponsor selected pupils at public schools only ever resulted in a very small number of such pupils taking up places. Frustrated that the Direct Grant Schools (which were in reality the most prestigious of the day grammar schools) were able to stand outside of the sweeping changes taking place at local level, Harold Wilson's second administration ended the Direct Grant arrangements in 1976, attempting to force these schools to pass under the aegis of the local education authorities and so participate in comprehensive reorganisation. This backfired spectacularly, as over 100 of these schools opted instead to join the private sector, thus reinforcing the distinction between state and private education. It was not until Margaret Thatcher's government announced its Assisted Places Scheme in 1981 that the state resumed its practice of sponsoring pupils through the private schools.

Changes in the examination structure matched these trends, although belatedly. In 1951 the General Certificate of Education (GCE) replaced the School Certificate examinations which had been in use since the early years of the twentieth century. To pass the old School

Certificate, whether at ordinary or higher level, pupils had to perform well in a range of subjects. The GCE enabled, for the first time, individual subject entry, a practice that has subsequently become almost universal. In 1965 the GCE examination was complemented by the Certificate in Secondary Education (CSE), aimed at the growing number of pupils who aspired to qualifications, but were not judged capable of succeeding at GCE. During the following 20 years a variety of schemes brought these two examinations into ever-closer co-ordination until, in 1986, the then Conservative government announced that they would be scrapped and replaced by a single General Certificate of Secondary Education (GCSE). However, this did not mean a 'once and for all' simplification of the examination system, since during the 1980s a growing number of B.Tec and GNVQ qualifications began to appear, catering in the main for technical and applied subjects, and inadvertently sustaining the tracking element within British secondary education. During the 1990s these have become a significant element in examinations in Britain for 16+ and 18+.

During the 1980s several developments made secondary schools more answerable to government and wider society. Publication of Inspectors' reports, new arrangements for local financial management, the weakening of the powers of the LEAs, and the specification that there could be no clearly defined catchment areas for secondary schools (forcing them to compete for pupils), all worked to transform the context within which secondary schools operate. Beyond this, the 1985/1986 teachers' industrial action had several consequences. It semi-permanently weakened the teachers' unions, it had a long-term deleterious effect on out-of-school activities, particularly team games, but most importantly, it resulted in the imposition of tight conditions of service for schoolteachers, including a prescription of the number of hours that they would be available. This, together with a significant increase in the bureaucratisation of the secondary system during the 1980s and 1990s, has resulted in a widespread perception that secondary schools in Britain are, at the close of the twentieth century, more tightly controlled and regulated than was the case in any earlier part of this century.

CURRICULUM

The 1904 Regulations for secondary schools demanded that all schools receiving financial support from the government must provide a general curriculum which 'should provide for instruction in English language and literature, at least one language other than English, geography, history, mathematics, science and drawing, with due provision for manual work and physical exercises, and in a girls' school, for housewifery'. These Regulations went on to specify precisely how much time should be devoted to each of these subjects. Since then, the curricula of secondary schools have remained remarkably stable over time, despite the many administrative changes that have taken place. It was widely assumed after 1944 that universal education would involve the development of three different kinds of secondary school – grammar, technical and modern. Each of these was to have its own curriculum. It was foreseen that the grammar schools would concentrate more on language, literature and the pure sciences. Technical schools were intended to place a greater emphasis on technical subjects and applied sciences: meanwhile, the modern schools were to have a more severely practical focus to their curriculum. In the event, as more and more schools of whatever type joined in a competitive scramble for success in external examinations, the differences between these three types of schools became less apparent, while the 'grammar school curriculum' which had been developed at the start of the century became steadily more universal. Under the influence of the Schools Council, established in 1964 and in existence for 20 years, debates came to focus more on the extent to which curricula should be child-centred (rather than heavily didactic) and less on the structure of the secondary school curriculum. None the less a number of Schools Council projects advocated greater fusion of such subjects, particularly within the field of social sciences, and the 1960s and 1970s did see some local attempts to redraw the map of the secondary school curriculum. This tension between 'progressive' and 'traditional' approaches to secondary school pedagogy has persisted down to the present time and was reflected in the recent demand by the Chief Inspector for Schools that teaching should be slanted more towards whole-class rather than individualised learning and study. The furore that this recommendation generated in the educational press is evidence of the controversial nature of this issue at the present time.

However, debates on the structure of the secondary school curriculum were largely ended by the introduction in 1988 as part of the Education Reform Act of a national curriculum. This prescribed a broad and balanced curriculum for all pupils which was to be offered by all state schools and taken up fully by each pupil. The national curriculum comprises the core subjects of English, mathematics and science, and alongside this technology (including information technology), history, geography, music, art, physical education and a modern foreign language. Secondary schools are obliged to offer at least one language of a European Union country such as French, German or Spanish. Within Wales, the national curriculum specifies the Welsh language as a core subject in Welsh-speaking schools and as a foundation subject in others. The national curriculum specified four key stages of schooling, with Key Stage 3 covering the ages 11–14 and Key Stage 4, ages 14–16. In this fourth stage art, music, history and geography are no longer compulsory, introducing an element of choice for pupils. Ironically, religious education is compulsory in all state schools, although it is not part of the national curriculum. Syllabuses for religious education have to be agreed locally and kept under regular review. Since September 1994 state secondary schools are also required to make provision for sex education for all pupils. The national curriculum also specifies attainment targets (i.e. the knowledge, skills and understanding that are to be acquired by pupils). Ten level grading systems have been introduced to enable the assessment of pupil progress in each of these subject areas. There is also a legal requirement that the results of these assessment procedures are made public through the publication of 'league tables' of schools, thus enabling parents to form judgements on the comparative effectiveness of schools in their area. These elements, together with the local financial management of schools (which was also introduced in 1998) and the abandonment of catchment areas, have meant that schools are involved in a very fierce struggle for pupils, with their perceived effectiveness in delivering the national curriculum as one of the key elements in their success.

Concerned at the furore concerning curriculum overload and the bureaucratisation of teaching which followed the introduction of the national curriculum, in 1993 Sir Ron Dearing was asked to undertake a major review of the national curriculum. This resulted in a significant 'slimming down' and streamlining, reducing the curriculum content in many subjects and offering schools greater flexibility, particularly for 14–16 year old pupils. For these older pupils, the ten level scale was scrapped and only English, mathematics and science, physical education, religious education and sex education remained compulsory. Up to 40 per cent of curriculum time was left open to individual choice for these older pupils.

These curriculum changes have also transformed the role of the Inspectorate. Since 1992, the Office for Standards in Education (OFSTED) in England, and OHMCI in Wales, have been responsible for the inspection of schools, with a brief to report specifically on the quality of the education provided and the educational standards attained. These inspection reports are in the public domain, so that the work of schools and teachers is placed under close scrutiny and parents are given further information against which to judge the comparative performance of schools. It is this element of public accountability and scrutiny which is probably the most significant curriculum change in recent years. In 1960, David Eccles, the then Minister of Education, referred in the House of Commons to 'the secret garden of the curriculum'. He announced a series of 'commando-like raids' by the government. By the end of the twentieth century, the process he initiated has resulted in the work of the secondary schools being exposed to public scrutiny to a greater degree than ever before. The question of whether or not these changes will prove to be irreversible is one of the most intriguing hanging over secondary education in the early twenty-first century.

MANAGEMENT

In recent years, a number of developments have impinged upon the management of secondary schools. In 1980 the Thatcher government responded to the 1977 Taylor Report by legislation that ensured parental representation on secondary school governing bodies. In 1986 the powers of these governing bodies were extended. They became responsible for school finances, for oversight of the curriculum and for staffing; they were also obliged to present annual reports to the parent bodies. In the same year, 1986, a new category of school was introduced, the City Technology College. These schools, located in inner-city areas, were an attempt to draw private sector sponsors into co-operation with the government to fund schools. Fifteen of these schools were set up.

The 1988 Education Reform Act saw further extensions to the power of secondary school governors. Now they assumed responsibity for ensuring that the national curriculum was delivered and were obliged to inform parents of pupil achievement. Also, and most significant, responsibility for school finances was delegated to school governing bodies. This local management of schools permanently weakened the power of the local authorities to influence what was going on 'on the ground', although the LEAs remain responsible for the payment of teachers. Another feature of the 1988 Act was the encouragement of schools to go for Grant Maintained status. All secondary schools were invited to consider whether they wished to ballot parental bodies with a view to the school being freed from local education authority control and placed under the aegis of the Funding Agency for Schools. Five years later, Independent schools were given the right to opt for Grant Maintained status on the same basis, thus blurring even more the distinction between the public and private sectors of secondary education.

The 1993 Education Act also allowed for the establishment of a new category of technology colleges. These would be schools that had a technical bias but were not necessarily located in inner-city areas. Another important clause of the 1993 legislation allowed for 'failing schools' to be taken over and put under new management. The judgement on which schools were 'failing' rested with the Inspectorate and this innovation had the effect of placing many schools under a permanent sense of threat. Also, a series of provisions between 1992 and 1994 resulted in secondary schools playing a much fuller part in the provision of initial teacher training than had been the case previously. They were now encouraged to establish much closer links with the Teacher Training Agency and were also given the right to establish their own school-centred initial teacher training schemes. This plethora of changes has transformed the management of secondary schools in the final years of the twentieth century. They now find themselves more directly answerable to their local communities, and under direct public scrutiny to a greater degree than ever before.

SCOTLAND AND NORTHERN IRELAND

Many of the characteristics of secondary schools which have been described above are shared by schools in Scotland and Northern Ireland. However, since the legal framework for education is different in both of these countries, there are significant points of contrast with secondary schooling in England and Wales. The existence of the Scottish General Teaching Council ensures that the teaching profession retains greater autonomy in Scotland than elsewhere in the United Kingdom. The Scottish school boards, which are the equivalent of the English governing bodies, are obliged to have a majority of parent members, thus ensuring an even greater element of community involvement in control of the schools. Devolved school management is less well developed in Scotland, although the government has announced plans for a greater degree of financial autonomy for schools. Secondary schools in Scotland are answerable to the Scottish Consultative Council on the Curriculum. The two main examining bodies are the Scottish Examination Board and the Scottish Vocational Education Council. The existence of these two examining bodies has resulted in a clear distinction between academic and vocational routes through secondary education in Scotland. The Scottish Higher remains the main route into university. It is taken by students in the equivalent of what is the lower sixth year in England and Wales and involves a wider range of subjects, with three passes being seen as a minimum level for university entry, although most students are entered for more subjects than this.

Schooling in Northern Ireland is the responsibility of the Department of Education for Northern Ireland and this recognises a variety of schools. There is a significantly greater proportion of schools under voluntary and denominational control in Northern Ireland and parents have well-established rights to express preferences for the secondary school they wish their children to attend. Arrangements for local school management and reporting back to parents are not dissimilar to those in place in England and Wales, although the Northern Ireland Council for Curriculum, Examinations and Assessment has introduced secondary school curricula which must include cultural heritage, education for mutual understanding, health education, information technology, economic awareness and careers education. Thus, the particular circumstances of Northern Ireland have resulted in school curricula which differ significantly from those in place elsewhere in the United Kingdom. It remains to be seen whether the coming of devolved government within the United Kingdom will result in even greater distinctiveness of secondary education in Wales, Northern Ireland and Scotland than is already the case in the early years of the twenty-first century.

CURRENT ISSUES

Secondary education has undergone massive change within the United Kingdom in recent years. It is impossible to be certain what the long-term impact of these changes will be as we enter the new millennium. However, several key issues can be identified and these raise significant questions for any student of education. In brief, will the shift to local management of schools, involving greater power for parent governors, prove to be 'once and for all' and irreversible in the twenty-first century? Will the enhanced power of the Inspectorate, together with the increased bureaucratisation for teachers in secondary schools which follows all these changes, result in a semi-permanent downgrading of the prestige of secondary education in modern Britain? Alternatively, will the introduction of new General Teaching Councils in England and Wales result in enhancement of the professional autonomy of teachers as we go into the next century? Will the curricula of secondary schools be responsive to the demands of the information age, the global network and the global economy, or will the relative historical stability of secondary school curricula in Britain persist? Will future governments identify ways of ensuring the accountability of secondary schools in modern Britain whilst, at the same time, ensuring the maintenance of the self-esteem and professional autonomy of those who teach in them?

Secondary education in the United Kingdom has become politicised in the closing years of the twentieth century to a greater extent than ever before. It remains to be seen how this will impact on the management and day-to-day working of the schools as well as the structure of the secondary education system as a whole. At the time of writing, it appears unlikely that we have yet reached the end of this period of kaleidoscopic change.

SELECT BIBLIOGRAPHY

Benn, C. and Chitty, C. (1996) *Thirty Years On: Is Comprehensive Education Alive and Well or Struggling to Survive?* London: Fulton.

Benn, C. and Simon, B. (1970) *Halfway There*. London: McGraw Hill.

Central Office of Information (1994) *Education Reforms in Schools*. London: HMSO.

Chitty, C. (ed.) (1987) *Redefining the Comprehensive Experience*. London: Institute of Education.

Chitty, C. (1989) *Towards a New Education System: The Victory of the New Right?* Lewes: Falmer Press.

Chitty, C. (1992) *The Education System Transformed: A Guide to the School Reforms*. Manchester: Baseline Books.

DfEE (1995) *The English Education System: An Overview of Structure and Policy*. London: DfEE.

Flude, M. and Hammer, M. (eds) (1990) *The Education Reform Act 1988*. Lewes: Falmer Press.

Gosden, P. (1983) *The Education System since 1944*. Oxford: Martin Robertson.

Kerckhoff, A. C., Fogelman, K., Crook, D. and Reeder, D. (1996) *Going Comprehensive in England and Wales: A Study of Uneven Change*. London: Woburn Press.

Leill, P., Coleman, J. and Poole, K. (eds) (1998) *The Law of Education* (9th edn). London: Butterworth.

Le Metais, J. (1995) *Legislating for Change: School Reforms in England and Wales, 1979–1994*. Slough: NFER.

Lowe, R. (1988) *Education in the Post-war Years*. London: Routledge.

Lowe, R. (ed.) (1989) *The Changing Secondary School*. Falmer, Lewes.

Lowe, R. (1997) *Schooling and Social Change, 1964–1990*. London: Routledge.

McCulloch, G. (1989) *The Secondary Technical School: A Useable Past?* Lewes: Falmer.

McCulloch, G. (1994) *Educational Reconstruction: The 1944 Education Act and the Twenty-First Century*. London: Woburn Press.

McCulloch, G. (1998) *Failing the Ordinary Child? The Theory and Practice of Working-class Secondary Education*. Buckingham: Open University Press.

Open University (1988) *Through the School Gates: A Guide for Parents, Teachers and Governors*. London: Channel Four Television.

Ranson, S. (1990) *The Politics of Reorganising Schools*. London: Unwin Hyman.

Sanderson, M. (1995) *The Missing Stratum: Technical School Education in England, 1900–1990s*. London: Athlone Press.

Simon, B. (1988) *Bending the Rules: The Baker 'Reform' of Education*. London: Lawrence & Wishart.

Simon, B. (1991) *Education and the Social Order, 1940–1990*. London: Lawrence & Wishart.

Simon, B. (1994) *The State and Educational Change*. London: Lawrence & Wishart.

Simon, B. and Chitty, C. (1993) *SOS: Save Our Schools*. London: Lawrence & Wishart.

Weeks, A. (1986) *Comprehensive Schools: Past, Present and Future*. London: Methuen.

37

LEARNING ALONG THE WAY

The evolution of adult and continuing education

Steven Weiland

Adult and continuing education is a vast and varied enterprise. Broadly defined it is part of the experience of virtually every mature individual around the world.[1] As the terms are generally used – with closely allied terms like 'recurrent education' favoured in Europe or 'lifelong learning' favoured in North America – adult and continuing education refers to:

1 the many and diverse educational activities in which individuals or groups engage, some activities deliberately organised for learning and some not;
2 the design and administration of educational programmes, and the instructional component of them, in post-secondary educational institutions and in organisations of many kinds (corporations, museums, churches, etc.);
3 an academic or scholarly speciality or field, primarily in colleges of education and the applied social or behavioural sciences, though many professors of adult education would prefer 'discipline', reflecting increasing sophistication in research in recent decades (Jarvis, 1991).

As the extensive literature on adult and continuing education reveals, it is difficult to generalise across policies, practices, issues, problems and scholarly methods (Houle, 1992).

In the 1920s and 1930s in the United States attempts were made to bring theoretical coherence to educational activities and initiatives for adults (e.g. in the work of Eduard Lindeman [1926] and others; see Kett [1994]). In recent decades international organisations (e.g. UNESCO) have sought unity in a global conception of adult education. But at century's end there appears to be little hope for realising the potential in such efforts.

> No grand design, no generally accepted definition unites the scholars, practitioners, and institutions of adult and continuing education. . . . No abstractions have transcended the various segments of this field of scholarship and practice. The whole remains less than the sum of the parts.
>
> (Pittman, 1989, p. 15)

An international overview of adult education asserts that 'the growing specialization and fragmentation of purposes and target audiences calls [*sic*] into question whether a comprehensive concept can be devised which has any practical utility' (Titmus, 1994, p. 119). A comprehensive study done in the United States makes a similar claim: 'At the brink of the 21st century, adult education appears more diverse and fragmented than ever before' (Merriam and Brockett, 1997, p. 79).

THE LEARNING SOCIETY

While no general theory of adult and continuing education may be feasible at present, one idea with potential for coherence or integration has captured the interest of many observers and scholars. According to them, the advent of the *learning society* – in which learning over the lifespan is increasingly understood as the essential individual and organisational endeavour – is a sign of the direction of social and economic life. For example, K. Patricia Cross begins her account of *Adults as Learners* (1981) – perhaps the most influential text in the field – with a forceful statement of the new social significance of education:

> The learning society is growing because it must. It would be difficult to think of some way to live in a society changing as rapidly as ours without constantly learning new things. When life was simpler, one generation could pass along to the next generation what it needed to know to get along in the world; tomorrow was simply a repeat of yesterday. Now, however, the world changes faster than the generations, and individuals must live in several different worlds during their lifetimes.
>
> (Cross, 1981, p. 1)

Such sentiments are ubiquitous among adult educators and theorists of adult learning (e.g. Apps, 1988). They supply a sense of historical urgency to their work and they bind the academic interests of scholars like Cross with those of organisational and corporate educational leaders (e.g. Senge, 1990) admired for guiding the business world towards recognition of its educational role and thus underlining the limitations of the traditional college or university as a site for adult learning, and for enquiry into its value and uses in society. Thus, the learning society houses the 'learning organisation', particularly corporations whose success in the marketplace reflects learning by employees and executives as the primary activity of the workplace, yielding gains for both the individual and the organisation (Watkins and Marsick, 1993).

Still, there is a historical tension at the heart of the learning society. Its oldest formal conceptualisation is the Greek *Polis*, or the ideal of an educated citizenry prepared for active and open participation in public affairs. Many of those who use the phrase today credit it to the famous educational leader and innovator Robert Maynard Hutchins of the University of Chicago and his book *The Learning Society* (1968) which actually reflects many ideas associated with the classical ideal. But this part of the original argument for the learning society – attention to *what is most worth knowing* in addition to what must be learned for success at work – is incompatible with the vocational orientation of much adult and continuing education, including its interest in the leadership that business might provide in the reorientation of the curriculum and research priorities of the university.

For Hutchins, the learning society was an extension of his belief in the possibilities of a democratic culture, in which educational activities of all kinds – those supporting citizenship and the arts, for example – would be seen as a check on the narrowing of education by the demands of the professions and the workplace. And to Hutchins's original impulse and the more recent contributions of the private sector, there must be added current interest among the middle classes of industrialised nations in individual 'growth' or 'self-improvement'. Thus, the learning society stands for a combination of historical, institutional, organisational and personal forces at work in the late twentieth-century world.

The general idea of the learning society has gained momentum since the 1970s, including the efforts of government agencies and private organisations in the United States, Canada and Great Britain, with complementary activities at UNESCO and other international groups (e.g. Apps, 1988; Husen, 1974). The durability of the idea in Europe at least is illustrated in an inventive life history enquiry into adult learning in Finland (Antikainen *et al.*, 1996) and in reports issued in 1995 by the European Union (Commission of the European Communities, 1995) and by university leaders, the Council of University Rectors (Cochinaux and de Woot, 1995).

The Dutch scholar Hendrik Van der Zee has asserted what he takes to be the international consensus on the features of the learning society. His own contribution is a classification of 'criteria' for its development, or strategic issues needing institutional and governmental attention. They are adapted below to suggest the strengths and limits of the learning society as a conceptual framework for understanding worldwide adult and continuing education.

1 *A broadened definition of learning* that seeks to 'harmonise' guided and unguided educational forms in recognition of their complementary relations, with institutions, organisations and agencies less preoccupied with and protective of their own prerogatives and more inclined to understand lifelong education in terms of the larger picture of an individual's learning career.
2 *Redirection of the goals of learning towards 'completeness' of the individual*, or human development that includes not only vocational attainment but aesthetic, moral, physical and other kinds of improvement and personal satisfaction over the life-cycle.
3 *Increasing collective competence*, or the ability to learn and act with the availability of support systems such as books, tools and technology, facilities (e.g. museums and libraries), networks and databanks, organised groups, proven and innovative procedures for learning, myths and legends, and other means of learning that augment our individual capacities as they enable us to do things collectively.
4 *Fostering autonomy*, or improving the individual's capacity for education by incorporating the capacity for independence in the activities of all learning institutions, particularly in strategies used for teaching adults which can recognise the mature learner's perspectives on subjects and methods, without oversimplifying the difference between learning at early and later stages in the life-cycle.
5 *Adopting a political approach to learning*, or guaranteeing opportunities for lifelong learning in all spheres – not only the vocational – and particularly via the strengthening of 'collective competence' or the joint and communal use of educational support systems over the life-cycle (as in 3 above).

(Based on Van der Zee, 1991, p. 215)

Meeting such criteria means institutional and policy reforms, and changes in social and individual attitudes towards learning. And even the best accounts of the learning society still leave the practice of adult and continuing education at a high level of generalisation and abstraction. The British scholars Christina Hughes and Malcolm Tight (1995) believe that to be, in effect, essential to the 'mythic' role of the learning society, a utopian image signifying mainly 'hopes' and 'promises' with yet to be discovered relations to the complexities of economic and social life, to the academic disciplines, and to the actualities of education.

In the United States and Canada the research universities have only ambivalently accepted the idea of the learning society – perhaps because of its association with adult and continuing education – and thus, because they set the tone for higher education generally, in the mid-1990s the learning society is still far from an institutional priority. Even so, there are those who foresee the transformation of the university according to the ideals of the learning society (e.g. Apps, 1988; Field, 1996). And as noted above, private sector advocates of the learning organisation supply a complementary approach to adult learning in higher education. The learning society is a useful and durable idea – as myths generally are – whose application to social and institutional change since 1970 still offers to many government leaders and academic critics an appealing vision of the role of higher education in society, in the US and around the world.

WHAT MATURE LEARNERS DO: TYPES AND DOMAINS OF ADULT AND CONTINUING EDUCATION

One obstacle to a general theory of adult and continuing education is, of course, the fact that learning itself is not a simple term to define, as is illustrated by the great variety of proposals accounting for why, when and how it happens – and with what results and meanings. A conventional definition of learning is *the processes by which behaviour changes as a result of experience*. Still, the experiences producing learning can be of many kinds, particularly as change comes with age. Thus, a more complete definition would recognise the many activities and forms of cognition, personality development and reflection which give rise to information and knowledge, abilities and capacities, and also changes in behaviour, ideas and attitudes. Some scholars in adult and continuing education favour limiting the use of the terms to those activities that are 'purposefully' educative, typically formal instructional programmes (Merriam and Brockett, 1997). I have adopted the broader view, favouring adult learning in whatever circumstances it takes place.

This section offers an account of 'types and domains of adult and continuing education'. 'Types' refers to educative activities favoured by adults (defined here simply as individuals beyond adolescence), while 'domains' refers to sites, settings and occasions for learning. From the perspective of the conventional study of adult learning, this classification moves from the familiar in 'highly structured learning', or what we most often recognise in the institutionally focused educational activities of adults, to what is less often recognised in learning that is 'moderately structured' and then 'unstructured', or what needs more attention to supply a complete picture of learning in adulthood. The terms 'formal', 'non-formal' and 'informal' are sometimes used to describe similar distinctions (e.g. Colletta, 1996).

Highly structured learning in adulthood typically reflects planning to learn, often in a sequence of activities leading to a diploma, degree, certificate or some other credential. Such learning generally takes place in:

656

- educational institutions, primarily colleges and universities, offering courses and programmes usually leading to credit or to a degree, certificate, or some other form of recognition of systematic study guided by an expert or teacher working with a curriculum or some other formal programme of study; or
- workplace, professional and other settings (e.g. churches, hospitals and museums) where, again, expertly designed and formal educational programmes are offered, typically focused on class or group instruction.

Varying by subject and setting, evaluation of individual performance and of programmes is often in keeping with formal recognition of learning (i.e. 'credentialling').

Moderately structured learning in adulthood takes place in a wide range of activities. Planning to learn is less formal, with greater variety of means and ends than in more structured forms of participation in education. Moderately structured learning derives from organised activities like those provided by museums, libraries, historical societies, churches, hospitals and voluntary associations. Such activities can be organised and designated as 'educational' by institutions or not. Often oriented towards individuals, learning opportunities of this kind can be observed in the self-guided mastery of tools and skills for household, artistic and other endeavours, or in the purposeful use of the print and electronic media for an understanding of and participation in civic affairs (e.g. elections). Moderately structured learning is often problem-focused. At times there are no teachers, or at least none who gives form to educational activities, as in highly structured learning. Learning can be self-guided, learners being free to adapt whatever has been organised on their behalf, for example, to browse in a museum exhibit or to undertake a programme aimed at improving one's health. There is no attempt to evaluate individual performance for purposes of credentialling, but the learner herself or himself may welcome or initiate evaluation, as may programmes themselves of the results of their activities.

Unstructured learning in adulthood refers to the unplanned experiences of everyday living from which we learn: in the workplace, and in family and community life, including entertainment, sports and other leisure pursuits. It is contingent, spontaneous, unexpected or even incidental (at the time at least) to other activities, including highly and moderately structured learning. Unstructured learning can derive from accepting certain social roles, or having particular age-related experiences (sometimes called 'life transitions'), or from ordinary human relationships at home or work. It can occur in groups but is often solitary. Learning, even if not identified as such at the time and difficult to measure, is often a by-product of other activities. It may be less purposeful than highly or moderately structured learning but no less useful or meaningful to the individual, particularly when the learning comes from deliberate reflection on experience.

Two additional points should be recognised in using this classification. First, with regard to the actual objects of learning, these can be 'weakly structured' even if the 'type' and 'domain' is 'highly structured'. The fact that learning in the classroom, for example, is organised in a syllabus is no guarantee that what is learned has the qualities of a complex or demanding cognitive or emotional structure. Likewise, the objects of learning in 'moderately structured' or even 'unstructured' settings can reflect a high degree of structure and of cognitive or emotional complexity. Second, while it is possible to distinguish among the three categories, there is considerable overlap as well. We may speak of a *ratio* in the activities of adult and continuing education among the categories: it may take place at any one time in a person's life, or during a period of life, or over the course of a whole life. For just as there is variety within each category, individual adult learners experience the opportunities described above in a variety of ways over the lifespan, with the types and 'domains' having different meaning, uses and consequences at different ages or stages.

TOPICS IN ADULT AND CONTINUING EDUCATION

Systematic attention to adult and continuing education with a focus on learning across the lifespan as an activity, practice and research subject appears in several forms: from skill-focused reports of work-related learning in professional publications and magazines of training and organisational development, to scholarly studies of education in adulthood using the empirical and experimental methods familiar to academic discourse in the social and behavioural sciences. A broad definition of adult learning would make the extensive literatures of corporate management advice and of personal therapeutic 'recovery' (especially popular in the US) part of an enquiry into why and how adults learn. There are also the familiar inspirational accounts in newspapers and magazines of successful older college students or of hobbyists who have mastered a particularly demanding skill or craft.

The chief topics and categories of enquiry into activities, practice and theory in adult and continuing education are described briefly below. They reveal how adult and continuing education can be understood from many perspectives, together representing the difficulties of integration and generalisation. But a cautionary word is necessary. The conventional distinction in accounts of adult and continuing education between practice (what participants, organisers and teachers do) and theory (what professors do) reveals how the gaps between categories of enquiry reflect a diverse enterprise with little opportunity for the 'top-down' planning, assessment or reform often characteristic of elementary and secondary systems of education, particularly in nations with centralised formats for schooling. Adult and continuing education has benefited in innovation and participation from its independence, while it has suffered in conceptualisation and reputation for its isolation from other sectors of the educational system, and the mainstream academic disciplines.

1 *History and philosophy* help us to understand the past and questions of value and meaning. It supplies a tradition or 'foundation' (as that term is used in educational studies generally) to adult learning and the study of it, sometimes identifying the formative educational activities of particular groups (e.g. factory workers), or illustrating the role of pioneer scholars working to gain legitimacy for the subject, or examining philosophical justifications for it (Elias and Merriam, 1994; Jarvis, 1987; Kett, 1994; Thompson, 1963).

2 *Motivation* refers to the choices made by adult learners to continue learning, particularly the configuration of personal (or cognitive and developmental) and professional forces that prompt participation in the great variety of educational activities, from formal or highly structured ones to those expressing 'self-direction' in learning (Candy, 1991; Courtney, 1991; Cross, 1981; Houle, 1961).

3 *Professional and occupational learning* is peculiar to the workplace (or 'practice'), to career

and professional development (including the profession of adult education), to what is sometimes termed 'knowledge utilisation', or to techniques for maintaining or enhancing competence in the context of technological and other changes in the learning environment (Eurich, 1990; Nowlen, 1988; Peters, Jarvis and Associates, 1991; Schon, 1987; Stern, 1983).

4 *Instruction* in adult and continuing education is concerned with the roles, assumptions, expectations and methods of teachers of adults. It examines the traditional structure of relations between faculty and students (and proposed innovations like 'andragogy' or the theory of teaching adults as a unique clientele), the classroom and other settings and circumstances for teaching and learning, strategies for special populations of adult learners, and the organisation and design of credit and non-credit programmes (Brookfield, 1986; Dirkx and Prenger, 1997; Hayes, 1989; Houle, 1972; Knowles, 1980; Mezirow and Associates, 1990).

5 *Adult cognition* is a key subject of learning theory, or the ways that the mind operates in adult education. It includes the mental structures sometimes called 'ways of knowing' or 'frames of mind', age-related change in abilities (e.g. information-processing, memory, problem-solving, etc.), and the potential for unique or 'transformational' educational experiences which have profound consequences for a person's intelligence or the ways that she or he thinks and sees the world (Belenky *et al.*, 1986; Gardner, 1983; Merriam, 1993; Mezirow and Associates, 1990; Sinnott, 1994).

6 *Adult development*, as a complement to cognition, directs us to what is distinctive about the affective dimensions of adult learning. In particular it focuses upon theories of personality and the ways that individuals change over time, the role of learning in 'life transitions' and movement towards a mature identity, and the 'well-being' associated with a satisfying and productive adulthood and old age (Erikson *et al.*, 1986; Ryff, 1995; Tennant and Pogson, 1995).

7 *Gender differences* (in cognition, personality, work opportunities, etc.) have consequences for learning over the lifespan, including the ways that women are socialised for learning of certain kinds, and the ways that male and female roles have shaped educational experiences in all categories (as above) across the life-cycle (Belenky *et al.*, 1986; Gilligan, 1982; Hart, 1995; Hugo, 1990; Rice and Meyer, 1989).

8 *Life history and biography* supply the perspective of the individual adult learner in the context of historical and social change. It directs attention to how – through the uses of narrative – the dynamics of an individual life and the role of education in it can suggest patterns of learning in a particular profession, culture or nation (Antikainen *et al.*, 1996; Cremin, 1988; Goodson, 1992; Houle, 1984).

9 *Higher education institutions* play a key role in policy or resource allocation. They recognise the needs of adults, particularly in programme, curriculum and instructional development. Moreover they increasingly focus on the workplace as a form of higher education's relations with society and the goal of local or regional economic development (Apps, 1988; Duke, 1992; Lynton and Elman, 1987; Matkin, 1990).

10 *Management* of adult and continuing education seeks effective techniques for leadership and administration (planning, marketing, finance, evaluation, ethics, etc.) of the adult learning organisation or continuing education programmes. This applies in particular to the college or university but also to the corporation, the museum, the hospital or other

organisation involved in adult education, and to relations between them (Caffarella, 1994; Edelson, 1992; Mulcrone, 1993; Senge, 1990).

11 *International and comparative adult and continuing education* designate the different national traditions, practices and problems in adult and continuing education. They also delineate the educational effects – on nations, regions and continents – of political, economic and social change, and current and potential forms of collaboration, including policy-making, resource-sharing, and the adoption and practice of a 'global perspective' (Charters and Associates, 1981; Charters and Hilton, 1989; Cunningham, 1991; Duke, 1994; Knox, 1993).

12 *Critical theory* directs us to the social, political and economic meanings of learning in adulthood and of the many practices making up the profession of adult education. It demonstrates how particular social structures organise, direct and constrain educational opportunities and results. It also shows the impact of feminist, post-modern and other perspectives on theory and practice in adult learning (Briton, 1996; Collins, 1991; Freire, 1973; Welton, 1995).

FUTURE DIRECTIONS IN ADULT AND CONTINUING EDUCATION

In a field as diverse and decentralised as adult and continuing education, what the future holds depends very much on particular national and local traditions, circumstances, interests and needs. Even so, there are essential issues and themes deserving attention because they will shape practice and enquiry in virtually every setting.

Demography: education in the ageing society

It is now frequently recognised that an ageing population across the globe will mean expanded and new roles for adult and continuing education. Developments in the past few decades have brought education in later life nearer to the centre of attention in any consideration of learning over the entire life course. There is first – among scientists and educators – recognition of the lengthening lifespan itself. In the industrialised world those born at the beginning of the twentieth century could have expected to live about 47 years. By 1950 scientific estimates of life expectancy had risen to 68 years and by 1990 they had reached 75 years. Thus, someone born in 1900 could anticipate only a few years of retirement and the opportunities they may bring to learn. But by the 1990s, and looking ahead to the next century, retirement years – newly defined to include more than simple leisure – could be as much as 20 per cent of an individual's life (Manheimer *et al.*, 1995 offer considerable relevant data). In less developed nations, life expectancy and the structure of work and retirement have not changed so dramatically, but there has been enough change to prompt a rethinking of the traditional roles of individuals and institutions. Indeed, with both fertility and mortality rates declining, what has been named the 'ageing society' (Pifer and Bronte, 1986) is a worldwide phenomenon attracting special attention at the United Nations and other international agencies now focused on its most rapidly growing segment, the 'oldest old', or those over 80 (Crossette, 1996).

So too has scientific and public understanding of ageing changed, though not surprisingly the latter has lagged behind the former. Thus the decrement model of ageing, which dominated views of the elderly – especially in biomedical research – has yielded to recognition that intelligence and the capacity for satisfying activities in many domains continue well into the seventh, eighth and ninth decades of life (Cole, 1992; Schaie, 1996). While definitions differ, 'successful' or 'productive' ageing is more the norm than the exception (Baltes and Baltes, 1991). Moreover, in the 1980s new conceptions emerged of ageing as a period of unique developmental potential and meaning for individuals, and of social transformation for communities and nations that recognise this to be the case (Moody, 1988). In an influential formulation, the 'Third Age' has been identified as one in which learning could have new significance and utility (Laslett, 1991).

New conceptions of learning in late life may now be seen as coterminous with society's goals for education generally. Still, without the conventional focus in adult and continuing education on the needs of the workplace, late-life learning can give priority to 'life enrichment' which capitalises on education as a source of 'renewed vitality, intellectual stimulation, fellowship [and] a shared sense of legacy with other generations' (Manheimer *et al.*, 1995, p. 219). Generational and other features of late life are set out by Manheimer *et al.* (1995, p. 222):

1 The realisation that ageing is no barrier to learning and that many and diverse opportunities to learn are available, from the traditional to the technological.
2 Intellectual stimulation that promotes continued growth and reflection on experience, and enables individuals to function in society as well-informed citizens.
3 A sense of personal meaning and life purpose – sometimes continuous with that of earlier years, sometimes considerably changed – through activities that engage the mind and body while often in fellowship with others.
4 Goals that generate self-fufilment and that may lead to contributions to a community or to society generally whether through artistic expression, volunteerism or social activism.

How may such ideals guide motivation to learn in later life? A 'new paradigm' rejects increasing preoccupation with the self and age peers and instead finds in the integration of lifelong learning, leadership and community service the opportunity for both personal satisfaction and 'intergenerational justice' (Manheimer *et al.*, 1995, pp. 29–31). Thus, late-life learning is not merely an individual matter – freed from its conventional associations with retirement for leisure – but is an indispensable resource for the welfare of the entire ageing society (Harootyan and Feldman, 1990).

Technology: work, learning and the post-modern 'self'

As is often asserted, the impact of technology is everywhere, including education, where the digital revolution promises to transform teaching and learning, the organisation and management of adult and continuing education, and the study of both domains. The personal computer is now ubiquitous, seemingly reinventing itself continuously with new hardware and software, and joining innovations in video and telecommunications to make 'technological literacy' an indispensable part of every adult's education. Indeed, far from being a barrier to learning in later life, technology is likely to be an indispensable resource for it (Lawhon *et al.*, 1996).

Current practitioners of adult and continuing education often focus on fresh adaptations to technology for today's mature learners. But the next generations of adult learners will already have been educated in an increasing technological environment, making it possible for them – and those organising programmes or teaching in continuing education – to incorporate technology into their activities with less attention to innovation and more to variety and mastery in utilisation.

In our current circumstances there are three primary kinds of technologically oriented change taking place. First, for many adults, achieving 'technological literacy' means keeping up with the latest applications in the workplace, from computer robotics in manufacturing to data management systems in the white-collar professions, to name just two of countless examples. A second way in which technology has taken hold in adult and continuing education is in the recognition by adult learners of its role in independent learning projects, from home finance to new forms of distance education offered by institutions of higher education, versions of what is now often called the 'virtual classroom'. But after its impact on the workplace, the home and the classroom, there is also the need to recognise the impact of the computer on the 'self', the third of the significant ways in which technology is permanently influencing the human mind, individual identity and learning. Technology plays an increasing role in defining who we are and what we are capable of, as individuals, societies and global communities (Turkle, 1984).

It is the accessibility and flexibility of the 'virtual classroom' that count the most in advancing adult and continuing education. More adult students can participate according to their own schedules and interests. Technology has always had a role in this domain, in computer assisted instruction (CAI) and in the various manifestations worldwide of 'educational television', or what is now generally called 'distance learning', in which courses and related activities have been broadcast as part of degree programmes. The famed British Open University perfected the latter medium but combined it with a demanding, text-based component. There are now new forms of 'visual' educational experience beyond the classroom in the CD-ROM, the laser disc, and certainly other innovations to come. These are part of the 'virtual classroom' – the classroom without an actual room and class – which not only provides seemingly unlimited variety in the representation of materials (in graphics, video simulation, animation, etc.) but also allows for a high degree of interactivity in distinguishing itself from the older forms of educational technology.

With the independence available to individual learners – including opportunities to take classes at home and at the workplace, and with increasing student expectations of technological literacy for the faculty – colleges and universities face a challenging period as providers of adult and continuing education. According to some proponents of technology-based adult and continuing education – in this case the Director of the US Public Broadcasting System's major distance learning initiative – the university will never be the same again:

> To excel in the 21st century, higher education must undergo a paradigm shift from an environment and culture that defines learning as a 'classroom process', shaped by brick-and-mortar facilities and faculty-centered activities, to an environment defined by 'learner-centered' processes and shaped

662

by telecommunications networks with universal access to subject content material, learner support services, and technology-literate resource personnel.

(Dubois, 1996, p. 20)

For such enthusiasts, technology, like the learning society, is a medium of institutional transformation.

But within the field of adult and continuing education itself there are also more moderate voices, those recalling the uneven record of previous technological innovations (the telephone and television) and how little we actually know of the consequences for learning of a dramatic shift in the nature of educational interactions across a great variety of subjects and programmes (Rose, 1996). Thus, even with the advent of the Internet and the Worldwide Web, and while there is a justifiable sense of urgency about the incorporation of technology into adult and continuing education, one authoritative observer notes that 'the reality is that several decades may pass before the full range of abilities of the information technologies is realized and before educators gain mastery in their application' (Lewis, 1989, p. 614).

Psychologists wonder what will the self be like in the new age of technology. According to Kenneth Gergen, we are already 'saturated' with media, the computer and the multiple voices they offer, which contribute to the 'breakdown of the . . . sense of self as a singular knowable essence' (Gergen, 1991, p. 16). He adopts an elegiac tone: 'The technologies giving rise to social saturation will be inescapable. And as they continue to expand and improve, so may the traditional mentalities and their related patterns of life slip away' (ibid., p. 200). Sherry Turkle is less pessimistic perhaps, but equally convinced that in the new and coming forms of 'virtual' experience – with their capacities to isolate us from the actual world – there is still the danger that we may be the victims as well as the beneficiaries of technological innovation. Another cause of concern is the uneven distribution of technological resources. Will the future of adult and continuing education in a technological era simply reproduce the differences between the educationally rich and poor, or will it widen the gap?

Despite the claims of educational futurists, and the concerns of those looking at things from a political or developmental perspective, there is far from a consensus in the matter of the role of technology in adult and continuing education. Fears of social isolation and passivity deriving from less contact between learners and teachers, and a widening of the gap between the rich and the poor are balanced by claims for the advantages of access and autonomy and (paradoxically perhaps) the possibilities for collaboration and teamwork among learners and teachers. Inevitably everything depends on how the new tools are used, including the images and examples leading institutions and individuals provide in the highly adaptive area of adult and continuing education.

Choices made to accommodate the impact of demography and technology on adult and continuing education will certainly be political ones, that is, expressions of institutional authority and the allocation of resources. No less than elementary, secondary and post-secondary education, learning in the adult years is part of a political system. How should the political meanings of the field be understood? For critical theorists, adult and continuing education is a site for political, professional and intellectual struggle. Thus, according to the former factory worker and now adult educator Derek Briton (1996, p. 6),

The commonplace assumption that the modern practice of adult education is a disinterested, *scientific* endeavor that need not, indeed *should not* concern itself with moral and political questions has become all but impossible to question because the field's normative base can no longer be addressed within its narrowly defined, depoliticised, dehistoricised, technicist, professional discourse.

'Critical theorists' of adult and continuing education find current practices and theory wanting in four respects. First, adult learning, as it is conceptualised mainly by developmentalists (in cognition or personality theory), provides an insufficient foundation for the field as a whole. Second, adult education has 'abandoned its once vital role in fostering democratic social action'. Third, the 'instrumental rationality' – with its focus on work, economic productivity and the competitive global marketplace – that dominates current educational practices, serves mainly the interests of business, industry and large organisations. Finally, self-directed learning, a popular formulation (Candy, 1991), is a misleading educational ideal because it is 'conceptually inadequate to serve the interests of the poor, oppressed, and disenfranchised' (Welton, 1995, p. 5). To be sure, there are differences among those accepting the label 'critical theorist' of adult and continuing education. Thus, Jack Mezirow, whose influential theory of 'perspective transformation' can be characterised this way, asserts that 'the dichotomy between individual and social development is a spurious one for educators' (Mezirow, 1995, p. 68).

An important source of new ideals in theory and practice is feminism. The key elements, deriving from influential work on women's development (Gilligan, 1982) and cognition (Belenky *et al.*, 1986), and from gendered applications of work in the international tradition of socially oriented 'radical' pedagogy (hooks, 1994), are recognition of the social construction of knowledge, women's distinctive voices, the need to reconfigure intellectual and classroom authority, and the impact of 'positionality' (see Tisdell, in press). The last, signifying the personal dimension in education and the mobilisation of self-consciousness about historical and contemporary social roles, asks that 'critical' adult educators make a place for gender as well as for class and race in understanding how educational relationships are made, used and changed. How women are situated in society and culture has consequences for them (and for men) as learners and teachers, and for the ways we understand home and work as sites for adult learning within the conventions – observable across cultures and nations – associated with the division of labour (Hart, 1992).

Feminism in adult and continuing education means identifying those features of these activities where gender is central and has been ignored, particularly by recognising the distinctive developmental patterns of women's lives, cognitive or learning styles, and the relation of learning over the life course to work in and out of the home. Thus women's perspectives and values (e.g. relational rather than competitive relations) would gain an equal share in adult-oriented classrooms and programmes, and in the individual learning careers of both men and women.

CONCLUSION: THE NEW UNIVERSITY AND 'LEARNING ALONG THE WAY'

Programmes of adult and continuing education will surely reflect demographic and technological change, and they will incorporate political and social ideals with the same diversity (and varied results) that have characterised the history of lifelong learning. Even so, we can satisfy at least one of the goals of critical theory by continuous and deliberate examination of premises and practices. Thus, as the American historian Paul Kennedy says in his provocative *Preparing for the Twenty-First Century*:

> Education in the larger sense means more than technically 'retooling' the workforce, or the emergence of the professional classes, or even the encouragement of a manufacturing culture in the schools and colleges in order to preserve a productive base. It also implies a deep understanding of why our world is changing, of how other people and cultures feel about those changes, of what we all have in common – as well as what divides cultures, classes and nations.
>
> (Kennedy, 1993, p. 340–341)

Such a view recalls the origins of the idea of the learning society and suggests how any new formulation of it must include more than adaptation to the needs of the organisation or workplace.

Where will the necessary ideals and practices come from for adult and continuing education? The twentieth century has been an age of the university, with industrial nations at least coming to rely, paradoxically perhaps, on higher education as a resource for tradition (in liberal education) and for adaptation (in its occupational and professional programmes). Accordingly, many of those contemplating the future of adult and continuing education imagine a reformed or 'new' university, able to accept the challenges presented by social, demographic, technological and other forms of change (e.g. Apps, 1988; Field, 1996). The cognitive psychologist Jan Sinnott adds to her disciplinary focus the problem of institutional reform, or attention to the 'big picture' and the long-term prospects for learning, more 'problem-centred' education, etc., since 'the university is the ideal mature-adult learning environment to incorporate new approaches to adult learning and adult learners over the next 50 years' (Sinnott, 1994, p. 460).

But there is another approach to the future of adult and continuing education. Anthropologist Mary Catherine Bateson's (1994) personal account of her professional career and life as a learner is designed to collapse distinctions between the two. 'Educators, even in universities', she says, 'are still strangely in thrall to the idea that education precedes participation, even though more and more adults are returning to study or working and studying simultaneously' (Bateson, 1994, p. 176). Bateson cites no studies proving as much because she believes there is no need to; she views adult learning beyond or outside of higher education (in its conventional forms at least) as widely accessible and observable, and probably a large part of the lives of her readers. It is, as she names it in the subtitle of her book *Peripheral Visions*, 'learning along the way'. Its scale and significance are such that the nature of adult learning in educational institutions and policy should be considerably greater than it is today.

> It is a mistake to try to reform the educational system without revising our sense of ourselves as learning beings, following a path from birth to death that is longer and more unpredictable than ever before . . . . The avalanche of changes taking place around the world, the changes we should be facing at home, all come as reminders that of all the skills learned in school the most important is the skill to learn over a lifetime those things that no one, including the teachers, yet understands.
>
> (Bateson, 1994, p. 212)

Identifying the resources for understanding of this kind from within the practice and theory of adult and continuing education is yet another task for this vast and essential global enterprise.

NOTE

1 The most widely cited definition is the 'global' one unanimously approved by representatives of 142 countries participating in the 1976 General Conference of UNESCO in their statement on the 'Development of Adult Education':

> The term 'adult education' denotes the entire body of organized educational processes, whatever the content, level, and method, whether formal or otherwise, or whether they prolong or replace initial education in schools, colleges, and universities, as well as an apprenticeship, whereby persons regarded as adult by the society to which they belong develop their abilities, enrich their knowledge, improve their technical or professional qualifications, or turn them in a new direction and bring about changes in their attitudes or behavior in the two-fold perspective of full personal development and participation in balanced and independent social, economic, and cultural development.

REFERENCES

Adult Learning (1996) Special Issue (September/October) on 'New Information and Communication Technology'.

Antikainen, A., Houtsonen, J., Huotelin, H. and Kauppila, J. (1996) *Living in a Learning Society: Life-Histories Identities and Education.* London: Falmer.

Apps, J. (1988) *Higher Education in a Learning Society.* San Francisco, CA: Jossey-Bass.

Baltes, P. and Baltes, M. (1991) *Successful Aging: Perspectives from the Behavioral Sciences.* New York: Cambridge University Press.

Bateson, M. C. (1994) *Peripheral Visions: Learning along the Way.* New York: HarperCollins.

Belenky, M. F., Clinchy, B. M., Goldenberger, N. R. and Tarule, J. (1986) *Women's Ways of Knowing: The Development of Self, Voice, and Mind.* New York: Basic Books.

Briton, D. (1996) *The Modern Practice of Adult Education: A Post-Modern Critique.* Albany, NY: State University of New York Press.

Brookfield, S. D. (1986) *Understanding and Facilitating Adult Learning.* San Francisco, CA: Jossey-Bass.

Caffarella, R. S. (1994) *Planning Programs for Adult Learners: A Practical Guide for Educators, Trainers, and Staff Developers.* San Francisco, CA: Jossey-Bass.

Candy, P. C. (1991) *Self-Direction for Lifelong Learning: A Comprehensive Guide to Theory and Practice.* San Francisco, CA: Jossey-Bass.

Casey, K. (1995–1996) 'The new narrative research in education'. *Review of Research in Education*, 21, 211–253.

Charters, A. N. and Associates (1981) *Comparing Adult Education Worldwide.* San Francisco, CA: Jossey-Bass.

Charters, A. N. and Hilton, R. J. (eds) (1989) *Landmarks in International Adult Education: A Comparative Analysis.* London: Routledge.

Cochinaux, P. and de Woot, P. (1995) *Moving Towards a Learning Society.* Geneva/Brussels: Conseil de Recteurs d'Europe/European Round Table.

Cole, T. (1992) *The Journey of Life: A Cultural History of Aging in America.* New York: Cambridge University Press.

Colletta, N. J. (1996) 'Formal, nonformal, and informal education'. In A. C. Tuijnman (ed.), *International Encyclopedia of Adult Education and Training.* (2nd edn). New York: Pergamon.

Collins, M. (1991) *Adult Education as Vocation: A Critical Role for the Adult Educator.* London and New York: Routledge.

Commission of the European Communities (1995) *Teaching and Learning: Towards the Learning Society.* Luxembourg: Office of Official Publications.

Courtney, S. (1991) *Why Adults Learn: Toward a Theory of Participation.* London: Routledge.

Cremin, L. (1988) *American Education: The Metropolitan Experience*. New York: Harper & Row.

Cross, K. P. (1981) *Adults as Learners*. San Francisco, CA: Jossey-Bass.

Crossette, B. (1996) '"Oldest Old", 80 and over, increasing globally'. *New York Times*, December 22, 1996, Section I, 7.

Cunningham, P. M. (1991) 'International influences on the development of knowledge'. In J. M. Peters and P. Jarvis (eds), *Adult Education: Evolution and Achievements in a Developing Field*. San Francisco, CA: Jossey-Bass.

Dirkx, J. and Prenger, S. (1997) *Planning and Implementing Instruction for Adults: A Theme-Based Approach*. San Francisco, CA: Jossey-Bass.

Dubois, J. R. (1996) 'Going the distance: A national distance learning initiative'. *Adult Learning*, September/October, 19–21.

Duke, C. (1992) *The Learning University: Towards a New Paradigm*. Milton Keynes: Open University Press.

Duke, C. (1994) 'International adult education'. In T. Husen and T. N. Postlewaite (eds), *The International Encyclopedia of Education*. (2nd edn), vol. 5. New York: Pergamon.

Edelson, P. J. (ed.) (1992) *Rethinking Leadership in Adult and Continuing Education*. New Directions for Adult and Continuing Education, No. 56. San Francisco, CA: Jossey-Bass.

Elias, J. L. and Merriam, S. B. (1994) *Philosophical Foundations of Adult Education* (2nd edn). Malabar, FL: Krieger.

Erikson, E. H., Erikson, J. M. and Kivnik, H. O. (1986) *Vital Involvement in Old Age*. New York: Norton.

Eurich, N. (1990) *Corporate Classrooms: The Learning Business*. Princeton, NJ: Carnegie Foundation for the Advancement of Teaching.

Field, John (1996) 'Universities and the learning society'. *International Journal of University Adult Education*, 35 (1), 1–12.

Freire, P. (1973) *Education for Critical Consciousness*. New York: Seabury.

Gardner, H. (1983) *Frames of Mind: The Theory of Multiple Intelligences*. New York: Basic Books.

Gergen, K. (1991) *The Saturated Self: Dilemmas of Identity in Contemporary Life*. New York: Basic Books.

Gilligan, C. (1982) *In a Different Voice: Psychological Theory and Women's Development*. Cambridge, MA: Harvard University Press.

Goodson, I. (1992) *Studying Teachers' Lives*. New York: Teachers College Press.

Harootyan, R. A. and Feldman, N. S. (1990) 'Lifelong education, lifelong needs: Future roles in an aging society'. *Educational Gerontology*, 16 (4), 347–358.

Hart, M. (1990) 'Critical theory and beyond: Perspectives on emancipatory education'. *Adult Education Quarterly*, 40 (3), 125–138.

Hart, M. (1992) *Working and Educating for Life: Feminist and International Perspectives on Adult Education*. London and New York: Routledge.

Hart, M. (1995) 'Motherwork: a radical proposal to rethink work and education'. In Michael Welton (ed.), *In Defense of the Lifeworld: Critical Perspectives on Adult Learning*. Albany, NY: State University of New York Press.

Hayes, E. (ed.) (1989) *Effective Teaching Styles*. New Directions for Continuing Education, No. 43. San Francisco, CA: Jossey-Bass.

Heermann, B. (ed.) (1986) *Personal Computers and the Adult Learner*. New Directions for Continuing Education, No. 29. San Francisco, CA: Jossey-Bass.

Heermann, B. (1988) *Teaching and Learning with Computers*. San Francisco, CA: Jossey-Bass.

hooks, b. (1994) *Teaching to Transgress*. London and New York: Routledge.

Houle, Cyril (1961) *The Inquiring Mind*. Madison, WI: University of Wisconsin Press.

Houle, Cyril (1972) *The Design of Education*. San Francisco, CA: Jossey-Bass.

Houle, Cyril (1984) *Patterns of Learning: New Perspectives on Lifespan Education*. San Francisco, CA: Jossey-Bass.

Houle, Cyril (1992) *The Literature of Adult Education: A Bibliographic Essay*. San Francisco, CA: Jossey-Bass.

Hughes, C. and Tight, M. (1995) 'The myth of the learning society'. *British Journal of Educational Studies*, 43 (3), 290–304.

Hugo, J. M. (1990) 'Adult education history and the issue of gender: Toward a different history of adult education in America'. *Adult Education Quarterly*, 41 (1), 1–16.

Husen, T. (1974) *Towards the Learning Society*. London: Methuen.

Hutchins, R. M. (1968) *The Learning Society*. New York: Praeger.

Jarvis, P. (ed.) (1987) *Twentieth Century Thinkers in Adult Education*. London: Croom Helm.

Jarvis, P. (1991) 'Growth and challenges in the study of adult education'. In J. Peters, P. Jarvis and Associates (eds), *Adult Education: Evolution and Achievements in a Developing Field of Study*. San Francisco, CA: Jossey-Bass.

Kennedy, P. (1993) *Preparing for the Twenty-First Century*. New York: Random House.

Kett, J. F. (1994) *The Pursuit of Knowledge under Difficulties: From Self Improvement to Adult Education in America. 1750–1990*. Stanford, CA: Stanford University Press.

Knowles, M. S. (1980) *The Modern Practice of Adult Education: From Pedagogy to Andragogy*. (Rev. edn). New York: Association Press.

Knox, A. B. (1993) *Strengthening Adult and Continuing Education: A Global Perspective on Synergistic Leadership*. San Francisco, CA: Jossey-Bass.

Laslett, P. (1991) *A Fresh Map of Life, the Emergence of the Third Age*. Cambridge, MA: Harvard University Press.

Lawhon, T., Ennis, D. and Lawhon, D. (1996) 'Senior adults and computers in the 1990s'. *Educational Gerontology*. 22, 193–201.

Lewis, L. H. (1989) 'New educational technologies for the future'. In S. B. Merriam and P. M. Cunningham (eds), *Handbook of Adult and Continuing Education*. San Francisco, CA: Jossey-Bass, 613–617.

Lindeman, E. C. (1926) *The Meaning of Adult Education*. New York: The New Republic.

Lynton, E. A. and Elman, S. E. (1987) *New Priorities for the University: Meeting Society's Needs for Applied Knowledge and Competent Individuals*. San Francisco, CA: Jossey-Bass.

Manheimer, R. J., Snodgrass, D. D. and Moskow-McKenzie, D. (1995) *Older Adult Education: A Guide to Research, Programs, and Policies*. Westport, CT: Greenwood Press.

Matkin, G. (1990) *Technology Transfer and the University*. New York: Macmillan.

Merriam, S. B. (ed.) (1993) *An Update on Adult Learning Theory*. New Directions for Adult and Continuing Education, No. 57. San Francisco, CA: Jossey-Bass.

Merriam, S. B. and Brockett, R. G. (1997) *The Profession and Practice of Adult Education*. San Francisco, CA: Jossey-Bass.

Mezirow, J. (1995) 'Transformation theory of adult learning'. In M. R. Welton (ed.) *In Defense of the Lifeworld: Critical Perspectives on Adult Learning*. Albany, NY: Suny Press.

Mezirow, J. and Associates (1990) *Fostering Critical Reflection in Adulthood: A Guide to Transformative and Emancipatory Learning*. San Francisco, CA: Jossey-Bass.

Moody, H. (1988) 'Late life education'. In H. Moody, *Abundance of Life: Human Development Practices for an Aging Society*, Baltimore, MD: Johns Hopkins University Press, 190–212.

Moody, H. (1990) 'Education and the life-cycle: A philosophy of aging'. In R. Sherron and D. B. Lumsden (eds), *Introduction to Educational Gerontology* (3rd edn). New York: Hemisphere, 23–39.

Mulcrone, P. (ed.) (1993) *Current Perspectives on Administration of Adult Education*. New Directions in Adult and Continuing Education, No. 60. San Francisco, CA: Jossey-Bass.

Nowlen, P. M. (1988) *A New Approach to Continuing Education for Business and the Professions*. New York: Macmillan.

Peters, J., Jarvis, P. and Associates (1991) *Adult Education: Evolution and Achievements in a Developing Field of Study*. San Francisco, CA: Jossey-Bass.

Pifer, A. and Bronte, L. (1986). *Our Aging Society: Paradox and Promise*. New York: Norton.

Pittman, V. (1989) 'What is the image of the field today?' In B. A. Quigley (ed.), *Fulfilling the Promise of Adult and Continuing Education*. New Directions for Continuing Education, No. 44. San Francisco, CA: Jossey-Bass, 15–22.

Rice, J. K. and Meyer, S. (1989) 'Continuing education for women'. In S. B. Merriam and P. Cunningham (eds), *Handbook of Adult and Continuing Education*. San Francisco, CA: Jossey-Bass.

Rose, A. (1996) 'Telecommunications transformation'. *Adult Learning*, September/October, 6, 24.

Ryff, C. (1995) 'Psychological well being in adult life'. *Current Directions in Psychological Science*, 4, 99–104.

Schaie, W. G. (1996) 'Intellectual development in adulthood'. In J. Birren and K. W. Schaie (eds), *Handbook of the Psychology of Aging* (4th edn). San Diego, CA: Academic Press, 266–286.

Schon, D. (1987) *Educating the Reflective Practitioner*. San Francisco, CA: Jossey-Bass.

Senge, P. (1990) *The Fifth Discipline: The Art and Practice of the Learning Organization*. New York: Doubleday.

Sinnott, J. D. (1994) 'The future of adult lifespan learning: Learning institutions face change'. In J. D. Sinnott (ed.), *Interdisciplinary Handbook of Adult Lifespan Learning*. Westport, CT: Greenwood Press.

Stern, M. R. (ed.) (1983) *Power and Conflict in Continuing Professional Education*. Belmont, CA: Wadsworth.

Tennant, M. and Pogson, P. (1995) *Learning and Change in the Adult Years: A Developmental Perspective*. San Francisco, CA: Jossey-Bass.

Thompson, E. P. (1963) *The Making of the English Working Class*. New York: Pantheon.

Tisdell, E. (1993) 'Feminism and adult learning: Power, pedagogy, and praxis'. In S. B. Merriam (ed.), *An Update on Adult Learning Theory*. New Directions for Adult and Continuing Education, No. 57. San Francisco, CA: Jossey-Bass.

Tisdell, E. (In press) 'Poststructural feminist pedagogies: The possibilities and limitations of a feminist emancipatory adult learning theory and practice'. *Adult Education Quarterly*.

Titmus, C. J. (1994) 'Adult education: Concepts, purposes, and principles'. In T. Husen and T. Postlethwaite (eds), *The International Encyclopedia of Education* (2nd edn). vol. I. Oxford: Pergamon, 111–120.

Turkle, S. (1984) *The Second Self: Computers and the Human Spirit*. New York: Simon and Schuster.

Van der Zee, H. (1991) 'The learning society'. *International Journal of Lifelong Education*, 10 (3), 213–230.

Watkins, K. E. and Marsick, V. J. (1993) *Sculpting the Learning Organization*. San Francisco, CA: Jossey-Bass.

Welton, M. R. (1995) 'The critical turn in adult education theory'. In M. R. Welton (ed.), *In Defense of the Lifeworld: Critical Perspectives on Adult Learning*. Albany, NY: State University of New York Press.

38

ADULT EDUCATION
Social movements or public service?

Tom Steele

INTRODUCTION: THE VIEW FROM YORKSHIRE

When J. F. C. Harrison wrote his seminal study of the history of the English adult education movement, *Learning and Living 1790–1960* (1961) he had no doubt that adult education was a movement which had participated centrally in the shaping of the institutions of mass democracy in Britain. As such, Harrison added, it should be separated from the subordinate idea of the 'education of adults'. It was not simply a series of largely voluntary organisations but an instrument of personal liberation and social justice. Adult education was an earnest business not to be confused with the 'learning for leisure' rhetoric (then fashionable in ministerial quarters) because it entailed a great struggle on the part of people who had little leisure to enjoy. Harrison's approach took its tone from his source material, which was drawn largely from the county in which he worked and studied, Yorkshire, and owed a great deal to the seriousness of purpose of that great puritan of the movement, the founding District Secretary of the WEA Yorkshire District, George Thompson.[1] But for Harrison, Yorkshire could not help being the 'epitome of England'.

Following J. W. Hudson's *History of Adult Education* (1851), Harrison located the origins of the adult education movement in the late eighteenth century, when two distinctly different forms of educational enterprise came into being (Harrison, 1961: xii–xiii). The first, in 1792, was the promotion by the Corresponding Societies and the Societies for Constitutional Information, of groups to study the works of Tom Paine. The second was the first specifically adult school, which was established in Nottingham in 1798. These two foundations have proved an instructive duality which has revealed the ambivalent role of adult education in the successive century or so. The first was a largely oppositional grouping which was germinating the means of independent workers' education and, eventually, class struggle, while the second was a liberal initiative to promote social harmony and class reconciliation. Like Castor and Pollux, this iconic pairing tiptoed and, periodically, thundered through debates on the purpose of adult education for the next century and a half, never to be separated, never to be resolved.

670

BRITISH AND EUROPEAN ADULT EDUCATION FORMATIONS

By the late nineteenth century many of the informal initiatives in adult education of the earlier part of the century had developed into three main formations: British university extension, Danish folk high schools and the French *universités populaires*. Also associated were the *Volksheims*, university settlements, people's palaces, Spanish 'rationalist' schools and a variety of other national developments (Steele, 1993).

The most influential form of organised adult education was university extension. Founded by the Scot, James Stuart, Cambridge University Extension held its first classes in 1874 after exploratory classes for the Ladies' Educational Associations of Liverpool, Manchester, Sheffield and Leeds (Harrison, 1961: 222). Undertaken largely as a mission to the industrial north by liberal intellectuals, who had been under the tutelage of such men as John Ruskin and T. H. Green, university extension was the most pedagogically advanced and systematic form of adult popular education then devised. As the first systematic engagement of universities in extra-mural work, it had enormous influence in northern Europe, especially in the larger towns of Germany, Austria, Holland and Scandinavia, and in North America. It also inspired the Modern Universities movement which led to the founding of university colleges in the northern industrial towns which, in turn, became the civic redbrick universities. These adopted a significantly different organisational model from the universities of Oxford and Cambridge, in that they eschewed the medieval, college-based system and instead organised their teaching through new disciplinary departments, loosely grouped into faculties. With newly established departments of English, languages and embryonic social science departments, to chairs of which former university extension lecturers were frequently appointed, the new universities displayed a strong belief in social relevance and new subjects of knowledge.

In contrast, the folk high schools originated in Denmark in 1864 under the leadership of a Lutheran pastor called Gruntvicg, in opposition to German annexations of Danish territory. They were rural-based, residential and concentrated on the creation of folk-national identity among small farmers. At times fiercely anti-Enlightenment, they were both religious and traditional. As a social movement, however, the folk high schools were highly democratic and sociable. Concentrating on life-skills, they relied on residential courses of three or six months rather than university extension's weekly classes. The schools were also privately owned, entirely open and refused examinations. The folk high school was common in Scandinavia and German-speaking Europe but not emulated in southern Europe. In England, it became the model for a number of residential adult education settlements like Woodbridge and Fircroft.

A quite different model, the *universités populaires*, originated in Paris in the late 1890s, as the inspiration of Georges Deherme, an anarchist printer. In the period following the upheavals of the Dreyfus affair they multiplied rapidly, especially in the provinces, where they were often associated with radical, anti-clerical freemasonry and the trade-unionist, *bourses de travail*. Politically, socialist or anarchist/libertarian (depending on local affiliations) and independent of the moribund French universities, the movement was emulated in southern Europe, particularly in Italy and Spain. More politically radical than the folk high schools and university extension, and deeply sceptical of clericalism in any guise, especially Catholicism, this was primarily an urban workers' movement. With the exception

671

of the followers of Comtean social science, intellectuals were treated with a degree of scepticism. In Spain a related but separate development was the anarchist 'rational' schools, mainly in Catalonia and Andalusia, which were again ardently anti-clerical and anti-Catholic. In metropolitan centres university intellectuals were involved in setting up workers' athenaeums not unlike university settlements and *casas del pueblo*, whose main function was social rather than educational (Tiana-Ferrer, 1996).

In the nineteenth century, then, in Britain and Europe adult education was a distinct sociological formation characterised by affiliations to workers' movements, nationalist movements and, in England, to the campaign for women's higher education and modernising the universities. By the mid-twentieth century it was much more diffuse. As Harrison himself acknowledged towards the end of his history, even by the late 1950s adult education could not be neatly associated with any social movement. There were too many loose ends to tie into the main idea. It was more of a jumble, a jungle even, of different forms of learning much of which had come to embrace that 'education for leisure' which would have been so despised by its serious-minded founders. This chapter will therefore try to keep hold of the fact that there was a relatively clear formation called adult education, which was traditionally closely allied to social (especially labour) movements, while acknowledging the pluralism of later developments.

As a sociological formation (as manifested in the WEA [Workers' Educational Association], independent working-class education and the extra-mural departments) adult education was dominated by an ethic of social purpose, enlightenment and voluntarism. In the heroically *male* phase of the movement, the social science and political subjects were seen as the serious core of adult education while the arts and humanities were, if not frivolous, then best left to the women folk. Suspicion about the stealthy inculcation of bourgeois values through literature and art appreciation was never quite eradicated, even when they became the dominant subjects in WEA classes and when women formed the majority of students, after the Second World War. But as the latest of the Yorkshire historians of adult education, Roger Fieldhouse, has recently argued, by this time the idea of adult education as a social movement was being displaced in favour of it becoming a public service (Fieldhouse *et al.*, 1996). The long and bitter struggles during the 1930s between the class warriors of the provinces and the modernisers of the centre had loosened traditional class affiliations and moved adult education into the sphere of the 'national popular' (Steele, 1997). From this time the voluntary movement entered a period of decline and professional organisers steadily took over its functions.

Even in its heyday the social movement manner of adult education was complemented by another strand, which was that of the technical and vocational education or training. This was developed by the local government authorities who inherited the tradition of technical education begun in apprenticeship schemes and the mechanics institutes. They were charged with the duty of providing vocational and technical education in relation to the needs of local industry, according to national and professional criteria which led to the City and Guilds and various other skills awards. But this provision suffered from the peculiarly British cultural phenomenon which privileged liberal education over vocational and technical aspects. This may have been a legacy of the public school system and the elitist tradition which saw the education of the gentlemen as something of the spirit rather than the hand (Wiener, 1981). The distinction also drew strength from the revulsion to the cruder forms of utilitarian education graphically described by Dickens and generalised in the Romantic critique of capitalism elaborated forcibly by Carlyle, Ruskin, Morris and others (Williams, 1958). Although by comparison the social movement side of adult education was less generously funded, the endowment of Responsible Body (RB) status to the WEA and the extra-mural departments after the First World War gave their prescribed *non*-vocational education much greater prestige. A liberal education component was added to further education (FE) vocational courses after the Second World War.

Despite its relatively marginal and poorly funded position, British adult education has received regular scrutiny from government commissions and various pieces of legislation have periodically attempted to set new agenda. Until the late 1980s the shape of adult education owed much to the Russell Report of 1973 and the Alexander Report in Scotland, which drew attention to educationally disadvantaged groups and the need for compensatory education (DES, 1973). These reports stimulated the growth of community education programmes, access to higher education (HE), part-time higher education and a credit transfer system.

The latter drew on the success of the biggest postwar innovation in adult education, the Open University, the brainchild of Michael Young. Despite increasing demand from adults for higher education, traditional university adult education had become complacent and the Open University with its radical use of technology and distance learning methods, its part-time and modularised curricula and, crucially, its attention to the counselling and guidance needs of adults, made it seem jaded.

The introduction of market-orientated policies by the 1979–1997 Conservative government, however, revealed little sympathy for the community focus of the Russell priorities. Indeed, to Keith Joseph and his advisors this looked suspiciously like encouraging social dissidence when what was really required was workplace discipline. The result was that liberal adult education found itself increasingly starved of resources and required to orientate itself towards 'vocational' criteria. In the FE sector colleges were steadily colonised by short-term (and largely ineffective) vocational skills training projects sponsored by the Manpower Services Commission of the Department of Employment (the first moves in a policy which was ultimately to unite the departments of Education and Employment in 1994). It was part of a concerted strategy of severing the FE sector from local authority control, weakening the power of Her Majesty's (much too liberal) Inspectorate, and subjecting it directly to the authority of the newly created Further Education Funding Council.

COMMUNITY EDUCATION

Community education, however, did not immediately succumb and, especially in Scotland, it developed in radical directions. The origins of community education as an idea can be traced to Henry Morris in the 1920s and beyond him to the university settlement movement of the 1880s and 1890s. It received an injection of energy from community development experiments in the former British colonies between the wars and from Gandhi's 1936 Wardha Scheme of *nai telim* or basic education. These were attempts to educate largely illiterate adult communities through holistic approaches to practical activities, vocational skills and local self-government. Gandhi, who was wholly sceptical of British arts education and Western technologism, centred his educational scheme on the creation of village self-sufficiency through skills learning, mother-tongue literacy and citizenship education (Steele and Taylor, 1995). Following the Second World War many idealistic young European and American educators participated in Third World community education and development schemes funded by aid agencies like UNESCO and by a number of British extra-mural departments – Oxford, Durham, Leeds and Nottingham being the most prominent (Titmus and Steele, 1995). One of them, Professor Lalage Bown (pers. com.) recalled how the practical orientation of this form of 'development' education was brought back to suggest new forms of work with deprived communities in Britain itself.

A further Third World stimulus to community education came from the work of Paulo Freire, the Brazilian educator and theorist, whose *Pedagogy of the Oppressed* became canonical for community educators everywhere but especially in Scotland (Kirkwood and Kirkwood, 1989). Freire's influence is indeed global and so-called participative and trans-formative education schemes throughout the world claim descent from him, although, in fact, the origins of this kind of work can be traced back to Gandhi's basic education schemes, to Frank Laubach's imaginative 'each one teach one' literacy programmes and to Nyrere's *ujamaa* and 'nation building' community development in Tanzania. Nevertheless Freire's radical method of 'conscientisation' – which draws together strands from Marxist, existentialist and Christian thinking – has provided one of the clearest expressions of the transformative approach.

Significantly, the community education initiatives of the early 1970s were multi-agency. In Liverpool, for example, Tom Lovett's and Eric Midwinter's work involved the local further education colleges, the WEA, Liverpool University and the LEA (Lovett, 1975). These innovatory projects were greeted sceptically by older practitioners in adult education, who did not regard discussions in pubs around pints of beer as sufficiently serious. However, in the light of this work, many northern industrial local authorities developed community education and development services, the more radical of them developing local management groups which handled substantial budgets.

At this time ALBSU, the adult basic literacy project, was launched to cater for the estimated four million functional illiterate adults in Britain – a shocking figure for most educators. Although it managed to overcome some of the sense of shame which prevented illiterate adults from seeking help, it nevertheless failed to escape the 'deficit model' of education which tended to view educational failure less as structural to the system (despite arguments to show that the system only worked by failing most of those who entered it) and more as individual deficiency. In Fieldhouse's analysis it was squeezed between the two discourses of, on the one hand, disadvantage and compensation and, on the other, economic efficiency. This strand of provision was mainstreamed under schedule two of the Education Act (1992) and became known as Schedule Two work. However, because of competitive bidding and the short-term nature of the funding, it was less able to serve the liberatory agenda demanded by Freirean-influenced community educators or to act as a sufficient basis for lifelong learning.

In some local authorities such as Sheffield, however, literacy schemes have become an important way of overcoming educational disadvantage in ethnic minority communities where imaginative approaches have led to a high degree of participation. The Sheffield Unified Multi-cultural Educational Scheme (SUMES) has, for example, drawn the literacy workers from indigenous family groups rather than using college staff. At the same time it has given the young literacy workers access to a college education which they would not normally have received and has increased the participation rate of their communities in further and higher education, through their example. This flexible relationship between local authority and further education has taken literacy work beyond the 'deficit' model (Gurnah, 1992). Also, because the local community is funded by the local authority to undertake the work, it restores a degree of control over educational process to the social group and challenges the education institutions to meet its needs, rather than simply fitting in with the institution's curriculum.

TRADE UNION EDUCATION

In line with Russell Report recommendations, a dramatic growth in trade union education was stimulated by the 1974–1979 Labour government's industrial and social legislation. Under the Employment Act and the Health and Safety at Work Act, trade unions were given much greater scope to expand their membership education and to introduce programmes of training for shop stewards and safety representatives. With Tony Benn at the Department of Trade and Industry, it was a heady time for those involved in this work. Much excellent educational material and programmes of study were generated by the TUC while the teaching itself was carried out by the WEA, FE and university extra-mural staff. Indeed, had the Labour government remained in office, real prospects of integrated educational programmes for working people which involved further and higher education and residential courses, were in prospect.

In 1979 a combination of government hostility to trade union education (and trade unions), accelerated deindustrialisation and mass unemployment brought much of this work to an end. Yet, despite the new government's suspicions, much trade union education was exemplarily restrained and, if anything, enhanced workplace discipline by strengthening the policing role of the unions. More radical tutors complained that the TUC packages were largely 'unpolitical' containing nothing, for example, on how to initiate or lead a strike, shop steward committees, workers' councils as organs of dual power or how to overthrow capitalism (McIlroy, 1996). Nevertheless it stimulated the unions' own educational structures, which in the examples of UNISON and USDAW have gone well beyond simple role education and towards the more liberal education of members, by means of formal links with the WEA, universities and open college networks to accredit their courses and create pathways into higher education.

THE WEA

The current role of the WEA is uncertain; indeed, its continued existence is a matter of wonder. Yet it remains a national organisation with a federal structure and, if anything, it appears to be thriving. Its founders, however, may not recognise it as the same organisation, because like the three-year tutorial classes which were the association's main contribution to the cause of adult education, its partnership with universities through the joint committees has almost everywhere long since disappeared. The combination of high seriousness and puritan purpose, which drove the movement in its early decades and produced the 'earnest minority' Richard Hoggart could celebrate in *The Uses of Literacy* (1957), dwindled under the onslaught of 1960s popular culture and the deconstruction of the working-class movement.

In 1992 the WEA lost its Responsible Body status (as had the university departments of adult education some years earlier) and was incorporated into the FE sector. Under the FEFC it has received funding for work with disadvantaged and excluded communities – precisely the role it, or at least its professionals, sought through the Russell Report – and has become integrated into the community education network. However this has been at the expense of voluntarism and decentralisation and this has made the WEA directly account-able to the policy whims of the FEFC. This is the loss of an almost unique independent educational agency which both received direct state funding but also democratically con-trolled its own affairs. Fieldhouse indeed suggests the original WEA as a model for a radically revived adult education system, despite his earlier criticisms of the ideological parameters which constrained its activities (Fieldhouse, 1985). Other threats to the WEA's conventional student body come from associations like the University of the Third Age (U3A), which offer the retired a relaxed diet of lectures and less-demanding courses. U3A, however, does reinvigorate the voluntary democratic spirit in adult education and is commendably cheap.

THE UNIVERSITIES

With its links to an organised labour movement broken by the ending of RB status, and the channelling of funding first through the Universities Funding Council (UFC) and then the Higher Education Funding Councils for England and Wales (HEFCE) and Scotland (SHEFC), adult education in the universities is becoming fully mainstreamed. This long-term displacement is reflected in the title of the departments. In the 1960s, Extra-mural departments mutated into departments of Adult Education, reflecting a shift of policy away from traditional constituencies in the community and signalling a professionalisation of staff and courses. During the 1980s and 1990s these gave way to 'Continuing Education' which signified greater investment in continued *professional* education and more broadly in the (rather nebulous) idea of 'lifelong learning'.

Currently, these departments are being more closely integrated into the mainstream of university provision or (like those in Manchester and Liverpool) have found themselves surplus to requirements. Because the new funding regulations which were first introduced by HEFCE in 1994, and have been largely followed by SHEFC, have radically changed the basis on which departments are funded, only a handful of departments now provide an extensive liberal studies programme. The burden of the changes is that CE departments receive funding virtually only for accredited courses, with a small amount which can be attained through competitive bids for widening access. As a result CE departments have had to develop courses for credit with indecent haste (often in the face of resentment from internal departments who claim ownership of the subjects of knowledge) and to modularise their programmes. In most of the 'new' and civic universities, this process has been integrated into a general process of modularisation but many of the older universities have held out against it. Thus the shape of university adult education is increasingly a modular, part-time mode of 'lifelong learning' within HE, in what may pilot a new model of flexible, mass, higher education.

There are ambiguous benefits for this process. In the first place there is little evidence that there is any great demand for accredited courses among university adult education's older constituency, who for the most part are already well qualified. The universities most likely to benefit are the 'new' universities, which responded to the government's policy of minimally resourced HE expansion by targeting adults. These new universities have made spectacular progress; many have had modularised, part-time degree structures in place for over a decade and already include a high proportion of mature students. They have generally invested more resources in access and guidance structures which can respond reflexively to the needs of part-time students.

ACCESS

One of the more important educational initiatives of the last two decades has been the movement for wider university access. Initially an exercise in increasing participation among ethnic minority groups in London, it took root in north-west England and in Scotland as a means of targeting educationally deprived groups generally. Open Colleges quickly developed and constituted the Open College Network (OCN) and shortly the Council for National Academic Awards (CNAA) instituted a national validation system. This movement has created alternative pathways of entry to standard school-leaver qualifications and has produced a more sensitive environment for adult returners. Parry (1996) notes that access has taken various forms: the Open College federation which created alternative pathways to GCSEs; community-based 'Second Chance' education; Fresh Horizons and New Opportunities for Women; credit-based college courses and directly preparatory courses for higher education (especially in the former polytechnic/new university sector). The era of the dedicated access course is drawing to a close in part because of the new moves to credit-based funding. Since access courses are logically pre-university entrance courses, university funding councils find difficulty in accrediting them (although in Scotland some have achieved this) and south of the border many universities have phased them out.

But however successful these courses were in expanding mature student access, they are still premised on the concept of an 'elite' rather than a 'mass' university. And, despite their radical appearance, access courses have been criticised as essentially conservative because they have uncritically adopted the elitist assumptions of the existing university system and have matriculated only a relatively small proportion of students. Emphasis has now shifted away from discrete access courses towards *accessibility* generally. Although Britain is now entering an era of mass higher education, Scott (1995) maintains there is still great uncertainty about what exactly it involves. Although adults (over 21) now form the majority of all students, the proportion steeply declines after the age of 25, so much of it looks simply like delayed entrance. Also, the growth in mature entrance is heavily weighted towards the new universities, while the older universities have either made only token gestures to adults or have remained discreetly aloof (Robertson, 1997). Scott maintains that the now unitary higher education sector actually disguises a pluralistic system in which older hierarchies will still be preserved.

CURRENT ISSUES IN ADULT EDUCATION

Adult education is currently faced with both extraordinary new possibilities and life-threatening disease. Although the ideology of 'lifelong learning' offers a prospect of continuous upgrading of individual skills and personal development, it has disguised its social aspect by focusing on career development and by fetishising qualifications. The emphasis on 'continuing' education assumes that individuals possess an already adequate foundation, whereas the bulk of school-leavers will make only minimal use of non-compulsory education. For these, the real deficiency in the educational system is in the lack of an adequate skills foundation between the ages of 16 and 18.

WORK-BASED LEARNING

Access to learning which could remedy this deficit may become more available to working people under various work-based learning schemes (WBL). The Labour government's idea of a 'University of Industry' blurs the distinction between the workplace and the college, while the idea of accrediting prior learning (APL) and prior experiential learning (APEL) revalues the working life as a source of learning and qualifications. Workers will increasingly be offered opportunities to upgrade their skills and enter into longer programmes of learning at the workplace, 'the corporate classroom', which will be accredited by higher education and lead on to higher qualifications. Tax incentives to firms and the introduction of a 'learning account' scheme where employees save regularly into an account to which government and employers also contribute were also proposed in the report of the Dearing Committee (NCIHE, 1997).

The danger, of course, is that once separated from the colleges and universities, education loses its traditional independence. What counts as learning might be narrowly skills-based and lack the development of conceptual understanding. It is also feared that control over the learning needs of employees will fall increasingly into the hands of employers. However, projects in the larger companies like Ford's EDAP scheme suggest that a substantial liberal element informs provision and that the very act of returning to learning stimulates further engagement (Moore, 1994).

FROM DISTANCE LEARNING TO CYBERSPACE

It is sometimes forgotten that the development of public libraries in Britain and Scandinavia formed part of the original adult education movement. Again the reasons for it were ambivalent. Many local authorities saw the provision of reading material for workers as counter-revolutionary while paternalist firms were quick to see libraries as a way of diverting thoughtful workers from more radical activities. Against this, many skilled workers experienced a hunger for book-learning which would enable them to form their own understanding free of both priest and rabble-rouser. Still an essential tool for learning and relaxation, the book has been a genuine instrument of enlightenment and liberation for generations of adults. The book is what was turned to at the end of the lecture, to improve the shining hour, to develop imaginative flights or merely to prepare for sleep. Without the coming of the book the development of individual and private learning would not have been possible beyond the confines of a peasant society: cities would not have been founded; nations would not have been built; and technology would not have developed beyond animal power. Is its hegemony now coming to an end?

With books which could be taken away and read at the learner's leisure, distance learning at once became possible. Public libraries greatly facilitated this in the nineteenth century and the introduction of cheap editions such as Dent's Everyman series and Penguin paperbacks created a vast public for reading in the twentieth.

The arrival of relatively cheap microchip personal computers has resulted in a revolution in information technology on a comparable scale to that of the book. Combined with distance learning techniques pioneered in the Open University and the National Extension College, it has become increasingly possible for those with access to a networked computer to complete whole programmes of learning without leaving the house. Whether anyone would want to do this is questionable, but clearly those who could benefit most are the physically disabled and those in remote populations. This form of learning is not sociable and lacks the community of the classroom where the dialogue between students and tutor can be crucial. But multi-occupier sites (Moos) now enable students to 'talk' to each other over the Net, while e-mail allows immediate correspondence between students and tutors.

Distance learning using information technology reinforces fears about andragogy (Collins, 1991). According to Collins, andragogy and self-learning techniques do not increase learners' autonomy, as is claimed, but merely increase students' reliance on the institution that is providing the courses and material. Learners are instead encouraged to adapt their learning needs to what the institution can provide. They forgo the important communicative process which is brought about by argument and dialogue in real time and become increasingly privatised. This argument draws on theories of how meaning is constructed put forward by the German philosopher Jürgen Habermas (Habermas, 1984) and is popular amongst those who want to recover adult education's social purpose. But against this it could be argued that nothing was more private than reading a book and that never seemed to prevent subsequent communal action. Distance learning may also be the answer to the prayers of university administrators who need to cut teaching costs. The Open University has shown that, because of standardised courses and low capital costs, it is possible to produce graduates at a fraction of the cost of other universities. Open University graduates seem in no way inferior to other graduates (as the frequent finals of the TV quiz 'University Challenge' graphically demonstrate); indeed, they have often pursued more imaginative academic pathways. However, measures to make access to the hardware more widely available must be taken if it is not to become yet another means of exclusion.

CONCLUSION

Because of post-modernist scepticism of the value of enlightenment and the grand narratives of history and science, the idea of public adult *education* has to an extent been eclipsed by that of solipsistic *learning*. So the lament goes: the teacher has given way to the 'facilitator' and the 'change agent' and increasingly the VDU screen. Knowledge itself is fragmented into bite-size modules which can be quilted together. In all but the most ancient universities, the rhetoric of vocationalism, skills development and competencies has replaced the more traditional vocabulary of liberal education. The institutions of higher education creak through low investment and high demand, and demoralisation stalks the common-room. In terms of wages, teachers and lecturers are the least valued of the professions. At moments it seems that donnish dominion is in terminal decline and with it all that Western civilisation holds dear.

Against this, much of the mystique of education is evaporating. The 'corporate classroom', for example, is siting a good deal of learning away from the older institutions and into the workplace. Universities can no longer be assumed to be the monopoly repositories of knowledge or excellence in research nor can dons be deemed the sole guardians of what is to be known. The idea of 'graduateness' – that rite by which the children of the privileged pass on to their allotted place among the employed elite – may become redundant. Graduating from a single university will become as archaic as the medieval university itself (although a few of these may well persist on a privatised basis). In its place a higher educational system may evolve which is more geared towards adults than school-leavers, which will no longer comprise a continuous period of three or four years immediately following on from school but periodic immersions over a lifetime. With the introduction of a national and even international credit accumulation and transfer scheme (CATS) and a voucher system, where and when this education can be had could be infinitely variable. This could be a genuinely mass or even 'universal' system, and adult education would have come of age.

But what of the view from Yorkshire? If adult education becomes wholly mainstreamed into a system of credits for individual learners through networked institutions, what is left that might be called a 'movement' in the sense in which Harrison used it? The short answer is that the identity of adult education will have been erased. But adult education cannot in the end avoid its commitment to social purpose because that is what has made it distinct. It has once again to become extra-mural, to rediscover those links with community groups and social movements that gave it vitality. Adult education in this sense will inevitably reinvent itself because the social causes of inequality and exclusion have not disappeared and new social movements will emerge. A funding regime which directly grant-aided communities to establish their own educational needs in partnership with institutions might be a first step and adult educators might rediscover a sense of vocation (Collins, 1991).

NOTE

1 The University of Leeds Department of Extramural Studies in which he was Deputy Director has since contributed notable historians and professors of adult education, including Sidney Raybould, Norman Jepson, Stuart Marriott, Chris Duke, Dick Taylor and the author of the most recent study of British adult education, Roger Fieldhouse. Harrison's distinguished colleagues included E. P. Thompson, then writing *The Making of the English Working Class*, the sociologist John Rex, the philosopher J. M. Cameron and the literary critic Walter Stein.

REFERENCES

Collins, M. (1991) *Adult Education as Vocation*, London: Routledge.

DES (1973) *Adult Education: A Plan for Development* (The Russell Report), London: HMSO.

Dover Wilson, John (1928) 'Adult Education in North Yorkshire', *Journal of Adult Education*, III, October.

Fieldhouse, R. (1985) *Adult Education and the Cold War*, Leeds Studies in the Education of Adults, Leeds: University of Leeds Press.

Fieldhouse, R. *et al.* (1996) *A History of Modern British Adult Education*, Leicester: NIACE.

Gurnah, A. (ed.) (1992) 'Literacy for a change: A special issue on the Sheffield black literacy campaign', *Adults Learning* 3 (8).

Habermas, J. (1984) *Theory of Communicative Action*, vol. 1, Cambridge: Polity Press.

Harrison, J. F. C. (1961) *Learning and Living 1790–1960*, London: Routledge & Kegan Paul.

Hoggart, R. (1957) *The Uses of Literacy*, London: Pelican.

Hudson, James William (1851) *The history of adult education, in which is comprised a full and complete history of the Mechanics' and Literary Institutions, Athanaeums . . . Of Great Britain, Ireland, America*, London: Longman, Brown, Green & Longman.

Hunter, I. (1988) *Culture and Government: The Emergence of Literary Education*, London: Macmillan.

Jepson, N. A. (1973) *The Beginnings of English University Adult Education – Policy and Problems*, London: Michael Joseph.

Kirkwood, G. and Kirkwood, C. (1989) *Living Adult Education: Freire in Scotland*, Milton Keynes: Open University Press.

Lovett, T. (1975) *Adult Education, Community Development and the Working Class*, London: Ward Lock Education.

McGuigan, J. (1992) *Cultural Populism*, London: Routledge.

McIlroy, J. (1996) 'Independent working class education and trade union education and training' in R. Fieldhouse *et al.* (eds), *A History of Modern British Adult Education*, Leicester: NIACE, 264–289.

Marriott, S. (1984) *Extramural Empires: Service and Self-Interest in English University Adult Education, 1873–1983*, Nottingham Studies in the History of Adult Education, Nottingham: University of Nottingham Press.

Martin, I. (1996) 'Community education: The dialectics of development' in R. Fieldhouse *et al.* (eds) *A History of Modern British Adult Education*, Leicester: NIACE, 109–141.

Moore, R. (1994) 'Ford EDAP: Breaking through the barriers', *Adults Learning*, 5 (9), 225–226.

NCIHE (1997) National Committee of Inquiry into Higher Education, Chair, Sir Ron Dearing, *Education in the Learning Society*, London: HMSO.

Parry, G. (1996) 'Access education in England and Wales 1973–1994: From second chance to third wave', *Journal of Access Studies*, 11, 10–33.

Robertson, D. (1997) 'Growth without Equity? Reflections on the consequences for social cohesion of faltering progress on access to higher education', *Journal of Access Studies*, 13.

Rowbotham, R. (1981) 'Travellers in a strange country: Responses of working class students to the University Extension Movement, 1873–1910', *History Workshop Journal* 12, Autumn.

Scott, P. (1995) *The Meanings of Mass Higher Education*, Milton Keynes: SHRE and Open University Press.

Silver, H. (1965) *The Concept of Popular Education*, London: Macgibbon & Kee.

Steele, T. (1993) 'A Science for democracy: The growth of university extension in Europe 1890–1920' in Barry J. Hake and Stuart Marriott (eds) *Adult Education between Cultures, Encounters and Identities in European Adult Education since 1890*, Leeds Studies in Adult Education, Leeds: Leeds University Press, 61–85.

Steele, T. (1997) *The Emergence of Cultural Studies: Adult Education, Cultural Politics and the 'English Question'*, London: Lawrence & Wishart.

Steele, T. and Taylor, R. (1995) *Learning Independence: a Political Outline of Indian Adult Education*, Leicester: NIACE.

Thompson, E. P. (1968) *The Making of the English Working Class*, London: Pelican.

Tiana-Ferrer, A., (1996) 'University extension and popular universities in Spain at the turn of the century: An educational strategy for social reform' in Barry J. Hake, Tom Steele and Alejandro Tiana (eds), *Masters, Missionaries and Militants: Studies of Social Movements and Popular Education in Europe 1890–1939*, Leeds Studies in Continuing Education, Leeds: Leeds University Press, 13–38.

Titmus, C. and Steele, T. (1995) *Adult Education for Independence: Adult Education in British Tropical Africa*, Leeds Studies in Continuing Education, Leeds: Leeds University Press.

Wiener, M. J. (1981) *English Culture and the Decline of the Industrial Spirit 1850–1980*, Cambridge: Cambridge University Press.

Williams, R. (1958) *Culture and Society 1780–1950*, London: Pelican Books.

39

UNDERSTANDING EDUCATION AND WORK

Themes and issues

Murray Saunders

INTRODUCTION

This chapter will address how the practices and concerns of the workplace, and, by implication employment, intersect with education. Characteristic of this topic is the breadth and quality of writing accompanied by continued uncertainty and lack of consensus on appropriate theoretical tools and thus interpretations of evidence. I shall pursue some preoccupations which have developed over 20 years of work in this broad area as a practitioner, researcher and evaluator.

In the late 1970s I began work on a piece of research which was to become a PhD thesis. Its central theme was the way in which redefinitions of educational practice might play a part in the reconstruction and development of society in general. I took as a case study the influential policy statement of President Julius Nyerere of Tanzania on the interrelationship between work and education. By redefining the priorities and processes of educational institutions, he hoped to create a better match with what he understood to be the realities of life and work in a developing country. He wanted education to be a driving force for a change in culture, which, at the time of the publication of the policy of 'Education for Self-reliance' in 1967, valued education mainly as a means of upward social mobility for a small minority of successful school graduates with little other consideration. In other words, the 'exchange' value of education was paramount with virtually no attention to its potential 'use' for the common good or national development. This research generated some persistent interests in the way education connects with the workplace and it is these interests that will shape the issues I want to address here. I shall take the postwar period as the canvas, but mainly the last two decades, with the main focus on the UK experience. However, reference will be made to the international case for comparative purposes and I shall conclude with some speculations and prescriptions for the future.

The first part of this chapter will address how the connections between education and work have been conventionally understood or theorised. The intention of this overview is to give an introduction to four significant underlying or tacit theoretical assumptions which pepper debates on education and work links, but are not always given form or shape. The perspectives are

- functionalist
- marxist
- liberal
- progressive/emancipatory.

The second part of this chapter will address briefly five subthemes which can be interrogated by issues arising from the first. These themes attempt to capture the tone and scope of current debates and preoccupations in education and work connections:

1 the globalisation of markets
2 education and changes in the organisation of work
3 trends in the connections between higher education and work
4 competence and learning in the workplace
5 the integrative perspective and the future of education and work.

The last of these subthemes speculates that a fifth perspective is evolving through the fundamental impact of information and communication technologies on knowledge acquisition, circulation and capture in work and education.

PART 1: UNDERSTANDING THE EDUCATION AND WORK RELATIONSHIP

This section will outline perspectives which have been used over the last three decades to explain the nature of the connection between education and work. There is relative fluidity between words and phrases like vocational, work/education relations, work education connections and so on. As a generic category, this chapter considers the way work and education are understood to be socially, culturally and economically connected. These connections may be recognised at one end of a continuum as temporally stable, systemically determining or causal in nature or, at the other, as diffused, changing over time, uneven and highly situated. These types of theoretical considerations are often expressed in terms of the *relative autonomy* or not of education in its relation with other areas of society, in particular the way society is stratified and the economic domain. The connections are also expressed both prescriptively and descriptively. On the one hand commentaries state what the connections *ought to be* and on the other how the connections *are working*, irrespective of the wishes or intentions of actors (learners, practitioners, politicians, employers, etc.).

The term *vocation* or *vocational* is a subset of these broader considerations. Michael Young (1990, p. 218) for example, critically identifies the active domain of the 'vocational' in three ways, all of which he ultimately rejects. In the first place, he identifies the connotation given to the idea of vocation as a 'calling', which he claims is individualistic and backward looking. This use evokes the psychological attraction to a particular occupation usually associated with selfless commitment to and absorption in a set of values and practices above all other considerations. In contrast to this view and because of the conceptual and political baggage 'vocational' brings along with it, Skilbeck (1994, p. 235) suggests that we should revert to this 'traditional', earlier connotation and not refer to education and training linked to work by use of the term. In this way our attention would be unambiguously focused. He suggests a term like *work-oriented education* when talking about a vocational education. He argues that training of a specific kind should be as close to the labour process as possible and thus become the main responsibility of the employer.

The second connotation, argues Young, has been conflated with a form of 'occupationalism'. It developed through a series of governmental initiatives during the 1980s in the UK which became known as the 'new vocationalism'. Despite the stated aims of these initiatives, he argues that they tended to focus in practice on specific job preparation rather than adult life in any 'emancipatory' sense.

The third connotation is identified with 'behavioural occupationalism', which he pictures as an ideology of production regulating education where so-called generic skill requirements of the 'new work order' have produced a preoccupation with the identification of core, key or transferable skill in curricula designs. In attempting a new formulation, Young introduces VAAL ('vocational aspects of academic learning') in which academic subjects are charged with contributing to the examination and critical assessment of work practices. We shall return to this view later. Skilbeck, as I note above, ultimately rejects the notion of vocation as a category of work-related education, precisely because of its association with employment. He argues for a much wider definition and scope for a work orientation in the curriculum.

This chapter will not use the term 'vocational', either in its narrow sense or in the sense which links it to a form of work-oriented liberalism that Richard Pring proposes (Pring, 1992). The references above give a flavour of the kind of prescriptive polemic such an approach generates. However, there is a place for a new vocabulary where new forms of understanding are being attempted. I shall return to the issue of discourse at that point. This section will now identify the principal theoretical means through which educational practices and work practices are understood. While there are connections between aspects of these frameworks, each stands as a distinctive, although not homogeneous, perspective on how education connects to work.

Two of the perspectives, namely the functional and the marxist, are 'structural' frameworks. They are modernist theories in that they tend to emphasise the overall patterning of trends and features of societies and offer explanations which operate at the macro or 'whole-society' level. They suggest strong causal frameworks and tend to be reductive, i.e. to look for explanations derived from unitary or meta-theories. To that extent we can say that they paint the big picture and do not easily translate to the explanation of specific processes or circumstances at the sub-societal level. The liberal and progressive/emancipatory perspectives are both prescriptive and descriptive but frame the link between education and work from the standpoint of 'education'. Their main focus is not on the connectedness between education and work but more on what educational practice should be about and, *de facto*, its relationship with work. The unit of concern tends to be with the experience of the individual and how that might impact on curricular designs rather than whole societies. The imperative therefore comes from the drive to provide a rationale for action in the educational domain rather than explanatory theory. Of course the nature of the individual as a worker, citizen, parent, etc. is a large part of the consideration of these perspectives. The belief is that a 'proper education' will automatically result in an individual being effective in these roles. The connectedness to work in these perspectives is not explicit but is addressed incidentally alongside connections to other aspects of the learners' lives. Explicit connections with work through the learning process and by the pedagogic actions of teachers is not precluded and is explicitly encouraged in some versions of these perspectives.

FUNCTIONALIST PERSPECTIVES

This perspective has a view of society which invokes the analogy of a living organism and uses a direct parallel between how its different institutions, parts and practices intersect, combine and interact and the way the constituent elements of an organism function to maintain the whole. The analogy suggests a society in which its elements or parts are mutually dependent and tend towards cohesion. The 'normal' condition is one in which the processes of each part of society dovetail and integrate to secure the health of the whole. The logic of the dynamic embedded in social processes is towards 'system maintenance'. This metaphor has its roots in the social theory of Auguste Comte in the eighteenth century. As a social theoretical framework it has dominated for two and half centuries and still has its echoes in current policy debate. This fundamental stance is underscored in the aspirations of global policy in the area of education and work linkages. It is where description and prescription meet. It offers the possibility of a world in which education should logically co-ordinate with the requirements of work because that is how societies function. The lack of 'technical' congruence which appears to occur between educational and work processes is a matter of 'dysfunction' subject to better or more appropriate 'fixes' at the level of policy. Put crudely, if labour market requirements are not being met, we should be looking for policy which brings them into line. Critically, this view presupposes that requirements can be 'known', that they are of a 'technical' nature and the 'norm' is that they can be met through the choice of appropriate policies. Frank Coffield (1997), in a statement summarising recent policy in the UK, captures the functionalist argument, operating at the level of an individual economy, succinctly.

> [D]evelopments in technology, in methods of production and in the globalisation of world trade are said to require a more highly skilled workforce. As a result, employers begin to apply pressure for educational standards to be improved. The outcome of this pressure can be seen in the previous Government's three White Papers on Competitiveness (in HMSO, 1994, 1995, 1996).

Functional connections between education and work can be understood in terms of two key metaphors: *bonds* (see Watts, 1983) or the functions of education and the idea of *human capital*. Bonds or the functions of education described by Watts refer to the way education acts to 'service' social imperatives derived from employment. These functions fall into four categories:

1 selection
2 socialisation
3 orientation
4 preparation.

Importantly, the economic level of activity in this framework is logically prior to that of education and to some extent determines the educational experience.

He describes the way education functions by a process of *selection* (that is the allocation and selection of young people for positions in the social division of labour). The theory is that on the basis of the testing and examination of young people and their acquisition or not of qualifications at different levels, society is able to disperse them appropriately into employment. Watts and subsequently many others have indicated the way in which this 'technical' logic breaks down. Among the problems are the failure of qualifications accurately to reflect skills and abilities, the lack of access to different types of qualifications, the different status of varying types of qualifications, the way employers use qualifications to select, the way young people use qualifications as exchange, and the way different qualifications are valued on criteria other than usefulness at work.

The second function identified by Watts is that undertaken by the *socialisation* process embedded in pupils' experience of schools. This is a complex process which incorporates a continuation of highly differentiated cultural meanings developed through family, community and peer group. To some extent it refers to the ways educational institutions sustain images and expectations of the kinds of work and work role to which different 'types' of young person might aspire. Types of young person might be differentiated in terms of class, gender and race. It is functional in that there is 'continuity' between a stratified working environment and a stratified educational experience. These differences occur between and within schools: they can be both explicit and implicit processes and they can be passively and actively engaged in by all the key stakeholders in education. The net result is that individuals passing through the educational system will develop a deeply ingrained sense of their potential work persona or identity and this work persona is a result of the interactions of day-to-day school life. The main problem with this interpretation is that it attributes a great deal of theoretical power to educational systems as socialising agencies and it under-theorises the process of individual agency and choice. It may be that while educational systems are important, they are relatively weak agents of social control in comparison with other institutions such as the family, peer group, the media and work itself.

The third function of *orientation* moves from the implicit processes characterising socialisation to the deliberate curricular interventions designed to help young people understand the world of work. The most recognisable are those experiences in which careers guidance is given to young people to help them make career choices. Curricular interventions might also use the workplace in more general ways in which, to quote Jamieson (1993), the work-related curriculum might involve young people in learning *about* work (the workplace as an object of study, polytechnical education), *through* work (the workplace as a pedagogic aid or learning site in which the learning outcomes might not have any direct link to employment) and *for* work (in which there is an explicit attempt to socialise the young person into what are considered desirable, work-related attributes which might range from punctuality and tidiness to entrepreneurialism and enterprise).

The fourth function of *preparation* refers to the role education has in equipping young people with specific skills and knowledge required by the workplace. At its most general, these attributes might be numeracy and literacy. Watts argues there is consensus that it is inappropriate to introduce more occupationally oriented preparation with specific job-related activities in the compulsory school curriculum. This was before the development of the 'new vocationalism' of the 1980s in the UK and does not take into account the central policy of diversification in the national educational policies of many developing countries.

We have also entered a period of re-consideration of the idea of 'general education' as we confront the rapidly changing working environment of the next century. I shall return to this theme at a later stage.

Turning now to the second metaphor of 'capital', human beings or, more precisely, their latent labour power, can be understood in terms of human capital in which individuals and societies can invest. This investment will pay back, in societal terms, in increased wealth creation, productivity and competitiveness and in individual terms, in better jobs, more money, prestige and life chances. In functional terms, society and individual interests coincide as individual investment in education contributes to the health of the whole society and accrues advantage to the individual. In this way the market will function 'socially' naturally. So individuals will invest in their own education and defer gratification. They will also invest in those areas in which there is an economic demand for scarce skills or knowledge requirements because the market will pay them more and vice versa. It thereby creates a self-regulating system.

However plausible this view may be, at a whole-society and individual level it is simplistic and unravels under close inspection. For example, we can understand the massive expansion of higher education (HE) during the 1960s and early 1970s in the UK, as an application of a naïve human capital approach in which the existence of larger numbers of higher education graduates equated with economic and social gains. Socially the investment in HE has not produced the expected returns, as the market did not function effectively (students perversely wanted – and still want – to engage in esoteric study like sociology and cultural studies) and the expected transfer of general intellectual capability to economic verve and dynamism did not automatically meet the fast evolving requirements of new work processes. At the same time, the assumption (of human capital theory) that individuals would enrol in those subjects and degree programmes for which graduates are in demand in the labour market proved to be incorrect. The theoretical approach that follows the basic principles of market-governed investment on the basis of supply and demand simply breaks down in education and work relations. At other phases of education (i.e. primary and secondary education) there is plausibility in the argument that investment, at either individual or social levels (particularly basic literacy and numeracy), is a necessary condition for economic development or individual 'advancement'. However, while it may be a necessary condition for certain types of growth, it certainly is not sufficient. We know, for example, that low labour costs and low educational levels can combine to produce rapid growth in developing economies.

MARXIST PERSPECTIVES

As I note above, these perspectives share with the functionalists a focus on structure and on fundamental social forces or trends which shape and determine key aspects of life. While the focus is on the whole society, there have been many attempts to research the way in which these 'base' trends are played out in day-to-day activities or practices of real people in real time. These ethnographies, however, often have difficulty in connecting plausibly with the overarching theory. They appear reductionist and eschew the multidimensional explanations for social action which might be applied.

Classically, these perspectives presuppose a society that is understood by the way in which its members interconnect in the production of their means of existence. In other words, we need to look at the relations that exist between people as they work to clothe, feed and house themselves and their families. These relations differ depending on the moment of history being considered. At the present time we are living in the period characterised by the capitalist mode of production, in which the basic relationship is one in which classes of individuals buy or sell labour power. These are the 'great classes'. However, it is not an equal relationship. Those who buy labour power own the 'means of production' (factories, plant, etc.) and yield the forces of production (the technology). Those who sell labour power simply own their labour power and possibly their domestic capital (home). In order for surplus value to be created for the buyers of labour power, labour is underpriced and thus exploited. This is the great contradiction of interest in marxist theory. There are, of course, many critiques of this basic formulation. It is hugely reductive and, some have argued, bears little relationship to the complex web of global and national economic interests and interconnections which characterise societies in the very late twentieth century. However, debates informed by the idea that differences in society, particularly in power and economic advantage, are sustained through the education system, owe much to marxist precepts.

Now, where does education fit into this scenario and how might it connect to work? For some marxists, education is part of the state apparatus (the state in marxist theory broadly sustains the conditions under which the capitalist mode of production can continue) and plays an ideological role in reproducing a culture that accepts as natural the existing social framework. To this extent, it is very close to the functionalist formulation. This is hardly surprising in that both perspectives seek to explain the way in which 'order' is maintained in a society and refer to the same phenomena, however from polar opposite explanatory assumptions. Functionalist perspectives are built on integration while marxist perspectives are built on contradiction. Functionalists identify socialisation as a means of creating order; marxists identify it as a means of maintaining social control. Functionalists identify selection as means of distributing appropriate recruits into the division of labour. Marxists identify selection as a means of sustaining inequalities in the educational system and the advantage of one class over another in their access to power, prestige and life chances. Social control through different types of socialisation process and the resultant differences in cultural power are the enduring themes of marxist perspectives on education and work links.

Possibly the best-known application of the basic marxist standpoint on education and work is the work of the Americans Bowles and Ginntis (1975), later developed by another American Michael Apple (1993) and adapted by British theorists like Chris Schilling (1989) and Inge Bates (1989) who were writing on and researching the 'new vocationalism' of the 1980s. Bowles and Ginntis cultivated the metaphor of *correspondence* to capture the relationship between education and work in a capitalist economy. This metaphor, while heavily criticised and even made redundant by more sophisticated formulations (see Willis, 1977) has now undergone a resurgence in modified form. The metaphor refers to the way in which the social relations between teachers and pupils in schools produce deeply socialised work habits and attitudes (often described as the 'hidden curriculum') in pupils which correspond to those required by a disciplined and subservient labour force. Steeped in the assumptions of control and work practices of fordist forms of work organisation, this perspective emphasises the social control dimension of school-based practices and under-emphasises the extent to which 'useful skills' for employment might be developed through the educational system.

These theories tend to be reductive and overplay the power of the structure in their explanations of specific processes. Bowles and Ginntis's theory of correspondence depends on the capacity of schools actually to socialise pupils in the way it suggests. The evidence for this is uncertain. As noted above, schools are relatively weak in their socialising power in comparison with family, peers and media. The work of Paul Willis is a more authentic account of the way in which working-class boys (the 'lads') are 'prepared' for work. In this ethnographic research, he charts the progress of a group of working-class pupils in a comprehensive school in Britain as they go about their daily school life.

The connection between school and work is not via a simple socialisation process in which the values of the school are internalised by the lads who are thereby formed into compliant workers. It is almost the reverse of this account. The lads have a view of their future lives as masculine, working-class identities. Their experience of school consists of a rehearsal of the culture they assume they will inherit. It is hard, grafting and includes many ingenious, often humorous ways of undermining the authority of the 'boss'. Schools might correspond to work but not in the way envisaged by Bowles and Ginntis. It is the lads' version of correspondence rather than the school's which prevails. The school manifestly fails as an agency of occupational socialisation in a technical or functional sense but succeeds as a rehearsal of the lads' future work identities in which they collude in their own exploitation. The collapse of the youth labour market and the change in the manufacturing base of the UK economy give these analyses a historical feel. Bowles and Ginntis also fail to account for the way schools might prepare middle-class or studious pupils, while the female gender and race dimensions are completely absent. However, variations on the socialisation or induction theme which focus on the middle or ruling class have been influential. Of particular significance is the work of French theorists like Pierre Bourdieu (Bourdieu and Passeron, 1979), who have identified the way in which education can play a part in the production of the cultural capital on which middle-class young people can draw to enter successfully the division of labour and the social networks of the rich and powerful.

In structural terms, a more sophisticated formulation concerns the separation of mental and manual labour in the school process, which reproduces the relations that characterise the workplace. Interestingly, it offers insight into the marxist perspective on the current relationship between education and work. If we give broad credence to the view that work organisation is changing and the character of labour at all levels is shifting from overtly hierarchic, 'command' relations to more diffused, devolved responsibility, the educational system might be required explicitly to intervene in the socialisation of young people in an attempt to prepare them for the new work order. To the extent that systems like the General National Vocational Qualification (GNVQ) in the UK are designed around an integration of vocational and general academic processes and 'key' skills, we can sense a change in focus. If we add to this the dismantling of traditional stable, working-class cultures over the last two decades whereby class identities have become diffused and have been replaced in some geographical areas by localised unemployment cultures, then the relevance of Willis's analysis to present circumstances in our schools shifts. What we might now be negotiating is a neo-correspondence, in which the link between education and work is being expressed, not

690

in analytical descriptive terms but in a prescriptive language. In theoretical discourse, the structurally derived rehearsals of future work cultures (in either the active or passive sense) are being replaced by the inclusion of explicit curricular designs that evoke the changes embodied in the new work order. Explanation gives way to legitimation. This process is focused particularly on the post-compulsory rather than compulsory sector of education in the UK. These changes will be discussed in Part 2 below.

THE LIBERAL PERSPECTIVE

In an important sense the phrase 'liberal education' has come to signify an antidote to those conceptions of education which are justified by reference to extrinsic factors or processses and have a largely instrumental approach to decisions on content, teaching or learning. It is in this light that 'liberal perspectives' have entered the debate on education and work.

It is important to identify what kind of basic perspective it embodies. It can be traced to the Platonic dichotomy between the idea of a liberal education for its own sake, the preserve of an aristocratic class, and an education for the masses which, given their destiny as workers, should be shaped by the requirements of their future role in the division of labour. The legacy of this formulation is the retention of ideas concerning higher ideals and citizenry, learning for its own sake, and the notion of a general, unfettered, universalistic curriculum free from the sectoral interests of time, class, economics or politics.

What is important is the distinction between two dimensions of the analysis: what students might be doing in the name of a 'liberal curriculum' and second, how this might connect with their future working lives. Future work roles are important in the liberal view. What is axiomatic is that young people are best prepared for these roles by an educational experience which is 'broad, deep and informed by a whole culture'. The strategies employed to achieve the engagement with this 'traditional' curriculum might well involve interactions with work, not as direct preparation for particular occupations, but as pedagogic process. The defining feature of this perspective is that the link between education and work is expressed in terms of the educated person rather than work requirements. An educated person will be, *de facto*, an effective worker in this broad sense. Effectiveness, however, should not be understood in a narrow or short-term frame or be reducible to the requirements of particular employer interests or national economies. It is a much loftier sense of effectiveness linked to the civilising aims of good citizenship. It may well be the case that an educated person will eschew the mind-bendingly boring, the hierarchically restricting or the environmentally inappropriate elements of the workplace. In which case, being an effective worker might well involve resistance to such features within the courses of action implied by a democratic society.

The 'liberal perspective' considers as misconceived the explicit preparation for work through work-related activities as part of a general education. According to this view, explicit, functional preparation involving job-related skills and knowledge should be undertaken while at work or immediately prior to undertaking it. Interestingly, this broadly complies with the current World Bank view (Middleton *et al.*, 1993).

This perspective is arguing for what best prepares an individual for a rewarding and responsible life. Work is not perceived in terms of wealth creation or competitiveness but through the eyes of the educator. So Paul Hirst and Richard Peters (1975), probably the most influential British philosophers of the liberal curriculum tradition, are able to identify the kind of general objectives to which an educator might aspire, e.g. autonomy, creativeness and critical thought. However, they argue that underlying these general objectives are 'the achievements of objective experience' and further, the most fundamental objectives of all are those of a cognitive kind, on the basis of which, out of which, or in relation to which, all others must be developed' (Hirst and Peters, 1975, p. 61). These fundamental 'modes of knowledge and experience' can be divided, they argue, into seven areas which are irreducible and should form the basis of a general school curriculum. They broadly correspond to the compulsory core curriculum embodied in the national curriculum of the English system and would be recognisable, more or less, in any country in the world. What is important for this perspective is the democratic imperative that no child should be denied access to these forms of knowledge and experience in the mistaken belief that they are not 'relevant' either to them or an extrinsic interest like the needs of employers. Relevance is not a matter of compromise on forms of knowledge but a matter of pedagogic skill and design. A general induction into these forms of knowledge would constitute the basis of any other intellectual or 'practical' preparation, including work. In this formulation no explicit connection with work is denied in the educational experience of young people, providing it is undertaken in the pursuit of fundamental knowledge and understanding. Of interest in these formulations is that skills are not divorced from knowledge and understanding but rather problem-solving, reasoning powers, sifting and sorting the relevant from the irrelevant, checking generalisation against evidence, the capacity to communicate effectively in a variety of forms, etc. are embedded in the process of induction into the forms of knowledge.

The main problem for this perspective lies in the extent to which young people are successfully inducted into the forms in the way envisaged by the philosophers. The reality has been that on many occasions the forms of knowledge have been taught and learned in disembodied chunks of memorisable information for the later regurgitation in a literate-based exam. Only those students with the cultural means of accommodating the strategic importance of this process have benefited. The rest have sifted themselves out of the educational process.

THE PROGRESSIVE/EMANCIPATORY PERSPECTIVE

This perspective is associated with styles of learning leading to the personal and social goals of individual growth, civic participation and democratic emancipation. It is possible to distinguish two important subthemes. The first affiliates personal growth and 'learner centredness' and the second social reconstruction through empowered democratic participation. The meeting point is that the style and processes of learning undertaken by individuals are central to the achievement of either goal. The fundamental position of this perspective is optimistic. It positions education centrally in social and personal reconstruction. It tends to under-emphasise the social and political context or the structural determinants identified by functional and marxist perpectives. It also under-emphasises the nature of the knowledge and skill that the liberal perspectives see as a starting-point for deciding what should be learned. It attributes great transformative power to the educational process through the personal growth or cultural re-orientation of individuals.

Like the liberal perspective, the work/education link is not an explicit preoccupation for the 'learner-centred' subtheme. Its stance is generally justified by reference to a fusion of ideas containing elements of egalitarianism, i.e. the rights of the child or the learner should not be subsumed or repressed by the teacher or educator. The learner may well 'know' what is best for them, or what is in their best interests. The position of the educator is to 'enable' this process of discovery to occur rather than to direct it. This characteristic is concerned with a form of 'interactional politics' but the other, and possibly more profound, is derived from a tacit theory of learning in which familiarity, individual practice and the extent to which learning is 'situated' or 'contextualised' are hugely influential on the quality and level of learning that is taking place. The thinker and educationalist Paolo Freire (1992), for example, understood the power of situated learning in his ideas on the way literacy programmes might work in rural communities. There is not an explicit relationship between a concept of 'education' and effectiveness at work or any other area of practice. Like the liberal perspective, the emphasis is much more on the quality of learning, its role in the growth of the person, their sense of fulfilment and self-esteem as a result, and finally their capacity to take up a responsible, thoughtful and active role at work or in civic society. This is certainly a Freirean aspiration. However, this perspective does make a number of assumptions. The most problematic is the last. It may well be that, in the view of the individual, work is the last thing they would be fulfilled in doing and a meta-value or overarching value (like civic responsibility) might have no influence if the learner is in control and does not subscribe to it.

However, the idea of work is pivotal for the reconstructionists, not as an instrumental justification, but in terms of the learning process and the future or current role of learners as working people. What is particularly important is that this perspective, like the liberal perspective, is operating in the prescriptive theoretical domain rather than the descriptive/ analytical framework adopted by the structural perspectives. John Dewey's work (1963) stands as the most influential and still relevant exposition of the position of work as a vehicle for learning, personal growth and active citizenship. His emphasis, however, was the link between experience or 'doing' and learning and thinking. 'Doing' had its most useful expression in 'work' or more precisely, 'occupations'. He rejected the divisions between the mental and manual but was quite clear that 'work' should be complex enough to allow for 'intellectual' growth which was, for Dewey, the dominant aim of education. It was in the reflective process during and after experience that 'cognition' resides.

An important variant of this theme has been the diversified curriculum, which has characterised curriculum innovation in the post-colonial educational systems of developing countries. These innovations have proceeded in an uncertain environment. Education has often been the site on which anti-colonial movements had fought battles for equal opportunity during the late colonial period. An element in the political platforms of independence struggle had consistently been opposition to a dual educational system. The recent history of the politicisation of secondary schooling in South Africa is a case in point. These systems generally consisted of a schooling for the indigenous population which prepared the mass for work as agricultural labourers and for the few, an academic curriculum to prepare clerks and low-level administrators and, for a tiny minority, opportunity for higher education study either in the colonial 'mother country' or in a few institutions which evoked the system of the white minority on a much less resourced scale.

Liberation had its expression in the educational field, by an insistence on universal access to the academic curriculum. The attempts by the colonial powers to adjust the curriculum of colonial states to reflect the agricultural destinations of most young people were fiercely resisted. Once independence had been gained in the 1950s, 1960s and early 1970s, however, it was quite clear that an education based on the academic European system was glaringly inappropriate and fostered an elite, Eurocentric, cultural orientation as well as demonstrating a hopeless lack of continuity with the lives of up to 80 per cent of the population. Diversified systems soon began to appear. These systems developed curricula which included vocational elements and extra-curricular activities including work, school farms, etc. which were intended to evoke, more realistically, the likely work destinations of young people. At the same time, they attempted to encourage a more positive attitude amongst young people towards the rural way of life and nation-building. To that extent, the aim of these approaches was to reconstruct the consciousness of young people through the educational system. The central problem was, and still is, that young people and their families understand education individualistically as the principal route up and away from the harsh realities of rural life, not as a preparation for, or a commitment to, rural development, as Foster has so cogently argued (Foster, 1982). As noted in the introduction, President Nyerere of Tanzania provides the most eloquent and inspirational expression of this reconstructionist approach to education and work links in his policy of *Education for Self-reliance*. Cultural reconstruction was the pivotal aim in this policy. The 'structural' imperatives of selection and distribution so intrinsic to educational systems and so dominant in the minds of rural communities remain stubbornly subversive of these attempts to re-orientate the education/work connection.

So where does this overview take us? We have on the one hand perspectives that emphasise the way education and work connect at the level of the whole society. The general conclusions from these perspectives are that work and education do not connect very strongly in terms of the technical dimension of the jobs people end up in but connect quite strongly in terms of who does what job and how they might do them as social or interactional practices in the workplace. This is not good news for the policy-makers because it is precisely the 'technical match' between education and work which has driven global educational policy for more than three decades. More problematic is the interpretation of perspectives which see the education/work link through what and how individuals learn. There is common ground that education connects to work through the learning process rather than through specific content. It is this connection which might form the basis of a fifth perspective to which I shall return in the final section of Part 2. Ultimate judgements about the efficacy of the analyses offered by the structural perspectives and the prescriptions offered by the educational perspectives will depend to a great extent on the changing nature of work.

PART 2: TRENDS IN EDUCATION AND THE NATURE OF WORK

The second part of this chapter is divided into five sections, each of which addresses an important theme in the policy and practice of education and work connections. These themes are not, of course, definitive but are intended to capture the tone and content of current debates in the field.

GLOBALISATION

This chapter has argued that the efficacy of policy which depends on structuralist perspectives relies to a great extent on the accuracy with which they identify trends and changes in the nature of work. A key concept in describing these changes is the idea of globalisation. While some analyses are genuinely 'global' in nature (Dore, 1976; Middleton *et al.*, 1993), many view global changes in the nature of work from the perspective of the 'advanced' economy preoccupation with competitiveness.

It is important, however, to distinguish between global integration of markets from global homogenisation of modes of production and forms of work organisation. The two are not logically connected, indeed it may be that global market integration depends in some sectors (e.g. the leisure industry, textiles, fancy goods, electronic component production) on modes of work organisation which are extremely regressive in nature and reflect nineteenth rather than twenty-first century forms of work organisation. These forms are characterised by very low wages, long hours, low job security, poor health and safety regulations, child labour and non-existent employment rights.

Reference is made in the West to work changes in Japan and other South East Asian economies (just-in-time production techniques, flexible team working, quality management systems) and their connection to particular educational strategies (high time allocations to maths and science, large amounts of set homework and relentless testing regimes). This combination was associated with the production of high-quality products and global competitiveness. Of note however, is the experience of these economies during the late 1990s, in which shifts in the price of labour power and underlying investment and lending policies have resulted in many company closures with resultant social dislocation and political instability. This suggests that the quality and nature of education and skill preparation or particular forms of work organisation will not in themselves determine long-term economic and social health in the new market environment.

In using concepts like globalisation, it is important to identify its focus precisely. The term is used here to refer to the process by which forms of cultural, social and economic practices are becoming globally integrated. Commentary on global changes in the nature of work should be tempered by the knowledge that approximately 70 per cent of the working population of the world is involved with labour-intensive subsistence agriculture with traditional forms of organisation, using traditional technology and with a per capita annual income which would not feed a family in the 'advanced' economies for a week. What is disturbing about these facts is that this huge proportion of the world population increasingly shares with the much smaller population of the 'advanced' economies, an increasingly homogeneous global culture of expectations through access to the media and that they are locked into the same global trade cycle. To some extent there has been cultural and trading convergence on the back of these traditional forms of work organisation. Further, globalisation means that in every country, no matter how poor, there is an 'enclave' of individuals and families which not only identifies with the global culture but gathers its economic benefits to itself. Extreme differentiation then occurs both within and between national boundaries.

In the light of these observations, I consider most commentaries that refer to globalisation in connection with education and work to mean the way in which global economic markets have suggested different types of 'preparation' for young people, so that individual economies, particularly of the 'advanced' type, might compete effectively. To that extent the analyses see globalisation in functional terms. The proceeding discussion will focus in particular on the circumstances in the 'advanced' economies unless otherwise stated.

EDUCATION AND CHANGES IN THE ORGANISATION OF WORK

It is striking how work in the advanced economies has become increasingly 'casualised' and 'part-time'. This means that terms and conditions of employment for increasing numbers of workers involve contracts which are for a fixed term or may be varied in other ways, including only part of their available time for work. The advantage for employers is that they can respond relatively quickly to new circumstances and opportunities. The disadvantage for them is that such conditions do not foster longer-term loyalties and commitment amongst employees and in some cases militate against developing continuity in teams, as employees have no particular reason for staying with one employer. For the employee there does not seem to be any particular advantage to this tendency, apart from increased mobility. The disadvantages are clearly in the difficulties of longer-term domestic planning and feelings of self-worth. The higher the level of specialised skill and the strength of those skills in the labour market will determine the extent to which an employee is favoured by casualisation or part-time working. This type of work is very close to consultancy and might be associated with 'portfolio' working, in which an individual will have more than one employer who outsources or subcontracts services and functions hitherto contained within the organisation. Most casualisation and part-time work, however, is sector specific (e.g. retail, distribution, hotels, catering) in areas of work in which women are mainly employed for relatively low wages.

A second consideration concerns changes in the way in which the practice of work itself is organised. The view is that the advanced economies are experiencing a shift from work processes that were organised hierarchically (particularly between managing functions and production or operational functions), based on a strong internal division of labour in the production process with very different educational and training backgrounds held by the occupants of different positions within the enterprise. The shift has been a result of a crisis in this 'fordist' mode of organisation, which has characterised industrial production for at least the first three-quarters of this century. Fordist modes involve those characteristics outlined above but also the notions of mass production via assembly lines for mass consumption. This mode of organisation, almost now a metaphor for 'traditional organisation', is threatened by changes in consumption patterns, volatile markets and a need for flexible, innovative responses to rapid changes in requirements. This analysis suggests that, increasingly, firms are attempting to integrate rather than prescribe clear divisions of labour. Rather than sustain layers of management function, firms are looking for reductions in management layers. Rather than clear hierarchic lines of management, firms are seeing where decisions can be devolved and taken by teams organised around project goals rather than functional roles and so on. The discourse of 'post-fordism' is in line with this description. We have team leaders, team members and section co-ordinators. We have coaching rather than training and projects rather than assembly lines. It is certainly the case that the rhetoric of 'post-fordism' has become hegemonic. However, is this vision of change accurate? There are of course sceptics. As early as the 1970s, Braverman (1974) identified a malign tendency in which people in work were being deskilled and rendered increasingly powerless. Andrew Sayer and Richard Walker (1994) persuasively argue against the kind of dualist analysis offered above. The most relevant point they make in connection with education and work links, is that fordism might never have been a dominant mode of work-based organisation and forms of work organisation have always been far more differentiated and uneven than these theses suggest. *De facto*, if it is a mistake to characterise economies as fordist, how can they be post-fordist?

Educational policy development has addressed the fact that, however slim the evidence is for a widespread shift in organisation along the lines post-fordism suggests, we do know that many and varied forms of organisation are now characterising work. The discourse of work organisation, if not the forms of work organisation itself, has undergone a shift. We know that a preoccupation with the nature of work has helped shape the orientation of educational policy-making in the advanced economies for the last 30 years or so. This preoccupation has been mainly expressed in terms of the functional requirements work might have of its potential participants.

The dominance of the work preparation theme in educational policy is pronounced. In the developing economies, as indicated earlier, diversified curricular forms characterise many national approaches (see Middleton *et al.*, 1993). The question in the advanced economies has been how diversified (explicitly work-related) should the general or compulsory curriculum be? Most European systems have adopted the line that work is best served by future employees experiencing general education at compulsory schooling phase. The argument that preparation for work is a legitimate prescription for the design of educational policy as well as a functional description is dominant. What is interesting is that liberal justifications of curriculum policy are now recast and co-opted as justifications for forms of effective preparation for work rather than in terms of effective cultural reproduction or education for its own sake. That is not to say that work connectedness does not characterise curricular policy at the compulsory stage (through work experience, work shadowing, enterprise schemes, etc.), but that it is justified as a pedagogic process rather than as subject knowledge. The TVEI (Technical and Vocational Education Initiative) experiment in the UK during the 1980s, considered as a more explicit preparation for work, was superseded by the UK national curriculum, a subject-specific curricular framework, reflecting this emerging consensus. The presence of 'work' in the educational policy domain is also apparent through the various attempts to promote the interests and awareness of 'industry' by encouraging local employers' participation in governance, sponsorship and partnership arrangements with educational institutions.

PREPARATION FOR WORK IN HIGHER EDUCATION

Post-compulsory, transitional or work-based education policy presents a much more fractured and uncertain prospect with respect to education and work links. The liberal, general education thesis which distinguishes education/work policy at compulsory phases of education, gives way to the emergence of neo-correspondence in the further and higher educational system (post-compulsory). This is a curricular orientation which more explicitly prepares young people for teams, project work, flexibility, problem-solving, decision-making and a range of other generic or multidisciplinary activities which are driven by a vision of a post-fordist work order. This orientation is manifest in the key, core or generic skill components in General National Vocational Qualifications (GNVQs) and National Vocational Qualifications (NVQs), along with many other higher education initiatives in the UK educational system (e.g. Enterprise in Higher Education initiative).

Despite real difficulties in identifying just what graduate employment is like, there is a growing consensus about the nature of the emerging labour process for graduates. Brennan *et al.* (1996, p. 8) however, in a recent review of the available literature, confirm the scepticism indicated above. They point to the difficulties researchers have in researching jobs that require higher education levels. The major tasks of graduates are hardly accessible to direct observation and they are often intertwined with other tasks. Analysis of high-level jobs is by definition incomplete regarding 'requirements' because graduates are expected to shape, innovate and restructure work tasks actively, and errors of prediction and in planning are more frequent than for competencies which require shorter periods of training. However, the belief in the existence in a shift from mechanistic to more organic forms of organisation in graduate-level employment is enduring.

This profile of graduate requirements has become packaged and to some extent has washed back on the nature of the HE experience, producing some interesting effects. We can adapt and develop what Brennan *et al.* (1996, p. 8) suggest are pressures for change emerging from the division of labour into the following:

- As a consequence of the difficulties faced in matching specific competencies and work tasks, employers increasingly tend to emphasise broad knowledge and flexible attitudes of graduates.
- There is a widespread conviction that a growing number of jobs require knowledge from several disciplines, thus calling for new fields of study for interdisciplinary learning or for collaborative learning.
- There is a growing mistrust on the part of employers in many European countries as to whether traditional modes of HE are suitable for preparing graduates, who are able to go on to learn professional problem-solving on the job. Instead, HE is itself expected to train graduates explicitly for professional problem-solving. Most frequently modes of experiential learning are advocated in this context.
- Employers tend to place a high value on social skills, attitudes and motivation in recruiting graduates.

This functionalist analysis points to the emerging prescriptive theory of correspondence as a mode of interpreting the link between higher education and work. The question is to what extent has the new genericism moved away from the kind of 'academic genericism' formulated by writers like Ronald Dore (1976)? It is true that the new formulation has a much closer correspondence to the work profile identified by Teichler and Khem (1995), but in essence it is almost the same as generic scholarly traits. New elements, however, are the inclusion of the rehearsal of more explicitly work-oriented processes like work-based projects and learning, working in teams, interdisciplinarity, project work, social and communication skill development.

In other words, these curricula are rehearsing the *operationalisation of the social and work context* in which the traditional or liberal intellectual capacities were intended to be displayed. The functional deficit to which these writers refer is not in academic practices themselves but in their explicit connection to work practices. This latter process had been under-theorised and more or less seen as a form of organisational naturalism (it will just happen). The crucial change has been in the growing insistence that a range of bridging experiences must be provided for students which will enable their higher education experience to be more deeply coupled to their future work role. This explicitness has come from a crisis of confidence in the idea of the transfer of general intellectual capability. British government policy has reflected this lack of confidence and has absorbed tacitly the neo-correspondence analysis by the development of a range of interventions and pronouncements which are designed to edge HE teaching and learning towards these explicit *bridging* or reconstructionist activities.

The alternative, of course, is to operate a much tighter control over the supply of graduate labour to 'fit' the requirements of the labour market more precisely. This *manpower planning* approach, however, has its own problems. As Teichler and Khem suggest (1995, p. 117), it is based on the assumption that educational policies should be oriented at expected and formulated needs and demands in order to reinforce economic growth and technological development. Problems arise in three areas:

1 Manpower planning can only work on the basis of quite draconian controls over undergraduate recruitment and graduate employment opportunities. Neither is possible in a capitalist economy or a social democratic political state. Without these controls, other inducements are ineffective.

2 It has proved very difficult to predict manpower requirements on the basis of economic and social need analysis with any accuracy. This left the precise throughput of students impossible to co-ordinate.

3 In a quasi manpower planning environment, projections of student enrolments were often wildly out, leaving key areas either under- or over-subscribed.

The plausibility of manpower planning models to some extent rests on a tacit critique of naturalistic functionalism, i.e. leave it to the market and it will 'sort itself out'. The market could not deliver the perceived requirements. What is interesting to note is that neo-correspondence can be interpreted as the most recent form of manpower planning in that it does herald a relatively high degree of government interventionism. However, there is an important difference. Neo-correspondence is non-specific in its focus. It suggests that *all students* should internalise the new requirements, thus avoiding the problems of co-ordination we identified above with traditional manpower planning models.

COMPETENCE AND LEARNING IN THE WORKPLACE

Paradoxically, the new work order, which has been presented as essentially organic rather than mechanistic, is increasingly associated with an education and training approach based on the idea of units of competence (for a clear exposition of this approach, see Jessop, 1991). It is to the general issue of the way education, learning and work are becoming 'integrated' that I now turn. The extent to which the competence-based approach has accomplished global ascendancy is striking. This approach requires the functional analysis of jobs (within occupations) to derive elements and units of behaviour or performance which can be specified and 'evidenced' so that an individual can be declared or certified competent at a job and awarded a qualification. These specifications are identified by leading bodies of occupations who constitute the award-giving authority. In the UK system they are designed to cover five levels which are broadly analogous to the introductory competence of a novice through to post-graduate expertise. The approach has been extensively criticised over the last ten years.

Nigel Norris (1991) argues that competence-based approaches tend to reduce job competence to atomised, observable behaviours, which may not embody competence in the sense of generalisable or holistic capability or, indeed, situated competence. This argument rehearses some of the issues raised above in the context of the nature of work-based learning. It suggests that there is a conflation of the notion of an 'act' and a 'competence', so the charge is that such systems are behaviouristic and reductionist. As Hodkinson would have it: 'Role performance dominates, and is seen as a composite of skills, knowledge and understanding. Knowledge and understanding underpin performance and, where possible, are to be tested through it' (Hodkinson, 1992, p. 31).

This critique maintains that the competence approach isolates or dismembers job-related action and encourages an alienated, atomistic framework for work capability rather than holistic understanding. Unless specifically built in to redress this tendency, holistic understanding will be de-emphasised (see also Ashworth and Saxton, 1990). This argument seems particularly pertinent for pre-work vocational training in which competence approaches are being used instead of 'education'-driven courses. These approaches find that the broader knowledge base is unspecified and experientially derived situated knowledge is absent, potentially leaving a much denuded structure. Saunders (1995) argues that it may well be that vocational degree schemes linked to higher education will retain a broader knowledge component, even though the logic of a competence-based approach suggests it is not needed.

While the argument that competence-based systems embody a reductionist concept of the nature of work practice is plausible, it is important to distinguish whether this tendency operates in different types of work context. The danger of reductionism may be more acute at the higher levels of qualification and their associated training. Winter (1992), with reference to social work practices, suggests that work practice may embody complex and potentially non-routine aspects along with a wide range of associated knowledge. Research on this extended notion of professional and organisational knowledge produced and sustained through situated work practice (see Blackler, 1995; Eraut, 1994; Lave and Wenger, 1991) suggests a danger that competence frameworks are simplistic or unidimensional.

What does the competence-based approach imply for theories of social practice in general and work practice in particular? In specifying job-related activity by the use of competence statements, we are asserting that for the purposes of developing the capability of a workforce, work can be understood predominantly in terms of technical rationality, i.e. a set of linearly connected components functioning together logically towards a specified end. While it is clearly the case that most jobs have a technical dimension, 'being good at it' involves a lot of other kinds of competence loosely implied by the logic of a 'job in action'. We may find therefore that there are unintended outcomes to competence approaches. As Jones and Moore suggest, by reducing work practice to competence statements, through a process of functional analysis, 'skills and behaviour are disembedded from everyday social relationships and cultural practices. Culturally embedded collective skill is replaced by an individualised, technical competency' (Jones and Moore, 1993, p. 392). While this may be true, would it not be the case in any abstract qualification system which was not entirely experientially derived? The problem for the proponents of the competence approach is that it actually cannot deliver what it promises. Observable job performance can never yield the collection of abilities which constitute 'being good at your job'.

The list of specific competencies associated with narrow or naïve conceptions of work-based learning connect to actual 'job capability' in the way a cybernetic or robotic representation of a human being reminds us of a person but somehow fails to capture the essence of 'personhood'. Lists of competencies remind but do not reconstruct practice at work. What is involved in a job may be only obliquely informed by competence lists. It may be, for example, that employees become involved in a competence scheme, experience it and perceive its meaning in ways that have little to do with an immediate improvement of skill, i.e. technical rationality. Sue Otter reported that positive responses of many of those who have been involved in work-based assessments may be more connected to feelings of well-being because their work and skill were being publicly acknowledged but a direct improvement in work effectiveness was not necessarily a perceived outcome (Otter, 1994).

With higher-level qualifications we may find a different kind of issue associated with the basis on which an appreciation of competence may be understood. The difficulty arises from the extent to which competence is embedded in the implicit knowledge people use as a resource for work-based decision-making or problem-solving, which cannot be accessed in any simple way. The point here is that the observable behaviour itself or even the formal knowledge base available for a particular work domain may tell only part of the story of an individual's competence, or indeed, a different kind of story altogether.

THE INTEGRATIVE PERSPECTIVE AND THE FUTURE OF EDUCATION AND WORK

A recent report by Valerie Bayliss (1998) suggests there is a consensus that a shift has occurred in the structure of work of advanced economies towards the provision of services and the production, management and circulation of knowledge, particularly through the use of information and communications technologies (ICTs). The power of these technologies to transform knowledge circulation and the rapid growth of their use within education, the workplace and the home problematises the perspectives on education and work links outlined above. The perspectives are based on a view that education/learning, family, community, work, etc. happen in different places, at different times, with different people, i.e.

spatially, temporally and in terms of 'practice', logically distinct. The power and potential of the new information technologies (WWW, electronic and video mailing and conferencing technologies, multimedia learning and information resources) lie in their capacity to reconstruct radically and integrate work, education, community and family practices. In the light of these changes, a fifth perspective on education and work which *integrates* aspects of the existing perspectives becomes plausible.

Over the last decade consensus has been developing among commentators like Richardson and his team and earlier Michael Young, along with reconstructionists like Malcolm Skilbeck, that prescriptions that dichotomise work and education are unhelpful, if not conceptually confused (Richardson *et al.*, 1995; Skilbeck *et al.*, 1994; Young, 1990). They adopt broadly John Dewey's prescription that the emphasis in compulsory education and work interconnections should be on pedagogic and learning processes which develop intellectual, social, personal and creative capabilities. Paradoxically, there is a global tendency towards general rather than vocational education at compulsory school age which might be reconstructed as a social investment in general human capability. In this modernised form, the liberal and reconstructionist project lives on.

Work becomes a powerful site for educational processes and activities. As Howieson *et al.* (1997) suggest, within this frame a range of associations, partnerships and collaborations between schools and work practices outside schools, aided by ICTs, becomes possible. This integrative orientation is evident in the discourse of contemporary UK policy and EU initiatives which encourage partnership approaches for the provision of learning opportunities that focus on unemployment (New Deal) and on education (Education Action Zones, University of Industry and Lifelong Learning).

Structural perspectives accurately identify the way in which educational experience is part of the process by which societies sustain differentiation between groups and individuals by distributing them socially, culturally and economically. They suggest that the distributive efficacy of education lies in social and cultural rather than technical outcomes. They also suggest the way policy-makers and employers confuse these two effects but pupils and their families rarely do. However, more recent 'post-structural' theory, like those reviewed by Rudd (1997), indicates the re-emergence of individual agency, choice and risk-balancing in theorising education and work connections. In addition, the ICT revolution has brought about the mediation of the structural imperatives suggesting much wider and unpredictable implications for the way people experience the education/work connection.

There is an impending crisis of confidence in academic practice, in particular higher education, as a sufficient preparation for the rapidly evolving new work order. It is here that a form of neo-correspondence is emerging. Aided by ICTs, education is being redefined as learning. At first sight, this redefinition is in danger of stripping away education's higher emancipatory or civilising goals and being reconstructed as a technical fix. Learning at work and work itself become integrated activities as it is increasingly difficult to distinguish between projects, planning, information-handling and evaluation, quality or learning circles. Higher education is often called upon to validate learning in this new environment and asked to provide a qualification framework. At the moment this requires the reconstruction and production of the learning experience in such a way that it displays 'academic' characteristics or meets higher education aims. Higher education is struggling to determine precisely what these might be in an environment in which intellectual endeavour is increasingly unconfined to the physical space and institutional practices of educational institutions. As Ronald Barnett suggests (1994), knowledge production, circulation and use are no longer the preserve of the educational or dedicated research institution.

The example of higher education suggests a possible long-term future in which learning processes are the focus rather than education. Examples of this trend are already emerging with the technological infrastructure being established in areas like California, in the USA and in enclaves of innovative practice in both the north-west and north-east of England. As education becomes de-institutionalised, the physical institutions of learning cease to be as socially important. Learning opportunities become freely and easily available to most individuals and groups via ICTs in, for example, the home, community and work-based learning centres. A new discourse of *virtuality* is being created for communities, networks and collaborative knowledge production. The structurally derived social, cultural and economic power of differences between educational institutions begins to diminish. If these trends continue, it might be the way the socially excluded can seize opportunities for knowledge use. In this scenario, the way individual and group identities are presently constructed, defined and sustained by their educational experience is transformed. Learning will be integrated into a much wider range of practices, including work. Ivan Illich's (1973) 30 year old vision of a deschooled society becomes a possibility. If learning is no longer in the hands of providers but learners, its emancipatory (educational) potential lies not only in content and process but also in open accessibility and use. This perspective might sound naïve but it is not. It acknowledges that learning processes will not challenge power directly but that education or learning will gradually cease to be the site on which social and cultural disadvantages are centred.

REFERENCES

Apple, M. (1993) *Official Knowledge: Democratic Education in a Conservative Age*, London and New York: Routledge.

Ashworth, P. D. and Saxton, J. (1990) 'On Competence', *Journal of Further and Higher Education*, Summer Issue.

Barnett, R. (1994) *The Limits of Competence*, Buckingham: Open University Press.

Bates, I. (1989) 'Versions of vocationalism: An analysis of some social and political influence on curriculum policy and practice', *British Journal of Sociology of Education*, 10, (2), 215–232.

Bayliss, V. (1998) *Redefining Work*, London: RSA.

Blackler, F. (1995) 'Knowledge, knowledge work and organisations: An overview and interpretation', *Organisation Studies*, 16 (6), 1021–1045.

Bourdieu, P. and Passeron, J. C. (1979) *The Inheritors: French Students and their Relation to Culture*, Chicago: University of Chicago Press.

Bowles, S. and Ginntis, H. (1975) *Schooling in Capitalist America*, London: Routledge.

Braverman, H. (1974) *Labour and Monopoly Capitalism: The Degradation of Work in the 20th Century*, New York: Monthly Review Press.

Brennan, J., Kogan, M. and Teichler, U. (1996) *Higher Education and Work*, London: Jessica Kingsley.

Burnhill, P. and McPherson, A. (1983) 'The Scottish university and undergraduate expectations', *Universities Quarterly*, 37 (3).

Coffield, F. (1997) 'Can the UK become a learning society?' Fourth Annual Education Lecture, School of Education, King's College London.

Dewey, J. (1963) *Democracy and Education*, New York: Macmillan.

Dore, R. (1976) *Human Capital Theory, Diversity of Societies and the Problem of Quality in Education*, London: Allen and Unwin.

Eraut, M. (1994) *Developing Professional Knowledge and Competence*, London: Falmer Press.

Foster, P. (1982) 'Education for self reliance: A critical evaluation' in R. Holly (ed.) *Education in Africa*, London: East African Publishing House.

Freire, P. (1992) *Pedagogy of the Oppressed*, Harmondsworth: Penguin.

Hirst, P. and Peters, R. (1975) *The Logic of Education*, London: Routledge & Kegan Paul.

Hodkinson, P. (1992) 'Alternative models of competence in vocational education and training', *Journal of Further Higher Education*, Summer issue.

Howieson, C., Raffe, D., Spours, K. and Young, M. (1997) 'Unifying academic and vocational learning: The state of the debate in England and Scotland', *Journal of Education and Work*, 10 (1), 5–37.

Illich, I. (1973) *Deschooling Society*, Harmondsworth: Penguin.

Jamieson, I. (1993) 'TVEI and the work-related curriculum', *Evaluation and Research in Education*, 7 (2), 51–65.

Jessop, G. (1991) *Outcomes: NVQs and the Emerging Model of Education and Training*, London: Falmer Press.

Jones, L. and Moore, R. (1993) 'Education, competence and the control of expertise', *British Journal of the Sociology of Education*, 14 (4).

Lave, J. and Wenger, E. (1991) *Situated Learning: Legitimate Peripheral Participation*, Cambridge: Cambridge University Press.

Middleton, J., Ziderman, A. and Adams, A. V. (1993) *Skills for Productivity: Vocational Education and Training in Developing Countries*, Washington, DC: Oxford University Press/World Bank.

Mill, J. S. (1867) *Inaugural Address delivered to the University of St Andrews*, 1 Feb. London: Longmans.

Norris, N. (1991) 'The trouble with competence', *Cambridge Journal of Education*, 21.

Nyerere, J. (1974) *Education for Self Reliance* in I. Lister (ed.) *Deschooling*, Cambridge: Cambridge University Press.

Otter, S. (1994) *Higher Level NVQs/SVQs: Their Possible Implications for Higher Education*, Sheffield: DfEE.

Pring, R. (1992) 'Academic respectability and professional relevance.' Inaugural lecture, University of Oxford.

Richardson, W., Spours, K., Woolhouse, J. and Young, M. (1995) *Learning for the Future*, London: Institute of Education, University of London.

Rudd, P. (1997) 'From socialisation to post-modernity: A review of theoretical perspectives on the school-to-work transition', *Journal of Education and Work*, 10 (3), 257–281.

Saunders, M. (1995) 'The integrative principle: Higher education and work based learning in the UK', *European Journal of Education*, 30 (2), 203–216.

Sayer, A. and Walker, R. (1994) *The New Social Economy*, Oxford: Blackwell.

Schilling, C. (1989) *Schooling for Work in Capitalist Britain*, London: Falmer Press.

Silver, H. and Brennan, J. (1988) *A Liberal Vocationalism*, London: Methuen.

Skilbeck, M., Connell, H., Lowe, N. and Tait, K. (1994) *The Vocational Quest*, London and New York: Routledge.

Teichler, U. and Khem, B. (1995) 'Towards a new understanding of the relationships between higher education and employment', *European Journal of Education*, 30 (2), 113–132.

Watts, A. (1983) *Education, Employment and the Future of Work*, Milton Keynes: Open University Press.

Willis, P. (1977) *Learning to Labour: How Working Class Kids Get Working Class Jobs*, Aldershot: Saxon House.

Winter, R. (1992) 'Quality management or the educative workplace: Alternative versions of competence-based education', *Journal of Further and Higher Education*, Autumn Issue.

Young, M. (1990) 'Beyond vocationalism: A new perspective on the relationship between work and education' in D. Gleeson (ed.) *Training and Its Alternatives*, Buckingham: Open University Press.

40

HIGHER EDUCATION IN A CONTEXT OF CHANGE

Tony Becher

Higher education is a vast topic: so no account of it within a reasonable compass can realistically aim to be encyclopedic. It is also heavily value-laden: so impartiality is an equally unattainable goal. The overview that follows, therefore, is both selective and personal. Its aim is to present the subject in a way that may be of interest to non-specialist readers, avoiding where possible the pervasive jargon and the abundant acronyms which characterise much of the relevant technical literature.

Bibliographical references have been limited, wherever possible, to sources which should be relatively easy to buy from, or order through, a good bookshop, or to access or borrow through inter-library loan, in a reasonably sized public library. All the titles listed are ones that are readable, clearly written and require no prior specialist knowledge.

MEANING AND PURPOSE

It might be supposed that, as a matter of principle, any account of higher education should begin by defining the term. As a matter of practice, however, any such attempt would be doomed to failure: what the term denotes is uncontrollably protean. Depending on the point in time and the location in space, higher education may be taken to refer variously to all post-secondary school courses, or more specifically to all programmes leading to recognised awards, or to those leading only to degrees, or – on the narrowest interpretation – to the offerings of fully fledged universities, to the exclusion of other types of institution. The constituents of a higher education system may be correspondingly varied. Although universities, in any given era and in any given country, would be seen as the central elements, there can be many other possible candidates for inclusion: technical colleges providing relatively low-level training for apprentices, sub-professionals and the like; monotechnics offering qualifications for a single profession or vocation (such as teachers' colleges, business schools, law schools, or schools of nursing); liberal arts colleges specialising in the provision of broad courses, mainly in the humanities and social sciences; polytechnics combining several vocationally oriented courses and often non-vocational ones as well, at degree or near-degree level; and some nationally specific institutions with high prestige outside the university network (such as the *grandes écoles* in France).

It follows that the purposes of higher education also defy any neat logical categorisation. At the individual level, those who enrol and subsequently pursue programmes are driven by the heterogeneous motives which characterise any educational activity, on a spectrum between uncontaminated love of learning and a utilitarian determination to improve career chances. For those who hold that institutions must have collective goals over and above those of their members, there is a further array from which to choose. Some institutions' mission statements (a currently fashionable genre in the UK in particular) emphasise the achievement of excellence in research; others give prominence to the quality of their teaching and their course provision; others focus on their roles in the community, their links with the industrial world or their commitments to participation in international scholarship. Given such diversity, there is little mileage in trying to identify either a single clear objective or a broad set of aims which uniquely characterise the academic enterprise.

But if higher education cannot be identified by tidy definition, or by the characteristics of its constituent elements, or in terms of a shared purpose, how can one know what it is? The response has to be a Wittgensteinian one: the concept is held together not by a single formula but by a set of family resemblances. There are important connecting likenesses, none of which applies universally but which none the less help severally to promote recognition. Whether a particular institution or type of institution is to be deemed a valid member of the higher education system depends in large part on how it relates to – what family characteristics it shares with – other institutions that are already accepted constituents of that system, bearing in mind both the current national context and the legacy of the past.

It is the universities within each higher education system – however wide its boundaries may be drawn – which both have the longest history and occupy the pivotal position. Moreover, they embody and illustrate well most of the problems and opportunities which confront present-day higher education. So although reference to other types of institution will not be excluded, it is inevitable that much of the subsequent discussion will tend to focus on them.

The annals of the academic world demonstrate that change is an endemic condition. The concept of the university has never remained constant for long: the path of its development has been a meandering one, and has at times doubled back on itself. In its early days in the mid-thirteenth century, the University of Bologna was controlled for some years by its student body, adopting a consumer-oriented stance to match the strongest wishes of the New Right in contemporary Britain. At more or less the same time, the University of Paris adopted a form of domination by the academic body which finds echoes in the post-communist universities of Eastern Europe. Higher education was at the outset uncompromisingly vocational, providing training for the clergy, the law and the medical profession (Cobban, 1975). It was not until much later that the notion of a liberal higher education came into vogue, with Cardinal Newman as its best-known proponent. Research emerged as a central feature of academic life – as against scholarship and teaching – in Germany and later the USA in the nineteenth century, but did not spread to Britain until the twentieth, and is still largely confined to specialist, non-teaching institutes and academies in much of the rest of Europe (Rothblatt and Wittrock, 1993).

It is appropriate, therefore, to see higher education as being in a constant state of flux, albeit with certain underlying continuities. In all its variant forms, it has been concerned with the accumulation and passing on of knowledge of an esoteric rather than an everyday kind. It has, except in its formative stages, been embodied in institutions, though not necessarily based in a single location. Its very existence presupposes students who have already attained a more than basic intellectual competence and academic staff who have the capabilities to teach at an appropriately advanced level. Its institutional form also requires non-academic staff to provide the administrative and other services necessary to support the central activities of teaching, learning and (where relevant) research.

That is about as much as can usefully be said by way of a general introductory account. What remains is to explore particular aspects of higher education which promise to offer indirect but relevant illumination to the topic, and which may serve collectively to promote a clearer understanding of a complex but fascinating set of activities. The following sections will examine, in turn, the nature and characteristics of the system as a whole; structural issues; financing and governance; institutional management; academic processes and practices; teaching provision; and quality demands. A final section will consider possible future directions for higher education as a whole.

EXPANSION OF THE SYSTEM

Higher education was, traditionally, an elitist phenomenon, attracting only a very small percentage of the relevant age-group. That age-group was in its turn largely circumscribed, with only a few aberrant students outside the 17–25 population (with the lower end mainly represented in the USA, and the higher in a number of continental European countries). Moreover, the use of the term higher education was confined to universities, to the exclusion, in more recent years, of a growing substratum of other post-compulsory institutions providing advanced level courses.

The relatively recent shift from elite to mass provision (see Scott, 1995) had its beginnings in North America, where the original land grant colleges, devoted to agriculture, engineering and the liberal arts, gradually came to offer a wider and steadily more academic provision. However, the floodgates remained tightly closed elsewhere until after the Second World War, when the returning conscripts were, in much of Europe and throughout the USA, given special opportunities, including financial incentives, to take degree programmes as an aspect of their rehabilitation schemes. The so-called GI Bill in America helped to extend still further the constituency for higher education, and at the same time to enlarge the number of institutions claiming university status.

The UK remained well behind its continental European counterparts, and even further behind the United States, until a sudden (but still carefully controlled) explosion took place in the 1960s, with the designation of half a dozen colleges of advanced technology as universities, and the creation of eight entirely new establishments. From that time onwards, there has been a more or less continuous, though by no means linear, increase in the number of students following degree courses in Britain, to a point at which they amount to roughly 33 per cent of the relevant group of school-leavers. The statistic is however misleading, since the actual student population includes as many students over as those under 25.

The growth in what is unquestionably the most expensive sector of education has been promoted by the engagement of national governments in a form of competitive bidding. The argument runs that any advanced nation must, in order to remain technologically and industrially competitive, have a large body of highly educated citizens: and that, in turn, requires a substantial investment in higher education. While this is seen as a welcome development by most of those whose livelihood depends on being employed in universities and other advanced level establishments, it raises two basic questions.

In the first place, the argument from international competition is clearly subject to Hirsch's paradox (Hirsch, 1977). This runs as follows: if, in a large crowd, one or more individuals stand on tiptoe in order to get a better view, it prompts others behind them (whose view is now further obscured) to stand on tiptoe themselves. Eventually, all or most members of the crowd find themselves standing on tiptoe, and are in that situation no better off *vis-à-vis* the rest than they were before. This phenomenon can be readily identified in the international jockeying for precedence, with French governments in particular setting higher and higher targets for the expansion of post-secondary numbers in a concern to better their European Union counterparts and to match up to the Americans and the Japanese. The predictable result is that their rivals are prompted to raise their own targets in response.

The second issue concerns the nature of the output (to use the fashionable jargon) from this seemingly limitless enterprise. Economic competitiveness tends to be defined mainly in terms of the development and provision of advanced technology and of scientifically based products, which in turn would seem to call for a workforce with a high proportion of qualified scientists and engineers. Unfortunately for the planners, however, in a large majority of advanced countries the choice of field of study is left to the applicants for higher level programmes, and – in nearly every case – courses in the humanities and social sciences, and vocational courses in non-scientific fields, are strongly preferred to those primarily required for a technologically dominated society. There seems to be something here equivalent to the economics of Passchendaele: vast numbers of inappropriately trained extra troops have to be thrown in simply to ensure the survival of those who are sufficiently experienced and competent to gain a few yards of ground.

Essentially similar problems can be seen to have beset less developed countries, many of which are only able to support a very limited number of universities, but which none the less devote a disproportionate share of the national education budget to their maintenance and expansion, leaving even basic primary education ill-provided. Again, there is often an element here of keeping up with one's neighbours, as well as of being seen to have a crown which is not altogether bereft of jewels.

There is also, according to Dore (1976), a problem about appropriate employment for graduates. What he termed 'the diploma disease' was the over-production in developing economies (Japan, his main subject, was still one at the time of his research) of highly qualified people who could find no jobs which made proper use of their intellectual capabilities and who were therefore forced to resort to occupations previously held by those who were less well educated. This served to create a downward spiral, leading to graduates beginning routinely to be taken on for less and less demanding and less and less well-paid jobs, while the non-graduates who previously held them had accordingly to lower their own occupational sights. The phenomenon is not, of course, entirely confined to less advanced economies, as the legendary New York taxi drivers with PhDs remind us.

Besides the frequently advanced economic justification for expansion, a more altruistic case is often made in terms of equality of opportunity. It has been rightly observed that social mobility is positively discouraged by demands for high admission qualifications. Entry to elite higher education is accordingly heavily biased towards the top end of the socio-economic scale, and the sons and daughters of professionals and other relatively wealthy members of society remain its major beneficiaries. Most taxpayers have therefore to contribute to a system that is subsidised in favour of those who least need subsidy, and which brings no benefit to their own children. Expansion, it was argued, would open up new educational opportunities to those with parents in lower-income groups, and so help to create a more egalitarian society. While this seemed an entirely reasonable case in theory, the outcome in practice has proved somewhat disappointing, in that in the UK and elsewhere in Europe much of the growth in numbers has been taken up by an increased percentage of entrants from well-to-do families and the children of white-collar workers, with only a relatively small proportion – albeit larger than before – of students from blue-collar and working-class backgrounds. In consequence, the gulf between the educated and the uneducated has widened. Such, alas, are the hazards of social engineering.

Arguably, the strongest case in favour of mass higher education is not in terms of its contribution to the national economy or its effects on levelling out social inequalities, but in virtue of its role in creating a more cultured and better educated citizenry, and thus in helping to promote a generally enhanced quality of life. Because that is not a proposition that will win obvious votes, it is not commonly advanced by politicians. However, it is one to which many academics – and probably a good proportion of graduates – would readily subscribe.

THE DECONSTRUCTION OF ACADEMIA

The consequences of the move from elite to mass higher education were first explored by Trow (1970), who argued that it called for radical changes in the structure and organisation of the system. Since mass institutions would by definition have to cater for a much more varied clientele than had been admitted to elite universities, they would have to provide a range of more flexible and less academically oriented courses. Moreover, since staff–student ratios were bound to be less favourable, given the need to limit costs, there would necessarily be changes in pedagogy as well. Further references to such changes will be made in the subsequent discussion of teaching programmes. At this point, another related set of considerations will be discussed, namely the loosening of the boundaries of academic activity.

British higher education has in the past been characterised as more tightly structured than its counterparts in other countries. In particular, it has involved relatively specialised undergraduate courses, covering a particular subject area in some depth over a limited timespan – characteristically three years of full-time study. It has been common to enter university straight from school, and to remain at the same institution throughout one's academic career. With the exception of Scotland, there has been no expectation that students should attend their local institution, so that the majority – following a long-established patrician tradition – have had to be accommodated away from home.

As the system has expanded, most of these constraints have disappeared. Courses in many institutions have ceased to be confined to a single discipline: what has sometimes been termed the 'pick and mix' approach associated for over a century with US universities has attracted a growing number of followers. Modular degrees, many of which enable students to take a series of self-contained short courses of their choice and to build them up through accumulated credits to the total required for a degree, clearly allow a greater flexibility than existed in the traditional system. Such programmes create the potential for locally based, part-time study (which is still relatively uncommon in conventional degree structures), and – through credit accumulation and transfer systems – also make it possible in mid-course to move between one institution and another to an extent unprecedented hitherto in Britain, though much more common in other European countries. The incidence of such mobility as yet remains modest, but has been further enhanced by special grants from European Union funds to enable students to spend a significant proportion – typically a year – of their total courses in an appropriate university in another member state (a detailed account is given in Maiworm *et al.*, 1991).

One consequence of what is sometimes inelegantly described as the massification of higher education has been to make it easier for those who, for one reason or another, missed out on going to university straight after school to take a degree course later in life. In particular, women of a generation in which higher education was considered to be a pre-dominantly male preserve have been able to demonstrate themselves very capable of aca-demic study. Overall, the undergraduate intake is now almost equally balanced in gender terms. Another related development has been to promote continuing education, in that it has become easier to adapt the system to allow for vocational, cultural and recreational part-time courses of varying lengths – from a day to a year or more – geared towards those who are motivated to go on learning at some stage after their formal education has been completed.

Distance education comprises a further break from the earlier pattern of provision. Given the acceptance of part-time courses for mature entrants, many of them in employment, it was perhaps a natural development to consider whether those concerned should necessarily be expected to have frequent contact with academic staff, or whether they might not be given the opportunity to study largely on their own. A major breakthrough in the concept of learning at a distance came in the form of the Open University in the UK, established in 1969. Although originally conceived to embody the then current ideas about educational technology, and in particular to concentrate on teaching by television, it soon – and, as it transpired, highly successfully – settled into a more straightforward pattern of high-quality, printed course books, carefully designed and painstakingly assessed written assignments, and a modest level of tutorial help and annual, week-long residential courses, aided to a fairly limited extent by broadcast and tape-recorded materials. Few other distance learning programmes – of which there are a steadily growing number, based on both university departments and commercial organisations – have been able to match the quality and professionalism of Open University provision: but several, particularly in vocational fields such as management, have proved to be economically viable and well subscribed.

Viewed collectively, the changes resulting from the advent of mass higher education have been dramatic, calling in question a whole variety of long-established traditions and taken-for-granted assumptions. Their effect can be likened to the deconstruction of art and music in the twentieth century, in which classical forms and structures have given place to a seeming freedom from any convention. None the less, there are important underlying continuities, maintained at least in part by the fact that the large majority of teachers in the system have themselves passed through it in the process of gaining the necessary qualifications and have, to that extent, assimilated the established values and assumptions of the relevant academic fields, even if they have later gone on to question them.

LINKS WITH THE WIDER SOCIETY

Within the higher education system, broadly defined, many of the institutions catering for subdegree qualifications have maintained a strong vocational bias, offering diplomas, certificates and the like geared to particular occupational qualifications. But although, as noted above, the early universities focused on training for the key professions of the time, they subsequently began to emphasise liberal and academic pursuits of a kind which distanced them from the everyday world and led them to be designated as 'ivory towers', set apart from society at large. As a rough and ready rule, in the elitist European universities of the late nineteenth century, and indeed into the second half of the twentieth, the more prestigious the establishment, the more concerned it was to guard its autonomy from external pressures, and hence to avoid commercial ties and community involvement.

The wider student clientele which characterises mass higher education has gradually, but in the end quite radically, altered the balance. It is only a minority of any year's intake which is ready to see higher education unequivocally as an end in itself or as a means to personal growth and fulfilment: for the most part, a degree has come to be viewed more profanely as a passport to a better job. Courses in hitherto unheard of fields (business studies, accountancy and the like) have multiplied apace at the expense of more traditional offerings, in the humanities, social sciences and science, while professional programmes (notably law) have also thrived.

One result has been to increase the degree of interchange between the universities and other social institutions. In particular, the professional bodies have been drawn in – or sometimes pushed themselves in – to discussions about the relevant curriculum programmes, while leading individual practitioners have been invited to act as part-time teachers on the practical aspects of professionally oriented courses.

For somewhat comparable reasons, commercial and industrial enterprises have begun to be more closely involved in academia than before. With a much increased proportion of graduates coming into the job market, the major employers have been concerned to promote the development of appropriate work-related skills as part of undergraduate provision, and have also sought to make more effective use of their graduate recruits. Another type of linkage, albeit on a relatively small scale, has been the development of academic courses containing an element of work experience – in some cases up to a full year – which involve students in the reality of doing a job and employers in creating some form of meaningful connection with their degree programmes. Boys *et al.* (1988) offer a balanced analysis of the pros and cons of such schemes.

On the technological side, universities are increasingly anxious to supplement their research funds from government sources with industrially sponsored projects, so opening up yet another avenue for outside contact. Indeed, there was a fashion, flourishing in the

1970s and 1980s, for some of the larger universities to set up 'science parks': geographical locations adjoining or near the main campus, which were intended to house applied research units and centres, run jointly with the sponsoring agencies concerned. Some but not all of these ventures have proved successful: the tendency more recently has been towards more flexible arrangements, but the emphasis on industrial collaboration remains.

A still more pervasive form of interconnection between universities and their regional communities derives from the opening-up of teaching programmes – referred to in the previous section – to part-time mature students. Continuing education, whether related to enhancing professional and vocational qualifications or to providing for a range of leisure interests, can draw in sectors of the population who were never previously involved in higher education, and rekindle a feeling – first manifested in Britain over a century ago, with the founding of the civic universities, and more recently with the creation of the former polytechnics – that academic institutions properly belong to their locality and its people.

In so far as the longest-established and most highly regarded foundations still hold themselves apart from any close community involvement, they have become the exceptions rather than the leaders of fashion: and even they can be seen to have given some ground. So here, too, is another departure from past practice and convention, consequent on the abandonment of elitism.

THE STRUCTURE OF THE SYSTEM

The first major wave of postwar expansion in the 1960s and 1970s saw the creation in Europe and elsewhere of sub-university institutions: the polytechnics in Britain, the IUTs (institutes of university technology) in France, the *Fachhochschulen* in Germany, the regional colleges in Norway, the tertiary education colleges in Australia and so on. The notion behind these was to avoid the larger expense of creating conventional universities by removing the costly research function. They tended to differ, too, in terms of their teaching conditions (larger classes, longer contact hours), the lengths of their courses (shorter programmes, leading to lower-level awards), and often their curricular context (a greater emphasis on technical and vocational subjects and an omission of provision for the liberal arts).

For a variety of reasons, there has been a recent tendency for the boundaries between such institutions and fully-fledged universities to become blurred, or to be removed altogether. In part, this can be ascribed to the phenomenon of 'academic drift': the progressive absorption by lower-level establishments of the values of those above them in the hierarchy, including an implicit redefinition of their original objectives, an increasing emphasis on advanced work, and a reorganisation of their course structures along more traditional academic lines. But even where this has happened with governmental connivance – where a hitherto formally stratified system has been subject to politically sanctioned destratification – differing levels of academic prestige may remain in evidence. In some cases, too, the institutions of the next stratum below that of the newly promoted sector may move upwards to fill the gap thus created, and become contenders for a further amalgamation. An emergent development of this kind could be observed in the late 1990s in relation to the colleges of further education in England.

Within most countries there remains some acknowledged or tacit hierarchy between the member institutions of the higher education system. Few classifications are as elaborate as that developed in the mid-1970s by the Carnegie Council on Policy Studies in Higher Education, which identified ten distinct categories of universities and colleges in the USA, topped by the major research universities. The boundaries here, as elsewhere, are in effect drawn in terms of the institutions' position on a spectrum between academic excellence (an 'elite' concept) on the one hand and social equality (a 'mass' concept) on the other. However, the differences are by no means clear-cut: some countries allow a more overt acknowledgement of relative prestige than others, and even within a given institution both values, of equality and excellence, may coexist (for example, a chemistry department may be less selective in its admissions policy than a department of history, because the pressure of student demand is lower). To talk of a national system as a whole is to draw attention to general tendencies, rather than to imply any uniformity of behaviour on the part of its constituent elements.

Those constituent elements form a pattern that is broadly similar across different countries (Becher and Kogan, 1992). First, there are the central authorities – national or state governments, their ministries and related agencies – who are held responsible for overall policy, resource allocation and system management (in the case of the private sector, these roles are usually played by a body of independent trustees). Next come the academic institutions, which have a largely co-ordinating and values-setting function, operating as mediators between the central authorities and the third level entities, the basic units, the most common form of which are subject departments. The latter can be defined as the smallest entities which operate with their own budgets and which have a distinctive role – be it in research, teaching or a service activity – within their parent institution. The fourth and final element comprises the individuals – whether staff or students, administrators or service personnel – who provide the human element in the system, and whose collective views and attitudes strongly influence what actually happens on the ground, as against what might be specified by the central authorities, the institutions, or even the basic units in which they operate.

In structural terms, a further distinction can usefully be drawn. In his masterly account of *The Higher Education System*, Burton Clark (1983) marks this by contrasting the discipline and the enterprise. By the latter he means the individual institution: a way of organising knowledge that brings together a diversity of specialist groups. The former, in contrast, denotes a specialised form or organisation, namely a particular knowledge domain which 'knits together chemists and chemists, psychologists and psychologists, historians and historians' (Clark, 1983, p. 29). He goes on to argue that disciplinary groupings can exercise a powerful influence on the system, in that many academics – especially those in heavily research-oriented institutions – give their first allegiance to their discipline rather than to their parent enterprise, and consequently allow it primacy in shaping their values and their behaviour.

GOVERNANCE AND FINANCE

The relationships between central authorities and institutions have become more complex and more changeable as the size of the higher education system has increased. There has never in any case been much uniformity of international practice. In the USA, for instance, the federal government has always had a very weak role, while individual states have varied in their degree of centralisation. Moreover, the whole picture has been further elaborated by the existence of a substantial private sector, a number of whose institutions enjoy high academic standing. In continental Europe, the tendency in the past has been for tight central control, with France offering the prime example of an education ministry determining virtually every aspect of university activity. In Britain, by fairly long but now defunct tradition, the government adopted a largely permissive stance, allowing a body controlled by senior academics, the University Grants Committee, to negotiate for resources and to distribute them in terms of its own priorities.

However, as the number of academic institutions and students has risen and costs have correspondingly escalated, there have been understandable pressures for greater account-ability in terms of both efficiency (the wise use of resources) and effectiveness (the quality of what has been achieved). This has resulted, in a number of Western European countries (excluding Britain), in new forms of governmental control: a useful analysis can be found in Neave and van Vught (1991). Previously, the emphasis was on a detailed specification of the processes which higher education institutions were required to follow, often with both undergraduate curricula and individual departments' budgets laid down on an annual basis. However, the point was eventually reached at which this became bureaucratically impos-sible. The common response was to shift the focus of control from processes to outputs. In effect, universities in the countries concerned have been given considerably greater freedom in how they choose to deploy their resources and shape their curricula, but are then subject to judgement of the results they achieve: at the crudest level, funding is related to the numbers of students who graduate successfully rather than to the size of the student intake.

If, in some respects, institutions in the countries with a hitherto centralised system have been allowed greater autonomy than before, their counterparts in the UK, which once enjoyed a fair measure of self-determination, have found themselves more tightly con-strained. Funding is based increasingly on measures of research competence, and teaching is subject to periodic inspection whose results are made publicly available (see also below, under 'The demand for quality'). The Higher Education Funding Council, the controlling body for the system, operates as an arm of central government in a way that its predecessor, the University Grants Committee, generally managed to avoid.

In the end, most of the changes come down to money. It would be a very exceptional system that has been allowed to expand without demands from the national treasury that universities should do more for less. But as with patterns of system-wide management, there is no consistency on an international scale about how higher education is funded. As already noted, there are some systems with a significant proportion of private institutions. These present few problems for the public purse, in that they rely on high student fees, endowments, donations, research grants and usually a modest number of government-funded scholarships. There are other systems in which the nationally funded institutions also call for students to make at least a contribution (varying considerably from one country to another) towards the costs of their tuition: a demand which may be ameliorated by means-tested grants or loans for those who could not otherwise meet such costs. The pattern in the UK has in the past been more generous than most, in that virtually no tuition fees have been recouped from full-time undergraduate students, and the latter have even had all or part of the costs of their maintenance met from the state: a situation which it proved increasingly difficult to sustain, and which eventually resulted in a much enlarged facility for student loans in the place of direct state subsidies.

MANAGEMENT IN INSTITUTIONS

Every aspect of higher education represents a delicate balance between competing demands: at the level of the system as a whole, as has already been noted, there is a conflict between quantity and quality, equity and excellence. Institutions embody another tension as well, namely that between corporate manageability and intellectual freedom. The need for some degree of hierarchy emerges most clearly in the role of the institutional leader, who must act as a key channel of communication between his or her academic colleagues and the outside world. In some cases (as in post-Thatcherite Britain) the head is uncompromisingly desig-nated as an organisational manager, sometimes with tenure from appointment to retirement; in others (as in some continental European universities) the post is largely symbolic, with a two- or three-year timespan. But whatever the case, coherent institutional policies must somehow be forged out of a diverse set of priorities. This is likely to require the co-ordination of views at a number of different levels, and hence a hierarchy of responsibility, if not of power.

At the same time it is a fundamental credo within the academic community that the trade in ideas should be free, and that every individual should have an equal right to test his or her own views against those of fellow professionals. The consequence is a strong sense of collegiality, in which scholars must respect each other's independence regardless of age or position. Even if this value is not always observed in practice, it calls for an organisational structure in which members have equal authority to participate in decisions, and individual discretion to conduct their affairs in their own way, subject only to minimal collegial controls.

Thus, particularly in settings in which academics have a strong sense of their profes-sionalism, and a consciousness of their authority in their chosen field, they are liable to question edicts from above, especially where these are considered to impinge on their expertise. The problems of maintaining a manageable balance between hierarchy and col-legium can still be clearly identified in the older-established universities, which have become especially difficult to govern at a time when scarce resources have to be tightly managed and external demands from governments are increasingly frequent, urgent and peremptory. Institutions that have been promoted to university status as part of the expansion of the system are in a better case here, because their traditions have generally been authoritarian, with considerable powers vested in the principal.

There seems little doubt that managerialism is becoming a permanent feature of academic life. Perhaps this is inevitable as institutions become larger and less personal, and instrumental values are brought in from society at large through students who have –

understandably enough – come to see higher education as a right rather than a privilege, and often as a passport to a better job rather than as an experience yielding intrinsic rewards. In contemporary universities it is not only the vice-chancellor or rector who is called upon to fulfil a managerial role. All down the line, from pro-vice-chancellors to deans of faculties to heads of departments, primarily academic concerns have had to give place to administrative duties (the change is well documented by Middlehurst, 1993). By no means all academics, having been reared in a different tradition, find the new situation easy to adapt to, and there has accordingly grown up a training structure for academic management in which newly appointed academic leaders are encouraged to engage. As so often, North American universities are an exception, in that their tradition has been to separate the administration and financing of the university as sharply as possible from its academic affairs, by appointing a fairly autocratic president with a retinue of staff to look after the former while the faculty are able to limit themselves to the politics and practice of teaching and research.

ACADEMIC WAYS OF LIFE

Teachers in higher education institutions are not in most countries especially well paid (though nor are they for the most part too badly off). It has usually been held that the job has enough other attractions to ensure a good level of recruitment. Especially in the more prestigious institutions, academics enjoy considerable freedom to pursue their own interests and to plan their own time: indeed, they have been likened to people running their own one-man businesses. That most of them work longer hours than their counterparts outside is a consequence of the highly competitive nature of the occupation. Recognition comes from being seen by one's peers to be making a worthwhile research contribution; reputation derives from doing something outstanding. This, far more than money, is the currency in which the inhabitants of academia are paid, and which they strive to earn.

But again, the values are changing. One well-known commentator (Halsey, 1992) has lamented what he terms the proletarianisation of 'the donnish dominion', charting a decline in both social status and the quality of occupational life. His research documents yet another manifestation of the move from elite to mass higher education, in that large-scale demands for teaching a heterogeneous and not always well-motivated student body, and the corresponding requirements for regular and careful assessment, inevitably take up more time than before and tend to offer less rewarding, because lower-level, work.

There has always been – at the level of the individual as of the institution and the system – a balance to be negotiated. Here, it takes the form of a tug-of-war between research on the one hand and teaching on the other. As already remarked, research is what brings professional visibility, if not the glory that is given to few. But teaching is generally what academics are appointed to do; it is an obligation they cannot easily escape. The relative valuation of the two is indicated in the common reference to teaching loads on the one hand and research opportunities on the other.

In any case, it seems highly unlikely that research funding will keep pace with the expansion of student numbers, so resources will inevitably be spread more thinly, or deployed more selectively; or both. And that means that fewer and fewer university academics will have the scope to do any research at all. In this regard, they will find themselves on all fours with teachers in lower-level colleges, who have never been able to combine research with teaching. Where once it may have seemed that rapid growth would raise institutions from below, it would now appear to be lowering them from above: another aspect of Halsey's proletarianisation process.

It is however hazardous to generalise about the nature of academic life and work, because of the great variations in context, not only between but within individual institutions. One crucial set of distinctions lies in the differing cultural patterns of different disciplinary areas. Becher (1989) argues that these are related in some degree to the nature of the knowledge being pursued within the fields in question. Thus, for example, those working in the humanities are not concerned with a rapid pace of publication because, unlike their scientist counterparts, they are rarely competing with rival academics for the solution of a particular problem: the texture of knowledge is less dense and less evidently cumulative, so that research is scattered across a wide field rather than focused on relatively few current areas of concern.

The wide variety of academic ways of life is evident not only in the physical surroundings of different groups (large workshops in engineering, laboratories in chemistry, libraries of reference texts in law, displays of artefacts in anthropology) but in the language, customs and assumptions embodied in each disciplinary community. This pervasive feature of institutions of higher education makes them particularly difficult to manage. The central administration has the uneasy choice of imposing exactly the same requirements on every constituent unit, even where they are quite evidently inappropriate to some (for example, giving favourable support to collective research, which suits physics very well but is quite alien to history); or instead, of responding to the need for differential treatment at the cost of being labelled as unfair and partial in its treatment.

To complicate matters still further, disciplinary groupings tend to be resistant to central initiatives, for two main reasons. The first is that, with only very limited exceptions, each enjoys a monopoly of expertise in its own intellectual field, and can accordingly reject external interference in its strictly academic affairs. The second is that those in any one institution are able to establish solidarity with counterpart groups in other institutions, on a national and often on an international basis, and are thus able where necessary to invoke the support of the relevant disciplinary population as a whole.

TEACHING PROVISION

In traditionally organised universities on the British model, undergraduates were normally admitted to a particular department and held captive there, following a predetermined programme (though in some cases with permitted options) until they graduated. There were, however, exceptions to this pattern even before the expansion of the 1960s, but especially after, of which Squires (1987, 1990) offers a useful overview. Some universities provided specifically designed interdisciplinary courses covering a number of different fields (European studies was one case in point, environmental studies another). A further pattern comprised joint degrees (for instance, in economics and French), in which the student followed selected parts of two different departments' programmes. The major growth in modular degrees (see 'The deconstruction of academia' above) which came later, was in full sway by the 1990s.

The adoption of modularity has inevitably affected the relations between students and staff, as well as between student cohorts themselves. Instead of being part of a stable year-group in the same department, and hence coming to know one's teachers and one's con-temporaries quite well, groups on modular programmes form and re-form every few months, with little or no constancy of membership. Modularity has also changed the pattern of teaching, in that each unit has to be self-contained, and cannot refer back to earlier material. Each has also to be separately examined, which results in a higher level both of assessed work for students and of marking for staff.

It is, however, the increased ratio of undergraduate students to staff rather than the change in course patterns *per se* which has moved British universities nearer in teaching style to their Continental and North American counterparts. The traditional one-to-one tutorial has virtually disappeared except in Oxford and Cambridge (and even there, it survives to a decreasing extent). Teaching by small seminar or laboratory demonstration group is no longer seen in many universities as a viable proposition, except if it is delegated (not always successfully) to graduate students. What remains as the staple fare is the large-scale lecture – usually presented as a one-hour monologue – supplemented by a substantial amount of self-study.

But again here, as in relation to research, conventions vary considerably between one discipline and another. In many science-based courses, students are expected to attend several lectures a day, and a number of lab classes in addition; in the humanities and many of the social sciences, they may have no more than at most a dozen lectures in a week. In the latter groups of disciplines, critical questions tend to be encouraged; in the former, ques-tions are only expected on matters of clarification. Evans (1988, 1993) gives highly readable accounts of what it is like to study in two different but related fields: modern languages and English.

Significant contrasts can also be identified in students' learning styles. Marton *et al.* (1984) provide an interesting review of research on student learning, with particular emphasis on the distinction between 'deep' and 'surface' approaches. The former reflects a concern to reach a personal understanding of academic material, interacting critically with it and relating it to previous knowledge. The latter derives from a conception of learning as memorisation and as relatively unrelated to personal interest. Although there does not seem to be a clear connection between the student's learning approach and the disciplinary subject matter or the stage reached in the undergraduate programme, it can be affected by assessment requirements and by lecturers' teaching styles.

The extent to which academics' research impinges on their teaching, and hence on their students' learning, has long been a matter for debate. In those institutions or for those individuals who undertake little or no research, the question is not at issue: but many commentators have been sceptical about the extent to which any connection exists, even in the most strongly research-oriented universities. An empirical study by Neumann (1994) has however clearly shown that there are a number of direct and indirect links between the two which enhance the students' motivation and interest.

Post-graduate students raise a different set of issues. In some countries (see Clark, 1993) they are given relatively little teaching support; in others they are expected to complete a quite substantial body of courses. At the master's level their work tends to be an extension of undergraduate study, though more focused and specialised. Doctoral students, especially in the later stages of their programme, are involved in a unique and novel piece of research and are to that extent necessarily self-sufficient, even in subject areas where teamwork is the norm. At best, they have access to one or two supervisors who can offer encouragement and comment: but except where (as in the USA) organised graduate schools exist, their life takes the form of a rigorous and lonely initiation into the academic community. To make matters worse, though post-graduate education has expanded significantly alongside that for under-graduates, the employment opportunities in higher education have not kept pace. So more and more of those who successfully complete their doctoral studies are left to survive in a wider job market which does not particularly value their skills.

However, the worth of a university education is in general not best measured in monetary or vocational terms. Even where a degree may bring its owner a lucrative or interesting job, that is arguably not the sole or the most important justification for acquiring it: there are intrinsic benefits, in terms of the development of personal qualities, which outweigh the more obvious extrinsic and utilitarian rewards. One that is widely remarked upon by gradu-ates themselves is an increase in personal confidence, linked to a recognition that they have achieved something difficult and worthwhile. Another consequence – discussed eloquently and convincingly by Barnett (1990) – is the ability to adapt intellectually, because a degree programme helps one to learn how to learn, and encourages one to reflect critically on what one is told, rather than swallowing it whole. Not all graduates, of course, can be said to possess these virtues, but enough are recognised to do so to make the case a convincing one.

THE DEMAND FOR QUALITY

One of the most noticeable changes in higher education has been the advent of govern-mental demands that institutions of advanced study should be subject to a critical scrutiny of the quality of their work. The sources of this widespread movement are diverse, and its rationale is open to interpretation. From the perspective of the traditional academic, it may represent a cunning conspiracy framed by unscrupulous politicians who, foreseeing the inevitable decline in quality brought about by expanded numbers and reduced resources, seek to pass on the blame by calling universities to account instead of themselves accepting responsibility. From the standpoint of those who represent the public interest, however, it may be argued to stem from a proper concern with the efficient use of the taxpayer's money at a time when the total higher education budget is – as in most countries – at an unprecedentedly high level. On either view, the quality movement represents an erosion of the trust once granted to academia, which was in the past considered capable of maintaining and policing its own standards without external intervention.

The means used to assess the performance of individual institutions and their component units have varied over the years and across national boundaries. There was a short phase when so-called 'performance indicators' were in vogue – that is, pre-specified criteria, usually quantitative, whose validity was assumed to be independent of context. However, this bizarre assumption was eventually seen not only to produce nonsensical results but also to encourage inappropriate and often unproductive changes in the behaviour of those anxious to achieve high scores. Subsequent approaches have for the most part depended on some variant of peer review – the informed judgement of fellow specialists on those being assessed.

Of the various national quality procedures in operation in the mid-1990s, that of the UK would seem the most demanding, since it required not only regular and frequent inspection of teaching in all subject areas and a periodic audit of each institution's quality assurance mechanisms, but also a department-by-department evaluation of research performance on a four-yearly cycle. This has given rise to an increase in the endemic tension between teaching and research (already remarked upon in the section on 'Academic ways of life' above), in that good grades in research assessment carry substantial monetary rewards, whereas teaching assessments do not – though, less tangibly, reports of poor performance may discourage applications from the better qualified students. In most other countries, research is left to be judged by traditional methods and the governmental requirements are limited to teaching.

In practice, the verdict on assurance procedures for teaching quality has to be an equivocal one. There is no question that, even at their most enlightened, they cause an excessive amount of paperwork, an unwanted increase in bureaucracy, and an incursion into academics' time that might be better spent improving, rather than documenting, the quality of their activities. However, there is also evidence to show a resulting benefit to students. It was one of the established features of elitist higher education systems that members of staff saw themselves as teachers of their subject rather than of their students. A mastery of disciplinary knowledge was essential, but it mattered little how it was put across: students were themselves expected to make sense of what they were given. Paradoxically, those who were described as university teachers were not in the least expected to have learned how to teach. Moreover, in the humanities and social sciences, the individualist tradition in research was carried over into teaching, so that different lecture courses – and even different contributions to the same lecture series – were in general very loosely correlated one with another. What independent scrutiny has done is to compel academics to be more conscious of communicating effectively with their students and more aware of the need to plan courses on a collective basis.

In addition, most quality assurance schemes call for a critical examination of the course documentation with which students are provided (which tended in the past to be sketchy at best) and insist on a clear opportunity for them to comment on their courses. When it works well, student involvement in a critical review of what they have learnt can become an integral part of the education process, reinforcing the opportunity which higher education should afford of learning how to learn.

FUTURE DIRECTIONS

If predicting the future is always a hazardous business, it is particularly so in the case of higher education. As has been emphasised in the preceding discussion, the advent of a mass system greatly increases the scope of, and the temptation for, political intervention: so institutions can no longer count on shaping their own destinies, as against having them shaped for them by education ministers keen to establish their own reputations for creative administration. One characteristic feature of the recent past, which seems all too likely to persist in times to come, is the pervasive effect but modish nature of management practices. The litany of techniques confidently guaranteed to produce lasting improvement is as long as their individual lives are short – ranging from Planning Programming Budgeting Systems in the 1970s through Management by Objectives and Zero Budgeting to Performance Indicators and – in the vanguard of late 1990s fashion – to Total Quality Management. In that connection, there seems little doubt that the present emphasis on quality assurance procedures will gradually fade into oblivion, partly at least because the emphasis on teaching competence seems likely to become a reasonably permanent component of the academic value system, and will consequently cease to call for external reinforcement. There were signs that this had begun to happen before the end of the century in countries as far apart culturally and geographically as Sweden and Australia.

What is particularly intriguing, but not easy to explain, is why changes in higher education spread with such rapidity from one country to another and why they take the form they do. The development of mass systems calls to mind an analogy – which is not as far-fetched as it might sound – with the world of men's or women's tailoring. While social classes remained highly stratified, the best and most stylish clothes remained the prerogative of the elite. However, with increasing prosperity, the hitherto less privileged had growing access to a range of reasonably designed, as well as badly designed, mass-produced garments. When this happened, the bespoke tailors and couturiers found themselves in a markedly less favourable position than before. Those who survived did so by finding (in the contemporary cliché) a niche in the market, specialising in a particular line which did not compete with mass products and for which there was a steady demand.

So too, to some extent, with universities. As with clothiers, there is more differentiation than before in the nature and quality of their offerings, and those institutions which still see themselves as catering for the intellectual elite have found themselves unexpectedly on the defensive. The identification of niche markets which they can safely occupy in their determination to remain relatively unchanged is a matter which increasingly occupies them. For the rest of the system, too, the need to attract customers remains active. As the demand for conventional first degree courses stabilises, which seems highly probable as the number of mature students who previously missed out on a university education dwindles, there will be less lip-service to the myth of uniform standards in academic awards and a greater public readiness – as there has always been in the USA – to accept that the qualifications from some universities are better than those from others. For similar reasons, the growth in sub-degree programmes is likely to be sustained.

Above all, however, higher education institutions are destined to face an increasing level of mutual competition: the artificial market economy forced on them in many countries by their political masters is likely to become a real market economy, in which students are required to pay a large share of the costs of their programmes, and thus have every reason to regard themselves as consumers. One might indeed see the wheel of university fortunes returning full circle, to the early days in which the students in Bologna set the demands with which the academics had little choice but to comply.

That may be too extreme a scenario, given that North American institutions of higher education already operate in a competitive, differentiated mass system with only the rare outbreak of student power. But whatever the future brings, it is safe to say that universities have proved themselves resilient enough, over their 750 years or so, to survive in one form or another well into the second millennium.

REFERENCES

Barnett, R. (1990) *The Idea of Higher Education*, Milton Keynes: Open University Press.

Becher, T. (1989) *Academic Tribes and Territories*, Milton Keynes: Open University Press.

Becher, T. and Kogan, M. (1992) *Process and Structure in Higher Education* (2nd edn), London: Routledge.

Boys, C., Brennan, J., Henkel, M., Kirkland, J., Kogan, M. and Youll, P. (1988) *Higher Education and the Preparation for Work*, London: Jessica Kingsley.

Clark, B. R. (1983) *The Higher Education System*, Berkeley, CA: University of California Press.

Clark, B. R. (ed.) (1993) *The Research Foundations of Graduate Education*, Berkeley, CA: University of California Press.

Cobban, A. B. (1975) *The Medieval University*, London: Methuen.

Dore, R. P. (1976) *The Diploma Disease*, London: Allen & Unwin.

Evans, C. (1988) *Language People*, Milton Keynes: Open University Press.

Evans, C. (1993) *English People*, Buckingham: Open University Press.

Halsey, A. H. (1992) *Decline of Donnish Dominion*, Oxford: Clarendon Press.

Hirsch, F. (1977) *Social Limits to Growth*, London: Routledge.

Maiworm, F., Steube, W. and Teichler, U. (1991) *Learning in Europe: The ERASMUS Experience*, London: Jessica Kingsley.

Marton, F., Hounsell, D. and Entwistle, N. J. (eds) (1984) *The Experience of Learning*, Edinburgh: Scottish Academic Press.

Middlehurst, R. (1993) *Leading Academics*, Buckingham: Open University Press.

Neave, G. and van Vught, F. (1991) *Prometheus Bound: The Changing Relationship between Government and Higher Education in Western Europe*, Oxford: Pergamon.

Neumann, R. (1994) 'The teaching-research nexus', *European Journal of Education* 24 (3), 323–338.

Rothblatt, S. and Wittrock, B. (eds) (1993) *The European and American University since 1800*, Cambridge: Cambridge University Press.

Scott, P. (1995) *The Meanings of Mass Higher Education*, Buckingham: Open University Press.

Squires, G. (1987) *The Curriculum beyond School*, London: Hodder & Stoughton.

Squires, G. (1990) *First Degree: The Undergraduate Curriculum*, Buckingham: Open University Press.

Trow, M. (1970) 'Reflections on the transition from mass to universal higher education', *Daedalus* 90 (1), 1–42.

41

TECHNOLOGY IN HIGHER EDUCATION
Altering the goalposts

Robin Mason

ISSUES AND PERSPECTIVES

There is no sector of professional life so susceptible to cyclical patterns, approaches and trends, as education. Readers will be well aware of the current *Zeitgeist* informing educational views at the tertiary level: student-directed learning, interaction with other learners and with the learning material, and concomitantly, teachers as facilitators rather than all-knowing fonts of knowledge. It is no surprise, therefore, that the technologies in vogue during the 1990s have been those that provide resources for the learner and communication with the teacher and other learners.

Another critical element in the education soup is the changing nature of the student body. The 18–22 year old is no longer the norm in post-secondary education. Diversity is the hallmark of the educational scene: women returnees, remote students, those in employment needing professional updating, those unemployed needing re-training, those with time and interest to learn for its own sake, disadvantaged students of all ages and types. In short, the tertiary field is a lifelong learning market.

Because of this change in who is to be educated, there is a change in what they need to be educated about. Many mourn the death of the printed book, and all of the skills associated with reading: linear buildup of knowledge and knowing, narrative approaches to understanding, and concentration spans appropriate to that medium of learning. Louder voices, however, are calling for the skills of team-working, browsing, selecting and synthesising information, and communication and presentation abilities – in short, learning how to learn appropriately in an information age.

Flexibility is now the key to programme design and media choice. The new learner needs to be able to fit study in and around a range of other commitments involving family, leisure and employment. Choice of what to learn, how to learn and when to learn is now a reality and reflects the growing competition amongst suppliers of tertiary education and training. Furthermore, this competition operates on a global scale through developments in telecommunications technology.

These and other changes (e.g. reduced funding from central government) have led to a crisis in universities, as the traditions for which they have always stood and the traditional ways in which they have regarded teaching, are disappearing. In short, the market, the funding and the mission of university education are changing. Communication and information technologies (C&IT) are contributing to both the demise of old traditions and the search for new solutions.

COMMUNICATION AND INFORMATION TECHNOLOGY

There are a number of different ways of categorising existing C&IT technologies. The most simple, if not simplistic, is to divide them into two camps: videoconferencing and the Internet. This divide reflects current usage. Videoconferencing largely replicates the traditional lecture at a distance; it relies on bespoke equipment, ISDN and satellite, and is a synchronous technology. In some contexts a video is made of the session which students can watch afterwards at their convenience. On the other hand, the Internet largely replicates print-based distance education. The web, as a subset of the Internet, is usually accessed as an individual, asynchronous technology, although increasingly it supports real time events. The winner in this division is clearly the Internet, which provides access to databases, the vast resources of the web and communication using text and increasingly, audio and video as well.

The outstanding success of the web rests on two facts – it is cross platform and it offers universal access (in theory). Consequently, other technologies have converged with it – major proprietary computer conferencing systems can be accessed through a browser; CD-ROM has become a storage facility for multimedia web courses; audio and video can now be delivered live and canned afterwards on the web. Furthermore, it supports all the elements of computer-based training simulations, quizzes and dynamic multimedia. Courses on the web can be restricted to specific users; they can be delivered on an internal network or they can be available globally and provide links to other sites.

Using videoconferencing as a means of increasing student numbers on courses, providing access to a wider curriculum for remote or distributed campuses, or for reducing travel by either students or lecturers, has less impact on the institution and on the students than the use of the Internet. Staff need far more support to design and tutor web courses, administrative systems need to be completely re-thought to manage a global student body, and students generally need different skills to work on the Internet. For these reasons, many speak of online teaching as being a 'new paradigm'.

One of the technologies which has emerged to ease the strain of this new paradigm is 'web in a box' software. This provides an integrated environment for the academic: design tools for preparing web materials, support tools for managing assignments, and conferencing systems for interacting with students. WebCT, developed at the University of British Columbia and TopClass, originally produced on an EU grant in Dublin, are typical examples. Companies have sprung up to help universities go online, providing a cradle-to-grave virtual environment from registration to graduation. Real Education, which has produced the University of Colorado's CUOnline environment is one such, and of course IBM also aims to provide this service through their Global Campus system.

724

EDUCATIONAL USES OF C&IT

There is hardly a tertiary educational institution anywhere that is not currently reconsidering its approach to the use of C&IT in its teaching or at least its administration and support of students. To have a technology strategy is now *de rigueur*, just as a mission statement was in the 1980s. The range of options typically under the microscope are:

- using computer-based multimedia teaching modules, either to reduce lecture hours or to enhance existing provision or to increase the student/lecturer ratio;
- converting existing print-based or lecture courses on to the web, to add flexibility, up-datability, or merely to keep up with the Jones's;
- exploiting telecommunications technologies – videoconferencing, computer conferencing, audioconferencing – to add interactivity to the learning environment;
- adopting a resource-based approach to course design, usually involving the web and/or CD-ROM to reflect a student-centred model of teaching and learning.

These illustrations point to another trend in higher education provision caused largely by developments in C&IT: the convergence of traditional campus-based teaching and traditional distance education. Dual-mode institutions in which the same course is taught face-to-face and at a distance (often with the same examination and assessment) have been common for some time, particularly in Australia. C&IT technologies – particularly the web and videoconferencing, have merged even these distinctions. Another example might be termed 'close distance education', in which students who live close to campus but who can't attend regular daytime lectures use the facilities of the campus (computers, library, video recordings of lectures) but may meet as a class infrequently or not at all. Finally, traditional print-based distance education providers are able, through technologies such as RealPlayer on the web, to offer synchronous events such as lectures and seminars, which students can access individually from their machines.

As technology has improved, and with it the potential of distance education to offer interactivity, a rich variety of learning materials and efficient administrative systems for supporting students, so the image and acceptability of online learning have been established. The Internet has facilitated yet another possibility – the globalisation of the student body. Many of the early web courses (prepared in most cases by an enthusiastic academic fascinated by the potential of the medium and offering the course free of charge) attracted students from all over the country and then expatriates or web surfers abroad who wanted to take the course as well. Soon courses were being written especially for the global market, charging fees and offering accreditation. Early adopters found the exchange of ideas amongst students from different countries had very positive educational benefits. Nevertheless, questions have been raised about the divisiveness this causes between the technology haves and havenots; about the social implications of largely first world courses subverting indigenous initiatives; and about cultural issues such as the dominance of mother-tongue speakers in online discussions. Despite these considerations, there are now many providers jumping on the global education bandwagon. It is common for North American higher education institutions to have arrangements to teach at least one course abroad; UK universities have many connections in the Pacific Rim, as do Australian and New Zealand institutions. Other obvious connections include France and Quebec; Spain and Central and

South America; Portugal and Brazil. These international connections are the beginnings of global initiatives.

INSTITUTIONAL RESTRUCTURING

As the distinctions between campus and distance education have blurred at the course level, so institutions have begun to rethink their position at the strategic level. One of the most notable trends is the rise of 'virtual universities'. These take many forms: some are new institutions altogether, reliant on C&IT (usually the Internet) to deliver courses; others are amalgamations of existing institutions.

The most common of these is the way in which universities are forming partnerships with industry, with other universities, with C&IT providers to increase efficiency, to expand markets and to share resources. The UK Open University is a good example of an institution relying on partners around the world to increase its market and make use of its vast store of high-quality teaching material.

'Green field' sites are also appearing on the scene regularly and though they lack the accrediting powers of universities, they do not suffer from the weight of tradition, the cost of funding research as well as teaching, or the need to offer a full curriculum. Examples include Microsoft Online Institute, Deutsche Telecom's Global Learning initiative and IBM's Global Campus.

Umbrella organisations which broker courses written by partner institutions, or which commission courses from various providers, are common. Most are heavily dependent on C&IT if not for the delivery of course content, at least for the tutorial support of students. The University of the Highlands and Islands Project in Scotland, the Western Governors University in the US and the University for Industry (LearnDirect) in the UK provide different models of this concept.

Finally, corporate universities are a phenomenon of the 1990s. In some cases through partnerships with existing universities, in others through upgrading existing 'stand-up' training, these new entities reflect the need for lifelong learning, the changing content of training and often a dissatisfaction with the offerings of traditional universities. Motorola University, Macdonald's University and British Aerospace University are only a few examples of this trend.

Current demand for 'virtual courses' is focused on particular areas of the curriculum. The largest of these is business and management qualifications, along with computing and IT courses generally. Language learning is appropriate and commonly taught, and open and distance education degrees and diplomas are abundant online. There are predictions that the leisure market will take off soon, but professional development and post-graduate courses are far more common as yet.

STUDENT UPTAKE OF TECHNOLOGY-BASED TEACHING

How do students react to these changes in the institutional, technological and pedagogical framework of higher education? At the course level, there is much evidence pointing to the

726

fact that resource-based, student-centred, technology-delivered teaching is more demanding, more time-consuming and more exciting than traditional forms of learning. On the whole, the brighter the students, the more self-directed, the more intrinsically motivated they are, the better they do, the more they benefit from the course and the more they enjoy it. Those with poor learning skills, with poor access to technology, with poor educational prerequisites or with very little time for studying, usually react against the technology, drop out of the course, or scrape through unenthusiastically.

Lack of time is without a doubt the primary reason for failure to complete technology-based courses. The paradox is that the new learner demands flexibility in the delivery of courses, but this very flexibility allows other demands than the course to dominate. Overcoming the remoteness of distance learning has largely been accomplished by communications technology. Time is the new distance!

In fact, most technology-based courses are *less* flexible than traditional print-based distance education. In many cases, students have to go to their local college for videoconference sessions, or to a study centre for access to computers and the web. If they own a computer and have access to the Internet at home, their study is still computer-centred and dominated by the screen and the whims of telecommunication for access to the system. This is all much less flexible than a book or printed study material which can be read in bed, on the train, waiting for an appointment, away on holiday, etc. For all these reasons, print continues to be a dominant delivery mode even on so-called technology-based courses.

As technology-based learning moves beyond the early adopter phase, and therefore beyond the cadre of people who naturally enjoy technology, there is a greater need on the part of course providers to help students develop the kind of skills and approaches required in a technology environment. The ability to take good notes from a lecture, to read sequentially through a teaching text, to reproduce course material in your own words in assignments – these are no longer as necessary as being able to search vast quantities of information, identify important or relevant ideas quickly, work with others to produce a joint report, contribute to discussions and comment on other students' work. While some students acquire these new skills easily, others will need help and guidance from teachers.

FACULTY REACTIONS TO TECHNOLOGY-BASED TEACHING

Many early adopters of new technology complain about the intransigence of their fellow academics, their Luddite reactions to the benefits of computers, their fears about losing their job, and their lazy satisfaction with the same lectures they have delivered for many years. Others point out the lack of incentives for lecturers to devote any time to re-thinking their teaching style or content. Furthermore, research shows that in many cases, moving to technology-based delivery takes more time than existing approaches – either preparation time, online tutoring time or software development time. There are some signs, however, that the role of teaching in academic life is being taken more seriously – for example, funding initiatives rewarding technology-based teaching; curriculum-focused research incentives for teaching; and institutional 'time off teaching' to develop software, become familiar with a new technology or to prepare an online course. Financial recognition, in terms of promotion or extra increments for remote students, is also on the increase.

At the other end of the spectrum, there is evidence of a new breed of academic – one who perhaps has no institutional affiliation, who prepares courses and teaches online for several educational providers, and who conducts research through the Internet, accessing journals, papers and databases, keeping in touch with colleagues and even attending virtual conferences. In many ways this scenario is the obvious result of the institutional changes and technology developments already described. It is commonly acknowledged amongst academics that they are 'closer' to their Internet colleagues around the world than they are to their colleagues on the same corridor. Virtual proximity has already replaced geographical proximity.

EXEMPLAR

The Masters in Open and Distance Education at the Open University exemplifies many of the trends already discussed. It has a global student body of about 50 students on each of the three years of the course. The second year of the course, (eight months long) entitled Applications of Information Technology, is delivered on the web using selected web resources and an enhanced web conferencing system. Significantly, core content takes the form of four set books sent to each student by post. Other media include two audiotapes, a videotape and a CD-ROM. The web pages give detailed guidance and resources for each section of the course and there are conference areas for each tutor group as well as a plenary area for general discussion. Figure 41.1 is a screen shot of a page from block 1, showing the design of the site, the tutor group areas at the top and the course content areas along the side.

Collaborative activities dominate the work of the first two blocks of the course. Students

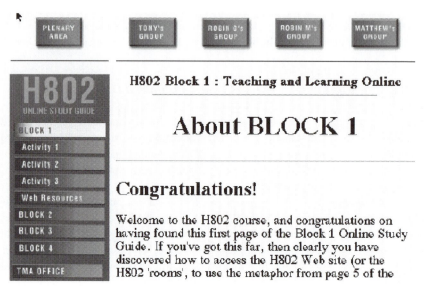

Figure 41.1 Web site for applications of information technology

are asked to work in small groups to investigate online media such as listservs, leading conferencing systems and web tools. They are each assigned a role in an online debate to consider questions about peer working, online moderating skills and collaboration as a learning tool. In block 2 they work collaboratively again to investigate the educational value of web courses: they agree a curriculum area, search for a course or teaching materials, and agree guidelines of good practice. Block 3 examines educational uses of multimedia, providing examples on the CD-ROM as well as on the web. Students discuss issues of navigation, interactivity and design in their tutor groups. Finally, block 4 reverts to a more traditional form with bespoke course material outlining the theory and practice of media use in open and distance education.

The conferencing system which supports these discussions and collaborative activities has been enhanced in-house to provide additional features important in an educational environment: a history function to enable tutors (and students) to see who has read messages; a file area where students submit their assignments; a series of editing functions for keeping the bulletin-board free from errors; and an option to e-mail all students on the course. Figure 41.2 shows the tool bar below the top level of discussion threads.

As no face-to-face meetings are possible with a student body dispersed over many continents, a number of real time events are held to provide telepresence and to aid motivation. The first event was a 'pan-synchronous' real time chat session held over 24 hours with each of the tutors taking a one-hour stint spread over the whole period. The focus of the event was the collaborative marking of an assignment just completed by the students.

A more high-tech event was held at the end of the course using KMI Stadium software, developed at the Open University, providing live audio out and a bulletin-board for student comments. The event is now 'canned' on the web site, as illustrated in Figure 41.3. The

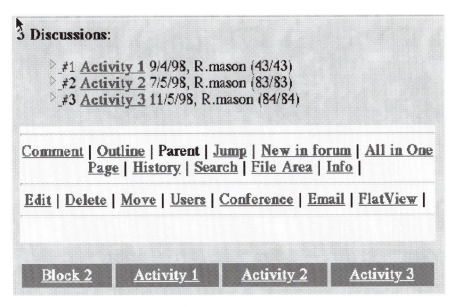

Figure 41.2 Enhancements to the bulletin-board

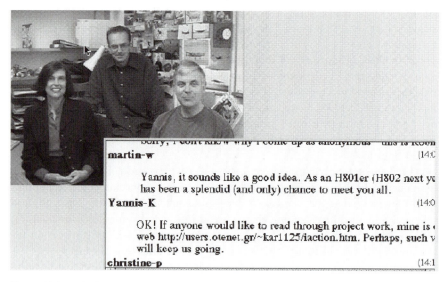

Figure 41.3 KMI Stadium event

tutors discussed the possibility of making all student assignments available for others to read. The session was completely interactive and very fast-paced with the tutors working hard to respond to the many comments from students on the board.

The undoubted successes of the first presentation of the course in 1998 included the recognition by many students of the value of peer learning, collaborative activities and interactivity as appropriate and important tools in education. The global student body gave a richness of perspective which no institutional print material could provide. Finally, the assessment system encouraged student participation through insisting that extracts from the online discussions were to be included in each assignment. This gave legitimacy and purpose to the interactions.

The difficulties encountered by students and tutors on the first year of the course centred around three areas. First, the holidays, job and other commitments of students caused problems in the collaborative activities, requiring tutors to substitute role allocations on short notice and some groups to be quite small. The term 'collaboration fatigue' was coined halfway through the course as students longed for the flexibility and individual activities of traditional print-based courses. Second, there were inevitably technical problems in accessing the web site in the early stages because of overloading and crashes, but latterly for no reason that could ever be discovered. With assignments requiring access to the bulletin-board, this was annoying for students working right up to the final deadline. Third, the tutors felt perpetually overwhelmed with marking and yet guilty about not taking a greater part in the online discussions. It seems there is a permanent tension between tutor as facilitator and as expert. Although many valued the comments of their peers, students still wanted more input, commentary and critique from tutors.

CONCLUSIONS

Despite all the changes and diversity in higher education provision suggested here, it is possible to make some generalisations. The most obvious and most obviously ignored rule of thumb is that technology should be used on a course or by an institution as a result of a needs analysis and a restructuring of educational provision, not because it is the latest gismo, or because it is cheaper to buy equipment than to re-engineer the organisation. Technology does not substitute for good course material. In fact, it highlights simplistic or uninspiring course design and magnifies poor lecturing skills. Technology is rarely the cause of failure in course delivery, but equally rarely is it the solution to educational or institutional problems.

Students will love the technology; they will resist the pedagogical changes it implies and will complain about having to pay for it. Faculty will jump on the technology bandwagon if there are clear incentives. And when they do so, the improvement in teaching will be the result, not of the technology, but of the extra effort and attention they have devoted to what and how they are teaching.

Technology is expensive; it alters the goalposts; itself it is constantly changing. Nevertheless, in higher education, it cannot be ignored.

SELECTED BIBLIOGRAPHY

Bates, A. (1995). *Technology, Open Learning and Distance Education*. London and New York: Routledge.

Collis, B. (1996). *Tele-Learning in a Digital World: The Future of Distance Learning*. London: International Thomson Computer Press.

Daniel, J. (1996). *Mega-Universities and Knowledge Media*. London: Kogan Page.

Ehrmann, S. (1996). *Adult Learning in a New Technological Era*. Paris: OECD.

Khan, B. (ed.) (1997). *Web-Based Instruction*. New Jersey: Educational Technology Publications.

Laurillard, D. (1993). *Rethinking University Teaching*. London and New York: Routledge.

Mason, R. (1998). *Globalising Education. Trends and Applications*. London and New York: Routledge.

42

TEACHER EDUCATION

From initial preparation to continuing professional development

Sharon Feiman-Nemser and Patricia J. Norman

The success of a nation depends on the quality of its educational system. Schools develop intellectual capacities, foster socially desirable values and lay the foundation for productive work and active citizenship. Moreover the quality of a nation's schools is directly linked to the quality of its teachers. What teachers know and can do is the single most important factor in determining what students will have an opportunity to learn. It follows that teacher education, the enterprise responsible for preparing well-qualified teachers and providing for their ongoing professional development, should be a highly respected, well-financed undertaking.

If teachers are so important, why have their education and continuing development been neglected for so long? Part of the answer lies in public perceptions of teaching. How teachers are prepared, where this takes place and who is in charge reflect beliefs about the nature of teaching and the role of teachers in society (Judge *et al.*, 1994). Historically, policy-makers have not devoted adequate resources to teacher education because they did not believe that teachers needed specialised training (Herbst, 1989). Common myths about teachers and teaching reflect this belief: 'Teachers are born, not made.' 'Teaching is easy to learn and simple to pull off.' 'All teachers really need to know is subject matter.' The fact that teachers work with children and youth, the least powerful and most vulnerable members in a society, further diminishes their status.

In addition, the rocky history of university-based teacher education strengthens the view that it is a weak intervention unworthy of substantial investment. In an effort to gain professional stature and academic respectability, teacher education moved from normal schools and training colleges to the university. In the process it lost touch with practitioners in the field without finding a congenial home in the university. Academics the world over consider teacher education to be at odds with the culture of the university. Unlike other professions such as law or medicine which have strong academic grounding, teacher education only partially satisfies this criterion. Without the political or intellectual clout that faculties in the arts and sciences and in other professional schools enjoy, many schools and colleges of education operate as second-class citizens in the university community (Clifford and Guthrie, 1988; Tom, 1997).

Still, as technology transforms society and contributes to new and higher expectations for student learning, as countries experience a shortage of well-qualified teachers, and as the global economy expands, we may at last be entering a historic period when teachers and their learning take centre-stage in educational reform. That seems to be the case in the US, where reform-minded policy-makers and educators have reached a consensus that what matters most to the nation's future is providing caring, competent and qualified teachers for all students. A report of the National Commission on Teaching & America's Future (1996, p. 5) puts it this way:

> What teachers know and can do makes the crucial difference in what teachers can accomplish. New courses, tests, curriculum reforms can be important starting-points, but they are meaningless if teachers cannot use them productively. Policies can improve schools only if the people in them are armed with the knowledge, skills and supports they need.

In this chapter we adopt a broad definition of teacher education which includes pre-service preparation, beginning teacher induction and continuing professional development. Rather than limit ourselves to initial teacher preparation, we have chosen to examine the broad continuum of teacher development. We did this for several reasons. First, we want to stretch our readers' understanding of what learning to teach well entails and how teacher education can support that process over time. Second, we want to highlight new trends in beginning teacher induction and professional development. Third, we want to underscore a basic connection between teacher learning and student learning. Pre-service preparation lays a necessary foundation for professional teaching. Unless teachers have access to rich learning opportunities and intellectual resources throughout their teaching careers, they cannot remain vital and responsive to new challenges and expectations for student learning.

The concept of teacher education as a broad continuum of learning opportunities geared to different stages in a teacher's career is still mostly an idea. While teacher educators are fond of talking about the pre-service/in-service continuum, there are few conceptual and structural links connecting the different stages in a teacher's career. Still, reform-minded educators and government leaders are beginning to conceive of teacher development in career-long terms because they recognise that teachers will not be able to promote ambitious, socially desirable goals for student learning without opportunities to acquire and develop knowledge, skills and normative understandings throughout their careers.

In discussing each stage of the teacher development continuum, we consider three questions:

1 What are the central learning tasks for teachers at this stage in their careers?
2 What structural arrangements and learning opportunities are typically provided and how well do they meet teachers' learning needs?
3 What are some promising new directions and reforms?

The first question suggests that each phase in a continuum of teacher development has a unique agenda shaped by the requirements of good teaching and by teachers' stage of development. Delineating some of the central learning tasks of pre-service preparation, induction and professional development allows us to see the special challenges associated with each phase as well as the threads of continuity that make up a continuum of professional education. The second question invites description and appraisal of current practice, while the third calls for an overview of new trends and developments. In answering these questions, we are influenced by our knowledge of and experience with teacher education in the US. Still, where possible, we refer to policies and practices in other countries.

PRE-SERVICE TEACHER EDUCATION

Pre-service teacher education includes both general education and professional studies. Since teachers introduce students to the life of the mind they should be among the best-educated persons in a society. From that perspective, all of a teacher's education is part of his or her preparation for teaching. There was a time when liberal arts education and teacher education were synonymous, especially for secondary teachers (Borrowman, 1956). Currently most people recognise that teaching demands specialised knowledge of children, learning, curriculum and pedagogy. Despite general agreement about broad domains of knowledge for teaching and surprising uniformity in programme components, there is no consensus about precisely what teachers need to know or how they should be prepared.

Teacher preparation has been the object of criticism by insiders and outsiders alike. Researchers have documented the weak impact of pre-service preparation on teachers' beliefs and practices compared with the socialising influence of early schooling and on-the-job experience. Fortunately, there is growing evidence that powerful and coherent pre-service programmes can make a difference.

In this section we discuss five tasks of pre-service preparation. The first four tasks relate to core knowledge, skills and dispositions that lay a foundation for teaching and learning to teach. The fifth task highlights a special challenge teacher educators face because teacher education students, unlike students in other professions, have spent many years watching what teachers do. Next we consider the components and structure of a typical pre-service programme, highlighting some of the problems associated with this configuration. Finally we examine some promising new directions which attempt to address some of these problems.

Central tasks of pre-service teacher education

Dewey (1938) warned that 'preparation' was a 'treacherous' idea when applied to education. Dewey believed that every experience should prepare a person for later experiences of a deeper, more expansive quality; however, he argued, educators should not use the present simply to get ready for the future. 'Only by extracting the full meaning of each present experience are we prepared for doing the same thing in the future' (ibid., p. 49).

Pre-service preparation takes place after prospective teachers have spent many years watching what teachers do as elementary and secondary students and before they enter the classroom as beginning teachers. Teacher educators must take into account what teacher candidates bring to their professional preparation as well as what they need to learn. Instead of trying to prepare students to perform as beginning teachers, teacher educators would do well to concentrate on those tasks that provide a foundation for learning in and from teaching.

Developing connected and meaningful subject matter knowledge for teaching

Most people agree that subject matter knowledge is the *sine qua non* of teaching. If teachers are responsible for helping students learn worthwhile content, they need to know and understand the subjects they teach. They also need to develop habits of mind such as critical thinking and openness to diverse perspectives associated with liberal learning if we want teachers to foster these habits in their students.

In conceptualising teachers' subject matter knowledge, scholars have identified three aspects:

1 knowledge of central facts, concepts, theories and procedures within a given field;
2 knowledge of explanatory frameworks that organise and connect ideas; and
3 knowledge of the rules of evidence and proof in a given field (Shulman, 1986).

Besides knowing the content itself, teachers must understand the nature of knowledge and enquiry. What is involved in 'doing' history, mathematics, science, writing? How is new knowledge established in different fields? Teachers' views of knowledge and knowing shape their practice in subtle ways, influencing the questions they ask, the tasks they set, the ideas they reinforce. If teachers do not understand how scholars working in these fields think about their subjects, they may misrepresent them to students (Ball and McDiarmid, 1990).

In addition to conceptual and connected knowledge of the subjects they teach, teachers need to know their subjects from a pedagogical perspective (Wilson *et al.*, 1987). This means understanding what students may find confusing or difficult and having an initial repertoire of explanations, models and analogies to represent core concepts and processes. It includes knowing how concepts connect across fields and how they relate to everyday life. It means thinking about the purposes for studying particular content, since teachers' views about why it is important to learn a subject influence their instructional decisions and strategies.

Developing an understanding of learners, learning and issues of diversity

In order to connect students and content in developmentally appropriate ways, teachers need to know about human development and learning. What are children like at different ages? How do they make sense of their physical and social worlds? How are their ways of thinking and acting shaped by language and culture? How do children gain new knowledge, acquire skills and develop confidence in themselves as learners? What role do prior experience, social interaction and modelling play in learning? Pre-service preparation is a time to develop foundational understandings and perspectives on these questions.

A related task is learning how to learn about the cultures that students bring to school. Increasingly many teachers find themselves teaching students whose racial, cultural and socio-economic backgrounds differ markedly from their own. Some educators advocate teaching about different cultures; others emphasise the value of cultivating self-knowledge through attention to the teachers' own experiences with diversity. All recognise the need to help prospective teachers develop the disposition and tools to learn about students, families and communities and to build on these resources in teaching (Zeichner and Hoeft, 1996).

Developing an initial repertoire for planning, teaching, managing and assessing

In order to teach effectively, teachers must be able to organise and manage groups of students and engage them in appropriate and purposeful learning activities. Learning to do this complex and challenging work involves learning how to frame goals and objectives, adapt curricular materials, plan and sequence lessons, assess student learning, provide clear explanations, lead discussions and organise small and large group work effectively. Prospective teachers can work on different aspects of the complex art of teaching and begin building a repertoire of approaches to planning, instruction, assessment and classroom management. Still, learning to put it all together in practice is a central task of teacher induction.

Developing the tools for ongoing study of teaching and learning

Pre-service preparation is a time to begin forming skills and habits necessary for the ongoing study of teaching in the company of colleagues. Pre-service teachers must come to see that learning is an integral part of teaching and that serious conversation among colleagues about teaching is a valuable resource in developing and improving their practice.

The ongoing study of teaching requires skills of observation, interpretation and analysis, the habit of raising questions, the ability to support claims about learning with evidence, and openness to alternatives. Pre-service students begin to develop these skills and dispositions by analysing student work, comparing different curricular materials, exploring and designing learning tasks, interviewing students to uncover their thinking about particular concepts, studying how different teachers work towards the same goals, and what impact their instruction has on students' thinking and understanding. If this work is carried out in the company of others, pre-service teachers will come to value professional discourse with colleagues as a way to develop and improve their teaching (Ball and Cohen, 1999).

Developing professional perspectives on the teacher's roles and responsibilities

As pre-service teachers learn about subject matter, students, learning and teaching, they must make a transition from layperson to professional educator. This task takes on special meaning at the pre-service level because prospective teachers are no strangers to classrooms. Long before future teachers begin their formal preparation for teaching, they have spent thousands of hours as elementary and secondary students watching what teachers do. From this extended, informal 'apprenticeship of observation' (Lortie, 1975), they have formed images and beliefs that influence what they learn during pre-service preparation. Unless teacher educators engage prospective teachers in a critical examination of their entering beliefs, they may be less open to forming new ideas and entertaining new possibilities.

For example, many prospective teachers enter teacher preparation thinking that teaching is a straightforward process of passing on information and learning a process of memorising and repeating what one has heard. These views conflict with ideas about teaching and learning that undergird current instructional reforms. If teacher educators want teachers to create classrooms where students construct understandings and teachers act as coaches and facilitators of learning, they need to help prospective teachers examine their taken-for-granted beliefs in relation to compelling alternatives.

The 'typical' pre-service programme and its limitations

Teacher preparation usually consists of general studies and professional studies. The former includes subject matter learning and educational foundations. The latter includes methods courses and field experiences (Ben-Peretz, 1994). Most often these four components are structured within a three- or four-year programme; however, post-baccalaureate programmes are also popular in some contexts (Goodlad, 1994).

Subject matter studies

Whatever else teachers need to know, they need to know the subjects they teach. Traditionally, subject matter knowledge is taught in the various disciplinary departments of the university. Secondary teachers often major in their teaching subjects; compared with elementary teachers, they take more discipline-based courses. In fact, most of their university course work occurs in arts and sciences, not education. Elementary teacher candidates take a range of disciplinary courses that roughly correspond to the subjects they will teach. Thus a core component of knowledge for teaching is in the hands of the liberal arts faculty, not teacher educators.

For a long time teacher educators took subject matter knowledge for granted, relying on the fact that teacher education students completed a specified number of courses in the arts and sciences. Recently serious questions have been raised about the adequacy of teachers' subject matter preparation. Some studies show that even when teachers major in their teaching subject, they often have difficulty explaining basic concepts in their discipline (National Center for Research on Teacher Learning, 1991).

In addition, teacher education students find that liberal arts professors rely mainly on lectures and rarely model the kind of pedagogies they are supposed to adopt in their own teaching. To strengthen subject matter preparation for teaching, prospective teachers need fewer lectures and more opportunities to engage with 'big ideas' within and across disciplines and to experience first-hand the modes of enquiry associated with different fields of study.

Educational foundations

Educational foundations, the second component of the pre-service curriculum, build on disciplines in the humanities and social sciences that provide a broad and critical understanding of teaching and learning, education and schooling. Traditionally, educational foundations have included psychology, history, philosophy and sociology of education. What unifies foundations scholars is a strong commitment to the development of interpretative, normative and critical perspectives on education. According to the Council of Learned Societies (1986), foundational studies should help future teachers:

- analyse the meaning, intent and effects of educational institutions;
- develop their own value positions on the basis of critical study and reflection;
- understand how major decisions and events have shaped educational thought and practice over time.

Foundations courses are supposed to help prospective teachers deepen their understanding of their role and responsibilities as professionals, but teachers often criticise them for being too theoretical and too remote from the practical realities of teaching. 'What does this have to do with actual teaching?' is a common refrain. Too often the important connections between educational foundations and teaching practice are lacking.

Another criticism of educational foundations courses is that much of the core disciplinary content has fallen by the wayside. Rather than taking a course in the history or philosophy of education, teacher candidates take an 'Introduction to Education' course, which does not explore the moral imperatives and ethical considerations of teaching. When asked what they remembered from their foundations courses, many pre-service teachers have great difficulty recalling their substance (Goodlad, 1994).

Professional studies

Professional studies include methods courses, curriculum courses and courses based on knowledge from research on teaching. This component of teacher education has a direct bearing on professional practice, providing teachers with techniques and strategies as well as ideas and frameworks to guide their work. Common topics addressed in professional studies courses include instructional planning, classroom management and discipline, assessment of student learning, issues of professionalism.

While management, planning and assessment are critical topics, knowing *about* them does not enable teachers to act in principled ways. Research on teacher thinking and reflective practice suggests that propositional understanding and skilful practice are different forms of knowledge (Carter, 1990; Schon, 1987). If skilful practice is the desired goal of professional studies, then the curriculum must be designed to foster the acquisition and use of intellectual and practical skills.

Two avenues for skill development in teaching are possible – laboratory experiences and field-based practice. Laboratory approaches such as micro-teaching and simulation exercises offer controlled opportunities for prospective teachers to practise specific techniques or apply theory-based strategies in a simplified context (Howey, 1994). Field-based practice involves either short or extended experiences in schools under the guidance of experienced practitioners. First-hand experience offers the advantage of reality, but it is not always possible to provide appropriate modelling, coaching and support.

Field experiences

Most pre-service programmes require prospective teachers to complete a period of supervised practice in an experienced teacher's classroom. Student teaching is considered a culminating experience, a time to apply what has been learned and to demonstrate one's readiness for independent teaching. Usually student teachers take on teaching responsibilities at a fairly rapid rate which may not allow time for them to get to know students as learners or get inside the curriculum. Too often the focus is on independent performance rather than on the thinking behind the performance or the learning from it.

Guidance and support are largely in the hands of experienced teachers who agree to host a student teacher in their classroom. In some cases co-operating teachers do not model the kind of teaching advocated by the programme. This creates a tension for student teachers who are caught between the expectations of the programme and the realities of the field. Often the programme loses out as student teachers adopt prevailing norms and practices. Nor do co-operating teachers receive preparation or compensation for their work with student teachers. Despite evidence to the contrary, many assume that knowing how to teach qualifies one to help others learn how to teach. A major challenge for teacher education is trying to prepare future teachers for tomorrow's schools in schools as they exist today.

Promising directions in pre-service preparation

Recent reforms in teacher education are beginning to address some of the persistent problems that limit the impact of pre-service preparation. One effort lies in using student cohorts to intensify the socialisation experience. A second strategy lies in shaping the content and pedagogy of teacher education in ways that better fit our understanding of practical knowledge and ways of knowing in teaching. A third new direction lies in creating extended clinical experiences which support the integration of theory and practice. Often these extended internships occur in professional development schools, where university and schools work together to make schools better places for students and teachers to learn. School–university partnerships represent another promising direction.

The use of student cohorts

Most professional schools have mechanisms to educate and socialise students into a given field. While the explicit curriculum offers formal training, the 'hidden curriculum' helps enculturate students into the norms of a profession. Such enculturation may be strengthened by the use of cohort groups, which encourage interaction with peers and faculty outside formal course work. This kind of informal interaction allows students to explore matters of professional practice, ethics and tradition in ways that might not otherwise occur in their formal training and promotes an initial understanding of what it means to be a member of the profession.

At their best, cohorts provide mutual support and foster socialisation into desirable professional norms and practices (Goodlad, 1994; Tom, 1997). When students move through a pre-service programme in cohorts, they build lasting relationships and come to value professional collaboration. Thus the use of cohorts can help counter the highly personal, individualistic orientation towards teaching that prevails in many Western countries. Of course, grouping prospective teachers together will not automatically provide professional socialisation unless programmes develop a strong ethos and deliberately encourage informal interactions around professional issues.

Reshaping the pedagogy of teacher education

Studies of professionals at work have provided new insights into the kinds of knowledge and ways of knowing that characterise professional practice. We know, for example, that teaching is a complex, context-specific activity involving reasoning, decision-making and continuous reflection. While some aspects of interactive teaching lend themselves to routine problem-solving, other aspects involve dilemma management and reflection-in-action (Lampert, 1985; Schon, 1987). Teachers must weave together different kinds of knowledge as they size up situations, weigh competing goals, and figure out what to do.

Teacher educators have begun to experiment with new pedagogies that represent the intellectual work of teaching and provide opportunities for prospective teachers to practise the kind of analysis and practical reasoning that teaching entails. One prominent strategy, common in legal and business education, is the use of cases and case methods (Sykes and Bird, 1992). Cases are narratives or descriptions of teaching which capture the complex, contextualised, multifaceted nature of teachers' work. Some cases include a 'behind-the-scenes' look at what the teacher was thinking and feeling at the time. Others present problematic situations which invite analysis and decision-making or commentaries by educators who represent different perspectives.

Teacher educators may use long, detailed cases in order to help students think about the interplay of goals, students and contextual variables in teaching and learning, or they may use a set of smaller cases to illustrate particular principles or patterns of practice. Some researchers and teacher educators have experimented with getting teachers to write their own cases. Cases allow teacher candidates to explore *what* teachers do, *how* they do it and *why* they do it. Advocates claim that analysing second-hand encounters with teaching can help prospective teachers develop the disposition and skills to learn from their own first-hand experience (Merseth, 1996).

Extended clinical experiences

Providing prospective teachers with extended field experiences (such as a year-long internship) enables a more gradual and supported transition into teaching than a brief stint of student teaching. Extended field experiences allow teacher candidates to get to know the students, curriculum and school community, to see learning unfold over time, and to work on their own practice with assistance. When extended clinical experiences are co-ordinated with seminars in curriculum or subject matter teaching, they support the integration of theory and practice.

Sometimes extended field experiences reflect a shift in the locus of authority for teacher education from the university to the school. Sometimes extended field experiences are developed in the context of school–university partnerships, which link the reform of pre-service teacher education with professional development. Recent proposals for reform in teacher education advocate the creation of professional development schools (PDSs) where university and school personnel work together to support the learning of students, teachers and teacher educators (Carnegie Forum on Education and the Economy, 1986; Holmes Group, 1990). Envisioned as centres of learning and enquiry, professional development schools enable prospective and novice teachers to learn to teach in the company of experienced teachers who are engaged in the complex and messy business of reforming teaching. Under ideal circumstances these teachers model and explicate good teaching and provide the necessary guidance, coaching and support to help novices learn to 'teach against the grain' (Cochran-Smith, 1991).

Of course, the most effective pre-service programmes are those that incorporate student cohorts, the use of teaching cases, and extended clinical experiences into a coherent curriculum guided by a clear vision of good teaching and a strong sense of mission. Such programmes challenge the familiar criticism that teacher preparation is both too theoretical and too superficial by engaging prospective teachers in intellectually challenging learning opportunities. Instead of emphasising discrete skills and strategies disconnected from the content and contexts of teaching, they focus on foundational understandings and skills related to the central tasks of teaching.

TEACHER EDUCATION DURING THE INDUCTION PHASE

New teachers have two jobs to do – they have to teach and they have to learn to teach in the context of teaching. No matter how good a pre-service programme may be, some things can only be learned on the job. At best the pre-service experience offers 'practice' in teaching. The first encounter with 'real' teaching occurs when the novice teacher steps into his or her own classroom. This is when learning to teach begins in earnest.

Many regard the first early years of teaching as a unique stage in learning to teach, influencing not only whether people remain in teaching but what kind of teacher they become. As Bush (1983, p. 3) explains:

> [T]he conditions under which a person carries out the first years of teaching have a strong influence on the level of effectiveness which that teacher is able to achieve and sustain over the years; on the attitudes which govern teachers' behavior over even a forty year career; and, indeed, in the decision whether or not to continue in the teaching profession.

Recently, reform-minded educators and policy-makers have begun to acknowledge the importance of these early years of teaching. In some countries, programmes for novice teachers are being established which offer support and guidance during this formative stage in their professional development (Moskowitz and Stevens, 1997). Motivated by a variety of concerns, the creation of formal induction programmes for novice teachers represents a promising change in the teacher education landscape.

The central tasks of beginning teacher induction

What do beginning teachers need to learn? What are the central tasks of teacher induction? Some general answers to these questions can be offered based on an understanding of the nature of teaching. Still, the actual learning tasks which novice teachers face are shaped by the specific circumstances they encounter, mediated by the knowledge, skills and normative understandings they bring.

Researchers characterise the first year of teaching as a time of survival and discovery, adaptation and learning (Huberman, 1989; Nemser, 1983). According to one school of thought, novices rely on trial and error to work out strategies which enable them to survive without sacrificing all the idealism that attracted them to teaching in the first place. They continue to depend on these strategies whether or not they represent 'best practice' (Lortie, 1975). According to another, beginning teachers face personal concerns about acceptance, control and adequacy which must be resolved before they can move on to more professional considerations about teaching and learning (Fuller and Brown, 1975; Gold, 1996). Veenman's (1984) review of research on the perceived needs of novice teachers claims that classroom management is the major preoccupation; however, case studies of beginning teaching (e.g. Bullough, 1990; Grossman, 1990) provide a more dynamic and contextualised picture. Clearly, the experience of beginning teaching and the lessons learned derive from a complex interaction of personal and situational factors.

Charged with the same responsibilities as their more experienced colleagues, beginning teachers are expected to perform and be effective. Yet most aspects of the situation are unfamiliar – the students, the curriculum, the community, the local policies and procedures. Besides the newness of the situation, the complexities of teaching confront the novice with daily dilemmas and uncertainties. The fact that beginning teachers have limited experience and practical knowledge to draw on increases their sense of frustration and inadequacy. On top of all this, many teachers work alone in their classrooms isolated from their colleagues. This makes it difficult to ask for or receive help.

Teacher induction is often framed as a transition from the university to the school, from pre-service preparation to practice, from being a student of teaching to becoming a teacher of students. As these phrases imply, induction brings a shift in role orientation and an epistemological move from knowing about teaching through academic study to knowing how to teach by confronting the day-to-day challenges of teaching. Becoming a teacher involves the formation of a professional identity and the construction of a professional practice. Both aspects of learning to teach need to proceed in ways that strengthen the beginning teacher's capacity for further growth. Many novice teachers are recent college graduates facing their first full-time job. Thus the first year of teaching may represent both an initiation into the profession of teaching and an initiation into the world of adulthood.

The situation in which beginning teachers find themselves is inherently paradoxical. Like all beginning professionals, they must demonstrate skills and abilities which they do not yet possess and which they can only gain by starting to do what they do not yet understand (Schon, 1987). This places novice teachers in a vulnerable position. Moreover the work of teaching itself, complex, uncertain and full of dilemmas, sharpens the paradox by reminding beginning teachers at every turn of what they cannot yet do.

Some of the most important things teachers need to learn are local. Teachers need to find out how their students feel about particular learning activities and what they already know and believe about particular topics. Over time teachers develop an appreciation for the concerns and confusions, ideas and interests that students in a particular grade or given school are likely to have and they build up a repertoire of ways to respond. Novices do not have contextualised or local knowledge of students and curriculum. So an important part of learning to teach is learning to construct such knowledge and verify it in practice.

Beginning teachers must also form a professional identity which is personally satisfying as well as institutionally appropriate and productive. Often beginning teachers struggle to reconcile competing images or aspects of their role – for example, the need to be an authority in areas of discipline and classroom management with the desire to be perceived as a friendly person; the need to prepare students for the 'real world' with the desire to be a nurturing caregiver, responsive to individual differences (Ryan, 1970). Constructing a professional identity is an ongoing, complex process in which beginning teachers develop a coherent sense of themselves as professionals by combining parts of their past, including their own experiences in school and in teacher preparation, with pieces of the present in their current school context, with visions of the kind of teacher they want to become or the kind of classroom they want to create in the future (Featherstone, 1993).

Burden (1981) identifies seven characteristics of first year or 'first stage' teachers:

1 limited knowledge of teaching activities;
2 limited knowledge about the teaching environment;
3 conformity to an image of the teacher as authority;
4 subject-centred approach to curriculum and teaching;
5 limited professional insights and perceptions;
6 feelings of uncertainty, confusion and insecurity;
7 unwillingness to try new teaching methods.

We are only starting to understand how beginning teachers move from this initial stage through a second stage of consolidation somewhere around the third year of teaching to a third stage of mastery and confidence after five to seven years of teaching experience.

Based on a study of clinical teacher education, including beginning teacher induction, researchers at the University of Texas Research and Development Center on Teacher Education identified four areas of development and learning. They suggest that, under appropriate circumstances, beginning teachers should

1 increase their knowledge of subject matter, teaching activities and teaching environments;
2 develop their abilities to diagnose student needs and to plan and implement instruction according to those needs;
3 develop positive working relationships with colleagues, administrators and parents; and
4 become more secure in their roles as instructional leaders in the classroom.

'Beginning teachers should also emerge from their first year with a strengthened commitment to learn from teaching and an enlarged disposition to engage in exploration, experimentation and change' (Borko, 1986, p. 50). These goals would be difficult for beginning teachers to achieve on their own.

Sink or swim induction and informal buddy systems

Unfortunately, induction into teaching is often an abrupt and lonely process. The bridge from pre-service preparation to full-time teaching is short and the transition far from gradual. Student teaching can last anywhere from 2 weeks (in Japan) to 15 weeks (in the US). Even when teacher candidates have more extended field experiences, such as year-long internships, their learning occurs in someone else's classroom.

In far too many places beginning teachers must 'learn the ropes' by themselves. The practice of letting new teachers 'sink or swim' results in high rates of attrition and lowered effectiveness. Many teachers work alone in the privacy of their classroom. In Western countries, norms of autonomy and non-interference keep teachers from requesting and offering help and perpetuate the view that good teachers figure things out on their own.

Sometimes a beginning teacher will get some support and assistance from a well-meaning colleague who offers to take the novice under his or her wing. This kind of informal 'buddy' system may work for the fortunate novice who happens to get adopted, but it hardly represents a responsible approach to beginning teacher support and development. Relying on the goodwill of experienced teachers to reach out to new teachers on their own initiative ignores the well-documented learning challenges that beginning teachers face and the call for a more sustained and systematic approach to novice teacher support and development.

Formal induction programmes for beginning teachers

The emergence of formal programmes for beginning teachers in their early years on the job is a relatively recent phenomenon. Japan instituted a government-mandated teacher induction programme in 1988 with implementation occurring between 1989–1992. Chinese Taipei revised and intensified teacher induction programmes in conjunction with reforms in 1994 (Moskowitz and Stevens, 1997). In the United States, the first state-mandated induction programme was established in Florida in 1980. Currently 27 states have a formally approved and implemented state-wide support system for beginning teachers and most urban districts, especially the large ones, offer some induction programme for this group (Fideler and Haselkorn, forthcoming).

Various reasons account for the rising interest in beginning teacher induction. They include:

- stemming the tide of teacher attrition;
- retaining and rewarding good, experienced teachers by creating new roles for them as mentor teachers;
- retaining strong novice teachers;
- improving the quality of teaching;
- reducing the stress and problems experienced by beginning teachers;
- compensating for gaps in initial preparation or, put differently, building on and extending pre-service preparation.

Some reasons are complementary while others may conflict. Mentoring benefits both mentor teachers and novices; however, reducing stress through new teacher support may increase retention without necessarily improving quality. Still, these varied priorities and concerns have contributed to a growing consensus that support and assistance are essential to the retention and success of new teachers.

Deciding what counts as an induction programme is not as straightforward as it might seem. Some consider an informal 'welcome' arranged by the school principal to be an induction programme (Moskowitz and Stevens, 1997). However, this is precisely the kind of activity that Huling-Austin (1990), an expert on induction in the US, wants to exclude by defining induction as 'a planned programme intended to provide some systematic and sustained assistance specifically to beginning teachers for at least one school year' (p. 536). Another area of controversy is whether induction programmes should incorporate formal evaluation of beginning teachers along with support and assistance. Some programmes link induction to licensure through assessments that determine the beginning teacher's eligibility to continue teaching.

The impetus for teacher induction may come from the federal government, the state or provincial government, or the local school system. Many programmes mandate participation of all beginning teachers, but budgetary constraints make this difficult to enforce. Equity becomes an issue when new teachers in wealthier jurisdictions participate in induction programmes while teachers in poorer areas do not. Most programmes last one to two years. In rare cases, beginning teachers get reduced teaching loads. Some programmes involve partnerships with institutions of higher education, which opens up the possibility for greater continuity between pre-service teacher education and beginning teacher induction. Still, the lack of widespread participation by universities in teacher induction is frequently cited as a problem and future need (Gold, 1996; Huling-Austin, 1990; Moskowitz and Stevens, 1997).

Widely perceived to have a positive impact on teacher retention and teacher effectiveness, induction programmes have not been the subject of rigorous evaluation. Although programmes differ widely, some commonalities exist. The most prominent include support for new teachers as the primary goal, and mentoring as the favoured strategy (Fideler and Haselkorn, forthcoming; Gold, 1996; Little, 1990; Moskowitz and Stevens, 1997). Four distinct support concepts thread through the literature on induction:

1 emotional support to cope with stress and anxiety;
2 operational/technical support to deal with school policies, programmes and practices;
3 pedagogical support to help in organising classrooms, planning lessons and responding effectively to the needs of diverse students;
4 increased subject matter knowledge and pedagogical content knowledge to identify essential elements in the curriculum and make complex concepts accessible to students.

In most cases these different kinds of support are provided by an experienced teacher (mentor) assigned to work with one or more novice teachers.

Mentoring is usually organised into a formal programme. Selection, training, role definitions, working conditions and incentives for mentor teachers vary. For example, some mentor teachers are released full-time from their teaching responsibilities to work with novices. Other mentor teachers must fit in mentoring with the demands of full-time teaching. In some programmes mentors receive special training before they assume their new responsibilities; in other programmes no training is provided. In a few contexts, mentors participate in an ongoing study group where they continue to develop their practice as mentors. Clearly, these factors affect both the frequency and the quality of mentoring.

If mentor teachers induct novices into traditional teaching practices, then mentoring serves as a force for continuity. If mentor teachers induct novices into new forms of teaching, then mentoring serves as a force for change. In one comparative study of mentoring in two beginning teacher assistance programmes, researchers found striking differences in the way mentor teachers defined and enacted their roles. Mentors who functioned as 'local guides' concentrated on helping novices fit comfortably into a particular setting and learn to teach with minimal disruption. They explained local policies and practices, shared instructional materials and helped to solve immediate problems. They did not have a long-term view of their role. In fact, they expected to decrease their involvement as beginning teachers gained confidence and control. Mentors who functioned as 'educational companions' still helped novices with immediate problems, but they kept their eye on long-term, professional goals such as helping the novice learn to attend to student thinking and understanding and to develop sound reasons for their actions. They worked towards those ends by enquiring with novices into the particulars of their teaching situation and by asking questions such as, 'What sense did students make of that assignment?' 'Why did you decide on this activity?' 'How could we find out whether it worked?' A few mentors saw themselves as 'agents of cultural change'. They sought to break down the traditional isolation among teachers by fostering norms of collaboration and shared enquiry. They built networks among novices and between novices and their more experienced colleagues, arranged for visits to other classrooms and promoted conversations among teachers about teaching. Researchers connected these differences to variations in the formal expectations, working conditions, selection and preparation of mentors (Feiman-Nemser and Parker, 1993).

A major tension or debate in the field of induction concerns the role of assessment. The dominant position favours assistance over assessment on the grounds that the two functions are incompatible and should not be carried out in the same programme, or at least not by the same person. The argument is that new teachers, concerned about making a good impression, would be reluctant to share problems and ask for help if the person supporting them was also responsible for evaluating their competence. This position has its challengers. Some argue that formative assessment is an integral part of professional development. Others assert that induction programmes should play both a 'bridging' and a 'gate-keeping' function, helping new teachers make a successful entry into teaching and determining if they are qualified to teach.

Formative assessment is a central feature in California's Beginning Teacher Support and Assessment programme where it provides focus and direction for the creation of individualised professional development plans for beginning teachers. Summative assessment is incorporated into Connecticut's Beginning Educator Support and Training programme, where specially trained assessors evaluate teaching portfolios assembled by beginning teachers with the help of their support providers. A different approach is used in programmes built around a 'peer assistance and review model', in which consultant teachers provide initial assistance to beginning teachers but also make recommendations about the renewal of their teaching contracts.

The experience of induction programmes in some Pacific Rim countries offers a different perspective. According to a recent study, the most 'successful' programmes 'downplay' assessment without eliminating it as a goal. Rather informal assessments by fellow teachers are so frequent that beginning teachers get used to having their teaching observed and receiving feedback. Consequently, when more formal assessment for purposes of certification or licensing occurs, new teachers do not feel threatened (Moskowitz and Stevens, 1997).

In principle, good induction programmes have many of the features of effective professional development. They offer ongoing assistance, grounded in problems of practice, based in collegial relationships, and focused on teachers' needs, questions and concerns. They depend on observations of and conversations about teaching. They promote teacher learning in the service of student learning. In the face of growing teacher shortages and rising standards for student learning, induction programmes have emerged as a central component in systemic reform initiatives aimed at improving the quality of teaching and learning. If induction programmes acculturate beginning teachers to new goals for student learning and cultivate the skills of continuous improvement, they may serve as a model for a new kind of professional development.

PROFESSIONAL DEVELOPMENT FOR TEACHERS

Professional development refers to learning opportunities for practising teachers. Educators frequently invoke the idea of teachers as 'lifelong learners', but most schools lack well-developed structures or systems for providing serious learning opportunities to teachers. Writing about schooling in America, Sarason observes:

> public schools have never assigned importance to the intellectual, professional, and career needs of their personnel. However the aims of schools were articulated, there was never any doubt that schools existed for children. . . . It is impossible to create and sustain over time conditions for productive learning for students when they do not exist for teachers.
>
> (Sarason, 1990, pp. 144–145)

The most common form of professional development consists of short-term workshops and training sessions, usually sponsored by a school district and scattered throughout the year. Universities also participate in in-service education by offering courses for teachers after school, in the evening, or during the summer. These opportunities may introduce teachers to new information and ideas and even provide intellectual stimulation, but they do not help teachers transfer new ideas to the classroom or learn from the everyday experience of teaching. Nor are they well suited to help teachers change their practice in significant ways.

Increasingly researchers, policy-makers and educators have reached two conclusions:

- The kinds of changes in teaching and learning embedded in current reform initiatives require fundamental changes in teachers' knowledge and their working relationships with students and colleagues.
- Traditional forms of professional development are not adequate to the task.

State and federal governments, school districts, individual schools and a variety of professional organisations have launched professional development efforts that seem more compatible with the demands of contemporary reforms and with the contexts of teaching. While

747

a consensus is emerging about what form effective professional development should take, research on how new forms of professional development affect teachers' practice and their students' learning is still quite limited.

Central tasks of professional development

We can distinguish two learning tasks for practising teachers. The first centres on helping teachers add new skills and strategies to their existing repertoire. The second centres on helping teachers transform their perspectives and practice in fundamental ways. Each requires a different form of professional development.

Some aspects of teaching can be framed in terms of discrete skills and strategies and these lend themselves to well-designed training. According to Showers *et al.* (1987, pp. 85–86), the purpose of training is 'not simply to generate the external visible moves that bring that practice to bear in the instructional setting, but to generate the conditions that enable the practice to be selected and used appropriately and integratively'. Effective training includes opportunities to learn about the rationale behind the new strategy or technique, to see it modelled, to practise under simulated conditions, to receive classroom-based coaching and feedback from trainers and/or peers (Joyce and Showers, 1988). When all these components are present, training has the potential to change teachers' beliefs and their behaviour.

Many present reforms do not lend themselves to skills training because they cannot be easily expressed in terms of specific, transferable skills and practices. Rather they require teachers to figure out in practice what new visions of teaching and new standards for student learning look like. Instead of adopting or implementing practices designed by someone else, teachers must invent and adapt pedagogies that reflect broad principles and values. This task calls for new organisational structures and cultures that allow teachers to learn in and from their teaching with the help of colleagues and outside experts (Little, 1993).

In the past 20 years our understanding of learning and knowledge has changed and this has led to new models of teaching. Current reforms call for a kind of teaching that looks quite different from what most teachers experienced as students and what they now practice (Cohen *et al.*, 1993). 'Teaching for understanding' aims to promote active learning and deep understanding. It focuses on student thinking and collaborative problem-solving. It goes beyond the acquisition of facts and skills to emphasise 'big ideas' and real-world applications.

Moving from 'teaching as telling' to 'teaching for understanding' places new demands on teachers. Besides revising their images of teaching, teachers must develop new understandings of students and subject matter. They must also learn how to use their practice as a site for professional development. This means learning how to try out new practices, analyse the effects on student learning and frame new questions to further their enquiry.

The ongoing study and improvement of teaching is difficult to accomplish alone. It requires access to new ideas and perspectives, support and encouragement, help in solving problems and imagining possibilities, shared understandings and a collective sense of accountability. It depends on teachers' capacity to participate in serious and sustained conversations with colleagues about their work. Since most teachers work alone in the privacy of their classroom, they have few opportunities to develop the skills and dispositions for such professional discourse. Moreover, norms of politeness and non-interference limit the possibility of developing critical dialogue. Thus a third task of professional development is helping practising teachers cultivate the skills and the stance required for participation in the ongoing study and improvement of practice with other teachers.

Conventional models of professional development and their limitations

The conventional model of professional development is largely a dissemination activity based on a direct teaching model. Teachers attend full- or half-day sessions in which outside experts give inspirational lectures, report research findings and offer techniques and strategies. Teachers have little say about the content of these sessions which treat their development as an individual activity. There is minimal effort to promote interaction among teachers or to provide for continuous learning or changed practice. Teachers are expected to take what they have heard and apply it to their classroom without the benefit of on-site demonstrations, coaching or shared problem-solving.

Besides attending in-service workshops and conferences, teachers participate in professional development by taking courses at the university. Even when these courses provide intellectual stimulation, their content is rarely connected to teachers' practice. In addition, university professors, like in-service presenters, generally treat teachers as passive recipients of expert knowledge, which does little to encourage intellectual initiative or a sense of professionalism.

Many experts now agree that conventional approaches to professional development have little impact on teachers' instructional practice and students' learning and that they do not fit the requirements of contemporary reforms. The 'one size fits all' approach ignores the fact that teachers teach in different contexts and have different learning needs, interests and concerns. The lack of continuity and follow-up discourages serious efforts by teachers to adapt and use what they have heard about in the sessions. The fact that in-service education is rarely linked to district or school goals means that it may not support broader institutional initiatives.

New models of professional development

Research on learning, the realisation that teachers make a critical difference in what and how students learn, higher standards for student achievement and the unanimous agreement that in-service training is woefully inadequate, have all focused attention on professional development. New studies and research syntheses highlight design principles of professional development that are likely to yield improvements in teaching and learning. Based on a combination of research and rhetorical claims, these principles reflect a growing consensus about the kinds of learning opportunities that teachers need (Little, 1993; NCES, 1998).

1 Professional development provides meaningful, sustained engagement with colleagues, ideas and materials. New approaches to teaching require new levels of knowledge and

understanding. Effective professional development enables teachers to deepen their understanding of the subjects they teach, to investigate student work and to experience new forms of learning. This contrasts with the shallow content of most in-service activities and the passive role adopted by the teacher.

2 Professional development takes account of the contexts of teaching and the experience of teachers. Instead of treating teachers as blank slates, effective professional development helps teachers situate new ideas in relation to current practice. It acknowledges variation in teacher expertise and institutional setting and helps teachers consider the 'fit' between new ideas and prevailing norms and practices. It rejects the 'one size fits all' approach, which permits the delivery of standardised content.

3 Professional development supports critical discussion among colleagues. Instead of reinforcing consensus and discouraging critical thinking, effective professional development promotes the assessment of alternatives, the close examination of underlying assumptions, the search for evidence. These norms and practices are more likely to flourish in close collaborations and long-term partnerships, where there is time to develop the trust needed to question and disagree, to learn from failures as well as successes and to share uncertainties and problems.

4 Professional development places classroom teaching in the broader contexts of schooling and the surrounding culture. It helps teachers see their individual work in relation to the work of others and to consider leadership roles beyond the classroom. Effective professional development is organised around common concerns and collaborative problem-solving. It mobilises collective efforts on behalf of students and their learning. It is part of a larger, ongoing change process.

Contemporary examples of teacher development

Professional communities inside and outside schools have an important role to play in promoting serious, long-term teacher learning. Professional development should be an integral part of the life of a school. At the same time, there is growing evidence that organisational arrangements outside school (such as coalitions, partnerships and networks) provide valuable learning opportunities that differ in quality and kind from those available inside schools or in traditional in-service programmes (Lieberman and Grolnick, 1996).

Below we offer three brief descriptions of what these principles might look like in practice. The first example highlights a format for conversation among teachers that developed in one school and then spread to other contexts. The second illustrates a form of professional development – the teacher network – which has grown up alongside more conventional venues. The third outlines structures for local problem-solving which draw on outside expertise yet allow teachers in a school to work together on emergent problems.

The descriptive review

In an effort to support children's learning in ways that build on their strengths, Patricia Carini and her colleagues at the Prospect Center in Vermont developed a process called the 'descriptive review'. The 'descriptive review' brings teachers together to talk about particular students whom individual teachers may find difficult to reach or teach. It is a collaborative, reflective process for describing a child's experiences in school in order to determine how best to support and extend that experience (Carini, 1986). During a descriptive review, the presenting teacher provides a rounded description of a student, commenting on physical presence and gesture, emotional tone and disposition, relationships with children and adults, activities and interests and formal learning. Once the other participants feel they have a picture of this child, they suggest possible strategies for supporting his or her learning and addressing the focal problem or question which the presenting teacher identified.

The descriptive review embodies many of the guiding principles of effective professional development. It is grounded in the close study of individual students in order to cultivate teachers' capacity to see students, to notice their strengths and to design supportive learning opportunities. It promotes student performance by helping teachers identify strategies responsive to individual children. It enables teachers to share their knowledge, learn from one another, and take responsibility for the growth and development of all children in a school.

The descriptive review process has been adopted by groups of teachers in other settings. For instance, the Teacher Learning Cooperative, a group of progressive teachers in Philadelphia who work in various public and private schools, has met weekly during the school year for over 20 years to talk about teaching. Descriptive child reviews are a prominent feature of these sessions which are organised and sustained by a core of highly experienced teacher leaders who learned about descriptive review and other formats for looking at children and their work at summer workshops sponsored by the Prospect Center in Vermont.

The Foxfire Network

A second example of professional development, the Foxfire Network, grew out of one high school English teacher's discovery that in order to reach traditional literacy goals, he had to tap students' interests and provide them with meaningful choices (Wigginton, 1985). Named after the journal which Wigginton and his students published from their classroom, the 'Foxfire approach' involved students doing research on their own communities. To share this process with other teachers, Wigginton and a colleague created summer courses where they modelled what they did with students and talked about the theory of experiential learning. Participating teachers wanted opportunities for continued support and conversation, so the leaders sought outside funding to create regional networks where teachers could get support as they tried to practise what they had learned during the summer.

The Foxfire Teacher Outreach Network grew out of these developments. Teacher leaders in the summer courses became co-ordinators of regional networks. They developed criteria for new networks, explicating the principles that represented the Foxfire way of learning. Currently 25 networks, some connected to colleges and universities, function as centres for professional learning by teachers for teachers.

Networks, partnerships and coalitions are becoming an important alternative form of reform-minded teacher and school development. Despite their variety and fragility, they seem to have powerful effects on their members, who value the chance to work and learn with like-minded teachers and administrators from different schools on common problems. At the same time, researchers acknowledge the challenge of documenting members' involvement, learning and changed practice (Lieberman and Grolnick, 1996).

School-wide professional development

Perhaps the most promising approach to professional development involves a combination of school-based strategies that meet the evolving needs of teachers as they seek ways to increase student achievement. One example comes from an inner city school in Boston, where professional development led to major school-wide changes. The process began when teachers and parents came together to develop a shared vision for learning in their school. Comparing their vision with current programmes in the school, they recognised that the school had high expectations for regular students, but lacked such expectations for special education students. This realisation led to a major decision – the inclusion of special education students in regular classrooms.

The new policy meant that all teachers had to learn new ways to reach all students. At first, teachers visited other schools and attended workshops on ways to meet the needs of students with a wide range of abilities, but there was little carryover to classrooms. Next the school invited a consultant to work directly with teachers to build a good early childhood programme. When this began to pay off, other consultants were brought in to work with teachers during the school day, observing, coaching and demonstrating new instructional approaches. Teachers formed study groups which now meet regularly to deal with new priorities identified by the staff. All these efforts have transformed teachers' ways of looking at students.

Many educators have rejected traditional models of professional development in favour of a 'new paradigm of teacher development' which promotes sustained, collegial enquiry into teaching, learning and subject matter. Still, we know little about what teachers actually learn in and from these new professional development opportunities or how their learning shapes their teaching practice and their students' learning. Researchers are just beginning to examine the complex relationship between teacher learning and student learning which lies at the heart of contemporary reform initiatives. Such studies are needed if we hope to move beyond current rhetoric to create meaningful opportunities for experienced teacher learning.

CONCLUSION

We have tried to demonstrate that teacher education does not and should not end with initial preparation. Rather, teachers need regular opportunities for professional learning at every stage in their career. These opportunities must be grounded in the central task of teaching – helping all students learn significant knowledge and skills in meaningful ways. They must also be responsive to the evolving needs of teachers as they develop a professional identity and create a practice based on shared professional standards.

Ideally, pre-service preparation lays a foundation for learning to teach by helping pro-spective teachers develop defensible visions of good teaching and a strong foundation in subject matter, pedagogy and learning. Teacher induction helps new teachers develop contextualised knowledge of students, curriculum and community and connect this new knowledge to broader principles and understandings. Professional development enables practising teachers to consolidate a repertoire of instructional strategies, take on new roles beyond the classroom, and continue refining their practice. At every stage, teacher educa-tion should cultivate the skills and dispositions teachers need to study and improve their teaching.

This comprehensive vision of teacher education rests on the conviction that the quality of teaching and teacher learning affects the quality of student learning. Taking this belief seriously requires new policies and programmes directed towards teachers and the institutions that prepare, license and employ them. Such reforms would establish coherent programmes of teacher education and professional development based on professional standards and linked to structures for teacher assessment and accountability. This is the challenge facing all those concerned about making schools good places for students and teachers to learn.

REFERENCES

Ball, D. L. (1996). 'Developing mathematics reform: What don't we know about teacher learning – but would make good working hypotheses'. In S. Friel and G. Bright (eds), *Reflecting on Our Work: NSF Teacher Enhancement in K-6 Mathematics*. New York: University Press of America, 500–508.

Ball, D. L. and Cohen, D. K. (1999). 'Developing practice, developing practitioners: Toward a practice-based theory of professional education'. In G. Sykes and L. Darling-Hammond (eds), *Teaching as the Learning Profession: Handbook of Policy and Practice*. San Francisco: Jossey-Bass.

Ball, D. L. and McDiarmid, G. W. (1990). 'The subject matter preparation of teachers'. In W. R. Houston (ed.), *Handbook of Research on Teacher Education*. New York: Macmillan, 437–449.

Ben-Peretz, M. (1994). 'The curriculum of teacher education programs'. In T. Husen and T. N. Postlethwaite (eds) *International Encyclopaedia of Education*. Vol. 10, (2nd edn) Oxford: Pergamon, 5991–5995.

Borko, H. (1986). 'Clinical teacher education: The induction years'. In J. V. Hoffman and S. A. Edwards (eds), *Reality and Reform in Clinical Teacher Education*. New York: Random House, 45–63.

Borko, H. and Putnam, R. (1996). 'Learning to teach'. In D. Berliner and R. Calfee (eds), *Handbook of Educational Psychology*. New York: Macmillan, 673–708.

Borrowman, M. (1956). *The Liberal and the Technical in Teacher Education: A Historical Survey of American Thought*. New York: Columbia University, Teachers College Press.

Bullough, R. (1990). 'Supervision, mentoring and self discovery: A case study of a first-year teacher'. *Journal of Curriculum and Supervision*, 5 (4), 338–360.

Burden, P. (1981). 'Teachers' perceptions of their personal and professional development'. Paper presented at the annual meeting of the Midwestern Educational Research Association. Des Moines, IA.

Bush, R. N. (1983). 'The beginning years of teaching: A focus for collaboration in teacher education'. Paper presented to the World Assembly of the International Council on Education for Teachers. Washington, DC.

Carini, P. (1986). 'Building from children's strengths'. *Journal of Education*. 168, 13–24.

Carnegie Forum on Education and the Economy. (1986). *A Nation Prepared: Teachers for the Twenty-first Century*. New York: Carnegie Corporation.

Carter, K. (1990). 'Teachers' knowledge and learning to teach'. In W. R. Houston (ed.), *Handbook of Research on Teacher Education*. New York: Macmillan, 291–310.

Clifford, G. and Guthrie, J. (1988). *Ed School: A Brief for Professional Education*. Chicago: University of Chicago Press.

Cochran-Smith, M. (1991). 'Learning to teach against the grain'. *Harvard Educational Review*, 61, 279–310.

Cohen, D., McLaughlin, M. and Talbert, J. (1993). *Teaching for Understanding: Challenges for Policy and Practice*. San Francisco: Jossey-Bass.

Council of Learned Societies in Education. (1986). *Standards for Academic and Professional Instruction in Foundations of Education, Educational Studies, Educational Policy Studies*. Ann Arbor, MI: Prakken.

Darling-Hammond, L. and McLaughlin, M. (1995). 'Policies that support professional development in an era of school reform'. *Phi Delta Kappan*, 76 (8), 597–604.

Dewey, J. (1938). *Experience and Education*. New York: Simon & Schuster.

Featherstone, H. (1993). 'Learning from the first years of classroom teaching: The journey in, the journey out'. *Teachers College Record*, 95 (1), 93–112.

Feiman-Nemser, S. and Parker, M. (1993). 'Mentoring in context: A comparison of two US programmes for beginning teachers'. *International Journal of Educational Research*, 19 (8), 699–718.

Fideler, E. and Haselkorn, D. (forthcoming). *Urban Teacher Induction Practices in the United States*. Belmont, MA: Recruiting New Teachers, Inc.

Fullan, M. (1991). *The New Meaning of Educational Change*. New York: Teachers College Press.

Fuller, F. and Brown, O. (1975). 'Becoming a teacher'. In K. Ryan (ed.), *Teacher Education* (74th Yearbook of the National Society for the Study of Education, Pt II). Chicago: University of Chicago Press, 25–52.

Gold, Y. (1996). 'Beginning teacher support: Attrition, mentoring and induction'. In J. Sikula (ed.), *Handbook of Research on Teacher Education* (2nd edn). New York: Macmillan.

Goodlad, J. (1994). *Educational Renewal: Better Teachers, Better Schools*. San Francisco: Jossey-Bass.

Grossman, P. (1990). *The Making of a Teacher: Teacher Knowledge and Teacher Education*. New York: Teachers College Press.

Herbst, J. (1989). 'Teacher preparation in the 19th century: Institutions and purposes'. In D. Warren (ed.), *American Teachers: Histories of a Profession at Work*. New York: Macmillan, 213–236.

Holmes Group (1990). *Tomorrow's Schools: A Report of the Holmes Group*. East Lansing, MI: Holmes Group.

Howey, K. (1994). 'Designing coherent and effective teacher education programs'. In J. Sikula (ed.), *Handbook of Research on Teacher Education*. New York: Macmillan.

Huberman, M. (1989). 'The professional life-cycle of teachers'. *Teachers College Record*, 1 (91), 31–57.

Huling-Austin, L. (1990). 'Teacher induction programs and internships'. In R. W. Houston (ed.), *Handbook of Research on Teacher Education*. New York: Macmillan, 535–548.

Joyce, B. and Showers, B. (1988). *Student Achievement through Staff Development: Fundamentals of School Renewal*. White Plains, NY: Longman.

Judge, H., Lemosse, M., Paine, L. and Sedlak, M. (1994). *The University and the Teachers: France, the United States, England*. London: Triangle Books.

Lampert, M. (1985). 'How do teachers manage to teach? Perspectives on problems in practice'. *Harvard Educational Review*, 55 (2), 178–194.

Leavitt, H. (1992). *Issues and Problems in Teacher Education: An International Handbook*. Westport, NY: Greenwood Press.

Lieberman, A. (1995). 'Practices that support teacher development: Transforming conceptions of professional learning'. *Phi Delta Kappan*, 76 (8), 591–96.

Lieberman, A. and Grolnick, M. (1996). 'Networks and reform in American education'. *Teachers College Record*, 98, 7–45.

Little, J. (1990). 'The mentor phenomenon and the social organization of teaching'. In C. Cazden, (ed.), *Review of Research in Education*. Washington, DC: American Educational Research Association.

Little, J. (1993). 'Teachers' professional development in a climate of educational reform'. *Educational Evaluation and Policy Analysis*, 15 (2), 129–151.

Lord, B. (1994). 'Teachers' professional development: Critical colleagueship and the role of professional communities'. In N. Cobb (ed.), *The Future of Education: Perspectives on National Standards in America*. New York: College Entrance Examination Board, 175–204.

Lortie, D. (1975). *Schoolteachers: A Sociological Study*. Chicago: University of Chicago Press.

Merseth, K. (1996). 'Cases and case methods in teacher education'. In J. Sikula (ed.), *Handbook of Research on Teacher Education*. New York: Macmillan, 722–746.

Moskowitz, J. and Stevens, M. (1997). *From Students of Teaching to Teachers of Students: Teacher Induction around the Pacific Rim*. Washington, DC: Asia-Pacific Education Forum.

National Center for Education Statistics (1998). 'Networks and reform in American education'. *Teachers College Record*, 98 (1), 7–15.

National Center for Research on Teacher Learning (1991). *Findings from the Teacher Education and Learning to Teach Study: Final Report*. SR 6–91. East Lansing, MI: National Center for Research on Teacher Learning.

National Commission on Teaching & America's Future (1996). *What Matters Most: Teaching for America's Future*. New York: National Commission on Teaching & America's Future.

Nemser, S. (1983). 'Learning to teach'. In L. Shulman and G. Sykes (eds), *Handbook of Teaching and Policy*. New York: Longman, 150–170.

Ryan, K. (1970). *Don't Smile until Christmas: Accounts of the First Year of Teaching*. Chicago: University of Chicago Press.

Sarason, S. (1990). *The Predictable Failure of Educational Reform*. San Francisco: Jossey-Bass.

Schon, D. (1987). *Educating the Reflective Practitioner: Toward a New Design for Teaching and Learning in the Professions*. San Francisco: Jossey-Bass.

Showers, B., Joyce, B. and Bennet, C. (1987) 'Synthesis of research on staff development: A framework for future study and a state-of-the-art analysis'. *Educational Researcher*, 45 (3), 77–87.

Shulman, L. (1986). 'Those who understand: Knowledge growth in teaching'. *Educational Researcher*, 15 (2), 4–14.

Sykes, G. and Bird, T. (1992). 'Teacher education and the case idea'. In G. Grant (ed.), *Review of Research in Education, Vol. 18*. Washington DC: American Educational Research Association, 457–521.

Tom, A. (1997). *Redesigning Teacher Education*. New York: State University of New York Press.

Veenman, S. (1984). 'Perceived problems of beginning teachers'. *Review of Educational Research*, 54, 143–178.

Wigginton, E. (1985). *Sometimes a Shining Moment: The Foxfire Experiment*. Garden City, NY: Anchor/Doubleday.

Wilson, S., Shulman, L. and Richert, A. (1987). '"150 different ways" of knowing: Representations of knowledge in teaching'. In J. Calderhead (ed.), *Exploring Teachers' Thinking*. London: Cassell, 104–124.

Zeichner, K. and Hoeft, K. (1996). 'Teacher socialization for cultural diversity'. In J. Sikula (ed.), *Handbook of Research on Teacher Education*. New York: Macmillan, 525–547.

43

THE OPEN LEARNING ENVIRONMENT

A new paradigm for international developments in teacher education

Bob Moon

OVERVIEW

The central arguments of the chapter are threefold:

1 that the 'bricks and mortar' institutions developed around teacher education to serve the needs of the twentieth century will be wholly inadequate for the twenty-first;
2 that the implicit and explicit models of development, derived from such bricks and mortar institutions, are insufficient to meet the changed circumstances of most, if not all, national contexts;
3 that developing a research agenda to inform the processes of institutional change and rebuilding is now an urgent priority.

The scenario for development is explored with a focus on the interrelated but contrasting movements towards:

- the globalisation of debate in part provided by the emergence of new interactive technology;
- the localisation of action through giving greater prominence to making the school a more central 'site for learning' in the teacher education process;
- the emergence of new forms of professional 'communities of practice' working through new modes of communication.

This chapter concludes by an exploration of key dilemmas that will be faced in the transformation of teacher education and the institutions of teacher education in the coming decades.

SCENARIO

Teacher education across the world is undergoing significant rethinking and reform. Most, if not all, countries have teacher education at the forefront of national policies. Expanding populations continue to make huge demands on the institutions responsible for preparing teachers. In South Africa, for example, pre-service teacher training expanded at 15 per cent per year through the 1990s, and training by distance education by 23 per cent (South African Ministry of Education, 1996). The competition from a range of increasingly knowledge-based occupations is threatening the supply of teachers in many countries. In the UK the recruitment of teachers for subjects such as mathematics, technology and languages fell significantly short of need. In California decisions to reduce class sizes in K1– 3 schools has created a huge teacher demand in a context where recruitment was already problematic. The quality of teacher education is also now widely debated, professionally and more generally in the media. Finally there is widespread recognition that teacher education must be a career-long process of development, at least equal in form and status to that enjoyed in law, medicine and comparable professional groups. The scale of this demand, if recognised globally, is enormous.

From this it follows

1 that the 'bricks and mortar' institutions developed around teacher education to serve the needs of the twentieth century will be wholly inadequate for the twenty-first;
2 that the implicit and explicit models of development, derived from such bricks and mortar institutions, are insufficient to meet the changed circumstances of most, if not all, national contexts;
3 that the new generation of open learning systems will inevitably be integrated into the conventional institutional structures of teacher education: the development of a research agenda to inform this process is now an urgent priority.

Two important points of qualification; first, making this argument is not to suggest the demise of the existing institutional structures. There has been, after all, a worldwide trend towards placing teacher education within the university. Such institutions, however, must adjust and change to become part of a broader landscape if we are significantly to improve the access and opportunity that teachers have for dignified, relevant and high-quality professional development. The use of the word 'dignified' may seem out of place. Yet many people continually come across teachers trying to improve their knowledge and skills in the most appalling of circumstances: a group of over 300 teachers of literature in an unheated, poorly lit gymnasium in the Russian province of Nivishny Novgorod; the teacher of English who set off each morning, and returned each evening, on a three-hour journey in massively overcrowded buses, from Beni Suef to reach the in-service course in Cairo; primary teachers in a London borough meeting in a 'pub', the only free venue, to plan a literacy campaign. All over the world, just as children and schools are underdeveloped and under pressure, so the teachers take the strain.

This raises a second point. The literature and ideas of teacher education resolutely accept the division between the developed, mostly northern countries, and the resource-constrained regions to the south. This is the colonial inheritance of the nineteenth century transposed into the aid and dependency systems of the present century. But this will change, and change rapidly, in the coming decades. National educational systems will increasingly co-exist on greater terms of equality than ever before. The forms and quality of teacher education must evolve in similar ways, with the likelihood that development and co-operation will go beyond the boundaries of national systems.

The institutional structures of teacher education have been developed in this century primarily to provide a pre-service training for the expanding teaching force in national, state systems of education. The focus was usually on the primary sectors and only in the latter part of this century has formal teacher education touched those preparing to teach in secondary, often elite institutions. The way such institutions have evolved, particularly the way they have found their way into the embrace of the universities, has been much discussed (Neave, 1992). And they have certainly, in many countries, come to embrace a much broader vision of teachers' professional development than was originally the case. Few, however, would suggest that the scale and nature of demand can be met by the present structures.

A number of factors, however, are combining to open up new possibilities. First there is the increasing recognition that the 'school' should be a more central part of the development process. Unlike medicine, as the status of teacher education grew in the latter part of the twentieth century, so the process became less, rather than more, school based (Moon, 1996). In many countries, where professional development became almost synonymous with higher degrees and diplomas, teachers often left their school for a year or more at a time to obtain the new qualification. Perhaps the move away from the very instrumental apprenticeship that characterised much teacher education was a necessary correction. But it has served its time. For some years now there has been a powerful advocacy for a more school-based, action-oriented fusing of theoretical and practical perspectives on the development process. In a number of countries this is coming increasingly to command the interest and respect of policy-makers. Teacher support needs to acknowledge the authenticity of the context in which teachers work, however economically or philosophically challenged that might be.

Second there are the beginnings of a common global interest in the educational foundations of the teaching profession. Sharp contrasts remain. What a teacher can expect from the Danish Royal School of Educational Studies is very different from someone playing a parallel role in the Eastern Cape Province of South Africa or the Skhodra district of northern Albania. The debate about teacher education is, however, a global one. International organisations such as UNESCO and the World Bank, despite many caveats, have played a role in this process. The idea, however, that the twentieth-century models of teacher education created in the richer countries should be simply replicated all over the world is becoming increasingly challenged, a theme I want to make further reference to below.

Third, there is the explosion of new forms of communication with the widespread adoption of older technologies such as television and the possibly much quicker take-up of newer interactive technologies associated with the growth of the Internet and the World Wide Web. Almost at a stroke, significant new horizons have been opened up. The previously cherished and separate worlds of publishing, broadcasting and, dare we say it, even 'The University' are all challenged and threatened by a revolution that arguably is already more significant than Gutenberg.

Finally there is an increasing acceptance that learners of all sorts need a rich and diverse range of prompts and stimuli. The passive lecture format, even supplemented by some personal seminar support, looks increasingly threatened as a pedagogic strategy. The arrival into mainstream thought of what some have termed 'the cognitive revolution' has its echoes in the way we think of teachers' learning (Bruner, 1996). Yet the institutions of teacher education, like most schools, with classrooms and lecture theatres, are premised on the older forms of pedagogy. Although overhyped in some quarters, new ways of accessing information and forming dialogues create opportunities to revisit, review and rehearse learning in ways that hitherto were logistically and economically impossible.

In summary, therefore, the suggestion is that over the medium-term future teachers will expect to be offered and participate in more developed forms of professional development than is currently offered, that this will be significantly based in their own and local schools, that 'online' electronic communication will be an important aspect of this increasingly international experience. Given this scenario, it seems inevitable that all forms of flexible and open forms of learning will increasingly play a major role in teacher education.

The ugly duckling of distance education emerges swan-like in the high-tech environment of 1990s open learning. Teachers, of course, have been one of the main consumers of open and distance learning, interchangeable terms that need some conceptualisation. In the early parts of this century correspondence colleges proliferated in all parts of the world. In the former USSR, still today in China and throughout the apartheid era in South Africa, distance education was a major means of providing teacher education. It represented a first-generation attempt to create greater flexibility and greater access, but it was most often a poor relation to the real thing. Inadequate resources and insufficient personal support gave many correspondence courses a bad name; an image that lingers on today.

A second generation is represented by the development of specialist 'open' universities or colleges, primarily in the 1970s and 1980s. The British Open University was one of the first of these dedicated institutions, and its influence is seen in the development of a number of similarly national institutions across the world. The open universities added to the correspondence method, the resources of an emergent multimedia industry (television and radio) and, perhaps most significantly, argued that to think of anything as 'wholly at a distance' was mistaken and, therefore, that allied to high-quality teaching resources, there needed to be some form of local 'face-to-face' mediation. They also broadened the concept of distance education towards the greater reach of open learning. Impediments to access were seen as more than geography. Women at home, men and women tied to 9–5 earning, could live next door to educational institutions but without the opportunity to benefit from them. Teachers more than most profited from the open universities where they existed. In the UK the transformation of the teaching profession into effectively an all-graduate one was realised by a significant input from the Open University in the 1970s. In the 1980s and 1990s a similar process was enacted in the establishment of a widely taken up masters programme and the introduction of a national pre-service qualification, which significantly opened up access to teaching (Bourdillon and Burgess, 1998; Moon and Shelton Mayes, 1995a, 1995b).

The support provided for teachers was given a much stronger focus and conceptualised in a variety of ways. Leach (1996a, pp. 124–125), for example, has summarised this in suggesting six functions that can be served:

1 Support should provide model learning environments.

2 Support should build on existing frameworks as far as possible and be consonant with the culture in which it is developed.

3 Support should be developmental and exploratory, providing experience of a wide variety of teaching and learning opportunities.

4 Support should recognise and build on the variety of professional experiences of its participants.

5 Support should acknowledge both the private and professional aspects of learners' experiences and their interconnectedness in the development of learning.

6 Support should have a firm base in schools and classrooms.

Now emerging is a third generation of open learning programmes exploiting the interactivity and communicative possibilities of the new technologies and focusing more strongly on school-based development. Not all of these are working in state of the art, high-tech environments. The Kualida Project in Albania, for example, in focusing on the in-service training of teachers in history, geography, English, French and citizenship, is built strongly around the concept of collaborative development utilising locally based, high-quality television and text resources. The course structure, however, has been planned in such a way that it can accommodate the introduction of new technologies where technically feasible (Leach and Lita, 1998). In California, California State University launched its open learning teacher credentialling programme 'Cal State Teach' in 1999. This programme, aimed initially at the thousands of teachers in K1–3 classes, makes extensive use of web resources with support rooted in a network of regional centres.

The open universities provided a personal interactive element, but in small measures. For reasons of cost, tutorials are generally infrequent and groups relatively large. Reliance on one-way synchronous communication represented the main staple of teaching provision. The new programmes, whilst perhaps retaining a face-to-face tutorial element, are significantly enhancing this through the highly personal new modes of electronic conferencing.

THE GLOBAL DIMENSION OF OPEN LEARNING IN TEACHER EDUCATION

Open learning, like teacher education, is therefore in a phase of rapid evolution. New types of open learning programmes are emerging, built around the applications of new telecommunications and computer technology (Nipper, 1989). These are characterised by markedly increased interactivity, more control for learners, global networking, and the possibility of working within a highly cost-effective environment (Pelton, 1991). Bates (1991) has contrasted these with earlier models of programmes that developed during the twentieth century. These he sees as exhibiting the use of 'one-way' media such as text, broadcasting, cassettes, with 'two-way' communication provided by correspondence tutors or the more resource-intensive and more expensive, 'face-to-face' tutorials. The key aspect of the third generation of courses, destined to mushroom in the next millennium, is the fusing of the one-way/two-way dimensions of communication with forms of interactivity hitherto undreamt of. It follows that the divide that has existed between open, often distance, learning and conventional, bricks and mortar institutions will narrow significantly.

Over the past two decades there have been numerous analyses of the potential of open learning in teacher education from regional, national and international perspectives. In Europe the Treaty of Maastricht, which extended European co-operation into the field of education, makes specific reference to the importance of more flexible forms of provision (para. 126). In South Africa, a national audit of teacher education following the 1992 elections, advocated that: 'teacher education needs to be conceived of as an open learning system which enhances access to professional lifelong learning through a variety of delivery medias [*sic*] and accompanying learner support' (South African Ministry of Education, 1996, p. 14). A World Bank publication (Perraton and Potashnik, 1996), prepared for a colloquium on teacher education through distance learning in Toronto in June 1997, suggested that imaginative forms of distance education were essential if the needs of the 60 million teachers in the world were to be met.

One of the early 1990s international publications dedicated to teacher training has come from the International Council for Educational Media (Farkas *et al.*, 1993). Under the title 'From Smoke Screens to Satellite', the authors suggest there is a paucity of literature. They argue for greater research and development given that: 'whatever the forms and modalities, it is obvious that these new systems of training and in-service training of teachers are here to stay and will be more and more needed in developing and industrial countries' (ibid., p. ii).

A further international survey (Perraton, 1993) explores a diverse range of distance education contexts for teacher training, primarily with an orientation towards the developing world. In the concluding chapters Perraton examines the costs and effects of distance education and looks at the conditions for success in projects linking teacher education and distance programmes. He sets out four essential framing factors for consideration:

1 the importance of establishing a clear relationship between distance education programmes and the regular arrangements to support and train teachers;
2 the need to build up an appropriate expertise in the practice of distance education;
3 the importance of ensuring that courses embrace a variety of media in order to make them more effective;
4 the need to take account of the context in which students learn and the particular needs they bring to the process, if a successful learning outcome is to be assured.

THE DEVELOPING RANGE OF METHODOLOGIES

Communications in open learning can now be achieved through an expanding range of methodologies. The success of a programme often depends on the way these methodologies are interrelated and, as noted above, a crucial concern is the specific context within which implementation will take place. Well-tried methodologies can have as significant a role to play as new technological applications.

Reddy (1986), for example, has suggested that in certain contexts, and he is referring to the smaller island nations of the South Pacific, *radio* remains most effective, quickest, and most cost-effective of media. But he is critical of the still popular belief that radio can be seen as a substitute for face-to-face communication. He argues strongly that

radio is only an aid, a powerful resource . . . its usefulness is maximized if it is programmed to do those things which a teacher cannot do in an interesting manner. Radio is at its best when it is used to excite the imagination of the learner.

(Reddy, 1986, p. 34)

This documentary, rather than instructional, focus has been adapted by the Open University School of Education in the UK, using publicly broadcast radio as a background resource for all educational programmes rather than as a specific teaching aid for specific courses. *Audio cassettes*, however, can serve both an instructional and documentary purpose and have a very real advantage in flexibility of use. The almost universal availability of walkmans (and the increased use of radio cassettes in cars) suggests that the flexibility of use offered by audio cassettes is also likely to develop further. Audio versions of text materials, 'talking books', previously a minority provision for the elderly and those with sight impairments, are now increasingly used. The lifestyles of many people, including teachers, require the flexibility of opportunity, for example in commuting, that comes from audio availability of text.

Interactive radio has been developed in a number of countries. The US Agency for International Development, for example, has supported projects in Africa, Asia and Latin America, although with varied success. Certain types of course content, for example mathematics, appeared to work more successfully with this medium (Douglas, 1993). One of the most notable and interesting examples is the Mathematica Interactiva programme for primary schools in Venezuela, notable for the evaluation work which looks at links between the progress and improvements in pupil attainment.

Television has generated a voluminous literature in open and distance learning, much of which now seems obsolete in the forward progress of technology. The excitement of the moving image, as with sound 50 years earlier, led many to overstate the impact of the medium and fail to note the critical lack of interactivity. Over-ambitious perceptions of the power of television still exist in many countries despite well-established, and well-grounded, arguments against overstating the impact television can have. There is also some evidence that inappropriate uses of television are sustained in those contexts where television is only recently becoming available. Van Horn and Doris (1993) argue that television is one media source that can be used effectively if its limitations are recognised. Laurillard (1990) has shown, in a detailed evaluation of the use of television within course design, the form that such limitations can take.

Evaluations of *interactive television systems* are mixed with little evidence of applications in pre-service or in-service training for teachers. Research in Utah, USA, on the use of interactive television with teachers enrolled on a special education methods course, shows that in terms of course outcomes, the distance education groups reached similar levels of achievement as on-site groups (Egan, 1993). The off-site teachers, however, gave more negative course evaluations, particularly with respect to the sort of feedback they experienced. More successful claims, again in the USA, have been made by Russell (1993) and Platten and Bruce (1987). In Australia a number of projects developed under an umbrella organisation, the Regional Telematics Education Consortium (RTEC), established to promote teacher education in rural Victoria. Whilst claiming a measure of success, the evaluation evidence (Prain and Booth, 1993, p. 8) pointed to significant difficulties on the part of presenters and participants.

Interactivity is achieved traditionally in the classroom through subgroup or whole class discussion, written feedback and personalised attention in one-to-one talk between teacher and student. Presenters whose classroom teaching practices were built around these ways to establish and sustain interactivity believed satellite teaching was restrictive in this area . . . participants commented about the lack of personal and group interaction too. . . . Where presenters and participants diverged was over the technical problems they encountered . . . only two presenters wrote about technical problems . . . whereas a large number of participants did. For participants the problems detracted from the success of communication by electronic means.

Despite, therefore, some of the earlier hopes for the use of interactive television in teacher education (see, for example, Porter, 1983), the benefits have only partially been realised. Technical, logistical and organisational factors still inhibit development and the benefits of visual contact may be outweighed by the static nature of current settings. The experience appears to reflect two recurring dangers in open and distance systems:

- the overemphasis of, and over-reliance on, a new technological medium;
- the insufficiently adapted application of teaching methods from an established context to the context situated by the new technology.

EXPLOITING THE POTENTIAL OF INTERACTIVE TECHNOLOGIES

The increased potential of electronic communications for teacher education has led to a spate of national and international discussions. The Council of Europe (1989a, 1989b), OECD (1992) and US Senate Committees (Congress of the USA, 1993) have all explored the issues in depth. The focus of these discussions embraces both the training needs of teachers in utilising educational technology for pedagogic purposes, and the way these technologies can be used in the training process itself. This distinction is an important one that will be returned to later in the chapter. In a paper presented in the USA to a national conference on 'Creating the Quality School', Baker and Patti (1993) argue for teacher education programmes to include preparation in the use of electronic classrooms. Open learning centres, they suggest, incorporating all possible forms of telecommunications, should be established for teachers already in service. Fulton (1993) and Hedberg and Harper (1993) are recent examples of analyses that link developments in educational technology to the changing character of teacher education.

Computer applications are developing so quickly that well-grounded evaluations of systems are soon rendered redundant. In teacher education there have been a number of critiques of teacher awareness and skills with the new technologies. Recent reports in all parts of the world have pointed to the unrealised potential of new technology. Similar pleas have come from regions and countries less well endowed with equipment and resources. Kuznetsov (1991), for example, has analysed the significance of new technology to teachers in Russia. There is, therefore, an urgent need in teacher education, at pre-service and in-service levels, to train teachers in the use of the technologies. Teachers for their own classroom use need to be trained in the use of new technologies (Buchanan, 1993). Open and distance education have a role to play particularly in 'training the trainers'.

Attempts in this area go back more than a decade (McKinnon and Sinclair, 1987; Rhys, 1988; Robson *et al.*, 1992; Veen *et al.*, 1994) but only recently has the technical potential matched the need. The UK's OU teacher training project, which began in 1994, is making extensive use of computer conferencing and Chile's Enlaces Project (Potashnik, 1996) is wholly dependent on electronic communication. A number of studies are beginning to emerge that demonstrate the potential of computer applications to conventional and to open and distance contexts.

Harrington and Hathaway in the USA, for example, have evaluated computer conferencing and the impact it can have in challenging prospective teachers' assumptions. The process of conferencing becomes a key issue:

> Because there is some indication from this analysis that as the conference progressed more questions regarding assumptions were being raised by the participants, further study appears to be warranted concerning the relationships between the progression of the conference, the topics of discussion, and the identification and clarification of taken-for-granted assumptions.
>
> (Harrington and Hathaway, 1994, p. 552)

Electronic conferencing is a medium in its own right, distinct from the accepted conventions of the written and spoken word. One international study, involving Finland, Japan and the USA, gives useful pointers as to the direction that the new generation of Internet-based collaborative learning systems can take.

> New technologies are transforming the ways in which businesses operate and people work, boosting demand for new knowledge and new types of skills. They are providing new alternatives of learning, offering a potential solution to meet challenges such as demand for more flexibility in delivery of education in terms of time, location, content and form. Students need to be able to learn when they want, where they want, what they need (just-in-time), and in a format appropriate to them.
>
> Distance learning has traditionally been used to give educational opportunities to such groups of students for whom the conventional educational models are not suitable, such as people at work, those studying at home, living in isolated areas, or people with physical limitations. However, the methods that have primarily been used in distance education can also be used to supplement conventional education. For example, alternatives are available to students in large cities who spend much of their time commuting to institutions – or who, for other reasons, prefer completing part of their studies off-campus.
>
> (Watabe et al., 1995, p. 141)

The authors point to the limitations of conventional delivery media (mailed texts, video, radio, TV) that emphasised students' own activity rather than the collaborative learning that interaction among students can promote. The new technologies, they suggest, have the potential to overcome this divide.

By introducing computer-based collaborative learning systems, Watabe and others foresee the following benefits (see also Alexander, 1992):

1 The students benefit from different perspectives of the material they are learning. The group inherently brings with it a wider range of experience than does an individual member. This enables students to obtain help from their group to tackle larger projects than they could individually.

2 The learning experience can be structured so that students will find themselves presenting and explaining parts of the material to other students. Discussion with peers can be more relaxed and free than with a teacher. By communicating what they have learned to others, the material will become more integrated into their general understanding ('best way to learn something is to teach it').

3 Working with groups is highly motivating. A group provides the pace for its members. People want to be seen doing their best. The support and sense of identity provided by the group allays fears and builds confidence.

(Watabe et al., 1995, p. 142)

The new systems to promote this approach can challenge assumptions about the old distinctions that have been made in computer applications (i.e. asynchronous vs. synchronous, same place vs. remote places, collaborative activity vs. individual activity). These distinctions, it is proposed, will blur in the new models being developed:

> The distinctions that have been made among computer support of different work modes (i.e. asynchronous vs. synchronous, same place vs. remote places, collaborative activity vs. individual activity) need to be blurred. In the conceptual model and actual system implementation, we aim at achieving seamless integration of these different modes for efficient collaborative learning support.
>
> (Watabe et al., 1995, p. 147)

A conceptual model of collaborative distance learning is set out in Figure 43.1.

The designers point out that models for collaborative resource-based learning at a distance have already been planned, for example in the UK's OU (Alexander and Mason, 1994) but the new model:

> extends them by adding real-time multimedia communication and access to external information sources (i.e. such resources that have not specifically been developed for the course).
>
> The student has learning materials, such as course texts, as well as support material, such as dictionaries and encyclopaedias, available in the learning environment. The students have access to teachers (maybe the developer of learning materials), tutors (advisors), other students, and other

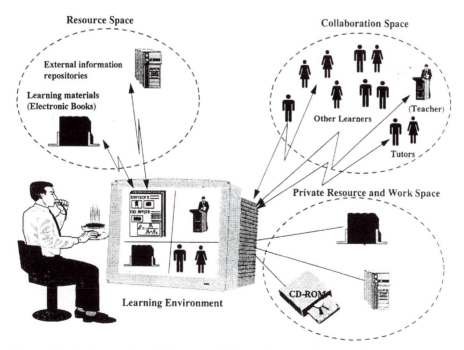

Figure 43.1 An Internet-based Collaborative Distance Learning System: CODILESS

information resources (such as online databases). For communicating with the outside world, the student has tools equivalent to a telephone, a fax machine, a TV set, and mail, as tools integrated within the learning environment.

(Alexander, 1992, p. 148)

The Open University's pre-service teacher education programme (the one year Post-graduate Certificate in Education) has over the last five years significantly extended understanding of the theoretical foundations upon which modes of electronic conferencing can be conceptualised. Leach (1996b, 1997), for example, has argued that computer-mediated communication supports an egalitarian style of communication in which everyone can participate. She argues that such communication promotes communities of practice very much in line with the theories of situated learning (Lave and Wegner, 1991), which see cognitive change as an attribute of pedagogical relationships in particular settings and contexts. For Leach this mode of dialogue raises three sets of questions:

- How relevant to the practice of e-pedagogy is the image of a traditional university community campus and its academic discourse?
- How useful are comparisons with traditional models of communication (reading, writing and speaking)?
- Why employ the metaphors of familiar teaching and learning strategies, recreating electronic versions of linear, 'real time' pedagogy such as lectures, seminars, claustrophobic classrooms? Should we be looking for alternative metaphors of practice?

(Leach, 1997, p. 8)

One of the most important tasks in the coming years is to develop a range of new models of teacher support that embrace the potential for interactive communication and the rapid delivery of a rich range of multimedia resources. The commercial imperative to exploit the uses of the media is already apparent. These developments now seem inevitable. The cost of hardware and software will fall significantly. The use of systems will become highly simplified and the speed of response will become almost instantaneous. These present barriers to teacher take-up and use will disappear. As teachers begin to use online facilities in their daily lives, for shopping, entertainment, advice service, travel and so forth, so professional use will evolve. For teacher educators a number of research questions arise. To what extent can a web environment of its own accord support teacher development? If forms of face-to-face mediation are appropriate, in what form, and in what contexts, should this be provided? To what extent can groups, or teams, of teachers exploit interactive technologies for mutual advantage? The next few years offer a rich research agenda to explore this, and other issues already mentioned, in advance of the widespread take-up of use envisaged at the turn of the century.

CONCLUSION: DILEMMAS

Four dilemmas need some resolution as we move to more loosely structured and open learning models of teacher preparation and development. The first is a transient issue, although significant in the short term. The lack of electronic and media literacy amongst policy-makers, and those playing related key roles, inspectors and school principals for example, presents real difficulties. Although the modes of working themselves are now fairly straightforward, there remain sufficient technical problems or folklore of problems, to create obstacles to empathy and understanding. The outcomes range from a total dismissal of the potential, to a total reliance on technical expertise which remains unlinked to the professional and cultural context in which it has to be embedded. Whilst a healthy scepticism can strengthen innovation, it can also stifle. Understanding how rapid developments in technology can be incorporated into the mind-frame of well-established leaders in any professional community represents an issue for research and study in its own right.

The second dilemma arises from the assertion above that any university can become an open university; indeed, an individual or institution will soon have the potential to attempt this. Should they? It is difficult in the anarchic liberalism of, for example a web environment, to say no to anything. But what follows, therefore, is the need for a much stronger articulation of the criteria for quality we might envisage for the new programmes (Moon and Shelton Mayes, 1995a, 1995b; SAIDE, 1996). In respect of the new interactive communities of resource and communication, this is relatively uncharted territory. Whilst there is a familiarity with the, admittedly debatable, criteria used for judging the contents of a bookshop or the books themselves, the human antennae in electronic environments remain relatively underdeveloped. Such criteria will evolve with time, but a debate needs joining.

It follows from the above that many institutions will need to develop new models of programme planning and support. It is difficult to envisage a programme for teachers that does not involve some face-to-face exchange with colleagues, through locally based, self-help groups, or through a more formal system of tutorials. Integrating the different aspects of programme planning and taking decisions that are sensitive to and go with the grain of local contexts is a complex process. This is more fully developed in a handbook developed as part of a recent survey of open learning and teacher education in Europe (Hobbs *et al.*, 1997). However, little training or support for these new forms of programme design and development and presentation exist currently outside the institutions of open learning.

The final dilemma is perhaps the most significant of all. Teacher education, as suggested earlier, is now a global process. In all parts of the world, encouraged in part by international organisations, programmes using new technologies and some form of open learning are developing. With this globalisation come dangers. First, the temptation to see this as the panacea for grave teacher inadequacies in many parts of the world is there. Satellite video conferencing, for example, has been funded in a range of countries with little thought as to how it might be used and developed. Second, the technology can be used to reinforce the invidious divide between richer and poorer nations, with the technical expertise of the former creating a new form of dependency or obligation that many of us are seeking to move out of as we move into a new millennium. Research and discussion around teacher education, like the communities from which it arises, still tend to reinforce the divide between North America and northern European concerns and those of the countries to the south. And from this comes a last concern. Scrutiny of the growing body of literature on teacher development, particularly that in English concerned with international programmes and projects, reveals a strong domination of models that have arisen from the debate now prevalent in Europe and North America. There are references to a 'new pedagogy' and the need to move away from traditional authoritarian models of teaching to create more autonomous learners, able to construct their own learning and with teachers playing a more individualistic or group-oriented role than was traditionally the case. There are many strengths in this analysis but there is also a growing concern about the way such a development orthodoxy fits alongside the very different cultural conditions we find in so many parts of the world and the very different economic circumstances we know exist. How does this approach sit in the context of mainstream Islamic traditions? Is it appropriate to try to reconceptualise the concept of teacher authority in certain ways where 'respect for elders' and that form of respect for teachers has far greater significance than in Birmingham Alabama or Birmingham UK? Advocacy of the need to develop stronger perceptions of group, or even project work, sound different to a teacher with a resourced class of 25 than to someone with a class of 70 or 80 in a room without books or adequate ventilation.

With global communities of interest beginning to emerge in teacher education, we need to watch cautiously for orthodoxies that fail to respect culture or place. The power of new technologies harnessed to more open forms of teaching and learning has the potential to contribute to the sorts of values espoused by the new South African government. Equally, however, orthodoxies can acquire unchallenged status.

The working out of these, and other, dilemmas will be an important feature of the development of the new generation of teacher education programmes. It will be necessary, as the opening to this chapter suggests, to think beyond the confines of present models and assumptions. New experience of practice must lead to a stronger theoretical basis of understanding the way teachers can be served by new, more dignified, models of support. The first few years into the new millennium represent an important opportunity for rethinking and redirecting open and distance forms of organisation. International co-operation in research and the sharing of experience will be a crucial element in this process.

ACKNOWLEDGEMENT

I would like to record my appreciation to staff from the Centre for Research and Development in Teacher Education at the Open University who provided very helpful critiques of this chapter in draft.

REFERENCES

Alexander, G. (1992) 'Designing human interfaces to promote collaborative learning', in A. R. Kaye, (ed.), *Collaborative Learning through Computer Conferencing: The Najaden Papers*, NATO ASI Series, New York: Springer.

Alexander, G. and Mason, R. (1994) *Innovating at the OU: Resource-based Collaboration Learning On Line*, CITE Report No. 195, Centre for Information Technology in Education, Buckingham: The Open University.

Baker, A. and Patti, R. (1993) 'Definitions of international learning: What we see is not what we get', *Journal of Instruction Delivery Systems*, 7 (3), 36–39.

Bates, A. W. (1991) 'Third generation distance education: The challenge of new technology', *Research in Distance Education*, 3 (2), 10–15.

Bourdillon, H. and Burgess, H. (1998) 'Open learning, new technologies and the development of a new model of pre-service education and training, The Open University UK experience'. Paper presented to the 1998 AERA Conference, San Diego, April 12–17.

Bruner, J. (1996) *The Culture of Education*, Cambridge, MA: Harvard University Press.

Buchanan, P. (1993) 'Project INSITE: Developing telecommunications skills for teachers and students', *Journal of Computers in Mathematics and Science Teaching*, 12 (3–4), 245–260.

Congress of the USA (1993) Technology for Education Act of 1993 seminar July 21, Congress of the USA.

Council of Europe (1989a) *The Information Society. A Challenge for Education Policies?* Strasbourg: Council of Europe.

Council of Europe (1989b) *The Information Society: A Challenge for Educational Policies? Policy Options and Implementation Strategies.* Strasbourg: Council of Europe.

Douglas, N. (1993) 'Interactive radio as a component of distance education in Third World countries', Paper presented at the National Third World Studies Conference, Oriana.

Egan, M. (1993) 'Rural pre-service teacher preparation using two way interactive television', *Rural Special Education Quality*, 9 (3), 27–37.

Farkas, P., Cornell, R., Saar, C. and Armstrong, J. (1993) *An International Survey of Distance Education and Teacher Training: From Smoke Signals to Satellites.* Report produced for the Innovation and Development Sub-Committee of the International Council for Educational Media, University of Florida.

Fulton, K. (1993) 'Teaching matters: The role of technology in education', *Educational Technology Review*, Fall/Winter, 5–10.

Harrington, H. L. and Hathaway, R. S. (1994) 'Computer conferencing, critical reflection and teacher development', *Teaching and Teacher Education*, 10 (5), 543–554.

Hedberg, J. G. and Harper, B. (1993) 'Supporting and developing teachers through telecommunications', *Educational Media International*, 30 (2), 88–93.

Hobbs, S., Moon, B. and Banks, F. (1997) *Open and Distance Education, New Technologies and the Development of Teacher Education in Europe: A Handbook*, Buckingham: Open University Press.

Kuznetsov, E. I. (1991) 'A new type of specialist is needed', *Soviet Education*, 33 (3), 15–23.

Laurillard, D. (1990) 'Mediating the message: Programme design and students' understanding', PLUM Paper No. 3, Institute for Educational Technology. Milton Keynes: Open University Press.

Lave, J. and Wegner, E. (1991) *Situated Learning: Legitimate Peripheral Participation*, Cambridge: Cambridge University Press.

Leach, J. (1996a) 'Learning in practice: Professional development through open learning', in A. Tait and R. Mills (eds) *Supporting the Learner in Open and Distance Learning*, London: Longman.

Leach, J. (1996b) 'Teacher Education – On-line!', *Educational Leadership*, 54 (3), November 1996.

Leach, J. (1997) 'Teacher education on-line: "The social" in the formation of teachers of English'. Paper presented at the European Educational Research Association conference, Frankfurt, September 24–27, 1997.

Leach, J. and Lita, Z. (1998) *Teacher Education in Adversity: Albania's Kualida Project, 1994–1998.* Paper presented to the 1998 AERA Conference, San Diego, April 12–17.

Leach, J. and Moon, B. (1997) 'Towards a new generation of open learning programmes in teacher education'. Paper presented at the Distance Education for Teacher Development Colloquium. Global Knowledge 97 Conference, Toronto, Canada, June 23–25.

Leach, J. and Swarbrick, A. (1996) 'Learning from each other: Computer mediated conferencing in an initial teacher education programme'. Paper presented at European Distance Education Network (EDEN) Conference, Poitiers, France, July.

McKinnon, D. K. and Sinclair, K. (1987) 'Teachers training teachers: A concerns based approach to computer inservice education', *Australian Educational Researcher*, 15 (2), 53–70.

Metz, J. M. (1994) 'Computer mediated communication. Literature review of a new context', *IPCT Interpersonal Computing and Technology: An Electronic Journal for the 21st Century, 2 (2), 31–49.*

Moon, B. (1995) *Teacher Education, Open Learning and the Use of Information Technology: an International Perspective.* Report prepared for UNESCO.

Moon, B. (1996). 'Practical experience in teacher education: Charting a European agenda', *European Journal of Teacher Education*, 19 (3), 217–250.

Moon, B. (1997) 'Open learning and new technologies in teacher education: New paradigms for development', *European Journal of Teacher Education*, 20 (1).

Moon, B. and Shelton Mayes, A. (1995a) 'Integrating values into the assessment of teachers in initial education and training', in T. Kerry and A. Shelton Mayes (eds) *Issues in Mentoring*, London: Routledge.

Moon, B. and Shelton Mayes, A. (1995b) 'Frameworks, competences and quality: Open learning dimensions to initial teacher education and training', in H. Bines and J. M. Welton (eds) *Managing Partnership in Teacher Training and Development*, London: Routledge.

Neave, G. (1992) *The Teaching Nation. Prospects for Teachers in the European Community*, Oxford: Pergamon.

Nipper, S. (1989) 'Third generation distance learning and computer conferencing', in R. Manon and A. Kaye (eds) *Mindweave: Communication, Computers and Distance Education*, Oxford: Pergamon.

OECD (1992) *Education and New Information Technologies. Teacher Training and Research*. A survey of co-operative projects between universities and schools. Paris: OECD.

Pelton, J. (1991) 'Technology and education: Friend or foe?' *Research in Distance Education*, 3 (2), 2–9.

Perkins, J. and Newman, K. (1995) *Lurkers and Virtuosos in E-Discussion*, Ontario: Lakehead University Press.

Perraton, H. (ed.) (1993) *Distance Education for Teacher Training*, London: Routledge.

Perraton, H. and Potashnik, M. (1996) *Teacher Education at a Distance*, Washington, DC: World Bank.

Platten, M. R. and Bruce, B. O. (1987) *Texas Tech University's Model of Teaching over Satellite*, Texas: Texas Technical University Press.

Porter, R. (1983) 'The implications of the domestic satellite for the in-service education of teachers in rural and remote areas', *The South Pacific Journal of Teacher Education*, 11 (2), 54–59.

Potashnik, M. (1996) 'Chile's learning network', *Education and Technology Series*, 1 (2), Washington, DC: World Bank.

Prain, V. and Booth, T. (1993) 'Using interactive television to deliver professional development programmes in rural Australia', *Education in Rural Australia*, 3 (2), 5–10.

Reddy, S. (1986) 'Educational radio: Directions in the Pacific', *Media in Educational Development*, 19 (1), 34–37.

Rhys, J. (1988) 'Teacher education and change. The first decade of IT', *European Journal of Teacher Education*, 11 (2/3), 195–205.

Robson, J., Routcliffe, P. and Fitzgerald, R. (1992) 'Remote schooling and information technology', *Education in Rural Australia*, 2 (2), 33–36.

Russell, T. L. (1993) 'A medium revisited: Televised distance education', in G. Davies and B. Samways (eds) *Teleteaching: Proceedings of the IFIPTC3 Third Teleteaching Conference*, Trondheim, Norway.

SAIDE (1996) *Teacher Education Offered at a Distance in South African*, Johannesburg: South African Institute for Distance Education.

South African Ministry of Education (1996) *National Policy on Teacher Supply, Utilization and Development*, Pretoria: South African Ministry of Education.

Van Horn, C. and Doris, A. (1993) 'Technology and the future of education'. Paper presented at the National Conference of the CSU Institute of Teaching and Learning. Quality, Creativity and Research, San Jose, California.

Veen, W., Collins, B., Devries, P. and Vozelzay, F. (1994) 'Telematics in education: The European case', *Academic Book Centre*, The Netherlands: De Lier.

Watabe, K., Hamalainen, M. and Whinston, A. B. (1995) 'An Internet based collaborative distance learning system: CODILESS', *Computers in Education*, 24 (3), 141–55.

Yates, S. (1996) 'Computer mediated English: Sociolinguistic aspects of CMC', in J. Maybin and N. Mercer, *Using English: from Conversation to Canon*, London: Routledge.

Part V

SUBJECTS

44

MOTHER TONGUE TEACHING

Jenny Leach

DEFINING MOTHER TONGUE

We do not speak one language, nor half a dozen, nor twenty or thirty. Four to five thousand languages are thought to be in current use. This figure is almost certainly on the low side. We have, until now, no language atlas which can claim to be anywhere near exhaustive. Furthermore the four to five thousand living languages are themselves the remnants of a much larger number spoken in the past. . . . One can only guess at the extent of lost languages. It seems reasonable to assert that the human species developed and made use of at least twice the number we can record today. . . . In many parts of the earth, the language-map is a mosaic each of whose stones, some of them minuscule, is entirely or partially distinct from all others in colour and texture. In 1845 a traveller came across five speakers of Kot. Today no living trace can be found. . . . Blank spaces and question marks cover the immense tracts of the linguistic geography of the [earth. . .] tongues remain unidentified or resist inclusion in any agreed category. . . . The language catalogue begins with Aba, an Altaic idiom spoken by Tatars, and ends with Zyriene, A Finno-Ugaritic speech in use between the Urals and the Arctic shore. . . . By comparison, the classification of different types of stars, planets and asteroids runs to a mere handful.

(Steiner, 1975, p. 54)

Muttersprache; jezyk ojczysty; ko makou alelo makuahine; langue maternelle; 한국어; *maay-boli*; 母國語; *moeder taal*; mother tongue: languages worldwide contain a phrase approximating to 'mother tongue'. Whilst the phrase is intuitively recognisable in many languages, as with so many 'common sense' interpretations, the term encompasses complex debates, competing definitions and differing uses both within and across cultures. The *Oxford English Dictionary* (OED) definition is 'one's native language', 'the language into which one was born'. The OED notes that the late Middle English (ME) derivation of 'mother' was an uninflected genitive, carrying the broad connotation of 'giving birth to' (c.f. mother land, mother [i.e. native] wit). However, Tulasiewicz and Adams (1998) argue that since medieval Latin contained the term '*lingua maternal*', it is possible to accept that the term denotes that in most European societies at least, it was the mother who was assumed to pass on her language to her children. 'Mother' is certainly integral to the concept in many European languages (e.g. *Muttersprache, langue maternelle, moeder taal*), but this is by no means the norm, either in Europe or elsewhere. Polish for example, refers to father tongue [*jezyk ojczysty*], Russian [*rodnoi yazyk*] to 'native language'. Welsh '*cymraeg*' and Korean 한국어 are literally 'Welsh' and 'Korean' – the language. Mandarin Chinese as spoken within Korea by contrast uses three interrelated concepts 'mother – nation – language': 母國語 whilst in China the term denotes three ideas, 'centre-nation-language', 中國語 embedding in its characters the ancient history and the power of the *Empire du Milieu*.

The association of 'mother tongue' with national language has a long history. Certainly the word's earliest appearances in medieval European texts indicate its use in relation to the legal language of the court and thus of governance. From the Renaissance onwards, as nation states emerged as the territorial basis for administration and cultural identity, internal lingua francas developed as both vehicles of governance and emblems of national identity. 'National' languages were thus constructed. Only two centuries later Humboldt (1972) was confidently articulating the view that every language expressed the 'spirit of the nation' that speaks it, possessing its own inner form [*innere Sprachform*]. Such a view was to become highly influential throughout Europe in the nineteenth and twentieth centuries. 'Language', he argued, makes 'man at home in the world', though he cautioned, 'it also has the power to alienate'. In the early twentieth century in England, moves to establish the English mother tongue as a school subject invoked this intimate relation between language and nationhood: 'English is not merely the medium of our thought, it is the very stuff and process of it. It is itself the English mind.'

Tulasiewicz and Adams (1998) have properly problematised the link between national language and home language, identifying three different uses of mother tongue:

- a private language used among intimate groups of speakers;
- a vernacular which may be used as a regional language; and
- a language which achieves national status, used on public occasions of the nation state.

There are, of course, many more mother tongues in the first two senses than sovereign independent states worldwide: indeed fewer and fewer national education systems in the twenty-first century are dealing with an homogeneous linguistic community. As Escarpit has commented 'la nationalité qu'on porte sur son passeport n'est pas donnée linguistique' (1979, p. 32). Escarpit's personal account of mother tongue and language learning provides an example of the complexities of multilingualism in practice:

- a language, French, acquired through imprintation from early childhood, then systematised by the school system that provided the written status for it;
- a language, 'Gascon', also acquired through imprintation from early childhood, ignored by both school and society and left in its oral state, only spoken by his grandmother in her native Béarn and totally forbidden at home by his father, a primary school teacher brought up in the republican tradition; and
- a third language, English, also learnt through early experience, because his mother used it with him, and later on it was systematised by his school and university education.

Many children may well have two or even three 'mother tongues' and acquisition of fluency in one (or more) of them will be determined by a combination of its status in the home, in school and society, as Escarpit's vignette illustrates. In Spain, for example, Catalan has 10 million users. In the UK, in addition to English, there are three other territorial languages: Welsh, Scottish Gaelic and Irish Gaelic; it is possible to add Cornish, Manx and Scottish English to this list of vernaculars. In the early 1990s, France's Minister for

Education stressed the importance of preserving 'the treasures of our common inheritance ['patrimoine'], to go out and speak in Basque, in Breton, Occitan or Alsation'. The Council of Europe's European Charter on minority or regional languages, published in 1992, was perceived by many as the first international document recognising the importance of the use and protection of home languages as a basic human right.

The term 'home language' has been preferred by some linguists to embrace the distinctive dialects and languages, often used solely in home contexts, and which may be predominantly oral, such as described in Escarpit's vignette. In a multilingual context, however, mother tongue might more properly be defined as the *preferred language*, one's personal choice of mother tongue. EU-funded research (Tulasiewicz and Adams, 1998), carried out in the UK for example, showed that in London the preferred language of school pupils was often English, even though their parents might not speak English. By contrast a large number of primary school students in Peterborough saw little point in learning English at all, as they live in communities in which it is possible to survive without seeing or hearing a single word of English, which they see as a foreign rather than second language.

Graddol (1997) has argued that since an increasing proportion of the world's population will be fluent speakers of more than one language in this century, the hierarchy of language implied by Tulasiewicz and Adams's definitions of mother tongue, becomes even more differentiated. In complex multilingual areas such as the Indian subcontinent, where nearly 2,000 languages exist, each with differing status, he locates four language categories: local vernacular; languages with widespread currency; scheduled languages; and national languages. In such contexts, he contends, whilst there may be many who remain monolingual in a local vernacular, those who speak one of the national languages will have better access to material success. Marathi for example, is the official language of the Maharashtra State, spoken by 70 million people, some of whom live in neighbouring states. If they know Hindi or English it is likely to be their fourth language. Yet the existence of a website '*Maayboli*' (mother tongue), to support the maintenance of Marathi, illustrates the potential fragility of language and the rapidly changing context for 'mother tongue teaching'.

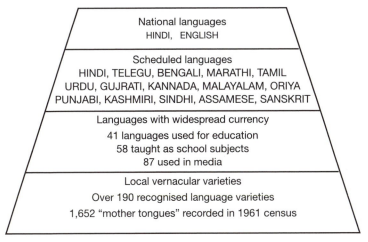

Figure 44.1   A language hierarchy for India
Source: Graddol, 1997, p. 12

As Graddol's model demonstrates (see Figure 44.1) many mother tongue languages do not enjoy status as an official language. A nation may have more than one language as a medium of communication, although one may be designated the 'national' or 'standard', as in England. Some countries such as Canada and Wales are officially designated as bilingual and law may require teachers to be fluent in both official languages. Singapore has boldly legislated a multi-language formula in setting up a new state, ensuring that Tamil, Malay and Mandarin Chinese all enjoy status as official languages. All are offered as part of the school curriculum, although English is the medium of instruction in schools. However, such enlightened legislation in relation to mother tongue maintenance is uncommon.

The term 'preferred language' thus implies a freedom of choice between two or more languages which can mask the complexities of context in which such choices are often made. As Tulasiewicz and Adams point out, the reasons for using a language are numerous:

> socio-political: the language is identified with some political and social classes of the population but not with others; cultural and religious: the language is used in predominantly artistic or denominational contexts; commercial: the language of business transactions; domestic: the language of the home; and linguistic: the language is small and not distinct enough, yet is different from the official language and has been used for a long time by people who are reluctant to change to another. In this they may be supported by experts who look upon such language as a cultural inheritance and object of study.

> (Tulasiewicz and Adams, 1998, p. 9)

Whilst choice of mother tongue may indeed be personal preference, the opportunity for using it will be largely dictated by societal considerations. As has been noted, languages are not equal in either political or social status and in reality the 'mother tongue' of many school curricula may well be more properly defined as the 'official language' of government or nation state. Indeed, in cases where a language is imposed upon an entire state, language becomes relegated to the instrumental function of communication used by a community. Graddol has proposed a further categorisation, which in his view expresses a 'world language hierarchy' (Figure 44.2). This hierarchy, he argues, will be increasingly significant in educational terms as more and more people learn languages in the uppermost layer, as a result of improved education and changing patterns of communication:

1 Private or what he terms *local vernacular varieties* (in Asia 1,652 'mother tongues' were recorded in a 1961 census) which are used within families and for interaction with close friends. These are usually geographically based and the first languages used by children;

2 *official languages within nation states*, found in the more formal and public domains and which have greater territorial 'reach', forming perhaps the basis of primary education, newspapers, local broadcasting and local commerce;

3 *national languages*: around 80 languages serve over 180 nation states;

4 *regional languages* which he defines as the 'languages of the United Nations'; and

5 the '*big languages*' of international communication.

Graddol argues that the majority of the world's mother tongues found in the base section of this diagram are likely to disappear from use, as languages higher up the hierarchy steadily 'colonise' the lower layers. One of the main linguistic issues facing the world this century he suggests, will be the extinction of a substantial proportion of the world's mother tongues (Foundation for endangered languages: http://www.bris.ac.uk/Depts/

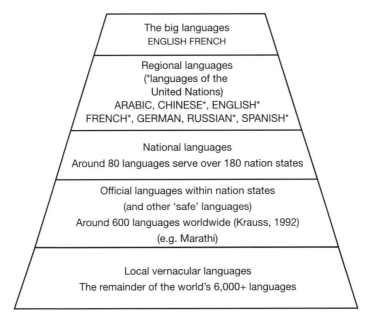

Figure 44.2 The world language hierarchy
Source: Graddol, 1997, p. 12

Philosophy/CTLL/FEL; Terra Lingua http://cougar.ucdavis.edu/nas/terralin/ home.html). Krauss (1992) thought it plausible this would be 90 per cent of world languages. The colonisation of mother tongues by 'big languages' is not a recent phenomenon. Although the Romans colonised England *c*. 55 BC, Latin survived as the official language of law and government, culture and university education throughout the Middle Ages, and in aspects of the educational system in England until the eighteenth century. This was also the case in many parts of Europe. In the early seventeenth century, Shakespeare powerfully articulated the colonisation of mind that the imposition of language can bring, through the voice of Caliban:

> You taught me language, and my profit on't
> Is I know how to curse. The red plague rid you
> For learning me your language!
> > (*The Tempest*, I, ii, 363–365)

Across the twentieth century these words reverberated in many post-colonial works of literature, as writers such as Derek Walcott, Sujata Bhatt and Maxine Hong Kingston articulated enduring and pressing dilemmas concerning their home language or dialect. Sujata Bhatt, for example, voiced the terror of losing a mother tongue:

Search For My Tongue

. . .
You ask me what I mean
by saying I have lost my tongue.
I ask you, what would you do
if you had two tongues in your mouth,
and lost the first one, the mother tongue,

and could not really know the other,
the foreign tongue.
You could not use them both together
even if you thought that way.
And if you lived in a place you had to
speak a foreign tongue
your mother tongue would rot,
rot and die in your mouth
until you had to spit it out.
I thought I spit it out
but overnight while I dream.

મને હતું કે આખ્ખી જીભ આખ્ખી ભાષા,
(*munay hutoo kay aakhee jeebh aakhee bhasha*)

મેં થું કી નાખી છે.
(*may thoonky nakhi chay*)

પરં તુ રાત્રે સ્વપ્નામાં મારી ભાષા પાછી આવે છે.
(*parantoo rattray svupnama mari bhasha pachi aavay chay*)

ફૂલની જેમ મારી ભાષા મારી જીભ
(*foolnee jaim mari bhasha mari jeebh*)

મોઢામાં ખીલે છે.
(*modhama kheelay chay*)

ફૂલની જેમ મારી ભાષા મારી જીભ
(*fullnee jaim mari bhasha mari jeebh*)

મોઢામાં પાકે છે.
(*modhama pakay chay*)
it grows back, a stump of a shoot
grows longer, grows moist, grows strong veins,
it ties the other tongue in knots,
the bud opens, the bud opens in my mouth,
it pushes the other tongue aside.
Everytime I think I've forgotten,
I think I've lost the mother tongue,
it blossoms out of my mouth.
. . .

(Sujata Bhatt, 1997, pp. 35–36)

Others focused on the potential resource of bilingualism or bidialectalism or, as in Walcott's poem below, on the importance of finding and reconstructing one's own language and culture:

Come back to me
my language.
Come back,
cacao,
grigri,
solitaire,
ciseau the scissor bird
no nightingales
except once,

778

in the indigo blue mountains
of Jamaica, blue depth,
deep as coffee,
flicker of pimento,
the shaft of light
on a yellow ackee
the bark alone bare
jardins
en montagnes
en haut betassion
the wet leather reek
of the hill donkey
(Walcott, 1986, p. 36–37)

This eloquent writing challenges better than any argument the rhetoric of choice with regard to mother tongue use for many peoples of the globe. It demonstrates the critical distinctions made by the terms 'preferred' and 'home' language, and underlines the impact of ideology on familial practices, educational curricula and government policy. Such work also emphasises the fluid, ever-changing nature of language. As Brodsky has commented, Walcott's poetry is

> Adamic in the sense that both he and his world have departed from paradise. He, by tasting the fruit of knowledge. His world, by political history. In this condition of fluidity, which is the authentic condition of language, the metropolitan, prescribed histories are displaced.
>
> (1994, p. 170)

Attempts to challenge imposed national language policies have, at their most extreme, led to imprisonment and death. The novelist Ngugi wa Thiong'o's home language of Gikuyu was banned in his Kenyan school under colonial rule, where 'language and literature were taking us further and further from ourselves to other selves, from our worlds to other worlds' (Ngugi, 1986). Ngugi's outspoken critique of the Kenyan government in 1978, allied with his public decision to write solely in Gikuyu or Kiswahili, Kenya's national language, rather than in English, resulted in his arrest and political imprisonment. In South Africa, prior to majority rule in 1996, neither of its two official languages – English and Afrikaans – was the mother tongue of the majority of the population. Bantu education was predicated on a specific, racist language policy:

> We believe that the teaching and education of the native must be grounded in the life and world view of the whites, most especially those of the Boer nation, as the senior white trustee of the native. . . . We believe that mother tongue must be the basis of native education and teaching but that the two official languages must be taught as subjects because they are the official languages, and to the native, the keys to the cultural loans that are necessary to his own cultural progress.
>
> (Janks, 1990, pp. 244–245)

The decision to introduce Afrikaans as a medium of instruction for 50 per cent of school subjects in the South African curriculum at primary level was to provide the flash-point for the 1976 Soweto uprising and the death of schoolboy Hector Peterson.

At the time of writing, 8 of 12 websites located by an Internet search engine relating to 'mother tongue' concern public debates about imposed language policies and mother tongue maintenance, marking a continued resistance to the imposition of official state languages in various locations and school systems globally. Competing uses of 'mother tongue'

– mirrored in the terms such as *national, home, first, preferred, official* language – thus demonstrate the linguistic, socio-political, economic, cultural and personal factors that underpin educational policies relating to mother tongue teaching. These factors provide the context in which any mother tongue teacher enacts choices in relation to both curriculum and pedagogy. In such contexts, and given increased linguistic diversity globally, mother tongue teachers are faced with some important questions: What is the students' view of this language? How is it viewed by parents? What additional languages and/or dialects are spoken within the school? In the local community?

BABEL TOWER: WORLDVIEWS OF MOTHER TONGUE

A second OED entry on mother tongue, 'an original language from which others spring', presents a definition which has been influential in the historical development of the philosophy of language and linguistics. It draws on metaphor and ancient worldviews that still find echoes in contemporary approaches to mother tongue teaching, national educational policy and literary theory. Raymond Williams has written, 'sometimes, the most basic concepts . . . from which we begin, are seen to be not concepts but problems, not analytic problems either, but historical movements that are still unresolved' (Williams, 1982, p. 78). Theories of an Adamic vernacular – a single primal language, which enabled all people to communicate with perfect ease, have underpinned 'common-sense' thinking as well as systematic language investigations from Genesis through to the early work of Ludwig Wittgenstein, for example the *Tractatus Logico-Philosophicus* (1961). Walter Benjamin founded his theory of translation on the concept of a universal language:

> a self identical thing that is meant, a thing which, nevertheless, is accessible to none of these languages taken individually, but only to that totality of all their intentions taken as reciprocal and complementary, a totality that we call Pure Language [*reine Sprache*]
>
> (Benjamin, 1955, p. 345)

Philosophers of language (Eco, 1997; Steiner, 1975) have traced the influence of the Babel story, a myth common to many world cultures (Borst, 1963), in the history of European thought. Until the Renaissance, they argue, many philosophers worked from the premise of an original common language or primordial language which had fragmented into many tongues; Hebrew was widely assumed throughout Europe to be the basis of an original, sacred language. This common search for a unique mother tongue, the 'monogenetic hypothesis', resulted in numerous, theoretical interpretations, viz. the search for a 'perfect language', mirroring the true nature of objects as sought by philosophers of language; the search for a language that everyone might or ought to speak; a study of the origin of language; the search for a primordial language (Eco, 1997).

The biblical account of Babel in Genesis: 11 prevailed in the collective imagination and in the minds of those philosophers who inquired into the plurality of languages at this time. Humanity, powerfully speaking a single language, came so close to Heaven that God himself felt threatened; the events that followed were a curse – the languages that so divide people a punishment. This view increasingly came under challenge as sixteenth- and seventeenth-century navigators discovered previously unknown civilisations, each with its own linguistic and cultural traditions. In 1699, for example, the philosopher John Webb advanced the idea that after the flood Noah had landed his ark in China; it was Chinese, he argued, that held primacy as a language. Attention began to move away from the problem of a primordial language to focus on *Matrices linguae*, or mother tongues. An alternative interpretation to that of Babel, the natural development of languages, found in Genesis: 10, thus took centre-stage. Scholars set about trying to understand this process by investigating grammatical structures common to all languages. As soon as ideas lost their quality as innate, Platonic entities, language itself lost its aura of sacrality, newly seen as an instrument for interaction – a human construct (Eco, 1997). The primal scattering of languages began to be reinterpreted as a natural and inevitable process. Thus the global explorations of the Renaissance period gradually ushered in modern linguistics. Pinker (1994), in popularising the Chomskian notion of Universal Grammar in *The Language Instinct*, uses the metaphor of Babel to convey the value of a common language which 'connects the members of a community into an information sharing network with formidable collective powers'. By contrast 'The Power of Babel', a language project in South Africa, takes the view that multilingualism and linguistic diversity are a resource, cultural diversity a national asset. Indeed, in the Republic of South Africa, in a strong repudiation of legislation prior to majority rule, 12 languages now have official status as the medium of school instruction. The right to mother tongue maintenance is enshrined in the constitution, and the South African Department of Education is tasked to promote multilingualism, the development of the official languages, and respect for all languages used in the country, including South African sign language. These differing responses to linguistic diversity can be seen to be informed by radically different worldviews. The former, Eco argues, has been 'a gesture of propaganda', in so far as it has historically provided a quite particular explanation of the origin and variety of languages, presenting it as a punishment and a curse. The second view not only accepts, but promotes diversity:

> If each language constitutes a certain model of the universe, a semiotic system of understanding, and if we have 4,000 different ways to describe the world, this makes us rich. We should be concerned about preserving languages just as we are about ecology.
>
> (Ivanov, 1992, p. 337)

Diversity and plurality are thus viewed as a means of providing access and participation, while mother tongue education is seen as an instrument of empowerment.

Here are to be found two strongly competing ideologies. The first worldview sees humanity as objects, without choice, being 'acquired by' a set of dividing languages. The second view proposes that humans are agentive, co-intentional, participating together in a creative, ever-changing practice of meaning-making. Both views influence language theory, debate about mother tongue teaching, national language policies and classroom practice.

THEORETICAL FRAMEWORKS IN MOTHER TONGUE TEACHING

The OED's definition 'the language into which one was born' dismisses any question that language is innate, emphasising rather the social nature of language development. Indeed, although neuroscientists are able to locate different active areas of the brain that can be linked to language tasks such as speech (see Figure 44.3 below), the neuroscientist

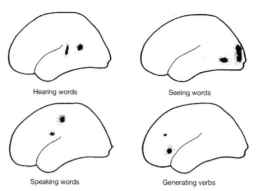

Hearing words   Seeing words

Speaking words   Generating verbs

Figure 44.3 The interactive brain. A positron emission tomography (PET) scan of a conscious human subject performing similar but subtly different tasks. Note that although the tasks are all linked to language, different brain regions will be involved according to the precise nature of the undertaking. Note also that at no time is just one brain region active completely on its own.
Source: Adapted from M. I. Posner and M. E. Raichle, *Images of Mind*, Scientific American Library Series, 1994.

Greenfield (1997, p. 30) argues that experience is a key factor in shaping the micro-circuitry of the brain itself.

More importantly, she suggests, it is experience which drives both the nature and development of language, irrespective of the physical capacity of the brain to mediate this complex process. The view of language as social practice has been influential in debates about the nature of mother tongue teaching for over half a century. It draws on one of two distinctive views of mind which predominate in any theory of first language acquisition and its development, centrally informing approaches to mother tongue teaching. Bruner (1996) has characterised these views of mind as the computational and the cultural. Bredo (1998) calls them the 'symbol-processing' and 'situated' views. (See Chapter 12, this volume, for further discussion.) The symbol-processing view sees the mind as a manipulator of symbols which are learnt and stored in the memory. There are different accounts of this process. At one end of the spectrum is the information-processing view, where the learner is seen as a passive processor of information. The more widely accepted situated view however, sees the learner as an active constructor of knowledge, agentive and intentional (Bruner, 1996). Chomsky's (1965) influential work on language, which owes much to the rationalism of Descartes and sixteenth-century grammarians, is based on a symbol-processing view of mind. It is essentially a working vision of a Universal Grammar – general ground rules of human cognitive and symbolic processes. From Chomsky's perspective 'Deep structures' are the innate components of the human mind that enable it to carry out 'certain formal kinds of operations in strings'. His theory that 'all languages are cut to the same pattern' is based on the notion of a 'language acquisition device' which, he posited, develops independently of other human capacities. The bulk and organising principles of the 'iceberg of language' thus belong to the subsurface category of universals, local languages being the surface-structure realisation of these. Chomskian theory acknowledges the creativity of a generative grammar, but also encourages the view of language as innate, the learner as processor of information, the process an essentially individual one. It has been a powerful influence in mother tongue teaching particularly in relation to the teaching of language through grammar, influencing the view that it is possible to lay down rules for the 'correct' use of language which students need to learn, often through the completion of spoken drills and written exercises, irrespective of purpose or context. Such interpretation ignores the distinction Chomsky made between deep and surface structure, as well as the essentially creative nature of language in practice.

A situated view of mind, by contrast, emphasises that language is part of a social semiotic – the exchange of meanings in interpersonal contexts. At the opposite end of the spectrum from Chomsky's rationalist linguistics lie Sapir (1921) and Whorf's (1956) comparative linguistic studies, which led them to claim that language wholly determines the way in which individuals see and experience the world, informing 'thinking as usual' (Schutz, 1971). The Hopi Indian language formed a major part of the language study on which this thesis was based, although the most commonly cited example of their 'linguistic determination hypothesis', is the suggestion that the Inuit have dozens of words for snow, compared to the mere three or four words (e.g. sleet, slush, hail) existing in English. Pullum (1991) has derisively called this the Great Eskimo Vocabulary Hoax, an 'anthropological anecdote which is bunk'. It appeals, he argues, to a patronising willingness to treat cultures as weird and exotic 'compared with our own'. Pullum's refutation of the theory, however, itself illustrates language interacting with social environment and the communities in which people live and work:

> [E]ven if there were a large number of roots for different snow types in some Arctic language, this would not, objectively, be intellectually interesting; it would be a most mundane and unremarkable fact. Horsebreeders have various names for breeds, sizes and ages of horses; botanists have names for leaf shapes; interior decorators have names for shades of mauve; printers have many different names for fonts.
>
> (Pullum, 1991, pp. 164–165)

Whilst most linguists would reject the Whorfian extremes of linguistic determinism, Slobin's (1982) accounts of the differently structured utterances of languages more subtly demonstrate the way in which language reflects and interacts with the different environments in which people live, thus playing a part in structuring experience. Many East African languages have two distinct past tenses – one for events in the recent past, the other for events in the distant past, whilst in Navaho there is a system for sub-classifying nouns according to the shape of the object which the noun denotes. This account of language as a heterogeneous phenomenon has been developed by linguists who take the functional aspects of language use as their major focus. Language evokes ideas; it does not represent them. Linguistic expression is thus not a natural map of consciousness or thought. It is a highly selective and conventionally schematic map (Slobin, 1982, pp. 131–132). Throughout the latter part of the twentieth century the unique relation between language, thought and experience, has been a major focus of research, impacting directly on mother tongue teaching. In the 1970s the comparative linguist Dell Hymes (1973), in rejecting Chomskian theory as inadequate and emphasising the role of social and historical forces in producing the multitude of mother tongues, placed language universals in a different perspective.

> the discovery of putative universals in linguistic structure does not erase the differences. Indeed, the more emphasis on universals, in association with a self-developing, powerful faculty of language within persons themselves, the more mysterious actual languages become. Why are there more than one, two or three? If the internal faculty of language is so constraining, must not social,

historical, adaptive forces have been even more constraining, to produce the specific plenitude of language actually found? For Chinookan is not Sahaptin is not Klamath is not Takelma is not Coos is not Siuslaw is not Tsimshian is not Wintu is not Maidu is not Yokuts is not Costanoan. . . . The many differences do not disappear, and the likenesses, indeed, are far from Chomskyan universals. Most of language begins where abstract universals leave off.

(Hymes, 1973, p. 63)

M. A. K. Halliday's (1973) work, like Hymes's, set him apart from Chomsky with its emphasis on language as a key element of the social semiotic. He referred to the process of first language acquisition as *learning how to mean*, stressing that language is text or discourse – the exchange of meanings in interpersonal contexts. Halliday's functionalist linguistics, which has informed approaches to mother tongue teaching for the last three decades, provides a systematic account of how speech situations or context are reflected in the linguistic choices made by the participants in those situations. Halliday proposed seven models of language which arise from the socio-functional nature of language in use (Instrumental; Regulatory; Interactional; Personal; Heuristic; Imaginative; Informative), focusing in his later work on three metafunctions of language: the ideational, the inter-personal and the textual (Halliday, 1985). His work raised teachers' awareness of the socio-functional nature of language; his contention that children must be taught how to operate in the school context, for example in the personal and heuristic language modes, was influen-tial. Functional linguistics thus moved thinking away from the individual perspective of symbol-processing, providing a framework for recognising language as a social phenom-enon. It has been highly influential in approaches to mother tongue teaching. In the UK, for example, the work of Halliday informed a national language project (Carter, 1990) in the late 1980s, while a new national curriculum (DES, 1989) included knowledge about language as integral to mother tongue teaching, requiring that students study aspects of language in its own right. In Australia, the highly influential genre theory (Kress, 1987) has emerged out of Halliday's work. Theorists argued that mother tongue teaching had placed too much emphasis on personal and narrative writing; they encouraged the explicit teaching of 'power-ful' genres, the impersonal genres of factual, expository and argumentative prose. The following possibilities for classroom practice, taken from the New Zealand curriculum, reflect the functional approach to mother tongue teaching:

- a study of the heritages of the children in the class;
- a language study on gender bias in language;
- a class investigation of ways in which language varies according to situation;
- learning about community meetings (include learning and enacting knowledge of meeting procedures);
- a study of topical issues such as health (includes strategies for note-taking);
- developing understanding of a new genre (includes exploration of cues to understanding, and conventions of writing such as text layout, punctuation, etc.);
- personal storytelling (students move between oral and written storytelling, focusing on ideas from own experience stimulated by teacher's own storytelling);
- a study of the language of film.

The work of Vygotsky (1962) also strongly influenced the theory and practice of mother tongue teaching. Social constructivism emphasised that through dialogue, knowledge is continually both socially constructed and transformed: thus when two or more people communicate, there is a real possibility that by pooling their knowledge and experience they achieve a new level of understanding beyond that which either had before (Edwards and Mercer, 1987). Vygotsky's (1978) concept of the zone of proximal development has been a central concept, an interactive system

> within which people work on a problem which at least one of them could not, alone, work on effectively. Cognitive change takes place within this zone, where the zone is considered both in terms of an individual's developmental history and in terms of the support structure created by other people and cultural tools in the setting.
>
> (Newman *et al.*, 1989, p. 61)

The process of learning from this perspective becomes a dialogue, a constant meeting of minds which Bruner has called a 'forum', in which teachers and learners engage in a negotiation of shared meaning: 'It is this that permits one to reach higher ground, this process of objectifying in language and image what one has thought and then turning around on it and reconsidering it' (Bruner, 1986, p. 129). This work has led to the strong foregrounding of oracy, particularly in the US and UK, focusing in research and practice on the importance of talk for learning, the use of pair and group tasks in the structuring and creating of knowledge, as well as the importance of peer collaboration in the development of mother tongue teaching. In the UK the National Oracy Project was influential in foregrounding talk for learning, whilst the Kualida project in Albania (Leach and Lita, 1998) is one example of projects in Eastern Europe which are exploring the centrality of pupil talk in the learning process, not only in mother tongue teaching but across the curriculum.

Literary theorists have also played a key role in shaping mother tongue teaching. Leavis and his Cambridge School of the 1930s and 1940s, in particular, have been influential in many English-speaking countries. Literature from a Leavisite perspective is a 'record of the experiences of the greatest minds'; books are the 'instruments through which we hear the voices of those who have known life better than ourselves'. Leavis advocated literature as a potent basis for social harmony, believing in the central value of 'great literature' in the university English studies curriculum and in the need for 'critical discrimination' in our 'debased cultural environment'. His voice dominated postwar mother tongue teaching in England – English literature was seen to equip pupils to withstand such evils as 'bad literature', the cinema, advertising and 'the popular press'. It was also seen to develop individual qualities of mind such as sensitivity, imagination, perception, sympathy, creativity and responsiveness – all Leavisite catchphrases. Such moralism was to be transmitted to followers such as David Holbrooke, whose personal mission was to extend Leavisism to the 'less able'. In the 1970s educators like Rosen and Barnes in the UK sought to shift this canonical tradition in mother tongue teaching. Influenced by the work of Vygotsky, Luria and Bruner, they moved the emphasis on 'great works' in the mother tongue curriculum to language and the learner, the pupil's daily life and 'authentic' experience. An emphasis was placed on the mother tongue teacher as anthropologist, mapping and collecting the values and cultures of differing groups, initially the working class (later girls and blacks). The notion of 'literature' thus became profoundly expanded to encompass 'all that can be said or written', to embrace oral language. This work also drew on Labov's (1970) studies of the language of black and Puerto Rican children in New York. Labov was developing, in the wake of Halliday, the notion that social context is the most powerful determinant of verbal behaviour. His research demonstrated that school discourse, in giving institutional authority to a standard language, lowered teachers' expectations of non-standard dialect users. Labov and his followers' rigorous research demonstrated that non-standard dialects are as logical and grammatically consistent as standard. Trudgill (1975), building on Labov's work in the United Kingdom in particular, argued that

> the teaching of higher status accents and of spoken Standard English in school is almost certain to fail. Children will in most cases learn to speak this dialect [Standard English] only if they wish to become associated with this group and feel that they have a reasonable expectation of being able to do so. Writing on the other hand, is a different matter. It is much easier to learn to write a new dialect than to learn to speak it.

(Trudgill, 1975, pp. 66–67)

Where socio-linguistics has been influential in mother tongue teaching, it has led to an emphasis on the 'standard language' as one among many varieties. There is an acceptance of dialects as valid linguistic and literary forms, and an emphasis on pluralism, which extends to a redefinition of literature to include a broader range of sources. Pupils' own work, popular literature, the poetry and fiction of 'other cultures and traditions', newspapers and comics made their appearance in some mother tongue classrooms, to be studied, discussed and written about rather than derided (Ball *et al.*, 1990).

In the last two decades of the twentieth century, post-structuralist literary theory challenged the notion of a literary canon in many parts of the world, problematising the relationship between text and meaning and shifting the focus within university literary studies from texts to 'readings'. Critics widely proposed that the literary canon had to be recognised as a 'construct', 'fashioned by particular people for particular reasons at a certain time. There is no such thing as a literary work or tradition which is valuable *in itself*, regardless of what anyone might have come to say about it' (Eagleton, 1982, p. 1).

The notion of intertextuality, inspired by the work of the Russian linguist Bakhtin (1981), challenged the dichotomy between 'literary' and 'nonliterary' language. The Open University's undergraduate course on the development of the English language graphically represents this shift as shown in Figure 44.4.

Increasingly, therefore, language has been seen not as a monolithic system, imposing a distinctive, homogeneous framework on its speakers, but as both functional and plural, mediating different modes of interpretation, allowing individuals to view their worlds from different positions and construct their interpretations through different linguistic practices. Language can be used to inform, to question, to persuade – in widely different contexts and for different purposes, as the Gaelic poet Caimbeul suggests:

Cànan	Language
Siursach is oigh	Whore, virgin
's tu agam an seo	with me here
ga do dhealbh	making you
ga mo dhealbh	making me.
Pogan naomh agus aingidh	Holy, wicked
thugad is bhuat	kisses
anns an dorcha	given and received
anns an t-solas	in the dark
thu a' cruin	the light
mar as miann leat	you create
fada o m' mhiann	as you wish

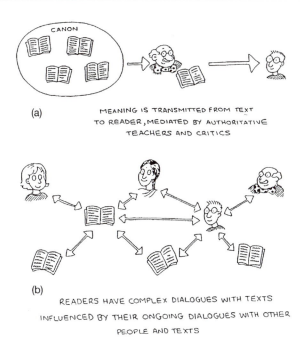

(a) MEANING IS TRANSMITTED FROM TEXT TO READER, MEDIATED BY AUTHORITATIVE TEACHERS AND CRITICS

(b) READERS HAVE COMPLEX DIALOGUES WITH TEXTS INFLUENCED BY THEIR ONGOING DIALOGUES WITH OTHER PEOPLE AND TEXTS

Figure 44.4 (a) Transmission model; (b) dialogic model
Source: Maybin and Mercer, 1996

'S co aig'tha fhios	far from my desire.
de thig asad–	And who knows
an e urnaigh, dan,	what you'll produce –
no ordugh bias	prayer, poem,
ann am belsen	or a death warrant
	in Belsen.

(Caimbeul, 1994, p. 37)

From this perspective the mother tongue classroom is inherently multi-voiced, not solely in terms of varieties of home languages and dialects, but in terms of a complex variety of discourses. Bakhtin argues that the taking on of different voices and their attitudes is part of the 'ideological becoming of a human being' (Bakhtin, 1981), thus a multiplicity of competing discourses is seen as being integral to the mother tongue itself. He has argued that the

> internal stratification of any single national language into social dialects, characteristic group behaviours, professional jargons, generic languages, languages of generations and age-groups, tendentious languages, languages of authorities, of various circles and of passing fashions, languages that serve the socio-political purposes of the day, even of the hour (each day has its own slogan, its own vocabulary, its own emphases).

(Bakhtin, 1981, pp. 262–263)

A more radical strand of situated theory has developed in the latter part of the twentieth century (Lave, 1988; Chaiklin and Lave, 1993). Meaning is seen to be created through participation in social activity; in this sense there is no individual notion of an idea or concept, but a distributed one. Collaboration is at the heart of this approach, and the development of intersubjectivity. Learning is seen as being developed through participation

787

in 'communities of practice' (Lave and Wenger, 1991). From this perspective, the home language community enculturates the individual into the mother tongue, also functioning as a mediator of worldview, thus providing a particular linguistic perception of the world. Also acknowledged from this situated perspective, however, are the different, frequently conflicting communities of practice to which individuals belong. This view is important in placing *identity* as central to the learning process and as the subject matter of all learning. It also challenges traditional dichotomies between abstract and practical knowledge, between procedural knowledge and conceptual understanding, between the individual and the social. The insights of this theory present important challenges and opportunities for the mother tongue teacher, which are explored in subsequent sections.

THE PRACTICE OF MOTHER TONGUE TEACHING: COMPETING VIEWS

Only in the closing decade of the twentieth century were any systematic comparative studies of the practice of mother tongue teaching carried out. The Kingman Inquiry (1988) investigated how the mother tongue was taught in England, drawing on data from a number of other European countries in its report. The following year the Chevalier and Janitza report (1989) worked to a similar brief in France, examining the purpose and nature of language education. A European Union (EU) funded comparative study of the teaching of mother tongue in France, England, Germany and Spain in 1993 was prompted by the growing necessity to consider the educational needs of a multilingual Europe. That decade also saw the launch of an international series of research papers (Gagne and Purves, 1993) devoted to mother tongue education, covering five continents and heralding a long overdue enquiry into comparative pedagogy in language teaching. Such research has demonstrated the variety of views of mother tongue teaching in different cultures and contexts, expressing itself in a wide range of traditional practices and conventions, inevitably strongly influenced by particular national examination and inspections systems.

The previous section outlined ideas that have informed strands in mother tongue teaching, across as well as within cultures. It is also important to acknowledge distinctive national traditions and philosophies of mother tongue teaching. McLean (1990), for example, argues that *humanism* and *encyclopaedism* are informing concepts in English and French education traditions respectively. Pepin (1999) used these principles (and the concept *Bildung* in German thought) to suggest common national traditions and conventions in the teaching of mathematics. Holmes and McLean (1989) argue that liberal humanism centrally informs the English education system – emphasising the interaction between teacher and pupil, child-centred philosophies and active teaching strategies. Such a view informs the stated aims of its statutory national curriculum for mother tongue teaching (DES, 1989), which identifies 'two different but complementary purposes' behind its broad aim of enabling pupils to develop their ability to use and understand English: (a) the personal development of the individual child and (b) the intellectual, emotional and aesthetic development of pupils. Research amongst mother tongue teachers in England has identified 'individualism' as a dominant theme. A study by Protherough and Atkinson (1991) exposed 'sensitivity to pupil needs', 'awareness of the centrality of the pupil', 'understanding of young people's sense of *their* world' as central to the thinking of one hundred 'effective' mother tongue teachers. They note:

> the heavy emphasis on personality and on relationships does seem to mark off [mother tongue] teachers from others. . . . The first significant official report on the subject in 1910 . . . formulated the difference in these terms. . . . 'No subject gives more scope for individuality of treatment or for varied experiment; in none is the personal quality of the teacher more important.' This stress on the individual and personal has remained significant in all subsequent discussions.
>
> (Protherough and Atkinson, 1991, p. 15)

Davies's (1996) more recent findings concerning the beliefs and attitudes of mother tongue teachers in the UK produced similar results which, he argues, 'whichever way you swing it . . . demonstrate a rather extreme form of liberal humanism'. Seventy-two per cent of respondents agreed that 'English, more than any other subject, can have an extremely humanising effect.' Morgan (1990) calls this view a secularised 'seminar of conscience', predominant also in the philosophy of 'personal growth' and 'developing personal values' to be found in Canada's *Guidelines for the Teaching of English* (Ontario Ministry of Education, 1997). Such a philosophy has also been honed through the Leavisite approach to the teaching of literature, also visible in many post-colonial mother tongue curricula globally, where despite espoused multiculturalism, 'the stress in mother tongue teaching continues to fall on a monochromatic and stable nationalism which espouses the use of "acknowledged classics" and "national literature"' (Morgan, 1990, p. 198).

By contrast, the philosophy underpinning French education, McLean (1990) suggests, emphasises encyclopaedism, with its associated principles of rationality, universality and *égalité*. The principle of utility is based on the idea that social change and improvement of the society is possible through rational knowledge; the principle of universality means on one hand that students study broadly the same curriculum (at broadly the same time); on the other hand that they gain what is perceived as general 'valued' knowledge. The principle of *égalité* aspires to remove social inequalities through education and promotes equal opportunities for all pupils. Convey's (1998) detailed account of the French mother tongue curriculum would seem to confirm these informing principles. Priority is given in major education policy documents in France (Bayrou, 1994; Jospin, 1989) to fundamental learning (*apprentissages fondamentaux*) in the elementary phase: French language, reading, mathematics and study skills. The first priority is the mastery of the mother tongue, both spoken and written; success in initial learning is regarded as essential, particularly in the area of reading. Official instructions are very detailed and specific. In the first year (*cours préparatoire*), the objective of the teaching of the French language is for pupils to master oral expression, the aim being to gain access to the written text. In the second and third years (*cours élémentaire*), the regular practice of reading and writing at a more demanding level aims to improve the quality of language. In the last two years (*cours moyen*), pupils learn to question, answer, explain and justify; their ability to read and write is expected to improve in quality and complexity and their enriched knowledge of language is expected to become more precise. Specific exercises are suggested, which include pronunciation exercises as well as exercises aimed at describing situations, narrating and commenting upon events, inventing and modifying stories, arguing and using a variety of registers.

Whilst the identification of national trends provides significant insights, these trends inadequately account for the complexity both of philosophy and practice within and across cultures in mother tongue teaching. Other studies have located a variety of informing approaches. The National Curriculum Orders for England and Wales (DFE, 1989), for example, located five different, though not necessarily mutually exclusive, views of mother tongue teaching: adult needs, personal growth, cultural heritage, cross-curricular and cultural analysis.

The *adult needs view* is clearly evident in all mother tongue models worldwide. It focuses on communication outside school, emphasising the responsibility of mother tongue teachers to prepare children for the demands of adult life, including literacy skills and the demands of the workplace in a fast-changing world. Students need to be able to deal with day-to-day demands of spoken language and of print; they also need to be able to write clearly and effectively. Whilst such a view has been shown to predominate in the French mother tongue elementary curriculum, as described earlier, it is clearly one important element of any mother tongue curriculum.

The *personal growth view* focuses on the child and emphasises the relationship between language and learning in the individual child and the role of literature in developing children's imaginative and aesthetic lives. As we have noted, this is the dominant view of mother tongue teachers in the United Kingdom, but it is also strongly represented in other contexts where English is the *lingua franca* or the medium of instruction, such as in Canada or South Africa. Literature offers the reader complex representations of the human condition for consideration and reflection, it is the means whereby individual experience can be imaginatively extended and sympathies enlarged. As well as an emphasis on literature, this view stresses the child's personal experiences and places an importance on attitudes, values and relationships in curriculum content. Pupils are helped to acknowledge and value their own uniqueness as individuals, whilst recognising that they share a commonality with others (Rosen, 1981). This view emphasises the affective aspects of experience and encourages, for example, autobiographical work with pupils and the exploration of issues significant in pupils' lives. Green (1990) has argued that all mother tongue teachers in Britain, whether specialist or not, have found themselves in a situation in which literature is significant and even critical to a proper sense of professional identity (p. 137).

The *cultural heritage view*, clearly overlapping with the personal growth view, is common to many mother tongue curricula worldwide, emphasising the responsibility of schools to lead children to an appreciation of 'great' works of literature. From this perspective, the works of 'great writers' are enshrined in the mother tongue curriculum. This is evident in widely differing educational systems such as South Korea, the Balkans and also in Egypt, where the Koran is a major focus for the teaching of Arabic. In all these contexts, the authority of text is paramount. What is recognised as great literature is regarded as obvious and in many curricula globally, the knowledge of 'great' books and writers is tested by public examination, thus enshrining them within the assessment system.

A *cross-curricular view* emphasises that all teachers have a responsibility to support students with the language demands of different subjects in the school curriculum, otherwise areas of the curriculum may be closed to them. This view became popular in the last decade, fuelled in particular by increased globalisation and the stress on what have been seen to be skills common across subject areas, emphasising both the ideational and interpersonal functions of language. The New Zealand National Curriculum put such a view into practice in its national curriculum in the 1990s, drawing up a 'coherent framework for learning and

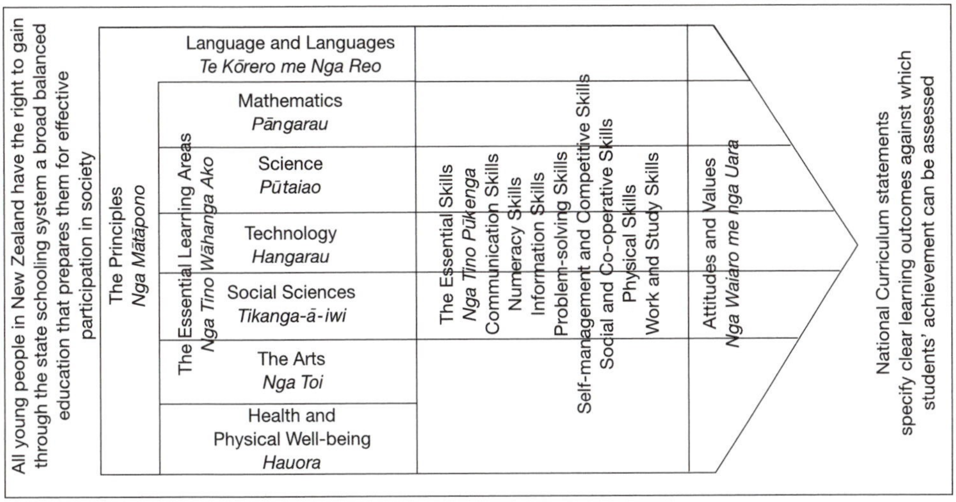

Figure 44.5 The New Zealand curriculum framework, Te Anga Marautango o Aotearoa
Source: New Zealand Ministry of Education, 1994, p. 6

assessment' which identified essential learning areas and skills. Figure 44.5 demonstrates this thinking. It names both Essential Learning Areas and Essential Learning Skills, which schools are encouraged to achieve in whatever ways they choose; traditional subject divisions are thus called into question by such categories. Mother tongue (English and Maori) teaching is located as a key element in the Essential Learning Area of Language and Languages and establishes language aims for the three 'strands of oral, written and visual language' (New Zealand Ministry of Education, 1994, p. 6).

The *cultural analysis view* emphasises the role of mother tongue teaching in helping students towards a critical understanding of the world and the cultural environment in which they live. Drawing to some extent on post-structuralist literary theory, this view starts from the premise that students should know about the processes by which meanings are conveyed, and about the ways in which print and other media carry value. This has increasing currency as a view, as information and communication technologies (ICTs) become a focus within the school curriculum. In Germany, for example, media literacy has become a key 'cultural educational concept'. Nationwide, projects are concerned with the development of pupils' ability within the mother tongue curriculum to:

- perceive and to recognise the impact of media;
- understand and to rate the message, and to select and to use media in a reflective way;
- create, construct and distribute media; and
- analyse and reflect on its societal meaning from a critical point of view.

These recommendations by the Scholastic Media Education (BLK) in Germany are underpinned by a view that the formation and utilisation of multimedia require the development of a variety of literacy skills, which include 'expanded analytical, evaluative and creative abilities' (Schulz-Zander, 1998).

Davies's (1996) in-depth study of 15 mother tongue teachers within the UK, uncovered

Table 44.1 Mainstream/liberal humanist versus radical/cultural theorist approach

Mainstream/liberal humanist	*Radical/cultural theorist*
Literature at the centre of English studies	Questioning the concept of literature
English studies for personal growth	The political dimension of language and literature studies
English as a means of educating taste and discrimination	Valuing popular culture and media study in English
Literary standard English as the ideal form of the language ('correctness')	Acceptance of students' own non-standard language use ('appropriateness')

Source: Davies, 1996, p. 26

'a patchwork' of approaches to mother tongue teaching. He argues that such plurality can be categorised within two overarching, competing lines, representing key areas of debate and contention about mother tongue teaching (Table 44.1).

It is useful to look at the other binaries that have emerged as major tensions throughout this overview: Babel as the fragmentation of a single, unifying language vs. Babel as product of a rich language resource; language as rule governed, generative universals vs. language as social semiotic; text as canon vs. text as social production. All reflect two underlying metaphors – the acquisition metaphor and the participation metaphor (Sfard, 1998) which demonstrate how learning and the nature of knowledge come to be understood. The acquisition metaphor represents knowledge as a commodity that can be developed or constructed, which the individual accumulates. The participation metaphor replaces knowledge with knowing, and having knowledge with participating, doing. It is the conflict between these two informing metaphors, underlying assumptions about *how* children develop expertise in mother tongue and of *what* that expertise consists, which so often surfaces in public rhetoric and acerbic debates about mother tongue teaching (e.g. 'back to basics' vs. a whole language approach; the 'teaching of grammar' vs. knowing about language).

Ball *et al.* (1990) have argued that the different versions of mother tongue teaching we have explored contain and inform a particular political epistemology: the learner is placed differently in relation to subject knowledge, their teachers and the state. Each produces different kinds of students (and citizens) with different kinds of abilities and relationships with peers. In each version the root paradigm of meanings *within* and *about* [the mother tongue] differs and conflicts (Ball *et al.*, 1990). We would additionally argue that mother tongue teachers and their views just as much reflect their own perceptions of their core task of teaching and learning the mother tongue, as they are the outcome of the mediating influences of the macro-politics of subjects at national and school level. The notion of a 'pedagogic setting' (Leach and Moon, 1999) enables us to conceptualise the way in which different settings call forth different knowledge and learning and therefore distinctively different language practices in the mother tongue classroom. The dimensions of a pedagogic setting which have been explored in preceding sections (educational goals; the knowledge which is the subject of the learning; learning and assessment activities, including roles and relationships; and of course discourse itself) serve to frame learners' activity. A pedagogic setting in which the nature of literacy knowledge is seen to be the development of discrete language skills, in which 'correct' forms of expression and presentation of self are of prime importance, operates from a symbol-processing view of mind in which learners are viewed as passive, rather than as active and intentional. Precedence is given to technical knowledge about language, pre-specified in terms of a serial progression through discrete items, largely separated from context, rarely allowing for reflection (metacognition) on the process. There is little if any room for feelings or emotions. By contrast, approaches to literacy that take a situated view of mind start from the belief that learners are agentive (Bruner, 1996), rather than empty vessels waiting to be filled with literacy 'items'. From this perspective, literacy cannot be understood as an autonomous, all-purpose one-size-fits-all set of skills for encoding and decoding (Morgan, 1999). Indeed, literacy from this perspective is nothing in itself, it must develop within particular social practices (Willinsky, 1991).

New analyses of situated learning (Lave and Wenger, 1991), as we noted earlier, challenge dichotomies which so bedevil debates about mother tongue teaching and the theories and metaphors underlying its practice (e.g. acquisition vs. participation; mind vs. body; individual vs. social; technical vs. functional; language as single/ideal/homogeneous vs. language as multifarious, plural, multi-voiced). From this perspective of 'participation in social practices', cognition is *always* distributed; 'stretched over, not divided among – mind, body, activity and culturally organised settings (which include other actors), across persons, activity and setting' (Lave, 1988). Such a view of learning demands a holistic, dynamic account of literacy, one which Morgan (1999) has called the 'three-dimensional model' of literacy learning. The model emphasises that in practice all three dimensions need to be attended to, more or less at the same time, no one of them taking priority:

- the *operational* (learning the language): students learn to acquire specific skills and content knowledge such as the basic skills of reading, the skills of drafting, editing, spelling, punctuation, using a dictionary or thesaurus; knowledge of prescribed literary texts, as well as grammatical and literary terminology;
- the *cultural* (becoming competent within the meaning system): students develop their understanding and expertise in the meaning-making functions of language and literacy as participants within differing literacy practices. Such an approach builds on individuals' language and identity, enabling the development of literacy in diverse ways, through a variety of contexts and for a variety of purposes, including the personal, imaginative and aesthetic;
- the *critical* (going beyond the socialisation to critique and transform through active production of text): students develop a critical understanding of the world and the environment in which they live. They are encouraged to investigate how different forms of knowledge are created in and through language and to ask how language might be put to different, more equitable uses; how texts might be re-created that would tell a different story of other possibilities in a more just world (Morgan, 1999, p. 3).

Shor calls critical literacy the process of developing

habits of thought, reading and writing, and speaking which go beneath surface meanings, first impressions, dominant myths, official pronouncements, traditional clichés, received wisdom, and mere opinions, to understand deep meanings, root causes, social context, ideology and personal consequence of any action, event, object, process, organisation, experience, text, subject matter, policy, mass media or discourse.

(Shor, 1992, p. 129)

793

It develops 'habits of mind' (Meier, 1995), encouraging students to constantly ask questions such as: How do I know? Whose point of view am I seeing? What causes what? How might things have been different? Who cares? It enables students to recognise the multifarious functions of language purposes both in their own lives and those of the society in which they live. It acknowledges conflicting viewpoints and interests and raises social and moral dilemmas. Freire (1974) called this literacy process 'reading the world', a 'pedagogy of knowing'.

THE FUTURE OF MOTHER TONGUE TEACHING: NEW LITERACIES, NEW DILEMMAS, NEW POSSIBILITIES

'This is a world . . . of fragmentation, of cultural diversity. . . . It is a world where there are thousands upon thousands of specialist magazines speaking in specialist tongues and where there are some cities that have sixty television channels for aficionados of all sorts of peculiar discourses from pentecostalism to pornography. It is a world where a dozen or more languages might be spoken on one city block, where the television brings live coverage to that same block of what is happening at the ends of the earth.

(Kalantzis and Cope, 1993, p. 38)

New literacies

Previous sections traced some dominant theories, models and metaphors which have influenced mother tongue teaching and its development in a variety of contexts worldwide. These have drawn on:

- views of how language and literacy develop, informed by differing views of mind (i.e. symbol-processing, situated);
- views of what counts as knowledge in mother tongue teaching (e.g. discrete literacy skills, the practice of meaning-making, the development of identity, metalinguistic knowledge, critical literacy); and
- views of learners (e.g. as passive receivers of language skills and information about literary texts and terminology, as active meaning-makers, as critical and creative communicators, involved in the creation of new texts, meanings and languages).

Earlier sections also outlined the increasingly multilingual, multicultural context of mother tongue teaching in the twenty-first century. In a new, digitised world, literacy can no longer be defined exclusively in linguistic terms, nor can information be seen as stable, located in fixed and bounded texts. The nature of texts, the process of reading and writing, contexts, audience and purpose are in flux. Indeed, new information and communications technologies are already showing that they transform the nature of mother tongue teaching. Texts written and read are no longer solely printed texts composed of words with a few illustrations. Electronic texts are composed using a number of modes integrating text, image, icons, sound, animation and video sequences. These texts can be nonlinear in format, often multi-authored, interactive and may not be the same on a subsequent rereading (Lanham, 1993). Images are becoming increasingly dominant as a form of communication (Kress and Van

794

Leeuwen, 1996), bringing to the fore the concept of 'visual literacy' (Raney, 1998). New literary genres are also being added to the range available, with electronic texts and print-based texts serving complementary functions. The distinction between author and reader is also blurred; there is a more immediate interface between writer and audience as well as an ease for collaborative compositions. The range of texts as well as how people access them has widened. All of this creates new demands, questions and challenges for mother tongue teachers, requiring a rethinking at every level of what it means to be literate and how to teach that.

The new millennium is also a time of global transition: a new world order is emerging, making it a singularly critical time for the development of mother tongue teaching. The Internet and related information and communications technology (ICT) call into question traditional patterns of communication upon which institutional and national cultures have been built. Graddol (1997) has argued that language will play a more central role than ever before in economic, political and social life. Many commentators, in the Adamic tradition, suggest that we are – and should be – moving closer to the time in which there will be a single global language of communication. In contrast the 'engco model' (Graddol, 1997) which provides predictions of global influences on key languages, suggests that the rationality of a rush towards a global language, such as English, is far from uncontested. Statistics about language collected by international bodies have been based on nation states, populations of speakers and relative sizes of economies, he argues. Yet Chaos theory suggests that the concept of flow may be better suited to understanding language in a borderless world. Complex systems of unpredictable cultural and economic shifts are invisible to statistical monitoring and a variety of cultural and political movements exists around the world promoting language maintenance. This shift towards a 'communication network' rather than a 'language hierarchy' Graddol argues, allows dispersed discourse communities to emerge, based on shared interests such as hobbies, criminality or support. Diasporic cultural and linguistic groups can share concerns, ideas and decision-making as never before. In the coming decades rapid urbanisation may well create new lingua francas, with not only a large number of speakers but also powerful cultural and economic support. The Hooke model, using economic indicators to predict language trends, forecasts that by 2010 the languages in greatest demand will be English, Mandarin, Spanish and Indonesian, and by 2050 Vietnamese is projected to be the fourth important language in the region's schools in Asia. Education in any multilingual country will need to cater for several languages used within that country. This will become a sensitive factor as the movement towards universal 'language rights' – including the right to a mother tongue education – grows around the world. (Graddol, 1997)

Dilemmas – and possibilities

This complex agenda presents mother tongue teaching with three major dilemmas:

1 *Mother tongue maintenance vs. the development of international lingua francas* The research on language focused in previous sections, demonstrates that mother tongue teachers must create pedagogic settings in which students develop self-esteem, including linguistic

identity and confidence. There must be opportunities for students to use and develop their preferred home language where appropriate – as well as developing fluency in a 'big' language which can provide access to the international community.

2 *The differential nature of access to technology worldwide* National governments have the responsibility to ensure access to information and communications technology, thus providing *all* students with knowledge of and access to new and changing literacies. Research (Castells, 1996) has already shown that the traditional distinction between 'North' and 'South' is no longer geographical, but is becoming a complex, virtual construct. Communities both within as well as across cultures have differential access to new technologies, new literacies and new possibilities for communication, blurring inequities previously represented by the traditional North and South geographical divide.

3 *What will mother tongue practice look like in a new context? How should new practices emerge?* How can students be enabled to be 'interactive' as opposed to being 'interacted' in the Information Age (Castells, 1996)? Three brief concluding case studies illustrate development in mother tongue practice in different parts of the world:

- **In the UK** 15 year old students work with a local elementary school and community television station to make a TV programme for local parents about the government's new approach to teaching literacy.
- **In Australia** Small 'network groups' involving teacher, school students and older youth, work on a face-to-face project for two hours each week, over 8 weeks, to produce one or more electronically mediated cultural texts. The choices include:
  - constructing a database for a community located in a particular school, the database to be available on line
  - engaging in a Geographic Information Systems mapping activity (e.g. mapping local skateboarding venues)
  - organising a 'computer Olympics' where the group works to get all participants up to a minimum skill level on a popular computer game within a certain time (Morgan, 1999).
- **Orillas network** Students are linked via electronic mail in the USA, Puerto Rico, Mexico, Canada and Argentina on a regular basis. Within this network, sister classes engage in two kinds of exchanges (a) monthly 'culture packages' of maps, photos, audio and video tapes, school work and local memorabilia and (b) collaborative projects planned jointly by teachers in different sites that involve interdependent, co-operative activity in small groups at both sites. These collaborative projects fall into several categories:
  - shared student publications (e.g. newsletters);
  - comparative/contrastive investigations (e.g. surveys of each community regarding topical issues such as pollution);
  - folklore compendiums and oral histories (e.g. collections of proverbs, children's rhymes and riddles, songs, etc.);
  - cultural explorations (e.g. students in the sister classes alternately play the role of anthropologist and cultural informant in order to explore each other's culture).

Among the issues addressed in similar case studies in different parts of the world are:

- A 'Food and Farming' Internet debate. Students shared ideas across the country and asked questions of experts in the field such as,

- Are supermarkets selling overpackaged, overprocessed and overproduced food or just meeting demand?
- What about genetically modified (GM) food? Is it just another profitable technology consumers could do without, or a real advantage?
- Will the poor lose out in every way – condemned to less choice, poor diets, ill health and shorter lives?
- Publication of an online international students' magazine focusing controversial issues of world importance (e.g. the Palestinian/Israeli conflict).

CONCLUSION

Language is a system of sounds, meanings and structures with which we make sense of the world around us. But it also functions as a tool of thought; as a means of social organisation; as the repository and means of transmitting knowledge; as the raw material of literature. It is the creator and sustainer – or destroyer – of human relationships. It changes inevitably over time and, as change is not uniform, from place to place. Because language is a fundamental part of being human, it is a crucial aspect of a person's sense of self. Because it is a fundamental feature of any community, it is a central aspect of a person's sense of social identity (based on DES, 1989). Since language is the enabler both of identity and agency, a mother tongue curriculum for the twenty-first century does not merely prepare students for their future, it also enables them critically to understand their present, in order to be able to make and shape their future. This chapter has argued that mother tongue teachers have the potential to be creators and enactors of literacy practices that are dynamic and creative, three-dimensional. These practices will enable students themselves to be agentive, responsible citizens – 'properly literate' in a new century.

REFERENCES

Bakhtin, M.M. (1981) 'Discourse in the novel', in Holquist, M. (ed.) *The Dialogic Imagination: Four Essays by M.M. Bakhtin*, Austin: University of Texas Press.

Ball, S., Kenny, A. and Gardiner, D. (1990) 'Literacy, politics and the teaching of English', in Goodson, I. and Medway, P. (eds) *Bringing English to Order*, London: Falmer Press.

Bayrou, F. (1994) *Tout sur la nouvelle école: le nouveau Contrat pour l'école*, Paris: Ministère de L'Education Nationale.

Benjamin, W. (1955 [1923]) 'Die Aufgabe des Übersetzers', in *Schriften*, Frankfurt: Suhrkampf.

Bhatt, S. (1997) *Point No Point*, Manchester: Carcanet Press.

Borst, A. (1963) *Der Turmbau von Babel. Geschichte der Meinungen über Ursprung und Vielfält der Sprachen und Volke*, Stuttgart: Hiersemann.

Bredo, E. (1998) 'Reconstructing educational psychology', in Murphy, P. (ed.) *Learners, Learning and Assessment*, London: Paul Chapman.

Brodsky. J (1994) *Less than One: Selected Essays*. New York: Farrar, Straus and Giroux.

Bruner, J. (1986) *Actual Minds, Possible Worlds*, London: Harvard University Press.

Bruner, J. (1996) 'Folk Pedagogies', in Bruner, J. (ed.) *The Culture of Education*, Cambridge, MA: Harvard University Press, pp. 44-65.

Caimbeul, M. (1994) 'Cànan', *Verse*, 11 (2), 37.

Carter, R. (1990) *Knowledge about Language*, London: Hodder & Stoughton.

Castells, M. (1996) *The Rise of the Network Society*, Oxford: Blackwell.

Chalklin, S. and Lave, J. (eds) (1993) *Understanding Practice*, Cambridge: Cambridge University Press.

Chevalier, J.C. and Janitza, J. (1989) *Rapport de la mission de réflexion sur l'enseignement du français, de la litterature et des langues vivantes et anciennes*, mimeo, Paris: Centre National de Documentation Pédagogique.

Chomsky, N. (1965) *Aspects of a Theory of Syntax*, Cambridge, MA: MIT Press.

Convey, F. (1998) 'Teaching the mother tongue in France', in Tulasiewicz and Adams (eds).

Cummins, J., and Sayers, D. (1995) *Brave New Schools: Challenging Cultural Illiteracy through Global Learning Networks*, Toronto: OISE Press.

Davies, C. (1996) *What is English Teaching?*, Buckingham: Open University Press.

DES (1989) *English for Ages 5–16*, London: Department of Education and Science.

Eagleton, T. (1982) *Literary Theory: An Introduction*, Oxford: Blackwell.

Eco, U. (1997) *The Search for the Perfect Language*, London: Fontana.

Edwards, D. and Mercer, N. (1987) *Common Knowledge*, London: Routledge.

Escarpit, R. (1979) 'Langue maternelle, langues étrangères', *Le Français dans le Monde*, 142.

Freire, P. (1974) *Education for Critical Consciousness*, Harmondsworth: Penguin.

Gagne, G. and Purves, A.C. (eds) (1993) *Papers in Mother Tongue Education 1*, Mother Tongue Education Research Series, vol. 1, Münster: Waxmann.

Graddol, D. (1997) *The Future of English*, London: The British Council.

Green, B. (1990) 'A dividing practice: "literature", English teaching and cultural politics', in Goodson, I. and Medway, P. (eds) *Bringing English to Order*, London: Falmer Press.

Greenfield, S. (1997) *The Human Brain: A Guided Tour*, London: Weidenfeld and Nicolson.

Halliday, M.A.K. (1973) *Explorations in the Functions of Language*, London: Edward Arnold.

Halliday, M.A.K. (1985) *An Introduction to Functional Grammar*, London: Edward Arnold.

Holmes, B. and McClean, M. (1989) *The Curriculum: A Comparative Perspective*, London: Unwin Hyman.

Humboldt, W. von (1972 [1836]) *Linguistic Variability and Intellectual Development*, Philadelphia: University of Pennsylvania Press.

Hymes, D. (1973) 'Speech and language: on the origins and foundations of inequality among speakers', *Daedalus*, C11, 63.

Ivanov, V. (1992) 'Reconstructing the past', *Intercom*, 15 (1), 1–4.

Janks, H. (1990) 'Contested terrain: English education in South Africa 1948–1987', in Goodson, I. and Medway, P. (eds) *Bringing English to Order*, London: Falmer Press.

Jospin, L. (1989) 'Loi d'Orientation sur l'Education'. *Loi 89–486 du 10 juillet 1989*. Paris: Gouvernment de la République.

Kalantzis, M. and Cope, B. (1993) 'Histories of pedagogy, cultures of schooling', in Cope, B. and Kalantzis, M. (eds) *The Powers of Literacy: A Genre Approach to Teaching Writing*, London: Falmer Press, pp. 38–62.

Kingman, J. (1988) *Report of the Committee of Inquiry into the Teaching of English Language*, London: HMSO.

Krauss, M. (1992) 'The world's languages in crisis', *Language*, 68 (1), 7–9.

Kress, G. (1987) 'Genre in a social theory of language', in Reid, I. (ed.) *The Place of Genre in Learning*, Geelong: Deakin University Press.

Kress, G. and Van Leeuwen, T. (1996) *Reading Images: The Grammar of Visual Design*, London: Routledge.

Labov, W. (1970) 'The study of language in its social context', *Studium Generale*, 23.

Lanham, R. (1993) *The Electronic Word, Democracy, Technology and the Arts*, Chicago: University of Chicago Press.

Lave, J. (1988) *Cognition in Practice*, Cambridge: Cambridge University Press.

Lave, J. and Wenger, E. (1991) 'Participation, Learning Curricula, Communities of Practice' in *Situated Learning*, Cambridge: Cambridge University Press.

Leach, J. and Lita, Z. (1998) 'Teacher education in adversity', paper presented at the American Educational Research Association Conference, San Diego, April 12–18.

Leach, J. and Moon, R.E. (1999) *Learners and Pedagogy*, London: Paul Chapman.

McLean, M. (1990) *Britain and a Single Market Europe*, London: Kogan Page.

Maybin, J. and Mercer, N. (1996) *Using English: From Conversation to Canon*, London/Buckingham: Routledge/The Open University.

Meier, D. (1995) *The Power of Their Ideas*, Boston: Beacon Press.

Mercer, N. (1995) *Talking and Working Together: The Guided Construction of Knowledge*, Clevedon: Multilingual Matters.

Morgan, R. (1990) 'The "Englishness" of English teaching', in Goodson, I. and Medway, P. (eds) *Bringing English to Order*, London: Falmer Press.

Morgan, W. (1999) *Digital Rhetorics: Literacies and Technologies in Education*, paper presented at the Centre for Language in Teacher Education seminar, The Open University, Milton Keynes, 16 February.

New Zealand Ministry of Education (1994) *New Zealand National Curriculum*, Wellington: Ministry of Education, p. 6.

Newman, D., Griffin, P. and Cole, M. (1989) *The Construction Zone*, Cambridge: Cambridge University Press.

Ngugi wa Thiong'o (1986) *Decolonising the Mind: The Politics of Language in African Literature*, London: James Currey.

Ontario Ministry of Education (1997) *Guidelines for the Teaching of English*, Intermediate Division Curriculum Guideline, Ottawa: Ministry of Education.

Pepin, B. (1999) 'The influence of national cultural traditions on pedagogy: classroom practice in England, France and Germany', in Leach and Moon (eds).

Pinker, S. (1994) *The Language Instinct*, London: Penguin.

Protherough, R. and Atkinson, J. (1991) *The Making of English Teachers*, Milton Keynes: Open University Press.

Pullum, G.K. (1991) *The Great Eskimo Vocabulary Hoax and Other Irreverent Essays on the Study of Language*, Chicago: University of Chicago Press.

Raney, K. (1998) 'Visual literacy', *The English Magazine*, Autumn.

Rosen, H. (1981) *Neither Bleak House nor Liberty Hall: English in the Curriculum*, London: Institute of Education.

Sapir, E. (1921) *Language*, New York: Harcourt, Brace and World.

Sayers, D. and Brown, D. (1987) 'Bilingual education and telecommunications: a perfect fit', *Computing Teacher, 17*, 23–24.

Schulz-Zander, R. (1998) 'Current trends in information and communication technology education in German schools', in Schulz-Zander, R. (ed.) *Information and Communication Technology Changing Schools and Teacher Education*, Dortmund: IFS-Verlag.

Schutz, A. (1971) 'The stranger: an essay in social psychology', in *School and Society*, London: Routledge & Kegan Paul.

Sfard, A. (1998) 'On two metaphors for learning and the dangers of choosing just one', *Educational Researcher, 27* (2), 4–13.

Shor, I. (1992) *Empowering Education: Critical Teaching for Social Change*, Chicago: University of Chicago Press.

Slobin, D.I. (1982) 'Universal and particular in the acquisition of language', in Gletman, L.R. (ed.) *Language Acquisition: The State of the Art*, Cambridge, Cambridge University Press.

Steiner, G. (1975) *After Babel: Aspects of Language and Translation*, London: Oxford University Press.

Trudgill, P. (1975) *Accent, Dialect and the School*, London: Edward Arnold.

Tulasiewicz, W. and Adams, A. (eds) (1998) *Teaching the Mother Tongue in a Multilingual Europe*, London: Cassell.

Vygotsky, L.S. (1962) *Thought and Language*, Cambridge, MA: MIT Press.

Vygotsky, L.S. (1978) *Mind in Society*, London: Harvard University Press.

Walcott, D. (1986) *Collected Poems 1948–1984*, New York: Farrar, Straus and Giroux.

Whorf, B. (1956) *Language, Thought and Reality*, Cambridge, MA: MIT Press and Wiley.

Williams, R. (1982) quoted in Green, M. 'The centre for contemporary cultural studies', in Widdowson, P. (ed.) *Re-reading English*, London: Methuen, pp. 17–31.

Willinsky, J. (1991) 'A literacy more urgent than literature: 1800–1850', in *Our Schools Our Selves*, 3 (1), 110–135.

Wittgenstein, L. (1961 [1922]) *Tractatus Logico-Philosophicus*, transl. Pears, D.F. and McGuinness, B.F., London: Routledge and Kegan Paul.

45

READING

Literacy and beyond

Bridie Raban

INTRODUCTION

The last quarter of the twentieth century has seen an unprecedented accumulation of research in reading, not only in quantity but also in variety. This variety has given rise to the development of teachers as researchers as well as academics and to the acceptance of a larger number of research paradigms, thus broadening the base of knowledge and information. Our vocabulary for talking about reading has also altered, giving us fresh ways of thinking about learning and teaching reading. The breadth of our understanding includes both the receptive and productive modes of the activity, through reading and writing, as well as its context; instructional, social, community and political. All these layers of investigation have challenged closely held assumptions and have the potential richly to illuminate our beliefs and practice. The story to be told is not a simple one. The development and refinement of reading ability is a feature of lifelong learning with facets reaching to every aspect of human experience. Because of these layers, research evidence has only increased as more sophisticated and ecologically valid methods of enquiry are being rigorously explored.

What follows is a brief indication of this wide variety of perspectives. Because these many perspectives from different academic disciplines coalesce around the skill and ability of reading and writing, it is not an easily accessed area of research and scholarship. It is, however, definitely a clear concern for everyone involved in education and, with the march of social and economic progress, it becomes more pressing that these issues are acknowledged, addressed and melded into a vision for progress in the future.

PERCEPTUAL TO CONCEPTUAL PROCESSES

Developments in the cognitive sciences have moved us forward to understand that early reading is more concerned with conceptual learning than the development of either auditory or visual perceptual skills. Hearing the sounds in words and seeing the similarities between different graphic marks were previously viewed as the hallmarks of early reading success. Initial training programmes were implemented to encourage young children to listen to familiar, everyday sounds and match these to illustrations, and pick out the same two pictures from distracters. These programmes were believed to support the first steps in learning to read. More recent research has pointed to the necessity to build young children's conceptions of reading and writing first, before this attention to detail. Understanding the purposes and functions of print in their own lives and the lives of others around them will be a powerful backdrop for later success in school-based instruction programmes. It is at this level of conceptual development that children can make sense of and pay attention to the kinds of perceptual knowledge both necessary and sufficient in learning to read and write.

The results of Victoria Purcell-Gates's study (1995) point out that the development of this conceptual framework is predictive of early literacy success in school, even for low socio-economic status children. Her research shows how this 'big picture' knowledge and understanding is affected by the frequency of experiences of print in use around them. By living and participating in an environment in which others use print for various purposes, children come to infer and understand the semiotic and functional nature of written language. Purcell-Gates claims that children who experience many uses of written language, which they attend to and personally experience, have more opportunities to build the important conceptual basis of beginning reading development – that print is symbolic and serves a purpose.

The development of this conceptual understanding gives children a framework within which to anchor and verify their increasingly detailed attention to print. Within this framework, learning individual letter – sound equivalence is considered item knowledge as opposed to this conceptual knowledge. It is the powerful interaction between these two knowledge bases which fosters the rapid reading development experienced by some children. Therefore, introducing children to print through letters, then words and sentences and so on will provide them with difficulties as they may not have had the chance to build up a conceptual framework which would enable them either to assimilate or to accommodate this new information.

Research in the future needs to acknowledge these layers of knowledge and their interrelationships. The clash of paradigms and methodologies with different messages for practice has been unhelpful in the education of our youngest children. Politically, a confusion between conceptual and item knowledge has been a powerful force for control of the reading curriculum, which has confused and bewildered teachers. For instance, teaching phonics or letter – sound relationships is an example of item knowledge, while its background conceptual knowledge of phonemic awareness is far more sophisticated and generalisable. Children remember words that are personal, private and picturesque, their own names being important in this regard. Finding other names that begin with the same letter or sound as their own name is a conceptual leap. Understanding that 'at' is part of the words 'pat' and 'sat' is also conceptual knowledge. Individual aspects of these types of information are item knowledge, and learning will only take place after the concept has taken root in the child's understanding. Practice in the new century needs to find a way of blending diverse methods of teaching which will support children's developing conceptual knowledge, not only their item knowledge, for the benefit of more rapid reading progress.

SPOKEN AND WRITTEN LANGUAGE LINKS

Children learn to speak seemingly effortlessly and if print is conceptualised as speech written down, then it has been argued that children may also be able to acquire reading in this natural way. This view has given rise to the 'immersion' view of reading development and some proponents have pressed this idea into practice with sometimes less than successful outcomes. However, there clearly are links between spoken and written language, but not at any superficial level. Conversational and interactive speech is deeply embedded within a context that is usually clear to both speaker and listener and, therefore, meanings are understood from many different clues, not only the words spoken.

Margaret Donaldson (1984) points out that while speech may be easily understood, written language is more difficult because it lacks a non-linguistic supporting context. The meanings in reading and writing are embedded in the text itself and disembedded from the immediate context of the participants. This is what makes learning to read so difficult for some children. They expect the feedback loop that is available in spoken communication to be there when they interact with text, and this is typically not the case. Because of this, Donaldson and others have argued for the need explicitly to teach young children the conventions and coded nature of text. Children will not be able to configure these for themselves without specific experience and instruction. We learn the conventions of our culture from more knowledgeable others and this includes features of the dominant and other orthographies.

However, there are important similarities between spoken and written language. Both involve arbitrary units which combine in non-arbitrary ways to form the features of language which conveys meaning. This notion of a rule-governed, interrelated set of systems gives the speaker/listener and reader/writer a common strategy for progressing through messages, either spoken or written. At these deeper levels of organisation, spoken and written language are more closely related. Key findings from the research of Ken and Yetta Goodman (1990), Marie Clay (1991) and others indicate how readers use their knowledge of grammar to anticipate the stream of language and gradually, as they gain control of the orthography, their accuracy improves. Even when the reading errors of novice readers are analysed, they are found to substitute the correct part of speech when attempting to read words they find difficult and during their self-correcting behaviours.

Nevertheless, little relationship has been found between children's oral language development and their reading development. This relationship appears to come later, as their experience of written language increases through school learning and the influence moves from the formal written language to speech. Therefore, one of the influences of schooling appears to be enabling people to speak a written language. This has consequences for those who join the professions through further education and can cause those who don't benefit from education in the form of schooling to be less able to enter the discourse of the dominant groups. This veil of formality in language needs urgent attention before large groups of diverse communities become increasingly disenfranchised.

ROLE OF PRIOR KNOWLEDGE

Cognitive science has heralded a shift of Copernican dimensions during the last years of the twentieth century. The conception of reading as an activity, learning to read and the teaching of reading have also changed because of this shift. It is now widely understood that readers 'construct' the meaning of texts in much the same way as listeners actively participate in the development of meanings. Learners are more successful if they understand what they are trying to learn, however little they may already know about the subject matter. Because of this insight, interest has been focused on learners' prior knowledge.

This view of necessary prior knowledge is based on the fact that it is easier to understand what people say or write when there is an existing understanding of what they are talking or writing about. In this sense, children who are categorised as low achievers in school are now deemed to have limitations in their prior knowledge rather than defective learning abilities. This has been an important breakthrough for practice. Questions are now asked concerning how best to create this prior knowledge and where does it come from, rather than condemning children and/or their families to various categories of uneducability because of learning difficulties.

What has been found is that prior knowledge does not come from systematic and specific instruction, because that in turn requires prior knowledge. It comes, therefore, from more general experience of the topic in which the learning takes place. It has become clear that we learn by engaging in activities where we are helped to understand what is going on, and helped by more knowledgeable others to understand and to engage in the activities themselves.

This insight has had a profound impact on practice, which has yet to become universal. We already know that children who come to school from literate homes are more likely to make rapid progress in learning to read through formal instruction. What is it about the literate home which gives them this head start? One of the things that is happening for these children is that they are included in an astonishingly high number of literate events – from joining in sending and signing cards to making shopping lists, owning books, listening and talking about stories and the like. It is through these experiences that children develop the conceptual knowledge concerning reading and writing which will help them to understand the item knowledge that is so much a part of school-based learning. We need to continue to help parents understand their significant role in children's early learning and to respect what they provide.

EMERGENT LITERACY

The notion of emergent literacy, a term coined by Marie Clay, has enabled a far more flexible approach to the early phase of learning to read to take place. Observations of young children show that they enter the world of those adults around them, playing with and exploring the same activities that they experience others doing. For instance, they use pens and pencils for making marks and they turn pages of books. They soon recognise that these are valued activities and that they are also powerful; if an object has a name on it, it belongs to that person, signing one's name is significant, leaving messages and taking notes can make things happen. Here we see the intricate relationship between reading and writing, creating the seed-bed for children's early experiences of written language and their growing ability to gain control over the activity for themselves.

As noted before, children from literate homes which include all the family members in the day-to-day reading and writing activities have an advantage in learning to read at school. Because of this, early compensatory programmes have been developed for those children who do not have these experiences in their preschool lives. However, the concentration on pre-reading and pre-writing skills which focused on perceptual knowledge rather than conceptual development, frequently failed to compensate for these children's lack of literate experiences. The notion of literacy and early literacy allows for the equal significance of writing in the development of early reading ability and also diverts attention away from those skill exercises which frequently had little print content. Emergent literacy has also been powerful in breaking down the concept of 'readiness', which has been differently interpreted by different school systems during different periods of time. Once it was believed that teachers should wait until children were 'ready' before being taught to read, typically about 6 years of age. Later it was believed that early experiences of a specific nature would promote successful development of reading ability. Now, it is clear that nothing can replace taking part in and generating activities themselves which include reading and writing for chosen purposes with the feedback from more knowledgeable others. Emergent literacy has paved the way for concepts surrounding the role of prior knowledge to be better understood. The challenge for the next century is to place these understandings at the centre of early childhood education practice. Notions of 'readiness', 'pre-reading' and 'pre-writing' are giving way to 'pretend' reading and writing. These ideas need further elaboration to account for the fact that, from the child's point of view, they *are* reading and writing, they do not see themselves as pretending at all. This needs to be acknowledged and valued during the preschool period so that children can benefit from the formal teaching reading programme they will experience on entering school.

PROGRESS AND INTERVENTION AT SCHOOL

Assessment of children's reading progress remains problematic. Traditional tests of reading through word recognition, for instance, have failed to capture the complexity of the task, while individual assessments using authentic passages have been too time-consuming to administer for large classes of students. Because these instruments have been inappropriate and because assessment across time has been non-systematic, a clear view of children's reading progress through the years of schooling has been elusive.

More recently, pressure from governments to make schools more accountable for their work has seen curriculum direction implemented nationally in many countries and progress pegged to descriptors for each year-cohort. With the advent of this move from irrelevant 'reading ages' to what are now known as 'benchmarks', the results that are currently being collected are still difficult to interpret. Large-scale sampling across year groups, to include teachers' assessments and standardised formats, is now becoming common and the lessons to be learned from this shift are yet to be realised.

It still seems possible for interpretation to be melded to the purpose of the reporting agencies, with some findings being couched in terms of 'at', 'above' and 'below' target, and others being referred to as 'above' and 'below' for all the scores. Clearly these ways of reporting findings give different pictures for different purposes. It is to be hoped that a more sophisticated and agreed upon procedure for collecting and reporting data will give a clearer picture of school progress against which major resource judgements can be made.

Regardless of the frailty of methods of assessment in reading and the mapping of student progress, there is still an unacceptable level of reading difficulty experienced by students in school. In particular it has been clearly documented that students who fail to make steady progress through their early years of schooling get left behind during the later school years and experience increasing school failure as the gap between the successful and unsuccessful students widens markedly. Because of this incidence of school failure, which appears intractable, and the increasing demands for literacy in a fast-moving world, the focus on the early years of schooling for successful reading progress is now crucial.

There is considerable research literature to indicate that there are three major factors associated with school progress. These three factors are: high expectations of students; deliberate, intentional, and systematic teaching programmes tuned to students' learning needs; and time dedicated to the literacy curriculum in each school day. In America, Robert Slavin's Success for All, in Australia, the Victorian government's Keys to Life initiative and in the UK, the National Literacy Project, are all successfully integrating these three factors in locally appropriate ways. What we are finding through these programmes is that government policy, teaching practice and theoretical understandings are coming together to influence what is happening in classrooms. However, it is clear, as national priorities and local concerns compete with each other for finite resources, that a system-wide reform of this kind is going to be difficult to sustain. The challenge for the twenty-first century is to document, support and monitor these programmes as they begin to impact on the gap between successful and unsuccessful students in our school systems. Beyond this we shall be looking for kinds of long-term gains which governments and communities can positively point to.

The pivotal point here concerns the kinds of professional development programmes that are available for teachers already in schools and how these can best be resourced. Also of major importance is the development of school teams that are significantly better informed concerning learning and teaching reading, with co-ordination across teams as professionals support each other. The view of one teacher for each group of primary students creates a heavy burden. We need to focus more on multi-professional teams rather than the single professional being responsible for every facet of student learning. Where reading development is just one of a number of responsibilities for a teacher, it remains difficult to keep the deliberate, intentional and high-quality programme in place that is necessary to impact early student learning.

CRITICALLY READING FOR MEANING

Having discovered that children do not simply learn to read and gather meaning as they progress through a text, we now understand how readers construct meanings of their own in collaboration with those found in the text. That is to say, it is now more generally accepted that the building blocks for the meaning of a text include not only the words on the page, but the reader's purposes and point of view, analysis of the context, and the author's intentions and already possessed knowledge and beliefs about the topic. Skilled readers swiftly and effortlessly integrate information from various sources as they build a representation of a text. Readers, through this process, 'construct' the meanings of texts.

Previously separate strands of research and theory have come to be considered together as 'social constructivism'. This view is not only expressed by developmental psychologists, but also by anthropologists, literary theorists, linguists, social scientists and the like. The key idea here is that the individual is a product of their culture and, therefore, that learning and development must be construed as socially situated. Children are seen to acquire the ways of thinking and behaving of those around them and these are deeply embedded in the language of communities and the family group. We now realise that language use, both spoken and written, reflects a wide variety of ideological assumptions, and that learning to read needs to include learning to read between the lines and beyond. Structuralist theorists have directed critical attention away from the writer and the text as repositories of values, towards the structures – the codes, the conventions and genre – which enable texts to be produced. Structuralists argue that everyone, speakers and authors, draws upon language which pre-dates them. Utterances and writing are, therefore, less the creation of the speaker or the author and more the product of language, and thus the culture, which is available to them. Structuralist theories have shifted many scholars' attention away from traditional concerns about authors' intentions, meanings and values to linguistic and stylistic analyses and, more recently, to psychological and sociological structures underlying texts.

Post-structuralist theorists and those who deconstruct are similarly interested in the contradictions and inconsistencies in literary texts, the unacknowledged assumptions in texts which illustrate the author's hitherto undiscovered and unchallenged ideologies, especially as these relate to issues of class, race and gender. Deconstructors' critical investigations set out to dismantle texts and to uncover bias or prejudice derived from the society at the time of writing. They are especially interested in ways in which, in the act of reading, everyone constructs new, equally valid products. However, there remains a dominant force in the conservative nature of schooling which influences how far these critical theories can be embraced in classrooms. This will be a challenge for different cultures and school systems in the coming century.

WAYS FORWARD

Ways of viewing children, their learning and, therefore, what should count as teaching are all being reconsidered at this time. Along with these changing understandings, ways of organising learning and teaching in classrooms, schools and national school systems are all providing policy-makers and practitioners with major challenges. The pace of modern progress will dictate a more radical approach to early years education especially, and the advent of technology will sharpen the focus for employment and lifelong learning, as well as school learning. One of the major concerns for all literacy educators in particular, and hence all educators, is the cycle of generational illiteracy and how to break into this pattern. People in remote communities, for instance, from cultures with no history of a written language, are becoming increasingly disadvantaged in the democracies of the world and this can no longer be ignored. It could be anticipated that new technologies may well provide a conduit for interest, change and development for these communities as they come to take what they need from, and contribute to, the knowledge base and understandings of the world.

SELECT BIBLIOGRAPHY

Adams, M. J. (1990) *Beginning to Read: Thinking and Learning about Print*. Cambridge, MA: MIT Press.

Barton, D. (1994) *Literacy: An Introduction to the Ecology of Written Language*. Oxford: Blackwell.

Brown, J., Goodman, K. and Marek, A. (1996) *Studies in Miscue Analysis: An Annotated Bibliography*. Newark, DE: International Reading Association.

Clay, M. (1991) *Becoming Literate: The Construction of Inner Control*. Auckland, NZ: Heinemann.

Donaldson, M. (1984) *Children's Minds*. London: Fontana.

Edwards, V. and Corson, D. (eds) (1997) *Encyclopedia of Language and Education. Vol. 2: Literacy*. Dordrecht: Kluwer Academic Publishers.

Goodman, Y. (1990) *How Children Construct Literacy*. Newark, DE: International Reading Association.

Goswami, U. and Bryant, P. (1990) *Phonological Skills and Learning to Read*. Hillsdale, NJ: Lawrence Erlbaum.

Hannon, P. (1995) *Literacy, Home and School: Research and Practice in Teaching Literacy with Parents*. London: Falmer Press.

Luke, A. (1994) *The Social Construction of Literacy in the Primary School S*. Melbourne: Macmillan Education Australia.

Olson, D. (1994) *The World on Paper: The Conceptual and Cognitive Implications of Writing and Reading*. Cambridge: Cambridge University Press.

Purcell-Gates, V. (1995) *Other People's Voices: The Cycle of Low Literacy*. Cambridge, MA: Harvard University Press.

Ruddell, R., Ruddell, M. and Singer, H. (eds) (1994) *Theoretical Models and Processes of Reading*. (4th edn). Newark, DE: International Reading Association.

Street, B. (1995) *Social Literacies: Critical Approaches to Literacy Development*. London: Longman.

46

MATHEMATICS AT THE CORE OF THE EDUCATIONAL PROCESS

Pearla Nesher

Although mathematics is an ancient discipline, studied systematically by students even in Pythagorean times, mathematics education as a discipline in its own right is very young, having originated as an independent field of research on the learning of mathematics about 30 years ago. Since then, many mathematics education departments have been founded at universities and many scientific congresses and conferences held. Numerous research journals appear regularly and dozens of books summing up the research are published every year. The feeling is that of a growing and constantly expanding field. In recent years many handbooks and summary books on maths education have been published (Bishop *et al.*, 1996; English, 1997; Grouws, 1992; Kilpatrick, 1994; Nesher and Kilpatrick, 1990; Steffe and Gale, 1995; Verschaffel, 1993a).

Motivation for this development was sparked by the Soviets' success in launching Sputnik in the 1950s, which shocked the Western world, bringing about a huge effort to promote the teaching of mathematics. Groups of mathematicians and educators joined in creating the 'new maths' agenda. SMSG and other curriculum materials were published and widely applied.

The euphoria of hopes was followed by disappointment of no lesser degree. Just as the 1960s were filled with innovations and an abundance of novel experimental materials, the 1970s were marked by feelings of disappointment and extensive criticism of the 'new maths'. Scholars working in the field began to understand that publishing new curricula is not enough and that research is required into uniting the factors that lead to failure in learning mathematics.

THE COGNITIVIST APPROACH

The 1970s marked a point of departure for research on learning mathematics. Contrasting with early, post-Second World War research that dealt with categories of difficulties in all sorts of algorithms and exercises, research in the 1970s and 1980s was characterised by resting on new emergent disciplines: a blend of psychology, educational psychology, information-processing, artificial intelligence, early childhood and classroom teaching and learning. The landmark Wingspread Conference (Wisconsin, 1979) (see Carpenter *et al.*, 1982) probably marked the transition from previous research of local difficulties and surface variables related to mathematical algorithms, to the 'cognitive' era.

Twenty years ago, in an introduction to a book on the Wingspread Conference, then a cornerstone of maths education, Tom Romberg wrote:

> During the past decade, the authors of these chapters have carried out a great deal of significant work which is now coming together. This volume clearly reflects the emergence of a 'normal science' approach to studying the development of addition and subtraction skills. What is important is to appreciate the growing consensus on the phenomena of interest, the acute problems to be studied, and the appropriate research methodology being used.
>
> (Carpenter *et al.*, 1982, p. 6)

Research in the 1970s and 1980s adopted the cognitive approach and stressed the need for learning mathematics to be meaningful and that problem-solving is driven by cognitive schemes. Thus, to solve a typical mathematical problem, one must first understand the semantic meaning of the task, and its underlying cognitive schemes. Next comes dealing with the numerical algorithms. Finally, the implied semantics in the problem must be expressed in the syntax of mathematics. The 1980s produced an optimistic belief that maths educators had founded a discipline that would enhance mathematics education.

Such optimism was based on real changes in teaching mathematics in primary grades. Early mathematical concepts regarding counting were thoroughly studied, introducing new notions such as, 'counting all', 'counting on', 'double counting' (Davydov, 1969; Fuson, 1982, 1992). At the same time Gelman (1978) challenged Piaget's (1952) approach to the development of the 'number concept'. A large group of researchers from various countries agreed on the characteristics of addition and subtraction situations and introduced the categories of 'combine', 'change' and 'compare' situations as universal findings (Carpenter *et al.*, 1982, p. 255; Davydov, 1969, p. 375; De Corte *et al.*, 1996, p. 50; De Corte and Verschaffel, 1981; Greeno, 1978b; Nesher, 1982; Vergnaud, 1983). With unbounded optimism, the results of the intensive research of the 1980s were immediately implemented in the classrooms.

Cognitive research performed within the subject matter of mathematics in the 1970s and 1980s used children's 'performance' to gain knowledge about their 'competence'. Literature in the 1980s claimed that knowledge is not the sum of isolated concepts, but is rather a connected system. 'Schemes', 'frames', 'microworlds' and 'semantic nets' used in cognitive psychology were introduced into the maths education research (Fischbein, 1997; Hershkovitz *et al.*, 1990; Hiebert and Carpenter, 1992; Nesher, 1989), with teaching materials also written in the light of these concepts.

Maths education research flourished in the 1980s as US federal funds were granted willingly and easily. In the early 1980s, another four conferences (ALA, Wingspread) were funded by the National Science Foundation under the heading of 'Research Agenda for Mathematics Education'. The general atmosphere was that of accumulated research findings and a need for more communication among researchers. Sowder, who initiated the Research Agenda in the 1980s, wrote: 'Most of us who do research would agree that our work is more likely to be profitable when it results from an accumulation of knowledge acquired through projects undertaken within a coherent framework rather than through single, isolated studies' (Sowder in Hiebert, 1988, p. vii).

Four monographs that emerged from this project contain the conference proceedings and are subtitled as follows: *The Teaching and Assessing of Mathematical Problem Solving* (Silver and Randall), *Perspectives on Research on Effective Mathematics Teaching* (Grouws and Cooney, 1988), *Research Issues in the Learning and Teaching of Algebra* (Wagner and Kieran, 1989), and *Number Concepts and Operations in the Middle Grades* (Hiebert and Behr, 1988).

CONSTRUCTIVISM

Concurrently, a theoretical basis for a new paradigm of research on learning mathematics began to flourish, known as 'constructivism'. It grew out of Piaget's perspective. Constructivists hold that mathematical knowledge for children is not 'perceived' or 'acquired'; it consists of those mathematical concepts and operations that children might learn through their own actions and reflections; and that a concept is 'nothing but a schema for action or operation' (Piaget, 1950).

Mathematics education researchers of the 1970s and 1980s became acquainted with constructivism primarily via arguments and debates on 'trivial constructivism' versus 'radical constructivism' (von Glaserfeld, 1984, 1991). In trivial constructivism, mathematics for children exists in an ontological reality. On the other hand, in radical constructivism, knowledge does not represent reality; one constructs a subjective reality, aiming to gain predictability and control. In radical constructivism, the mathematical knowledge of the *other* is seen to be relative to one's own frame of reference and can be understood only by interpreting the language and actions of the other.

Advocates of radical constructivism were concerned with the practice of teaching, claiming that the teacher comes to know the mathematical realities of the students through experimental encounters. Long-term experiential encounters with children are necessary when investigating mathematical learning, with its goal of constructing models of children's mathematical knowledge and observing how such models might change under directed adult guidance (Cobb, 1985; Cobb *et al.*, 1992; Steffe, 1996; Steffe and Gale, 1995).

Constructivism had an enormous impact on the practice of teaching. It changed the way in which teachers approached their students. Teachers learned to listen to their students and to understand their way of thinking. It was no longer a matter of 'errors', 'bugs' and 'misconceptions', but rather a different way of thinking, which the teachers must understand and take into account. In the constructivist view, to appreciate learning is to understand that knowledge is constructed from actions and abstract reflection (a key Piagetian notion) on one's own actions. The constructivist approach deepened the understanding of what is involved in performing a mathematical task from the learner's standpoint.

SOCIAL CONSTRUCTIVISM

The late 1980s and 1990s were marked by the influence of the Soviet psychologist Vygotsky (Vygotsky, 1962, 1978 [1930]). Vygotsky stressed the socio-historical basis of psychology, emphasising the role of language in developing higher cognitive functions. He introduced the concept of 'the zone of proximal development' which redefined the teacher's role. Investigations into classroom interactions and social practices replaced claims of individual constructions. Abundant descriptions of teacher – student interactions describe regularities and norms of speech while performing mathematical activity. It is claimed that 'Students arrive at what they know about mathematics mainly through participating in the social practice in the classroom, rather than through discovering external structures existing independent of the students' (Bauersfeld, 1995).

Under the Vygotskian influence, research in the late 1980s shifted to classroom practice, adopting anthropological methods and analysing many classroom episodes and protocols. A central tenet was that classroom discussions and peer interactions are important opportunities to learn, especially through 'negotiation of mathematical meanings' (Wood *et al.*, 1990, 1995).

For those supporting the social, cultural, theoretical and practical aspects, it was important to stress that their approach still accepts the constructivist views on learning and teaching:

> We question that either cognitive or social processes should be relegated to a secondary role as we attempt to understand mathematics learning and teaching in [US] public school classrooms. . . . These claims about the ahistorical, mind-independent essence of mathematics are incompatible with the epistemology that underpins both constructivism and symbolic interactionism.
>
> (Wood *et al.*, 1990)

Thus the emphasis on construction by one's own activity has evolved into other classroom modes such as 'co-operative learning' and a 'community of learners', stressing the communicative aspects of the mathematics classroom.

The 'radical constructivist' view as well as its younger sister, the 'social constructivist' view were criticised on several grounds: the epistemological, contending that knowledge is a representation system and not an interpretive and subjective one; and on the ground that knowledge is teachable even if it is constructed individually by each learner. In spite of some criticism the constructivist's influence in shaping the practice in the maths classroom cannot be underestimated.

SITUATED COGNITION

Another epistemology that developed concurrently with social constructivism is the approach that states that knowledge is embedded in context, being specific to the real-life situation in which knowledge is applied. The view that action is situationally grounded is the central claim of those who defend the notion of situated cognition. They claim that the potentialities for action cannot be fully described independently of the specific situation and that more general knowledge cannot and will not be transferred to real-world situations (Anderson *et al.*, 1996).

The most commonly quoted examples in support of situated cognition are those presented by Carraher *et al.* (1985) and Lave (Lave, 1988; Lave and Wenger, 1991). Carraher *et al.* produced an account of Brazilian street children who could perform mathematics when making sales in the street but were unable to solve similar problems when presented in a school context, while Lave gave several examples of workers performing maths activities in their workplace.

Anderson *et al.* (1996) argue against four central claims of situated learning with respect to education:

1 action is grounded in the concrete situation in which it occurs;
2 knowledge is not transferred among tasks;
3 training by abstraction is of little use; and
4 instruction must be carried out in complex social environments.

Although Anderson *et al.* cited abundant psychological research findings contradicting the above claims, in mathematics education of the 1990s, 'situated cognition' is still adhered to by many maths educators. Currently it strongly influences what is being taught in schools.

PROBLEM-SOLVING

Problem-solving was always an important issue. Research in the 1980s engaged in understanding and promoting the teaching of problem-solving. Two main streams dealt with problem-solving. The first stream stemmed from the work of Polya (1945, 1954, 1962, 1965, 1980), who engaged in trying to teach *heuristic* strategies. The second stream took the *linguistic* approach.

With the heuristic approach, the rationale was simple. Once the most important heuristic strategies were discovered and elaborated, the next step was obvious. One should provide direct instruction in these strategies, thereby saving students the trouble of having to discover strategies of their own.

A substantial amount of effort went into attempts to discover the strategies students use in attempting to solve mathematical problems. Most influential in this direction in the 1980s was Schoenfeld (1985, 1987, 1991, 1992), who devoted great efforts in teaching experiments accompanied by full protocols that had direct implications on mathematics teaching. Schoenfeld's teaching experiments were conducted within a specific context but ended with generalisations about the four main aspects needed to promote heuristic problem-solving: resources, heuristics, control and belief systems.

The second approach to word problem research adopted a linguistic approach dealing with the actual formulation of the problems, as well as their semantics and the actual situations they denote. This research paradigm was successful in clarifying differences between various types of situations calling for the same mathematical operations. It demonstrated, for example, that the same 'additive structure' can appear in various situations, whether they are static, dynamic or making comparisons (De Corte *et al.*, 1996; Greeno, 1978a; Greer, 1994; Kintsch, 1986; Kintsch and Kozminsky, 1977; Laborde, 1990; Nesher and Katriel, 1977; Nesher and Teubal, 1975; Nesher *et al.*, 1982; Paige and Simon, 1966; Verschaffel, 1993a).

The linguistic and semantic approach, although limited in scope, was readily adopted by teachers and implemented in the classrooms. At present, problems presented to students take into account the developmental trends that were identified in the research of the 1970s and the 1980s.

THE ROLE OF TECHNOLOGY

In the 1970s technology was employed mainly for 'drill and practice' or direct 'tutoring systems' that tried to imitate good teachers. The 1980s and the 1990s brought about a revolutionary shift in the technology available to schools. In addition to hand calculators that could free students from many arithmetic calculations, other, more advanced mathematical tools were developed. Now one can find on the market software that is capable (in a manner similar to the number calculator) of performing almost every operation that used to be included in the high school mathematics curriculum. A serious question now faces the maths education community: what should be the content of mathematics learning in the light of the above developments? (Bendaz *et al.*, 1996; Chazan, 1993; Confrey and Scarano, 1995; Confrey and Smith, 1994; Kaput, 1989; Reusser, 1992; Yerushalmy, 1995, 1997; Yerushalmy and Gilead, 1997).

Many discussions in the last decade dealt with this problem. Available technology with its graphics capability presented researchers with the challenge of using the graphics option and stressing an enquiry approach to many mathematical notions without needing to employ lengthy algebraic analytic manipulations. Yerushalmy wrote (Yerushalmy, 1998):

> When the purpose of the procedure is to have a 'result' then technology is capable of replacing human actions. Technology allows us to split the traditional meaning of 'solving an equation' into two parts which are no longer mutually dependent: manipulating equations and seeing solutions. Only the solution (the result) can be observed using symbolic manipulators or graphic software. . . . Understanding equations involves many aspects other than procedural aspects. We would like to explore what is involved in the evolution of 'a sense of equation; intuition and understanding', and what are possible relationships between actually performing the procedures and these aspects of understanding.

The major belief that maths educators currently share is that today it is possible, with the help of the available technology, to relax the requirements for procedural knowledge and that the core of mathematics learning should be *conceptual understanding*. This calls for a major reform in mathematics curriculum.

Experiments in this direction have already started. The collective use of mathematical language and the thinking strategies in class discussions are the most striking impressions gained from this new approach.

> During these discussions students often display what seems to be mathematician's mental habits. While confronting new problems, they are capable of visualizing in flexible ways, they see functions in unexpected places, they reason employing deductive and inductive methods, and finally, they experiment with the problem, raise questions about the problem and critically analyze its solution. The language they use is precise and organized around mathematical objects and processes.
>
> (Yerushalmy, 1998)

NCTM STANDARDS

The accumulated research findings on the learning and teaching of mathematics and the changes engendered by technology have affected mathematics curricula throughout the world. Calls for reform in school mathematics suggest that new goals are needed. All industrialised countries are experiencing the shift from the industrial society to the information society, a shift that transforms both the aspects of mathematics that need to be transmitted to students, as well as the concepts and procedures that they must master if they are to become productive citizens of the next millennium.

In 1989, the National Council of Teachers of Mathematics (NCTM) in the US issued a set of standards for the mathematics curriculum, assessment and teacher education. The Commission on Standards for School Mathematics was charged with two tasks:

- To create a coherent vision of what it means to be mathematically literate both in a world that relies on calculators and computers to carry out mathematical procedures and in a world where mathematics is rapidly growing and is extensively being applied in diverse fields.
- To create a set of standards to guide the revision of the school mathematics curriculum and its associated evaluation towards this vision.

The K–12 standards of 1989 articulate five general goals for all students:

1 that they learn to value mathematics;
2 that they become confident in their ability to do mathematics;
3 that they become mathematical problem-solvers;
4 that they learn to communicate mathematically; and
5 that they learn to reason mathematically.

These goals imply that students should be exposed to numerous and varied interrelated experiences that encourage them to value the mathematical enterprise, to develop mathematical habits of mind, and to understand and appreciate the role of mathematics in human affairs; that they should be encouraged to explore, to guess and even to make and correct errors so that they gain confidence in their ability to solve complex problems; that they should read, write and discuss mathematics; and that they should conjecture, test and build arguments about a conjecture's validity (NCTM, 1989).

The 1989 Standards were immediately adopted by many schools in the USA, in some cases to an extreme degree. Some goals were misunderstood. The backfire emerged in the form of states calling for a return to basics: California even enacted this into law. As a result, NCTM has initiated a process of revision in the form of Standards 2000, which are currently (1998) in process. As the basis for Standards 2000, NCTM presented its set of core beliefs about students, teaching, learning and mathematics, some of which are as follows:

- Every student deserves an excellent programme of instruction in mathematics that challenges them to achieve at the high level required for productive citizenship and employment.
- Computational skills and number concepts are essential components of the mathematics curriculum, and knowledge of estimation and mental computation is more important than ever. By the end of the middle grades, students should have a solid foundation in numbers, algebra, geometry, measurement and statistics.
- Learning mathematics is maximised when teachers focus on mathematical thinking and reasoning. Progressively greater formal reasoning and mathematical proof should be integrated into the mathematics programme as a student continues through school.

- Learning mathematics is enhanced when content is placed in context and connected to other subject areas.
- The widespread impact of technology on nearly every aspect of our lives requires changes in the content and the nature of school mathematics programmes. Students should be able to use calculators and computers to investigate mathematical concepts and to increase their mathematical understanding.

Standards 2000 reflects the shift of the pendulum towards a more structured curriculum based on technology that calls for understanding and thinking without giving up growth in the facility of using mathematical concepts and formal tools.

ASSESSMENT

One cannot conclude this brief description of the state of the art without attending to matters of assessment. As with research and curriculum, the pendulum effect is easy to detect here as well. The post-Second World War period brought about the flourishing of the psychometric testing methods. Mathematics is one of the easiest disciplines for employing multiple-choice tests. A special spread of psychometric tests is connected to the revision movement and the cry for 'back to basics' that demanded 'accountability' of the schools for the mathematics learned in the school.

However, along with the ease of using psychometric tests, came their limitations. This type of testing could not capture any of the innovations in the curriculum. Nor could it produce any informative results about understanding and meaningful learning that the cognitive, as well as the constructivist, research pointed out and directed to. As a result, alternative assessment tools began to emerge alongside conventional assessment, in the form of open-ended problems, portfolio, protocols, etc.

In Standards 2000 the demands for assessment are as follows: 'The assessment of mathematical understanding must be aligned with the content taught and must incorporate multiple sources of information, including standardized tests, quizzes, observations, performance tasks, and mathematical investigations.' At present, the psychometric methods continue to serve as accountability tests, to satisfy the policy-makers. However, increasingly schools are employing alternative assessment modes to support their actual teaching in the classrooms and to address curriculum planning.

INTERNATIONAL STUDIES: TIMSS

Public concern about mathematics learning also finds an outlet in international comparisons. The last TIMSS (Third International Maths and Science Study) drew considerable international attention. It was the most comprehensive (and expensive) assessment ever attempted.

International comparisons are problematic. The educational systems of individual countries are embedded in their respective cultural traditions and have developed in different ways over the last decades. They differ with respect to their school populations and curricula, their school organisation, financing, teaching methods, values, etc. TIMSS is comprised of five components that provide context to the achievement findings:

1 a study of the curriculum of each country (including books);
2 an achievement study;
3 interviews with principal on school organisation and culture;
4 case studies of some countries;
5 videotaping of 231 classes in Germany, US and Japan.

Three populations (primary, secondary level I and secondary level II) were examined. The research questions were as follows:

1 How do countries vary in the intended learning goals for mathematics and science (intended curriculum) and what characteristics of educational systems, schools, students influence the development of those goals?
2 What opportunities are provided for students to learn mathematics and science (implemented curriculum); how do instructional practices in mathematics and science vary among nations; and what factors influence these variations?
3 What mathematics and science concepts, processes and attitudes have students learned (attained curriculum); and what factors are linked to students' opportunity to learn?
4 How are the intended, the implemented, and the attended curriculum related with respect to the context of education and arrangements for teaching and learning, and the outcomes of the educational process?

The TIMSS results are currently being studied by many countries and this will probably be an additional factor in shaping their future curriculum.

FINAL COMMENTS

Mathematics education is a young discipline. As part of the education sphere, it is still struggling to find its identity and to establish its theoretical basis. Yet recent research in this field has contributed enormously to our understanding of the difficulties faced by students in learning mathematics.

The current shift from the industrial society to the information society places mathematics at the very core of education, since the various aspects of mathematics are a necessity for today's educated citizen. While technology can alleviate much of the mathematical drudgery, there are human beings behind the technology that drives the machines who must be mathematically literate. Today knowledge of mathematics should not be the prerogative of only the most capable students, mathematics must reach every child. This is the mission of mathematics educators for the years to come.

REFERENCES

Anderson, J. R., Reder, L. M. and Simon, H. A. (1996) 'Situated learning and education'. *Educational Researcher*, 25 (4), 5–11.

Bauersfeld, H. (1995) 'The structuring of the structures: development and function of mathematizing as a social practice'. In L. S. G. Steffe (ed.), *Constructivism in Education*. Hillsdale, NJ: Lawrence Erlbaum Associates, 137–159.

Bendaz, N., Kieran, C. and Lee, L. (eds) (1996) *Approaches to Algebra*. vol. 18. Dordrecht: Kluwer.

Bishop, A., Clements, K., Keitel, C., Kilpatrick, J. and Laborde, C. (eds) (1996) *International Handbook of Mathematics Education*. Dordrecht, Boston, London: Kluwer Academic Publishers.

Carpenter, T. P., Moser, M. J. and Romberg, T. (eds) (1982) *Addition and Subtraction: A Cognitive Approach*. Hillsdale, NJ: Lawrence Erlbaum Associates.

Carraher, T. N., Carraher, D. W. and Schliemann, A. D. (1985) 'Mathematics in the streets and in the schools'. *British Journal of Developmental Psychology*, 3, 21–29.

Chazan, D. (1993) 'F (x) = G (x)? An approach to modeling with algebra'. *For the Learning of Mathematics*, 13, 22–26.

Cobb, P. (1985) 'Mathematical actions, mathematical objects, and mathematical symbols'. *The Journal of Mathematical Behavior*, 4, 127–134.

Cobb, P., Yackel, E. and Wood, T. (1992) 'A constructivist alternative to the representational view of mind in mathematics education'. *Journal for Research in Mathematics Education*, 23, 2–33.

Confrey, J. and Scarano, G. H. (1995) 'Splitting reexamined: Results from a three year longitudinal study of children in grades three to five'. Paper presented at the PME-NA, 17th, Columbus, OH.

Confrey, J. and Smith, E. (1994) 'Exponential functions, rates of change, and the multiplicative unit'. *Educational Studies in Mathematics*, 26, 135–164.

Davydov, V. V. (1969) 'The psychological analysis of multiplication procedures'. In V. V. Davydov (ed.) *The Psychological Capability of Young Children in Mastering Mathematics*. Moscow: Prosveshchinie, 3–63.

De Corte, E. and Verschaffel, L. (1981) 'Children's solution processes in elementary arithmetic problems: Analysis and improvement'. *Journal of Educational Psychology*, 73 (6), 765–779.

De Corte, E., Greer, B. and Verschaffel, L. (1996) 'Mathematics learning and teaching'. In D. C. Berliner and R. C. Calfee (eds) *Handbook of Educational Psychology*. New York: Macmillan, 491–549.

English, L. D. (ed.) (1997) *Mathematical Reasoning: Analogies, Metaphors, and Images*. vol. 1. Hillsdale, NJ: Lawrence Erlbaum Associates.

Fischbein, E. (1997) 'The concept of schema and its relevance for the education of mathematics teachers' (draft).

Fuson, K. (1982) 'An analysis of the counting-on solution procedure in addition'. In T. P. Carpenter, M. J. Moser and T. Romberg (eds), *Addition and Subtraction: A Cognitive Approach*. Hillsdale, NJ: Lawrence Erlbaum Associates, 67–81.

Fuson, K. (ed.) (1992) *Research on Whole Number Addition and Subtraction*. New York: Macmillan.

Gelman, R. (1978) 'Counting in the preschooler: What does and does not develop'. In R. S. Siegler (ed.), *Children Thinking: What Develops*. Hillsdale, NJ: Lawrence Erlbaum Associates.

Greeno, J. G. (1978a) 'A study of problem-solving'. In R. Glaser (ed.), *Advances in Instructional Psychology*. Vol. 1. Hillsdale, NJ: Lawrence Erlbaum Associates.

Greeno, J. G. (1978b) 'Understanding and procedural knowledge in mathematics instruction'. *Educational Psychologist*, 12 (3), 262–283.

Greer, B. (ed.) (1994) *Extending the Meaning of Multiplication and Division*. Albany, NY: State University of New York Press.

Grouws, D. (ed.) (1992) *Handbook of Research on Mathematics Teaching and Learning*. Reston: NCTM.

Hershkovitz, S., Nesher, P. and Yerushalmy, M. (1990) *Schemes for Problem Analysis (SPA)*. Tel Aviv: Centre for Educational Technology.

Hiebert, J. and Behr, M. (1988) *Number Concepts and Operations in the Middle Grades*. Reston: NCTM.

Hiebert, J. and Carpenter, T. P. (1992) 'Learning and teaching with understanding'. In D. Grouws (ed.), *Handbook of Research on Mathematics Teaching and Learning*. Reston: NCTM, 65–97.

Kaput, J. J. (1989) 'Linking representations in the symbol systems of algebra'. In S. Wagner and C. Kieran (eds), *Research Issues in The Learning and Teaching of Algebra*. Hillsdale, NJ: Lawrence Erlbaum Associates, 167–194.

Kilpatrick, J. (ed.) (1994) *Mathematics Instruction: Contemporary Research*. Oxford: Pergamon.

Kintsch, W. (1986) 'Learning from text'. *Cognition and Instruction*, 3 (2), 87–108.

Kintsch, W. and Kozminsky, E. (1977) 'Summarizing stories after reading and listening'. *Journal of Educational Psychology*, 69 (5), 491–499.

Laborde, C. (1990) 'Language and mathematics'. In P. Nesher and J. Kilpatrick (eds), *Mathematics and Cognition*. Cambridge: Cambridge University Press, 53–70.

Lave, J. (1988) *Cognition in Practice: Mind, Mathematics, and Culture in Everyday Life*. New York: Cambridge University Press.

Lave, J. and Wenger, E. (1991) *Situated Learning: Legitimate Peripheral Participation*. Cambridge: Cambridge University Press.

Nesher, P. (1982) 'Levels of description in the analysis of addition and subtraction word problems'. In T. Carpenter, T. Romberg and J. Moser (eds), *Addition and Subtraction: A Cognitive Approach*. Hillsdale, NJ: Lawrence Erlbaum Associates.

Nesher, P. (1989) 'Microworlds in mathematical education: A pedagogical realism'. In L. B. Resnick (ed.), *Knowing Learning and Instruction*. Hillsdale, NJ: Lawrence Erlbaum Associates, 187–215.

Nesher, P. and Katriel, T. (1977) 'A semantic analysis of addition and subtraction word problems in arithmetic'. *Educational Studies in Mathematics*, 8, 251–269.

Nesher, P. and Kilpatrick, J. (eds) (1990) *Mathematics and Cognition*. Cambridge: Cambridge University Press.

Nesher, P. and Teubal, E. (1975) 'Verbal cues as an interfering factor in verbal problem-solving'. *Educational Studies in Mathematics*, 6, 41–51.

Nesher, P., Greeno, J. J. and Riley, M. S. (1982) 'The development of semantic categories for addition and subtraction'. *Educational Studies in Mathematics*, 13, 373–394.

Paige, J. M. and Simon, H. A. (1966) 'Cognitive processes in solving algebra word problems', *Problem Solving: Research, Method and Theory*, Chichester: Wiley, 51–119.

Piaget, J. (1950) *The Psychology of Intelligence*. London: Routledge & Kegan Paul.

Piaget, J. (1952) *The Child's Conception of Number*. New York: Norton.

Polya, G. (1945) *How to Solve It*. Princeton, NJ: Princeton University Press.

Polya, G. (1954) *Mathematics and Plausible Reasoning*. Vol. 2. Princeton, NJ: Princeton University Press.

Polya, G. (1962) (Vol. 1); (1965) (Vol. 2); (1980) (combined edition, paperback). *Mathematical Discovery*. New York: Wiley.

Reusser, K. (1992) 'From text to situation to equation: cognitive simulation of understanding and solving mathematical word problems'. *Learning and Instruction*, 2, 477–497.

Schoenfeld, A. (1985). *Mathematical Problem Solving*. London: Academic Press.

Schoenfeld, A. H. (1987) 'What's all the fuss about metacognition?' In A. H. Schoenfeld (ed.), *Cognitive Science and Mathematics Education*. Hillsdale, NJ: Lawrence Erlbaum Associates, 189–215.

Schoenfeld, A. H. (ed.) (1991) *On Mathematics as Sense-Making: An Informal Attack on the Unfortunate Divorce of Formal and Informal Mathematics*. Hillsdale, NJ: Lawrence Erlbaum Associates.

Schoenfeld, A. H. (ed.) (1992) *Learning to Think Mathematically: Problem Solving. Metacognition, and Sense Making in Mathematics*. New York: Macmillan.

Steffe, L. P. (1996) 'Radical constructivism: a way of knowing and learning'. *ZDM*, 6, 202–204.

Steffe, L. P. and Gale, E. J. (eds) (1995) *Constructivism in Education*. Hillsdale, NJ: Lawrence Erlbaum Associates.

Vergnaud, G. (1983) 'Multiplicative structures'. In R. Lesh and M. Landau (eds), *Acquisition of Mathematical Concepts and Processes*. New York: Academic Press.

Verschaffel, L. a. D. C., E. (ed.) (1993a) *Word Problems. A Vehicle for Authentic Mathematical Understanding and Problem Solving in Primary School?* Hillsdale, NJ: Lawrence Erlbaum Associates.

Verschaffel, L. a. D.C., E. (1993b) 'A decade of research on word problem-solving in Leuven: Theoretical, methodological and practical outcomes'. *Educational Psychology Review*, 5, 239–256.

Von Glaserfeld, E. (1984) 'An introduction to radical constructivism'. In P. Walzwlawick (ed.), *The Invented Reality*. New York: Norton, 17–40.

von Glaserfeld, E. (ed.) (1991) *Radical Constructivism in Mathematics Education*. Dordrecht: Kluwer.

Vygotsky, L. S. (1962) *Language and Thought*. Cambridge, MA: MIT Press and Wiley.

Vygotsky, L. S. (1978) [1930]) *Mind in Society*. Cambridge, MA: Harvard University Press.

Wood, T., Cobb, P. and Yackel, E. (1990) 'The contextual nature of teaching: Mathematics and reading instruction in one second-grade classroom. *The Elementary School Journal*, 90 (5), 497–511.

Wood, T., Cobb, P. and Yackel, E. (1995) 'Reflection on learning and teaching mathematics in elementary school'. In L. P. Steffe and J. Gale (eds), *Constructivism in Education*. Hillsdale, NJ: Lawrence Erlbaum Associates, 401–423.

Yerushalmy, M. (1995) *Visual Mathematics: Algebra and Calculus* (Software and Curriculum Units). Tel Aviv: Centre for Educational Technology.

Yerushalmy, M. (1997) 'On syntax, semantics and technology. *International Journal of Computers for Mathematics Learning*.

Yerushalmy, M. (1998) 'Organizing the post-arithmetic curriculum around big ideas: An idea turned into practice' (draft).

Yerushalmy, M. and Gilead, S. (1997) 'Solving equations in a technological environment: Seeing and manipulating'. *Mathematics Teacher*.

47

SCIENCE EDUCATION

Have enquiry-oriented science curricula failed?

Pinchas Tamir

INTRODUCTION

Twenty years later

In 1970 Lee Shulman was asked by Robert Travers to write a chapter on science education for the prestigious *Second Handbook for Research on Teaching*. Fortunately for me, he decided to spend his sabbatical in Jerusalem and asked me to be a co-author.

More than twenty years later I was invited by the editors of this Companion to discuss the contemporary problems and issues in science education. I decided to describe the state of affairs in 1993 by looking back at Shulman and Tamir (1973) and comparing it with Gabel (1993). Following are some interesting figures, based on the data reported in or extracted from the two handbooks.

Altogether there were about 5,000 authors in 1993 compared with about 500 references and 400 authors in 1973. Out of these 5,000 authors, only 50 (1 per cent) were cited more than 10 times, while most authors were cited just once. The dominance of 'single article researchers' can be seen in 1973 references as well. Only 40 authors out of 5,500 are cited in both years. Those 40 researchers constitute 8 per cent and 0.8 per cent of the authors in 1973 and 1993, respectively. These figures imply that the majority of the references from 1973 were no longer considered useful in 1993.

Basic questions

However, when looking more carefully at the contents, one may notice that, in spite of the differences, some basic issues and problems have remained in 1993 much as they were in 1973. What knowledge is more worthwhile? How to teach it? How can we arrive at meaningful learning? How often and in what manner should the laboratory be used? What kind of teacher education should be provided? What are the relationships between cognition and affect? Is critical thinking a genuine universal skill or domain-specific?

In this chapter we attempt to provide some answers to such questions in selected areas.

EDUCATION OF SCIENCE TEACHERS

The space available in a volume of this scope will not permit us to deal with all aspects of teacher education. Hence, we focus on two topics that have undergone substantial development in recent years, namely: teacher education *knowledge* and the use of *research* as a basis for pedagogical decisions.

Knowledge demands

If there is one lesson that I can single out as a consequence of the curriculum reform of the 1960s and its followers, including computer-based instruction, it is the indispensability of the teachers. In this context the question of what knowledge a professional science teacher should have is quite in order. By *professional knowledge* we refer to a body of knowledge and skills which is needed in order to function successfully in a particular profession.

In order to function successfully as a science teacher, the teachers have to know a lot. We shall mention three important areas. First, knowledge of the subject matter, namely major ideas and theories of the discipline. Second, pedagogical knowledge, both general (e.g. designing different types of tests) and content specific (e.g. common conceptions, alternative conceptions and how to deal with them). Third, relevant ideas from and concepts in other domains (such as history, philosophy and sociology of science as developmental psychology, and Piaget). Moreover, along with broadness and versatility of the knowledge, it must be active and creatively usable in actual teaching. This implies that it should be practical. Teachers develop much of their practical knowledge by experiences and reflections on their experiences. Through practice and reflection it becomes their own personal knowledge (Clandinin, 1989; Connelly and Clandinin, 1990; Elbaz, 1981).

Presumably, teacher educators are already experts and very experienced professional teachers. Certainly, many of them have been active as teachers and teacher educators for a number of years. During this time a lot of opportunities have occurred for applying professional and personal knowledge in a variety of settings and contexts. Teacher educators may be expected to have available a repertoire of learning experiences for student teachers. The broader the personal/professional knowledge of teaching they have, the better are their chances of developing sound learning activities for teachers' education.

Teacher educators confront a heavy task. Their student teachers expect them to be able to demonstrate high-level, interesting and sophisticated teaching. Hence the teacher educators have a responsibility to find ways and means to make their instruction exemplary. The ability to select and plan worthwhile activities and to carry out exemplary teaching along with guiding reflective discussion is an example of a special kind of pedagogy that I propose to designate as Teacher Educator Pedagogy Knowledge. This kind of pedagogical knowledge cannot be developed without the experiences that teacher educators undergo when they teach pre-service teachers.

RESEARCH ON TEACHER EDUCATION

There are two kinds of research that are pertinent to teacher education. The first is research on various aspects of teacher education itself (e.g. Swift, N. J., cited in Tobin and Capie, 1981; Tamir and Ben-Peretz, 1981). The second is research on teaching which bears implications for teacher education. A common statement is frequently found at the end of research studies suggesting that the findings have 'important implications for teacher education'. This kind of suggestion is often meaningless, unless the authors specify in detail what is the nature of these implications and, even better, design and actually carry out additional studies to find out if their suggestions indeed work.

Wait-time

I have chosen, as an example, the research on wait-time. This research deals with clearly defined variables which can be measured reliably and appear to be relatively easy to manipulate. Rowe (1974), the creative inventor of wait-time, discovered that the quality of the verbal interaction that occurred in the classroom was related to the duration of the pauses separating speakers. Two types of pauses were identified: wait-time 1, defined as the length of time a teacher pauses after asking a question; and wait-time 2, defined as the time a teacher waits after a pupil response before a comment is made and another question asked. Rowe studied more than 300 elementary science classes and found a mean wait-time 1 of one second and a mean wait-time 2 of 0.9 seconds.

Following teacher training, when mean wait-time was extended beyond 3 seconds, significant improvements were observed, such as increase in length of student responses, incidence of speculative responses, incidence of questions asked by students, and the incidence of responses of slow learners.

Based on her findings, Rowe suggested the possibility of a mean wait-time of 3 seconds as a threshold below which there are no detectable changes in teacher and students' behaviours. Further studies corroborated the existence of this threshold phenomenon as well as other findings of Rowe (Tobin and Capie, 1981). It seems that we have at our disposal an unusually clear prescription for improving classroom transactions. Yet, further studies have revealed considerable difficulties (De Ture, 1979; Esquivel *et al.*, 1978; Swift N. J., cited in Tobin and Capie, 1981).

Difficulties with innovations

Tobin and Capie (1981) suggest that one reason for the relatively poor results of wait-time training may be the fact that the teacher is unable to control the wait-time of students. Shulman (1979) observed that the tendency has been for teachers to increase their wait-times during the training period but, upon returning to the classroom, rapidly to shorten them to their original length. Shulman suggests two possible reasons for this reversibility:

1 As the classroom pace slows, the frequency of pupil-initiated disruptions increases.

2 The higher quality of cognitive response is intrinsically less predictable than the lower quality. Most teachers would not tolerate ambiguity and lack of control over classroom events and hence they retreat to their more familiar and less threatening environment.

CURRICULUM AND INSTRUCTION

Science curriculum reform

Science curriculum reform was described by Bruner (1960) in a highly influential book, *The Process of Education*. This barely 90-page book communicated more than any other book that 'radical changes in the teaching of science are imminent' (Shulman and Tamir, 1973, p. 1098).

The Process of Education emphasised four conceptions which characterise the science curriculum reform that had started in the late 1950s:

1 *Structure* of subject matter. This includes issues such as instructional objectives, the nature of science, substantive (content) and syntactic (process) structure of the discipline, the nature of explanations and what consists as evidence in science.
2 *Learning*. This is an active process involving manipulation of materials, discovery and enquiry. Learning in the laboratory is essential.
3 *Teaching*. This should employ guided discovery (enquiry) and problem–solving rather than relying on and/or providing facts to be memorised. Individualisation of instruction is desirable.
4 *Instructional technology*. A variety of instructional media, including innovative apparatus such as single-concept loop films and inexpensive equipment for laboratory work.

Traditional and new

Since the major curriculum reforms of the late 1950s/early 1960s, many terms have been used to characterise the various programmes that were developed. Usually a new programme differs from the traditional in particular attributes, such as the use of the laboratory, working in small groups, or employing a Science Technology Society (STS) approach. The evaluation of the 'new' programme often includes a comparison with the existing or previous programme, referred to as 'traditional'. Notice, however, that 'traditional' is *not* a uniform 'creature', equally representing content and pedagogy. Instead, it represents a programme that was taught in schools prior to the introduction of the new programme. Usually it lacks certain attributes that were included in the new programme. This may be the reason for continuing to relate to the programme of the 1960s as 'new'.

Table 47.1 presents a list of dichotomies that clearly distinguish between 'traditional' and 'new' programmes, as well as instructional practices. In real life, a move towards the extreme poles is never recommended. A student, a class or a course should find the optimum level for their learning. The levels may change according to needs and goals of the user. The decision at which level a particular task or class should be taught is essential for successful learning.

Table 47.1 The nature of learning in traditional and innovative programmes

Traditional	New
Reception	Discovery
Prior knowledge not considered	Prior knowledge stressed
Rote	Meaningful
Recitation	Constructivism
Rhetoric of conclusions	Narrative of enquiry
Memorising facts	Critical thinking
Chalk and talk	Hands-on, laboratory
Passive	Active
Mechanical	Conceptual
Algorithmic reasoning	Problem-solving
Assessment by multiple choice	Alternative assessment
Competition	Co-operation
Teacher-centred	Student-centred
Research ignored	Teachers as researchers
Test purpose is giving grades	Tests provide feedback

Alternative frameworks and conceptions

No other area has grown as rapidly as the area of alternative conceptions. This can be seen from the fact that 25 years ago a comprehensive review of the research in science education has no mention of this topic (see Shulman and Tamir, 1973).

I begin by explaining why the field has headings such as preconceptions, children science, alternative frameworks and alternative conceptions, before turning to the reasons for the popularity of research in this field. I then move on to describe the notion of this popular field of research and continue by providing some suggestions for dealing with the problems in the teaching of science. This leads smoothly to the general principle of the effect of prior knowledge on subsequent learning and instruction. Although the research started by searching for misconceptions, most researchers prefer the term 'attention conceptions' or 'alternative frameworks', because the term 'alternative conceptions' allows the status of an alternative explanation which might be valid, whereas misconceptions are treated simply as mistakes.

There may be several reasons for this rapid development of alternative conceptions research, the latest bibliography of which amounted to 2,500 studies published in less than 20 years (Pfundt and Duit, 1994). The major reasons are presented below.

Popularity of research

1 Alternative conceptions are very common; anyone can find them. Hence they lend themselves very well as topics for dissertations.
2 Conceptions are domain-specific so science educators whose main preparation is in their subject matter can more easily be identified with such topics.

3 The application of findings of research in this area appears to be straightforward.
4 It marries the two 'camps' of science education researchers. From the 'Piagetians' comes the basic method, namely the clinical interview, whereas the theoretical foundations reflect Ausubel's (1968) notions on prior knowledge. It is true that Ausubel stressed the effect of prior knowledge as facilitator, while the alternative conceptions are usually discussed as being barriers to learning. However, the principle, namely the effect of prior knowledge on subsequent learning, is equally valid in both cases.
5 Physics is considered to be a difficult school subject, more difficult than chemistry and biology. This probably explains the fact that two-thirds of the studies reported by Pfundt and Duit (1994) are in physics, 20 per cent in biology and 15 per cent in chemistry. Thus it may be hypothesised that the wide distribution of alternative conceptions is a major reason for the difficulty in studying physics.

Attributes of alternative conceptions

In a review (Wandersee *et al.*, 1993, p. 195) the reviewers summarise what we have learned from these studies by proposing eight claims:

1 Learners come to formal science instruction with a diverse set of alternative conceptions concerning natural objects and events.
2 The alternative conceptions that learners bring to formal science instruction cut across age, ability, gender and cultural boundaries.
3 Alternative conceptions are tenacious and resistant to extinction by conventional teaching strategies.
4 Alternative conceptions often parallel explanations of natural phenomena offered by previous generations of scientists and philosophers.
5 Alternative conceptions have their origin in a diverse set of personal experiences, including direct observations and perceptions, peer culture and language, as well as in teachers' explanations and instructional materials.
6 Teachers often subscribe to the same alternative conceptions as their students.
7 Learners' prior knowledge interacts with knowledge presented in formal instruction, resulting in a diverse set of unintended learning outcome.
8 Instructional approaches that facilitate conceptual change can be an effective classroom tool.

Dealing with alternative conceptions

Although these eight claims are based on research, they constitute only part of the information that teachers need for dealing with particular alternative conceptions. Ideally the following stages should be followed:

1 identifying alternative conceptions;
2 discovering their origins;
3 designing instructional strategies to overcome these misconceptions;

4 trialling the effectiveness of these strategies;

5 training teachers in using these strategies;

6 evaluating the success of these teachers in implementing these strategies and in inducing conceptual change in their students.

In practice, extant research rarely goes beyond stage 1. Examples of a complete account covering all the six stages are rare. Perhaps the closest is photosynthesis, the topic most studied in biology (Anderson *et al.*, 1990; Barker and Carr, 1989a, 1989b; Bell, 1985; Dreyfus and Jungwirth, 1988; Eisen and Stavy, 1988, 1989; Fisher, 1985; Roth *et al.*, 1983; Stewart *et al.*, 1990; Wandersee, 1983, 1984, 1986).

Prior knowledge

The most important aim of teacher education with regard to alternative conceptions is getting them to experience ways and means of assessing prior knowledge. By prior knowledge we refer to knowledge which may affect the learning and understanding of new learning material. Assessment of prior knowledge has become a focus of interest with the increasing number of studies on students' preconceptions and misconceptions. One of the implications of these studies is the need to assess prior knowledge in relation to any important concept that is to be learned. There are many ways to accomplish this task, both formal and informal. For example, exploratory activities such as those recommended in the learning cycle approach (Lawson *et al.*, 1989) are no longer considered as fulfilling simply a motivation function. Rather they are seen as providing students with the opportunity to reveal their knowledge, much of which has been learned through life experience out of school.

PROCESSES OF LEARNING

What is discovery learning?

We find discovery learning as the main cornerstone of the curriculum reform and a convenient focus for dealing with the learning and teaching of science.

A major problem with the concept of discovery has been its use in different contexts to describe different attributes. With regard to the process of learning, it refers to the unique individual experience by which concepts evolve in the mind of the learner rather than being transmitted ready-made.

> Discovery applies so long as a specific rule or generalisation is not mentioned by a teacher. It is usually confined to hierarchically arranged subject matter in which the learner has considerable background. With instructions he has a fairly high probability of deriving by himself correct answers and generalisations.
>
> (Wittrock, 1966, p. 44)

Discovery learning is the opposite of 'reception', 'being told' or 'being passive'.

Presumed advantages

Four major advantages have been attributed by Bruner (1960) and others to the method of discovery:

- Discovery learning is more meaningful and hence results in better retention. 'To be amenable to learning by discovery what is taught can never be meaningless, useless, or arbitrary. Instead, it must be somehow rational and structured' (Wittrock, 1966, p. 29). 'Instead of mechanically memorising isolated bits of information, the student thinks, understands and applies.'
- Discovery learning enhances motivation, interest and satisfaction. Satisfaction is associated with intrinsic motivation, which is derived from a drive towards competence.
- Discovery learning enhances the development of intellectual capacities, information and problem-solving skills. Students learn how to discover, how to learn, and how to organise what they have learned.
- A generalised heuristics of discovery, which has been developed, enables the students to solve problems in new contexts, thus increasing the transfer of learning.

Presumed disadvantages

Discovery learning has not gained easy access in most schools. Several reasons may have accounted for reservations and reluctance on the part of many teachers to adopt it (Harris and Taylor, 1983; Wellington, 1981), such as lack of experience on the part of teachers and time pressure to cover the mandated curriculum.

Discovery learning can arouse feelings of uncertainty in both students and teachers, shaking the self-confidence of both. The challenge of discovery learning – especially in physics when many concepts, laws and theories are counter-intuitive – may be too high and lead to failure and dissatisfaction.

Inductive learning

Discovery learning is commonly equated with inductive learning when the subject proceeds from the specific to the general. It is just as plausible, however, to assume that the learner begins with a high-order generalisation from which he or she derives more specific conclusions and thus discovers answers and even generalisations (Wittrock, 1966, p. 42).

> Discovery is something that the student does beyond merely sitting in his seat and paying attention. . . . Discovery is a process of search and selection. . . . What is sought for and selected varies with the kind of learning taking place.
>
> (Gagne, 1966, pp. 149–150)

Two dimensions

Much progress has become possible as people realise that discovery learning is not an 'all or nothing' phenomenon, and that reception and discovery should be looked upon as opposites on a continuum. Two dimensions have frequently been used to distinguish discovery from nondiscovery learning, each of which constitutes an independent continuum. These dimensions are *guidance* and *sequence*.

Guidance

A useful framework for viewing the question of guidance has been suggested by Schwab (1962) in describing the use of an enquiring laboratory for the teaching of biology. Schwab first distinguishes among three components of the learning situation: (a) problems, (b) ways and means for discovering relations, and (c) answers. As can be seen in Table 47.2, there are a number of possible ways to permute these components to arrive at different levels of guidance or 'openness and permissiveness', to use Schwab's terms.

Herron (as reported by Shulman and Tamir, 1973) added the most highly guided dimension, where all three levels are given, and designated it as Level 0: namely, discovery is missing altogether. Herron analysed the proposed laboratory exercises in the manuals of two secondary science programmes, Physical Science Study Curriculum (PSSC) and Biological Science Curriculum Study (BSCS).

Herron found more than 80 per cent at Level 0 with discovery teaching. Herron's analysis finds that there is a massive difference between theory and practice, despite the claim that the laboratory had changed from a verification-demonstration activity under traditional programmes to an enquiry activity under new programmes. Similar results were obtained by others with regard to different programmes (Tamir and Garcia, 1992).

Sequence of instruction

An 'inductive sequence', wherein examples or observations precede generalisations, is inevitably dubbed the discovery treatment, while a 'deductive sequence', in which generalisations are provided first, to be followed by illustrations, is labelled the expository or nondiscovery treatment. The facile manner in which inductive sequencing is identified with discovery reflects a prevalent misunderstanding of how science is conducted. It reflects the pervasive influence of a tradition usually attributed to Bacon and Mill.

Table 47.2 Levels of openness in teaching by discovery

	Problem	*Ways/Means*	*Answers*
Level 0	given	given	given
Level 1	given	given	open
Level 2	given	open	open
Level 3	open	open	open

Sequence has received considerable attention. Thus, in an enquiry-oriented course, the laboratory should lead and take place prior to the theoretical study of the topic in class, or to the presentation of its findings in the textbook (Schwab, 1962). Certain particular sequences have been employed and found to be particularly effective. A good example is the 'learning cycle', which has been described in detail and its effectiveness confirmed experimentally (Lawson *et al.*, 1989).

Discovery and enquiry

Learning by discovery is often considered to be identical to learning by enquiry. Indeed, there are many similarities between enquiry and discovery, yet they are different. Bruner's conception of the structure of the disciplines implies that any learner, if guided properly, can discover that structure. Schwab's conception of structure is fundamentally different. For Schwab, structure such as that of science is not an existing entity to be discovered, but rather a framework imposed by the scientist on the subject matter. Hence, one can talk about enquiry as a property of science or as an instructional method that is similar to discovery. As already observed by Shulman and Tamir (1973, p. 1104), Schwab's distinction between 'science as enquiry' and 'teaching-learning as enquiry' is an important one. The first defines the substantive focus of the classroom – what is taught and learned. The second refers to the syntax of the classroom and its consequences, the nature of the transactions that will be conducted, the enquiry skills that will be mastered, and the attitudinal 'meta-lessons' that will be learned. In this definition of teaching-learning as enquiry, the activity in which the student participates is not scientific enquiry *per se* but the critical analysis, interpretation and evaluation of reports of scientific enquiry. Although this simulates many of the processes in which the scientist engages reflectively during enquiry, it does not require the student to conduct original enquiries in a laboratory.

'Of the two components – science as enquiry and the activity of enquiring – it is the former which should be given first priority as the objective of science teaching in the secondary school' (Schwab, 1962, p. 71). Criticism and reservations have usually alluded to enquiry as a teaching method, namely discovery learning. The desirability of the conception of 'science as enquiry' rather than 'rhetoric of conclusions' has reached a high level of consensus among science educators.

Discovery and constructivism

There is now extensive research which shows that

> what pupils learn from lesson activities, whether these involve talk, written text, or practical work, depends not only on the nature of the tasks set but on the knowledge schemes that pupils bring to these tasks. . . . Learning involves progressive development and restructuring of learners' knowledge schemes.
>
> (Driver, 1989, p. 484)

Since it is assumed that knowledge schemes are constructed by the student, this process of learning has been broadly termed 'constructivist'.

Since knowledge construction is an active process of the learner, the learning process appears to be very similar to discovery learning. The constructivist approach realises that the socially and culturally constructed ideas, principles, theories, and models

> cannot all be discovered by individuals through their empirical enquiry. . . . Learning involves being initiated into the culture of science. . . . Learners need to be given access not only to physical experiences but also to the concepts and models of conventional science.
>
> (Driver, 1989, p. 485)

What research says

Shulman and Tamir concluded their review by cautiously stating that

> although it has repeatedly been noted that no firm evidence in support of the superiority of discovery learning exists, there are enough suggestive studies and strong advocates, such as Schwab, to maintain the seriousness of the hypothesis that under certain conditions, such as those in which highly transferable problem-solving proficiencies and attitudes towards enquiry in science are the objectives of instruction, those sorts of activities advocated by Bruner or Schwab are more likely to be fruitful than those so strongly supported by Gagne or Ausubel.
>
> (Shulman and Tamir, 1973, p. 1118)

The following review of 20 years of subsequent research supports that conclusion. Unfortunately, empirical research carried out since the early 1970s on discovery learning has been scarce.

The research mentioned above established that more than 80 per cent of the science classes were operating at Level 0, namely problems, methods and answers, all given. Its diametric opposite would be minimum guidance (problems, methods and answers all left to student invention or discovery) and undetermined sequences left to student control. Examples of such minimum guidance and a great deal of students' interdependence can be found in the exploration phase in the 'learning cycle' (Lawson *et al.*, 1989), the BSCS Second Course *Interaction between Ideas and Experiments*, and individual research projects carried out by students, usually after school hours.

It should be emphasised that between the two extremes of method just delineated lies an impressive variety of pedagogical procedures. Even though more research on discovery learning is available in the 1990s than in the 1970s, it is still difficult to make sense of the data and apply them in teaching, since few researchers bothered to define their instruction in terms of the dimensions described above.

Critical thinking

The development of critical thinking has been one of the major unfulfilled goals of the enquiry-oriented curricula of the 1960s for three reasons. First, the most widely used evaluation instrument was the Watson Glazer Critical Thinking Appraisal (WGCTA), in which items 'do not refer specifically to science, so changes in score may as readily be attributed to the social studies and the English course as to a particular science course' (Ramsey and Howe, 1969, p. 65). This explanation is supported by the findings that critical thinking is partially domain-specific (Perkins and Salomon, 1989). Second, many teachers are reluctant to lose time on activities other than covering more science contents. Third, even when teachers recognise the importance of developing reasoning skills, many do not know how to do that.

Recently, along with the rising popularity of performance-based assessment, there appears to be a new interest in the development of reasoning. Two major approaches to the developing of reasoning can be identified: (a) special courses in critical thinking aimed at developing general processes and strategies of reasoning; and (b) the infusion approach, namely developing thinking is infused within regular disciplinary courses. The infusion approach has been shown to make three major contributions: developing reasoning in a specific subject, enhancing transfer to other domains, and improving understanding of subject matter (Zohar et al., 1994).

GENDER DIFFERENCES IN SCIENCE LEARNING

General trends

Research on differences between the sexes in relation to schooling and learning has received much attention in the last two decades. It is widely accepted that, as far as general intellectual ability is concerned, there are no differences between the sexes. Differences were found, however, in three cases:

1　In verbal ability females have the advantage, whereas males excel in numerical and spatial abilities (Maccoby and Jacklin, 1974; Steinkamp and Maehr, 1984).
2　Girls tend to succeed more in elementary school and less in high school. The 'breaking point' is the beginning of adolescence and this has caused researchers to explain the gender gap by the entry into sex roles (Nash, 1979). At this stage, girls show lower cognitive achievement in 'masculine' fields (Garratt, 1986) as well as lower aspirations towards future achievements.
3　There is greater motivation on the part of boys to achieve academically (ensuring superior occupational status) and lower motivation among girls, together resulting in the formation of an achievement gap at this stage (Kfir, 1988).

Importance of the issue

A number of major books have been published pointing at issues such as curricular differences for boys and girls (Department of Education, 1975), women in science (Kahle, 1985), schooling and sex roles (Hannan et al., 1983) and girls in physics (Royal Institute of Physics, 1982).

The rich information provided by the sources mentioned above has indicated that, in general, boys show higher achievement, are more interested in, and tend to have more positive attitudes towards science. Usually the differences are lowest at age 10 and greatest at age 17. For example, in the First International Science Study, the difference was about a quarter of a standard deviation at age 10, half a standard deviation at age 14 and three-quarters of a standard deviation at age 17 (Comber and Keeves, 1973). An increase in the gap with age is reported also by Johnson and Murphy (1986). In some countries, such as

India (Sansanwal, 1983), Singapore (Chy-Tin, 1986) and Canada (Ben-Peretz *et al.*, 1985) boys achieve better in all science subjects including biology. In other countries, such as the UK, boys were found to achieve better in chemistry and physics but not in biology (Johnson and Murphy, 1986).

It may be seen that there are indeed differences between boys and girls; however, this is no basis for assuming that all these differences are in favour of boys. Instead it is possible to identify certain features that clearly distinguish between boys' version of science on the one hand and girls' version of science on the other.

The various dimensions are interrelated in many ways and these relationships may vary under different circumstances and contexts. For example, career choices are affected by out-of-school activities and interests developed in young children as well as by role stereotypes, a history of success in studying science in school, social images and personal characteristics.

Equal achievement

With regard to achievement at senior high school, it appears that in biology and chemistry girls achieve as well as or better than boys. Although in physics boys still achieve more than girls, the gap is half of that which exists in grade 9. Still the under-achievement of girls in physics remains a puzzle.

Girls have emerged as showing significantly more favourable orientation towards enquiry and practical work in the laboratory. It may be speculated that if physics were taught with greater emphasis on enquiry, girls' achievement might improve and the sex-achievement gap would disappear.

The crucial period

Although the underachievement of grade 12 girls in physics needs attention, the most important implication of this research is the urgent need to improve the achievement and attitudes of girls at junior high school.

It appears that the junior high school plays a crucial role in distracting girls and pushing them away from science. The negative experiences during this crucial period may be one of the main reasons why two-thirds of the students who stay away from science in grades 11 and 12 are girls.

By grade 10, when students make their choices for specialised fields of study in grades 11 and 12, we begin to see the interaction between sex and the different science disciplines. At this time the biology–physics polarity emerges, with chemistry occupying a place in the middle. This is also the time when another polarity is at work, namely the plants–animals polarity. Thus, on average, males are more oriented towards physics and engineering, while females are more oriented towards biology. Within biology, females have a higher preference than males for plants, and stronger reservations regarding the use of live animals in the study of biology.

Conclusions about gender

Five major conclusions are set out below.

1 In elementary school there are no sex differences in attitudes and only a small advantage to males in achievement in the physical sciences.

2 Very large sex differences in all areas exist at the end of junior high school and only 34 per cent of the students who elect to take specialised science subjects in senior high schools are girls.

3 Among students who specialise in science in senior high school there are, on average, no sex differences in biology and in chemistry, but males excel in physics.

4 Two sex polarities were found, namely, biology (females)/physics (males) and botany (females)/zoology (males).

5 Females' orientation to science is enhanced by enquiry and laboratory-based instruction.

EVALUATION IN SCIENCE LEARNING

New trends

This chapter on assessment and evaluation could not have been written even ten years ago. Some of the well-established routines of assessment (e.g. multiple-choice items, norm-referenced test scores) have been shaken and new terms (e.g. performance-based assessment, self-assessment, portfolios) have become dominant in the field of education.

Purpose of evaluation

Evaluation has always been an important cornerstone of education. The main reason for this is the basic need of educators to know whether their educational intentions are realised, to what extent their educational activities achieve their goals, how these activities affect different students, and how best to plan for a continuous and optimal instruction.

Student assessment

Student assessment may be defined as a systematic collection of information about student learning and other variables that are associated with particular learning experiences. Student assessment has traditionally relied on measures, instruments and methodologies developed by measurement experts and based on measurement theories that yield quantitative data that served to rank-order individuals within given groups such as a classroom, a school or a particular age-cohort. The results of assessment have been typically used for selection and classification, for example serving as criteria for admitting candidates to prestigious schools.

Multiple choice criticised

Traditional multiple-choice achievement tests in science have been criticised in several ways (e.g. Shavelson *et al.*, 1990). Despite their efficiency (economical to develop, administer and score), they do not measure some aspects of the knowledge that are valued in science education, such as the ability to formulate a problem or carry out an investigation. Consequently, they provide only limited information about what the students know and can do in science.

Performance assessment

Performance-based assessments have caught public attention in recent years as an alternative to multiple-choice tests. Performance assessments are assumed to tap 'higher-order thinking processes' and to be more directly related to what students do in their classroom and what scientists actually do – observe, hypothesise, record, infer and generalise.

The promising advantages of performance assessments led educators and policy-makers to assume that educational progress can be achieved and monitored by this 'new' testing technology. Consequently, many educators are trying to move towards the 'new' technologies. At the same time, however, some people are beginning to have second thoughts regarding the wisdom of making hasty and unfounded decisions concerning multiple-choice items.

Based on a long history of performance-based tests in medical education, Swanson *et al.* (1995) identify eight lessons. Listed below are four of these lessons:

- No matter how realistic a performance-based assessment is, it is still a simulation and examinees do not behave in the same way as they would in real life (p. 7).
- It is difficult to develop scoring keys that appropriately reward alternate answers that are equivalent in quality (p. 8).
- Performance in one context does not predict performance in other contexts very well (p. 8).
- Neither traditional testing nor performance-based assessment methods are a panacea. Selection of assessment method should depend on the skills to be assessed and, generally, the use of a blend of methods is desirable (p. 11).

Framework

The most widely used framework for evaluation of student attainment was for 30 years the taxonomy of educational objectives in the cognitive domain (Bloom *et al.*, 1956) and in the affective domain (Krathwohl *et al.*, 1964). While this framework can be and was applied to science students, it has soon been realised that, for many purposes, it is too general. Consequently, special science taxonomies have been designed (e.g. APU, 1981; Tamir *et al.*, 1982). Today, Bloom's taxonomy seems outdated and there are several other frameworks for evaluating students' achievement (e.g. the framework used in the Third International Mathematics and Science Study (TIMSS); Beaton *et al.*, 1996).

Curriculum reform and student assessment

For many decades, assessment has acted as a barrier to many innovations. There are at least two major reasons why testing would act as a barrier. First, teachers teach and students study towards success in the tests. *Innovations that compete with tests are bound to fail.* Second, tests that do not match the innovation fail to reveal the impact of the innovation. The commonly heard statement that the 'new' curricula of the 1960s have failed to achieve their goals has been based on results of paper and pencil, multiple-choice questions that favour rote learning and memorisation and, consequently, cannot reveal gain in higher-order thinking. Finally, quite often the implementation of innovations has not been actual-ised even when the class was using the 'new' text. In these cases the teachers continued to teach in their traditional manner with the new text. Consequently the intended opportun-ities to learn have not taken place. Under these circumstances no wonder that the intended has not been attained.

A balanced student assessment

Ideally, an assessment programme should reflect the goals and experiences of the curric-ulum to such an extent that when students study towards the tests, they will be doing what they are intended to do in their school studies. For example, high school students who specialise in biology in Israel have been assessed at their graduation from school by a series of external examinations, as well as by their teachers. The final grade is the average of the two grades.

Table 47.3 presents the entire assessment programme. An examination of Table 47.3 shows how studying towards various components of the assessment programme is likely to result in an in-depth, comprehensive and balanced operational curriculum.

SPECIAL ISSUES

THE TEACHING OF EVOLUTION

Importance of the theory of evolution

The teaching of Darwin's theory of evolution is one of the controversial issues in the biology curriculum. For biologists, ignoring the theory of evolution has the same effect as depriving a mammal of its backbone, namely, weakening the framework which makes biol-ogy unique and coherent. The teaching of evolution poses two dilemmas, one concerned with faith and the other with instruction.

The faith dilemma

Many religious people conceive the theory of evolution as challenging and calling into question the truth of the biblical story of the Creation. This often results in deleting the

Table 47.3 The assessment components of high school students who specialise in biology in Israel

Teacher's grade (50%)	*External examination grade (50%)*	
Teacher-made tests	**Paper and pencil**	
Homework	30 items multiple choice	30
Participation in class	3 items multiple choice with	
Individual ecological project	justifications	6
Other	3 data based and/or essay	39
	1 unseen passage of research to be	
(*Note:* Teachers are free to decide how	analysed and plan a next step	25
to assess and what weight to assign to		
each component)	Total	100
	Practical	
	Planning and carrying out an	
	investigation in the laboratory	50
	Oral examination on individual	
	ecological project	38
	Identifying unknown plant with a	
	dichotomous key	12
	Total	100
	(*Note:* The paper-and-pencil test constitutes 60% and the practical 40% of the matriculation final score)	

topic from the biology course. Schwab (1963, p. 33) observed that 'the usage of the Theory of Evolution is often taken to mean that evolution is but an envisaged possibility, something uncertain and unproved'. However, Schwab continues: 'this interpretation . . . is due to a mistaken idea about the meaning of "theory" and its place in science'.

The instructional dilemma

Often the study of evolution takes place at the end of the high school biology course, when the mechanism of evolution can be explained and understood in terms of various processes and concepts such as mutation, genetic recombination, homology versus analogy, population, adaptation and so on. Students need to have the opportunity to study the relevant topics before embarking on a systematic study of Darwin's theory and comparing it with competing views such as Lamarckism.

There are, however, at least two compelling reasons for studying the theory of evolution rather early in the course. The first is that in order to make sense of what they learn, students should be able to interpret much of the material covered in earlier parts of the course in terms of the theory of evolution. The second reason is that the theory of evolution can serve as an excellent advance organiser for the study of biology (Ausubel, 1968). Understanding the main ideas and assumptions of the theory will facilitate the learning of many biological concepts and principles such as classification, the complementarity of structure and function, or the relationship between organisms and their environment.

Conclusion

It is therefore recommended that a brief account of the theory of evolution be studied early in the course and be built up on the knowledge and experience that students had while studying natural history in the elementary and middle schools. In addition, an extended study should take place towards the end of the course in grade 12.

Tamir (1993) describes four possible approaches to the teaching of evolution in grade 12, and, based on research results, particularly recommends the historical approach.

THE SCIENCE TECHNOLOGY SOCIETY (STS) APPROACH

Increased emphasis on STS

There are many good reasons for adopting an STS approach. Some of these are presented in the following citation:

> Progress in science and technology (genetic engineering and nuclear weaponry, for example) forces us to confront rapid changes and raises what were once intellectual abstractions to the level of hard, often painful reality for individuals, families and nations.

STS and enquiry

Since hands-on activities have been one of the unique features of learning science and they constitute a major component of an enquiry-oriented STS programme, it is especially useful to compare and identify the differences between traditional activities and STS enquiry-oriented activities.

The increasing interest in STS and its success, especially when it integrates an enquiry approach, justifies the prediction that its popularity and adoption will continue to grow.

Decision-making

The STS approach starts with the students, with their interests, and with what is relevant to their lives. It builds on local resources and it has assigned to the teachers the role of the decision maker regarding the curriculum structure and the instructional approaches used. Although the teacher is the decision maker regarding the curriculum and instruction, this does not negate the central position of the students. The decisions teachers make relate to the use of student questions and ideas and how they help meet course and curriculum goals. Teachers as decision makers does not mean decisions concerning the concepts and processes to which students will be exposed. It does not mean didactic teaching based on the textbook. Although the teacher is a decision maker about the curriculum framework and teaching strategies, students are encouraged to make decisions regarding issues and questions, how to pursue them, how to get needed information, how to use information, and what actions to take.

Like any other major reform, the STS approach requires special attention in pre-service and in-service education of teachers as well as continuing support and guidance to teachers.

RECENT TRENDS

Different emphases for different ages

Whereas the 1960s emphasised the development of process skills, including a demand for abstract reasoning that was beyond the capability of many students, the most popular view in the 1990s, according to the National Research Council, Committee on High School Biology Education (1990, p. 17), is that biology in the elementary school 'should focus on natural history, be integrated with other subjects whenever possible, and emphasise observation, interpretation and hands-on involvement, rather than memorisation of facts'. Thus, when entering the middle or junior high school, students are not expected to have mastered particular concepts, but rather 'to have developed "intuitive" understanding of biological diversity and relationships of living organisms' (ibid., p. 14).

In the middle school, the specific needs and interests of early adolescents who are especially curious about themselves point directly at a human biology course, which will have biological, cultural and social dimensions (ibid., pp. 18–20).

More choice, more depth

In the high school, 'we need a much leaner biology course that is constructed from a small number of general principles that can serve as scaffolding on which students will be able to build further knowledge' (ibid., p. 21). Moreover the concepts must be presented 'in such a manner that they are related to the world that students understand' and must be taught 'with ample time for discussion with peers and with the teacher' and be 'based on observation or experimentation confronting the essence of the material' (ibid., p. 25).

To achieve these aims, two interesting and almost opposite directions have been taken by different countries. In the United Kingdom and the United States, with their decentralised education, national and/or state curricula have been implemented. In many centralised educational systems, on the other hand, the trend is towards less control by the centre. In Israel, for example, increased in-depth study of fewer subjects has been instituted by offering an 'all-elective' curriculum in high school biology. This means that teachers do not have to cover the 15 topics that appear on the syllabus. Rather they have to choose nine topics, and they can teach for in-depth understanding by using a variety of instructional approaches such as investigations, discussions and problem-solving.

REFERENCES

Anderson, C., Sheldon, T. and Dubay, J. (1990) 'The effects of instructions on college non-majors' concepts of respiration and photosynthesis'. *Journal of Research in Science Teaching*, 27, 761–766.

Assessment of Performance Unit (APU) (1981) *Science in Schools, Age 11, Report No. 1*. London: HMSO.

Ausubel, D. P. (1968) *Educational Psychology: A Cognitive View*. New York: Holt, Reinhart & Winston.

Barker, M. and Carr, M. (1989a) 'Teaching and learning about photosynthesis. Part I: An assessment in terms of students' prior knowledge'. *International Journal of Science Education*, 11, 49–56.

Barker, M. and Carr, M. (1989b) 'Teaching and learning about photosynthesis. Part II: A generative learning strategy'. *International Journal of Science Education*, 11, 141–152.

Beaton, A. E., Martin, M. O., Mulis, I. V. S., Gonzales, C. J., Smith, T. A. and Kelly, D. L. (1996) 'Science achievement in the middle school years'. IEA Third International Mathematics and Science Study (TIMSS), Chestnut Hill, MA, Boston College, Boston.

Bell, B. (1985) 'Students' ideas about plant nutrition. What are they?' *Journal of Biological Education*, 19, 213–218.

Ben-Peretz, M., Menis, J. and Raphael, D. (1985) 'Biology in the upper school: Achievement, intentions and perceived opportunities to learn'. Unpublished report. Toronto, The Ontario Institute for Studies in Education.

Bloom, B. S., Krathwohl, D. R. and Masia, B. B. (1956) *Taxonomy of Education Objectives: The Classification of Educational Goals, Handbook I: Cognitive Domain*. New York: McKay.

Bruner, J. (1960) *The Process of Education*. Cambridge, MA: Harvard University Press.

Chy-Tin, L. (1986) 'Attitudes and learning behavior correlates of science performance of secondary school students in Singapore'. Unpublished Master's dissertation, National University of Singapore.

Clandinin, D. J. (1989) 'Developing rhythm in teaching: The narrative study of a beginning teacher's personal practical knowledge of classrooms'. *Curriculum Inquiry*, 19 (2), 121–141.

Comber, L. C. and Keeves, J. P. (1973) *Science Education in Nineteen Countries*. Stockholm: Almquist & Wiskell.

Connelly, F. M. and Clandinin, D. J. (1990) 'Stories of experience and narrative inquiry'. *Educational Researcher*, 19 (5), 2–14.

De Ture, I. P. (1979) 'Relative effects of modeling on the acquisition of wait time by chemistry teachers and concomitant changes in dialogue patterns'. *Journal of Research in Science Teaching*, 16, 553–562.

Department of Education (1975) *Curricular Differences for Boys and Girls*. London: HMSO.

Dreyfus, A. and Jungwirth, E. (1988) 'The cell concept of 10th graders: Curricular expectations and reality'. *International Journal of Science Education*, 10, 221–229.

Driver, R. (1989) 'Students' conceptions and the learning of science'. *International Journal of Science Education*, 11, 481–490.

Eisen, Y. and Stavy, R. (1988) 'Students' understanding of photosynthesis'. *American Biology Teacher*, 50, 208–212.

Eisen, Y. and Stavy, R. (1989) 'Development of a new science study unit following research on students' ideas about photosynthesis'. In P. Adey (ed.), *Adolescent Development and School Science*. London: Falmer Press, 295–302.

Elbaz, F. (1981) 'The teacher's "practical knowledge": Report of a case study'. *Curriculum Inquiry*, 11 (1), 43–71.

Esquivel, J. M., Lashier, W. S. and Smith, W. S. (1978) 'Effect of feedback on questioning of preservice teachers in SCIS micro-teaching'. *Science Education*, 62, 209–213.

Fisher, K. (1985) 'A misconception in biology: Amino acids and translations'. *Journal of Research in Science Teaching*, 21, 53–62.

Gabel D. (ed.) (1993) *Handbook of Research in Science Teaching and Learning*. New York: Macmillan.

Gagne, R. E. (1966) 'Varieties of learning and the concept of discovery'. In L. S. Shulman and E. R. Keislar (eds), *Learning by Discovery: A Critical Approach*. Chicago: Rand McNally.

Garratt, L. (1986) 'Gender differences in relation to science choice at A level'. *Educational Review*, 38, 67–77.

Hannan, D., Breen, R., Murray, B., Hartman, N., Watson, D. and O'Higgins, K. (1983) *Schooling and Sex Roles: Sex Differences in Subject Provision and Student Choice in Irish Post Primary Schools*. Dublin: The Economic and Social Research Institute.

Harris, D. and Taylor, M. (1983) 'Discovery learning in school science: The myth and the reality'. *Journal of Curriculum Studies*, 15, 277–289.

Johnson, S. and Murphy, P. (1986) *Girls and Physics*. APU Occasional Paper 4. London: Department of Education and Science.

Kahle, J. B. (ed.) (1985) *Women in Science*. New York: Falmer Press.

Kfir, D. (1988) 'Achievements and aspirations among boys and girls in high school: A comparison of two Israeli ethnic groups'. *American Educational Research Journal*, 25, 213–236.

Krathwohl, D. R., Bloom, B. S. and Masia, B. B. (1964) *Taxonomy of Educational Objectives, Handbook II: Affective Domain*. New York: McKay.

Lawson, A., Abraham, M. R. and Renner, J. W. (1989) *A Theory of Instruction: Using the Learning Cycle to Teach Science Concepts and Thinking Skills*. NARST Monograph No. 1.

Maccoby, E. E. and Jacklin, C. N. (1974) *The Psychology of Sex Differences*. Stanford, CA: Stanford University Press.

Nash, S. C. (1979) 'Sex role as a mediator of intellectual functioning'. In M. A. Wittig and A. C. Peterson (eds), *Sex Related Differences in Cognitive Functioning*, New York: Academic Press, 263–302.

National Research Council, Committee on High School Biology Education (1990) *Fulfilling the Promise: Biology Education in the Nation's Schools*. Washington DC: National Academy Press.

Perkins, D. and Salomon, G. (1989) 'Are cognitive skills context bound?' *Educational Researcher*, 18, 16–25.

Pfundt, H. and Duit, R. (1994) *Students' Alternative Frameworks and Science Education* (4th edn). Kiel: Institute of Science Education, University of Kiel.

Ramsey, G. A. and Howe, R. E. (1969) 'An analysis of research on institutional procedures in secondary school science. Part I: outcomes of instruction'. *The Science Teacher*, 37 (3), 62–70.

Roth, K., Smith, E. and Anderson, C. (1983) *Students' Conceptions of Photosynthesis and Food for Plants*. East Lansing, MI: Institute for Research on Teaching, Michigan State University.

Rowe, M. (1974) 'Relation of wait-time and rewards as instructional variables and their influence on language, logic and fate control'. *Journal of Research in Science Teaching*, 11, 502–556.

Royal Institute of Physics (1982) *Girls in Physics*. London: Royal Society and Institute of Physics.

Sansanwal, D. N. (1983) 'Sex differences in attitude to, interest in and achievements in science – a review of Indian research'. In *Contributions to the Second GASAT Conference*. Oslo: Institute of Physics, 152–162.

Schwab, J. J. (1962) 'The teaching of science as enquiry'. In J. J. Schwab and P. F. Brandwein (eds), *The Teaching of Science*. Cambridge, MA: Harvard University Press.

Schwab, J. J. (1963) *Biology Teachers' Handbook*. New York: Wiley & Sons.

Shavelson, R. J., Carey, N. B. and Webb, A. M. (1990) 'Indicator of science achievement: Options for a powerful policy instrument'. *Phi Delta Kappan*, 71, 692–697.

Shulman, L. S. (1963) 'Research on teaching: The missing link in curriculum implementation'. In P. Tamir, A. Hofstein and M. Ben-Peretz (eds), *Preservice and Inservice Education for Science Teachers*. Rehovot: Balaban, 77–84.

Shulman, L. S. and Tamir, P. (1973) 'Research on teaching in the natural sciences'. In R. M. W. Travers (ed.), *Second Handbook of Research on Teaching*. Chicago: Rand McNally, 1098–1140.

Steinkamp, M. W. and Maehr, M. L. (1984) 'Gender differences in motivational orientation towards achievement in school science: A quantitative synthesis'. *American Educational Research Journal*, 21, 39–59.

Stewart, J., Hafner, B. and Dale, M. (1990) 'Students' alternative use of meiosis'. *American Biology Teacher*, 52, 228–232.

Swanson, D. B., Norman, G. R. and Linn, R. L. (1995) 'Performance based assessment: Lessons from the health professions'. *Educational Researcher*, 24 (5), 5–11.

Tamir, P. (1993) 'The curriculum potential of Darwin's theory of evolution'. *Interchange*, 24, 73–86.

Tamir, P. and Ben-Peretz, M. (1981) 'Source of knowledge and curriculum material used by preservice teachers in Israel'. *Studies in Education*, 31, 85–98 (in Hebrew).

Tamir, P. and Garcia, P. (1992) 'Characteristics of laboratory exercises included in science text in Catalonia, Spain'. *International Journal of Science Education*, 14, 381–392.

Tamir, P., Nussinovitz, R. and Friedler, Y. (1982) 'The design and use of practical tests assessment inventory'. *Journal of Biological Education*, 16, 42–50.

Tobin, K. G. and Capie, N. (1981) *Wait Time and Learning Science*. Burlington: American Association for the Education of Science Teachers and North Carolina Supply Co.

Wandersee, J. H. (1983) 'Students' misconceptions about photosynthesis: A cross-age study'. In H. Helm and J. D. Novak (eds), *Proceedings of the International Seminar on Misconceptions in Science and Mathematics*. Ithaca, NY, 451–466.

Wandersee, J. H. (1984) 'Why can't they understand how plants make food? Students' misconceptions about photosynthesis'. *Adaptation*, 6 (3), 13–17.

Wandersee, J. H. (1986) 'Can the history of science help science educators anticipate students' misconceptions?' *Journal of Research in Science Teaching*, 23, 581–597.

Wandersee, J. H., Mintzes, J. J. and Novak, J. D. (1993) 'Research on alternative conceptions in science'. In D. Gabel (ed.), *Handbook of Research on Science Teaching and Learning*. New York: Macmillan.

Wellington, J. J. (1981) 'What is supposed to happen, Sir? Some problems with discovery learning'. *School Science Review*, 63, 167–173.

Wittrock, M. C. (1966) 'The learning by discovery hypothesis'. In L. S. Shulman and E. R. Keislar (eds), *Learning by Discovery: A Critical Approach*. Chicago: Rand McNally.

Zohar, A., Weinberger, J. and Tamir, P. (1994) 'The effect of the Biology Critical Thinking Project on the development of critical thinking'. *Journal of Research in Science Teaching*, 31, 183–196.

48

THE PAST, PRESENT AND FUTURE OF HISTORY TEACHING IN SCHOOLS

Tony Taylor

INTRODUCTION

Of all school activities, history has acquired a contradictory reputation for being the most robustly controversial, the least immediately relevant and, at the same time, one of the most consistently boring subjects in the curriculum. These peculiar contradictions have become more, rather than less, apparent during a century and a half of popular education and, since the mid-nineteenth century, history as a school subject has advanced, retreated, recovered and then been forced back yet again by successive waves of debate, ideological change and curriculum reform. This state of flux has not been helped by some very poor teaching of a subject which is often regarded by school authorities as more an amalgam of civic instruction and general knowledge than a reputable specialist discipline.

Nevertheless, whilst sometimes at the centre of the curriculum, sometimes on the margins, history retains, in a new millennium, the potential to be at once the most empowering and the most oppressive single subject in the school curriculum. Empowerment may come from developing in students a rational capacity for examining evidence, comprehending the relationships that existed (and still exist) between individuals, ideology and historical change. Oppression may come when, as has so often happened in the past, history becomes merely a means of political or religious self-justification. This article will discuss some developments in the teaching and learning of history, focusing on three democratic states: the United Kingdom, the United States and Australia, but will also make reference to school history as it is taught to other kinds of political systems.

FROM THE OLD TO THE NEW HISTORY

A major feature of history in schools during the first half of the twentieth century was the primacy of factual knowledge. A second important feature was the selection of facts which focused on civic justification of the dominant political culture, even in progressive democracies. Thus, in the United States for example, a survey of history in elementary schools during the 1960s indicated that a disproportionate period of time was devoted to the Colonial Period and to the American Revolution whilst in the United Kingdom, as late as the early 1960s, lists of early kings and queens (with attached anecdotes) featured strongly in the school history curriculum, to be replaced, when examining the nineteenth and twentieth centuries, by lists of prime ministers and governments, all moving inexorably towards a better world. As a further demonstration of the link between school history and ruling cultures, in Australian schools, until the 1940s, a major focus of historical syllabuses was on the colonising mother nation Britain, rather than on Australia, which had already gained almost complete independence in 1901.

The consequence was that, because of this traditionalist view of school history, generations of elementary and high school students in the United States, the United Kingdom and Australia were the victims of an obsession with facts, but facts with a specific political context. Moreover, this political/traditional approach to the construction of the history curriculum was not just a characteristic of the USA, the UK and Australia but was also a widespread phenomenon in all democratic states, mainly because it was regarded as ideologically sound and comfortable but partly also because there seemed to be no valid alternative.

The 1960s, however, saw the development of a new and liberating movement in political and educational circles across the Western world, a change of attitude to authority, a growth of internally directed criticism and even protest. Accordingly, in conjunction with a better understanding of the relationship between psychology and the study of history and reformist initiatives in social studies teaching, an opportunity arose for progressive history teachers to move on from simple, fact-based syllabuses and turn to an alternative kind of historical study, labelled 'New History', founded on critical analysis of the past through the development of classroom-based historical methodology.

PSYCHOLOGY AND THE STUDY OF HISTORY IN SCHOOLS

Until the 1960s, it had been the philosophers and philosopher/historians (for example, Collingwood, Oakeshott and Walsh) who had dominated the debate about what constituted historical thinking. A change came in the mid-1960s, when the growing importance of educational psychology saw the removal of the debate from narrow rationalist epistemological discourse about the conflict between narrative post-Hegelian idealists on the one hand and post-Marxist covering law theorists on the other, and the placing of the discussion more firmly in mainstream deliberation about the cognitive aspects of the historical process. Unfortunately, the debate then lost its way as psychologists with a little history joined argument with historians who had acquired a little psychology.

One of the major problems faced by 1960s teachers of history when they attempted to establish a relationship between psychology and the study of history in schools was the dearth of relevant, psychological studies apart from those of Piaget and co-worker Barbara Inhelder. These Piagetian studies, with their emphasis on visuo–spatial and linguistic experiments, were quickly adopted by some early researchers and used to develop a model of the historical conceptual development of children. In summary, some researchers asserted (Hallam, 1971; Peel, 1967) that the three Piagetian stages (pre-operational/

concrete operational/formal operational) seemed to correspond to stages in the development of historical thinking and understanding. At the pre-operational stage for example, young school students often failed to make sense of historical information. At the concrete stage, students could describe historical events. At the formal operational stage, students could make effective inferences from limited information and hypothesise as to motivation and causation. Peel termed the latter two stages descriptive (concrete) and explanatory (formal operational).

However, the post-Piagetian researchers were criticised for trying too hard to slot children's historical conceptual development into the Piagetian three-stage model of chronological development. The Piaget/Peel model was considered to be (a) restrictive – in that it seemed to be tied to chronological age, (b) inappropriate – in that it related to scientific rather than humanistic modes of thought and (c) over-convenient – in that teachers could all too easily grasp a fairly simplistic and possibly facile explanation of what might be happening in their history classes.

Later research studies revised the model into a more complex series of conclusions which suggested that historical understanding was a much more intricate process than had been at first thought. Generally, categories of historical thinking and understanding fell under these major headings.

- an understanding of the use and value of different forms of evidence;
- a capacity to establish causal links between events;
- an understanding of change over time;
- an ability to see events from the point of view of participants (empathy);
- an ability to sift through evidence, produce a working hypothesis and produce conclusions (historical explanation) that are open-ended, i.e. not necessarily conforming to the teacher's interpretation;
- an ability to report conclusions and place events in a proper historical context.

These attributes required quite advanced cognitive and affective skills which, the research indicates, were evident at most levels in school, albeit at a very basic level in young primary school students. A child's ability to demonstrate these modes of thought is commonly found to start between the ages of 7–10 (prior to the 7–8 age range concepts of time, causality inference and reporting were difficult for young primary school students), to develop substantially between the ages of 10–14, and to reach a more sophisticated level of operation between the ages of 14–16. As earlier researchers had found, this is broadly in line with Piaget's stages but later research had indicated that students at quite early ages were able to demonstrate some aspects of historical thinking notwithstanding their chronological position in the Piagetian model (Cooper, 1994).

REFORMING THE HISTORY CURRICULUM AND NEW HISTORY

A significant change of attitude and practice in the teaching and learning of history has taken place during the last quarter of the twentieth century. Once, the idea that elementary and high school students should work from source materials of various categories (e.g. documents/artefacts/film) was considered risible by professional historians and some

845

history teachers; now it is almost axiomatic that the starting-point for historical learning lies in examining evidence (Shawyer *et al.*, 1988; Knight, 1993). Students of mid-elementary school/senior high school are encouraged to examine change over time.

The New History movement flourished particularly in the United Kingdom where the Schools Council History (13–16) Project began in 1972 as a major national history programme and became an emblematic focus for radical changes in the teaching of secondary school history. The Schools Council History (13–16) Project (or SCHP, later SHP) had its roots in the curriculum reforms of the 1950s and 1960s which had been instigated by three United States educators. It was during this period that Edwin Fenton, Jerome Bruner and Harold Bloom constructed new curricular concepts which began to inform almost every aspect of the school curriculum in education systems which were prepared to take a lead from the United States.

Fenton introduced the notion of generic social studies with an enquiry-based emphasis, which would encompass history (as well as other humanities disciplines) and which would develop a child's understanding of not just historical facts but also concepts and generalisations. This was a starting-point in the development of knowledge, skills and values in the field of social studies. Fenton's epistemological template could be laid across any humanities subject, including history, and it provided a far greater strength to the justification of history than did the traditionalist arguments which had been based on the need for civic knowledge.

Bruner's contribution was to justify the teaching of history in school at a time when many professional historians regarded the simple provision of dates, names and anecdotes as the only goal of school history. A well-known proponent of this minimalist view of school history was Geoffrey Elton, a major British constitutional historian and a leading conservative in the debate, who put forward the view that 'the whole concept of historical study in the schools is distorted by being assimilated to a concept proper to quite another compartment of historical studies, namely that rightly prevalent at universities'. In other words, history was a study of the adult world and therefore, because of the sophisticated conceptual issues involved, was a subject fit only for adults. It was Bruner who confounded this view with his spiral theory of the curriculum, a development which allowed history teachers to see a justification for what they were attempting to achieve by introducing adult activities into a child's world.

Bloom's taxonomy strengthened teachers' ability to construct an epistemological framework of knowledge and skills which would allow children to make sense of what they were seeing, hearing and doing in their history classes. Previously there had been no universally accepted set of principles to define the construction of school history syllabuses, each national history curriculum had been at the mercy of individual political whim rather than any educational agenda. In this context, there was an increasingly urgent need for a systematic approach to the teaching of history and a desire for an objective justification for its place in the curriculum. The urgency came from the recent 1960s work on the education of the rational child (Hirst, 1966; Peters, 1966) which had been heightened by a long-term, post-1945 revulsion against education as mere nationalistic indoctrination, the worst aspects of which had been seen in the schools of the Axis powers.

If history was not then to be a simple absorption of a chronology of national triumphs and betrayals, what *was* it to be? It was the answering of this question that led to the construction of 'New History', which, following Bloom's work, moved away from an emphasis on content and more towards a balance between content and methodology. In the United Kingdom, it was Coltham and Fines who provided the initial stimulus for this change of direction in their influential 1971 study *Educational Objectives for the Study of History.*

All of these developments influenced the thinking behind the construction of the SCHP, which attempted to balance methodology and content. Methodology in history implied several concepts.

1 The notion of the use of evidence as part of the enquiry process. Here, students could be introduced to simple detective exercises before tackling more complex historical case studies.
2 The importance of studying causal relationships, motivation and the idea of historical empathy. Students could be asked to examine historical topics in depth to allow them the luxury of getting to grips with a historical topic. These in-depth studies permitted a close examination of causality, motivation and empathy.
3 The SCHP dealt with the idea of history as a study of change over time. Here, instead of asking school students to engage in a chronological race which frequently resulted in a half-comprehended understanding of large slabs of history, it would be enough to select a self-contained historical topic as an exemplar. In the SCHP, the history of medicine was chosen as an ideal topic which dealt with change over time, a key component of historical study.
4 Students were encouraged to examine their own landscape as a topic of historical study. This applied equally to students who inhabited a landscape which was filled with ancient historical features and to students who lived in large, modern, urban suburbs.
5 The importance of a systematic process in studying the evidence but of open-endedness in a range of enquiries and in conclusions. This, to some extent was a reflection of Walsh's (1958) position that history was a study that had no objectivity in its conclusions but could claim some objectivity in its methodology: in other words, there might be commonly agreed upon strategies for studying a topic even if the conclusions were to vary (Shemilt, 1980).

From the 1960s onwards, content in New History became subservient to the demands of methodology, a position that was seen as radical by the fact-based traditionalists but which was willingly seized upon by the progressives, so much so that by the 1980s there was significant controversy, especially in the UK, about the dominant role of methodology at the expense of content.

Nevertheless, whilst limited in its curricular scope (ages 13–16), confined to the United Kingdom and only broadcast piecemeal overseas, the SCHP acted as a source of inspiration for many secondary and some primary history teachers in the UK. The SCHP was a slow agent of change however for, in 1978, a report of Her Majesty's Inspectors stated that 80 per cent of primary school history remained superficial, with too much emphasis on traditional textbook sources. A second wave of change took place in the late 1980s which saw a renaissance of 'new history in countries as far apart as Canada, France and the United States' (Knight, 1993).

In the United States there was no Schools Council to provide a national focus and three major local factors affected the position of history in the curriculum. In the first place, New

History developed less completely in the United States because the subject content and methodology varied from state to state and from school district to school district and often the debate was more about content than methodology. Second, history in the schools of the United States was to be found in a much broader social studies syllabus, a position which weakened its political base in the wider curriculum debates. Finally, arguments about history's place in the curriculum were but one small corner of a much larger 1980s debate (still current) about the apparent failure of the national education system beset by low literacy and numeracy levels, high levels of unemployment, racial tension and a growing urban drugs crisis.

Nevertheless, the disappearance of history, particularly in the elementary schools, was a matter of such concern amongst US educators that four curriculum reform reports in 1989 asked for the establishment of core requirements in the social studies to replace the allegedly vague and outmoded 'Expanding Environments' approach to the curriculum. Expanding Environments was the broad label attached to a social studies framework which had grown in importance in US schools since the First World War and which was based on the notion that the child relives the cultural history of his/her race as he/she develops.

The most significant critic of the expanding environments approach was the Bradley Commission's 1989 *Historical Literacy: The Case for History in American Education*, which was itself a follow-up to the much briefer *Building a History Curriculum: Guidelines for Teaching History in Schools*, a report published in the previous year. The Bradley Commission document followed the radical California Framework (1988), which was based on a critique of the expanding environments approach to elementary history and argued for a central place in the elementary school curriculum for history (and geography).

Kenneth Jackson, chair of the Bradley Commission, stated that 'History is typically a forgotten subject in the elementary schools, where an "expanding environments" approach assumes that preadolescents cannot understand historical concepts.' Jackson's own research showed that 15 per cent of high school students did not take a course in US history and approximately 50 per cent did not study European or world history. The Commission's report, however, only renewed a debate which then centred around the premise that history and geography should be at the core of a social studies syllabus in both elementary and high schools. Although Jackson was optimistic, remarking that 'the political and psychological climate in the final decade of the twentieth century may be more receptive to curricular reform than at any time in the past eight decades', arguments about what constitutes the core of an integrated curriculum still continue. Nevertheless, a California Frameworks approach quickly became the focus for changes adopted by several other states (for example, the Texas, New York and Florida Frameworks) as a reaction away from Expanding Environments.

The current status of school history in the United States, as ever, varies from state to state but, following the debates of the 1980s, a National Centre for History in the Schools (NCHS) was established as a joint research venture of the University of California Los Angeles and the National Endowment for the Humanities, and, in 1992, the NCHS produced a collaboratively written benchmark volume *Lessons from History: Essential Understanding and Historical Perspectives Students Should Acquire* (Crabtree et al., 1992).

Lessons from History outlines a case for school history, discusses the factors that underpin the selection of content in school history, and finally outlines suggested themes and topics which include a US focus (for example, the Colonial Era 1600–1754 and the Emergence of the United States as a World Power 1890–1920) as well as world history topics (e.g. the Early Modern World 1450–1800 AD and the World in the Contemporary Era).

A US National Standards for History K-12 project (again funded by the NEH) followed on from the NCHS's work and from the National Education Goals adopted by the nation's Governors at Charlotesville (Va.) in 1989. The work of the National History Standards project bore some relationship to the work of a national curriculum History Working Group in the United Kingdom which, during roughly the same period (Gardiner, 1990), had been struggling with similar issues – namely, what history should be taught in schools and to what standard? The UK experience was initially much more traumatic than that of the US because there was direct interference by Prime Minister Margaret Thatcher in the construction of the History Working Group's final report. Thatcher's insistence on more British history was supported by her Minister of Education Kenneth Clarke, who also demanded an embargo on any topic being introduced which was less than 20 years old.

In the US, the National History Standards project did not initially encounter such robust political interference but its final report, published in 1994, did attract what was considered to be politically motivated criticism (Nash and Dunn, 1995) and caused considerable controversy in the national press, amongst professional historians and amongst educators (Bell, 1994).

The Australian experience has been less controversial. In Australia, where the national curriculum is diluted by separate state and territory educational systems, the newly elected Liberal (1996) conservative Commonwealth Prime Minister John Howard spoke against the 'politics of guilt', claiming that there was too much emphasis in schools on remembering European settler massacres, dispersals and appropriations of indigenous Australians. In this debate, he adopted the term 'black armband history' but, unlike the British system which allowed direct governmental interference in a national curriculum, apart from creating a temporary storm, Howard's pronouncements had no particular effect on Australian school history syllabuses. The Australian national curriculum was based on key learning areas (KLAs) which were modified by the states and territories in a way that put them outside Commonwealth government control.

Although educationalists working in the area of reforming school history in each of the three nations endured varying degrees of political interference in the construction of their school history programmes, a common thread remained: school history was seen by politicians as being too important to be left to the historians.

IDEOLOGY, POLITICS AND THE STUDY OF HISTORY IN SCHOOLS

History's contentiousness lies in its close relationship with politics. Sir John Seeley, the Cambridge historian and imperialist, once remarked that 'history fades into mere literature when it loses sight of its relationship with politics' and it is this relationship which has given the study of history in schools a special tension.

Whilst other subjects may have their particular political crises (science and creationism; English and standards of literacy; mathematics and standards of numeracy; biology and sex education), history, because of its very nature, is all about political issues or it is not history.

In this context, the study of history in schools is almost a litmus test for a society's political openness and democratic strength, since there is a clear distinction between the open study of history in schools as a discipline and the narrow study of history as indoctrination. We can even determine a nation's commitment or lack of commitment to democratic ideals and the principles of human rights by examining its school history syllabuses. In Nazi Germany, to take an extreme example, a recommended history curriculum for the German youth of the 1930s (from *The National Socialist Educator*) focused on two aspects of the past. First came Germany's relations with the world and second, relations with the Jews. Thus, an ideal topic for study was 'The stab in the back [*Dolchstoss*] 1918' followed by 'Jews as leaders of the November insurrection'. As far as the Nazis were concerned, history was at the core of a strongly politicised curriculum in which the purpose of the subject was to inculcate in German youth militarism and anti-semitism.

Not all nations have quite such a blatantly distorted view of the past, but nevertheless there is this apparently close correlation between the open or closed nature of historical study in schools and the open or closed nature of a political system and its capacity for self-examination. Broadly, there are three categories of political systems which have quite different approaches to historical studies in schools, namely, totalitarian states, paternalistic democracies and pluralistic democracies.

In totalitarian societies ideology was, and remains without exception, the master of the one-eyed history curriculum. In modern totalitarian states, such as the People's Republic of China, the retelling of a past is a carefully controlled, sanitised part of a national curriculum packaged for despatch to schools via government-approved textbooks. School students in totalitarian societies may only study history which justifies the existence of the current regime, which denigrates any political/social/ethnic/religious alternatives, and which glorifies heroes of the ruling ideology. There is no room for a free and open examination of the evidence nor is there any room for an explanation of the past which conflicts with state ideology.

In the middle ground lie the paternalist democracies, such as Japan, Malaysia and Indonesia. They allow slightly more room for comment and disagreement but, even in these supposedly democratic societies, a strong link has traditionally existed between political ideology and history teaching. In Japan, for example, a nation which considers itself to be a leading democracy, history textbooks of the 1980s and 1990s, which have to be screened by the government, avoided reference to notorious Japanese wartime atrocities such as the Rape of Nanking. For the Japanese authors of officially adopted school textbooks, imperial Japanese conquests of the 1930s and 1940s were merely 'advances' rather than invasions, a position which aroused protest both inside and outside Japan. In 1997, Professor Saburo Ienaga, who had fought a heroic 30-year campaign against this textbook vetting system, finally struck a major blow for freedom of expression in Japanese schools. The Supreme Court of Japan was persuaded by Ienaga that the Ministry of Education had acted illegally in telling him that, if he wanted his textbooks to be adopted, he had to remove references to Japanese war atrocities: in this case it had not been the victors who rewrote history but the vanquished.

The third model can be found in more genuinely pluralistic democratic societies, but even here the prevailing ideology has played an interfering role. For example, in the United States, prior to the 1960s, Manifest Destiny (the opening/exploitation of the American

West as a civilising necessity) was once taught without much criticism. Similarly, in British schools during the first half of the twentieth century, the benefits of Empire took centre-stage in a history curriculum which spent little or no time on such major colonial atrocities as the Amritsar massacre (1919) or Boer War concentration camps. In the 1980s, however, following the brief interim reign of New History in the 1960s and 1970s, this traditionalist view was replaced in the United Kingdom by 'heritage history', a nostalgic look at the achievements of a once great national past. Heritage history is promulgated through a national curriculum at the insistence of conservative governments who are reacting to what they consider to be the formless excesses of New History (lack of content and rigour) and the widespread problem of social/civic amnesia (school students cannot name the king who signed the Magna Carta). Some would argue that the United Kingdom has been particularly afflicted with heritage history as part of a post-imperial readjustment to a changed world order and a hankering for a golden age.

There is, in contrast, another and more radical approach to historical debate in pluralistic democracies. In this case, historical arguments are owned and broadcast by a variety of ideological factions, religious groups, races and ethnic associations within these societies. Such an approach can be found in France, for example, where, according to Robert Gildea, historians from different political groups compete for control so that they might 'win acceptance for their own presentation of French history' and in France it is the Revolution which is at the heart of French historical debate. In modern pluralistic societies, every political, religious, racial and ethnic group now claims a single voice striving for legitimacy, a situation which, it has been suggested, has produced an emphasis on cultural and ideological mythology rather than any advance towards genuine historical investigation and explanation.

In the United States, these debates are much more polarised than in other major democracies and they exist between two major competing ideological interests. One group, labelled 'multiculturalists', is very clearly based on a sympathetic approach to racial and ethnic minorities. Multiculturalists argue that a world history approach to teaching the subject in schools reflects the diversity of American culture, places the contribution of minority groups in their proper historical context, and helps redress past political wrongs. The opposing camp, predominantly conservative-liberal, argues first, that the European contribution to American culture and history is being lost in a rising tide of varying and fragmented minority narratives; second, that students are ignorant of basic historical facts which are central to the American experience; third, that schools are emphasising skills over content; and finally, that 'world history' is politically biased (Ravitch, 1994). This debate is likely to continue into the new millennium in a society that has to take into account very large minorities including African American, Spanish American and indigenous American groups but interestingly, more recently there has been something of a backlash against the perceived over-politicisation of school history (Kramer *et al.*, 1994), a backlash which has extended to some conservative representatives of minority groups entering the multicultural debate (Faryna *et al.*, 1997).

The danger here is that whereas in totalitarian and paternalist states, the dominant ideology explains the past in a direct and unfiltered fashion, in non-totalitarian states competing ideologies contest to own an explanation of the past. The single paternalist myth is therefore replaced by a variety of myths and cultural justifications and mythology makes for bad history. The essence of history, examining the evidence according to broadly agreed methodologies, being aware of and incorporating a variety of interpretations, producing a clear and accessible explanation, quickly becomes corrupted under ideological pressure – a development which makes history in schools very vulnerable.

HISTORY UNDER THREAT IN THE NEW MILLENNIUM

The present and future vulnerability of history in schools has three causes and, paradoxically, the first of these is the very curriculum reform movement of the 1950s and 1960s which gave rise to New History. Although Fenton's New Social Studies movement did indeed produce a renaissance in the teaching of history, these reforms also allowed teachers to move away from specialist historical study towards, some would argue, a cross-disciplinary compendium of facts and methodology which could also be taught by non-specialists whose loyalty to the study of history is more of an obligation than a vocation. In the integrated social studies curriculum, geographers teach history and vice versa, historical skills are dealt with summarily, and history disappears in a welter of geographical, literary, anthropological, sociological and psychological information. For example, in the Victorian (Australian) social studies syllabus 'Study of Society and the Environment', history is reduced to a mere part of the whole and, to the delight of school timetablers, may be taught by a range of non-specialist teachers. This dilution of historical specialisation in schools can lead to inaccuracy in a subject where evidence is paramount, carelessness where rigour in methodology is vital, and incoherence where clarity in explanation is supreme.

The second problem lies in the proliferation of university courses in the arts and other faculties, a development which has eroded the nature of history as a major undergraduate field of study in the arts and humanities. This process started in the 1960s when the social sciences began to replace history as the general-purpose field of study for undergraduates, a phenomenon which saw the continuation of the decline of history as a core humanities discipline in the 1970s and 1980s, when law and business courses began to dominate non-scientific university study. Cultural studies too, with its reliance on the orthodoxies of post-structuralism (a feature of the 1980s and 1990s), has, by questioning the basis upon which history is founded and by attracting a cohort of students who identify with the post-modern world, led to a further decline in the position of history as a single discipline in the universities. This has reduced the proportion of students undertaking major studies in history, thus producing a shortage of future specialist history teachers.

Associated with this phenomenon is a late twentieth-century student preference for applied university areas of study such as economics, business studies, applied science and information technology. These courses are seen as prerequisites for survival in a post-modern world and this emphasis on the value of applied subjects at the expense of 'pure' science and arts subjects is, amongst many students, combined with a strong drive towards vocational outcomes. There is little room therefore for the study of a discipline which concerns itself with the past rather than with the future, which demands a rigorous examination of evidence rather than rationalist attempts at theory or supposition, and which requires advanced explanatory skills rather than superficial journalistic skimming.

A third threat is the growth of religious fundamentalism both in whole societies and in sections of other non-fundamentalist societies. The disempowered, the subjugated and the dissatisfied who had previously turned to anti-colonialism and to revolutionary Marxism have, more recently, become increasingly alienated from the politics of radicalism and have turned instead to the politics of religious fundamentalism. This is particularly true in the Middle East and in the United States, where the spread of Islamic fundamentalism has had a profound effect on the politics of the Middle East and on the internal politics of the United States. At the same time, in pluralist societies which espouse multiculturalism and which also have absorbed large migrant populations, religious fundamentalism has been seized upon as an anti-assimilationist barrier which will prevent rising generations of migrant children from adopting the ways of their host society. Both of these developments have seen ideological mythology replace history and, in the United Kingdom, accusations that some Islamic schools are teaching Holocaust denial, a particularly pathological form of anti-history.

In the end, a free and open society will accommodate a free and open examination of history in its schools, however uncomfortable that may be at times. In the new millennium, the growth of personal computers, access to the Internet and the growth of a globalised, satellite-based media will allow the students and the citizens of even the most rigorously controlled society, to make up their own minds about the past.

REFERENCES

Bell, E. (1994) *Response to the Proposed United States History Standards*, Chicago: Organisation of History Teachers.

Bradley Commission (1988) *Building a History Curriculum: Guidelines for Teaching History in Schools*, Westlake, OH: Educational Excellence Network.

Collingwood, R. G. (1946) *The Idea of History*, Oxford: Oxford University Press.

Coltham, J. and Fines, J. (1971). *Educational Objectives for the Study of History*, London: Historical Association.

Cooper, H. (1994) 'Historical thinking and cognitive development in the teaching of history' in H. Bourdillon (ed.) *Teaching History*, London: Open University Press and Routledge.

Crabtree, C., Nash, G., Gagnon, P. and Waugh, S. (1992) *Lessons from History: Essential Understandings and Historical Perspectives Students Should Acquire*, Los Angeles: National Center for History in the Schools.

Faryna, S., Stetson, F. and Conti, J. (eds) (1997) *Black and Right: The Bold New Voice of Black Conservatism in America*, Westport, CT: Praeger.

Gagnon, P. (ed.) (1989) *Historical Literacy: The Case for History in American Education* (A Bradley Commission Report), New York: Macmillan.

Gardiner, J. (ed.) (1990) *The History Debate*, London: Collins.

Hallam, R. N. (1971) 'Piaget and thinking in history' in M. Ballard (ed.) *New Movements in the Study and Teaching of History*, London: Temple Smith.

Hirst, P. H. (1966) 'Educational theory' in J. W. Tibble (ed.) *The Study of Education*, London: Routledge & Kegan Paul.

Knight, P. (1993) *Primary Geography, Primary History*, London: Fulton.

Kramer, K., Reid, D. and Barney, W. (eds) (1994) *Learning History in America: Schools, Cultures and Politics*, Minneapolis: University of Minnesota Press.

Nash, G. and Dunn, R. (1995) 'National history standards: Controversy and commentary', *Social Studies Review* (USA) 34 (2), 4–12.

Oakeshott, M. (1983) *On History and Other Essays*, Oxford: Blackwell.

Peel, E. A. (1967) 'Some problems in the psychology of history teaching' in W. H. Burston and D. Thompson (eds) *Studies in the Nature and Teaching of History*, London: Routledge & Kegan Paul.

Peters, R. S. (1966) 'The Philosophy of Education', in J. W. Tibble (ed.) *The Study of Education*, London: Routledge & Kegan Paul.

Ravitch, D. (1994) 'Standards in US history: An assessment', *Education Week* (USA) 7 December.

Shawyer, G., Booth, M. and Brown, R. (1988) 'The development of children's historical thinking', *Cambridge Journal of Education*, 18 (2).

Shemilt, D. (1980) *History 13–16 Evaluation Study*, Edinburgh: Holmes McDougall.

Walsh, W. H. (1958) *An Introduction to Philosophy of History*, London: Hutchinson.

ADDITIONAL READINGS

Carretero, M. and Voss, J. (eds) (1994) *Cognitive and Instructional Processes in History and the Social Sciences*, Hillsdale, N. J: Lawrence Erlbaum.

Dickinson, A. and Lee, P. (eds) (1980) *History Teaching and Historical Understanding*, London: Heinemann.

Stearns, P. (1993) *Meaning over Memory: Recasting the Teaching of Culture and History*, Chapel Hill: The University of North Carolina Press.

49

EXPERTISE AND THE
TEACHING OF HISTORY

Richard J. Paxton and Sam Wineburg

It is first period of the school day, and the class of some 35 teenagers turn to their high school history teacher as he is about to begin his lecture:

> In 1930, the Republican-controlled House of Representatives endeavored to alleviate the effects of the – Anyone? Anyone? – Great Depression. Pass the – Anyone? Anyone? – the tariff bill. The Hawley-Smoot Tariff Act, which – Anyone? Raised or lowered? – Raised tariffs in an effort to collect more revenues for the federal government. Did it work? Anyone? Anyone know the effects? It did not work and the United States sank deeper into the Great Depression. Today we have a similar debate over this. Anyone know what this is? Class? Anyone? Anyone? Anyone seen this before? The Laffer Curve. Anyone know what this says? It says that at this point on the revenue curve, you will get exactly the same revenue as at this point. This is very controversial. Anyone know what Vice-President Bush called this in 1980? Anyone? Something 'D-O-O' economics? Voodoo economics.
>
> (*Ferris Bueller's Day Off*, 1986)

HISTORY TEACHING: THE GOOD, THE BAD AND THE MEDIOCRE

The characteristics of poor history teachers are by now well known. Taken together, these singular traits amount to society's stereotype of what a bad (some might say typical) history teacher is. The movie actor in *Ferris Bueller's Day Off* has the distinguishing attributes down pat: the monotone presentation; the mind-numbing march through historic times; the burned-out persona delivering an absurd Socratic monologue; the blackboard dense with notes – all facts to be written down, committed to memory, and later regurgitated. The students, for their part, sit mute and glassy-eyed, scribbling notes frenetically or, more likely, yawning and nodding in boredom. This image is well fixed in society's collective mind – whether it got there through bitter experience or sheer repetition in the media.

The question then arises: If the actor in this scenario is the icon of poor history teaching, where is his opposite – the master history teacher at work? Is this an image that comes readily to mind? Perhaps not. Although the call for scholarly examination of the complexities of teaching history goes back to the beginning of this century (Bell and McCollum,

855

1917; Collie, 1911), only recently has research emerged that speaks to the nature of accomplished history teaching.

This research focuses not on the failures of history teachers, but on their successes. It looks not only at the results of large-scale standardised tests, but at real teachers and real students in the act of teaching and learning. It is research that examines the practice of real historians, using them as role models for the kind of thinking and habits of mind to which students should aspire and teachers should nurture.

When we turn to this emerging body of research, a picture of what the master history teacher looks like begins to take shape. But let us be clear: it is here that we diverge from popular culture's myths and icons. This is not the movies, nor is it golden memories of schools remembered: this is real life, a topic all too often ignored by film-makers and media critics. This research reveals pedagogical approaches far more varied and complex than any simplified icon can capture. Though it may be impossible to fit the master history teacher into a single, made-to-order icon, a few standard characteristics can be discerned. For this teacher, these elements seem important:

- That the essential questions of history are the same at all academic levels, whether first grade or graduate school. These questions, and not some inevitably incomplete list of facts and events, constitute the core of historical learning (cf. Shemilt, 1983; Wineburg, 1999).
- That history is first and foremost an evidentiary quest. A history class that does not acquaint students with the epistemological pillars of the discipline – the tools of warrant, justification, evidence; the ability to discern sound from slippery narrative – risks doing more harm than good (Brown, 1966; Dickinson et al., 1978; Wineburg, in press).
- That students' prior understandings – including their misunderstandings – must be explored, not ignored (Barton and Levstik, 1996; Seixas, 1993a).
- That the fundamental component of historical learning should be authentic historical documents and artefacts. These serve both as a source of engaging students in the exercise of judgement, and as palpable evidence that must be examined before meaningful judgement can take place. A history course in which primary evidence is peripheral should be viewed with suspicion (Ashby et al., 1997; Rouet et al., 1996; Scott, 1986; Shemilt, 1980; Stahl et al., 1996; Wineburg, 1991a; Yeager and Davis, 1995).
- That the job of the teacher includes serving as an exemplar for what it means to think historically and to demonstrate the habits of mind that allow us to make sense of the past (Gabella, 1995; VanSledright and Brophy, 1995; Wineburg and Wilson, 1988; Wineburg, 1998).
- That history, to a large degree, is made up of competing narratives, not single truths, and that we determine the quality of any one of these narratives by asking how it accounts for the available evidence (Cronon, 1992; Tetreault, 1986; Wineburg, 1991b; Paxton, 1999).
- That there is no such thing as *a* history but there are instead multiple histories that account for the perspectives of the triumphant and the vanquished, the powerful and the marginalised, the mainstream and the minority, the enslaved and the enslavers, and so on (Fournier and Wineburg, 1997; Kerber, 1989; Lerner, 1975; Nash, 1974; Zinn, 1995).
- That knowing facts about history is vitally important, but should serve as a beginning of study, not its conclusion (Sellers, 1969).
- That focusing exclusively on memorising historical facts, while putting off the learning

of 'higher-order' thinking skills, is contrary to the discipline itself, to what we know about human learning, and is something that quashes students' desire to learn (Paxton, 1997; Wilson and Wineburg, 1993).

- That 'covering' huge spans of history during brief classroom periods runs counter to the achievement of genuine historical understanding (Newmann, 1988; Wiggins, 1989).

- That methods of assessment should be seen as powerful tools that often convey unintended messages to students about what matters most in making sense of the past (Boix Mansilla and Gardner, 1997; Gardner, 1985).

ACCOMPLISHED HISTORY TEACHING

Many of these characteristics – these central tenets of accomplished history teaching – are exemplified in the classrooms described by Thomas Holt (1990), a professor of history at the University of Chicago, who has devoted considerable effort to his teaching. Holt, like many university historians, is well aware that students come to him with historical knowledge that is not just insufficient, but erroneous.

'Before I can teach them history, they have to unlearn what they think history is,' he writes. Holt's students arrive at college believing the practice of history is inseparable from the collecting of historical facts; the process of historical writing simply an act of assembling a sufficient number of facts and putting them in chronological order. The facts are self-evident and the process of writing about them unvarying.

But there is another way. Taking advantage of what students already know is the starting-point. No matter what the grade level, students already possess some of the skills historians use – they simply do not associate these skills with creating historical knowledge. Holt attempts to re-educate students by furnishing them with contrasting historical documents, rather than a comprehensive textbook. He is interested not just in having them read these texts, but in *how* they read them.

To Holt, the essential skills of the historian amount to a set of questions one puts to historical documents. The point is not simply to read and remember, but to use documents to create a personal historical narrative. All historical writing is essentially human narrative about the past, Holt believes, no matter what form that writing takes. Therefore, students must write their own histories, and thus come to understand that all historians essentially face a set of parallel questions.

Of course, while students may already possess some of the essential tools of the historian, this does not mean they will put them to use. Simply giving students a selection of documents and expecting them magically to come up with the skills necessary for thoughtful research and writing is as effective as hoping that memorisation of content will spontaneously lead to a grasp of process. Likewise, while a solid disciplinary knowledge may be one essential element for the accomplished history teacher, it does not stand alone. Master teachers must surely know their subject matter, but they must also know how to teach it – and this, too, is no skill that springs automatically from the knowledge of subject matter (McDiarmid, 1994). Rather, it comes from careful attention to the motivations and concerns of learners, and the teacher's ability to tailor pedagogical techniques to real students.

David Kobrin (1992) lays out these issues in his description of several 'students-as-historians' projects in public high school classrooms in the United States. Kobrin contends that student historians have the same right to interpretation and intentionality as professional historians – but only so long as students follow 'appropriate standards and procedures for historical research' (ibid., p. 330). This is a key point, demarcating the line between history and opinionated rhetoric. While exploring this complex landscape, Kobrin found that simply asking students to generate questions and search for their own answers neither led to satisfactory results, nor engendered overwhelming interest. Giving students the authority to be historians may be a powerful idea, but it does not go far enough. Rather, it is important for the teacher to create a classroom atmosphere supportive of the structure of historical research. If students are to learn the skills and habits of mind of the experienced historian, it is up to teachers to create a curriculum that supports this effort.

One way this might be done is the approach of Kevin O'Reilly (1991), a teacher in Massachusetts who created a structured curriculum for teaching critical thinking skills to high school students. O'Reilly begins with current-day problems with which students are already familiar. Skills are first represented in the context of everyday use (on subjects students already know). Then, gradually, students learn to apply these skills to the evaluation of oral and written historical evidence – initially by evaluating others' historical reasoning, and then by creating their own historical interpretations from source materials. O'Reilly makes the case that thinking skills are analogous to athletic skills, and should be taught in a similar fashion – breaking them down into component parts, offering guided practice, repetition and further coaching (cf. Gagné, 1976). The idea is to move students from naïve consumers of history to discerning historical reasoners.

O'Reilly's approach to teaching history differs from the more holistic approaches of Kobrin or Holt. Just as the discipline of history itself has branched out in recent years to encompass new questions, topics and methods (Seixas, 1993b), so too has the spectrum of pedagogical approaches to teaching experienced healthy growth.

Two different, and yet apparently effective, approaches to history teaching were profiled by Wineburg and Wilson (1988). The two teachers they described were particularly noteworthy for the way they bridged the gap between their own understanding of subject matter and the emerging understandings of their students. The methods they used differed markedly. One teacher, called the 'invisible teacher', sculpted an entire class unit around the legitimacy of British taxation in the American colonies, saying little as her students debated the pros and cons. The other, called the 'visible teacher', covered similar ground in a more traditional, teacher-directed lecture. Yet despite dramatic differences in the outward appearance of this instruction, there was a fundamental similarity in both classrooms. Students encountered a vision of the subject matter that challenged them to consider alternatives, forced them to confront uncertainty, and invited them to consider how interpretative frameworks affect their perception of the past.

Studies of accomplished teachers reveal that they possess rich networks of factual and conceptual knowledge of the disciplines they teach. But they possess much more: they also possess a coherent and well-organised understanding of the epistemology of their disciplines – the canons of warrant and proof that are brought to bear on knowledge claims. They are also acquainted with the major interpretive schools and substantive theories that provide alternative frameworks for viewing the same historical subject. These knowledge structures provide expert teachers with cognitive road maps that guide the assignments they give students, the assessments they use to gauge student progress, and the questions they ask in the give and take of daily classroom life.

For example, Leinhardt (1993, 1994) spent two years studying a highly accomplished teacher of AP history in an urban high school in Pittsburgh. Ms Sterling, a veteran of over 20 years, began her school year by having her students ponder the meaning of the statement, 'Every true history is contemporary history.' In the first week of the semester, Sterling thrust her students into the kinds of epistemological issues that one might find in a graduate seminar: 'What is history?' 'How do we know the past?' 'What is the difference between someone who sits down to "write history" and the artefacts that are produced as part of ordinary experience?' The goal of this extended exercise was to help students understand history as an evidentiary form of knowledge, a notion that ran counter to the images of reified names and dates that students brought to the classroom.

Given the varied topics in the history curriculum, one might wonder about the efficacy of spending five days 'defining history'. But it is precisely Sterling's framework of subject matter knowledge – her overarching understanding of the discipline as a whole – that permits students entry into historical sense-making. By the end of the course students move from passive spectators of the past to enfranchised agents who can participate in the forms of thinking, reasoning and engagement that are the hallmark of skilled historical cognition. So, for example, in early October, Sterling asked her students a question about the American Constitutional Convention and 'What were men able to do?' Paul, one of her students, takes the question literally: 'Uh, I think one of the biggest things that they did, that we talked about yesterday, was the establishment of the first settlements in the Northwest area states.' Paul responded at a literal level to the teacher's question, and did not tie his response to the abstract issues Sterling sought.

But after two months of socialising students into considering history as a way of thinking, Paul starts to catch on. By January his responses to questions about the fall of the cotton-based economy in the South are linked to British trade policy and colonial ventures in Asia as well as to the failure of Southern leaders to read public opinion in Great Britain. Sterling's own understanding of history as a way of knowing allows her to create a classroom in which students not only master concepts and facts but use them to craft their own historical explanations.

It is tempting to reduce the skilled teaching that we see in a teacher like Sterling to two components: deep knowledge of the subject matter and a generic ability to manage children in a classroom. However, many of us sense that the scene is more complex: we have all languished in classrooms where the teacher, clearly an expert in his or her field, taught a class that soared far above students' understanding. The subject matter knowledge of such teachers is rarely in doubt: the key question is whether they can communicate their knowledge in ways that induct students into unfamiliar intellectual terrain.

The word 'communication' here masks the complexity and active nature of this process. Careful case studies of expert teachers have documented how teaching is an act of *cognitive transformation*, in which skilled teachers transform their knowledge into activities, examples, demonstrations, analogies and explanations that reflect their understanding of subject matter and what they know of the internal world of students. In other words, what separates the garden-variety expert from the expert *teacher* is that the teacher possesses something in addition to rich subject matter knowledge. Expert teachers know how to bridge the gap between their own richly elaborated knowledge base and the emerging and often inchoate knowledge bases of their students.

Without such knowledge, which Shulman (1986) has called 'pedagogical content knowledge', teachers are forced to rely upon textbook publishers for decisions about how best to organise content for students. Elizabeth Jensen, the 'invisible' teacher featured in Wineburg and Wilson (1988), knows that her 15 and 16 year olds cannot begin to grasp the complexities of the debates between Federalists and Anti-Federalists (two groups which debated the nature of government in the new American republic) without first understanding that these disagreements were rooted in fundamentally different conceptions of human nature. This point was glossed over in two paragraphs in the history textbook used in her class. Rather than beginning the year with a unit on European discovery and exploration, as her text dictates, she begins with a conference on the 'Nature of Man'. Students in her 11th-grade history class read excerpts from the writings of philosophers (Hume, Lock, Plato and Aristotle), leaders of state and revolutionaries (Jefferson, Lenin, Gandhi), and tyrants (Hitler, Mussolini), presenting and advocating these views before their classmates. Six weeks later, when it is time to study the ratification of the Constitution, these now-familiar figures – Plato, Aristotle and others – are reconvened to be courted by impassioned groups of Federalists and Anti-Federalists. It is Jensen's understanding of what she wants to teach and what adolescents already know that allows her to craft an activity that helps students get a feel for the domain that awaits them.

Another key element of pedagogical content knowledge is a teacher's ability to create *representations* of content – analogies, simulations, metaphors, demonstrations – that serve as bridges between the teacher's advanced level of knowledge and understanding and the inchoate knowledge base of students. As an example of a representation by a skilled teacher, consider the approach of William Bigelow (1989), a high school teacher in Portland, Oregon. Bigelow begins his year-long course on American history with Christopher Columbus, but this is not what students hear about when they walk in the first day. Instead, Bigelow accosts one of his students (who has been forewarned, unbeknownst to her classmates) and grabs her purse. 'This is my purse', he claims, dumping its contents on his desk, grabbing hold of the money, the lipstick, the address book. He then asks students who the rightful owner of the purse might be. If it is the student, what is the warrant for her ownership? Once students have specified a list of claims on the student's behalf, Bigelow makes the connection to Columbus with the statement: 'I have *discovered* this purse, it is mine.'

Representations such as this provide students with a powerful and vivid entry to a new subject, and in this instance help them move beyond a one-sided perspective still preserved in holidays and cultural myths. However, the danger of such an approach is that it risks substituting one reductionism for another. Without careful follow-up to push students beyond either/or thinking, powerful representations can be the source – rather than the antidote to – entrenched misconceptions. Bigelow's opening activity is followed up with an examination of primary materials describing the 'quota' Columbus placed on the Arawaks, the indigenous people he encountered in Hispaniola: if a 'hawk's bell' of gold dust was not provided every three months, the Arawaks were hunted down and their hands amputated. After an examination of other primary accounts, students are sent to find a textbook account of Columbus, and thrust into the position of critic: What does the book include and what does it leave out? What is its 'narrative position', from whose perspective is the story told? What is the subtext of the narrative? In this way, students become acquainted with the Columbian encounter but, even more, they become thinkers who possess powerful ways to reason about how these stories are constructed – and for whom.

Although talented teachers of history are present in many schools (as has always been the case), there has rarely been any attempt to create an entire curriculum around the ideas and methods advocated here. The most ambitious attempt to do so took place in the United Kingdom during the 1970s. The Schools Council History 13–16 project (cf. Boddington, 1984; Shemilt, 1980) united some 60 schools in an effort to revitalise the teaching of history as an independent subject in the schools.

Teachers and project organisers collaborated to create a curriculum arranged not as a chronological jaunt through the ages, but as a debatable subject based on a wide range of source materials. The project stressed the nature of history as an academic subject and the active participation of pupils in the construction of historical knowledge. The resulting curriculum featured teaching, learning and assessment objectives that included a small-scale local history project, the study of a historical theme over an extended period, the study of a limited topic in-depth, and the examination of a modern (twentieth-century) issue or crisis. The project set lofty goals, and the results were controversial (Booth, 1994). However, a comparison of some 500 pupils from the project with approximately 500 students from more traditional history classrooms showed that project students consistently outperformed control students in their understanding of key concepts (Shemilt, 1983). The ambitious goals and the enduring achievements of the Schools Council History Project have set a standard that has yet to be matched in any other venue.

CONCLUSION: A BRIGHT FUTURE FOR THE PAST?

Today we have a much better understanding of accomplished history teaching than we did only a few short years ago. But whether the future is bright for learning about the past is still an open question. After all, this is a subject that is typically more influenced by politics than by any pedagogical wisdom. History courses regularly serve as vehicles for passing on national myths, icons and shibboleths, rather than teaching a mature awareness of history (cf. Blackburn, 1985; Hobsbawn, 1993; Lowenthal, 1996). Nevertheless, the body of research discussed here does offer a measure of hope. So, too, do a number of other developments. We end this essay by examining the problems and possibilities of a much-touted development: the use of computer technology in history education.

In history, as in other subjects, the promise of new technologies has been heralded as an aid – and even a fix – to the inherent difficulties of classroom education. But if computers are to be a central tool for the student of history, the software they run on will have to exhibit some of the same characteristics as the good history teachers mentioned above. Few programs now available rise to this challenge (cf. Rosenzweig, 1995). Many of the CD-ROMs that spring so plentifully to market cling to the same outmoded pedagogical approaches that have been so criticised in the mass media and the professional literature. Often 'edutainment' programs do a better job of entertaining than educating. And still other history 'learning' programs are apparently slap-dash efforts produced, one suspects, more as money-makers than as serious educational tools. Computer technology does, however, hold untapped potential along with its seductive allure.

The computer's ability to archive vast quantities of information is an auspicious starting-point. With the capacity to store not only text, but pictures, film images and sound, computers can put more historical documents at the fingertips of students and teachers than was ever before possible. But the ability to store huge quantities of information does not in itself commend CD-ROMs as a breakthrough tool in the teaching and learning of history. If this technology is to change the history classroom, it must do more than bury students with historical documents: it must suggest ways to interpret and understand them.

For this to occur, new technologies should be founded on a solid understanding of what it means to think historically, and be arranged in a way that best represents these complex skills to students. Computers must serve as a tool of enhancement for teachers and classroom communities, not as a substitute for them, or as a 'history toy' that detracts from the communal nature of knowledge construction. This requires much more than chronologically or alphabetically organised archives. A few programs have begun to explore this new territory (Britt *et al.*, 1996; Rosenzweig, 1995; Rouet *et al.*, 1996; Spoehr and Spoehr, 1994). But many others seem stuck in a region dominated by the drill and practice of discrete historical facts.

Computer technologies are not a panacea for what ails history teaching. Any classroom tool – whether it is a textbook, a video or a piece of software – is filtered through the minds of the adults we call teachers. One unintended consequence of these new technologies might be that they deflect our attention from the preparation of teachers and the forms of knowledge they must possess. If this happens, computers will act to degrade the educational experience, not to enhance it.

REFERENCES

Ashby, R., Lee, P. and Dickinson, A. (1997) 'How children explain the "why" of history: The Chata research project on teaching history'. *Social Education*, 79, 17–21.

Barton, K. C., and Levstik, L. S. (1996) '"Back when God was around and everything": Elementary children's understanding of historical time'. *American Educational Research Journal*, 33 (2), 419–454.

Bell, J. C. and McCollum, D. F. (1917) 'A study of the attainments of pupils in United States history'. *The Journal of Educational Psychology*, 8, 247–274.

Bigelow, W. (1989) 'Discovering Columbus: Rereading the past'. *Language Arts*, 66, 635–643.

Blackburn, G. W. (1985) *Education in the Third Reich: A Study of Race and History in Nazi Textbooks*. Albany, NY: State University of New York Press.

Boddington, T. (1984) 'The Schools Council History 13–16 project'. *The History and Social Science Teacher*, 19, 129–137.

Boix Mansilla, V. and Gardner, H. (1997) 'Of kinds of disciplines and kinds of understandings'. *Phi Delta Kappan*, 78, 381–386.

Booth, M. (1994) 'Cognition in history: A British perspective'. *Educational Psychologist*, 29, 61–69.

Britt, M. A., Rouet, J. F. and Perfetti, C. A. (1996) 'Using hypertext to study and reason about historical evidence'. In J. F. Rouet, J. J. Levonen and A. Dillon (eds), *Hypertext and Cognition*. Mahwah, NJ: Erlbaum, 44–68.

Brophy, J. and VanSledright, B. (1997) *Teaching and Learning History in Elementary Schools*. New York: Teachers College Press.

Brown, R. H. (1966) History as discovery: An interim report on the Amherst project'. In E. Fenton (ed.), *Teaching the New Social Studies in Secondary Schools: An Inductive Approach*. New York: Holt, Rinehart & Winston.

Collie, F. (1911) 'The problem method in the history courses of the elementary school'. *Journal of Experimental Pedagogy and Training College Record*, 1, 236–239.

Cronon, W. (1992) 'A place for stories: Nature, history and narrative'. *Journal of American History*, 1347–1379.

Dickinson, A. K., Gard, A. and Lee, P. J. (1978) 'Evidence in the history classroom'. In A. K. Dickinson and P. J. Lee, *History Teaching and Historical Understanding*. London: Heinemann Educational Books.

Ferris Bueller's Day Off (1986) [Film]. Paramount Pictures Corp. Producers J. Hughes and T. Jacobson. Director J. Hughes.

Fournier, J. E. and Wineburg, S. S. (1997) 'Picturing the past: Gender differences in the depiction of historical figures'. *American Journal of Education*, 105, 160–185.

Gabella, M. S. (1995) 'The art(s) of historical sense'. *Journal of Curriculum Studies*, 27, 139–163.

Gagné, R. M. (1976) 'The learning basis of teaching methods'. In N. L. Gage (ed.), *The Psychology of Teaching Methods: Seventy-Fifth Yearbook of the National Society for the Study of Education*. Chicago: University of Chicago Press, 21–43.

Gardner, H. (1985) *The Mind's New Science: A History of the Cognitive Revolution*. New York: Basic Books.

Hobsbawn, E. (1993) 'The new threat of history'. *The New York Review*, 16 Dec., p. 63.

Holt, T. (1990) *Thinking Historically: Narrative, Imagination and Understanding*. New York: The College Entrance Examination Board.

Kerber, L. (1989) ' "Opinionative assurance": The challenge of woman's history'. *Magazine of History*, 2, 30–34.

Kobrin, D. (1992) ' "It's my country, too": A proposal for a student historian's history of the United States'. *Teachers College Record*, 94 (2), 329–342.

Lee, P. J. (1978) 'Explanation and understanding in history'. In A. K. Dickinson and P. J. Lee (eds), *History Teaching and Historical Understanding*. London: Heinemann Educational Books.

Leinhardt, G. (1993) 'Weaving instructional explanations in history'. *British Journal of Educational Psychology*, 63, 46–74.

Leinhardt, G. (1994) 'History: A time to be mindful'. In G. Leinhardt, I. L. Beck and C. Stainton (eds), *Teaching and Learning in History*. Hillsdale, NJ: Lawrence Erlbaum Associates, 209–255.

Lerner, G. (1975) 'Placing women in history: Definitions and challenges'. *Feminist Studies*, 3, 5–14.

Lowenthal, D. (1996) *The Heritage Crusade and the Spoils of History*. New York: Free Press.

McDiarmid, G. W. (1994) 'Understanding history for teaching: A study of the historical understanding of prospective teachers'. In M. Carretero and J. F. Voss (eds), *Cognitive and Instructional Processes in History and the Social Studies*. Hillsdale, NJ: Lawrence Erlbaum Associates, 159–185.

Means, B. and Knapp, M. S. (1991) 'Introduction: Rethinking teaching for disadvantaged students'. In B. Means, C. Chelemer and M. S. Knapp (eds), *Teaching Advanced Skills to At-risk Students: Views from Research and Practice*. San Francisco: Jossey-Bass, 1–26.

Miller, M. M., and Stearns, P. N. (1995) 'Applying cognitive learning approaches in history teaching: An experiment in a world history course'. *The History Teacher*, 28, 183–204.

Nash, G. B. (1974) *Red, White and Black: The Peoples of Early America*. Englewood Cliffs, NJ: Prentice-Hall.

Newmann, F. M. (1988) 'Can depth replace coverage in the high school curriculum?' *Phi Delta Kappan*, 69, 345–348.

O'Reilly, K. (1991) 'Informal reasoning in high school history'. In J. F. Voss, D. N. Perkins and J. W. Segal (eds), *Informal Reasoning and Education*. Hillside, NJ: Lawrence Erlbaum Associates.

O'Reilly, K. (1994) 'Informal reasoning in high school history'. In M. Carretero and J. F. Voss (eds), *Cognitive and Instructional Processes in History and the Social Studies*. Hillsdale, NJ: Lawrence Erlbaum Associates, 361–379.

Paxton, R. J. (1997) ' "Someone with like a life wrote it": The effects of a visible author on high school history students'. *Journal of Educational Psychology*, 86, 1–16.

Paxton, R. J. (1999) 'A deafening silence: History textbooks and the students who read them'. *Review of Educational Research*, 69, 371–395.

Rosenzweig, R. (1995) ' "So, what's next for Clio?" CD-ROM and historians'. *Journal of American History*, March, 1621–1640.

Rouet, J-F., Britt, M. A., Mason, R. A. and Perfetti, C. A. (1996) 'Using multiple sources of evidence to reason about history'. *Journal of Educational Psychology*, 88 (3), 478–493.

Scott, J. (1986) *Energy through Time*. Oxford University Press.

Seixas, P. (1993a) 'Popular film and young people's understanding of the history of Native American-White relations'. *History Teacher*, 26, 351–369.

Seixas, P. (1993b) 'Parallel crises: History and the social studies curriculum in the USA'. *Journal of Curriculum Studies*, 25 (3), 235–250.

Sellers, C. G. (1969) 'Is history on the way out of the schools and do historians care?' *Social Education*, May, 509–515.

Shemilt, D. (1980) *Schools Council History 13–16 Project*. Glasgow: Holmes McDougall Ltd.

Shemilt, D. J. (1983) 'The devil's locomotive'. *History and Theory*, 22, 1–18.

Shulman, L. S. (1986) 'Those who understand teach: Knowledge growth in teaching'. *Educational Researcher*, 15, 4–14.

Spoehr, K. T. and Spoehr, L. W. (1994) 'Learning to think historically'. *Educational Psychologist*, 29, 71–77.

Stahl, S. A., Hynd, C. R., Britton, B. K., McNish, M. M. and Bosquet, D. (1996) 'What happens when students read multiple source documents in history?' *Reading Research Quarterly*, 31 (4), 430–456.

Tetreault, M. T. (1986) 'Integrating women's history: The case of United States history in high school textbooks'. *The History Teacher*, 19, 210–261.

VanSledright, B. A., and Brophy, J. (1995) ' "Storytellers," "scientists," and "reformers" in the teaching of U.S. history to fifth graders: Three teachers, three approaches'. *Advances in Research on Theory*, 5, 195–243.

Wade, S., Thompson, A. and Watkins, W. (1994) 'The role of belief systems in authors' and readers' constructions of texts'. In R. Garner and P. A. Alexander (eds), *Beliefs about Text and Instruction with Text*. Hillsdale, NJ: Lawrence Erlbaum Associates.

Wiggins, G. (1989) 'The futility of trying to teach everything of importance'. *Educational Leadership*, November, 44–59.

Wilson, S. M. and Wineburg, S. S. (1993) 'Wrinkles in time: Using performance assessments to understand the knowledge of history teachers'. *American Educational Research Journal*, 30, 729–769.

Wineburg, S. S. (1991a) 'Historical problem solving: A study of the cognitive processes used in the evaluation of documentary and pictorial evidence'. *Journal of Educational Psychology*, 83, 73–87.

Wineburg, S. S. (1991b) 'On the reading of historical texts: Notes on the breach between school and academy'. *American Educational Research Journal*, 28, 495–519.

Wineburg, S. (1998) 'Reading Abraham Lincoln: An expert/expert study in the interpretation of historical texts'. *Cognitive Science*, 22, 319–346.

Wineburg, S. (1999) 'Historical thinking and other unnatural acts'. *Phi Delta Kappa*, 80, 488–499.

Wineburg, S. (in press) 'Making historical sense'. In P. Stearns, P. Seixas and S. Wineburg (eds), *Knowing, Teaching, and Learning History: National and International Perspectives*. New York: New York University Press.

Wineburg, S. S. and Wilson, S. M. (1988) 'Models of wisdom in teaching history'. *Phi Delta Kappa*, 70, 50–58.

Yeager, E. A. and Davis Jr, O. L. (1995) 'Between campus and classroom: Secondary student-teachers' thinking about historical texts'. *Journal of Research and Development in Education*, 29, 1–8.

Zinn, H. (1995) *A People's History of the United States: 1492–Present*. New York: HarperPerennial.

50

WHAT IS THE PURPOSE OF TEACHING GEOGRAPHY IN SCHOOL?

Simon Catling

INTRODUCTION

Informed citizenship requires a geographical education. A knowledge of the world, locally, nationally and globally, a critical awareness of the information and issues concerning places and the environment, and the skills to examine the facts and values involved are essential to every individual to enable them to play an active role in their communities, where they live, through work and in leisure (Johnstone, 1996). The Commission on Geographical Education of the International Geographical Union (IGU/CGE, 1992) has argued for and encouraged research, publication and the dissemination of effective practices to support the development of geographical curriculum in schools, innovative and varied teaching strategies and techniques, and the production of accurate, balanced and up-to-date resources to enable effective geographical education to be provided in schools at all levels.

GEOGRAPHY IN SCHOOLS AT THE START OF THE TWENTY-FIRST CENTURY

The state of geographical education around the world varies (Haubrich, 1996a). Geography appears to be regarded in most countries as an essential part of the education of their children, whether as a separately timetabled subject or, more likely, subsumed within a social studies context (Conolly, 1996). Though geography teaching has a long history, particularly in Europe, and appears as part of the primary (5–11 age-group) curriculum in some countries (such as England and Wales), in most countries geography is taught only to children from age 10 upwards. Though there are countries that would challenge this, geography teaching is only tentatively established in many parts of the world in the 11–14 year age-group in secondary education. While it is usually integrated with social sciences or science in the primary phase, geography is more often taught as a single subject at secondary level (Haubrich, 1996a; Kunavar, 1997; Maksakovsky, 1995; Meyer *et al.*, 1992; Ostuni, 1998). Where the opportunity exists, less than half of older secondary age students (14–18 year olds) opt to take geography for further study. While many secondary geography teachers are geography graduates, the large majority of primary teachers, even in developed countries, have little or no training in geography teaching.

It is hardly surprising that the picture of geographical education at the start of the twenty-first century is one dominated by a didactic approach to classroom-based teaching (Haubrich, 1996a). Drawing largely on textbooks as key resources, nationally approved and provided in a number of countries, the emphasis is on passing on factual knowledge about the home country and selected regions of the world (e.g. Gorbanyov, 1995, 1998; Kunavar, 1997). Traditional teaching approaches dominate where geography has a weaker place in the school curriculum and where resources are limited. Inevitably innovation in curriculum development and teaching occurs where the subject is strongest, sometimes in the context of a national curriculum, though this can also have a numbing effect. Given the limitations to both material and teacher resources, it is understandable – if not acceptable to geography as a school subject – that fieldwork is weak in many countries, and that the study of environmental and development matters and issues is under-represented in geography curricula.

The development of geographical education is not static, as reference to the range of research in geographical teaching and learning testifies (Foskett and Marsden, 1998; van der Zijpp *et al.*, 1996; Williams, 1996). Research and debate concerning curriculum development, children's geographical understanding, resource development (particularly of textbooks), teaching methods and managing change in geography teaching in schools have been developed on an international basis in recent years (see Ferreira *et al.*, 1998; Gerber, 1992b; Gerber and Lidstone, 1988; Gerber and Williams, 1996; Haubrich, 1987; Hill, 1992; Naish, 1998; Schettenbrunner and van Westrhenen, 1996; Scoffham, 1998; Smit, 1998; van der Schee *et al.*, 1996; see also the journals *International Research in Geographical and Environmental Education*, and *Environmental Education Research*). Though there is evidence that developments are under way in many countries as new curricula have been or are being devised and implemented during the 1990s and into the twenty-first century, it is still the case that what goes on in the myriad of classrooms around the world is only changing very slowly, even in those countries where resources and support might be thought to be most available to encourage change.

Rather than summarise the state of play or attempt a bare outline of the variety of developments, this chapter offers a direction and approach for geography teaching. It makes the point that geographical education is as much about perceptions as about knowledge. It identifies the need to take account of the variety of geographical perspectives that influence the way we understand and act upon the geographical stage. Drawing on views about geographical education, it puts forward a set of aims, a sequence of experiences and/or outcomes and an approach to teaching and learning in geographical education that should influence the choice of geography content, activities and assessment. The purpose is to encourage the recognition of geography as a key subject in pupils' education for the future.

GEOGRAPHY AS VIEWS OF THE WORLD

Among the variety of topics included in many geography syllabuses is the study of *natural hazards*. This topic usually covers the physical processes that lead to hazardous natural events, such as hurricanes, earthquakes and floods, and examines the impact on people and their responses and needs following such events. Approaches to teaching about hazards tend strongly to present them in the context of disasters, because the emphasis is on the negative impact on people's lives (Lidstone, 1996a), a view which also comes through strongly in media reports. In some curricula, the geography content then introduces pupils to the variety of ways in which national and international agencies work to understand, predict, prepare for and respond to natural hazards. Given the dramatic nature of and, admittedly, damage and devastation often caused to settlements and livelihoods by natural hazards, it is hardly surprising that the messages pupils take from such study units is that hazards are to be feared and that certain case study parts of the world can be seen to be risky places in which to live or visit.

In effect, natural hazards have come to be seen in most cultures as enemies, and this perspective is readily passed on through geography curricula and teaching. Refer to a hazard and you imply disaster. The geography of floods is usually presented in this way. Appropriate in many situations though it is, it is not the only way floods are responded to by those who experience them. A balanced view of flooding can be presented by looking, for example, at the replenishment of soil following the flooding of cultivated land in the flood plain. Indeed, it is possible to celebrate flooding as a friend, which benefits naturally both the physical environment and, as a result, people's lives (Namafe, 1997) because a fertile soil can provide for higher crop yields and, perhaps, disposable cash for the farmer. Thus, an alternative cultural response is to celebrate flooding as reinvigorating and sustaining, as providing for people and as a positive environmental event. In effect, while the flood is recognised as hazard, it is not seen as a disaster but is valued.

A fundamental point emerges here about the nature of geographical education. What must be recognised is that school geography, while helping pupils develop knowledge and understanding about the world, is essentially about developing pupils' perceptions and images of the world around them through the study of a selection of topics and real places. These perceptions and images have cultural settings. An effective geographical education recognises and explores the meanings and values of different cultural perspectives (McDowell, 1999; Massey *et al.*, 1999; Morgan, 1996; Slater, 1996). Alongside the study of the common dynamics of natural events and human activities reflected in landscape patterns and changes, for example, it recognises that there is a plurality of experiences and sets of values, considered through studies based in an appreciation of cultural diversity. This raises the issue that geographical education within any nation state is very likely to be culture-bound and that its development inevitably is problematic, given the limited education in teaching geography of many of those who do and will teach the subject in school.

Geography teaching travels a fine line between developing pupils' geographical knowledge and geographical imagination. By geographical knowledge is meant the information about real places and the ideas and concepts which geography uses to structure its way of examining places and the natural and social environment. It does this through looking at the impact of spatial location and patterns and of the processes involved in creating and changing such aspects of our world as weather, land forms, settlements, land-use, transport and resources, as well as by examining the way in which places and environments are managed and protected. In effect, this is the intended curriculum of geographical education. Geographical imagination covers the understandings and images of the world which each of us takes from our formal and informal geographical experience. These are influenced not just by school but also through daily life with family, friends and the media. These are what might be called the received and residual curricula that stay with us.

While geographical knowledge attempts to help us understand how the world works geographically, geographical imagination is about how each of us experiences and sees the world and the way in which our perceptions, values and attitudes are shaped through this experience, which in turn shape how we continue to view the world. Thus, while pupils can be informed about the processes and impacts of natural hazards (geographical knowledge), they will also develop attitudes to such hazards that will see them as enemy or friend or both, or as neutral (geographical imagination). The importance in geography teaching lies in recognising that the interplay of geographical knowledge and imagination forms part of every teaching session and that it is the received and residual curricula of geographical imagination that pupils will carry with them throughout life and which will influence their appreciation of the world and their actions in and for it (Lambert and Matthews, 1996; Lidstone, 1997).

The teaching of geography in schools requires clarity about its aims, consideration about the balance of content in terms of progression through schooling, the use of a variety of teaching strategies and activities, concern for the selection of resources, and appreciation of the need to help pupils appreciate what they understand from their geographical learning.

TRADITIONS IN GEOGRAPHICAL EXPLANATION

The selection of geographical perspectives, aims and content reflects the ways in which geography explains its views of the world (Slater, 1996), as well as politicians' (Rawling, 1996a, 1996b) and practitioners' self-interested or utilitarian ambitions for the subject (Gerber, 1992b; Goodson, 1988; Lidstone, 1996b). That is in the nature of every educational enterprise, for geography is no different in its service of social purposes as a curriculum subject. Over the years geography has developed a number of traditions to describe, analyse and explain the world. Within geographical education its long-standing and evolving traditions (NGS, 1994; RGS, 1998) maintain a concern to:

- study places, as localities and as physical and cultural regions, including nations, in order to be informed about the nature of area in geography and to foster both a sense of place and local, national and even international identity (Johnstone, 1996);
- study both natural processes, such as those creating land forms, and human activities (e.g. settlement, transport and resource development and change) and their outcomes, to develop an understanding of thematic approaches and systems analysis in geography (NGS, 1994);
- describe and explain locations and patterns at local, regional and global scales, to develop

an appreciation of the way spatial analysis can describe and explain how the world works, both naturally and through human impact (NGS, 1994);

- examine the impact of people's actions on the social and natural environment and of the natural environment on people's lives and activities, to appreciate the nature of the people–environment interaction (Naish *et al.*, 1987).

To these older approaches can be added the following concerns:

- to explore issues, including such matters as environmental quality and management, resource use and waste, sustainable development and decision-making processes to draw on issues-based approaches to geographical study (Naish *et al.*, 1987);
- to consider and identify standpoints, including one's own, in relation to matters such as inequalities in gender, disability and race and in social justice linked to wealth and power distribution as these affect the use of space, places and the environment;
- to appreciate that geography implies understanding of personal, local and global diversity and difference, and obligations in terms of social responsibility (Massey *et al.*, 1999; Stoltman, 1995);
- to examine ways in which action is to be taken personally, through lifestyle and community involvement, to address concerns about places and the environment;
- to recognise that people are active geographical agents directly affecting and changing places and environments, social and natural, locally, at a distance and globally through day-to-day actions, taking an ecoethical stance in their personal actions in terms of their effects on others, the community and nature (Haubrich, 1996b).

Alongside the development of its variety of perspectives, geography has evolved methods and skills to support effective geographical observation, description, analysis and explanation. Thus, in geographical education there is a concern to develop competence in:

- the key geographical skills of:
  – graphicacy, particularly map, photograph and sketch reading and interpretation, to enable the analysis of appropriate resources to help develop geographical knowledge and understanding (Gerber, 1992a);
  – fieldwork investigation, fundamental to geography's study of the real world, using a range of techniques and instruments to carry out research in the natural environment (e.g. a river study); in urban and rural environments (e.g. land-use surveys); and in the social environment, including surveys of attitudes to different environments and places (Bland *et al.*, 1996);
- an enquiry-based approach to geographical study, which takes an investigative approach drawing on physical and social sciences to develop effective questions to explore place, space and environmental matters, for example: 'What are the features here like?' (description); 'How is this place changing and why?' (description and analysis); 'How can the patterns in the environment be explained?' (analysis and explanation); and 'What might the impact be of this new development?' (prediction) (Naish *et al.*, 1987).

Geographical education draws on a wide range of resources, on literacy, numeracy and other skills. This will include the use of many types of text, including descriptions, reports, newspapers, posters, stories and poetry, as well as numbers, charts, graphs, diagrams and models.

Geographical education seeks to

- develop knowledge *about* places and the environment;
- build conceptual understanding and skill competence *through* the study of places and the environment reinforced by first-hand fieldwork undertaken *in* real localities;
- develop in pupils positive feelings, attitudes and values *for* people, places and environmental issues.

The role of geographical education is to inform and help pupils appreciate the world around them so that they develop a strong sense of responsibility, concern and commitment to a just world and to environmental protection and improvement (Cox, 1992; Fein, 1996; Hart, 1997). This involves helping pupils to recognise the variety of sources that inform their images and values, to realise that their understanding is limited and incomplete, and to appreciate their perspective can develop and change (Lambert, 1997). This implies the need to develop a critical approach within pupils to their learning in geography (Fisher, 1998; Gerber, 1998; Morgan, 1996).

AIMS FOR GEOGRAPHY TEACHING

Given the points made above, a number of aims for school geography can be identified, drawing on both the *International Charter on Geographical Education* (IGU/CGE, 1992) and other sources (for example, AICE, 1998; DES, 1990; IBO, 1996; Johnstone, 1996; Lidstone, 1997; Naish *et al.*, 1987). These aims reflect the older traditions and more recent approaches in geography, and they also address the balance of geographical imagination and geographical knowledge. They concern geographical attitudes and values, as well as knowledge, understanding and skills. The aims are set out below.

Geographical attitudes and values

- to stimulate and develop pupils' interest in their own surroundings and the variety of natural and human environments and places on the surface of the Earth, and to engage pupils' sense of wonder and appreciation of the beauty and variety of the world, in order to open their eyes to the value of observing and studying the world;
- to develop in pupils informed concern about human impact on the quality of places and the environment in order to enhance their appreciation of their role in the care of the Earth as an ecosystem and human habitat;
- to foster pupils' appreciation of the contribution of geography to the analysis, evaluation and problem-solving of contemporary issues on a variety of scales;
- to encourage in pupils readiness and commitment to use geographical understanding and competence responsibly in daily life, personally and in the local and global community;
- to promote a global perspective and pupils' commitment to international understanding, appreciation of cultural diversity and interrelationships, and respect for the rights of all people to equal treatment and to justice, on the basis of the Universal Declaration of Human Rights.

Geographical knowledge, understanding and competence

- to develop pupils' knowledge and understanding of the spatial locations, relationships and patterns of natural and human features;
- to develop pupils' knowledge and understanding of natural and social processes and systems in creating and changing patterns and relationships in different landscapes, cultures and human activities. This should include the study of such aspects of the environment as the natural environment; the impact of and responses to natural hazards; economic growth and development; manufacturing and service industry development; urban and rural environments; food supply and agriculture; population dynamics; communication and transport systems; resource and energy sustainability and management;
- to develop pupils' sense of place so that they appreciate what it means to live in one place rather than another, and to understand the cultural richness in the diverse societies over the Earth. This should include study of the interplay of natural and social environments and their impacts on each other, in the context of differing cultural and religious values, political systems and technical and economic structures;
- to develop in pupils knowledge and understanding of their own locale, home region and nation, and their capacity to set local, national and international events within a global framework;
- to build pupils' competence in using the methods of geographical enquiry and the skills of fieldwork, mapwork and picture study, as well as the use of written texts and numerical and graphic data and information, acquired from primary and secondary sources.

A CONTENT FOR THE GEOGRAPHY CURRICULUM

There are a variety of ways in which content is and can be selected for the geography curriculum. These include:

- national or local determination on the curriculum, set out in some detail and becoming common in an increasing number of countries, such as England (DfE, 1999; Naish, 1997);
- national guidance on the standards to be achieved, but which might be adopted or modified variously within a nation's states, for example in the USA (NGS, 1994, and see late 1990s issues of the *Journal of Geography*);
- the requirements of nationally or internationally recognised curricula and examination syllabuses, used by a number of countries and independent schools around the world, for example the International General Certificate of Secondary Education (IGCSE, 1998), though these too can be controlled (Naish, 1997);
- the access schools, teachers and pupils have to particular resources, such as a textbook, which may be nationally determined or the result of very limited or moderately generous resources;
- the decisions of individual schools and teachers about what they feel it is important to introduce pupils to, for example in a number of independent schools.

Inevitably geographical content, concepts, themes and case studies will be chosen for specific ideological purposes. These might include promotion of, for example, a particular belief system, a particular set of competencies and knowledge (such as those related to national economic security and the development of a workforce), or personal attitudes (such as a sense of enquiry, the capability to plan and see through an investigation and the independence to make up one's own mind). Content may be selected and arranged for these or other purposes to meet a degree and/or focus of breadth and balance in the national and global coverage of places and environmental themes and issues, to ensure a level and depth of study that will enable progression in the development of ideas and skills relevant to the world today and to pupils' needs, and to provide a coherent programme of study during schooling or within a school. These are all vital factors in effective curriculum planning (see Bailey and Fox, 1996; Carter, 1998; Powell, 1997).

Given the influence of these factors on the selection of particular content and coverage of the world, it is worth considering what pupils at particular points in their geography schooling should have had the opportunity to experience and achieve. The following list summarises a set of directions and a possible sequence for progression in geographical learning. It is intended to support the traditions, purposes and aims of geography outlined above.

1 By *5–6 years old*, through initial educational opportunities, geographical experience should have helped pupils to:

- identify a variety of features in the environment, both at first hand and in photographs;
- talk about their experience of one or more places, in terms of what is there and what some people do;
- be aware of some of the purposes of local features;
- express their own views about their environment;
- begin to ask and respond to questions about places and the environment;
- use a variety of resources, including photographs, toys, picture maps and the local environment, to find out about places and the environment;
- respond to and ask questions about places and the environment, make forays into the environment locally and develop a basic everyday vocabulary of environmental words.

2 By *10–11 years old*, towards the end of primary schooling, geographical studies should have helped pupils to:

- describe and explain the natural and human features and activities that give a particular place its character;
- describe personal and others' ideas of place;
- use maps and globes to locate places, locally, nationally and globally;
- show awareness of the interdependence of people and places and of valuing the diversity of ways in which people live;
- describe how some natural and social processes create and shape places and the environment;
- recognise and describe some ways in which spatial location, links and patterns can be affected by and have an impact on features and activities in an area;
- identify and describe the nature and impact of some changes on places and the environment;

- compare places, identifying some obvious similarities and differences;
- examine an environmental or place issue from more than one point of view;
- put forward alternative solutions to geographical problems;
- ask and structure the sequence of questions in geographical enquiries, and to use maps, photographs, fieldwork skills and appropriate vocabulary in investigations in the environment and of secondary sources.

3 By *14–15 years old*, towards the end of secondary schooling geographical studies should have helped pupils to:

- explain how changes in natural and human processes can affect the way the character of a place evolves;
- describe and evaluate the similarities and differences between places and explain how these have an impact on their interdependence with other places and future development;
- describe and explain a personal sense of place;
- describe and explain the impact of spatial location, links and patterns on places and human activities;
- describe and explain ways in which a variety of natural and social processes work and how they influence the nature and development of places and environments;
- recognise the significance of different views and levels of power in influencing decisions about places and environmental changes;
- show understanding and appreciation of the interdependence of people and places across the world and of the diversity of cultural approaches to places and the environment;
- identify and describe the nature of geographical problems and issues and put forward soundly evidenced alternative solutions;
- relate geographical understanding to personal experience and reported topics and put forward appropriately supported personal perspectives and commitment;
- select and sequence appropriate geographical questions and use a variety of geographical skills and techniques, including appropriate maps and photographs at a range of scales, fieldwork and suitable texts and numerical data, to plan enquiries, investigate them and draw conclusions about geographical topics, and use geographical terminology accurately.

4 By *18–19 years old*, at the end of advanced schooling and in preparation for higher education, geographical studies should have helped students to:

- explain and predict how changes will have impacts on the nature and character of places and people's lives;
- explain the nature and complexity of interactions between natural and human processes and their impact on places and the environment at a range of scales;
- analyse and evaluate the relative importance of spatial location, relationships and patterns at local, regional and global scales;
- understand and value the idea of global interdependence, and evaluate the relative merits of alternative approaches to development and environmental sustainability and the implications for the quality of life for different people in different places;

- appreciate and analyse the role and impact of perceptions and values on decision-making as it affects people, places and environments;
- present and support credibly a personal viewpoint about a matter of personal geographical interest and/or concern;
- apply the ideas and approaches of geography to everyday real-life situations;
- select and use appropriately relevant geographical skills, techniques and resources to identify appropriate geographical topics and questions, plan and undertake investigations, and analyse, evaluate and communicate the findings and conclusions, distinguishing evidence and opinions, in geographical enquiries through fieldwork and with secondary sources;
- explain and sustain their view of the nature, role and value of geography;
- demonstrate critical awareness of the geographical ideas, theories and evidence they encounter and use.

AN ENQUIRY-BASED APPROACH TO TEACHING GEOGRAPHY

The teaching of geography should always make use of (a) first-hand investigation in the environment through fieldwork and (b) the study of secondary sources of information. The importance of fieldwork is twofold. It demonstrates that geography is about real places and that a great amount of data gathered on the environment comes from studies undertaken in that environment. It provides an opportunity for pupils to develop their competence in using some of the techniques employed in studying in the environment. The examination of secondary sources of information, such as maps, satellite photographs, census data, geographic information systems, reports and summaries, provides pupils with experience in using a range of techniques to read and interpret such sources. Both fieldwork and secondary sources provide opportunities for pupils to describe, analyse and evaluate information about spatial and environmental matters. However, the use of these approaches needs to be within a teaching and learning framework for geographic education.

The aims and the structure for progression in geographical learning outlined above indicate that pupils, even in the earliest years, are encouraged to be active participants in their own learning. This approach implies an increasing level of pupil autonomy in learning, as well as the development of critically enquiring and reflective understanding and skills. An enquiry-based approach (Fisher, 1998; Naish *et al.*, 1987; QCA, 1998; Slater, 1982) offers such a basis for geographical teaching and learning.

An enquiry-based approach to geographical education uses questions about environmental and place matters and concerns to focus and structure investigations. It develops pupils' skills in identifying appropriate geographical questions such as 'What is the pattern of land-use in this town or city?'; 'How can the road and rail patterns be explained?'; 'How do the resources we use at home reach us and from where do they come?'; 'What is the impact of producing raw materials on the natural environment and on the lives of the people who produce them?' and 'What alternative ways are there to sustain and improve this environment?' An enquiry-based approach requires pupils to use a range of intellectual skills, including identification, description, analysis and evaluation as they develop, carry out, draw conclusions from and communicate findings about their investigation.

While the enquiry-based approach might be strongly guided and structured by the teacher in the early years, increasingly as pupils develop knowledge, understanding, skills and values, they will contribute more directly to the planning and investigation of the topic and build their confidence through undertaking their own enquiries. Yet at all stages, the teaching and learning approach will involve work that will be teacher guided and motivated (as well as involving pupils in independent enquiries, in both groups and individually), knowledge-seeking and problem-oriented (Gerber, 1998). Teacher demonstration and support will be essential when new ideas and techniques are introduced, but pupils can be involved in making choices when they can select from their repertoire of knowledge and competencies.

In all of this, geographical enquiry will remain clearly structured. In essence, a geographical, enquiry-based approach will move pupils from description, through analysis and evaluation to personal responses, as the sequence in an enquiry framework indicates, whether asked about a place, an environmental matter or an issue (Table 50.1).

Table 50.1 An enquiry framework for geography teaching

Focused questions	*Enquiry structure*
• What is it?	Identification and description
• Where is it?	Description
• What do I know/think it is like?	Description and perception
• What is it like?	Observation and description
• Why is it like this?	Analysis and explanation
• How and why is it changing?	Analysis and explanation
• What might it be like to be there?	Evaluation
• What might happen, with what impact?	Evaluation and prediction
• What do I think and why?	Personal judgement
• What would I do?	Personal response

Undertaking an enquiry involves a sequence of six steps:

1 Consider the topic of study and generate appropriate questions (and/or hypotheses).
2 Decide on the information to collect and the techniques to use.
3 Gather and record the information through fieldwork and/or secondary sources.
4 Process and analyse the information and draw conclusions.
5 Explain and communicate the results.
6 Evaluate the process and recognise what has been learnt.

This approach might be used in exploring the way in which land is used in the school grounds through fieldwork, just as readily as in drawing on text, maps, photographs and data in a textbook spread on river flooding. It can involve identifying the focus for a study of energy provision, need and use using library sources and information gathered from energy providers, as well as role play about a road development using information obtained from the planning office and developers. It might involve pupils in developing a questionnaire for other pupils and their families about how a new out-of-town shopping centre is changing their shopping habits. Or they may be preparing a tourist brochure to attract visitors to a location in Africa; or making a poster to attract new industries to an area in Eastern Europe;

or preparing the storyboard and script for a radio report on environmental degradation in South East Asia. Pupils could undertake research in order to make a model of an upgraded play area in school or to compare their microclimate with another school's, using e-mail or fax to share data. The point is that geographical enquiries can, indeed should, include a variety of tasks and styles of working to challenge pupils to identify and explain their ideas and understandings (Leat, 1998).

An enquiry-based approach requires that some thought be given to the assessment of pupils' learning. In turn, this implies a clear relationship with the learning objectives of the units studied (Daugherty, 1996). Thus, a unit for older pupils on life in an earthquake zone might require them, as a summative assessment, to draw up a chart about the advantages and disadvantages for people, in order to assess their knowledge and understanding of earthquake causes and impacts, human responses and why major urban destruction may or may not occur. During the unit pupils might have been assessed on their skills in reading and interpreting photograph and map information, as well as on their ability to use questions to identify a variety of suitable case studies.

CONCLUSION

The teaching of geography in schools is focused on three goals:

1 To develop in pupils their capacity to act with responsibility for the whole Earth, its natural environment, its human inhabitants and habitats and use, and the way in which it is developed and sustained, so that it can be passed to the next generation as an improved rather than impoverished home.
2 To provide pupils with a basic knowledge and understanding about places and the environment, and the natural events and human activities that affect the Earth's processes and patterns, in order to understand and view the Earth in more than one way and to contribute to ways to manage and sustain it.
3 To enable pupils to make their own enquiries, with confidence in their skills in doing so, in order that they can fulfil their responsibilities to the Earth and their co-inhabitants.

These goals are founded on a set of values that are grounded in social responsibility and ecological ethics (IGU/CGE, 1992). Furthermore they espouse an issues-based approach to teaching, which accepts guided learning teaching strategies as well as structured teamwork and independent study by pupils. This approach recognises learning as a social and experiential activity, and it understands education as culturally contextualised while arguing that it must support the values of multiculturalism, equal opportunities and human rights. Geography is not a value-free subject; indeed, it is imbued with the values of the cultures in which it is taught. This implies that geographical education is politically sensitive, and in many cases its inclusion, focus and content in the curriculum are the result of ideological stances and decisions. What is included in the geography curriculum and how it is taught reflect those values. In this chapter the core value is that teaching geography can achieve purposeful and positive changes in pupils' attitudes and values, knowledge and understanding and competences in relation to their experience and studies of places and the environment of the Earth. This can help pupils develop a viewpoint that is grounded in personal decision-making based on informed appreciation and choice and which recognises personal responsibility for and to others.

REFERENCES

AICE (Advanced International Certificate of Education) (1998) *Geography Syllabus*, Cambridge: University of Cambridge Local Examinations Syndicate.

Bailey, P. and Fox, P. (eds) (1996) *Geography Teachers' Handbook*, Sheffield: The Geographical Association.

Bland, K., Chambers, W., Donert, K. and Thomas, A. (1996) 'Fieldwork', in P. Bailey and P. Fox (eds), *Geography Teachers' Handbook*, Sheffield: The Geographical Association.

Carter, R. (ed.) (1998) *Handbook of Primary Geography*, Sheffield: The Geographical Association.

Conolly, G. (1996) 'Setting the curriculum: A place for geography', in R. Gerber and J. Lidstone (eds), *Developments and Directions in Geographical Education*, Bristol: Channel View Publications, 37–52.

Convey, A. and Nolzen, H. (eds) (1997) *Geography and Education*, Munich: University of Munich.

Cox, B. (1992) 'Geography for education', in R. Gerber (ed.), *Geography in Society*, Brisbane: Royal Geographical Society of Queensland, 65–68.

Daugherty, R. (1996) 'Defining and measuring progression in geography', in E. Rawling and R. Daugherty (eds), *Geography into the Twenty-First Century*, Chichester: Wiley, 195–216.

DES (Department of Education and Science) (1990) *Geography for Ages 5 to 16*, London: DES.

DfE (Department for Education) (1999) *The National Curriculum for England: Geography*, London: HMSO.

Fein, J. (1996) 'Teaching to care: A case for commitment in teaching environmental values', in R. Gerber and J. Lidstone (eds), *Developments and Directions in Geographical Education*, Bristol: Channel View Publications, 77–92.

Ferreira, M., Neto, A. and Sarmento, C. (eds) (1998) *Culture, Geography and Geographical Education – Proceedings: Volume 1*, Lisbon: University of Aberta.

Fisher, A. (1998) *Developing as a Teacher of Geography*, Cambridge: Chris Kington Publishing.

Foskett, N. and Marsden, W. (eds) (1998) *A Bibliography of Geographical Education 1970–1997*, Sheffield: The Geographical Association.

Gerber, R. (1992a) *Using Maps and Graphics in Geography Teaching*, Brisbane: Queensland University of Technology Press.

Gerber, R. (1992b) 'Geography: An essential component of our society', in R. Gerber (ed.) (1992), *Geography in Society*, Brisbane: Royal Geographical Society of Queensland.

Gerber, R. (1998) 'Understanding and promoting learning in geographical education in multicultural societies', in M. J. Smit (ed.), *Geographical Education in Multicultural Societies*, Stellenbosch: University of Stellenbosch Press, 35–46.

Gerber, R. and Lidstone, J. (eds) (1988) *Developing Skills in Geographical Education*, Brisbane: Jacaranda Press, 1–4.

Gerber, R. and Williams, M. (eds) (1996) *Qualitative Research in Geographical Education*, Armidale: University of New England Press.

Goodson, I. (1988) *The Making of Curriculum*, London: Falmer Press.

Gorbanyov, V. (1995) 'The renovation of geographical education at Russian secondary schools', in J. Lidstone, E. P. Romanova and A. Kondakov (eds), *Global Change and Geographical Education*, Moscow: Moscow State University Faculty of Geography, 113–117.

Gorbanyov, V. (1998) 'Perspectives on secondary geographical education in Russia', in M. Ferreira, A. Neto and C. Sarmento (eds), *Culture, Geography and Geographical Education – Proceedings: Volume 1*, Lisbon: University of Aberta, 146–148.

Hart, R. A. (1997) *Children's Participation*, London: Earthscan Publications.

Haubrich, H. (ed.) (1987) *International Trends in Geographical Education*, Freiberg: Paedagogische Hochschule Freiburg.

Haubrich, H. (1996a) 'Geographical education 1996: Results of a survey in 38 countries', *IGU/CGE Newsletter* 32 (June), I–XXVIII.

Haubrich, H. (1996b) 'Global ethics in geographical education', in R. Gerber and J. Lidstone (eds), *Developments and Directions in Geographical Education*, Bristol: Channel View Publications, 163–174.

Hill, D. A. (ed.) (1992) *International Perspectives on Geographic Education*, Skokie: Rand McNally.

IBO (International Baccalaureate Organization) (1996) *Geography*, Cardiff: IBO.

IGCE (International General Certificate of Secondary Education) (1998) *Geography Syllabus*, Cambridge: University of Cambridge Local Examinations Syndicate.

IGU/CGE (International Geographical Union Commission on Geographical Education) (1992) *International Charter on Geographical Education*, Brisbane: Queensland University of Technology.

Johnstone, R. (1996) 'A place in geography', in E. Rawling and R. Daugherty (eds), *Geography into the Twenty-First Century*, Chichester: Wiley, 59–76.

Kunavar, J. (1997) 'Recent trends in geography teaching in Slovenia: a transnational and European perspective', in A. Convey and H. Nolzen (eds), *Geography and Education*, Munich: University of Munich, 159–168.

Lambert, D. (1997) 'Geography education and citizenship: Identity and intercultural communication', in F. Slater and J. Bale (eds), *Reporting Research in Geography Education: Monograph No. 5*, London: London University Institute of Education, 1–13.

Lambert, D. and Matthews, H. (1996) 'The contribution of geography to personal and social education', in E. Rawling and R. Daugherty (eds), *Geography into the Twenty-First Century*, Chichester: Wiley, 339–356.

Leat, D. (ed.) (1998) *Thinking through Geography*, Cambridge: Chris Kington Publishing.

Lidstone, J. (ed.) (1996a) *International Perspectives on Teaching about Hazards and Disasters*, Clevedon: Channel View Publications.

Lidstone, J. (1996b) 'Professionalism in geographical education', in R. Gerber and J. Lidstone (eds), *Developments and Directions in Geographical Education*, Bristol: Channel View Publications.

Lidstone, J. (1997) 'The essence of geographical education: An essential issue to discuss', in A. Convey and H. Nolzen (eds), *Geography and Education*, Munich: University of Munich, 169–188.

Maksakovsky, V. P. (1995) 'Modern problems of school geography in Russia', in J. Lidstone, E. P. Romanova and A. Kondakov (eds), *Global Change and Geographical Education*, Moscow: Moscow State University Faculty of Geography.

McDowell, L. (1999) *Gender, Identity and Place: Understanding Feminist Geographies*, Oxford: Polity Press.

Massey, D., Allen, J. and Sarre, P. (eds) (1999) *Human Geography Today*, Oxford: Polity Press.

Meyer, J. W., Kamens, D. H. and Benavot, A. (1992) *School Knowledge for the Masses*, London: Falmer Press.

Morgan, J. (1996) 'What a Carve Up! New times for geography teaching', in A. Kent, D. Lambert, M. Naish and F. Slater (eds), *Geography in Education: Viewpoints on Teaching and Learning*, Cambridge: Cambridge University Press, 50–70.

Naish, M. (1997) 'Geography and education – knowledge and control', in A. Convey and H. Nolzen (eds), *Geography and Education*, Munich: University of Munich, 199–208.

Naish, M. (ed.) (1998) *Values in Geography Education*, London: University of London Institute of Education.

Naish, M., Rawling, E. and Hart, C. (1987) *Geography 16–19: The Contribution of a Curriculum Project to 16–19 Education*, London: Longman.

Namafe, C. (1997) 'Cultural differences in response to environment', in F. Slater, D. Lambert and D. Lines (eds), *Education, Environment and Economy: Reporting Research in a New Academic Grouping*, London: University of London Institute of Education, 115–134.

NGS (National Geographic Society) (1994) *Geography for Life*, Washington: National Geographic Society.

Ostuni, J. (1998) 'Geography texts and the new curricula', in M. Ferreira, A. Neto and C. Sarmento (eds), *Culture, Geography and Geographical Education – Proceedings: Volume 1*, Lisbon: University of Aberta, 64–68.

Powell, A. (ed.) (1997) *Handbook of Post-16 Geography*, Sheffield: The Geographical Association.

QCA (Qualification and Curriculum Authority) (1998) *Geographical Enquiry at Key Stages 1–3*, London: QCA.

Rawling, E. (1996a) 'The impact of the National Curriculum on school-based curriculum development in secondary geography', in A. Kent, D. Lambert, M. Naish and F. Slater (eds), *Geography in Education: Viewpoints on Teaching and Learning*, Cambridge: Cambridge University Press, 100–132.

Rawling, E. (1996b) 'A school geography for the twenty-first century? The experience of the National Curriculum in England and Wales', in J. Stoltman (ed.), *International Developments in Geography Education: Preparing for the Twenty-First Century* (special issue), *International Journal of Social Education*, 10 (2), 1–21.

RGS (Royal Geographical Society) (1998) *Geography: An Essential Contribution to Education for Life*, London: RGS.

Schrettenbrunner, H. and van Westrhenen, J. (eds) (1996) *Empirical Research and Geography Teaching*, Amsterdam: University of Amsterdam Centre for Geographical Education.

Scoffham, S. (ed.) (1998) *Primary Sources: Research Findings in Primary Geography*, Sheffield: The Geographical Association.

Slater, F. (1982) *Learning through Geography*, London: Heinemann.

Slater, F. (1996) 'Values: towards mapping their locations in a geography education', in A. Kent, D. Lambert, M. Naish and F. Slater (eds), *Geography in Education: Viewpoints on Teaching and Learning*, Cambridge: Cambridge University Press, 200–230.

Smit, M. J. (ed.) (1998) *Geographical Education in Multicultural Societies*, Stellenbosch: University of Stellenbosch Press.

Stoltman, J. (ed.) (1995) *International Developments in Geography Education: Preparing for the Twenty-First Century* (special issue), *International Journal of Social Education*, 10 (2).

Van der Schee, J., Schoenmaker, G., Trimp, H. and van Westrhenen, J. (eds) (1996) *Innovation in Geographical Education*, Amsterdam: University of Amsterdam Centre for Geographical Education.

Van der Zijpp, T., Van der Schee, J. and Trimp, H. (eds) (1996) *Innovation in Geographical Education: Proceedings*, Amsterdam: University of Amsterdam Centre for Geographical Education.

Williams, M. (ed.) (1996) *Understanding Geographical and Environmental Education: The Role of Research*, London: Cassell.

51

CIVIC/CITIZENSHIP EDUCATION AND THE SOCIAL STUDIES IN THE UNITED STATES OF AMERICA

Mary Jane Turner and Scott M. Richardson

INTRODUCTION

Most Americans have assumed, since the founding of the first colonial institutions of learning, that all United States (US) schools should train young people in the duties and responsibilities of citizenship. The basic principles of republican citizenship in the USA were developed during two distinct historical periods: the classical era of the Greek city states and the Roman Republic, and the revolutionary era of Western Europe and America, which saw the growth of the modern nation states.

These two intellectual streams influenced the founders of the USA about such ideas as human nature, individual rights, and the relationship between the citizen and the polity. The founders also distinguished between a 'subject' and a 'citizen'. To them, only well-educated citizens and not passive subjects could be trusted to protect the rights proclaimed in the Declaration of Independence. Alexander Hamilton, John Adams, James Madison, Thomas Jefferson and Benjamin Franklin, among others, all felt that the education of citizens should not be left to chance or individual initiative, but taught and nurtured in the educational institutions of the new nation.

For example, in 1796 George Washington stated in an address to Congress:

> [A] primary object . . . should be the education of our Youth in the science of *Government*. In a Republic, what species of Knowledge can be equally important? And what duty, more pressing on its Legislature, than to patronize a plan for communicating it to those, who are to be the future guardians of the liberties of the Country?

In a similar vein, Thomas Jefferson wrote in 1820:

> I know of no safe depository of the ultimate powers of the society but the people themselves; and if we think them not enlightened enough to exercise their control with a wholesome discretion, the remedy is not to take it from them, but to inform their discretion by education. [1]

Unfortunately, all the interest in preparing citizens to assume their 'proper' role in society largely failed to produce a coherent civics curriculum, particularly at the pre-collegiate level. Textbooks prior to the 1880s were primarily concerned with morals and patriotism, strongly reflecting the nationalistic values of the new nation.[2]

THE PRE-EMINENCE OF HISTORY

Between 1880 and 1900, with the advent of compulsory attendance laws, increased attention was given to systematising public education. During this period, many began to believe that the discipline of history should form the core of what citizens needed to learn. Early on, the goal of the history courses was to 'exercise' the faculties of the mind through 'memory work' and to give students an adequate store of essential historical facts in order for them to function as good citizens.[3] Obviously, this rationale has been modified and amended over the years, but most historians still maintain today that a thorough understanding of history is a prerequisite for understanding the present and should compose the bedrock of citizenship education.

THE EMERGENCE OF SOCIAL STUDIES

By the early decades of the 1900s, social scientists – particularly those representing the discipline of political science – began to question the validity of focusing entirely on history as the sole tool for teaching citizenship. In large measure, the concerns of the political scientists were well founded. They, like the historians, accepted the responsibility of 'training for citizenship'. The political scientists, though, called for more intensive instruction about American government, the role of the presidency, procedures in Congress, questions about the judiciary, and examination of the Constitution. They also noted that information about local government, a subject that historians tended to ignore (and which continues to receive short shrift today), should constitute an integral dimension in any instruction for citizens.[4]

The political scientists, followed by other academics, began to issue reports[5] and make recommendations concerning better ways to structure the field of citizenship education. This general area has become known as the 'social studies', the purpose of which was 'to develop effective, critically thinking, and participatory citizens through the study of history and the social sciences'.[6]

Did all of this mean that coherent courses of study and teachers qualified to develop responsible and active citizens magically began to appear? No, of course not. Not everyone agreed with the stated purpose of the social studies, and not many knew how to achieve that purpose. Few conceptual tools, coherent methodologies, or useful generalisations emerged from any of the disciplines. Worse, an interdisciplinary approach was of little interest to the individual academic fields.

Even institutional structures and departmental rivalries within single universities prevented the kind of co-operation that was necessary. Historians could identify little benefit in talking to political or other social scientists. Schools of education, often working with modest budgets, were not inclined to use their limited funds to involve other academics in teaching methods courses, but few social studies educators had the content expertise to design adequate programmes.[7]

THE NEW SOCIAL STUDIES

Throughout the 1930s, 1940s and 1950s, citizenship education usually occurred by happenstance. Most people still believed that the schools existed primarily for the purpose of educating citizens, but there was no clear vision about what this meant. Furthermore, the field of social studies, that part of the curriculum that supposedly had the principal responsibility for educating citizens, was clearly in retreat. Whatever social studies was, or purported to be, it was judged by most to be 'soft' and ineffective, if not downright dangerous. The public, the Congress and the media were outraged about the poor performance of education in general.

The era that followed, which lasted from the 1960s until the 1980s, was known as the 'new' social studies, because it focused on the methodologies of the social sciences and history – the 'hard' sciences. This movement differed from those preceding it because of the people who tried to effect change, the approach that was taken, and the massive amounts of money that became available to the new 'change agents'.

In the past, the various professional associations had shown little sustained interest in making recommendations for educational programming. By the 1960s, the American Historical Association, the American Political Science Association, the American Anthropological Association, the American Sociological Association, the American Economic Association, the Association of American Geographers and the National Council for Geographic Education all had task forces to study and develop action plans. These associations did not make recommendations for changing education that were intended for implementation by 'someone else', however. Each association developed a curriculum itself, and each brought to the task senior, tenured professors who represented the 'best and the brightest' in their profession. The array of curriculum development projects was largely supported by the National Science Foundation and the US Office of Education.[8]

As might be expected, the academics approached their curriculum development task in what seemed to be a purely rational way. The materials would, first of all, be based on learning theory and research findings, then field-tested, and finally introduced as replacements or supplements for courses that were already in the schools – history, geography, government and so on. The consequence of this approach was that materials were designed to be ends in themselves. For example, history was taught as the process of historiography, and sociology as the scientific method of enquiry. Very few of the materials provided an explicit connection of the content to citizen behaviour, although they included a variety of exciting new ways to present content, such as simulations and the use of primary sources. Initially, the 'new social studies' programmes did little to prepare students for responsible citizenship.

Towards the end of this era, a number of scholars began trying to link the social studies/ social sciences and citizenship. Others – many of whom had started out promoting a single-discipline approach to instruction – began to seek useful concepts from other disciplines to strengthen their programmes. Unfortunately, these efforts did not produce exemplary curricula.

BACK TO 'THE BASICS'

By the mid-1980s, the general public believed that the 'new social studies' had not produced a new cohort of competent students ready to assume their citizenship tasks. Neither test scores nor measures of civic involvement showed any improvement over previous eras. Many recommended that educators stop teaching young people how to apply the concepts and methodologies of the social sciences. Rather, they should teach the facts (or 'the basics') and instil in students the values of good citizenship, focusing on the ways good citizens should act.

This approach has always been, and continues to be, the most prevalent in US schools. The public's demand for 'back to the basics' is totally congruent with what most teachers have done and are doing. There is scant evidence that other approaches – reflective enquiry or social science investigations – have ever been widely used. According to data collected by the National Assessment of Educational Progress in 1990, text-and-lecture was the predominant instructional strategy used by social studies teachers.[9]

Even so, the US is a huge country characterised by differences among the many school districts and the schools within them. Some tend to be more progressive or quicker to embrace new approaches; others follow more closely the traditional patterns of instruction. Susan Griffin of the National Council for the Social Studies (NCSS), which is the largest association representing social studies teachers in the USA, estimates that as of 1998 there are at least 145,000 educators in the USA who identify themselves as social studies professionals. Each can approach the educational task somewhat differently, so there are doubtless some who encourage enquiry and a more active pedagogy.

CIVIC/CITIZENSHIP EDUCATION IN THE 1990s

Pressures to change educational practices in the USA have often emerged because of a public perception that American students are not 'first' in the world in terms of academic ability. In 1957, Sputnik ignited the call for better science education and the consequent emergence of the new social studies. The fact that US students did not score well on international science and mathematics assessments in the late 1980s energised the business community and powerful political constituencies to push for change.

As a result, President George Bush announced in April 1991 that past education reform efforts had failed. In his view, the time had come for an educational 'revolution'. This announcement was the product of an education summit held with the 50 state governors in 1989. The introductory statement on national education goals, adopted by the National Governors Association in 1990, refers to citizenship education a number of times:

> If the US is to maintain a strong and responsible democracy and a prosperous and growing economy into the next century, it must be prepared to address and respond to major challenges at home and in the world. A well-educated population is the key to our future. Americans must be

prepared to: . . . Participate knowledgeably in our democracy and our democratic institutions; . . . Function effectively in increasingly diverse communities and states and in a rapidly shrinking world. . . . Today a new standard of an educated citizenry is required, one suitable to the next century. . . . [All students] must understand and accept the obligations of citizenship.[10]

Among the first groups to begin serious work on reconceptualising a new civic/citizenship curriculum were the Center for Civic Education and the Council for the Advancement of Citizenship. As early as 1988, staff at the Center had analysed more than 40 state curriculum frameworks dealing with civic education. The findings supported the contention that instruction in the schools needed serious repair and that the best thinking of earlier decades was either not sufficient or had not filtered down to the schools. Among the findings were the following:

- The question of what citizenship means was seldom addressed.
- Little was said about the aims of citizenship education.
- Descriptions of civic education as a subject tend towards conceptual fuzziness and diffusion.
- In only a few instances could a specific rationale for civic education be found.[11]

In response to these findings, the Center for Civic Education and the Council for the Advancement of Citizenship assembled some of the best minds in the USA. They were charged with the task of suggesting

guidelines for the development or enhancement of civic education instructional programs in public and private elementary and secondary schools in order to promote civic competence, civic responsibility, and the widespread participation of youth in the social and political life of their communities and the nation.[12]

The resulting document, *Civitas: A Framework for Civic Education*, eventually involved 44 contributing writers, a 19-member Framework Development Committee, a 24-member National Review Council and a 59-member National Teachers Advisory Committee.

Civitas is by far the most comprehensive and scholarly attempt to codify and illustrate the themes and subthemes of civic education. The writers believed that these themes should be woven into every social studies instructional programme in the US, from kindergarten through the 12th grade. The framework is divided into three parts, each of which contains model formats, commentary and background information:

Part I: Civic virtue
Goal: To foster among citizens *civic dispositions* and commitments to fundamental values and principles required for competent and responsible citizenship.

Part II: Civic participation
Goal: To develop among citizens the *participatory skills* required to monitor and influence the formulation, implementation, adjudication, and enforcement of public policy, as well as to participate in voluntary efforts to solve neighborhood problems.

Part III: Civic knowledge and intellectual skills
Goal: To provide citizens the *knowledge and intellectual skills* required to monitor and influence the formulation, implementation, adjudication, and enforcement of public policy, as well as to participate in voluntary efforts to solve neighborhood and community problems.[13]

The same impetus for reform that energised the Center for Civic Education and the Council for the Advancement of Citizenship to develop *Civitas* led to Congressional action in 1992. The Goals 2000: Educate America Act codified educational goals and sanctioned the development of national standards as a means of encouraging and evaluating student achievement. The Act provided for standards in most disciplines, including civics and government, [14] economics, geography and history. Though the Act overlooked social studies as an aggregate discipline, the NCSS successfully developed its own social studies standards, *Expectations of Excellence*, in 1994.

The relationship between the social studies standards and those of its individual disciplines is intriguing. The authors of the social studies standards intended for them to address general curriculum design and comprehensive student expectations. The discipline standards, on the other hand, present content detail. Curriculum decision-makers are advised by NCSS 'to establish their program framework using the social studies standards as a guide', and then to use the standards from history, geography, civics, economics and others to develop grade-level standards and courses.[15]

The framework of the social studies standards consists of ten themes:

- Culture;
- Time, Continuity and Change;
- People, Places and Environments;
- Industrial Development and Identity;
- Individuals, Groups and Institutions;
- Power, Authority and Governance;
- Production, Distribution and Consumption;
- Science, Technology and Society;
- Global Connections;
- Civic Ideals and Practices.[16]

These themes span grade levels from early to middle grades through high school. The framework also specifies student performance expectations throughout each theme, and it gives examples of classroom activities that will enable students to achieve those expectations.

One of the most interesting aspects of *Expectations of Excellence* is the definition of social studies. The document clearly and unequivocally states that the primary goal of social studies is citizenship education.

> Social studies is the integrated study of the social sciences and humanities to promote civic competence. Within the school programs, social studies provides coordinated, systematic study drawing upon such disciplines as anthropology, archaeology, economics, geography, history, law, philosophy, political science, psychology, religion, and sociology, as well as appropriate content from the humanities, mathematics, and natural sciences. The primary purpose of social studies is to help young people develop the ability to make informed and reasoned decisions for the public good as citizens of a culturally diverse, democratic society in an interdependent world.[17]

THE OUTLOOK FOR STANDARDS

It is difficult to predict exactly where the so-called standards movement is going in the US. While state governors promoted standards as the vehicle for improving education, many of them are now hostile to the idea. They cite the fact that education in the US is not now, and never has been, a national prerogative. The states and local school districts are largely responsible for funding the American educational machine. Indeed, the federal contribution towards educational programming is only about 11 per cent of the total expenditure on education. This small amount has not stopped the numerous demands for Congress to dismantle the US Department of Education, because many states want no involvement by the federal government.

Originally, it was proposed by the governors that the standards be accompanied by high-stakes assessments that would determine what students were learning and which school districts were meeting performance goals. If national standards angered the school districts and the states, national assessments made them apoplectic. With the exception of the National Assessment of Educational Progress (NAEP) – a survey or trend assessment mandated by Congress, and first carried out in the 1975–1976 school year – there has been little movement towards national testing. As the NAEP assessment involves only representative samples of students, the results cannot be used to determine the achievement of individual students or compare results classroom to classroom.

States, of course, are free to develop their own tests, and many are doing so. Supporters of this approach suggest that a combination of 'voluntary' state-designed tests and the NAEP can be a useful measure of how well schools are doing.

Most states are also developing their own frameworks and standards. These are quite different in content and format. Some contain content standards, others performance. In many cases, the development process has become highly politicised and rancorous. In some, the professional organisations have become involved in the debate. For example, in 1997 the National Council for History Education recommended the following guidelines for state social studies/history frameworks:

- history as continuing core, K–12;
- substantive historical content as well as historical thinking that goes beyond critical thinking skills;
- continuing themes and questions that will engage students and pull courses together across the grades;
- specific rather than abstract content, but also not overly detailed;
- at least four full years of formal history instruction between grades 7 and 12, and a K–6 programme that is history-centred.[18]

Such guidelines would be unlikely to accommodate the ten themes recommended by the National Council for the Social Studies.

Another problem in the standards movement is the sheer number of performance expectations that are included in the various standards documents. It is unlikely that all, or even most, of them can be addressed by schools given the hours in a school day, the years in a pre-collegiate career, and the configurations of courses taught. Some of the standards would appear to be most useful in designing courses – history, for example. Others, such as those for civics and government, should be infused or integrated into ongoing courses throughout the entire K–12 experience. But even if educators follow the suggestion of NCSS to use its plan as a general guide, they will find it nearly impossible to meet all the performance expectations combined.

A final problem is the vague nature of the relationship between the social science disciplines and civic action. There is no clear consensus among the academic disciplines about what citizens should know and be able to do. Lacking this determination, many teachers have no idea about what content they should be teaching in order to enhance students' civic competency. The unfortunate result is that teachers often end up teaching a discipline for its own sake, rather than teaching those elements that will best inform civic behaviour.

NEW APPROACHES TO SOCIAL STUDIES/CITIZENSHIP EDUCATION

This section offers a brief look at several approaches to social studies/citizenship instruction that go beyond the traditional course offerings. Some of these – law-related education, economic education and global education – are characterised by a particular content focus that its proponents submit is lacking in the core curriculum. As a group, these are characterised as 'special interest' social studies. They tend to be implemented as part of the elective programme. Economic education as described here is quite different from the traditional economics course that is usually offered at grade 12.

Other approaches – such as service learning, character education, multicultural education and experiential education – are really strategies that are designed to improve and enhance required classes. Service learning, for example, is a strategy that can and should be used in history, geography and government courses, because students apply what they learn in class to community settings. Similarly, multicultural education emphasises the contributions of minorities in many disciplines and reflects the diversity of the school population.

Although these approaches are being widely discussed in the literature and are attracting more and more proponents, most are not really 'new' at all. It is more correct to say they are being recycled or renamed from an earlier time. Character education has previously appeared as moral education and values education. Community service/service learning was being promoted in 1916.

Law-related education[19]

Civics and government teachers provide instruction about the political system, but offer little about the legal system. As a result, most young people graduate with no notion about the nature or function of law, its role in society, its techniques, or its limitations.

According to Dr David T. Naylor, Professor of Education at the University of Cincinnati and former member of the National Advisory Commission of the American Bar Association's Special Committee on Youth Education for Citizenship, instruction about the law can and has been successfully implemented at every grade level to correct this deficiency.

Generally speaking, the purpose of providing instruction about the law to students is 'to encourage each generation to reinvent the republic and to internalize the principles of democracy', according to Naylor. This is particularly challenging now because of the level of apathy and cynicism provoked by political scandals and alleged wrong-doing by government officials, increasing fragmentation and polarisation of racial groups, and a dreary litany of past non-compliance with civil rights legislation. Adds Naylor, 'There is tension between *pluribus* and *unum*[20] that has been exacerbated by unfortunate media attacks that have equated accusations of wrong-doing with proof of guilt.'

Naylor indicates that many of the law-related materials have focused on the Bill of Rights, and he believes that these provided a basic understanding of individual rights. He is not sure that enough attention has been paid historically to the 'responsibilities' side of the equation. Thus, he is pleased to note that in recent years more instruction is being offered that focuses on the twin concepts of the common good and public virtue. Says Naylor: 'An important role of schools is to help students sort out exactly what is a social good and to develop in them a social consciousness about others and about the environment.'

Naylor also points out that the strategies most law-related educators use – such as case studies, mock trials, moot courts and analyses of primary documents – allow students to 'produce' knowledge. They learn to tolerate ambiguities, appreciate complexities, and understand that different actions can lead to multiple consequences. He is unwilling to estimate the number of students involved in such instructions.

> Probably more than in any other 'special interest' content, but still not enough. We still need to get more pre-service teachers involved, develop a research base, get the content integrated into basic textbooks, and design thematic approaches that will involve teachers of literature, for example. Oh yes, there is still much to do.

Global education[21]

Every politician and observer agrees that the USA is now more a part of the high-technology 'global economy' than ever. Likewise, few dispute the global scope of environmental problems. Yet with few exceptions, television and newspaper coverage in the USA of international events becomes more sparse each year. Although citizens' well-being is increasingly affected by global issues, they have less access to reliable world news. Schools are thus having to assume the responsibility for providing students with a sophisticated understanding of world affairs. Most districts, however, do not require a course on contemporary world events.

For that reason, many propose the integration or infusion of global issues into traditional civics and government classes. Although citizens need to have a basic understanding of global issues in order to evaluate public policies in the international arena, scant attention has been paid to international topics in the past – according to Susan Graseck, director of the Choices for the 21st Century Education Project at Brown University. Choices was developed to teach the habits and skills of citizenship through a deep engagement with international issues. It is used each year by approximately 650,000 students in more than 3,500 US schools.

Graseck hopes that Choices in particular and global education in general will bring about a subtle evolution in the definition of effective civic action. Specifically, Graseck says Choices is intended to help students think for themselves 'about contested international issues'. Graseck also feels Choices gives students the opportunity to develop mental habits that are conducive to effective citizenship. For Graseck, effective citizenship education must have a global component, lest Americans 'close in on ourselves'.

Choices promotes serious thinking among students by focusing its materials on discrete citizenship competencies. Students are challenged to 'appreciate the history that has shaped current issues, weigh national priorities, consider diverse perspectives, and decide for themselves the direction they think US policy should take'. Lessons are also structured to encourage co-operative group work and role-playing among students. This style of teaching helps students analyse historical data, assess diverse views, identify logical inconsistencies, make and defend judgements, and debate issues based on evidence. The substance is global affairs, but the skills are immediately useful in the local civic arena.

Like many initiatives, global education is hampered by the intense demands on teachers' time. Thus, in her Choices workshops, Graseck concentrates on helping teachers infuse global content into their existing courses. She also ensures that Choices materials explicitly support the existing social studies curriculum. The teacher resource books spell out numerous core content areas supported by the Choices unit. Programme expansion depends on whether teachers can be convinced that Choices, instead of diverting precious teaching time, is a worthwhile strategy to teach existing material.

Economics education[22]

In the view of Patricia Elder of the National Council for Economics Education (NCEE), the purpose of citizenship education is to 'empower people to make responsible choices'. She sees great crossover between economics education and civic empowerment. The process of making choices in market economies resembles the skill set used by effective citizens in public life. Economics and citizenship education both emphasise making decisions, anticipating consequences, weighing costs and benefits, and assessing evidence. Power in democracy and in the marketplace accrues to those who know how to broaden their choices and learn from their bad decisions.

One of the NCEE's programmes is designed to reduce the dropout rate among secondary students. When addressing other economists, Elder knows how to promote education as an 'investment in human capital'. But convincing students that staying in school has tangible benefits requires a more concrete approach. Elder titles this approach 'Choices and Changes' and says it lets students understand the consequences of investing in themselves. Elder strongly believes that abstract concepts in economics and citizenship must be taught experientially.

One 'Choices and Changes' activity is titled 'The Market Game'. Students take assigned roles and simulate the process by which people set prices within markets. Students learn that market prices are not established by government, conspiracy or divine guidance. Rather, by role-playing producers, consumers, shippers, retailers and others involved in pricing, students begin to understand the human decisions that constitute 'market forces'. Demystifying the market in this way is the first step towards showing students that they have economic power based on the decisions they make every day. Two key outcomes of 'Choices and Changes', enhanced decision-making and increased efficacy, are equally crucial elements of effective civic action.

According to Elder, the NCEE leads the nation's most comprehensive economic education network. Nearly one-half of all secondary teachers have taken either one or no college-level economics courses. Because '28 states now mandate either a separate course or the infusion of economics', Elder focuses much of NCEE's energy on teacher training and a trainer-of-trainers approach.

Experiential education[23]

Experiential education was described by Mortimer Adler in *The Paideia Proposal: An Educational Manifesto* as an approach that 'is active, not passive. It involves the use of the mind, not just the memory. It is a process of discovery, in which the student is the main agent, not the teacher.'[24]

Maureen McDonnell of the Close Up Foundation argues that civic educators should focus primarily on strategies. She believes that civics content can be defined within the broad framework of a few key questions (for example: What is the role of government in a democracy? What is the role of citizens as individuals or in groups?). Such a framework for civic education allows the topic to be woven throughout all grade levels and a number of courses.

McDonnell is more concerned with the types of experiences provided to students and with how teachers teach. To her, the crucial civic responsibility is informed action, so civics instruction must be active. In McDonnell's view, too few teachers use experiential methods, irrespective of subject and grade level. She is not surprised to see that surveys of college freshmen indicate greater levels of apathy than ever. Text-and-lecture strategies have separated young people's everyday concerns from the local, national and global issues that affect them.

Field experiences in civics can reverse these negative trends, says McDonnell. She believes that civics programmes like Close Up Washington, which is a week-long residential programme in the nation's capital for American high school students, can and should be replicated in communities everywhere. There is no guaranteed formula for creating a successful field experience in civics instruction, but McDonnell suggests some principles used by Close Up that increase the likelihood of success:

- Involve students of different backgrounds (racial, religious ideological, etc.) to reflect the diversity of the community.
- Explore field sites that help students see the connection between their private concerns and their public responsibilities.
- Build adaptability into the content so that it reacts to student choice.
- Ensure that all content provided is rigorous.
- Provide time for students to reflect on their experiences through discussion, writing, acting or other means.
- Set and enforce norms requiring respect, listening and participation.
- Provide students with conflicting views and allow them to draw their own policy or historical conclusions.

Many of these recommendations can be used in classroom settings as well as in field experiences. A classroom with norms that promote respect, choice and reflection will increase student motivation. Teachers, though, should not avoid dealing with controversial issues to promote harmony in the classroom. Controversy in the classroom serves two purposes: it engages student interest, and it can illustrate how policy emerges from the clash of ideas, interests and views. As the culture becomes more polarised, schools need to provide concrete models of dealing with controversy that are civil and peaceful. These models must then be reinforced by structured learning experiences in the community.

Service learning[25]

Dawn Bova, who manages service learning programmes for the Close Up Foundation, also suggests that civic educators should regard skills and attitudes as the equal of content. Effective civic education must prompt students to exercise their responsibilities if they are to understand and internalise content, says Bova. Service learning activities give students a structure in which to exercise their civic responsibilities.

Service learning can help prepare students for the 'office of citizen' in three additional ways, according to Bova. First, service learning exposes students to people with whom they would otherwise have little interaction, such as those from different age-groups and socio-economic strata. Second, service learning activities provide an immediate answer to the common student question, 'Why do we have to know this?' Finally, service learning demon-strates that there is much more to citizenship than voting and obeying the law – such as keeping informed, addressing community problems and promoting a point of view.

Service learning reaches a growing number of students each year. According to figures from the US Corporation for National Service (CNS), one and a half million students in grades K-12 and 500,000 college students are involved in service learning activities, as of 1997. CNS supports programmes with federal funds; privately funded programmes are not included in the CNS totals.

Bova is concerned about improving the quality of projects defined by their organisers as service learning. Some schools errantly refer to their community service efforts – which have no connection to the curriculum – as service learning. Training for educators is crucial to help them understand that service learning is a teaching strategy to be used within the curriculum.

Bova also stresses that service learning is not necessarily the best teaching strategy for all topics. She emphasises that service learning projects can vary as much as communities and problems do; no single model works best everywhere. Quality improves, however, when service learning creates partnerships between teachers and communities, parents and schools, and students and communities.

To have any lasting impact, service learning must engage students in solving community problems, according to Donna Power. Power is the Curriculum Director for the Earth Force programme Community Action and Problem Solving (CAPS), an environmental education and service learning programme for young teens (ages 10–14).

CAPS encourages teachers to teach civics and ecology through service learning. Service learning engages students in community problem-solving that makes use of core course concepts and academic skills. In Power's terms, CAPS 'is experiential education applied to the community'. Power says teachers in other disciplines can effectively use CAPS materials because the original rationale for US public schools was to produce constructive citizens.

CAPS teachers challenge students to take positions on key issues, defend their opinions, conduct surveys and debate the public good. Power says these civic skills help students move beyond altruism, which is the aim of many service programmes, to 'enlightened self-interest'. Power adds that CAPS teaches students 'society is as it is because people made it that way', specifically by pursuing their interests. Upon seeing that community problems stem from people's action or inaction, students learn they can choose either to shape the world or react to it.

Power has specific ideas about sustaining service learning as a national citizenship education strategy. First, she says administrators, community agency personnel and teachers must participate equally in staff development sessions about service learning. Second, administrators must experiment with new scheduling schemes that encourage collaboration among teachers and field experiences among students. Third, community agencies must work with teachers to provide meaningful service experiences for students. Finally, service learning programmes must explicitly support the curriculum as it currently exists. Power insists that service learning collapses when teachers view it as another ancillary activity.

Multicultural education[26]

In the view of Howard University Professor Russell Adams, the rationale for citizenship education is changing dramatically. The change is being driven by a national attempt explicitly to define the aims of citizenship education. Adams asserts that the US has abandoned decades of citizenship education based on a tautology: 'Why did we teach citizenship? To promote good citizenship.' Little consideration has been given to what constitutes civic competency. Rather, Adams points out, there was an unspoken consensus about effective citizenship, which has emphasised deference, respect for institutions, nationalist pride and a 'melting pot' view of ethnic difference.

The attempt to spell out the aims of citizenship education has effected a sensitive political debate involving race, gender, religion and ethnicity. 'Traditionalists' promote a civic education that stresses the common heritage of Americans as one people. They argue that nourishing a common national identity supersedes promoting an appreciation of cultural differences. 'Multiculturalists' counter that racial, sexual, religious and other forms of discrimination continue to deny large groups of Americans their full citizenship opportunities. This discrimination stems from people's ignorance about the traditions and contributions of groups such as African Americans, Hispanic Americans, American Indians and Asian Americans. Civic education must promote knowledge and appreciation of America's diverse groups, say the multiculturalists.

While the traditional reason for civic education was unarticulated, says Adams, the multicultural rationale has now become 'self-conscious to the point of having a political edge'. Two national organisations have joined the debate. The National Academy of Scholars (NAS) argues for traditionalism, while the National Council for the Social Studies (NCSS) promotes multiculturalism. The NAS acknowledges diversity, but they stress the contributions of minority groups to the common good. They also continue to focus on common history and ritual: the Gettysburg Address, the Pledge of Allegiance, Pearl Harbor and *America the Beautiful*. The NCSS gives multiculturalism 'a strong vision', says Adams, advocating awareness of cross-cultural rituals and history viewed from multiple perspectives.

The debate is having an impact on the practical, everyday teaching of citizenship. According to Adams, many schools will continue to seek the appropriate balance between *pluribus* and *unum*. Such public behaviours as saluting the flag will continue to be passed along to students of all ethnic backgrounds. However, Adams believes that parts of the 'face-to-face culture', such as recognising that different people pray differently, will be taught as part of citizenship as well.

While traditional citizenship training denied the tension between *unum* and *pluribus*, Adams says some educators are becoming 'explicit about the duality'. Adams labels this evolving definition of civic education 'critical patriotism'. According to Adams, critical patriotism teaches that 'the US is our parent, [but] with due respect of group experience and cultural nuances'.

Consequently, many teachers of critical patriotism fear a backlash in their communities from parents or others in communities who received traditional civic education. Adams has seen a number of teachers who taught critical patriotism once, received complaints and quickly returned to traditionalism. Thorough training for teachers is an essential part of successfully teaching critical patriotism.

Adams acknowledges that teaching critical patriotism places enormous stress on teachers – who must learn new cultural content, adapt their strategies and find the time to cover traditional and multicultural material. Therefore, he has trained teachers in Maryland to weave respect for diversity and cultural information into their social studies courses. As more teachers gain skills in teaching critical patriotism, civic education will become, in Adams's phrase, 'a sharing of functions, not a competition for content'.

Character education[27]

In some ways, character education appears to have erupted upon the educational scene recently. Certainly, the topic has received more prominence since the former US Secretary of Education, William Bennett, used his office as a 'bully pulpit' to promote explicit instruction about virtue. Bennett's *The Book of Virtues*[28] has been developed into a television series targeted at young people and has been widely viewed across the nation. There is also now an association, the Character Education Partnership, which includes a variety of organisations that are developing character curriculum materials.

However, moral education and values education have been around for many years. What may be different today is the deliberate linking of private morality and public virtue. Dr James S. Leming, Professor of Curriculum and Instruction at Southern Illinois University, has noted that of the three sets of outcomes for civic education – knowledge, skills and attitudes – the last has been the least successful:

> The biggest weakness that I see with civic education is with regard to the formation of 'habits of the heart'[29] or civic virtue. I think we social studies educators are doing a terrible job of instilling the basic dispositions necessary for civic life.

A Task Force on Character Education in the Social Studies, of which Dr Leming was co–chair, developed a position paper entitled 'Fostering civic virtue: Character education in the social studies'. This statement, which was approved by the Board of Directors of the National Council for the Social Studies in the autumn of 1996, attempted to build a rationale for including character education in the schools and linking private and public virtues. The rationale portion of this position paper points out that the US is the first nation not founded on bloodlines or kinships, but on a shared commitment to fundamental ideals and principles.

The task force linked civic virtue to individual character. It defined character as the regular display of virtuous behaviours.[30] Many virtues, both private and public, when consistently and regularly demonstrated, are considered relevant not only to personal but also to public life.

Studying the traditional subject matter of the social studies is believed to provide the necessary conceptual framework for an understanding and appreciation of the democratic way of life. However, study alone is not enough. Leming emphasises that the school itself should become the model of a just community. Parents, clergy, business people and local government officials should all involve themselves in displaying the private and public behaviours of virtuous citizens.

> It is essential that young people be exposed to attractive models of civic virtue and have the opportunity to produce civic virtue in a meaningful and rewarding manner. Schools need to recognize the different learning processes shaping the civic 'habits of the heart'.[31]

CONCLUSION

For the foreseeable future, most people continue to agree that educating for citizenship is the primary goal of social studies. However, R. Freeman Butts, one of the foremost scholars in the field, notes that

> this historic purpose of public education has been muted in most of the recent arguments and controversies about national education goals, standards, and testing. The emphasis has all too often been confined to the need for better teaching of science and math, a speeded-up technology, and better training for jobs.[32]

As a principal contributor to *Civitas*, Butts sees that document and its companion, *The National Standards for Civics and Government*,[33] as the best hope for the future of civic education. 'These documents', he says, 'have been widely adopted or adapted by educational authorities throughout the US and more recently in many of those newly independent countries of the world that are seeking to become truly democratic societies.'[34] Butts concludes with a warning to US schools: 'Preparing democratic citizens is your fundamental goal. American democracy is at stake.'[35]

NOTES

1 Letter of Thomas Jefferson to William C. Jarvis, 28 September 1820.
2 See Barr, Robert D., James L. Barth and S. Samuel Shermis (1977) *Defining the Social Studies*. Arlington, VA: National Council for the Social Studies, and Turner, Mary Jane Nickelson (1978)

'Political education in the United States: History, status, critical analysis and an alternative model'. University of Colorado, doctoral dissertation.

3 National Education Association (1892) *Report of the Committee [of Ten] on Secondary School Subjects with the Report of the Conferences*. Washington, DC: United States Bureau of Education.

4 Turner, op. cit., pp. 17–21.

5 See, for example, 'Report of the Committee of Five of the American Political Science Association and Instruction in American Government in Secondary Schools', proceedings, *American Political Science Association V* (1908). National Education Association (1916) 'The social studies in secondary education: A report on the reorganisation of secondary education of the National Education Association', *Bulletin*, 28, Washington, DC: Bureau of Education.

6 Barr, Barth and Shermis, op. cit., p. 32.

7 Turner, op. cit., pp. 40, 44.

8 Barr, Barth and Shermis, op. cit., p. 41.

9 Anderson, Lee *et al.* (1990) *The Civic Report Card*. Washington, DC: US Department of Education; National Education Goals Panel (1994) *The National Educational Goals Report*. Washington, DC: US Government Printing Office.

10 Cited in Bahmueller, Charles F. (ed.) (1991) *Civitas*. National Council for the Social Studies, Bulletin No. 86. Washington, DC: National Council for the Social Studies, p. xx.

11 Ibid., p. xxi.

12 Ibid., Introduction.

13 Ibid.

14 Although the Center for Civic Education developed the *Standards for Civics and Government*, it is a different document than *Civitas*, which was discussed above.

15 National Council for the Social Studies (1994) *Expectations of Excellence: Curriculum Standards for Social Studies*, Washington, DC: NCSS, pp. viii, ix.

16 Ibid., pp. x–xii.

17 Ibid., p. vii.

18 Bailyn, Bernard (1997) 'On the teaching and writing of history', *History Matters: Ideas, Notes and News about History*. Westlake, OH: National Council for History Education, Inc, 9 (6), February.

19 Information in this portion of the essay is based on a telephone interview with Dr David T. Naylor in 1997.

20 *E Pluribus Unum* [From many, one] is the national motto of the United States, referring to the country's goal of unity in the midst of diversity.

21 Information in this portion of the essay is based on a 1996 telephone interview with Susan Graseck, Director of Brown University's Choices for the 21st Century Education Project, and from the Choices prospectus.

22 Information in this portion of the essay is based on a 1996 telephone interview with Dr Patricia Elder, Vice President for International Programs at the National Council for Economics Education.

23 Information for this portion of the essay is based on a 1998 interview with Maureen McDonnell, Training and Educational Design Specialist at the Close Up Foundation.

24 Adler, Mortimer (1982) *The Paideia Proposal: An Educational Manifesto*, New York: Macmillan.

25 Information for this portion of the essay is based on interviews with Dawn Bova, Active Citizenship Today Manager for the Close Up Foundation, 1998, and Donna Power, Curriculum Director for Earth Force, Inc., 1996.

26 Information for this portion of the essay is based on a telephone interview with Dr Russell Adams, Professor of Afro-American Studies and Co-Editor of *Common Quest*, the magazine of Black-Jewish Relations, 1996.

27 This portion of the essay is based upon a telephone interview and a letter from Dr James S. Leming dated 26 September 1996, and a Task Force Position paper.

28 Bennett, William (ed.) (1993) *The Book of Virtues: A Treasury of Great Moral Stories*, New York: Simon and Schuster.

29 Bellah, Robert (ed.) (1985) *Habits of the Heart: Individualism and Contentment in America*, Berkeley: University of California Press.

30 Ibid., p. 3.
31 Ibid.
32 Butts, Freeman (1998) *Education Week*, Feb. 18, p. 37.
33 *National Standards for Civics and Government* (1994) Calabasas, CA: Center for Civic Education.
34 Butts, Freeman (1998) *Education Week*, Feb. 18, p. 37.
35 Ibid.

52

CIVICS AND MORAL EDUCATION

Marvin W. Berkowitz

Civics and moral education encompass a rather broad and diverse set of educational phenomena, so it is necessary to begin by explaining the specific foci of this essay. The primary focus is on moral education, and this term is explained in some detail. Secondarily, the relation of moral education to civics education or citizenship education is explored, particularly from the vantage point of educating for democratic citizenship. Included in this section is a discussion of the elements of successful moral education for democracy. Finally, integrated throughout the discussion are considerations of new and impending trends in the field of moral education.

DEFINING CIVICS AND MORAL EDUCATION

Moral Education

It is important to note at the outset that the term for this field varies both between cultures and historically within cultures; for example, with diverse current preferences of character education (USA), values education (Great Britain), etc. For this discussion, the term *moral education* will be used simply because it is one of the widest internationally recognised rubrics. Here moral education is intended to mean any form of intentional education aimed at promoting the growth of moral functioning; i.e., to increase an individual's capacity to function as an effective moral agent. The specific aim of moral education may be an increase in the ability to reason about right and wrong, an increase in the motivation to do pro-social work or engage in pro-social behaviours, an increase in knowledge about right and wrong, etc. Or it may focus on a combination of these and other related aims.

There is also great diversity and disagreement about what comprises moral education. For some scholars, such as those from a virtue ethics orientation, moral education is a matter of instilling desirable behavioural habits (e.g. Carr, 1991; Wynne and Ryan, 1993). For others, moral education reduces to a form of attitude change; i.e., inculcating specific values. For yet others, such as those from a more liberal cognitive orientation, moral

897

education is essentially the stimulation of the development of the capacity to reason about right and wrong (e.g. DeVries and Zan, 1994; Power *et al.*, 1989; Reimer *et al.*, 1983). As Damon and Colby have argued,

> formal knowledge systems that rely on logic, reasoning and reflection play an important role but they are incomplete and insufficient as the basis of moral behaviour without practice-orientated systems such as goals, habits, affect and commitment. [. . .]
>
> [W]e should not have to choose between promoting clearer moral thought, more humane moral emotions, or more admirable moral habits. . . . We should pursue programmes and practices that contribute to all of these and also promote their integration.
>
> (Damon and Colby, 1996. pp. 32, 34)

More recently, numerous scholars have promoted such a comprehensive and integrative conceptualisation of moral education, one that entails all of these aspects (e.g. behaviour, character, values, reasoning) and more (Berkowitz, 1995; Damon and Colby, 1996; Lickona, 1991; Walker *et al.*, 1995). Such models are both very promising and very challenging. They underscore the need to (a) conceptualise the goals of moral education as multifaceted and psychologically comprehensive, and (b) design moral education initiatives that should effectively address these complex sets of goals rather than being limited to only one or two of them.

Civics education

Moral education and civics education are not synonyms, so it is important to define civics education. There are two common ways to understand civics education: education *about* civics and education *for* citizenship. They are not unrelated, but neither are they redundant. The former concerns the traditional didactic presentation of information about one's society; e.g. the particular form of government, the roles and obligations of citizens, etc. The latter is more a matter of nurturing the development of the individual, in this case the development of those attributes necessary to function as an effective citizen of the society; e.g. the ability to understand and evaluate relevant issues, the willingness to advocate for the society and the civic process, etc. Given the diversity of forms of society, civics education can take quite different forms itself and orient to quite different outcome goals. A totalitarian society may wish to implement civics education for obedience to a rigid and narrow set of behaviours, for example, whereas a democratic society may wish to promote independent thinking and political activism. More authoritarian societies may emphasise loyalty, patriotism and group cohesion, whereas more democratic societies may emphasise critical thinking, conscience and participation in governance. In this essay, we shall focus exclusively on democratic civics education, or what we shall term, 'educating for democracy'.

Educating for democracy

Educating for democracy is any form of intentional education aimed at instilling the skills and knowledge necessary to function effectively in, and thereby contribute to, the democratic political process. At the most mundane level this includes literacy to allow one to be aware of issues and components of the democratic process. At a somewhat more direct level, it entails teaching about the democratic process. More fundamentally, however, educating for democracy includes the fostering of the psychological development of citizens, so that they may be able to understand, evaluate and advocate for the citizenry, the state and the democratic process. Damon and Colby (1996, p. 32) have criticised contemporary schooling for being too 'disconnected from essential outside sources of moral influence such as family, workplace, church or past and present cultural traditions'. Educating for democracy offers a means of bridging this gap between schools and society. None the less, as Damon and Colby suggest, the complete moral education of a future citizen must transcend the school to include the community. It also must begin well before schooling and include parenting for moral development (Berkowitz and Grych, 1998).

RELATION BETWEEN MORAL EDUCATION AND EDUCATING FOR DEMOCRACY

It is this last aspect, fostering development, that underscores the considerable overlap between moral education and educating for democracy. Educating for democracy promotes character development and requires elements of moral education. Whereas some experts focus on the *practice* of democracy as the central ingredient in preparation for citizenship, Patricia White, in her book *Civic Virtues and Public Schooling: Educating Citizens for a Democratic Society* (1996), argues that it is the character of the citizenry that truly defines a democracy. Indeed, many experts believe that left to nature, humans would be ultimately hedonistic. Plato's *Republic* was explicitly intended to offer an antidote to rule by hedonists, a theme echoed by his teacher, Socrates, and student, Aristotle. If humans are to develop democratic (or any moral form of) character, then society must intervene and foster it.

> When government and law urge me to support the common good, they may find an ally in my reason and my soul, but they must expect resistance from my body and my senses. . . . Civic virtue requires that we govern some of our strongest feelings and desires. In that sense, Aristotle argued, to rule free men – and hence, to be a citizen of a democracy – one must first learn how to be ruled.
>
> (McWilliams, 1980, p. 84)

Regardless of how pessimistic one is about fundamental human nature, it is clear that moral character is part of democratic functioning. Thomas Jefferson argued that democracy depends upon the cultivation of 'public-spiritedness' which will not flourish spontaneously, but must be educated. Benjamin Franklin stated that 'only a virtuous people are capable of freedom' and Theodore Roosevelt claimed that 'educating a person in mind and not in morals is to educate a menace to society'. When Alexis de Tocqueville came to explore American character to find out how this great experiment in democracy was working, he observed that 'America is great because she is good; but if America ever ceases to be good, she will cease to be great.' Thomas Lickona, has argued that

> Educating for virtue is especially crucial in a democracy in which people govern themselves. A democratic people, the American founders believed, must grasp and be committed to democracy's moral foundation: respect for the rights of others, concern for the common good, voluntary compliance with law, and participation in the public life.
>
> (Lickona, 1994, p. xii)

899

Furthermore, Lawrence Kohlberg (Power *et al.*, 1989) has argued that a democratically run school is the ideal context for moral education, just as John Dewey (1966) argued that a democratically run school is essential for educating for citizenship. Kohlberg's 'Just Community Schools' are based in part upon the structure of a direct democracy, which is justified by the argument that participation in collaborative egalitarian governance is a rich context for the development of moral maturity. Beckerman and O'Rourke argue that educating for democracy has the

> potential for character-building, for promoting basic democratic values, and for developing patterns of responsible citizenship behavior. Well-designed programs . . . can enhance the social, psychological and intellectual development of youth and help them to become informed, engaged, and effective citizens.
>
> (Beckerman and O'Rourke, 1996, p. 25)

Verba and colleagues (1995), in a study of political participation, conclude that it is the 'hands-on training' in US schools, rather than 'teaching about' democracy, that promotes political participation.

Clearly these ideas about democracy are neither unique nor original to the United States of America. Their roots are traceable back to ancient Greece (Plato, 1945). Socrates clearly articulated the need for citizens and politicians to be virtuous. He felt that the only means of creating a just society was through the development of just citizens. Plato, although construing the solution through enlightened leaders (philosopher kings), echoed the refrain that character was the essential ingredient in building a just and effective republic. Furthermore, other longstanding contemporary democracies are utilising character education as a means of promoting democratic self-governance. In Scotland (which recently won its own parliament after centuries of being included in the English parliament), the 1998 annual conference on values education focused on 'Values education for democracy and citizenship' (Christie *et al.*, 1998).

Currently, many nations (e.g. throughout Eastern Europe, the former Soviet Union, Indonesia and in South and Central America) are confronting the transition from authoritarian rule to democracy, and are exploring the value of character education in facilitating this transition. In Colombia, for example, an organisation called Participación Cuidadana [Citizen Participation] is attempting to facilitate such a transition by both (a) developing a network of civic associations and citizen groups and (b) promoting democratic character education.

Not only is character routinely included in models of citizenship, but citizenship is often included in models of character. The Josephson Institute for Ethics' Youth Summit meeting of 30 experts in youth character in 1992 identified six core character traits that were assumed to be universal goals of moral education. The sixth of these was 'civic virtue and citizenship'.

Clearly there are many intimate links between moral education and educating for democracy. But the overlap between moral education and educating for democracy is not complete. There are some important differences as well, to which we now turn. First of all, the goals are different. For moral education, character is the end. For educating for democracy, character is a means towards the end, which is effective citizenship in a democratic society. Second, character development is only one of the targets of educating for democracy.

Educating for democracy, to be comprehensive and effective, must also target practical skills such as literacy and knowledge of the structure of government and the legal processes of democratic law-making. Third, moral education may choose as an option to include participation in democratic education as a means towards the end of character development (most moral education initiatives do not choose this option), whereas it has been argued that educating for democracy *must* include democratic participation as part of its curriculum to provide practical experience in what is the end goal of educating for democracy; i.e. democratic competency. As Mosher *et al.* lamented in their 1994 book *Preparing for Citizenship: Teaching Youth to Live Democratically*, 'Students have been taught about democracy, but they have not been permitted to practice democracy' (pp. 1–2).

Whereas some non-character aspects of educating for democracy will be included here, the primary focus will be on the overlap between educating for democracy and moral education; hence the primary emphasis will be on the character-specific aspects of educating for democracy.

GOALS OF EDUCATING FOR DEMOCRACY

Ultimately, the goal of educating for democracy is to produce future effective citizens of the democratic state. But what exactly comprises such a citizen? In addition to the 'bedrock' democratic values such as justice, tolerance and personal autonomy that undergird the democratic enterprise, Patricia White (1996) identifies seven traits or dispositions of democratic character: hope and confidence; courage; self-respect and self-esteem; friendship; trust; honesty; and decency. She goes so far as to argue that it is the values of the democratic institutions and the dispositions of its citizens, and not the democratic procedures or 'machinery', that comprise a democracy. David Sehr (1997) argues that public, not private, democracy is the legitimate conceptualisation of democracy. Public democracy requires active commitment to and participation in the public arena and rests upon five characteristics of the democratic citizen:

- an ethic of care and responsibility;
- respect for the equal right of everyone to the conditions necessary for their development;
- appreciation of the importance of the public;
- critical/analytical social perspective;
- capacities necessary for participation in public democracy (e.g. verbal analytical skills, habits of active listening, self-confidence, co-operation, etc.).

In essence, democracy rests on the character of both its institutions (including its schools) and its citizens, or as John Dewey stated

> Government resting upon popular suffrage cannot be successful unless those who elect and who obey their governors are educated. . . . A democracy is more than a form of government; it is primarily a mode of associated living, of conjoint communicated experience.
>
> (Dewey, 1966, p. 87)

Dewey further felt that the way students experience their schools is central to the way they will learn to experience and relate to their broader social contexts when they are adults.

Schools are therefore obliged 'to reorganize curriculum and instruction to teach the knowledge, participation skills, and civic values that students need to become responsible citizens' (Minkler, 1998, p. 2).

Four elements of educating for democracy

Educating for democracy therefore requires at least four central elements:

1 the need for learning *about* democracy and the role of citizens in a democratic state;
2 the need to *experience* or practise democracy;
3 the need for more general education as a foundation for the capacities of democratic participation;
4 the need for the development of character, especially moral character.

Government quells our selfish nature and education makes us both governable and governors. The intersection of personal moral development and citizenship is apparent. Moral education is intended to promote moral development of students but it is also critical to the formation of citizenship, which requires moral agency as one of its components.

IMPLEMENTING MORAL AND CIVICS EDUCATION

The four elements of educating for democracy (foundational capacities, knowledge about democracy, practice at democracy, moral character), provide a framework for how these outcomes can best be achieved through education.

Foundational capacities for democratic functioning

Lawrence Kohlberg (1980) has argued that the right to an education in the US is really the right to read the founding documents of our democratic republic and thereby to sign the social contract that undergirds a true democracy. Literacy becomes necessary for optimal functioning as a citizen in a democracy. This is one example of a foundational capacity for democratic functioning. As noted above, David Sehr (1997, p. 79) lists other such capacities:

1 analysis of written, spoken and image language;
2 clear oral and written expression of one's ideas;
3 habits of active listening as a key to communication;
4 facility in working collaboratively with others;
5 knowledge of constitutional rights and political processes;
6 knowledge of the complexities and interconnections of major public issues to each other and to issues in the past;
7 self-confidence, self-reliance and the ability to act independently (within context of the community);
8 ability to learn more about any issue that arises.

Items (5) and (6) are more appropriately included in the category of democratic knowledge (see below) and others of these capacities may be better construed as aspects of character, e.g. item (7). None the less it should be clear that there are certain skills of communication and social co-operation, among others, that schools need to instil in students in order to successfully accomplish the central goals of moral and civics education.

Skill-building such as this is a fundamental goal of education in general and should not be difficult to implement, nor will it be examined in detail here. It may require some less traditional forms of education to foster specifically democratic skills. Such forms may be service learning, co-operative learning, etc., which embody the communicative and co-operative competencies required for citizenship in a democracy (Andersen, 1998; Watson *et al.*, 1994).

Educating for democratic knowledge

This is probably the simplest of the four goals of educating for democracy, as it is most centrally what educators know how to do; i.e., the transmission of knowledge. Of course, this assumes that the educators are professionally familiar with the knowledge domain. This is a bit trickier in newly democratised nations. One of the typical constraints on implementing educating for democracy in such cultures is that the socialising agents (parents, teachers, etc.) have little familiarity with democracy. They don't know what the practices and institutions of a democracy are, nor can they articulate their nuances or justifications. Hence, educating for democratic knowledge may presuppose professional training of educators and altering the teacher preparation curriculum.

In addition to this is the problem of motivation. Do citizens who have not previously experienced a democracy value the new democracy? If they are not committed to its value and future success, then they may be fairly ineffective in teaching about democracy. Obviously this qualification is not limited to this element.

Practising democracy

It has already been demonstrated that most experts agree that one cannot foster democratic character and skills without allowing for the practice of such skills. As Beckerman and O'Rourke argue, 'social studies teachers have long recognized that civics is no less a laboratory science than, say, chemistry or biology' (1996, p. 26). Unfortunately, schools have historically not been places where students can legitimately exercise their democratic rights of self-governance. Schools have traditionally been authoritarian and hierarchical in structure. Hence, advocates of educating for democracy tend to argue for alterations in the traditional structure of schools. On the more extreme end are experts like Kohlberg (Power *et al.*, 1989), who has designed the Just Community Schools to function as direct democracies. Similarly Berman (1997) and Mosher (Mosher *et al.*, 1994) have argued for increasing the democratic nature of schools, in Berman's case to instil social responsibility and activism and for Mosher to prepare future citizens in a democracy. Others rely on somewhat less direct means, such as role-playing or a limited weekly open forum.

John Dewey (1966) strongly argued that experience lies at the core of education, and that educating for democracy means participation in democratic processes (Mosher *et al.*, 1994). For this to succeed, however, educators need to embrace the philosophical justifications for such a form of education and to confront their own fears and misgivings about doing so. Educators often fear either that giving up control will lead to anarchy and chaos, or that they are somehow violating their professional obligations to 'run' schools by allowing students to take some control for the functioning of the classroom or school.

First, there are degrees of implementing educating for democracy. Some programmes merely use periodic open discussions of school issues. Others run the school as a complete direct democracy, with one vote per 'citizen' whether they be teacher or student. Some teachers clearly delineate the domains that are open to student decision-making and those that are not. Indeed, even Kohlberg's Just Community approach (Power *et al.*, 1989) has been successfully implemented in prisons (Hickey and Scharf, 1980), where limits are clearly placed on the domains that are under inmate control (e.g. inmates cannot vote themselves parole).

Second, when students are given control of their schools, they are less likely to be alienated from them and therefore more likely to take responsibility for them. When one has a say in forming legislation, then one is more likely to respect and obey that legislation. Hence schools with democratic aspects do not become anarchies, just as democratic nations do not become anarchies. Indeed, the Child Development Project reports that the development of a sense of community in the school relates to better academic motivation as well as a decrease in problem behaviours (Battistich *et al.*, 1995).

Building democratic character

This fourth and final piece of the puzzle is the most complex. This is partly so because it invokes all of the complexities and controversies in the field of moral or character education. Some experts differentiate between moral character and non-moral character; others do not (Berkowitz, 1995). Some view character as holistic and others see it as a list of disparate traits. Some believe that character is formed before school begins (in the family); others believe school can be a significant force in shaping character. Most disagree as to what comprises character. And most disagree to some degree on how to foster character development, however it is defined. Therefore it is important to understand that what will be argued here is far from consensual.

There is little doubt, either today or at the very roots of democracy, that the character of a nation's citizens will determine the nature of its democracy. We have already described some of the character traits that experts have identified as central to democratic functioning. Patricia White (1996) cited hope and confidence, courage, self-respect and self-esteem, friendship, trust, honesty and decency. The Josephson Institute of Ethics (Josephson, 1993) elaborates its sixth 'pillar of character' civic virtue and citizenship as comprised of six elements:

- recognition of and living up to social obligations;
- participation in democratic process;

- law abidance;
- protection of the environment;
- community service;
- doing one's share.

However one defines the character components of democratic citizenship, it is clear that educating for democracy must consider how to foster those aspects of character.

Moral educators are unfortunately in great disagreement as to how to foster moral development in schools. Some rely on teaching and lecturing. Others rely on active experimentation. Some use specific curricula; others do not. Some alter the governance structure of schools, etc. We shall argue here, from an admittedly biased perspective, that (a) character is a complex set of psychological attributes and (b) moral education requires a pervasive and differentiated set of educational initiatives. It is important, at this point, to raise the empirical issue. Unfortunately the amount of research dedicated to moral education pales in comparison to the amount of discussion about moral education. The state of the field is that relatively little is known about what works. There are some exceptions; e.g. much research has been dedicated to exploring what educational practices impact on the development of moral reasoning capacities (e.g. Berkowitz, 1985; Mosher, 1980; Power *et al.*, 1989; Rest and Thoma, 1986; Solomon *et al.*, in press). But much less is known, for example, about what effectively impacts on character, values, conscience, etc. The field is beginning to recognise this deficiency and to address it; e.g. the Character Education Partnership has established a task force on this issue. None the less, much of the educational prescription offered here is based on limited scientific evidence.

Numerous theorists have argued for a comprehensive model of character (Damon and Colby, 1996; Lickona, 1991; Walker *et al.*, 1995). Berkowitz (1995) has described a model of character referred to as the 'moral anatomy'. Essentially it argues that there are seven interrelated parts of the moral person (person with moral character):

- moral behaviour;
- moral values;
- moral personality;
- moral reasoning;
- moral affect;
- moral identity;
- meta-moral characteristics.

All of these models support the perspective that being a good person is not a unitary phenomenon and certainly not a simple one.

Because character is complex, moral education is also complex and multifaceted. Promoting moral reasoning requires educational components that challenge one's existing moral reasoning capacities. Such components may be the periodic classroom discussion of moral problems or the experience of having collectively to solve real problems in the classroom, school or community. Promoting moral values relies more heavily on role-modelling and reinforcement as well as guided introspection. Nurturing moral behaviour relies on role-modelling and learning, but is also derivative of all the other components of the moral anatomy; i.e. a student with moral values, personality, reason, etc. is more likely to engage in moral behaviour. Little is currently known about how to educate for moral identity, a rather recent addition to the moral education landscape.

GENERIC AND TARGETED MORAL EDUCATION FOR DEMOCRACY

There are two basic approaches to designing moral education for democratic functioning. The first is generic. Simply implement a successful moral education programme and assume that moral character will support democratic functioning. The second is targeted. Identify those character attributes that are considered essential and specific to democratic functioning and implement an intervention designed specifically to promote their development. It may seem at face value that the 'targeted' option is decidedly preferable; however, there are three reasons for the preferability of the 'generic' option. First, there is disagreement on what comprises specifically democratic character, as can be seen from the examples offered above. Second, the 'science' of moral education is too new to be able validly to identify which moral education components specifically produce which moral development outcomes; thus greatly reducing the likelihood of accurate 'targeting'. Third, many of the character traits associated with democratic functioning tend to be outcomes of many generic moral education initiatives. For example, the Child Development Project (1998), frequently cited as a model moral education programme, reports increased spontaneous prosocial behaviour, democratic values and social competence in students, all of which are identified by others as aspects of democratic character. This is accomplished through a comprehensive approach which includes the development of a vision of character education among administrators, staff development, curriculum reform, behaviour management reform, parent involvement, etc. Moral curriculum content, collaborative learning and the building of a caring school community are central components, as are both process and outcome evaluation.

What then is generic moral education? A six-facet model of moral education will be presented. First it relies on the climate of the school. Recent studies of the Child Development Project (1998) suggest that schools where the perception of a sense of community in the school increases are also schools that promote social competency, critical thinking, democratic values, prosocial motivation and reduced violence and substance use. Kohlberg (Power *et al.*, 1989) argued for the formation of communities of justice and caring in schools. At the minimum, how people treat each other in the school is critical to the effectiveness of moral education (DeVries and Zan, 1994). This clearly includes how students treat each other and how teachers treat students, but also must include how teachers treat each other, how other staff and administrators treat each other and how they treat teachers and students, etc.

This leads to a second dimension of effective moral education; i.e. role modelling. Educators cannot effectively promote character if they do not manifest character; e.g. a dishonest teacher will not effectively promote honesty in students. Identifying other role models in the local community is a popular addendum to moral education programmes.

Third, students also need to develop the capacity for ethical reflection and analysis. They need to develop mature moral reasoning capacities. Furthermore, it is difficult to enter into and contribute to civic debate in a democracy without such capacities. It has been well demonstrated that guided peer discussions of moral issues and problems (Berkowitz, 1985) and participation in democratic governance promote the development of such capacities (Power *et al.*, 1989).

Fourth, exposure to moral ideas and examples is also central. Formal curricula are often very useful here, and are often targeted to specific character outcomes; e.g. courage, honesty, responsible sexuality, etc. Even where such curricula are not available, however, the traditional curriculum is rife with adaptable examples. Every history or social studies or civics curriculum is full of examples of desirable and undesirable character traits. Literature is also a rich source of such examples. Teachers can readily develop their own curricula from such existing sources.

Fifth, because parents are the primary influences on the development of character, it is important to include them in any comprehensive moral education initiative. The Child Development Project has found it valuable to include families in the curriculum (Watson *et al.*, 1994). They have developed extensive curricula to be taken home and completed with family members. As noted earlier, parents in a newly democratised nation may not have the inclinations and/or skills to aid in educating for democracy. Then training of parents may be necessary before including them in the educating for democracy initiative.

Finally, just as practice at democracy is critical for educating for democracy, practice at being moral is critical for moral education. In the US, a currently very popular form of this is service learning, which although quite variable in implementation, is basically using community service as a means of learning about educational content (Andersen, 1998). For example, if students are studying environmental conservation in science class, then a service learning component would be to have them either join an existing conservation initiative in the local community or start their own initiative aimed at a real existing local environmental problem. Co-operative learning is another form of moral education practice. Whereas schools, at least in the US, tend to be very competitive, recent advances in education have tried to promote team learning and small group co-operative projects and classroom exercises. Such activities tend to require co-operation, sharing, altruism, effective communication, etc.

In summary, then, a generic moral education initiative would include the following key elements:

- promotion of a moral atmosphere in the school and/or classroom;
- role modelling of good character by school members and community members;
- guided peer discussions of moral issues and/or participation in school or classroom governance;
- learning about character through the curriculum;
- inclusion of families, especially parents, in the moral education initiative;
- practical experience in moral behaviour.

REFERENCES

Andersen, S. M. (1998) *Service Learning: A National Strategy for Youth Development*. Washington, DC: Institute for Communitarian Policy Studies, George Washington University.
Battistich, V., Solomon, D., Kim, D., Watson, M. and Schaps, E. (1995) 'Schools as communities,

poverty level of student populations, and students' attitudes, motives and performance: A multi-level analysis'. *American Educational Research Journal*, 32, 627–658.

Beckerman, M. and O'Rourke, T. G. (1996) 'Democracy is as democracy does: Citizenship Education Clearinghouse at UM-St. Louis'. *Missouri ASCD Journal*, 6, 25–29.

Berkowitz, M. W. (1985) 'The role of discussion in moral education'. In M. W. Berkowitz and F. Oser (eds), *Moral Education: Theory and Application*. Hillsdale, NJ: Lawrence Erlbaum, 197–218.

Berkowitz, M. W. (1995) *The Education of the Complete Moral Person*. Aberdeen: Gordon Cook Foundation.

Berkowitz, M. W. and Grych, J. H. (1998) 'Fostering goodness: Teaching parents to facilitate children's moral development'. *Journal of Moral Education*, 27, 371–391.

Berman, S. (1997) *Children's Social Consciousness and the Development of Social Responsibility*. New York: State University of New York Press.

Carr, D. (1991) *Educating the Virtues: An Essay on the Philosophical Psychology of Moral Development and Education*. London: Routledge.

Child Development Project (1998) *The Child Development Project: Summary of the Project and Findings from Three Evaluation Studies*. Oakland, CA: Developmental Studies Center.

Christie, D., Maitles, H. and Halliday, J. (eds) (1998) *Values Education for Democracy and Citizenship: Proceedings of the Gordon Cook Foundation Conference*. Glasgow: University of Strathclyde.

Damon, W. and Colby, A. (1996) 'Education and moral commitment'. *Journal of Moral Education*, 25, 31–37.

DeRoche, E. F. and Williams, M. M. (1998) *Educating Hearts and Minds: A Comprehensive Character Education Framework*. Thousand Oaks, CA: Sage.

Developmental Studies Center (1998) *The Child Development Project: Summary of the Project Findings from Three Evaluation Studies*. Oakland, CA: Developmental Studies Center.

DeVries, R. and Zan, B. (1994) *Moral Classrooms, Moral Children: Creating a Constructivist Atmosphere in Early Education*. New York: Teachers College Press.

Dewey, J. (1966) *Democracy and Education*. New York: The Free Press.

Hickey, J. and Scharf, P. (1980) *Toward a Just Correctional System*. San Francisco: Jossey-Bass.

Josephson, M. (1993) *The Six Pillars of Character*. Marina del Rey, CA: Josephson Institute of Ethics.

Kohlberg, L. (1980) 'High school democracy and educating for a just society'. In R. L. Mosher (ed.), *Moral Education: A First Generation of Research and Development*. New York: Praeger, 20–57.

Lickona, T. (1991) *Educating for Character: How Our Schools Can Teach Respect and Responsibility*. New York: Bantam Books.

Lickona, T. (1994) 'Foreword'. In R. Mosher, R. A. Kenny Jr. and A. Garrod, *Preparing for Citizenship: Teaching Youth to Live Democratically*. Westport, CT: Praeger, xi–xv.

McWilliams, W. C. (1980) 'Democracy and the citizen: Community, dignity, and the crisis of contemporary politics in America'. In R. A. Goldwin and W. A. Schambra (eds), *How Democratic Is the Constitution?* Washington, DC: American Enterprise Institute for Public Policy Research, 79–101.

Minkler, J. (1998) 'Civic responsibility assessment'. Invited address to the Character Education Assessment Forum, Fresno, CA.

Mosher, R. L. (ed.) (1980) *Moral Education: A First Generation of Research and Development*. New York: Praeger.

Mosher, R., Kenny Jr, R. A. and Garrod, A. (1994) *Preparing for Citizenship: Teaching Youth to Live Democratically*. Westport, CT: Praeger.

Plato (1945) *The Republic of Plato* (trans. F. M. Cornford). New York: Oxford University Press.

Power, F. C., Higgins, A. and Kohlberg, L. (1989) *Lawrence Kohlberg's Approach to Moral Education*. New York: Columbia University Press.

Reimer, J., Paolitto, D. P. and Hersh, R. H. (1983) *Promoting Moral Growth: From Piaget to Kohlberg* (2nd edn). New York: Longman.

Rest, J. R. and Thoma, S. J. (1986) 'Educational programs and interventions'. In J. R. Rest (ed.), *Moral Development: Advances in Research and Theory*. New York: Praeger, 59–88.

Sehr, D. T. (1997) *Education for Public Democracy*. New York: State University of New York Press.

Solomon, D., Watson, M. S. and Battistich, V. A. (In press) 'Teaching and schooling effects on moral/

prosocial development'. In V. Richardson (ed.), *Handbook of Research on Teaching* (4th edn). Washington, DC: American Educational Research Association.

Verba, S., Schlozman, K. L. and Brady, H. E. (1995) *Voice and Equality: Civic Voluntarism in American Politics*. Cambridge, MA: Harvard University Press.

Walker, L. J., Pitts, R. C., Hennig, K. H. and Matsuba, M. K. (1995) 'Reasoning about morality and real-life moral problems'. In M. Killen and D. Hart (eds), *Morality in Everyday Life: Developmental Perspectives*. New York: Cambridge University Press, 371–407.

Watson, M., Schoenblum, A. and Zubizarreta, R. (1994) 'Cooperative schoolwide communities for teachers, parents, and students'. *Cooperative Learning: The Magazine for Cooperation in Education*, 14, 9–13.

White, P. (1996) *Civic Virtues and Public Schooling: Educating Citizens for Democratic Society*. New York: Teachers College Press.

Wynne, E. A. and Ryan, K. (1993) *Reclaiming Our Schools: A Handbook on Teaching Character, Academics, and Discipline*. New York: Merrill.

53

TECHNOLOGY EDUCATION
Towards a new school subject

Marc J. de Vries

INTRODUCTION

Probably there is currently no school subject around which there is so much debate as there is around technology education. To a large extent this is because technology education is a relatively new subject in the school curriculum, when we mean technology as a contribution to general education for all pupils (of course there is also vocational, technical education, which does have a long tradition; in this article we shall focus on technology education as general education). Although technology education in all countries has a sort of historical background – usually in craft education – the changes towards technology education are so fundamental that one could easily be justified in calling it a new subject. Of course, other school subjects go through major changes also. Science education, for example, has become increasingly linked to everyday life phenomena that pupils directly experience for themselves. Furthermore, there has been a growing sense of awareness of the role played by pupils' preconceptions which they bring to science, and how these can be transformed into more scientifically valid concepts by creating effective educational situations. But even with these sorts of changes, science education remains science education in a recognisable way. And maybe more importantly: the changes are made by teachers that have been specifically educated to teach science. In that respect the situation is different for technology education, where in most countries teachers of other subjects have been retrained to become technology teachers (often in addition to their other teaching roles). These teachers often do not have much more than a basic knowledge of the subject, which is sufficient to teach technology adequately, but does not enable them to create a new school subject. But in a way the same holds for the teacher trainers, who in most cases have their background in other subjects too. An additional problem for technology education is that, contrary to most other school subjects, it has no directly equivalent discipline in the academic world. Science educators can draw from the academic disciplines of physics, chemistry and biology to get a conceptual basis for their teaching. For technology education, one could of course think of the various engineering disciplines in the academic world, but it is generally felt that following those would create too narrow a scope for teaching technology. And other than

910

those disciplines, there are no others that combine all the different aspects that one would like to bring together in technology education.

In such a situation – a relatively new school subject without a direct academic equivalent – it is hardly surprising that the emergence of technology education causes a lot of fundamental discussions with respect to curriculum content, teaching strategies and ways of assessment, just to mention a few aspects.

AIMS OF TECHNOLOGY EDUCATION

The motivation for creating a school subject that focuses on technology as a discipline and as a phenomenon in our culture, has been for most countries that (future) citizens ought to have a good concept of what technology is and the skills to deal with it effectively. The importance of this is, in the first place, that it will enable them to live in a modern society in which technology has come to play such a vital role. 'Living' in this respect means more than surviving. They ought to have control over technology rather than vice versa. That means that they should not only have the skills to use technology in a safe and proper way, but also know how technology is developed, what decisions are made in that process, and what roles they can play in influencing those decisions, either as technologists or as non-technologists. Second, it enables them to make a well-based choice to opt either for a technological or a non-technological career. Several countries have implemented technology education because of the concern for an adequate national technological workforce. Even though the social debates of the 1970s, which often had a negative image of technology as a background, have faded away, for many people it is still not an attractive option to work in the field of technology. Enrolment in engineering training programmes, both in the academic and in the vocational sectors, in several countries is too low to guarantee the technological workforce these countries need. Attitude research has shown that there is a relationship between a narrow concept of technology, which envisions technology mainly in terms of the *outcomes* of technology, i.e. products, and a negative attitude towards technology. In particular, this results in gender differences: boys more often seem to feel comfortable in dealing with machines and equipment while girls show more interest in the human and social aspects of technology, which in their concept of technology plays only a minor role. This tends to result in a general lack of interest in technology on the girls' part (Raat and De Vries, 1986). If both boys and girls would acquire a better, more balanced concept, that encompasses technology as knowledge, as artefacts, as skills and as volition (Mitcham, 1994), rather than as artefacts only, this would result in a more sophisticated attitude towards technology and more sophisticated career choices. This implies that in technology both products and processes need to be given sufficient attention. In the third place, specific areas of technical knowledge and skills can be seen as aims for technology education, but then we are already making a transition to vocational education, which aims to prepare pupils for specific technological careers, and as stated before, here we shall focus on technology education as general education.

These considerations in many countries have resulted in adequate political support for the introduction of technology education, often as a compulsory school subject.

911

ISSUES IN THE DEVELOPMENT OF TECHNOLOGY EDUCATION

In different countries with their different economic and social situations, different approaches to technology have emerged. It would be impossible to describe them all, but one way to gain an impression of the variety is to describe the extremes in which specific aspects of technology have been given a strong emphasis. They can be seen as specific wavelengths in the whole spectrum of possible approaches: one will hardly ever find them as such, but all existing approaches can be seen as either close to one of these wavelengths or as a combination of wavelengths (a similar strategy has been used in an OECD project on Science, Maths and Technology education; see Black and Atkin, 1996). Thus the following approaches can be identified (De Vries, 1993):

- a craft-oriented approach
- an industry-oriented approach
- a science-oriented approach
- a 'high-tech' approach
- an engineering concepts approach
- a key competencies approach
- a design-oriented approach
- a social issues approach.

Through increasing international contacts, the differences among the approaches we find in various countries gradually become less prominent than the categorisation above suggests. But each of these extremes causes a discussion about the proper role of the aspect that it has overemphasised. We shall now consider each of these aspects in more detail.

The role of craft skills

As stated earlier, in most countries technology education has its roots in craft education: often this is still noticeable in current practice. Technology education to a large extent means making workpieces. Whatever else may be involved around those workpieces, the skills for making simple technical devices still is present in most programmes. In general it is felt that making products remains an essential element in technology and that pupils should experience this aspect. There are, however, situations in which this idea is abandoned. In the United States so-called modular curriculum programmes can be found in which production tools and equipment have been replaced by computers and – often automated – equipment for experimenting with sophisticated technological devices. There is a debate ongoing about the pros and cons of these modular programmes. One of the objections against them is that vendors rather than educationalists seem to determine the content of technology education. But primarily the fact that pupils no longer get any feeling or *Fingerspitzengefühl* for technical materials and tools, is seen as a serious disadvantage of these modular programmes.

The role of industry

In particular, in the former Eastern bloc in Europe, one could see a technology education approach that was strongly biased towards industrial production. Pupils in 'polytechnic education' had to learn the various industrial production processes, including work preparation. This was motivated by the strong ideological role of industry in those countries at that time. The political changes at the end of the 1980s have resulted in a substantial decrease in the importance of technology education (for example, in Hungary), mainly because of their ideological flavour. But in the USA too the direct precursor of what is nowadays called 'technology education' was called 'industrial arts' and thus in its very name showed a certain bias towards industrial aspects of technology (Hayles and Snyder, 1982). As curriculum organisers, the social systems of construction, production, transportation and communication were used in this approach and the same headings were used under the new name of 'technology education'. In Germany, one of the options for technology education is called *Arbeitslehre/Technik*. The term *Arbeitslehre* relates to the world of work and the *Arbeitslehre* stream claims to be able to combine technology, economy and home economics into one school subject (Brauer-Schröder and Sellin, 1996). In France textbooks for the subject *Technologie* showed similar interests: often they started by making pupils consider what is needed to start a technological business company. In the UK traditionally there is a good relationship between technology and industry. Industries and educationalists work together to produce learning materials and mutual visits take place between companies and schools. Although industrial aspects should not be overemphasised, as if business interests should be prominent in technological developments, it is yet necessary that pupils gain a good insight into how technology is practised in industry. Therefore technology education programmes should be kept up to date in terms of developments in industry. In that respect there is a current need to pay more attention to quality aspects in technology education. Quality has become a key issue in industry, not only in the sense that finished products need to be checked for possible failures, but even more that quality encompasses every aspect of customer satisfaction. That starts with the identification of the requirements for the product (the so-called 'design-inbuilt' quality) and stretches out to the service that is offered to the customer in the user phase of the product life-cycle and even to the final phase when the product is discarded by the user and may be recycled or re-used. This life-cycle perspective on quality is mirrored in the life-cycle approach to environmental awareness in industry: here too the whole life-cycle needs to be taken into account. This development in modern industries too needs to be implemented in technology education programmes.

The role of science and mathematics

The role of science and mathematics is a most complex matter in technology education (Layton, 1993). In the first place most countries have technology teachers with a non-scientific background (they often came from craft and/or arts education). For those teachers it is difficult to deal with science concepts effectively in their technology lessons. Alternatively science teachers in their science teaching often claim to deal with technology, but then appear to take technology as 'applied science' and pay insufficient attention to the complicated process that leads from scientific knowledge to a technical device or system (apart from the fact that in principle this process does not even start with scientific knowledge). Thus there seems to be a dichotomy here which is not easy to overcome. Finland is an example of a country where this split has led to struggles between science educators and craft educators. Yet, as science plays an important role in many current technological developments, there is a need to make pupils aware of this relationship. Knowledge from science about the properties of materials, energy and information as the basic 'stuff' with which technologists work is crucial to a good understanding of the development of new devices and systems. In this respect there is a pressing need for in-service training of both science and technology teachers to ensure a more effective relationship between science education and technology education to reflect the real-world relationship between science and technology. But there is a more fundamental problem here: philosophical and historical studies into the development of new products have shown that scientific concepts often need some sort of transformation in order to be usable for the engineers. This complicates the relationship between science and technology substantially (De Vries, 1994b). Similar problems can be expected when technology teachers in their lessons try to use the abstract scientific concepts that have been learnt in science education. Here too a certain transformation is needed that requires input from both science educators (and mathematics teachers) and technology educators.

The role of information technologies

As with the previous aspects of technology, the aspect of information technologies can be and has been overemphasised in the practice of technology education. The so-called modular curriculum programmes in the USA have been mentioned already. In particular, in countries with strong electronics industries, like France and Israel, we see the danger of making pupils use information technologies in such a way that they are amazed by them rather than gaining a good understanding of the nature of technology. In such cases pupils build constructions that are controlled by a computer, learn which button to push at which point, but do not acquire an understanding of the basic system concepts behind those constructions. At the same time, experiences in these countries have shown the enormous potential of information technology as a learning tool. Computers can do simulations and calculations, and can yield access to worldwide data (e.g. through the Internet) which pupils can use when doing their (design) project work. And besides that, the use of information technologies in technology education contributes to a realistic concept of technologies, because they play an increasingly important role in all phases of technological developments.

The role of engineering concepts

The quest for a conceptual basis for technology is an ongoing concern (De Vries and Tamir, 1997). This debate is often coupled to the issue of whether or not technology education should be taught as a separate school subject. Those who favour a separate subject rather than integration into science or other subjects often use the argument of technology having its own body of knowledge and methodologies. This debate is particularly concerned with technology education at the level of secondary education. In primary education there is a different culture in the curriculum and there is more or less general agreement that here technology education should not be taught as a separate subject. Several individuals in various countries have suggested conceptual bases for technology education (people like DeVore [1980] and Todd [Todd *et al.*, 1985] in the USA and Blandow [1993], Lutherdt [1995] and Wolfgramm [1994/95] in Germany, just to mention a few). In the project Technology for All Americans, an effort is made to base new national technology education standards on such a conceptual basis (Dugger, 1997). But the generality of the concepts they come up with, according to others, conflicts with the specificity of the concepts that engineers seem to use most in practice. One of the concepts that generally come out as basic is the systems concept. Systems process materials, energy and information by basic functions like transforming, connecting, separating, transporting, storing and retrieving. Even though the concept of systems may not always play a dominant role in the work of engineers, from a didactical point of view it can be useful, because it helps pupils to gain a more fundamental insight into the technologies they see around them rather than detailed knowledge about specifics. Moreover it frees technology educators from the need of constantly trying to keep up to date in terms of introducing the newest technologies. Especially in countries that cannot afford high-tech equipment (such as African countries), this would be an approach to teach technology effectively without necessarily spending a lot of money on resources. In The Netherlands this and other basic concepts have become the basis for technology education textbooks.

The role of key competencies

The idea of competencies that have a general and transferable character has come from industry, in particular in Germany (there the term *Schlüsselqualifikationen* is used and sometimes we find this inadequately translated as 'key qualifications'). Industry has stated the need for a workforce that has skills like co-operating, problem-solving, innovative thinking, communicating: technology education would be a subject *par excellence* where such competencies could be acquired. Teaching those competencies in the eyes of industrialists would be much more useful than teaching specific skills with school equipment that, compared to industry standards, mostly is outdated anyway. There is, however, serious doubt about the claim that doing specific technology project work would 'automatically' yield transferable skills, and even the mere existence of such skills is sometimes questioned. Research by McCormick and others has shown that teaching and learning 'general' skills can never be separated from specific content areas. This is reflected in design methodological research, which has shown that designing a corkscrew is really something different from designing a television camera. Hence it can be questioned whether there exists such a thing as 'general design skills'. On the other hand, various design processes do show common features that could be related to linked skills. Further research is needed to reveal the nature of such commonalities.

The role of design

The example of design skills and general competencies brings us to our next aspect: the role of design as such in technology education. Here the UK is the most prominent example of a country in which we find an approach that is evidently biased towards this aspect. In the past this has even resulted in a criticism by professional engineering associations in the UK that design in 'Design and Technology' education could be about anything and totally lacked content focus. On the other hand, the history of technology education in several countries shows a resistance against design activities in technology education that was fed by the false assumptions that designing would not be possible with pupils of primary and secondary school ages. Here practice in the UK has been very valuable in proving the feasibility of real design work in schools. Through international contacts we can now see other countries importing this aspect from the UK. A major drawback here has been discussed already in the previous section: schoolbooks often use very general flowcharts for design processes that suggest that any design can be made by following such a general scheme. Here we should be careful not to use these schemes too rigidly, but rather as a checklist of activities that somewhere in the process need to be given attention.

The role of social issues

By including the design phase of a product in technology education programmes, almost automatically social issues come into our scope. Design requirements are directly related to human and social needs. On the other hand we find human and social norms and values in the using phase of technology. Technology Assessment has been developed as a policy tool for decision-making with respect to technological developments. In general one can say that in some Scandinavian countries, in particular Sweden, this has played a visible role in technology education programmes. In countries such as the USA and Canada, we have seen the emergence of so-called STS (Science, Technology and Society; see Solomon and Aikenhead, 1994) programmes that usually focused on specific 'trendy' social issues (nuclear power, environmental pollution and genetic engineering can be mentioned as examples of such issues which, in the past, have attracted the interest of science educators in STS programmes). Often the decrease in interest in such specific and time-dependent social issues caused the disappearance of STS programmes. Another problem with the STS programmes in the past was that, as in the 'applied science' approach, the technology component had not been developed strongly in terms of the process of creating new techno-logical devices and systems. It was only the existing technology as such that was the target of social debate: the way decision-making in those development processes could be influenced by social concerns was hardly dealt with. Enhancing this aspect (i.e. combining social issues with design activities) could repair this weakness.

CONDITIONS FOR TECHNOLOGY EDUCATION

From the previous sections it has become evident that various aspects of technology need to be combined in technology education programmes. This makes them multidimensional, which places high demands on teachers and resources. Many conditions need to be met in order to allow adequate teaching and learning about technology. In this section we shall discuss the following conditions:

- the availability of well-trained teachers;
- the availability of sufficient and adequate facilities (including teaching and learning materials);
- educational research to support the further development of technology education;
- international co-operation to enable countries to gain from each other's experiences.

Teacher education

Whatever wonderful programmes can be developed for technology education, in the end it all depends on the willingness, knowledge and skills of teachers to implement them. The fact that associations for technology educators flourish is an indication that, in general, technology educators have a positive attitude towards renewing their programmes. However, they often lack the expertise to design the renovations themselves. In this area there is evidently a role for universities and (other) teacher training institutes; indeed, some of these have produced useful collections of articles for technology teachers (e.g. Banks, 1994; McCormick et al., 1994; Williams and Williams, 1997). Some countries (e.g. the UK and The Netherlands) in addition have an elaborate system of support centres to help teachers to implement changes in their teaching practice. In addition, the technology teacher associations often are a valuable source of support for teachers.

Training programmes for teachers usually have the following components: courses on technological content, courses on educational issues, school apprenticeships and industrial visits (De Vries, 1994a). The difference between technology teacher training programmes and those for other subjects is that for the former the student teacher often has to build up the school subject almost from scratch (e.g. writing their own teaching and learning materials and designing and equipping a technology lab).

Learning materials and facilities

As technology education activities almost constantly require materials and tools, it is a challenge for technology educators to work with a limited budget and yet keep pupils working on practical design-and-make activities. As technology education in many cases still has to fight for its position in the school, this budget is limited indeed. In order to establish a sound position in the school, the teacher has to get rid of the misconception, often held by school boards and parents, that technology is just about tinkering and handicraft. This can be done by developing a technology education programme that reflects the true nature of technology and then communicating about this with the school management and with parents.

Educational research

In terms of supporting educational research, the situation is still inadequate in a number of countries. Probably the best situation can be found in Germany, in France and in the UK, where several universities have good educational research programmes for technology education. In the USA we also find several universities with such a research programme, but recent surveys of the content of those programmes have shown that there is a strong tendency to focus on curriculum content and that there is hardly any research focused on pupils (Zuga, 1997). Furthermore, universities seem to compete rather than co-operate, which often causes inefficient use of means from a nationwide perspective. In general, education research for technology education can relate to three fields:

- the aims and content of curricula (*what to teach*);
- the characteristics of pupils, like preconceptions and attitudes (*whom to teach*);
- the creation of adequate educational situations in which the right content is conveyed to the learner (*how to teach*). This field also includes assessment strategies and tools.

This last-mentioned topic is one of particular importance, given both the complexity of assessing the various activities (like project work in which all sorts of aspects need to be evaluated) and the relevance of proving that the aims of technology are somehow realised in practice (Mottier and De Vries, 1997). It is desirable that an international agenda for educational research in technology education be established (Jenkins, 1992).

International co-operation

As the development of technology is a constant struggle that is complicated by the relative newness of the school subject, international co-operation is an almost indispensable condition for a successful development. Although each country has a specific background and situation, much can be learnt from experiences abroad, both in terms of successes and pitfalls. In the past decades this feeling has resulted in the emergence of some international organisations that enable contacts between experts from various countries. In some cases existing international bodies, like OECD, NATO and UNESCO, have extended their scope of interests to include technology education; in other cases new dedicated organisations were initiated, like WOCATE (the World Council of Associations for Technology Education), EGTB (the European Association for Technology Education, EGBT is the German abbreviation; see Kussmann and Tyrchan, 1994) and PATT (Pupils' Attitudes Towards Technology, a small foundation that biennially organises international conferences on various aspects of technology education). In some cases national technology education organisations, such as the ITEA (International Technology Education Association) and the EPT fraternity (Epsilon Pi Tau) in the USA and DATA (Design And Technology Association) in the UK, have included international aspects in their activities. Not only conferences but also scholarly journals provide a platform to exchange experiences. *The International Journal of Technology and Design Education*, the *Journal of Technology Studies*, and the *Journal of Technology Education* are examples of journals with international authorship and readership.

TECHNOLOGY EDUCATION IN THE TWENTY-FIRST CENTURY

It can be expected that most trends in technology education of the late twentieth century will be continued in the twenty-first century. Partly thanks to increasing international contacts, technology education will become more mature (i.e. richer combinations of the various issues dealt with above will emerge) and as a result, technology education will be able to establish a sound position in schools. The low-level image of technology education will gradually disappear and technology education will be taken more seriously as a contribution to the general education of all future citizens by policy-makers, industries, school boards and parents. It is to be hoped that this will also result in the allocation of more resources for educational research to support technology education developments, in particular in those countries that at the moment hardly have any. The still ongoing fundamental debates on curriculum content, teaching and learning strategies (including assessment) call out for such resources and thus justify this allocation of means. Given the dynamic character of technology itself, it can be expected that technology education will always remain a dynamic field of teaching and learning. This presents a challenge to all parties involved.

REFERENCES

Banks, F. (ed.) (1994) *Teaching Technology*. London: Routledge.

Black, P. and Atkin, M. (1996) *Changing the Subject: Innovations in Science, Mathematics and Technology Education*. London: Routledge.

Blandow, D. (1993) 'Innovation and design for developing technological capabilities in general education', in M. J. de Vries, N. Cross and D. P. Grant (eds), *Design Methodology and Relationships with Science*. Dordrecht: Kluwer Academic Publishers.

Brauer-Schröder, M. and Sellin, H. (eds) (1996) *Technik, Ökonomie und Haushalt im Unterricht. Arbeitsorientierte Allgemeinbildung in Europa*. Baltmannsweiler: Schneider Verlag Hohengehren GmbH.

DeVore, P. W. (1980) *Technology: An Introduction*. Worcester: Davis Publications.

Dugger, W. E. (1997) 'Technology for all', in T. Kananoja (ed.), *Seminars on Technology Education*. Oulu: University of Oulu.

Hayles, J. A. and Snyder, J. F. (1982) 'Jackson's Mill industrial arts curriculum theory: A base for curriculum derivation'. *Man Society Technology*, 41 (5), 6–10.

Jenkins, E. W. (1992) 'Towards an agenda for research in technology education', in D. Blandow and M. J. Dyrenfurth (eds), *Technological Literacy, Competence and Innovation in Human Resource Development*. Erfurt/Columbia: WOCATE/AEA.

Kussmann, M. and Tyrchan, G. (eds) (1994) *Technology Education: On the Way to a Eurocurriculum School Technology*. EGTB Report 2. Düsseldorf: Europäische Gesellschaft für Technische Bildung.

Layton, D. (1993) *Technology's Challenge to Science Education*. Buckingham/Philadelphia: Open University Press.

Lutherdt, M. (1995) 'Key qualifications – Content of general and vocational education', in I. Mottier,

J. H. Raat and M. J. de Vries (eds), *Teaching Technology for Entrepreneurship and Employment*. Proceedings PATT-7 Conference. Eindhoven: PATT-Foundation.

McCormick, R., Murphy, P. and Harrison, M. (eds) (1992) *Teaching and Learning Technology*. Wokingham: Addison-Wesley and the Open University.

McCormick, R., Murphy, P. and Harrison, M. (eds) (1992) *Technology for Technology Education*. Wokingham: Addison-Wesley and the Open University.

McCormick, R., Murphy, P. and Hennessy, S. (1994) 'Problem solving processes in technology education: A pilot study', *International Journal of Technology and Design Education*, 4 (1), 5–34.

Mitcham, C. (1994) *Thinking through Technology. The Path between Engineering and Philosophy*. Chicago: University of Chicago Press.

Mottier, I. and M. J. de Vries (eds) (1997) *Assessing Technology Education*. Proceedings PATT-8 Conference. Eindhoven: PATT-Foundation.

Raat, J. H. and M. J. de Vries (1986) *What Do Girls and Boys Think of Technology?* Eindhoven: University of Technology.

Solomon, J. and Aikenhead, G. (eds) (1994) *STS Education. International Perspectives on Reform*. New York: Teachers College Press, Columbia University.

Todd, R. D., McCrory, D. L. and Todd, K. (1985) *Understanding and Using Technology*. Worcester: Davis Publications.

Vries, M. J. de (1993) 'Approaches to technology education and the role of advanced technologies: An international orientation', in A. Gordon, M. Hacker and M. J. de Vries (eds), *Advanced Educational Technology in Technology Education*. Heidelberg: Springer Verlag.

Vries, M. J. de (1994a) 'Teacher education for technology education', in Maurice Galton and Bob Moon (eds), *Handbook of Teacher Training in Europe*. London: David Fulton and Council of Europe.

Vries, M. J. de (1994b) *Science and Technology Teacher Training: What Training for What Type of Teaching?* Paris: Council of Europe.

Vries, M. J. de and Tamir, A. (eds) (1997) *Shaping Concepts of Technology: From Philosophical Perspectives to Mental Images*. Dordrecht: Kluwer Academic Publishers.

Williams, J. and Williams, A. (eds) (1997) *Technology Education for Teachers*. Melbourne: Macmillan.

Wolfgramm, H. (1994/95) *Allgemeine Techniklehre*. Hildesheim: Verlag Franzbecker.

Zuga, K. F. (1997) 'An analysis of technology education in the United States based upon an historical overview and review of contemporary curriculum research', *International Journal of Technology and Design Education*, 7 (3), 203–217.

54

FOREIGN LANGUAGE EDUCATION

Balancing communicative needs and intercultural understanding

Rosamond Mitchell

INTRODUCTION

Language education can be seen as a continuum, running from the further development in school of the language variety first encountered in the home (the 'mother tongue'), through the teaching of standard languages related to the home variety or dialect, or the teaching of a second, unrelated language which none the less has currency in the local community, and finally to instruction in languages not typically to be met with in the learner's everyday environment.

A range of different labels is commonly applied to different points on this continuum. 'Mother tongue' education refers to the further development in school of the language of the home, whether this be the standard national language (e.g. English in England or the United States), or the heritage language of a minority group (e.g. Maori in New Zealand, Quechua in Peru). 'Second language' education is used to describe the case where students must learn a second language current in their own community to a high level, in order to achieve mainstream academic and vocational goals; this case is common in many ex-colonial states in Africa, for example, where French or English retain key roles as languages of higher education, administration and business. The term 'bilingual education' is used to describe educational programmes which use more than one locally relevant language as media of instruction, e.g. a standard national language plus the heritage language of a local community or minority group (such as Spanish–English bilingual programmes serving the Hispanic community in the United States). Finally, 'foreign language' education refers to one end of the continuum described above, that is to the case where languages are systematically taught as a classroom subject, though they lack immediate local roots and are not to be met with in the everyday environment of the learner. This chapter is primarily concerned with foreign languages in this particular sense.

As described here, foreign language learning most usually involves an organised classroom encounter with the 'high' or standard form of someone else's national language, which may also function as a language of wider international communication. For example, a recent IEA study conducted in 25 countries, mostly European, found that English, French,

German and Spanish were the most commonly taught foreign languages, with English overwhelmingly the most popular (Dickson and Cumming, 1996). In other regions of the world, languages such as Arabic, Chinese, Russian, Japanese or Portuguese are more likely to be taught, though again with English as a strong competitor today.

HISTORICAL ROOTS

The organised teaching of foreign languages can be traced back at least to classical times, when Latin and/or Greek were taught as languages of learning and of public life in the different regions of the polyglot Roman Empire. In Europe Latin continued as the main language of the Christian Church and of learning more generally throughout the Middle Ages, and was taught as a second language in schools and universities with the aid of written grammars, specially written dialogues and excerpted texts. Practical needs to learn contemporary spoken languages were met at this time outside the church-run schools, with phrasebooks and dual-language collections of dialogues useful for travellers, merchants, etc. (Howatt, 1984, pp. 3–10).

The Renaissance period saw the production of descriptive grammars and dictionaries for the major contemporary European languages, which was a key step in their standardisation, and a symptom of their rising status as languages of learning, high culture and public life. This also made possible a much more systematic approach to the teaching of these languages to foreigners; for example, the *Nouvelle Méthode* of Guy Miège (1685) combined a grammar, a compact dictionary and a dialogue manual for teaching English as a foreign language (Howatt, 1984, pp. 54–60).

However, it was only in the course of the nineteenth century that modern foreign languages became generally established in the academic secondary school curriculum, initially alongside the classical languages which had held a pre-eminent position since the Middle Ages. In German *Gymnasien*, for example, French became a compulsory subject alongside the classical languages in the early years of the century, and both French and English were compulsory in *Realschulen* from 1859. In England, the establishment of university-run school examinations in the 1850s was the lever which established modern languages on the grammar school curriculum. However, the most prestigious private schools in England continued to concentrate on Greek and Latin, and the universities of Oxford and Cambridge established modern languages degrees only at the end of the century (Cambridge in 1886, Oxford in 1903). Indeed, the later nineteenth-century history of foreign language teaching in English schools has been described as 'a record of an upward thrust for status constantly hampered by the stigma of utilitarianism' (Radford, 1985, p. 211).

Outside the school systems, the greatly increased mobility and trade of the later nineteenth century created a mass demand for practical foreign language instruction. This provided a receptive audience of adult learners for the so-called Reform Movement, headed by scholars such as the German Viëtor and the Dane Jespersen, which drew on the new science of phonetics to support the teaching of spoken language (Hawkins, 1981, pp. 117–153; Howatt, 1984, pp. 169–189).

In the course of the twentieth century, modern foreign languages have decisively replaced Classical Greek and Latin in the schools of Europe, and figure as a compulsory element of the secondary school curriculum virtually everywhere (Dickson and Cumming, 1996). Upsurges of interest in foreign language learning, and concomitant periods of innovation in methodology and in the organisation of foreign language teaching, have followed major political events. Thus, for example, the Second World War was a big impetus to innovation in the United States, leading to the development of so-called audiolingual methods for language teaching based on behaviourist learning principles, because of the country's greatly expanded military and political role around the world. The postwar enthusiasm for greater political integration in Europe was the background to the successive modern languages projects of the Council for Cultural Co-operation of the Council of Europe (Brumfit, 1995; Council for Cultural Co-operation, 1996; Trim, 1988). This Council of Europe activity proposed new, functional-notional syllabus models for foreign languages, which have become internationally influential. But above all, the postwar rise of English as the pre-eminent language of international communication has created global demand for practical skills in English as a foreign language. Crystal (1997, p. 61) estimates that up to a billion people are learning and using English as a foreign language today, and the recent IEA study shows it as overwhelmingly the most commonly taught language in the schools of the 25 countries surveyed (Dickson and Cumming, p. 1996, p. 131). Correspondingly, English as a foreign language has been a powerhouse of innovation in language curriculum design, teaching methodology and assessment, in both public and private sector institutions.

RATIONALES FOR FOREIGN LANGUAGE EDUCATION

Practical and utilitarian need has always been a strong strand in the motivation to learn a foreign language, and has sustained traditions of foreign language teaching to adults more or less regardless of what was happening in schools. However, in the period when modern foreign languages were struggling to become established on the school curriculum alongside Latin and Greek, the rationales advanced for foreign language study tended to imitate those already well established for the classical languages. (These, by the later nineteenth century, were largely useless vocationally, and had to defend their curriculum place on general educational grounds.) So, the inclusion of modern languages in the school curriculum was often justified partly by presenting them as vehicles providing access to great literature and high culture (this applied particularly to French), and partly on the grounds that analytic study of grammar provided a training in logical and systematic thinking (Radford, 1985, pp. 212–216).

Contemporary rationales for foreign language learning in school once more place a central emphasis on meeting current and future practical and vocational needs, through the development of communicative proficiency (Clark, 1987). Typically this emphasis is associated with a re-ordering of priorities among the different language skills, and in many contexts, placing a new stress on the development of oral skills. (The current reorientation of English language programmes in countries such as Korea and Malaysia provides some very clear examples.)

However, this central goal of communicative proficiency is typically complemented by supplementary goals, which may include:

- the systematic study of the culture(s) associated with the target foreign language;
- the development of knowledge about language/language awareness, through the explicit study of the target language system, and comparisons with that of the mother tongue;
- the development of attitudes of tolerance and openness towards cultural difference.

For example, the National Standards in Foreign Language Education (1996) recently articulated by a national project in the United States, are organised around five themes:

- *Communication:* communicate in languages other than English;
- *Cultures:* gain knowledge and understanding of other cultures;
- *Connections:* connect with other disciplines and acquire information;
- *Comparisons:* develop insight into the nature of language and culture;
- *Communities:* participate in multilingual communities at home and around the world.

Perhaps the most remarkable change which has taken place in such overall rationales for FL education this century is the international decline in literary studies (though with exceptions in some school systems at higher secondary level, and in higher education), and their replacement with broader goals for intercultural understanding. As Byram (1997, p. 6) points out, however, it is rare for aims other than the development of practical language proficiency to be supported by any systematic assessment of development/change in learners' cultural knowledge and attitudes, so that in many programmes they receive comparatively little systematic attention.

SYLLABUS MODELS FOR FOREIGN LANGUAGES

A range of different syllabus types have been proposed in twentieth-century debates on foreign language teaching. These derive from different underlying views on the nature of language and the language learning process and include the following:

- the structural syllabus;
- the functional-notional syllabus;
- the situational syllabus;
- the task-based (or procedural) syllabus.

The structural syllabus organises the language content to be taught as a sequence of grammatical items and patterns, e.g. verb tenses, or how to form questions or relative clauses. This type of syllabus follows from the traditional view of language as an abstract system of linguistic relationships. It has most affinities with the grammar-centred teaching of classical languages, though modified and updated through the influence of twentieth-century structural linguistics, and adopted in modernised form to support audiolingual methodology (see below).

The functional-notional syllabus, popularised by successive Council of Europe modern languages projects, views language as action rather than as grammatical system (Wilkins, 1976). That is, the syllabus seeks to identify the speech acts or language functions which the learner may wish to perform (acts such as 'advising', 'requesting', 'offering', 'informing', etc.), and teaches the typical exponents (language expressions) for individual functions, regardless of their perceived grammatical (un)relatedness. Similarly, this syllabus model seeks to identify semantic 'notions' which may be useful to the learner (such as the notion of 'future time'), and to teach the means of expressing these notions (e.g. in English, future time may be expressed through use of modal auxiliary verbs and/or through adverbial expressions).

This model for syllabus design could clearly be much more responsive to an analysis of learners' presumed communicative needs, and was highly significant for the future development of 'languages for specific purposes' (Richterich, 1980). From these various theoretical proposals the Council of Europe team sponsored and promoted the production of actual model syllabuses for a range of languages, which have proved extremely influential internationally ('*Threshold Level*' for English, '*Niveau Seuil*' for French, etc.; see van Ek, 1977).

The situational syllabus specifies expressions and sequences of utterances seen as relevant to particular conversational contexts and roles; these are often presented in the form of situational dialogues. This model can be traced back a long way, in fact to medieval dual language phrasebooks, whose prime concern was to provide a core of immediately usable and useful language routines. It is still commonly used in utilitarian/leisure-oriented foreign language teaching for adults, and with school students at elementary levels, as in the British Graded Objectives for Modern Languages movement of the 1970s and 1980s (Page, 1996).

The task-based (or procedural) syllabus abandons any formal specification of language content. Instead, the syllabus is conceived as a sequence of tasks to be undertaken or problems to be solved, which have some meaningful, non-linguistic outcome (Crookes and Gass, 1993). The foreign language elements, whether vocabulary or grammatical structures, are introduced and practised as necessary for the successful completion of the task. This highly experiential approach raises numerous problems to do with selection, grading and sequencing of tasks, and it has found only a limited role in formal school education, the best-known example being an English teaching project in Bangalore, India (Prabhu, 1987). However the approach has achieved somewhat more popularity with private and public institutions serving more advanced, adult learners (see Legutke and Thomas, 1991).

In practice, many educational systems today adopt mixed syllabus models, in which structural, functional and situational strands can be identified in varying proportions. In particular, the enthusiasm for functional syllabuses which underpinned many FL curriculum reform projects in the 1970s and 1980s has been tempered, as they failed to live up to high expectations. Such syllabuses have been criticised for producing students who were fluent but inaccurate, and often could not move with confidence beyond a stock of rote-learned expressions. This has led to renewed interest in structural syllabuses, with the lexical syllabus a new variant, supported by the new field of corpus linguistics (the computerised analysis of the links between words and their grammatical and textual context, in very large databases of natural language; see Wichmann *et al.*, 1997).

METHODS FOR FOREIGN LANGUAGE TEACHING

Just as a range of syllabus models has been tried in the quest for more effective foreign language education, so in the course of the twentieth century a wide range of teaching methods has been proposed, with varying rationales drawn from change and development in language learning theory. A selection of the most significant includes:

- the grammar-translation method;
- the audiolingual method;
- communicative language teaching;
- naturalistic and immersion methods;
- humanistic methods.

The grammar-translation method (Howatt, 1984 pp. 131–146). In its nineteenth-century origins, the grammar-translation method was a development of the traditional approach to the teaching of classical languages, centring on the study of grammar and of literary texts. However, as updated by German scholars – for Prussian secondary schools in the first instance – the method typically centred on the explicit study of grammar rules, followed by the completion of grammar exercises and the translation of sentences illustrating particular grammar points, to and from the foreign language. This approach to foreign language teaching, with its emphases on grammatical understanding, on accuracy and on written rather than spoken language, dominated the academic secondary school curriculum until at least the Second World War. The Reform Movement of the late nineteenth century, with its accompanying oral teaching methods and de-emphasis on formal grammar, had considerable success in private language teaching institutions (such as the Berlitz schools), but had much less impact on the school curriculum.

The audiolingual method (Lado, 1964; Richards and Rogers, 1986, pp. 44–63). During the Second World War, American linguists achieved considerable success in rapidly developing the practical language skills needed by military personnel, by the application of behaviourist principles to language learning. In the postwar period this led to the widespread advocacy and adoption of so-called audiolingual methods. Explicit grammar study was seen as diversionary, and foreign language grammar and pronunciation were to be learned by habit formation, through intensive oral repetition and pattern practice (oral exercises where minimal word-level changes are rung on basic sentence patterns). The 'four skills' of speaking, listening, reading and writing were separated out for discrete attention. However, spoken language was given priority, and accurate production was emphasised, for fear 'bad habits' would become entrenched. Thus new material was introduced in a very controlled manner, and correction was thorough. The method was typically supported and delivered using the new technology of the language laboratory, which became widespread in the 1960s.

Communicative language teaching (Brumfit, 1988; Brumfit and Johnson, 1979; Widdowson, 1978). In their different ways, both grammar-translation and audiolingualism treated the control of sentence grammar as the central element of foreign language learning. However, by the 1970s language educators were increasingly dissatisfied with such formalistic views, which seemed increasingly out of line with the needs and interests of the new mass audiences for foreign languages. Behaviourism was also theoretically discredited as a model for the learning of grammar, with the rise of Chomskian generative linguistics. Second language acquisition research was rehabilitating the concept of 'error', no longer seen as a bad habit to be eliminated through drilling, but as the product of learners' creativity and developing interlanguage systems (Davies *et al.*, 1984; Mitchell and Myles, 1998, pp. 22–41).

Language educators were thus very receptive to the theoretical proposals of the American anthropological linguist Dell Hymes, who popularised the objective of 'communicative competence' as the proper goal of language pedagogy (Hymes, 1979). This downgraded grammar to just one component of a broader construct, variously defined also to include sociolinguistic, pragmatic, discourse and strategic competences (see McNamara, 1996 for review).

The broader goal of communicative competence was quickly adopted as a key element in the communicative language teaching movement, popularised internationally partly through the promotional English language teaching efforts of the British Council. Other elements in the CLT movement were the adoption of functional-notional syllabuses, and an accompanying experiential pedagogy, which emphasised the use of authentic target language texts in place of artificial, structurally controlled exercises, and the meaning-oriented use of the target language in activities such as role play. Communicative pedagogy was also to be more learner centred, with for example the fine-tuning of syllabuses in line with students' needs, and the incorporation of group work into foreign language lessons; error correction was downplayed, in the interests of learner fluency (for overviews, see Brumfit, 1988; K. Johnson, 1982).

Naturalistic and immersion methods (Johnson and Swain, 1997; Richards and Rogers, 1986, pp. 128–141; Snow, 1990). The communicative language teaching movement represented a clear shift towards more experiential modes of foreign language learning, by comparison with its predecessors. However this shift has been taken considerably further by advocates of naturalistic and immersion approaches to foreign languages. The psycholinguist Stephen Krashen is the theorist most prominently associated with the idea that the classroom learning of foreign languages is most effective where it reflects most closely the 'natural' situations and processes of first language acquisition. For Krashen, these learning processes are distinctive to language, and not open to introspection nor capable of being modified through conscious control. Therefore, defined language syllabuses, explicit grammar instruction, practice and correction contribute little to the acquisition of foreign language competence. Instead, the teacher following Krashen's so-called 'Natural Approach' provides a constant flow of target language input in pursuit of communicative goals, around topics relevant and interesting to the students. After a silent period, they start to join in, selecting from the rich input on offer the vocabulary and grammar relevant to their needs and developmental stage, in order to achieve immediate communicative goals (Krashen and Terrell, 1983).

Full or partial immersion programmes are also optimistic that naturalistic learning processes can be recreated for foreign languages in a classroom setting. In such programmes, the foreign language is itself used as a medium of instruction for one or more of the other academic subjects on the school curriculum. As in Krashen's Natural Approach, this ensures that the foreign language is encountered primarily as a means of communication rather than an object of study. However, the cognitive demands of the academic content dealt with are considerably higher than those of the everyday topics, games, etc. which provide the communicative stimulus in most 'methods' where FLs are taught as a subject only.

For several decades, Canada has been the main centre of innovation concerning immersion programmes (mainly providing French-medium schooling for English-speaking Canadians, with the long-term goal of promoting personal and societal bilingualism in these languages). Extensive long-term research has also been undertaken, which has demonstrated the generally positive learning outcomes of these programmes. The Canadian programmes commonly involve full immersion for intact cohorts of English L1 students, i.e. the entire school programme is delivered through the medium of French (except for English Language Arts). However, in the United States and in parts of Europe partial immersion programmes are also growing in popularity; in such cases, just one or two subjects (e.g. history, geography, science) are taught through the foreign language.

Humanistic methods (Richards and Rogers, 1986, pp. 99–127; Stevick, 1976). The mainstream approaches to foreign language pedagogy outlined so far draw their rationales from varying models of language itself, and from a range of current psycholinguistic theories about the language learning process. None the less a number of 'alternative' approaches to language pedagogy have also been promoted in recent decades, which draw their rationale from broader, non-linguistic models of learning. Examples are the Silent Way, based on a general theory of student-centred discovery learning (Richards and Rogers, 1986, pp. 99–112), and Community Language Learning, which applies psychological counselling techniques to the problem of foreign language learning (ibid., pp. 113–127).

As the foregoing descriptions show, a wide range of methods have been argued for in foreign language debates, often very polemically. In practice, language teachers' observed classroom practices do not often reflect any one method in a pure form, and activities sometimes strongly criticised on theoretical grounds (such as grammar explanations, or behaviourist repetition and rote learning) retain their place (see Mitchell and Martin, 1997). This pragmatic approach on the part of classroom teachers is justified in so far as it has proved very difficult to demonstrate empirically the overall superiority of any one 'method' over another. Given time and adequate motivation, it seems that foreign languages are broadly 'learnable' by any or all of the methods described, though the acceptability of particular pedagogic procedures is certainly dependent on the particular socio-cultural context and the related aspirations of the learner.

ASSESSMENT OF FOREIGN LANGUAGES

Assessment in foreign language education has unsurprisingly reflected the changing educational aims and rationales for the subject. In the twentieth century broad trends in foreign language assessment have led away from an elite preoccupation with literary knowledge and critical ability, towards a clear focus on language proficiency. Language testing has developed as a specialised profession, increasingly accountable in terms of the reliability and the validity of its instruments, though traditional essay-style examinations continue to play an important role, especially in many national higher education systems.

Reform movements in the earlier part of the century were greatly influenced by the growth of psychometrics, and can be seen as prioritising reliability in the attempt to develop more adequate test instruments (Spolsky, 1995). The objective language testing movement concentrated on core areas of language knowledge such as grammar, pronunciation and vocabulary, treating separately the 'four skills' of listening, speaking, reading and writing. The best-known product of this tradition is the Test of English as a Foreign Language (TOEFL), a test battery developed and administered by the Educational Testing Service at

Princeton, which is widely used around the world as an objective measure of English language proficiency, e.g. for purposes of admission to higher education. (This test, together with its main British competitor, the International English Language Testing Service [IELTS] test, is taken by around one million candidates each year.)

The rise of the communicative language teaching movement, with its broader objective of 'communicative competence', has led though to an increased emphasis on construct validity in language test design, and the attempt to broaden the scope of assessment instruments, e.g. to include the assessment of conversational skills (ignored in TOEFL). There have been numerous attempts to operationalise the construct of 'communicative competence' for testing purposes (reviewed by McNamara, 1996). One current influential example is that offered by Bachman and Palmer who argue that communicative competence comprises the following (Bachman and Palmer, 1996, pp. 61–82):

1 *Language knowledge*, subdivided into

- grammatical knowledge: how individual sentences or utterances are organised;
- textual knowledge: how utterances or sentences are organised to form texts;
- functional knowledge: how utterances or sentences and texts are related to the communicative goals of language users;
- sociolinguistic knowledge: how utterances, etc. are related to features of the language use setting;

2 *Metacognitive strategic use*, subdivided into

- goal setting;
- planning;
- assessment.

This renewed concern for construct validity is accompanied in language testing research and development with increased sensitivity to the need for face validity. Thus for example Bachman and Palmer (1996) argue for 'authenticity' in the selection of assessment tasks, and face validity is also a concern in continuing development of the IELTS testing system (Spolsky, 1995, pp. 337–347).

One byproduct of the move to the use of more holistic and integrative tasks in foreign language assessment has been an active interest in the development of criterion-referenced assessment scales. Typically, such scales divide language proficiency into a number of dimensions, and devise level descriptors for the steps on an achievement 'ladder' for each dimension. One well-known example is the *Proficiency Guidelines* produced by the American Council on the Teaching of Foreign Languages (ACTFL, 1989), which offer ten-point scales and accompanying level descriptors for each of the traditional 'four skills' of listening, speaking, reading and writing. Increasingly such scales are being used to set exit standards for secondary school foreign language programmes, e.g. in certain states within the USA such as Oklahoma, Oregon and Pennsylvania (Glisan and Foltz, 1998). Scales may be drafted a priori by expert committees (as was the case, for example, with the British scales for modern foreign languages in the present national curriculum; see DfE, 1995). Alternatively they may be the product of extensive programmes of empirical research, as is the case with the scales proposed by the Council of Europe for its Common European Framework for modern languages (CCC, 1996).

FOREIGN LANGUAGES IN SECONDARY EDUCATION

Since the mid-nineteenth century, modern foreign languages have had a secure place on the secondary school curriculum at least for sections of the academic elite (though in varying degrees of competition with the classical languages). In the twentieth century the growth of mass secondary school systems in the developed world has led to a big expansion of the audience for school foreign language learning. The main challenge for curriculum developers and researchers at this level has been to identify curriculum models, teaching methods and assessment procedures that are appropriate for the complete secondary school population. This has frequently involved the downgrading of grammar study and the teaching of literature, and a concentration on relevance in specifying language learning objectives, and on more experiential and learner-centred classroom activities. The tenets of 'communicative language teaching' have proved attractive, and have been widely adopted as the principles which should drive secondary school programmes aiming at 'languages for all'. (Hawkins, 1996 provides a good account of this process in the UK setting.)

FOREIGN LANGUAGES IN PRIMARY EDUCATION

The inclusion of foreign languages in the curriculum of the primary school has been a more recent development. In the 1960s and 1970s, both the United States and Britain experimented with centrally funded primary school foreign language programmes, on largely behaviourist principles. However, these programmes were largely abandoned when they did not lead to immediately measurable success (Hawkins, 1996). Canadian immersion programmes launched at a similar time, which typically started in the primary years, have proved more robust. More recently there has been a great international expansion of interest in foreign languages at primary level, largely fuelled by the rise of English as an international language. English is appearing on the primary curriculum of many countries; thus 20 out of the 25 countries recently surveyed by the IEA reported starting English as a primary school subject by age 10 or earlier (Dickson and Cumming, 1996, p. 131). In contrast, only five countries reported that the teaching of French had started by this age. This push for primary school English is often driven by parental demand, and may follow a period of growth of uncoordinated private instruction outside school (as in Korea, for example, where primary English was introduced as a full curriculum subject in 1997).

Research and development on primary school foreign language teaching typically concentrates on the teacher supply problem on the one hand, and on devising experiential and activity-based programmes appropriate to the primary age range (Edelenbos and Johnstone, 1996).

FOREIGN LANGUAGES IN FURTHER AND HIGHER EDUCATION

The foreign language curriculum in higher education has become increasingly heterogeneous in the course of the century. Today, HE foreign languages students spend variable amounts of time on the development of their practical language skills, on theoretical linguistic studies, and on a greatly diversified menu of literary and cultural studies. The results in terms of language proficiency are equally diverse (Coleman, 1996), though a period of residence in the target language environment significantly enhances language progress. Students specialising in foreign language studies have become rarer, and languages are increasingly taught in combination with other vocational subjects, which may range from business to engineering. Partly because of resourcing difficulties, there is great current interest in the promotion of learner autonomy in HE foreign language programmes, with the development of self-access centres and open learning systems relying on new information and communication technology (Esch, 1994). There is interest in institution-wide language programmes to develop and support students' foreign language skills outside the framework of their core studies (Little and Ushioda, 1998); again, this applies especially to English language support in many international HE settings, in the form of 'English for Academic Purposes'. However, integrative motivation and the desire to travel remain strong factors promoting foreign language study in higher education, alongside the instrumental/ vocational motivation which is most characteristic of students of English as a foreign language (Coleman, 1996; Grosse *et al.*, 1998).

Adult and continuing education has historically been perhaps the most innovative sector in foreign language teaching, being unhampered by the need to mimic the classics, and responding to changing vocational and/or leisure needs among the general population. Nineteenth-century private language schools such as Berlitz adopted oral 'reformed' methods at an early stage. Similarly in the twentieth century, private sector language schools were early converts to versions of communicative language teaching, and have also promoted language teaching for specific purposes (e.g. languages for business communication; see C. Johnson, 1993). Private language schools continue to innovate, being among the most enthusiastic users of new technologies such as computer-based instructional programmes, multimedia and the Internet.

FOREIGN LANGUAGES: THE FUTURE

The future shape of foreign language instruction will be influenced substantially by a range of broader cross-curricular issues. For example, the international movement towards the use of standardised tests as levers intended to raise attainment, and the setting of target standards against which teachers as well as students are held accountable, touches foreign languages as other subjects. Will this movement bring real results in terms of language proficiency, or will it deprofessionalise and alienate our teachers, while failing to alter learning outcomes significantly (Crookes, 1997)? Similarly, developments in information technologies, and particularly on the Internet, potentially make a large range of language learning resources more immediately available to teachers and students (Finnemann, 1996). The longer-term consequences for classroom practices, and for self-access learning, are likely to be profound in foreign languages as in other areas.

Looking at issues more distinctive to the foreign language field, there is a continuing lack of consensus among second language acquisition theorists about the learning processes that underpin the development of foreign language proficiency (Mitchell and Myles, 1998). This has led to continuing uncertainty about teaching methodology, for example on such issues as

931

the place of explicit grammar teaching, or the potential of task-based programmes in mainstream education. The development of assessment procedures which can adequately record learners' communicative proficiency in valid, reliable and practical ways remains a challenging task where consensus has not yet been achieved. These issues are all currently receiving active research attention, and this can be expected to continue into the next century.

However, the broader future of foreign language education will not in the end depend on the resolution of such technical matters. There is increasing recognition of the socially situated nature of the language learning enterprise, and of the need for foreign language instruction to become more culturally sensitive and socially engaged if it is to serve the best interests of the large new publics for languages. There is also recognition that the future shape of foreign language teaching will depend significantly on the social forces, which in recent decades have promoted English as the seemingly unstoppable global language (Graddol, 1997). Will increased mobility and globalisation of the economy continue to drive the spread of English, or will they lead ultimately to increased multilingualism, intercultural understanding and more pluralistic identities? Will satellite television and the Internet bind us all irrevocably to English, or will they in the longer term become vehicles for the projection of many local languages into wider spheres? As the economic balance of power changes, will languages such as Chinese, Spanish or German achieve greater regional significance, and correspondingly become more important players on the foreign language curriculum? Foreign language education has historically been based on a mix of utilitarian need and higher cultural aspirations, and has flourished where it has proved open and adaptable to such changing social needs and expectations.

REFERENCES

American Council on the Teaching of Foreign Languages (ACTFL) (1989) *Proficiency Guidelines*. Yonkers, NY: ACTFL.

Bachman, L. F. and Palmer, A. S. (1996) *Language Testing in Practice*. Oxford: Oxford University Press.

Brumfit, C. (ed.) (1988) *Communicative Language Teaching. Annual Review of Applied Linguistics*, Vol. 8. Cambridge: Cambridge University Press.

Brumfit, C. (ed.) (1995) *The Work of the Council of Europe and Second Language Teaching*. London: Macmillan.

Brumfit, C. and Johnson, K. (eds) (1979) *The Communicative Approach to Language Teaching*. Oxford: Oxford University Press.

Byram, M. (1997) *Teaching and Assessing Intercultural Communicative Competence*. Clevedon: Multilingual Matters.

Clark, J. L. (1987) *Curriculum Renewal in School Foreign Language Learning*. Oxford: Oxford University Press.

Coleman, J. A. (1996) *Studying Languages: A Survey of British and European Students*. London: Centre for Information on Language Teaching and Research.

Council for Cultural Co-operation (1996) *Modern Languages: Learning, Teaching, Assessment. A Common European Framework of Reference*. Strasbourg: Council of Europe.

Crookes, G. (1997) 'What influences what and how second and foreign language teachers teach?', *Modern Language Journal* 81 (1), 67–79.

Crookes, G. and Gass, S. M. (eds) (1993) *Tasks in a Pedagogic Context: Integrating Theory and Practice*. Clevedon: Multilingual Matters.

Crystal, D. (1997) *English as a Global Language*. Cambridge: Cambridge University Press.

Davies A., Criper, C. and Howatt, A. (eds) (1984) *Interlanguage*. Edinburgh: Edinburgh University Press.

Department for Education (DfE) (1995) *Modern Foreign Languages in the National Curriculum*. London: HMSO.

Dickson, P. and Cumming, A. (eds) (1996) *Profiles of Language Education in 25 Countries*. Slough: National Foundation for Educational Research.

Edelenbos, P. and Johnstone, R. (eds) (1996) *Researching Languages at Primary School: Some European Perspectives*. London: Centre for Information on Language Teaching and Research.

Esch, E. (ed.) (1994) *Self-access and the Adult Language Learner*. London: Centre for Information on Language Teaching and Research.

Finnemann, M. D. (1996) 'The World Wide Web and Foreign Language Teaching', *ERIC/CLL News Bulletin*, 20 (1), 1–8.

Glisan, E. W. and Foltz, D. A. (1998) 'Assessing students' oral proficiency in an outcome-based curriculum: Student performance and teacher intuitions', *Modern Language Journal*, 82 (1), 1–18.

Graddol, D. (1997) *The Future of English?* London: British Council.

Grosse, C. U., Tuman, W. V. and Critz, M. A. (1998) 'The economic utility of foreign language study', *Modern Language Journal*, 82 (4), 457–472.

Hawkins, E. W. (1981) *Modern Languages in the Curriculum*. Cambridge: Cambridge University Press.

Hawkins, E. W. (1996) 'The early teaching of modem languages – a pilot scheme', in E. W. Hawkins (ed.) (1996) *Thirty Years of Language Teaching*, London: Centre for Information on Language Teaching and Research, 155–164.

Hawkins, E. W. (ed.) (1996) *Thirty Years of Language Teaching*. London: Centre for Information on Language Teaching and Research.

Howatt, A. P. R. (1984) *A History of English Language Teaching*. Oxford: Oxford University Press.

Hymes, D. (1979) 'On communicative competence', in C. Brumfit and K. Johnson (eds) *The Communicative Approach to Language Teaching*, Oxford: Oxford University Press, 5–26.

Johnson, C. (1993) 'Business English', *Language Teaching*, 26 (4), 201–209.

Johnson, K. (1982) *Communicative Syllabus Design and Methodology*. Oxford: Pergamon Institute of English.

Johnson, R. K. and Swain, M. (eds) (1997) *Immersion Education: International Perspectives*. Cambridge: Cambridge University Press.

Jung, U. O. H. (1992) 'Technology and language education in the twenty-first century', *AILA Review*, 9, 21–38.

Krashen, S. D. and Terrell, T. (1983) *The Natural Approach: Language Acquisition in the Classroom*. Oxford: Pergamon.

Lado, R. (1964) *Language Teaching: A Scientific Approach*. New York: McGraw-Hill.

Legutke, M. and Thomas, H. (1991) *Process and Experience in the Language Classroom*. Harlow: Longman.

Little, D. and Ushioda, E. (1998) *Institution-Wide Language Programmes*. London: Centre for Information on Language Teaching and Research.

McNamara, T. (1996) *Measuring Second Language Performance*. Harlow: Longman.

Mitchell, R. and Martin, C. (1997) 'Rote learning, creativity and "understanding" in the foreign language classroom', *Language Teaching Research*, 1 (1), 1–27.

Mitchell, R. and Myles, F. (1998) *Second Language Learning Theories*. London: Arnold.

National Standards in FL Education Project (1996) *Standards for Foreign Language Learning: Preparing for the 21st Century*. Lawrence, KS: National Standards Project.

Page, B. (1996) 'Graded Objectives in Modern Languages (GOML)', in E. W. Hawkins (ed.) *Thirty Years of Language Teaching*. London: Centre for Information on Language Teaching and Research, 99–105.

Prabhu, N. S. (1987) *Second Language Pedagogy*. Oxford: Oxford University Press.

Radford, H. (1985) 'Modern languages and the curriculum in English secondary schools', in I. Goodson (ed.) *Social Histories of the School Curriculum*, Lewes: Falmer Press, 203–237.

Richards, J. C. and Rogers, S. (1986) *Approaches and Methods in Language Teaching*. Cambridge: Cambridge University Press.

Richterich, R. (1980) *Identifying the Needs of Adults Learning a Foreign Language*. Oxford: Pergamon.

Snow, M. A. (1990) 'Language immersion: An overview and comparison' in A. Padilla, H. H. Fairchild and C. M. Valadez (eds) *Foreign Language Education: Issues and Strategies*. Newbury Park, CA: Sage Publications, 109–126.

Spolsky, B. (1995) *Measured Words*. Oxford: Oxford University Press.

Stevick, E. W. (1976) *Memory, Meaning and Method: Some Psychological Perspectives on Language Learning*. Rowley, MA: Newbury House.

Trim, J. L. M. (1988) 'Applied linguistics in society', in P. Grunwell (ed.) *Applied Linguistics in Society*. London: Centre for Information on Language Teaching and Research/British Association for Applied Linguistics, 3–15.

Van Ek, J. (1977) *The Threshold Level*. London: Longman/Council of Europe.

Wichmann, A., Figelstone, S., McEnery, T. and Knowles, G. (1997) *Teaching and Language Corpora*. Harlow: Longman.

Widdowson, H. G. (1978) *Teaching Language as Communication*. Oxford: Oxford University Press.

Wilkins, D. A. (1976) *Notional Syllabuses*. Oxford: Oxford University Press.

55

THE PLACE OF PHYSICAL EDUCATION IN THE CONTEMPORARY CURRICULUM

Len Almond

INTRODUCTION

One of the dilemmas in the enterprise of reviewing a wide subject field like physical education is what to select and what to reject. My own prejudices reflect a concern for curriculum
and teaching in schools and a narrow view of research in higher education. Much of the
research endeavours within this in higher education centre on the sports sciences, which
have little real relevance for physical education; I have therefore chosen not to include them
in this essay. Even though I believe that much of the current research in physical education
has little significance for most teachers, it is quite clear that much of the best work in schools
reflects the collaborative endeavours of key figures in higher education who believe in
promoting informed practice. In this chapter I shall explore current developments in the
curriculum and their association with teaching and learning. This will be followed by an
exploration of some research initiatives in higher education.

CURRICULUM AND TEACHING

Physical education encompasses a whole range of physical activity areas such as dance,
sports, outdoor and adventurous activities as well as individual exercise programmes. However, there has been considerable debate about the connections between these physical
activities. The dance world has tried to move out of physical education and seek a stronger
association with the world of the Arts and, in particular, the performing arts. In England the
historical association with physical education has ensured that dance retains a compulsory
component up to the age of 16, whereas the Arts have lost this at 14 years. This is particularly important in the primary years where the introduction of numeracy and literacy hours,
together with a concern for ICT, has meant that the Arts receive little practical support
whereas physical education is seen as an important element of the curriculum. In other
countries this is less of a problem, though the dance world would prefer to be associated
with the Arts. Outdoor and adventurous activities have led a chequered life because a

commitment by a school to promoting associated activities requires specialists, extra time outside of the curriculum as well as inside, in addition to a heavy cost burden. As a result commitment has waned considerably, and a lobby to support the development of outdoor and adventurous activities has been conspicuous by its absence – hence the decline of any real initiative to restore its value as an entitlement for all children at key stage 2 or 3.

In effect this has meant that in the UK the physical education curriculum is dominated by activities that are associated with sport. Despite the aborted challenge to competition in the 1970s by advocates of a more co-operative approach to physical education, sport has emerged with greater strength, assisted in part by considerable support from political parties and patronage by prime ministers. In a thorough discussion of this issue, Evans and Penney (1995) have provided a comprehensive review of this fascinating debate. The sports world has responded positively and governing bodies of sports, such as association football, rugby, basketball, tennis and cricket have attempted to provide schools with comprehensive support materials. In addition, the physical education curriculum in English primary schools has benefited from the introduction of a programme called TOP Sport, which has provided practical support to teachers through resource cards and equipment but also through much needed in-service training courses. However, the key feature of this development has been the collaborative networks that have evolved, which have the potential for uniting the profession and enabling it to respond positively to the scenario of a changing national curriculum. The development of TOP Sport has been influenced by developments in Australia called Aussie Sport and by Kiwi Sport in New Zealand. However, the southern hemisphere developments have been evaluated (Kirk, 1997) whereas in England there has been little coherent attempt to monitor and evaluate the impact of such developments.

In recent years, sport has become the focus for a new innovative curriculum. Daryl Siedentop (1994) in North America proposed that teachers should refocus their teaching of individual sporting activities and highlight six key features of sport in inter-school contexts such as seasons, affiliation, formal competitions, culminating events, record keeping and festivity. Siedentop believes that this approach highlights equal participation by all players throughout the season, developmentally appropriate competition with a deliberate emphasis on fair play, as well as the learning of diverse roles. Traditional approaches to the teaching of individual sporting activities have focused simply on performance and the development of competent performers. Sport needs officials, organisers as well coaches; consequently in sport education modules, students need to learn these important roles in addition to that of performer. The hidden curriculum of this approach is that students become more informed and intelligent participants for adult sport cultures. For Siedentop, sport education helps students become competent, literate and enthusiastic sportspersons.

Nevertheless, perhaps the most exciting feature of sport education is the pedagogical stance that it takes. Responsibility for management of learning is transferred to young people as they become collaborators in their own learning and derive satisfaction from participation. Students are central to the process of planning and making decisions about what they do next. Conflict resolution mechanisms are necessary to resolve the inevitable interpersonal conflicts that arise during competitions. The teacher becomes a resource that students draw upon. It is this approach that challenges teachers to adopt a different pedagogy and to move beyond the directive, class-based approach which fails to account for differentiation and the need for students to feel fully involved in the course of their own learning. It is interesting to note at a time when there is a movement to emphasise more class teaching with a more directional teacher role, that innovations in physical education are beginning to adopt a different stance.

A significant feature of this innovation is the growing literature on research into its effectiveness. In North America, Hastie (1996, 1998) has looked at the student role involvement in sport education, whereas Alexander *et al.* (1996, 1998) in Australia and Grant (1992) in New Zealand have explored its impact on primary and secondary teachers. This literature clearly supports the role of sport education in transforming teachers' pedagogical skills and making the enrichment of young people's sporting experiences much more of a collaborative venture for all students, as opposed to an overemphasis on the more able student. The legacy of sport education may well be the turning point for showing teachers how to involve young people in their learning and to demonstrate very clearly how learning can be a genuine sharing process. Nevertheless, Alexander does acknowledge that one of the key ingredients in the success of sport education has been the requirement in the Australian national curriculum for all teachers to incorporate a concern for self-directed learning and independence and the student's involvement in the learning process.

The sport education movement has been preceded by the 'teaching games for understanding' approach, which Siedentop acknowledges has similar value commitments in terms of striving to promote more intelligent and informed consumers of sport as players and spectators. However, much of the research into games teaching, mainly in North America, has focused on comparing what is seen as a technique-based approach with a more game-centred tactical focus that is associated with teaching games for understanding. One whole edition of *The Journal of Teaching Physical Education* (vol. 15, 1996) edited by Judith Rink, provides a comprehensive portrayal of this comparison together with a valuable critical review. Nevertheless, sport education and teaching games for understanding represent viable solutions to the same problem: How can we provide all young people with more productive sporting experiences and help them to appreciate the contribution that sport can make to enriching their lives? At the same time both approaches invite the teacher to consider alternative ways of organising learning and helping young people play a significant part in the development of their own learning.

It is this dimension which is intriguing because much of the research in physical education has focused on teaching whilst very little attention has been directed towards learning. One exception has been Luke's doctoral study into learning strategies. Nevertheless, a number of books (Hellison and Templin, 1991; Mawer, 1995; Pieron and Cheffers, 1989; Siedentop, 1991) have had a powerful impact on teaching. Mawer (1995) provides an excellent introduction for those who wish to study the teaching process, and together with Silverman's (1991) review of research on teaching physical education, this presents a thorough insight into the problems and dilemmas of teaching. Academic articles in books or journals continue to be published but there is little evidence of their impact on teachers, although the American Alliance for Health, Physical Education, Recreation and Dance, through its professional publications, does strive to embed the teaching–learning process with informed practice guided by much of the research from academic journals.

In many respects, distinguished researchers like Siedentop, who have contributed a great deal to enhancing teaching research in physical education through doctoral students and publications, may have taken an important step forward by providing teachers with frameworks for developing their understanding of sport education and teaching. These frameworks provide the means for teachers to develop their teaching and create real learning opportunities for their students and, in the process, to transform their thinking about pedagogical possibilities. The challenge of innovations like sport education takes teachers into new dimensions and away from a reliance on didactic and class-paced lessons. It is important to recognise also that students are being asked to enter into new forms of learning which may move them away from comfortable modes of working and therefore create potential conflicts unless such situations are handled with sensitivity and tact. Just as teachers may require in-service training, perhaps we should consider the need for students to be inducted into new forms of organised learning.

HEALTH AND FITNESS

Besides sport, the major focus for debate has been a concern for promoting health and its association with exercise, though a number of terms are often used interchangeably. Health-related fitness is the preferred term and this is used in most countries. In England the national curriculum for physical education referred to health-related exercise to dissociate it from fitness, which is mainly associated with preparation for performance in a sport and fitness testing. Critics (Armstrong, 1992; Health Education Authority, 1995) of this approach have proposed that it is inappropriate to use fitness testing as a motivator and as a focus for developing curriculum materials with young people. From the World Health Organization (WHO) a new term has recently emerged: health-enhancing physical activity. This debate reflects changes in the recommended levels of activity that young people need to maintain a healthier lifestyle. In the past five years there has been a wealth of data (Armstrong, 1992; Cale and Almond, 1992) to show that large numbers of young people are not engaging in vigorous exercise. However, a number of authors (Corbin et al., 1994) have suggested that there is a need for a re-examination of the messages associated with promoting health-enhancing physical activity. In England the Health Education Authority (HEA) held an international consensus conference in 1997 in order to generate a policy framework as well as practical suggestions for the teaching profession (Biddle et al., 1998).

In North America the Center for Disease Control (CDC) Guidelines for Promotion of Physical Activity and Reduction of Sedentary Lifestyles in Youth serves as an important document for shaping new policy decisions about exercise, health and behaviour (see also McKenzie, 1998). The CDC document emphasises the development of self-efficacy, decision-making and behavioural skills needed to adopt and maintain positive lifestyle behaviours. This document is important because it completes the shift from health-related fitness to health-enhancing physical activity and voices a concern for lifestyle behaviours rather than fitness and also for all young people instead of only those interested in sports performance.

In addition to the CDC document, Corbin (NASPE, 1998) has produced a comprehensive set of guidelines for teachers who need to implement the new proposals for promoting health-enhancing physical activity and to match them with the developmental needs of children. These are important documents for teachers because they represent guidelines that need to inform practice and enable intelligent practice to emerge.

In Australia the new health and physical education curriculum highlights a socio-cultural view of health, and students are encouraged to question contrasting interpretations of health and critically to examine the role of the media in presenting stereotypical and distorted images of the body.

Nevertheless, a concern for health hardly challenges the hegemony of sport in the curriculum – a subject that has received much debate in the academic literature (Evans, 1990, 1993; Evans and Davies, 1997; Kirk, 1992; Penney and Evans, 1999). What is interesting is the link between developments in sport and health-enhancing physical activity. In both cases there is a shift towards an approach in which young people are closely involved in the development of their own learning. This connection probably reflects a concern that the personal development of young people should be highlighted more clearly and the need to promote citizenship and personal responsibility.

THE CONTEXT OF PHYSICAL EDUCATION

I propose (see Almond, 1997) that in addition to the *content* of physical education (e.g. activity areas) that we present to young people which makes accessible the 'goods of accomplishment', there are other important goods of which we need to be aware. These 'goods' emerge from the *context* of physical education. It is this context that generates 'goods' from interaction with others. These represent the 'goods of relationships'. Thus, within the context of physical education, I argue that there are important interpersonal dispositions which can be acquired, shaped and appreciated. However, it is the environment of learning (and caring) that teachers create which is necessary to make available the 'goods of accomplishment and relationships'. In this nurturing and cultivating process, teachers are engaged in developing and creating a community (in this case within a school) in which this can unfold. This is an important condition for ensuring that both the content and context of physical education can bring about real learning. We need to create the conditions that generate collegiality and solidarity. All of this is based on an understanding that within such a community, teachers of physical education need to adopt a caring pedagogy which encompasses a set of procedural principles to guide their practice and help to protect and promote children's interests and welfare.

These sentiments are expressions of an idealised version of physical education and very little attention has been given to disaffected youth. In North America there has been a significant focus on underserved youth in response to concerns about the kind of environments that breed disadvantage, disaffection and exclusion. Martinek and Hellison (1997), Hellison (1995) and Lawson (1997) have articulated ways in which we can begin to redress the risks associated with exclusion, namely being poor and living in deprived neighbourhoods. They have used sport as a vehicle for promoting growth and renewed optimism. In England there is no research in this area although there is an interest by the English Sports Council to initiate work and to monitor its effects.

When one examines professional journals, assessment is clearly visible as a real issue but it has hardly touched the academic world and there is very little literature to examine. Carroll (1994) explored the world of assessment for examinations and his book thoroughly explores many of the issues, though Mawer (1995) provides clear guidance for teachers on pupil assessment and monitoring progress. In North America the term 'authentic assessment' has emerged in recent years. It is here that the notion of standards has risen and excellent guidance is provided by the National Association for Sport and Physical Education (NASPE) through the publication of a number of booklets: *National Physical Education Standards: A Guide to Content and Assessment* (1995); *Professional and Student Portfolios for Physical Education* (1998); *Assessment Series* (1999); *Assessing Student Learning: New Rules, New Realities* (1999).

NEW DIRECTIONS

The academic literature in physical education has tended to focus on a few small areas. There are a number of significant articles on the justification of PE in schools. Reid (1997), McNamee (1998), Parry (1998) and Arnold (1997) have argued that the activities of physical education are valued cultural practices of some significance and they propose that we direct our activities in physical education to promoting personal well-being. These authors present convincing cases based on critical analysis of competing arguments, and the reader will gain much from their deliberations. In addition to these authors, Meakin (1994) and Carr (1991) have explored the ethics of competition and the notion of fair play, which are issues that play a major part in national and international competition. The concern about bad behaviour and unfair play by adult players in association football and rugby, together with concerns about drugs abuse in sport, raises a potential danger for young people. The media highlight these incidents and there is a danger that such behaviour will transfer to younger players at school who see cult figures behaving inappropriately. Thus, it is important that these issues are brought to the attention of all teachers and provide the opportunity to appreciate the complex ethical dilemmas that they raise. It is essential that students in initial teacher training have the opportunity to reflect critically on these articles and seriously to debate these concerns. Nevertheless, it is difficult to ascertain what impact these deliberations have on the teaching of physical education. There is little evidence in professional publications that these issues are taken seriously or that they represent practical concerns in schools.

Looking forward to the new millennium and forecasting the trends in curriculum and teaching as well as research is a complex task but there are clear signs that provide important clues. There are clear 'hot topics' in the literature as 'cold topics' begin to wane and lose favour with both teachers and researchers. Lawson's (1997) excellent analysis of physical education in North America provides ample scope for looking forward.

The role of sport will grow as lottery funding will provide more support to develop extra-curricular opportunities. After-school clubs, particularly in primary schools, will emerge as crucial opportunities to challenge young people to adopt a more active lifestyle in a world of increasing automation and computer technology. Citizenship and the need for greater social responsibility will influence physical education and lead to much more student-directed activities. The voices of young people will be listened to and they will have a wider impact on community provision. Youth Physical Activity Forums will emerge and provide opportunities for young people to contribute significantly to how their communities evolve. However, the starting-point will be schools, where young people can acquire the skills to co-ordinate their own intra-mural programmes for sport, dance and other physical activities.

The school intra-net will provide the basis for consultation and discussion. This experience will provide the basis for local authorities or communities to consult with young people.

In many cases disadvantaged communities and disaffected youth will benefit from a substantial government commitment to use sport and physical activity as a vehicle for tackling inequalities and social exclusion. Young people will have the opportunity of acquiring transferable skills which will have value beyond the context of sport.

Dance teachers will form a stronger association with the Arts but they will see their role developing into the leisure field. The Arts (in their broadest sense) in the theatre, radio, television and community represent important features of many people's lives. People value music and the visual arts, and dance will forge a new, more practical role within the leisure field in response to a growth in the Arts. At the same time, teachers will recognise that young people need to learn how to plan, organise, manage and run their own clubs during their time in schools. They will learn that they have the capacity to generate initiatives within their own communities. The dance field will benefit from these initiatives as self-help groups bring dance, music and movement within the compass of everyone. In the same way, sport could also benefit from such a movement. These movements will generate new forms of learning strategies and how to relate more to students' needs and interests.

Electronic forms of communication will mean that young people can be consulted more widely and present their views. They will have access to a wide range of ideas and events which will widen their perspectives about new forms of sport and individual activities. This is something that may generate the demand for new activities in the curriculum. One of the major developments in the future which will have a crucial influence on teachers is the role of the Internet in providing comprehensive in-service training programmes and access to a wide range of teaching and learning ideas. There are numerous Internet communities and websites that provide access to every aspect of the physical education profession. Publications such as a recent text in Australia (Kirk, 1997) provide an Internet service that enables teachers and their students to access a whole range of new avenues and contacts. The scope is enormous. This kind of service will become commonplace and it will enable curriculum developers to make accessible new teaching resources, alternative learning strategies and provide comprehensive advice on almost any issue that concerns teachers. For researchers the Internet provides a new challenge for creating partnerships with teachers. Already, the author is engaged in providing support for an intervention study in five schools in the Far East through e-mail and the Internet.

What about research initiatives? Much of the research community in physical education will be involved in monitoring and evaluation in order to demonstrate the effectiveness and efficiency of particular schemes. In particular, disaffected youth will be a major focus. The need to engage in applied research will become a necessity as accountability forces researchers to seek scarce funds far and wide. So far, evidence-based practice has had little impact on physical education but this will change rapidly as teachers feel the need to demonstrate that their practice is informed and intelligent. This will probably be the major reason for practice to improve as teachers respond to the call for greater accountability.

The profession will generate a range of networks and co-operatives in order to share ideas and support one another. In England, the Youth Sports Trust through the Sports Colleges movement has already created such a network. The success of this venture may well encourage other networks to form relationships for mutual support. There is ample evidence of local authority groups emerging in the absence of adequate in-service support but also through advisers, who have recognised the need to supplement their efforts at a time when there are plenty of ideas but a culture of scarce resources.

One of the 'hot spots' of research in physical education has been the work of Evans and Penney (1995) on policy and the national curriculum in England. This work conceptualises policy research as a process which deconstructs the divide between policy-makers and practitioners as well as policy and implementation. They see the need to report their research throughout an evaluation rather than in retrospect. This work is interesting and provides a wealth of insights into the process of curriculum-making and the problems of implementation. Nevertheless, one of the authors (Penney, 1997) bemoans the fact that their work has had little impact on either policy or practice in the UK. This clearly illustrates a real dilemma for much research and scholarship, and here physical education is no different than any other subject. Nevertheless, physical education does need to develop a strong research basis that will inform the best endeavours of its teachers. How it can achieve this status represents the real challenge of the new millennium.

References

Alexander, K., Taggart, A. and Luckman, J. (1998) 'Pilgrim's Progress: The sport education crusade down under'. *Journal of Physical Education, Recreation and Dance*, 69 (4), 21–23.

Alexander, K., Taggart, A. and Thorpe, S. (1996) 'A Spring in their steps? Possibilities for professional renewal through sport education in Australian schools'. *Sport, Education and Society*, 1 (1), 23–46.

Almond, L. (1997) *Physical Education in Schools*. London: Kogan Page.

Armstrong, N. (1992) 'Are British children and youth fit?' in *Are American Children and Youth Fit? Research Quarterly for Exercise and Sport*, 63 (4), 449–452.

Arnold, P. J. (1994) 'Sport and moral education'. *Journal of Moral Education*, 23 (1), 75–90.

Arnold, P. J. (1997) *Sport, Ethics and Education*. London: Cassell.

Biddle, S., Cavill and Sallis, J. (1998) *Young and Active? Young People and Health-enhancing Physical Activity – Evidence and Implications*. London: Health Education Authority.

Cale, L. and Almond, L. (1992) 'Physical activity levels of secondary aged children: a review', *Health Education Journal*, 51 (4), 192–197.

Carr, D. (1991) *Educating the Virtues*. London: Routledge.

Carroll, B. (1994) *Assessment in Physical Education: A Teachers' Guide to the Issues*. London: Falmer Press.

Corbin, C. B., Pangrazi, R. P. and Welk, G. J. (1994) 'Toward an understanding of appropriate physical activity levels for youth'. *The President's Council on Physical Fitness and Sports Research Digest*, 8, 1–17.

Evans, J. (1990) 'Defining a subject: The rise and rise of the new PE?'. *British Journal of Sociology of Education*, 11 (2), 155–169.

Evans, J. (ed.) (1993) *Equity, Education and Physical Education*. London: Falmer Press.

Evans, J. and Davies, B. (1997) Editorial introduction. 'Physical education, sport and the curriculum'. *The Curriculum Journal*, 8 (2), 185–197.

Evans, J. and Penney, D. (1995) 'Physical education, restoration and the politics of sport'. *Curriculum Studies*, 3 (2), 183–196.

Grant, B. C. (1992) 'Integrating sport into the physical education curriculum in New Zealand secondary schools'. *Quest*, 44, 204–216.

Hastie, P. A. (1996) 'Student role involvement during a unit of sport education'. *Journal of Teaching Physical Education*, 16, 88–103.

Hastie, P. A. (1998) 'Participation and perceptions of girls during a unit of sport education'. *Journal of Teaching Physical Education*, 17, 157–171.

Health Education Authority (1995) *Fitness Testing for Health Promotion*. London: Health Education Authority.

Hellison, D. R. (1995) *Teaching Responsibility through Physical Activity*. Champaign, IL: Human Kinetics.

Hellison, D. R. and Templin, T. J. (1991) *A Reflective Approach to Teaching Physical Education*. Champaign, IL: Human Kinetics.

Kirk, D. (1992) *Defining Physical Education*. London: Falmer Press.

Kirk, D. (1997) 'Physical education in the health and physical education statement and profile', *ACHPER Healthy Lifestyles Journal*, 44 (1), 5–7.

Kirk, D., Burgess-Limerick, R., Kiss, M., Lahey, J. and Penney, D. (1999) *Senior Physical Education: An Integrated Approach*. Champaign, IL: Human Kinetics.

Lawson, H. (1997) 'Children in crisis, the helping professions, and the social responsibilities of universities'. *Quest*, 49 (1), 8–33.

Luke, I. T. (1998) 'An examination of pupils' metacognition ability in physical education'. Unpublished doctoral thesis, Loughborough University, Leicestershire.

Martinek, T. and Hellison, D. (1997) 'Fostering resiliency in underserved youth through physical activity'. *Quest*, 49 (1), 34–49.

Mawer, M. (1995) *The Effective Teaching of Physical Education*. London: Longman Group.

Meakin, D. (1994) ' The emotions, morality and physical education'. *Physical Education Review*, 17 (2), 106–116.

McKenzie, T. (1998) 'School health-related physical activity programmes: What do the data say?' *Journal of Physical Education, Recreation and Dance*, 70 (1), 16–19.

McNamee, M. (1998) 'Philosophy and physical education: Analysis, epistemology and axiology'. *European Physical Education Review*, 4 (1), 75–91.

NASPE (1998) *Physical Activity for Children: A Statement of Guidelines*. Reston, VA: National Association for Sport and Physical Education.

Parry, J. (1998) 'Reid on knowledge and justification in physical education'. *European Physical Education Review*, 4 (1), 770–774.

Penney, D. (1997) 'Playing different games, speaking different languages: Policy makers, practitioners and researchers in health and physical education'. In J. Wright (ed.) *Researching in Health and Physical Education*. Wollongong: Faculty of Education, The University of Wollongong, Australia, 53–64.

Penney, D. and Evans, J. (1999) *Politics, Policy and Practice in Physical Education*. London: E. and F. N. Spon.

Pieron, M. and Cheffers, J. (eds) (1989) *Research in Sport Pedagogy: Empirical Analytic Perspective*. Schorndorf: International Council of Sport Science and Physical Education/Verlag Karl Hofman.

Reid, A. (1997) 'Value pluralism and physical education'. *European Physical Education Review*, 3 (1), 6–20.

Siedentop, D. (1991) *Developing Teaching Skills in Physical Education*. (3rd edition) Mountain View, CA: Mayfield.

Siedentop, D. (1994) *Sport Education: Quality P.E. through Positive Sport Experiences*. Champaign, IL: Human Kinetics.

Silverman, S. (1991) 'Research on teaching in physical education'. *Research Quarterly for Exercise and Sport*, 62 (4), 353–364.

56

THEATRE AND DRAMA EDUCATION
Themes and questions

Shifra Schonmann

In everyday life, *if* is a fiction, in the theatre *if* is an experiment. In everyday life, *if* is an evasion, in the theatre *if* is the truth. When we are persuaded to believe in this truth, then theatre and life are one. This is a high aim. It sounds like a hard work. To play needs much work. But when we experience the work as play, then it is not work any more. A play is a play.

Peter Brook, 1968, pp. 140–141.

Why do theatre and drama continue to claim their place in the educational landscape? Why is it that theatre and drama play a powerful cultural role in society but are not required as part of the compulsory school curriculum? Why do they have to battle to secure a legitimate place in the curriculum? This chapter seeks to answer these questions by providing an overview of the main orientations and critical issues in drama/theatre education, and by examining the current ideas of the central leaders in the field, including their ways of knowing and teaching *through* drama/theatre and *within* this art form.

THE SCOPE OF THEATRE/DRAMA IN EDUCATION

What comes to mind when we talk about theatre/drama in schools? We naturally think of staging a play in which the children are the actors and their friends, teachers and parents are the audience. Our thinking has been limited by seeing only a narrow part of a developing phenomenon in education, which only recently is becoming more acceptable as another mode of knowing that we can use very effectively in the school's curriculum.

When drama educators meet, they engage in extensive discussion, usually exchanging experiences and successful strategies. Quite some time can pass before they realise that their concepts of drama education differ considerably. This ranges from completely spontaneous activities (i.e. improvisational exercises) to very carefully planned work (i.e. staging written scripts).

944

A controversial topic in drama education, as Bailin argues, has been how to distinguish drama and theatre and how to clarify the relationship between them. Bailin claims that the essential difference is 'that drama is seen as having to do with the experience of the learner whereas theatre is about communication with an audience' (Bailin, 1993, p. 423). In the last decade it has become clear that it is not necessary to choose between drama and theatre in education. In fact, the use of both in the curriculum is essential in providing a comprehensive aesthetic experience and facilitating full modes of expression. Drama and theatre both use time and place in a symbolic way, focusing on the person as the central medium of expression. Both depend on the person's ability to develop roles and characters within the framework of an 'as if' situation. They also both depend upon voice and physical gestures which are the primary modes of expression. Bolton, a central contemporary leader in drama education, claims that,

> Drama and theatre are essentially the same dramatic art form. There is no difference of status between them even though there is a difference of intention and technique. . . . All good drama and theatre seek the simple action to embody significance.
>
> (Bolton, 1986a, p. 224)

USES OF THEATRE/DRAMA ACROSS THE CURRICULUM

In clarifying what is meant by the term 'theatre/drama education', we need to differentiate between education *for* theatre and education *through* theatre. Education for theatre refers to the theatrical medium as an art form. As an end in itself, it functions as 'master'. Education through theatre refers mainly to theatre as a means to achieve educational objectives, such as improving learning skills, social skills, self-image, etc. In this respect, it functions as 'servant', helping individuals to improve in areas that are external to the artistic-aesthetic medium. The current hotly debated issue of learning through the arts as opposed to learning art forms for their own sake is a particularly contentious one for theatre/drama education. As Best (1996) reflects, it is hard to understand why it is assumed that we have to choose between them; the two options are essentially complementary.

In schools, in fact, drama/theatre education as a field for teaching and learning includes both the aesthetic and the utilitarian. Although many courses, workshops and seminars are available to teachers, the use of drama as a medium for integrating learning across the curriculum still remains relatively unknown to many. In *Arts in Their View*, a 1995 study of youth participation in the arts in England, an interesting outcome was that references to drama as important decreased with age. Participating in plays and drama was often recalled as a particularly enjoyable activity in primary school, and 'drama is the arts activity which, in retrospect, would have been most welcomed by respondents when younger' (Hill, 1996, pp. 290–291).

A closer look into the field is necessary to understand more thoroughly what constitutes theatre/drama education, why its importance decreases with the age of the students, and what are the main themes and questions to be discussed.

MAIN ORIENTATIONS

For many years, drama/theatre education has been influenced by leading teachers who have led the way with new ideas and set the tone in the field. Prominent in the area of *creative drama* (or *child drama*) are pioneers like Caldwell Cook in the 1920s and, in the 1950s, Winifred Ward from the US and Brian Way and Peter Slade from England. Creative drama is a term referring to dramatic activity that is spontaneous. It overlaps with improvisation and cannot always be distinguished from it. It is commonly used with elementary school children. The influence of Dorothy Heathcote and Gavin Bolton from England in the 1960s is still dominant today in the area of *dramatic play*. Dramatic play is a term referring to metaphoric acts. Its assumption is that the entire classroom space in which the activity occurs is the stage, and the participants, who are engaged in the dramatic playing, perform for one another. From the same time period, associated with the concept of *developmental drama* is the name of Richard Courtney from Canada. Developmental drama is a generic term for the academic study of dramatic activity, the study of the transformations achieved through dramatic action.

In the last few years, the field of drama/theatre education has attempted to rely less on its leading teachers, as evidenced at the proceedings of the congress of the International Drama/Theatre and Educational Association (IDEA) in Portugal (1993) and in Brisbane (1995), the conference of the American Alliance for Theatre and Education (AATE) in 1996, and the 1997 Exeter conference in England.

Following is a discussion of the three interrelated orientations in the field of theatre/drama education: the artistic-aesthetic; the pedagogical-educational; and the sociological-cultural. Theatre/drama education operates within an artistic medium, and drama as pedagogy cannot be separated from drama as art. For clarification purposes it will be helpful to consider each orientation.

The artistic-aesthetic

Theatre is an art form that addresses the senses and awareness of the individual. It has a language of its own. Participating in theatre/drama is learning to use this language, and achieving new modes of communication. Theatre, like every other art form, has a process and a product and, as an artistic-aesthetic field of learning, it is attuned to both. The aesthetic functions of theatre and drama help us to understand their nature as an art form and to make judgements which contribute to our understanding of the process and product. Aesthetic modes of knowing, as Eisner (1985) argues, are:

> motivated by our own need to give order to our world. To form is to confer order. To confer aesthetic order upon our world is to make that world hang together to fit, to feel right, to put things in balance, to create harmony.
>
> (Eisner, 1985, p. 29).

'We know more than we can tell', Polanyi says, and leads us to question how can we tell when experience is dramatic and when it is not. Therein lies the challenge of dramatic art. In theatre we seek to communicate what we know but cannot say, i.e. deep structures of knowledge. In this context it is reasonable to ask, as Courtney (1990) suggests: Does dramatic activity affect the way we think? Does it improve our ability to think? These questions and others regarding the nature of human cognition suggest that we need to examine what is unique about theatrical 'ways of knowing'.

The pedagogical-educational

What are the difficulties classroom teachers face if they want their pedagogical foundation to be theatre? This main question leads to others posed by Cooper. What forms of theatre can be suitably taught within the classroom? What constitutes an appropriate pedagogy to teach students about theatre in a practical way? Can such a pedagogy effectively educate tomorrow's theatre audiences (Cooper, 1996)?

In order to answer questions like those raised by Cooper, it is necessary to create a pedagogical environment that is safe and controlled, enabling students to develop an identity with characters and situations. In a climate free of fear and shame, students must be allowed to develop their self-identity, strengthen their self-image, build their self-confidence and share their emotions. Interactions among students and between students and teachers in this pedagogical environment are unconventional and critical to developing the learning process.

The sociological-cultural

Is this drama, social studies or something else? This is the frequently asked question in theatre/drama when we are faced with social/political controversies. The answer is to be found in the assumption that drama is a social art form. Drama/theatre, due to its very nature, demands meaning-making both for individuals and for society. O'Farrell in his 1994 monograph *Education and the Art of Drama*, shows how close the art of drama is to the process of ritual and to the structure and motifs of critical events in the social and political arenas. He claims: 'Any curriculum which professes to teach the art of drama must take these accordances into account if students are to be enabled to resist social manipulation and to control the course of social dramas which affect their lives' (O'Farrell, 1994, p. 36). The most salient issues related to the sociological-cultural orientation are addressed in the following topics: education for life in a multicultural society (Dalrymple, 1996); involvement in current political events (Schonmann, 1996); gender issues (Errington, 1994; Nicholson, 1996); and value-based education (O'Toole, 1995).

The most dominant movement now in theatre/drama education is to expand the practical uses of theatre/drama in the curriculum, thereby realising its full potential. Drama is now being viewed as a multilevel discourse. The current argument that theatre/drama is primarily an art form, involving process and product, needs to be strengthened, as does the basic claim that art should be a central component of the educational curriculum.

THE PLACE OF THEATRE/DRAMA IN THE CURRICULUM

Curriculum theorising

Curriculum development in theatre/drama education has its own logic. It follows the rationale of not separating theory from practice. The sources of theory lie in drama teachers' practice. Theoretical frameworks for drama education are described in books like: *Towards a Theory of Drama in Education* (Bolton, 1979), and *Gavin Bolton Selected Writings* (Bolton, 1986b); *Drama and Intelligence Cognitive Theory* (Courtney, 1990); *Dorothy Heathcote: Collected Writings on Education and Drama* (Johnson, L. and C. O'Neill (eds), 1988); *Making Sense of Drama* (Neelands, 1984); *The Process of Drama* (O'Toole, 1992); *Researching Drama and Arts Education: Paradigms and Possibilities* (Taylor 1996a); and *Drama and Theatre in Education: Contemporary Research* (Somers, 1996a). These frameworks contain ideas about how reality in drama can be defined and researched (i.e. classroom-based enquiry; reflective practitioner design; multiple ways of constructing the world; belief systems that are constructed out of the historical frameworks). The list of contemporary writers interested in curriculum theory is much longer. We can only share Taylor's (1996a) surprise that Hornbrook, a well-known British researcher, ignores the above-mentioned research when he claims that for years the drama in education community 'has been conventionally instrumental, in just this way, generally preferring to discuss and progress working methods rather than to worry too much about their theoretical or ideological implications' (Hornbrook, 1989, p. 3).

What characterises the development of theory in theatre/drama education is that it emerges from within practice, not outside of it. Many scholars – the above mentioned as well as O'Farrell, Davis, Somers and O'Neill, to name a few – concentrate their main efforts on practice as the basis for theorising. According to Britzman, the sources of many theories in education lie in the practice of classroom teachers. Educational theory, as she claims, is derived from the 'lived lives of teachers in the values, beliefs, and deep conventions enacted in practice' (Britzman, 1991, p. 50). From a historical point of view, teachers had worked in drama for a long time before an overarching theory of the subject evolved to encompass its teaching.

The most influential twentieth-century theorists in theatre/drama education are Bertolt Brecht, Augusto Boal and Eugenio Barba. Their different perceptions about the nature of performance inspired innovative thinking and led to revolutionary ways of teaching theatre/drama in school. Their influence on drama teachers has been considerable, both at the primary and secondary levels. Brecht's Epic Theatre was a contrast to naturalism. It says that the job of theatre is to inspire the spectators to participate in reform. Brecht was convinced that only those who understood the principles of the world could change it. He compared the theatre to a scientific endeavour in which the audience participates in the experiment. He 'alienated' his dramas by setting them in the past or in an exotic milieu. Boal wanted to achieve what Brecht dreamt of. Theatre of the Oppressed was his way of suggesting that anyone can act and that theatrical performance should not be solely the province of professionals. Barba's ways of performance brought to the educational drama a vast range of interactive and chaotic ways of working. The theatre of Brecht, Boal and Barba seeks to challenge and provoke. Their forms of theatre are suitably taught within the classroom and they constitute an appropriate pedagogy, allowing students' practical engagement with theatre forms.

948

Many of the world's greatest theoreticians of the past, including Aristotle, Plato, Rousseau and Dewey, considered theatre/drama education to be important in the development of intellectual and emotional resources. This line of thought is echoed in the ideas of the leading figures of contemporary educational philosophy and aesthetics – Maxine Green and Elliot Eisner. They both seek new directions in an artistic aesthetic curriculum. They appealed to educators to construct learning experiences where students can struggle with contradictions of life. Yet this appeal does not resonate with the common public understanding of the primary importance of the dramatic art, which is entertainment. Commonly, drama is regarded 'as merely a bit of fun, catharsis, and relaxation from serious learning, because it is assumed to be merely a matter of feeling' (Best, 1996, p. 12).

INTEGRATING THEATRE/DRAMA EDUCATION INTO THE CURRICULUM

Given the tendency to regard theatre only as fun and games, integrating theatre/drama education into the curriculum is a never-ending challenge. It is a continual struggle to influence the educational policy of decision makers, at both the national and local levels. Moreover schools face a constant search for qualified teachers who have the kind of broad experience in the field of theatre/drama education that is needed.

The concepts in the field of theatre/drama education are diverse, unconventional, tend to be ambiguous, and therefore, they may be potentially threatening to those who want to integrate theatre/drama into the curriculum. Moreover, the knowledge base involved is not clearly defined, and the question of the place of theatre in the curriculum is not self-evident. Therefore, more disciplinary, philosophical research needs to be done that focuses on the question: What is the main body of artistic knowledge and experience that we need in theatre/drama education? Once it is recognised that theatre as an art form holds a valid cultural position in society and can be an effective vehicle for integrating multiple disciplines in the school curriculum, theatre/drama education can add richness and diversity to the school environment rather than being viewed as a potentially threatening element.

IS THERE SUBJECT MATTER TO BE STUDIED IN THEATRE/DRAMA EDUCATION?

What is the core of theatre/drama in education? What is it that we do not want to lose sight of? These questions cannot be answered easily. A close look at the conceptual framework for teaching of and learning about and through theatre, prepared by the Getty Education Institute for the Arts in 1996 (Wheetley, 1996), may shed some light on these concerns.

This document professes that theatre must be an academic discipline relevant for all students rather than an extra-curricular activity for a select few. As an academic discipline, theatre/drama education should teach the history of theatre; aesthetic and philosophical enquiry to understand how people make judgements about dramatic texts and performances; theatre criticism, to be able to analyse, interpret and evaluate dramatic texts; and to be able to analyse, interpret and evaluate theatre production. Intrinsic to the discipline-based approach is the understanding that works of dramatic texts may be 'play scripts, stories, or poems from or about a variety of cultures and historical periods. They can also include improvisational scenarios, personal life experiences, contemporary and historical events, social issues, themes, images, and concepts' (Wheetley, 1996, p. 57). Furthermore, in order for students to comprehend the complexity and interrelated nature of the theatre and fully to understand and appreciate selected dramatic texts, they 'must have the opportunity to engage in production activities that enable them to explore the texts from the various perspectives of the researcher, playwright, director, designer, technician and actor' (Wheetley, 1996, p. 1). The Getty document, the most current conceptual framework for the teaching of and learning about and through theatre, can serve as a basis for further debate.

THE THEATRE/DRAMA TEACHER

The role of the theatre/drama teacher is critical. She/he must create a safe acting environment so that the student will not feel threatened in any way. Teacher training should include both theatre and education. One of the common misconceptions among drama teachers is that their role is to discover future 'stars' and to prepare students to become professional actors. This is definitely not the aim of theatre/drama education. Rather, its goal is to serve students by helping them develop perspectives on the art and skills needed in the real world. The emphasis is on the intimate work done in the classroom, and when this work is taken outside of the classroom as a performance, the goal remains the same. The authentic teacher continues to be connected to her/his students in a live experience and her/his personal signature becomes evident.

Typical to the field is that many of the leaders in theatre/drama education are teachers as well as researchers who are committed to increasing the recognition of the role of the arts in education. They focus on the realities of the classroom. In teacher training groups, they share their ideas and strategies regarding the use of dramatic play as a tool for integrating student learning.

DRAMA STRATEGIES IN THE CLASSROOM

In the classroom the teacher can use various strategies in dramatic contexts to encourage learning on many levels – intellectual, emotional, social, aesthetic and sensory-motor. According to Heathcote (1988b), a well-known leader in theatre/drama education for more than 30 years, drama is anything that involves people in active role-taking situations in which attitudes and not characters are the chief concern. She developed the idea that role-playing gives children the opportunity to interpret knowledge for themselves. The origin of Heathcote's 'mental of the expert' approach to education lies in her work with her students. Before focusing on their topic of study as a class, each student acquired knowledge (i.e. expertise) in an area related to that topic. Then, when the class came together as a team to study the topic in depth, each 'expert' was able to contribute to an understanding of the key issues.

Many drama strategies can be used in the classroom: *teaching in role* is a way to engage the students' and the teacher's interest in dramatic playing; *small group improvisation*, where a class may separate into small performance groups, each exploring a facet of an overall theme; *forum theatre*, which is Boal's technique whereby the audiences can take the place of the actor; *freeze-frame exercises*, where students are extending the movement or the idea into tableaux; and *role-play activities* with or without predetermined outcomes are only a few of them. All convey the essence of dramatic action in different ways.

Dramatic action

Dramatic action is always a physical, concrete expression of a role. It is the conversion of thoughts and feelings into form, and so it is significant and symbolic. It may be completely spontaneous, improvised or well planned, but its nature is always to be expressive and communicative. Based on Bolton's views, it can be argued that the more students lose themselves in their fictitious roles, the closer they approach to reality.

Dramatic action helps students fully to experience the environment through the senses and to give meaning to their interpretation of fiction and facts. Creating meaning in drama is a complex process, involving actual and fictional worlds. The 'as if' situation is not merely a matter of putting yourself in someone else's shoes; it also requires the avoidance of stereotypes and learning to interpret the fiction of drama in imaginative ways. When students act in drama, they are typically actively involved in learning new ways of thinking and doing things. The activity of moving in and out of the 'as if' role helps students gain an understanding of different levels of meaning in dramatic action. This playing between virtual and actual *as if* transformation is the main knowledge gained out of the dramatic action.

Dramatic playing

Dramatic playing is based on dramatic action. It is a basic concept we learned from Gavin Bolton, already mentioned above, who alongside Heathcote has set the tone in the field during the last 30 years. Dramatic playing is a process that uses role-playing focusing on a student's feelings and intellect to achieve educational goals. These goals, as Bolton defined,

> are generally to do with the development of the mind and especially to do with understanding the 'content' of particular dramatic experience. This experience is created by pupils and teachers together, working within the unit of a drama lesson or session in which often undifferentiated dramatic and non-dramatic elements (for instance, discussion or writing) are part of a total process.
> (Bolton, 1986b, p. 18)

The aim is to create, through symbolic forms, situations that have not been resolved. It is a way of negotiating meaning and is characterised by a high degree of spontaneity on the one hand, and a high degree of control on the other. The ability to think and feel through control of the medium is a central understanding in Bolton's work. Two underlying principles form the basis of dramatic activity (game or play). The first is that the starting-point of the game or play is always known to the participants. The second is that every form of dramatic activity has a way out, in contrast to reality, and is therefore safe. The stage or playing area is the entire classroom space in which the activity occurs, and the participants who are creating the dramatic event perform for one another. Students bring their own prejudices, stereotypes, thoughts and feelings to every dramatic activity. Heathcote claims that, 'drama cannot properly function unless the children agree to tolerate generously, and to put to work, different personalities, points of view, information, speed of working and level of attention' (Heathcote, 1988a, p. 56).

Performance

In contrast to dramatic playing there is the performance-centred perspective. Performance is a form of drama that is rehearsed and scripted. Performed by actors for an audience, it is a manifestation of drama that we are used to seeing in professional or amateur theatre. Hornbrook, who has written extensively about performance, stresses the need to explore ways in which students can become stage literate, i.e. better readers of drama/theatre and therefore better audiences (Hornbrook, 1991). The school play has been the subject of many attacks. Yet, the persuasive argument in favour of producing a school play is in the understanding that it can become a meeting point of teachers and students in a joint creative process, striving towards a shared goal as an educational benefit. It requires interdisciplinary co-operation and provides an opportunity for experiencing genuine theatrical communication.

Pedagogic improvisation

The common denominator in all classroom drama strategies is improvisation, which can be defined as an unplanned sequence of activities in which we react on the spur of the moment to what others are doing or saying. In theatre the meaning of improvisation is far more complicated. Improvisation is creating drama without the help of a script. As students improvise, they rely on their cognitive foundation to make impromptu responses within a dramatic context. It is working within the two extremes of spontaneity versus controlled inspiration. Improvisation without planning leads to chaos, while overplanning can kill spontaneity and originality. These views make us aware of the enormous potential of improvisation, which has become a popular tool in education.

Improvisation is not often discussed by educators because the unspoken assumption is often that 'while jazz musicians and actors may improvise, educators plan' (Donmoyer, 1983, p. 39). Improvisation, as a tool for teaching life-skills, can help students develop their ability to apply knowledge to solve real-life problems. In addition, as a tool for increasing interpersonal skills, it encourages the formation of trust and bonding between teacher and students.

Assessment: a controversial issue

The assessment of learning in dramatic play is a controversial issue. What are the components of theatre/drama in education that have to be evaluated? Is it performance?

Pedagogy? What are the benefits to students? to society? What tools can be used to evaluate the many complex factors that are involved? Would it be of value to use different methods of evaluation for different parts of the curriculum?

Since the mid-1980s, the culture regarding assessment changed, creating new opportunities for investigating. Redington (1983), Robinson (1980) and O'Neill and Lambert (1982), among others, sought solutions to the above questions, but the questions are still unanswered. It is a common belief that the arts contribute significantly to an individual's emotional and intellectual growth. However, in order for the arts to gain more recognition and support as an integral part of the school curriculum, it is essential that we prove its value in terms of student achievement. This can only happen if we develop more imaginative approaches to evaluating student performance. Taylor claims: 'There is a danger in promoting a neo-positivist view of research which promotes technical modes of inquiry when describing artistic process' (Taylor, 1996b, p. 11). Somers argues that in order to assess drama in education: 'we now have a more mature and rounded view of the relationship of drama in education and performance and in the same way it is time for the usefulness of quantitative approaches to be contemplated when we consider our choice of methodology' (Somers, 1996b, p. 169).

When it comes to influencing decisions about curriculum and ensuring that drama has a place in the educational process, much depends upon being able to prove that theatre/drama education has a positive impact on cognition. We need to conceptualise ways that challenge the traditional epistemology of educational assessment.

CONCLUDING COMMENTS AND FUTURE ORIENTATIONS

Theatre/drama education is no longer a matter of choosing between education *for* theatre or education *through* theatre. Both paradigms offer ways of knowing that must be studied in this age of plurality of world views and cultures. Yet the artistic-aesthetic dimension is the foundation upon which the field of theatre/drama education is constructed. The essence of the field is that it is an art form. Upon accepting this view, we must ask ourselves: As we approach the twenty-first century, what are the major issues facing theatre/drama educators? What are the objectives? Seeking answers to these questions requires that we continually look for new ways of working and knowing.

Consider Csikszentmihalyi's ideas about enjoyment:

> In the first place, it is necessary to have something to do, to face some opportunities for action or challenge. Next, it is necessary for the person to have appropriate skills or the capacity to respond to the challenges at hand. When the challenges and skills balance each other, the situation usually produces an intrinsically motivating experience.
>
> (Csikszentmihalyi, 1985, p. 491)

These are good guidelines to follow as we strive to make learning in the classroom an enjoyable experience for students – one of the most neglected issues in education.

The two metaphors: theatre/drama education – master or servant, that were introduced as opening up the two different approaches for theatre/drama education, can be considered here as emphasising that both are needed in the future. The master metaphor is a call for a strong artistic-aesthetic curriculum that has to be supported by a large range of research.

Academic thinking opens up minds to seeing drama as a vital subject in its own right, not merely as an embellishment to the curriculum. The servant metaphor is a call for using theatre/drama as a tool for holistic education. It is an essential part of values-based education in our world of multiple realities.

REFERENCES

Bailin, S. (1993) 'Theatre, drama education and the role of the aesthetic', *Curriculum Studies*, 25 (1), 423–432.

Best, D. (1996) 'Research in drama and the arts in education: The objective necessity – proving it'. In J. Somers (ed.), *Drama and Theatre in Education: Contemporary Research*. Ontario: Captus Press, 4–23.

Bolton, G. (1979) *Towards a Theory of Drama in Education*. London: Longman.

Bolton, G. (1986a) 'Drama in the curriculum'. In D. Davis and C. Lawrence (eds), *Gavin Bolton Selected Writings*. London: Longman, 224–231.

Bolton. G. (1986b) 'Freedom and imagination and the implication for teaching drama'. In D. Davis and C. Lawrence (eds), *Gavin Bolton Selected Writings*. London: Longman, 18–22.

Britzman, D. (1991) *Practice Makes Practice: A Critical Study of Learning to Teach*, Albany, NY: SUNY Press.

Brook, P. (1968) *The Empty Space*. New York: Macmillan.

Cooper, R. (1996) 'Priorities in drama research: An agenda for the next decade', *Research in Drama Education*, 1 (2), 261–264.

Courtney, R. (1990) *Drama and Intelligence Cognitive Theory*. Montreal: McGill-Queen's University Press.

Csikszentmihalyi, M. (1985) 'Reflection on enjoyment', *Perspective in Biology and Medicine*, 28 (4), 489–496.

Dalrymple, L. (1996) 'Lifestyle education in Kwazulu-Natal, South Africa'. In J. Somers (ed.) *Drama and Theatre in Education: Contemporary Research*. Ontario: Captus Press, 87–98.

Donmoyer, R. (1983) 'Pedagogical improvisation', *Educational Leadership*, 40 (4), 39–43.

Eisner, E. W. (1985) 'Aesthetic Modes of Knowing'. In E. W. Eisner (ed.) *Learning and Teaching: The Ways of Knowing*. Chicago: Chicago University Press, 23–36.

Errington, E. (1994) 'Dramatising gender issues: A qualitative approach to educational inquiry'. In J. Grenfell and R. Steven (eds) *Directions in Arts Education: Reader and Study Guide*. Geelong, Australia: Falmer Press

Heathcote, D. (1988) 'Subject or system?' In L. Johnson and C. O'Neill (eds) *Dorothy Heathcote: Collected Writings on Education and Drama*. London: Hutchinson.

Hill, R. (1996) 'Arts in their view: A study of youth participation in the arts', *Research in Drama Education*, 1 (2), 289–291.

Hornbrook, D. (1989) *Education and Dramatic Art*. Oxford: Basil Blackwell.

Hornbrook, D. (1991) *Education in Drama*. London: Falmer Press.

Johnson, L. and O'Neill, C. (eds) (1988) *Dorothy Heathcote: Collected Writings on Education and Drama*. London: Hutchinson.

Neelands, J. (1984) *Making Sense of Drama: A Guide to Classroom Practice*. London: Heinemann.

Nicholson, H. (1996) 'Performing gender: Drama, education and identity'. In J. Somers (ed.), *Drama and Theatre in Education: Contemporary Research*. Ontario: Captus Press, 75–86.

O'Farrell, L. (1994) *Education and the Art of Drama*. Geelong, Australia: Deakin University Press.

O'Neill, C. and Lambert, A. (1982) *Drama Structures*. London: Hutchinson.

O'Toole, J. (1992) *The Process of Drama*. London: Routledge.

O'Toole, J. (1995) 'The rude charms of drama'. In P. Taylor and C. Hoepper (eds) *Selected Readings in Drama and Theatre Education*. Brisbane: NADIE.

Polanyi, M. (1964) *Personal Knowledge: Towards a Post-Critical Philosophy*. New York: Harper and Row.

Redington, C. (1983) *Can Theatre Teach?* Oxford: Pergamon Press.

Robinson, K. (ed.) (1980) *Exploring Theatre and Education*, London: Heinemann Educational.

Schonmann, S. (1996) 'Jewish–Arab encounters in the drama theatre class battlefield', *Research in Drama Education*, 1 (2), 175–188.

Somers, J. (ed.) (1996a) *Drama and Theatre in Education: Contemporary Research*. Ontario: Captus Press.

Somers, J. (1996b) 'Approaches to drama research'. In J. Somers (ed.) *Drama and Theatre in Education: Contemporary Research*. Ontario: Captus Press, 165–173.

Taylor, P. (ed.) (1996a) *Researching Drama and Arts Education: Paradigms and Possibilities*. London: Falmer Press.

Taylor, P. (1996b) 'Introduction: Rebellion, reflective turning and arts education research'. In P. Taylor (ed.) *Researching Drama and Arts Education: Paradigms and Possibilities*. London: Falmer Press, 1–21.

Wheetley, K. A. (1996) 'A discipline-based theatre education handbook'. In *The Getty Education Institute for the Arts* (The Southeast Center for Education in the Arts.), National Advisory Board Meeting, October 25, 1996, The University of Tennessee at Chattanooga.

57

THE SHAPING OF VISUAL ARTS IN EDUCATION

Douglas G. Boughton

ORIGINS

The history of visual arts education in state-supported education systems is a relatively short one, beginning in Europe, the United States and other Western nations less than 200 years ago. Other, more traditional apprenticeship methods of artist education have a much longer history, probably as long as the history of art itself. The difference between apprenticeship training of artists and the more recent, school-based notion of visual arts education, is that the former was directed towards preparing the apprentice to become an artist or art worker, while the latter has encompassed a shifting array of educational goals throughout its short history. State-supported education systems have typically taken the view that it is important for students to understand art, but not necessarily to develop highly refined skills of production, since not all students will become artists or art workers.

The transition from the European guild apprenticeship system of art instruction began before the end of the eighteenth century, and by the early 1900s the only institutions offering drawing instruction were the academies of art. Instruction in these institutions was carried out by professional artists, and their students were talented individuals destined to become artists themselves (Efland, 1983). By the end of the nineteenth century in Europe and most of the Western world, art instruction was provided by a range of institutions including high schools, some primary (elementary) schools, vocational institutions such as schools of decorative arts, and trade schools (Aland, 1992; Young, 1985). While the academies continued into the nineteenth century with the preparation of artists, the major difference between them and schools was that art teachers in school systems were not themselves practising artists.

The emergence of visual arts education as a discipline has been attributed to the Industrial Revolution (Efland, 1983). The practical concerns of the world of industry were not seen to have been served well by fine art education. Consequently a split developed between fine and applied arts instruction. Both continued through the nineteenth century, with applied arts focusing upon the practical application of technical and design drawings suitable for industrial utility, while the fine arts served the upper-class pretensions of those seeking access to the higher ideals of aesthetic endeavour. The twin schemes of education for fine and applied art at this time reflected the European class system – applied art for the working classes; fine art for the aristocracy.

Through the twentieth century artist education has continued in various institutions as a relatively minor enterprise in comparison to the majority of visual arts education, which has been conducted in schools, museums, community centres, and privately for numerous purposes.

THE CONTENT OF VISUAL ARTS EDUCATION

During the twentieth century the term '(visual) art education' embraced both the practice of art teaching and research into teaching, learning and related issues. In schools, visual arts curricula have included many topics, including art appreciation, art criticism, art history, design history, aesthetics, and an almost limitless range of production skills. The list of skills taught in art programmes around the world is extensive and impossible to list in its entirety. Some of the most popular are: drawing (expressive and technical); lettering; calligraphy; print-making; painting; sculpture; mixed media; bricolage; environmental, graphic and product design; film and electronic media ceramics; and various handcrafts such as *slöjd*, fibre arts and jewellery.

In contemporary literature, discourse about visual arts education has included discussion of teaching and learning, not only in schools but in all educational contexts from pre-school ages to university level, and in various social institutions including state and private schools, art schools, universities and other institutes of further education, museums and community centres. Since the late 1950s growing interest in systematic enquiry has contributed a body of research literature to the field. Methods of research were initially derived from the natural sciences, but by the late 1960s they more frequently shared common approaches with the social sciences and humanities.

Research has attempted to develop an understanding of the ways in which humans come to understand, produce and attribute value to artistic forms. Some research effort has focused upon human development, positing models to describe and predict artistic behaviours in students. Other investigation has examined adult behaviour to determine the difference between the performance of novices compared with experts in the ways they handle artistic symbols. A third approach has examined alternative strategies to enhance individuals' capacity to decode and respond sensitively to artistic forms (Gardner, 1983). Various themes have engaged researchers with different degrees of urgency since the late 1950s. Dominant amongst these have been: creativity; the relationship between personality variables and artistic performance; aesthetics and the visual aesthetic response; drawing; and perception (including physiological and psychological orientations). Since the mid-1980s philosophic research has addressed central questions about the nature of art, and the transition between modernist and post-modern conceptions of the discipline of art and art education.

INFLUENCES THAT SHAPE THE FIELD

The visual arts are amongst the most dynamic of disciplines studied in schools, responding to various interrelated influences which shape its content and practices. These influences include:

- social changes;
- economic imperatives;
- political pressures;
- ideological changes in education and the art world;
- research findings;
- technological developments.

(Boughton, 1989)

Social changes

World societies have changed rapidly since the Industrial Revolution, with the pace of change increasing significantly since the Second World War. New world countries like Canada, the USA and Australia have been faced with problems generated by the rapid immigration of peoples from all over the world into new, rapidly expanding multicultural communities. The role of the arts education in these communities has been directed towards the service of various social purposes such as the creation and maintenance of national identities (Freedman and Hernández, 1998); the rediscovery of traditional cultures lost by indigenous, colonised peoples (Rogers, 1994); and the development of cultural awareness and sensitivity in new world contexts. Other colonised countries, like Latin America and Africa, have suffered problems of lingering cultural dependency on colonising nations (Barbosa, 1999).

Since the Second World War in Western European countries large numbers of immigrants from former colonies have challenged long-standing conceptions of nationality, class and race. The traditional feudal base of authority and nationality in these countries is no longer practical as the major reference against which national heritage and cultural iconography can be measured. Hegemonic views of education and cultural values are beginning to flounder in European communities discovering cultural democracy and the limitations of monistic approaches to education. Art education literature from countries such as Spain, Portugal, the United Kingdom and even Hungary and Lithuania calls for revisionist approaches to the teaching of art and art history in order to reflect the changing ethnic texture of these communities.

Asian nations have responded to the industrial imperatives of economic development by recognising the need to embrace elements of Western society, while at the same time maintaining traditional Eastern values and cultural practices, so creating a kind of cultural schizophrenia in the maintenance of dual cultural ideologies. The educational problem in Asia has been significant, with many nations reflecting strong Western influence in schools. In Singapore and Hong Kong art education practices have been dominated by British constructions of art and education. In Japan and Taiwan the notion of internationalisation has created tensions between traditional Asian and Western artistic values.

In Western developed nations an increase in the level of general education and ageing population profiles have affected the pattern of arts education. Both the level of education and advancing average age of these populations are factors influencing increased levels of participation in arts activities (Hillman-Chartrand, 1986). The future effect of these changes is likely to be increased demand for continuing education, and community arts education programmes for adults.

Economic imperatives

Rapid post-Second World War industrial development has exerted considerable influence upon visual arts curricula in those countries competing for a share of the international marketplace. With the growth of advertising as the lubricant of the market economy (Hillman-Chartrand, 1986), visual arts programmes in schools have experienced two developments. The first has been a growth of programmes intended to develop in students design skills likely to be useful in industry. The belief underpinning this development is that design schools, and subsequently industry, will benefit from the pool of potential designers exiting from schools. The second development has been the advent of design programmes intended to increase awareness in students of the qualities of good design, hence preparing a future population of discriminating consumers. Presumably, informed consumers will in turn place pressure upon industry to produce well-designed products, thus improving their capacity to compete successfully in the international marketplace.

Design, as part of visual arts education, can be traced back to the late eighteenth century when drawing was taught to serve the needs of industry, particularly in the United Kingdom (Chalmers, 1990). The most powerful influence in art education came from South Kensington. South Kensington was the home of the School of Art and Science, formerly the British Department of Practical Art. The South Kensington philosophy of art education drew from German ideologies which tended towards utilitarian orientations. The proponents of this approach 'believed and espoused a view of drawing as being utilitarian, ornamental and mechanical as opposed to an aesthetic atelier training in the French and Italian academic traditions' (MacDonald, 1970, p. 227). Based upon geometry and technical drawing, this drawing syllabus demanded mechanistic processes of imitation. The basic intention was to discipline and train the hand and the eye.

Design disciplines, particularly environmental, graphic and product, re-emerged and burgeoned through the 1980s, particularly in Europe, the United Kingdom and Australia, where it was frequently linked with craft and technology in the curriculum. It has not been so evident in the United States and Canada as a distinct curriculum presence.

Political influence

The relationship between industry and governments became closer as international competition for markets increased in the 1980s. From the late 1980s most industrialised countries engaged in systematic reforms of their industrial infrastructure with a view to improving competitiveness in the international marketplace. This took the form of widespread micro-economic reforms in all levels of industry, the public service and professions.

Industrial reforms were accompanied by sweeping national curriculum revisions designed to bring schools into line with the needs of industry. Most industrialised and newly developing nations shared a common agenda – to achieve and sustain economic growth, successfully to accommodate technological change, and to achieve social stability (Skilbeck, 1992). The basis for reform was to provide industry with more appropriately prepared workers, and to define more clearly the pathways between education and the workforce.

In conjunction with curriculum revisions, many governments exercised political power in an attempt to achieve predictability, uniformity and reliability of high standard educational outcomes. These outcomes were expressed in remarkably similar ways in most industrialised countries. Agreed curriculum 'standards' or 'profiles' were developed to describe typical student trajectories and expected outcomes for the arts, creating some problems of conception and implementation for arts educators.

Ideological changes in education and the art world

A major ideological transition in the late twentieth century affected education, the art world and visual arts education. This was the movement from modernist to post-modern ideologies. The debate began in the mid-1970s and by the late 1980s it had split visual arts educators into two loosely grouped ideological camps: those maintaining the value of modernist assumptions, and those embracing a more eclectic, politically and socially based set of beliefs about the nature of cultural evolution, society, and the place of the visual arts within it.

Modernism was exemplified by practices in the arts that promoted individualism, and which embraced the principles of evolutionary progression in human cultural development. 'Aesthetic modernism' arose from the general condition of 'cultural modernism', the origins of which have been traced by contemporary social theorists to the eighteenth-century Enlightenment (Efland *et al.*, 1996). Modernist views held disinterested aesthetic experience as the centrepiece of artistic contemplation, elevating artworks to an elite position while condemning mundane and popular tastes. Abstraction was valued as a pure form of aesthetic expression, and knowledge of formalist principles of visual organisation were thought to provide purchase on the secret to both the production of significant aesthetic form and the ability to understand it.

The nature of post-modernism cannot be neatly defined, and is best described as an attitude of scepticism about modernist concepts of progress, scientific assumptions of objectivity, and hierarchies of knowledge and art. By the end of the 1990s post-modernism still was not regarded as a cohesive ideology, but was sufficiently well established to indicate the emergence of a powerful challenge to established orthodoxies in visual arts education (Efland *et al.*, 1996; Fehr, 1994; MacGregor, 1992; Wolcott, 1996). Differences in views held by modernists and post-modernists raise questions for educators about central pedagogical issues like the virtue of originality in image-making (Freedman, 1994a; MacGregor, 1992), the relationship of art and context (Blandy and Hoffman, 1993; Chalmers, 1985), the relative merits of popular art and fine arts (Duncum, 1996), the influence of new technologies upon expression (Freedman and Relan, 1992), the relative value of Eurocentric forms of expression for cultural minorities (Anderson, 1995; Garber, 1995; Hart, 1991; Stuhr, 1994) and gender issues in art and education (Freedman, 1994b; Sandell, 1991).

Influence of research findings

Like all fields of education, the arts have been responsive to the findings of research. Psychological research has held considerable interest for the field, specifically in relation to developmental theory, clinical psychology and cognitive processes (Freedman, 1995), and it can be seen that different psychological perspectives have sustained different approaches to art teaching. During the early twentieth century the progressive movement in education initially focused upon the natural unfolding of students' creative potential, thereby promoting the view that freedom of expression in children provided a sound foundation for the democratic personality (Freedman, 1995). Expressive freedom was thought to promote psychological health (Lowenfeld, 1957) and in that sense clinical psychology provided the crucible for a therapeutic approach to the teaching of visual arts which gained widespread acceptance in both Eastern and Western countries after the Second World War.

The writings of John Dewey, also in the early years of the twentieth century, had a profound influence upon the ways in which the mind of the child was regarded, and the kinds of educational experiences thought to be appropriate to stimulate learning. Dewey's proposition – that the child's interests should be exploited in education – led to the practice by some progressive educators to let children do whatever they wanted in art. A second effect was to forbid the teacher to intervene in instruction in order to preserve the developing character of the child. A third result, prevalent in the work of some art educators at this time, was to translate Dewey's interest in promoting the creative intelligence of children into a bold claim for art education. That claim, not sustained by later research, was that the study of art would first improve creative artistic behaviour, and second would transfer that capacity for creative thought into the child's general intelligence (Eisner, 1972).

Supporting these educational developments were the findings of psychological research (particularly in the area of child development) and creativity. It was noted by researchers that children appeared to progress through predictable stages of artistic development in the absence of instruction. Various models of artistic development were generated by researchers in order to describe and predict the expected artistic trajectory of children as they matured. In general terms these models claimed universality of development; charting progress from children's spontaneous artistic production (uninhibited psychomotor activity) through schematic to stylised representations (Freedman, 1995). The nature of that development was interpreted by researchers as 'U' shaped, in the sense that early uninhibited work was valued as fluent and expressive, while the products of the middle years of development demonstrated growing inhibition and struggles to achieve realism. The middle years were viewed as an aesthetic low point in artistic development, recoverable by only a few who complete the second leg of the 'U' with a greater facility for making artistic decisions in the later years of adolescence. The notion of 'U'-shaped artistic development, particularly in drawing, still has currency in the research literature (Davis, 1997).

In the late 1970s early psychological research was reconsidered in the light of some alternative perceptions challenging the assumptions of universality in patterns of children's artistic growth, and questioning the uniqueness of individual creative performance (Freedman, 1995). No longer was it clear that children followed similar patterns of development in different cultural contexts. Moreover, the values that shaped the interpretation of developmental research were shown to be tangled with conceptions of art anchored in modernist, Western frameworks. Duncum (1986) argued that the similarity between abstract expressionist art of the 1960s and the art of young children led to a culturally biased interpretation of value in children's artistic production. For those who hold abstract expressionism as the paradigm for aesthetic performance in art, the diminution of free expressive abstract forms during the middle years of development is regarded as an aesthetic decline. In another cultural context, in which abstraction is not regarded as an artistic virtue, development theory may well assume a different profile. In short, the assumptions of earlier psychological research have promoted a view of artistic development which may well be nothing more than a cultural artefact (Korzenik, 1995; Pariser, 1997; Wilson and Wilson, 1981).

Technological development

The impact of rapid technological development in the visual arts has affected the nature of images made by artists and students, the manner in which they have been made, and the ways in which they are exhibited. Scanning hardware and sophisticated software developed in the 1990s, has made it possible for artists to recycle and manipulate images borrowed from other sources. Digital records make it possible rapidly and accurately to reproduce an original image. Galleries are required to assume very different configurations of display spaces with dim lighting, smaller spaces and consoles to allow interactive engagement of patrons with keyboards and visual displays.

In schools students have begun to work collaboratively on the production of computer images (Freedman and Relan, 1992), whereas previously they tended to work independently using traditional artistic methods. The Internet has provided students with access to a greatly increased source of resource materials and images. The nature of images created by students has changed as a consequence of graphics programmes which have removed dependence on drawing skills to enable them to create the illusion of realism in their representations.

Of even greater consequence are the questions raised about the nature of art, the value of originality, what counts as an art work, and who takes credit for the creative activity (Efland *et al.*, 1996). Are digital images produced on a computer appropriate as works of art? Does originality matter, or is it acceptable for images to be recycled? If so, to what degree must the original be altered before it assumes artistic value? What is the original image anyway, when one contemplates a work of art – that displayed on the screen or the digital record on disk, or does it matter? Who can legitimately take credit for an art work – the artist, or the team that developed the graphics software used by the artist? Technological development is very much an instrument of post-modern ideology, and these questions reflect many of the issues embedded in that debate.

Technology has also been instrumental in the spread of popular culture and cultural colonisation (Duncum, 1995). In most of the rest of the world, cultural invasion from the West has been ideological and electronic, and has crossed borders as a consequence of the pervasive influence of the popular media, since the ideology of Western capitalism is wrapped in the images of television advertising. Access to the Internet in conjunction with interactive multimedia, has accelerated the promulgation of information and advertising, increasing the pace of change. Cultural colonisation by electronic means has raised fundamental questions about cultural identity in both Western and non-Western nation states, and has emerged as an issue for visual arts education.

THE PATTERN OF INTERNATIONAL DEVELOPMENT

Curriculum in various world regions can be regarded as a patchwork quilt of ideas, reflecting different emphases and rationales in response to the forces acting upon art and education in that specific region. The influences so far described have coincided in particular ways in particular world regions, resulting in some similarities and many regional differences in the local character of visual arts education. Ideas about art curriculum and teaching have sometimes taken peculiar routes, and there has often been a considerable time-lag between the emergence of similar ideas in different world regions.

There have been a number of significant movements in art education that have achieved almost universal appeal. In the late 1800s schools in Western countries included drawing in the curriculum to develop hand–eye co-ordination and provide skilled workers for industry. The impetus for this came from South Kensington in the United Kingdom and spread to the United States and most of the British colonies of the time. In the early 1920s interest in rigid copying gave way to the promotion of more expressive work in children, due largely to the work of Franz Cizek, an Austrian whose ideas were embraced in England and exported to the United States and the British Colonies. The ideology of *free expression* gained impetus through the work of psychologists, such as G. Stanley Hall's investigation of children's interests, and James Sully and Earl Barnes's belief that children's artistic development replicated human cultural development.

The creativity movement reached its peak after the Second World War, bolstered by the political impetus of the space race and the belief that study of the visual arts promoted creative growth in children that would transfer to other domains of human intellectual functioning. The writings of Viktor Lowenfeld were widely read and internationally accepted as doctrine for almost 20 years. Additional credence was afforded the creativity doctrine by the coincidental emergence of abstract expressionism in the 1960s. The outward appearance of abstract work resembled the images made by young children, suggesting that creative capacity was innate in all children.

With the failure of the creativity movement to deliver the benefits claimed for it, the interests of art educators turned to a more disciplined approach to teaching, where the pedagogical interest switched from process to content. The Getty-funded Discipline-Based Art Education (DBAE) movement in the United States derived a curriculum framework from the professional art world which promoted a four-strand structure modelled on the professional roles of artist, critic, historian and aesthetician. The growth of DBAE survived into the 1990s as a consequence of generous funding from the Getty Center for Education in the Arts, but its history was dogged by considerable criticism from many scholars concerned about elitist, modernist orientations reflected in its philosophy.

Postwar social changes, coupled with an emerging interest in issues of race, culture, gender, and a commitment to cultural democracy, have threatened the survival of DBAE in the United States. Outside the USA, DBAE is not as significant in its presence as are concerns about art as a means to generate *cultural understanding*, the analysis of *social issues*, and art and design as *vocational skills*.

Other rationales for art education since the Industrial Revolution have existed in varying degrees of prominence, sometimes in parallel with conflicting arguments supporting art in the curriculum. These reasons range from the conservative to reactionary, and from the bizarre to the logical, depending upon one's perspective of the time and context. Some of these include arguments that the visual arts will develop:

- skill in genteel accomplishments (like china painting and embroidery) for the children of the wealthy;
- standards of good taste among potential consumers of manufactured goods;
- an appreciation of the beautiful;
- aesthetic understanding;
- an improved society;
- visual literacy;
- hemispheric balance in cerebral functioning;
- citizens trained to make productive use of their leisure time;
- international understanding and world peace;
- a means to explore moral alternatives in human relationships;
- a means to assist learning in other areas of the school curriculum;
- access to the great artistic achievements of human cultures;
- critical skills for the analysis of visual culture and/or social reconstruction.

THE FUTURE OF THE VISUAL ARTS IN EDUCATION

At a time in human history when people are moving around the globe in unprecedented numbers, issues of cultural identity have become increasingly important in arts education. In many countries, in many ways, cultural groups are experiencing a collision of their own deeply embedded values with the values held by different cultural groups. Twin themes are evident in the writings of scholars concerned with multiculturalism: *concern about cultural colonialism* and *rediscovery and preservation of traditional cultural heritage as a means to maintain national identity*. There are many different manifestations of these themes country by country.

In New Zealand biculturalism is a long-standing issue with enormous attention paid to the problem of maintaining the integrity and distinctiveness of traditional Maori culture, outside, alongside and within the mainstream Western culture, consistent with the treaty of Waitangi.

In Spain, despite a long multi-ethnic and multi-religious history, multiculturalism is a new debate sparked to some extent by that country joining the European Union in 1985. New immigrants from South America, Magreb (Morocco and Algeria), and Africa South Sahara (Guana, Senegal and Guinea), although small in overall percentages, have brought a new awareness of cultural relationships (Hernández, 1999).

Hungary is a country in which folk culture is valued as an important knowledge base for patriotism. The new Hungarian national curriculum (published in 1995) identifies for the first time a discipline called *design and crafts*, recognising the need to establish a new Hungarian conscience in the face of cosmopolitan ideals which have become the norm for young people in that country. More seriously, revival of traditional folk culture has become a matter of survival in that country (Kárpáti, 1999).

Singapore, the crossroads of Asia, is a country with a long history of multiracial coexistence. It is populated by Chinese, Malay, Indian and a mix of other cultures, including a small proportion of European. With four principal languages – Chinese, Malay, Tamil and English – the current challenge for educational authorities in that country is the development and implementation of politically sensitive policy that accommodates the diversity of cultural views.

First nation peoples in North America and Australia argue that the notion of multiculturalism ignores the fact that they are first people of the land, which they believe affords them rights and privileges that are different to those of the newer immigrants. 'Contemporary leaders in these communities are studying their pasts in an effort to forge new directions for policy development at all levels of institutions . . . and are influencing the direction of art education in both Australia and Canada' (Irwin *et al.*, 1999).

In Japan there has been lively debate about the need to internationalise the culture. The equivalent of the Japanese national curriculum, the 1990 'Course of Study', prescribes four principles aimed at internationalist education reform, one of which is to develop international understanding, together with respect for Japanese culture and traditions. This principle clearly illustrates a concern with cultural transformation (Iwano, 1999).

The collision of disparate influences from social/cultural changes, new technologies, design and the marketplace, and the ideas of post-modern theorists (who argue that pejorative distinctions between popular and high art, the original and the eclectic, ought to be removed) has brought about the need for a significant reconsideration of the nature of art education, and the ways in which its outcomes are expressed and assessed.

Considerable rethinking of the field has resulted in many changes of emphasis, which will directly affect assessment practices. The traditional view of 'art for art's sake' is now challenged in some places by the role of design (environmental, product and graphic), which more appropriately serves the needs of industry, and is more directly in line with government reform agendas. In the past the place of art in the curriculum (in Western countries at least) rested upon 'essentialist' arguments. Art does not serve other purposes, leaving the artist free to generate new visions, to be a social critic, or to provide new insights into the human condition. The designer on the other hand operates in a client–employee relationship, with a specific responsibility to serve the interests of the client. In the current economic climate there is pressure upon design to serve the interests of both industry and government . . . and hence, tacitly, to accept and support the values of the capitalist system.

Social and cultural change, brought about by changing demographics, increased education and increased activism by cultural subgroups, has in many places contributed to a broadened conception of the arts that is consistent with the new mood of post-modernism. It is argued that Eurocentric forms of art should become less dominant in education (Freedman, 1994a), that distinctions between popular arts, craft and fine arts are no longer helpful (ibid.), that critical-social theories have provided new ways to interrogate traditional

hegemonic views of art in education (Freedman, 1994b), and that technological developments have opened vast new possibilities for visual expression and have provided pathways
for connection with other art forms (Duncum, 1995). The post-modern age of eclecticism,
aided by the wizardry of modern electronic image retrieval devices, has provided a new
playground in the past for artists; the need to search always for a new definition of the
'original' may have gone.

The potential impact of these changes in art education reveals a minefield of difficulties
for those who have to assess the outcomes of art learning. Artistic production does not
always result in simple, predictable outcomes that can be adequately defined in reductionist
terms. Art learning is often concerned with unpredictable outcomes, with the exploration of
new combinations of ideas, with subtleties and complexities, and with newly emerging
forms of cultural expression. Art learning, unlike maths, science and technology, requires
the engagement of human feelings in concert with perceptual sensitivities, and the range of
ways this can be done cannot be effectively captured within the reductionist framework of
competency-based (behavioural) curriculum statements. The outcomes of learning in the
visual arts are not easily described in behavioural language, or other kinds of language for
that matter.

The potential effect of forces shaping the field of arts education in the future are these.
First, changing demographics within the composition of societies, coupled with the post-
modern trend towards removal of old cultural distinctions, suggest a broader and more
eclectic approach to the selection of content for art study, with a concomitant decrease in
emphasis upon Western 'fine art' traditions. Similarly the distinction between 'high art' and
'popular art' has blurred, leading to a more serious study of the imagery contained within
art forms of all kinds.

Second, in the post-modern world, changing views about what should be valued as an art
expression have increased the status, and changed the role, of the critic in both the world of
art and the arts classroom. Social/cultural changes, ideological changes and technological
changes have all contributed to an increased uncertainty about what counts as a work of art,
which means that the disciplined manner in which the debate will be conducted, in and out
of the classroom, is more important than it ever was before. It is no longer sufficient for
students to accept the interpretations of historians and critics. Now they should be able to
interpret art work on their own terms, and actively to interrogate the interpretations of
others.

Third, because of the impact of new technologies, studio practice in art classrooms has
assumed a new range of physical possibilities, particularly in terms of the potential offered
through electronic image generation. Coupled with the post-modern interest in the past as a
rich source of ideas for imaginative reinterpretation, the output of studio products from
school art classrooms should reflect a distinctly different technological profile in the next
few years.

Fourth, recent economic influences have promoted the development of design in various
guises within school curricula over the past decade. In some countries 'Design' is located
within the art curriculum, and in some instances it is not. The tension between the instrumental interests of design and the essentialist values of art is not yet resolved. This issue will
constitute a significant debate over the next decade with the possibility that many teachers
will become involved at some stage. If one views the possibilities for the study of design,

both content and pedagogy offer a wide range of alternatives. The teaching of product design simply to satisfy the demands of an industrial client has little in common with the values of art education, whereas the critical analysis of graphic design does. If design is to be woven into the art curriculum, care ought to be taken to develop socially critical perspectives consonant with the values of art education. Much will depend upon the pedagogy developed for the delivery and assessment of this content.

Fifth, political influence from the governments of industrialised nations has demanded that the outcomes of schooling ought to be clearly defined and accurately measured through assessment. To make sure this occurs, governments need to maintain control of the reform agenda and typically this has resulted in highly uniform assessment and reporting practices (Boughton, 1993). The fact that no evidence exists to demonstrate any relationship between the performance of schools and the success of industry has not deterred governments (Boughton, 1995). The problem is that *uniformity* and *predictability* are the key elements of evaluation strategies useful to governments as a surveillance and control mechanism to ensure schools and teachers meet government goals. Uniformity and predictability are not necessarily the most desirable elements to build into arts curricula for the most interesting or appropriate outcomes.

In theory there are many potential gains to be made from national curriculum and assessment practices, provided the approach is sensitive to the character of the discipline and responsive to regional variations. In practice the development of national curricula and concomitant assessment practices tends to be flawed in both concept and process when applied to the arts.

Assessment practices in the future will have to accommodate the above-mentioned rapid changes. The form of practical expression in the visual arts, which is increasingly influenced by electronic technology, will place new demands upon established patterns of centrally controlled assessment and moderation. Post-modern eclecticism will also require considerable debate about the place of originality in determining the value of a student's ideas and visual expression.

REREFERENCES

Aland, J. (1992) 'Art and design education in South Australian schools, from the early 1880's to the 1920's: The influence of South Kensington and Harry Pelling Gill'. Unpublished Master's thesis. Canberra: University of Canberra.

Anderson, T. (1995) 'Toward a cross-cultural approach to art criticism'. *Studies in Art Education*, 36 (4), 198–209.

Barbosa, A. M. (1999) 'Cultural identity in dependent countries: The case of Brazil'. In Doug Boughton and Rachel Mason (eds) *Beyond Multicultural Art Education: International Perspectives*. European Studies in Education, Vol. 12. München and New York: Waxmann.

Blandy, D. and Hoffman, E. (1993) 'Toward an art education of place'. *Studies in Art Education*, 35 (1), 22–33.

Boughton, D. G. (1986) 'Visual literacy: Implications for cultural understanding through art education'. *Journal of Art and Design Education*, 15 (1 and 2), 125–142.

Boughton, D. G. (1989) 'The changing face of Australian art education: New horizons or sub-colonial politics'. *Studies in Art Education*, 30, 197–211.

Boughton, D. (1993) 'Will the national art curriculum be stillborn or resuscitated through research?' *Australian Art Education: Journal of the Australian Institute of Art Education*, 16 (1).

Boughton, D. (1995) 'Six myths of national arts curriculum reform'. *Journal of Art and Design Education*, 14 (2).

Chalmers, F. G. (1985) 'Art as a social study: Theory into practice'. *Bulletin of the Caucus on Social Theory and Art Education*, 5, 40–50.

Chalmers, F. G. (1990) 'South Kensington in the farthest colony'. In Don Soucy and Mary Ann Stankiewicz (eds), *Framing the Past: Essays on Art Education*. Reston, VA: The National Art Education Association, 71–85,

Davis, J. (1997) 'Drawing's demise: U-shaped development in graphic symbolisation'. *Studies in Art Education*, 38 (3), 132–157.

Duncum, P. (1986) 'Breaking down the alleged "U" curve of artistic development'. *Visual Arts Research*, 12 (1), 43–54.

Duncum, P. (1995) 'Art education and technology: These are the days of miracles and wonder'. Unpublished paper, Central Queensland University, Rockhampton.

Duncum, P. (1996) 'From Seurat to snapshots: What the visual arts could contribute to education'. *Australian Art Education*, 19 (2), 36–45.

Efland, A. (1976) 'The school art style: A functional analysis'. *Studies in Art Education*, 17 (2), 37–44.

Efland, A. (1983) 'School art and its social origins'. *Studies in Art Education*, 24 (3), 149–157.

Efland. A. (1996) 'Art education programmes'. In Torsten Husén and T. Neville Postlethwaite (eds) *The International Encyclopedia of Education*, (2nd edn). Vol. 11. Oxford: Pergamon Press, 338–343.

Efland, A., Freedman, K. and Stuhr, P. (1996) *Postmodern Art Education: An Approach to Curriculum*. Reston, VA: The National Art Education Association.

Eisner, E. (1972) *Educating Artistic Vision*. New York: Macmillan.

Fehr, D. (1994) 'Promise and paradox: Art education in the postmodern arena'. *Studies in Art Education*, 35 (4), 209–217.

Freedman, K. (1994a) 'Guest editorial: About this issue: A social reconstruction of art education'. *Studies in Art Education*, 35 (3), 131–134.

Freedman, K. (1994b) 'Interpreting gender and visual culture in art classrooms'. *Studies in Art Education*, 35 (3), 157–170.

Freedman, K. (1995) 'Learning and instruction of visual and performing arts'. In Torsten Husén and T. Neville Postlethwaite (eds), *The International Encyclopedia of Education* (2nd edn). Vol. 11. Oxford: Pergamon Press, 6616–6618.

Freedman, K. and Hernández, F. (1998) 'A sociological framework for international education', in Kerry Freedman and Fernando Hernández (eds) *Curriculum Culture, and Art Education: Comparative Perspectives*. NY: State University of New York Press.

Freedman, K. and Relan, A. (1992) 'Computer graphics, artistic production, and social processes'. *Studies in Art Education*, 33 (2), 98–109.

Garber, E. (1995) 'A study in the borderlands'. *Studies in Art Education*, 36 (4), 218–232.

Gardner, H. (1983) 'Artistic Intelligences'. *Art Education*, 36 (2), 47–49.

Hart, L. (1991) 'Aesthetic pluralism and multicultural art education'. *Studies in Art Education*, 32 (3), 145–159.

Hernández, F. (1999) 'Cultural diversity and art education: The Spanish experience'. In Doug Boughton and Rachel Mason (eds) *Beyond Multicultural Art Education: International Perspectives*. European Studies in Education, Vol. 12. München and New York: Waxmann.

Hillman-Chartrand, H. (1986) 'The Arts: Consumption skills in the postmodern economy'. *Journal of Multicultural and Cross-cultural Research in Art Education*, 4 (1), 30–45.

Irwin, R., Rogers, T. and Farrell (1999) 'Irrelevance of multiculturalism to the realities of aboriginal artists'. In Doug Boughton and Rachel Mason (eds). *Beyond Multicultural Art Education: International Perspectives*. European Studies in Education, Vol. 12. München and New York: Waxmann.

Iwano, M. (1999) 'Japanese art education: From Internationalisation to Globalisation'. In D. Boughton and R. Mason (eds) *Beyond Multicultural Art Education: International Perspectives*. European Studies in Education, Vol. 12. München and New York: Waxmann.

Kárpáti, A. (1999) 'When pedagogy becomes politics: Folk art in Hungarian art education'. In

Doug Boughton and Rachel Mason (eds) *Beyond Multicultural Art Education: International Perspectives*. European Studies in Education, Vol. 12. München and New York: Waxmann.

Korzenik, D. (1995) 'The changing concept of artistic giftedness'. In C. Golomb (ed.) *The Development of Artistically Gifted Children*, Hillsdale, NJ: Lawrence Erlbaum Associates.

Lanier, V. (1972) 'Objectives of teaching art'. *Art Education*, 25 (3), 15–19.

Lowenfeld, V. (1957). *Creative and Mental Growth*. (3rd edn). New York: Macmillan.

MacDonald, Stuart (1970) *The History and Philosophy of Art Education*. London: University of London Press.

MacGregor, R. N. (1992) 'Post-modernism, art educators, and art education'. *ERIC Digest ED348238*. Bloomington, IN: ERIC Clearinghouse.

Pariser, D. (1997) 'The mind of the beholder: Some provisional doubts about the U-curved aesthetic development thesis'. *Studies in Art Education*, 38 (3), 158–178.

Rogers, T. (1994) 'Art and aboriginal cultures'. *Australian Art Education*, 17 (2), 12–20.

Sandell, R. (1991) 'The liberating relevance of feminist pedagogy'. *Studies in Art Education*, 32 (3), 178–187.

Skilbeck, M. (1992) 'National curriculum within the OECD', *UNICORN*, 18 (3), 9–13

Stuhr, P. (1994). 'Multicultural art education and social reconstruction'. *Studies in Art Education*, 35 (3), 171–178.

Wilson, B. and Wilson, M. (1981) 'Review of *Artful scribbles: The significance of children's drawings*, by H. Gardner'. *Studies in Visual Communication*, 7 (1), 86–89.

Wolcott, A. (1996) 'Is what you see what you get? A postmodern approach to understanding works of art'. *Studies in Art Education*, 37 (2), 69–79.

Young, M. (1985) 'A history of art and design education in South Australia'. Unpublished Master's thesis. Adelaide, Flinders University.

58

MUSIC EDUCATION: WHERE NOW?

Keith Swanwick

Early in the twentieth century, Jacques-Dalcroze drew attention to a tendency of music education to detach itself from the mainstream culture.

> Before everything else, always make sure that the teaching of music is worthwhile. And there must be no confusion as to what is understood by 'music'. There are not two classes of music: one for adults, drawing rooms, and concert halls, the other for children and schools. There is only one music, and the teaching of it is not so difficult a matter as scholastic authorities are apt to suggest at their congresses.
>
> (Jacques-Dalcroze, 1967 [1915], p. 98)

Jacques-Dalcroze might not have thought the matter quite so simple had he been exposed to the range of music to which we all now have access. In principle though he is surely right. School and college education can become a closed system that leaves behind or gets left behind ideas and events in the wider world. And the teaching of music does have to be worthwhile, whatever that may mean.

INSTITUTIONALISING MUSIC EDUCATION

Music education is not obviously problematic until it surfaces in schools and colleges, until it becomes 'formal', institutionalised. If we want to strum a guitar, get into the plot of a Wagner opera, play a sitar or sing in a chorus, then finding a teacher, reading a book or joining a performing group may be all that is required. There is no need to form a curriculum committee, produce a rationale or declare a list of objectives. The informal music 'student' can copy jazz riffs from recordings, ask friends about fingering or chord patterns, learn by imitation – 'sitting next to Nelly' – or widen musical experience by watching television, listening to the radio or exploring record shops. Formal instruction may not be necessary. Yet for some this may be a crucial point of access. For others though, the contribution of educational institutions to their personal music education will be negligible and could even be negative. In Britain there is a history of research reporting negative attitudes to music in the curriculum compared with other subjects (Francis, 1987; Ross, 1995; Schools Council, 1968).

Unlike most if not all other school and college curriculum subject areas, in the case of music many alternative avenues of access are open. The easy accessibility of music from the ends of the earth, high levels of music-specific information technology – including sound generation, recording and reproduction – these developments, along with the rapid dissemination of popular musics, compete with conventional curricula in schools. The consequence is that students may have very little time for 'school music' and are likely to see it as a quaint musical subculture.

For example, beginning in the 1950s, the introduction of Orff instruments into school music classrooms resulted in the creation of a musical subculture, characterised by decorative *glissandi* and circling *ostinati*, played on specially designed classroom instruments and based on pentatonic materials. This was music designed for children, music bearing little relationship to music elsewhere, except when it begins to approximate the Indonesian gamelan. In the late 1960s came the influence of modernism. In Britain and elsewhere we encouraged children to become performers and composers of 'texture' pieces and to use aleatoric devices, randomised lists of numbers and so on. Pulse, tonality and modally defined pitch relationships were suspended. So children made sound *collages*, recorded 'found' sounds in their environments and constructed graphic scores. The word 'music' was frequently dropped altogether from books for use in schools and the word 'sound' was substituted: *New Sounds in Class*; *Sound and Silence*; *Exploring Sound*; *Make a New Sound*; *Sounds Fun*; *Sounds Interesting*. Here was an attempt to begin again, to make a new start without the clutter of inherited classical traditions which are so easily seen as opposed to the popular music industry and the alternate musical preferences of many students. Metrical rhythms and tonal pitch relationships were discarded and attention was switched to levels of loudness, texture and tone colour. But in the evenings – after these distinctive school experiences – the students went home and played the Beatles and the Rolling Stones.

> Many teenagers for instance elect to teach themselves to play a musical instrument – the drums perhaps or the guitar. What do they do? They usually know already the kind of sound they are interested in. They insist on the right equipment. They listen to their mentors and try to emulate them, running into problems of sound production and control, figuring their own way through them, comparing notes with fellow practitioners, following the example of preferred models.
>
> (Ross, 1995, p. 196)

More recently and in an attempt to recognise the reality of music 'out there', popular musics have entered the formal education scene. Even so, popular music has to be reduced, abstracted and modified to fit into classrooms and timetables and becomes what Ross calls 'pseudo music'.

An alternative way of creating a school musical subculture is discernible in North America as the high school band, and especially when given over to marching at ball games with a purpose-made repertoire, uniforms, parade ground routines and majorettes. Yet on graduating from school or leaving the band, a large proportion of students appear to put it all behind them. There appears little sign among adult communities of continued engagement with instrumental music. The same appears true for the choral programmes. The main aim of the class is often to get a programme of music in shape for public performance, rather than to provide a rich musical and educational experience. The teaching method is accordingly very directive and there is considerable repetition in rehearsal of a very small repertoire, often giving rise to boredom. The real musical interests of these students are likely to lie elsewhere.

Reservations about performance programmes in North America have been raised by several writers. These include Leonard and House (1959), Kirchhoff (1988) and Reimer (1989), who warn against an overemphasis on performing ensembles and a concentration on technique which works against musical understanding. The relevance of such activities has also been questioned. The band movement, with its old military connections, hardly reflects the contemporary world of music 'out there'.

> The result has been that students spend an increased amount of time performing on instruments that are foreign to the mainstream of music making in this country and abroad. . . . The increased emphasis upon marching band and marching band contests has meant that greater numbers of students are leaving high school band programs literally overloaded and burned out. They have been victims of an educational curriculum that has placed its entire emphasis on the short term reward of winning. . . . The marching band is not the only group that stands in the way of students' achieving an aesthetic music education. The jazz ensemble and the concert band have also been guilty.
>
> (Kirchhoff, 1988, p. 265)

This critical stance has a long history. Boethius, writing in the sixth century, distinguished between performers, composers and those who listen in audience and appraise the music.

> But the type which buries itself in instruments is separated from the understanding of musical knowledge. Representatives of this type, for example kithara players and organists and other instrumentalists, devote their total effort to exhibiting their skill on instruments. Thus, they act as slaves, as has been said: for they use no reason but are totally lacking in thought.
>
> (Boethius cited in Godwin, 1986, p. 48)

Against this polemical background and alongside the tension between music in schools and music 'out there', a debate has recently been rekindled, distinguishing the claims of the daily round of 'music for all' in general classes and the greater public status and higher musical rewards for teachers of extra-curricular performance activities. In an attempt to 'situate' the formal music curriculum in relation to 'viable music cultures', David Elliott urges us to affirm the centrality of performance in music education (Elliott, 1995, p. 99). In this he chimes with most actual practice in North American music education – focused as it is on bands and choirs. To do this he counters what he sees as an inadequate philosophy of music education, a philosophy articulated most consistently in the USA by Bennett Reimer. Elliott sees as his initial task the demolition of this 'aesthetic philosophy' of music education.

This deficient 'philosophy' Elliott (1995, p. 23) sees resting on four common, basic and profoundly wrong assumptions:

- that music is a collection of objects or works;
- that these musical works are for listening to and that there is only one way of listening, aesthetically and with attention to the structure of the work;
- that the value of these works is always intrinsic, internal;
- that if we listen correctly to these pieces we may achieve a distinctive aesthetic experience.

This is something of a caricature of the views of Reimer and misrepresents several other writers whom he seeks to cluster together as promoting the 'aesthetic concept of music education', including the present author. In an earlier book I was critical of the formalist view taken by Meyer.

> The problem is that it fails to connect musical experience with other experience in any direct way. Music has once again been removed from life, turned into a kind of game, if of an intellectual kind. It seems more likely that expectation and surprise are part of the *mechanism of engagement* with the work. It is how we are kept interested and involved, is how we are brought into action with prediction, speculation and ideas about what is happening and what is likely to happen, and in all this there is obviously likely to be a trace of excitement. But it is *not* the prime source of high aesthetic pleasure. The peak of aesthetic experience is scaled only when a work relates strongly to the structures of our own individual experience, when it calls for a new way of organizing the schemata, or traces, of previous life events. This experience of seeing things by a new light is called by Koestler 'bisociation' (1949). It is a 'eureka' experience, what Langer calls the triumph of insight: we discover in the work a 'point of view' that seems to us at the moment to be a kind of revelation.
>
> (Swanwick, 1979, p. 36)

If this is Elliott's 'distinctive aesthetic experience', then I plead guilty to finding it desirable. Seeing arts activities as part of the aesthetic also gives them a much needed educational rationale. However, it is too easy to conflate the aesthetic with the artistic, a confusion which Elliott rightly castigates. Such a conflation tends to essentialise artistic experience into a single entity instead of recognising distinctive forms of discourse.

AESTHETIC VERSUS ARTISTIC EDUCATION

There is now a multiplicity of definitions as to what is meant by the aesthetic, and an unsatisfactory mingling of several different concepts, including the aesthetic, aesthetics, the artistic and the affective. For example, Malcolm Ross (1984) characterises aesthetics as 'the general field of sensuous perception' while Bennett Reimer (1989, p. xiii) thinks of 'aesthetic', 'artistic' and 'intrinsic' as interchangeable. Peter Abbs sees aesthetic experience as signifying the memorable or overwhelmingly affective, which leads him to the idea of a 'generic community' of the arts. This aesthetic community is seen to have three shared characteristics that distinguish it from other areas of human activity (Abbs, 1994, p. 92).

1 All the arts 'create forms expressive of life'.
2 All for their meanings 'depend upon their formal constructions that cannot be extracted or translated without significant loss'.
3 They require 'not a critical response but an aesthetic response – a response through feeling, the senses, and the imagination'.

The first and second of these defining statements must surely apply to *all* forms of knowing, unless a very restricted meaning is placed upon the phrases 'expressive of life' and 'formal constructions'. The third definition, the idea of aesthetic response, seems more distinctive, though it is difficult to imagine artistic participation – let alone arts teaching – divorced entirely from critical response. There is also a problem about relating response through the senses directly to the idea of symbolic processes, a concept that is also important for Abbs. Symbolic forms develop within traditions of use and involve cognitive elements; making connections and comparisons, the ability to read expressive conventions and to recognise structural exceptions and deviations. As Dewey reminds us: 'The odd notion that an artist does not think and a scientific inquirer does nothing else is the result of converting a difference of tempo and emphasis into a difference in kind' (Dewey, 1934, p. 15).

All three of Abbs's aesthetic propensities appear to be shared with other forms of human discourse. The aesthetic is only a part of artistic experience, a necessary but not sufficient condition for artistic understanding. Furthermore, aesthetic response is often an unlooked-for gift having little to do with the arts; the flash of light on water, a sunset, a fine shot in a ball game, an elegant experiment, a tight argument; all these may qualify as partaking of the aesthetic. Ross stretches the concept even further until it becomes a generic life-force. 'A good aesthetic education, a healthy aesthetic development, will, by definition, increase the life-force, empower the life-drive, release all our instincts and savour life and live life to the full. It will be strengthening – virtuous' (Ross, 1984, p. 65). For Ross, aesthetic education should not be an induction into what he calls the 'artistic predilections of a privileged social minority'.

> The classes would be jam sessions and the public events community happenings. Arts lessons would generate an artistic dimension in the school's life – not merely function as yet another variation on an academic or vocational theme. There would be room for cartoon, comic strip, food, film, make-up, D.I.Y., clothing, the fairground, muzak, Boots Art, pop, electronic games, cars, bikes, hair, graffiti, advertising, entertainment, politics. The esoteric practices of the studio, the theatre, the concert hall, the gallery would be replaced by an altogether more robust, more plebeian, more ephemeral range of activities – all imbued with what I have called the vernacular spirit.
> (Ross, 1984, p. 46)

It may be encouraging for arts teachers to see aesthetic experience as celebratory, illuminating every corner of life, vitally pulsing through the curriculum and communities of schools. But this vitality is not necessarily confined to the arts. All lively and significant experience can be seen as aesthetic, as indeed it is by John Dewey (*Art as Experience*, 1934). The emphasis by Ross on day-dreaming, cordiality and the vernacular principle are certainly in opposition to educational 'standards', vocational attitudes to the school curriculum and school timetables. But even in this context of our contemporary schools, we should be looking for *eventfulness* in the curriculum rather than low-pressure sequences of dull routines.

Essentially though, aesthetic experience has to be seen in a dialectical relationship with traditions and conventions. This relationship is not a simple matter of transmitting a culture or a set of cultural values. There are, of course, obvious connections between the music of particular groups and their lifestyle and social position. But this is not to say that music in some way embodies a social order. As Peter Martin puts it, 'there is a relationship between social class and the hierarchy of musical styles, but this does not mean that the latter is determined by the former' (Martin, 1995, p. 180). Distinctive musical styles are maintained and developed through an *interpretive community*. Musicians work in a dialogue with other musicians and with their audiences.

> Artworks are the product of activities shaped by a constant process of decision-making, of innumerable choices through which their creators imaginatively take account of the likely responses of others. This does not imply that artists will simply conform to such expectations – on

the contrary, they may consider their whole purpose to be the challenging or subverting of established conventions.

(Martin, 1995, p. 193)

Music thus takes place within a cultural environment without being culturally determined. Rejecting the dichotomy of mass culture versus high art, Gans conceives of what he calls 'taste cultures' and 'taste publics', pluralistic value groups rather than a heterogeneous society. An individual subscribes to any number of such groups at the same time and changes allegiance over time (Gans, 1974).

This comes close to the work of Habermas, who sees the importance of divergencies that may in time become important for survival and development. Variations occur which change the potential of individuals and communities: 'In the case of social evolution the learning process takes place not through changes in genetic makeup but through changes in knowledge potential' (Habermas, 1991, p. 171) This cultural margin of manoeuvre is kept open by systems of discourse which facilitate the growth of knowledge for any individual, and through individuals to society. In music its essence consists in being multilevel, engaging us from the particularity of the sensory, through expressive metaphors to the relationships of structured argument. At any of these levels, the interaction of aesthetic subjectivity and artistic traditions is potentially rich in bringing about what Habermas calls 'divergent phenotypes' (ibid., p. 170): witness the richness and range of musical idioms and the multitude of distinctive individual musical voices.

Music is a distinctive form of discourse. By definition, all discourse takes place within a nexus of cultural conventions and all discourse also makes it possible for individuals to make a unique contribution.

> As civilised human beings, we are the inheritors, neither of an enquiry about ourselves and the world, nor of an accumulating body of information, but of a conversation, begun in the course of centuries. . . . Education, properly speaking, is an initiation into the skill and partnership of this conversation.

(Oakeshot, 1992, pp. 198–199)

Music is one way of joining in such a conversation.

SUSTAINING MUSICAL CONVERSATIONS

What then are the educational activities that sustain and develop musical conversation? Here again there are variations of view. The pivot of the British secondary classroom is composing, whereas Elliott lays his stress on performance, which matches the status quo of North American curriculum practice.

> Composing is also an important way of developing musicianship and immersing students in musical practices. But unless or until students come to know the essential nature of music works as performances, composing should not be the primary way of developing musicianship. Instead (and time permitting) I suggest that composing is a reasonable and important supplement to the development of students' musicianship through performing and improvising.

(Elliott, 1995, p. 173)

It could be argued, however, that composing gives more decision-making to the participant: it allows more scope for cultural choice and is more likely to avoid the snare of treating

975

music as 'object'. This ought not to be a question of 'time permitting' but a necessity, giving students an opportunity to bring through their own work to the micro-culture of the classroom ideas from the music 'out there' in their experience.

In many of the best British classrooms – and not all are good of course – composing is a highly developed musical process, though where it amounts to no more than playing around with sounds it is hard to justify. Performing too can be a mixed educational blessing. Work in large groups can often stifle individual contributions and the repetition of rehearsal for public display can produce a state of mindlessness or boredom. The larger and more centrally directed the performing group, the more likely this is. To counter this, Elliott advocates breaking whole classes and choruses into smaller groups to identify and solve performance problems for themselves.

Even so, both composing and performance as single educational activities will limit us to what we can ourselves play or sing. If formal music education is to help us into ongoing, 'situated' musical discourse, it should offer more than this. Also, in the world outside of classrooms is the 'conversation' of musical thinking from other times and places, recorded and in live performance. Access to this must also be part of the experience of students in formal education. Composing, performing and audience-listening all have their part to play. In this way individual differences of students can be respected, for we all ultimately find our own way into music.

But how is this to be achieved? There has to be radical re-thinking of how time and resources are used. I can only hint at them here. Smaller groups than whole class, whole band or whole chorus are essential for student interaction, musical decision-making and individual choice. There also has to be openness to wider musical encounters, a recognition of the plurality of musical discourse. To avoid the tendency to create 'school music' sub-cultures, students should sometimes work alongside musicians, composers and performers.

There are two parallel strands in present educational provision and they affect the arts in general and music in schools in particular. One strand is the evolution of national curricula; the other is the growth of *ad hoc* educational projects initiated by agencies working outside of the formal educational framework.

> Represented here are two distinct approaches to curriculum innovation which appear to be in tension – the one a nationally engineered, standardised approach to a curriculum devised in non-school settings and imposed with the force of law; the other a locally diverse basket of activities devised in collaborations between professional musicians in school and joined on a voluntaristic basis.
>
> (Kushner, 1994)

Children also visit centres outside of schools to work alongside musicians, including visiting composers and performers from opera companies or members of orchestras. Kushner's point is that these events are negotiated for particular children in a specific locality rather than nationally imposed. They are also educationally potentially rich activities, permitting children to engage with music in their own way and at their own speed. There is no curriculum sequencing towards pre-specified learning outcomes. These events tend to be broadly process-based rather than geared to narrowly defined and standardised 'products'. Complex music may be 'deconstructed'; for example, involvement over time with an opera production can have different levels of meaning for different individuals. This is thought to be unlike the supposedly cumulative and incremental teaching that characterises a specified curriculum with attainment targets focused on particular age-groups (Kushner, 1994).

These 'authentic' musical activities are increasing in scope and availability. In 1993 the London Arts Board located 50 collaborations between professional music organisations and the statutory education sector in its region. This is probably not exhaustive but points to new forms of collaboration between musicians and young people that take professional performers and composers into classrooms.

ENSURING THAT THE TEACHING OF MUSIC IS WORTHWHILE

In a world where music teaching means so many different things it seems necessary to hold in mind the exhortation of Jacques-Dalcroze to make music teaching worthwhile and to identify some working principles to apply whatever the educational setting. We start from the basic premise *that music educators should respect and promote music as a form of discourse.* This has a number of consequences.

1 *Care for music*: By care I do not mean just generalised concern for the school subject 'music' or for music as a 'good' thing. I mean that when music sounds, however elementary the resources and techniques may be, the teacher is receptive and alert, is really *listening* and expects students to do the same.

2 *Care for the pupil, for his or her achievement and autonomy*: Discourse – musical conversation – is not a monologue. Each student brings a realm of musical understanding with them into our educational institutions. We have to try to ensure that this is given scope for expression while at the same time acknowledging that for an educator, to care is to teach.

3 *Always work for expressiveness*: Whether we see the music as being closely linked to its particular cultural setting or to the psychological profile of an individual, music has a peculiarly expressive power. The *phrase* and not the note or bar is the smallest musical unit. In the work of the best educators, including Kodály, Orff and Jacques-Dalcroze, there is never a moment where a *phrase* – an expressive gesture – is not looked for.

4 *Promote fluency before literacy*: This is clearly the position of Orff and Jacques-Dalcroze but I think it should be said too of Kodály that a rich background of singing 'by ear' is assumed before children begin to read music in the choral method. Literacy is not the ultimate aim of music education, it is simply a means to an end in some music and is often unnecessary. In any event (on an analogy with language) the order of development is listen, articulate, then read and write. We might consider how this would affect the first few piano lessons, classroom instrumental work, choral rehearsals and composing.

We can see how these simple and perhaps obvious working principles might inform current developments. For example, take the necessity of broadening the cultural range of music teaching, of engaging in intercultural work or 'world musics'. The first principle, that we care for the particularity of musical experience, will help us avoid using multicultural resources as a kind of musical 'coach-tour'. Having fairly recently escaped from the clutches of the history of Western classical music, we must be careful not to replicate this state of affairs with music from India, the Caribbean, Africa, China or the Pacific region. If we are to stay close to music and to the principle that we should work for music's expressiveness, then we shall sometimes have to cut off cultural labels and help shift the barriers of cultural possessiveness and exclusiveness. One way through is to recognise that in spite of the apparent diversity of much of the world's music, we can still identify musical elements which, though they appear in quite different contexts, are common to much music. We can think, for example, of repeated melodic or rhythmic patterns, the use of scales or modes, of chorus or antiphonal effects, dance rhythms, drones, changes of texture, qualities of timbre, and so on. We extend our idea of what Orff called limited structures, to take in ragas, whole tone scales, note-rows, jazz and blues chord sequences. In these ways we can extend our potential expressive range, and in handling these elements, come to have a better understanding of the minds of other people by entering into their musical procedures.

In this handling and listening we are also, of course, extending the scope of musical imagination, getting the sounds 'in our ears' (the second principle). Music from outside of the Western classical tradition has a great deal to offer us in terms of the fourth principle, of musical fluency taking precedence over what is sometimes called musical literacy. It is precisely this fluency, the aural ability to image music coupled with the skill of handling an instrument (or the voice) that characterises jazz, Indian music, rock music, music for steel-pans and folk music anywhere in the world. These musicians have much to teach about the virtues of playing 'by ear' and the amazing possibilities of memory and collective improvisation and composition.

Finally, what are we to make of the emerging world of the microchip and the computer? How do these stand the test of our principles? We can divide the possible contribution of micro-technology into three broad areas. One obvious development is the extension of individualised learning. The second area of development is the extension of instrumental resources in a radical way, giving us instant accompaniments, quite new tonal effects and undreamed of combinations of sounds. The third and most significant (and most expensive) possibility is the development of computers to assist the processes of musical composition and performance.

The first of our principles, care for music, is at risk only if we forget that micro-technology is a tool and not an end in itself. It is the principle of expressiveness that seems most at risk. It is very easy to mechanise human diversity out of existence and to use pre-recorded loops and patterns which, whilst they may serve the purposes of instant music-making, certainly do not develop expressive range. But the computer can be used to stimulate compositional processes, can translate visual metaphors of music into sound, and can enhance performance. If technology delegates some of the tedium to machines – especially notation – this would be an advance. Let us hope that technological progress can release teachers and students from drudgery, leaving us free to create lively *events*, promoting conviviality and extending sensibility.

Where microchip technology is a boon is in connection with the principle of care for student autonomy. Headphones help to create and sustain private worlds. However, an emphasis on individual work may not suit everyone. Those of us with extrovert tendencies will prefer to be with groups of people, taking part in events together, rather than being shut away with a piece of apparatus. We would be wise to look at the fate of many language laboratories, and at the return to the face-to-face group interaction. We shall have to safeguard some space that is not sectioned up into boxes. Music is not like that, it is not that kind of activity.

I conclude with one more quotation from my own writing which I think still encapsulates my own view of music education and suggests where we might look in working out the future role of formal education.

> [The] first and unique aim of music education in schools and colleges is to raise to consciousness and purposefully and critically explore a number of musical *procedures*, experienced directly through the reality of various inter-cultural encounters. A second aim is to participate in creating and sustaining musical events in the community, events in which people can *choose* to be involved and thus contribute to the rich variety of musical possibilities in our society.
>
> In these ways, we avoid transmitting a restrictive view of music and of culture and may help to keep prejudice at bay. Human culture is not something to be merely transmitted, perpetuated or preserved but is constantly being reinterpreted. As a vital element of the cultural process, music is, in the best sense of the term, *recreational*; helping us and our cultures to become renewed; transformed.
>
> (Swanwick, 1988, pp. 118–119)

This idea is captured by Margaret Mead, who also worried about the separation of education from the world of communities outside of institutions. There is a positive side to schooling! As she says,

> out of the discontinuities and rapid changes which have accompanied these minglings of people has come another invention, one which perhaps would not have been born in any other setting than this one – the belief in education as an instrument for the creation of new human values. . . . the use of education for unknown ends.
>
> (Mead, 1973, p. 107)

REFERENCES

Abbs, P. (1994) *The Educational Imperative*, London: Falmer Press.

Dewey, J. (1934) *Art as Experience*, New York: Capricorn Books.

Elliott, D. J. (1995) *Music Matters: A New Philosophy of Music Education*, New York and Oxford: Oxford University Press.

Francis, L. J. (1987) 'The decline in attitudes towards religious education among 8–15 year olds', *Educational Studies*, 13 (2).

Gans, H. J. (1974) *High Culture and Popular Culture*, New York: Basic Books.

Godwin, J. (1986) *Music, Mysticism and Magic: A Sourcebook*, London: Routledge.

Habermas, J. (1991) *Communication and the Evolution of Society* (trans. T. Macarthy), Cambridge: Polity Press.

Jacques-Dalcroze, E. (1967) [1915] *Rhythm, Music and Education* (trans. H. F. Rubinstein), London: Riverside Press.

Kirchhoff, C. (1988) 'The school and college band: Wind band pedagogy in the United States', in J. T. Gates (ed.) *Music Education in the United States: Contemporary Issues*, Tuscaloosa: University of Alabama Press.

Kushner, S. (1994) 'Against better judgement: How a centrally prescribed music curriculum works against teacher development', *International Journal of Music Education*, 23, 34–45.

Langer, S. (1942) *Philosophy in a New Key*, New York: Mentor Books.

Leonard, C. and House, R. W. (1959) *Foundations and Principles of Music Education*, New York: McGraw-Hill.

London Arts Board (1993) *Musicians in School. Collaboration between Music Organisations and the Statutory Education Sector in London*, David Pratley, Gwynn Rhydderch and John Stephens.

Martin, P. J. (1995) *Sounds and Society*, Manchester: Manchester University Press.

Mead, M. (1973) [1942] 'Our educational emphases in primitive perspective', in Keddie (ed.) *Tinker, Tailor*, Harmondsworth: Penguin.

Meyer, L. B. (1956) *Emotion and Meaning in Music*, Chicago: University of Chicago Press.

Oakeshot, M. (1992) *Rationalism in Politics and Other Essays*, London: Methuen.

Reimer, B. (1989) [1970] *A Philosophy of Music Education*, Englewood Cliffs, NJ: Prentice Hall.

Ross, M. (1984) *The Aesthetic Impulse*, Oxford: Pergamon.

Ross, M. (1995) 'What's wrong with school music?', *British Journal of Music Education*, 12 (3), 185–201.

Schools Council (1968) *Enquiry One: The Young School Leavers*, London: HMSO.

Swanwick, K. (1979) *A Basis for Music Education*, London: Routledge.

Swanwick, K. (1988) *Music, Mind and Education*, London: Routledge.

Swanwick, K. (1994) *Musical Knowledge: Intuition, Analysis and Music Education*, London and New York: Routledge.

INDEX

Note: Page numbers in italic type refer to tables; page numbers followed by 'n' refer to notes.